D0116906

# Homemade

## The Heart and Science of Handcrafts

## Carol Endler Sterbenz

SCRIBNER

New York   London   Toronto   Sydney   New Delhi

SCRIBNER
A Division of Simon & Schuster, Inc.
1230 Avenue of the Americas
New York, NY 10020

*To my twin sister,*

*Nancy,*

*with love*


May time be thick as honey
and no one saying good-bye.

—Robert Hass
*The Apple Trees at Olema*, 2010

# Contents

Introduction     xi

## Chapter One: Beading     I

The Heart     1

    French Lessons     1

    A Brief History of Beads     4

The Science     5

    All About Beads     6

    Materials and Tools     19

    Wiring Beads     33

    Stringing Beads     46

    Off-Loom Weaving:
      The Peyote Stitch     55

Projects     62

    Moonlight: A Pair of Earrings     62

    Rainbow: A Bangle Bracelet     63

    Princess: A Choker     65

    Blue Ice: A Pendant     66

    Gold Band: A Peyote Ring     68

    Frothy Silver: A Necklace     69

    Vieux Nice: A Charm Bracelet     71

    Swing: A Pair of Earrings     73

    Blue Topaz and Pearls:
      A Necklace     75

    Spring Leaf: A Peyote Bracelet     76

    Gold Disk: A Ring     78

    Rock Crystal: A Bracelet     79

    Heirloom: A Miniature
      Christmas Tree     81

## Chapter Two: Floral Arts     87

The Heart     87

    Family Roots     87

    A Brief History     90

The Science     91

    The Principles of Floral Design     92

    Fresh Flowers and Foliage     104

    Dried and Preserved Flowers
      and Foliage     109

    Silk Flowers and Artificial Fruit     123

    Wiring Stems, Adding False
      Stems, and Using Floral Picks     125

    Bouquets to Carry and to
      Display     133

    Container Arrangements     136

    Wreaths     144

    Garlands     155

    Topiary     159

    Natural Care for Body and Soul     165

Projects     191

    Floral Arch: Pitcher Bouquets     191

    Forest: Winter Wreath     191

    Clouds: Hydrangea Wreath     193

    Rose and Berry Pineapple:
      A Table Centerpiece     194

Confetti: Summer Wreath 196
Della Robbia: Autumn Wreath 197
Untamed: Summer Garland 198
Harvest: A Dried Topiary 199

## Chapter Three: Paper Crafting 201

The Heart 201
   Woven Baskets 201
   A Brief History 204
The Science 205
   All About Paper 206
   Materials and Tools 209
   Essential Techniques 212
   Greeting Cards and Invitations 225
   Gift Packages 243
   Making Paper Flowers 253
   Memory Keeping: Albums,
     Books, and Scrapbooks 268
Projects 277
   Woven Heart: A Paper Basket 277
   Priceless: A Die-Cut Card 278
   Memories: Mini Photo Album 279
   First Love: A Soft-Cover Photo
     Album 280
   The Deluxe Book of Butterflies:
     A Flag Book 282

## Chapter Four: Hand Printing 285

The Heart 285
   Through Immigrant Eyes 285
   A Brief History 288
The Science 291
   Stamping 292
   Block Printing 300
   Traditional Stenciling 321
   Screen Printing 324
Projects 344
   Cord-and-Bead: Post Cards 344
   Butterfly: A Gift Bag 346

Leafy Branch: A Place Mat 348
Chandelier: An Art Print 349
Chrysanthemum: Printed Fabric
   for a Box Book 352

## Chapter Five: Decoupage 355

The Heart 355
   November Roses 355
   A Brief History 358
The Science 361
   Materials and Tools 361
   Selecting and Preparing the
     Prints 366
   Decoupage on Wood and Metal 375
   Decoupage on Glass 398
Projects 410
   Zebra: A Decorative Platter 410
   Head Shots: Theme-and-Variation
     Dessert Plates 412
   Swimming Lessons: A Vase 413

## Chapter Six: Decorative Embellishing 415

The Heart 415
   One Pathway to Joy 415
   A Brief History 418
The Science 419
   Glass Etching 419
   Gilding 437
   Dry Embossing 449
   Ribbons and Trims 456
   Decals and Heat-Transfers 467
   Candle Making and Decorating 480
   Chandeliers: Restoring and
     Recycling 517
   Picture Frames: Restoring and
     Recycling 523
   Picassiette: Restoring and
     Recycling 534

Projects     544

     Tuxedo: An Etched Decanter
        and Tumbler     544

     Polka Dots: A Gilded and
        Bejeweled Glass Vase     545

     The Golden Sparrow: A Gilded
        Bird     547

     Golden Leaves: A Gilded Box
        with Embossed Leaves     548

     Wind: An Embossed-Velvet
        Pillow     550

     Zebra: A Throw with Tassels     551

     English Garden: A Ribbon-Rose
        Lampshade     551

     Juliet: A Vase with Rose Decals     553

     Portrait: A Block-Shaped Candle     555

     Hopewell: A Cottage-Style
        Mirror Frame     556

**Chapter Seven: Children's Arts
and Crafts**     **561**

     The Heart     561

        Home for Christmas     561

        A Brief History     564

     The Science     566

        Getting Started     566

        Children's Ages and
          Developmental Stages     573

        Working with Paper     584

        Working with Crayons, Paint,
          Chalk, and Markers     610

        Working with Clay     631

        Working with Glitter     638

Projects     643

     Polka Dot: A Kaleidoscope     643

     Katie and Charlotte: Pom-Pom
        Chicks     645

     Robert: The Nuts-and-Bolts
        Robot     646

     Sox Martin: Sock Monkey     649

     Izzie and Andrew: Jointed
        Clay Dolls     651

     Glitter Feet: Mary Jane Shoes     654

     Harry: A Jumpy Spider     655

     Little Miss Muffet: Small
        Spider on a Spiderweb     657

     Mardi Gras: A Feather Mask     659

     Starlight: A Magic Wand     662

     Bumblebees and Ladybugs:
        Halloween Headgear     664

     Monster with Wiggly Eyes:
        Halloween Headgear     665

     Flower Girl: Halloween
        Headgear     667

     Imperial: Eggshell Gift Boxes     668

     Easter Parade: Hollowed-Out
        Eggshell Ornaments     669

Patterns and Original Art     681

Resources     725

Bibliography     741

Advisory Board     747

Acknowledgments     751

Credits and Notes     753

Index     755

# Introduction

YOUNG ADMIRER: Papa Bach, how do you manage to think of all these
new tunes?

J. S. BACH: My dear fellow, I have no need to think of them. I have the
greatest difficulty not to step on them when I get out of bed in the
morning and start moving around my room.

—Laurens van der Post,
*Jung and the Story of Our Time*, 1975

I've heard it said that a carpenter with a hammer sees nails everywhere. I say a crafter
with imagination sees handcrafts everywhere. I know I do. I see sparkling bracelets
in a scattering of beads, keepsake journals in sheets of handmade paper, and jointed
dolls in a lump of clay. An ever-present part of my childhood, handcrafts were my

playthings. They were part of my home education. I was encouraged from an early age to express my ideas freely, and I took readily to arts and crafts materials, which were supplied in abundance. I was expected to know how to embroider, draw, paint, cultivate a garden, and take care of a home with resourcefulness and discipline. Through a lifelong practice of making things by hand, I have come to understand my world and my place in it, first as a daughter of immigrant parents, then as a wife and a mother, a teacher of schoolchildren, a craft designer, and an author of books about handcrafts. Handcrafts are central to who I am; they are part of the rhythm of my everyday life.

It all began with my parents. My mother was born in Finland at the beginning of the twentieth century and spent her early childhood in Kolhola, a little village near a lake where fir trees outnumbered the people. In winter, she skied across a field to a one-room schoolhouse on finely crafted skis made by her oldest brother. There were four grades in one room. Discipline was strictly enforced. After the academic fundamentals, the girls and boys were divided into two groups. Girls were taught needlework, with more sophisticated handwork introduced as the girls got older: hand sewing and knitting in the first grade, embroidery in the second and third, and by fourth grade, using a treadle sewing machine to make a man's dress shirt. Boys were taught woodworking and cabinetry.

After school my mother returned home to a long dwelling made of hewn logs cut from the forestland owned by her father's family. Once inside the door, hand-loomed runners painted bands of color along the wood floor, which was made of smooth planks cleaned once a week by hand using brushes and fine sand until they were as white as birch bark. Oil lamps and lighted faggots of wood that protruded from specially made holes in the log walls were used to light the rooms during the long winter evenings. On many of these evenings my mother would sit in their glow, embroidering alphabets, geometric patterns, and simple flowers onto thick handwoven linen cloth. The thread for the cloth was spun from flax that grew in the family's fields. On Saturdays, she would help her mother make the beds, pinching the corners of the stiff, snow-white linen into knife-sharp folds and making sure the panels embroidered with monograms were carefully positioned over the blankets.

Her mother and teachers were not the only ones who believed that children should uphold high standards in the home arts. The importance of taking pride in one's work and avoiding idleness were enduring values of social custom that the elders of the village upheld by keeping children under their watchful eye. One summer while my mother was babysitting an infant, soothing him to sleep by pressing her foot against the rocker of a hand-carved cradle, the child's grandfather complained that certainly she could be doing *something* with her hands, too. And summer was certainly the time to try an ambitious project as daylight lasted until midnight, and only heavy woolen shades made from blanket-like cloth could keep the sun from streaming through the windows. Women took advantage of the natural light to sew, knit, crochet, bake, and keep their homes scrupulously organized and well-functioning. In winter, an eerie twilight brightened the sky for only two hours around noon, after which darkness enveloped the land again and all handwork had to be done by the light of an oil lamp or on weekends after chores.

My mother left Finland when she was twelve, immigrating to Canada, and finally finding her way to New York City, where she met and married my father. Born in Dresden, Germany, to a German father and a Danish mother, my father came to America in 1933 when he was twenty-five years old. When he first arrived in New York, he and a friend opened a photography store and portrait studio on Broadway in Manhattan. When the business closed several years later, he turned his trained eye and exacting standards to carpentry, a craft which provided for his growing family.

Although his daily work as a carpenter required large power tools, planes, and rasps, his evenings and weekends were spent making small pieces of furniture and carving sculptures of figures, street scenes, and sailing ships. He would spend hours deftly wielding his gouges, chisels, files, and rifflers, one time carving a small country village that he then painted with oils and set into a frame. I watched, utterly absorbed. Enveloped in the scent of linseed oil and turpentine, I learned how to sharpen a gouge like a razor by moving the tool in a circular motion, pushing the gouge forward before easing up on the tool on the way back across a sharpening stone. I learned to mix paint, experimenting with color on the wooden lids of cigar boxes. One year my father made three wooden banks for my two sisters and me. Each bank was an architectural model of a 1940s-style cottage with a chimney through which we could drop our allowance, listening for the sharp "tink" of the coins as they landed on the rising heap of money inside.

Of the many disciplines my father introduced to me, photography was the one I pursued with the greatest interest. I loved the chemistry involved in processing film and making prints and was enthralled each time a hidden image conjured itself, ghostlike, on a sheet of photo paper. My father and I worked together in our home in Bellerose, New York, where a darkroom was built in our basement and outfitted with the professional equipment originally used in his photography store. During the many hours spent there, my father taught me about the art of photography, as well as about the tools and techniques of printing black-and-white photographs. I also learned, by my father's example, about the importance of commitment to good workmanship, which he explained as a seamless mix of discipline and imagination. He promised that if I put time and effort into learning a skill, I would be rewarded with moments of deep satisfaction, which, in turn, would motivate me to search further for the undiscovered possibilities in the materials with which I worked. I also would discover unexpressed potential in myself and be able to produce work that was beyond my expectations. He was right, but at that time, caught in the confusing labyrinth of rules and cautions and sorting out the variables of taking good pictures and making good prints, I didn't see that as clearly as I do now.

My father's practical philosophy and methodical approach to photography found a complement in my mother's approach to handcrafts. As a child I would sit next to her and practice my embroidery; I would hold a piece of linen and a threaded needle and try to sew straight lines or form the letters of the alphabet, ultimately progressing from a modest sampler to small tablecloths and pillowcases. Today, I'm keenly aware of how my mother ensured an everlasting tie between us by passing on to me the traditions she learned growing up. What stands out is her resourcefulness—like the time she made a ballerina tutu in the style of a Degas sculpture from real parachute silk saved after the war—a quality I was to inherit from her. Encouraged to look to my surroundings for craft supplies, I learned to braid the stems of flowering clover into a bracelet, weave strips of paper into heart-shaped baskets, glue toothpicks together to make a miniature log cabin, and carve bars of Ivory soap into polar bears and rabbits.

My sisters and I led very structured lives that did not include much television. Our weekly viewing was limited to half an hour. An early favorite was *I Remember Mama,* a show about a Scandinavian family that had immigrated to America. Our home life was centered on becoming "well-rounded" and the American dream of getting a good education. When I was in my early twenties, I received my bachelor of science and master of science degrees in elementary education and spent five glorious years in the classroom, weaving crafts into the curriculum as often as they would support learning. It was during those years that my belief that crafts opened children to discovery was forged.

During my second year of teaching I married John Sterbenz, coupling my life and my name with his. John taught mathematics in a suburban high school, but then he became a stockbroker and we moved into our first house in East Setauket, New York. Our lives shifted seismically with the birth of our first daughter, Genevieve. Suddenly, I saw life through the lens of motherhood, and I began to measure my free time in baby naps and dryer loads. When our son Rodney was born, we moved to a house by the bay in Huntington, Long Island, where we would also welcome our second daughter, Gabrielle. As far back as I can remember, my children did arts and crafts of some sort. While still in a high chair, each began to finger-paint and squish clay. As they got older, craft activities like drawing, painting, and model-making moved to the kitchen table, or to the basement or the backyard, and sometimes to the beach across the street from our house where they tie-dyed T-shirts and made sand candles. Crafts seemed to maroon us on these small domestic islands where time slowed down. The kids had fun. I had fun. Boredom disappeared. Joy took hold. As the children became engrossed in their projects, it was as if they entered an inner world and came back out with ideas that went on to be revealed impeccably in 3-D and Technicolor. I kept their projects for years, *years,* not wanting to part with a single one.

During the period when I was fully engaged in child-rearing and home-keeping, I also got together with my friends, meeting weekly at one of our houses to catch up with what was going on in our lives while doing crafts. Whether gathered around a kitchen table or spread out in a living room, I felt the uncomplicated pleasure of belonging, the comfort of sharing laughs and worries, advice, and know-how. Through crafts our friendships deepened and our crafting repertoire grew. Each of us had a special skill that we shared with the others—quilting, sewing, beading, or whatever seemed like fun. One year we made beaded Christmas trees, sitting together for hours and hours, painstakingly counting and threading tiny beads on wire branches and adding ornaments that were only one seed bead wide. As intricate as the maneuvers were, I only remember the easy camaraderie. I look back and wonder how among the demands of organizing a home and raising my children I could focus on so small a project, but I did.

As I look back, I can see that I always carried an unbridled love for making things by hand. I know that I am not alone in this. There are countless numbers of crafters who persist in making things by hand in spite of the fact that our super-automated society can supply us with material goods to meet our every need. We leave these mass-produced items on store shelves and retreat in goodly numbers to work spaces tucked under attic eaves, to kitchen tables cleared of the evening meal, or to professional studios to take up our handwork and make something brand-new. I believe we are motivated to make things by hand for several reasons, but being practical isn't really one of them. Frankly, it is often easier, quicker, and less expensive to simply buy stuff, but we don't. I believe that, in part, we enjoy creating something from scratch, one at a time, no two exactly alike. We take pride in our ability to transform raw materials into objects of aesthetic and functional value that help us realize and express our personal style. We like knowing precisely how to apply a smooth coat of finish, how to restore a chandelier with good bones, or how to wrap a gift and tie a loopy bow.

I believe we draw closer to the heart of the matter when we speak about connection. Connection is a powerful motivator for picking up our set of paints or turning off the television to teach a young child to mold clay. We present our handmade things as gifts, we show them off at fairs, we affix them to our refrigerator doors. We use our hands to establish and solidify the connection to ourselves, to our loved ones, and to the spaces we inhabit. Making something by hand makes us part of a community of kindred spirits who speak the same language. Sitting with friends hour after hour, week after week, gluing photographs and embellishments onto the pages of our scrapbooks or waking before sunrise to pick out the most perfect green roses for a daughter's wedding bouquet when a New York City floral designer would gladly have done it seems, well, excessive . . . and yet necessary, because doing these things keeps us connected.

But the crafting instinct goes even deeper. I believe we are driven by an innate ambition to express ourselves. Creativity powers our search for the perfect bead, the right color paint, the secret to unblemished gilding. While we strive for expert craftsmanship, it is not for its own sake, but rather, to bring a project as perfectly close to our vision of it as we can. When we give our handcrafts to others, we pass on more than a tangible object, we pass on our ideas, initiating a transgenerational relay that is endless and soothing. Making something by hand is our way of announcing our human presence, to become known and to leave a witness of our presence here on earth.

Over my many years of crafting, I made some discoveries that remain as true today as they were when I was a total beginner. Foremost was my interest level; I discovered that when I had a genuine interest in a craft, I had more fun doing it and was likely to achieve better results. The more I learned and practiced, the more accomplished I became.

The materials used in crafting were a definite draw. When I allowed my senses to guide me, I tended to choose new crafts that held my interest for years to become fulfilling, long-lasting pursuits. The strong connection I felt with certain materials motivated me to continue working through the difficult parts of a technique or to try to find out what a particular craft material could do. Photography pulled me in from the moment I saw a sheet of photo paper change from the color of moonlight to layered tones of gray and black and finally to a recognizable image—I never tired of making pictures. The shimmering hand of rayon velvet inspired me to try embossing it with a coil of wire and a household iron.

A particularly appealing aspect of crafts is their accessibility. Any craft I ever tried always had a nonintimidating point of entry. I could begin at an elementary level, or I could build on an existing foundation of experience and skills. I could always proceed at my own pace. If I got stuck, I knew I could find another crafter who would be willing to help me. Crafters consider themselves part of a sharing artistic community. Being a part of a crafting group always made my crafting experiences richer, so I made a habit over the years of starting or joining crafting groups wherever I lived.

Following my intuition has proved reliable in crafting. Intuitive choices unfailingly felt right, not just in surface things like color or pattern, but right in deeper ways too, like choosing to do what was important to me. Intuition told me that it was impossible to create and judge at the same time. Creativity and critique are both essential, each at the appropriate time, but put together, they work against each other. Judgment shut down my creative flow and slowed my work, so I stopped listening to judgment from myself and others and turned instead to my own creative voice.

Of course, I made a lot of mistakes in the beginning. Frankly, I still make them; they are fewer in number than before but often more complicated in nature, though rarely catastrophic enough to warrant starting a project from scratch. I have come to appreciate mistakes as an inevitable part of the crafting process and have also been pleasantly surprised to find that some "mistakes" aren't mistakes at all, simply unexpected outcomes that I end up liking better than the result I first pictured. The ordinary, obvious precautions—practice on scrap materials, read project directions thoroughly, take my time, stay organized, keep my tools in good working order— become so easy to forget as I become engrossed in the creative process. Mishaps of any nature always raise my awareness, providing insights into how I might do something differently next time.

As I continue to craft, I am sure I will make new discoveries to direct and guide me. No doubt, you will develop your own inner guidance system as you go along. Learn to connect with your inner voice, gravitate toward materials you love, and you will find that your crafting hours are filled with fun and satisfaction.

The idea for this book first came to me a decade ago, and it finally took shape in the last four years when a series of serendipitous events moved all the cosmic tumblers into place at one time. I wanted to write a comprehensive one-volume reference work that informed and inspired the crafter, that was based on extensive firsthand experience and in-depth research, that presented a broad cross section of hand-crafts, and that took the crafter from the beginning level of each particular craft to the more advanced. It was a book I looked for and couldn't find anywhere.

My many years of making things revealed that while there would always be new and evolving styles to influence the outward appearance of my craft designs, the underlying set of technical sequences remained fundamentally the same. Alter-ations usually came through advancements made in technology, tool design, or chemical formulas. With this in mind, I decided that instead of presenting a synop-sis of traditional handcrafts or focusing on the hip craft du jour, I would take a deep look at techniques that had stood the test of time, often longer than two centuries, along with those that were developed recently, and present an amalgam of both in a style that was fresh, reliable, and contemporary. To that end, I reexamined many traditional crafts, reinterpreted archaic methods, and when it seemed wise to do so, updated the methods and techniques to arrive at the best methods for ease of craft-ing and the highest possible standard of workmanship and beauty.

The book is organized into seven broad chapters, each featuring a handcraft category that is popular and easy to learn. All that is required to practice any of them is an interest (or better, an enthusiasm), some basic dexterity, and a bit of time. The book works for both the beginner and the veteran crafter, providing a dependable working manual from which to learn a craft from the ground up or develop the expertise to advance to the next level.

The following handcrafts are featured: beading, floral arts, paper crafting, hand printing, decoupage, decorative embellishing, and children's arts and crafts. Each chapter is composed of two distinct parts. "The Heart" speaks to the personal and historical practices of the handcraft, and "The Science" is an illustrated guide to all the salient materials, tools, and techniques. A collection of original projects based on the featured techniques rounds out each chapter. The techniques and projects are presented in easy-to-follow step-by-step directions and are often accompanied by hand-drawn illustrations and diagrams. Each numbered step begins with a one-line synopsis of *what* you are going to do, followed by a clear explanation that details *how* to accomplish the task, including some of the pertinent reasons behind the instruction. Of course, there are many ways to do things; I am presenting techniques that have worked consistently for me. At times, there may appear to be a lot of information, but the format of the book is designed to give you an immediate choice by separating the general crafting goal from the in-depth explanatory text; you can skim the headings to get a sense of what to do next or you can read all of the text. Proceeding in this way, you can establish your own crafting rhythm based on your level of experience. Working tips, troubleshooting guides, and cautions call attention to the more arduous or complicated parts of the crafting process to help you avoid pitfalls. Original patterns and artwork, referenced throughout the text, begin on page 681.

It is my hope that this book will become a trusted resource, one that you reach for when you are seeking reliable information, inspiration for new projects, or just some company along the way as you pursue your crafting.

# Homemade

# CHAPTER ONE

# Beading

## THE HEART

### French Lessons

Even if heaven were real, and measured as
Revelation says, so many cubits this way
      and that,
how gimcrack a place it would be, crammed
      with
its pavements of gold, its gates of pearl and
      topaz,
like a gigantic chunk of costume jewelry.
                    —Margaret Laurence,
                    *The Stone Angel,* 1964

I awoke early one Saturday morning, determined to arrive at the market in Vieux Nice before the inevitable crowds clogged the parking lots and the paths that crisscrossed the central square. I was hoping a particular *vendeuse* (saleswoman) from the previous year would be there, without her impatient scowl but with her jumble of cardboard boxes, lidded tins, kitchen bowls, and worn packets filled with trinkets, beads, and vintage costume jewelry. There was no guarantee, of course, as vendors moved from town to town, but even the possibility of finding beads of any kind was reason enough for me to venture onto the roads in the south of France on a market day in August, a prospect more than a little *effrayant* (frightening) for me. I dressed carefully, hoping to look French, grabbed my dictionary, and walked out to the car carrying a straw basket I found in the kitchen.

The trip to Nice was short but a nail-biter. I had to travel a narrow road that was carved into a steep mountainside. Even before I reached the most treacherous section of the route, my top lip was misted with perspiration, my heart was pounding, and my hands were damp on the steering wheel, which I gripped as tightly as the roots of the ancient olive and cypress trees lining the side of the road. I kept my eyes fixed on every passing kilometer, negotiating the curves and often driving perilously close to the edge of the road where a low stone wall was the only barrier to keep me from plummeting down the jagged stone cliffs to the fields below. I imagined my little Citroën flying out of a turn, straw basket ripping through the air, my scarf fluttering dramatically behind me. Admittedly, five miles per hour was far too slow a speed for any kind of takeoff, but it was enough to annoy the horn-honking driver of the red car that zipped past me at a dizzying speed and the *moto* (motorbike) that tried to overtake us both. *Incroyable!* (Unbelievable!)

I drove into Nice and followed a long line of vehicles to an underground parking lot, which was already choked with cars and *motos* tilted onto kickstands. Improvising, I eased my car into a narrow space, breathed deeply, and began to relax.

A cobblestone path cut a narrow corridor between tall stone-walled houses. I was wearing heels and a dressy skirt, but tottering gracelessly on the cobblestones, I regretted my choice. I arrived at the central square crowded with smartly dressed women carrying baskets. I immediately bought a pair of sandals, and as I changed into them a little dog strained at his collar, nudging my ankle with his wet nose. I reached out to pet him, and he nipped at my hand. His master wagged a finger in my direction, closed his eyes, and shook his head from side to side. *"Elle est méchante,"* he said in a warning tone as he pulled at the leash. I felt scolded, but the man was smiling and I smiled back. I leafed through my dictionary: *méchante*, nasty.

Canvas awnings dappled with sunlight shielded long tables and glass display cases. I walked from one stall to another carried on a current of people. I loved being a part of the bustle and hearing the sound of spoken French. Some people gathered at the back of a van, its banged-up doors flung open, revealing crates of just-picked vegetables and buckets filled with field flowers. The gleam of kitchen paraphernalia caught my eye, and I turned off the main aisle, but it was the flash of silver jewelry that drew me. There were rings and bangles, handwrought and modern in style, embellished with cabochons of black onyx in bezel settings. There were heaps of necklaces made from dyed shells and hammered brass, carved bracelets in fake ivory, and sunglasses. But none of it was what I was looking for. The aisle ended at a table stacked high with American T-shirts and Italian jeans. A *vendeur* (salesman) dressed in a plaid shirt and gray sweater stood wedged knee-deep between a mattress and box spring laid on footed platforms and encased in sagging plastic that seemed to inhale and exhale with the breeze. He announced a sale, between puffs on a cigarette, but no one stopped. It was lunchtime.

The peals of the church bells broke over the marketplace like a wave, folding hollow sounds over one another and pouring across the rooftops. Vendors were packing up for the day, and the outdoor tables in a restaurant across the square were beginning to fill. I had found *no* vintage jewelry. I had not spoken *one word* of French. And I had already begun to dread my torturous drive home. Heading toward my car, I passed a crowd in front of a handwritten sign that announced *Brocante, perles, bracelets, colliers* 1, 2, 3 *rangs, boucles d'oreilles*.

As I mouthed each of the words, I saw the

familiar face of the *vendeuse* from the previous year. Angling my body, I slipped to the front of the crowd and saw the dustiest collection of the most magnificent beaded things on the table. At first, I wanted everything I saw: glass teardrops hanging from a chain, pearls the color of rain threaded on a knotted cord, crystal bracelets in cerulean blue and chartreuse that cast sharp blades of light onto the square of cardboard to which they were pinned. I lifted molded glass berries in a raspberry color attached to a yellowing card and held on to them, adding a dozen strands of round glass beads, a few packets of crystal bicones, and a tarnished silver chain and clasp to my stash. I even closed my fist around a hank of seed beads just to feel the granules of smooth glass, releasing them when my eyes landed on the *bijou* (piece of jewelry) I wanted most.

It was a bracelet threaded with a faded velvet ribbon and laden with charms that looked like miniature porcelain vases with shiny lids. Suddenly a hand reached in and picked up the bracelet, causing its beads to click together sharply. I felt a stab of fear. In a moment, the bracelet was paid for and carried off. Disappointment swam over me.

When I looked up, I met the staring eyes of the *vendeuse* who was gesturing toward the beads that cascaded from my hands. I laid them on the mat in front of her and asked, "*Combien pour le tous?*" ("How much for all?") I heard the rise and fall of her voice, but she spoke so rapidly, all of her words seemed to be touching one another. Flustered, I held out my hand, and with a thumb and two fingers, she picked from the coins scattered on my palm, counting out loud and making disapproving clicking sounds with her mouth as she did. After an elongated "*Voi—là,*" she passed me the bag of beads. I walked away, remembering my new vocabulary word *méchante* and then adding *incroyable*, thrilled that I had found what I was looking for.

As I drove home, I began to plan a bracelet with charms shaped like miniature vases.

My design approach would be simple. First I would spill the loose beads on a cloth to see what random groupings formed on their own. I would squint my eyes to see their color only, pushing some beads together and rolling others apart to create more unusual pairings. Next I would consider the relationships between the shapes and sizes of the beads and change out beads or add others until the beaded stack had a vaselike silhouette. At this point, I would be impatient to start the actual construction of the charms, but I also knew it would be important to walk away from the arrangements to gain a fresh perspective. When I was ready to proceed, I would lose myself completely in the subtle manipulations needed to shape the wrapped-wire loop that would hold the beads of one charm together—gripping the head pin between the jaws of the pliers just so, guiding the wire around its conical nose with a finger, wrapping the wire around the main stem, and smoothing its snipped end with a file to complete a perfectly round wrapped-wire loop, one for each charm. For me, it was the methodical rhythm and exacting nature of the work, simultaneously practical and calming, that drew me back to beading every time.

I was so preoccupied with planning the charm bracelet that it wasn't until I pulled up to our back door that I realized my return drive hadn't been *le voyage infernal* (the trip from Hades) after all. When I got inside, I spread the beads on the dining room table and rolled them around, intending to come

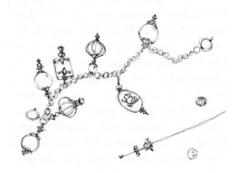

back to them the following morning, but that is not what happened. By midnight, fifteen charms dangled from the silver chain, each one with a wrapped-wire loop that was not perfect, but neat and beautiful enough that I could take pride in it. I was sorry there weren't any more beads to work into charms. Perhaps I would venture out to the market again the next week.

## A Brief History of Beads

For forty thousand years, people have worn beads as adornment, sought healing and protective powers from them, and acquired them as symbols of wealth and faith. Originally produced one at a time, the bead evolved into a mass-produced commodity that has survived the rise and fall of civilizations. That such a small cultural artifact continues to be prized century after century is proof of its universal beauty and appeal.

Archaeologists believe that the first beads were items like seedpods, teeth, bits of ivory, and shells that could be gathered and strung on grass or sinew and worn as adornment and as talismans. Beads found in France made of teeth and shells have been attributed to Neanderthals who lived thirty-eight thousand years ago. In Africa and India, beads made from the shells of ostrich eggs date from 10,000 BC. In North America, native tribes wove the wings of beetles, porcupine quills, feathers, and shells into ceremonial strips or belts, called wampum, that were used as a medium of exchange.

In early agrarian societies, bead making was a domestic pursuit practiced by local artisans. In Neolithic Africa, clay used to make cooking vessels and utensils was hand-shaped into beads and scratched with designs. Holes were pierced with blades of grass and the beads were sun-dried, baked in a fire, and strung. More advanced technology followed. Clay beads called faience were made from finely glazed ceramic in Egypt in 4000 BC. Faience is cited as the forerunner of true glass, an invention of the Bronze Age that would revolutionize bead making. By 1000 BC, a bead-making economy was developing in India.

The thirteenth century began a period of great exploration and migration. Trade routes through Mesopotamia, the Indus Valley, and Central Asia brought together diverse cultures from three continents and created a network for the exchange of goods that extended from the British Isles to China. Precious minerals and metals from local sources became available to distant markets. As commerce developed and flourished, knowledge of bead-making methods spread and helped to establish the intrinsic value of beads as a medium of exchange. India became famous for its lampwork beads and for developing mass production methods that allowed it to supply beads to Africa and Asia and ultimately to the Americas. Several cities in strategic positions along the established trade routes, notably Venice and the Italian island of Murano, Cambay (present-day Khambhat in India), and Morocco, became centers of glassmaking, stonecutting, and jewelry making. India's bead economy suffered from the enormous output of beads from Venice, which by the sixteenth century had become the world capital of glassmaking.

To guard trade secrets and protect the populated city from the threat of fires from the glass furnaces, Venetian guild artisans worked on the island of Murano, a name that has become synonymous with a style of thin-walled glass with colorful whorl patterns. Glass beads were first fashioned to imitate precious jewels; after the Crusades, laws prohibiting the wearing of decorative jewelry led glassmakers to produce rosary beads in quantities that made them a profit. Venetian-produced millefiori, chevron, and lampwork beads were exported worldwide, especially to Africa, where they were bartered for slaves, gold, and ivory.

The demand in Africa for glass beads did not obviate the evolution of indigenous bead-making techniques. Ancient silverwork traditions were practiced in northern Africa.

Ebony beads were carved and decorated with inlays of silver wire in Mauretania, and lacy wire filigree was advanced in Egypt. Explorers who crossed the Atlantic brought trade beads with them. Native American tribes replaced shells, seeds, and quills with European glass seed beads, incorporating the beads into their indigenous decorative arts with hide and sinew and later with cloth and thread.

In the seventeenth century, as the demand for more intricately designed beads grew, master glassmakers established new bead-making centers in Bohemia, Germany, France, the Netherlands, Hebron in Israel, and Purdalpur in India. Of particular note was Bohemia, a city in the Czech Republic, where artisans had been making glass beads of incomparable quality and variety since the ninth century.

Beads also came to be used as ornamentation on clothing; beaded styles changed from decade to decade. During the Victorian and Edwardian eras, couturiers sewed thousands of tiny jet beads onto gowns and royal garments. In European fashion houses and passementerie workshops, the smallest beads, sometimes the size of a grain of sand, were hand-sewn to fabric, producing patterns with gradient color and sparkle. Flappers in the 1920s popularized garments with long beaded fringe.

An American innovation that transformed the beading industry was the development of plastic, credited to Alexander Parkes, who demonstrated it at the Great International Exhibition in London in 1862. Plastic was an affordable and versatile product that could be used to simulate the look and feel of more valuable materials, such as tortoiseshell, horn, and ivory. Costume jewelry made of Bakelite, an early plastic, would become highly collectible in the late twentieth century.

As developments in bead manufacturing took place, beading gained momentum as a social pastime. Inspired by the availability of beads and beading kits, women's magazines began supplying instructions and patterns.

Beading fads included loom weaving in the 1950s, love beads in the 1960s, and beaded macramé in the 1970s. Later, the Japanese bead manufacturer Miyuki introduced Delicas, a small, evenly sized drawn-glass bead distinguished by its cylindrical shape, large hole, and exceptional uniformity; this little bead spurred a revival of bead weaving techniques common to earlier cultures, especially to Native Americans.

Today, beading is practiced in America, Europe, and Asia by crafters and also by needleworkers who combine embroidery, crochet, and knitting techniques with those of beading to embellish or to construct purses, sweaters, bracelets, and earrings. Runway styles consistently elicit fashionable responses in the beading community. Bead artisans rise to the challenge to interpret trends such as the "chunky" look, supported by information supplied in how-to books, personal blogs, and crafting groups and drawing on an unlimited supply of beading materials and tools from all corners of the world.

## THE SCIENCE

Beading is one of the most addictive crafts I have ever practiced. In mere moments, the color and sparkle of crystal beads or the soft luster of pearls can captivate me, inspiring my imagination and my desire to collect beads of every description. Although I usually begin a bead shopping expedition with a fairly clear idea of the kind of jewelry I want to make, I find that as soon as I am in a bead store, I depart from the plan and fill my tray with all of the enticing orbs I see. I buy beads that I have no immediate plans for, telling myself that I will find some way to string or wire them. I am ready to learn whatever new beading technique is needed to justify buying a splendid find. My shopping philosophy has given me shelves stacked with partitioned boxes of beads and findings, drawers brimming with vials and containers, and bowls of beads that I can set out on the table to urge me to sit down and begin beading.

Certain beading maneuvers must be practiced again and again to do them well. Frustration is natural when you are learning new skills, and patience has never been my strength; it was my sheer love of beads that gave me the discipline to keep working at new techniques until I improved. For example, you'll need to work wire loop after wire loop in order to get one as perfectly round as you want it to be. There was the time I endured the tedium of unraveling row after row of a bead weaving project in order to replace one tiny cracked bead, but in doing so, I finally understood the weaving technique. This technical breakthrough made me a better crafter.

Repetition also has its downside. I find that when I try to force a design decision or rush through a project, I am inevitably disappointed in the result. Merely finishing a project cannot be the goal if you are to do your best work. If you're tired or stuck, take a break and come back to your project when you are rested and have a fresh perspective. It is likely that in the interim creative solutions will serendipitously present themselves when you are not thinking about beading at all.

I have included many effective shortcuts in this chapter along with a broad range of straightforward techniques that will enable you to make a nearly infinite number of pieces of beaded jewelry—from a crystal cuff bracelet to a pendant necklace to a gold ring with a tiny jewel—and establish a foundation from which you can design your own originals.

This chapter is meant to teach and inspire. It includes three methods of beading: wiring, stringing, and weaving. All three methods have certain beads, findings, and tools in common, and these are introduced first. Once you venture into a particular method, however, you'll need to know about additional materials and tools that are required for more specialized techniques. If you are new to beading,

you may prefer to begin with stringing, one of the most elementary techniques, but one from which you will be able to create an infinite number of unique jewelry designs. Stringing beads is easy to visualize and learn; you may find it takes you a bit more effort to grasp some of the technical or more subtle aspects of wiring and weaving. As you become more skilled, your preoccupation with the mechanics will recede and your creativity will emerge, resulting in beautiful pieces of jewelry. When the transition from learning to creating is made, you will see beads everywhere; you will be on the lookout for a perfect little bead or clasp; and you might even conjure beaded charms for a bracelet after seeing a pretty bracelet at a village market.

## All About Beads

Advancements in bead manufacturing have placed a large variety of affordable, gemstone-quality beads within easy reach. But having so many colors, textures, shapes, and sizes to choose from can also be a bit overwhelming. Knowing the distinguishing characteristics of different beads can help you make good choices for your projects.

I have found that the best way to choose beads is to handle them. The first thing I notice about any bead is its color and finish; beads made from naturally occurring minerals have color gradations, whereas dyed beads are nearly perfect in their color distribution. Texture is another important design consideration, and I inspect the surface of the bead quite carefully. Fluorite beads, for instance, have natural occlusions and hairline cracks that are visually appealing, but molded glass beads with cracks are vulnerable to shattering, so I leave these behind. The weight of a bead will affect my choice of strand material and also drives the kinesthetic value of a piece. Consider, for example, the heaviness of chunky quartz beads as compared to the weightlessness of pearls—each one is pleasurable in its own way.

## Types of Beads

There are times when a bead is so well made, it is difficult to know what it is made of. Simply tap the bead gently on a hard surface. Broadly speaking, glass makes a higher-pitched "tink" than plastic, which sounds dull. High-quality glass and plastic beads are seamless. Of course, cost plays a role in any buying decision, and you will notice that beads made from semiprecious stones are more expensive than most comparably sized glass beads; however, within these classifications, quality and cost vary widely. When buying metal beads, you'll find it helpful to know the differences between such terms as *plated, filled, washed,* and *vermeil,* because appearances do not reveal them. Finally, always buy good-quality beads. Good-quality beads assembled with technical expertise will result in more beautiful pieces of jewelry.

## Working Tips: Getting Ready to Bead

Beading is easier when your materials are organized and your tools are in good working condition.

- **Organize your supplies.**
  Smooth a flat-weave cotton cloth or a rubberized or flocked bead mat over your work surface to prevent your beads from rolling and bouncing and to make it easier to pick up single beads. Organize your beads in partitioned boxes with lids that shut tightly or keep them in separate vials with screw tops. Consider using a beading board, which will allow you to lay out your bead designs before stringing or wiring them. Keep your tools within easy reach, either mounted on hooks on a wall or laid out on your work surface.
- **Work in good light.**
  Beads and bead holes are small so good light is essential. Work in a nonglare light and use magnification to avoid eyestrain. If you do a lot of work with tiny beads or fine wire, consider getting a special lamp. I use one that has a magnifying glass attached to a flexible arm that allows me to move the lens wherever I need it.
- **Plan ahead for errors.**
  As careful as you try to be in your work, assume that you are going to make some errors and plan ahead. Resist the temptation to rush through your work. Measure and measure again. Double-check a stringing sequence. Head pins and crimp beads cannot be reused if you make a mistake; keep extras on hand so you can start fresh.
- **Think about safety.**
  While beading does not pose industrial-sized dangers, some beading tasks do require extra precautions. Wear safety glasses to protect your eyes when working with wire, as snipped wire ends can go flying. When working with glues or adhesives, keep the room well ventilated. Maintain your tools, using them for the tasks they are designed to do. Use nippers to cut thin wire only, not extremely hard memory wire, which can ruin a nipper blade. Keep children and pets away from tools and supplies.

## Glass Beads

Glass beads are the most abundant kind of bead. They are reasonably priced and available in a wide variety of shapes, sizes, and colors. All glass beads are made in an annealing process. In this process, glass is heated and melted with a torch or in a kiln and then allowed to cool slowly over a mandrel (or core wire) or in a mold that determines the size, shape, and surface character of the bead.

- **Lampwork (or flamework) beads**
  Made one at a time by hand, each lampwork bead is formed when colored glass cane is heated by a torch until it melts and then wrapped around a thin rod called a mandrel. When colored glass canes are melted and drizzled in patterns onto the glass bead base, they can form intricate and raised designs in the shape of flowers, stripes, polka dots, and geometric patterns. You will recognize well-made lampwork beads by their raised designs in glass; those that are the widest and thickest where they connect to the bead base are best because the added designs are much less likely to break off when the bead is handled.
- **Fused beads**
  Produced by hand or machine, fused beads are made by melting layers of glass together in a vacuum or kiln. Fused beads show the areas where the layers of colored glass are joined. Typical of this type of bead are white-heart beads, which are made from white cane over which a thin coating of colored glass is applied. Also in this category are dichroic glass beads in which two planes of colored glass are fused and often coated with a random pattern of metal oxide and then covered with a smooth glass layer. *Dichroic* is a gemological term that refers to any mineral that naturally presents two colors when viewed from different angles.

- **Molded (or pressed) beads**
  Produced by machine, molded beads are formed by pouring molten glass into a mold and allowing it to cool slowly; when the glass is cool and hard, the bead is removed. Molded beads are available in a broad variety of shapes and sizes, including flowers, leaves, and animals. The Czech Republic and Germany are well known for their high-quality molded beads. Druk beads, which are perfectly round, are very popular pressed glass beads from the Czech Republic. In lesser-quality molded beads, the seams from the molds can be seen.
- **Fire-polished beads**
  Made by machine, fire-polished glass beads are faceted and then placed in a kiln to melt and soften the sharp angular edges. They come in the same shapes and sizes as leaded crystal beads, but they do not contain lead and are generally less expensive.

## Seed Beads

Produced by machine, seed beads are made when glass rods are fed into a steel die that casts their slightly rounded shape while a mandrel forms their holes. Available in a wide variety of colors, sizes, and finishes, seed beads are sold on hanks (bundles of 8 to 12 beaded strands) and by the gram in vials and in bags.

- **Czech and Japanese seed beads**
  Known for their donut shape, the majority of high-quality seed beads, also called rocailles, comes from the Czech Republic and Japan. Those made in the Czech Republic are rounder in shape, and those from Japan are known to be more angular. Czech seed beads are suited to looser stitches in bead weaving, while Japanese seed beads are suited to tighter stitches. It is important to note that both Czech and Japanese seed beads are known for

their consistency in shape and size; if you intend to use seed beads manufactured in other countries, or are doing tight bead weaving stitches, be sure to edit your beads carefully, picking out misshapen beads to avoid weaving them into the beaded fabric.

- **Cylinder (or tubular) beads**
While often classified as seed beads, Japanese cylinder beads, or Miyuki beads, are unlike round donut-shaped seed beads; rather, they are cylindrical in shape—short tubes that have sharper, more precise edges. Prized by weavers, the bead has a flat end that allows the beads to line up in precise rows and columns. Extra-large holes and thin walls make it possible to pass a thread through this bead several times, a necessity in weaving.

- **Bugle beads**
Bugle beads are longer than they are thick, giving them the shape of tubes. Although they come in a variety of lengths, they are approximately ⅛" (0.3 cm) or longer. A faceted bugle bead comes in a two-cut style, which has two flat sides, and a three-cut style, which has an uneven number of sides. Available in a wide variety of colors and finishes, bugle beads are typically used for making tassels or for the square stitch.

- **Crow and pony beads**
Crow beads look like oversized seed beads and are available in glass and plastic. Cut from tubes and then tumbled and polished, crow beads are commonly found in two sizes: 6 mm diameter with a 3 mm hole and 9 mm diameter with a 5 mm hole. Pony beads also look like large seed beads but are smaller than crow beads. They are available in many colors and finishes and are sometimes referred to as size 8/0 or 6/0 seed beads.

## Crystal Beads

Made of lead-infused glass, crystal beads are available in a wide range of sizes, cuts, and colors. Valued for their sparkle and transparency, crystal beads have faceted surfaces that are cut by machine or by hand in a process that is made easier because of the lead content. Often referred to by their shapes, such as a bicone, briolette, and teardrop, crystal beads are one of the most popular bead types. Austrian and Czech crystals are particularly sought after, although their high quality makes them costly. Japanese crystals are of a good quality overall but have less precisely cut facets. Chinese crystals are of a lower quality and have unsubstantiated lead counts.

## Cubic Zirconia (CZ) Beads

A crystalline form of zirconium oxide, cubic zirconia beads are synthetic, yet convincing, substitutes for natural gemstones. In its early development, CZ, as it has come to be known, looked too bright and fake. Scientific advances helped produce a CZ that is more lustrous and diamond-like. Beads made of CZ are prized for their sparkle, cut, and color range.

## Precious and Semiprecious Stones

According to the Gemological Institute of America, a gemstone must be beautiful and possess a number of quantifiable attributes: durability, rarity, and portability. Of the more than three thousand different crystals, minerals, and biogenic materials known, diamonds, rubies, sapphires, and emeralds are four of the most well-known gemstones. Because the value of any gemstone is dependent upon its quality, not its name (a sapphire, for example, can sell for less than $100 per carat and a tourmaline can sell for $20,000 per carat), the Gemological Institute of America does not use the terms *semiprecious* or *precious* in its descriptions of stones.

# Matching Months and Birthstones

Gemstones are said to be imbued with mystical properties. Most scholars trace the tradition of associating a month of the year with a gemstone to a biblical reference to the breastplate of Aaron, a religious ceremonial garment that featured gemstones representing the twelve tribes of Israel. The gemstones also corresponded to the twelve signs in the zodiac. Through the centuries and across different cultures, different lists that match month and gemstone have been devised.

| Month | Traditional | Modern | Old Testament | Spanish | Jewish |
|---|---|---|---|---|---|
| January | Garnet | Garnet | Jasper | Hyacinth Yellow zircon Red zircon | Garnet |
| February | Amethyst | Amethyst | Sapphire | Amethyst | Amethyst |
| March | Aquamarine Bloodstone | Aquamarine | Chalcedony | Jasper | Jasper |
| April | Diamond | Diamond | Emerald | Sapphire | Sapphire |
| May | Emerald | Emerald | Sardonyx | Agate | Agate Carnelian Chalcedony |
| June | Pearl Alexandrite Moonstone | Alexandrite | Sardonyx | Emerald | Emerald |
| July | Ruby | Ruby | Chrysolite | Onyx | Onyx |
| August | Peridot Sardonyx | Peridot | Beryl Emerald Aquamarine | Carnelian | Carnelian |
| September | Sapphire | Blue sapphire | Topaz | Chrysolite | Chrysolite |
| October | Opal Tourmaline Rose zircon | Rose zircon | Chrysoprase | Aquamarine | Aquamarine |
| November | Golden topaz Citrine | Golden topaz | Bloodstone | Topaz | Topaz |
| December | Turquoise Blue topaz Blue zircon Lapis lazuli | Blue zircon | Amethyst | Ruby | Ruby |

Chart © 2006–2007 Jewelry-Design-Gemstone.com. Printed with permission.

The term *semiprecious* is widely used, however, throughout the beading industry to distinguish beads made of naturally forming materials from those made of glass, leaded crystal, metal, and plastic. The "big four" gemstones are almost never made into beads, but semiprecious stones are made into beads in an array of shapes and sizes and are widely available from bead suppliers.

- **Quartz**
  Quartz is a crystalline mineral that comes in a vast and affordable variety of transparent, translucent, and opaque stones that can be cut, sanded, and polished and made into beads that are often used instead of more expensive stones. Amethyst, citrine, and ametrine are examples of transparent quartz crystal that are known for their exquisite color. Amethyst ranges in color from pale lilac to deep purple; citrine is a golden to lemon yellow; and ametrine is a mix of purple and yellow. Quartz stones can also be permanently dyed in an irradiation process that infuses permanent color.
- **Rock crystal**
  Valued for its water-clear transparency, rock crystal, while not flawless, is a popular choice for cut-crystal glassware, as well as for beads used in jewelry making.
- **Rutilated quartz**
  While beads made of rock crystal are prized for transparency, those made of rutilated quartz are valued for their inclusions—needlelike rutiles (a titanium dioxide mineral) that are scattered in patterns inside the beads.
- **Chalcedony quartz**
  Quartz that is formed from a number of finely grained microcrystals is called chalcedony. Beads made from this mineral have even color, opacity, and patterns, as seen in such examples as agate with its parallel bands of color and moss agate with its plantlike patterns. Some chalcedonies include quartz stones that are translucent and have patterns, such as carnelian with its brownish-orange color and chrysoprase with its translucent bright apple-green color.
- **Jade**
  Jade has enjoyed a rich cultural history. As early as 3000 BC, jade was known in China as *yu* (royal gem). Having a greasy luster, jade is most recognized for its distinct green color; it also comes in shades of white, black, gray, yellow, orange, and violet. There are two forms, nephrite and jadeite; both have similar properties, but jadeite (the imperial jade) is more valued.

### Pearls

Several kinds of pearls are used in beading. Each one is distinguished by its origin: natural, cultured, freshwater, or faux.

- **Natural pearls**
  Natural pearls are grown inside an oyster or other mollusk and are known foremost

## Defining Nacre

Nacre is secreted by oysters and mollusks to both smooth the inside of their shells and to defend against the irritation caused by a foreign object; when nacre builds up in layers around an irritant, such as a grain of sand, a pearl forms. The value of a pearl is judged by the quality of its orient (the soft iridescence caused by the refraction of light through the layers of nacre) and its luster (the reflection of light off the surface of the nacre).

for their color, ranging from champagne, peach, rose, and purple; they are also dyed other colors, such as bright orange and metallic green. Pearls are valued for their luster and surface made up of nacre, whose quality and thickness determine the value of the pearl.

- **Cultured pearls**
  Cultured pearls are artificially cultivated in saltwater pearl farms found predominantly in Japan. An irritant, such as a shell bead, is introduced into a mussel, which is returned to the water. The mussel secretes layers of nacre around the bead, resulting in a cultured pearl. It can take from 2 to 5 years for the pearl to form.
- **Freshwater pearls**
  Freshwater pearls are artificially cultivated in freshwater pearl farms found predominantly in China. They are available in such forms as stick, angel wing, cross, and coin shapes, as well as in near-round, drop, oval, button, nugget, rich, and baroque shapes.
- **Faux pearls**
  Faux pearls are made completely by machine from glass, ceramic, shell, and plastic that is coated with materials that mimic the iridescence (nacre) of natural pearls. The coating on glass beads is a mixture of ground-up fish scales and varnish (known as pearl essence), formulated by a seventeenth-century Frenchman named Jacquin. The pearl essence is actually called guanine, which gives fish scales their color. Today synthetic pearl essence is produced through a chemical process and is used to introduce luminosity in lipstick and eye shadow.

## Organic (or Biogenic) Beads

Beads made from living (or once living) organisms are characterized by their unique shapes, color, and sizes. The substance for a biogenic bead may be found on the surface of the land or under the sea, or harvested from a plant or animal, but the manufacture of the bead is a human enterprise.

- **Coral**
  Coral is a marine organism that exists in a colony that secretes calcium carbonate to form its hard polyp-shaped skeleton, building up coral reefs in tropical waters. Prized for its distinctive shapes that look like the twigs and branches of a young sapling, coral is available in rich colors—cardinal red, red-orange, deep pink, and, most rare, black.
- **Shell**
  Inexpensive, light-weight, and abundant, beads made of shell have appeared in many guises across the centuries—as perfectly round, iridescent mother-of-pearl beads, which are made from the pearlescent inner nacre layer of a mollusk shell, to the thinly sliced disks and tube-shaped beads made of heishi shell.
- **Resin**
  Made from the secretions discharged in the sap of the pine tree, resin beads often retain tiny insects and random bits of flora that are caught in the hardening sap. Difficult to find and expensive to buy, resin beads move in and out of popularity.
- **Bone and horn**
  Many beads made from bone and horn originate in the Philippines and Indonesia. The raw material is harvested from such animals as cows and goats and shaped by hand to make a wide variety of light-weight beads in natural and dyed colors.
- **Ivory**
  Harvesting natural ivory from elephants is illegal, making vintage ivory pieces rare and expensive; scrimshaw is one surviving form of carved and engraved ivory, but it is difficult to find and expensive to buy. A convincing substitute for

ivory is vegetable "ivory," a plant material derived from the South American palm nut that is used to make decorative items, including beads.

- **Ebony and other woods**
  The dense, dark, hardwood called India ebony or Ceylon ebony, depending upon its origin, is prized for its rich black color and fine grain that can be polished to a satin finish. Made in small geometric and sculptural shapes, ebony beads have understated elegance. Other woods, such as maple, bamboo, and teak, are also used to make beads in a wide variety of geometric shapes and sizes.
- **Jet**
  Hard jet is an organic material derived from wood that has decomposed under extreme pressure over thousands of years. Black in color, jet is easy to cut and polish. Jet was used in making mourning jewelry and was especially popular during the reign of Queen Victoria.
- **Paper**
  Paper beads are often made by hand of recycled paper, a process that reveals their humble beginnings through bumpy textures. Patterned paper can be layered over paper beads and the surface coated with varnish in a decoupage process to create the illusion of a smooth, porcelain finish.
- **Clay**
  Ceramic and polymer clays play popular roles in bead construction. Requiring little previous sculpting experience, clay beads can be fashioned by hand and cured in a home oven or in a kiln. Beads made of porcelain clay can be bisque-fired and glazed.

### Plastic Beads

Machine made and relatively inexpensive, plastic beads are available in many shapes, sizes, and colors. Many are designed to replicate the characteristics of more expensive stones and minerals. Handsome plastic beads can be used to create pieces of jewelry with glamorous and vintage style. Light-weight and easy to work with, good-quality plastic beads can be combined with other types of beads to reduce the weight of an elaborate piece of beaded jewelry and to lower the overall cost.

### Metal Beads

Easily shaped in hand and machine processes, metal beads are available in an extremely wide variety of shapes, sizes, textures, and patinas. Familiar metals for beads include sterling silver, silver plate, gold plate, gold-filled, pewter, copper, and brass. Metal beads have a unique hand—they are cool to the touch. Beads made of precious metals are usually tooled and polished to highlight their natural color. Less expensive metals, such as brass and pewter, are often molded into balls, ovals, rods, and charms that have patterns in relief on their surfaces. Base metals might be concealed by a thin layer of electroplated silver or nickel or disguised by a web of intricate wirework, glazed enamel, or machine work, as seen in such beads as Bali, cloisonné, and crenulated brass.

## Defining Cloisonné

*Cloisonné* is a French term that refers to a colorfully patterned metal-based bead that uses wire soldered to the surface to define the design and hold the enameled colors apart. The wire is manipulated to form the outlines of a simple design. The spaces are filled with powdered glaze, which is fired to a smooth, porcelain-like finish.

Bead Sizes and Shapes

Beads come in many sizes and shapes. Bead sizes are measured in millimeters. Use the actual-size chart below to measure the diameter of round beads. You can place a round bead directly on top of the circles printed on the page until you find the best match.

Round Beads in Millimeters
(shown actual size)

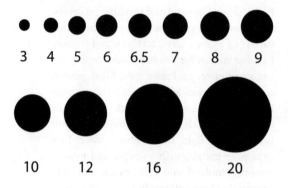

3  4  5  6  6.5  7  8  9

10  12  16  20

One or more measurements may be given to indicate the size of a bead that is not round. For example, a 2 mm cube is denoted in only one measurement because all sides of the cube are equal, but a leaf-shaped bead may be identified as 8 mm wide × 11 mm long × 2 mm thick. A traditional ruler marked with millimeters can give you a rough estimate of a bead's dimensions, but accurate sizing is done with a micrometer, a tool designed for precise measuring of beads in millimeters and inches. A bead can be measured from one end of the drilled hole to the other, as well as across its length, width, and thickness.

The shape of a bead often appears in its name, for example, crystal briolette. It is helpful to understand bead shapes and standard measurements when ordering beads online because photos can be misleading. New bead shapes are being developed all the time by designers and gem cutters who make unique geometric shapes and sculptural forms.

## Common Bead Shapes

| Shape | Name | How to Measure |
|---|---|---|
| | Bean | Length × width × thickness, measured roughly |
| | Bicone (or lantern-cut) | Diameter × length |
| | Briolette | Diameter × length × thickness when flat; diameter × length for teardrop shapes |

| Shape | Name | How to Measure |
|-------|------|----------------|
|  | Cabochon | Across the dome |
|  | Chip | Diameter × length or width × thickness, measured roughly |
|  | Corrugated | Diameter × length, measured roughly |
|  | Cube | From one end of the bead hole to the other |
|  | Dagger | Length × width |
|  | Disk | Diameter × thickness |
|  | Donut | Inner and outer diameters, thickness |
|  | Keishi | Width × thickness, measured roughly |
|  | Keystone | Length, width at narrow end, and width at wide end |

## Common Bead Shapes

| Shape | Name | How to Measure |
|---|---|---|
| | Melon | Diameter × length |
| | Nugget | Length × thickness, measured roughly |
| | Oval | Length × width × thickness |
| | Pipe | Length × diameter |
| | Potato | Length × thickness |
| | Pressed glass bead | Length × width, measured roughly |
| | Rectangle | Length × width × thickness |
| | Rondelle | Diameter × thickness |

| Shape | Name | How to Measure |
|-------|------|----------------|
| | Round (or druk) | Diameter |
| | Rice | Length × thickness |
| | Seed bead | Diameter |
| | Square | Length of one side |
| | Teardrop | Diameter × length |
| | Teardrop, faceted | Diameter × length |
| | Tube (also called cylinder) | Diameter × length |

## Seed Bead Equivalents

Seed beads come in a range of sizes from 1/0 to 24/0; however, beaders typically work with seed beads in sizes from 6/0 to 15/0. Because there is a lack of standardization among manufacturers, it is helpful to handle seed beads before choosing them for a project.

| Aught Size | Diameter in Millimeters |
|:---:|:---:|
| 6/0 | 3.3 |
| 8/0 | 2.5 |
| 9/0 | 2.2 |
| 10/0 | 2.0 |
| 11/0 | 1.8 |
| 12/0 | 1.7 |
| 13/0 | 1.5 |
| 14/0 | 1.4 |
| 15/0 | 1.3 |

## Common Bead Hole Placements

The position of the hole in the bead is determined by the material from which it is made, the bead shape, and the aesthetic effect desired. Foremost, a bead hole must facilitate the security of the bead and orient it attractively on the beaded construction. For example, hole placement on metal and plastic beads is more varied because these materials are more durable than beads made of crystal and glass. Beads shaped like keystones and briolettes, which are commonly head-drilled, are more prone to breaking than beads drilled through their centers, requiring extra care as strand material is passed through their holes whose size determines both the thickness and kind of strand material that can be threaded through them and which, in turn, affects the bead's orientation on the jewelry—a head-drilled briolette hangs lower on a strand than a center-drilled round bead.

Center drilled: the hole runs through the middle of the bead.

Axis drilled: the hole runs through the longest axis of the bead.

Side drilled: the hole runs through a wide axis of the bead.

Diagonally drilled: the hole runs through the bead on a diagonal.

Head drilled: the hole runs through the tip of the bead.

Top drilled: the hole runs through the top of the bead.

Bottom drilled: the hole runs through the bottom of the bead.

## Bead Finishes

The surface texture and sheen of a bead are design elements that can be utilized to great advantage. Refer to the chart for common terms used to describe the patina and finish of beads. Some terms are strictly technical and others are descriptive of the beads they identify.

## Materials and Tools

Beads may define and characterize your project, but certain other supporting components are essential to your jewelry creations. Metal pieces that join the beads to one another are called findings. Various specialized tools are used to cut, shape, and attach findings, and even to make them from wire, if you are so

## Common Bead Finishes

| Term | Description |
|---|---|
| Crazed or checked | Appearance of hairline cracks on the surface of the bead. |
| Dyed | Permanent color artificially infused into the bead material. |
| Etched | Fine lines, patterns, and shapes scratched into or engraved onto the surface of the bead. |
| Feathered | Appearance of white jagged and irregular fractures in the interior of the bead. |
| Fire | The play of light and color on or within a bead as a result of light dispersion. |
| Frosted | Appearance of an ice-colored film or coating on the surface of a bead. |
| Greasy | Smooth, cool, slippery quality of a bead. Jade is greasy. |
| Iridescent | Appearance of spectral colors in the interior of the bead and on its exterior; seen in rainbow beads (also called aurora borealis or AB) and iris beads. |
| Lustrous | Glowing quality of light as it is reflected off or refracted through a bead. Pearls are lustrous. |
| Metallic | Appearance of shine and luster as found on metals through polishing, coating, or electroplating a surface. |
| Mirrored | Appearance of a bright surface illuminated by reflected light, as seen in silver-lined rocailles, Czech fire-polished beads, and precious-metal beads. |
| Opalescent | Appearance of a shimmering milky or cloudy color in the bead. |
| Satin | Shiny, smooth finish, similar to satin fabric. |
| Transparence | Quality and intensity of light as it passes through a bead. |

## Findings at a Glance

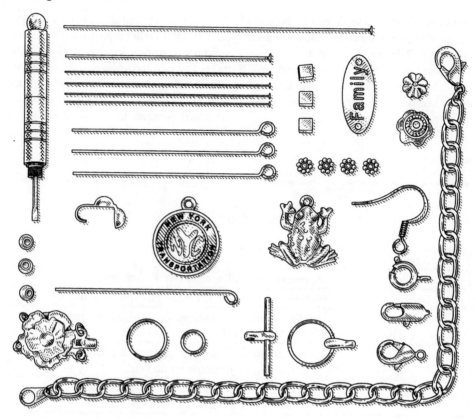

inclined. Bead stringing and weaving techniques use thread, cord, and other natural or synthetic fibers to join beads together, and pieces made by these methods may include metal findings as well. This section provides an overview of the various supplies and tools you will need to begin beading.

### Findings

While small in size, findings play a pivotal role in determining the movement and security of all the separate parts of a finished piece. Choose findings that coordinate with the size, scale, proportion, and style of your piece of jewelry, matching metals and finishes.

- **Jump rings**

Jump rings are small metal hoops that are used to connect different components together in a piece of jewelry, such as a wire-looped bead to a link on a chain. Available in a variety of gauges and finishes, jump rings come in three styles: open, closed, and split.

An open jump ring has a split in the

hoop, which allows the ring to be opened and closed with two pairs of pliers at any point in the design process.

A closed jump ring is a continuous hoop with no split. This ring cannot be opened or closed, but separate components can be secured to it. It can handle weightier components than open jump rings can.

A split jump ring resembles a key ring with a one-and-a-half wind of stiff wire that must be pried apart to attach other components to it. A split jump ring can be added or removed at any point in your designing. Split ring pliers make this type of jump ring much easier to manipulate.

- **Head pins and eye pins**
Head pins and eye pins are used to attach beads to a chain, an ear wire, or to other beads. Available in a variety of gauges, lengths, and finishes, both kinds of pins resemble large straight pins with one blunt end and one shaped end.

A head pin has a flat, ball-shaped, or decorated metal stop at the opposite end of the pin to hold the beads in place.

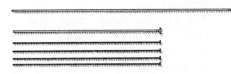

An eye pin has an eye-shaped loop at one end to hold the beads on the pin. Use the eye-shaped loop to attach additional jump rings, chains, or beaded components.

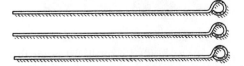

- **Clasps**

Clasps are two-part components that are attached to opposite ends of beaded strands to secure the ends together when the jewelry is worn. Available in a wide array of sizes and finishes, clasps can be either mechanical, such as spring-ring, box, barrel, and lobster-claw clasps, or nonmechanical, such as toggle, hook-and-eye, and S-shaped clasps. Mechanical clasps are more secure for attaching necklaces; nonmechanical clasps are suited to bracelets as they require just one hand to latch and unlatch.

- **Chains**

Made of connecting links, chains are available in an infinite number of styles and finishes. The end links are connected to a two-part clasp. Decorative beads, charms, and other ornaments are attached to the links with wrapped-wire loops and jump rings.

- **Earring clasps and hooks**

Clip-ons, leverbacks, posts, French, kidney, and fishhooks are popular components for connecting beaded earrings to the ear.

- Bails

Bails, such as hook-and-loop bails and fold-overs, are connectors that allow a single bead designed as a pendant to be suspended from a strand. Bails can be made by hand from wire.

- **Crimp beads and tubes**
Crimp beads and tubes are hollow and are made in a variety of metals, including base metal, sterling silver, silver-plated, gold-plated, and gold-filled, as well as copper and brass. They are used to secure the ends of nylon-coated beading wire to another finding, such as a clasp, or to fix a bead in place anywhere on its length. Although crimp beads and tubes can be used on some other stringing materials, they are generally used on strands that cannot be knotted. Choose a crimp bead diameter large enough to accommodate a double pass of beading wire when attaching a clasp or a closed jump ring. Crimps can be concealed with a crimp bead cover.

- **Crimp-style fold-over clamps**
Suited to finishing off the ends of ribbon or other flat strand material, crimp-style fold-over clamps are made in narrow widths and work by trapping the ends of a strand material between their parts when they are clamped shut.

- **Crimp bead covers**
Resembling small, round, hollow beads that are open on one side, crimp bead covers are used to enclose crimp beads and tubes that are already secured to the strand material, concealing them and adding a professional finish.

- **Scrimp findings and Scrimp tool**

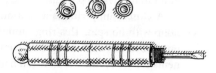

Available in round, oval, and bullet shapes, Scrimp findings serve the same purpose as crimp beads or crimp tubes. To secure a Scrimp finding, a tiny set screw is loosened using a Scrimp tool to allow the wire to pass through the barrel and then tightened to secure it inside the barrel.

- **Clamshell with hook**

Used to cover an end knot on a strand, this finding opens like a clamshell and has a hook that connects the closed clamshell to other findings, such as a jump ring or a clasp.

- **Bead tips**
Available in a narrow range of sizes, bead tips are used to attach strands to clasps while concealing the cut end of the strand material. Bead tips come in conical, barrel, and dome shapes that have hooks or loops onto which a clasp can be attached. Some bead tips are called bead caps.

- **Spacer beads**

Spacer beads are small, flat beads that are placed between two beads to keep them from rubbing against one another.

They are made in a variety of metals and finishes and come in decorative shapes and surface textures, such as twisted hoops, flowers, and embossed patterns, that can add a decorative accent between beads.

Metal Wire

An alternative to buying findings and components to connect separate parts of your jewelry designs is to fashion your own findings from metal wire. Wire for findings is chosen for its metal composition, gauge or thickness, finish, and hardness. Techniques and projects in this chapter use round wire in their construction, but novelty shapes, including half-round, triangular, and square, will give you new options. The type of metal a wire is made from affects its color and sheen, not to mention its price.

- **Gold**
  The purity of gold is measured in karats. A hallmark debossed in the gold itself denotes the number of karats, indicated by a number followed by the abbreviation *kt*. Gold marked *24kt* has twenty-four parts of or is 100 percent pure gold; it is the standard by which all other gold is measured. Because pure gold is soft,

the gold components used in jewelry are usually an alloy composed of gold and some other metal. The alloy hardens the gold and facilitates bending and shaping by hand or tools. Commonly, 14-karat gold, which has 14 parts pure gold and 10 parts of some another metal, is used. It is the other metals added that give gold its beautiful range of color, introducing such alloys as green gold, which is a mix of 75 percent gold, 20 percent silver, and 5 percent copper.

- **Gold-filled**
  A gold-filled wire is accompanied by a reference to its metal content. For example, a gold-filled wire that is marked *10kt/20* means that one-twentieth of the weight of the overall piece is 10-karat gold, and this amount has been bonded or electroplated to the core wire, which can be made of copper or sterling silver. Gold-filled wire is less expensive than pure gold.

- **Gold-plated and silver-plated**
  Plated wire consists of a wire core made of a base metal, such as copper, nickel, or aluminum, that has been coated or bonded with a micron-thin layer of precious metal, such as gold or silver, in a standardized thickness. Because plated metal can be worn away with handling, it is viewed as less durable than gold or sterling silver.

- **Sterling silver**
  For a metal to be stamped *sterling silver*, it must be made of 92.5 percent pure silver and 7.5 percent copper or some other metal. Quick to tarnish, sterling silver wire should be kept in a protective soft flannel bag. Vermeil is sterling-silver wire electroplated with 22-karat gold.

- **Niobium and titanium**
  These two industrial alloys have been adopted by jewelry makers. Appealing colors can be added through an anodizing process, and they are hypoallergenic.

- **Stainless steel**

  Stainless steel is most widely sold as memory wire. A unique and appealing alternative to flexible beading wire, memory wire is stiff and preformed into coils that retain their shape after being manipulated, making the wire an appealing choice for choker-style necklaces, bangle-style bracelets, and rings. Because the wire is so stiff, it requires special memory wire cutters, which are stronger than traditional wire cutters. Memory wire can be completely concealed with beads, even heavy ones, or narrow rubber tubing, and it can be finished by bending and flattening a tiny loop in each end or by concealing the cut ends with end caps.

Gauge refers to the thickness or diameter of a wire, which is measured in millimeters, abbreviated *mm*. The higher the gauge, the finer the wire; the lower the gauge, the thicker the wire. Most of the wires used for the projects in this chapter range from 26-gauge to 20-gauge, or 0.4 mm to 0.8 mm in diameter. I like working within this range because the wires pass easily through most of the bead holes, they are easy to manipulate, and the results are aesthetically pleasing.

**Common Wire Gauges**

**Diameter**

| In Inches | In Millimeters | Actual Size | |
|---|---|---|---|
| 14 gauge = .0641 inches = 1.63 mm | | | |
| 16 gauge = .0508 inches = 1.29 mm | | | |
| 18 gauge = .0403 inches = 1.02 mm | | | |
| 20 gauge = .0320 inches = 0.81 mm | | | |
| 22 gauge = .0253 inches = 0.64 mm | | | |
| 24 gauge = .0201 inches = 0.51 mm | | | |
| 26 gauge = .0159 inches = 0.40 mm | | | |
| 28 gauge = .0126 inches = 0.32 mm | | | |

The color of the wire used to make findings plays a defining role in the look and style of the completed piece of jewelry. For exam-

## Beading Tools at a Glance

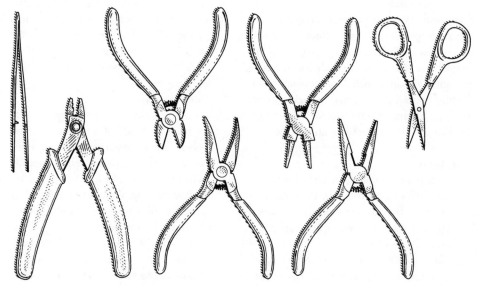

ple, the high polish of sterling silver will highlight the cool refracted light of a crystal bead, and the warm glow of gold-plated wire goes well with a leaf-green faceted crystal. There are inexpensive wires that come in a wide range of party colors, as well as wires made from copper, brass, and steel.

The hardness of wire refers to the resistance it has to bending. Half-hard wire is an appealing choice for making components—it bends into sharp angles, maintains its shape when manipulated, and is satisfying to work with. Ring bands and earring wires that must maintain their rigidity should be made from half-hard wire. By contrast, dead-soft wire is very malleable and easy to manipulate, making it well suited to forming eye loops, wrapped-wire loops, and bails.

## Hand Tools for Wire Work

The tools used for wirework are specifically designed to cut, bend, or shape wire and to attach findings in the neatest and most efficient way possible. You needn't buy the most expensive tools; there are well-made, dependable tools that are affordable, effective, and easy to use even for beginners.

I have purchased many tools over time. At first, I simply shopped by price, but I quickly discovered that a cheap wire cutter was a bad investment—it would work well at first, but then its cutting edge would become nicked and dull. Now when I buy a tool, I select one according to the metal from which it is made and the process used to make it—two factors that directly affect both the longevity of the tool and the quality of wirework I will be able to produce with it. Metal tools can be made of hardened tool steel or die-cast stainless steel. Hardened tool steel is forged for durability, is nick-proof, and is the longer-lasting metal; however, extra maintenance is needed to prevent rust. Stainless steel provides rust resistance, but it isn't as strong as hardened tool steel and will develop pits and chips, especially

on its cutting surface, after prolonged use. Regardless of your choice of metal, make sure the jaws of the tool align and the inner surfaces are smooth before you make a purchase. If you are left-handed, take note that the jaws of some wire cutters are designed for right-handed crafters.

An equally important factor when choosing a tool is its ergonomic functioning, or the way the tool fits in your hand and the ease with which you can use it. Tools that are lightweight, compatible with your hand size, and easy to use are best. Because wirework often requires repetitive actions that can strain and tire your hand muscles, you might want to consider pliers with springs that automatically return the handles to the open position after you press them closed. In all cases, make certain that the handle spread is comfortable; test the tool beforehand, working it as you would under actual beading circumstances to get an idea of the way the grip feels in your hand.

- **Wire cutters**

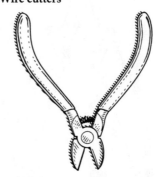

Wire cutters are used to cut both wire and nylon-coated beading wire. If purchasing only one pair of cutters, choose a pair that will cut the widest range of wire gauges. Manufacturers will usually specify on the packaging what cutters are best for various gauges and tempers of wire. Look for cutters that come to a point so that you can snip off short ends of wire in recessed spaces. As you become more serious about beading, you will appreciate expanding your tool repertoire, buying specialized tools for particular jobs. For example, you will love the clean efficiency of a pair of nippers to cut thin-gauge wire in tight spaces, a pair of medium cutters for gauges of dead-soft wire, and chain cutters for thick-gauge wire or heavy chain. Cutters suited to particular tasks range from end cutters (with straight cutting edges across a wide, rectangular nose), side cutters, also called flush cutters (one side produces a flat, flush cut and the other side produces an angled cut), and small nippers (with short, sharp blades designed to make neat cuts on thin wire). When using any wire cutter, position the blades so that the side that produces the flush cut faces the project wire.

- **Crimping pliers**

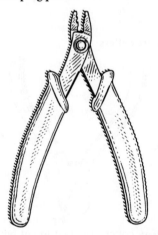

This specialized tool is designed to secure nylon-coated beading wire to findings using a crimp tube. Crimping pliers have two "wells" aligned on their jaws. When squeezed, one well turns a crimp tube into a crescent shape, and the other folds it in half, securing the beading wire inside. Crimping pliers can be used with crimp beads but work best with tubes.

- **Round-nose pliers**

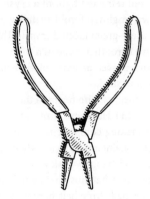

One of the "must-have" jewelry-making tools, a pair of round-nose pliers is indispensable when shaping wire loops. Round-nose pliers have a tapered nose with two cone-shaped jaws designed to make loops in a variety of diameters, depending on where on the jaw the wire is placed—the narrow tips make small loops and the wider area near the joint makes large loops.

- **Chain-nose pliers**

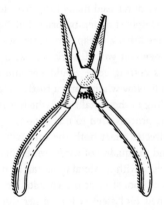

Incredibly versatile, chain-nose pliers are suited to a broad range of tasks—from opening and closing jump rings and links in a chain to making bends in wire, gripping wrapped loops, and reaching into narrow spaces. Chain-nose pliers have a slight curve on the outside of the nose that tapers at the tips. Inside, the jaws are smooth and flat so that the surface doesn't mar or groove the metal or wire it is working. Needle-nose pliers are chain-nose pliers with long noses that are suited to reaching into small or recessed spaces.

- **Bent-nose pliers**

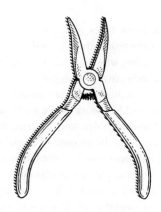

Also called bent chain-nose pliers, these pliers have a sharply angled nose with tapered ends that provides better leverage for reaching into narrow spaces. This tool is also used for wrapping wire and opening and closing jump rings.

- **Needle file and emery cloth**
Long and tapered, a needle file smooths the cut end of a wire to remove any sharp or rough edges. To smooth the wire end further and make the jewelry safe for wearing, use emery cloth, a mineral-coated cloth that resembles sandpaper but is made for metal. Emery cloth can be laid flat and a cut wire end dragged and rolled over its surface until it is smooth.

- **Bead reamer**
Available in bead supply or hardware stores, bead reamers are packaged in a set that contains a handle and different files suited to the degree of abrasion desired. The files are embedded with diamond dust and are suited to grinding away material inside a bead hole that would abrade the strand material. One of the files is thin enough to pass through the full length of the hole to enlarge it and another file will allow you to grind the jagged edges of the bead to help prevent thread or cord from fraying when it is drawn through the bead hole. Bead reamers can crack and break glass and crystal beads, so careful pressure is highly recommended; however, they work well on softer materials like pearls and some semiprecious stones.

- **Clamps**
Available in a wide variety of styles, alligator and photo clamps can be used to temporarily secure the ends of stringing material to prevent beads from slipping off while the strand is being worked on.

- **Ruler and tape measure**
Any tool that helps you take accurate measurements can be used in beading. Small rulers marked with millimeters can measure the length and width of single beads to help you plan your designs. For more precise measurements, use a micrometer, a handy ruler with calipers that comes in plastic or brass. A micrometer is very helpful for ordering items online because it gives you a visual size reference. A tape measure is handy for measuring the length of a flexible strand of beads for bracelets and necklaces.

- **Beading board**
Used to lay out beads when planning a design, a beading board can be made of molded and flocked plastic or from wood lined with velvet. The board is marked with measurements to aid in the making of neck-

laces and bracelets. Several channels let you lay out the beads for multi-strand designs.

- **Flat-weave cotton towel or felt mat**
  A cotton dish towel or felt mat on your work surface can prevent beads and findings from bouncing or rolling around.

- **Storage boxes and vials**
  Stackable storage containers with screw tops, partitioned boxes with snap-close lids, even recycled jars and plastic containers are suited to organizing and safeguarding beads. Bags made of soft cloth can protect loose beads and finished pieces of beaded jewelry.

- **Safety glasses**
  Recommended when cutting wire and when reaming beads, safety glasses are essential to protect your eyes.

- **Magnifier lamp**
  Prolonged work with small beads requires focus and concentration that can cause eyestrain. A magnifier lamp provides both a magnifying glass through which to view beads and delicate maneuvers and a light source that simulates daylight.

## General Beading Supplies

Tools for measuring, cutting, and keeping your work organized are useful for all types of bead wirework, stringing, and weaving.

## Stringing and Off-Loom Weaving

Three different types of strands are popular for stringing beads: thread, cord, and nylon-coated beading wire. Each strand type is available in a wide range of materials, both organic and synthetic. The appropriate strand material is determined by the weight of the beads, the size of the bead holes, and aesthetic considerations such as the amount of drape desired and the look envisioned for the finished piece. Pearls, for example, are traditionally strung on silk thread or cord, a fiber that supports the lighter weight of the pearls while supplying sublime drape to maximize their elegance. Glass beads, which are heavier than pearls, must be strung on strong nylon-coated beading wire that resists abrasion from the sharp edges of the bead holes. Seed and cylinder beads used in off-loom weaving require synthetic thread that can hold up to stretching and fraying.

Visiting a bead store will allow you to examine and compare strand materials firsthand. When I am shopping for a stringing material, I take my beads along. I can make a better choice if I am able to take into account the actual weight, shape, and color of the beads.

Once you've done some beading with conventional strands, try a few of the less common materials, such as ribbon, leather, neoprene rubber, and plastic, according to the stylistic effect you are trying to achieve. Beading needles, scissors, and a few other items will round out the small number of supplies you need to begin stringing or weaving beads.

## Thread and Cord

- **Silk thread**

A natural fiber, silk thread is suited to stringing pearls and light-weight beads made from gemstones. Noted for its luster, strength, and range of available colors, silk thread is sold on spools and on cards that often come with needles attached. Silk thread is strong, knots well, and has an appealing drape, all desirable characteristics, especially when stringing pearls. Silk thread needs to be conditioned, or prestretched and coated with wax, before it is used to prevent stretching and fraying, which in turn causes tangles and kinks. Please note that silk will begin to degrade, fray, and weaken within 3 to 5 years of use; if you use silk thread to string your beads, expect to eventually restring them.

- **Nylon thread**
A synthetic strand material, nylon thread is made from long fibers that are strong and flexible. The thread is available on bobbins and spools in a broad range of colors and diameters, ranging from size 000 (the thinnest) to sizes 00 and 0 and up to A, B, C, D, E, F, FF, and FFF (the thickest). Sizes B and D are recommended for weaving, especially for woven bracelets and necklaces, depending upon the size of the bead hole. To prevent fraying, twisting, and kinking, nylon thread should be conditioned, or prestretched and coated with wax, before it is used for stringing. Use knotting, clamshells, end bars, and clasps to finish this thread.

- **Silk cord**
Pliable and with a soft hand, 100 percent silk cord is made up of tight, twisted strands of silk and is sold on cards that often come with a twisted-wire beading needle attached. Kinks can be pressed out with a household iron, and the cord should be stretched by hand prior to use. Meant to be a visible design element, silk cord is suited to stringing single or multiple focal beads, as in a "tin cup" necklace. Named after a Hollywood film, this style of necklace features bead stations separated by bare silk cord, which gives the beads the appearance of floating. Silk cord can be finished with knots, clamshells, bullion, and clasps.

- **Waxed cotton cord**
Available on spools, this cotton cord is treated with wax to prevent fraying and to aid knotting. The cord has little stretch; two strands of monofilament at the core make it strong, but the organic material will degrade. Commonly available in a diameter of 0.5 mm to 2.0 mm, this uniformly dyed cord comes in many colors. The cord can be finished using knots, clamshells, bullion, and clasps.

- **Satin cord**
Having a smooth hand, satin cord comes in many colors and in three diameters: 2 mm rattail, 1.5 mm mousetail, and 1 mm bugtail. Suited to straightforward, minimal stringing, satin cord can be a prominent element in the design and is especially suited to pendants or necklaces that feature only one or a few focal beads. It is important to choose beads with smooth bead holes that will not abrade and fray the satin. It is a good idea to smooth rough or sharp edges of the bead holes with a bead reamer prior to stringing. Satin cord is light-weight and is finished by knotting or using fold-over bead tips.

- **Stretch cord**
Elastic stretch cord is suited to casual jewelry featuring light-weight and

medium-weight beads. The cord itself can be used to string beads that have large holes, but a flexible, collapsible-eye beading needle is often needed for beads with small holes. Heavy beads require a double strand of stretch cord. Because jewelry made with elastic cord is stretched when slipped on and off, the cord can degrade and break over time. To avoid these outcomes, make the jewelry loose enough to reduce the tension on the elastic. In general, plastic stretch cord can be finished with a square knot or with a crimp tube, eliminating the need for a separate clasp.

*Nylon-Coated Beading Wire*

Nylon-coated beading wire is known for its flexibility, resistance to stretching and kinking, and durability. It comes in a wide variety of overall diameters, tensile strengths, colors, and metal finishes, but because there are so many different kinds on the market, choosing the right one can be confusing. There are several factors to consider. Beading wire comes on spools that are clearly labeled with the strand count, overall diameter, name of the color or metal finish, and tensile strength of the wire, written in pounds. Tensile strength is the weight in pounds that the strand can support before breaking. All of these factors combine in different ways to produce beading wires with distinctly different properties, including flexibility, resistance to kinking and breaking, aesthetic qualities of color and luster, and kinesthetic qualities such as hand and weightlessness that make a piece of jewelry comfortable to wear.

## Working Tips: Stringing with Ribbon

Available by the yard or wrapped on cards or around spools, ribbon is available in an extremely wide assortment of fabrics, widths, colors, patterns, weaves, and finishes. Because it is subject to stretching and wear, ribbon for bead stringing should be carefully chosen; it must support the weight of the beads without drooping and be able to resist the abrasive effects of sharp bead holes. It is common to use a flexible twisted-wire needle with a collapsible eye or a big-eye needle when using ribbon as a strand material. Hinged, clamp-style findings are often used to finish the raw edges of cut ribbon and to attach clasps.

- **Strand count and flexibility**
  Nylon-coated beading wire is composed

of bundled and twisted strands of stainless steel wire coated in a nylon sheath. It is available in 3-strand, 7-strand, 19-strand, and 49-strand. The 49-strand beading wire has seven bundles of wires, each with seven twisted strands, that are collected together and coated in nylon. The greater the number of strands, the more flexible the wire and more graceful the drape.

- **Diameter and threadability**
  Beading wire comes in a wide variety of diameters from .010" (0.25 mm), which is suited to seed beads, to .036" (0.90 mm), which is suited to beads with large holes. General-purpose diameters are .015" (0.38 mm) and .018" (0.46 mm). Choose a beading wire that is thin enough to pass through the bead but thick enough to fill the hole without getting stuck.
- **Tensile strength and bead weight**
  Beading wire comes in a practical range of strengths that make it possible to string heavy, medium-weight, or light-weight beads. Choose a beading wire that can withstand the cumulative weight of your beads without breaking. In addition, consider the amount of wear and tear your piece of jewelry will encounter and the value of the beads to ensure a safe wearing experience. Beading wire in general is especially suited to stringing medium- and heavy-weight beads in glass and ceramic that may have rougher bead holes that could easily abrade a strand made of natural fiber.
- **Color and metal finish**
  The color of a beading wire is determined by the nylon coating on the wire. A wide range of colors, including tangerine and lavender, is available. Clear nylon coating reveals the color of the metal finish on the wire; it could be gray (stainless steel), silver (silver-plated), or yellow (gold-plated).

## Beading Needles and Other Tools

The tools for bead stringing and weaving are few and simple. In traditional bead stringing with thread, a needle is required because the strand material is not stiff enough on its own to pass through the bead holes. Beading wire and some cords can be strung without a needle. A needle is required for bead weaving. Scissors, tweezers, thread conditioner, and a few general beading supplies round out what you will need.

- **Beading needles**

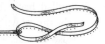

  Unlike sewing needles, beading needles are designed so that the eye end of the needle is equal in diameter to the shaft of the needle, thus allowing the entire needle to pass easily through the bead hole. Always choose a needle with a diameter that is smaller than the diameter of the bead hole and test-fit the beading needle in the bead hole before beginning work. Choose a needle length that gives you the control you need; a shorter needle will allow you to pass through one or two beads at a time— needles between 1¼" (3.2 cm) and 2" (5.1 cm) work well. Large-eye, twisted wire, and flossing needles are suited to stringing a greater number of beads at one time.
- **Flexible large-eye and collapsible-eye beading needles**
  Made of twisted stainless steel, the flexible shaft and collapsible eye of this style of needle make it practical for wider and thicker strand materials, such as ribbon and cord.
- **Carpet needle**
  Used to hand-knot beads on a strand, a carpet needle has a strong, sharp point

that allows you to place a knot accurately on a strand of thread. The carpet needle is a convenient substitute for a beading awl. A darning needle can be used for the same purpose.

- **Needle threader**
Used to aid in threading a needle, a threader is composed of two parts: a handle and a collapsible loop made of very fine wire. The pointed end of the loop is inserted through the eye of the needle, collapsing and then opening again as it passes through. The thread is fed through the loop, which is then pulled back through the eye, drawing the thread with it. A needle threader can also be inserted through a bead hole to aid in stringing it.

- **Thread scissors**

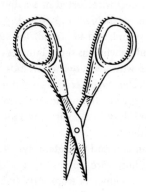

Thread scissors are approximately 4" (10.2 cm) long with finely honed blades that come to extremely sharp points. Unlike traditional household scissors, which can leave thread ends frayed, thread scissors are designed to make precise and sharp cuts. They are particularly valuable for cutting thread that will be fed through

## Working Tips: Threading a Needle without a Needle Threader

To thread a needle, cut one end of a length of thread on a sharp diagonal. Flatten the end of the thread with your fingers and then hold the thread between your thumb and index finger so that only the cut end of the thread can be seen. Move the eye of the needle *toward* and onto the thread end. When a bit of thread protrudes through the eye, grab the end and pull the thread through.

## Quick & Easy: Stiffening the Strand Material to Make a Needle

Suited to cord and thread, this technique is an efficient way to stiffen the end of the strand material so that it can pass through the bead hole. Use clear nail polish to coat ½" (1.3 cm) of one end of the beading cord or thread. Pull the coated section of the cord or thread through your fingers to flatten it. Instant glue (cyanoacrylate) can be used as a stiffener instead of nail polish; just flatten the glued end with a toothpick instead of your fingers. Once the nail polish or glue is dry, insert the stiff end through the bead holes just as you would a needle.

the eye of a needle or for trimming short lengths of excess thread. In bead weaving, thread scissors are used to quickly and precisely refresh the end of the working thread, which is prone to fraying as it is worked through the beaded fabric.

- **Tweezers**

Stainless steel bead tweezers and cup-style bead tweezers are practical for picking up single beads and for making knots between beads.

- **Thread conditioner**
Particularly important in bead weaving, beeswax or a thread conditioner like Thread Heaven helps guard against a thread's natural tendency to fray, knot, and tangle. Use a conditioner sparingly on nonwaxed threads to avoid making the thread sticky.

- **Instant glue (cyanoacrylate) and nail polish**
Of the various glues suitable for securing knots in bead weaving, I prefer instant glue (cyanoacrylate) because it sets up quickly and dries clear. Read the manufacturer's directions before using this glue, work in a well-ventilated space, and avoid getting the glue on your skin. Work carefully; if glue runs inside a bead hole and hardens, the hole will become impassable for stringing or weaving. Both instant glue and clear nail polish

are also extremely effective in stiffening the fibrous ends of thread and cord for stringing without a needle. Instant glue can degrade some synthetic materials, such as elastic stretch cord, so use it sparingly and always wipe away excess.

## Wiring Beads

Wiring is a method in which bare metal wire is used to make small parts for individual beads so they can be connected to other beads and to the strand material. Wiring beads allows freedom to place the wired beads anywhere on the strand or chain, easily allowing for changes in the design.

The wiring techniques in this chapter are straightforward and easy to learn but require practice to perform with competence. Establishing good work practices from the start will enable you to achieve a level of craftsmanship you can take pride in. If you are a beginner, I recommend that you practice with scrap wire. After you have a better feel for the wiring techniques, you can switch to wires made of precious metals and work on an actual project.

---

## Quick & Easy: Transferring Seed Beads to a Wire

Stringing seed beads one at a time is extremely tedious and also unnecessary. Seed beads come on a thin thread that can be laid along the index finger on one hand with holes facing out. While holding the thread taut along your finger, use your other hand to feed the end of the beading wire through the seed beads, sliding them onto the wire and pulling the thread out of the beads as you work.

---

## Technique: Smoothing Cut Wire Ends

Smoothing cut wire ends is one of the techniques I use again and again. Learn it, master it, and give all your pieces the same high level of attention to detail practiced by professional jewelry makers. For loose wire that has just been cut, use emery cloth, which looks like dark gray sandpaper and has a very fine texture. It is available in coarse (40–70), medium (80–100), and fine (120, F, and FF) grits. On wires that scratch easily, use the fine-grit emery cloth.

MATERIALS AND TOOLS
Wire
Wire cutters
Emery cloth

**Step 1**
Cut the wire.
Use wire cutters to cut your wire to the desired length.

**Step 2**
Smooth the wire end.
Lay a piece of emery cloth on a flat surface. Drag the cut end of wire along its surface, rotating the wire end until it is smooth.

## Technique: Smoothing Cut Wire Ends on a Wrapped-Wire Loop

For wire that is wrapped and then cut, as in a wrapped-wire loop, use a needle file to smooth the cut end.

MATERIALS AND TOOLS
Wrapped-wire loop, in progress
Wire cutters
Chain-nose pliers
Needle file

**Step 1**
Wrap the end of wire three or four times down the wire stem. Use wire cutters to trim off the excess wire close to the stem.

**Step 2**
Use a needle file to smooth the cut end of wire, being careful not to scratch the bead. Use bent-nose pliers to press the wraps flush against the stem.

### Eye Loops and Stops

Suited to beads that are light-weight, the simplest loop to add to the end of a head pin or to one or both ends of a length of wire is the eye loop. Having a round shape, the loop can be used to connect other findings or beaded elements.

An eye loop can also serve as a stop to prevent a bead threaded on the pin from sliding off. A stop is essential on any wire that will hold a bead. Stops come in many styles, from the simple metal disk that is soldered on the end of a head pin to a coil that is shaped at the end of a length of wire.

## Technique: Making an Eye Loop on a Head Pin

A head pin already has a stop at one end. Adding an eye loop at the opposite end will allow you to attach it to another finding, such as an ear wire to create dangly earrings. Round-nose pliers are used to shape the loop; the inner diameter of the loop is determined by the location on the cone-shaped nose that wire is placed for shaping.

MATERIALS AND TOOLS
Round bead
Head pin (in a gauge that passes
    easily through the hole in the
    bead)
Wire cutters
Chain-nose pliers
Round-nose pliers
Emery cloth
Ruler

**Step 1**
Thread on the bead.

Thread the blunt end of the head pin through the hole in the bead, sliding it down to the stop. Use wire cutters to cut the wire that extends beyond the top of the bead hole to ½" (1.3 cm), or the length required to make the eye loop. For a large loop, leave a longer wire. Use an emery cloth to smooth the cut wire end.

**Step 2**
Make the first bend.

Use the tips of the chain-nose pliers to grip the head pin where it exits the bead hole. Rotate the pliers, bending the head pin at a 90-degree angle.

**Step 3**
Shape the eye loop.

Grip the cut end of the head pin with the round-nose pliers and rotate the pliers toward the bend to begin shaping a loop. When your wrist can no longer rotate comfortably, stop. Remove the round-nose pliers.

**Step 4**
Finish shaping the eye loop.

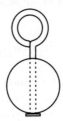

Grip the cut end of the head pin with the round-nose pliers again, positioning the wire on the jaws of the pliers at the same location as in step 3. Rotate the pliers until a round closed loop is formed.

## Working Tips: Determining Loop Size

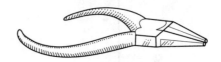

Eye loops can be made in various sizes by using round-nose pliers with cone-shaped jaws. When the eye loop is formed close to the tip of the jaw, the circumference of the loop will be small. When the wire is placed closer to the box (or joint) on the pliers, the circumference of the loop will be larger. Use 22- or 24-gauge wire that is strong but thin enough to bend and wrap, varying the position of the wire on the jaws to make eye loops in different sizes. Use a permanent marker to make a line on the jaws to indicate a desired circumference. The mark can be easily removed with rubbing alcohol.

## Technique: Making a Concealed Wire Stop

This is an easy way to hide a handmade stop inside a bead. The technique can also be used to make a stop that will be covered by a Scrimp bead, as in the Blue Ice: A Pendant (page 66).

### MATERIALS AND TOOLS

Bead, 8 mm or larger
Length of wire (in a gauge that passes easily through the bead hole)
Instant glue (cyanoacrylate)
Wire cutters
Round-nose pliers
Chain-nose pliers
Ruler

### Step 1

Make an eye pin with a stop.

Use a ruler and wire cutters to measure and cut a length of wire 1½" (3.8 cm) longer than the diameter or length of the bead. Use the tips of the round-nose pliers to make a tiny eye loop at one end of the wire. Use chain-nose pliers to flatten the loop into a long oval.

### Step 2

Thread the bead onto the eye pin.

Insert the blunt wire end into the bottom of the bead and pull the flattened loop into the bead hole until the end of the loop is flush with the bottom of the bead. If the flattened loop does not fit in the hole, use pliers to further flatten the wire and reinsert the wire into the bead until the loop is flush with the bottom of the bead. Apply a drop of instant glue (cyanoacrylate) to the bottom of the bead to secure the wire stop inside the bead.

## Technique: Making a Decorative Wire Stop

Use a length of wire to make a decorative head pin by shaping one end of the length into a coil. The appeal of this technique is that you can transform straight wire into an effective stop for beads of any size; some standard head pins, either plain or fancy, are not long enough for larger beads.

### MATERIALS AND TOOLS

Round bead
Length of wire (in a gauge that passes easily through the bead hole)
Wire cutters
Round-nose pliers
Chain-nose pliers
Emery cloth, medium-grit (#400) or fine-grit (#600)
Ruler

### Step 1

Make the coil-shaped stop.

Lay the emery cloth on a protected surface and drag each end of the wire on its surface, turning the wire to smooth it. Use the tips of the round-nose pliers to make a tiny eye loop at one end of the wire. Use chain-nose pliers to grip the loop and then use your fingers to coil the long wire around the outer edge of the first eye loop. Continue to coil the long wire around itself, spiraling it as tightly as possible.

### Step 2

Make the head pin.

Use the chain-nose pliers to bend the wire end that extends from the spiral at a 90-degree angle so that the spiral is centered beneath the wire stem. Thread the wire end through a bead. Use wire cutters to trim the wire that extends above the bead to a desired length.

## Technique: Making a Seed Bead Stop

This unique finding is suited to wiring beads with small bead holes, such as pearls and crystals.

### MATERIALS AND TOOLS

Seed bead
Round bead with small hole
Length of wire (in a gauge that passes easily through the bead hole)
Wire cutters
Ruler

### Step 1

Prepare the wire.

Cut a 4" (10.2 cm) length of wire. Thread on a seed bead and slide it to the midpoint. Bend the wire in half.

### Step 2

Make the head pin.

Hold the seed bead with one hand while twisting the wires together with the other. The bead will become trapped at the bottom of the twisted stem. Thread the wire ends through a bead. The seed bead will act as a stop to prevent the bead from slipping off. Use wire cutters to trim the wire that extends above the bead to a desired length.

## Technique: Making a Stop on Memory Wire

To keep beads from sliding off memory wire and to prevent the cut ends from catching on clothing, make a stop on each cut end of the wire.

### MATERIALS AND TOOLS

Memory wire
Beads, as desired
Memory wire cutters
Chain-nose pliers
Needle file
Emery cloth, medium-grit (#400)
Safety glasses

### Step 1

Prepare the wire ends.

Put on safety glasses. Use memory wire cutters to cut off the desired number of turns from a coil of memory wire. Smooth the cut wire ends with a needle file. Then lay an emery cloth on a flat surface and drag each end of wire on the emery cloth to further smooth the ends.

### Step 2

Bend one wire end.

Grip one wire end with the tips of the chain-nose pliers. Rotate the pliers against the natural curve to bend a ⅛" (0.3 cm) section at a 90-degree angle.

**Step 3**

Flatten the bend.

Place the bent wire in the widest part of the jaws of the chain-nose pliers and squeeze the pliers to flatten the bend so the wires are flush against one another.

**Step 4**

String on the beads and make the second stop.

Thread the desired beads on the memory wire. Use memory wire cutters to cut off all but ⅜" (1.0 cm) of the excess wire. Grip the wire ⅛" (0.3 cm) beyond the last bead with the chain-nose pliers. Rotate the pliers against the natural curve (as in step 2) to bend a ⅛" (0.3 cm) section into a long oval loop. Use the pliers to flatten the loop.

Wrapped-Wire Loops

Several features of handmade jewelry immediately distinguish good workmanship. One is the quality of the wrapped-wire loops. Wrapped-wire loops are secure connector loops that are added to a single bead, or group of beads, using a head pin or wire. Practical and utilitarian, they provide ways to connect the beads to the links in a chain, to other findings, or to themselves. Wire loops are also a design element and are traditionally made from metals that match the other design elements. For example, a gold wrapped-wire loop is traditionally used with a gold chain.

There are several styles of wrapped-wire loops: a single wrapped-wire loop, a double wrapped-wire loop, a bail with a wrapped-

wire loop, and a wrapped-wire bail-and-loop combination. Some types of loops, such as the single wrapped-wire loop, can be made using either a cut length of wire or a head pin. A cut length of wire is used to make a double wrapped-wire loop, in which both ends of the wire are made into loops.

**Technique: Making a Single Wrapped-Wire Loop from a Head Pin**

For this technique, choose a head pin that will extend at least 1½" (3.8 cm) beyond the bead hole.

MATERIALS AND TOOLS

Round bead
Head pin
Chain-nose pliers
Round-nose pliers
Bent-nose pliers
Wire cutters
Needle file
Ruler

**Step 1**

Thread on the bead.

Thread the blunt end of the head pin through the hole in the bead, sliding it down to the stop. Allow the head pin wire to extend 1½" (3.8 cm) above the bead hole.

**Step 2**

Make the first bend.

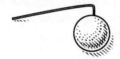

Use the tips of the chain-nose pliers to grip the head pin approximately ⅛" (0.3 cm) above the bead hole. Rotate the pliers, bending the head pin wire at a 90-degree angle.

## Step 3

Shape the loop.

Use the round-nose pliers to grip the wire ⅛" (0.3 cm) from the bend. Rotate the pliers toward the bend to begin shaping the loop. When your wrist can no longer rotate comfortably, stop. Do not remove the pliers but use the fingers of your opposite hand to wrap the head pin wire around the jaw of the round-nose pliers until it crosses in front of the head pin wire and completes a round loop.

## Step 4

Wrap the wire around the stem.

Use the chain-nose pliers to grip the wire loop. Use your fingers to wrap the wire tail around and down the stem of the head pin until it touches the top of the bead. Be sure to make tight, even wraps. As the wire stem shortens, the wraps will become more difficult to make; use the bent-nose pliers instead of your fingers to make the last few wire wraps, if necessary. Trim away the excess wire using the wire cutters. Then use a needle file to smooth the wire end, being careful not to scratch the bead. Use bent-nose pliers to gently squeeze the cut wire end flush against the stem.

## Technique: Connecting a Wrapped-Wire Loop to a Link in a Chain

A charm or bead with a wrapped-wire loop can be attached directly to a link in a chain using its loop, but only if the wire is threaded through the link before the wrapped-wire loop is completed. A finished wrapped-wire loop can be attached to a chain link with a separate finding, such as a jump ring; however, the jump ring will add length, causing the wired bead to hang lower than one attached directly to the link.

### MATERIALS AND TOOLS

Round bead
Head pin
Ruler
Round-nose pliers
Chain-nose pliers
Bent-nose pliers
Wire cutters
Needle file

## Step 1

Thread on the bead.

Thread the blunt end of the head pin through the hole in the bead, sliding it down to the stop. Allow the head pin wire to extend 1½" (3.8 cm) above the bead hole.

## Step 2

Make the first bend.

Use the tips of the chain-nose pliers to grip the head pin approximately ⅛" (0.3 cm) above the bead hole. Rotate the pliers, bending head pin wire at a 90-degree angle.

## Step 3

Shape the loop.

Use the round-nose pliers to grip the wire ⅛" (0.3 cm) away from the bend. Rotate the pliers toward the bend to begin shaping the loop. When your wrist can no longer rotate comfortably, stop. Do not remove the pliers but use the fingers of your opposite hand to wrap the head pin wire around the jaw of the round-nose pliers until it crosses in front of the head pin wire and completes a round loop.

## Step 4

Attach the loop to the chain link.

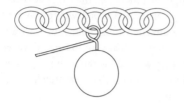

Thread the end of the head pin wire through a link in the chain.

## Step 5

Wrap the wire around the stem.

Use the chain-nose pliers to grip the wire loop. Use your fingers to wrap the wire tail around and down the stem of the head pin until it touches the top of the bead. Be sure to make tight, even wraps. As the wire stem shortens, the wraps become more difficult to make: use the bent-nose pliers instead of your fingers to make the last few wire wraps, if necessary. Trim away the excess wire using the wire cutters. Then use a needle file to smooth the wire end, being careful not to scratch the bead. Use bent-nose pliers to gently squeeze the cut wire end flush against the stem.

## Technique: Making a Single Wrapped-Wire Loop from a Length of Wire

When you want to make a single wrapped-wire loop using a length of wire, you will have to make a stop at one end. This method shows a stop that is concealed inside the bead hole.

### MATERIALS AND TOOLS

    1 bead, center-drilled
    Wire (in a gauge that fits through bead hole)
    Instant glue (cyanoacrylate)

    Ruler
    Wire cutters
    Emery cloth
    Round-nose pliers
    Chain-nose pliers
    Bent-nose pliers
    Needle file

## Step 1

Prepare the wire.

Measure and cut a length of wire that is long enough to accommodate the bead and extends at least 1½" (3.8 cm) from each bead hole. Drag the ends of the wire on a piece of emery cloth, rotating the ends to smooth them.

## Step 2

Make a stop on one wire end.

Use the tips of the round-nose pliers to make a tiny eye loop at one end of the wire. Use chain-nose pliers to flatten the loop into a long oval. Insert the blunt wire end into the bead and pull the flattened loop into the bead hole so the end of the loop is flush with the bottom of the bead and a length of wire above the bead extends 1½" (3.8 cm) above the bead hole. Apply a drop of instant glue (cyanoacrylate) to the bottom of the bead to secure the wire stop inside the bead.

## Step 3

Make the first bend.

Use the tips of the chain-nose pliers to grip the wire approximately ⅛" (0.3 cm) above the bead hole. Rotate the pliers, bending the wire at a 90-degree angle.

**Step 4**

Shape the loop.

Use the round-nose pliers to grip the wire ⅛" (0.3 cm) away from the bend. Rotate the pliers toward the bend to begin shaping the loop. When your wrist can no longer rotate comfortably, stop. Do not remove the pliers, but use your fingers on your opposite hand to wrap the head pin wire around the jaw of the round-nose pliers until it crosses in front of the head pin wire and completes a round loop. You can thread the wire through a link in a chain at this point, if desired.

**Step 5**

Wrap the wire around the stem.

Use the chain-nose pliers to grip the wire loop. Use your fingers to wrap the wire tail around and down the stem of the head pin until it touches the top of the bead. Be sure to make tight, even wraps. As the wire stem shortens, the wraps get harder to make: use the bent-nose pliers instead of your fingers to make the last few wire wraps, if necessary. Trim away the excess wire using the wire cutters. Then use a needle file to smooth the wire end, being careful not to scratch the bead. Use bent-nose pliers to gently squeeze the cut wire end flush against the stem.

## Technique: Making a Double Wrapped-Wire Loop

Neat and pretty, the double wrapped-wire loop allows you to connect each end loop to another bead or to a length of chain.

### MATERIALS AND TOOLS

Round bead
Wire (in a gauge to fit bead hole)
Ruler
Wire cutters
Emery cloth
Needle file
Round-nose pliers
Chain-nose pliers
Bent-nose pliers
Needle file

**Step 1**

Prepare the wire.

Measure and cut a length of wire that is long enough to accommodate the bead and extend at least 1½" (3.8 cm) from each bead hole. Drag the ends of the wire on a piece of emery cloth, rotating the cut ends to smooth them.

**Step 2**

Wire the bead.

Insert the wire through a bead and center it. Use the round-nose pliers to make a small wrapped-wire loop at each end, ⅛" (0.3 cm) from the bead hole. Use a needle file to smooth the wire ends.

## Technique: Connecting Double Wrapped-Wire Loops for a Beaded Chain

Making a strand of beads in which single beads are connected to one another with wrapped-wire loops requires that a double wrapped-wire loop be made on the first bead. After that the beads are attached by connect-

## Fun for Kids: Making a Beaded Bug

Beading requires a certain degree of coordination, but with an adult's guidance, a school-age child will be able to make bugs by wiring plump beads together. In principle, the bug is composed of segments, and each segment is made up of a bead. The beads are threaded with wire to keep them together. Help a child follow the diagram and choose any combination of beads to make a fantasy bug. You will need a spool of 18-gauge beading wire, 6 medium to large beads to string the body, wings, and head, and 4 small beads to secure them. You will also need wire cutters or junky scissors.

- **Make the wings.**

Working from the spool of wire, thread the end of the wire through 2 leaf-shaped beads so their narrow ends are facing one another. Thread on a small bead and then reinsert the wire back through the leaf-shaped beads and a small bead. Bring the wires around the small bead, tightening the wire to move the beads together to secure the wings. Cut the wires. Set the wings aside.

- **Make the segmented body.**

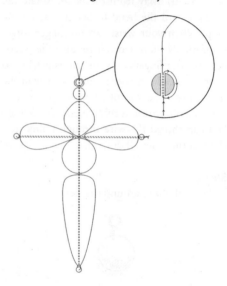

Working from the spool of wire, thread the end of the wire through 1 small bead, 1 medium bead, 2 large beads, and 1 long leaf-shaped bead. Thread on a small bead and then reinsert the wire back through the long leaf-shaped bead and the other beads, exiting out the small bead at the top of the body. Bring the wires around the small bead, tightening the wires to move the beads together to secure the body. Leave long wires for antennae. Then cut the wire from the spool. Center the wing section over the center wire between the large beads and wrap the wire on the wings around the center wires on the body.

ing the new loop to the previous loop to make a continuous chain in any length.

## MATERIALS AND TOOLS
Round bead
Wire (in a gauge that fits through bead hole)
Ruler
Emery cloth
Round-nose pliers
Chain-nose pliers
Bent-nose pliers
Wire cutters
Needle file

### Step 1
Prepare the wire.

Measure and cut a length of wire that is long enough to accommodate the bead and extend at least 1½" (3.8 cm) from each bead hole. Repeat to cut wire lengths for each bead in your design. Drag the ends of the wire on a piece of emery cloth, rotating the cut ends to smooth them.

### Step 2
Wire the first bead.

Make a double wrapped-wire loop at each end of the first bead.

### Step 3
Make one wrapped-wire loop on the second bead.

Make a single wrapped-wire loop on one end of a second length of wire. Thread the opposite end of the wire through the hole of the second bead.

### Step 4
Bend the wire.

Use the tips of the chain-nose pliers to grip the wire stem approximately ⅛" (0.3 cm) above the bead hole. Rotate the pliers, bending the wire at a 90-degree angle.

### Step 5
Shape the loop.

Use the round-nose pliers to grip the wire ⅛" (0.3 cm) from the bend. Rotate the pliers toward the bend to begin shaping the loop. When your wrist can no longer rotate comfortably, stop.

### Step 6
Thread the unfinished loop through one loop in the first bead.

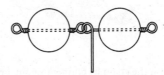

Thread the long wire through one of the loops on the first bead to connect them. Use the chain-nose pliers to grip the unfinished wire loop. Use your fingers to wrap the wire tail around and down the stem of the wire until it touches the top of the bead. Be sure to make tight, even wraps. As the wire stem shortens, the wraps get harder to make: use the bent-nose pliers instead of your fingers to make the last few wire wraps, if necessary. Trim away the excess wire using the wire cutters. Then use a needle file to smooth the wire end, being careful not to scratch the bead. Use bent-nose pliers to gently squeeze the cut wire end flush against the stem.

### Step 7
Add the remaining beads.

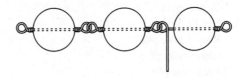

Repeat steps 3–6 to add more beads until the chain is as long as you desire.

## Step 8
Connect the beads.

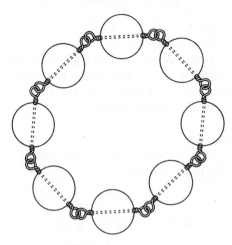

Finish the chain by connecting the first and last beads, threading the wire tail from the last bead through the loop on the first bead and completing a wrapped-wire loop.

## Technique: Making a Bail with a Wrapped-Wire Loop

In this design, a bail is shaped from wire, allowing a bead with a head-drilled hole, such as a briolette, to hang like a pendant from earrings or a necklace. The wire is threaded through the bead hole and forms a triangle above the tip of the bead that ends with a wrapped-wire loop.

MATERIALS AND TOOLS
1 bead with head-drilled hole,
 such as a briolette
Wire (in a gauge that fits bead hole)
Ruler
Wire cutters
Needle file
Round-nose pliers
Chain-nose pliers
Bent-nose pliers

## Step 1
Prepare the wire.

Measure and cut a length of wire that is long enough to accommodate the briolette and extend at least 3" (7.6 cm) from each bead hole.

## Step 2
Thread on the briolette.

Thread one end of the cut wire through the hole in the briolette, sliding the bead to the midpoint of the wire.

## Step 3
Begin to shape the bail.

Bend both wires up along the sides of the briolette toward the top. Cross the wires just above the tip to make an X. Grip the front wire with chain-nose pliers where the wires cross just above the tip of the bead and bend it straight up to make a stem.

## Step 4
Wrap the wire around the stem.

Grip the wires just below the point where they cross using the chain-nose pliers. Wrap the longer back wire tail around the front of the wire stem, continuing three or four times around and up the wire stem. Be sure to make tight, even wraps. As the wrapping wire shortens, the wraps may get harder to make; use the bent-nose pliers instead of your fingers to make the last few wraps, if necessary. Trim away the excess wrapping wire using the wire cutters. Then use a needle file to smooth the wire end, being careful not to scratch the bead. Use bent-nose pliers to gently squeeze the cut wire end flush against the stem. Rotate the now completed wire bail back above the bead tip.

## Step 5

Make a single wrapped-wire loop.

Grip the long wire stem ⅛" (0.3 cm) above the wire wraps using the chain-nose pliers and bend the wire at a 90-degree angle.

## Step 6

Begin to shape the loop.

Use the round-nose pliers to grip the wire ⅛" (0.3 cm) away from the bend. Rotate the pliers toward the bend to begin shaping the loop. When your wrist can no longer rotate comfortably, stop. Do not remove the pliers, but use your fingers on the opposite hand to wrap the wire around the jaw of the round-nose pliers until it crosses in front of the wire stem and completes a round loop.

## Step 7

Wrap the wire around the stem.

Use the chain-nose pliers to grip the wire loop. Use your fingers to wrap the wire tail around and down the wire stem until it touches the first wire wraps (or the top of the optional accent bead). Be sure to make tight, even wraps. As the wrapping wire shortens, the wraps get harder to make: use the bent-nose pliers instead of your fingers to make the last few wire wraps, if necessary. Trim away the excess wire using the wire cutters. Then use a needle file to smooth the wire end, being careful not to scratch the bead. Use bent-nose pliers to gently squeeze the cut wire end flush against the stem.

## Technique: Making a Wrapped-Wire Bail-and-Loop Combination

Suited to a head-drilled bead, this technique features a wrapped-wire loop, but instead of snipping off the excess wire, the tail is wrapped around the top of the bead to create a bail that conceals the bead hole. This wrap technique works very well with 24- to 28-gauge wire because the pliability of the wire makes it easy to manipulate it into neat wraps that conform to the shape of the bead tip.

MATERIALS AND TOOLS

    1 bead with head-drilled hole, such as a
      briolette
    Wire (in a gauge that fits through bead
      hole)
    Ruler
    Wire cutters
    Round-nose pliers
    Chain-nose pliers
    Bent-nose pliers
    Needle file

## Step 1

Prepare the wire.

Measure and cut a length of wire that is long enough to accommodate the briolette and extend at least 3" (7.6 cm) from each side of the bead hole.

## Step 2

Thread on the bead (a).

Thread one end of the cut wire through the hole in the briolette, leaving a ¾" (1.9 cm) length of wire on one side. Bend both wires up along the sides of the briolette toward the top.

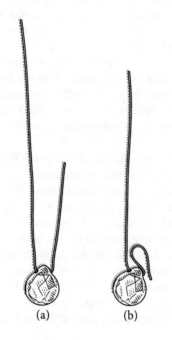

(a)          (b)

## Step 3

Make an open loop (b).

Grip the short wire with round-nose pliers and rotate the pliers to make an open loop over the tip of the briolette; use your fingers to gently push and flatten the short wire end against the sloping side of the briolette. Trim away the excess wire so that the short end is even with the hole in the briolette. (This end of the wire will be concealed by the wire wraps.)

## Step 4

Begin to shape the wrapped-wire bail.

Grasp the loop with the chain-nose pliers. Use your fingers to wrap the long wire against the base of the loop, around to the back of the briolette, and then around to the front.

## Step 5

Finish the wrapped-wire bail.

While continuing to grasp the loop with the chain-nose pliers, wrap the long wire down and around the tip of the bead. Be sure to make tight, even wraps. As the wire stem shortens, the wraps get harder to make: use the bent-nose pliers instead of your fingers to make the last few wire wraps, if necessary. Trim away the excess wire using the wire cutters. Then use a needle file to smooth the wire end, being careful not to scratch the bead. Use bent-nose pliers to gently squeeze the cut wire end flush against the bead.

## Stringing Beads

Stringing is one of the most straightforward and intuitive methods for making beaded jewelry. All you need are beads, a strand to string them on, and some kind of closure, even if it is just a square knot.

The strand provides a simple way to keep beads together in a particular order. A strand can be concealed completely, or it can play a prominent role in the jewelry design, such as in an illusion necklace, a design in which beads are strung in groups, or stations, on a sheer strand material that gives the illusion the beads are floating. A strand must be strong enough to support the beads and be in keeping with the style of the beads. It is rare to see crystals strung on a length of twine, for example, because the twine would obstruct the clearwater colors and would likely fray from contact with the sharp bead holes.

The kind, number, and order of the beads being strung, as well as the number of strands used, affects the jewelry design. A single kind of bead or several groups of beads may be strung onto a single strand, or beads in any configuration can be threaded onto several strands that are combined in one design. Clearly, the number of designs possible when combining beads, strands, and findings is limited only by your imagination.

The stringing technique is essentially the same whether you are stringing beads onto a thread, a cord, or a wire. However, the techniques used to secure and finish a strand are different for each strand material. Silk cord is secured to a clasp with a knot. Beading wire is secured to a clasp with a crimp bead. On some pieces, a jump ring may be used as a connector. This section describes skills and techniques for stringing and securing beads on a strand.

## Technique: Opening and Closing a Jump Ring

The most effective way to open and close a jump ring is to use two pairs of pliers. Proper use of the pliers will prevent twisting, distorting, or weakening of the wire ends. When closing a jump ring, be sure to align the two wire ends so they meet; otherwise the clasp or other finding that is threaded onto the ring won't be secure.

MATERIALS AND TOOLS
Jump ring
Chain-nose pliers
Bent-nose pliers

**Step 1**
Position the tools.

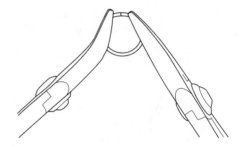

Grip opposite sides of the jump ring using the chain-nose pliers and bent-nose pliers with the ring's opening between them. Avoid using the tips of the pliers.

**Step 2**
Open the jump ring.

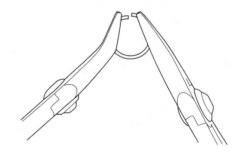

Rotate one pair of pliers away from you and one pair of pliers toward you to open the ring.

**Step 3**
Close the jump ring.
Reverse the motion in step 2, allowing the cut wire ends of the ring to meet.

## Working Tips: Tying Knots

- **Single overhand knot**

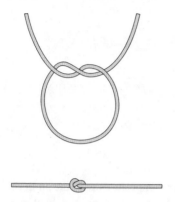

- **Double overhand knot**

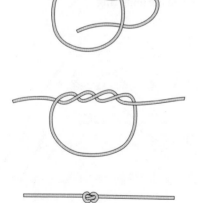

- **Square knot**

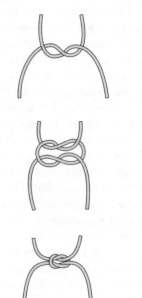

- **Surgeon's knot**

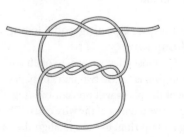

## Technique: Conditioning Thread

If the stringing material will be hidden by the beads, condition the beading thread prior to stringing to prevent fraying, kinking, and twisting.

### MATERIALS AND TOOLS

Beading thread
Thread scissors
Thread conditioner

### Step 1

Cut a length of thread.

Pull a length of thread from the card or spool and use thread scissors to cut it to the desired length.

### Step 2

Stretch the thread.

Use your hands to pull the thread at opposite ends to stretch it.

### Step 3

Coat the thread.

Apply a *very* thin film of thread conditioner, such as Thread Heaven, or beeswax over the thread; avoid an excessive coating, which will cause the thread to become sticky.

## Technique: Stringing and Knotting Beads on a Cord

Silk cord is best suited to stringing light-weight beads. It is most often used to make knotted pearl necklaces. A knot between two pearls keeps them from rubbing against one another and at the same time adds a decorative element to the beaded strand. Beads strung and knotted on cord are traditionally finished with a clamshell and a clasp.

### MATERIALS AND TOOLS

Beads, as desired
Silk cord on a card with a twisted wire
    needle attached
2 clamshells
2 jump rings
Clasp, as desired
Instant glue (cyanoacrylate)
Carpet needle
Beading board
Household iron
Chain-nose pliers
Round-nose pliers
Bent-nose pliers
Thread scissors
Ruler

### Step 1

Arrange the beads and prepare the cord.

Lay out the beads in the desired order on a beading board. Unwind the cord from the card. Use a household iron to straighten out the folds in the cord, being careful to keep the needle attached. Prestretch the cord. Make a double knot in the end of the cord, leaving a 1" (2.5 cm) tail.

### Step 2

Attach the clamshell.

Insert the needle into the *interior* of the clamshell. Slide it down the cord until the knot sits inside the clamshell. Add a drop of glue to further secure the knot; trim away the excess cord. Use chain-nose pliers to close the clamshell around the knot.

### Step 3

Knot the cord.

Make a loose single overhand knot next to the clamshell. Place the tip of the carpet needle through the knot and slide it 1/16" (0.2 cm) from the clamshell. Remove the needle and tighten the knot.

## Step 4

String on the first bead and knot the cord.

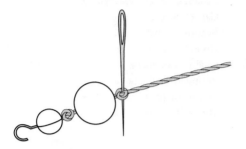

Thread a bead onto the needle and down the cord until it is next to the knot. Make a loose single overhand knot on the opposite side of the bead. Use the carpet needle to slide the knot as close to the bead as possible. Remove the needle and tighten the knot.

## Step 5

String on the remaining beads.

Continue to add the remaining beads to the cord, following each one with a knot, until all of the beads are strung.

## Step 6

Attach the second clamshell.

Insert the beading needle into the *exterior* hole of the second clamshell. Slide the clamshell down to the last knot tied. Make a loose single overhand knot in the cord and insert the carpet needle through the knot. Slide the knot into the open clamshell; remove the needle and tighten the knot. Add a drop of glue to secure the knot further. Trim away the excess cord with scissors.

## Step 7

Attach the clasp.

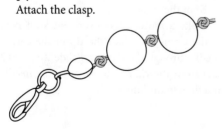

Close the clamshell using chain-nose pliers, trapping the knot inside. Open one jump ring using the chain-nose pliers and the bent-nose pliers. Thread one end of the jump ring through the loop on one half of the clasp. Close the jump ring. Bend the hook end of the clamshell around a closed jump ring using round-nose pliers. Repeat to attach the second half of the clasp to the remaining jump ring and clamshell on the other end of the beaded and knotted strand.

## Technique: Attaching a Clamshell and a Clasp to Beading Thread

Cord is easily secured to a clamshell with a knot and a drop of glue. A finer stringing material like beading thread is best secured by knotting it to a seed bead first. The seed bead adds bulk to the knot so it remains securely inside the clamshell.

### MATERIALS AND TOOLS

Beads, as desired
Seed bead
Beading thread
2 clamshells
2 jump rings
2 spacers, as desired (optional)
Clasp, as desired
Instant glue (cyanoacrylate)
Thread conditioner
Beading board
Beading needle
Carpet needle
Chain-nose pliers
Round-nose pliers
Bent-nose pliers
Thread scissors
Ruler

## Step 1

Arrange the beads and prepare the thread.

Lay out the beads on a beading board, as desired. Cut double the desired length of thread from the spool. Prestretch the thread. Double thread the beading needle and make a double knot at the end of the thread. Condition the thread.

**Step 2**

Thread on the seed bead and attach the first clamshell.

Insert the needle into the seed bead and slide it down to the knot, tying a double knot to trap the bead. Insert the beading needle into the interior of the clamshell. Slide the clamshell down the thread until the knotted bead sits inside the clamshell. Add a drop of

---

## Working Tips: Using Bullion to Safeguard Thread and Cord

Instead of a clamshell, bullion—tightly coiled fine wire—can be slipped over the end of the thread or cord that is attached directly to a clasp. Bullion protects the exposed loop of cord by preventing abrasion and subsequent fraying where the cord is attached to the clasp. To use bullion, cut a short section with wire cutters, slide it onto the cord until it rests against the loop, and then attach the clasp.

---

instant glue (cyanoacrylate) to further secure the knot; trim away the excess thread. Use chain-nose pliers to close the clamshell around the knotted bead.

**Step 3**

String on the beads.

Thread on one spacer bead, if desired, followed by all of the beads on the beading board, ending with a second spacer bead, if desired.

**Step 4**

Attach the second clamshell.

Insert the beading needle into the exterior hole of the second clamshell. Slide the clamshell down to the last bead strung. Make a loose single overhand knot in the thread and insert the carpet needle through the knot. Slide the knot into the open clamshell; remove the needle and tighten the knot. Thread on a seed bead. Tie a double knot to trap the bead. Add a drop of glue to secure the knot further. Trim away the excess thread, using scissors.

**Step 5**

Attach the clasp.

Close the clamshell using chain-nose pliers, trapping the knotted seed bead inside. Open one jump ring using the chain-nose pliers and the bent-nose pliers. Thread one end of the jump ring through the loop on one half of the clasp. Close the jump ring. Bend the hook end of the clamshell around a closed jump ring using round-nose pliers. Repeat to attach the second half of the clasp to the remaining jump ring and clamshell on the other end of the beaded and knotted strand.

## Technique: Attaching a Crimp Bead or a Crimp Tube to a Strand of Nylon-Coated Beading Wire

Nylon-coated beading wire is best secured with a crimp bead or tube at the beginning and end of the strand. Crimp beads and crimp tubes differ in appearance both before and after crimping, but they function in the same way. Either type can be concealed with a crimp-bead cover. Match the metal, finish, and diameter of a crimp bead or tube to the beading wire to harmonize the design elements. Use this crimping technique if you plan to add a jump ring and a clasp *after* the end of the beading wire has been secured with a crimp bead.

## MATERIALS AND TOOLS
Nylon-coated beading wire
Crimp bead or tube
Crimping pliers
Wire cutters

### Step 1
Thread on the crimp bead.

Use wire cutters to cut the nylon-coated beading wire from the spool in the desired length. Thread one end of the beading wire through the crimp bead. Slide the crimp bead down the wire ½" (1.3 cm) from the end. Bend the short end of the beading wire around and insert the tip back through the crimp, pulling the beading wire until there is a ⅛" (0.3 cm) loop.

### Step 2
Make the crimp oval-shaped.

Rest the crimp bead in the oval-shaped space near the tips of the crimping pliers, making certain the wires are parallel to one another. Squeeze the pliers closed to shape the crimp bead into an oval.

### Step 3
Make the crimp crescent-shaped.

Lift the crimp bead out of the oval-shaped well in the pliers and transfer it to the crescent-

shaped space near the joint of the crimping pliers, making certain the wires are parallel to one another. Squeeze the pliers closed to shape the crimp into a crescent.

### Step 4
Finish securing the crimp bead.

Return the crimp bead to the oval-shaped space in the crimping pliers, but at a 90-degree

# Working Tips: Standard Lengths for Beaded Jewelry

While any piece of jewelry may be sized to suit the wearer, standard lengths are followed for the strands in bracelets and necklaces. A bracelet, for example, should be long enough to be comfortable, but not so long that it slips off the wrist. There is greater latitude when making necklaces. For example, an opera-length necklace can be wrapped around the neck or knotted to shorten it.

Bracelet, 7" (17.8 cm)
Anklet, 10" (25.4 cm)
Necklaces:
   Choker, 16" (40.6 cm)
   Princess, 18" (45.7 cm)
   Matinee, 22" to 24" (55.9 to 61.0 cm)
   Opera, 30" to 32" (76.2 to 81.3 cm)
   Rope (or lariat), 45" (114.3 cm) or longer

angle. Squeeze the pliers closed to fold the crimp bead in half.

## Technique: Attaching a Crimp-Bead Cover to a Crimp Bead

Although a pair of chain-nose pliers can be used to secure a crimp bead cover around a crimp bead or tube, the oval-shaped well of the crimping pliers also works, conforming to the round shape of the cover.

### MATERIALS AND TOOLS

Beading wire with crimped end
Crimp bead cover
Crimping pliers

**Step 1**

Position the crimp bead cover.

Open the jaws of the crimping pliers. Place a crimp bead cover in the front oval-shaped well with the open portion of the cover facing out.

**Step 2**

Secure the crimp bead cover.

Place the finished crimp bead secured to the beading wire into the crimp bead cover. Squeeze the jaws of the crimping pliers closed to secure the crimp bead cover around the crimp bead.

## Working Tip: Coordinating Crimp Bead Sizes and Nylon-Coated Beading Wire

Insert both cut ends of a length of nylon-coated beading wire into the crimp bead or tube. If the pair of wire ends fits snugly without any gaps, the crimp bead is the correct size. For more guidance, consult the manufacturer's recommendations on the package of beading wire.

## Technique: Attaching a Clasp to a Strand with a Crimp Bead

This technique is recommended when stringing heavy beads on nylon-coated beading wire. Instead of a jump ring, a clasp is strung onto nylon-coated beading wire *before* the wire is secured with a crimp, ensuring that the clasp cannot accidentally come loose and fall off.

### MATERIALS AND TOOLS

Nylon-coated beading wire
Crimp bead or tube
Clasp with loop
Crimping pliers
Wire cutters
Beads, as desired
Wire nippers

**Step 1**

Thread on the crimp bead and the clasp.

Use wire cutters to cut the nylon-coated beading wire from the spool in the desired length. Thread one end of the beading wire through the crimp bead and the loop on one half of the clasp. Fold over ¾" (1.9 cm) of beading wire and insert the tip back through the crimp, pulling the beading wire until there is a ⅛" (0.3 cm) loop that traps the clasp. Be sure to leave some room between the crimp and the clasp so that the clasp can move freely.

**Step 2**

Make the crimp oval-shaped.

Rest the crimp bead in the oval-shaped space near the tips of the crimping pliers, making certain the wires are parallel with one another. Squeeze the pliers closed to shape the crimp bead into an oval.

**Step 3**

Make the crimp crescent-shaped.

Lift the crimp bead out of the oval-shaped well in the pliers and transfer it to the crescent-shaped space near the joint of the crimping pliers, making certain the wires are parallel to one another. Squeeze the pliers closed to shape the crimp into a crescent.

**Step 4**

Finish securing the crimp bead.

Return the crimp bead to the oval-shaped space in the crimping pliers, but at a 90-degree angle. Squeeze the pliers closed to fold the crimp bead in half.

**Step 5**

String the beads.

String one to three beads onto the nylon-coated beading wire, sliding them down to the crimped end. Hide the short end of the beading wire in the bead holes. Use wire nippers to trim off any excess wire. String on the remaining beads. Repeat steps 1–5 to secure the opposite end.

## Technique: How to Keep Beads from Binding

When beads are strung on nylon-coated beading wire, they usually touch one another. The close proximity causes the beads to grate against one another and possibly crack. To provide ease, a temporary seed bead is added to the strand, the strand is secured with a crimp bead as usual, and then the seed bead is crushed and removed.

MATERIALS AND TOOLS

Beads strung on beading wire
Crimp bead or tube
Seed bead
Chain-nose pliers
Crimping pliers
Safety glasses
Paper towel

**Step 1**

Thread on the seed bead and the crimp bead.

At the end of the beaded strand, thread on one seed bead; slide it against the last bead. Thread on the crimp bead and slide it against the seed bead. Fold over ½" (1.3 cm) of beading wire and insert the tip back through the crimp to form a ⅛" (0.3 cm) loop. Secure the crimp bead using the crimping pliers.

**Step 2**

Break off the seed bead.

Cover the seed bead with a paper towel. Grasp the seed bead between the tips of a pair of chain-nose pliers. Squeeze the pliers to carefully crush the seed bead and break it off the strand without scratching the adjacent bead. Tuck the end of the beading wire into the hole in the last bead.

## Working Tips: Securing Bead Stations

Use crimp beads to secure a single bead or a group of beads on a strand in a particular place (called a bead station). Place crimp beads like bookends on both sides of the bead or bead group. Then flatten the crimp beads using chain-nose pliers to secure them, permanently fixing the bead or beads in place on the strand.

## Off-Loom Weaving:
## The Peyote Stitch

The method for weaving beads into a fabric without the use of a loom is known as off-loom weaving. The weaving is done by hand, one bead at a time. Thread is pulled through a sequence of small beads to make a beaded row. As the process is repeated, row joins to row in an established sequence and a beaded fabric is formed.

The flat, even-count peyote stitch is one of the easiest bead weaving patterns to learn because it always uses an even number of beads. (There are flat, odd-count peyote stitches, but they are not covered here.) The possibilities of this simple little weaving stitch go well beyond its deceivingly easy looks, as the stitch can be used to create a seemingly endless variety of patterns by changing the size, shape, and color of the beads. You will sail through learning the stitch and be ready to try your own designs and move on to other bead weaving stitches to produce fanciful designs of every description. This stitch will simply start your weaving adventures.

Traditional peyote stitch weaving is done using either seed beads or cylinder beads and a needle and thread. For the best results, beads should be consistent in shape and size and the holes must be uniform and free of sharp edges. The thread must be sturdy and resilient enough to stand up to the stresses of weaving, thin enough to pass through the bead hole several times, and resistant to fraying and tangling. Many types of thread have the desired properties; my personal favorite is nylon thread. The best way to make a selection is to try several brands until you find one that works for you.

The importance of working with a good thread cannot be overemphasized as a weaving is only as strong as the thread used to make it. Manufacturers produce a wide array of synthetic beading threads that are suited to weaving. Made from long fibers that are strong and flexible, the thread is available on bobbins and spools in a broad range of colors and diameters—from size 000 (the thinnest) to sizes 00 and 0 and A, B, C, D, E, F, FF, and FFF (the thickest). Sizes B and D are most commonly used for weaving, especially for woven bracelets and necklaces, depending upon the size of the bead hole. The needle is equally important. Choose one that is smaller than the diameter of the bead hole, testing it first to make certain it passes through the holes in your beads.

You will also need thread conditioner (a synthetic conditioner such as Thread Heaven, natural beeswax, or both), instant glue (cyanoacrylate), thread scissors, and a flat towel. Findings for woven pieces include crimp-style fold-over clamps, multistrand bar clasps, and tube bar clasps, as well as buttons that fit into slits in the beaded weaving.

If you have never done bead weaving before, begin with a manageable project, such as a ring, to get a feel for the technique. A ring can be made using a flat, even-count peyote stitch; the narrower the band, the easier and faster it is to weave. Pour small piles of seed or cylinder beads, organized by color, onto a flat-weave cotton towel or a piece of felt. I find it easier to pick up single beads when they are placed in a smooth layer on a cloth; some weavers prefer to work from a low, flat dish.

You can work with either a single strand or a double strand of thread; I always work with a double strand to give the finished piece extra security. The double strand must be able to pass through the bead hole a minimum of two times so adjust the size of your thread accordingly. Thread that is too long twists and tangles easily so keep the double strand of thread a workable length, approximately 24" (61.0 cm). Remember to condition each length of thread you use by pulling the length at opposite ends to stretch it and by applying a very fine film of a thread conditioner. Synthetic conditioner is a silicon-based product that is lighter than natural beeswax, but both work well. Apply only the lightest coating to avoid a sticky thread that leaves residue inside the beads.

## Common Charted Design for Off-Loom Weaving

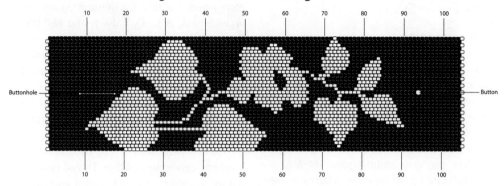

Equipped with all your supplies, you are ready to begin bead weaving—but first, a few words of encouragement about the flat, even-count peyote stitch. When you are establishing the first few rows of your weaving, they will appear uneven. Do not stress; as more beaded rows are added, these first few rows will become uniformly even and straight and the woven piece will begin to take shape. Keep the working thread taut, rather than loose and droopy, as you add new beads to your weaving. After a bead is seated, place your thumb gently against the thread where it exits the bead. Insert the needle into the next bead hole, drawing the thread through the second bead in a direction that is away from the hole while gently pressing against the thread to keep it from tangling. With the thread taut, you will be able to neatly seat the new bead, which in turn ensures uniform rows and columns in the weaving. Work in the same direction, either from left to right or from right to left, and from top to bottom or vice versa. Generally, right-handed weavers (which I am) work all the rows from right to left (which I do), and left-handed weavers work the rows from left to right. Each row (except for row 1) is made by working across the row to add half of the beads and then flipping the piece over and working back to the starting point to add the remaining beads in the row.

Charted designs are indispensable for woven designs that are more complex. If your weaving project includes a charted design that requires counting beads and changing colors, make an enlarged copy of the design chart and refer to it often. I keep track of the rows and the attendant changes in bead color using a straight pin. I prick the paper at the edge of the row on which I am working and move the pin as I go along, especially when a color change is coming up. Although following a chart can get tedious, the extra effort is worth it. That said, you may find that despite your concentrated efforts, you weave in a bead in the wrong color. Don't worry—simply incorporate the color change into your design, using a marker to make a note on the chart. If the mistake is one you feel you must correct, stop weaving. If the mistake is on the working row, back the needle, eye first, through the row. If the mistake is in another row, cut off the needle and draw the thread back through the beaded rows until you reach the mistake, and then begin weaving again from there. Note that you are raveling the weaving in order to get to the problem bead; the beads that are removed must be rewoven into the beaded fabric.

Regardless of the design of your bead weaving, you will need to know how to begin a thread using a stop bead. You will also need to know how to end a thread and begin a new one because on larger projects it is unlikely that you will be able to complete a weaving using only one length of thread.

## Technique: Attaching a Stop Bead

Begin a peyote stitch weaving by attaching a stop bead. It will keep newly added beads from sliding off the thread. The stop bead is not a permanent part of the design but is removed when the weaving is finished. The extra length of thread is woven into the beaded fabric or used to add a closure.

### MATERIALS AND TOOLS

Seed bead in a contrasting color (for stop bead)

Thread, such as Nymo nylon thread, size B

Thread conditioner

Beading needle, #10

Scissors

Ruler or tape measure

### Step 1

Prepare the thread.

Measure and cut a double strand of thread 24" (61.0 cm) long. Use your hands to stretch the thread by pulling on opposite ends and use a thread conditioner.

### Step 2

Add a stop bead to the thread.

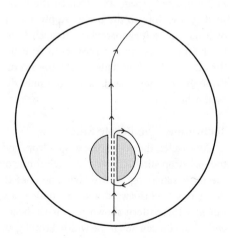

Insert one end of the thread through the beading needle and pull the ends even; do not make a knot. Insert the needle through the stop bead. Slide the bead to within 6" (15.2 cm) of the cut ends of thread. Draw the needle around the bead and reinsert it into the bead hole in the same direction as before. Pull the thread snug. Repeat to secure the stop bead.

## Technique: Ending a Thread

A working thread eventually becomes too short to maneuver easily through the beads. The beading can be finished or still in progress, but in either case, a neat, secure finish is essential. The technique to end off a thread involves weaving in the thread end and making overhand knots to anchor it.

### MATERIALS AND TOOLS

Peyote weaving in progress (featuring cylinder beads, size 11/0)

Thread, such as Nymo nylon thread, size B

Beading needle, #10

### Step 1

Reweave the thread.

Weave the needle in a zigzag pattern back through several beads, emerging at a lower row.

### Step 2

Knot the thread.

Use the needle to make a single overhand knot around the thread that is between two beads and gently pull the thread taut; refer to Tying Knots (page 48). Reweave the thread through a few more beads, then repeat to make a second overhand knot. Then weave the thread through a few beads, exiting on the underside of the weaving and leaving a thread tail.

### Step 3

Weave in the tail.

When the weaving is complete, thread the tail and weave it into the woven fabric, zigzagging across and down to lower rows.

## Technique: Beginning a New Thread

If you have ended a thread and you need to continue weaving to finish the pattern, you will need to weave in a new thread that emerges where you left off.

### MATERIALS AND TOOLS

Peyote weaving in progress (featuring cylinder beads, size 11/0)
Thread, such as Nymo nylon thread, size B
Thread conditioner
Beading needle, #10
Thread scissors
Ruler or tape measure

### Step 1

Begin the new thread.

Thread a needle with a new length of stretched and conditioned thread, pulling the ends even; do not knot the thread. Beginning on a lower row than where you stopped weaving, thread the needle through three or four beads that are already woven into the beaded fabric. The thread will naturally be in a zigzag pattern.

### Step 2

Knot the thread.

Use the needle to make a single overhand knot around the thread that is between two beads and gently pull the working thread taut. Go through a few more beads and then make a second overhand knot, as before. Weave the thread through more beads, emerging where you left off weaving.

### Step 3

Continue the established pattern.

Use the newly threaded needle to add additional rows to the weaving.

## Technique: Joining a New Thread to an Old Thread

Every bead weaver develops a particular style of working with thread. Here is a unique way to contend with the inevitable ending of an old thread and beginning a new one by using knots to join them together.

### MATERIALS AND TOOLS

Peyote weaving in progress (featuring cylinder beads, size 11/0)
Thread, such Nymo nylon thread, size B
Thread conditioner
Instant glue (cyanoacrylate)
Beading needle, #10
Thread scissors
Ruler or tape measure

### Step 1

Stop weaving.

When approximately 5" (12.7 cm) of the working thread remains on the needle, stop weaving. Cut off the needle. Thread the needle with a new double strand of stretched and conditioned thread 24" (61.0 cm) long. Pull the ends even; do not knot the thread.

### Step 2

Join the old threads to the new threads.

Use a square knot to tie each end of the new thread to one end of the old thread; refer to Tying Knots (page 48). Tighten the knots so they are close to the beads. Apply a drop of instant glue (cyanoacrylate) to each knot; let them dry. Use thread scissors to trim the thread ends to short tails. Insert the needle through the next bead, and continue the established pattern.

## Technique: The Peyote Stitch

Also called the gourd, the single-drop, and the one-drop stitch, the peyote stitch is one of the most satisfying bead weaving stitches to do. It is straightforward and can be learned quickly. The pattern shown here is six beads wide, but you can adapt the width, keeping an even-count number of beads and making a weaving in any length you wish.

## MATERIALS AND TOOLS

Cylinder beads, size 11/0
Seed bead in a contrasting color (for stop bead)
Thread, such as Nymo nylon thread, size B
Thread conditioner
Instant glue (cyanoacrylate)
Beading needle, #10
Flat-weave cotton towel (or dish)
Ruler
Thread scissors

### Step 1

Prepare the thread.

Cut a double strand of thread 24" (61.0 cm) long. Prepare the thread by stretching it and applying a conditioner. Attach a stop bead 6" (15.2 cm) from the cut ends. Spill a low pile of cylinder beads onto a flat-weave cotton towel.

### Step 2

Make row 1.

String on 6 cylinder beads (#1–#6), sliding them along the thread until they touch the stop bead.

### Step 3

Begin row 2.

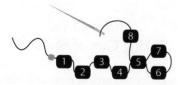

String on bead #7. Insert the needle into bead #5 (in row 1) and pull the thread taut to seat bead #7. String on bead #8.

### Step 4

Complete row 2.

Insert the needle into bead #3, and pull the thread taut to seat bead #8. String on bead #9 and insert the needle into bead #1. String on bead #10. Turn the weaving over.

### Step 5

Begin row 3.

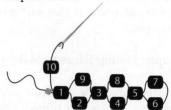

Insert the needle into bead #9 (in row 2) and pull the thread taut to seat bead #10. String on bead #11.

### Step 6

Complete row 3.

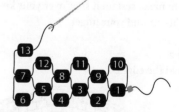

Insert the needle into bead #8 to seat bead #11. String on bead #12 and insert the needle into bead #7 to seat bead #12. String on bead #13. Row 2 is now complete. Turn the weaving over.

### Step 7

Continue adding beads.

Insert the needle into bead #12 and pull

the thread taut to seat bead #13. Continue to add beads, working across the row and back to complete each row until the weaving is the desired length.

## Technique: Joining Edges to Make a Ring

When opposite ends of peyote weaving are joined at their edges, it is much like fitting the bricks in a wall together. Where there is a bead on one side, there is no bead on the other, opposite, side. When the edges are sewn together to create a continuous band, no seams are apparent.

### MATERIALS AND TOOLS

Peyote-stitch ring in size 11/0 cylinder beads, woven but not joined
Thread, such as Nymo nylon thread, size B
Beading needle, #10
Thread scissors
Instant glue (cyanoacrylate)

### Step 1

Test-fit the ring.

Bring together the short edges so that the beads on the first row and the last row interlock neatly to form a ring. If the ring does not fit, add or remove a row of beads, test-fitting the ring to make certain it slips over your knuckle and fits around your finger.

### Step 2

Join the edges.

Insert the double-threaded needle into the first bead on the opposite edge and then into the next bead on the first edge. Continue working back and forth to secure the edges together, alternating the beads of the first and the last rows and pulling the thread taut and ending on the same side of the band as the stop bead.

### Step 3

Tie the weaving and stop bead threads together.

Use a spare needle to remove the wrap of thread on the stop bead. Working close to the edge of the weaving, tie the working thread and the stop bead threads in a snug square knot; refer to Tying Knots (page 48). Apply a drop of instant glue (cyanoacrylate) to the knot; let the glue dry.

### Step 4

End the thread.

Thread the tail ends into a needle and weave the needle in a zigzag pattern through a few

## Working Tips: Taking Care of Yourself

Bead weaving requires intense concentration and focus. To avoid fatigue and eyestrain, get up from your worktable from time to time, stretch, and change your posture.

beads in nearby rows to reinforce the joined edges. Bring the needle to the underside of the band and cut off the needle. Make a double knot close to the weaving. Apply a scant drop of instant glue (cyanoacrylate) to the knot; let the glue dry. Trim the excess threads close to the knot.

## Technique: Making a Buttonhole

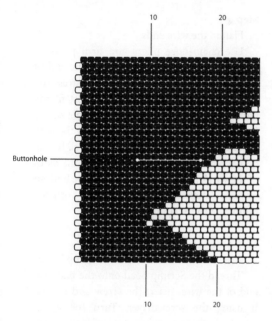

Some bracelet designs call for a slit in the beaded fabric so that a button can be inserted through the weaving to create a closure. Making a buttonhole involves separating a full width of woven beads into two separate segments to form the buttonhole opening and then rejoining the segments to complete the weaving.

### MATERIALS AND TOOLS

Peyote-stitch band in progress, size 11/0 cylinder beads

Thread, such as Nymo nylon thread, size B

2 beading needles, #10

Thread scissors

Instant glue (cyanoacrylate)

### Step 1

Weave the beaded band up to the beginning of the buttonhole.

Follow the beading diagram for your chosen project to complete all the rows up to the beginning of the buttonhole row.

### Step 2

Begin the buttonhole slit.

Work across the next row until you reach the position marked on the diagram for the buttonhole. Turn the work over, thread on a new bead, and work back to finish the row. Continue beading this segment only, working the rows across and back, until you reach the row count that corresponds to the end of the buttonhole slit on the diagram. Turn the work over and leave the needle and thread attached.

### Step 3

Complete the buttonhole slit.

Weave a second threaded needle through the beaded section, exiting at the beginning of the slit. Slip a bead onto the needle and proceed from this point to begin a new row, working across and back. Continue making rows for this beaded segment until you reach the row count that corresponds to the end of the buttonhole slit on the diagram. To end off the thread, weave the needle through several rows of the band in a zigzag pattern, exiting between any beads. Cut off the needle and tie the thread in a double knot. Apply a drop of instant glue (cyanoacrylate); let the glue dry. Cut off the excess thread.

### Step 4

Join the segments together.

Use the attached needle and thread and follow the beading diagram. Work straight across the full row to join the two beaded segments together and close the buttonhole slit. Turn the piece over and work back across the row. Continue weaving according to the beading diagram.

## PROJECTS

### Moonlight: A Pair of Earrings

Scrimp cylinder-and-screw findings are usually used to crimp beading wire, but here they add an industrial touch that gives these silver ball earrings contemporary style.

### MATERIALS AND TOOLS

Wire, sterling silver, 20-gauge
2 hollow round beads, center-drilled,
    sterling silver, 14 mm diameter
2 Scrimp findings, oval, 3.5 mm and
    1.04 mm inside diameter
Instant glue (cyanoacrylate)
Chain-nose pliers
Wire cutters
Screwdriver (for eyeglass repair)
Emery cloth, medium-grit (#400)
Ruler
Fine-tip marker
Rubbing alcohol
Cotton swab
Masking tape (optional)

### Step 1

Prepare the wire.

Use a ruler and wire cutters to measure and cut two 3" (7.6 cm) lengths of sterling silver wire.

### Step 2

Smooth the wire ends.

Lay the emery cloth on a flat surface. Drag each cut end of one wire across the cloth, rotating the end until it is smooth. Repeat for the second wire.

### Step 3

Prepare the Scrimp oval findings.

Remove the screws from the scrimp beads and set them aside in a safe place, such as an upturned jar lid, so that they will not roll or get lost.

### Step 4

Flatten the wire ends.

Use chain-nose pliers and firm pressure to flatten a ³⁄₃₂" (0.2 cm) length at one end of each wire, being careful not to overstress the wire, which can make it brittle. Test-fit the flattened end of each wire in the hole of the Scrimp bead as you work. Stop when the wire fits snugly inside the hole in the barrel. It may be necessary to use nippers to trim the sides of the wire's flattened end. Do trim the bottom of each flattened wire so it is flush with the bottom of the Scrimp finding.

### Step 5

Insert the wire ends into the Scrimp beads.

Thread the Scrimp bead onto the flattened end of the wire. Insert the screw and tighten it using the screwdriver. Turn the barrel upside down and apply a drop of instant glue (cyanoacrylate) into the hole; let the glue dry. Repeat on the second wire.

### Step 6

Add the silver balls.

Thread one silver ball onto the opposite end of the wire, sliding the ball down until it touches the Scrimp bead. Repeat on the second wire.

### Step 7

Mark the ear wires.

Use a ruler and a marker to measure and mark a point on each wire 1⅛" (2.9 cm) above the top of the silver ball.

## Step 8
Shape the ear wires.

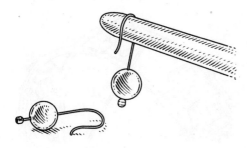

Position the marked point on one wire against the barrel of the marker. Pull both wire ends downward to form an upside-down U shape. Repeat on the other wire.

## Step 9
Bend the wire ends.

Use your thumb and forefinger to make a soft curve at the cut end of the wire so that it flares away from the straight wire. Repeat for the second ear wire. Use a cotton swab dipped in rubbing alcohol to remove the marker from the metal.

## Step 10
Test-fit the earrings.

Use a pencil to test-hang the earrings to make certain that they hang straight. If they do not, apply masking tape to the jaws of the chain-nose pliers; then use the tips of the pliers to grip and bend the ear wire a scant ¹⁄₁₆" (.2 cm) from the top of the silver ball. The masking tape will prevent damage to the wire.

## Rainbow: A Bangle Bracelet

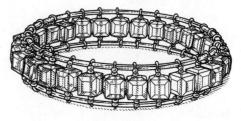

The sparkle of cut crystal is shown to great advantage in a bracelet composed entirely of crystal cubes in all of the colors of the rainbow. Each cube is secured with gold wire to purchased gold-tone bangle bracelets.

### MATERIALS AND TOOLS
2 round bangle bracelets in 14-gauge gold-tone wire, 3" (7.6 cm) diameter
30 crystal cubes, 7 mm, in multiple color ranges
6 pale pink to red
4 orange to yellow
6 pale lime to leaf green
6 aqua to cobalt blue
5 lavender to purple and maroon
2 frosted to clear crystal
1 black (if needed to fill out space)
Vial of gold seed beads, 1.5 mm (120 beads may be used in bracelet)
Gold-plated wire, 20-gauge
Scrap wire
4 round wooden beads, 12 mm (for placeholders)
Wire cutters
Round-nose pliers
Bent-nose pliers
Wire nippers
Safety glasses
Soft cloth or beading board
Emery cloth, medium-grit (#400)
Ruler
Marker
Rubbing alcohol
Cotton swab

**Step 1**

Arrange the beads.

Arrange all of the crystal cubes on a flat, cloth-covered work surface or a beading board. Follow the color sequence in the materials list, beginning with pale pink and ending with clear crystal.

**Step 2**

Prepare the bangle bracelets.

Put on safety glasses. Use a ruler and wire cutters to measure and cut four 4" (10.2 cm) lengths of scrap wire. Use a marker to mark four evenly spaced points on each bangle, dividing it into quarters. Center one length of scrap wire over one bangle at a marked point and bend the wire in half. Thread both wire ends through a 12 mm round placeholder bead and then wrap them around the second bangle at a marked point. Both bangles should align and be separated by the bead trapped between them. Repeat to secure the remaining three wooden placeholder beads to the marked positions on the bangles.

**Step 3**

Affix the first bead on the wire.

Measure and cut a ¼" (0.6 cm) length of 20-gauge gold-plated wire. Use an emery cloth to smooth one end. Use round-nose pliers to make a hook on the smoothed end with an inner diameter of 2.5 mm. (The hook should fit the width of the bangle wire.) Hang the hook on one bangle. Use bent-nose pliers to gently squeeze the hook against the bangle wire, using just enough pressure to hold it in place. Do not tighten the hook completely but allow the wire to swing.

**Step 4**

Thread on the small accent beads and the crystal cube.

Hold the wire at a right angle to the bangle and insert the cut end into 2 gold seed beads, 1 pale pink crystal cube, and 2 gold seed beads.

**Step 5**

Secure the beads.

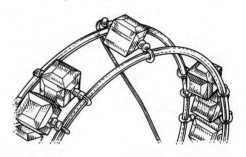

Position the unsecured end of the wire against the top of the second bangle and bend it around the bangle wire, using bent-nose pliers if necessary, to create a second hook. Use wire cutters to trim the wire end on the hook to ⅛" (0.3 cm). Use bent-nose pliers to crimp the wire flush against the bangle. The end of the wire does not need to form a continuous loop around the bangle wire; there can be a slight gap.

**Step 6**

Trim the wire end.

Use wire nippers to trim the opposite wire hook, if necessary. Use the emery cloth to smooth both wire ends.

**Step 7**

Thread on the remaining cubes.

Repeat steps 3–6 to secure the remaining crystal cubes and seed beads to the bangles, sliding the round placeholder beads along the bangles as you work and eventually removing them, one by one, to make room for new crystal cubes. The bangles will tend to shift until the row of crystal beads is established, so be careful not to twist them.

**Step 8**

Distribute the crystals around the bangles.

Adjust the crystals so the sides of the cubes are adjacent and perpendicular to the bangle bracelets. If there is a gap between the crystals after 30 cubes are wired and the space is large enough to fit another crystal cube, add it. However, if the gap is too small to accommodate another cube, adjust all of the cubes around the bangles, distributing them to minimize the gap.

## Princess: A Choker

Pearls in a variety of sizes and pastel colors produce a piece of jewelry with delicate style. Here, pearls are threaded onto memory wire in a random pattern to make a single-wrap choker. A tassel made up of plump pearls and a crystal cube suspended on sterling silver chains adds a swingy detail that makes the choker fun to wear.

### MATERIALS AND TOOLS

**For the necklace:**
51 round glass pearls in assorted colors
    and sizes
    2 pale pink, 10 mm
    2 white, 7 mm
    2 white, 5 mm
    42 white, 4 mm
15 freshwater pearls, 6 mm × 7 mm,
    in soft peach
7 freshwater pearls, 4 mm × 5 mm,
    in white
5 seed beads, silver-lined, size 11/0,
    in lime green

1 seed bead, size 11/0, in dark color (to be
    broken off)
1 spool of memory wire, necklace weight,
    in bright silver

**For tassels:**
1 round glass pearl, 11 mm, in white
1 round glass pearl, 11 mm, in cream
1 round glass pearl, 9 mm, in clear pastel
    green
1 crystal cube, 7 mm, in clear pale green
4 head pins, sterling silver, 24-gauge,
    1½" (3.8 cm) long
7" (17.8 cm) cable-link chain, sterling
    silver, 2 mm links
2 jump rings, sterling silver, 2 mm
Crystal seed beads, 11/0 (optional;
    for large-hole pearls)

Chain-nose pliers
Round-nose pliers
Bent-nose pliers
Memory wire cutters
Wire nippers
Wire cutters
Emery cloth, medium-grit (#400)
Beading board or soft cloth
Safety glasses
Ruler
Paper towel

### Step 1

Arrange the beads.

Lay all of the pearls and seed beads for the necklace in a random order on a soft cloth or beading board. Put on safety glasses. Unspool one-and-a-half hoops of memory wire and cut with memory wire cutters. Drag the ends across the emery cloth to smooth them.

### Step 2

Make a stop on one wire end.

Following the natural curve of the wire, use the chain-nose pliers to make a 90-degree bend ⅛" (0.3 cm) from one end of the memory wire. Position the widest part of the plier jaws on the bend and squeeze the end flush against the wire. This flattened bend will keep the pearls from sliding off the wire.

### Step 3

Thread on the beads.

Insert the opposite cut end of memory wire through the pearls and the seed beads, sliding them along the wire until all of the beads are strung. End with a dark seed bead (to be broken off later).

### Step 4

Make a stop on the second wire end.

Use memory wire cutters to cut off the excess memory wire ⅜" (1.0 cm) beyond the seed bead. Hold onto the beads and drag the cut end across the emery cloth to smooth it. Following the natural curve of the wire, use chain-nose pliers to make a 90-degree bend ⅛" (0.3 cm) from the end of the wire. Use the chain-nose pliers to squeeze the bent end flush against the wire.

### Step 5

Remove the end seed bead.

Wrap a piece of paper towel around the end seed bead and use pliers to break it off the wire. The extra space will prevent the beads from binding. Set the necklace aside.

### Step 6

Make and attach the tassel.

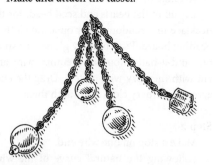

Thread the cream 11 mm pearl onto a head pin; if the pearl slips off the head pin, add a seed bead as a stop. Make a wire-wrapped

loop at the other end. Repeat for the other two pearls and the crystal cube. Referring to the chart, use a ruler and wire nippers to cut 4 lengths of silver chain. Use the chain-nose and bent-nose pliers to open one end link on each chain, thread on the wire loop of the corresponding bead, and close the link. Secure the opposite ends of the chains in pairs to two jump rings. Position each jump ring between two beads on the necklace and close to secure.

| Length of Chain | Bead |
|---|---|
| 2⅛" (5.4 cm) | Cream pearl, 11 mm |
| 1" (2.5 cm) | Pastel green glass pearl, 9 mm |
| 1¾" (4.4 cm) | White pearl, 11 mm |
| 2" (5.1 cm) | Clear green crystal cube, 7 mm |

## Blue Ice: A Pendant

The appeal of this pendant is its simplicity. A faceted crystal in clear blue is accented with sparkling silver findings that highlight the cut of the crystal.

## MATERIALS AND TOOLS

- 1 faceted quartz nugget, 18 mm wide × 27 mm long × 6 mm thick, in pale blue
- 1 oval bead, brushed sterling silver, 5 mm × 12 mm long
- 2 round beads, sterling silver with stardust finish, 4 mm
- 2 spacers, sterling silver with stardust finish, 7 mm
- 1 neck wire with removable ball-and-tube end caps, silver, 16" (40.6 cm) circumference
- 1 bead-and-loop pendant bail, silver, with 4 mm bead, 3 mm loop
- 3" (7.6 cm) wire, sterling silver, 20-gauge
- Instant glue (cyanoacrylate)
- Wire cutters
- Round-nose pliers
- Bent-nose pliers
- Chain-nose pliers
- Emery cloth, medium-grit (#400)
- Ruler

### Step 1

Make a wire stop.

Cut a 3" (7.6 cm) length of 20-gauge wire. Drag each end along the surface of a piece of emery cloth, rotating the end to smooth it. Use round-nose pliers to make a 1/16" (0.2 cm) bend at one end of the wire. Use chain-nose pliers to squeeze the end flush against the wire to make the stop.

### Step 2

Thread on the first two beads.

Thread one 4 mm silver bead and one 7 mm spacer bead onto the wire. Slide the beads down and onto the stop to conceal it. Apply a drop of instant glue (cyanoacrylate) to secure the beads; let the glue dry.

### Step 3

Thread on the large crystal and the remaining beads.

Thread the crystal bead onto the wire, followed by a silver spacer bead, a round bead, and the oval bead.

### Step 4

Make an eye loop.

Use wire cutters to trim the top of the wire to 1/4" (0.6 cm). Drag the cut end over emery cloth, rotating the wire to smooth it and holding on to the beads so that they do not slip off the wire. Use round-nose pliers to make a small loop at the top end of the wire; do not close the loop.

### Step 5

Thread the pendant onto the bail.

Use bent-nose pliers to feed the open loop into the loop on the pendant bail. Then use chain-nose and bent-nose pliers to close the loop.

### Step 6

Thread the bail onto the neck wire and add the end cap.

Remove one ball-and-tube cap from the neck wire. Insert the end of the wire through the bead on the pendant bail, sliding the pendant to the center of the neck wire. Apply a drop of instant glue (cyanoacrylate) to the end of the wire and insert it into the tube end of the ball-and-tube cap. Let the glue dry.

## Gold Band: A Peyote Ring

Perfect for a beginner, this elegant ring is made using 24-karat gold cylinder beads that are woven in flat even-count peyote stitch. The finished band for the ring is 6 beads wide and 37 rows long; however, it is easy to custom-fit a ring because the Delica beads allow changes in small increments to the length of the woven band. A matching bracelet can be made by weaving a band that is 7" (17.8 cm) long; test-fit the band around your wrist and add an inch or so if needed to slip the closed band on and off your wrist.

### MATERIALS AND TOOLS

1 vial (4 g) of Delica cylinder beads, 24-karat bright gold-plated, size 11/0 (approximately 222 beads are used)
1 bobbin Nymo thread, gold, size B
Stop bead
Thread conditioner or beeswax
Instant glue (cyanoacrylate)
Beading needle, #10
Crystal rondelle, 3mm, in emerald green (optional)
Flat-weave cotton towel (or a dish)
Ruler
Thread scissors
Straight pin

### Step 1

Begin beading.
Thread the needle with a double strand of Nymo thread, 24" (61.0 cm) long. Attach a stop bead 5" (12.7 cm) from the thread ends. String on 6 gold beads (#1–#6), sliding the beads to a point 5" (12.7 cm) from the stop bead.

### Step 2

Make rows 2 and 3.
String on a new bead (#7), insert the needle into bead #5 from the previous row, and pull the thread taut to seat the bead. Continue across row 2, adding two more new beads. There are now three completed rows. Turn the strip over.

### Step 3

Make rows 4–37.
Continue adding rows of gold beads until the band measures 2½" (6.4 cm) long, or a length that wraps around your finger and your knuckle. When the band fits, stop adding rows of beads. Do not cut off the needle.

### Step 4

Connect the edges.
Bring the edges of row 1 and row 37 together, matching up the beads so that they interlock neatly, forming a ring shape. Note that every row has "up" beads and "down" beads, names that identify the position of the beads in the row. If the "up" and "down" beads do not come together and interlock, add or remove a row of beads, making certain the finished length will wrap around your finger and slip over your knuckle.

### Step 5

Weave the edges together.

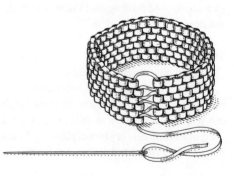

Weave the needle in a zigzag pattern through the "up" beads in row 1 and the "down" beads in row 37 (or vice versa), pulling the thread taut to join the beaded edges together and ending at the outside edge of the ring.

### Step 6

End the thread.

Insert the needle into the hole of the bead on the opposite edge and weave the needle in a zigzag pattern through a few beads in nearby rows to reinforce the joined edges. Bring the needle to the inside of the band and cut off the needle. Tie a double-knot close to the weaving. Apply a drop of instant glue (cyanoacrylate) to the knot; let the glue dry. Trim the excess threads close to the knot.

### Step 7

Weave in the stop bead thread.

Use a pin to open the knot on the stop bead from step 1 and slide it off. Thread both thread ends through the needle and weave the needle in a zigzag pattern through the band to anchor the threads. Exit on the inside of the band. Tie a double knot close to the weaving. Apply a drop of glue to the knot; let the glue dry. Trim the excess threads close to the knot.

### Step 8 (optional)

Secure a stone to the band.

Thread the needle with a double strand of thread 10" (25.4 cm) long; do not make a knot. Insert the needle through the outside of the band between beads 3 and 4 of row 18, leaving a 2" (5.1 cm) tail on the right side of the band. Insert the needle between beads #3 and #4 on row 19 from the underside. Pull the needle through, bringing it back to the right side of the band. Thread on the green rondelle and a gold Delica bead. Pull the thread taut, holding the beads against the band. Insert the needle back through the rondelle (skipping the gold bead) and through to the inside of the band between beads #3 and #4 of row 18. Repeat to reinforce the rondelle, ending with the needle on the

inside of the band. Tie a double knot close to the weaving. Add a drop of glue; let the glue dry. Trim the excess threads close to the weaving.

## Frothy Silver: A Necklace

A frothy collar of sparkling silver is made from twisted wire and an assortment of clear crystal and silver beads. The necklace is tied with a sheer ribbon that echoes the light and playful style of the beading.

### MATERIALS AND TOOLS

Round beads, silver-plated with stardust finish, on 9" (22.9 cm) strands
    5 strands of 6 mm beads (108 beads)
    3 strands of 5 mm beads (90 beads)
Wound-wire beads, silver-plated, on 9" (22.9 cm) strands
    3 strands of 7 mm beads (75 beads)
    1 strand of 7 mm beads (25 beads)
14 crystal cubes, clear, aurora borealis (AB) finish, 4 mm
25 Swarovski bicone crystals, 6 mm
50 round pearls, in white, 4 mm
50 pony beads, clear glass, 3 mm
4 round beads, in silver finish, 8 mm
2 jump rings, sterling silver, 8 mm
2 bails (or spools) of sterling silver wire, 26-gauge (for twisted strands)
Two 2½" (6.4 cm) lengths nylon-coated 7-strand beading wire, .015" diameter

2 bead caps
4 crimp beads, silver, size #2
4 crimp bead covers
1½ yards (1.4 m) sheer ribbon, 1½"
   (3.8 cm) wide, in white
Wire cutters
Chain-nose pliers
Bent-nose pliers
Round-nose pliers
Crimping pliers
Safety glasses
Scissors
Large bowl
Ruler

**Step 1**

Prepare the beads.

Use wire cutters or scissors to cut the strands on all of the beads, sliding them into one bowl. Mix them thoroughly.

**Step 2**

String on the beads.

Working from one spool of silver wire, string on all the beads in a random pattern, placing different kinds, sizes, and textures next to one another. Slide the beads down the wire toward the spool, leaving 3" (7.6 cm) of bare wire on the loose end. Do not cut the wire from the spool.

**Step 3**

Twist the wires together to trap each bead.

Loosen the wire end from the second spool. Join this plain wire end with the end of the beaded wire by twisting them together for 2" (5.1 cm). To make the first strand in group A, slide one bead up the wire to the twist. Run the plain wire over the bead. Twist the two wires together at the base of the bead for ½" (1.3 cm), trapping the bead within the wires.

**Step 4**

Add more beads and twist the wires.

Slide another bead up the wire and twist to trap it between both wires. Continue in this way, spacing the beads at ½" to ¾" (1.3 to 1.9 cm) intervals until the twisted, beaded strand measures 13½" (34.3 cm) long; twist the next 2" (5.1 cm) of the wire without adding any beads. Use wire cutters to cut the strand from the bail of wire; set the 15½" (39.4 cm) beaded strand aside.

**Step 5**

Make the remaining strands.

Repeat steps 3–4 and follow the chart below to make 12 beaded strands total, adding a twisted 2"-long (5.1 cm) section to the beginning and end of each strand. Make a wrapped-wire loop using the tips of the round-nose pliers at both ends of each beaded strand. The wrapped-wire loops should be as small as possible.

| Group | Number of Strands | Strand Length |
|---|---|---|
| A | 1 | 15½" (39.4 cm) |
|  | 1 | 16½" (41.9 cm) |
|  | 1 | 17" (43.2 cm) |
| B | 3 | 18" (45.7 cm) |
|  | 1 | 18½" (47.0 cm) |
|  | 2 | 19" (48.3 cm) |
| C | 3 | 21" (53.3 cm) |

**Step 6**

Secure the wire ends.

Insert one end of the 2½"-long (6.4 cm) nylon-coated beading wire through two crimp beads, a jump ring, and back through both crimp beads. Slide the top crimp bead up the wires toward the jump ring to form a ¼" (.6 cm) loop. Secure the crimp bead. Slide the second crimp bead to ½" (1.3 cm) below the first to trap the excess wire tail. Secure the crimp bead. Use wire cutters to trim away the excess wire tail below this second crimp bead. Do not cut the long beading wire.

**Step 7**

Gather all of the strand groups in alphabetical order. Insert the opposite end of the nylon-coated beading wire through two crimp beads, the loops on 12 twisted strands, and back through both crimp beads. Slide the top crimp bead up the wires toward the loops on the twisted strands so that a ½" (1.3 cm) loop is formed. Secure the crimp bead. Slide the second crimp bead to ½" (1.3 cm) below the first. Secure the crimp bead. Use wire cutters to trim away the excess wire tail below this second crimp bead.

**Step 8**

Repeat steps 6 and 7 to join the opposite ends of the strands to the other piece of beading wire. Use pliers to cover the crimp beads on both ends with crimp bead covers.

**Step 9**

Shape the necklace.

Use your hands to scrunch the wires so that they tangle and "shrink." Thread the ribbon through the jump rings, tying the ends to secure the necklace when worn.

## Vieux Nice: A Charm Bracelet

Inspired by a bracelet I saw at a French market, my *Vieux Nice* design is hung with charms composed of beads and findings that are threaded onto head pins in unique combinations. The head pins are made into single wrapped-wire loops and secured to a silver chain using jump rings. Each "charm" contains four or five beads and three to five bead caps. The list of materials provides a wide choice of alternatives so that beads and bead caps can be arranged according to your taste, with pieces left over for another project.

MATERIALS AND TOOLS

    5 round beads, 16 mm
        1 faceted crystal, in clear pink
        2 opaque quartz, in orange and rose
        1 dyed jade, in robin's-egg blue with crazing
        1 jasper, in rust brown and red with whorls
    1 round carnelian, 6 mm, in rosy pink
    5 fused-glass rondelles with vertical stripes, 16 mm × 12 mm
        1 raspberry and lime green
        1 deep rose and medium pink
        1 medium rose and pale pink
        1 pale pink and pale leaf green
        1 white and medium sky blue
    2 fused-glass lampwork rondelles,

14 mm diameter × 8 mm thick,
in raspberry and mint green
1 fluorite rectangle, 14 mm wide ×
20 mm long × 6 mm thick, in icy
blue
1 carnelian rectangle, 13 mm wide ×
18 mm long × 5 mm thick, in tobacco
brown
1 long oval, axis-drilled, 18 mm wide ×
25 mm long × 4 mm thick, in opaque
cream
60 assorted crystals
30 Swarovski bicone crystals, 3 mm,
in fuchsia, leaf green, turquoise,
and orange
30 faceted crystal rondelles, 6 mm,
in pale green, blue, lavender,
purple, and rose
30 seed beads in colors, as desired
2 sterling silver charms with flat backs
20 filigree bead caps, antiqued silver,
16 mm diameter
36 filigree bead caps, antiqued silver,
8 mm diameter
15 spacer beads, silver, 4 mm diameter
15 ball-tipped head pins, sterling silver,
3" (7.6 cm) long
15 open jump rings, sterling silver, 4 mm
7½" (19.1 cm) round-link chain,
16-gauge, sterling silver, 4 mm links
Spring-ring clasp, sterling silver,
14 mm diameter
Closed jump ring, sterling silver, 10 mm
Instant glue (cyanoacrylate)
Chain-nose pliers
Bent-nose pliers
Round-nose pliers
Wire cutters
Emery cloth, medium-grit (#400)
Flat-weave cotton towel

## Step 1

Arrange the beads for each charm.

Place all the beads on a flat covered surface. Arrange 15 groups of beads and bead caps in a row, placing one large focal bead in each group.

To each group, add 2 large filigree bead caps, 2 small filigree bead caps, 2 crystal rondelles, and 2 bicone crystals. Combine the smaller accent beads and findings with the large focal beads, alternating bead colors and shapes. Pair long bead caps with the fluorite rectangle and the carnelian rectangle. Use instant glue (cyanoacrylate) to adhere one metal charm to the center of the carnelian rectangle and one charm to the center of the cream oval. Let the glue dry.

## Step 2

Attach a clasp to the chain.

Drape the sterling silver bracelet on your wrist to ensure that it fits comfortably. If the bracelet is too big, use wire cutters to remove one or more links. Attach the spring-ring clasp directly to one end link on the bracelet; use the chain-nose and bent-nose pliers to open the link, insert the clasp, and close the link. Attach the large jump ring to the opposite end link in the same manner.

## Step 3

Thread the beads on the head pins.

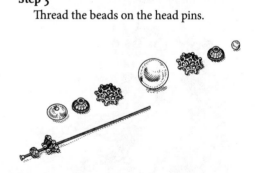

Insert a head pin through the beads arranged in step 1. Repeat to make 15 stacked bead-and-cap head pins. Make certain that no configuration is longer than 1½" (3.8 cm).

## Step 4

Make the first bend.

When you are satisfied, carefully lift one bead-stacked head pin. Use chain-nose pliers to grip the wire stem approximately ⅛" (0.3

cm) above the top bead. Rotate the pliers, bending the wire at a 90-degree angle.

### Step 5

Shape the loop.

Use round-nose pliers to grip the wire ⅛" (0.3 cm) away from the bend. Rotate the pliers toward the bend to begin shaping the loop. When your wrist can no longer rotate comfortably, stop. Do not remove the pliers, but use your fingers on the opposite hand to wrap the head pin wire around the jaw of the round-nose pliers until it crosses in front of the head pin wire and completes a round loop.

### Step 6

Wrap the wire around the stem.

Use the chain-nose pliers to grip the wire loop. Use your fingers to wrap the wire tail around and down the stem of the head pin until it touches the top of the bead. Be sure to make tight, even wraps. As the wire stem shortens, the wraps get harder to make: use the bent-nose pliers instead of your fingers to make the last few wire wraps, if necessary.

### Step 7

Finish the wrapped-wire loop.

Trim away the excess wire using the wire cutters. Then use an emery file to smooth the wire end, being careful not to scratch the beads. Use bent-nose pliers to gently squeeze the cut wire end flush against the stem. Repeat steps 4–7 to add wrapped-wire loops to the remaining head pins.

### Step 8

Attach the charms to the bracelet.

Lay the bracelet on a flat work surface and arrange the charms along its length. Use a jump ring to attach each charm to a link in the bracelet, spacing the charms at even intervals.

## Swing: A Pair of Earrings

Earrings with pendants that swing when you move are fun to wear. These earrings are made from the hoops of two toggle clasps, each of which holds three dangling pendants made of cube crystals and a delicate faceted teardrop.

### MATERIALS AND TOOLS

4 crystal cubes, 8 mm
  2 deep turquoise
  2 deep fuchsia
2 crystal teardrops, head-drilled, peridot,
  8 mm diameter × 12 mm long
2 Austrian crystal bicones, 3 mm diameter
6 silver beads, 2 mm
4 ball pins, sterling silver, 2" (5.1 cm)
Wire, sterling silver with copper core,
  20-gauge
Wire, sterling silver, 24-gauge
2 ring-shaped sections from toggle clasps,
  sterling silver
2 ear wires with ball ends
Instant glue (cyanoacrylate)
Wire cutters
Chain-nose pliers
Bent-nose pliers
Round-nose pliers
Emery cloth, medium-grit (#400)
Ruler

**Step 1**

Make the turquoise cube pendants.

Cut two ball pins to 1¾" (4.4 cm) long. Drag the cut ends on a piece of emery cloth, rotating them to smooth them. Thread an 8 mm turquoise cube and a silver bead onto one ball pin. Slide the silver bead up against the turquoise cube and use a dab of instant glue (cyanoacrylate) to secure it in place. Let the glue set. Use the round-nose pliers to make an eye loop at the cut end. Open the eye loop using the chain-nose and the bent-nose pliers, attach it to the hoop-shaped portion of the toggle clasp, and close the loop. Repeat with the other ball pin and the second hoop-shaped portion of the toggle clasp.

**Step 2**

Make the fuchsia cube pendants.

Cut two ball pins to 1½" (3.8 cm) long. Drag the cut ends on a piece of emery cloth, rotating them to smooth them. Thread an 8 mm fuchsia cube and a silver bead onto one ball pin. Slide the silver bead down the stem until it rests on the cube and use a dab of instant glue (cyanoacrylate) to secure it in place. Let the glue set. Use the round-nose pliers to make an eye loop above the silver bead. Open the eye loop using the chain-nose and bent-nose pliers, attach it to the right of the turquoise cube on the toggle clasp, and close the loop. Repeat with the other ball pin and toggle clasp.

**Step 3**

Begin the teardrop-bicone pendants.

Use wire cutters to cut two 3" (7.6 cm) lengths of 24-gauge wire. Insert 1" (2.5 cm) of one wire through a crystal teardrop. Bring both wires to the center top of the teardrop and cross them. Wrap the short wire up the long wire for ⅛" (0.3 cm). Cut off any excess short wire. Use chain-nose pliers to press the cut end flush against the wire. Thread a 3 mm bicone crystal onto the long wire, sliding it down to the wire wrap. Make a wrapped loop ¼" (0.6 cm) above the bicone using the round-

nose pliers, wrapping the wire down the stem stopping just short of the bicone. Trim away the excess wire. Press the end flush against the wire. Repeat with the second wire and the remaining bicone.

**Step 4**

Complete the teardrop-bicone pendants.

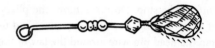

Measure and cut two 1" (2.5 cm) lengths of 20-gauge wire. Drag the cut ends on a piece of emery cloth, rotating them to smooth them. Use the round-nose pliers to make an eye loop on one end of each piece. Open the eye loop using the chain-nose and the bent-nose pliers and thread on a teardrop-bicone made in step 3; use the pliers to close the loop. Thread on one silver bead. Use the round-nose pliers to make an eye loop on the cut end. Open this eye loop using the chain-nose and the bent-nose pliers, attach it to the right of the fuchsia cube on the toggle clasp, and close the loop. Repeat these steps with the other wire and attach it to the other toggle clasp.

**Step 5**

Add the ear wires.

Thread the cut end of an ear wire through the ring in the toggle clasp until you reach the ball stop at the opposite end. Repeat to finish the second earring.

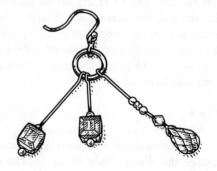

## Blue Topaz and Pearls: A Necklace

A straightforward stringing technique is all that is needed to make this luxurious and sparkling necklace in clear blue faceted topaz in briolette shapes and freshwater pearls in lustrous white.

### MATERIALS AND TOOLS

1 beaded strand, 9" (22.9 cm) long,
   of blue topaz in faceted briolettes in
   graduated sizes from 5 mm wide ×
   5 mm long × 2 mm thick to 8 mm
   wide × 12 mm long × 2 mm thick,
   in pale blue (70 briolettes)
1 beaded strand, 16" (40.6 cm) long,
   of freshwater pearls, head-drilled,
   6 mm diameter × 7 mm long,
   in white (75 pearls)
Nylon-coated beading wire, 7 strands,
   very fine, .013" (0.33 mm) diameter
Clasp, box-style, sterling silver, 5 mm
   diameter
Jump ring, closed, sterling silver,
   5 mm
2 crimp beads, sterling silver,
   1 mm diameter
French bullion wire, medium, silver
Wire cutters
Crimping pliers
Ruler

**Step 1**

Arrange the beads.

Use wire cutters to cut two ¼" (0.6 cm) lengths of bullion; set them aside. Cut a 24" (61.0 cm) length of beading wire; set it aside. Lay the strand of briolettes on a flat surface. Use wire cutters to cut off one end of the stringing material that holds them; slide off the briolettes, laying them out in the same order as they are on the strand. Repeat to lay out the pearls.

**Step 2**

Attach one half of the clasp.

Thread one end of the beading wire through a crimp bead, a ¼" (0.6 cm) length of bullion, and the loop on the clasp. Thread the end back through the crimp bead, centering the bullion in the loop of the clasp. Use the crimping pliers and the crimp bead to secure the clasp to the beading wire.

**Step 3**

Thread on the beads.

Use the opposite end of the beading wire to thread on three freshwater pearls, the first small briolette, and another pearl. Continue to string the briolette-and-pearl pattern until all of the briolettes are used. Then thread on the remaining two pearls.

**Step 4**

Finish attaching the clasp.

Repeat step 2 to attach the second half of the clasp to the end of the beading wire.

## Spring Leaf: A Peyote Bracelet

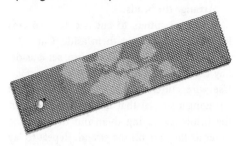

This bracelet is a very satisfying project for a bead weaver with some experience. The challenge is to keep track of the cream-colored beads that need to be added to create the abstract leaf pattern. Make an enlarged copy of the beading layout and use a straight pin to mark the rows on the chart as you work. I used Japanese seed beads because they are reasonable in cost. I selected the beads very carefully as I worked to make certain the weaving remained even. Miyuki Delica beads could also be used, but the band woven from them would be slightly larger.

### MATERIALS AND TOOLS

Japanese seed beads, size 12/0, one
   5-gram bag each
   Pale turquoise, opaque with luster
   Cream, opaque with luster
1 round dyed-jade bead, center-drilled,
   cream, 8 mm
1 spool Nymo nylon thread, cream,
   size D

Stop bead (in a different color than the
   seed beads)
Instant glue (cyanoacrylate)
Thread conditioner
Flat-weave cotton towel or small bowls
   (for beads)
Beading needles, #10
Thread scissors
Ruler or tape measure

**Step 1**
Prepare the beads and thread.
Pour a small amount of each color bead into a separate mound on the towel and use your hand to make a smooth layer. Move the towel within easy reach. Cut a double strand of thread 24" (61.0 cm) long. Prepare the thread by stretching it and applying a conditioner. Attach a stop bead 6" (15.2 cm) from the cut ends.

**Step 2**
Make row 1.
String on 17 turquoise and 17 cream beads, beginning with turquoise and ending with cream and alternating the colors across the row. Slide the beads to a point 5" (12.7 cm) from the stop bead. Note that only row 1 (the first row) and row 105 (the last row) have a "lace" edge that is made using cream beads.

**Step 3**
Make row 2.
String on a turquoise bead; skip over the

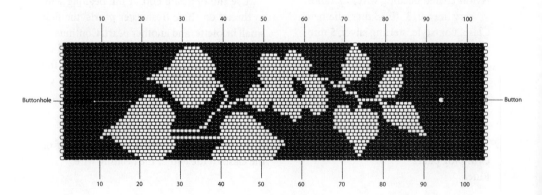

next bead (turquoise bead from row 1) and insert the needle into the next cream bead from row 1. Pull the thread taut to seat the new bead. Continue across, adding and seating a turquoise bead on every cream bead until 17 new turquoise beads have been added. Turn the weaving over. String on a turquoise bead, skip over the next bead, and work back across, adding a turquoise bead in every other bead. Turn the weaving over.

## Step 4

Make rows 3–10.

Repeat step 3, working across and then back with turquoise beads, to add 8 new rows.

## Step 5

Begin leaf pattern with row 11.

Referring to the beading diagram, seat 3 turquoise beads and 1 cream bead; continue across using turquoise beads only. Turn the work over and follow the diagram to work back, seating 13 turquoise beads, 1 cream bead, and 3 turquoise beads. Turn the work over.

## Step 6

Continue the leaf pattern on rows 12–90.

Referring to the beading diagram, work the leaf pattern across and back to complete rows 12–90.

## Step 7

Begin the slit for the buttonhole.

Begin row 91, beading halfway across with 8 turquoise beads. Turn the weaving over, thread on a new turquoise bead, and work back, skipping every other bead and pulling the thread taut as you go to seat each new bead. Turn the work over. Work rows 92–100 across and back in the same way. Turn the work over and leave the needle and thread attached.

## Step 8

Complete the buttonhole slit.

At row 91, weave a second threaded needle across the first segment, exiting in the center where the first section ended. Add 9 new turquoise beads, working across to the opposite edge of the band. Turn the weaving over and work back across to the slit location. Continue weaving with turquoise beads to complete rows 92–100 of the second segment. To end off the thread, weave the needle through several rows of the band in a zigzag pattern, exiting between any beads. Cut off the needle and tie the thread in a double knot. Apply a drop of instant glue (cyanoacrylate); let the glue dry. Cut off the excess thread.

## Step 9

Join the segments.

Begin at row 101 with the attached needle and thread and follow the beading diagram. Work straight across the full row in turquoise beads to join the two segments together and close the buttonhole slit. Turn the work over and work back across the row. Continue weaving to complete rows 102–104.

## Step 10

End with the lace pattern.

To create the lace pattern at the end, work row 105 across using 17 turquoise beads and then work back using 17 cream beads. Cut off the needle and tie the ends together in a square knot. Apply a drop of glue; let the glue dry. Snip off any excess thread.

## Step 11

Sew on the bead closure.

Test-fit the woven band around your wrist to see if the proposed position for the bead closure (at rows 3 and 4) is comfortable for you; adjust as necessary. Double-thread the needle with a 14" (35.6 cm) length of thread; don't knot the ends. Insert the needle between two beads at the center of row 3 on the right side. Pull the thread through, leaving a 4" (10.2 cm) tail on the right side of the band. Insert the needle between two beads at the center of row 3 on the wrong side to bring the needle back to the right side. Thread on 2 turquoise seed beads, 1 round 8 mm bead, and 1 turquoise seed bead; pull the thread taut. Insert the needle back through the round bead and the two blue seed beads and through the band to the wrong side. Repeat the stitching path to reinforce the bead closure. Remove the needle and use it to thread the 4" (10.2 cm) tail on the right side of the band. Insert the needle between two beads to either side of the center of row 3 to bring the needle back to the wrong side. Remove the needle. Tie the threads in a double knot. Apply a drop of glue; let it dry. Trim away excess threads.

## Gold Disk: A Ring

A delicate gold disk and gold wire can be used in a simple winding technique to make a ring in a spare, but sophisticated style. Use any cylinder-shaped item that will make a ring that fits you, using the item to make the windings.

MATERIALS AND TOOLS

1 Austrian crystal bicone, 3 mm, in turquoise

1 seed bead, 11/0 (1.8 mm), in gold

Gold disk, brushed gold vermeil, 10 mm diameter × 2 mm thick

22" (55.9 cm) wire, gold-plated, 24-gauge

10" (25.4 cm) wire, gold-plated, 34-gauge

Wood dowel, ⅝" diameter × 6" long (1.6 cm × 15.2 cm)

Wire cutters

Chain-nose pliers

Bent-nose pliers

Emery cloth, medium-grit (#400)

### Step 1

Make the first half of the wire coil.

Position the midpoint of the 24-gauge wire on the dowel. Hold the wire against the dowel with one hand. Use the other hand to grasp one wire end and bend it around to the opposite side. Then wind the same wire end four more times around the dowel, ending with the wire on top.

### Step 2

Make the second half of the wire coil.

Repeat step 1 with the second wire end.

### Step 3

Bend the wire stems.

Slip the ring off the dowel and test-fit it to your finger. Adjust the coil as necessary. Use the chain-nose pliers to bend each long wire at a 90-degree angle toward the center of the ring, crossing over the wire coil.

### Step 4

Wind the wire around the coil.

Bend one long wire into a curve and thread it through the center of the ring. Then pull the wire around the wire coil, winding it around the band three times. Repeat these steps to wind the remaining long wire around the band on the opposite side.

### Step 5

Finish the wraps.

Use wire cutters to cut off the wire tails and smooth the ends with emery cloth. Use bent-nose pliers to press the cut ends flush against the band.

## Step 6

Attach the beaded accent.

Slide the gold seed bead to the midpoint of the 34-gauge wire; bend the wire in half. Insert both wire ends through the bicone crystal and the gold disk. Separate the wires and wrap them in opposite directions around the band, pulling the disk against the band. Then wrap the wires around the underside of the disk to form a shank. Cut away excess wire. Then press the excess wire in between the coils.

## Rock Crystal: A Bracelet

Easy and surprisingly quick to make, this bracelet is encrusted with a wide variety of beads in shimmering pastels. Each pretty crystal, pearl, or glass bead is "stitched" in a random pattern to a foundation of crocheted silver wire.

### MATERIALS AND TOOLS

93 assorted crystal beads
  1 faceted teardrop, 23 mm long ×
    14 mm wide × 11 mm thick,
    in pale blue

2 faceted rectangles, 23 mm long ×
  16 mm wide × 8 mm thick, in pale
  blue
6 faceted briolettes, 12 mm long ×
  9 mm wide × 5 mm thick, in pale
  pink
6 faceted tube beads, 12 mm long ×
  6 mm diameter, in pale pink
10 faceted round beads, 5 mm,
  in deep rose
10 faceted round beads, 5 mm,
  in pale rose
12 faceted round beads, 6 mm,
  in pale pink
12 faceted bicones, 2 mm, in fuchsia
6 faceted teardrops, 2 mm long ×
  7 mm wide, in pale yellow
6 faceted teardrops, 2 mm long ×
  7 mm wide, in amber
6 faceted teardrops, 2 mm long ×
  7 mm wide, in purple
4 cubes, 7 mm, in pale yellow
4 cubes, 7 mm, in lavender
4 cubes, 7 mm, in purple
4 cubes, 7 mm, in leaf green
30 assorted pearls
  2 round pearls, 14 mm, in white
  2 round pearls, 10 mm, in white
  14 round pearls, 6 mm, in white
  4 round pearls, 10 mm, in rose
  6 oval pearls, 9 mm high × 7 mm
    diameter, 2 in pink, 2 in pale green,
    and 2 in olive green
Wire, sterling silver, 24-gauge
Lobster-claw clasp, sterling silver,
  15 mm long × 5 mm wide
Closed jump ring, silver-plated, 10 mm
Wire cutters
Bent-nose pliers

### Step 1

Crochet the silver wire bands.

Cut two 36" (91.4 cm) lengths of silver wire. Make a slipknot at the end of one wire, leaving a ½" (1.3 cm) tail. Use your fingers to shape the wire next to the knot into a ½" (1.3 cm) loop and insert it through the slipknot. Make a new loop and insert through the previous loop. Continue making loops until the band is 7" (17.8 cm) long. Insert the wire end through the last loop and pull it taut. Use wire cutters to cut off the excess wire, leaving a 1" (2.5 cm) tail. Crochet the second piece of wire in the same way.

### Step 2

Lash the crocheted bands together.

Lay the crocheted bands side by side, one long edge against the other. Cut a 14" (35.6 cm) length of wire. Wrap one end of the wire around both crocheted bands at one end, lashing them together. Use an overcast stitch to "sew" the bands together along the entire edge. Finish by wrapping the wire end around the opposite end of the crocheted bands. Cut away the excess wire.

### Step 3

Sew on the first bead.

Lay the crystals and pearls in a random order on a flat surface, mixing up the sizes and colors. Distribute the large blue crystals within the central part of the bracelet. Cut a 36" (91.4 cm) length of wire and wrap it around one end of the bracelet until it is secure. Thread the opposite end through one crystal (or pearl) and then into the crocheted band, exiting out the back and leaving a loose loop with the crystal on the front. Push the crystal into the crocheted band so it nestles in the wire.

### Step 4

Continue sewing on the beads.

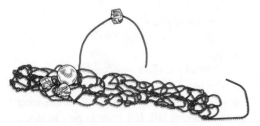

Thread the wire up through the band, add another crystal or pearl, and draw the wire through to the back. Continue adding beads, zigzagging back and forth until the band is encrusted. Wrap the end of the sewing wire around a loop in the crocheted band to anchor it securely and clip off the excess. Bring any beads that have slipped to the underside back up to the right side. Use your hands to scrunch the wire so the beads gather in a tight cluster on the right side of the bracelet.

### Step 5

Attach the clasp.

Insert the end wire into the connector loop on the lobster-claw clasp. Wrap the wire around the loop to reinforce it, using bent-nose pliers to ensure a tight wrap. Cut away any excess wire. Use a separate length of wire to attach the jump ring to the opposite end of the bracelet.

## Heirloom: A Miniature Christmas Tree

This is one of my favorite beading projects of all time. No matter how many of these little trees I have made over the years, I continue to be amazed at the delicate beauty of the branches and ornaments as I begin yet another one. The preparation steps are somewhat tedious; seed beads come on lengths of thread and must be transferred to wire. But even this effort will be forgotten as you become engaged in the fantasy of shaping the branches and decorating your own beaded holiday tree. Design miniature ornaments using any leftover beads you have from other projects.

### MATERIALS AND TOOLS

12 ounces (340.2 g) glass seed beads, size 11/0, on beaded strands totaling 268" (680.7 cm), in green

23 seed beads, in red
23 bugle beads, in white
23 sequins, in gold
Silver glass star, ½" (1.3 cm) high
Spool wire, green, 28-gauge
Beading wire, brass, 34-gauge
Stem wire, 16-gauge
Miniature terra-cotta pot, without drainage hole, 2" (5.1 cm) high
Florist tape, brown
Acrylic craft paint, in pale turquoise (optional)
Plaster of Paris
White craft glue
Instant glue (cyanoacrylate)
Paintbrush (optional)
Chain-nose pliers
Wire cutters
Scissors
Smooth, flat-weave cotton cloth
Small paper cup
Craft stick
Ruler

### Step 1

Transfer the green seed beads to the spool wire.

Lay a piece of fabric on your work surface to keep the seed beads from rolling and bouncing. Pull about 20" (50.8 cm) of 28-gauge green wire from the spool; do not cut it. Transfer approximately 16" (40.6 cm) of green seed beads (I used 267 beads) from the strand onto the wire, 1" to 2" (2.5 cm to 5.1 cm) at a time.

### Step 2

Make an 11-loop beaded piece.

Lay a ruler on the scrap fabric. Press your thumbnail against the wire 2" (5.1 cm) from the end, slide the beads against it, and measure a 1" (2.5 cm) segment of beads (approximately 17 beads). Bend this section back on itself to

form a beaded loop and then twist the wires twice at the base to secure the loop. Slide some loose beads up to the base, count off 5 beads, set your thumbnail against the wire, and measure a second 1" (2.5 cm) segment. Bend this segment into a loop and twist it once to secure it. Repeat the process to form 11 loops. To secure the end loop, twist the wires twice and then use wire cutters to cut the wire 1" (2.5 cm) from the twisted base.

## Step 3

Make more beaded pieces.

Repeat steps 1 and 2 and follow the chart below to make 26 beaded pieces total.

| Number of Loops | Number of Pieces to Make | Length or Number of Beads to Start |
|---|---|---|
| 11 loops | 6 | 16" (40.6 cm) or 267 beads |
| 9 loops | 6 | 12" (30.5 cm) or 201 beads |
| 7 loops | 6 | 9" (22.9 cm) or 151 beads |
| 5 loops | 8 | 7" (17.8 cm) or 117 beads |

## Step 4

Shape the branches.

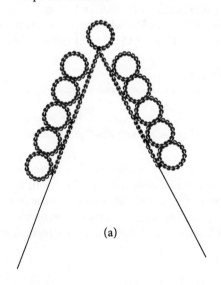

(a)

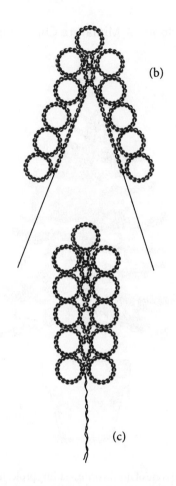

(b)

(c)

For each branch, bend a beaded piece in half so the middle beaded loop forms the branch tip (a). Give the branch a half twist between the pair of loops below the center loop (b). Continue making half twists between the remaining loops until the loops from each side of the branch are interlaced. Twist the cut wire ends together into a tight spiral, using pliers, if necessary (c).

### Beaded Branches at a Glance

The beaded branches of the tree are bound onto a central stem in a downward spiral according to the number of loops, beginning with a cluster of 5-loop beaded branches at the top of the tree and ending with a cluster of 11-loop branches at the bottom of the tree.

5-loop branch

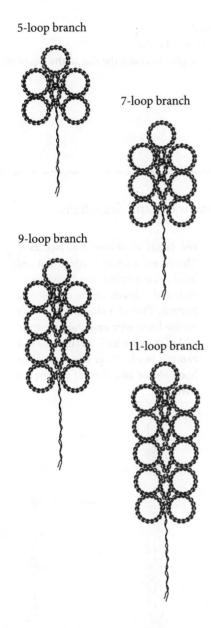

7-loop branch

9-loop branch

11-loop branch

them together using florist tape. Cluster 3 five-loop branches around the trunk ⅛" (0.3 cm) below the top branch and bind them in place with tape. Cluster 4 five-loop branches around the stem another ⅛" (0.3 cm) down and bind them in place with tape. Continue binding the remaining branches to the trunk in a downward spiral about ⅛" (0.3 cm) apart, increasing the branch size as you descend. Leave 2" (5.1 cm) of the wrapped trunk free at the bottom.

### Step 6

Make the tree stand.

Paint the outside of the terra-cotta pot, if desired, with two coats of turquoise paint, letting the first coat dry before applying the second. Let the second coat dry completely. Use a craft stick to mix water and plaster in a paper cup, following the manufacturer's directions. Transfer the plaster to the pot. Insert the trunk of the tree into the plaster and prop the tree, keeping the stem straight, until the plaster is set, about 10 minutes.

### Step 7

Make and attach the candles.

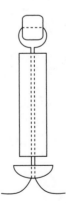

### Step 5

Attach the branches.

Lay the 26 completed pieces on a clean surface in order of size. Cut a 5½" (14.0 cm) length of 16-gauge stem wire and wrap it with brown florist tape for the tree trunk. Choose a five-loop branch for the tree top. Touch the stem of the branch to the trunk and bind

For each candle, cut a 1¾" (4.4 cm) length of brass wire. Thread a red seed bead onto the wire, slide it to the midpoint, and bend the wire in half. Insert both wire ends through a white bugle bead and a sequin, concave side first. Push the beads toward the seed bead and separate the wires. Use the wires to attach the candle to the tip of a tree branch and secure with a dab of instant glue (cyanoacrylate). Make and attach 22 more candles.

**Step 8**

Attach the star.

Use glue to attach the star to the top of the tree.

## Quick & Easy: Candy Canes, Snowmen, and Snowballs

Miniature beaded ornaments take just minutes to make. Follow the beading diagrams as a reference. You'll need 33-gauge brass beading wire, seed beads, pearls or round white beads, and sequins.

- **Candy cane**

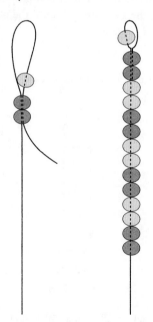

Cut a 4" (10.2 cm) length of brass wire. Thread on 1 white seed bead and 2 red seed beads. Insert the end of the wire back through the

red beads as shown and pull taut. Thread on 2 white beads and 2 red beads, concealing the loose wire end; add 8 beads in the same color pattern. Thread a single white bead on the loose wire end and insert the end of the wire back through the last two red beads. Bend this end into a hook shape and clip off the excess wire.

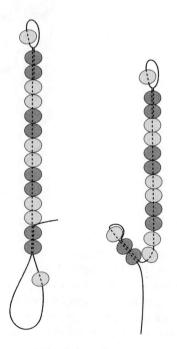

• **Snowman**

• **Snowball**

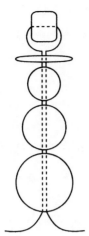

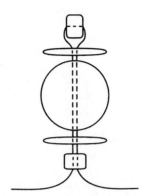

Insert a length of brass wire still connected to the spool through 3 pearls in graduated sizes (largest to smallest), followed by 1 black sequin and 1 black bead for a hat. Thread the loose wire end back through the sequin and the pearls, exiting the last pearl. Use the wire ends to attach the snowman to the beaded tree.

Insert a length of brass wire still connected to the spool through 1 white seed bead, 1 white sequin, 1 round white pearl, 1 white sequin, and 1 white seed bead. Thread the loose wire end back through the sequins and pearl, exiting the seed bead. Use the wire ends to attach the snowball to the beaded tree.

CHAPTER TWO

# Floral Arts

## THE HEART

### Family Roots

> "It is in believing in roses that one
> brings them to bloom."
> —French proverb

It was July and my whole family was back together, making the familiar drive from Nice airport to the same two-story farmhouse we had stayed in over the last three summers. We passed fields carpeted with sunflowers and lavender and arrived in Seillans with a high-desert heat baking the hillside. As we readied for bed, the wind began as a low hum at the outside corner of the house. Its strong angular bursts pushed the tree branches in ragged arcs and lifted a few tiles from the roof, looking for any opening it could find, leaving shutters swinging on their hinges and doors banging shut.

The next morning, all was soundless. I opened the French doors and sunlight filled the room. I stepped onto a narrow balcony rimmed by a wrought-iron fence tangled in a thick bramble of roses that perfumed the air. Petals were scattered over the stone, and a few branches, one with a cluster of pale pink roses, were torn from their canes. I used my sewing scissors to make a diagonal cut across each stem and placed the stems in a water glass on the bedside table. It was such a simple bouquet, and yet, it changed the way I related to the room—I felt more like I belonged there.

In the center of the kitchen was a long farm table made from a ten-foot-long door. Over the last half century the history of a family had been chronicled in fine scratches—a toddler learning to wield a fork, a young daughter learning to write, her mother sitting nearby with knitting needles clicking rhythmically—marks worn smooth by elbows of friends who stayed for supper and rags smeared with beeswax.

John and Rodney returned from the market, carrying wrapped packages and crusty baguettes. Gabrielle and Genevieve fluttered a thick linen cloth over the table. Heavy silverware, oversize plates, and large platters were laid, and the glass of roses was retrieved from upstairs.

We sat around the table in, oddly, the same places as the previous year. Genevieve and Gabrielle were laughing about something; Rodney and John were engaged in conversation; and I was acutely aware of a deep sense of belonging.

After lunch, I plucked a rose stem out of the glass and found a little patch of earth behind the house where it wouldn't get too much sun.

I sifted some soil and sand through a piece of screen found in the shed and planted the cutting, poking a hole in the ground and using my cupped hands to make a mound around the stem. I sprinkled on some water and covered the sprig with a clean glass jar.

Every day, I checked the cutting. The jar had developed a little weather system of its own—beads of moisture clung like a lace veil to the sides of the glass, and large drops on the top of the jar fell under their own weight, watering the soil below. On the day we were leaving, I knelt down on the ground for the last time to inspect the plant for any signs of new growth, and through the glass, I saw a pair of tender leaves, clasped together like praying hands.

Knowing what to do to try to coax new growth from a small cutting made me think of my parents. They had set down roots in Bellerose, New York, in the mid-1950s, moving from the city to the suburbs to establish our family's version of the peaceable kingdom. My parents believed in the importance of conservation and recycling and cultivated every square foot of land that surrounded our house, which was set on a small forty-by-one-hundred-foot lot. We planted vegetables and flowers, setting up an ecosystem that produced a hearty and abundant yield. The soil was rich, nourished with the vegetable peelings, coffee grounds, and eggshells that we folded into the earth along with peat moss and organic fertilizer. Taught that bugs were beneficial, we handled them without squeamishness, going so far as to mail-order ladybugs to feed on the aphids.

Vegetables grew from seeds or seedlings started indoors in the section of the yard that received the most direct sun. It wasn't until I was older that I understood the pleasure of standing between rows of staked vines and eating a tomato still warm from the sun. We used to travel upstate to Hopewell Junction to see my parents' friends, who had loaned us a plot of land that we would cultivate. One weekend we were busy with hoes, rakes, and twine for trellises, while the next we were watching tender green sprouts poke up through the brown soil. By midsummer we were marching in single file between the rows of beans, spinach, lettuce, beets, and tomatoes. Even though we were young and no taller than the vines ourselves, we thought it perfectly natural to pick the plump fruit right from the vine and eat it where we stood, sun beating down and juice dribbling onto our shirts.

However, what captured my heart completely were our flower gardens in Bellerose, which offered a veritable feast for my senses. Unsparing in our attention, we cultivated the soil and planted narrow bands, odd-shaped beds, and borders. Plants sprouted buds, blossomed, and went to seed, just as other plants sent up sun-seeking shoots. Leaves uncurled, showing their shiny surfaces. Stalks grew sturdy and reached high above the back fence. There was something important to do in the gardens throughout the seasons. I enjoyed it all: choosing the plants, preparing the soil, sowing the seeds—and cutting the flowers. I loved the loamy fragrance of the newly turned earth, the neatness of planted and weeded rows, and the colors and shapes of the flowers. There was something blooming every week. In spring, flowering bulbs, such as grape hyacinth, ranunculus, daffodils, parrot tulips, and lily-of-the-valley, refreshed the yard with vivid blotches of color while our apple and pear blossoms fragranced the air; in summer, cosmos, blanket flowers, and poppies opened like little parasols while foxgloves and prairie gentian stood sentry; zinnias and dahlias filled the beds with a rainbow of near unbroken color; and roses with names like "Chrysler Imperiale" and "Queen Elizabeth" mingled with other plants, while hydrangeas and asters took us into autumn when the weather turned cooler and chrysanthemums briefly filled the borders; in late winter, when the garden lay dormant, the arching stems of snowdrops could be seen bending over the melting snow.

While flowers grew naturally outdoors, fresh flowers were cut and brought inside to fill our vases throughout the year. First a vase was filled with water (with an aspirin thrown in to retard the growth of bacteria). No Oasis floral foam was installed, no metal frogs pushed into clay, no latticework of tape stuck to the vase opening. Instead, my mother taught us to use common sense and allow the vase to determine the arrangement or to use the stems themselves to form a supportive framework. Sometimes, roses filled my mother's favorite vase, made of cream-colored porcelain in the 1930s, or lilies-of-the-valley or sweet peas were neatly snipped at the ends of their stems and threaded into charming little vases from Denmark shaped like children fishmongers. Sometimes, a mix of wild flowers was gathered willy-nilly in an old Mason jar or a drinking glass.

There continue to be many natural signals that call me back to those early years when I was surrounded by gardens: the colors, in shades and hues so numerous, many don't have names; the fragrance of daffodils and hyacinths, brought to my nose for an indulgently long sniff; the pink or white petals that rain down on the ground from a flowering branch; the metamorphosis from bud to blossom; the chance that a lone rose stem will take root and grow again.

## A Brief History

People have been growing, cutting, and displaying flowers for millennia to bring beauty, scent, and inspiration to civic events, spiritual worship, and public and private celebrations. Stylistic approaches to floral design have changed and evolved according to the century and the country in which they have been practiced. In Europe and the Western world, flowers of rich and varying colors were amassed close together to celebrate the fruits of gardening and horticulture. In a second style, just a few flowers are used and the arrangement is linear and uncluttered. This style originated in China as a spiritual practice and was developed artistically in Japan. These two approaches came in contact with one another in modern times and have inspired new forms.

Ancient civilizations that actively cultivated flowers took various paths when it came to using and displaying them. Carved stone reliefs and painted walls from Egypt show vases of lotus flowers or water lilies, papyrus, and palms arranged in simple, repetitive patterns. Flowers were customarily left at tombs, and the symbolic meanings of various flowers enhanced burial ceremonies and processions. Egyptian floral artisans created exotic new forms by sewing together blossoms and fruits grown in the Nile Valley.

The ancient Greeks and Romans reveled in flowers and foliage. They fashioned wreaths and garlands for every occasion, from athletic competitions to funerals. Each plant had a symbolic meaning, such as the laurel wreath as a sign of victory. Vases were rarely used, but flowers might be gathered into baskets or cornucopias. Loose rose petals, strewn across the ground or floor, released their scent when stepped on; indoors, this was a way to perfume a bedroom. At lavish banquets, the petal accumulation on the floor could measure up to two feet deep, and more petals would be released from ceiling height to float down upon guests.

As the ancient world passed away, new floral forms emerged. Dense cone-shaped arrangements of flowers and fruit and stylized trees and topiary came out of the Byzantine Empire. Pilgrims returning from the Crusades introduced these new styles to the European continent and brought back new plants as well. Simple bouquets of flowers and herbs started appearing in chapels and interiors during the Middle Ages. The devotion to individual flowers and their symbolism would continue through the Renaissance and influenced the choice of flowers for bouquets.

The prosperity of the Baroque period, particularly in Holland, introduced a brand-new way of displaying flowers. Plants, seeds, and bulbs were expensive and highly collectible. Wealthy burghers commissioned paintings of exuberant bouquets to trumpet their savvy as collectors as well as their net worth. Horticultural models for such paintings were physically impossible, since growing conditions did not allow all of the flowers pictured to bloom at once. Instead, as each flower bloomed, the artist would make sketches and small paintings in a series of colorways to use as models for the future painting.

Floral arrangements over the next three hundred years followed the changing fashions in clothing and interior furnishings. The French Rococo bouquet used pastel colors and allowed more space between flowers and foliage, for a light and airy look. The Neoclassical period emphasized symmetry and harmony rather than contrasting colors; sensitivity to spacing allowed the beauty and form of individual flowers to be appreciated. Arrangements from the Romantic and Victorian eras were colorful, lush, and naturalistic, spilling over the edges of their containers as if growing freely. Lovers and would-be lovers could use the language of flowers to communicate their sentiments in bouquets, tussie-mussies, nosegays, and boutonnières. Heated glass greenhouses made it possible to grow more varieties, including tropical plants, all through the year.

The Japanese approach to flower arranging, called *ikebana,* originated in China. The ancient Chinese stood cut flowers in containers of water next to temple altars as a sign of adoration. Buddhist teachings forbade the taking of any life form, so cuttings were taken sparingly and with reverence. The practice reached Japan in the sixth century and developed over time, culminating in large upright arrangements called *rikkas* that used seven or nine materials to represent full landscapes of mountains, waterfalls, villages, and streams. Strict rules governed their construction, and by the sixteenth and seventeenth centuries, nobles and warriors were studying the art in order to adorn their castles and homes. *Rikkas* were also featured at festivals. Japan's rising mercantile class embraced a smaller form, the *shoka,* constructed of three branches representing heaven, man, and earth. A third style, called *nageire,* was less formal and more naturalistic. For the first time, branches were allowed to cross, and rules were relaxed to allow for more individual expression. The many classifications of *ikebana* were all practiced as a spiritual meditation. Artistic isolation was believed to reveal the plant's essence more fully than its natural setting.

Japan remained a virtually closed society through the end of the Edo period (1615–1868), but once trade with the West commenced, cultural exchange was rapid. International exhibitions in Europe and the United States showcased new products, art, and inventions. Westerners were mesmerized by the simplicity and elegance of Japanese floral design and its foundation in meditation and reflection. The aesthetic character was totally new and stood in sharp contrast to the abundant colors and profuse blooms in Victorian arrangements. *Ikebana* influenced the Art Nouveau movement and became even more popular after World War I through garden clubs, flower shows, and classes.

The general prosperity of the twentieth century saw an increase in middle-class homeowners who tended flower gardens in their own yards. They turned to magazines for advice on what to grow and how to make floral arrangements. Flower arrangement contests featured a variety of categories for competition, including the mass-line arrangement, in which Western and Japanese principles were combined. Following World War II, advances in refrigeration and transportation made it possible to ship flowers around the world. The international flower market is centered in The Netherlands, and it has become a source not only of plant material but also of styles and design trends that reach all corners of the globe. Floral designers such as Jane Packer and Paula Pryke, both from Great Britain, and Americans Arturo Quintero and Grayson Handy are leading the way by creating naturalistic, elegant floral designs that draw on all the historical styles while adding something new to enjoy and reflect upon.

## THE SCIENCE

Flower arranging is such a satisfying pursuit, whether you are putting a single stem in a vase of water or constructing an arrangement of architectural proportions. With only a few essentials, you can make the smallest bouquet to the largest; master a few simple construction basics and you will be on your way to making an infinite variety of bouquets, wreaths, garlands, and topiaries.

As few as five construction techniques—bouquets, container bouquets, wreaths, garlands, and topiary—form the foundation of practically any floral design you can imagine. These techniques, a few carefully chosen plant materials, and readily available tools—some of them right in your kitchen drawer—will allow you to arrange fresh, dried, and preserved flowers and stems, as well as silk flowers and foliage. Even if you are a beginner, you will find arranging flowers and foliage to be both satisfying and intuitive; over time you will notice that you have developed a firm foundation, based on practice and experience, that propels you to generate floral designs that will enhance any space. No room need be neglected, no nook or cranny ignored, no occasion overlooked.

Florals provide a way for us to harmonize our spirits with the season, changing the palettes of our arrangements according to our personal taste and style. When spring bursts through in flowering plants and trees, we are cheered by flowers in soft pastels and luminous greens. In summer, we can create a centerpiece bursting with colorful flowers in butter yellow and poppy red. In autumn, we can combine rich earth colors of burnt orange and copper in an untamed garland made of bittersweet harvested from a walk along a roadside. And when winter wraps the back steps in snow, we can use nature's more limited palette to draw closer to the hearth, draping a mantel with balsam and pine, infusing the air with the fragrance of an entire forest.

Nature will always provide you with all the inspiration you need if you but take a closer look at the world around you. This chapter offers a dependable foundation for working with nature's bounty—from bouquets to bath oils, from wreaths to potpourri.

## The Principles of Floral Design

A working knowledge of the principles of good design will help you work more confidently with both live and artificial plant material so that you can take genuine pleasure at all stages of creation, from the initial preparation of your materials to their final arrangement.

Good design means knowing how to apply certain principles to create an arrangement that is beautiful to look at, that displays each floral element to its best advantage, and that is structurally sound. Some of the principles pertain to the aesthetics of the arrangement, and some, perhaps the more crucial, to the mechanics: Will the container topple over?

Will the style of the arrangement make the flowers wilt prematurely? Key considerations are size, proportion, scale, balance, and form. The design elements must work together; achieving harmonious interrelationships involves physical choices, beginning with the flowers themselves.

Your arrangements will look more natural when you choose flowers in season. Just about any fresh flower can be purchased outside of its growing season or geographic range because of the thriving international floral trade that ships flowers of every kind all over the world. But fresh flowers and foliage are more abundant in the season in which they naturally grow and also more reasonably priced. When working with artificial silk or fabric flowers and foliage, choose varieties that are in season to replicate the colors and shapes of the fresh plant material they imitate.

An arrangement should be appropriate to the occasion—a plump nosegay of roses to say "thank you," an exuberant garland of evergreens to decorate a holiday mantel. Floral arrangements are made for every occasion imaginable and involve very personal relationships. Having a clear idea about the purpose of the arrangement will direct many of your choices regarding size, scale, and color. The arrangement must work coherently and fit comfortably in the display space, with enough "air" around it so as not to appear cramped or crowded. Keep the social setting in mind; don't erect a centerpiece with tall line flowers, such as curly willow and tuberose, that will keep dinner party guests from seeing and conversing with one another at a dining room table. For a low table centerpiece that looks beautiful from all angles, choose mass flowers, which are round and full-faced and come with only one flower at the end of a stem.

If you are designing an arrangement for placement in a container, choose a container that is in proportion to the flowers and the space in which the arrangement will be displayed. Containers come in a wide range of styles, sizes, and shapes and are made in materials as divergent as cut crystal and Plexiglas. Containers can be made of terra-cotta, porcelain, metal, or woven vines; do not use containers made of steel or iron as they can rust. Choose a vase that doesn't leak in a size that provides enough space to hold the flowers and an opening that accommodates the stems. The height of the vase should be approximately one-half to one-third as tall as the flowers. Tall vases are harmonious with line flowers, such as gladiolus, snapdragons, and delphiniums. Plump, squat vases are suited to mass flowers, such as roses, lilies, and tulips, and filler flowers, such as baby's breath, asters, alstroemerias, alliums, and leucadendron berries. Containers do not have to be traditional in style, of course, but they do need to be capacious enough to hold an adequate water supply, according to the amount and size of plant material placed inside. If you choose to recycle a vintage pail, bucket, or tin, use a plastic liner or a sheet of cellophane inside the container to prevent leaks. Water is essential for live flowers and foliage and will prolong their life whether supplied in a vase or a block of floral foam. Single blooms can also be inserted into floral water tubes.

Look to creative solutions when arranging your flowers. Although you may not have the perfect vase at home, you may have other vessels that offer a stylish solution. I have been inspired by Prudence Designs, whose simple yet innovative choices of containers are beautiful and witty although not originally designed for flowers at all; they include a Chinese takeout container, recycled food packaging, such as coffee cans (a colorful label can cue the colorway of the arrangement), and a rhinestone purse. Use a plastic liner with any container that is not meant to hold a water supply. Select a container that is substantial enough to support the flowers in proportion to the overall design.

Once the flowers and a container are chosen, think about the overall form or shape of the arrangement. The form of the arrangement establishes a focal point that sets a visual rhythm, moving the eye along an axis from side to side or from top to bottom. Form can be strict and linear, loose and free-form, or a mix of both. I prefer a mixed approach in which I combine a structured, compact arrangement with floral elements that mimic their natural growing patterns as a counterpoint, such as a mass bouquet of roses with dangling tendrils for an organic contrast. In a larger display, I like to combine flowers and foliage in a loose arrangement with contrasting heights and textures and allow draping flowers or vines to break the line of the container or touch down on the display surface. I try to pose a flower or a branch in a way that replicates how it might grow in nature.

While many forms are limited to what the plant material can do naturally, the form of the arrangement can also be manipulated using

## Working Tips: Adding Floral Food to Water

Floral food dissolves in warm water, making a solution that supplies plant stems with essential nutrients that can extend the display life of fresh flowers by several days. I have always used a solution of food and water as part of my conditioning ritual, to prepare foam for a container arrangement, and to get the water ready for a vase arrangement. Individual packets of floral food, such as Floral Life, are usually available wherever cut flowers are sold. Follow the directions on the packet of food, mixing enough solution according to how you are going to use it. Always mix a fresh batch every time you change the water in your vase or add to the water level in the foam.

# Working Tips: Green Floral Foam

Green floral foam, known by the brand name Oasis, is a highly porous material that has a wicking property, allowing it to absorb water until it is completely saturated. The wet foam provides hydration and nutrients to the cut flowers and foliage that are inserted into it and helps them stay fresher longer. Here are some tips for working with green floral foam.

- **To saturate green floral foam**
  Mix floral food and water in a plastic bucket large enough for the foam to float freely. Place the foam in the solution on whatever side exposes the greatest surface area. Different types of foam absorb water at different rates; Instant Oasis is known for its fast absorption. Don't push down on the foam in an attempt to speed up water absorption; you will only leave permanent depressions in the surface that weaken the foam and cause layers of foam to lift off the block. When the foam is fully saturated, bubbles will stop rising to the surface.
- **To sculpt the foam to your container**
  Place the saturated foam on a protected work surface. Use your container as a template, inverting it and pressing it onto the foam to create a cutting pattern. Use a serrated knife to trim the foam to the size, shaving off slices of foam to sculpt it into the shape of the container. Install the sculpted foam into the container, trimming the top either even with the rim of the vase or allowing it to extend above it, according

to your floral design. An extended lip of foam will provide a hydrated place to insert flowers and foliage that conceal the rim and the foam. If the container has a tapered base, add chunks of foam in the narrow end before installing a larger block on top. The space around the loose foam will act as a reservoir for water.

- **To use foam without a container**
  Some arrangements call for free-standing blocks of saturated foam. To contain the water supply, minimize water loss, and protect the display surface, use a plastic liner or, in a pinch, wrap the block with aluminum foil.
- **To use foam in a container or plastic liner**
  Cut a narrow wedge-shaped vertical groove along one side of the foam to expose an interior area of the foam to a water supply and help with water absorption. If your container is an unusual shape that does not accept a standard-size liner, improvise with a sheet of clear cellophane.

- **To keep floral foam hydrated**
  Continue to add water fortified with floral food to the foam to keep the flower arrangement fresh and hydrated as long as possible. The broader the expanse of foam, the greater and faster will be the rate of evaporation.

- **To discard floral foam**
  When an arrangement has matured past its prime, remove the flowers from the foam and compost them. Drain the water from the used foam and throw the foam in the trash. Do not reuse floral foam because it will not completely resaturate.

certain base materials, such as floral foam and preconstructed cages made of vine or metal that are installed in the container. Floral foam provides both a water source for the plant material and a way to anchor flowers in a fixed position; a "field" of wild poppies in a narrow windowsill garden in your kitchen becomes a possibility, if you wish.

Color is perhaps the most prominent feature of any floral arrangement. When color is used well, it stirs the emotions. Clearly, you are not going to be mixing liquid color, as in painting, but you will be making color choices and color placements in ways that affect the harmony and appeal of the arrangement. Knowing the basics of color theory and understanding the relationships between colors on a color wheel can help you decide what colors to put together to bring out the shape, texture, and definition of the floral materials. There are several approaches. When flowers are all in one color, the arrangement is monochromatic. When the colors of the flowers are in one shade or colorway and vary only slightly, such as red-orange, orange, and yellow-orange, they are analogous, or next to one another on the color wheel. When two colors in an arrangement are opposite one another on the color wheel, such as red and green, they are complementary. Complementary colors have the highest contrast and are visually stimulating.

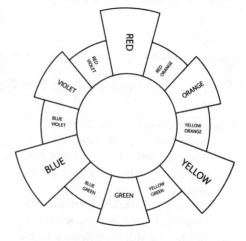

Color does not exist independently of the size and scale of the individual or groups of flowers. A single flower placed in an arrangement is always in a relationship to all of the other flowers, whose number, size, and texture affect how prominent any flower—and its color—is going to appear. Will it attract attention or heighten the impact of other flowers? For example when one kind of small flower is scattered throughout an arrangement, each flower is reduced in impact; however, if these same small flowers are grouped together in a block, they attract attention. A block of color can be composed of one large flower, such as a peony, or several flowers in the same kind and color whose mass is equal to the size of one large flower. The effect of a color block changes according to the other flowers that are near it. Red roses next to red peonies will call out the differences in their textures, whereas red roses next to white lilacs will shift the attention to the color, scale, and proportion of the "opposing" flowers. Texture works together with color, and mixing flowers with different textures is one way to establish depth and movement in the design. For example, mixing velvet roses, shiny berries, and fluffy viburnum will enhance the individual textures and provide definition between blooms, allowing each to shine.

The size of single floral elements works within a design whole, and it is important that the size of the different flower heads be in a balanced relationship. An arrangement can effectively present flowers of one size, such as a vase filled with mophead hydrangeas, or it can mix flowers in different sizes and scale, playing off the contrast between large-headed blooms, such as lilies, and frothy-headed flowers, such as wax flowers. Using a variety of flowers with different shapes and textures—large blooms with smooth petals, slender stalks with spiky offshoots, branchy stems with sprays of small flowers, each arranged at a different angle and height—is an altogether effective way to create a strong design.

## Working Tips: Two Types of Arrangements

Arrangement Seen from the Front Only
- Insert a row of plant material, one flower at a time or in wired bunches, in a soft fan shape at the back of the container.
- Working from back to front, add flowers of varying textures and shapes in rough lines with some flowers angled forward slightly, decreasing the height of each new row so as not to obscure the flower heads in back.
- Step away from the arrangement occasionally as you work to get an overall sense of the design and then rearrange flowers or cluster others to create a stronger design.
- When satisfied with the arrangement of the primary floral components, add foliage or filler flowers to fill in or accent empty spaces, placing some shorter-stemmed foliage near the front of the arrangement to conceal any bare stems and to "break" the line of the container.

Arrangement Viewed from All Sides
- Insert the tallest plant material in the center of the prepared container first.
- Add flowers and foliage to the sides to form a soft dome shape with the highest point in the center of the arrangement.
- Vary the texture and shape of the plant material, mixing tall and spike-shaped components with plump and wispy selections.
- Allow the natural curve of the stems to suggest their placement; place materials with strong curves at the rim of the container to "break" the hard line.
- Fill in spaces, inserting the stems of plant material at low angles if the arrangement will also be seen from below and add extra flower heads or foliage to sparse plant material.

## Floral Arts Materials and Tools at a Glance

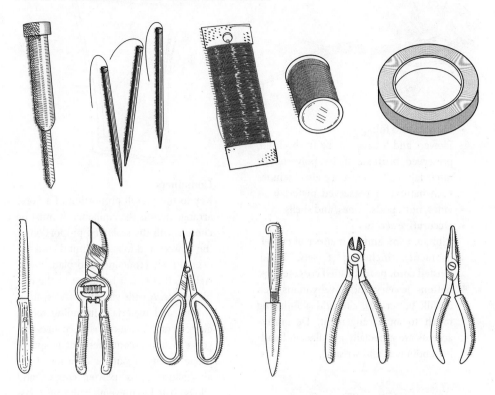

Finding plant material is easy—it is everywhere—in your own garden or a friend's, at a florist, a garden center, a local grower, even a grocery store. Of course, there are countless retail and online craft stores that offer a wide selection of dried and silk flowers as well as all the materials needed for the mechanical operations, from wiring a stem to covering a foam base. While there are distinct technical considerations to observe when preparing each kind of material (fresh stems are conditioned in water whereas dried flowers with fragile stems are supported with wire), you can employ a set of common techniques when it comes to arranging and decorating with florals, whether they are fresh from the garden or made of silk.

The essentials for a simple fresh arrangement are few: flowers and foliage and a cutting tool, such as a floral knife. A pair of floral scissors or pruning shears can be used in some cases, although if not scrupulously sharp, they can grind and bruise tender stems, compromising their ability to absorb water. Materials such as stem wire and floral tape are needed for fresh flowers with heavy heads or dried flowers with slender, brittle stems, whereas neither is needed to arrange silk flowers, which are composed of wire stems and lightweight silk floral heads. You will find that as your skills and interests grow and you venture into arrangements with more complex structures, you will be adding to your supplies. Wreath frames, picks, pins, and foam will become essential. The form of your arrangement will determine what other materials you will need.

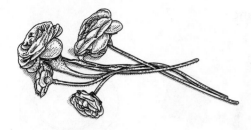

- **Flowers and foliage**
  Flowers and foliage can be fresh, dried, preserved, or made of silk, polyester, or other fabric. The category also includes such natural or preserved materials as vines, nuts, pods, cones, and shells.
- **Decorative accents**
  Ribbon, trim, and all manner of embellishments, including tassels, braid, twisted cord, pearl-headed corsage pins, buttons, jewelry, and novelty items such as silk butterflies, can add a finishing touch to an arrangement. Decorative accents are especially popular on handheld bouquets and wreaths.

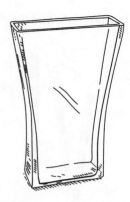

- **Containers**
  Key to the overall proportion of a floral arrangement is the container. It must be chosen with the scale and proportion of the flowers and foliage in mind, and the overall scale (container and plant material together) must be suited to the display space. A wide variety of styles, sizes, shapes, and materials, including metal, glass, terra-cotta, and plastic, ensures that you can find a container that is appropriate to any season or occasion. Metals include brass, pewter, copper, and alloys coated to prevent tarnishing. Glass vases can be handblown or molded, and the glass can be clear, colored, or etched. Terra-cotta can be painted, faux-finished, or left plain. A clear Lucite container can visually disappear, to keep the focus on the flowers. Containers that are not leakproof, such as wooden trays and boxes, vintage pails and tins, and woven baskets, can be fitted with plastic liners or lined with cellophane or heavy plastic in order to support fresh floral arrangements that require a water supply. The base container for a tall topiary is often weighted with plaster of Paris to make it more stable.
- **Floral foam**

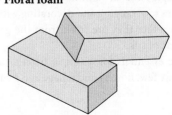

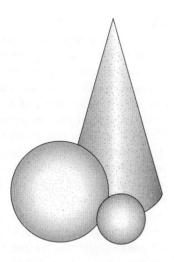

Several types of foam are used in floral design. Green floral foam, often referred to by the brand name Oasis, comes in blocks that can be saturated with water, making it suitable for live plant material. Another kind of foam is brown and used dry; it is suited for dried and artificial flowers. Both types of foam can be carved into shapes and joined together using wooden skewers to provide support for large arrangements. Styrofoam is stiffer than floral foam and is suited to holding the stems of dried and silk flowers and foliage. It is available in a wide assortment of shapes, including rings, cones, spheres, and planks, and comes in a pale green color that blends in easily with most arrangements. However, it dents easily, breaks into irregular chunks, and melts easily under hot glue. A preformed sphere of Styrofoam or floral foam is used for the head of the traditional topiary.

- **Foam anchor**
  Particularly important for top-heavy constructions, a foam anchor is a plastic disk with four upright prongs that is used to secure foam to the floor of a container. The disk is held to the container with a wad of floral clay, and the foam is impaled on its prongs.

- **Wood dowel**
  Straight and strong, a dowel can be used as a trunk that connects the topiary head and the base container. The diameter of the dowel can range from ¼" to 1" (0.6 to 2.5 cm), depending on the scale of the other components, with a more slender trunk being used for a smaller, more delicate design and a thicker trunk being use for a larger, more muscular design. A natural thick branch can also be used for the trunk.

- **Plaster of Paris**
  Used for weighting containers and anchoring the trunk of a topiary, plaster of Paris provides a stable base and counterweight for the top-heavy weight of the decorated topiary head. A respirator mask, disposable gloves, and protective eyewear are recommended when working with plaster.

- **Wreath frames**

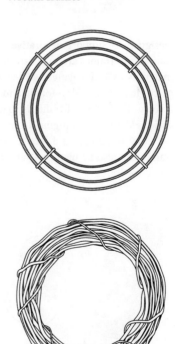

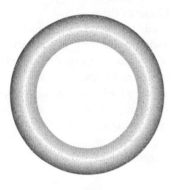

Designed to support decorative material, wreath frames are made from such materials as heavy-gauge welded wire, grapevines, straw, dry foam, and Styrofoam. Each kind of frame is made in various diameters, ranging from 6" to 24" (15.2 to 61 cm) and larger. Wreath frames can also be made by hand using vines or wire.

- **Wire**
  Wire is used extensively in the construction of wreaths and garlands, and it plays a supporting role in dried flower arrangements. It is also the internal support system of the stems of artificial flowers, allowing them to be articulated. Wire is available in fine, medium, and heavy gauges. The higher the gauge, the thinner the wire: 24-gauge (0.6 mm) is considered medium-gauge and is the most commonly used wire in this chapter; 20-gauge (0.9 mm) is the thickness of a standard paper clip; 18-gauge (1.2 mm) is slightly thicker than a standard paper clip; 12-gauge (2.7 mm) is the thickness of a wire coat hanger. Paddle wire or spool wire for floral work comes prewound on wooden or plastic paddles; it ranges from 20- to 26-gauge and is unwound directly from the holder in continuous lengths to bind plant materials together or onto frames. Stem wire or stub wire comes in stiff precut lengths that can range from 12" to 18" (30.5 to 45.7 cm) and typically ranges from 18- to 24-gauge. Stem wire is used to reinforce fragile stems by forming a kind of supporting "stake" or a false stem, and it is sometimes used to support fresh flowers with heavy floral heads. Both types of wire can be cut into lengths to support stems, form floral pins by hand, and perform other support or binding tasks.
- **Waxed string or twine**
  Suited to tying bunches of foliage together, binding stems, and hanging plant material, waxed string is strong and water-resistant. It won't cut into stems, and the waxy surface ensures that a knot won't slacken so that bound materials remain secure.

- **Floral picks**

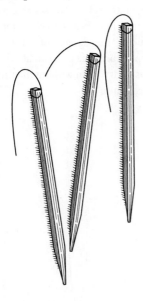

A floral pick is a pointed wooden stick, dyed green for camouflage, with a pair of fine, strong lengths of wire attached at one end. The wire can be used in a number of ways: to bind a small cluster of stems, to wire cones or pods, or to extend short stems or strengthen the stems of fragile plant material. The pointed end of the pick is sharp enough to be inserted into a foam or straw base to anchor plant material at a precise location. Sometimes hot glue or glue from a low-temperature glue gun is used to reinforce floral picks.

- **Floral pins**

  Floral pins look like large staples. Sharp, long-pronged, and made of stiff metal, they can be pushed into a base, such as a straw wreath frame, to secure floral material to it. Floral pins can be made in any size from medium- and heavy-gauge paddle wire and used to anchor fragile stems in floral foam.

- **Floral tapes**

Many kinds of tape are used in flower arranging. Floral tape, or stem tape, is wrapped around stems or wire to conceal them. It comes in green, brown, white, and lavender. Floral adhesive tape (also called Oasis tape) is water-resistant and has a sticky side that can secure floral foam to a container. Floral clay tape is used to plug holes in flower and plant pots and to adhere light-weight materials together or to their containers. Double-sided tape is used to adhere two materials together, such as ribbon to the stems of a bouquet.

- **White craft glue**

  White craft glue is used primarily with dried flowers. It has the consistency of thick cream and is suited to bonding porous materials to one another. It has a longer drying time than glue applied with a hot-glue gun or low-temperature glue gun.

- **Spray mister**

  Suited to applying a fine mist of water to large flower heads and foliage, such as hydrangea, lilacs, and viburnum, a spray mister is filled with water and supplements the water supply in the container of a fresh floral arrangement.

- **Plastic liners**

  Plastic liners are added to decorative containers that leak, such as baskets and vintage boxes, pails, and tins. Clear plastic liners come in a variety of standard sizes suited to shallow and deep containers. Inserted into a container and filled with floral foam, a plastic liner will contain the water supply and prevent water from damaging the container or the display surface. When a standard-size plastic liner does not suit your needs, you can line a container with a sheet of cellophane and trim the top edge even with the container rim.

- **Water tubes**

This enclosed vial delivers a water supply to individual thin-stemmed flowers, such as grape hyacinth, sweet peas, anemones, and ranunculus, that are inserted into it through a hole in its cap or stopper. Made from plastic or glass, water tubes are available in different lengths from 2½" to 4" (6.4 to 10.2 cm); some have sharp picks that make it easy to pierce foam or other support material. A water tube is recommended for hydrating daffodils, which are poisonous; the discrete water supply will prevent contamination of the water supply for other flowers.

- **Glue gun and glue sticks**
  A hot-glue gun dispenses a stream of molten glue that sets up in seconds to bond both porous and nonporous materials. Hot-glue guns can be used to attach material to a wreath frame made of straw, vine, or metal; it is also suited to a moss-covered surface, regardless of the construction material underneath. A hot-glue gun must be used with caution,

as the hot molten glue can burn. A low-temperature glue gun uses glue sticks that become liquid at a lower temperature, reducing the danger of burns. A low-temperature glue gun can attach decorations to dry foam without melting it.

- **Floral knife**

A floral knife is generally recommended for cutting the stems of fresh flowers, but any knife, especially Swiss knives, are ideal for making sharp cuts in floral stems without bruising or crushing them. A stem that is bruised or crushed will have difficulty drawing water from a foam- or water-filled container. In a pinch, a general-purpose knife with a straight, sharp blade is acceptable for cutting natural materials, such as stems and leaves; use it on a cutting board or protected cutting surface.

- **Floral scissors**

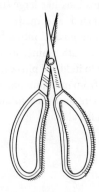

Floral scissors are designed with short, sharp blades that won't grind or compress floral material as it is being cut. Floral scissors are suited to cutting thin-stemmed flowers and foliage. A better alternative for this type of cutting, however, is a sharp floral knife.

- **Pruning shears**

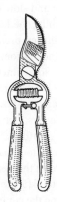

The workhorse of cutting tools for live plant material, pruning shears have short handles and heavy-duty jaws that cut easily through medium-thick woody stems and branches. It can also be used to cut wood skewers.

- **Hammer**

A hammer is used to smash the ends of thick, woody stems and branches of such flowering plants as lilacs and hydrangea in order to spread apart the fibrous material and improve its ability to absorb water from a water supply.

- **Serrated knife**

A serrated knife is used to cut and shave floral foam and Styrofoam. Rubbing both sides of the blade on a bar of soap will help the blade move through the foam more easily.

- **Scissors**

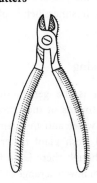

General-purpose household scissors are used to cut light-weight to medium-weight materials, such as paper and ribbon. Scissors can also cut through fine-gauge wire.

- **Wire cutters**

Indispensable for cutting through most gauges of wire, wire cutters have strong, angled jaws that will snap a clean cut on thin- and medium-gauge wire with little pressure. Always wear safety glasses when using them.

- **Chain-nose pliers**

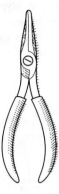

Suited to bending and shaping wire, chain-nose pliers have a flat interior jaw surface that will grip wire. The tip of the pliers can be used to make a small loop in one end of a false stem so the wire does not slip through the flower head.

## Fresh Flowers and Foliage

The moment a flower is cut from the plant, it begins to wilt and die. While there is no way to stop the natural progression from full bloom to wilted flower head, measures can be taken to prolong the lifespan of a stem and maximize its beauty and freshness before placing it in an arrangement.

### Conditioning

Conditioning is the general term used to describe treatments of the crucial hydration system—the water and the stem structure—that keep all fresh plant material alive and thriving. Although there is no fixed lifespan for any kind of flower, a range of 7 to 10 days is a realistic expectation for fresh flowers. Some slender-stemmed flowers with notable fragrance have a shorter display life than thicker-stemmed, nonfragrant kinds. It is important to put fresh flowers in water as soon as possible after buying them or cutting them in the gar-

den. Immediately recut the stems on a diagonal, using a sharp knife. Some professionals hold the stems underwater as they are cutting them to avoid introducing air bubbles, which can clog the delicate system of stem fibers. In all cases, the most important factor is the quality of the water supply. The water must be clean and free of debris and bacteria, elements that can clog the stem and slow or stop the water supply from reaching the leaves and flowers, resulting in wilting or premature aging. As flowers mature, they become less efficient at absorbing water—sometimes the bottoms of the stems become blocked, reducing the water supply to the foliage and flowers. To lengthen the life of fresh flowers, I change the water in the vase every 2 or 3 days, replacing it with water to which floral food has been added. At the same time, I recut the stems, using a sharp knife to cut off 2" to 3" (5.1 to 7.6 cm) from the bottom and angling the cut in order to expose as much of the cell structure as possible so there is a good flow of water up the stem and to the leaves and flower head.

If you are harvesting flowers and foliage from a garden, clean the bucket in which you will collect them with a disinfectant, such as household bleach, to ensure that no harmful debris or bacteria lingers. Use a clean, sharp floral knife, floral scissors, or clippers to cut the flowers late in the evening or early to mid-morning when the plant is hydrated but not overly wet; avoid cutting flowers during the hottest part of the day. After cutting the flowers or foliage from the plant, strip off the lower leaves and set the stems in a clean bucket filled with lukewarm water to which floral food has been added. Leaves that are submerged underwater will begin to rot, so double-check that all the foliage is above the waterline.

If you are buying fresh flowers, select fresh-looking stems with robust foliage and flower heads that have unblemished color and no wrinkles or tears. Vibrant green stems and leaves signify a very fresh flower. If the leaves are turning yellow or the petals are wrinkled, the flower is old—do not buy it. After making and purchasing your selection, remove the packaging and condition the plant material as soon as possible. Don't leave flowers out of water or wrapped in paper or cellophane any longer than necessary. A florist will have already conditioned the plant material, but it is wise to repeat some of the measures, especially recutting the ends of the stems and hydrating them to maximize water absorption and extend their display life.

## Technique: Conditioning Fresh Flowers and Foliage

The goal of conditioning is to support the display life of any live plant material, a task that can be accomplished with ease. While there is no guarantee that flowers or foliage will thrive for a given time, conditioning provides a hospitable environment that maximizes their potential.

### MATERIALS AND TOOLS
Fresh flowers
Floral food
Clean bucket
Floral knife
Sink with hot and cold running water

### Step 1
Mix the floral food.
Mix the floral food with warm water in a clean bucket to make a solution, following the directions on the packet or jar.

### Step 2
Cut the stems.
Set the stems in the bucket with the floral food solution. Take out one stem at a time, hold the stem under running water, if desired, and use a clean, sharp floral knife to cut off 1" to 2" (2.5 to 5.1 cm) from the end. Cut on the diagonal to maximize the surface area of the stem that takes up water.

## Herbs for Floral Arts

- **Annuals**
Annual herbs bloom for only one season, usually summer, and then die.
Anise
Basil (sweet)
Borage
Chervil
Coriander
Dill
Marjoram (sweet)
Savory (summer)
- **Perennials**
Perennial herbs bloom year after year; they lay dormant in winter, once they are established.
Catnip
Chives
Fennel
Horehound
Hyssops
Lovage
Oregano (wild majoram)
Rosemary
Sage
Savory (winter)
Spearmint
Tarragon
Thyme
Woodruff
- **Biennials**
Biennial herbs live for two seasons, blooming only in the second season.
Caraway
Lavender
Parsley

| Plant Type | Spring | Summer | Fall | Winter |
|---|---|---|---|---|
| Flowers | Allium | Ageratum | Alstroemeria | Allium |
| | Alstroemeria | Allium | Andromeda | Alstroemeria |
| | Anemone | Alstroemeria | Astilbe | Amaryllis |
| | Anthurium | Aster | Calla lily | Andromeda |
| | Astermarium | Astilbe | Carnation | Anemone |
| | Astrantia | Bachelor button | Celosia cockscomb | Aster |
| | Bleeding heart | Black-eyed susan | Chrysanthemum | Carnation |
| | Carnation | Calendula | Cockscomb | Gypsofila |
| | Chrysanthemum | Celosia cockscomb | Cosmos | Hellebores |
| | Daffodil | Clematis | Freesia | Leucadendron |
| | Euphobia | Cockscomb | Hydrangea | Lily |
| | Fritillarias | Dahlia | Hypernicum | Narcissus |
| | Grape hyacinth | Daisy | Lysimachia | Orchid |
| | Hellebores | Delphinium | Orchid | Paper whites |
| | Hydrangea | Evening primrose | Sunflower | Poinsettia |
| | Iris | Hibiscus | Thistle | Rose |
| | Leucojum | Hydrangea | Wax flowers | Stephanotis |
| | Lily-of-the-Valley | Jasmine | Zinnia | Tulip |
| | Lisiantus | Lily | | |
| | Narcissus | Limonium | | |
| | Orchid | Lisianthus | | |
| | Pansy | Marigold | | |
| | Phlox | Orchid | | |
| | Poppy | Phlox | | |
| | Ranunculus | Rose (including tea, garden, rambling, old) | | |
| | Snowdrop | Salvia | | |
| | Sweet pea | Strawflower | | |
| | Tulip | Sunflower | | |
| | Tweedias | Veronica | | |
| | Veronica | Zinnia | | |
| | Viburnum | | | |

| Plant Type | Spring | Summer | Fall | Winter |
|---|---|---|---|---|
| Flowering bushes, shrubs, and trees | Almond | Hydrangea | | |
| | Azalea blossom | Lilac | | |
| | Crabapple | Mountain laurel | | |
| | Dogwood | | | |
| | Fruit trees (apple, apricot, cherry, quince) | | | |
| | Gardenia | | | |
| | Magnolia | | | |
| | Lilac | | | |
| Foliage | Cedar | Cedar | Beech tree | Balsam fir |
| | Fern | Coin grass | Blueberry bush | Cedar |
| | Fiddle-head fern | Dusty miller | Burning bush | Pine |
| | Hosta leaves | Foxtail | Cedar | Spruce |
| | Ivy | Salvia | Coleus | |
| | Jasmine | Solidaster | Dusty miller | |
| | Maiden-hair fern | | Hosta leaves | |
| | Plum leaves | | Moss | |
| | | | Oak leaves | |
| Fruit, berries, pods, nuts | Hypernicum berries | Blueberries | Acorns | Eucalyptus berries |
| | | Brown echinacea seedpods | Apple | Juniper berries |
| | | Crabapple | Artichoke | Leucodendron berries |
| | | Early thistle | Bittersweet | Pinecones |
| | | Hypernicum berries | Crabapple | |
| | | Meadow grasses (amaranths, fountain grass, foxtail, oats, penstemmon, sedums, wheat) | Grapes | |
| | | Queen Anne's lace | Nuts | |
| | | Rosehips | Ornamental cabbage | |
| | | Sunflower | Pomegranate | |

### Step 3

Strip off the foliage.

Before returning the stem to the bucket, strip off any leaves, thorns, or plant matter that would fall below the waterline to prevent decay that can foul the water.

### Step 4

Allow the flower to fully hydrate.

Store the flower bucket in a cool, well-ventilated area between 40°F and 45°F (4.4°C and 7.2°C). Flowers draw in a lot of water. If you are storing the flowers overnight, check the water level in the bucket before retiring and replenish it, if necessary. Then check it again first thing in the morning. If the water level is low, add more water.

### Preventing Premature Aging

There are many simple ways to maximize the display life of fresh plant material after it has been placed in an arrangement. Light, temperature, nutrients, even the air quality of the immediate environment will affect how long cut flowers last.

Try to display an arrangement out of direct sunlight, either away from sunny windows or in the shade if outdoors. Bright sunlight will heat the cellular plant material and accelerate the evaporation of moisture from leaves and flower heads. Dehydration from heat can stress the plant material and cause it to age prematurely. A room temperature environment, approximately 70°F (21.1°C), or a temperature comparable to that of the plant's natural habitat, is ideal. Tropical flowers need warm environments to thrive and will discolor when placed in conditions that are too cold. Avoid areas near heating vents or under ceiling fans.

Once the flowers and foliage are cut from their plants, keep their stems hydrated and fed and change the water every 2 days, adding fresh floral food according to package directions. Whenever you do a water change, also recut the stems on a diagonal, removing

approximately 2" (5.1 cm) to expose fresh cellular material so the stem can absorb more water efficiently; some people advise holding the stem underwater during cutting to prevent air from entering the plant cells. If an arrangement is anchored in floral foam, keep the foam saturated and wet to the touch. Water evaporates quickly on broad foam surfaces, so you may need to add water (fortified with plant food) every day. All plant matter emits the hormone ethylene gas as a part of the natural aging process. Keep the floral arrangement away from bowls of fruits or vegetables, which will add to the gas in the atmosphere and cause the flowers to age prematurely.

## Technique: Using Water Tubes to Keep Flowers Fresh

The small plastic water tube holds a fresh flower stem, providing hydration that will extend the display life of a flower in an arrangement. Check and replenish the solution periodically to prolong the life of the flower.

MATERIALS AND TOOLS

Rose stems, or other thick-stemmed
    flower
Water tubes
Plant food
Floral knife
Cutting board
Bucket

**Step 1**

Cut the stem.

Place a stem on a cutting board (or underwater) and use a floral knife to cut the end of the stem on the diagonal.

**Step 2**

Fill the floral tube with water.

Remove the flexible rubber cap from the floral tube. Fill the tube with a solution of plant food and water. Recap the tube.

**Step 3**

Insert the stem.

Carefully insert the cut stem through the slit in the cap. If the stem is too large to fit in the hole, slice the cap with a sharp knife to make the hole larger. Set the tube aside; it is not necessary to stand a water-filled tube upright as the slit will form a seal around the stem so that the tube does not leak. Repeat steps 2 and 3 to prepare the desired number of tubes.

## Dried and Preserved Flowers and Foliage

There is little to compare to the beauty of fresh flowers, yet our pleasure in them is destined to come to a natural end as soon as the flowers and foliage begin to wilt and discolor. To prolong the enjoyment of flowers and foliage, consider giving them a new life, albeit in a different form, by drying them. Drying preserves enough of the color and shape of certain kinds of flowers, such as roses and hydrangea, to make them suited to unique arrangements as well as to wreaths, garlands, and topiary. Flowers and foliage are not the same and do not all dry at the same rate, making it necessary to use a method of drying that suits the kind of flowers you are working with. First, you need to gather the live plant material that you wish to dry.

### Harvesting

Because all dried plant material begins as living matter, it is important to harvest flowers and foliage before they reach their peak. Plant material will continue to ripen and change after it has been detached from the plant; unfortunately, there is no fail-safe way to guarantee a plant's color or shape in the natural drying process. If you have a flower garden, cut the flowers just as you would if gathering for a fresh arrangement—ideally in the evening or early to mid-morning when the plant is not overly wet, has taken in and stored all of the vital nutrients, and is fully hydrated and has not begun to wilt from the heat of the sun. If you are making your selection from a vase arrangement, avoid material that is wilted, discolored, or torn because these imperfections will become more pronounced in the drying process. If you are harvesting roses, for example, make certain the roses have not opened completely. Cut the stems of stalk-style flowers, such as larkspur and delphinium, when the lower buds are flowering and the top buds are closed. Eucalyptus, lemon leaves, boxwood, and yarrow are very easy to dry, as are cones, seed pods, acorns, reeds, and grasses, which can be found in great abundance along

## When to Make a Straight Cut Instead of a Diagonal Cut

All live stems need to be cut at their ends to expose a fresh part of the stem to a water supply and improve water uptake. While a diagonal cut is suited to most flower stems, especially roses and other stiff-stemmed flowers, a straight cut is suggested for flowers with hollow stems. These include dahlias, daffodils, amaryllis, and delphinium.

country roadsides and in fields, as well as in garden centers, flower markets, and florist shops—their cost, of course, varying significantly according to the source. Berries can add beauty, but they turn black and fall off their stems, making silk berries preferable.

If you wish to harvest plant materials from farther afield, the task is as simple as carrying a pair of floral scissors or a floral knife with you while taking a walk. While you can harvest plant material in other seasons, autumn presents beautiful specimens standing at the ready. Deep russet, burnt sienna, and burnt umber are common hues in autumn's natural palette that can be found in arching branches and vines and the softly twisting grasses that grow in the wild. They are promising choices as long as they are picked before they have withered. Be certain to get permission from the landowner to snip the plant material, if you are strolling on someone else's property. Take small bouquets of grass or weeds from different clumps, being careful not to rip the plants by their roots, and train yourself to recognize dune grass and other protected plants that are illegal to cut. You will find many grasses grow in abundance in fields and along roadsides and can be collected with a clear conscience. Because grasses tend to shrivel unevenly

---

## Protecting Endangered Species

Take care to ensure that you do not harvest plants illegally by removing them from their natural habitats. For a list of rare plants in your area, check with your local library or contact the field office of The Nature Conservancy in your state or region. For a program that focuses on endangered animals and plants, contact your state government Natural Heritage program.

---

while drying, press the blades between layers of absorbent paper to maintain their shape, unless you prefer the look of soft twists and curls natural to dried long-blade grass. Use a newspaper-lined cardboard box to dry your finds until you are ready to use them.

### Drying Flowers and Foliage

Air-drying, drying with a desiccant, and drying in a microwave are three easy, yet different, methods to use for drying live plant material. The choice of drying method is largely dependent on the character of the plant material and the speed with which you want to dry it. Air-drying is the slowest and microwave-drying is the fastest, with drying with a desiccant being somewhere in between. Air-drying is applicable to most flowers and foliage, but drying with a desiccant is superior for thin flowers and foliage as the desiccant provides a supportive bed of granules that maintains the shape and position of petals while drawing out the moisture at a rate that can be monitored, preventing overdrying. Microwave-drying also dehydrates plant material, but it is my least favorite method as seconds count; careful vigilance is necessary to prevent overheating that can make delicate plant structures brittle.

The choice of drying method is also an artistic consideration as it affects the appearance and character of the dried material in different ways. Some floral material, such as roses, can be dried using all three methods, with different aesthetic results. Fresh roses darken in color and become slightly wrinkled when air-dried, keep more of their natural color and shape when dried in a desiccant, and become pale in color and somewhat brittle when dried in a microwave. No drying method can ensure a perfect result, but generally, dried flowers and foliage present unique decorating options for arrangements that are beautiful and long-lasting. Pods and cones that have dried naturally can introduce unique shapes, textures, and natural color to an arrangement that cannot be achieved with dried flowers alone.

## Air-Drying

Of the three methods for drying plant material, air-drying is the slowest and most intuitive and requires the least effort. It is a great way to salvage flowers that are gathered on a walk or about to peak in a vase. The method works on the principle of evaporation. As moisture leaves the cells of flowers or foliage, the plant material naturally dehydrates and shrinks. Air-drying is least suited to thin flowers and foliage, which will wither and curl as their moisture evaporates; a better drying method for these materials is a drying agent, such as a desiccant. Some air-dried flowers and foliage retain much of their color, but others become very pale or bleached. Through observation and testing, you will be able to assess the efficacy of air-drying for various plant materials.

It is important to air-dry plant material according to its shape, weight, and how you wish to use it in your floral design. Plant material can be air-dried hanging upside down, right side up, or lying flat. Most flowers are hung upside down so the flower heads remain in a semiclosed position and the stems remain straight. If a rose were to stand upright for air-drying, the petals could drop open and fall off the flower head. Light- and medium-weight materials, such as roses and field flowers, should be hung upside down. Tall floral materials with stalks, such as delphinium, and foliage with flat or broad leaves, such as magnolia and lemon leaves, are best laid flat on absorbent paper, such as newspaper, or a window screen. Heavy plant materials, such as hydrangea and artichokes, are best dried on a supportive framework, such as chicken wire. The drying time will be determined by the thickness of the stems, leaves, and flower heads, as well as by the temperature and humidity in the drying area; it generally takes a week or two for most flowers to dry. Ultimately, the orientation of the plant material and the time needed to dry it will involve some trial and error.

Most flowers that are dried undergo a change not only in texture but also in color to varying degrees. Roses that are bright pink or magenta dry to a color that is close to their natural shade, while others change markedly; yellow and orange roses turn pale yellow, and red roses darken and appear reddish-black when completely dry. Flowers that remain true to their original color when dried include statice (shades of lavender, yellow, and white), yarrow (shades of mustard yellow), sunflowers (shades of deep brown at their centers with orangey-yellow petals), everlastings or strawflowers (garnet, gold, white, and yellow), lavender (pale purple), and cornflowers (shades of marine blue).

## Growing Flowers for Drying

The following flowers can be grown easily from seed and are good choices for dried arrangements. Read the directions on the packet of seeds to plant them.

> Cockscomb
> Everlasting or strawflower
> Globe amaranth
> Glove thistle
> Gypsophila (also known as baby's breath)
> Large-flowered sunray
> Larkspur
> Lavender
> Love-in-a-mist
> Mophead hydrangea
> Russian statice
> Safflower
> Tea rose
> Yarrow

## Technique: Air-Drying by Hanging Upside Down

This air-drying technique is suited to roses, globe amaranths, goldenrod, delphiniums, lavender, grasses and cereals, such as wheat, oat, and barley, and plants with papery flower heads, such as Chinese lanterns and statice.

### MATERIALS AND TOOLS

Light-weight and medium-weight plant material
Rubber band
String
Wire hanger or pushpin
Floral scissors

### Step 1

Prepare the flowers.

Arrange the flowers on a flat, protected work surface. Inspect the stems, especially the leafy parts. Use floral scissors to trim off a few leaves from thickly clustered parts along the stem to thin them out. Strip off all of the leaves from the bottom 3" to 4" (7.6 to 10.2 cm) of the stems, as dense plant matter can trap moisture that will encourage mold to form.

### Step 2

Make small bouquets.

Arrange 6 to 8 stems of your flowers in a loose bouquet so that their heads are just touching. Wrap a rubber band around the lower stripped part of the stems to hold them together. The stems will contract and shrink as they dry.

### Step 3

Dry the flowers.

Choose a cool, dry, well-ventilated, dimly lit place, such as an attic eave (in cool seasons only) or a spare closet, for drying the flowers. Tie a length of string around the rubber band and use a pushpin to secure the opposite end of the string to a beam or other support so that the bouquet hangs upside down. Another arrangement is to tie several bouquets onto the lower bar of a wire hanger and hang it on an empty clothes bar. If the flowers are heavy, lash a dowel to the lower bar before attaching the bouquets. Suspend a bouquet so that the flowers do not lean on a wall. If the flowers do touch the wall, rotate the bouquet from time to time so that it maintains a uniform shape.

## Technique: Air-Drying on Chicken Wire

Stems of large-headed flowers, such as mophead hydrangeas and sunflowers, can be inserted through the openings in chicken wire so that the flower heads rest on the mesh. The honeycomb mesh has hex-shaped openings, ½" to 1½" (1.3 to 3.8 cm) wide, that allow air circulation and can support the weight of a large flower head as it dries. The method requires space to set up a length of chicken wire, which is available in 45"-wide (114.3 cm) rolls in hardware and garden centers. The wire can be cut in short pieces, such as ½ yard (45.7 cm) long.

### MATERIALS AND TOOLS

Mophead hydrangea, or other plant with large flower head
Chicken wire
Newspapers
Work gloves
Pliers

### Step 1

Prepare the chicken wire.

Put on work gloves. Use the pliers to bend under the sharp wire ends along the cut sides of the chicken wire. Lay the chicken wire on a protected work surface, propping up the sides with wads of crumpled newspaper and leaving the center area free of obstruction to accommodate the stems of the flowers or plants being dried.

### Step 2

Dry the flowers.

Insert the woody stem of each hydrangea

into the chicken wire, choosing any opening in the center of the expanse and allowing the head of the flower to rest on the surrounding mesh.

## Drying with a Desiccant

A desiccant is a fine-particle substance that slowly absorbs moisture from the plant material but leaves it looking lifelike and colorful. It is ideal for thin plant material, such as buttercups and cosmos, and for flat-faced flowers, such as pansies and daisies, whose petals would curl up if air-dried. It can preserve the delicate trumpet and bowl shapes of thin-petaled flowers, such as daffodils and narcissi. Silica gel is a popular desiccant that is available in two forms: white crystals and crystals with color indicators that turn from blue to pink when they have absorbed moisture. Household borax and sand are two other desiccants, but I prefer silica gel because it is convenient and can be reused indefinitely. Borax is light in weight, but it is difficult to get into narrow crevices. Sand must be washed thoroughly before it can be used as a desiccant.

Drying times are determined by the thickness and density of the plant material and the amount of silica gel used to fill the container in which the plant material is placed. The average drying time for flowers dried in silica gel is between 2 and 7 days. The thinner the petal, the faster the petal will dry. Fragile flowers, such as anemones and crocus, need more careful watching because dehydration occurs rapidly, and overdrying will make the petals brittle. The color indicator in the silica gel aids in this monitoring. Overall, it is wiser to choose flowers that are sturdier, such as roses or zinnias, for drying with a desiccant.

Small flowers can be dried in a plastic container. Long-stemmed flowers, such as bleeding hearts, need to be laid horizontally in a container that is longer than the stems to prevent breakage. Experiment with different flowers and foliage and keep track of the time needed to dry the material to ensure consistently pleasing results. Silica gel is ideal for drying flowers with full or open, flat faces, such as pansies, to preserve a distinct arrangement of petals around a calyx. The flat face of the flower is laid on the gel and the crystals are sprinkled around it little by little until the flower is covered, thereby protecting the shape and condition of the delicate petals. With a hearty flower, such as a rose, the shortened stem is inserted into the desiccant, which supports and pre-

## Common Flowers for Drying by Any Method

Astilbe
Bells of Ireland
Celosia cockscomb
Chinese lantern
Cockscomb
Coreopsis
Globe amaranth
Globe thistle
Goldenrod
Gypsophila
Heather
Heliopsis
Larkspur
Lavender
Liatris
Love-in-a-mist
Mophead hydrangea
Rose
Safflower
Sage
Statice
Strawflower, or everlastings
Tansy
Yarrow, golden-headed
Yarrow, small-headed
Zinnia

serves the shape of the flower head, which is covered with more crystals. Plant material with flowers along the stem, such as lily-of-the-valley and statice, are laid flat for drying.

### Technique: Desiccating with Silica Gel

Although desiccating with silica gel is particularly suited to delicate flowers (or those that readily wilt), such as buttercups and daffodils, it also works very well with flowers that have a more dense arrangement of petals, such as chrysanthemums and peonies, although more time will be needed for the granules to absorb their moisture. To speed up the drying process, prepare the flowers with silica gel in a microwave-proof container and follow the steps for "Drying in a Microwave Oven" on page 116. Be careful when working with silica gel as it releases very fine particles into the air while you are working with it. To avoid breathing the dust or getting it on your skin, work outdoors or in a well-ventilated space and wear a respirator mask, safety glasses, and disposable gloves. Wear clothing that covers your arms and legs.

<><><><><><><><><><><><><><><><><>

## Quick & Easy: Drying Decorative Citrus Fruit Slices

Lemons, limes, and oranges can be sliced and air-dried on a fine-mesh screen for ornamental use in dried floral arrangements or homemade potpourri. Use a sharp knife to cut the fruit into $1/8$" (0.3 cm) slices, revealing a radial pattern. Place the slices on the screen in a single layer without touching; the screen should be slightly elevated off the work surface to allow even air circulation. Turn each slice over every 2 or 3 days. When the slices are dry and hard, they can be stored in a container until you are ready to use them.

<><><><><><><><><><><><><><><><><>

MATERIALS AND TOOLS
Sturdy flowers, such as roses
Silica gel with color indicators
Airtight plastic container with lid
Tablespoon
Plastic tape
Floral scissors
Narrow soft-bristle brush
Respirator mask
Safety glasses
Disposable gloves
Craft stick
Bowl
Blunt-nose tweezers
Chipboard box
Tissue paper

**Step 1**
Clip each flower from the stem.
Use floral scissors to clip off each stem to 1" (2.5 cm) below the calyx of the flower head.

**Step 2**
Add the flowers to the silica gel.
Put on a respirator mask, safety glasses, and disposable gloves. Pour an even layer of silica gel, 1" (2.5 cm) deep, into the plastic container. Arrange the flowers so they do not touch one another. For flowers with thin petals and a flat face, lay the flowers, facedown, on the silica gel. For flowers with sturdy and dense petal configurations, insert the cut stem of each flower into the silica gel so the flower heads rest on top.

**Step 3**
Surround the flower heads with silica gel.
Use a tablespoon to sprinkle silica gel around each flower, building up granules on top or under the petals and at their edges until the silica supports the flower. Use a craft stick to gently lift the petals so that you can sprinkle silica gel underneath. Continue to fill until the spaces between the petals and the flower heads are completely covered by a 1" (2.5 cm) layer of crystals.

**Step 4**

Seal the container.

Close the container tightly. Wrap plastic tape around the lid and container to seal the edges. Store the container in a cool place. Let the silica gel work undisturbed for 2 or 3 days, depending on the fragility or density of the plant material, before checking the progress.

**Step 5**

Check the flowers for dryness.

Put on the respirator mask, safety glasses, and disposable gloves. Peel off the tape seal and open the container. Carefully pour off enough silica gel into a bowl so that the top petals of one flower are showing. Use a gloved finger to test the flower. If the exposed petals and center bud are papery dry, or if the color indicators have turned from blue to pink, proceed to step 6. If the petals and center bud are pliable, or if the color indicators are still blue or purplish, replace the silica gel, close the lid, and reseal with new tape. Check again the next day and every succeeding day until the petals and buds are dry before proceeding.

**Step 6**

Remove the flowers from the silica gel.

Gently pour off the silica gel to expose more of the flowers. Use blunt-nose tweezers to lift out one exposed flower by its stem. Hold the flower upside down by its stem. Tap the hand that is holding the stem with your other hand to gently dislodge and shake off any excess crystals. Use a soft-bristle brush to carefully sweep the silica gel crystals from between the petals. Repeat for each flower.

**Step 7**

Store the dried flowers.

Line the bottom of a chipboard box that is spacious enough to prevent overcrowding or overlapping of the dried flowers and deep enough when the lid is on to accommodate their heights. Place the flowers, faceup, on a supportive layer of crumpled tissue paper.

Close the lid and store the box in a cool, dry place, out of direct sunlight.

## Technique: Reviving Silica Gel for Reuse

In order for silica gel to absorb moisture from plant material, it must be complete dry. You can revive silica gel for reuse by heating it.

### MATERIALS AND TOOLS

Silica gel with color indicators turned pink
Plastic storage container with lid
Shallow baking pan
Aluminum foil
Home oven
Wire rack
Respirator mask
Safety glasses
Disposable gloves

## Common Flowers for Desiccating

African violet
Anemone
Aster
Buttercup
Calendula
Climatis
Columbine
Cornflower
Cosmos
Daisy
Daylily
Geranium
Hollyhock
Iris
Pansy
Queen Anne's lace
Snapdragon
Zinnia

**Step 1**

Preheat the oven.

Preheat the oven to 200°F (93.3°C). Line a baking pan with aluminum foil.

**Step 2**

Heat the silica gel.

Put on a respirator mask, safety glasses, and disposable gloves. Pour the used silica gel into the pan. Set the pan into the oven, close the oven door, and heat the gel for 30 minutes, or until the color indicators turn from pink to blue.

**Step 3**

Cool and store the silica gel.

Remove the pan from the oven and set it on a wire rack. Allow the silica gel crystals to cool to room temperature. Wearing a respirator mask, safety glasses, and disposable gloves, transfer the silica gel to a plastic container and seal the lid. Discard the aluminum pan.

*Drying in a Microwave Oven*

A microwave oven delivers waves that dry plant material in seconds, accelerating the drying process to such an extent that extra vigilance is needed to prevent overdrying. A trial-and-error approach is required because drying times will vary according to the kind of microwave you have, the power level at which the oven is set, the kind of flowers, and the number of flowers and foliage being dried at the same time. Keep a notepad handy to keep track of drying times.

To make certain you understand the way your microwave works, specifically how quickly it dries your flowers, pretest your settings with sample material to establish the power levels and drying times that deliver the results you are looking for. For delicate flowers that dry quickly, begin with a lower setting for a longer time; if the microwave is set at high power, you will only have a narrow margin of a few seconds before a flower head becomes overly dry. Flowers that are naturally sturdy and resilient are better able to hold up to the accelerated process of microwave-drying and the rigors of the testing procedure. As an extra safeguard, place a small microwave-proof cup filled with water in the oven to prevent over-drying the plant material. Choose plant material that is all natural—no wired stems, please, as metal of any kind will cause a dangerous electrical arc to form that will damage the oven and can cause serious injury. After the flowers have been dried, allow them to cool before handling.

## Technique: Drying in a Microwave Oven

Follow the steps below as a guideline and perform tests to determine which settings on your microwave will produce results you like. Begin with a medium-low power level and limit the time to small increments, testing for dryness after each try. Always allow the plant material to cool before handling it.

MATERIALS AND TOOLS

Sturdy flowers, such as roses
Microwave oven
Airtight container
Floral scissors
Paper towels
Tissue paper

**Step 1**

Clip each flower from the stem.

Use floral scissors to clip off each stem to 1" (2.5 cm) below the calyx of the flower head.

**Step 2**

Microwave the flower heads.

Lay paper towels on the oven turntable to absorb the moisture that will build up at the base of the flowers. Lay two or three flower heads near the edge of the turntable, spacing them a few inches apart. Cover them with a second paper towel. Microwave the flowers at medium-low for 60 seconds. Let them rest in the oven for 15 minutes.

## Step 3

Check the flowers for dryness.

Open the oven and gently touch the petals and the center buds to see if they are dry. If moisture remains, change the paper towels and repeat step 2, heating the flower heads in 15-second increments until they are dry. Lift the paper towel like a little hammock to remove all of the flower heads from the oven at one time and let them cool to room temperature.

## Step 4

Microwave the remaining flower heads.

Repeat steps 2 and 3 with the remaining flowers, adjusting the times according to how your microwave performed.

## Step 5

Store the flower heads.

Crumple tissue paper and place it in the bottom of an airtight container to provide support for the flower heads. Carefully place the dried flowers on the paper, close the lid to seal out moisture, and store in a cool, dry place for future use.

### Caring for Dried Floral Arrangements

Dried and preserved plant materials are fragile and subject to breaking and fading. You can protect them from damage by following a few simple rules of thumb that are practical and easy to remember. The cautions are based on basic principles that sunlight and dust will fade and dull color; jerky movement and rough direct contact into hard objects will break dried material. If a pretty element breaks off, it can be recycled even if the rest of the arrangement has gotten shabby.

Foremost, keep your dried arrangements out of direct sunlight and free of dust, as ultraviolet light and particles of dust will fade the colors. You can apply a fine coat of acrylic spray to protect flowers and foliage, if you wish, but don't use hairspray as it will scent the air on humid days in an unpleasant way. If you are drying or displaying a bouquet of flowers upside down, insert the free end of the hanging string through a sheet of tissue paper in snowy white or a pastel color and slide the paper canopy down the string and over the flower heads. The canopy will shield the flowers from light and dust and add a flower-market style to your bouquet while disguising your more practical intentions.

Display a dried arrangement in an area that will bring out its best features, moving it as infrequently as possible. Dried materials are fragile and moving an arrangement from

## Common Flowers for Microwave-Drying

African daisy
Aster
Bachelor's button
Calendula
Carnation
Chrysanthemum
Clematis
Cornflower
Dahlia
Delphinium
Hydrangea
Marigold
Pansy
Peony
Poppy
Rose
Statice
Tulip
Violet
Yarrow
Zinnia

place to place simply increases the possibility of breakage. This is especially true of large arrangements with spiky branches that easily can be broken off if swiped against a doorway or wall in the moving process. Pets, especially cats, seem to like the play value of dried flowers—our cat Minou did. Although there was never a place safe from his gentle paw, I did listen for dry rustling and kept a keen eye for his whereabouts.

Despite your best efforts at preservation, dried arrangements will eventually get old and brittle and the colors will fade. Old arrangements have a way of looking stylistically boring. These detractors need to be dealt with. You can rejuvenate a faded arrangement (and your delight in it) by adding new dried plant material to brighten it up or by introducing a faded or pale-colored ribbon that supports the softer, muted palette. A light coat or two of spray paint can recolor and revitalize an entire arrangement in a most appealing way. A garland of leaves, for instance, can be sprayed gold or copper and placed around a frame or mirror for a sparkling, festive decoration during the holidays. If the full arrangement is not salvageable, you can pick out certain elements and fashion them into a miniature version of the original or recycle them into new arrangements. Loose flower petals and flower heads can be saved for potpourri.

Store any loose dried flowers and foliage in a shallow cardboard box that is long enough for the stems to lie flat. Line the box with newspaper, use tissue paper to wrap flowers of similar type, and lay the parcels side by side without crowding, alternating the flower heads and stem bottoms. Use a knife to cut holes in the sides of the box for air circulation and add a packet or two of desiccant to absorb moisture. Store the box in a cool, dark place.

### Preserving Foliage

Live foliage from trees, such as beech, maple, and oak, and shrubs, such as boxwood and holly, can be preserved using a glycerin and water solution. The proportion of glycerin and water is determined by the thickness of the leaves—the thinner the plant material, the more water that is needed to take up the solution into the plant material. Thick leaves, such as magnolia, take a 1:2 ratio of glycerin to water; whereas thin leaves, such as beech, take a 1:3 ratio of glycerin to water. The freshly cut branch absorbs the glycerin carried by the water, replacing the natural moisture in the foliage, helping it to keep its natural form and texture. A trial-and-error approach is required here, too, but the method is so simple and the leaves turn out so lustrous and soft to the touch, I find it worth my time to try. The most suitable season to harvest the foliage is in the summer when the leaves are at their peak of maturity and still absorbing water. This approach will not work on branches harvested in the fall, when plants are slowing down their water absorption in preparation for a dormant period during winter, or in the spring, because fresh young leaves are unable to absorb glycerin.

Condition the freshly cut branches by scraping off the bark at the bottom of the woody stem and cutting a 2" (5.1 cm) split in the stem to further expose the wood fibers. Place the stems into a clean bucket that contains the well-mixed glycerin solution so the level reaches approximately 2" (5.1 cm) high on the base of the stems, or the area of the exposed wood. Allow the stems to remain in the solution as long as it takes for the leaves to become pliable. Glycerin often changes the character of the leaf: ivy will keep its green color, but beech leaves will turn brown; boxwood will turn gold; and the colors of the maple and oak leaves will deepen.

### Pressing Flowers and Foliage

Flower pressing may be considered old-fashioned by some, but I find the craft simple and delightful, reminding me of country walks or a child's delight upon finding a flower to pick.

Pressed flowers and foliage retain much of their original color but lose contours and dimensionality, making thin-petaled, open-face flowers and low-relief foliage the most suitable for this treatment. The flattened specimens can be used to advantage to decorate handmade greeting cards, note cards, gift tags, and journal pages. Pressing flowers is an educational way for children to study different kinds of flowers, identify and scrutinize particular characteristics, such as petal shapes and patterns, and record notes on their harvests, observations, and specimens in a small journal of their own.

Pressing plant material can be accomplished in the pages of a heavy book or in a flower press. Successful pressing requires an absorbent layer to draw moisture from the plant material along with consistent pressure across the layer of plant material to flatten it evenly. Ideally, the flowers and foliage you choose to press will be of a uniform thickness so pressure is distributed equally without any gapping. Regardless of whether you are using a book or the padded layers of a flower press, separate and organize individual blooms so that thin material is on one layer and thicker material is on another. For example, lay thin violets and buttercups between one set of pages or layers and lay daisies, which are thicker, between a different set of pages. Full-blown roses are extremely difficult to press; however, individual petals can be pressed flat and then reconfigured into a composition.

Pressing is a drying method and thus

## Troubleshooting: Pressing Flowers

- Maintain approximately $1/2$" (1.3 cm) of space between the individual flowers and foliage. Pieces that are touching during pressing will stick together as they dry and be impossible to separate without tearing.
- Do not lift a dried pressed flower or leaf with your fingers and do not pull on a pressed flower; it may tear.
- Single petals can be pressed individually and be reconfigured into an original flower design.
- If you pick your own flowers and foliage, gather your choices on a late afternoon on a dry day, using a floral knife or floral scissors to cut the material and leaving a 1" (2.5 cm) stem.
- Before laying the flowers and foliage between the pages of a book, lay them between two sheets of waxed paper or thicker paper, such as blotter paper, paper towels, or blank newsprint.
- If you are using a book to press the material, open up the pages to where the items lie, tilt the book, and allow the items to slide from their position onto a clean sheet of paper.
- If you are using a handmade flower press, keep the number of padded layers to two or three for best results.
- The longer the plant material is trapped in a damp environment with little air circulation, the greater the chance that mold or decay can develop on the plant matter.

requires evaporation of the moisture from the plant material. Because some warmth is needed to support the drying process, pressing flowers is most successful when there is warm air circulating in the environment. Place your pressing equipment (book or press) in a dry attic or a garage. The length of drying time will depend on the ambient temperature and humidity, the kind and thickness of the plant material, and the material chosen for the absorbent padding. Padding options include the pages of a book, blotting paper, paper towels, and layers of fiberfill. Lighter-weight flowers and foliage require 4 or 5 days to press flat. Heavier or thicker material may require up to 9 days.

## Technique: Pressing Flowers and Foliage in a Heavy Book

The simplest method for pressing flowers is to lay the items between the pages of a heavy book, such as a telephone book or a dictionary. To avoid staining the pages or, conversely, transferring ink to the flowers and foliage, layer thin, light-weight plant material, such as a buttercup or lily-of-the-valley, between sheets of waxed paper and layer denser medium-weight pieces, such as ferns, between sheets of non-embossed paper towels, blotter paper, or newsprint. An even simpler method is to sandwich

---

## Working Tips: Newsprint vs. Newspaper

Newsprint is a plain off-white paper that can be purchased on rolls or in pads. It is good for making rough sketches and can be crumpled up and used as padding. Newspapers are printed on newsprint. Sheets of newspaper are less versatile than newsprint, and the ink can rub off onto other surfaces.

---

the items between sheets of absorbent paper and lay a heavy book on top.

### MATERIALS AND TOOLS
Flowers in full bloom
Foliage
Blunt-nose tweezers
Heavy books
Newsprint or wax paper
Sheet of white paper

### Step 1
Organize your plant material.

Lay your collected specimens on a clean, flat work surface and select the pieces that you want to press. Organize them into groups according to their thickness.

### Step 2
Arrange the plant material on a page.

Open the book and lay a double layer of plain newsprint or wax paper on the facing page. Place items of like thickness on the layered paper, spacing them at least ½" (1.3 cm) apart. Cover the specimens with a double layer of the same type of paper. Turn over a ¼"-thick (0.6 cm) section of book pages onto the layered pieces.

### Step 3
Arrange another layer of plant material.

Lay a double layer of plain newsprint or wax paper on the new facing page. Prepare another layer of plant material, choosing pieces of equal thickness, cover the pieces with a double layer of paper, and lower a ¼"-thick (0.6 cm) section of the book pages onto it. Continue in this manner to sandwich the remaining plant material between the pages of the book. Close the book and place several heavy books on top. Set aside for 4 days to dry.

### Step 4
Check the plant material for dryness.

Carefully open the book and turn to a page where the pressed material was placed. Lift up the layer of newsprint or wax paper. Use your finger to touch the material. If the plant material is dry, it will feel like paper. Gently grasp a stem or other part of the plant, using blunt-nose tweezers, and slowly move the flower or leaf laterally to ensure that no parts are sticking to the drying material. Then carry the specimen to a piece of white paper.

### Technique: Making a Flower Press

The principles that guide the construction of a commercial flower press can be applied to one you make yourself using sheets of chipboard padded with polyester batting and covered with nylon fabric. The fiberfill allows air to circulate and moisture to evaporate, and the chipboard keeps the plant material supported and flat against the padding. A heavy book adds evenly distributed weight. The capacity of one flower press is limited—fitting perhaps four or five medium-size flowers—so it makes practical sense to prepare more than one press to accommodate more flowers and foliage at one time. The presses can be stacked together and a heavy book can weight them down. To identify the plant material on each set, hot-glue a long paper tab on one edge of the press so that when they are stacked you can identify the specimen you are looking for.

#### MATERIALS AND TOOLS
Polyester batting, two 5½" × 8½" (14 × 21.6 cm) pieces
Chipboard, two 5½" × 8½" (14 × 21.6 cm) pieces
Sheer nylon fabric, two 7" × 10" (17.8 × 25.4 cm) pieces
Spray adhesive
Wide packing tape
Chemical cartridge respirator mask
Cardboard carton (for spray booth)
Scissors

#### Step 1
Apply spray adhesive to the chipboard and the batting.

Work outdoors or in well-ventilated space and wear a chemical cartridge respirator mask. Lay the polyester batting on a protected work surface inside the spray booth. Apply a light even coat of spray adhesive to the facing surface of each piece. Repeat for the chipboard pieces. Let the adhesive dry.

#### Step 2
Adhere the chipboard and batting.

Lay a piece of batting on a piece of chipboard, adhesive sides together, and press to adhere. Repeat to adhere the second pair.

#### Step 3
Apply spray adhesive to the batting and the fabric.

Lay the chipboard/batting pieces inside

---

## Common Flowers and Foliage for Pressing

Ageratum
Alyssum
Azalea
Bleeding heart
Buttercup
Columbine
Daisy
Geranium
Hydrangea
Larkspur
Lily-of-the-valley
Mint leaves
Pansy
Queen Anne's lace
Rose petals
Strawberry leaves
Sweet peas
Verbena
Violet
Violet leaves

the spray booth with the batting side facing up. Apply a light even coat of spray adhesive to the batting. Repeat for the nylon fabric. Let the adhesive dry.

**Step 4**
Adhere the fabric layer.

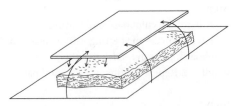

Lay the fabric adhesive side up. Center a chipboard/batting piece on it, batting side down, and press to adhere. Repeat to adhere the second pair.

**Step 5**
Tape the fabric to the chipboard.

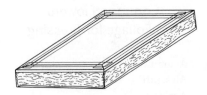

Fold the short edges of the fabric onto the back of the chipboard and secure with tape.

---

## Working Tips: Selecting Fiberfill for Flower Presses

The fiberfill padding on a handmade botanical press should be $1^1/_2$" thick (3.8 cm) for pressing large flowers like roses, daisies, dahlias, delphiniums, and zinnias and $^1/_2$" thick (1.3 cm) for pressing small or delicate flowers such as forget-me-nots, pansies, buttercups, and violets.

---

Fold the long edges onto the chipboard and secure with tape. Reinforce the overlapping fabric at the corners with tape.

## Technique: Pressing Flowers and Foliage in a Handmade Flower Press

If your harvest yielded more flowers and foliage than can be accommodated by a single handmade flower press, make several presses so all of your materials can be dried at the same time. Three or four presses can be laid with flowers and then stacked together and weighted with one heavy book as long as it doesn't topple the stack. Presses can also be prepared individually with plant material and weighted with one heavy book each.

### MATERIALS AND TOOLS
3 handmade flower presses
Floral material for drying
Heavy books

**Step 1**
Set out the flower presses.
Lay the pairs of components of each flower press side by side on a protected flat surface, padded side up.

**Step 2**
Sort and arrange the plant material.
Arrange the flowers and foliage according to their size and thickness, grouping like elements together.

**Step 3**
Layer the material in the presses.
Place floral items from one group on the padded side of one press, spacing them ½" (1.3 cm) apart. Set another press on top, padded side down. Repeat to layer plant material in the remaining presses.

**Step 4**
Weight with a heavy book.
Stack the layered presses and set a heavy

book on top. If the stack is wobbly, make several shorter stacks instead. Let dry undisturbed for 4 days before checking for dryness. Thick floral material may require up to 9 days to dry.

## Silk Flowers and Artificial Fruit

Silk flowers and foliage require little to no preparation before they are arranged. Although all kinds of artificial floral decorations are referred to as "silks," most kinds found in the market today are not made from silk at all but from strong synthetic fibers and resins that are manufactured to look like convincing substitutes for the real thing. Usually, there is a direct link between cost and quality, which varies widely, so inspect the pieces you are thinking of purchasing closely. One of the most telling parts of an artificial piece is its stem; stems that are stiff and fake-looking (bright green and plasticky) should be passed by. Look instead for stems that are flexible and that have the same characteristics as their natural counterparts, such as thorns and stem hairs. In floral pieces, subtle textural variations, such as frosted and dewy patinas and variegated color, help to reinforce the illusion that the sample is fresh.

Certain craft chains carry a wide selection of artificial flowers, foliage, berries, and fruit, with most kinds presented according to season, although many varieties, such as roses, chrysanthemums, and flowers associated with bridal bouquets are available all year long. If you are familiar with artificial flowers, it is also worthwhile to check out the myriad number of online sources. Before making an online purchase, be certain that there is a return policy so if you are not satisfied with your purchase, you can send the merchandise back to the seller for a refund.

The care of silk floral arrangements, whether majestic or diminutive, is similar to that of dried arrangements. Silk and fabric flowers and foliage absorb moisture from the air, which can encourage the growth of mildew, and ultraviolet rays from direct sunlight can quickly fade colors. Once you create an arrangement, display it in a space that is cool and dry. Keep the arrangement at room temperature or cooler, avoiding spaces with high humidity. If you want to store a seasonal arrangement till the next season, choose a dry, dust-free, dimly lit space and cover the arrangement with a light-weight layer of fabric, such as an old cotton sheet. Don't use plastic sheeting as a dust cover, as it can trap moisture in the enclosed spaces around the flowers and create an environment where mold can grow.

Try to keep dust from accumulating on the fabric flowers; if dust gets embedded in the fibers, the arrangement will look dull and dirty. To blow off surface dust, place the arrangement outdoors or in a well-ventilated space and use a hair dryer set to "cold" and "low." Flowers or foliage made of a synthetic fiber, such as polyester or rayon, can be swooshed in a sink filled with warm water and then allowed to air-dry. Handling can begin to wear the petals and leaves at their edges, and after a while, you may notice that they are beginning to fray; to make repairs, apply a thin dab of fabric glue along the frayed edge, using your finger to smooth the fibers flat against the edge of the petal or leaf, and let the glue dry completely. Minor stains can be spot-cleaned with a fabric-compatible stain remover and a cotton swab.

Although I recommend buying good-quality artificial flowers and foliage, there are occasions when I have been able to bring a mediocre flower to a more beautiful level using a painting technique. As long as the petals are made of fabric, you can add color and pattern to create more exotic kinds of flowers, ones that are always much more expensive to buy. I have discovered that with a bit of watercolor paint or traditional fabric dye and washable markers, I can add variegated color to create cerise-tinged roses and the patterning on parrot tulips. You'll find it helpful to refer to color photographs or illustrations of the kind of flower you are reproducing, and it is easy to find vivid examples with up close details online.

## Technique: Enhancing Fabric Roses with Paint and Markers

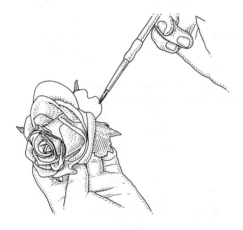

One of the features that distinguishes fine silk flowers are the delicate color variations on the petals of the flower. You can replicate those effects on fabric flowers, especially roses, which grow in an infinite number of colorways in nature. You can re-create the cerise-tinged rose with its soft moiré color that changes from saturated color at the edges of the petals to faded pastel in the interior of the flower, beautiful in any kind of floral display, whether a single hand-painted bloom or a huge bouquet of full-blown flowers and buds. Consider painting only a few roses to learn this technique and add to your collection over time.

### MATERIALS AND TOOLS
Fabric rose, either polyester or nylon
Watercolor paint or ink, in burgundy, wine, red, or dark pink, or other colors, as desired
Washable markers, in scarlet and maroon
2 watercolor paintbrushes
Disposable gloves
Small dish of water
Paper towels

### Step 1
Tint one petal.

Put on disposable gloves. Hold the rose, petals up, and isolate one petal so it lies on your gloved hand. Use a paintbrush dipped in water to saturate the top third of the petal. Dip the tip of the paintbrush into the red, burgundy, or wine paint or ink and dab the color onto the moist petal so the color spreads. If the paint makes a hard line on the fabric, use a clean brush soaked in water to add plain water to the surface of the petal to spread the color.

### Step 2
Dampen and tint all the petals.

Repeat step 1, working around the flower to tint the edge of each petal. Tap the painted flower on a paper towel to shed excess moisture so that the flower is damp but not dripping.

### Step 3
Add darker stain to the petal tips.

Choose a marker in a darker shade than the paint color. Add more color to the edges of each petal and to the center bud. Let the flower dry completely.

## Technique: Enhancing Fabric Tulips with Paint

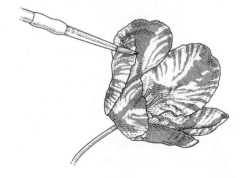

Noted for the rich veins of color that radiate from the base and the top edge of each petal, the parrot tulip seen in nature exhibits signature patterning in such bold color combinations as red and white and red and yellow. The edges of the petals on the live flower are curly and scallop-shaped. You can mimic the silhouette by using manicure scissors to cut the edges of an artificial tulip to re-create the distinct edges that make the parrot tulip so prized.

### MATERIALS AND TOOLS

Fabric tulip, either polyester or nylon, in yellow
Watercolor paint, in red and orange
Tapered watercolor paintbrush
Disposable gloves
Manicure scissors
Small dish
Paper towels

### Step 1

Prepare the paint.

Put on disposable gloves. Use a paintbrush to mix a few drops of bright red and orange paint in a small dish to make a red-orange color. Rest the brush on a paper towel to drain off any overload of paint on the bristles.

### Step 2

Paint the first petal.

Hold the tulip, petals up, and isolate one petal so it lies faceout on your gloved hand. Dip the tip of the paintbrush into the red-orange paint and paint a vertical line up through the center of the petal, beginning at the base and stopping three-quarters of the way up. The color should appear as a hard line on the fabric.

### Step 3

Add a feathered pattern to the petal.

Add feathery strokes that radiate out from each side of the painted line. Then paint the top edge of the petal, using thin lines that begin at the edge and go toward the base of the flower.

### Step 4

Paint all of the petals.

Repeat steps 2 and 3 to paint the remaining petals on the tulip. Let the paint dry.

### Step 5

Scallop the edges of the petals.

Use manicure scissors to trim the edge of each petal in small scallop shapes.

## Wiring Stems, Adding False Stems, and Using Floral Picks

This section covers essential techniques that are used to prepare smaller design elements, which can then be combined into larger floral arrangements. The techniques can be used for live or dried plant material as well as for silk flowers and foliage. Wiring a stem allows you to strengthen and lengthen the stem. Adding false stems to flowers, foliage, fruit, pods, and cones that do not have stems provides a way to add and secure those elements to an arrangement. A floral pick can be used to bind the stems of small plant materials together in a bunch, reducing the number of punctures in the surface of foam and permitting more efficient coverage of a large surface. Once you are acquainted with the essential techniques, you can apply them as the occasion arises.

Wiring involves running a length of wire along an existing stem and binding the stems together with wire or floral tape. The wire strengthens the stem and also can extend it. The wire can be a precut length of stem wire (also called stub wire) or it can be unwound from a paddle or spool in a desired length and cut. Wire can be plain, painted green, or wrapped in green thread. The technique is used mostly with dried plant material and silk flowers. Fresh flowers are not generally wired, except for stems with heavy, droopy flower heads that could use some support. Floral tape can also be used alone to protect tender stems from bruising or breaking when they are inserted into an arrangement or to make the stems more attractive, as in a boutonnière or a corsage.

## Technique: Wiring a Stem and Binding It with Wire and Floral Tape

The wiring and wrapping steps of this technique can be used in various combinations, depending on the plant material and the floral design. A wire stem can be bound to a floral stem using spool wire, floral tape, or both. Multiple stems may be bound individually with spool wire and then held together and wrapped with floral tape to create a small bouquet. This technique can be used to strengthen a stem and to extend its length, depending on the length of the wire that is used.

### MATERIALS AND TOOLS

Dried or silk flower
Precut stem wire, medium-gauge
Spool wire, fine-gauge
Floral tape, in green
Ceramic cup or bowl (optional)
Wire cutters

**Step 1**

Position the stem wire.

To strengthen the stem or to extend its length, use wire cutters to cut a length of wire that is equal to the desired length. Place the stem wire against the stem of the flower, resting the top end of the wire under the flower head and the bottom end of the wire either even with it or extended beyond the end of the floral stem.

**Step 2**

Bind with fine-gauge spool wire.

Place the spool of fine-gauge wire in a cup to keep the spool from rolling around. Draw out the loose end and hold it against the stem wire just under the flower head. Wind the spool wire around both the stem wire and the flower stem in a downward spiral for the full length of the stem. Use wire cutters to cut off the spool of fine-gauge wire.

**Step 3**

Bind the stem with floral tape.

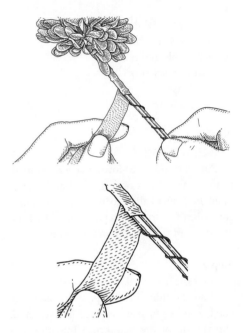

Use one hand to hold the end of the floral tape (do not cut it from the roll) against the stem just under the flower head. Use the other hand to wrap the tape around the stem, rotating the stem and angling the tape so that it wraps around the entire length of the stem in a downward spiral. Stretch the tape slightly as you wrap. When you reach the end of the stem, cut the floral tape from the roll, and press the loose end against the stem to secure it.

There are occasions when a flower head does not have a stem and one must be added before the flower can be used in an arrangement. The stems of flowers dried in desiccant are purposely cut short to make the drying easier;

adding false stems opens up the design options for using these types of flowers. Sometimes a fresh flower has broken off its stem, leaving a bare spot in the arrangement. A false stem on a fresh flower can allow you to return it to its spot in the arrangement for the remainder of the display life.

The repair of accidental breaks is not the only occasion for false stems on fresh flowers. Sometimes, you will want to remove fresh stems and replace them with false stems on purpose. When I designed my daughter's bridal bouquet—a sumptuous gathering of pink and super-green roses—it was clear that the collective circumference of all the stems would have been far too large for her to hold comfortably. Instead of removing flowers from the bouquet and altering the design, I replaced the live stems with false wire stems on a number of the roses (they were hardy and well-hydrated and would last the day). The wiring techniques used to add false stems to both dried and fresh flower heads are essentially the same, although a different gauge wire may be required for each, depending on the weight of the flower head.

## Technique: Creating a False Stem on a Dried Flower Head

Use this technique to add long stems to flower heads that have been dried in a desiccant or to give new purpose to air-dried flower heads that have broken off their thin, brittle stems.

### MATERIALS AND TOOLS

Dried flower head
Stem wire, fine- or medium-gauge (to suit flower head)
Floral tape, in green
Wire cutters
Chain-nose pliers

### Step 1

Prepare the stem wire.

Use the chain-nose pliers to bend a tiny loop at one end of a stem wire.

### Step 2

Install the stem wire in the flower head.

Insert the straight end of the wire through the top center of the dried flower head, carefully pulling the wire through the head and wrapping it once around the calyx (the inverted cone shape just under the flower head).

### Step 3

Secure the wire stem with floral tape.

Hold the real and false wire stem together just under the calyx. Press the end of the floral tape (do not cut it from the roll) onto both stems. Use the other hand to hold the tape against both stems. Begin rotating the stems and angling the tape so that it wraps around both pieces in a downward spiral. Stretch the tape slightly as you wrap. Continue wrapping down the entire length of the single wire stem. Cut the floral tape and press the loose end against the stem to secure it.

## Technique: Creating a False Stem on a Fresh Flower Head

Heavy flower heads that are fully hydrated may need some added support, or you may simply want a large quantity of fresh flowers, but not the added volume of their stems, in a bouquet or arrangement. This method involves inserting medium-gauge wire through the head of the flower and wrapping it around the stem. For a flower with a large calyx, such as a rose or a carnation, you can pierce its side and then bend the wire down so it is parallel to the stem before wrapping the wire around the stem.

## MATERIALS AND TOOLS

Flower head, fresh, or as desired
Paddle wire, medium-gauge, green
Wire cutters
Chain-nose pliers

### Step 1

Prepare the stem wire.

Unspool a length of stem wire and use wire cutters to cut a piece that is 6" (15.2 cm) longer than the length of the stem. Use chain-nose pliers to bend a tiny loop at one end.

### Step 2

Install the stem wire in the flower head.

Insert the straight end of the wire through the top center of the flower head, carefully pulling the wire through the head and wrapping it once around the calyx (the inverted cone shape just under the flower head).

### Step 3

Bind the stem with wire.

Continue to wind the wire around the stem. When you reach the end of the stem, use wire cutters to clip off the excess wire even with the end of the floral stem.

False stems are also useful on fruits, vegetables, pinecones, pods, and similar materials. These items can add color and texture to an arrangement, but unlike flowers and foliage, they have no existing stems that can be used to attach them. Lady apples, lemons, limes, oranges, figs, brussels sprouts, pomegranates, and artichokes are just a few of the fruits and vegetables that can be wired individually. In cases where a heavier fruit or vegetable is displayed over the rim of a container, it is wise to provide extra support underneath it so that the fruit or vegetable does not rip out of the wire under its own weight.

An alternative to real fruits and vegetables are pieces made of styrene, a light-weight plastic that has some flex and is easy to pierce with the end of a wire and fit with a false stem. Avoid plastic fruits that have a hard shell, which can be difficult to penetrate with the wire and are sometimes coated with a thin latex shell that can peel off.

## Technique: Creating a False Wire Stem on a Fresh Fruit or Vegetable

Adding a wire stem to a piece of fresh fruit will allow you to position pieces safely in an arrangement. Because fresh fruit and vegetables are relatively heavy compared to other plant materials such as flowers and foliage, it is common for heavy items to be wired to create strong stems, which are then secured to floral picks or to sturdy branches.

# Quick & Easy: Adding Shimmer and Shine to Plastic Fruit

Plastic fruit may come in realistic shapes, but the surface finish is not very elegant. A coating of reflective glass beads or micro glitter can make plain fruits worthy of more sophisticated designs. Choose fruits made of styrene, as this material takes well to paint and glue. Use a foam brush to apply a coat of metallic paint in a natural hue, such as peach or plum, to all of the surfaces of the fruit. When the paint is completely dry, use a soft-bristle brush to coat the surface with decoupage medium. Hold the fruit over a bowl filled with tiny reflective glass beads and use a large soupspoon to stream glass beads over the wet glue. Rotate the fruit until the entire surface is coated. The same coating technique works well with micro glitter. The finished fruit can be placed in a glass bowl or wired for use in floral arrangements.

MATERIALS AND TOOLS
    Fresh fruit, such as a lady apple
    Paddle wire, medium-gauge
    Floral tape, in green (optional)
    Wire cutters
    Ruler

**Step 1**
    Cut the wire.
    Use a ruler and wire cutters to measure and cut a 12" (30.5 cm) length of wire.

**Step 2**
    Insert the wire in the fruit.
    Use one end of the wire to pierce the skin of the fruit within the bottom third of the fruit.

Push the end of the wire completely through the fruit so that it exits out the opposite side. Pull the wire through so that the ends extending at each side are even.

**Step 3**
    Shape the false stem.

Bend down both wires, bring them together under the fruit, and cross one wire over the other. Use your hands to twist the wires together in a spiral to form a false stem. Wrap the stem with floral tape, if desired.

## Technique: Creating a False Wire Stem on Plastic Fruit

Adding a wire stem to a piece of plastic fruit allows you to position the fruit wherever you want in an arrangement. The fruit can be nestled in the other decorative materials or it can hang low near the edge, depending on the length of the false stem wire. Fruits made of soft, flexible styrene are the easiest to pierce. Hard plastic fruit has to be gouged out to insert the wire, which can break the plastic coating and cause the interior to crumble.

MATERIALS AND TOOLS
    Plastic fruit
    Stem or spool wire, medium-gauge
    Hot-glue gun and glue stick
    Wire cutters
    Chain-nose pliers
    Scissors
    Ruler

---

## Working Tips: Supplying Water to a Boutonnière

A boutonnière with a delicate flower such as a stephanotis will stay dewy and fresh-looking all day if you use a false stem that has a special cotton tip. The cotton tip is soaked in water and then placed inside the flower. The stem is wrapped in floral tape, concealing the water source.

**Step 1**

Pierce the plastic fruit.

Use the pointed blade of a pair of scissors to pierce a small hole in the base of the plastic fruit.

**Step 2**

Cut the wire.

Use a ruler and wire cutters to measure and cut a 6" (15.2 cm) length of wire.

**Step 3**

Attach the wire to the fruit.

Use chain-nose pliers to bend a narrow hook at one end of the wire. Apply a dab of hot glue to the hook and immediately push the glued end into the hole in the plastic fruit.

## Technique: Creating a False Wire Stem on a Pinecone

Pinecones add texture and earthy color to a floral arrangement, but before they can be added, you need to create a false stem, because they do not have sturdy stems of their own. The most suitable kind of pinecone is one that has overlapping scales with spaces between them that will allow a piece of wire to slip between the rows of scales and wrap around the cone, anchoring the stem.

MATERIALS AND TOOLS

Pinecone
Stem or spool wire, medium-gauge
Floral tape, in brown (optional)
Wire cutters
Ruler
Chain-nose pliers
Scissors

**Step 1**

Cut the wire.

Use a ruler and wire cutters to measure and cut a 9" (22.9 cm) length of wire.

**Step 2**

Position the wire stem.

Hold the wire against the cone, pushing it between the scales within the bottom third of the cone and leaving a 2" (5.1 cm) tail extending at one side.

**Step 3**

Secure the wire.

Bring the long end of the wire around the cone, concealing it between the scales, until it meets the shorter end of wire. Use pliers to twist the wires together, forming a 1" (2.5 cm) twisted length.

**Step 4**

Bend the stem.

Bend down the wire that is extending from the pinecone to form the false stem. Wrap the wire stem with brown floral tape, if desired.

Gathering and binding wired plant material into small bunches has broad applications, both practical and aesthetic, regardless of whether you are working with fresh, dried, or silk materials. By joining several stems of plant material together at one time, it is possible to achieve full coverage of broad areas, from the foam head of topiary to the foam surface of a large container arrangement, in a short time. Consolidating the stem count means fewer holes are made in the foam base, which helps to keep it strong and viable as a support. Small bouquets of flowers and bundles of foliage can also be assembled for garlands and wreaths.

A wooden floral pick with an attached set of wires is another option for binding stems together. The wires are wrapped around the stems of the floral material and the pick is inserted into the floral foam. A small bouquet of six or more stems attached to a single wooden pick allows for precision placement in an arrangement. Wooden picks are thicker than stem wire and make bigger holes, so avoid inserting picks into foam in congested groups, which can weaken the foam and cause it to crumble.

## Technique: Wiring Bunches and Making a Wire Pick for Flowers and Foliage

This simple technique will allow you to use one length of wire to secure the stems of a bunch of flowers or foliage and to form a pick that can be bound or inserted into an arrangement. Heavy-gauge wire is better because it is stiffer, allowing you to use the extension as a pick. Choose an appropriate cutting tool for this technique—a floral knife or floral scissors to cut fresh plant material, scissors of any type to cut dried plant material, and wire cutters to cut the stems of silk flowers and foliage.

### MATERIALS AND TOOLS

4 to 6 stems natural, dried, or silk flowers and foliage

Stem wire, 18-gauge, 14" (35.6 cm) long

Floral tape, in green

Cutting tool

Ruler

Pliers

**Step 1**

Prepare the floral stems.

Use an appropriate cutting tool to trim the stems of the flowers and foliage to 3½" (8.9 cm) or another desired length. Strip away all of the foliage on the stems except for any leaves around the bloom. On stems that contain only foliage, strip the lower part of the stem, leaving a leafy top.

**Step 2**

Bind the stems in a bouquet.

Hold the stems together in one hand and use your other hand to wrap floral tape around them, beginning at the top and wrapping down in a spiral. Tear the tape from the roll when the stems are concealed.

**Step 3**

Add the pick.

Hold the wire against the back of the taped stems, allowing 3½" (8.9 cm) of wire to extend below the cut ends of the stems and the other end of the wire to extend above the flowers and foliage. With your free hand, bend the top wire down so the bend that forms in the wire is hidden between the flower heads and the foliage. Wind the remaining wire around the straight wire and the stems, moving on a diagonal as you wrap the wire around and along the full length of the stems. Use pliers to twist the wire ends together to form the pick.

## Technique: Wiring onto a Wooden Floral Pick

False stems formed by wood picks are thicker than the false stems made of wire. Floral picks come in several lengths ranging from 3" to 18" (7.6 to 45.7 cm) long with and without a pair of same-length binding wires. Be sure to choose a cutting tool appropriate to your floral material.

### MATERIALS AND TOOLS

3 to 4 stems natural, dried, or silk flowers and foliage
Floral pick, in length longer than cut stems
Cutting tool

### Step 1

Prepare the floral stems.

Use an appropriate cutting tool to trim the stems of the flowers and foliage to 3½" (8.9 cm) or another desired length. Strip away all of the foliage on the stems except for any leaves

## Quick & Easy: Making Your Own Floral Picks

Although floral picks come in a variety of precut lengths—3", 4", 6", 7", 12", and 18" (7.6, 10.2, 15.2, 17.8, 30.5, and 45.7 cm)—it is easy to make your own wired picks using common and inexpensive materials. A long wooden skewer can be cut into short sections that are wired individually, or its entire length can be wired at the blunt end.

- Cut a 12" (30.5 cm) wooden skewer into approximately three equal lengths. Use a pair of scissors to nick a groove in the skewer ¼" (0.6 cm) from one end (don't cut all the way through). Cut three pieces of fine-gauge wire, approximately 4½" (11.4 cm) long. Center each wire in the groove on one of the picks and wrap the wire around once, twisting the wires tightly against the wood.

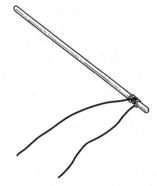

- Use the wire on the pick to bind the chosen floral material and then wrap with floral tape.

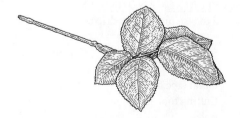

around the bloom. On stems that contain only foliage, strip the lower part of the stem, leaving a leafy top.

### Step 2

Bind the stems in a small bouquet.

Hold the stems together in one hand and use your other hand to wrap floral tape around them, beginning at the top and wrapping down in a spiral, overlapping the edges of the tape. Tear the tape from the roll when the stems are concealed.

### Step 3

Attach a pick to the small bouquet.

Hold the pick against the stems with the blunt end of the pick just under the flower heads and the point extended below the ends of the stems. Wrap one of the wires on the floral pick around the stems of the bouquet in one direction and wrap the other wire in the opposite direction, spiraling down the stems so the wires meet. Twist the wire ends to secure the bunch.

## Bouquets to Carry and to Display

A bouquet can be defined as an arrangement of flowers and foliage that is formed by gathering stems together in a loose free-form arrangement, in a compact mound, or anything in between. A bouquet can be carried in the hand or displayed in a vase or other container. A hand-tied bouquet can be as simple as a small bunch of wildflowers tied with a ribbon or as complex as rows of different flowers organized in a tight mound with stems wrapped in tight bands to form a handle.

The flower stems of formal handheld bouquets for weddings are usually arranged so that they are straight and parallel with one another and evenly trimmed at the bottom. The number of flowers is a feature of the floral design but is often determined with practicality in mind. The bouquet handle must

have a small enough circumference to carry comfortably. Wrapping the stems with ribbon holds the stems secure, keeps the fresh plant material from staining the hands, and adds a touch of style. Ribbon wrappings can conceal the entire stem length or a portion of it. One style is to wrap the upper three-quarters of the stems and allow 1½" (3.8 cm) of the cut ends to show at the bottom. Another style is to wrap about half of the stem length and allow ½" (1.3 cm) to show at the bottom. There is no technical reason to choose one approach over the other; it is entirely a matter of personal taste.

## Technique: Making a Handheld Bouquet Using Hand-Tying

This classic bouquet design begins with a central mound of flowers and adds different kinds of flowers in rounds around it. The number of floral rounds can be as few as two and as many as five or six, depending on the size and shape of the flower heads and the overall circumference of the stems, which needs to remain small enough to be comfortable to hold and carry. Fresh flowers can be gathered into this hand-tied bouquet, or you can use silk flowers (as specified below) in kinds that reflect the natural growing season.

## MATERIALS AND TOOLS

- 7 silk open roses on 8" (20.3 cm) stems, in pale pink
- 14 silk tulips on 7" (17.8 cm) stems, in peach
- 18 tulip fronds
- 18 stem wires, medium-gauge, 6" (15.2 cm) long
- Paddle wire, medium-gauge
- Floral tape, in green
- 1 yard (91.4 cm) wire-edged ribbon, 1½" (3.8 cm) wide, in black-and-white plaid
- Wire cutters
- Scissors
- Ruler or tape measure

### Step 1

Prepare the wire for wrapping.

Use a ruler and wire cutters to measure and cut a 24" (40.6 cm) length of paddle wire. Wrap the wire with floral tape. Cut the wrapped wire in thirds.

### Step 2

Prepare the roses, tulips, and leaves.

Lay the roses on a flat surface. Working one stem at a time, use your hands to strip off all of the foliage. Lay the tulips on a flat surface. Working one stem at a time, use wire cutters to cut the leaves where they meet the stems. Use stem wire and floral tape to make a false stem on each leaf, extending each existing stem so that it is equal in length to the length of the tulips.

### Step 3

Begin to form the central mound.

Hold one rose stem in your hand. Use your other hand to cross a second rose stem over the first, positioning its rose head to the left of the first rose. The crossover point is where the bouquet will be tied. The lower the crossover point on the stems, the greater the circumference of the floral part of the bouquet.

### Step 4

Add roses to the central mound.

Continue to add the roses, one stem at a time, to the ones in your hand, placing each

---

## Suggested Flowers for Hand-Tied Bouquets by Season

| Summer | Fall | Winter | Spring |
|---|---|---|---|
| Alstroemarium | Chrysanthemum | Calla lily | Delphinium |
| Dahlia | Cosmos | Carnation | Peony |
| Daisy | Hydrangea | Rose | Ranunculus |
| Rose | | Sweet pea | Tulip |

new rose head to the left, crossing the stems, and twisting the stems slightly so that the stems splay and the roses form a dome.

**Step 5**

Bind the stems of the bouquet together.

Hold the stems securely at the crossover point. Use one of the wrapped wires made in step 1 to bind the stems together at that place.

**Step 6**

Add the tulips to the bouquet.

Repeat steps 3–5 to add the tulips to the bouquet, turning the flower heads outward to form a collar. Use the second length of wrapped wire made in step 1 to bind the tulip stems together at the crossover.

**Step 7**

Assess the bouquet's shape.

Assess the arrangement. Hold the bouquet securely and view it from the top, making sure the flowers form neat rounds and the bouquet is dome-shaped. Adjust the stems to reposition any flower head to maintain uniform rounds.

**Step 8**

Add the leaves to the bouquet.

Position the leaf section of the wired leaves around the central dome of flowers to form a leafy collar, pressing the wire extensions against the floral stems. Use the remaining wrapped wire to secure the leaves, arranging them so the tips of the leaves are on the same line.

**Step 9**

Tie the ribbon bow.

Place the midpoint of the ribbon on the stems, just below the tulips and the leaves. Wrap the ribbon once around the bound stems and tie it into a bow, allowing the streamers to cascade down. Use the wire cutters to trim the center rose slightly shorter than the surrounding tulip and leaf stems for a bouquet that will stand upright.

## Technique: Wrapping the Stems of a Handheld Bouquet with Ribbon

Ribbon can be used to conceal the stems of a handheld bouquet as long as the stems are straight and parallel with one another. Any opaque ribbon you like can be used from grosgrain and satin to velvet; however, the number of yards you need will be determined by the circumference of the handle on the bouquet and the width of the ribbon. As a general rule of thumb, the larger the circumference and the narrower the ribbon, the more ribbon you will need to wrap around the stems. I am generous in my designing and love long cascading ribbons, so I often over-buy, knowing I will use the excess in another project.

MATERIALS AND TOOLS

Bouquet, with stem handle 2" (5.1 cm) in diameter

3 yards (2.7 m) ribbon, ⅜" (1 cm) wide

Pearl-headed pins

Double-sided tape

Scissors

**Step 1**

Apply tape to the stem handle.

Cut two lengths of double-sided tape, each equal to the height of the stems of the bouquet. Position and press the strips to opposite sides of the stems, pressing one end of the tape under the petals of the bouquet and extending the tape all the way down to the end of the stems.

**Step 2**

Begin the ribbon wrap.

Place the midpoint of the ribbon on the front of the bouquet handle near the bottom of the stems. Wrap the ribbon ends around the handle, twist them at the back, and bring the ends forward again.

---

## Working Tips: Using Plant Material at Various Stages of Growth

All flower species progress through many stages as they mature from unopened bud to a flower head in full bloom. Consider adding flowers to your arrangements that represent various stages of growth. Your arrangement will not only feature a variety of textures, shapes, and colors but will also reveal the unfolding beauty of the life cycle itself.

---

**Step 3**

Finish the ribbon wrap.

Wrap and return the ribbon ends to the back of the stems, crisscross the ends to form a neat twist, and bring the ribbon ends forward. Continue wrapping the ribbon up the bouquet handle until there is a neat and even line of twists at the back of the handle (which will be the new front). Tie the ends together in a tight double knot and make a ribbon bow with streamers (which is now the back of the bouquet).

**Step 4**

Add the decorative pearls.

Insert a pearl-headed pin into each twist, angling the pin so that the point doesn't protrude on the other side of the handle, where it can prick hands. Hold the bouquet with the pearls facing front.

## Container Arrangements

The container in which a flower arrangement is placed or made serves both a mechanical and an aesthetic purpose. It should be of a size and scale that supports the flowers and in a compatible style, shape, and color, but even working within those parameters, you'll find you have a lot of design latitude when it comes to choosing a container. I own many vases and containers in unique shapes and in different colors and patinas, but I also keep several clear glass vases for those occasions when I receive loose flowers. In all cases, choose a container that is waterproof or insert a waterproof liner when working with live plant material.

The style of a container can be traditional, modern, vintage, or any other look you choose. You may wish to coordinate the style of the container with the flowers themselves or with the room setting in which the floral arrangement will be displayed. The shape of a container should enhance the floral materials. The curves of an urn can play to the arching stems of tulips and the subtle line of softly draping foliage. Conversely, the hard lines of a rectangular vase can become a foil to softly arching stems. Similarly, the container color can be in close concert with the flowers or introduce a stark contrast. To create an uninterrupted flow of color in an arrangement, choose flowers and a container in the same color or a similar colorway, but vary the kinds of flowers to add drama and textural interest. For example, choose a variety of red-orange flowers and berries, such as red spray roses, leucadendrum, viburnum berries, and dahlias, and place the arrangement in a cherry red vase. To accentuate and offer contrast to the floral heads of pink tulips, consider using a glazed ceramic pot in robin's-egg blue. When I buy flowers, I usually have a particular vase in mind on which to base my selection. One simple rule of thumb: flowers can be twice as tall as the vase. I feel free to break this rule, however, as long as the center of gravity is low and the container is heavy enough to support taller flowers.

Several approaches are followed to place flowers in a vase or container. A compact bouquet of hand-tied flowers can always be placed into a container as is, keeping the bindings in place. Releasing and removing the bindings lets the flowers fall into a loose arrangement. Compact and loose arrangements can also be accomplished by setting the flowers inside the container one stem at a time, using either the tripod method or floral foam, for maximum control and structure. In the tripod method, stems of the floral material are arranged in a supportive framework inside the container.

## Technique: Using a Tripod Construction for a Container Arrangement

In the tripod method, flowers with the thickest stems and largest heads are placed first to create a framework. Flowers with thinner stems and smaller heads are placed within the framework in descending size and fragility,

forming a sturdy teepee of stems. A clear vase will help you see the tripod more clearly as you learn the technique. Remember to condition fresh flowers before you use them to keep them at their peak.

### MATERIALS AND TOOLS
40 conditioned roses, in pink and yellow
Vase, 10½" (26.7 cm) high, with a 4½"
    (11.4 cm) opening, or as desired
Floral knife
Cutting board
Floral food
Bucket
Sink with hot and cold running water

**Step 1**
Cut the flowers.
Assess the desired height of the flowers and use a floral knife to cut the stems on a diagonal to that measurement.

**Step 2**
Make the tripod.
Insert 3 rose stems into the vase, crossing the stems at the rim of the vase and splaying the ends.

**Step 3**
Add more flowers to the tripod.
Hold the stems where they cross with one hand. Continue to add stems, one at a time, crisscrossing the new stems into those

## Working Tips: Styling for Abundance

To give the impression of a fuller bouquet, display a floral arrangement in front of a mirror.

previously placed to form a network of stems. Continue until all the stems are inserted.

**Step 4**

Add floral food to the water.

Mix floral food and room temperature water in a bucket, according to the directions on the package, swishing the solution to blend it. Pour the solution into the vase.

**Step 5**

Add water to the vase.

Pour clean, room temperature water into the solution in the vase.

Floral foam inserted into a container supports the stems of flowers and foliage and fixes their position in the arrangement. Foam-based designs run the gamut, from billowing, arching blooms to tight, highly organized grids. Each bloom can be inserted into the foam in an orientation that shows the flower to its best advantage. I find that I use floral foam when I want to control the line of a floral arrangement or orient the position of a stem or flower head in a way that best serves the floral design.

Arranging flower stems in a grid pattern requires little effort yet produces stunning results. Garden flowers such as daisies, asters, and roses, which have hearty heads and sturdy stems, can be arranged in neat grids of color. The stems can be cut short and "planted" in the foam in rows to create a low carpet of color, or the stems can be left longer so the flowers stand higher. To establish neat rows and columns, the flower heads should be the same size as nearly as possible and the stems should be cut to the same length. The color can be uniform or alternate from one row to the next. The grid pattern seems to enhance and bring out the beauty of the individual flowers.

To support live flowers and foliage, use green floral foam, known by the brand name Oasis. The dry foam is easily carved to a size

## Adjusting the Span of the Tripod

For a squat vase:

For a tall vase:

and shape that fits the container. Once the carved foam is fitted snugly inside the container, it is saturated with water (including a solution of floral food, if desired) and the plant material is added. When working with a container that is tapered on the top, fill the bottom of the container with loose chunks of foam and then cut and push in a sculpted piece of foam to rest on top. The foam at the bottom of the container will provide a handy reservoir of water.

To support dried and silk material, use dry, brown floral foam, which is denser than green floral foam and holds slender stems easily; this foam is not designed to hold a water supply. Styrofoam for floral use is pale green in color; its tough texture makes a good support for dried and silk material with wire stems. Hot glue will melt Styrofoam, but some glues from a low-temperature glue gun are safe to use. If you want to use a glue gun, experiment on a foam scrap first.

## Technique: Filling a Container with Foam

Use this method for green floral foam, brown foam, or pale green Styrofoam, depending on the floral material being supported. A container that is large or shapely may take more than one block of foam to fill it; joining two or more blocks together will provide the needed volume. The foam may need to be trimmed to fit through the mouth of the container.

### MATERIALS AND TOOLS

Container
Floral foam blocks
Wooden toothpicks or skewers
Floral clay
Floral adhesive tape
Foam anchor
Respirator mask
Safety glasses
Serrated knife
Pruning shears
Cutting board
Bar soap

### Step 1

Fit the foam to the container.

Determine how many blocks of foam are needed to fill the container. If the container is small and one block of foam can fill it, go to step 2. For larger containers, stack the foam blocks vertically or place them side by side to construct a base that approximates the volume of the container. Insert toothpicks or wooden skewers into the blocks to join them together. Use clippers to trim off any excess from the skewers.

### Step 2

Impress the foam.

Set the foam on the cutting board. Invert the container onto the foam and press it down so that the rim of the container makes an impression on the foam.

### Step 3

Shape the foam.

Put on a respirator mask and safety glasses. With the rim impression as a guide, use a serrated knife to gradually shave the foam block into a shape that will fit into the container. For smoother cutting, periodically run the knife blade over a bar of soap.

### Step 4

Install the foam in the container.

Place blobs of floral clay at even intervals across the bottom of the container. Push a foam anchor into each blob of clay. Impale the shaved foam block onto the prongs of the foam anchors, pushing down until the foam rests ½" (1.3 cm) below the rim of the container.

### Step 5

Secure the foam.

Crisscross two strips of adhesive tape over the center of the foam and secure the tape ends to the outside of the container.

⁂

## Working Tips: Cleaning Floral Containers

Bleach, antibacterial soap, a bottle brush, and a nylon scrub pad are the necessary items for cleaning and maintaining floral containers. For light cleaning, use antibacterial liquid soap, water, and a bottle brush. To remove caked-on mold or plant matter or for other heavy cleaning, dissolve ¼ teaspoon (1.2 ml) bleach in 1 gallon (3.8 L) of water, pour some of the solution into the container, and place the whole container into the bucket with the rest of the solution, leaving it to soak. Use a bottle brush to reach into the inside of the container to clean it and use using a nylon scrub pad to clean the outside. After cleaning a container with soap or bleach, flush it thoroughly with clean water to remove all traces of the cleaning agents. Let it dry before adding fresh flowers.

⁂

## Technique: Making a Mound-Shaped Monochromatic Silk Floral Arrangement

One of the prettiest, simplest, and fastest container arrangements to make uses silk flowers in all one color. Inspired by Prudence Designs, the featured flower is the ranunculus, a flower known for its rich color and delicate petals. The flowers are placed in a ceramic vase filled with Styrofoam, which is then concealed with wads of green sheet moss. Because the vase is tall and the flowers are not top-heavy, no tape was needed to secure the foam in the container. Create the same arrangement with fresh flowers using green floral foam.

### MATERIALS AND TOOLS

Container, 4½" × 3¼" × 6" (11.4 × 8.3 × 15.2 cm), prepared with green Styrofoam
35 to 40 silk ranunculus buds and flowers on 8" (20.3 cm) stems, in deep strawberry pink
Sheet moss, in green
Wire cutters
Ruler
Craft stick

### Step 1

Cut the stems.
Lay the silk flowers and buds on a flat

surface. Use a ruler and wire cutters to cut each stem to 7" (17.8 cm).

## Step 2

Arrange the flowers in the center of the foam.

Insert approximately 15 flower stems into the center of the foam, making a mound of flower heads that touch one another with the highest point of the arrangement at the center.

## Step 3

Fill in the perimeter of the arrangement.

Add the remaining flowers and the buds around the mounded arrangement. Push some stems slightly deeper into the foam to vary the heights and give texture to the arrangement. Tilt the flower heads so they radiate outward for a natural look.

## Step 4

Conceal the foam.

Tear small pieces of moss from the sheet. Use a craft stick to carefully press the moss between the stems of the flowers, concealing the foam completely. Tuck in the moss at the rim of the container.

## Technique: Arranging Tall Silk Flowers in a Styrofoam Base

Styrofoam is strong enough to support tall silk flowers and foliage that rise above the container. Be sure to anchor the foam securely inside the container using floral clay and a foam anchor before inserting your floral material. Then use lengths of adhesive tape to further stabilize the foam and to keep it from lifting up after the flowers have been inserted; see Technique: Filling a Container with Foam (page 139).

## Quick & Easy: Using a Tape Grid to Support Tall Stems

To steady long-stemmed flowers in a vase, use narrow lengths of clear strapping tape (or floral adhesive tape) to make a grid on the mouth of the vase. Stretch lengths of tape across the vase from edge to edge in one direction, parallel to one another and approximately $3/4$" (1.9 cm) apart. Then lay another set of strips perpendicular to the first set to create a grid pattern. Stand one flower stem in each grid opening.

## MATERIALS AND TOOLS

Glazed celadon urn, 10" (25.4 cm) high with 6" (15.2 cm) opening, prepared with Styrofoam

25 silk tulips on 12" (30.5 cm) stems, in apricot

8 silk tulips with closed buds on 12" (30.5 cm) stems, in apricot

10 partially opened silk roses on 12" (30.5 cm) stems, in pink

8 small silk viburnums with foliage on 9" (22.9 cm) stems, in white

10 silk lilacs on 10" (25.4 cm) stems, in blue

12 silk rose leaves on 10" (25.4 cm) false stems

Stem wire, medium-gauge, 10" (25.4 cm) long

Sheet moss, in green

### Step 1

Arrange the tulip stems.

Insert a cluster of 3 or 4 mature tulip stems at the left side of the urn with the flower heads bending over. Insert another cluster at the right side with the flower heads in a soft arch. Place the remaining mature tulips in a radial pattern across the center. Add single tulip bud stems to the radial pattern, pushing the stems into the foam between the mature tulips at different heights and orienting the flower heads so that they face different directions for a natural look.

### Step 2

Arrange the rose stems.

Insert 2 roses into the right front side of the arrangement, 1 rose to the left of center, and the remaining 7 roses throughout the arrangement, referring to the illustration on page 141 for more details.

### Step 3

Arrange the remaining stems.

Distribute the viburnum throughout the arrangement. Insert the lilacs throughout the arrangement so that they are higher than the surrounding flowers. Insert the rose leaves next to the roses.

### Step 4

Conceal the foam.

Tear small pieces of moss from the sheet. Use a craft stick to carefully press the moss between the stems of the flowers, concealing the foam completely. Tuck in the moss at the rim of the container.

## Technique: Making a Grid Arrangement in Floral Foam

Fresh floral heads with short stems are inserted into green floral foam to make this pretty grid arrangement. Choose a rectangular or square container to fill with floral foam. You can follow the same geometric principle to design a radial pattern in a round container.

The low, compact design also makes effective use of dried floral heads, which already have short-clipped stems.

## MATERIALS AND TOOLS

Rectangular container, 8½" × 4¼" × 2½" (21.6 × 10.8.4 × 6 cm), or as desired
15 fresh roses with leafy stems, flower heads 2" to 2¼" (5.1 to 5.7 cm) across
Sheet moss
Green floral foam
Cutting board
Serrated knife
Floral knife
Ruler
Pencil

Respirator mask
Safety glasses

### Step 1

Shape and install the foam.

Put on a respirator mask and safety glasses. Place the foam block on a cutting board and use a serrated knife to trim it to fit snugly in the container. Insert the foam into the container, pushing it down so it rests ½" (1.3 cm) below the rim. Saturate the foam completely with water before moving to the next step.

### Step 2

Make a grid pattern in the foam.

Use a ruler and a sharp pencil to incise a

---

## Fun for Kids: Planting a Teacup Garden

Kids will love the near-instant results they get when arranging flowers in a potted garden of their own. They will learn a few basics of flower arranging at the same time. The floral design features 10 to 15 daisies, but

carnations and marigolds would also be suitable.

- Press the rim of a teacup into a block of green floral foam to make an impression. Use a plastic knife and follow the indentation to sculpt the foam so it fits inside the teacup. Slice across the foam so it is level with the rim.
- Crisscross two strips of adhesive tape over the center of the foam, pressing the ends against the cup. Pour water onto the foam, saturating it completely.
- For an adult to do: Cut each daisy stem to about 5½" (14.0 cm), or a height that allows the flower head to stand higher than the rim of the teacup.
- Insert the stems of the daisies into the foam, one at a time, to make a loose mound of flowers.

three-by-five grid pattern on the surface of the foam.

## Step 3

Prepare the roses.

Using a knife and submerging the roses in water, cut the stems diagonally so that each stem, including the flower head, equals the height of the container plus 1½" (3.8 cm). (For a taller arrangement, leave longer stems.) Strip off the thorns and leaves from the stems of the roses. Cut off and reserve 20 to 25 large leaves with stems.

## Step 4

Add a leafy border.

Insert a leaf between the container and the foam, going around the entire rim to make a leafy collar. Use small wads of sheet moss between the stems to conceal any visible foam.

## Step 5

Decorate the grid.

Insert the stem of one rose into the center of each marked section, working from one row to the next until there are 15 roses in a grid pattern.

## Wreaths

We usually associate wreaths with Christmas or winter, but wreaths can be interpreted in seasonal flowers and foliage for display throughout the year. The traditional wreath is a ring of fresh, dried, or silk plant material, but modern wreaths also come in heart and square shapes. Shapes and sizes can be designed to suit one's personal style and display goals.

How the wreath is displayed will depend on its overall weight and size as well as the character of the decorative material. A wreath can be hung on a door or a wall, suspended in front of a mirror, secured to the arms of a chandelier or candelabra, or placed flat on a table as a centerpiece. If a wreath is decorated with fresh flowers and foliage, it will need a water supply, which will add substantial weight. It is recommended that such wreaths be displayed flat on a tabletop or other supportive surface. Wreath frames made of vines or welded wire are intrinsically light-weight and can support a variety of decorative materials, from preserved plant materials to dried flowers and silks. Heavier material, such as evergreen branches and fresh fruit, must be well anchored to a sturdy wreath base. Ornamental items, chosen to enhance the aesthetics of the design, are usually light-weight; they include ribbons, feathers, raffia, high-quality plastic fruit, and dried materials such as seeds, grasses, and pods. The collective size, scale, and weight of the floral elements and embellishments will determine which type of frame to use. By having a general understanding of the interrelationship between the decorative material and a wreath base, you will be able to design wreaths with greater confidence and achieve better results.

### Making or Preparing a Wreath Frame

A wreath frame in the traditional ring shape can be made using any flexible material that can be shaped into a hoop while remaining rigid enough to support the added decoration. The appeal of making your own wreath frame is that you choose the diameter. Using grapevine to make a wreath frame is one approach. Freshly cut, hydrated grapevine is naturally flexible and very easy to bend and shape into a wreath. The wreath will dry and stiffen naturally, becoming woody and strong enough to hold decoration without sagging. Another method uses a wire coat hanger and a large plastic trash bag. The hanger is bent into a circle shape and wrapped with the plastic bag, which bulks up the form to make a base for the decorative material. Wreath bases made of welded metal, packed straw, green Styrofoam, or plastic bags are intended to be covered with sheet moss or a carpet of leaves to make an attractive stage for the design elements that follow.

## Technique: Making a Wreath Frame with Grapevines

A relatively even hoop shape is obtained by shaping the grapevines around an armature or form, such as an overturned bucket, in the desired size. Use long lengths of freshly cut vine that bend easily. If the vine is stiff, soak it in water to make it more pliable. Vine is available at garden stores and florists, and it also grows wild. Get permission to harvest wild vine you come across on private property.

### MATERIALS AND TOOLS

8 natural grapevines, each 4' (121.9 cm) or longer
Paddle wire, medium-gauge
Bucket
Wire cutters
Spring-type clothespins

**Step 1**
Soak the stiff vines.
Soak the grapevines overnight in a bucket of water to make them as pliable as possible. Be aware that some of the bark may come off the vines.

**Step 2**
Wrap the bucket with the longest vine.
Take the bucket outdoors. Turn the bucket over on a flat work surface so that the tapered end faces up. Choose the longest vine and wrap it around the base of the bucket, interweaving the end back into the vine circle. Use clothespins to clip the vine to itself to hold the wrap in place.

**Step 3**
Weave in the remaining vines.
Repeat step 2 to interweave each of the remaining vines into the main vine, one at a time, tucking in the ends behind the main vine, until the desired wreath thickness is achieved. Rotate the bucket occasionally to ensure the vines are evenly placed all around.

**Step 4**
Let the vine dry in place.
Leave the vine on the bucket. Let it dry in a protected place for a week or more, or until completely dry. Lift the wreath off the bucket and remove any clothespins.

**Step 5**
Bind the grapevine wreath with wire.
Pull a 12" (30.5 cm) length of wire from the paddle (do not cut the wire). Use your hand to hold the end of the wire against the vine anyplace on the hoop. Use your other hand to hold the paddle and wrap the wire around the vines, continuing around the wreath until you reach the starting point. Repeat to make a second pass. Twist the wires together three or four times and use wire cutters to cut the wire from the paddle. Wrap the excess wire around the vines.

## Technique: Making a Wire-and-Plastic-Bag Wreath Frame

This frame is perfectly suited to spontaneous wreath designing, because you make it from items you have on hand. The plastic trash bag naturally traps air as it is wrapped around the wire, adding volume and loft to the wreath.

### MATERIALS AND TOOLS

Wire hanger
Kitchen trash bag, large
Paddle wire
Tape
Wire cutters

### Step 1

Shape the hanger.

Use the wire cutters to cut the hook from the hanger and discard it. Use your hands to stretch and shape the hanger into a hoop, being careful to avoid scratching yourself on the cut wire end.

### Step 2

Wrap the wire hoop with a plastic bag.

Lay the plastic bag on a flat surface and fold it lengthwise into a long band. Wrap the band around the wire hoop, making snug overlapping wraps, until the entire wreath frame is wrapped with an even layer of plastic. Use a strip of tape to secure the plastic to itself at the overlap.

### Step 3

Bind the plastic bag to the frame with wire.

Pull a 12" (30.5 cm) length of wire from the paddle (do not cut the wire). Use your hand to hold the end of the wire against the overlapping bands of plastic bag. Use your other hand to hold the paddle and wrap the wire around the wreath frame and the plastic bag, continuing until you reach the starting point. Twist the wires together three or four times and use wire cutters to cut the wire from the paddle. Bend the twisted wires into a hanging loop.

## Technique: Concealing a Wreath Frame with Moss

Use this technique on any wreath frame that is meant to be concealed, such as a metal frame, a straw frame, or one you make yourself from a wire coat hanger and a plastic trash bag. Moss provides an attractive foundation for the decorative material, which can be attached using a glue gun or wire.

### MATERIALS AND TOOLS

Metal wreath frame, or as desired
Sheet moss or sphagnum
Paddle wire, medium-gauge
Wire cutters

### Step 1

Attach the wire to the frame.

Pull a 12" (30.5 cm) length of wire from the paddle (do not cut the wire). Use your hand to hold the end of the wire against the inside ring of the wreath frame. Wrap the wire end around the frame, continuing around a second time to secure the binding. Twist the two wires together.

### Step 2

Prepare the moss.

Lay the moss on a protected work surface. Pull off large wads of moss until you have laid out enough to cover the top and sides of the wire frame in a thick layer.

### Step 3

Begin to bind the moss to the frame.

Lay several wads of moss on the section of the wire frame where the paddle wire is joined. Pat the moss flat against the sides and top of the frame. While holding the paddle in your hand, wrap the wire around the frame to secure the wads of moss. Stop wrapping when you get to the bare part of the frame.

### Step 4

Finish binding moss to the frame.

Repeat step 3 to add more wads of moss to the frame and bind it with paddle wire. Continue working around the wreath, covering the top and sides in a thick layer of moss, until you reach the starting point and the paddle wire meets the loose wire secured in step 1. Twist the wires together three or four times and use wire cutters to cut the wire from the paddle. Wrap the excess wire around the frame or shape it into a hanging loop.

## Technique: Concealing a Wreath Frame with Lemon Leaves

To make this wreath base, harvest fresh, leafy branches from your garden or buy them from a local garden center or florist. Start with a moss-covered frame. The wreath form will be completely concealed. For a wreath that's less earthy and more regal, spray the leaves metallic gold, silver, or copper before attaching them to the wreath base, and then use a wide metallic ribbon to tie a decorative bow with long streamers. Attach the leaves with a bull's-eye configuration in mind, adding leaves to the outer ring, followed by the inner ring, and the middle ring last.

### MATERIALS AND TOOLS

Wreath frame, covered in moss
10 to 12 branches of lemon leaves
Floral pins
Wire cutters

### Step 1

Add lemon leaves to the outer ring of the wreath.

Pull the lemon leaves off of the branches. Beginning at the outer circumference of the wreath, use floral pins to apply the leaves in tiers around the outside surface of the wreath; overlap the stems of the previously pinned leaves with the tips of the new leaves.

### Step 2

Add lemon leaves to the inner ring of the wreath.

Continue to add leaves in tiers around the inner surface of the wreath, overlapping the stems of the previously pinned leaves with the tips of the new leaves.

## Quick & Easy: Making a Moss-Covered Ball

A moss-covered ball can add a touch of decorative greenery to a table, shelf, windowsill, or mantel. Moss will stay green and fresh-looking if misted daily.

- Lay green sheet moss on a protected work surface and mist it lightly with water until it is flexible.
- Wrap the sheet moss around a green Styrofoam ball, pressing the moss against the foam and fitting the edges together to form a smooth layer. Tear away the excess moss to avoid clumpy seams. Secure the moss with floral pins. Add more wads of moss until the ball is concealed.
- Wrap a fresh ivy vine or a slender grapevine around the moss-covered ball for accent.

**Step 3**

Add lemon leaves to the center ring of the wreath's surface.

Continue as before, pinning leaves in tiers over the bare center portion of the wreath and filling in any bare spots with single leaves.

## Technique: Adding a Hanging Loop to a Wreath Frame

If you intend to hang your wreath on a door or wall, you will need to add a wire hanging loop. The loop can be added before or after the decoration has been applied to the wreath. The easiest frames to work with are grapevine and wire-welded frames, because there are openings in the frame for anchoring a hanging loop. If you are working with a straw or Styrofoam wreath base, simply wrap and secure the wire around the wreath before shaping it into the hanging loop.

MATERIALS AND TOOLS

Grapevine or welded-wire wreath frame, decorated
Spool or paddle wire, medium-gauge
Wire cutters
Pliers

**Step 1**

Determine the hook location.

Lay the wreath faceup on a protected work surface. Orient the wreath so that the top of the wreath is at the 12 o'clock position.

**Step 2**

Make the hanging loop.

Cut an 8" (20.3 cm) length of spool wire. Thread it through some vines or a wire hoop at the back of the wreath at the 12 o'clock position. Use your hands to twist the wire ends together and then use pliers to crimp the wire ends back on themselves until secure.

### Decorating a Wreath Frame

The items used to decorate a wreath frame are prepared as they might be for any floral arrangement. There might be stems to reinforce with wire, flowers to attach to picks, or false stems to add to flower heads or artificial fruit. A wreath may be a showcase for a bevy of tiny bouquets, each made with a wide variety of fresh flowers, or it may be a large Della Robbia–style display with enough fruit for a bacchanalian feast.

For a wreath with beauty and stylistic impact, try to envision the kind of decoration you want and then choose an appropriate wreath frame to support it. Heavy decoration requires a very sturdy frame, such as a straw or welded wire, while most light-weight decoration can be applied to wreaths made of vine or Styrofoam. To supply fresh flowers and foliage with fresh water, use a special wreath frame of green floral foam installed in a molded plastic frame.

While there are no strict rules for applying decoration, several tried-and-true approaches ensure a coherent, well-balanced, beautiful design. One approach is to visualize the wreath as a clock face and orient the placement of the materials in quadrants (or three-hour sections). A symmetrical design in which the same or similar materials are evenly distributed in each quadrant creates a balanced movement of colors and shapes around the wreath. In a bull's-eye design, the decoration is attached in the concentric rings, outer ring first, followed by the inner ring, and finally building up and filling the area in between. For an asymmetrical design, you choose an off-center focal point, such as the 4 o'clock position, and apply the decorative material there so it radiates outward, opening up the design. Of course, you can always create a design spontaneously, adding decorative materials randomly and evaluating their color, texture, and size as you go. Wreath designs can be very spare, with just a small cluster of flowers accenting one spot, or they can be sumptuous with flowers that cover the wreath base completely.

When you have your design plan in mind, attach one type of material at a time. Begin with heavier or larger elements and progress to those that are smaller and more delicate. This approach will create a strong, cohesive design, and it will also safeguard the smaller, more fragile materials from damage during wreath assembly and decoration. Your objective is to ensure that each element is displayed to its best advantage and that everything is well-anchored, especially fresh fruit or clusters of plastic fruit. A lush apple attached with a fine strand of thread is just waiting to fall; securing it with medium-gauge wire will prevent the Newtonian inevitability.

Wire is one of the most versatile materials for attaching decorative material to a wreath frame. The wire in the stem of a silk flower can facilitate the direct insertion of the flower into foam or it can be woven between the branches on a grapevine wreath or the hoops on a wire frame. When I am working with fresh delicate stems, I wrap them with floral tape first to protect them before adding the wire, which can cut into plant matter. Stub wire (precut lengths of painted or thread-wrapped wire) can be wound around bendable stems, such as those found on tulips, to support and stiffen them so that they can stand upright in a vase or foam. Continuous lengths of spool wire or paddle wire are used to bind fresh and voluminous material, such as evergreen branches, around a wreath frame that is either concealed with moss or left bare.

Waxed string and twine are also used for binding and for tying. Strong, waterproof, and more pliable than wire, waxed string is particularly suited to fresh flowers and foliage. Other attachment methods include the use of hot glue, low-temperature glue, and floral picks. Ultimately, the suitability of a particular attachment method rests on the material used to make the wreath frame and the type of material being attached.

## Fresh Plant Materials that Can Dry in Place for a Long-Lasting Display

Many kinds of flowers and foliage can be attached fresh and allowed to dry in place, progressing through natural changes in color and texture that continue to remain attractive on a wreath, garland, or topiary. Be aware that the stems of fresh plant material shrink and become brittle and wrappings and binding can loosen around the stems. Here are a few hardy types to try.

| Flowers | Celosia cockscomb |
|---|---|
| | Globe amaranth |
| | Larkspur |
| | Rose |
| | Sea lavender |
| | Statice |
| | Strawflower |
| | Yarrow |
| Foliage | Beech |
| | Boxwood |
| | Caspia |
| | Cypress |
| | Eucalyptus |
| | Lemon |
| | Magnolia |
| | Oak |
| Berries and pods | Acorn |
| | Bittersweet |
| | Pink pepper |
| | Poppy |
| | Viburnum |
| | White pepper |

*Vine Wreaths*

The natural, spindly character of tangled and gnarled vines lends a rustic quality to the wreath when the vine is allowed to show. Keep the natural character of this plant material in mind when choosing the decoration. To me, there is a natural harmony between the muted hues of dried flowers and the rich brown of the vine's bark. A bare and beautiful vine wreath is especially suited to autumnal arrangements of dried foliage, pods, cones, nuts, and a variety of silk and plastic fruits and berries. The elements can be hot-glued to the wreath or they can be wired directly to the vines. Autumnal colors and cornucopia-style arrangements of plastic fruit look beautiful wired to a vine wreath, whether the vines show through the arrangement or not. Always choose high-quality artificial materials that will look like convincing substitutes for the real thing.

The use of silk flowers and foliage on a vine wreath is a matter of personal taste. While technically a breeze to attach (just interweave the wire stems through the vines), the overall look of delicate silk materials on a rustic vine can be jarring. I find that live plant material is more stylistically compatible with a vine wreath and can look beautiful whether it is arranged in clusters or covers the entire wreath. Plants that continue to look attractive as they dry on the wreath, such as fresh-cut stems of hydrangea

or branches of autumn leaves, make them an even more appealing choice. Leafy stems can be intertwined with the vines, lashed in place with waxed string or wire, or hot-glued at strategic locations as their weight and length allows. As plant material dries, it shrinks, so be ready to fill in any gaps or bare spots that develop. I have also covered a vine wreath with a thick blanket of moss, which has opened up a whole new range of design possibilities, from adding clusters of dried flowers or stems of silk berries to sprigs of fresh flowers set in water tubes to keep them hydrated.

## Technique: Binding Small Bouquets to a Vine Wreath

Use this binding technique to completely conceal the grapevine wreath with small bouquets. A grapevine wreath is naturally sturdy and holds up well even when the decoration is heavy. Bouquets of fresh flowers and foliage can be bound with nonskid waxed string or thread-wrapped spool wire, but live plant material, especially flowers, will have a more limited display life than silk decoration as there is no plentiful water supply, other than misting. Silk decoration can be bound onto the wreath using the same binding technique and paddle wire painted green. Once the first bouquet is in place on the wreath, new bouquets are added in an overlapping sequence until the wreath is covered.

## MATERIALS AND TOOLS
Flowers and foliage
Vine wreath
Floral scissors
Floral tape, in green
Thread-wrapped spool wire
Wire cutters

### Step 1
Arrange a bouquet.

Lay the plant material on a flat surface, stems facing the same way. Pick up several stems of flowers and foliage in the desired kinds and colors and assemble them into a small bouquet, adding or removing material, until the bouquet is full enough to cover a third to half of the width of the wreath. Keep the back of the bouquet as flat as possible, for placing against the wreath.

### Step 2
Bind the bouquet.

Hold the bouquet firmly in one hand to maintain the arrangement and use a floral scissors to cut the stems to the same length. Wrap floral tape around the stems to conceal and protect them and then use thread-wrapped spool wire to bind the stems together snugly. (If you are working with dried flowers, keep the binding *just* snug, but not too tight, which will break them; whereas, when working with silk material, make the binding tight.) Twist the wire ends together and cut the wire off the spool.

### Step 3
Make more bouquets.

Repeat steps 1 and 2 to make enough bouquets to go around the vine wreath.

### Step 4
Attach the binding wire to the vine wreath.

Pull a 10" (25.4 cm) length of thread-wrapped wire from the spool (do not cut the wire). Use your hands to wind the free end of the wire around an inside branch of the grapevine wreath. Twist the wire to itself until secure.

### Step 5
Bind on the first bouquet.

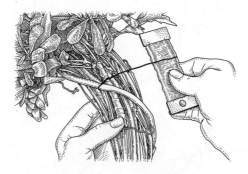

Position one bouquet against the vine to the right of the fixed wire from step 4. Holding the spool in your hand, bring the wire over the bound stems, just below the flower heads, and wrap the wire once around the wreath to make the bouquet secure.

### Step 6
Bind on the second bouquet.

Lay the head of the second bouquet over the stems of the first bouquet. Wind the wire over the stems of the second bouquet and around the wreath to bind it in place.

### Step 7
Continue binding on bouquets.

Working side to side for full, even coverage, continue to bind bouquets to the wreath one by one until the entire wreath is concealed. Thread the wire end through two vines at the back of the wreath and wrap the wire three or four times around one vine to end it. Add a hanging loop using the binding wire.

## Fun for Kids: Making a Miniature Wreath with Wired Leaves

Kids will love the ease with which a wreath can be made using prewired velvet leaves. These two simple wreaths are made in the same way, by wrapping the wire leaf stem around a wire wreath form. The only difference is that one has thirty leaves and other has twice as many. The more leaves added to the wire frame, the fuller the wreath.

*Foam Wreath Frame*

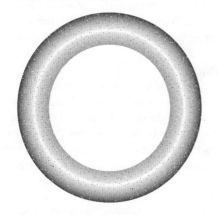

Foam of all kinds is ideally suited as a support for light-weight and medium-weight decorative material; it is less suited to heavy materials, which can pull out of the foam (as would be the case if a foam wreath is hung), or to tall stems, whose higher center of gravity makes them prone to falling over if the foam cannot support their top-heavy floral heads. Carefully evaluate the cumulative weight of the decorative material before choosing a foam base. Be aware that a lot of heavy materials inserted into a small section of foam can cause the foam to crack, crumble, and break down. For dense arrangements of heavy materials, it is better to choose frames made of welded-wire, vines, or straw. That said, heavy materials can be inserted into a plain wreath frame or one filled with wet floral foam if the wreath is displayed on a flat surface.

Live flowers and foliage need a water supply to remain fresh and appealing in a wreath. One type of tabletop frame is composed of a molded-plastic ring into which floral foam is fitted and secured in place with bands of floral adhesive tape. Stiff flower stems, such as fresh rose stems, can be cut on a diagonal and inserted directly into the wet floral foam. To reinforce stems that are fragile, long, or flexible, wind a length of fine- to medium-gauge spool wire around the stem or use a stem wire, binding it in place with either a second length of wire or floral tape before inserting the stem

into the wet foam. Be sure to keep the foam saturated to prolong the life of the live plant material inserted into the wreath.

Brown dry foam and Styrofoam are suited to dried and silk materials, which can be inserted directly into the foam or attached using floral pins and picks. Trim the end of a dried stem on an angle so that it pierces the foam cleanly. If a dried stem appears fragile or flexible, long, or brittle, reinforce it with spool wire or stub wire as you would a fresh floral stem. Silk flowers and foliage have wire stems concealed in a sheath of colored plastic, making their stems naturally stiff and resilient so they are easy to insert into the foam. Hot glue may be used on brown floral foam, but experiment on a small section first to make sure the foam won't melt. Styrofoam is sturdy and stiff, but it will melt on contact with hot glue.

*Straw Wreath Frame*

A straw wreath base is "home-sweet-home" for dried flowers and foliage. The sturdy straw structure can support a full covering of dried plant material, which can be affixed with floral pins, floral picks, hot glue, white craft glue, waxed string, or paddle or spool wire. Floral pins look like large, stiff metal staples; they are pushed into the straw, straddling the decorative material and trapping the decoration against the wreath frame. A glue gun can direct hot molten glue around stems or parts of a decoration, trapping the decoration in the glue when it cools. Hot glue is ideal for securing light-weight dried and silk material to a straw base, but there is always the annoying issue of dealing with threads of glue. I have had success by storing my glue sticks in the freezer, which seems to prevent long thin threads from forming. Waxed string and spool wire work by lashing materials in place. A floral pick is useful for attaching single blooms or small bouquets or other decorations, such as nuts and cones. Stems are usually gathered into clusters or small bouquets, wired together or wrapped with floral tape, and secured to the wreath with floral picks or floral staples. Sometimes hot glue is used to reinforce floral picks.

Fresh flowers and foliage, especially those with weak or floppy stems, such as cornflowers, are ill suited for use on a straw wreath frame. Most live plant material simply wilts too quickly without an active water supply. Exceptions include branches of balsam, pine, Israeli ruscus, and lemon leaves; secured to a straw wreath, these will survive when misted with water, especially if the wreath is placed outdoors and away from the dehydrating effects of home heating.

## Technique: Using Floral Picks on a Straw Wreath Base

A straw wreath is composed of short and long cuts of dried straw that are compacted into a molded hoop shape and bound with nylon twine. It is easy for sharp picks and floral pins to pierce the straw.

### MATERIALS AND TOOLS
Straw wreath base
Dried or silk floral stems
Floral picks
Floral tape, in green

### Step 1
Make small bouquets.

Make a small bouquet of dried or silk materials, trimming the stems as short as desired. Wrap the stems with floral tape. Repeat to make more bouquets, as desired.

### Step 2
Secure the bouquets to the floral picks.

Hold the bouquet in one hand and wrap the wire on the floral pick around the wrapped stems of the bouquet, twisting the wire ends together. Repeat to make, wrap, and attach the desired number of bouquets to floral picks.

### Step 3
Insert the picked flowers into the straw.

Hold a pick at a slight angle to the straw base and push firmly on the pick to drive it into the straw. Position the next bouquet in the desired position, with the pick at an angle, and push the pick into the straw. Continue in this manner to attach all the picks with the bouquets.

## Technique: Using Floral Pins and Hot Glue on a Straw Wreath Base

Light-weight material can be hot-glued directly to a straw wreath base. Bunches of flowers or other heavier decoration can be secured with both floral pins and hot glue. This double measure will prevent pieces from loosening and dropping off.

### MATERIALS AND TOOLS
Straw wreath base
Dried or silk floral stems
Floral tape, in green
Floral pins
Hot-glue gun and glue sticks

### Step 1
Prepare a small bouquet.

Make a small bouquet of dried or silk materials, trimming the stems as short as desired. Wrap the stems with floral tape. Repeat to make more bouquets, as desired.

**Step 2**

Pin a bouquet to the base.

Lay a bouquet in any position on the straw wreath base. Hold the bouquet with one hand and use the other to position the floral pin over the stems, so the legs of the pin straddle the stems. Push down on the pin on a slight angle, allowing the pin's crossbar to press against the stems with enough pressure to hold but not break them.

**Step 3**

Reinforce the floral pin with hot glue.

Apply a blob of hot glue over the pin to further secure the stems to the straw.

## Garlands

One of my favorite floral forms is the garland because it is so easy to create a sumptuous boa of decorative material using one simple technique called binding. In the binding technique, clusters of decorative material are wrapped and wired together at their stems and then attached to a base to make one continuous length of flowers and foliage. The width of the garland is determined by the length and fullness of the floral material. Bouquets of roses and berries will create a more compact garland than bunches of wild grasses and dangling vines. Regardless of the style—plump and compact or straggly and flowing—every garland is made the same way. The stems of flowers and foliage are gathered and wired into small bouquets, or bundles. Then they are bound onto a base made of wire, twine, or rope, using wire or waxed string.

Binding the flowers and foliage into a bouquet is the first use of the binding technique when making a garland, and there are several approaches. If the stems are fragile, I wrap them in floral tape first and then use spool or paddle wire to hold them together. The floral wrap protects the stems so they don't bruise or break. If the stems are sturdy, I wrap them with wire first, and sometimes, I use floral wrap to conceal the wire, especially for single flowers that are meant to be viewed up close like a boutonnière. Basically, whatever method works for you is all right as long as it doesn't alter the condition of the stems.

Designing single bouquets for a garland is fun and rewarding. You are actually arranging flowers in miniature and have creative latitude to express your ideas with each one you make. A bouquet can be composed of fresh, dried, preserved, or silk materials. Dried materials need to be handled carefully to avoid breaking off fragile stems and flower heads, but you will develop an accommodating touch once you begin work. Live flowers and foliage need to be conditioned before they are gathered into bouquets so they are fully hydrated. Silk floral materials are sturdy, requiring little preparation.

Once the decorative bouquets are made, use a continuous length of wire, string, twine, or rope to secure the bouquets, one at a time, to a base that is strong enough to support the material without breaking and long enough to span the intended location. The weight and length of the garland are inextricably linked. A base will sag under the weight of water-saturated bouquets of fresh flowers. If the garland is long and suspended across a wide span, it will benefit by some kind of support, such as hooks spaced along a doorway opening. Lightweight flowers and foliage can be used to make a long garland providing the base is strong. A general rule of thumb is to use a rope or wire for heavy- and medium-weight decorations and string or twine for light-weight decoration.

Garlands can be displayed along banisters

and railings or draped across window frames, with the excess, called the drop, allowed to hang down gracefully at each end. To determine an appropriate garland length, determine where you want to display the garland, and then measure the path of the garland as accurately as possible using a string or a tape measure. You can drape a string across the expanse between two doorways, for example, or wind it around the banister of a staircase. Record the measurement of the tested length and add an allowance for drops or to accommodate the drape if you didn't include these in your testing string. A garland is usually not displayed as a taut line of decoration but in a softly arching drape.

## Technique: Making Bouquets for a Garland

The color, texture, and scale of the floral material will determine the finished look of a garland. For a garland that focuses on subtle textural contrasts, mix materials in a similar colorway, such as the dark greens of fresh pine, spruce, juniper, and cedar branches. To accentuate individual shapes and colors, select materials with distinctly different silhouettes, such as pink roses and purple hydrangeas. Although you can plan the arrangement of bouquets ahead of time, you can also design them as you work, interspersing dark colors and light and deciding in which sequence to bind them onto the base.

### MATERIALS AND TOOLS

Silk or fresh flowers and foliage, as desired
Wire, twine, or rope, in precut lengths (for base cord)
Paddle wire or thread-wrapped spool wire, medium-gauge
Floral tape, in green
Tape measure or ruler
Floral knife or scissors
Wire cutters

**Step 1**

Arrange a bouquet.

Lay the plant material on a flat surface, stems facing the same way. Pick up several stems of flowers and foliage in the desired kinds and colors and assemble them into a small bouquet, adding or removing material, until the bouquet is full enough to cover half of the width of the base. For a garland that will rest on a table or against a wall, keep the back of the bouquet as flat as possible.

**Step 2**

Bind the bouquet.

Hold the bouquet firmly in one hand to maintain the arrangement and cut the stems to the same length. Use paddle wire or thread-wrapped spool wire to bind the stems. Twist the wire ends together and cut the wire off the paddle or spool. Use floral tape to conceal the wired stems. Repeat steps 1 and 2 to make 4 or 5 bouquets.

**Step 3**

Estimate the number of bouquets needed.

Lay the base cord on a flat surface. Place the bouquets on the cord, overlapping them so that the head of one bouquet conceals the stems of the previously laid bouquet. Set a ruler alongside the cord and count the number of bouquets needed to fill a 1' (30.5 cm) length of the base. Fractions are possible; you might find, for example, that the bouquet count is neither 4 nor 5 but 4½. Multiply the bouquet count by the length of the base cord in feet to determine the total number of bouquets to make for the garland. For example, if the bouquet count is 4½ and the base cord is 6', the total number of bouquets to make is 27. [For metric conversion, measure the base cord in centimeters, divide the base cord length by 30.5 cm, and multiply that number by the bouquet count.] If your answer includes a fraction, round up to the nearest whole number.

**Step 4**

Make the needed number of bouquets.

Repeat steps 1 and 2 to until you have the number of bouquets estimated in step 3.

## Technique: Binding Bouquets onto a Braided Twine Base

To support dense sprays of flowers and foliage, three strands of twine can be braided together. The surface of a braided base cord is broader and stronger than a single strand of twine. Add an extra 1" (2.5 cm) allowance for every 12" (30.5 cm) of the cut strands as braiding will shorten the overall length.

### MATERIALS AND TOOLS

Decorative floral bouquets, wrapped with floral tape

Twine, 3 precut lengths, slightly longer than estimate for garland

Paddle wire, medium-gauge

Wire cutters

**Step 1**

Make the braided base.

Hold the 3 lengths of twine together at one end and tie an overhand knot, leaving a short tail. Weight the knotted end with a heavy book or ask a friend to hold it. Hold the 3 strands side by side and slightly separated. Cross the strand on the right side over the middle strand. Cross the strand on the left over the new middle strand. Cross the new strand on the right over the new middle strand. Continue working in this way, alternating from left to right and pulling the strands snug after every few wraps, to braid the strands together. When you reach the end, make an overhand knot and leave a short tail.

**Step 2**

Bind on the first bouquet.

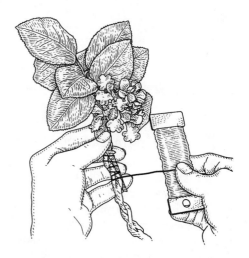

Pull a 10" (25.4 cm) length of wire from the paddle (do not cut the wire). Use your hands to wind the free end of the wire around the braided core near one knot and twist the wire to itself until secure. Hold one bouquet against the braided base, blooms overlapping the knot. Hold the paddle in your other hand and wrap the wire once around the stems and braided base to secure the bouquet.

**Step 3**
Bind on the remaining bouquets.

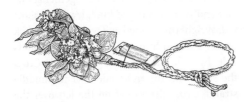

Lay the head of the second bouquet over the stems of the first bouquet. Wind the wire over the stems of the second bouquet and around the braided core to secure the bouquet. Continue in this way, binding new bouquets along the braided base until all the bouquets are used and the base is concealed. Cut the wire from the paddle, leaving a 6" (15.2 cm) tail. Weave the wire tail through the braided twine to secure it.

**Step 4**
Cover the ends.
Gather the remaining loose plant material into a bouquet and bind it over the bare end of the braided twine to conceal the knot.

### Technique: Binding Heavy Bouquets to a Galvanized Wire Base

Boughs of fresh evergreen and similar heavy decorative material require a sturdy, nonskid base that can withstand the added stress and tension without stretching or breaking. Galvanized wire is strong, flexible, and rustproof, making it suitable for fresh plant material. The wire is wrapped with floral tape to keep the plant material from sliding along the smooth wire or bunching together. Use hooks or nails at even intervals to support long or heavy garlands and to prevent the wire from snapping in two.

## Quick & Easy: Monogram Garland

Use pliers to bend a length of galvanized wire into the shape of a script letter of the alphabet, doubling back over sections of the basic letter as needed to form the crossbars on letters *B, E, F, H,* and *T.* Use medium-gauge wire to wrap the double wires to keep them together. Use wire cutters to cut the monogram from the coil of wire. Wrap the wire in floral tape to give it a nonskid surface. Decorate the armature with overlapping bouquets, attaching them as you would for a garland. Mount the monogram on a wall or door with cup hooks anchored in strategic locations to help the monogram keep its shape. A monogram can also be displayed flat on a tabletop.

## Working Tips: Making a Garland with a Central Spray of Flowers

To create a garland with a medallion of flowers at the midpoint, bind bouquets of foliage to each end of the base cord, working toward the center until the stems of the last two bouquets meet. For the center spray, make a small, plump bouquet, trimming the floral stems so they radiate from the center of the bouquet outward and are the same height as the surrounding foliage, and wire it to the garland.

MATERIALS AND TOOLS

    Wired evergreen bouquets

    Extra floral material

    Galvanized wire, in precut length (for base cord)

    Paddle wire, medium-gauge

    Floral tape, in green

    Chain-nose pliers

    Wire cutters

**Step 1**

Wrap the wire.

Wrap floral tape around the full length of the wire to prevent the bound bouquets from slipping.

**Step 2**

Make end loops in the base wire.

Use chain-nose pliers to form one end of the galvanized wire into a loop, sized to hold the stems of one bouquet; twist the wire back on itself to secure the loop. Repeat to make a loop on the opposite end of the paddle wire.

**Step 3**

Attach the paddle wire.

Thread the end of the paddle wire through one of the end loops and twist it to secure it to the base. Do not cut the paddle wire.

**Step 4**

Bind on the first bouquet.

Insert the stems of one bouquet into the loop at the end of the base, stems first. Use the paddle wire to bind the bouquet in place; do not cut the paddle wire. Lay the floral head of the second bouquet over the loop in which the stems of the first bouquet were inserted and bind the stems of the new bouquet in place on the base wire.

**Step 5**

Bind on the remaining bouquets.

Continue binding new bouquets to the entire length of the base wire until all of the bouquets are used and the base is concealed.

**Step 6**

Conceal the second end loop and fill in any bare spots.

Gather extra plant material in a loose bouquet and wrap the stems with floral tape. Insert the stems into the second loop at the end of the base and secure with the paddle wire, cutting the wire off the paddle, leaving a 6" (15.2 cm) tail of wire. Wrap the tail around the main wire and make a slip knot to tighten the bind. Fill in bare spots along the length of the garland with accent flowers or other decoration, as desired, attaching them with separate lengths of wire.

## Topiary

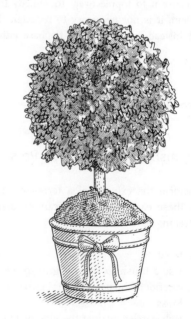

Reminiscent of royal gardens where obelisks and larger-than-life animals, birds, and human figures are sculpted from live foliage, topiaries evolved from the Roman practice of clipping and training trees and shrubs into ornamental shapes. For the home crafter, cultivating a live bush and having the patience and skills to shape a live topiary may remain an unrealized fantasy; however, there is a very easy way to make small topiary that require little to no mainte-nance using flowers and foliage of all kinds.

The design of a topiary re-creates the look of a real tree, albeit a highly stylized and man-icured one. The traditional topiary is com-posed of three parts: the head, the trunk, and the base container. These components must be visually and physically balanced. The usual ratio is 2:1:1, or one-half head, one-quarter trunk, and one-quarter base. The one cru-cial mechanical requirement, true of all flo-ral arranging, is that the topiary be physically stable. When the head of the topiary is dec-orated, it becomes larger and heavier; when a heavy head is elevated above the container on a trunk, it can make the topiary top-heavy and cause it to topple over. To remedy this problem, it is not necessary to redesign the head. Instead, you can rethink the base, either enlarging it or adding weight to counterbal-ance the heavy decorated head.

Making the traditional ball-head topiary progresses through three stages: preparing the base container, attaching a foam sphere for the head, and decorating the sphere. A Styrofoam ball is impaled on a thick dowel and secured with strips of tape and glue. The dowel serves as the trunk of the topiary and is anchored in a pot weighted with hardened plaster of Paris. The plaster stabilizes the trunk and provides the necessary counterweight. Variations on this basic construction principle abound. For example, a topiary can be assembled by adher-ing a ball of light-weight dried tea roses to the candle cup of a heavy candlestick that serves as both trunk and base container. A very large sphere decorated with dried foliage can be secured to a twisted stem made from natu-ral branches or it can simply rest on a wide-mouthed urn, doing away entirely with the need for a trunk.

---

## Quick & Easy: Natural Finishes for Terra-Cotta Pots

Transform the exterior of a terra-cotta pot with these easy surface applications using natural ingredients.

- **Mold**
  Use a brush to apply yogurt to the exterior of the pot. Let the yogurt dry.
- **Moss**
  Rub parsley against the side of the pot to add a green tint and glue on thin sections of dried sheet moss.
- **Sand**
  Apply a coat of white craft glue to the exterior of the pot and pour on a thin layer of fine sand. Let the glue dry completely. Shake off any excess sand.

---

## Technique: Preparing the Base Container and Topiary Trunk

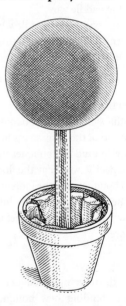

The base container for a topiary is pre-pared with plaster of Paris to lower the center of gravity and add stability. Plaster of Paris expands as it cures and becomes permanent in the container, so choose an inexpensive pot, such as a terra-cotta flowerpot, for the base. If your topiary base is a more valuable decorative container, such as a ceramic bowl or brass urn, use a large can or other container that fits inside it as a liner to hold the plaster.

## MATERIALS AND TOOLS

Terra-cotta flowerpot, 6" (15.2 cm) tall, 6" (15.2 cm) in diameter
Floral foam scraps
Floral clay
Plaster of Paris
Packing tape
Dowel or thick tree branch, 16" (40.6 cm) long, 1" (2.5 cm) in diameter
Respirator mask
Tape measure
Disposable plastic container (for mixing plaster)
Large craft stick (for mixing plaster)
Disposable gloves

### Step 1

Prepare the container.

Place a piece of packing tape in the bottom of the pot to cover the drainage hole. Line the interior wall and floor of the pot with wedge-shaped scraps of floral foam and secure them with small wads of floral clay.

### Step 2

Make a batch of plaster.

Work outdoors or in a well-ventilated space and put on a respirator mask and disposable gloves. Use a stirring stick to mix a batch of plaster of Paris in a disposable plastic container, following the package directions.

### Step 3

Add the plaster to the flowerpot.

Pour the plaster into the flowerpot until it is ½" (1.3 cm) below the rim, using the stirring stick to scrape the plaster out of the container.

Then run the stirring stick through the wet plaster in the flowerpot to level the plaster.

### Step 4

Set the dowel in the flowerpot.

Insert the dowel into the plaster, making certain it is centered and straight when viewed from all angles. Hold the dowel in place until the plaster begins to cure, about 3 to 4 minutes. Let the plaster continue to cure and harden for 1 hour without disturbing it.

## Technique: Attaching a Foam Head to a Topiary Trunk

The foam head forms the core of the decorated head of the topiary and it must support the weight of the added decorative material and remain securely attached to the trunk. One of the best ways to ensure a secure installation is to impale the foam head on a dowel.

## MATERIALS AND TOOLS

Base container prepared with plaster and a dowel
Foam sphere, 6" (15.2 cm) in diameter
Floral adhesive tape
Low-temperature glue gun and glue sticks
Knitting needle

### Step 1

Make a hole in the foam sphere.

Use a knitting needle to pierce a starter hole in the foam sphere, pushing the needle straight through the center of the foam sphere on the axis and exiting out the other side. Work the needle to increase the diameter of the hole, stopping when it is slightly smaller in diameter than the dowel.

### Step 2

Impale the sphere on the trunk.

Hold the sphere with two hands over the dowel. Guide the top of the dowel into the hole and push down on the sphere with gentle, even pressure until the top of the sphere and the top of the dowel are even. Use two long strips of floral adhesive tape to secure the sphere to the trunk, crossing each strip over the top, bringing the strips under the ball, and wrapping the ends around the dowel.

### Step 3

Reinforce the join between the sphere and the trunk.

Tilt the topiary and apply melted glue to the underside of the ball where it joins the trunk. Let the glue cool.

Adding a layer of decorative floral material to the foam sphere will make the topiary head larger. Cut the stems of your decorative material short, leaving just enough stem length, about 3" (7.6 cm), to insert into the foam, depending on the circumference of the sphere. A layer of rosebuds will add a low, compact carpet of color. Boxwood adds a spiky layer that noticeably increases the size of the topi-

ary head. Long, thick tufts of dried foliage will add even more to the girth, increase the sense of movement, and cause the foam sphere to lose definition.

### Technique: Decorating a Topiary Head with Boxwood

The length of the boxwood stems determines the overall look of the topiary. For a compact look, trim the boxwood stems short, about 3" (7.6 cm) long. Approximately 1" (2.5 cm) of the stem will be inserted into and concealed by the foam. For a fuller, fluffier appearance, cut stems that will extend 5" to 6" (12.7 to 15.2 cm) from the foam. For more texture, vary the lengths and alternate them as you create the topiary head.

MATERIALS AND TOOLS

Topiary base prepared with foam sphere
15 to 20 branches of preserved boxwood, in dark green
Sheet moss, in green
Floral scissors

### Sculpting a Block of Green Floral Foam to Make a Topiary Head

A topiary with live plant material is beautiful and can be made using the principles of making any topiary. What is important is that the head of the topiary be made using absorbent floral foam, which will hydrate the flowers and foliage you insert into it. The block of green floral foam can be sculpted into a small sphere approximately $4^{1}/_{2}$" (11.4 cm) in diameter. Use a serrated knife to cut the foam into a cube and then sculpt the cube into a rough sphere, slicing away the corners of the block until it is a ball shape.

**Step 1**

Prepare the foliage.

Arrange the boxwood branches on a protected work surface. Use floral scissors to cut the branches into leafy stems that measure 4" (10.2 cm) long, or another length of your choice. Use your fingers to strip off the bottom 1" (2.5 cm) of leaves from the stem.

**Step 2**

Decorate the topiary head.

Insert the boxwood stems one by one into the foam, pushing gently to prevent the stems from breaking. Cover all surfaces of the sphere, angling the stems so that they radiate from the center. Turn the container as you work to ensure even coverage.

## Technique: Decorating a Topiary Head with Moss

Sheet moss is a simple, attractive covering that conceals a foam sphere and provides a rich green foundation for decorations that are added next. New decorations can be attached using floral pins, which are pressed through the moss into the foam sphere, or with a low-temperature glue gun. Try using three different shades of moss to cover a single foam sphere, as shown in the topiary on the cover.

MATERIALS AND TOOLS

Topiary base prepared with foam sphere
Sheet moss or reindeer moss, in green
Spray adhesive
Floral pins
Low-temperature glue gun and glue sticks
Old newspapers
Safety glasses
Chemical-cartridge respirator mask
Floral scissors

**Step 1**

Prepare the moss.

Work outdoors or in a well-ventilated space. Remove the sheet moss from the package and use your hands to flatten the sections. Pick out any sticks or debris. Select unbroken sections of moss and set them, soil side up, on a layer of newspaper.

**Step 2**

Adhere one piece of moss to the foam.

Put on a respirator mask. Apply a light coat of spray adhesive to the wrong side of one piece of unbroken sheet moss. Immediately place the moss, adhesive side down, on the foam sphere and press firmly until it adheres. Insert floral pins into the moss to further secure it.

**Step 3**

Cover the entire sphere with moss.

Repeat step 2 to adhere and pin additional moss sheets to the foam sphere. Continue until the foam sphere is fully covered with an even layer of moss. Use a low-temperature glue gun and glue stick to secure any loose pieces.

## Quick & Easy: Making a Dome Topiary

A topiary can be made without a stem or trunk simply by wedging the bottom quarter of a foam sphere in a flowerpot and decorating the exposed part of the sphere. To secure the foam sphere, line the top inside rim of the flowerpot with floral adhesive clay, set the sphere over the opening, and push down gently to wedge it in place. Surface decoration that is subtle and low, such as a layer of sheet moss or small tea roses packed tightly together, will accentuate the sphere shape. Stems of dried foliage cut to varying lengths will appear feathery and fluffy, and the silhouette will be airy and less precise.

## Technique: Making a Topiary with Live Flowers and Foliage

For a topiary head to hold live plant material, it must function both as a supporting surface and as a water source. A green floral foam sphere saturated with water can serve this purpose. The stems of the live plant material are inserted directly into the foam head. A word of caution: This type of head becomes heavy when saturated. A shorter trunk will lower the center of gravity, for better overall balance.

### MATERIALS AND TOOLS

Live flowers and foliage, conditioned
Topiary base prepared with green floral foam sphere
Floral adhesive tape
Floral adhesive clay
Floral food
Bucket
Serrated knife
Bar soap
Sharp knife
Cutting board

### Step 1

Secure the foam sphere.

Use two long strips of adhesive tape to secure the foam sphere to the dowel, crisscrossing the strips over the center top of the ball and bringing them under the ball and wrapping the ends around the dowel. Press a narrow collar of floral clay against the dowel just under the foam ball to further secure it.

### Step 2

Saturate the foam.

Fill a bucket with enough room-temperature water to saturate the foam. Fortify with floral food, following the package instructions. Invert the topiary and submerge the foam sphere in the water until it is saturated, 5 minutes or longer, depending on the size of the piece. Stand the topiary in the sink and wait until the foam stops dripping. Tip the pot to pour off any standing water. Move the topiary to a protected work surface.

## Working Tips: Choosing between an Essential Oil and a Fragrance Oil

The difference between an essential oil and fragrance oil goes beyond cost (essential oils are more expensive). Essential oil is 100 percent pure, while fragrance oil is a blend made of essential oil, sometimes up to 80 percent, and synthetic oil. Synthetic oils are formulated to replicate the scents of pure oils. The modern scent industry has professional smellers who can combine chemicals so expertly, they can chemically reproduce the smell of practically anything imaginable, from roses and butter to baked cookies and fresh laundry. The formulas for fragrance oils are not protected by patents, but they are kept secret. Ordinary users can tell what something smells like, but not exactly what is in it. The label on a fragrance oil will indicate those FDA-designated raw materials that are unsafe for use in perfumes, cosmetics, and personal care products—in other words, not safe for use on the skin.

**Step 3**

Prepare the live flowers and foliage.

Cut the flower and foliage stems on a diagonal on a cutting board (or underwater) to the desired length. Insert the stems partway into the foam, one at a time, pushing some deeper into the foam than others and angling some of the pieces to create texture and movement. Continue until the foam sphere is concealed.

**Step 4**

Check the topiary daily.

Use a finger to feel the foam to ensure that it is damp. Use a spray mister to hydrate the plant materials. If the topiary is displayed outdoors or in direct sunshine, use a cup filled with water to drizzle water onto the dry areas, holding the topiary on an angle with the head supported. Do not resoak the foam completely as the foam may crumble along the holes.

## Natural Care for Body and Soul

Using botanicals to support body and soul is an ancient practice. Today it is very easy to make healthful preparations that combine natural herbs and flowers with ingredients you already have at home, such as olive oil, milk, and sea salt. Herbs are easy to grow in window boxes and in small pots planted with seedlings. Flowers can also be started from seed and cultivated in a window box or a small outdoor plot of soil. Small amounts of the harvested plants can be used to add texture and fragrance to potpourri and handmade soaps. Herbs and flowers can be combined with other natural materials to make soothing bath oils, bath and scrubbing salts, and facial scrubs and masks. Each of these homemade products gets a fragrance boost from highly concentrated essential oils.

## Working Tips: Using and Cleaning an Eyedropper

An eyedropper is comprised of two parts, the bulb and the pipette; the pipette is submerged in the bottle of oil and the bulb rests on top of the pipette. When the bulb is squeezed, a column of oil is drawn into the pipette, and when the bulb is released the oil remains in the pipette until it is squeezed in a stop and start motion, dispensing the oil in single or multiple drops. When you buy an essential oil, you may find that many are sold in amber or cobalt-colored bottles that have an eyedropper. The eyedropper has a plastic collar so it can be screwed onto the bottle's neck; the bottle also comes with a plain cap that replaces the eyedropper to avoid keeping the eyedropper submerged in oil, which can degrade a plastic pipette, and to seal the bottle so the fragrance does not evaporate. Some oils do not have an eyedropper and one must be purchased. I recommend a glass eyedropper because it doesn't absorb the oil, making it suitable for use with several different oils as long as it is cleaned thoroughly after each use. Separate the glass pipette from the rubber (or neoprene) bulb. Pour rubbing alcohol into a glass bowl and soak the pipette for about 5 minutes; then wash the pipette in hot soapy water, allowing the water to irrigate the inside of the pipette. Reserve the use of the eyedropper for your botanical projects; do not use it with food or beverages.

## Potpourri

Potpourri infuses the air with fragrance. It is composed of three basic ingredients—natural materials, a fixative, and decorative accents— that can be mixed in small batches to suit your personal scent preferences.

Finding natural materials that smell good is as easy as stepping into your garden or opening your kitchen cupboard. Fresh herbs, including chamomile, eucalyptus, thyme, mint, sage, rosemary, and lemon verbena offer distinctive scents, as do spices such as clove and cinnamon. Certain plant materials can contribute green, sweet, pungent, musky, or sharp scents that fill out and layer the overall fragrance. Freshly cut peels of citrus fruit initially add both scent and color, but the color contribution outlasts the scent.

To boost a scent, essential oil (pure and natural) or fragrance oil (a blend of oils, some pure and some synthetic) is used. Derived from the root, bark, wood, seed, fruit, leaf, or flower of a single plant, an essential oil is chosen to support the aromatic notes set by the natural materials. Often, several oils are used together to create a more complex scent. Blending fragrances requires a sensitive nose; if you are new to using essential oils, begin with the featured recipes to become familiar with formulations that consistently yield a pleasant layering of scents.

As you compare essential oils, you will find yourself gravitating toward certain fragrances. Take note of what appeals to you as you shop and test the samples. Take a break between sniffs as the nose can become fatigued, making it difficult to discern one fragrance from another. Essential oils are potent, and the more potent the oil, the more it will dominate or override the other scents. Oils can vary in potency from one supplier to another; you can always increase the number of drops used according to your assessment. Refer to Health and Safety Precautions (page 190) before handling the oils. Various perceived benefits are ascribed to essentials oils or fragrance oils and their carriers, such as potpourri and base oils. It is said that certain fragrances inspire happiness or sensuality, that they reinvigorate the mind, soothe aching muscles, and promote healing, or that they provide myriad other physical and emotional benefits. The effects of any olfactory experience are very personal, varying according to one's own body chemistry and spirit. We do know that fragrance can stir the emotions and instigate subtle changes in the way we think and react, although there is little hard scientific data to prove definitively that a particular essential oil produces a predictable effect for everyone. For this reason, it is wise to simply check in with yourself, noticing how you feel before and after you expose yourself to any fragrance, and draw your own conclusions.

A fixative is an absorbent, fibrous material that binds the fragrance so it lasts longer. All scent ultimately dissipates when exposed to air, becoming weaker in potency. A fixative enhances the scent by absorbing and binding with the oil, which slows down the evaporation. A popular plant-derived fixative is orris-root, made from the bulb of an iris. Cellulose is a less expensive commercially prepared fixative that is available in hypoallergenic preparations. The fixative is mixed with the essential oil in a glass jar and allowed to cure for 48 hours, during which time it is stirred or shaken to distribute the oil. Only then is it added to the rest of the ingredients. The oil is thoroughly absorbed by the fixative, keeping the more delicate and colorful plant materials, especially dried petals and leaves, from getting oil-stained.

Once all of the potpourri ingredients are mixed together, the potpourri is set aside in a closed container and allowed to cure for several weeks. The cured potpourri can be displayed in a small, open china bowl or basket, put into small pouches and sachets to scent linen, drawers, and closets, or extended with decorative materials. Decorative materials enhance the appearance of the potpourri by adding color, texture, and bulk. Dried flowers, particularly roses, carnations, violets, lavender, bachelor's buttons, and larkspur, add hints of vivid or pale color for greater textural contrast. Some flower petals retain a lot of their original color as they dry and some do not. Other natural accents that can be added to potpourri include pods, nuts, wood shavings, and sticks. Gilded ornaments, ribbon, and similar decoration can be added in small amounts to support the theme or scent of the potpourri. For example, if your potpourri is scented for the winter holidays, you may wish to add miniature pinecones or snippets of ribbon in seasonal colors. Although not an intrinsic ingredient in the potpourri, the dish or container in which the potpourri is placed also plays a decorative role in the presentation.

Basic ingredients and tools used to make potpourri are annotated below.

- **Essential oil**
An essential oil is a very complex substance with fragrant properties made up of hundreds of distinct molecules that combine to create a particular scent. Essential oil is extracted from the root, bark, wood, seed, fruit, leaf, or flower of a single plant using such methods as steam distillation or hydro-distillation, although newer technologies also use carbon dioxide. An essential oil can be used in many ways, but primarily to enhance and strengthen the fragrance of other ingredients, including potpourri, that provide scent, such as herbs and spices. Because essential oils are so highly concentrated, they should always be used sparingly. An essential oil is traditionally sold in a small bottle made of colored glass, which retards the effects of light that can break down the oil, and often comes with its own eyedropper for accurate dispensing and a second bottle cap that seals the bottle to prevent evaporation. Essential oils are said to have aromatherapeutic benefits, but some are considered toxic, so caution is mandated.

- **Fixative**
A fixative binds the scent of the essential oil and fragrance oil, making the scent last longer. A fixative can also add bulk. Cellulose fiber chips, whole oak moss, and orrisroot are natural fixatives used in potpourri. Orrisroot comes in dried chunks or powder. It has been known to cause allergic reactions in some people; if it troubles you, try a hypoallergenic commercial fixative, such as Fiberfix, instead.

- **Decorative plant material**
Decorative plant materials add color and texture to potpourri. They include flower petals, foliage, seeds, and pods. Some may also infuse their own scents or serve as a fixative, absorbing and slowly emitting the fragrance. The petals of dried flowers and herbs should be lightly crushed. Dried spices, such as whole cloves, nutmeg, cinnamon sticks, and vanilla bean, and dried fruit, such as orange rind, should be broken into small pieces, crushed using a mortar and pestle, or finely chopped before being added to potpourri. Treat potpourri containing decorative plant material carefully, as these materials will naturally lose their color and fragrance when exposed to air and direct sunlight.

- **Large glass mixing bowl**
The ingredients for potpourri are tossed together in a bowl. A bowl made of glass or ceramic will not absorb essential oils as the ingredients are mixed.

- **Airtight glass jar with a screw top**
Mixed potpourri ingredients need to be cured and stored in an airtight container that does not absorb the essential oils or the plant color. Glass is impermeable and will absorb neither the oils nor stain of any colorant used. The screw top will safeguard the fragrance, preventing it from vaporizing.

- **Wooden spoon**
  A wooden spoon will not bruise the plant material during gentle stirring. Because wood can absorb essential oil, do not use the wooden spoon for anything except your potpourri concoctions.
- **Stainless steel measuring spoons and equipment**
  When working with essential oils, use stainless steel measuring spoons. Do not use any equipment with copper, aluminum, cast-iron, or Teflon finishes.
- **Eyedropper**
  An eyedropper is a two-piece apparatus with a glass (or plastic) pipette and a rubber bulb at one end. The rubber bulb is squeezed and released to draw the oil into the pipette. Squeezing the

bulb again dispenses the oil drop by drop with precise control. Keep a separate eyedropper, preferably made of glass, to dispense essential oils from bottles that do not come equipped with a dropper. Clean an eyedropper after each use to avoid contamination between different oils.

## Technique: Making Potpourri with a Sweet Fragrance

Rose is the predominant scent of this potpourri. The fixative is oak moss. Dried rose petals, statice, eucalyptus, and chamomile flowers are added as colorful accents.

Yield: About 1¾ cups (414 mL)

### INGREDIENTS
10 drops rose essential oil*
Fixative: ⅛ cup (29.6 mL) whole oak
  moss
Dried flowers and foliage
  ½ cup (118.3 mL) pink rose petals
  ¼ cup (59.1 mL) red rose petals
  ¼ cup (59.1 mL) yellow rose petals
  ¼ cup (59.1 mL) white statice flowers
  ⅛ cup (29.6 mL) purple statice flowers
  ⅛ cup (29.6 mL) chamomile flowers
  ⅛ cup (29.6 mL) eucalyptus leaves
*See Health and Safety Precautions (page 190)

### EQUIPMENT
Glass jar with airtight screw-on lid
Large glass bowl
Wooden spoon

### Step 1
Two days ahead: Add the essential oil to the whole oak moss.

Tear the whole oak moss into ragged ½" (1.3 cm) pieces. Place the moss in a thin layer on the bottom of a glass jar. Dispense the rose essential oil on top. Screw the lid on the jar and shake the jar to distribute the oil throughout the moss. Set the jar in a cool place, out of

---

## Working Tips: Safeguarding the Fragrance Potency of Potpourri

To keep potpourri from losing its fragrance, store it in an airtight screw-top glass jar until you are ready to set it out. Potpourri displayed in an open container can be tossed with a wooden spoon (designated for craft use) to reinvigorate the scent. If tossing doesn't produce the desired effect, return the potpourri to the glass jar, add a few drops of essential oil or other herbal ingredients, and stir or shake the mixture over a day or two as it cures.

direct sunlight. Shake the jar a few times a day for the next 2 days.

## Step 2

Combine the dry ingredients.

Place the rose petals, statice flowers, chamomile flowers, and eucalyptus leaves into a glass bowl. Use a wooden spoon to gently toss the ingredients together. Add the scented moss made in step 1 and toss until combined.

## Step 3

Cure the potpourri.

Use a wooden spoon to transfer the potpourri mixture back to the glass jar. Screw on the top. Store the jar in a cool, dark place for 2 weeks. During that time, stir or shake the potpourri every 2 to 3 days to disperse the oil throughout all of the dried ingredients.

## Step 4

Use the potpourri.

Using ½ to ¾ cup (118.3 to 177 mL) at a time, fill a pretty open dish with a loose mound of potpourri, adding dried floral material for accent, if desired. Refresh the mixture, as needed, by returning the potpourri to the jar and gently stirring the ingredients to reinvigorate its fragrance.

## Technique: Making Potpourri with a Spicy Fragrance

The predominant scent in this recipe comes from the essential oils and the ground cloves and the allspice. The fixative is orrisroot.

Yield: About 1½ cups (473.2 mL)

INGREDIENTS
Essential oils*
    4 drops rose
    6 drops lavender
    4 drops neroli
    4 drops patchouli
    8 drops sandalwood
Fixative: ¼ cup (59.1 mL) orrisroot powder
Spices
    2 tablespoons ground cloves
    4 tablespoons ground allspice
Fresh floral material
    1 cup (236.6 mL) lavender buds
*See Health and Safety Precautions (page 190)

---

## Caution: Essential Oils Can Cause Adverse Reactions and Be Toxic

Be aware that some essential oils can cause an allergic reaction. Place a drop of the essential oil you want to test on a piece of absorbent cotton, rest the cotton in the crook of your elbow, and tape it in place; if after 48 hours the skin has reddened or broken out in a rash, do not use the oil. Refer to Health and Safety Precautions (page 190) for related information.

According to the International Fragrance Association (IFRA), some essential oils are considered toxic and should be completely avoided. Among those on the banned list are almond bitter, boldo leaf, calamus, camphor, cassia, horseradish, jaborandi leaf, mugwort, mustard, pennyroyal, rue, sassafras, savin, southernwood, tansy, thuja, wintergreen, wormseed, and wormwood.

EQUIPMENT
Glass jar with airtight screw-on lid
Large glass bowl
Wooden spoon

**Step 1**

Two days ahead: Add the essential oils to the orrisroot.

Divide the orrisroot in five roughly equal portions. Place one portion into the bottom of a glass jar and dispense the rose essential oil on top. Add the next portion of orrisroot to the jar and dispense the lavender oil. Continue layering orrisroot and the neroli, patchouli, and sandalwood oils. Screw the lid on the jar and shake to break up the layers and distribute the oils. Set the jar in a cool place, out of direct sunlight. Shake the jar a few times a day for the next 2 days.

**Step 2**

Combine the dry ingredients.

Place the lavender buds into a glass bowl. Sprinkle the ground cloves and allspice on the mixture, gently stirring the spices throughout the lavender buds. Add the scented orrisroot to the mixture, using a wooden spoon to gently toss the ingredients together.

## Chart of Fragrance Groups

Essential oils are divided into eight broad categories, according to their predominant scent. Some essential oils fall into more than one category. The chart below will help you select essential oils that enhance your natural materials.

| Citrus | Floral | Herba-ceous | Campho-raceous | Spicy | Resinous | Woody | Earthy |
|--------|--------|-------------|----------------|-------|----------|-------|--------|
| Bergamot | Chamo-mile | Basil | Cajuput | Anise-seed | Benzoin | Cedar-wood | Angelica |
| Grape-fruit | Gera-nium | Clary sage | Eucalyp-tus | Black pepper | Elemi | Cypress | Patchouli |
| Lemon | Jasmine | Hyssop | Pepper-mint | Carda-mom | Frankin-cense | Juniper berry | Valerian |
| Lime | Lavender | Marjo-ram | Tea tree | Cinna-mon | Myrrh | Pine | Vetiver |
| Orange | Neroli | Melissa | | Corian-der | | Sandal-wood | |
| Tangerine | Rose | Pepper-mint | | Cumin | | | |
| | Ylang-ylang | Rose-mary | | Ginger | | | |
| | | | | Nutmeg | | | |

## Step 3

Cure the potpourri.

Use a wooden spoon to transfer the mixture back to the glass jar. Screw on the top. Store the jar in a cool, dark place for 2 weeks. During that time, stir or shake the potpourri every 2 to 3 days to disperse the oil throughout all of the dried ingredients.

## Step 4

Use the potpourri.

Using about ¾ cup (177 mL) at a time, fill a pretty open dish with a loose mound of potpourri, adding dried floral material for accent, if desired. Refresh the mixture, as needed, by returning the potpourri to the jar and gently stirring the ingredients to reinvigorate its fragrance.

## Technique: Making Potpourri with a Winter Holiday Fragrance

The predominant fragrance in this potpourri is balsam. The fixative is orrisroot. The colorful plant material includes evergreen needles, eucalyptus leaves, rosehips, and miniature pinecones, for seasonal color as well as fragrance.

Yield: About 2 cups (473.2 mL)

### INGREDIENTS

Essential oils*
    8 drops balsam
    2 drops orange
    1 drop clove
Fixative: ⅛ cup (29.6 mL) orrisroot
Fresh flowers and foliage
    ¼ cup (59.1 mL) bayberry leaves
    ¼ cup (59.1 mL) evergreen needles
    ⅛ cup (29.6 mL) eucalyptus leaves
    ¼ cup (59.1 mL) rosehips
    ½ cup (118.3 mL) miniature pinecones
    ¼ cup (59.1 mL) white statice flowers
    ½ cup (118.3 mL) pink rose petals
    ¼ cup (59.1 mL) red rose petals
*See Health and Safety Precautions (page 190)

### EQUIPMENT

Glass jar with airtight screw-on lid
Large glass bowl
Wooden spoon

## Step 1

Two days ahead: Add the essential oils to the orrisroot.

Divide the orrisroot in three roughly equal portions. Place one portion into the bottom of a glass jar and dispense the balsam essential oil on top. Add the next portion of orrisroot to the jar and dispense the orange oil. Add the third portion of orrisroot and dispense the clove oil. Screw the lid on the jar and shake to break up the layers and distribute the oils. Set the jar in a cool place, out of direct sunlight. Shake the jar a few times a day for the next 2 days.

## Step 2

Combine the dry ingredients.

Place the bayberry leaves, evergreen needles, eucalyptus leaves, rosehips, and pinecones into a glass bowl. Use a wooden spoon to gently toss the ingredients together. Fold in the statice and the rose petals. Then fold in the scented orrisroot.

## Step 3

Cure the potpourri.

Use a wooden spoon to transfer the mixture back to the glass jar. Screw on the top. Store the jar in a cool, dark place for 2 weeks. During that time, stir or shake the potpourri every 2 to 3 days to disperse the oil throughout all of the dried ingredients.

## Step 4

Use the potpourri.

Using about 1 cup (236.6 mL) at a time, fill a pretty open dish with a loose mound of potpourri, adding dried floral material for accent, if desired. Refresh the mixture, as needed, by returning the potpourri to the jar and gently stirring the ingredients to reinvigorate its fragrance.

## Technique: Making Potpourri for Gift Giving Year-Round

In this potpourri, floral petals, leaves, and crushed spices create an interplay of color and texture. The predominant scent is lavender with woodsy notes. The fixative is both orrisroot and the dried petals and leaves. The spices are crushed instead of pulverized to keep their rough texture, which also serves to retard the dissipation of scent. If you prefer, you can use powdered versions of the spices. The recipe makes enough potpourri to share with friends. Mark a special occasion or say thank-you by presenting a stack of potpourri-filled paper sachets tied with satin ribbon or buy small bags made in sheer fabric and fill them with your special blend.

Yield: About 3½ cups (828.1 mL)

## Working Tips: Mellowing Scent

In the beginning, the scent of the potpourri made with essential oils and spices is strong and sharp. After the mixture cures for two or three weeks, the fragrance becomes more delicate and subtle.

### INGREDIENTS
Essential oils*
    10 drops lavender
    10 drops rose geranium
    6 drops sandalwood
Fixative: ¼ cup (59.1 mL) orrisroot
1 orange
Spices
    1 tablespoon (14.8 mL) whole cloves, lightly crushed
    1 tablespoon (14.8 mL) whole allspice, lightly crushed
Dried flowers and foliage
    1 cup (236.6 mL) dried rose petals
    1 cup (236.6 mL) dried lavender buds
    1 cup (236.6 mL) dried geranium leaves
*See Health and Safety Precautions (page 190)

### EQUIPMENT
2-quart (1.9 L) glass jar with airtight screw-on lid
Sharp knife
Mortar and pestle
Large glass bowl
Wooden spoon

**Step 1**

Two days ahead: Add the essential oils to the orrisroot.

Divide the orrisroot in three roughly equal portions. Place one portion into the bottom of a glass jar and dispense the lavender essential oil on top. Add the next portion of orrisroot to the jar and dispense the rose geranium oil. Add the third portion of orrisroot and dispense the sandalwood essential oil. Screw the lid on the jar and shake to break up the layers and distribute the oils. Set the jar in a cool place, out of direct sunlight. Shake the jar a few times a day for the next 2 days.

**Step 2**

Two days ahead: Prepare strips of orange zest.

Use a knife to score the orange in eighths.

Peel the rind off the flesh in pieces and trim away the white pith, leaving the orange zest. Use a knife to cut narrow strips of orange zest. Let the strips dry for 2 days, or until they curl and stiffen.

### Step 3

Crush the whole cloves and the allspice.

Place the whole cloves in a mortar and use the pestle to crush and split them open; set them in a small dish. Crush the allspice and add to the cloves.

### Step 4

Combine the ingredients.

Place the dried rose petals, lavender buds, and geranium leaves into a glass bowl. Use a wooden spoon to gently toss the ingredients together. Fold in the orange strips. Then fold in the scented orrisroot.

### Step 5

Cure the potpourri.

Use a wooden spoon to transfer the mixture back to the glass jar. Screw on the top. Store the jar in a cool, dark place for 2 weeks. During that time, stir or shake the potpourri every 2 to 3 days to disperse the oil throughout all of the dried ingredients.

### Step 6

Use the potpourri.

Using about 1 cup (236.6 mL) at a time, fill a pretty open dish with a loose mound of potpourri, adding dried floral material for accent, if desired. Refresh the mixture, as needed, by returning the potpourri to the jar and gently stirring the ingredients to reinvigorate its fragrance.

## Technique: Making Fragrant Paper Sachets

Sachets made of silk paper and filled with potpourri can be used directly in bathwater, or they can be slipped between layers of folded linen to add a subtle whiff of fragrance to sheets. The potpourri is mixed one day ahead so that the oil has time enough to be absorbed by the fibrous ingredients without dissipating the potency, ensuring that the fragrance will infuse a large volume of water. After one use in the bath, the sachets will lose much of their potency and can be discarded. When making a sachet for placement between fabrics, double the layer of silk paper to keep the oil from staining. Tucked between sheets, the sachets will last for weeks. Do not use the sachet with pillowcases, as the ingredients, especially essential oils, may irritate the eyes. Match the essential oil to a single dried plant material, such as lavender buds, rose petals, balsam needles, or orange zest.

Yield: 10 sachets

### INGREDIENTS

8 drops lavender essential oil, or as desired*

Fixative: ½ cup (118.3 mL) whole oak moss

20 tablespoons (295.7 mL) dried lavender buds, or as desired*

*See Health and Safety Precautions (page 190)

### EQUIPMENT

Sheet of silk paper, 22" × 30" (55.9 × 76.2 cm)

Glass jar with airtight screw-on lid

Glass bowl

Wooden spoon

Ruler

Pencil

Pinking shears or scissors

Sewing machine with zigzag function

### Step 1

One day ahead: Add the essential oil to the whole oak moss.

Tear the whole oak moss into ragged ½" (1.3 cm) pieces. Place the moss in a thin layer on the bottom of a glass jar. Dispense the lavender essential oil on top. Screw the lid on the jar and shake the jar to distribute the oil throughout the moss. Store the jar in a cool, dark place overnight.

### Step 2

Combine the ingredients.

Place the lavender bud in a glass bowl. Add the scented moss and toss gently with a wooden spoon until combined.

### Step 3

Make the silk paper sachets.

Use a ruler, pencil, and scissors to mark and cut three 3" × 30" (7.6 × 91.2 cm) strips from the silk paper; cut each strip into five 3" × 6" (7.6 × 15.2 cm) rectangles. Save the excess paper for another project. Fold each rectangle in half to make a square. Use a sewing machine to straight-stitch two sides of each square, ¼" (0.6 cm) from the edge, to make a pouch. For sachets that will be placed in drawers with linens, use a double layer of paper for each pouch.

### Step 4

Fill the sachets with potpourri.

Fill each pouch with 2 tablespoons (29.6 mL) of potpourri. Machine-stitch the open end of each pouch closed. Use pinking shears to trim the edge along each side. Store the sachets in the jar and screw on the lid to keep the fragrance from evaporating.

## Scented Bath Oil, Bath Milk, and Bath Salts

Another use for essential oils is to add scent to a variety of personal bathing products you can make at home. Essential oils are highly concentrated plant extracts that are said to have aromatherapeutic properties that can influence your mental and physical well-being. However, sensitivities and toxicities are associated with the use of essential oils, especially for pregnant women, children, and the elderly, so be especially careful when choosing an essen-

tial oil for a preparation that will touch your skin. See Health and Safety Precautions (page 190) and read the manufacturer's label on the bottle. Essential oils vary widely in potency according to the extracts from which they are derived, and the same scent can have different potencies depending upon the supplier. Essential oils will affect individuals differently. The chart on page 175 lists popular essential oils and their ascribed health benefits. Of course, you should consult a qualified physician for the care of any ailment.

Scented bath oil soothes the psyche as well as the skin. In addition to the essential oil, which provides the scent, you will need a base oil, which is often composed of several unscented oils. A base oil, or carrier oil, is the liquid in which ingredients such as essential oil and dried herbs are carried or suspended. Base oils extracted from seeds and nuts are the closest to our own body oils and the ones you should consider for your bath oil preparation. Oils that are cold-pressed or expeller-pressed (a mechanical process) have had less exposure to heat and thus retain more of their nutritious properties than oils extracted through heat processes. Oils can become rancid if exposed to heat and light, so it is better to purchase smaller quantities and to store them in a cool, dark place, such as your refrigerator. Products that contain synthetic oils, mineral oils, or petroleum do not allow the skin to breathe and are not recommended as they do not nourish the skin like the base oils listed here.

- **Almond oil**
  Pressed from almonds, this general, all-purpose base oil is very light, virtually odorless, and one of the most versatile of oils, suited to all skin types. It is known for its softening and soothing properties. It is often combined with heavier oils.
- **Apricot kernel oil**
  Made from the kernels of apricots, this oil is light and slightly aromatic and is used to condition dry and inflamed skin;

## Popular Essential Oils and Their Characteristics

| Name | Scent | Aromatherapy Effects | Health Claims |
|---|---|---|---|
| Anise | Sweet, licorice | Warming, clarifying | Antispasmodic. Provides relief from respiratory congestion. Good for digestion and head-clearing. |
| Basil | Sweet, floral, spicy | Uplifting, refreshing; good for concentration | Alleviates nervousness. Improves memory. Strengthens resistance against infectious diseases. |
| Bergamot | Lemony | Refreshing, uplifting, clarifying | Good for anxiety, depression, and insomnia. Avoid sunlight after use. |
| Black pepper | Warm, sharp, spicy | Stimulating to the appetite and mental processes | Alleviates muscle aches and pains. |
| Cedarwood | Woodsy | Calming, soothing, harmonizing | Astringent properties good for dry skin. Digestive stimulant used to remediate nausea. |
| Chamomile | Italian-grown kind has fresh apple | Relaxing, calming; alleviates anger | Soothing anti-inflammatory. Regenerates new skin cells. Helpful for insomnia. Balances the female system. Good for digestion. |
| Cinnamon | Sweet, spicy | Strong but soothing, warming | Antiseptic. Good for rheumatism, digestion, respiratory system, and warts. Acts as an aphrodisiac. |
| Citronella | Citrusy | Use in humidifier as an insect repellant | Good for clearing the head and treating rheumatic pain. |
| Clary sage | Woodsy, evergreen | Warming, relaxing, uplifting, calming | Helps ease muscle pains. Alleviates depression, counters insomnia. |
| Clove | Strong, spicy | Warming | Antiseptic. Antioxidant. Good for respiratory and digestive systems. |
| Cypress | Woodsy | Relaxing, refreshing | Helps clear the head. Good for circulatory system. |
| Eucalyptus | Menthol | Stimulating, uplifting, cooling, invigorating | Antiseptic. Antimicrobial. Good decongestive. Encourages oxygen uptake. |
| Fennel | Spicy, licorice | Sweet, invigorating | May relieve nausea and improve digestion. Good muscle relaxant. |
| Frankincense | Woodsy | Relaxing, rejuvenating, confidence-building | Immunostimulant. Good for coughs. Nourishes mature skin. |

| Name | Scent | Aromatherapy Effects | Health Claims |
|------|-------|---------------------|---------------|
| Geranium | Sweet floral | Refreshing, relaxing, balancing | Antimicrobial. Antidepressive. Acts as anti-inflammatory. Good for eczema. |
| Ginger | Spicy | Warming | Acts as an anti-inflammatory; good for aches and pains. Aids digestion and motion sickness. |
| Grapefruit | Citrusy | Refreshing, invigorating, stimulating; good for creating euphoria | Good for acne, cleansing oily skin, and reducing cellulite. |
| Jasmine | Sweet floral | Relaxing, soothing, confidence-building, stimulating sensuality | Good for treating depression and hoarseness. |
| Juniper | Woody and green | Refreshing, balancing, relaxing | Detoxifies and cleanses oily skin. Relaxes muscles and stimulates appetite. |
| Lavandin | Sweet floral, stronger than lavender | Relaxing | Helpful for muscle stiffness and healing wounds. |
| Lavender | Very clean, floral | Relaxing, calming, soothing | Acts as muscle relaxant and antidepressant. Counters insomnia. |
| Lemon | Tangy, citrusy | Cooling, refreshing, stimulating, uplifting; helps focus concentration and sharpen senses | Astringent. Antiseptic. Good for the circulatory system. |
| Lemongrass | Citrusy | Refreshing, toning | Antiseptic. Antibacterial. Astringent. Good for headaches. |
| Lime | Citrusy | Uplifting; helps clear mind | Antibacterial. Antiseptic. Astringent. Good for depression. |
| Litsea | Strong citrus | Improves moods | Good for oily skin. Calms bronchial irritation. |
| Mandarin | Sweet citrus | Calming | Aids digestion. |
| Marjoram | Herbal | Warming, sedating, calming, relaxing | Good muscle relaxant. Nerve tonic. |
| Melissa | Fresh, sweet, herbaceous | Calming, refreshing | Acts as antidepressant, counters anxiety. Antiseptic. |
| Myrtle | Sweet herbal | Calming; aroma may cause drowsiness | Astringent; aids in clarifying skin and treating breakouts. |
| Neroli | Strong citrus with floral notes | Relaxing, calming; dispels fears | Sedative; relieves insomnia. Helps heal the skin and can be used as antidepressant. Antibacterial. |

| Name | Scent | Aromatherapy Effects | Health Claims |
|---|---|---|---|
| Orange | Sweet mild citrus | Refreshing, relaxing | Anti-inflammatory. Relieves depression. Remediates colds. Good antiseptic. |
| Oregano | Strong herbal | Stimulating | Good antiseptic. Antimicrobial. Aids respiration. |
| Palmarosa | Lemony, green, with hints of rose | Calming, instilling of trust, adaptability, and security | Aids neuralgia, sciatica. Helps with anxiety. Antifungal. |
| Patchouli | Strong musk, earthiness | Sensual, regenerative | Helps alleviate depression, reduce stress. Acts as aphrodisiac. |
| Peppermint | Minty | Stimulating, refreshing, invigorating, cooling | Acts as muscle relaxant. Good for indigestion, headaches, nausea, and painful muscles. |
| Petitgrain | Woodsy, with floral and fruity notes | Relaxing, calming, strengthening | Antibacterial. Good for digestion and breakouts on the skin. |
| Pine | Woodsy | Fresh and invigorating; good for deodorizing stuffy spaces | Aids in relieving muscle aches and pains. |
| Rose | Sweet, floral | Relaxing, soothing, sensual; uplifts emotions | Helps alleviate irritability, stress, anger. |
| Rosemary | Strong herbal | Invigorating, refreshing; aids memory and concentration | Good for stimulating circulation. |
| Rosewood | Sweet, woody | Calming | Good for skin. Relieves headaches and nausea. |
| Sage | Fresh herbal | Invigorating, stimulating | Astringent. Antiseptic. Good for healing skin, reducing large pores, relieving muscle soreness. |
| Sandalwood | Woodsy, exotic, sweet | Relaxing, warming, grounding; helps relieve stress | Good for overall balance of nervous system. |
| Spearmint | Strong and minty | Stimulating, uplifting | Good for digestive issues and headaches. |
| Tangerine | Sweet, citrusy | Calming; promotes happiness and well-being | Aids in digestion. |
| Tea tree | Clean, spicy, antiseptic | Invigorating | Good decongestive, helps respiratory system. Acts as antifungal. |

| Name | Scent | Aromatherapy Effects | Health Claims |
|---|---|---|---|
| Thyme | Herbal and antiseptic | Refreshing, stimulating; aids memory | Good muscle relaxant. Good for circulatory and respiratory systems. |
| Valerian | Strong earthy | May cause drowsiness | Sedative; good for headaches and insomnia. Diuretic. |
| Vanilla | Sweet with calming notes | Warming, sensual, soothing | Acts as an aphrodisiac. |
| Ylang ylang | Exotic, floral | Relaxing, soothing, sensual; helps alleviate anger and irritability | Acts as aphrodisiac. |

suited to all skin types. It is often combined with heavier oils.

- **Avocado oil**
  Derived from the flesh of the avocado, this oil is emollient, rich in essential fatty acids and Vitamins B1 and B2, A, D, and E, and is suited to sensitive skin. It is relatively thick and is best when combined with lighter base oils. It also has antioxidant properties.

- **Canola oil**
  Made from the seeds of the rape plant, this oil is light and good for most skin types. It works best when combined with a more emollient oil, like avocado oil.

- **Grapeseed oil**
  Pressed from the seeds of grapes, this oil is the lightest and least greasy of all the oils. It can be drying. It works best when combined with heavier oils.

- **Jojoba oil**
  Extracted from the leaves of a small desert shrub, this oil is technically a liquid wax that closely resembles our skin's natural protective oils. It is effective in moisturizing dry or damaged skin and has antioxidant properties.

- **Olive oil**
  Pressed from olives, this oil is heavy, emollient, and fragrant. It works best when combined with lighter oils, such as almond or apricot kernel oil.

- **Sesame oil**
  Derived from sesame seeds, this is a heavier oil with a strong aroma. The oil is slightly drying. It has natural antioxidants and natural sunscreen properties.

- **Vitamin E oil**
  This oil can be used alone or in combination with almond or jojoba oil. Use only 100 percent natural d-alpha tocopherols as other vitamin E oils are synthetic.

- **Wheat germ oil**
  Extracted from the germ of the wheat kernel, this oil has a strong aroma and is very heavy. It is nourishing for the skin.

## Technique: Making an Unscented Base (or Carrier) Oil

Use this recipe to make an unscented carrier oil. The carrier oil will become the base for essential oils and other ingredients to make a scented bath oil.

Yield: 12 ounces (354.8 mL) unscented base oil

### INGREDIENTS

5 ounces (147.9 mL) sweet almond oil
2½ ounces (73.9 mL) olive oil
2 ounces (59.1 mL) canola oil
1 ounce (29.6 mL) apricot kernel oil
1 ounce (29.6 mL) sesame oil
½ ounce (14.8 mL) wheat germ oil

### EQUIPMENT*

Glass jar with airtight screw-on lid
Large glass measuring cup
Stainless steel measuring spoons

*Do not use copper, aluminum, cast-iron, or Teflon finishes.

**Step 1**

Measure the ingredients.

Use a large glass measuring cup or stainless steel measuring spoons to measure the oil quantities listed and add them to a glass jar.

**Step 2**

Blend the ingredients.

Shake the jar to blend the oils together. If you are not using the unscented base oil

---

## Working Tips: Equivalent Measures for Drops

As a general rule of thumb, ¹/₄ teaspoon (1.2 mL) equals 10 to 15 drops of essential oil.

---

immediately, screw the lid on the jar and store it in a cool, dark place.

## Technique: Making a Relaxing Lavender-Blend Bath Oil

The fragrance of this bath oil is fresh and mild. Made from a blend of lavender, bergamot, and cedarwood, the oils are swooshed into bathwater (not applied directly to your skin). Keep in mind that bergamot (and also citrus oils) can cause photosensitivity, so do not expose your skin to sunlight after you bathe with this preparation. Store the oil in a dark glass container (blue or brown); avoid plastic containers as they will absorb some of the oil.

### INGREDIENTS

12 ounces (354.8 mL) unscented base oil, prepared in a glass jar
Essential oil*
1 teaspoon (4.9 mL) lavender
½ teaspoon (2.5 mL) bergamot
½ teaspoon (1.2 mL) cedarwood

*See Health and Safety Precautions (page 190)

### EQUIPMENT**

Stainless steel measuring spoons
Rubbing alcohol
Paper towels

**Do not use copper, aluminum, cast-iron, or Teflon finishes.

**Step 1**

Add the essential oils to the base oil.

Use measuring spoons to measure the essential oils and add them to the jar of base oil. Use a paper towel and rubbing alcohol to clean the oil off the spoons.

**Step 2**

Blend the oils.

Secure the cap on the jar. Shake the jar to blend the oils. Store the bath oil in a cool, dark place. To use the bath oil, add 1 tablespoon (14.8 mL) to your bathwater and swoosh the water with your hand to blend in the oil.

## Technique: Making a Warming Vanilla-Blend Bath Oil

Vanilla is a gentle and reassuring scent that makes for a relaxing bath.

### INGREDIENTS

12 ounces (354.8 mL) unscented base oil, prepared in a glass jar
Essential oils*
   ½ teaspoon (2.5 mL) vanilla
   ½ teaspoon (2.5 mL) sandalwood
   2 drops patchouli

*See Health and Safety Precautions (page 190)

### EQUIPMENT**

Stainless steel measuring spoons
Rubbing alcohol
Paper towels

**Do not use copper, aluminum, cast-iron, or Teflon finishes.

### Step 1

Add the essential oils to the base oil.

Use measuring spoons to measure the essential oils and add them to the jar of base oil. Use a paper towel and rubbing alcohol to clean the oil off the spoons.

### Step 2

Blend the oils.

Secure the cap on the jar. Shake the jar to blend the oils. Store the bath oil in a cool, dark place. To use the bath oil, add 1 tablespoon (14.8 mL) to your bathwater and swoosh the water with your hand to blend in the oil.

Another easy-to-make bath formula is the milk bath. Instead of a carrier oil, this preparation uses a dairy product that contains fat, which is known for moisturizing and nourishing the skin. Prepare the mixture and pour it directly into the warm bathwater, swooshing the water with your hand to blend it in. Soak your body for at least 20 minutes to feel the soothing effects.

## Technique: Making a Scented Milk Bath

This bath uses whole milk and honey. Mix it just before you use it or make it a few hours ahead and store it in the refrigerator so it stays fresh. Add 20 drops of essential oil to the 4½ cups of milk and honey.

Yield: One bath

### INGREDIENTS

1 quart (0.9 L) whole milk
¼ cup (59.1 mL) honey
Essential oil*
   16 drops chamomile
   2 drops bergamot
   2 drops vanilla

*See Health and Safety Precautions (page 190)

### EQUIPMENT**

Glass or stainless steel measuring cup
Eyedropper
Large glass bowl
Stainless steel spoon

**Do not use copper, aluminum, cast-iron, or Teflon finishes.

### Step 1

Combine the milk and honey.

Combine the milk and honey in a glass bowl. Stir with a stainless steel spoon.

### Step 2

Blend in the essential oil.

Add the essential oil with an eyedropper. Stir the ingredients with the stainless steel spoon until well blended.

### Step 3

Make a milk bath.

Pour the mixture into a tub full of warm water, swooshing the water with your hand to blend.

Bath salts are added directly to the bathwater. They do more than add fragrance; the minerals have a drawing effect that detoxifies the skin. After you bathe, apply a moisturizer, as bath salts have a slightly drying effect on the skin.

## Technique: Making Scented Bath Salts

This recipe can be made ahead of time and stored in a tightly closed glass jar.

Yield: Three baths

### INGREDIENTS

1 cup (236.6 mL) coarse sea salt or kosher salt
Rubbing alcohol
3 to 5 drops liquid colorant (optional)
5 drops tea tree, eucalyptus, peppermint, or rosemary essential oil*

*See Health and Safety Precautions (page 190)

### EQUIPMENT**

Glass mixing bowl, medium size
Glass measuring cup
Stainless steel spoon
Glass eyedropper
Glass storage container with screw-on lid

**Do not use copper, aluminum, cast-iron, or Teflon finishes.

### Step 1

Measure the salt.

Use a measuring cup to measure and pour the sea salt or kosher salt into a glass bowl.

### Step 2 (optional)

Add color.

Add 2 drops of the desired color to the salt, stirring it with a stainless steel spoon to blend the ingredients. For more intense color, add a few more drops, one at a time, and blend well. The liquid food colorant will not stain your skin but may stain any cloth made of natural fibers.

### Step 3

Add fragrance.

Use an eyedropper to add the desired essential oil. Mix well to distribute the oil. Use alcohol to clean the dropper.

### Step 4

Use and store the bath salt.

Add about 3 heaping tablespoons (about 50 mL) of bath salts to warm bathwater as you are filling the tub. Store the remaining preparation in a glass container.

Salt scrubs are fine-grained exfoliates that are massaged into the skin and rinsed off, usually while you are in the bath or shower. The abrasive action of the salt removes dead skin cells and also opens the pores, allowing them to breathe. Natural oils in the scrub provide a soothing lubricant that reduces the abrasive quality of the salts while nourishing the skin.

Apply a small amount of salts onto your damp skin and rub it in with your fingers and hands. Work in a circular motion, starting at your extremities and moving toward your heart—scrub your hands and arms first, then your feet and legs, concentrating on rough spots like heels and elbows. Be gentle when scrubbing your skin, paying attention to the way you feel, and avoid sensitive areas. Do not apply salt scrub to any cuts or to newly shaved skin, to avoid skin irritation. Leave the scrub on your skin between 5 and 10 minutes, depending on how much moisturizing you need, before rinsing off with cool, clean water. As beneficial as salt scrubs can be, they are known to have a drying effect, so use a light moisturizer after you towel off.

## Technique: Making Scented Salt Scrub

While in the shower or tub, when your skin is damp, scoop out a tablespoon or two of the fragrant sea salt, and begin to massage the salt onto your skin. Rinse off with clean, cool water.

Yield: About 15 applications

INGREDIENTS

3 cups (709.8 mL) fine sea salt
¾ cup (177 mL) olive oil
¾ cup (177 mL) sweet almond oil
Any two of the following essential oils*
    ¼ teaspoon (1.2 mL) tea tree
    ¼ teaspoon (1.2 mL) eucalyptus
    ¼ teaspoon (1.2 mL) peppermint
    ¼ teaspoon (1.2 mL) rosemary
*See Health and Safety Precautions (page 190)

EQUIPMENT**

Rubbing alcohol
Stainless steel measuring spoons
Glass measuring cups
Glass bowl, large
Stainless steel spoon
Glass container with a lid
Paper towels

**Do not use copper, aluminum, cast-iron, or Teflon finishes.

**Step 1**

Combine the salt and base oils.

Add the sea salt, olive oil, and almond oil to a large glass bowl. Stir with a stainless steel spoon to combine.

**Step 2**

Add the essential oils.

Measure and add the essential oils to the scrub mixture. Use rubbing alcohol and a paper towel to clean the measuring spoon when changing scents. Stir until all of the ingredients are blended.

**Step 3**

Store the salt scrub.

Store the scented salt scrub in a tightly sealed glass container.

### Facial Scrubs and Masks

Composed of natural ingredients, such as ground nuts or grains, and a creamy ingredient that holds the ground material together, facial scrubs are easy to make. It is key that a facial scrub be mildly abrasive, just enough to remove dead skin cells, improve circulation, and close pores. Use fine-grained seeds, such as crushed grape or cranberry seeds, apricot seed powder, and finely ground walnut seed to make a concoction that gently exfoliates and moisturizes.

## Technique: Making a Facial Scrub with Oats, Nuts, Honey, and Apples

The ingredients in this gentle facial scrub are easily found in any grocery store. Buy rolled oats and whole almonds and grind them individually in a food grinder. While not an exact science, 1½ tablespoons of rolled oats produces about 2 tablespoons of ground oats and 1 teaspoon of almonds produces about 1¼ teaspoons of ground almonds. The grinder will change the oats and almonds into light granular powders and when they are mixed with the honey and apples, the combination will be a mild exfoliating paste. Mix up a batch an hour or so before you use it. It can be stored in the refrigerator for a day or two, but be aware that the chopped apple will turn brown.

Yield: One treatment

INGREDIENTS

½ medium apple, peeled, cored, and
    chopped
1 to 1½ tablespoons (14.8 to 22.2 mL)
    honey
1½ to 2 tablespoons (22.2 mL) ground
    oats
1½ teaspoons (7.4 mL) ground almonds

EQUIPMENT

Blender or food processor
Large bowl
Spoon
Glass jar with airtight screw-on lid

**Step 1**

Make an apple-and-honey paste.

Put the apple pieces into a blender or a

food processor. Add the honey and blend the ingredients until they are smooth.

## Step 2

Fold the ingredients together.

Combine the ground oats and almonds in a bowl. Fold the apple-honey paste into the oat-and-almond mixture with a spoon. If the mixture is too wet, add more ground oats; if the mixture is too dry, add more honey.

## Step 3

Store and use the facial scrub.

Use a spoon to transfer the facial scrub into a jar. To use the scrub, scoop up some paste with your fingers and rub it onto your face, using gentle pressure and a circular motion. Rinse with warm water and gently pat your skin dry.

A facial mask can help to remove dead, dry skin cells. It also can moisturize, rejuvenate, heal, or repair skin, depending on the skin type and the ingredients used. A facial mask is applied to the skin and allowed to remain for about 20 minutes before being rinsed off.

## Technique: Making a Skin-Specific Facial Mask

A facial mask should be matched to the skin type, either normal, dry, or oily, to ensure a blend of ingredients that will restore the proper balance. Apply the freshly made mixture to your face, avoiding your eyes completely. Leave the mask in place for 20 minutes and then rinse your face with warm water and pat dry.

### For Normal Skin

Yield: One application

#### INGREDIENTS

1½ teaspoons (7.4 mL) honey
3 drops lavender essential oil*

*See Health and Safety Precautions (page 190)

Combine the honey and lavender essential oil in a glass bowl, stirring thoroughly with a stainless steel spoon.

### For Dry Skin

Yield: One or two applications

#### INGREDIENTS

2 tablespoons (29.6 mL) avocado, scooped from a freshly cut avocado
1½ tablespoons (22.2 mL) whole-wheat flour
½ teaspoon (2.5 mL) jojoba oil
½ teaspoon (2.5 mL) honey
1 tablespoon (14.8 mL) distilled water

Place the avocado in a glass bowl and mash it with a fork. Mix in the flour, oil, and honey; then add the distilled water. Stir with a stainless steel spoon until well combined.

### For Oily Skin

Yield: One to two applications

#### INGREDIENTS

1 tablespoon (14.8 mL) whole-wheat flour
1½ tablespoons (22.2 mL) green clay
1½ tablespoons (22.2 mL) apple cider vinegar
1 tablespoon witch hazel
¼ teaspoon (1.2 mL) vitamin E oil
1 drop grapefruit essential oil*

*See Health and Safety Precautions (page 190)

Combine all the ingredients in a glass bowl and stir with a stainless steel spoon. If mixture is too wet, add more flour; if it is too dry, add more witch hazel.

## Air Fresheners

Infusing the air with scent helps freshen up a room. Air fresheners are especially welcome in spaces that have been closed up. While there are commercial products on the market, it is healthier to make your own air fresheners with natural ingredients that don't depend on propellants or synthetic ingredients. An air freshener can be simmered in a pot, using evaporation to infuse the air with fragrance, or it can be mixed and put into an atomizer to be used selectively according to need.

A simmering air freshener is a short-term solution to adding fragrance to a room. The technique uses heat from a stove to vaporize the water, whose tiny droplets carry the scent of the fresh ingredients. The ingredients in this air freshener are likely to be in your kitchen cupboard or the fruit drawer of your refrigerator. Once the ingredients are combined, they are allowed to steep in a pot over low heat. It is important not to let the water evaporate completely to avoid scorching the pot or causing a fire. Never leave the simmering freshener unattended.

## Technique: Making a Simmering Air Freshener

This simmering air freshener is a perfect way to add moisture and fragrance to the kitchen and to nearby rooms and hallways, especially in winter when home heating can dry out the air. The natural air currents in your home will dissipate the scent of the ingredients simmering together in the pot.

INGREDIENTS
3 or 4 lemons
2 or 3 oranges
1 cup (236.6 mL) whole cloves
1 cup (236.6 mL) whole allspice
6 bay leaves
5 cinnamon sticks

EQUIPMENT
Sharp knife
Cutting board
Mortar and pestle
Measuring cup
Small bowl

Pot
Stove

**Step 1**
Peel the citrus fruit.

Use a knife and a cutting board to cut each lemon into 8 wedges. Use the tip of the knife to separate the yellow peel from the white pith and the fruit. Cut the lemon peels into smaller pieces to make ¼ cup (59.1 mL) of chopped lemon peel. Cut the orange peels in the same way to make ½ cup (118.3 mL). Reserve the fruit for another use.

**Step 2**
Crush the spices and break up the cinnamon sticks.

Place the whole cloves in the mortar and use the pestle to crush them until they are split and squashed, but not pulverized. Repeat with the allspice. Use your hands to crush the bay leaves. Break the cinnamon sticks into pieces. Put the spices and pieces of cinnamon stick into a small bowl.

**Step 3**
Add the citrus, spices, and cinnamon sticks to simmering water.

Add 1 cup (236.6 L) of water to a pot, bring to a boil, and reduce to a simmer. Carefully place the ingredients prepared in steps 1 and 2 into the pot. Place the pot cover loosely over the rim to create a vent and allow the fragrant vapor to freshen the air. Do not leave the pot unattended. Add more water to the mixture, if desired, as the water evaporates, but note that the fragrance will become weaker when the freshener is reconstituted.

## Technique: Making an Atomizing Air Freshener

An atomizer filled with natural ingredients is a healthy way to infuse fresh scent into the air, especially stuffy spaces without ventilation or with stagnant air. Instead of buying a commercial preparation made of unknown ingredients in an aerosol can, make your own customized scent and do your part to reduce the emissions in the air. You can buy a glass atomizer in a home store or pharmacy. When an air freshener is sprayed, the alcohol and water solution is propelled in a fine mist that carries the essential oils. The mist evaporates, leaving behind a lovely lingering scent. Do not spray on wood or fabric surfaces to avoid marring and staining them.

## INGREDIENTS

6 ounces (177.4 mL) distilled water
1.5 ounces (44.4 mL) vodka
Essential oils*
    ¼ teaspoon (1.2 mL) bergamot
    6 drops clove
    5 drops lemon
*See Health and Safety Precautions (page 190)

## EQUIPMENT

Measuring cup
Stainless steel measuring spoons
Jigger (for measuring)
Eyedropper
Rubbing alcohol
Clean glass jar, 16 ounce (473.1 mL), with
    screw-tight cap
Glass atomizer

**Step 1**

Combine the ingredients.

Fill a measuring cup with 6 ounces (177.4 mL) of distilled water. Using a jigger, measure and add the vodka. Use a measuring spoon to add the bergamot essential oil. Use an eyedropper to add the clove and lemon essential oils. Clean the eyedropper with rubbing alcohol followed by a wash in hot soapy water; set the dropper aside. Pour the ingredients into a clean, glass jar. Screw the lid on the jar. Let the air freshener cure for 2 days in a cool place.

**Step 2**

Fill the atomizer.

Pour the air freshener into a clean measuring cup and then into the atomizer. Use the spray, as desired, to freshen the air.

## Soapmaking

The traditional approach to making soap by hand involves combining melted fatty acids and a solution of sodium hydroxide, or lye, when both are at precisely the same temperature. The mixture is stirred continuously by hand until a creamy trace forms, indicating that saponification has begun to take place. At that time, the soap is poured into a mold and allowed to set for 3 or 4 days. The soap must cure, which takes another month or longer, before it can be used.

My approach is easier and faster. I avoid direct contact with the very caustic lye (which is an ingredient in all soap), and because there is no need for a long curing time, I can use my handmade bar or cake of soap within hours of making it. I begin by purchasing clear unscented glycerin soap that has already gone through the saponification process. This block of soap is ready to melt and pour, and I can add color, fragrance, and textural ingredients according to my personal tastes. The materials and tools for melt-and-pour soapmaking are described here.

- **Melt-and-pour soap base**
  Conveniently formulated, a melt-and-pour soap is ready to make into bars or cakes of soap. The base soap is made of glycerin that comes in blocks that are clear, white, or tinted, ready to melt and pour into a soap mold. Melt-and-pour soap takes color very well.
- **Soapmaking colorants**
  Three kinds colorants are suited to melt-and-pour soapmaking.
  —Pigments, consisting of oxides and ultramarines, are stable mineral colors that used to be mined naturally, but which are now manufactured in a laboratory in liquid and powdered form to ensure safety. Powdered pigments can be

mixed with liquid glycerin in a 3:7 ratio, which makes them easy to add to liquid soap. Liquid pigments are composed of crushed pigments dispersed in pure vegetable glycerin.

—Food, Drug, & Cosmetic (FD&C) dyes are synthetic colorants that come in powdered and liquid form and are certified by the FDA as safe for use in food, drugs, and cosmetics. These colorants are created in a laboratory, are easy to use, are available in an extremely wide range of colors, are usually water-soluble, and do not change the degree of transparency when added to clear melt-and-pour soap; however, they are known to bleed.

—Mica powder can be used to add shimmering color to soap. It blends easily into the liquid soap with no clumping. A naturally lustrous material that is mined, mica is coated on one side with a FD&C colorant, making it safe for use in soapmaking.

- **Fragrance**
Essential oils or fragrance oils (a blend of essential oil and other ingredients) are used to scent soap. The oil is dispensed one drop at a time from an eyedropper to the melted soap. It is best to add fragrance sparingly as it is very concentrated. A dropper with a suction bulb will hold about ¾ teaspoon (3.5 mL) of fragrance oil.

- **Eyedropper**
Many essential oils come in a bottle with a pipette whose bulb, when squeezed and released, will draw oil from the bottle and, when squeezed slowly, will dispense one drop of oil at a time. Do not keep the eyedropper in the bottle, but use the solid screw cap that comes with the bottle to prevent dissipation of the fragrance. If the bottle of oil you have purchased does not have an eyedropper, buy a glass eyedropper in a pharmacy.

- **Textural ingredients**
Textural additives are mixed into molten soap for various effects. Some add pretty visual effects, such as mica, which shimmers with color. Some add skin-care benefits, such as ground oatmeal and almonds that gently exfoliate. Some add natural rusticity, such as lavender buds and dried herbs. Some additives, such as ground oatmeal and almonds, remain suspended in the soap as it hardens, but others, such as lavender buds, have a tendency to float to the top of the soap or to settle on the bottom, depending on their weight and size.

- **Molds**
Hard molds and soft, flexible molds are used to contain and shape the molten soap. Molds come in a wide variety of sizes and shapes. They include molds

## Quick & Easy: Making Hand-Molded Soap

Instead of pouring molten soap into a mold to shape it, allow the liquid soap to cool in the glass measuring cup and use your gloved hands to shape it into a ball. When the liquid soap is a soft mass that is warm to the touch, pull on rubber gloves and apply olive oil to the palms. Scoop up a clump of the warm soap and shape it into a round ball (or a flat patty). Set the soap on a flat surface to harden, reshaping it every hour or as often as needed until the soap is hard and keeps its shape. If the soap has cracks, use a finger dipped in warm water or vegetable oil to smooth over the crack. Polish the surface of the hardened soap by rubbing it on a ceramic plate, rotating the surface that comes into contact with the plate, until the exterior is smooth and glossy.

with embossed surfaces, two-part molds that create a three-dimensional object, and loaf-shaped plastic molds that form a large block of soap that can be cut into slices of any thickness.

- **Microwave-proof measuring cup**
  A measuring cup that can be used safely in a microwave oven is suited to melting hard blocks or chunks of soap and pouring the liquid soap into molds.
- **Cutting board and sharp knife**
  Suited to cutting a loaf-shaped block of hard soap, a plastic cutting board protects the work surface from damage and is easy to clean after use.
- **Nonstick cooking spray**
  Eco-friendly and noncaustic, nonstick cooking spray is a vegetable product that is safe to use with soap-making molds and ingredients. Applied to the interior of the mold, the spray acts as a mold release so that the hardened bar can be removed easily.
- **Plastic wrap**
  Plastic wrap is used when melting soap in a microwave oven. Placed over the container that holds the chunks of soap being melted, the wrap keeps the moisture in the soap base from evaporating.

## Technique: Making Soap in a Microwave Oven

In this quick and easy technique, the base soap is melted in a microwave oven, treated with color and fragrance, and poured into a mold in the shape of a bar or a round cake. If you don't want to use a microwave, the base soap can be melted in the top half of a double boiler.

Yield: Ten 4-ounce (113.4 g) bars of soap or sixteen 2½-ounce (70.9 g) round cakes of soap

### INGREDIENTS
Soap base: 2½ pounds (1.1 kg) clear, unscented glycerin
Soapmaking colorant

Liquid cosmetic-grade pigment or mica
¼ teaspoon (1.2 mL) mica powder, in color as desired (optional)*
½ teaspoon (2.5 mL) essential oil, in desired scent, divided**

*For use in hand soap only; mica powder can irritate the eyes
**See Health and Safety Precautions (page 190)

### EQUIPMENT
Plastic soap molds (choose one type)
  10 bars, each 3¼" × 2¼" × 1⅛"
    (8.3 × 5.7 × 2.9 cm)
  16 round cakes, each 2½" diameter
    (6.4 cm) × 1" (2.5 cm) deep
Microwave oven
2 microwave-proof 4-cup (946.2 mL) measuring cups with spouts and handles
Nonstick cooking spray
Spray bottle with rubbing alcohol
Cutting board
Saucer
Knife
Fork
Spoon
Wooden skewer
Clear plastic wrap
Paper towels

## Working Tips: Removing the Soap Skin

As hot liquid soap begins to cool, it forms a thin skin over its surface. To ensure that the soap is perfectly smooth and liquid, use a wooden skewer to lift off and remove the skin before you pour. Another option is to hold back the skin with a spoon as you pour the liquid soap into the molds. The scenario to avoid is having the skin come loose and plop down into the molds during pouring.

**Step 1**

Prepare the molds.

Apply a very thin film of cooking spray on the interior of each mold. Use a paper towel to wipe off any excess.

**Step 2**

Cut the soap base into cubes.

Place the block of glycerin soap on a cutting board. Use a knife to cut the soap into thick slices. Cut the slices into strips and cut the strips into cubes. Divide the soap cubes into two equal piles and place one pile into each measuring cup. Cover each cup with plastic wrap.

**Step 3**

Melt the soap.

Microwave one batch of soap on medium

for 20 seconds. Open the microwave oven and use a spoon to stir the soap. Continue to heat for another 10 seconds, then 5 seconds, stirring the soap until it is fully melted. Do not let the soap boil. When the soap is liquefied, remove the measuring cup from the microwave and remove the plastic wrap.

**Step 4**

Add the colorant.

Add a single drop of color to a saucer. Dip a tine of a fork into the color and use the fork to stir the melting soap, blending in the color until it is evenly distributed. Repeat to darken the soap.

**Step 5 (optional)**

Add mica powder.

Add mica powder, and use a spoon to blend it thoroughly into the melted soap. If bubbles form on the surface of the soap, spray on a fine mist of rubbing alcohol to dissipate them.

## Quick & Easy: Swirling Loaf Soap

To make one large block of soap using a ceramic loaf pan as a mold, follow the ingredients and melting instructions for Technique: Making Soap in a Microwave Oven (page 187). Make a full batch of clear or tinted soap, using two measuring cups to melt the full amount of soap at one time. Pour the soap into the loaf pan, stopping $1/4$" (0.6 cm) from the top rim. Use an eyedropper to drizzle a vivid line of colorant down the center of the soap. Insert a wooden skewer into the soap at one side of the loaf pan and move the skewer back and forth across the color to create a marbled pattern. Let the loaf soap harden for 2 to 3 hours and remove it from the mold. Use a ripple-blade vegetable cutter or thin-blade knife to slice the soap into cakes of any thickness.

**Step 6**

Add the fragrance.

Add essential oil to the liquid soap, stirring gently to blend the ingredients.

**Step 7**

Pour the soap into the mold.

Use a wooden skewer to skim off and remove the thin skin of soap on the surface. Immediately pour the blended soap into the prepared molds until the soap is ¼" (0.6 cm) from the top rim. Apply a light spray of rubbing alcohol if any bubbles form on the surface of the soap. Allow the soap to rest undisturbed until it is firm, about 30 minutes.

**Step 8**

Melt the second batch of soap.

Repeat steps 3–7 to melt the second batch of soap cubes, adding colorant, mica, and essential oil, as desired.

**Step 9**

Remove the soap from the mold.

When the soap is hard, release it from the mold by turning the mold over and hitting it hard against a protected work surface. The soap should fall out of the mold, but if it doesn't, place the mold in the refrigerator for an hour and try again.

**Technique: Making Hand Soap Balls**

Here is a resourceful way to recycle any kind of worn-down soap. You can reconstitute slivers of soap by adding olive oil and hand-molding the pieces into a ball shape. Sensual to use, the soaps fit in your cupped hands.

## Creating Textural and Colorful Variations in Handmade Soap

Adding natural grains and buds, such as lemon rind or lavender, to melted soap and letting the soap harden provides an effective and fragrant way to transform a plain bar of soap into an emollient hand scrub. Adding surface treatments, such as inscriptions and photos, can personalize soap and give it style.

- **Layered colors**

  Tint two batches of melted soap different colors. Pour one color batch into a mold halfway to the rim and allow it to set. Pour in the second color batch, stopping $1/4$" (0.6 cm) from the top rim of the mold.

- **Layered citrus**

  Follow the directions for layered color, adding grated lemon rind to the first batch of soap that is in a yellow color and adding grated lime rind to the second batch of soap that is in a pale green color.

- **Floral**

  Pour soap into the mold halfway to the rim. Gently lay a flat silk flower or a pressed fresh flower with a flat face, such as an anemone or pansy, on the surface and allow the soap to set. Melt and pour a new batch of clear soap and pour it into the mold, stopping $1/4$" (0.6 cm) from the top rim.

- **Portrait découpage**

  Make a laser print of a child's face and cut it out. Insert the portrait between the layers of poured soap, as for Floral above, to encourage personal care.

- **Inscribed**

  Use a pointed skewer to inscribe a word or a saying, such as *Love* or *Joy*, on a hardened bar of soap. Remove the soap layer to a depth of $1/8$" (0.3 cm). Add curlicues, serifs, or other decorative accents to stylize the letters, a perfect favor for baby and wedding showers.

- **Embedded**

  Pour clear soap in the mold, filling it partway. Add a three-dimensional object, such as a charm, or cubes of hard soap in a vivid color, and then continue pouring clear soap over the object, stopping $1/4$" (0.6 cm) from the top rim of the mold.

INGREDIENTS

    10 ounces (283.5 g) leftover soap ends and
        shavings (or new bars of soap)
    8 to 9 tablespoons (118.3 to 133.1 mL)
        olive oil
    2 drops essential oil, as desired*

*See Health and Safety Precautions (this page)

EQUIPMENT**

    Handheld cheese grater
    Plastic cutting board
    Heavy pot
    Wooden spoon
    Stainless steel measuring spoons
    Stove
    Rubber gloves
    Wax paper

**Do not use copper, aluminum, cast-iron, or Teflon finishes.

Step 1

    Grate the soap.
    Lay the cutting board on a protected work surface. Use the grater to pulverize all of the slivers of soap, allowing them to form a pile on the cutting board. Transfer the pile to a pot.

Step 2

    Heat the olive oil and soap.
    Use a measuring spoon to add the olive oil to the pot. Place the pot over a stove burner, turn the heat to medium-high, and stir the mixture constantly with a wooden spoon until it is the consistency of cookie dough. Add a drop or two of olive oil, if necessary. When the soap is doughy and slightly mealy, remove it from the heat.

Step 3

    Add the essential oil to the mixture.
    Dispense the essential oil into the mixture. Turn your face away from the pot to avoid directly breathing in the vapors as you stir the ingredients together.

Step 4

    Make soap balls.
    Lay a sheet of wax paper on a flat surface. Put on rubber gloves, apply a drop of olive oil to each palm, and rub the palms together to distribute the oil. Scoop out a clump of soap and pack and shape it like a snowball. Set the ball on the wax paper. Repeat to make more soap balls. Allow the soap to harden overnight.

Health and Safety Precautions

Essential oils are potent and should be treated and stored like any other medicine. They should be kept out of the reach of children. If you are pregnant and in your first trimester, avoid *all* essential oils. Thereafter, pregnant women and the elderly should consult a doctor before using them. In all cases, essential oils should be used with the following cautions:

- **Always dilute**
  Never use essential oils full-strength as they can cause burning and irritation to the skin. Avoid any contact with mucous membranes and eye areas. Always dilute essential oil in a carrying agent like a base oil or water and mix them in a safe proportion, such as a bathtub full of water, as directed in the specific recipes.
- **Do a skin-patch test**
  Before using essential oils, be sure to do a patch test, especially if you have sensitive skin or are prone to allergies. Blend together 5 drops of the essential oil and ½ ounce (14.8 mL) of base oil. Dab a little of this mixture on the inside of your elbow or the back of your neck. Wait 12 to 24 hours. If redness or itching occurs, dilute further, or change to another essential oil, and repeat the patch test. Cinnamon, clove, dwarf pine, oregano, savory, spearmint, and thyme are known skin irritants even with dilution.

- **Avoid the sun**
  Certain essential oils cause photosensitivity. Avoid exposure to the sun at least 12 hours after using bergamot, cold-pressed lime, neroli, lemon, and grapefruit oil.
- **Never take internally**
  Do not ingest essential oils. Even a couple of drops can be toxic.

## PROJECTS

### Floral Arch: Pitcher Bouquets

If you have only a few fresh flowers, you can still create an arrangement with style and impact by distributing the blooms in several coordinating containers and placing them together as one. Here, a few roses are placed in a trio of Fiestaware pitchers, creating a unified arrangement of flowers in a soft arch. As an alternative to roses, you can use peonies, ranunculus, or dahlias.

#### MATERIALS AND TOOLS
    8 stems fresh roses, in pink
    8 stems rose of Sharon, in dark pink
    3 Fiestaware pitchers in graduated sizes,
        each in a different color, or as desired
    Cutting board
    Floral knife
    Floral food
    Bucket
    Access to water

**Step 1**
Prepare the flowers.
Lay the roses on a cutting board and use a floral knife to cut each stem on a diagonal (or cut stems underwater). Repeat to cut the stems of the roses of Sharon.

**Step 2**
Arrange the roses of Sharon.
Insert a few rose of Sharon stems into the opening of each pitcher, positioning the stems close together with blooms facing upward and outward.

**Step 3**
Add the pink roses.
Insert single stems of pink roses between the roses of Sharon to fill in the arrangement. Distribute the flowers evenly throughout the arrangement, blooms facing up.

**Step 4**
Display the arrangement.
Set the vases together in the display area, arranging them in ascending order so the flowers form a soft arch.

### Forest: Winter Wreath

Fresh and fragrant, evergreens are perfect for wreaths displayed outdoors because they keep their needles and leaves throughout the cold months. Mix evergreens, such as blue spruce and cedar, with leafy foliage, such as boxwood and holly, for rich texture and color. In all cases, make your wreath as soon as you have gathered your greens, while they are springy and fresh. Holly is sharp even when it is fresh, and it dries quickly and becomes brittle and difficult to work with. Wear gloves to protect your hands from sharp edges and from sap, which can stain your skin and be difficult to remove.

MATERIALS AND TOOLS
    Wire wreath frame, 18" (45.7 cm)
        in diameter
    Sphagnum moss
    Evergreen branches, 16" (40.6 cm) long
        30 arborvitae
        30 balsam pine
        30 cedar
    10 sprigs holly berries
    10 tea roses, in red
    12 sprigs white bruneia berries
    12 everlastings (strawflowers), in red
    4 silk poinsettias, in red
    Floral tape, in green
    Floral picks, 4" (10.2 cm) long
    1 yard (91.4 cm) wire-edged ribbon,
        3" wide (7.6 cm), in strawberry-red,
        or as desired (optional)
    Paddle wire, 22-gauge, in green
    Garden gloves
    Pruning shears
    Scissors
    Wire cutters
    Spray mister

Step 1
Prepare the moss.
Lay the moss on a protected work surface. Use your hands to carefully pull it apart into large wads, picking out any sticks or debris.

Step 2
Attach the wire to the frame.

Pull a 10" (25.4 cm) length of wire from the paddle (do not cut the wire). Wind the end of the wire around the inside ring of the wreath frame several times and twist the wire to itself to make it secure.

Step 3
Cover the wreath frame with moss.
Lay several wads of moss on the wreath frame, making a 1½"- to 2"-thick (3.8 to 5.1 cm) layer, and bind the moss in place using the paddle wire. Continue to bind wads of moss to the frame until there is an even layer all around. Make a second pass with the wire to ensure that the moss is secure. Use wire cutters to cut the wire, leaving a 10"-long (25.4 cm) tail. Wrap the wire tail around a ring of the wreath several times to secure it and push the end into the moss. Shake the wreath gently to release any loose particles.

Step 4
Prepare the greens and make bouquets.
Put on garden gloves. Lay the evergreen branches on your work surface. Divide the greens by type into separate piles. Select three or four stems from each pile and assemble them into a leafy bunch, staggering the length of the stems and keeping the back of the bouquet flat. Use wire to bind the base of each bouquet; set it aside. Continue to make enough bouquets to go around the wreath frame.

Step 5
Bind on the first bouquet.
Secure the end of the paddle wire to the outside ring of the wreath frame (do not cut the wire from the paddle). Lay the first bouquet on the wreath and bind it in place. Lay the next bouquet on the wreath frame, so the foliage overlaps the stems and binding of the first bouquet. Hold on to the bouquet and wrap the paddle wire around the foliage and the frame two or three times, pulling the wire toward you on each wrap for a tight bind.

**Step 6**

Bind on the remaining bouquets.

Continue binding bouquets onto the wreath frame. When you reach the starting point, place the stems of the last bouquet under the head of the first bouquet and bind them in place, winding the wire around the stems several times until secure. Cut the wire from the paddle, leaving a 10" (25.4 cm) tail. Bind the tail securely around the frame.

**Step 7**

Add the decorative accents.

Read Creating a False Stem on a Dried Flower Head (page 127) and Wiring onto a Wooden Floral Pick (page 132) to familiarize yourself with those techniques. Lay out the flowers and berries on a flat surface, grouping like materials together in groups of three or four stems. Assess the length and condition of the live stems, which should be 2" to 3" (5.1 to 7.6 cm) long. Make individual bouquets using the materials in one group, securing their stems with medium-gauge wire concealed with stem wrap; attach the stems of the bouquet to a wire pick, using the wires on the pick. Insert the picked decorative bouquets into the wreath, distributing them evenly, or as desired. Use wire cutters to cut the wire stems of the silk poinsettias to 4" (10.2 cm). Then make a hanging loop at the back of the wreath, using wire cutters to cut a 10" (25.4 cm) length of paddle wire. Thread the wire through the center of the wreath, bring the ends together at the top, and twist them together. Use pliers to crimp the wires together and wind them around the wreath frame. Turn the wreath face up. Distribute the poinsettias evenly around the wreath, pushing in the stems so the flowers rest on the greenery. Weave the entire length of ribbon between the branches of greenery, making short swags and tucking the ends to finish.

## Clouds: Hydrangea Wreath

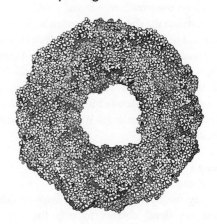

The mophead hydrangea has large, fluffy heads of smaller florets; even when dried, this flower head is sumptuous and beautiful, making it ideal for covering large surfaces. Single heads are light-weight and airy in appearance, yet surprisingly sturdy. They can be broken up into smaller clusters and used to carpet a straw wreath. Alternatives to hydrangea are coxcomb, magnolia, and boxwood.

### MATERIALS AND TOOLS

Straw wreath base, 16" (40.6 cm) in diameter

30 heads dried mophead hydrangea

Sheet moss, in green

30 floral pins

Hot glue-gun and glue sticks

Paddle wire, medium-gauge

Wire cutters

Floral scissors

Pliers

**Step 1**

Make the hanging loop.

Work on a protected work surface. Cut a 10" (25.4 cm) length of paddle wire. Thread the wire through the center of the wreath, bring the ends together at the top, and twist them together. Use pliers to crimp the wires together and wind them around the wreath frame.

**Step 2**

Cover the wreath with moss.

Separate the sheet moss into wads. Anchor one end of the paddle wire to the straw frame. Lay wads of sheet moss on the frame and bind them in place with wire, working around the wreath frame until you reach the starting point. For more detailed instruction, refer to Technique: Concealing a Wreath Frame with Moss (page 146).

**Step 3**

Prepare the hydrangeas.

Lay the hydrangeas on the work surface and use floral scissors to snip the stems 1½" (3.8 cm) below the floral head.

**Step 4**

Attach the hydrangeas to the outer edge of the wreath.

Use a floral pin to secure one hydrangea to the outside edge of the wreath at the 12 o'clock position. Moving clockwise, position and pin hydrangeas around the entire outer circumference of the wreath. Apply a short squirt of hot glue to each floral pin and the stems of the hydrangeas to ensure a secure bond to the wreath base.

**Step 5**

Attach the remaining hydrangeas.

Repeat step 4, positioning and pinning hydrangeas to the inside edge of the wreath. Then fill in the center section of the wreath as before.

**Step 6**

Fill in any bare spots.

To fill in any gaps or bare spots, snip small florets from areas that are fuller and use hot glue to attach them to the wreath where needed. Let the hot glue cool.

## Rose and Berry Pineapple: A Table Centerpiece

Blocks of floral foam can be glued together to achieve a desired size, carved into a simple three-dimensional shape, and covered in a layer of flowers and berries to resemble a real fruit. This pineapple shape carved out of two blocks of floral foam is decorated with a layer of dried roses and artificial berries. A dried froth of foliage from a real pineapple accents the top.

### MATERIALS AND TOOLS

2 blocks floral foam, each 2¼" × 4" × 8" (5.7 × 10.2 × 20.3 cm)

180 dried roses, each flower head about 1" (2.5 cm) in diameter

50 stems small artificial berries in clusters

Fresh pineapple with leafy top

Pliers

Floral scissors

Serrated knife

Respirator mask

High-tack glue

2 wooden skewers

Scissors

Wire cutters

**Step 1**

Prepare the pineapple top.

Twist off the leafy top of a fresh pineapple. Use a pair of pliers to push the sharp end of a wooden skewer into the fresh pulp at the bottom of the pineapple top. Use the wire cutters to trim the skewer to 5" (12.7 cm).

**Step 2**

Glue the blocks of foam together.

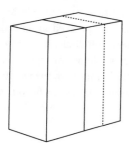

Use wire cutters to cut a wooden skewer into two pieces. Lay one block of foam on a protected work surface so the side with the broadest area faces up. Insert each skewer into the central area of the foam, spacing them a few inches apart. Apply a thick squiggle of glue to the matching side on the second block of foam. Press the blocks of foam together. Let the glue dry completely.

**Step 3**

Sculpt the basic pineapple shape.

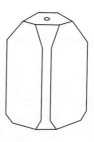

Put on a respirator mask. Stand the joined foam blocks upright on a flat surface. Using the real pineapple as a model, slice away the corners of the foam with a serrated knife and cut the top and bottom edges on an angle to create a rough pineapple shape.

**Step 4**

Prepare the flowers and berries.

Use floral scissors to cut the stems of each of the dried roses to 1" (2.5 cm). Use the wire cutters or scissors to cut the berry stems to 1" (2.5 cm).

**Step 5**

Decorate the foam with roses.

Insert the short stem of a rose on the base of the glued blocks, gently pushing until the rose head touches the foam. Continue to insert roses in the same way until the sides of the pineapple shape are covered with roses. Do not insert roses into the bottom of the pineapple. Leave a 1½" (3.8 cm) circular area on the top of the pineapple undecorated.

**Step 6**

Add the berry accents.

Insert the stems of the berries to fill in the gaps between the roses.

**Step 7**

Install the leafy top on the pineapple.

Insert the skewer with the leafy top into the center top of the foam pineapple. Fill in the bare foam around the plume with dried roses, nudging berries between the roses to fill in any bare spots.

## Confetti: Summer Wreath

Colorful and summery, this zinnia wreath is made of silk flowers in vivid magenta, acid yellow, strawberry red, and purple. The construction couldn't be simpler—weave the wire stems of the silk zinnias into the wire wreath frame, keeping the flower heads close to one another, until the entire surface of the frame is lush with flowers. The appeal of the weaving technique is that you can articulate the direction of the flower heads, clustering them together for thick coverage or adjusting their position to fill in any gaps. The technique can also be used for wreaths composed entirely of foliage, such as magnolia and lemon leaves gathered into bouquets.

### MATERIALS AND TOOLS
> Wire wreath base, 20" (50.8 cm)
> in diameter
> 35 to 40 silk zinnias, in assorted
> colors: magenta, purple, acid yellow,
> and strawberry red
> Spool wire, medium-gauge
> Wire cutters
> Ruler

**Step 1**
Prepare the silk zinnias.
Use wire cutters to trim each zinnia stem to 8" (20.3 cm). Sort the zinnias by color, making a separate pile for each.

**Step 2**
Weave in the first zinnia.
Lay the wire wreath frame faceup on a flat surface. Thread one zinnia stem between the wires on the frame, pushing the end of the stem under one spoke and over an adjacent spoke and pulling it through until the flower head rests on top of the frame.

**Step 3**
Weave in the remaining zinnias.
Select a different color zinnia, place its head next to the first zinnia, and weave its stem in between the wires, as in step 2. Continue adding new zinnias over the woven stems, weaving all of the stems in the same direction and working from side to side for full, even coverage as you proceed around the wreath. As you come full circle, it may be necessary to weave new stems through already-woven stems instead of through the wreath base. Use any remaining zinnias to fill out the wreath where needed.

# Della Robbia: Autumn Wreath

Although plastic fruit and berries have enjoyed a less-than-enthusiastic following, there are some kinds that are so realistic, it is difficult to distinguish them from their fresh counterparts. Here, an exuberant mix of berries, cones, fruit, and silk foliage make a wreath that resonates with the abundance of a fall harvest. When buying plastic fruit, choose pieces made of styrene, which is easily embedded with wire should you need to add stems. For added sparkle around the holidays, coat the fruit in a layer of reflective beads. (See page 128 for details.)

## MATERIALS AND TOOLS

Wire wreath base, 8" (20.3 cm) in diameter
Plastic fruit
  20 sprigs with pea-sized berries
  20 sprigs with olive-sized berries
  8 cherries
  4 miniature apples
  4 miniature oranges
  4 sprigs grapes
  8 miniature pears
  4 miniature pomegranates
  6 strawberries
8 pinecones, dried
14 sprays assorted silk leaves
Paddle wire, medium-gauge
Floral wire, 18-gauge
Floral tape, in green
Ruler
Wire cutters

### Step 1

Add false stems to the pinecones and pomegranates.

Use the paddle wire to make false stems on the pinecones and the pomegranates; set them aside.

### Step 2

Create false stems for plastic fruits, as needed.

Use a ruler and wire cutters to measure and cut 6" (15.2 cm) lengths of floral wire for the false stems. Add a false stem to any plastic fruit that needs a stem.

### Step 3

Make 14 mixed bouquets.

Lay out the decorative items (except the pinecones and pomegranates) on your work surface. Select one spray of foliage, two sprigs of berries, and two fruits, combining items with strong contrasts in color and shape. Bind the stems of the bouquet with wire and wrap with floral tape. Repeat to make 14 assorted bouquets.

### Step 4

Bind the bouquets to the base.

Anchor the end of the paddle wire to the wreath base. Bind the bouquets onto the wreath, continuing around the wreath until the frame is concealed. Secure the wire and cut it free.

### Step 5

Attach the pinecones and pomegranates.

Wire the pinecones and pomegranates to the wreath, distributing them evenly. Use any remaining pieces of fruit or foliage to fill in any bare spots.

## Untamed: Summer Garland

A casual walk along a roadside can yield all kinds of grasses and weeds for a garland with an untamed look. Collect long-blade grasses and flowering weeds and combine them with any other light-weight foliage you find along the way. For added color, consider adding dried flowers—most can be purchased—such as globe amaranth (in bright pink), sea lavender (in snowy white), and artemisia (in silvery green). Sea grass, wheat grass, and Queen Anne's lace are possibilities. Display the finished garland over a doorway or window, allowing it to dry in place.

### MATERIALS AND TOOLS

Waxed twine (for base)
40 to 60 blades wild grass with long blades
20 to 30 stems flowering weeds
Other dried material, purchased if desired
    20 to 30 stems globe amaranth, in
      bright pink
    40 sprigs gypsum, in green
    40 sprigs artemisia, in silvery green
    40 sprigs sea lavender, in snowy white
Raffia, in wheat color

Spool wire, fine-gauge
Stem wire
Scissors

### Step 1

Prepare the twine base.

Use scissors to cut a length of waxed twine, keeping in mind that the length of the twine will determine the length of the finished garland. Tie a loop at one end that is large enough to insert the ends of one bouquet. Attach one end of the spool wire to the loop.

### Step 2

Prepare the plant material.

Lay the plant material on a protected work surface, separated into groups by kind. Use stem wire to strengthen or replace any fragile or missing stems on the flowers.

### Step 3

Make the bouquets.

Gather 10 to 14 stems in your hand, combining grass, foliage, and flowers of varying textures, to make a bouquet that is full and straggly. Use scissors to snip the ends even. Bind the bouquet with spool wire at its cut end. The bouquets illustrated are approximately 4" to 5" (10.2 to 12.7 cm) long with blades of grass dangling lower. Continue to make bouquets until you have enough for the full length of the twine base.

### Step 4

Bind the bouquets onto the base.

Insert the cut ends of one bouquet into the loop, laying the flower heads over the loop, and bind in place with spool wire (do not cut the wire from the spool). Lay the head of the second bouquet over the stems of the first bouquet and bind the stems in place. Continue binding new bouquets along the entire length of twine until it is concealed. Gather loose plant material, and bind it over the bare end of twine.

## Step 5

Make the raffia bow.

Use strands of raffia to tie a straggly bow at the cut end of the garland. Drape the garland over a window or a doorway.

## Harvest: A Dried Topiary

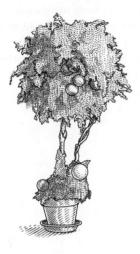

The appeal of this topiary is its wild, natural beauty. Dried and faded boxwood and goldenrod create a full head of decoration. The trunk of the topiary is a thick, natural branch that appears to be rooted in a pot piled with moss. Artificial peaches in velvety pink and yellow add subtle color accents in a wheat-colored palette. To make the topiary base, the natural stem is secured in the pot with plaster of Paris and the foam ball is impaled, taped, and glued securely on the top of the natural stem. For details on the construction, refer to Technique: Preparing the Base Container and Topiary Trunk (page 160) and Technique: Attaching a Foam Head to a Topiary Trunk (page 161).

### MATERIALS AND TOOLS

Prepared topiary base
  Foam ball, 6" (15.2 cm) in diameter
  Natural stem, 20" (50.8 cm) long
  and approximately ⅞" (2.2 cm) in diameter
Terra-cotta flowerpot, 6" (15.2 cm) high and 6¼" (15.9 cm) in diameter
Dried foliage and flowers, 6" (15.2 cm) long
  90 to 120 sprigs boxwood
  30 to 40 stems goldenrod
20 faded lemon leaves
5 artificial peaches with silk leaves
Grapevine, approximately 20" (50.8 cm) long
Sheet moss
Sphagnum moss
Wire cutters
Scissors
Pruning shears
Low-temperature glue gun and glue sticks
Hot-glue gun and glue sticks
Ruler

### Step 1

Attach the grapevine.

Use pruning shears to cut the grapevine in half. Use a low-temperature glue gun to secure one end of the vine to the left side of the foam ball and the other end to the base of the tree trunk. Gently wrap the second length of vine around the first vine, gluing one end just under the foam ball next to the first vine and the other end to the base of the tree trunk.

### Step 2

Prepare the dried materials.

Arrange the boxwood and goldenrod on a protected work surface. Use scissors to cut the stems to 6" to 7" (15.2 to 17.8 cm); approximately 1" (2.5 cm) will be concealed in the foam ball.

### Step 3

Add the boxwood and goldenrod to the topiary head.

Select a boxwood stem and insert 1" (2.5 cm) of the stem into the foam ball, pushing carefully to prevent the stem from breaking. Continue selecting and inserting stems of boxwood, angling the stems so they radiate from the center of the ball until the head is full, turning the pot so that it can be viewed from all angles. Add the stems of goldenrod, distributing them evenly throughout the boxwood stems.

## Step 4

Add the leaf and peach accents.

Hot-glue all but one of the lemon leaves between the branches, nestling the leaves so they show on the outer leafy surface. Glue two peaches to the lower left center of the topiary head, nestling them together so they touch; then add one to each side of the pair.

## Step 5

Conceal the plaster in the pot.

Arrange sheet moss over the plaster, building up a mound around the base of the tree trunk. Add wads of sphagnum moss to one side of the sheet moss, trailing the moss around and up the topiary stem. Glue one remaining peach to the bottom left of the mound of moss and the other peach near the pot's rim.

# CHAPTER THREE

# Paper Crafting

## THE HEART

### Woven Baskets

"I have everything I need. . . . a page, a pen, and memory raining down on me in sleeves."

—Harriet Doerr,
*The Tiger in the Grass: Stories and Other Inventions*, 1995

One Christmas, my mother gave me a slender box, unadorned except for a ribbon and a small card inscribed in her slightly unsteady script, "For Carol." I lifted the lid and in an instant I was young again, fiddling with paper strips, weaving them into the heart-shaped baskets that now lay flat in the bottom of the box. My mother had collected several of the baskets I had made when I was a child, thinking they would be the perfect gift now that I had a family of my own.

Following Scandinavian tradition, our woven paper baskets were hung on our tree on Christmas Eve long after my sisters and I had gone to bed. By morning, they would be filled with candy—sugared fruit slices, dark chocolate rings with sprinkles, and marzipan shaped like little potatoes. One Christmas Eve before bedtime, I lay on the floor under the tree and looked up through the branches, wishing I could sleep there all night so I could be the first one to taste the sweet confections, but that wasn't to be. When I awoke on Christmas morning, I found myself snuggled under the covers in my own bed. My sisters and I crept quietly downstairs to the tree, whispering conspiratorially as we filled our mouths with candy, emptying most of the baskets before my parents awoke.

I remember the year my mother taught us how to make heart-shaped baskets out of paper. We sat together in our little kitchen, the soft hiss of the radiator forcing heat into the room. Snow was falling silently on roofs and on newly planted evergreens and pudgy hydrants in a just-built postwar neighborhood in the mid-1950s. A pair of scissors and sheets of shiny red and white paper were set out for each of us. Holding up two folded sections of paper, my mother showed us how to interlace the paper strips, saying to "thread and loop, thread and loop" as she deftly guided the bands through and around each other until the weaving was done. At first, she guided my fingers as I tried to thread and loop the bands together without twisting or wrinkling the paper. Then I tried it alone, *thread and loop, thread and loop,* making a reasonably similar version of the paper basket. My mother thought my basket was beautiful. I simply hoped it was sturdy enough to hold the candy.

Christmas wasn't the only time I did arts and crafts as a child. I always seemed to have some kind of art supply in my hands—a box of pastel sticks swathed in a layer of felt, a two-tiered box of watercolors that included fluorescent orange, pink, and green, which I used

sparingly to make the dried tablets last longer, and a red fountain pen with a gold lever recessed into the side of the barrel to draw ink into the reservoir. I painted my own greeting cards and sometimes I decorated my homework, even though more than one teacher reminded me that I wasn't in art class.

Of all the craft supplies I had growing up, paper was in the most constant and generous supply—thick pads of drawing paper with a pebbly texture, packages of loose construction paper in a rainbow of dull colors, and pads of paper with sheets as white as snow—everything I needed to make a greeting card, a little folder, and a simple bound book at a moment's notice. There was also a supply of crepe paper and tissue paper, as well "special" paper—folded cards for writing thank-you notes, onionskin for airmail letters to my grandparents in Denmark, bond paper for our little Underwood typewriter with ivory keys, and lined pads of loose-leaf paper for our homework. Little was thrown away. Postcards were saved for their photographs and stamps; letters that fell through our mail slot were ceremoniously read aloud by my father at dinner and then saved in his desk drawer; greeting cards were tied in a bundle with ribbon; and drawings and paintings from school were saved in a large envelope the color of rust. Even wrapping paper was saved—carefully ironed flat, using a warm household iron—and then used again to wrap gifts for the immediate family or to include in impromptu collages.

I carried forward the tradition of making things to my own children, keeping all sorts of supplies handy, especially at Christmas, when it was our custom to exchange one gift that was handmade. One year, John and I decided that the little heart baskets would bear that tradition. As with all traditions, I decided to add something of our lives together, so I included a handmade woven basket together with some shiny paper in bright colors so the kids could make their own heart baskets. The paper had two sides, one shiny and the other dull. Before

I slipped the paper into the gift box, I wrote little messages on the dull side of each of the bands of paper, composing sentiments with each of the children in mind. I was hoping that, woven into their baskets, the words might symbolize the inseparable nature of the philosophy and the traditions of our family. I was pretty sure they would view the inscriptions as far too sentimental, but I also hoped the words would have more meaning one day.

Here are the messages I wrote:

Fall in love—again and again and again; love helps you grow. And don't forget to turn it in equal measure toward yourself.

Do the hard thing—choose the challenging path; it will strengthen you for life's journey ahead.

Tell the truth—you won't have to wonder what it is, you'll know it by the peace that it brings.

Sing—even if you have forgotten the words; hum past the forgotten lyrics or make some up, for a song will heal the heart and make you happy.

Believe in miracles—they happen every single day in untold numbers. Some will say "luck," others will say "coincidence," but actually, there is a heavenly conspiracy to bring you all you need; just ask.

Give thanks—not because you have more or less than someone else, but because you are here, and knowing the immensity of this gift, life, will instill in you humility and gratitude, as well as help you spend your time on this sweet planet more wisely.

Make something by hand—it will be a dwelling place for your spirit for all time. A simple ornament to hang on a tree, yes, but over time, more than that, it will stand as a symbol of tradition, a little place holder in life that embodies all you were and all you were meant to become.

The paper hearts have long since been stored away, slipped between the pages of our family scrapbook along with letters, notes, and cards I have collected over the years. Yes, there were woven paper baskets on our tree that Christmas many years ago, but it wasn't my children who made them. It was my mother and I, sitting by the light of candles still burning from dinner, intoning the familiar *thread and loop, thread and loop* at the little table in our kitchen in Bellerose.

## A Brief History

Since ancient times, paper has been a sign of civilization and literacy. Paper allowed transactions of commerce, government, and learning to be conducted with ease and decorum and conferred status on writers and readers. The industrial age brought technological advances that dramatically changed the way people produced, used, and thought about paper. Mass market paper products, from newspapers and catalogs to disposable products like drinking cups and facial tissue, made paper seem less exalted. It is during this breakthrough period in manufacturing that paper crafting emerged as an affordable pastime and hobby.

The word "paper" comes from the Greek word *papyrus,* the name given to the reeds that grow abundantly along the banks of the Nile. As early as 2400 BC, the Egyptians began cutting very thin slices of the papyrus flower stem and pressing them together to make a surface for writing or drawing. In other civilizations, people cleaned, stretched, and scraped animal hides, such as those from calves, sheep, and goats, to produce very thin, strong sheets, known as parchment or vellum (the finer of the two), for writing upon.

True paper is made in a different way than papyrus and parchment. Cellulose fibers, such as cotton, hemp, or flax, are soaked, pulverized into a liquid slurry or sludge, and suspended on a fine screen that allows the water to drain away. When the water is completely evaporated, a sheet of paper remains behind. Paper making originated in China and is first mentioned in the imperial court records of 105 AD. Over the next 1,300 years, paper-making techniques spread west through the Islamic world and eventually reached Europe. Early paper mills were powered by people or animals, but by the High Middle Ages, water power came into use. The Industrial Revolution led to more mechanized paper production at an even lower cost. Beginning around 1838, people in various locations were exploring ways to make

newsprint from wood pulp alone, at a lower cost than paper with rag content, and the circulation of newspapers and periodicals soared.

The appearance of paper crafts in the Western world coincided with the industrial advances. Paper kites appeared in the second half of the eighteenth century, as did simple toys made from folded sheets of paper: birds, animals, toy soldiers, and boats and ships that floated. Manufacturers began turning out all kinds of inexpensive paper items, including paper for drawing and crafting. Popular magazines supported the public's love affair with paper by including project directions for paper crafts. Mothers and children could learn how to create holiday decorations, model towns, paper flowers, masks, party hats, and much more. The development of chromolithography, or color printing, gave rise to novelties such as paper dolls and die-cut pictures, called scraps, which consumers collected, pasted in their scrapbooks, and traded with friends. Utilitarian paper products, including kraft paper, corrugated cardboard, paper bags, paper plates, paper cups, and drinking straws, would also find their way into craft projects.

Hands-on learning through paper crafting became standard in early childhood education through the mid-nineteenth-century work of Friedrich Froebel, founder of the kindergarten movement in Germany. The kindergarten movement spread to the rest of Europe, to North and South America, and to Japan. Froebel and his followers encouraged paper folding to teach geometry, mathematical proportions, and decorative patterns. The kindergarten curriculum included elementary color theory and various paper "construction" projects that included folding, embroidering, perforating, weaving, and cutting. Manufacture of colored paper for kindergartens began in the nineteenth century, and a Prang Company supply catalog introduced the term *construction paper* in 1911.

The abundance of manufactured papers for crafting—crepe paper, tissue paper, cardstock, foil paper—has helped revive traditional and regional paper crafts. Scrapbookers and collage artists use centuries-old hand bookbinding techniques to make one-of-a-kind blank books, journals, diaries, and scrapbooks. From Japan comes *origami,* the art of paper folding, and *kirigami,* which allows cutting as well as folding. Poland's *wycinanki* uses cutting, clipping, punching, tearing, carving, and pasting to create three-dimensional stars, birds, flowers, and tableaux for Easter and Christmas. Originally, *wycinanki* was done with tree bark or leather; the paper version emerged in the nineteenth century. *Scherenschnitte,* or "scissor snipping," was practiced in the sixteenth-century Germanic world although it probably originated in China. This technique is used to create intricate two-dimensional cutout designs. Silhouette cutting, practiced in the late eighteenth and early nineteenth centuries, was an affordable alternative to the painted portrait. Quilling features narrow strips of paper that are rolled, shaped, and glued together to create filigree designs. Quilling was originally practiced during the Renaissance to decorate religious articles but by the eighteenth century it had become a pastime for well-to-do ladies. These and other paper crafts are even more affordable in our day than when first practiced because of modern paper manufacturing.

Paper crafting for young children enjoyed a surge of interest in the 1950s and 1960s as baby boomers entered kindergarten, and adults experimented with greeting cards and gift wrap during this period. Paper chains, lanterns, tissue paper flowers, and other bold paper decorations were popular during the 1960s. Decoupage was popular in the 1970s. Paper crafting kept a low profile until the late 1990s, when rubber stamping, scrapbooking, journaling, collage art, and alternate art exploded on the craft scene, popularized in part by new business ventures such as Stampington & Company's *Somerset Studio* and Making Memories' retail and online stores. Like the scrapbookers of earlier generations, paper crafters incorporated family photographs, vintage photography, documents, ephemera, and other archive-worthy memorabilia into their work, except now the focus was on art and not simply sentimental recordkeeping. Paper artists who developed signature styles began blogging, showcasing their work on the Internet, and selling it directly to the customer through sites like Etsy. Artist Trading Cards (ATCs) are already becoming highly collectible because of their personal, handmade, tactile quality. As the more mundane documents of daily life and commerce are increasingly consigned to digital files, interest in paper artifacts and artwork continues to grow.

## THE SCIENCE

As a crafter, I have a weakness for paper of any kind—single sheets, bound sheets, decorated, plain, even the heft of a ream of copy paper excites me. I love to handwrite notes and letters with a fountain pen, eschewing ball-point pens for everything except shopping lists and notes scribbled on my way out the door. I buy stationery whenever I see a design I like. I store love letters from my husband in a polished wood box, and I have bought more blank books than I could ever fill. On a separate shelf, sheets of handmade paper await my ministrations.

I believe one reason paper crafting is so popular is because the essential material, paper, is available in such variety and abundance. Paper is everywhere and it is not intimidating. We began working with it long before we developed any preconceived notions about it. It is an emotional staple that we reach for with purpose in mind—to jot down a telephone number, make a list, write to a friend, and enter into all manner of exchange between our own thoughts and those of others.

What is remarkable about paper is its simplicity. Not meant to remain in its natural state, paper is about change—we can crease it, apply a thin line in shapely swirls that become meaningful words, brush on swaths of color, or cut out new shapes. At its heart, paper is about communication. Paper carries new and old ideas on the pages of a book; it reveals our innermost thoughts when we set our pen upon its surface; it enfolds the letters we write and wraps the packages we send or present in person. With a new and pristine sheet of paper in hand, we may hesitate just slightly before making that first crease or drafting that first line, but once we've crossed that threshold, there is little to curtail our progress as we manipulate or decorate paper to create beautiful keepsakes to be treasured for a lifetime.

## All About Paper

Various kinds of paper can be used to make greeting cards, tags, little books, and journals. While project design is always a matter of personal choice, certain practical considerations will steer you to the kinds of paper that will ensure good crafting results. What is important is that the paper serves the intended purpose and holds up to the crafting process.

Used dry, most papers are easy to work with. In general, the sturdier the paper, the more appropriate it will be for projects that are handled a lot or that have to protect other lighter-weight papers. A sheet of copy paper is too floppy and insubstantial for the cover of a handmade book, but a sheet of handmade paper is both sturdy and elegant. Textured paper is an option for many paper crafts as long as the texture does not get in the way of your design; a heavily textured surface, for example, could interfere with the necessary mechanics of drawing a smooth, unbroken line. Glossy papers take on fingerprints at the slightest touch. Some papers, depending on thickness, can be used interchangeably; chipboard and mat board can be used for the cover of a book, and laser printer paper or fine rag paper can work equally well for greeting cards, depending on the style and occasion of the card. The resiliency of rag paper may come

as a happy surprise. You can use the heat of an iron to transfer prints and photographs to its surface and you can stitch designs on it using a sewing machine.

Knowledge of your paper repertoire becomes even more important when the paper will be treated with glue, paint, or other decoration. Glue introduces moisture that will alter the paper, causing it to shrink and twist and then finally relax and flatten once it is saturated and the moisture distributed. For a decorative covering that will be glued in place, paper with some rag content is desirable because the long rag fibers resist tearing and allow the paper to stretch over and around corners and curves. Most sheer papers tear easily and disintegrate when wet and are therefore not suitable for wet techniques.

Ultimately, the best way to gain a sense of what paper can do (beyond the basics) is to experiment with as many kinds as you can. Don't shy away from papers that you haven't worked with before. Experimentation will help you uncover paper's best-kept secrets.

### Grain

Paper is made up of fibers, and it is the direction in which the fibers lie that determines the paper's grain. Grain directly affects how a paper behaves when it is folded, torn, and glued. For example, it is always easier to tear or fold along the grain of the paper than across it. When two pieces of paper are glued together in a laminating process, they will dry flat without twisting if the grains of both papers run in the same direction.

The direction of the grain occurs as a result of the manufacturing process. In machine-made paper, the grain runs in a single direction. Slurry, a fibrous pulp suspended in water, floats on a large moving belt made of mesh. As the belt speeds along, the paper fibers travel in the direction in which the belt is moving, creating a long sheet of paper that is subsequently cut into single sheets.

Handmade paper is produced by the same process, only one sheet at a time. Slurry floating in a small vat is scooped up on a fine mesh screen, called a *mold*, and contained by a raised frame, called a *deckle*. The pulp settles in multiple directions and creates a random grain that resists tearing and folding. A tear in any direction will run across the grain and create a jagged edge, and folds will not be as sharp and precise as those made in machine-made papers.

Most of the techniques and projects in this chapter use machine-made paper, with its more predictable folding properties, but there are a few exceptions.

## Weight

Weight refers to the density and thickness of the fibrous pulp that settles on the mold, which in turn affect the transparency and strength of the paper. Paper weight is measured in grams, written as *gsm* or *g/m2* (grams per square meter), a notation that refers to the amount of paper needed to fill a square-meter area. This reference will help give you a feel for the paper's relative thickness. The appeal of the g/m2 measurement is that you can compare any paper, regardless of sheet size, and eliminate guesswork when ordering online. Most paper is sold in sheets, and prices vary a lot, depending on whether the paper is machine-made or handmade, with handmade paper being more expensive.

You will also see paper weight expressed as *pounds (lbs.) per ream,* which refers to a standard ream of 500 sheets of paper, regardless of the dimension of the paper. Generally, lightweight paper, such as tracing paper, ranges from 25 to 55 lbs. per ream, medium-weight paper, such as drawing paper, ranges from 55 to 90 lbs. per ream, and heavy-weight paper, such as bristol, ranges from 100 to 120 lbs. per ream. Choosing paper by weight alone can be misleading, however, because paper weight is affected by three factors: size, thickness, and density.

## Finish

Finish refers to the look and feel of the paper's surface, which can range from the smooth feel of satin to the rough feel of tiny gravel. Finish is expressed in such terms as *hot-pressed* or *H.P.* and *not* (meaning not hot-pressed); these terms refer to surface effects produced by subjecting the paper to pressure between either hot glazing rollers or cold highly polished rollers. Cold-press paper has a medium to coarse finish and a high level of absorbency that is suited to traditional watercolors. Hot-press paper has a smooth finish and is less absorbent, making it a good choice for pen and ink or charcoal, and for writing and drawing in general. Some hot-press rollers are designed to emboss a pattern, such as the woven threads of fine linen, into the surface of the paper.

Texture can also be introduced earlier in the process when the paper fibers are still floating in the slurry. Because textural additives either bond to or are trapped by the paper fibers, they are permanent, changing how the paper feels to the touch and affecting the quality and character of a drawn line or applied media. Paper with a pronounced texture is more suited to projects where texture is a desired part of the design, such as in watercolors and collages. Additives can be an important feature in handmade papers.

## Absorbency and Color

Two other properties that affect the behavior and appearance of a sheet of paper are absorbency and color. Absorbency refers to the paper's capacity to hold or repel moisture, whether in the form of applied liquid (such as paint or ink) or moisture in the environment (humidity). If the paper absorbs too much moisture, colors can bleed and the paper can warp.

To prevent excessive bleeding and warping, many papers are treated with size. Size decreases a paper's absorbency, causing ink to

## Paper Crafting Materials and Tools at a Glance

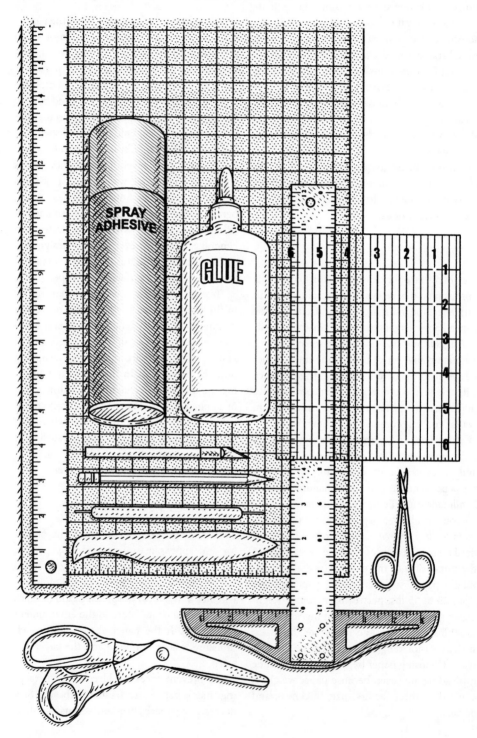

stay on the surface, and it increases the paper's smoothness, making it easier to crease.

Color refers to the pigment that is used to dye the cellulose fibers that make up the paper; pigment can either bond with the fibers or coat them. Color remains one of the more obvious and alluring characteristics of paper, since the range of available hues seems nearly infinite.

## Materials and Tools

While there are countless papers to consider for your paper crafting, only a few standard adhesives are needed for most techniques. Your choice will depend on the kind of paper you are working with, its weight and thickness, its degree of absorbency, the size of the area to be glued, and the weight and porosity of the items being adhered. A few implements for cutting, measuring, and folding will round out your materials for paper crafting.

- **White craft glue**

Also called PVA (polyvinyl acetate), this all-purpose white glue is smooth and strong and dries to a transparent, flexible finish. The creamy consistency makes it suitable for medium- and heavy-weight papers; it is a particularly effective adhesive when used on chipboard. White craft glue is washable when it is wet. It can be squeezed directly from the bottle, or it can be applied to large areas with a brush. Drying time can vary from 1 hour to overnight, depending upon the materials being glued.

Most brands of PVA glue come in a bottle with a dispenser tip. On a new bottle, you may need to snip off the tip of the dispenser to create a hole that regulates the flow of glue. Some bottles have a twist cap that unscrews along a threaded stem to control the size of the opening and the glue flow. After use, always replace the cap and wipe the dispenser tip with a damp cloth so that glue does not dry inside the tip and clog it.

- **Paste**

Paste comes in a broad range of consistencies; it can be runny (flour or starch paste) or thick (school paste). Used primarily for adhering sheets of paper to large surfaces, flour paste, wallpaper paste, and a flour paste/white glue

---

## Working Tips: Handling Paper

- Work in good light to avoid messy cuts, folds, and glue jobs.
- Always work with clean hands, washing them often to avoid transferring hand oils or dirt to the surface of the paper.
- Use a sharp craft knife and change to a fresh blade often to avoid ragged cuts and torn paper.
- Make an indented line before folding medium- to heavy-weight papers.

combination are applied with a brush. Water-soluble paste creates a tight bond between porous materials; however, due to its high moisture content, paste can warp and curl paper.

- **Glue stick**
  Made from a solid cylinder of paste housed in a push-up tube, a glue stick is convenient for small jobs, such as sticking a small piece of paper to a surface and adhering photo corners. Glue sticks are available in both washable and permanent formulations. Dyed glues let you see the glue during application but they dry clear.

---

## Working Tips: Reading Product Labels to Ensure Safe Use

Some products are hazardous to your health and can cause toxic reactions if breathed in, spilled on your skin, or used improperly. It is very important to read the product label. In the United States, a manufacturer must provide information on a Material Safety Data Sheet (MSDS) if the product has toxic ingredients. If the product is nontoxic, the label will state that the product conforms to ASTM D 4236. In Europe, nontoxic products print CH-BAGT T on the label. Products that have been endorsed by the Art & Creative Materials Institute (ACMI) will have seals that indicate that the product has been evaluated and certified to be nontoxic by a qualified toxicologist for both acute and chronic hazards.

---

- **Cellophane, double-sided, and masking tape**
  Many kinds of tape work well with paper, but they have different purposes. Transparent cellophane tape, which comes in either a high-gloss or a translucent finish, is used to attach light-weight materials, such as gift wrap paper. Most cellophane tapes are applied on the surface of an item and remain visible; because cellophane will discolor, lose adhesion, and stain paper over time, it is not recommended for mounting valuable materials, such as those used in scrapbooking. For these applications, acid-free tape is preferable. Double-sided acid-free tape has a bonding adhesive on both sides of the strip. Available in a range of bonding strengths, from heavy-duty and permanent to removable and repositionable, double-sided tape will not show because it is applied between materials, such as between the backs of photos and a page in an album. Masking tape, which is highly acidic, is a paper tape that is available in high- and low-tack versions and is used to temporarily position artwork.
- **Spray adhesive and rubber cement**

Rubber and solvent-based adhesives are effective in dry-mounting two materials together, such as sheets of paper or chipboard; however, these adhesives *must* be used with extra caution. When spraying an adhesive, work outdoors or in a very well ventilated space and wear a chemical-cartridge respirator mask. A cardboard carton can act as a spray booth to contain the inevitable overspray. Follow the same safety precautions when using rubber cement (although small glue jobs in a room with cross-ventilation can be all right for a short period). Both adhesives are toxic in that they accumulate in your body with prolonged exposure.

- **Novelty glues and adhesives**
Liquid glues of varying consistencies are designed for specific tasks, such as adhering glitter, metallic foil, fabric, and glass beads. Some are available in unique containers with narrow dispenser tips. Small containers are designed to prevent loss through fast evaporation rates. Other adhesive materials, commonly used in card making and scrapbooking, include convenient and mess-free double-sided foam tape, which allows adhered art to be elevated by the thickness of the foam, and adhesive-backed tabs, such as glue dots and photo corners.

- **Craft knife**

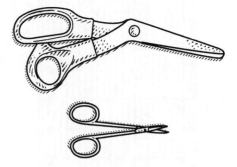

Indispensable and versatile, a craft knife is suited to making precise and intricate cuts on most papers with ease. Used together with a steel (or steel-edged) ruler to make straight cuts, a craft knife can also be used freehand to cut curved lines and shapes. The craft knife is recommended for cutting photos; when thick photo paper dulls the cutting blade, simply replace it with a new blade.

- **Scissors**

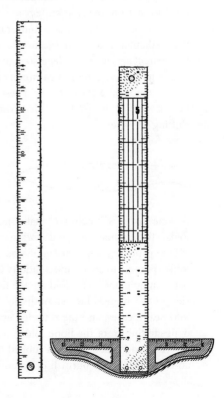

A good-quality pair of scissors is a must-have tool for producing smooth, even cuts in paper. Manicure scissors are suited to small cutting jobs where control is needed, such as precise cuts around intricate silhouettes or shapely details on the interior of a larger piece of paper.

- **Rulers**

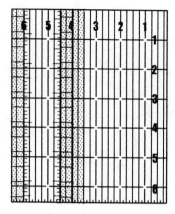

Besides being a prime measuring tool, a steel ruler is used as a guide for cutting straight lines with a craft knife. A wood ruler with a steel edge can also be used, but it may not lie flat to the surface. A plastic ruler or a wood ruler without a steel edge is not suitable as a cutting guide because of the potential for damage from the craft knife blade. A T square allows you to assess and draw perpendicular lines with accuracy. A transparent acrylic grid ruler also makes it easy to view and align measurements and ensure square corners; a skid-resistant underside keeps this ruler from shifting on paper.

- **Bone folder**

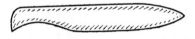

A bone folder will help you make neat folds—the hallmark of good workmanship in paper crafting. The tip of a bone folder is used to make indentations in paper in preparation for folding; the flat side of the bone folder smooths folds into neat creases; and the rounded end opposite the tip of the bone folder can placed flat against a fold and rubbed in an ovoid motion to burnish or smooth the crease without abrading the paper's surface. Viable substitutes for a bone folder are a stylus (for indenting paper) and the convex side of a stainless steel spoon (for making and burnishing smooth creases).

- **Stylus**

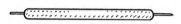

Used on medium- and heavy-weight papers, a stylus compresses the fibers in paper, resulting in an indented line. The more pressure applied to the tip, the deeper and glossier the embossed line. A substitute for a stylus is a dry ball-point pen.

- **Self-healing cutting mat**

Made of hard rubber, a cutting mat protects the work surface from scratches and cuts while providing a firm, yet slightly yielding, surface for smooth cutting with a craft knife or rotary cutter.

## Essential Techniques

There are so many ways to work with paper, it would be impossible to account for all of them here. Following are essential techniques for manipulating paper so that it behaves in a prescribed way. Consider them as guidelines, as starting points. As you work with paper, it will reveal its characteristics in surprising ways sure to ignite your imagination and creativity.

### Folding and Scoring

Most folding involves bending a sheet of paper along the grain and then smoothing the bend flat. On medium- and heavy-weight paper, folding is easier and far more accurate when an indented line or score line is made first to guide the fold.

## Technique: Making an Indented Line (Dry Embossing)

Suitable for medium-weight paper, such as the bristol or cardstock used to make greeting cards, an indented line helps guide the paper into a neat fold. A good tool for making an indentation is a bone folder or a stylus. These tools compress the paper, flattening the fiber into a shallow trough. Making an indentation in paper requires just enough firm pressure to reduce bulk along the fold line. The fold is made backward and away from the indented line.

MATERIALS AND TOOLS
    Bristol or cardstock
    Steel ruler
    Bone folder
    Pencil

**Step 1**
    Mark the fold line.
    Lay the bristol or cardstock on a flat work surface. Use a steel ruler to measure the position of the fold line at the top and bottom edges of the paper and make light ticks with a pencil as a guide.

**Step 2**
    Indent the fold line.
    Lay the ruler on the paper so it connects the ticks. Run the pointed tip of a bone folder along the ruler's edge, beginning just slightly above the top edge of the paper and ending just slightly below the bottom edge, to create an indentation the length of the fold.

**Step 3**
    Fold the paper.
    Bend the paper *backward* and away from the indented line, beginning at the center of the fold and working out toward the edges. Lay the folded paper on a flat surface and use the flat side of the bone folder to smooth and flatten the fold.

## Technique: Making a Score Line

Suitable for heavy paper, such as chipboard, a score line is actually a cut made along the fold line. Scoring slices through the topmost layer of paper fibers only, releasing the fibers on either side of the cut so that the paper can bend backward and away from the score line. Just the right amount of controlled pressure is needed to avoid cutting completely through the paper.

MATERIALS AND TOOLS
    Chipboard
    Steel ruler
    Craft knife
    Self-healing cutting mat
    Bone folder (optional)
    Pencil

**Step 1**
    Mark the fold line.
    Lay the chipboard on the cutting mat. Use a steel ruler to measure the position of the fold at the top and bottom edges of the chipboard and make light ticks with a pencil as a guide.

**Step 2**
    Score the fold line.
    Lay the ruler on the chipboard so it connects the ticks. Run the craft knife against the ruler's edge, from just slightly above the top edge of the chipboard to just slightly below the bottom edge, using light but even pressure to make a shallow cut in the surface.

**Step 3**
    Fold the chipboard.
    Bend the chipboard *backward* and away from the score line and smooth the fold flat with your hand.

**Step 4 (optional)**
    Burnish the fold.
    Lay the folded chipboard on a flat surface. Use the bone folder to smooth and flatten the fold.

Folds are often used in paper crafting to make greeting cards and insert folios for stationery and books. All folds divide the paper in some way, and while it is usual to fold a sheet of paper along the grain, folds can also cross over the grain to create interesting sculptural effects. A series of parallel folds alternating between front and back produces an accordion-folded or pleated sheet of paper. Accordion folds can be used to make greeting cards; pleated sheets can also be used to form the pages of a memory journal. The width of the pleats can be altered simply by increasing or decreasing the distance between the folds. It is also possible to vary the width to achieve unique folds, such as those in a pop-up card. Ultimately, the width and number of pleats are determined by the dimensions of the sheet of paper; the longer the paper, the greater the number of pleats or the width of each folded panel.

Accordion folds can be made in most kinds of paper as long as the paper has some structure. Bristol and cardstock hold up well to the rigors of folding, whereas thin tissue paper does not. Mat board and chipboard may be difficult, if not impossible, to fold neatly without first making an indentation line or score line to guide the fold into a neat crease. Some recycled paper will split, its short fibers breaking apart and tearing along the fold, when undergoing the pressure of a stylus. To avoid mistakes, test-fold a small section of a sheet of paper to make sure it folds to your satisfaction.

---

## Working Tips: Creating a Faux Deckle

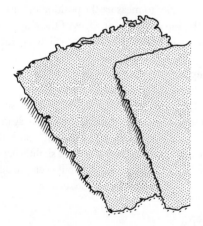

Here's a way to mimic the characteristic ragged deckle edge of handmade paper on a sheet of machine-made paper. Use a ruler and a bone folder to make an indentation in the paper along the grain. Dampen the fold using water and a cotton swab. Hold the ruler along the wet indented line with one hand and use your other hand to pull up and tear the paper against the ruler's edge.

---

### Technique: Making Accordion Folds

There are two approaches to pleating a length of paper. The less precise method (one we practiced as children) is to make the first fold and use it to guide the subsequent folds. A more accurate method, recommended for lengths of paper with many folds, is to indent all of the fold lines first. By making the indented lines on both sides of the paper and alternating the folds, you can easily create the "mountains" and the "valleys" that are characteristic of accordion pleats. Use your accordion-folded paper to make a little flag book.

MATERIALS AND TOOLS
   Bristol
   Chipboard or mat board
   White craft glue
   Steel ruler
   T square
   Bone folder
   Pencil

**Step 1**

Indent the first fold line.

Lay the bristol on a flat surface with the grain running vertically, top to bottom. Decide on a pleat width, for example, 2" (5.1 cm). Use a steel ruler to measure the position of the first fold line at the top and bottom edges of the paper and make light ticks with a pencil. Use a T square to confirm that the fold line will run perpendicular to the edge. Align the ruler on the ticks and use the tip of a bone folder to indent the fold line.

**Step 2**

Indent the second fold line.

Turn the paper over. Use a ruler to measure 2" (5.1 cm) from the indented line (an impression will be visible) and make ticks on the top and bottom edges. Align the ruler on the ticks and use a bone folder to indent the fold line.

**Step 3**

Indent the remaining fold lines.

Repeat step 2 to make indented fold lines across the full length of the paper, alternating from one side to the other.

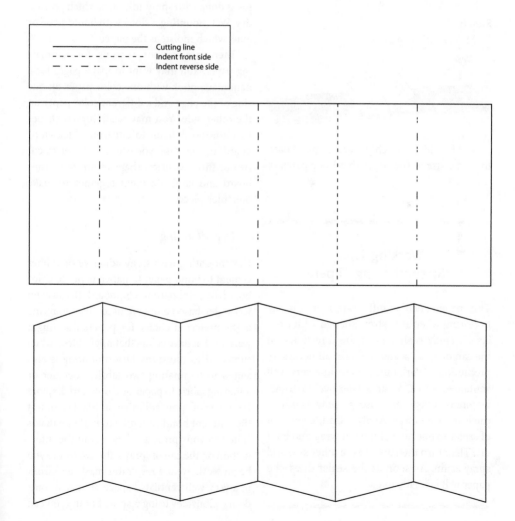

**Step 4**

Make the first two folds.

Fold the first 2" (5.1 cm) section backward along the indented line, smoothing the fold from the center toward the outside edges. Turn the paper over and fold the second section of the paper backward along the indented line, smoothing the fold as before.

**Step 5**

Make the remaining folds.

Repeat step 4, folding the paper along each indented line to make accordion pleats across the paper.

**Step 6**

Make a little flag book.

Cut two pieces of chipboard or mat board the same size as (or larger than) one panel of the pleated paper. Glue the chipboard pieces to the first and last panels of the accordion-pleated paper to form the front and back covers of a flag book. Decorate the covers as desired.

## Laminating

Laminating is a way of strengthening light- to medium-weight paper by backing it with another sheet of light- to medium-weight paper or with a thicker, stiffer sheet of paper, such as chipboard. Laminating can be done by dry mounting or wet mounting. Dry mounting is done with spray adhesive, which goes on dry. Wet mounting is done with liquid paste or glue, which moistens the paper.

There are various reasons for laminating paper. You may want to make pages for a handmade book with one color paper on one side of the page and a different color paper on the other side. You may need curved shapes that are too difficult to cut from thick chipboard; in this case, you'll find it easier to cut two or three identical shapes from thin chipboard and laminate them together to make one thick piece.

### Dry Mounting

Dry mounting uses spray adhesive or rubber cement to bond paper to paper, paper to chipboard, or chipboard to chipboard. Because no wet water-based glues are used, dry mounting is the preferred choice for papers that might warp or that have colors that might bleed when subjected to moisture. Dry mounting is also suited to laminating two fabrics together or adhering fabric to paper or chipboard. Explore the range of spray adhesives available and test the different bond strengths to find one that is suited to your project. Always read the information on the can of spray adhesive before you begin work, wear a respirator mask, and work in a very well ventilated space or, ideally, outdoors. Consider using a spray booth (you can

---

## Working Tips: Strengthening Paper

Thin paper, such as gift wrap, is less prone to tearing when it is strengthened with clear acrylic spray sealer. Read the directions on the can of spray sealer and take all necessary precautions. Work outdoors or in a very well ventilated space, wear a chemical-cartridge respirator mask, and use a spray booth to catch the overspray. Apply a thin, even coat of sealer to one side of the gift wrap and let it dry. Then turn the paper to the other side and spray again. As soon as the sealer dries, the paper will be ready to use.

make one from a large cardboard carton) to contain the inevitable overspray.

Overall, I prefer dry mounting to wet mounting because the method is nearly foolproof. It produces a tight bond with no buckling. Both spray adhesive and rubber cement allow some repositioning, if you proceed promptly. Generally, repositioning can be done only once before running the risk of tearing the papers; trying to peel papers apart once the bond is set can cause tearing and wrinkling, especially for thin papers and large sheets that can't be peeled apart in one smooth motion.

## Technique: Dry-Mounting Porous Materials

### MATERIALS AND TOOLS
Two sheets of paper or chipboard (or one of each)
Spray adhesive
Chemical-cartridge respirator mask
Cardboard carton (for spray booth; optional)
Low-tack masking tape (optional)

### Step 1
Lay out the paper.

Work outdoors or in a very well ventilated space and wear a chemical-cartridge respirator mask. Lay both sheets of paper or chipboard wrong side up on a protected surface (or in a spray booth), with their grains running in the same direction. Use short strips of masking tape to secure the corners of light-weight papers so that the aerosol spray doesn't blow the paper around.

### Step 2
Apply the spray adhesive.

Apply a thin, even coat of spray adhesive to both sheets of paper or chipboard, spraying beyond the edges. Wait a minute or two to allow the adhesive cure slightly.

### Step 3
Lay the papers together.

Lift one sheet of paper at opposite edges. Hold it adhesive side down over the second sheet of paper and lower the center of the paper onto the center of the second sheet. Once contact is made at the center, allow the sides to roll smoothly until both sheets are joined. Check the placement of the paper. If you need to reposition it, proceed to step 4. If it is correctly positioned, use your hand to smooth the papers together, working from the center outward in all directions to press out any air bubbles.

### Step 4 (optional)
Reposition the paper.

If you are dissatisfied with the placement, carefully peel the papers apart. Then without applying more spray adhesive, repeat step 3. Note that the papers can be repositioned one time only.

### Wet Mounting

In wet mounting, water-soluble glue is used to bond porous materials. There are many different kinds of water-soluble glues, and your choice will be determined by the weight of the papers being laminated. White craft glue, applied full strength, can be used to laminate two sheets of chipboard, whereas thinned white glue or a flour paste/white glue mixture can be used to laminate paper to chipboard. Always test the adhesive on samples of your paper and adjust the thickness of the glue as needed.

In general, wet mounting requires a thin application of glue to avoid saturating the paper, which can cause it to tear. The short fibers in recycled papers are especially prone to tearing and disintegrating when wet. Even when wet glue is applied in a thin layer, the paper will absorb some moisture and begin to expand, stretch, and warp. This effect is normal and is not permanent. After a few minutes, the paper will relax and straighten and you can proceed to adhere it to another surface. Be sure to match the grains of the two papers in wet mounting; if the grains run in different directions, the laminated papers may warp and cockle as the glue dries.

## Technique: Wet-Mounting Bond Paper to Chipboard

Wet glue can be used to adhere two pieces of porous material, such as paper and chipboard, together. Always apply a thin, even coat of glue. Allow time for the paper to absorb the moisture in the glue and relax before handling it further.

### MATERIALS AND TOOLS

Sheet of paper
Sheet of chipboard
Wallpaper paste, or flour paste/white craft glue mixture
Paintbrush with acrylic bristles

### Step 1

Apply the glue.

Lay the paper wrong side up on a protected work surface. Use a brush to apply wallpaper paste to the paper, beginning at the center and working out and just beyond the edges. Give the paper time to absorb the moisture in the paste and to relax.

### Step 2

Adhere the paper.

With the grains of the paper and the chipboard running in the same direction, lay the sheet of paper paste side down onto the chipboard. Smooth the paper from the center to the outside edges to keep air bubbles from being trapped underneath. Let the glue dry completely.

### Embossing

Embossing is a method that permanently alters the physical surface of the paper by introducing texture and contour. There are two basic ways to emboss paper: dry embossing, which

works by heat or pressure, and wet embossing, which uses moisture to stretch and expand the paper around a relief object. Sometimes both methods are used in one paper project.

### Dry Embossing with Heat

Dry embossing with heat requires a heat gun and heat-sensitive embossing powder. The powder—which comes in several grades, from ultrafine to thick—is made up of plastic particles that turn to molten liquid when they reach their melt point. In the dry embossing process, a design is applied to paper using a rubber stamp and dye-based ink (or a special pen). Embossing powder is sprinkled over the wet inked image and the powder that doesn't stick is shaken off. When a stream of hot air is directed on the image, the remaining powder melts and bonds to the paper fibers, forming a raised impression of the image. The appeal of this process lies in the wide and beautiful range of stamps and the colors and patinas of the embossing powders. To learn more about this technique, see Heat Embossing (page 297).

### Dry Embossing with Pressure

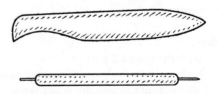

Dry embossing through pressure produces actual physical changes in the surface of the paper. Pressure embossing requires a stylus with a ball tip, a dry ball-point pen, or a bone folder. When a stylus is pressed into the paper, it stretches the fibers, leaving a dent or an impression. A stylus can be moved freehand over the surface of the paper, providing creative latitude for designs with curves, circles, and geometric shapes and patterns, or it can be run against the edge of a steel ruler for precise linearity. While color can enhance an embossed design, the sculptural effects and contours are often quite effective on their own.

### Wet Embossing

Wet embossing is a method in which wet 100 percent rag paper or raw paper pulp is molded around a dimensional object. The paper is allowed to dry around the object, producing a low-relief replica that highlights the sculptural form. Choose a waterproof object that will not rust or discolor when wet.

## Technique: Wet Embossing on 100 Percent Rag Paper

Wet embossing lets you create impressions of familiar objects in 100 percent rag paper.

Rag paper is thick, strong, and absorbent, allowing it to hold up to the moisture that swells the paper fibers and the stretching and shrinking that occurs as the paper dries and conforms to the contours of the embossing object. Choose something waterproof with a flat side that can lie against the surface. I chose a pair of stainless steel scissors. The finished embossing can be slipped into a window card or placed in a shadow box frame. Be sure to allow a generous margin of paper to highlight the textural contours.

### MATERIALS AND TOOLS
Sheet of 100 percent rag paper, 8" × 10" (20.3 × 25.4 cm)
Relief object, not to exceed 4" × 5" × ½" high (10.2 × 12.7 × 1.3 cm)
Sheet of foam, ½" (1.3 cm) thick, in a size to support relief object
Plastic cutting board, in a size to support foam
Clean sponge
Plastic wrap
Heavy weight, such as a stack of books

**Step 1**
Soak the paper.
Work on a waterproof surface. Use a wet sponge to saturate the piece of paper with water. Let the paper buckle and then relax. Use the sponge to sop up any pools of water remaining on the paper surface.

**Step 2**
Begin the embossing process.
Lay the foam on the plastic cutting board. Place the relief object on the foam. Center the wet sheet of paper over the relief object. Lay a sheet of plastic wrap over the wet paper and stack heavy books on top, balancing them against a wall if necessary. Leave undisturbed for 48 hours.

**Step 3**
Allow the embossed paper to cure.

Remove the books and plastic wrap and check the paper. If it is still damp, replace the plastic wrap and the books and continue checking at 24-hour intervals. When the embossed paper is completely dry, store it on a flat surface until you are ready to use it in a project.

## Cutting

Clean cuts are the hallmark of professional-level paper crafting. For general cutting, sharp scissors are fine. For more precise, straight cuts, a craft knife is recommended, especially when making greeting cards, gift tags, insert folios for books, and book covers. A craft knife is also good for targeted cutting of hard-to-reach interior shapes in a larger sheet of paper. Manicure scissors are used for intricate cutting on both the perimeter and interior areas of paper shapes.

### Technique: Cutting Straight Edges on Paper with a Craft Knife

A single clean cut is generally sufficient to slice through light-weight or medium-weight paper. If the paper is thick and your cut does not go through on the first pass, run the blade through the first cut again, tracing its path as carefully as you can without wobbling the blade or lifting it out of the cut, until the paper is cut through.

MATERIALS AND TOOLS
   Paper, light- to medium-weight
   Steel ruler
   Craft knife
   Self-healing cutting mat

**Step 1**
   Lay out the materials.
   Lay a cutting mat on a flat surface and place the paper on top. Lay the ruler on the paper in a position that delineates the cut you want to make.

**Step 2**
   Make one long cut.
   Run the blade of the craft knife along the edge of the ruler, beginning and ending the cut slightly beyond the edge of the paper. Use steady pressure and avoid lifting the blade to make a continuous cut through the paper.

**Step 3 (optional)**
   Make a second cut.
   Repeat step 2, if necessary, pressing down on the craft knife and following the score line until the paper is cut through.

### Technique: Cutting Straight Edges on Chipboard with a Craft Knife

You will most likely need to make more than one pass of the blade to cut completely through the thickness of chipboard. The secret to a clean second cut is to make a clean first cut, or score line, to guide it. Use medium pressure on the first pass; too much pressure can cause the ruler to shift and misdirect the cut. You can increase the pressure on the craft knife as the track deepens.

MATERIALS AND TOOLS
   Chipboard
   Steel ruler
   Craft knife
   Self-healing cutting mat

**Step 1**
   Lay out the materials.
   Lay a cutting mat on a flat surface and place the chipboard on top. Lay the ruler on the paper in a position that delineates the cut you want to make.

**Step 2**
   Score the chipboard.
   Use medium pressure to run the blade of the craft knife along the edge of the ruler, beginning and ending the cut slightly beyond the edge of the chipboard and using steady

pressure to cut through the top layer of board without picking up the blade.

## Step 3

Make additional cuts.

Repeat step 2, pressing down harder on the craft knife as you cut on the score line. Continue to deepen the cut until the chipboard is cut completely through.

## Fun for Kids: Elephant Parade

Children can stage a little circus at the kitchen table by making their own simple puppets from paper cutouts. Use the Elephant pattern (page 683) or have a child draw a favorite animal on paper and cut it out. Then tape a pencil or a wooden skewer to the back of paper animal and watch the imaginative play unfold.

## Technique: Cutting Curved Edges with a Craft Knife

It is difficult to cut clean curves and full circles with a craft knife unless you have a jig with a blade. However, if you take your time, you can cut curved shapes freehand or with a template.

### MATERIALS AND TOOLS

Cardstock marked for curved cut
Craft knife
Self-healing cutting mat

### Step 1

Make a score line.

Lay a cutting mat on a flat surface and place the cardstock on top. Hold the craft knife like a pencil and place the blade at the beginning of the curved line. Follow the curved line with the blade, using a flexible wrist and applying medium, steady pressure as you draw the blade toward you.

### Step 2

Make a second cut.

Follow the curved score line, pressing down on the craft knife to deepen the cut until the cardstock is cut completely through.

## Sewing

Sewing is a simple way to add decoration, texture, and dimension to a paper's surface. You can hand-sew beads, buttons, and trims to paper using an ordinary needle and thread. A sewing machine can help you emblazon a paper surface with sweeping stitches or attach ribbons, fabric scraps, and textured papers collage-style. You can use a threadless hand or machine needle to perforate paper with a pattern of tiny holes.

Choose a paper for sewing that is sturdy enough to withstand the pressure and piercing of the needle. The holes made by sewing or perforating should not be spaced so closely that the paper splits apart. You can sew almost any weight paper except for tissue paper, which tears easily. Adjust the size of your needle according to the paper thickness, choosing a thinner needle for one layer of paper and a thicker needle for several layers.

*Hand Sewing*

A suitable needle for hand sewing depends on the thickness and weight of the paper and the fiber being threaded through it. Choose a needle that pierces the paper neatly and easily without leaving gaping holes that may weaken the paper. An embroidery needle can be used with floss, and a darning needle can be used with most threads and light-weight yarn. Use a threadless needle to perforate the design path before sewing with thin thread. To make holes for cord and ribbon, use a hole punch.

### Technique: Hand-Sewing Paper

Hand sewing gives you a lot of control over the placement of the stitches and decorations you sew on the paper's surface. You can eas-

## Working Tips: Making Clean Cuts with a Craft Knife

- Always cut on a protected surface, such as a self-healing cutting mat.
- Always cut toward you, being careful to keep your fingers clear of the blade's path.
- To cut straight lines, use a steel (or steel-edged) ruler as a guide and run the blade of the craft knife against it. Avoid swerving into the metal edge, which can dull the knife blade.
- To cut curves, move the blade slowly along the marked line, cutting through thin layers of paper at a time. Slowly rotate the paper as you cut so that your wrist on the cutting hand does not take on an awkward angle, which in turn can cause you to lose control and miscut.
- For neat cuts at the edges, start the cut beyond the edge of the paper and pull the knife toward you and past the second edge of the paper.
- To cut heavy-weight paper or thick chipboard, cut a score line first to provide a pilot groove for the blade to follow. Make additional passes until the blade cuts through the paper layers.
- Change blades as soon as the knife begins to drag.
- Use a T square or carpenter's square to check right-angle cuts.
- Keep the cap on the blade when the craft knife is not in use and store the capped knife with the blade down.

ily change the direction, length, and kind of stitches you sew, and you can switch from one weight thread to another as you add buttons, beads, and similar findings to create an interesting surface texture on the paper.

MATERIALS AND TOOLS
Single-fold greeting card in cardstock
Collage materials: scraps of paper, button
Thread
Needle
Scissors
Glue stick
Tape

**Step 1**

Arrange the collage.

Arrange the scraps of paper and the button in a pleasing design. Use a glue stick to tack them in place on the front panel of the card.

**Step 2**

Secure the thread end.

Thread a needle with a double strand of thread and make a knot at the end. Insert the needle from the underside into the card front and slowly pull the thread through until the knot rests against the paper. Use a short strip of tape to secure the knot to the paper.

## Quick & Easy: Decorating a Card with Sewing

You can use machine stitching to add picturesque details to a printed image. Here a bird print is glued to the front panel of a single-fold card and machine stitches form the nest. The bird on the inside panel is not stitched.

All you need are a blank single-fold card, one or two printed bird images (page 683), white glue, and a threaded sewing machine.

- Cut out the bird prints, following the contours of each image. Glue one cutout to the front panel of the card and glue the other cutout to the inside facing panel of the card. Let the glue dry.
- Open the card flat. Slide the front panel under the presser foot of the sewing machine, position the needle on the print, and lower the presser foot. Slowly sew back and forth, raising the presser foot and pivoting at the end of each line of stitching, to add curving lines of stitches to the card to create the shape of a nest. Use the edge of the cutout to guide the placement and density of the nest stitches.

**Step 3**

Sew on the collage materials.

Position the needle on the top side of the card front in a desired position for the first stitch; push the needle down through the paper, gently resting your finger against the paper to keep the thread from tangling as you pull it through the hole. Continue making stitches to attach the paper pieces and the button to the card. End the sewing on the back of the paper and secure the end of the thread with tape.

### Machine Sewing

Using a sewing machine is an efficient, secure, and attractive way to add texture and decoration to a paper surface. Plain machine stitching can mimic patterns found in textiles, and different colored threads can add contrast and texture to your design. Applied materials, such as ribbon and paper, can create collage-style designs. Tack down loose collage pieces with a glue stick to prevent shifting while you sew.

If you do not have an electronic sewing machine that automatically corrects the tension, practice stitching on a piece of scrap paper from your project. To begin, use a 10/70 sharp needle threaded with cotton or polyester thread. After the machine is threaded, raise the presser foot, slip the paper under the needle, and use the handwheel to lower the needle into the paper at the desired position. Then lower the presser foot to hold the paper against the needle plate. The needle plate has two rows of teeth (called *feed dogs*) that will pull the paper backward. If the paper is stiff or has a slick surface, it may not feed automatically and you may need to gently coax it to start the stitching.

Because a sewing machine is powerful, you will need to control its speed in order to guide the direction and density of the stitches. Always use the handwheel to guide the placement of the first stitches in the paper. Use light pressure on the foot pedal or turn the handwheel to carefully control the speed of the sewing.

Experiment sewing on different kinds of paper. Tissue paper can be sewn if stabilized, appliqué-style, with a backing paper. Avoid handmade paper containing dried leaves, stems, or thick plant material that could break the sewing machine needle. Although lightweight needles are often chosen for sewing on paper because they do not leave big holes, you may need a heavier needle, such as those made for sewing leather, to pierce through heavier-weight paper or to sew through several layers of lighter-weight paper, such as the folios for a book. Do not attempt to sew more than three sheets of cardstock together at once. A heavier needle is also good if you want the stitching to be a prominent feature of the design. Avoid dense machine embroidery stitches, which will only chew up the paper.

### Technique: Machine-Sewing Paper

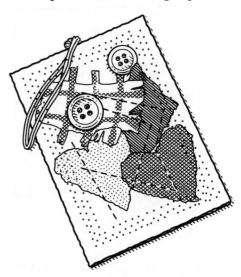

Sewing by machine on paper is enormous fun. It takes very little time to machine-stitch designs or to secure ribbons, paper, and other appliqués to paper.

## MATERIALS AND TOOLS

Cardstock
Collage materials: scraps of paper, button
Sewing machine
Thread
Glue stick
Scissors

### Step 1

Set up your machine.

Install an appropriate size needle according to the thickness of the paper and the trim you have chosen. Thread your machine and make sure the bobbin is full. Set the machine for a long stitch length, such as 3.5 mm, to avoid tearing or weakening the paper.

### Step 2

Arrange the collage.

Lay the scraps of paper in a pleasing design on the front panel of the card. Use a glue stick to tack them in place.

### Step 3

Sew on the collage materials.

Begin in an inconspicuous place on the paper, using your hand to turn the handwheel and insert the needle into the paper. Sew the first few stitches with the presser foot down and the feed dogs up. Then lower the feed dogs to sew a loose, freestyle design, moving the paper in soft arcs or zigzags. You can cover the first few stitches with an embellishment later, if desired.

## Greeting Cards and Invitations

In order to select appropriate paper and design for a greeting card, consider first for whom and for what occasion the card is intended. So many sentiments can be conveyed through paper choice alone. For an urban chic look, you can fold a sheet of newspaper into a card and add your text using stencils and paint. For a formal occasion, you can fold a sheet of 100 percent rag paper in soft ivory and slip a vellum folio inside.

Your paper choice must support the mechanics of your format. Will there be a cutout window or an accordion fold? Will you attach embellishments, such as ribbon or charms, to convey a particular tone or message? As long as your card holds together and reaches its destination, you have fairly wide latitude in your design. If your card is an odd shape or heavy and you plan to send your creation through the mail, be sure to visit the post office to purchase any additional postage that is required. If you attached an embellishment that adds bulk, you can ask for hand stamping so the decoration does not get crushed going through the postal machine.

Techniques for decorating and embellishing paper greeting cards and invitations abound, and mixed-media approaches add to the fun and creativity of making your own. This section includes techniques for cutting, embellishing, photo transfer and printing, and making multiples, such as invitations and birth announcements. But your first task is to make a basic card and envelope.

## Technique: Making a Single-Fold Card

The easiest card to make is one with a single fold—a rectangle of paper is folded in half, instantly creating a front and an inside back panel that is seen when you open the card. Both panels of the card can be decorated in any way you choose, including any text or illustrations that you decide are compatible with the card's occasion.

MATERIALS AND TOOLS
100 percent rag stock paper
Steel ruler
Craft knife
Self-healing cutting mat
Stylus, or dry ball-point pen
Bone folder
Pencil

**Step 1**

Cut out the card.

Lay the paper on a cutting mat so the grain runs in the direction of the intended fold. Use a ruler and a stylus (or a pencil) to mark four points that define a 10" × 7" (25.4 × 17.8 cm) rectangle. Use a ruler to connect two points that mark one side and cut along the edge of the ruler with a craft knife. Repeat until all four sides are cut.

**Step 2**

Indent the center fold line.

Use a ruler and a pencil to measure the top and bottom edges of the rectangle and make ticks at the middle. Lay the ruler on the paper to connect the marks. Run the tip of the bone folder against the edge of the ruler from a position slightly above the top edge of the paper to a place slightly below the bottom edge, using firm pressure to make a straight and even indentation in the paper.

**Step 3**

Fold the card in half.

Bend the card backward along the indented line to fold the card in half. Then lay the folded card on a flat surface and press down the fold, beginning at the center and smoothing toward each edge. Use a bone folder to flatten the fold into a neat crease.

**Step 4**

Decorate the card front.

Embellish the front panel of the card, following the illustration or referring to Quick & Easy: Adding Embellishments (page 236) for ideas.

## Technique: Making an Envelope

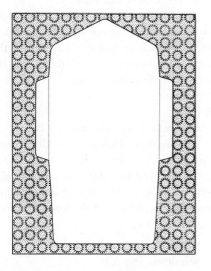

Use the Standard Envelope pattern (page 684) to fit a card that measures 5" × 7" (12.7 × 17.8 cm). You can draft a similar pattern to make a custom-size envelope to fit any card you make. Simply use your finished card as a guide to make an envelope from a sheet of decorative paper.

### MATERIALS AND TOOLS

Greeting card
Decorative paper
Glue stick or double-sided tape
Scrap paper
Steel ruler
Scissors
Bone folder
Pencil

### Step 1

Make a custom-size pattern.

Lay the scrap paper on a flat work surface. Place the closed greeting card on it and use a pencil to trace around it. Set the card aside. Use a steel ruler and a pencil to redraw the shape, adding a ⅜"-wide (1.0 cm) margin all around. Sketch in two narrow side flaps and a bottom flap that is slightly tapered along the side edges, as shown in the illustration. Then sketch in a peaked top flap. Use the ruler and pencil to true up your lines and to round corners, if desired.

### Step 2

Test the pattern.

Use scissors to cut out the paper pattern along the outside lines. Fold the pattern along the inside lines. Make sure the flaps overlap with enough allowance for gluing. Test-fit the pattern to your card and make any necessary adjustments.

### Step 3

Make the envelope.

Use your custom-size pattern as a template to cut out an envelope shape from decorative paper. Use a ruler and a bone folder to indent fold lines for the side flaps, bottom flap, and top flap on the right side of the paper. Fold in the side flaps and fold up the bottom flap. Use dabs of glue from a glue stick or pieces of double-sided tape to secure the bottom flap to the side flaps.

### Step 4

Seal the envelope.

Insert the card into the envelope, fold down the top flap, and seal it with dabs of glue or pieces of double-sided tape.

## Technique: Making a Liner for an Envelope

To coordinate an envelope and card, make an envelope liner from light-weight paper. Suitable papers for liners include gift wrap designed for holidays and special occasions such as birthdays and anniversaries, individual art papers filled with color (look for ombré, variegated, plain, or patterned papers), and textured papers such as Japanese rice paper and velveteen.

### MATERIALS AND TOOLS

Envelope
Light-weight decorative paper
Scrap paper
Steel ruler
Craft knife
Self-healing cutting mat
Glue stick
Pencil

### Step 1

Make a pattern.

Lay a sheet of scrap paper on a cutting mat and lay the envelope with flap open on top. Use a pencil to trace around the entire shape. Set the envelope aside. Use a ruler and pencil to reduce the size of the flap section by approximately ¼" (0.6 cm) to provide room for the strip of glue on the envelope flap. Use a craft knife and a steel ruler to cut out the paper pattern.

### Step 2

Make the decorative liner.

Lay the pattern on a sheet of decorative paper. Line up the edge of the ruler along each side of the pattern and run the blade of the craft knife along the edge of the ruler to cut through the decorative paper.

### Step 3

Adhere the liner to the envelope.

Slip the liner, decorative side facing out, into the envelope. Use a glue stick to tack the liner to the envelope flap. Use a ruler and a bone folder to make a lightly indented line along the flap fold. Fold the lined flap along the indented line.

## Windows, Pop-Ups, and Other Hand-Cut Features

One of the simplest hand-cut decorations to add to the front panel of a card is a window. The window can be placed anywhere on the front panel as long as there is enough of a margin to maintain the physical structure of the card. Once the window is cut, a separate paper is slipped inside the card to provide a place to attach a photo or a charm. When the card is closed, the window frames the embellishment. Other features, combined with folding, can add dimension and movement to a card. A pop-up band cut into the card works when the card is opened. More fanciful cutting with a craft knife or scissors can create silhouettes that mimic the look of expensive die-cut cards.

## Technique: Making a Cutout Window Lined with Vellum

A cutout window can be placed anywhere on a card as long as a sturdy margin of paper remains around the cutout area to support the structure of the card. Use this technique to cut out a window on the front panel of any card. Slip a piece of vellum inside the card and add a small charm or emboss an image so that the window frames the decoration.

### MATERIALS AND TOOLS
Single-fold card
Cardstock
Vellum
Rubber stamp
Ink pad with dye-based ink
Embossing powder and heat gun (optional)
Glue stick
Graph paper
Scrap paper
Clear grid ruler
Steel ruler
Craft knife
Self-healing cutting mat

Bone folder
Stylus, or dry ball-point pen
Pencil

### Step 1
Make a template of the window.

Draft a rectangle on graph paper to represent the actual size of the card's front cover. Cut out the graph paper template. Work on a cutting mat and use a steel ruler and a craft knife to cut a piece of vellum to this size.

### Step 2
Mock up the image on the template.

Use the rubber stamp to print an image onto scrap paper. Cut out the stamped image and center it on the graph paper rectangle, using the grid as a guide. Draft a small rectangle, no larger than 2" (5.1 cm) across, around the image to represent the window.

### Step 3
Cut out the window.

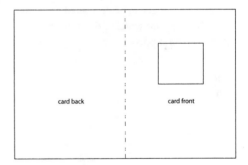

card back          card front

Open the card and lay it flat on the cutting mat. Place the graph paper template on top of the front cover only. Use a steel ruler and a craft knife to cut out the window through both layers.

### Step 4
Stamp the image on the vellum.

Lay the graph paper template over the vellum, so that the vellum shows through the cutout window. Position the test print made in step 2 under the vellum as guide for stamping. Stamp a fresh image onto the vellum. Remove the template. Use embossing powder and a heat gun to make a raised design, if desired.

### Step 5

Secure the liner.

Open the card and lay it flat on a clean work surface so the inside faces up. Lay the vellum liner face down on the window panel. Secure the edges with dabs of a glue stick. Cut and add a second liner from cardstock to conceal the vellum liner, if desired.

## Technique: Making a Double-Fold Card with a Cutout Window

A double-fold card is a simple variation of the single-fold card; instead of one fold, it has two. A rectangle of paper is folded twice to create three panels, two for the card front and one for the card back. A window is cut into the center panel and then an adjacent panel is folded behind the window, providing a ready-made backing that can be decorated or formed into a "sleeve" into which a sheet of decorated vellum can be slipped.

### MATERIALS AND TOOLS

100 percent rag stock paper
Steel ruler
Craft knife
Self-healing cutting mat
Stylus, or dry ball-point pen
Bone folder
Pencil
Graph paper

### Step 1

Cut out the card.

Lay the paper on a cutting mat so the grain runs in the direction of the intended fold. Use a ruler and a stylus or pencil to mark four points that define a 15" × 7" (38.1 × 17.8 cm) rectangle. Use a ruler to connect two points that mark one side and cut along the edge of the ruler with a craft knife. Repeat until all four sides are cut.

### Step 2

Indent the fold lines.

Use a ruler and a pencil to measure the top and bottom edges of the rectangle and make two sets of ticks 5" (12.7 cm) and 10" (25.4 cm) from the left edge of the rectangle. Lay the ruler on the paper to connect each

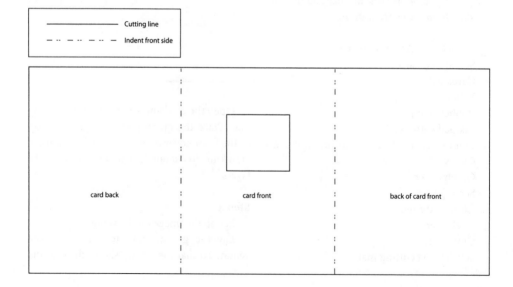

| ——————— | Cutting line |
| — ·· — ·· — ·· — | Indent front side |

card back          card front          back of card front

set of marks. Run the tip of the bone folder against the edge of the ruler from a position slightly above the top edge of the paper to a place slightly below the bottom edge, making straight and even indentations in the paper and using firm pressure.

## Step 3

Fold the card in thirds.

Lay the card flat on a cutting mat. Lay a steel ruler ⅛" (0.3 cm) from the right edge, parallel to the indented lines, and trim off this sliver of paper. Bend the card backward along the indented lines to fold the card in thirds so that the first and third panels overlap the center panel. The third panel, which was trimmed, should fold neatly behind the center panel, which will become the cover of the card. Lay the folded card on a flat surface and press down each fold, beginning at the center and smoothing toward each edge. Use a bone folder to flatten each fold into a neat crease.

## Step 4

Add a cutout window to the center panel.

Draft a rectangle on graph paper to represent the actual size of the card's front cover. Cut out the graph paper template. Draft a small square, approximately 2" (5.1 cm), to represent the window. Open the card and lay it flat on the cutting mat. Place the graph paper template on top of the center panel. Use a steel ruler and a craft knife to cut out the window through the paper. Add a vellum insert to the card, as desired.

## Technique: Making a "Die-Cut" Card

*Die-cut* is a term that refers to the use of a die to guide the blade of a cutting machine through multiple layers of paper or fabric to create a particular shape. For the crafter, *die-cut* has come to describe a card that has a defined silhouette made by precise hand cutting.

The secret to this fun and flirty paper purse with a hidden Velcro closure is the piece of one-ply chipboard that provides the needed structure. It is sandwiched between two decorative papers—an animal print on the outside of the card and a stripe pattern on the inside. You can mix contrasting styles and patterns of paper on your card purse as you wish. Add a key on a chain or any other embellishment that dangles. Glitz up the clasp or leave it plain.

### MATERIALS AND TOOLS

Key to My Heart purse pattern (page 685)
2 decorative papers, with animal print and with stripes
One-ply chipboard
Ornaments: gold chain with key, oval plastic rhinestone, felt flower
Velcro closure, ½" (1.3 cm) diameter
Spray adhesive
Hot-glue gun and glue stick
Glue stick
Chemical-cartridge respirator mask
Photocopier
Craft knife
Scissors

**Step 1**

Cut out the purse.

Photocopy the Key to My Heart purse pattern and transfer it to chipboard. Use scissors to cut out the chipboard purse shape.

**Step 2**

Laminate the chipboard and the animal print paper.

Work outdoors or in a very well ventilated space and wear a chemical-cartridge respirator mask. Lay the animal print paper, wrong side up, on a protected surface. Apply a thin, even coat of spray adhesive to the paper. Lay the chipboard purse made in step 1 on the paper, flip it over, and smooth the paper flat from the center to the outside edges. Use a pair of scissors and a craft knife to cut out the purse, following the directions on the pattern. Be as accurate as possible when cutting the handle and the purse flap because they share a cutting line.

**Step 3**

Laminate the purse to the striped paper.

Repeat step 2 to affix the striped paper to the other side of the purse. Use scissors or a craft knife to trim off the excess.

**Step 4 (optional)**

Create an insert folio.

Use the pattern to trace the purse shape on a piece of plain paper. Use scissors to cut out the shape ¼" (0.6 cm) inside the marked line. Lay the purse card open on a flat surface. Use a glue stick to attach the folio inside the card, matching the fold lines.

**Step 5**

Fold the purse and add the key chain.

Fold the purse in half and bring the flap through the handle opening. Position and hot-glue the Velcro closure pieces, loop and fuzzy surfaces facing, to the underside of the flap and the front of the purse. Thread the chain with the key around the purse handle and secure the Velcro flap.

**Step 6**

Add a rhinestone accent and a felt flower.

Position and hot-glue the rhinestone accent to the purse flap and the felt flower to the bottom left edge of the purse.

## Technique: Making a Pop-Up Card

The pop-up effect is created by combining cutting and folding techniques in one card. A section of paper is cut, but part of the section remains attached to the background paper. The cut section is folded in the opposite direction from the rest of the paper so that when the card is opened, the cut section pops up or to the side.

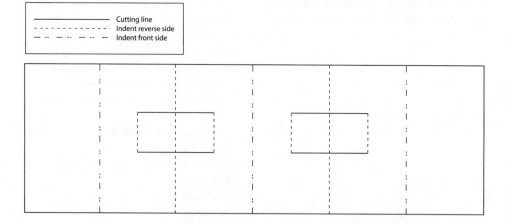

## MATERIALS AND TOOLS

Cardstock, 12" wide × 3½" high
  (30.5 × 8.9 cm), in any color or pattern
Computer with printer
Glue stick
Steel ruler
Craft knife
Self-healing cutting mat
Bone folder
Pencil

### Step 1

Mark the accordion folds.

Use a pencil and a ruler to lightly mark six 2"-wide (5.1 cm) panels at the top and the bottom edge of the 12" × 3½" (30.5 × 8.9 cm) cardstock.

### Step 2

Indent the folds on the front of the cardstock.

Use a ruler and a bone folder to indent the fold lines on the first, third, and fifth set of marks, beginning slightly higher than the top edge of the paper and ending slightly lower than the bottom edge.

### Step 3

Indent the folds on the back of the cardstock.

Turn the paper over and use a ruler and a bone folder to indent fold lines on the second and fourth set of marks, beginning slightly higher than the top edge of the paper and ending slightly lower than the bottom edge. The cardstock will have five indented lines, each 2" (5.1 cm) apart.

### Step 4

Make the accordion folds.

Fold the paper backward on the first indentation. Continue folding on the indented lines, alternating the direction of each fold, to make accordion pleats across the cardstock.

### Step 5

Mark and cut the pop-ups.

Lay the cardstock flat. Use a ruler and a pencil to mark two parallel horizontal lines, 2" (5.1 cm) long and 1" (2.5 cm) apart, on the second and third panels; the lines should straddle the middle of the center fold. Repeat to mark two parallel horizontal lines across the fourth and fifth panels. Lay the cardstock on a cutting mat and use a steel ruler and a craft knife to cut along the marked lines.

### Step 6

Fold the pop-ups.

Ease forward the paper bands formed in

step 5 and begin to close the card. Make a crease to mark the fold that forms when the band moves completely forward as the paper is folded flat. Use a bone folder to reinforce the crease.

**Step 7**

Print the paper messages.

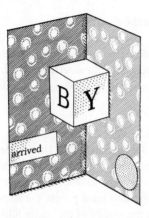

Use a computer to compose a message and print it out on paper. Trim the messages to fit the card, as desired, and then use a dabs of glue from a glue stick to attach the paper messages to the card.

## Technique: Making a Side Pop-Up

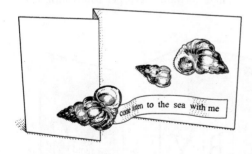

Caption: Folded size: 6" wide × 4½" high (15.2× 11.4 cm). Greeting: *Come listen to the sea with me.*

This pop-up card is made by stamping or gluing an image on a fold and cutting around part of the image so its edge pops out when the card is opened.

### MATERIALS AND TOOLS

Seashell original art (page 686)
Cardstock, 12" wide × 4½" high
(30.5 × 11.4 cm), in any color
Rubber stamp with shell image
Ink pad with dye-based ink
Embossing powder and heat gun
Calligraphy pen and paper or computer
with printer
Photocopier
Steel ruler
Craft knife
Self-healing cutting mat
Bone folder
Manicure scissors
Paintbrush

### Step 1

Make the center fold.

Lay the cardstock horizontally on a cutting mat. Use a steel ruler and a pencil to measure for a center fold and make ticks at the top and bottom edges of the paper. Connect the marks with a ruler and use the tip of a bone folder to indent the line. Fold the paper backward and away from the indented line and smooth the crease flat.

### Step 2

Mark the second fold.

Open the card and lay it flat, forming a valley fold. Measure the left panel for a center fold and make ticks at the top and bottom edges. Connect the marks with a ruler and use the tip of a bone folder to indent the line.

### Step 3

Stamp and emboss a shell image.

Center an inked rubber stamp on the marked second fold and make a seashell print. Sprinkle clear embossing powder over the stamped image. Shake off the excess onto a sheet of scrap paper and use the tip of a dry paintbrush to carefully sweep off any remaining powder from the stamped image; return all the excess powder to the container. Use the heat gun to melt the embossing powder on the stamped image.

### Step 4

Die-cut half of the shell and make the fold.

Use manicure scissors to cut around the right side of the shell, following the outline. Fold the paper backward and away from the indented line. Do not fold the shell.

### Step 5

Add more shell images to the card.

Photocopy several seashell prints in different sizes. Use scissors to cut out the images along their outlines. Open the card flat with the inside of the card facing up. Place the seashell images on the right panel of the card and use dabs from a glue stick to glue down the prints.

### Step 6

Make a pop-up band.

Use a calligraphy pen to handwrite a message or use a computer and printer to print a message on a sheet of copy paper. Trim the message to make a narrow strip of paper and then glue one end, message facing out, behind

the shell and the second end to the right inside panel of the card.

### Step 7

Bring the band forward.

Ease the paper band formed in step 6 forward and begin to close the card. Make a crease to mark the fold that forms when the band moves completely forward as the paper is folded flat, using your hands to flatten the fold.

## Applied Embellishments

An embellishment is a small accent added to the paper surface to create visual interest. The surface might be a panel on a greeting card or a page in a scrapbook. To be effective, an embellishment should support the established theme, reflect the emotional appeal of all the design elements, and be in balance with the overall layout. Some embellishments come ready-made and can be applied immediately to the paper. Others require that you take a few crafting steps first. The array of embellishments available is absolutely stunning, and their use is limited only by your imagination.

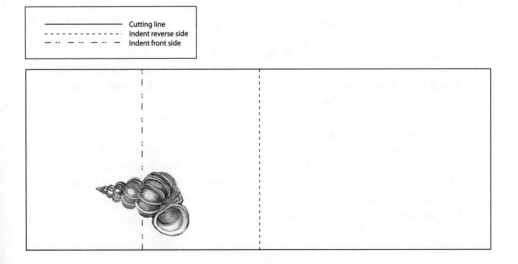

| | |
|---|---|
| ——————— | Cutting line |
| - - - - - - - - - - - | Indent reverse side |
| — ·· — ·· — — ·· — | Indent front side |

**Technique: Writing with Glue and Glitter**

Writing or making designs with glitter is a fun and sparkly way to add glamour to paper. All that is required is white glue or a glue that is designed specifically for use with glitter, metallic foil, or glass. Typically, glue containers have slender nozzles with fine tips that allow you to apply glue in small dots and skinny lines, perfect for writing or making detailed designs. You can also pour glue into a small saucer and use a tapered brush to apply the glue wherever you want it.

MATERIALS AND TOOLS
Glitter
White craft glue or specialty glue
Paper for project
Scrap paper

**Step 1**
Apply the glue.
Start the glue flowing slowly and evenly on a piece of scrap paper and then move onto your project paper to write your inscription. Avoid squeezing the container too hard as an unwanted blob of glue may burst from the bottle's tip.

**Step 2**
Apply the glitter.
Sprinkle the glitter onto the wet glue. Allow the glue to dry completely. The glue will contract as it dries, drawing the glitter to the paper surface.

**Step 3**
Shake off the excess glitter onto a sheet of copy paper and funnel it back into the container.

## Quick & Easy: Adding Embellishments

Here are quick and easy ways to add color, texture, and form to your paper designs.

- Elevate individual photos using lengths of flexible foam tape.
- Draw on shrink plastic and bake it to miniaturize a drawing and intensify its color.
- Attach a row of eyelets to provide neat holes through which to thread lace or yarn.
- Make a small envelope out of paper and sew on snaps or buttons that actually work.
- Glue a small photo on paper and frame it with a concho.
- Create a "room with view" by cutting a single photo into equal-size squares and gluing the tiles in a neat grid to simulate the view from a multipaned window.
- Use a sewing machine to stitch lengths of ribbon in the shape of a letter of the alphabet.
- Use small hardware, such as a brass hinge or buckle, to add realistic accents to drawings or printed images of items that have those working elements.
- Use clear or colored nail polish to add a high-gloss finish to part of an illustration, such as drops of rain or a pair of red shoes on dancing feet.

## Technique: Gilding a Hand-Drawn Design

Gilding with composition metal leaf adds soft luster to your work. Use a brush or a glue pen to apply the size and to draw the shape of this leafy garland. Anywhere you apply the glue, the metal leaf will adhere, so be as neat and precise as possible when you are drawing with the size to prevent the leaf from adhering to the wrong area of the paper.

### MATERIALS AND TOOLS

Purchased blank cards and envelopes
Engraved print of girl's head, or as desired
Spray acrylic sealer
Composition gold leaf
Water-based size, or adhesive pen
Laser photocopier
Chemical-cartridge respirator mask
Cardboard carton (for spray booth; optional)
Tapered paintbrush
Soft-bristle brush
Cotton gloves
Tweezers
Tape

### Step 1

Size the print.

Enlarge your image, sizing it to fit the front panel of your blank card. Use a laser copier to print a test image on copy paper, fitting it to your card to confirm the size. When you are satisfied, use a laser copier to print the image on the right front panel of the blank card.

### Step 2

Seal the paper.

Work outdoors or in a very well ventilated space and wear a chemical-cartridge respirator mask. Lay the card flat on a protected work surface or in a spray booth. Place a scrap of paper over the left front panel of the card, using short strips of tape to keep the paper from blowing off when you spray. Apply a thin, even coat of acrylic sealer to the front panel of the card. Let the sealer dry.

### Step 3

Draw the leafy garland.

Use a pencil to sketch two slender branches with leaves on the girl's head to resemble a garland.

### Step 4

Apply the size.

Use a tapered paintbrush to apply a thin coat of size to the pencil sketch, filling in the leaves and drawing the stem. Allow 15 to 30 minutes for the size to reach tack.

### Step 5

Tear the leaf into small pieces.

Put on cotton gloves. Working in a room without any air currents, remove a sheet of metal leaf from the book and place it on a protected work surface. Use your fingers to tear the leaf into small, postage-stamp-size pieces.

### Step 6

Apply the leaf to the garland.

Use tweezers to carry a piece of leaf to the card and place it on the sized surface. Use the handle of the tapered brush to tamp the leaf in place. Use tweezers to pick up another piece of leaf and place it on the sized surface, overlapping the leaf already laid. Use the handle of the brush to tamp down the new piece of leaf. Continue to position and overlap pieces of metal leaf until the leafy garland is concealed. Lay a sheet of orange paper from the book of gold leaf over the leafed surface and smooth all of the pieces of leaf so they adhere. Let the size dry overnight.

**Step 7**

Remove the excess gold leaf.

Use a dry soft-bristle brush to gently sweep off the excess pieces of leaf (called *skewings*) and save them in an envelope for another project.

---

## Working Tips: Metal Leafing on Paper

Gilding paper is virtually the same as gilding other porous surfaces (see Chapter Six), with a few caveats. Small designs and motifs are more suitable than large surfaces. The paper must be sturdy enough to support the adhesive size and the metal leaf that is applied to it. Cardstock is the ideal paper weight, but thinner papers can be leafed if they are first sealed or laminated to another sheet of paper to strengthen them. Use water-based rather than oil-based size to avoid staining the paper.

---

## Technique: Making Paint-Chip Polka Dots

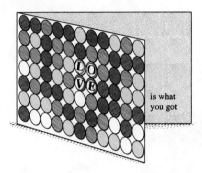

Polka dots in subtle pastels can be punched from paint samples and placed in a simple grid. You can find an array of rich colors on paint company brochures. Using colors that are light in value, such as pale pastels, for the polka dot background will set off a design formed in dots cut from a darker color.

### MATERIALS AND TOOLS

Bristol, 13⅞" × 4½" (35.2 × 11.4 cm)
Vellum, 13¾" × 4½" (34.9 × 11.4 cm)
Paint chip samples, in baby pink, lime green, baby blue, and brown
Beading glue
Circle hole punch, ⅝" (1.6 cm) diameter
Steel ruler
Craft knife
Self-healing cutting mat
Bone folder

**Step 1**

Punch out the circles.

Use the hole punch to cut out circle shapes from the paint chip samples. For the heart design, cut 77 assorted pastel circles and 16 medium color circles.

**Step 2**

Glue on the first circle.

Lay the bristol horizontally on a protected work surface. Use beading glue to glue a pastel circle to the bottom right corner of the paper, so that the edge of the circle touches the right and bottom edges of the paper.

**Step 3**

Glue on the remaining circles.

Glue another pastel circle directly above the first one so it touches the first circle and the right edge of the paper. Working from the bottom to the top and from right to left, continue gluing pastel circles to the paper until there are 7 rows and 11 columns. Let the glue dry.

**Step 4**

Glue on circles in a heart shape.

Place 16 medium color circles on top of the grid circles to make a heart outline. Glue the new circles in place. Let the glue dry.

**Step 5**

Fold and trim the card.

Use a ruler and a bone folder to score the edge of the left column of circles. Fold the card along the score line. Use a craft knife and a ruler to trim the card so the front and back panels are the same dimensions.

## Technique: Making Magnified Letters

The look of letters under a transparent dome adds an optical illusion to a greeting card. You can spell out a message or the name of a friend, printing the letters or words you need on a piece of copy paper. When the domes are placed over individual letters, they are magnified, making them easy to read.

**MATERIALS AND TOOLS**

Handmade greeting card
Clear glue-on solid-plastic domes with flat backs, 14 mm diameter
Beading glue
Computer with printer
Manicure scissors

**Step 1**

Print out the letters.

Use a computer to type the letters for a word or short message, keeping the letters five spaces apart. Experiment with different fonts and styles to get the look you want (I typed *love* in Times New Roman, bold, point size 26). Make a laser print of your final version.

**Step 2**

Glue on the domes.

Lay the printout on your work surface. Center one dome over each letter, which will magnify it, and secure the dome to the paper with a dab of glue. Let the glue dry completely.

**Step 3**

Cut out the domed letters.

Use manicure scissors to trim the excess paper from around each dome.

**Step 4**

Glue the letters to the card.

Glue each domed letter to the greeting card to spell your message.

## Photo Transfer and Printing

Using modern technology to make multiple prints of your favorite images on greeting cards, informal notes, and postcards is easy and affordable. A computer scanner and printer (either ink-jet or laser) or even an old-fashioned photocopier can help you reproduce fine images that can be printed directly on your own choice of paper or on printable cards you can buy.

You can use a scanner to convert any

printed picture into a digital file that you can store in your computer and print at a later time. There are two kinds of printers, either of which make beautiful reproductions: an ink-jet printer, which lays down drops of ink, and a color laser printer, which lays down powdered toner that needs heat to set. A photocopier can also be used to reproduce and print your images. Even the least sophisticated printer can resize your images, adjust tonal quality, and make multiple prints.

A scanner and printer or a photocopier can be used to print images onto almost any paper, but papers of high quality will give you richer color and better ink retention and will be preserved longer. Always use papers that are coated for an ink-jet or a laser printer for good results. Specialty papers can be fed through a printer or copier as long as the machines can adjust for paper thickness. Cardstock, laminated silk, vellum, and photo transfer paper are just a few of the papers that will provide unique effects. I recommend that you experiment with different images and settings to see what effects you can achieve. Photo transfer paper, for example, allows you to bond an image to a sheet of rag stock paper. I love transferring old family photos to cream-colored stock for both aesthetic and practical reasons. As with all reproduction processes, this technique allows you to make use of your valuable old photographs without subjecting them to processes or products that can destroy them.

Hand-printing methods can also be used to create greeting cards and invitations. For a very special occasion, such as a wedding or a birthday dinner, you may wish to use a fine engraving for the decorative image on the card. The photo emulsion method allows you to capture such fine detail on a screen, which is used to print. Images can be screen-printed on separate sheets of paper and then trimmed and dry-mounted on blank cards (see Chapter Four for more on this technique).

## Technique: Making Multiple Prints from Original Art

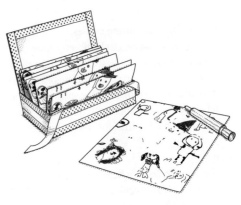

The easiest way to make multiples of children's artwork is to use a photocopier or a computer scanner and printer. Even a child can get involved in the joy of creating personal stationery using original drawings.

### MATERIALS AND TOOLS
Child's original line drawings
Sheets of white copy paper, 8½" × 11" (21.6 × 27.9 cm)
Business-size envelopes
Cigar box with attached lid
Stickers and ribbon
Markers, colored pencils, and watercolor paints (optional)
Photocopier, or computer with scanner and printer
Tracing paper
White craft glue (optional)
Glue stick

### Step 1
Create a composite of your child's illustrations.

Use a computer scanner or copier to resize the individual illustrations so that you can fit six to eight on a single sheet of copy paper. Cut out the copies and arrange them on a sheet of copy paper. Lay a sheet of tracing paper over them and secure it with dabs of glue from a glue stick to keep the paper from shifting.

### Step 2

Print the sheets of copy paper.

Place the master design, tracing paper facedown, on the bed of a photocopier or scanner and make a test print. The tracing paper will lighten the intensity of the drawings so that they can become a background design on the stationery. Print as many copies of the master design as desired on sheets of copy paper.

### Step 3

Decorate a recycled box.

Decorate the cigar box with stickers and lengths of ribbon. Store the stationery and the envelopes inside the box until ready to use.

## Technique: Making a Photo Transfer

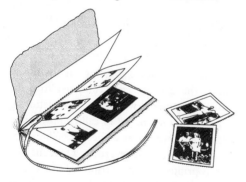

Original photographs, especially those of years long gone, provide unique glimpses of a family's heritage. Too fragile to use directly on a card, old photographs can be reproduced using a photo transfer technique. Photo transfer paper is usually used to transfer artwork to fabric; however, in this application it is used to transfer artwork to paper. Note that this technique causes the original image to print in reverse, which will make letters and numerals appear backward. To ensure the correct orientation of the type, work from a mirror image photocopy of the photograph instead of the original.

### MATERIALS AND TOOLS

Paper with high rag content, in ivory
Sheet of copy paper, 8½" × 11"
 (21.6 × 27.9 cm)
Photographs, black-and-white or color
Photo transfer paper designed for white cloth
Computer with scanner and ink-jet printer
Steel ruler
Craft knife
Self-healing cutting mat
Household iron
Flat-weave cotton fabric (such as an old pillowcase)
Glue stick

### Step 1

Lay out the photographs.

Sort through your photographs and arrange your favorites on a sheet of copy paper, fitting as many as you can without overlapping to avoid wasting transfer paper. Secure the photos with a scant dab of a glue stick.

### Step 2

Make a printout onto transfer paper.

Place the photo transfer paper grid side up in the paper tray of the ink-jet printer. Place the sheet with the photos facedown on the scanner bed. Scan the images and make one copy on the photo transfer paper. Allow the printout to dry for 30 minutes.

**Step 3**

Cut out the prints.

Lay the photo transfer sheet on a cutting mat. Use a ruler and a craft knife to cut out each photograph, trimming it to the desired size.

**Step 4**

Transfer the prints.

Empty the iron of all water and preheat to high. Place several layers of fabric (or a pillowcase folded once) on a flat, hard, heat-resistant surface. Lay the ivory paper on top.

Position a trimmed photo transfer facedown on the ivory paper. Lightly touch your fingertips to one corner of the photo transfer to prevent shifting as you place the tip of the iron on another corner to start the transfer process. Press the paper for 60 to 90 seconds, moving the iron constantly and in overlapping passes and concentrating on the corners and the edges. Do not remove the paper backing. Let the image cool. Repeat to transfer additional images.

**Step 5**

Peel off the backing paper to reveal the transferred image.

Use the tip of a craft knife to carefully pry up one corner of the paper backing; then use your fingers to peel off the paper backing in one continuous motion to reveal the transferred image. Repeat for each image.

## Working Tips: Transferring Photos

- Always use a dry iron set to the highest temperature to transfer the image.
- Iron on a flat, hard, heat-resistant surface covered with a flat, evenly woven fabric, such as a folded pillowcase or a sheet. Avoid uneven surfaces, which can keep the iron from coming into contact with some part of the transfer, resulting in a partial print.
- If you plan to transfer more than one print to the same sheet of good paper, keep the backing papers on to protect the transfers until all the prints are made. Transfers that are not protected may melt and gum up your iron.
- Let the paper cool completely before peeling off the backing sheet to avoid a partial or wrinkled print.

## Technique: Printing a Greeting on an Insert Folio

When you make a folded card, it is traditional to include a greeting on the inside panel. You can use your computer to compose a sentiment with decorative lettering (simulating the fine art of calligraphy, if you desire) and print it on a sheet of vellum that is hand-fed into a laser printer. Once the vellum is printed, it can be trimmed to size and tipped, or glued, into the card along the center fold. The size of the vellum should be slightly smaller than the size of the card so that the edges of the vellum do not extend beyond the edges of the card when the card is folded flat. This technique makes a tip-in for one panel of a card. Another option is to set your printer software to landscape and print a message on a sheet of vellum that is large enough to span the width of the open card. The vellum can be folded and glued along the inside fold of the card, or it can be held in place with a length of narrow ribbon that is wrapped around the fold of the card and tied on the outside for a pretty accent.

## MATERIALS AND TOOLS
  Folded card
  Sheet of vellum
  Ribbon
  Computer with laser printer
  Copy paper
  Steel ruler
  Craft knife
  Self-healing cutting mat

### Step 1
Compose your greeting.

Select a pleasing typeface and use it to type a greeting on your computer. Line up the text on the right-hand side of the page. When you are pleased with your layout, make a test print on plain copy paper.

### Step 2
Print the inside folio.

Print the greeting on vellum by hand-feeding the paper into the laser printer. Let the ink dry.

### Step 3
Trim the folio.

Working on a cutting mat, use a steel ruler and a craft knife to trim the printed vellum so that it is slightly smaller than the right inside panel of the card. Open the card and lay it flat. Use a scant dab of glue to secure the left edge of the vellum tip-in alongside the fold in the card.

### Step 4
Add a decorative ribbon.

Lay a ribbon in the center fold. Bring the ends of the ribbon around the fold to the outside of the card and tie a bow or a square knot. Let the ribbon ends cascade down.

## Gift Packages

Gift packages can be wrapped to rival the excitement of the gift inside. Whether you are wrapping a small box with paper or adding a handmade decoration to an unwrapped gift box, making original gift wrap is easy, regardless of your previous craft experience.

### Gift-Wrapping Paper

Although there are many beautiful wrapping papers to buy, it is nice to wrap a gift in a sheet of paper you have decorated yourself. (You can also avoid a last-minute dash to a store when you know a few artistic tricks for making your own wrapping paper.) Making an overall, random design is easy. Just unfurl a length of kraft, shelf, or butcher paper and decorate a length that wraps around your box. Kraft paper is a soft brown color, uncoated, and very absorbent; shelf paper is white and coated on one side; butcher paper comes in the largest continuous white sheet and is coated on one side. All three papers are utilitarian on their own, but adding decoration or metallic luster will raise the glamour index. Choose a paper that will make a good background for the decoration you plan to add and be sure to adapt the size and scale of your printed pattern to the size and scale of your gift package.

### Quick & Easy Technique: Shining Stars Gift Wrap
  White butcher paper
  Rubber stamp with a star image
  Ink pad with metallic silver ink

Use a rubber stamp to print metallic silver stars on a piece of white butcher paper. Let the ink dry. Perfect for the holidays or anytime you want to add sparkle to paper.

### Quick & Easy Technique: Fruit Cocktail Gift Wrap
  White butcher paper or shelf paper
  Acrylic craft paint in orange, red,
    and turquoise
  Fresh citrus fruit, such as lemon, orange,
    and grapefruit, cut in half
  Watercolor paintbrush
  3 old dinner plates
  Paper towels

Pour each color of acrylic craft paint onto a separate plate. Use a watercolor paintbrush to mix the paint until there is a smooth coating on the plate. Press a half lemon onto a paper towel to blot the excess moisture and then press its surface onto the paint on one plate, coating it evenly. Use the lemon to print a sparse overall pattern on a length of white butcher paper. Repeat to print with the orange and the grapefruit, changing the paint color each time. Let the paint dry completely. Fruit Cocktail is the perfect paper design for year-round gift giving.

## Quick & Easy Technique: Gold Rush Gift Wrap

Kraft paper
Sheet of clear cellophane
Composition gold leaf
Spray adhesive
Chemical-cartridge respirator mask

Work outdoors on a calm day and wear a chemical-cartridge respirator mask. Apply a thin coat of spray adhesive to the surface of brown kraft paper. Crumple sheets of composition gold leaf onto the surface of the paper. Lay a sheet of cellophane over the gilded paper and smooth the layers together using your hands. The flakes of composition gold leaf covered in shimmering cellophane makes for a glamorous presentation year-round.

## Quick & Easy Technique: Glitter Scribbles Gift Wrap

Kraft paper
Fine glitter in three different colors
Specialty white glue designed for glitter

Use the nozzle on the bottle of glue to draw a series of parallel squiggles and individual coil shapes on a sheet of brown kraft paper. Sprinkle fine glitter in different colors over the wet glue, being careful to establish a broad swath of each color glitter; let the glue dry completely. Pour the excess glitter into one container as the colors will have blended. Use this festive paper to wrap a New Year's gift.

## Quick & Easy Technique: Triangles Gift Wrap

White butcher paper or shelf paper
Acrylic craft paint in orange and robin's-
egg blue, or colors as desired
Watercolor paintbrush
Large household sponge
2 saucers
Scissors

Pour each color of acrylic craft paint onto a separate saucer. Use a watercolor paintbrush to mix the paint until there is a smooth coating on the saucer. Use scissors to cut the sponge into three or four triangle shapes in different sizes. Press one triangle onto one color paint and print a sparse overall pattern on a length of white butcher paper. Repeat with a different triangle to print the second color. Use this cheerful geometric pattern to wrap a child's birthday gift.

## Quick & Easy Technique: Fern Print Gift Wrap

Kraft paper
Acrylic printer's ink in hunter green
Several fresh ferns or large leaves
Brayer (or household sponge)

Lay a fresh fern on a protected work surface. Use a brayer to apply a thin coat of acrylic printer's ink to one side. Lift the fern by the stem and press it, paint side down, onto the kraft paper. Repeat to make an overall pattern. Let the paint dry. The neutral brown and green tones are suited to informal occasions.

Wrapping a Gift

Wrapping a gift is easy when the package has straight, flat sides; any other shape, especially one with a rounded contour, will challenge your creativity. If stuck, place a plump gift in a box and follow the straightforward and easy directions for wrapping a box. Once you feel comfortable with the basic folding technique, consider pleating the paper before wrapping and taping the paper to the box. Experiment with small packages first.

## Technique: Wrapping a Gift Box

Gift wrap is sold as large single sheets, in prepackaged folded sheets, and by the roll. All these packaging formats provide gift wrap that can be used to wrap a box, but gift wrap on rolls may be the only option for large gift boxes. Use the sequence of steps detailed here to wrap any rectilinear box—from a cube-shaped box to a shirt box to a flat square. Test-fit the paper to make sure it is ample enough to wrap around the gift before proceeding to fold and tape the flaps.

### MATERIALS AND TOOLS
Gift wrap
Double-sided cellophane tape
Scissors

**Step 1**
Position the gift box on the paper.

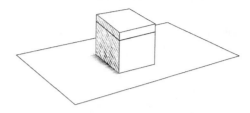

Lay the gift wrap wrong side up on a flat work surface. Invert the gift box and center it on the paper. Lift the paper around the box to make certain the paper is large enough to conceal the box with some overlap.

**Step 2**
Fold up the sides of paper.

Bring one side of the paper around and on top of the box. Use a strip of double-sided tape to secure the paper's edge to the box. Fold up a narrow hem on the other long side. Bring the hemmed side of the paper around the box and pull the paper taut. Use tape to secure the edge to the gift wrap.

**Step 3**
Fold the top flap.

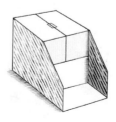

With the box still inverted, fold down the top flap at one end of the box, using the edge of the box to guide the crease.

## Step 4
Fold the side flaps.

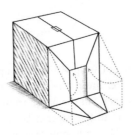

Fold in the sides, using the edges of the box to guide the creases.

## Step 5
Make a hem.

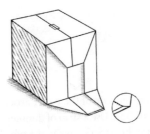

Fold up a narrow hem along the cut edge of the bottom flap for a neat finish.

## Step 6
Fold the bottom flap.

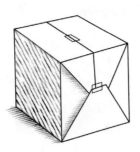

Fold up the whole bottom flap and use tape to secure the folded paper to the gift wrap on the box.

## Step 7
Fold the flaps on the opposite side.
Repeat steps 3–6 to fold and seal the other end of the box.

### Bows, Gift Tags, and More

After a gift box is wrapped in paper, it generally receives the further adornment of a ribbon bow and gift tag. Gift-wrapping ribbon is available in a variety of textiles, both natural and synthetic, in widths ranging from ⅛" (0.3 cm) to 4" (10.2 cm). The array of prints, patterns, and colors is virtually limitless. When choosing ribbon, be guided by your imagination and your budget.

Tying a simple shoelace bow (the first bow we learned) is easy, but you can quickly graduate to a more exuberant multiloop bow with cascading streamers. The technique for a multiloop bow is based on folding a length of ribbon back on itself. It is important to use

### Working Tips: Ribbon Width and Loop Sizes

The ribbon width will affect the number and length of loops needed for a beautiful bow. As a rule of thumb, the wider the ribbon, the greater the number and size of the loops required to make a bow with good proportions; conversely, the narrower the ribbon, the smaller the size and fewer the number of loops. The key is to avoid loops that look floppy or skimpy.

double-faced ribbon—ribbon made to be seen from both sides—so your loops don't look inside out.

The featured bow has six loops that are made by laying a length of ribbon on a flat surface and doubling back to form the first loop and one of the two streamers. More loops are formed in the same way until all of the ribbon is used. The stack of loops is tied at the center with a separate length of ribbon, adding two more ribbon streamers. The ends of the streamers are notched for a decorative finish.

## Technique: Tying a Multiloop Ribbon Bow

Generally speaking, a bow with four to eight full loops is attractive on a large box. When small boxes are beribboned, the span of the loops and the width of the ribbon should naturally be smaller and narrower. This bow has six loops and four streamers.

### MATERIALS AND TOOLS
3⅓ yards (3.0 m) wire-edged ribbon,
  2" (5.1 cm) wide
Ruler
Scissors

### Step 1
Cut and notch the ribbon tie.

Cut a 24" (61.0 cm) length of ribbon. Fold one end in half lengthwise and make a diagonal cut across the ribbon, angling the scissors toward the fold to make a notch. Repeat at the opposite end; set the tie aside.

### Step 2
Make a six-loop bow.

Locate a point approximately 12" (30.5 cm) from one end of the remaining ribbon and press one finger on that point. Extend the ribbon 6" (15.2 cm) beyond that point, and then fold the ribbon back on itself, pressing your finger on the ribbon to hold the loop in place. Extend the ribbon 6" (15.2 cm) in the other direction,

---

## Quick & Easy: Cutting a Notch on the End of a Ribbon

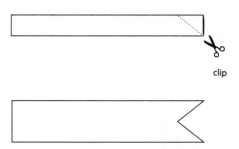

clip

Lay the ribbon flat on a work surface. Fold the end of the ribbon in half lengthwise, smoothing the fold with your hand. Use scissors to cut the ribbon end on a diagonal toward the fold. To prevent the ribbon's edge from raveling, use your finger to apply a scant film of liquid fray preventer on the cut edge of the ribbon and allow it to dry before handling the ribbon further.

and then fold the ribbon back on itself, coming back to first point and pressing your finger down to hold the loop in place. Continue to go back and forth across that point accordion-style to make six 6" (15.2 cm) loops, three on each side. Use your hand to hold the stack of ribbon at the center of the loopy bow, making sure there is a ribbon streamer on both sides of the stack of loops. Squeeze the center of the stack to crimp the ribbon loops.

**Step 3**
Tie the streamer around the bow.

Wrap the ribbon streamer cut in step 1 once around the center of the bow, tying it to secure the six-loop bow.

## Technique: Making a Gift Tag

A gift tag is generally made from medium-weight paper, such as cardstock. The tag can be a rectangle with angled corners, a square, or a shape cut from a pattern. To make a rectilinear tag, you will need a steel ruler, a craft

knife, and a cutting mat. You can cut multiple gift tags from one sheet of paper. A gift tag can be suspended from a length of string sewn directly through the paper or from a length of ribbon threaded through a punched hole.

### MATERIALS AND TOOLS
Sheet of cardstock, 8½" × 11" (21.6 × 27.9 cm)
2¼ yards (2.1 m) satin ribbon, ⅜" (1.0 cm) wide
Steel ruler
Craft knife
Self-healing cutting mat
Hole punch, ¼" (0.6 cm) diameter
Scissors

**Step 1**
Cut the gift tags.

Lay the sheet of cardstock on the cutting mat. Use a ruler and a craft knife to cut eight 2½" × 3½" (6.4 × 8.9 cm) rectangles from the cardstock.

**Step 2**
Trim the top corners of the tag and punch a hole.

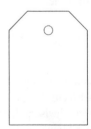

Use a craft knife and a steel ruler to cut away the top left and top right corners of each tag. Use a hole punch to make a hole in the center of the top of each tag ½" (1.3 cm) from the top edge.

### Step 3

Decorate the gift tags.

Add a design to the tag; refer to the Quick & Easy Techniques (this page to page 252) or create a design of your own.

### Step 4

Add the ribbon ties.

Use scissors to cut the ribbon into eight equal lengths. Attach a ribbon to each tag, making a cowslip knot or a ribbon bow (see pages 250 and 252).

Adding decoration to a gift can be as simple as tying on a ribbon and a handmade gift tag. All of the featured gift tags use scraps of material—from fabric and wire to gold leaf, plastic buttons, and magazine illustrations. Use a collage approach to design your own little tableaux. Keep a supply of blank gift tags on hand to embellish gifts as the occasion arises. Each sheet of cardstock is large enough to fit five tags.

## Quick & Easy Technique: Wet Paint Gift Tag

Gift tag with ribbon tie
Scrap of blue plastic
Scrap of cardstock
White craft glue
Marker

Use a marker to draw a freehand illustration of a paintbrush on the top left corner of the tag. Cut a piece of transparent blue plastic in the shape of a sweeping brush mark of paint. Glue it over the bristles of the brush and the card, extending the sweep of plastic beyond the edge of the tag. Make a little "wet paint" sign out of scrap paper and glue it to the tag. Let the glue dry and then trim the plastic brush mark even with the edge of the card.

## Quick & Easy Technique: Mended Hearts Gift Tag

Gift tag with ribbon tie
Scraps of construction paper and plaid
    fabric
2 small shirt buttons
White craft glue
Sewing machine

Tear the shapes of two hearts and one square from construction paper in different colors. Trim a scrap of plaid fabric to the size of a postage stamp. Use glue to attach the hearts and fabric scrap to the gift tag. Use a sewing machine set to a long stitch to sew over the paper in a loose "scribble." Glue on two small buttons.

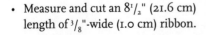

## Quick & Easy: Tying a Cowslip Knot

The way you attach a ribbon to your gift tag can add another element of beauty to your wrapped package. The cowslip knot secures a piece of ribbon to a gift card so that the card can be attached to a gift. All you need is a card-stock tag with a punched hole and a length of narrow ribbon or cord to tie in a pretty knot.

- Measure and cut an $8^1/_2$" (21.6 cm) length of $^3/_8$"-wide (1.0 cm) ribbon.

- Fold the ribbon in half and thread the loop through the hole from the back of the tag.
- Bring the ends of the ribbon around the card and draw them through the loop, pulling the ribbon ends to make a neat, snug knot against the tag.

## Quick & Easy Technique: Coffee Break Gift Tag

Gift tag with ribbon tie
Picture of a cup of coffee (cut from a magazine)
Wire, 22-gauge
Thread
Chain-nose pliers
Needle

Cut out the picture of the cup of coffee. Use chain-nose pliers to shape the word *love* from 22-gauge wire, ending the word in a serpentine shape. Glue the coffee picture to the tag. Use a needle and thread to tack the wire *love* sign perpendicular to the cup. Use a black marker to draw a frame around the card, omitting the bottom edge.

## Quick & Easy Technique: Love and Time Gift Tag

Gift tag with ribbon tie
Pictures of clockfaces (cut from a home goods catalog)
Text blocks (cut from a magazine)
White craft glue
Thread
Small button
Small heart charm
Gold pen
Red marker
Needle

Cut a block of text that is a ¼" (0.6 cm) smaller all around than the gift tag; glue on the text. Cut out pictures of two or three clockfaces and glue them to the tag in a reverse L shape at the bottom right corner. Use a gold pen to write *love* and use a red marker to draw two hearts on opposite sides of the card near the top of the text block. Using a knotted thread, sew through the card just below one clockface, thread on a button, and tack the thread to the card so that the button hangs down like a pendulum; make a second pendulum from a heart charm.

### Quick & Easy Technique:
### Golden Pears Gift Tag

Gift tag with ribbon tie
Scraps of cardstock
Picture of pears (rubber-stamped image or
    cut from a magazine)
Composition gold leaf
Acrylic size

Apply size to one side of the gift tag and let it reach tack. Apply small pieces of composition gold leaf to the size, concealing the tag completely; let the size dry. Cut a large square of cardstock and a slightly smaller square of construction paper; center and glue the smaller square to the larger one. Cut out the pear image and center and glue it on top of the construction paper.

## Quick & Easy: Tying a Ribbon Bow on a Gift Tag

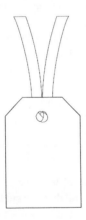

A ribbon bow is a traditional way to accent a gift card that is glued to a gift. Make a gift tag with a hole punched in the top center.

- Measure and cut an $8^{1}/_{2}$" (21.6 cm) length of $^{3}/_{8}$"-wide (1.0 cm) ribbon.
- Fold the ribbon in half and make a knot at the center point.

- Thread both cut ends through the hole from the back of the tag and pull until the knot rests on the back of the tag.
- Tie the ribbon ends into a neat bow that rests on the front of the tag.

## Making Paper Flowers

A beautiful variety of paper flowers can be cut and shaped by hand to resemble flowers found in nature. Paper flowers are made by wiring petals and a floral center, called a stamen, to a stem or stalk made of stiff wire. The petals can be wired to the stamen one at a time (which can add bulk) or they can be attached to a length of wire that is wrapped around a stamen already attached to a wire stem; they can also be made in a continuous strip of paper that has petal tips cut along the top edge and that is wrapped around a stamen. Although paper flowers will always look artificial, no matter how artfully they are made, even those that are graphic and stiff can add style and beauty when attached to gift packages, wired together to make garlands and wreaths, or adhered to place cards and napkin rings for table settings.

Choice of paper is key to making a flower that closely resembles its natural counterpart. The paper should be malleable enough to replicate the characteristics of the main components (the petals and leaves). Crepe paper can be used to make most flowers. It has natural stretch, texture, and malleability and is especially suited to flowers with sculptural characteristics, such as the contoured petals and rolled edges of roses. However, some caution is needed. Saturating crepe paper with glue will permanently stain it and may cause the paper to fall apart; to avoid discoloration, especially when gluing a length of wrapped or thread-covered wire to a leaf, apply a thin film of glue to the wire and then press it onto the crepe paper.

Another option is tissue paper. Lightweight and translucent, it is suited to delicate flowers like narcissus, lily of the valley, and snowdrops; however, tissue paper is fragile—it can tear and fall apart when exposed to moisture, so it needs careful handling. Another, albeit nontraditional, choice is plain white copy paper. Its opacity and stiffness produce crisp cut edges, and its smooth texture is suitable for flowers with spiky flower heads, such as asters, inulas, and spider mums, that highlight, rather than disguise, the paper's inherent qualities. I like using copy paper to make all-white arrangements of flowers for gift boxes wrapped in white paper. The effect is graphic, clean, and sculptural.

No matter what paper you choose, you will need to prepare four basic parts for each flower: the petals, the center stamen, the leaves, and the stem or stalk. The petals are the most prominent feature; their shape, size, color, and texture define the silhouette and identify the flower. For example, a daisy has long petals with rounded tips that radiate from a button-shaped stamen; a chrysanthemum has short pointed petals so tightly clustered around the stamen that the stamen appears to be part of the flower; a lily has softly arching petals that reveal prominent "anther-and-filament" stamens; a poppy has cup-shaped petals around a stamen that looks like a combination of a button stamen and

---

## Working Tips: Using the Grain of Crepe Paper to Advantage

Crepe paper has a grain that can help you shape the parts of the flower more realistically. On the Rose Petal pattern (page 689), you will notice a line with an arrow at each end to indicate the grain direction. To cut this petal from crepe paper, lay the pattern on the paper so that the grain line on the pattern matches the visible vertical grain line in the crepe paper. When the petal piece is oriented in this way, you will be able to stretch the paper petal across the grain to give it a soft bowl-shaped contour.

---

anther-and-filament stamens; a gardenia has petals with edges that are rolled toward the center of the flower and that fall away from a bud-shaped stamen; a rose has bowl-shaped petals that hug the bud-shaped stamen and then curl out at the edges.

Although there are several methods for making flowers, two methods are featured here: the wired strand of single petals and the continuous strip of petals. For flowers with large individual petals, such as anemones, roses, gardenias, and poppies, I use a pattern to make individual petals, add them one petal at a time to a length of wire, and then wrap the wired petals around the center stamen. For flowers with a full head of closely packed petals, such as daisies, asters, chrysanthemums, and carnations, I make a paper strip of continuous petals that is the full height of the flower and cut the top edge in the shape of the petal tips; the strip is wrapped around the center stamen and secured with a dab of glue or, for a thicker wrap and more security, a length of fine wire that is later concealed with floral tape.

There are many styles of stamens, depending upon the kind of flower. Featured here are the button, the bud, the brush, the anther-and-filament, and a combination button and anther-and-filament. Premade stamens are also an option; they come in a variety of sizes and lengths, most of them resembling skinny wires with grain-shaped heads.

Each of the featured stamens is matched with a particular kind of flower. All of the components of the flowers are made in crepe paper, although the flowers can also be made in tissue paper and copy paper, according to the look you want. You do not have to make an exact replica of a real flower. Experiment with other kinds of paper—velveteen, rice paper, metallic paper, and gift wrap—to see how the paper alters the character of the flower. Use your imagination to create fantasy flowers, such as an oversized crepe paper rose.

Flower stems or stalks can be made from stiff precut lengths of wire that are already wrapped with thread or that can be wrapped with floral tape. Stems can also be made from paddle wire that is cut to a desired length and wrapped with floral tape. Most floral stems have leaves of some kind, which can be cut from crepe paper and wired directly to the floral stem. Paper leaves can be supported with wire so that the leaf can be bent or a twisted in a way that resembles the movement of a leaf found in nature. A few basic leaf shapes are included here, but there are many others with unique silhouettes. Study the shape and contour of the natural leaves found on flowers and make paper versions by using the actual leaf as a template.

## Working Tips: Choosing Wire

You will need two different gauges of wire for your paper flowers: thick wire, from 14- to 18-gauge (the lower the number, the thicker the wire), and thinner wire, from 20- to 26-gauge (the higher the number, the thinner the wire). The thick wire is used to form the stem of the flower, which must be stiff enough to support the flower head without bending (unless drooping is an effect you want). The thin wire is used to attach the petals, leaves, and stamens to the main stem without adding bulk and to form spines on the leaves so that they can be articulated into natural-looking bends and twists. Stem wire can be purchased in precut lengths or by the spool. Thread-wrapped stem wire is nonabrasive to paper and its soft green color blends well with the green of the foliage. Painted stem wire should be wrapped with floral tape to blend nicely with the natural elements of the flower and also to provide a nonslip surface so the added elements stay where you place them.

## Making Stamens for Different Flowers

There are several basic styles of flowers featured here, and each corresponds to a particular kind of flower. The names I've given the stamens are descriptive, not scientific. In nature, stamens are more complex; as you examine real flowers, you will be able to create versions that more accurately represent them.

### GENERAL MATERIALS AND TOOLS

Stem wire wrapped with floral tape or
thread
Fine-gauge spool wire
Floral tape
White craft glue (optional)
Wire cutters
Scissors

### Technique: Making a Button Stamen for a Daisy

### ADDITIONAL MATERIALS AND TOOLS

Crepe paper, in yellow or another color,
as desired
Cotton or polyester fiberfill

**Step 1**

Make a cotton bun and cut the crepe paper.

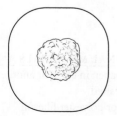

Place a small bun of cotton in your palms and roll it into a ball. Rough-cut a 2½"-diameter (6.4 cm) circle of crepe paper. Place the cotton ball in the center.

**Step 2**

Form the button stamen.

Gather and pinch the paper ends together, trapping the cotton ball and forming a dome-shaped button. Wrap a length of fine wire around the gathered paper, leaving a 2" (5.1 cm) tail.

**Step 3**

Attach the button stamen to the floral stem.

Lay the button stamen against the end of a length of stem wire and wrap the excess wire around the stem. Use floral tape to conceal the binding.

## Technique: Making an Anther-and-Filament Stamen for a Lily

ADDITIONAL MATERIALS AND TOOLS

Crepe paper, in black or another color, as
desired

**Step 1**

Cut and twist the paper strips.

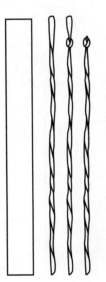

Cut a ⅜" × 3½" (1.0 × 8.9 cm) strip of crepe
paper along the grain; twist the strip into a
tight stick, tie a knot at one end, and trim off
the knot's paper tail. Repeat to make several
more twisted sticks.

**Step 2**

Bind the twisted sticks together to make a
stamen.

Hold the twisted sticks in one hand and
wrap fine wire around the bottom ends,
leaving a 2" (5.1 cm) tail of wire.

**Step 3**

Attach the stamen to the floral stem.

Place the stamen against the end of a length
of stem wire and wrap the excess wire around
the stem. Wrap with floral tape to conceal the
binding.

## Technique: Making a Combination Button and Anther-and-Filament Stamen for a Poppy

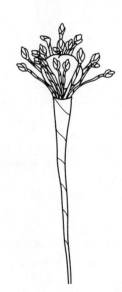

ADDITIONAL MATERIALS AND TOOLS

Crepe paper, in black or another color,
as desired

Cotton or polyester fiberfill

**Step 1**

Make a button stamen.

Make a button stamen and attach it to the end of a length of stem wire.

**Step 2**

Make 25 twisted sticks.

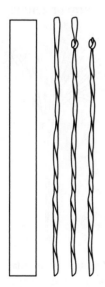

Cut 25 strips of crepe paper along the grain, each ⅜" × 3½" (1.0 × 8.9 cm). Twist each strip into a tight stick and tie a knot at one end.

**Step 3**

Combine the button stamen and twisted sticks.

Hold the button stamen in one hand and gather the twisted sticks around it, distributing them evenly and allowing the knots to extend slightly above the button stamen. Use wire to bind the knotted stamens to the base of the button stamen, leaving a 2" (5.1 cm) tail of wire. Trim the ends of the stamens. Then use floral tape to conceal the binding.

**Technique: Making a Bud Stamen for a Gardenia or a Rose**

ADDITIONAL MATERIALS AND TOOLS
Crepe paper, in white or another color,
  as desired
Cotton or polyester fiberfill
White craft glue

**Step 1**

Cut a square of crepe paper and line it with fiberfill.

Rough-cut a 2½" (6.4 cm) square of crepe paper. Place a very thin layer of cotton or fiberfill on the square.

**Step 2**

Fold the lined crepe paper.

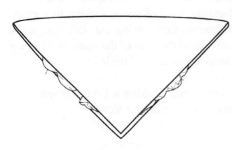

Fold the square in half to form a triangle, pressing the fold flat.

**Step 3**

Shape the bud stamen.

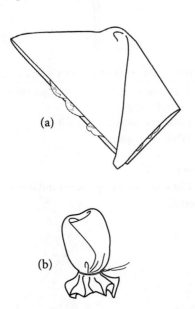

(a)

(b)

Fold over each side of the triangle (a). Pinch the paper ends together to form a bud and secure the ends with wire (b).

**Step 4**

Add the stem.

Place the bud against the end of a length of stem wire and wrap the excess wire around the stem. Use floral tape to conceal the binding.

## Technique: Making a Long Brush-Style Stamen for a Chrysanthemum or Zinnia

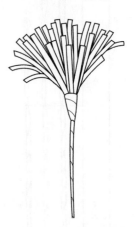

A brush stamen can be made in any size. The long style is suited to larger flowers, such as chrysanthemums. The short style is suited to smaller flowers, such as zinnias. Here the stamen is made in a long style.

ADDITIONAL MATERIALS AND TOOLS
Crepe paper, in magenta, orange,
or another color, as desired

**Step 1**

Make deep cuts that run parallel to the grain of a wide strip of crepe paper.

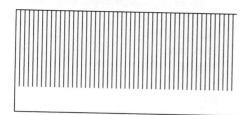

Cut a 2½" × 10" (6.4 × 25.4 cm) piece of crepe paper. Snip deep parallel cuts into the top edge of the strip at ⅛" (0.3 cm) intervals to make fringe along the full length of the strip. Repeat on a second strip of paper for a fuller stamen, if desired.

**Step 2**

Roll the strip into a brush.

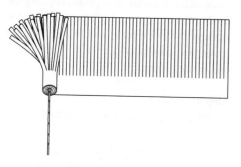

Use your finger to apply a scant dab of glue along one end of the strip and press it to one end of the stem wire. Roll the paper strip around the stem wire to make a snug tube-shaped brush. Apply a scant dab of glue at the overlap to secure the strip. Add a second strip for more fullness, if desired. Then wrap a piece of fine wire around the base of the paper tube, leaving a 2" (5.1 cm) tail of wire.

**Step 3**

Attach the stamen to the floral stem.

Place the stamen against the end of a length of stem wire and wrap the excess wire around the stem. Use floral tape to conceal the wire binding.

**Step 4 (optional)**

Trim the stamen.

Use the tips of the scissors to snip the top of the stamen so that it resembles a spiky brush.

## Making Flowers

A flower can be made by one of two methods. One way is to cut a long strip of paper into continuous petals and wrap it around a stamen. The other way is to cut individual petals, wire them into a continuous strand, and wrap the strand around the base of a stamen. In both cases, the stem wire to which the petals are attached is concealed with floral tape to provide a nonslip surface.

### Continuous-Petal Flowers

The construction method behind this style of flower is to cut a strip of paper, snip the top edge of the strip into the shape of the petals, and then wrap the strip around a stamen that is already attached to a stem wire.

## Quick & Easy: Making a Short Brush-Style Stamen

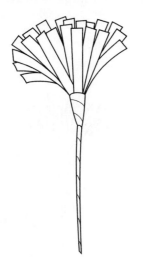

Cut a 1¹/₄" × 10" (3.2 × 25.4 cm) rectangle from crepe paper. Follow steps 1–3 for making a long brush-style stamen. Omit the trimming described in step 4; instead, leave the tips of the stamen straight.

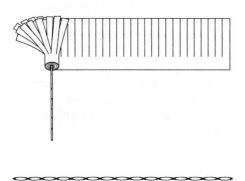

## Technique: Universal Method for Continuous-Petal Flowers

### MATERIALS AND TOOLS
Flower pattern, as desired (page 686)
Crepe paper, in desired color
Prepared stamen on floral stem wire,
   14- to 18-gauge, wrapped with thread
   or floral tape
Fine-gauge wire
Floral tape
White craft glue

### Step 1
Cut a continuous strip of paper petals.

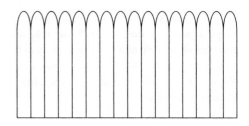

Use the petal pattern to make two or three strips of continuous petals, aligning the double-tipped arrow on the pattern with the grain of the crepe paper and being careful to make neat cuts around the tips of the petals and between them.

### Step 2
Wrap the petals around the stamen.

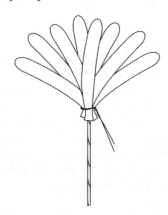

Wrap one continuous strip of petals around the base of the stamen, pleating the straight edge of the paper to keep the petals radiating out and flat against the stamen's base; use a scant dab of glue to secure the end where it overlaps the wrap.

### Step 3 (optional)

Add more petals to the flower head.

Repeat step 2 once or twice until the head of the flower is full and the petals are evenly distributed around the stamen.

### Step 4

Secure the petals to the stamen and the stem wire.

Use a length of fine wire to secure the wraps. Conceal the base of the stamen and the full length of the wire using floral tape.

## Technique: Making Daisies, Black-Eyed Susans, and Sunflowers with Button Stamens

Follow the Universal Method for Continuous-Petal Flowers. The daisy flower with its yellow button stamen and white petals represents a basic construction technique that can form the foundation of other kinds of continuous-petal flowers that have a loose fringe of many slender petals, such as black-eyed Susans and sunflowers. Often a change of color is all

that is necessary to create a different kind of flower—for example, changing a daisy's button stamen from yellow to black (or dark brown) and its petals from white to bright yellow to configure the black-eyed Susan. Sometimes a change of size is all that is necessary to create a new kind of flower; for a sunflower, you would simply make a saucer-sized button stamen in medium brown and surround it with a short fringe of orangey-yellow petals. (See patterns for a daisy on page 686.)

## Technique: Making Chrysanthemums, Zinnias, Cornflowers, and Carnations with Brush Stamens

Follow the Universal Method for Continuous-Petal Flowers. The chrysanthemum flower with its orange spikey brush stamen and petals represents a basic construction technique that can form the foundation of other kinds of densely packed continuous-petal flowers with lots of texture, such as zinnias and carnations. Elongating the size of the brush stamen and the petals gives you a spider mum; rolling a short brush stamen and shorter petals makes a zinnia. Snipping into the tips of the petals with straight-blade scissors creates a spike-shaped fringe such as that found on a cornflower; using pinking shears to cut the edges of the continuous petals produces the modified sawtooth profile of a carnation. (See patterns for a chrysanthemum on page 686.)

*Single-Petal Flowers*

The principle behind this construction is to secure individual petals to a length of fine wire and then wrap the wired petals around the base of the stamen. This technique can be used to make gardenias, poppies, and lilies, or other flowers with small, medium, or large petals, such as petunias, tulips, runuculus, and hibiscus.

## Technique: Universal Method for Single-Petal Flowers

Flower pattern, as desired (pages 687–88)
Crepe paper, in desired color
Prepared stamen on floral stem wire,
    14- to 18-gauge, wrapped with thread
    or floral tape
Fine-gauge wire
Floral tape
White craft glue

### Step 1

Cut out the individual petals.

Use the petal pattern to cut out the desired number of petals, aligning the double-tipped arrow on the pattern with the grain of the crepe paper and being careful to make neat cuts around the shape of the petal.

### Step 2

Attach the petals to a length of wire.

Cut a length of fine wire. Gather the end of one petal and wrap the wire around twice,

pulling the wire tight. Repeat to attach the remaining petals, spacing them about ⅜" (1.0 cm) apart at their gathered ends, but allowing the widest part of the petals to overlap slightly.

### Step 3

Secure the length of wired petals to the stamen.

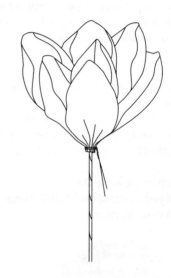

Wrap the wire and the petals around the base of the stamen and twist the wire ends together to secure them. Use floral wrap to conceal the base of the stamen and the wire.

## Technique: Making a Poppy with a Combination Button and Anther-and-Filament Stamen

Follow the Universal Method for Single-Petal Flowers. To suggest the character of the stamen found in the poppy, you can combine the techniques used for making a button stamen and those used to make an anther-and-filament stamen, framing the center button stamen with tall anther-and-filament stalks in black and then surrounding it with delicate petals in scarlet or some other analogous color. This combination of techniques for forming the stamen suggests the value of taking a more careful look at nature's offerings. (See patterns for a poppy on page 687.)

## Technique: Making a Lily with an Anther-and-Filament Stamen

Follow the Universal Method for Single-Petal Flowers. What is remarkable about the lily is the tapered shape and graceful curve of the individual petals juxtaposed with slender stalks of the anther-and-filament stamen that extend above the flower head. By simply changing the size of the petal pattern and the color of the crepe paper used to make the petals, you can make different kinds of flowers, such as tiger lilies and stargazer lilies, which are yellow or deep pink with speckles, and lilies of the Nile, which are pale purple. (See patterns for a lily on page 687.)

## Technique: Making a Gardenia with a Bud Stamen

Follow the Universal Method for Single-Petal Flowers. The single-petal construction technique provides a lot of creative latitude in affixing petals of different sizes to a single stamen. In the gardenia, the size of the individual petals varies within one flower—there are small cup-shaped petals in white near the stamen and larger, more open white petals on the outer ring of petals. By wiring the first collar of small petals, followed by a second collar of larger petals, the flower head looks more natural. (See patterns for a gardenia on page 688.)

### Oversize Crepe Paper Rose

The fun of making an oversize crepe paper rose is imagining the garden in which a rose with a 5½"-diameter (14.0 cm) flower head might grow. Roses of varying sizes can be made simply by changing the size of the Rose Petal pattern (page 689). Consider making roses in different colors and sizes for a lush bouquet or for binding into a garland or onto a wreath frame.

To add body to the petals of an oversize rose, use several layers of crepe paper for each petal. Layering also provides an easy way to make two-tone flowers. If you add a third layer of white crepe paper over a two-layer petal, you can create more subtle pastels. Coordinate the colors so they are close in hue or choose papers in wildly contrasting colors. For example, the petals on a pink rose can be dark pink on the outside and light pink on the inside; or the petals can be wired so the individual petals change from dark to light with dark pink petals positioned as inner petals and light pink petals positioned as outer petals.

When you are cutting individual petals, lay the pattern along the grain of the crepe paper so that the petal can stretch widthwise and bring more natural contour to the rose. When working with a double layer of crepe paper, align the grains so each petal stretches in the same direction. Then add realistic features such as curled edges. In the featured rose, inner petals are curled along the length of their top edges, middle petals are curled on each side to create a pointed tip, and outer petals are curled along the top edge. These details mimic the way roses open up as they bloom.

### Technique: Making an Oversize Crepe Paper Rose

MATERIALS AND TOOLS
Rose Petal pattern (page 689)
Crepe paper, in rose and pink, pink and
    yellow, pale pink and white, or any two
    colors, as desired
Thread-wrapped spool wire, 24-gauge
Floral tape
Cotton or polyester fiberfill
Paper leaf with thread-wrapped wire stem
Wire-edged ribbon, 1½" (3.8 cm) wide, in
    chartreuse or another color, as desired
Wire cutters

Scissors
Pencil

**Step 1**
Cut out the petals.

Photocopy the Rose Petal pattern and cut it out. Unfurl the rolls of crepe paper and lay one color over the other with the grains running vertically. Rough-cut a 5" × 5" (12.7 × 12.7 cm) square through both layers. Lay the pattern on top, matching the grain lines, and trace around the perimeter of the petal with a pencil. Cut on the marked line through both layers. (For faster cutting, try holding the pattern against the paper layers and cutting around the shape without marking). Cut out 10 two-layer petals.

**Step 2**
Curl the top edge of the petal.

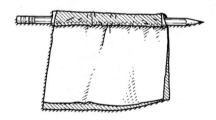

Lay a double-layered petal on a flat surface. Use a pencil to curl the top edge, rolling the paper toward you and around the pencil two or three times. Push the crepe paper toward the center of the pencil to crimp the curl and then slip out the pencil.

**Step 3**

Curl one side edge at the top of the petal.

Hold the pencil at an angle on one side of the curled edge and roll the paper toward you and around the pencil two or three times. Push the crepe paper toward the center of the pencil to crimp the side curl and then slip out the pencil. Repeat for the remaining petals.

**Step 4**

Curl the opposite side edge at the top of the petal.

Repeat step 3 to curl the opposite side edge of the petal, rolling and crimping the paper as before. Slip out the pencil. Repeat for the remaining petals.

**Step 5**

Shape the petals.

Hold a double-layer petal in your hands and use your thumbs to gently stretch the petal to form a bowl shape. For three inner petals, form the bowl shape closer to the upper edge. For four middle petals, form the bowl in the middle of the petal. For three outer petals, form the bowl closer to the base of the petal.

**Step 6**

Make a bud stamen.

Roll a wad of cotton or fiberfill (or crumple a scrap of crepe paper) into a 1"-diameter (2.5 cm) ball. Place the ball in the center of a rough-cut 6" × 6" (15.2 × 15.2 cm) square of crepe paper. Fold the paper on a diagonal to trap the ball, wrapping the side "wings" around the ball to make a tight bud. Wind spool wire around the cut edges of the bud to secure it; do not cut the wire.

**Step 7**

Enclose the bud with petals.

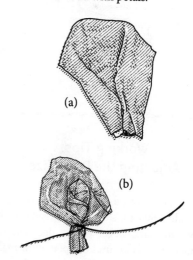

Fold in the sides of a petal at the base so the petal flares at the top (a). Hold the button stamen by the wire, and press the pleats of the petal against the base, allowing the petal to form a cup around the bud (b). Add a second inner petal, overlapping the edge of the first petal and winding the wire around the base of the petals to secure them. Bind on the third inner petal.

**Step 8**

Add the remaining petals.

Continue to bind petals to the bud, positioning larger petals as you go and staggering their placement around the stem. When 10 petals are bound to the center bud, add the leaf and then wrap the wire around the base four more times. Cut the wire. Use floral tape to wrap the base of the rose. Tie a ribbon bow around the stem of the rose.

**Step 9**

Shape the rose.

---

## Working Tips: Adjusting the Petal Size

Rose petals around a center bud tend to be smaller that those on the outside of the flower. To make larger petals, decrease the number of curls around the pencil; to make smaller petals, increase the number of curls.

---

Gently separate the petals of the flower so the rose appears more open. Bend the lower petals down and tighten the curls of any middle petals to highlight the contrasting shapes.

### Making and Attaching Leaves

There are many different leaf shapes that you can make to add realistic detail to your flowers; choose from among the patterns on pages 690–92. Select a leaf shape that naturally grows on the kind of flower you are making or create a leaf in a fantasy style, if you prefer.

### Technique: Making and Attaching a One-Ply Leaf

MATERIALS AND TOOLS

Leaf pattern (pages 690–92)
Crepe paper, in green or another color, as desired
Prepared floral stem
Medium-gauge wire
Floral tape
White craft glue
Wire cutters
Scissors

**Step 1**

Cut out the leaf.

Use the leaf pattern to cut out one leaf from crepe paper, aligning the double-tipped arrow on the pattern with the grain of the crepe paper and being careful to make neat cuts around the shape of the leaf.

**Step 2**

Prepare the wire.

Measure and cut a length of wire according to the desired length of the stem you wish to attach to the leaf, allowing extra length for attaching the leaf to the floral stem. Wrap the wire in floral tape.

**Step 3**

Attach the wire to the leaf.

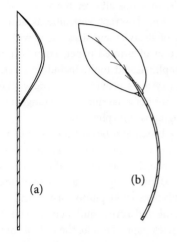

(a)     (b)

Apply a scant film of glue to the wrapped wire. Position and press the wire lengthwise along the center of the paper leaf. Fold the leaf in half around the wire and press the fold with your finger so that the paper at the fold adheres to the wire and conceals it (a). Keep the leaf folded as the glue dries. When the glue is dry, carefully open the leaf and press the fold flat (b).

**Step 4**

Attach the leaf to a floral stem.

Lay the end of the leaf stem against the floral stem at the desired position. Wrap floral tape around both wires to secure the leaf. Use your fingers to bend the leaf. Make and add more leaves to the floral stem as desired.

## Technique: Making and Attaching a Two-Ply Leaf

MATERIALS AND TOOLS

  Leaf pattern (pages 690–92)
  Crepe paper, in green or another color,
    as desired
  Prepared floral stem
  Medium-gauge wire

Floral tape
White craft glue
Wire cutters
Scissors

**Step 1**

Cut out the leaf.

Use the pattern to cut out two leaf shapes from crepe paper, aligning the double-tipped arrow on the pattern with the grain of the crepe paper and being careful to make neat cuts around the shape of the petal.

**Step 2**

Prepare the wire.

Measure and cut a length of wire according to the desired length of the stem you wish to attach to the leaf, allowing extra length for attaching the leaf to the floral stem. Wrap the wire in floral tape.

**Step 3**

Attach the wire to the leaf.

Apply a scant film of glue to the wrapped wire. Position and press the wire lengthwise against the center of one paper leaf. Lay the second leaf over the first, all edges even, and press down to adhere the second leaf along its center. Let the glue dry.

**Step 4**

Attach the leaf to the floral stem.

Lay the end of the wire on the leaf against the floral stem in a position as desired. Wrap floral tape around the wires to secure the leaf. Use your fingers to bend the leaf, as desired. Add more leaves, as desired.

## Memory Keeping: Albums, Books, and Scrapbooks

Crafters are communicators by nature. Using decorative elements and paper, we can share our cherished experiences and memories with the most important people in our lives, lavishing pages with photos and embellishments every spare chance we get. Witness the growth of the scrapbooking industry, which has grown to global proportions in the last decade. In shops all over the world an array of ready-made scrapbooks, albums, and blank books of all styles and sizes, along with a vast collection of printed paper, embellishments, and sophisticated tools, including electronic cutting systems, provide ever more ways for us to tell our personal stories in arrangements of photographs and ephemera.

The broad and beautiful choice of ready-made materials available today was nowhere to be seen decades ago. Crafters then relied on a narrow range of commercial materials—black or white photo corners and maybe white ink and a crow-quill pen to write on the coal-black paper. Despite the lack of supplies, however, there was no shortage of the yearning to record life's important moments in all their poignancy and simplicity using photographs and hand-inscribed notations written with imagination and ingenuity. I remember my mother's photo albums, each one containing a packet of plain black photo-filled pages secured by a long lace and interleaved with protective sheets of embossed vellum. I learned at an early age how to handle an album—how to set it on a flat surface (clean hands a must) and how to lift the pages, supporting them as they were turned so they did not bunch at the binding and threaten photographs that had remained pristine through decades of careful handling. When I was a Girl Scout, I filled my first personal photo album with photos, hand-drawn illustrations, letters, and sentimental mementos. As I grew older, my albums reflected my life in other ways—movie tickets from a first date, foreign stamps soaked off an envelope, a lock of baby hair tied with a pale ribbon, a handmade greeting card from one of my kids—items for safekeeping saved within the pages of a book in a timeless tradition of remembering our lives.

It is a return to those fundamentals that informs the designs of each small book, album, and journal in this section, formats that have endured for generations and that depend only on your imagination and a few materials that you may already have at home—paper and a box, a scrap of fabric, a length of ribbon, needle and thread. This was our original starting place, and this is where I begin.

## Technique: Making a Soft-Cover Travel Journal

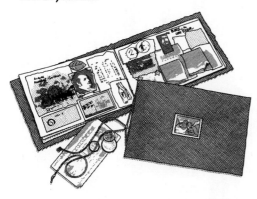

The soft, flexible cover of this travel journal is crafted from handmade paper. You can make the paper for the cover yourself (see Making Paper in Chapter Seven) or you can purchase it an art supply store or online. The folios are light-weight paper, and the bindings can be sewn by hand or by machine. Using a sewing machine is fast and easy and will give you time left over to make several little journals in which to record highlights of a trip—your itinerary, impressions, and memories—and paste in souvenirs like stamps, ticket stubs, and an envelope to keep foreign currency, that will bring back memories in years to come. Carry a journal (along with a glue stick) in your bag and add short notes while your experiences are still fresh in your mind.

### MATERIALS AND TOOLS

3 sheets of paper with some rag content, 7⅞" × 9¼" (20.0 × 23.5 cm), in ivory
1 sheet of handmade paper, 8" × 10" (20.3 × 25.4 cm), in pale blue
Thread, in ivory
Pen, markers, and colored pencils
Glue stick
White craft glue
Sewing machine
Needle with large eye
Steel ruler
Craft knife
Self-healing cutting mat
Bone folder
Paper clips

### Step 1

Prepare the pages and the cover.

Lay a sheet of ivory paper on a flat work surface. Use a ruler and a bone folder to indent a fold line and fold the paper in half widthwise; repeat for the remaining ivory sheets. Fold the blue handmade paper in half widthwise for the cover, using a bone folder and ruler to make a neat fold.

### Step 2

Make the journal.

Lay the pages of the journal on a flat surface, aligning the center folds. Use paper clips to secure the stack of paper. Thread a sewing machine with ivory thread and set the stitch length to long. Sew the pages together along the fold line. Remove the clips from the pages. Fold the pages and use the flat side of a bone folder to burnish the fold so that it lies flat. Open and lay the journal cover on a flat surface. Run a thin line of white glue along the inside fold and set the outside fold of the sewn pages along the glued fold; let the glue dry. Close the cover of the journal and use the flat side of a bone folder to burnish the fold so that it lies flat.

### Step 3

Embellish your journal.

Decorate the cover with embellishments, as desired. Bring the journal with you on your next trip.

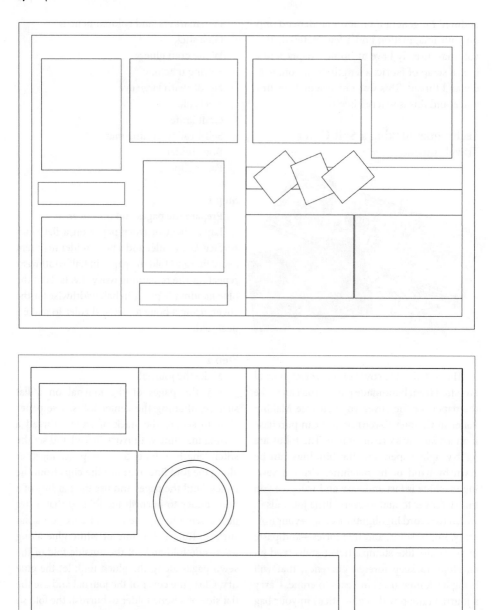

Regardless of the format chosen to tell our personal stories, all crafters need to decide how to organize the separate elements (titles, embellishments, page accents, borders, journal entries, photographs, mats) in a heartfelt, original, and coherent way that is visually beautiful and balanced. Here are two layouts to inspire you.

## Technique: Making an Album Cover

Customizing the cover of a store-bought album is fun, especially when you apply quirky, but meaningful, embellishments you make yourself. A decorative cover can be made from paper if the original album covers are flat; however, if the covers are padded, as mine were, use fabric instead as it will stretch and ease around padded corners without tearing.

### MATERIALS AND TOOLS

Purchased album, 9¼" wide × 9½" high (23.5 × 24.1 cm), or as desired
2 pieces of fabric, 10½" × 11½" (27.7 × 29.2 cm), in cotton print, or as desired
2 sheets of cardstock, 17½" wide × 9" high (44.5 × 22.9 cm)
Scraps of fabric
Fusible web
Spray adhesive
Sewing machine
Household iron and ironing board
Chemical-cartridge respirator mask
Cardboard carton (for spray booth; optional)
Steel ruler
Craft knife
Rotary cutter
Self-healing cutting mat

### Step 1

Cut the fabric covers.
Lay one fabric piece on the ironing board.

Fold over one short side to make a ⅜"-wide (1.0 cm) hem and press flat with an iron. Repeat for the second piece of fabric.

### Step 2 (optional)

Decorate the fabric.

To strengthen the fabric, use a sheet of fusible web trimmed to the size of each album cover. Use an iron and follow the manufacturer's instructions to fuse the web to the wrong side of the fabric. Cut out letters from scraps of fabric and arrange them on the fabric piece for the front cover. Use a sewing machine set to a zigzag stitch to sew the raw edges of the letters to the fabric cover through all layers.

### Step 3

Mark the guidelines for the fabric placement.

Use a ruler and a pencil to mark a line on the front and back covers of the album that is 1" (2.5 cm) from and parallel to the spine.

### Step 4

Adhere the fabric pieces.

Work outdoors or in a very well ventilated space and wear a chemical-cartridge respirator mask. Lay the fabric pieces wrong side up on a protected work surface or in a spray booth. Following the manufacturer's recommendations, apply a thin, even coat of spray adhesive to the wrong side of each piece of fabric, spraying over the edges. Place the front cover fabric piece, adhesive side down, on the album cover so that the hemmed edge just conceals the marked guideline. Smooth the fabric flat from the center outward. Repeat to affix the second piece of fabric to the back cover.

### Step 5

Trim and adhere the flaps to the inside covers.

Open the front cover. Use scissors to trim the fabric at the top left and bottom left corners in a gentle arc about ⅜" (1.0 cm) beyond each corner. Fold the flaps at the top, bottom, and left side onto the inside cover, smoothing them until they adhere. Repeat to trim and adhere the flaps to the inside back cover.

### Step 6

Trim the endpapers.

Open the front cover of the album. Lay the top edge of the 17½" × 9" (44.5 × 22.9 cm) paper even with the top of the book pages and use a pencil to make a light tick on the paper even with the bottom of the book pages. Remove the paper from the book. Draft a line through the tick that is parallel to the top edge. Use a cutting mat and a craft knife to cut along the line. Reposition the paper on the book ⅛" (0.3 cm) in from the left edge of cover and make a tick even with the book pages at the far right. Remove the paper, draft the line at the mark, and cut along the line. Repeat for the inside back cover.

### Step 7

Adhere the endpaper to the inside front cover.

Fold one of the endpapers in half, using a bone folder to make a neat crease. Lay the folded endpaper flat, fold facing left, and apply spray adhesive to the paper on the exposed half. Lay the endpaper on the inside front cover, smoothing it to adhere the paper against the cover and the inner spine.

### Step 8

Adhere the endpaper to the inside back cover.

Fold the remaining endpaper in half, using a bone folder to make a neat crease. Lay the folded endpaper flat, fold facing right, and apply spray adhesive to the paper on the exposed half. Lay the endpaper on the inside back cover, smoothing it to adhere the paper against the cover and the inner spine.

## Technique: Making a Ribbon Badge

This book contains no formal sewing instruction, but I still had the urge to include great-looking cotton prints in some way. Here a band of lively print fabric in bright colors forms a pleated ruffle around the center button, creating a badge inspired by the blue ribbons awarded to champions at sporting events. I glued my badge to an album cover, but it could also be worn on a lapel as a fun pin.

### MATERIALS AND TOOLS

Fabric, 15" × 1½" (38.1 × 3.8 cm)
Satin ribbon, 22 pieces, each 9" (22.9 cm)
   long and ⅛" to ⅜" (0.3 to 1.0 cm) wide,
   in assorted colors and patterns
Round, flat button, 1" (2.5 cm) diameter
Scrap of chipboard
White craft glue
Hot-glue gun and glue stick
Scissors
Pencil
Compass

### Step 1

Cut a chipboard circle.

Use a compass to draw a 3"-diameter (7.6 cm) circle on chipboard. Use scissors to cut out the circle along the marked line. Use the compass to draw a 1"-diameter (2.5 cm) circle in the middle of the large circle.

## Step 2

Glue on the fabric strip.

Use white glue to secure one long edge of the fabric strip around the inner marked circle, pleating the edge with your fingers to ease it around the curve. Let the glue dry.

## Step 3

Glue on the ribbon streamers.

Turn the circle to the wrong side. Use glue to attach one end of each ribbon to a 1" × ½" (3 × 1.3 cm) area at the bottom edge of the chipboard circle.

## Step 4

Turn the badge to the right side. Use a glue gun to attach the button to the center of the circle so it is surrounded by the pleated strip.

## Technique: Making a Box Book

Boxes provide handy storage for many things, but they needn't look plain and ordinary. Here the bottom half of a two-part box is enclosed inside a pretty cover made of chipboard laminated with floral fabric, transforming the plain box into an attractive "book." The box book can be made in any size—simply adjust the measurements of the covers to fit the dimensions of your box. Designed to keep stationery neat and ready to use, the little volume can also be used to store a set of journals or anything else you wish to keep in one special place. To screen-print the fabric for this technique, see Chrysanthemum: Printed Fabric for a Box Book (page 352).

## MATERIALS AND TOOLS

White or light-colored fabric:
    2 pieces screen-printed, each 10" × 10"
      (25.4 × 25.4 cm)
    1 plain piece, 10" × 4" (25.4 × 10.2 cm)
Sheet of decorative paper, such as
    strengthened gift wrap
½ yard (45.7 cm) satin ribbon, ⅜" (1.0 cm)
    wide, in color as desired (optional)
Box, 6⅜" × 6⅜" × 1½" (16.2 × 16.2 × 3.8 cm)
Chipboard
Spray adhesive
Chemical-cartridge respirator mask
Cardboard carton (for spray booth;
    optional)
Steel ruler
Acrylic grid ruler
Craft knife
Rotary cutter
Self-healing cutting mat
Pencil

## Step 1

Cut the chipboard.

Working on a self-healing cutting mat, use a craft knife and a steel ruler to cut two cover pieces from chipboard that are ¼" (0.6 cm) larger all around than the box. Cut one spine piece from chipboard the same length as the cover pieces and in a width equal to the depth of the box plus ¼" (0.6 cm).

## Step 2

Cut the fabric.

Lay the fabric, wrong side up, on a flat surface. Lay the cut chipboard pieces from step 1 side by side on the fabric, with the spine in the middle; allow a ³⁄₁₆" (0.5 cm) space between each cover and the spine. Use a pencil to mark the placement of the covers and the spine on the fabric; then mark a 1" (2.5 cm) allowance around all three pieces. Remove the chipboard pieces from the fabric. Use a cutting mat, a rotary cutter, and an acrylic grid ruler to cut the fabric on the outer marked line.

### Step 3

Laminate the fabric to the book covers and spine.

Work outdoors or in a very well ventilated space and wear a chemical-cartridge respirator mask. Lay the fabric rectangle from step 2 facedown on a protected work surface or in a spray booth. Following the manufacturer's recommendations, apply a thin, even coat of spray adhesive to the fabric. Reposition the chipboard spine and cover pieces on the fabric as marked. Press down on the pieces to adhere them. Turn the cover over and smooth the fabric with your palm, then turn the cover over again.

### Step 4

Trim the corners and press down the flaps.

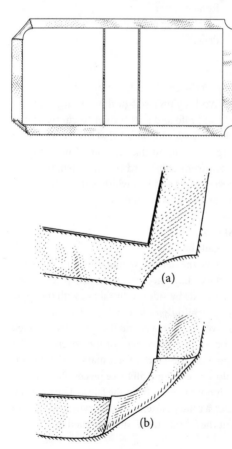

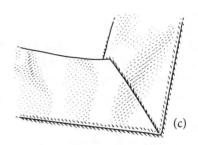

Use scissors to trim away the fabric corners in a gentle arc about ⅜" (1.0 cm) from the chipboard (a). Fold each arc-shaped edge onto the cover (b). Fold the remaining allowances onto the cover and press down until they adhere (c).

### Step 5

Cut and glue the paper liners.

Working on a cutting mat, use a craft knife and a steel ruler to cut a piece of decorative paper that is equal in measurement to the open book cover less ¼" (0.6 cm). Cut a second piece to fit the box bottom. Lay the pieces on a protected work surface in your spraying area and apply a thin, even coat of spray adhesive. Center the liner paper, adhesive side down, on the cover, pressing to adhere. Use your finger to gently press down the paper between the spine and the covers. Adhere the remaining piece to the floor of the box.

### Step 6

Glue the box bottom to the inside cover.

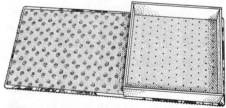

Use a brush to apply a coat of white glue to the bottom of the box. Center the box, glue side down, on the right inside cover and press down to adhere.

## Technique: Making an Altered Book

Altered books are inviting landscapes for artistic jottings and illustrations; they can also serve a practical need by providing a place to secret away trinkets or valuables. The transformation requires some rigorous cutting and gluing, but after the more muscular efforts, you can decorate the first few pages of your altered book in any way you wish.

### MATERIALS AND TOOLS

Old book, approximately 6" × 9¼" × 1¾" thick (15.2 × 23.5 × 4.4 cm)

Chipboard jewelry box, 2⅛" × 3" × 1" deep (5.4 × 7.6 × 2.5 cm), or another size, as desired

Watercolor set and brush (optional)

White craft glue

Foam brush

Steel ruler

Craft knife

Wax paper

Rubber band

Heavy weight, such as a stack of books

### Step 1

Glue the pages together.

Count off the first 30 pages of the book and use a rubber band to hold them against the front cover. Use a foam brush to apply glue to the outside edges of the remaining book pages, smoothing the glue with your finger so it seeps between the pages. Lay a piece of wax paper over the facing page, remove the rubber band, and close the book. Lay a heavy weight on top of the book and let the glue dry overnight.

### Step 2

Mark the box shape in the center of the pages.

Open the book and use a rubber band to hold back the first 30 pages. Center the box top on the right-hand facing page and use a pencil to trace around the perimeter. Set the box top aside and use a ruler and a pencil to redraw the outline, adding a scant ⅛" (0.3 cm) all around.

### Step 3

Cut out the box shape.

Working carefully, use a steel ruler and a craft knife to cut on the marked lines to make a 1⅛"-deep (2.9 cm) cavity; remove the cut paper and test-fit the box *top* in the cavity as you go. The walls of the cavity will not be perfectly straight or even, but once the box is installed, any messy or uneven cutting will be concealed. Continue cutting until the box top fits inside the cutout. Apply glue to the floor and sides of the cavity and the outside surfaces of the box *bottom*. Install the box bottom in the cavity, centering it so that there is easement for the addition of the box top; let the glue dry. When the glue is completely dry, put on the box top.

### Step 4

Make a flap to conceal the box.

Cut out one page from the pages reserved in step 2. Measure and cut a 2½" × 3½"

(6.4 × 8.9 cm) piece of chipboard for the flap. Use the cut page to cover the chipboard flap, adding a paper tab to one short side and a strip to the opposite short side for a hinge. Position the flap over the box lid and glue down the hinge to the top book page. Let the glue dry. To access the box, lift the flap by its paper tab.

**Step 5**

Decorate the pages.

Use watercolor or any art supplies to decorate the first loose pages in the book, as desired.

## Quick & Easy: Modifying the Pages in an Altered Book

Here are some ways to customize an altered book by treating the printed pages as an artist's canvas.

- Apply strips of low-tack masking tape around all four edges of the page. Use watercolor paint and a tapered paintbrush to draw your illustration, painting over the edge of the tape. When the paint dries, remove the tape to reveal the plain frame. You can also arrange the strips of tape in a grid, in vertical or horizontal bars, or in zigzags, spilling (writing or illustrating in a spontaneous freeform style) in the spaces left open.
- Use a fountain pen to handwrite passages in tiny script or cut texts from a printed source. Glue them on the page and use stencils or adhesive-backed letters and numerals to add contrast.
- Paste a collage of materials on a page or add new pages or tab dividers in different papers to add texture to the existing pages in the book. To accommodate the added bulk, remove a page or two, depending upon the thickness of the paper being added. Slip a thin cutting mat under the page to be removed, pushing its edge as close to the binding as possible, and use a craft knife and a steel ruler to cut the page from top to bottom $1/2$" (1.3 cm). Cut the new paper to the size of the page, adding a tab to the right edge of the paper, if desired, and glue the new page along the $1/2$" (1.3 cm) strip left next to the binding.

# PROJECTS

## Woven Heart: A Paper Basket

Simplicity itself, this woven heart-shaped basket is modeled after the heart-shaped baskets that hung on our family's Christmas tree when I was a child. The basket can be made in papers in any color combination. Use the pattern to make a small basket or enlarge the pattern to make a basket in any size you wish.

### MATERIALS AND TOOLS

Woven Heart pattern (page 693)
Paper, in two colors
Photocopier
Steel ruler
Craft knife
Self-healing cutting mat

### Step 1

Cut out the paper pieces.
Photocopy the Woven Heart pattern and use it as a template to cut out two pieces from paper, one piece in a dark color and the other piece in a light color. Lay the pieces on a cutting mat. Use a steel ruler and a craft knife to slash each piece along the solid lines.

### Step 2

Begin the weaving.

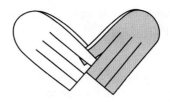

Fold each basket section in half, right side out, along the dash line. Position the folded shapes on your work surface as shown and begin threading a flattened loop into an open loop.

### Step 3

Complete the weaving.

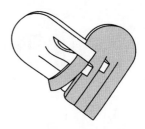

Continue weaving the first loop and begin weaving the second loop. Continue in this way until all the loops are woven.

### Step 4

Shape the basket.
Straighten the woven sections by pulling gently in both directions, being careful not to tear the paper.

### Step 5

Make the handle.

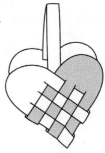

Cut a 1¼" × 7½" (3.2 × 19.1 cm) strip of paper for the handle. Fold the strip in half lengthwise, using a dab of glue to secure the fold. Glue the ends inside the basket at the inner point of the heart.

### Step 6

Add a hanging ribbon (optional).

Thread a ribbon through the handle of the basket to attach it to a wrapped package. Use a calligraphy pen to write a special note to the recipient and tuck it into the basket.

## Priceless: A Die-Cut Card

Glitter is not just for kids. Available in a wide spectrum of rich colors, fine glitter is the perfect material for glamorizing greeting cards. The glue is applied through a stencil and the glitter is sprinkled onto the glue, creating crisp and sparkling edges. Cut your own shoe stencil from acetate, sizing it fit the front panel of the card.

### MATERIALS AND TOOLS

Red Shoe, a Strappy Sandal pattern
(page 697)
Bristol, 12" × 12½" (30.5 × 30.5 cm)
Striped scrapbook paper or gift wrap
Scrap paper
Envelope to fit card
Magenta glitter
Metallic flower
Satin ribbon, ⅛" (0.3 cm) wide, in lime
green
White craft glue
Spray adhesive
Masking tape
Computer with printer
Acetate (for stencil; see step 2)
Steel ruler
Craft knife
Self-healing cutting mat
Bone folder
Hole punch, ¼" (0.6 cm) diameter
Stencil brush
Craft stick

### Step 1

Cut out the card.

Measure and cut the bristol to make 12" × 6" (30.5 × 15.2 cm) rectangle. Fold the paper in half widthwise.

### Step 2

Make the stencil.

Photocopy the Red Shoe pattern, sizing it to fit the right front panel of the blank card. Print a test image on copy paper and check the size. Use your final pattern to cut a stencil from plastic film; refer to Traditional Stenciling in Chapter Four.

### Step 3

Position the stencil.

Squeeze some white glue into a dish. Open the card flat on a clean work surface. Position the acetate stencil over the outside front right panel of the card, aligning the heel of the shoe with the fold and the sole of the shoe approximately ¼" (0.6 cm) from the bottom edge of the paper (this allowance will be trimmed off later). Use short strips of masking tape at the corners to keep the stencil from shifting.

**Step 4**

Apply glue through the stencil.

Pick up some glue on the stencil brush and gently stroke the bristles on a paper towel to ensure they are only lightly loaded. Use a gentle up-and-down pouncing motion to apply glue to the cutout areas of the stencil, working the glue from the outer edges to the inner area and using a craft stick to press down any edges to prevent the glue from seeping under the stencil and to ensure a crisp line.

**Step 5**

Apply the glitter.

Lift off the acetate stencil and set it aside. Pour a thick layer of glitter directly from the container over all of the glued sections on the paper. Let the glue dry completely, preferably overnight. Clean the stencil with warm soapy water. The next day, lift the card and tap the excess glitter onto a sheet of scrap paper. Carefully transfer the glitter back into the container.

**Step 6**

Make the die-cut shoe.

Use scissors to carefully cut away the paper that lies to the right of the glittered sole and straps, beginning at the sole of the shoe and ending at the top of the shoe and using the marked pattern as a guide.

**Step 7**

Laminate the striped paper to the inside of the card.

Measure and cut the striped paper so the stripes run vertically and the piece measures 6" × 5½" (15.2 × 14.0 cm). Lay the paper, stripes facing down, on a protected work surface and apply spray adhesive, following the manufacturer's precautions for safe use. Position and press the striped paper, adhesive side down, onto the inside right panel of the card.

**Step 8**

Make a hang tag.

Use a computer printer to print *$ Priceless* or any other message on a sheet of paper. Glue the message to scrap paper and trim it to 2½" × ¾" (6.4 × 1.9 cm). Use a hole punch to make a hole in the hang tag. Open the card and punch a hole through the front panel at the heel area of the shoe, as shown. Fold an 8" (20.3 cm) length of ribbon in half, thread the loop through the hang tag, and tie a cowslip knot. Thread the ribbon ends from the inside of the card through the hole near the heel. Tie a double knot, leaving 3½" (8.9 cm) ribbon ends. Glue a metallic flower to the hang tag.

## Memories: Mini Photo Album

If you have no idea what to do with the collection of jewel cases that originally stored your CDs, consider using them to hold photographs. I had many photos from my parents' old albums that I wanted to share with other family members. By slipping copies of the photos into an empty jewel case and enclosing the case in a handmade card, I had a special way to pass on the memories. I pasted a coordinating photo on the front of the card to complete this miniature keepsake album.

## MATERIALS AND TOOLS

    CD Card pattern (page 693)
    Photo (for front of card)
    Bristol, at least 12" × 13" (30.5 × 33.0 cm)
    Jewel case, CD and packaging removed
    Rubber cement
    Photocopier
    Craft knife
    Steel ruler
    Self-healing cutting mat
    Bone folder
    Pencil

### Step 1

Mark the pattern on the bristol.

Photocopy the CD Card pattern. Cut out the pattern piece and test-fit it around the jewel case to confirm the size. Lay the pattern on the bristol and use a pencil and a ruler to trace around the perimeter. Remove the pattern to add the interior fold lines.

### Step 2

Cut out the card.

Lay the bristol on a self-healing cutting mat. Use a steel ruler and a craft knife to cut out the card around the perimeter. Use a steel ruler and a bone folder to mark and score the fold lines. Clip to form the flaps.

### Step 3

Assemble the card.

Fold on the score lines, tucking in the flaps. Use rubber cement to seal the flaps.

### Step 4

Glue on a photograph and message.

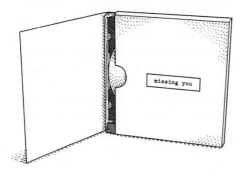

Glue a photo or other image to the front panel of the card. Write a personal message on the inside panel.

## First Love: A Soft-Cover Photo Album

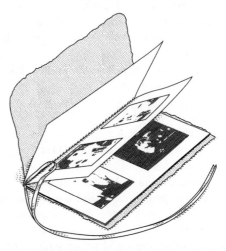

You can create a memory album for family and friends with a few easy-to-find materials, your photos, and a unique application of the photo transfer technique. Originally designed for use on white cloth, the transfer technique can be used to print photographs on the pages of a handmade album. This little album uses a single sheet of handmade paper (see Making Paper on page 606) and two sheets of ivory rag paper. The folder and insert folio formats would also work for wedding invitations or birth announcements.

### MATERIALS AND TOOLS

    Photos, in black-and-white or color
    1 sheet of handmade paper, 8" × 10" (20.3
        × 25.4 cm), in pink
    2 sheets of paper with some rag content,
        7⅞" × 9¼" (20.0 × 23.5 cm), in ivory
    ¾ yard (68.6 cm) silk cord or narrow rib-
        bon, in ivory
    Ivory sewing thread
    Photo transfer paper (designed for white
        cloth)

Sewing machine

Computer with scanner and ink-jet printer

Hand-sewing needle with large eye

Steel ruler

Craft knife

Self-healing cutting mat

Pillowcase (for cushioning)

Household iron

Low-tack masking tape

Glue stick

### Step 1

Prepare the photos.

Arrange your photographs on a sheet of copy paper, fitting as many as you can without overlapping, and secure with a scant dab of a glue stick. Place the arrangement on the bed of your computer scanner, select the mirror image function, and scan the photos into your computer.

### Step 2

Make the photo transfer.

Place the photo transfer paper, grid side up, on the paper tray of your computer's ink-jet printer. Make a printout of your photographs on the transfer paper. Allow the printout to dry for 30 minutes.

### Step 3

Cut out the photo transfers.

Lay the sheet of photo transfers on a cutting mat. Use a steel ruler and a craft knife to cut out each photo transfer, trimming it to desired size.

### Step 4

Make the album cover.

Fold the pink handmade paper in half widthwise, using a ruler and a bone folder to make a neat fold. Open the paper and lay it flat.

### Step 5

Create a layout for the album pages.

Lay a sheet of ivory paper on a flat work surface. Use a ruler and a bone folder to fold the paper in half widthwise. Fold the second ivory sheet and slip it inside the first one, matching the folds to make a folio. Place one or two photo transfers on one side of each page, arranging them as desired. Use a small piece of masking tape to secure one corner of each photo transfer. Use a pencil to make very light ticks at each corner.

### Step 6

Transfer the photos to the folio pages.

Empty the iron of all water and preheat it to high. Place a folded pillowcase on a heat-resistant surface. Lay one sheet of ivory paper on the smooth area of the pillowcase, away from seams and hems. Remove the tape from the corner of the photo transfer on the page and turn the photo transfer facedown in the same position. Hold down one corner of the photo transfer with your fingertips to keep it from shifting as you place the hot iron on another corner of the same image. Press down on the transfer paper with the hot iron for 60 to 90 seconds, moving the iron continuously in overlapping passes and focusing on the corners and the edges. Let the image cool. Do not remove the backing paper. Transfer additional images to this page or other pages in the same way.

### Step 7

Peel off the backing papers.

Use the tip of a craft knife to carefully pry up one corner of the paper backing and then use your fingers to peel off the rest of the backing paper in one continuous motion to reveal the transferred image. Repeat.

### Step 8

Make the album.

Lay the ivory folio pages flat, aligning the center folds and using paper clips to hold the pages together. Thread the sewing machine and set the stitch length to long. Sew the pages together along the fold line. Run a thin bead of glue along the inside fold of the album cover.

Set the folded outside edge of the sewn ivory folio pages into the glued fold, secure the pages with paper clips, and allow the glue to dry completely.

### Step 9

Decorate the album pages.

Embellish the pages by writing sentiments around the photographs and gluing on mementos, as desired.

### Step 10

Add the ribbon accent.

Open the book so that the center fold of the ivory folio pages faces up. Lay the midpoint of the ribbon on the midpoint of the fold, bring the ribbon ends around to the outside of the album cover, and tie a square knot, allowing the ribbon ends to cascade.

## The Deluxe Book of Butterflies: A Flag Book

This flag book combines the best of folding, cutting, and painting in one project. The butterflies are made by copying a butterfly image in pairs. Some butterflies were enlarged and some were reduced to create a variety of sizes. Pairs of butterflies were painted in bright colors, wired, and glued to the paper pleats so they would rise out of the book when the covers opened.

## MATERIALS AND TOOLS

Butterfly image (page 694)
Scrapbook paper, 8" × 10" (20.3 × 25.4 cm)
Mat board, 8" × 10" (20.3 × 25.4 cm)
Gift wrap, as desired
Cotton cord (optional)
Brass wire, 26-gauge
Watercolor paints and tapered paintbrush
Spray adhesive
Spray acrylic sealer
Chemical-cartridge respirator mask
White craft glue
Cellophane tape
Steel ruler
Craft knife
Self-healing cutting mat
Manicure scissors
Pencil

### Step 1

Make the covers of the book.

Use spray adhesive to dry-mount a piece of gift wrap to each side of the mat board following manufacturer's cautions. Measure and cut two 5½" × 8¾" (14.0 × 22.2 cm) rectangles from the laminated board for the covers.

### Step 2

Make the pleated band.

Use a ruler and a craft knife to measure and cut a 12½" × 5½" (31.8 × 14.0 cm) band of scrapbook paper or bristol. Mark and score nine 1¼"-wide (3.2 cm) folds, alternating the folds backward and forward.

### Step 3

Make the card.

Lay the laminated covers horizontally on a flat surface, with short sides aligned. Overlap and glue one 1¼"-wide (3.2 cm) end panel of the pleated band to the laminated cover on the left, aligning the first fold in the pleated band with the inside edge of the cover. Overlap and glue the other end of the pleated band to the other cover in the same way.

## Step 4

Paint the butterflies.

Copy the butterfly image in a variety of sizes using a laser copier or computer scanner and laser printer. Use the printouts to make twenty pairs of butterflies in different sizes on laser copy paper. Use watercolors and a tapered brush to paint each pair of butterflies with the same color, selecting any colors desired; let the paint dry. Working outdoors on a protected surface and wearing a chemical-cartridge respirator mask, apply a thin, even coat of acrylic sealer to all of the butterflies; let the sealer dry.

## Step 5

Cut out and wire the butterflies.

Use manicure scissors to cut out each butterfly. Layer each pair back to back, painted sides facing out and edges even; trim off any excess paper so each pair matches exactly. Measure and cut a 5½" (14.0 cm) length of wire and use your fingers to make a small loop at each end. Use tape to secure one of the loops to one butterfly in the pair. Apply white glue to the plain side of the second butterfly and press it onto the first butterfly with edges even. Repeat to make 19 more wired butterflies.

## Step 6

Attach the butterflies to the pleated band.

Stand the wire loop on one butterfly between two pleats and use a strip of tape to secure the wire. Repeat to position and tape the remaining 19 butterflies, arranging them randomly in the other pleats. Glue the pleats closed, concealing the taped wire loops. Bend the wires in soft arches so butterflies fly at different heights.

## Step 7 (optional)

Finish the edges of the covers.

Use glue to add a length of cotton cord to the edge to each cover, butting the ends together; let the glue dry.

## Step 8

Add your message.

Use a calligraphy pen to write a message on a narrow band of copy paper. Glue one end to the card front, as desired.

# CHAPTER FOUR

# Hand Printing

## THE HEART

### Through Immigrant Eyes

"En Far er mere end hundrede lærere."
(One father is more than a hundred
teachers.)

—Danish saying

I found two cigar boxes in my closet, each with
an embossed label that was torn in a ragged
split where the lid opened. *Negatives, '37–'48*
was written over each label in a bold hand.
I raised the lid of one box, revealing glassine envelopes golden with age and stacked
sidewise like *mille feuille* pastries. I slipped
out one glass negative and held it up to the
light—a silvery image of a horse-drawn hay
wagon bathed in eerie light. I flipped through
images from the far edge of the last century—

a behemoth hull of a ship roped to a foreign pier; the Statue of Liberty, her extended arm rising into a cloudy sky; a small house under construction, its foundation wrapped high in snow drifts. When I saw the smiling face of my father, I stopped. These pictures were a gift. Through them, I witnessed an immigrant's journey. I saw the world through my father's eyes. Even though I had never seen any of the images before, they dovetailed with stories he used to tell me when I was growing up, suddenly bringing them to life.

My father was a storyteller, and his stories grew out of his rich and varied life; about the hyperinflation in Germany in the early 1920s, when he saw his mother hand over thick packets of paper money to pay for groceries; the predictable crow of the rooster that set him on a path to the barn to milk the cows; and his little photography shop on Broadway in Manhattan. His stories grew out of Dresden, Germany, where he was born, Denmark, where he spent summers on his grandparents' farm, and New York City, where he immigrated in 1933, bringing ambition, imagination, and a dream of becoming a photographer.

When I was fifteen, I held my father's camera for the first time. It was a 35-mm single-lens reflex. I placed its worn leather strap around my neck and grasped the camera with one hand, surprised by its weight. My father explained the relationships between its mechanical parts as my hands struggled in an awkward ballet with the light meter and the metal collar on the lens.

"Take pictures from your heart," he urged. I looked through the viewfinder for a subject and pressed the shutter release. My father believed that understanding the alchemical processes of photography would make me a better photographer, so we visited his darkroom that afternoon. It was a small, quiet chamber built in one corner of a large, open basement. Thick black velvet covered two high windows. Only the ticking of a clock was audible at first, but then the sound of my mother

calling to my sisters upstairs seeped between the floor joists. My father was consulting a notebook filled with neatly ruled tables that correlated exposure times, lens openings, and developer temperatures, and he was running his finger down the page as he referred to test strips taped to the margin. There was the faint smell of chemicals. Meticulous order was imposed on every space. The parts of a plastic developing tank rested on a mat along with measuring cups, thermometers, and a timer, all precisely laid out like surgeon's tools. Strips of drying film were hanging by clips from an overhead line. Glass bottles the color of burnt sugar were pasted with labels—*Developer, Stop Bath, Fixer*—and situated on a low shelf.

At my father's instruction, I turned off the overhead lamp and a single safelight automatically came on, washing the room in crimson. As my eyes adjusted, the ghostly profiles of a premonitory enlarger and a long table set with trays and tongs appeared. Elbow to elbow, my father and I made short side steps from the enlarger to a tray of developer, and I slid a sheet of newly exposed paper under its surface. Time moved differently there; it was measured in fractions of a second and in the rhythm of the stories my father curled around his small admonishments to use a different set of tongs for the developer and the stop bath or to make a test print each time I printed a new photograph. As he would begin a new story, the tone and cadence of his voice would change as if he were translating his memories from an original text laid down in the idioms and syntax of his mother tongue. Filled with intrigue, his narratives were shaped by flourishes and details, aimed at illustrating an important lesson or moving the story along, but I believe now that his stories from the old country also helped keep the early years of his life at a bridgeable distance. That day he recounted a story about a sea voyage he took on a passenger liner with his parents and older sister after World War I. The ship was heading across the Baltic Sea from Germany to Sweden where the family had relatives. It was January, and they were warned that the crossing could be rough.

On the day of their departure, there was a light snow falling as my father and his family made their way up the gangway to the main deck. His leather shoes kept slipping, and his mother tried to take his hand, but he pulled it away. There were a few blasts from the ship's horn that smothered any other sound, and the ship left port with seagulls, unbothered, screeching and flying against the wind near the stern. By dinnertime, the snow had turned to a pouring rain and a planned promenade on the deck was called off, much to my father's dismay.

"Well, you know your father. I am obstinate. I was more so then. I put on my wool coat and my cap. My sister started to cry, worried I would get in trouble, but I said I would be all right. The ship was pitching and rolling, and I walked along the corridor and up a narrow gangway like a drunken man. I reached the main deck and didn't see a soul. I wanted to stand by the railing near the lifeboats, but I didn't make it that far."

My father interrupted his own story when an image began to ghost through the developer—first a nose and an eye appeared, then the remaining features of my father's face developed rapidly on the paper, a moment of pure magic to me. I carefully gripped the edge of the print with the second pair of tongs and transferred it to the stop bath and then to the fixer. My father looked at me without speaking. Then he smiled and continued his story.

My father explained that the gusts of wind were so strong, he lost any steps he gained. A wave crashed over the railing in the place he would have been standing had the wind not forced him back. "The wave hit with such force that it burst into a heavy spray that filled the air, soaking my clothes and freezing my bones. It was fantastic! I was shaking with cold as I waited for another wave, which came with the same force as the other. I made my way back to

our cabin. Your grandmother and grandfather were standing outside the door, speaking to a ship's officer. I knew, of course, I was in trouble, but I wasn't afraid. I was happy.

"Carol, looking back, I know I learned something important that day. Courage is a cumulative thing. It builds on itself. You will have enough for each challenge that comes your way. Always pursue what is important to you and you will find the courage you need inside." My father and I hung the prints to dry and I turned off the light in the darkroom. Over time, with diligent practice, I would learn to develop film in complete darkness and advance to using the subtleties of different print papers to interpret my negatives, producing black-and-white photographs that told my own story.

There was a knock at the door. I looked down at the last glassine envelope in my hand. I didn't know how long I had been sitting in my kitchen. It was my nephew Dennis who had come to learn photography. My large kitchen had already been converted—black velvet hung across the windows and an enlarger, three enamel trays, and two pairs of black tongs rested on the long counter next to the sink. I darkened the room, turned on the safelight, and we began the methodical sequence I learned so long ago. As I explained the rudiments of developing film and printing pictures, I heard myself repeating my father's words, interspersing details of my life in New York in the 1960s and a bit of philosophy about the joy of seeing something emerge from effort and courage.

I was sad that my teacher was no longer there to fill in the details. I missed my father. I missed hearing the tone of his voice and the way he spoke, using words and sentences still caught in the gravitational pull of the German language. His role as teacher had been passed to me. Dennis listened eagerly as he lifted a piece of photo paper from the enlarger and submerged it in the developer. In seconds, an image took form—first a nose and an eye appeared, and then the whole of my father's face appeared through the clear liquid. My father was smiling with kind eyes. Dennis turned to me and said, "I remember grandpa. He looks so young."

My father once said, "Teach someone something. You will have no idea whose life will be changed by the teaching." It's true. Today, all these years later, I am making prints by projecting high-contrast line art onto a screen prepared with photo-sensitive emulsion so that I can print fabric for a project featured in this chapter. At first I was surprised that the photo-emulsion process came so easily to me, but then, as if for the first time, I became aware of who I was and who I had become—a daughter of immigrant parents who learned well that creation isn't an act of the will, but one of the heart.

## A Brief History

The history of printing dates back to a time when humans first used their hands to transfer color pigment to a surface. Some of the earliest surviving relief prints of human hands and feet were made twenty thousand years ago on the walls of Kenniff Cave in Australia. Early civilizations also understood the principle of using a raised surface to print. In Mesopotamia circa 3000 BC, carved cylinders made of hard stone, glass, or *faience* were used to imprint a two-dimensional surface, usually wet clay, to make cylinder seals, which were used as magical amulets, jewelry, and admin-

istrative notary seals. In ancient Egypt, hand-carved wooden stamps were used to print on cloth. Single impressions were made on papyrus, parchment, and vellum, but it wasn't until the invention of paper that relief printing was used to print multiples of the same design.

The earliest paper prints were made in China in the second century in a technique called dab printing; damp paper was placed over a stone carving and burnished with ink to create a relief image. As the technique evolved, the stone tablets were replaced by wood blocks, an innovation that paired the hospitable properties of paper (resilience and flexibility) with the benefits of wood (it was plentiful and easier to carve than stone). Beginning in the sixth century, woodcuts were used to illustrate sacred texts. The printed sheets were bound into books, an innovation that had a monumental impact. After the first millennium of Chinese printing, the use of paper and relief printing spread through Japan, the Islamic world, and Europe.

In the fifteenth century, Germany established itself as a center of printing. The style and character of German woodcuts became more refined, and bold, stark graphics were printed in black ink. Images were printed on playing cards that also included color and on the pages of block books, short books, up to fifty folios in length, that were printed on only one side of a sheet of paper using cut blocks; almost all were religious in nature. At first, text and images were carved together into the same wood block. The introduction of movable metal type in the mid-fifteenth century by Johann Gutenberg allowed texts to be composed from individual letters and punctuation marks. After a book or pamphlet was printed, the metal type, made in individual molds from an alloy of lead, tin, and antimony, could be disassembled and sorted, ready to be arranged in a new configuration of text to print a new document.

While technological advancements in relief printing allowed for mass production, the value and popularity of the individual print, called a *single-leaf print,* also grew. Through the sixteenth century, advances in woodcut technology furthered the expressiveness of the medium, allowing artists to realistically depict light, shadow, and perspective, and even to add some coloring. The work of German artist Albrecht Dürer is characterized by fine detail and complex textures and represents some of the most beautiful woodblock work ever produced. The popularity of relief printing declined for several centuries and then reemerged in the nineteenth century when Commodore Perry opened up trade with Japan. An influx of exceptionally beautiful Japanese woodcuts into the Western world influenced Vincent van Gogh, Paul Gauguin, Henri de Toulouse-Lautrec, Edvard Munch, and the German expressionists Emile Nolde, and Ernst Ludwig Kirchner.

In the twentieth century, artists adapted newly invented linoleum for printing. Linoleum responded well to the artist's forceful gouges that gave linocuts distinctive graphic power and immediacy. Since its invention, linoleum has made its way into both high art and home crafts—from Picasso's *Still Life with Glass under the Lamp* to schoolchildren across the world whose first experience with printmaking is cutting designs into a linoleum block.

Stenciling is even older than relief printing. In stenciling, part of the printing surface is masked off and colored pigment is applied to the open nonmasked areas. Stenciled prints have been found all over the globe and come from many different time periods. The earliest recorded examples of stenciling are prints found in Paleolithic caves that date back to 30,000 BC. Humans pressed their hands against the rock surface with fingers splayed and blew powdered pigments through a reed to create an image of the hand as a negative space. Hands stenciled on the stone walls of the Cueva de las Manos in Argentina are dated three thousand to nine thousand years

ago. A study of the early history of the Fiji Islands shows that stencils were used to print textiles; natives cut perforations in bamboo and banana leaves and applied vegetable dyes through the openings onto *tapa,* a cloth made of bark. In ancient Egypt, stencils were used to decorate tombs, and the Greeks and the Romans employed stencils to paint murals and to outline mosaic designs.

Both the Chinese and the Japanese advanced stenciling as an art form. Among their many innovative technologies, the Japanese improved the quality and efficiency of the stenciling method by using paper stencils, which ensured a more accurate print by stabilizing the floating parts of the stencil using strands of hair to connect them to other parts of the stencil. The hairs were sandwiched between identical pieces of thin stencil paper to keep the floating design elements in place. So fine were these connecting ties that they were almost invisible in the printed image. Silk thread was substituted for hair in the system that eventually became silk screening. In another advancement, the Japanese created more durable stencils for printing on textiles by using stacked sheets of thin mulberry bark cured and waterproofed in persimmon juice. The Chinese contributed a technique of using a dye-resist technique, producing a stenciled fabric called *blue nankeen.* A thick paste made up of soya-bean flour and slaked lime was applied through hand-carved stencils made of wood and allowed to dry on the underlying white cotton fabric. After the fabric was dipped in large vats of indigo dye, it was dried and the paste was scraped off, leaving simple patterns in white on a rich blue field.

Although many innovations originated on the Silk Road, stenciling technology spread from Asia to the Middle East along the trade routes and reached Europe during the Crusades. In Europe, stencils were used to decorate church walls and screens with images of the Virgin Mary and the saints. By the seventeenth century, the textile industry was employing stenciling and block-printing techniques to decorate furniture and wallpaper. In England, stencils were used to make flocked wallpaper; in this adaptation, adhesive was applied through the cutouts in the stencil and fine wool flock was sprinkled over the sticky pattern to replicate the look of appliqué and embroidery.

In North America, stenciling became an economical way to reproduce the look of ornamental trim and braiding found on expensive wall coverings or in carved decoration. A stiff brush was used to apply oil- or water-based paint mediums through stencils made of oiled paper. Itinerant artists carried their brushes, paint, and stencils with them as they traveled from one New England town to another, stenciling walls and floors, as well as textiles, furniture, and small household accessories. Traditional stenciling fell out of favor by the mid-nineteenth century but reemerged in the mid-twentieth century with the revival of colonial and folk art styles of decorating. Prefabricated plastic stencils and water-soluble paints made do-it-yourself stenciling accessible and popular for the home crafter.

Screen printing is an advanced and more recent form of stenciling. In late-nineteenth-century France, stencils, or *pochoir*, were affixed to silk and used in fine-art stenciling, a forerunner of modern silk-screen art. The "Jazz Series" collage cutouts of Henri Matisse were rendered for publication in an art book using *pochoir*. To make a silk screen, a stencil is attached to or incorporated into a fine mesh screen that is stretched across a frame. Color pigment, either ink or paint, that is pressed against the screen passes through the unmasked areas of the mesh to print a paper or textile surface laid underneath.

The transition from stenciling to screen printing as we know it today was complete by 1907 when Samuel Simon was awarded the patent for the modern silk screen. A few years later, John Pilsworth patented a multicolor screen process that could be used to produce large quantities of banners, posters, show cards, billboards, and labels used in advertising. A cluster of additional technologies helped to popularize screen printing as a viable system for commercial use as well as for artistic experimentation. The ingeniously conceived squeegee replaced the stiff brush used to push ink through the screen, newly formulated substances replaced paper as a masking material, and synthetic fabrics, such as polyester and stainless steel mesh, replaced silk to form the screen.

Because of its association with commercial mass production and advertising, screen printing was initially rejected as a medium for fine art. Nonetheless, artists continued to explore it. They found that new technologies, especially photomechanical processes, freed the screen print from its textural limitations and allowed the painterly effects and details of halftone and continuous-tone images. Distinguishing between the fine-art print and the commercially reproduced print became an important issue for artists who produced signed, limited editions of multiple originals. Artists were adamant that each hand-pulled print was unique and not a copy. Carl Zigrosser, a curator for the Philadelphia Museum of Art in the 1930s, originated the term *serigraphy* to differentiate fine-art screen prints from prints mass-produced for commercial use.

Not until the pop art movement in the mid-twentieth century did screen printing gain full acceptance as a respected medium in the graphic arts. Using the mechanics of screen printing and the advancements made in photography, Andy Warhol created his well-known work *Campbell's Soup Can* and Roy Lichtenstein replicated the look of an old-fashioned comic strip in *The Kiss*. Screen printing is very popular among crafters, who see how easy it is to reproduce prints of extraordinary detail and tonality using readily available materials and techniques that were once the province of studio and commercial artists.

## THE SCIENCE

Printing by hand is very satisfying to do. Designs expressed in bold graphics, crisp contours, and flat swaths of vibrant color distinguish hand printing from designs that are drawn or painted directly on paper. In that final suspenseful moment, the stamp or stencil is lifted, the screen is raised, and the printed design is seen for the first time. It is this moment of revelation that continually brings me back to hand printing, but each stage of the process delights me in a unique way. When I am block printing, I like carving the block and watching the curl of linoleum or pink soft-carve material develop in front of the cutter. When I am screen printing, I enjoy watching the screen turn from snowy white to chocolaty brown as I squeegee liquid filler across it. I have learned to take my time when preparing a block or stencil because everything I do in the early stages affects the look and quality of the finished print. Working slowly also allows time for my ideas to develop.

It was predictable that I would begin my printing experience at age five with the easiest approach, relief printing with a cut potato. I quickly graduated to linoleum block printing when I was in elementary school, but only recently did I take a new interest when I worked with a pink soft-carve block. This medium is so receptive to the cutting tool that, for the first time, I was able to carve smooth curves and swirls with complete ease. I like the neat containment of block printing. There is no time-consuming setup—all you need is a block and a cutter—and the carving goes quickly. In a short time, I can cut out a design on a block and use it to print gift wrap, informal notes, and postcards. Silk-screen printing requires a bit more planning and careful setup, but the visual effects created with a screen and a stencil—from smooth layers of color to fine line work—are well worth the extra effort. Once you make a screen, you can keep it for future use. I made a screen years ago that I still use to print paper and fabric. A good cleaning after each use will keep a screen in good printing order.

If you are a beginner, relief printing is a good place to start. Relief printing includes rubber stamping and printing with a hand-carved linoleum, pink soft-carve, or high-density rubber block. The raised areas of the inked block come into direct contact with the paper surface to produce a print in mirror image. Only the raised surfaces print; the carved-out, recessed parts of the block do not pick up any ink and will not print. Successful designs for a hand-carved block are graphically strong

---

### Four Categories of Fine-Art Prints

- **Relief printing**
  Ink is applied to the raised surfaces on a block or plate. The block or plate is pressed against paper to make the print.
- **Intaglio**
  An image is incised or etched on a metal plate. These recessed areas hold the ink that produces the print.
- **Lithography**
  A drawing is made with a greasy crayon on a smooth slab of limestone. When the stone is wetted with water and coated with ink, the ink adheres only to the greasy areas to make the print.
- **Screen printing**
  A stencil is made on a fine mesh screen. Ink is forced through the fine mesh but is blocked by the stencil to print the design. This method is also known as silk screen, serigraphy, and stencil printing.

## Hand-Printing Materials at a Glance

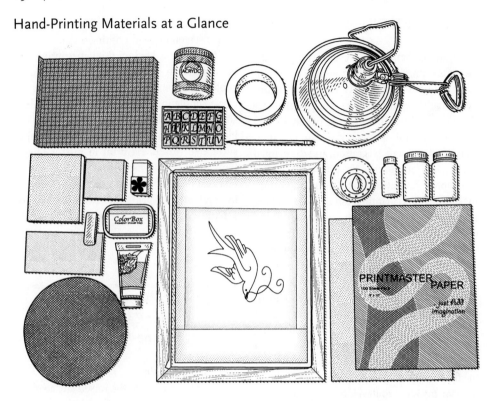

and characterized by high contrast and well-defined shapes. This is not to say that you cannot render details when cutting a block (or manipulate the ink on its surface for color effects), because you can. It simply requires greater facility with the carving tool, especially when you are working with linoleum, which is more resistant to the cutter than the pink soft-carve material or high-density rubber. I recommend that you begin with a slab of pink soft-carve for your block because it is extremely easy to cut, allowing for intricate details, and it produces neat prints.

Screen printing is a popular method of hand printing because it provides a lot of creative latitude and allows for potentially more interesting graphic effects than block printing. A stencil is attached directly to the screen, or the screen itself can become a stencil with the application of a liquid mask, such as screen

filler or drawing fluid. Photo emulsion can be used to create a screen negative. Each material produces a distinct graphic effect. Screen prints are suitable for decorating paper and fabric; you can make holiday cards and party invitations with vellum inserts, art prints to frame, and prints on fabric to use in personal or home accessories, such as a tote bag with a screen-printed monogram or a comfy oversized pillow for your couch or for a dog's bed.

### Stamping

The principle behind stamping is that an image can be reproduced innumerable times using an ink-coated die that carries a design. The die is coated in ink and pressed onto the desired surface. When the stamp is lifted, the design appears on the printing surface in mirror image. Multicolor stamped effects

## Hand-Printing Tools at a Glance

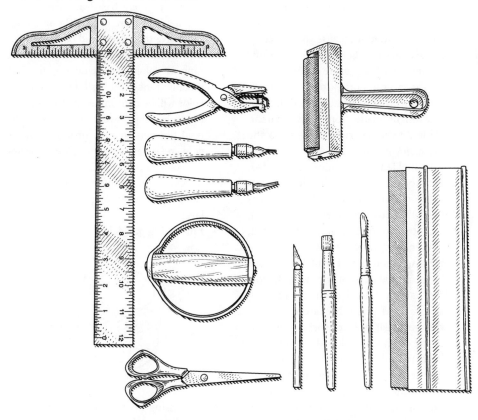

can be created using a stamp with masks. Dimensionality can be created by varying the amount of ink and the pressure exerted on the stamp or by combining stamping with a heat-embossing process to create a raised print that mimics traditional steel-plate engraving. In the heat-embossing process, a stamped design is sprinkled with fine embossing powder while the pigment-based ink is still wet. The embossing powder adheres to the stamped image and is melted with a heat gun to permanently bond to the paper's fibers. Embossing powder comes in small vials and jars and is available in a wide array of colors, from rich primary colors and jewel tones to pastels, and patinas that include transparent, pearlescent, neon, and metallic.

## Materials and Tools

The materials and tools needed for stamping are simple and few.

- **Stamp**

A stamp is composed of a die that carries a design affixed to a backing or mount. The mount can be made of hardwood, plastic, or acrylic. A clear plastic or acrylic mount makes it much easier to position and print the design exactly where you want it because you can actually see through the plastic to the printing surface while you are stamping.

The most important part on a stamp is the die, which is glued to a thin foam cushion or made from a transparent, gel-like material trimmed close to the perimeter of the die. Early stamp dies were molded from opaque gum rubber, but modern producers use clear plastics that look and feel like a firm yet flexible jelly. Look for stamps with printing areas that are smooth and unblemished, as even tiny imperfections, such as bubbles and pinholes, will print. Dies should be sturdy and deep. Stamps with shallow dies have a greater likelihood of printing an obscured image because the barely recessed areas of foam cushion or plastic gel can hit the ink pad when the die is being loaded, picking up ink that can transfer as an unwanted smudge during printing, especially when too much pressure is applied to the stamp which can cause a low-relief rubber stamp to "bottom out" on the printing surface.

- **Ink pad**

A stamp needs an ink supply. The most convenient form is an ink pad, which can be made of foam, felt, or fabric-covered foam, depending upon the kind of ink used. Dye-based ink, which can be used for general stamping, comes on a pad made of fabric-covered felt. Pigment-based ink is required for heat embossing because it remains wet long enough for the embossing powder to adhere. Pigment-based ink comes on a pad made of foam or felt. Though more expensive than dye-based pads, they are available in a wider and more brilliant range of colors that includes pastels and metallic tones. The visibility of the ink color will be determined by the color of the embossing powder used with it: colored powders that are opaque, such as gold and silver, will conceal the underlying color of ink, but powders with clear or opalescent finishes will allow the ink color to show through the embossed layer.

- **Embossing powder**

Embossing powder is available in several finishes, from clear and opalescent to metallic, tinsel, and enamel. Made of tiny particles of plastic, embossing powder works best with pigment-based ink.

- **Heat gun**

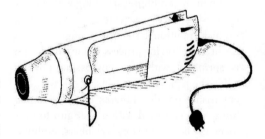

A heat gun is a convenient and useful tool for drying stamped images and for melting embossing powder. The nozzle on the heat gun directs a stream of hot air to the stamped image that is gentle enough not to blow the powder granules off the print and hot enough to melt the powder, so the molten powder when cooled permanently bonds to the paper or other printing surface.

- **Paper**

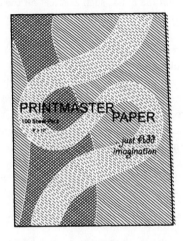

Smooth papers of all kinds and weights can be used for stamping. The texture and absorbency of the paper, along with the type of ink used, will determine the quality of the visual effect you achieve. Generally, the smoother the paper, the sharper and cleaner the image. Very glossy papers may cause a rubber stamp to slide, causing a blurred print. Textured papers often produce a stamped image with broken or missing parts because the die does not lie flat against the paper.

## Beginner Stamping Techniques

Stamping is an intuitive printing method that requires only downward pressure with a steady hand on the stamp to avoid a smudged print.

## Technique: Basic Stamping

### MATERIALS AND TOOLS
Stamp
Ink pad
Scrap paper
Printing paper

### Step 1
Load the stamp.

Lay the scrap paper on a clean flat surface. Hold the stamp in one hand and use your other hand to hold the ink pad. Press the stamp against the ink pad until the die is coated with ink.

### Step 2
Test your stamping technique.

Press the inked surface of the stamp firmly against the scrap paper without rocking or sliding the stamp. Lift the stamp straight up to reveal the image. Repeat several times and evaluate your technique. A good-quality stamp shows shape and details clearly. A partial print may be caused by uneven pressure on the stamp. A light image may be caused by insufficient inking or not enough pressure. Too much pressure or moving the stamp after it has come into contact with the printing surface can result in a blurred or smudged print.

### Step 3
Stamp a series of images in a straight line.

Load the stamp with ink. Align the bottom edge of the stamp and the bottom edge of the printing paper and print one image. Reload the stamp and make a second print next to the first one. Continue stamping in one direction along the paper's edge.

## Technique: Overprinting with a Mask

You can achieve interesting decorative effects, including printing in two (or more) colors and reconfiguring a design, using a masking technique and one stamp. A design can be masked randomly using scrap paper, which will block a part of the design, or you can cut a piece of paper to mask a particular feature.

### MATERIALS AND TOOLS
Stamp with large graphic image
Ink pad
Scrap paper
Printing paper
Manicure scissors

---

## Working Tips: Inking a Rubber Stamp with a Brayer

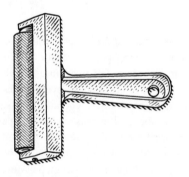

A brayer is a special roller with a handle that is used to coat a flat surface with pigment. Traditionally used to ink a carved linoleum or soft-carve block, a brayer can also be used to apply a coat of ink onto a large stamp. Roll the brayer across a large ink pad to pick up the ink. Then roll the inked brayer over the surface of the stamp in one continuous motion. Do not go back and forth over the stamp to avoid overloading the die.

---

### Step 1
Make the mask.

Make a stamped print on a piece of scrap paper. Use manicure scissors to cut out the print along the outline. Snip the stamped image in half, following a random line that divides the design, or carefully snip away a part of the image on the mask, such as a leaf on the edge of a flower, using the stamped lines as a guide.

### Step 2
Make a partial print in one color.

Lay the cut mask on the smooth printing paper and align the reinked stamp so that it is as precisely positioned as possible; the stamp will straddle the mask and the printing paper. Use the stamp to print the image: part of the image will print on the printing paper but the rest of the design will overprint on the mask instead.

### Step 3
Use the mask to make a partial print in a second color.

Lay the snipped-away section of the mask on the printed image to block that part of the design. Clean the stamp and reload it with a second color ink. Align the stamp as closely as possible over the mask and press down and lift up to stamp the second part of the design on the printing paper. Lift off the mask to reveal the multicolor stamped image.

## Technique: Registering a Print with a Right-Angle Ruler

For a neatly positioned stamped impression, line up the stamp backing on a transparent right-angle ruler, also called a "stamp positioner."

### MATERIALS AND TOOLS
Stamp
Ink pad
Tracing paper
Printing paper
Transparent right-angle ruler

**Step 1**

Make a pattern on tracing paper.

Lay the tracing paper on a protected flat surface. Line up the right-angle ruler on the bottom left corner of the tracing paper. Invert an inked stamp over the corner, aligning the backing with the ruler, and press down to print an image on the tracing paper.

**Step 2**

Position the pattern on the printing paper.

Place the image on the tracing paper over the printing paper, sliding the tracing paper around until you like the position of the stamped image.

**Step 3**

Stamp the image.

Lay the right-angle ruler at the bottom left corner of the tracing paper. Hold the ruler securely against the printing paper and pull the tracing paper away. Use the ruler as a guide to position the inked stamp on the printing paper. Press down on the stamp to make the print.

## Heat Embossing

In heat embossing, an inked stamp is pressed on paper and the printed image is sprinkled with embossing powder while the ink is still wet. An electric heat-embossing tool, which looks like a small hair dryer with a gunlike nozzle, directs a stream of hot air onto the powder to melt it. It is always fun to see the granular powder transition to a molten layer of raised color on the paper. Keep the gun's nozzle moving to avoid scorching the paper. Before applying any heat, be sure to tap off any stray granules from around the stamped image so that they do not melt and spoil an otherwise neat print.

## Technique: Embossing with a Heat Gun

The special heat gun used in heat embossing delivers a controlled flow of hot air that will melt the embossing powder without blowing it off the stamped print because it adheres well to pigment-based ink, which is required in this technique. Be sure to apply the embossing powder to the stamped image while the pigment-based ink is still wet in order to achieve a complete print.

MATERIALS AND TOOLS

Stamp

Pigment-based ink pad

Embossing powder

Paper for printing

Heat gun

Teaspoon

Tapered watercolor paintbrush

Copy paper

**Step 1**

Make a print.

Press a stamp onto the ink pad. Press the loaded stamp onto the paper.

**Step 2**

Apply the embossing powder.

Pour some embossing powder into a teaspoon and sprinkle the powder evenly over the wet ink. Lift the paper and tap off the excess powder onto a clean sheet of copy paper. Blow gently on the image or use the tip of a tapered paintbrush to sweep off any stray particles of embossing powder that remain around the image. Return the excess embossing powder to its container.

**Step 3**

Melt the powder.

Turn on the heat gun and use it to melt the embossing powder, moving the nozzle constantly from side to side, monitoring the change in the embossing powder, whose surface will go from a relatively dull, granular texture to a glossy molten liquid that will solidify quickly, and removing the heat when all of the powder has changed over.

### Making Your Own Stamps

Despite the seemingly infinite number of commercial stamps available, it is still fun to print your own graphic designs using stamps made from common office and art supplies, such as art erasers, adhesive-backed foam sheets, and high-density rubber (or cloth-lined computer mouse pads).

### Technique: Making a Stamp from an Eraser

For a small icon, symbol, or monogram, an art eraser, such as an Artgum eraser by Sanford, is the perfect medium from which to carve your own stamp. You can carve a geometric or abstract shape in little time and then use the stamp to sign off on cards and letters. A design can be represented in either a positive space or a negative space, depending on what area of the design you carve in relief. For more complex images, make several eraser stamps or stamp in several different colors. With a set of small geometric shapes, such as circles, triangles, and squares, you can make up simple animals or figures or you can create an overall pattern. Three round circles can be the beginning of a snowman and a tear shape can be stamped in a radial pattern to make the petals of a flower. Make a continuing collection of unique stamps and store them in a small box so they are ready to use when you are feeling artistic. For larger designs, consider buying high-density rubber slabs made especially for carving stamps.

### MATERIALS AND TOOLS

Art eraser
Craft knife with replaceable blades
Tracing paper
Soft #2 pencil

**Step 1**

Draw the design.

Use a pencil to draw a small bold shape, such as a flower or a star, onto a piece of tracing paper, sizing it so that it fits within the surface of one side of the eraser and allowing enough room for a small margin. Use a pencil to color in the printing parts of the design, which will not be cut.

**Step 2**

Transfer the design to an eraser.

Lay the tracing facedown on one surface of the eraser. Use a pencil to rub the back of the tracing to transfer the design to the eraser.

**Step 3**

Cut out the design.

Use a craft knife to cut into the eraser, first removing any details in the interior of the design. Then use the knife to outline the shape of the image. Cut away from the outline toward the outer edges of the eraser to remove all of the parts of the eraser that will not print.

---

## Working Tips: Cleaning and Storing Stamps

Be sure to clean your stamps after each use to keep them in good condition. To clean water-based inks, wipe the printing surface or die with a damp sponge. To clean pigment-based inks, use a stamp cleaner or a baby wipe, which has a mild detergent. If a stamp has caked-on ink, remove it with a soft toothbrush, gently scrubbing the crevices on the die to loosen and remove the ink and then wiping the stamp clean with a baby wipe. Never submerge a stamp in water, as soaking can cause the mount and the die to separate.

## Technique: Making a Stamp from an Adhesive-Backed Foam Sheet

A foam sheet is easy to cut with scissors. It is also easy to use a large decorative punch with a simple contour although you will probably have to manipulate the edge of the foam sheet between the closely spaced jaws of the punch, but you should be able to cut out a complete shape. The adhesive back on the foam makes it easy to affix cutouts to a mount. A standard hole punch can be used to cut circles for a polka dot pattern. Clear plastic boxes make perfect mounts for this type of stamp—the containers are easy to hold and, because they are transparent, you will be able to see where you are stamping the image. For a deeper stamp that doesn't bottom out, cut out several identical foam shapes and stack them together on the surface of the mount.

### MATERIALS AND TOOLS

Decorative punch with a simple, bold shape, approximately 1" (2.5 cm) wide
Foam sheet with adhesive backing, $\frac{1}{16}$" (0.2 cm) thick
Clear plastic box with a lid, slightly larger than the cutout shape
Scissors

### Step 1

Cut out a shape using a punch.
Slide one edge of the foam sheet between the jaws of the punch, metal template facing up, tugging gently on the foam until the entire cutting die covers the foam. Keep the foam flat. Squeeze the punch to cut the shape. Release the jaws, which should release the shape or use your fingers to lift the shape from the die. Use sharp scissors to trim off any jagged edges from the cutout shape.

### Step 2

Make more foam cutouts.
Repeat step 1 to make two more identical shapes.

### Step 3

Make a stack of foam cutouts.
Peel off the paper backing from one foam cutout to expose the adhesive. Press the cutout, adhesive side down, onto the foam side of the second cutout. Add the third cutout to make a stack.

### Step 4

Make a stamp.

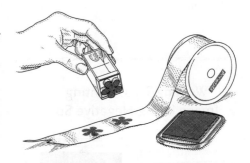

Stand the plastic container upright on a flat surface, lid facing up. Peel off the paper backing from the bottom cutout in the foam stack. Center the stack on the plastic lid and press until it adheres. Use your foam stamp to print images as desired.

## Technique: Making a Stamp from a Slab of High-Density Rubber

High-density rubber is an ideal material for making stamps of your own design. You can use a purchased slab or adapt a rubber mouse pad; both materials are easy to cut. A plain rubber slab has a smooth surface on both sides, whereas a mouse pad may have one fabric-coated side. Simple details can be scored or cut into both surfaces. The fabric layer is a good feature because it can absorb more ink or paint for printing, allowing you to print more images before having to reload. Rubber pads are thick and flexible, making them suited for printing on contoured surfaces, such as the outside of a pail. For more control when stamping on flat surfaces, mount the stamp on a piece of stiff chipboard.

MATERIALS AND TOOLS
Paper cutout of pattern
High-density rubber slab or mouse pad
Chipboard, slightly larger than cutout
    (optional)
Rubber cement (optional)
Permanent marker or soft #2 pencil
Craft knife
Self-healing cutting mat
Scissors

## Working Tips: Printing an Image Using Negative Space

You can use a punch to cut out a foam shape and use it to print with, or you can use the foam that surrounds the cutout to make a print instead.

**Step 1**
Mark the pattern.
Lay the rubber slab or mouse pad on a flat surface; if using a mouse pad, place it fabric side up. Place the cutout pattern on top, remembering that the stamp will print in reverse, and trace around it with a pencil or a permanent marker

**Step 2**
Cut out the stamp.
Cut on the outside marked line, using a craft knife and self-healing cutting mat to cut a plain rubber slab, and scissors to cut a mouse pad. Cut through the entire thickness of the pad. Pull on the mouse pad, if necessary, to cut through the fabric layer.

**Step 3**
Add details to the stamp.
Use a craft knife to cut surface details into the rubber or fabric surface. Cut only halfway through the pad's thickness. These cuts will add texture and dimension to the stamp.

**Step 4 (optional)**
Mount the stamp on chipboard.
Use rubber cement to mount the rubber stamp to a piece of chipboard. Apply the rubber cement to the chipboard and to the side of the stamp without the detail cuts. Wait 5 minutes and then press the pieces together for a firm bond.

## Block Printing

The block-printing sequence proceeds in four stages: marking a design on the block, cutting the block, applying ink to the block, and printing the design. Bold shapes with little to no detail can be cut into the surface of a block or more intricately cut forms with slightly more detail can be incised, depending on whether the cutting surface is linoleum, soft-carve material, or high-density rubber. Of the three block-printing materials featured, linoleum is generally considered the most difficult to cut, offering resistance to the cutter, so it's advisable to keep the design simple. For block prints with greater detail, choose a block made from soft-carve material. The cutter glides easily through this material, giving you more control over the design with less effort and opening up such design possibilities as sweeping curves and curlicues. As you become acquainted with the different materials, you will notice small but discernible crumbling on the edges of a gouge made in linoleum and, to a lesser degree, high-density rubber. This slight crumbling will affect the sharpness of a printed line. Pink soft-carve material is far less prone to this phenomenon.

## Fun for Kids: Easy Stamping with Thin Foam

Although it may be difficult for young hands to operate a decorative punch without help, it is supereasy for kids to make stamps once the foam shapes are cut out. Both the positive shape (the foam cutout) and the negative shape (the foam frame that remains after the cutout is removed) can be used. Clear plastic containers for the mounts come in a range of sizes—from a small size perfect for little hands to hold to larger sizes for mounting an array of adhesive-backed shapes. Use a brayer to apply ink to a large stamp composed of multiple foam cutouts.

Materials and Tools

- **Linoleum printing block**

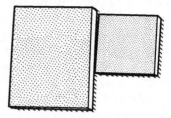

Mounted on a block of wood or particleboard, linoleum is a naturally stiff and sturdy material that is somewhat difficult to cut. It is suited for designs that are bold and graphic in character rather than intricate or detailed. Unmounted linoleum with a jute or burlap back is also available, but it tends to warp.

- **Pink soft-carve printing block**

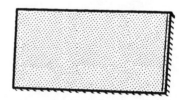

Pink soft-carve blocks are available in ¼"-thick (0.6 cm) slabs. This material is durable, flexible, and not prone to crumbling at the edge of a cut. It is easy to cut, allowing for designs with flowing curves and a moderate to high level of detail.

- **High-density rubber printing block**

Clay or cream-colored high-density rubber is available in ¼"-thick (0.6 cm) slabs of varying dimensions. High-density rubber is a durable material that is easy to cut, making it suited to designs with moderately dense line work when gouges are spaced about ⅛" (0.3 cm) apart. Intricate cutting where gouges cross over one another or are close together may cause the edge of the gouged line to crumble slightly. Some computer mouse pads are manufactured of high-density rubber in a variety of shapes, including those that are coated with fabric, making them suited to bold designs with some detail.

- **Block printing ink**

## Fun for Kids: Making a Multicolor Bird Print

Work together with a child to make this cute two-part bird print using the Bird pattern (page 694). Cut stamps from a slab of high-density rubber. The legs on the bird are purposely long to provide convenient "handles" for the child who is printing.

- Cut out the two stamps yourself with a craft knife or a pair of scissors. Eye and feather details can be cut with a craft knife or they can be added to the stamped print using a marker or paint. Omit the chipboard mount—it's fun for children to press their fingertips over the entire back of the soft stamp when making the print.
- Show your child how to brush acrylic craft paint onto the surface of the stamp. The tabs are intended to provide handles for printing; leave them free of paint so that they don't print.
- Let your child press the stamp, paint side down, onto the printing surface. Print the bird first. When the paint is dry, overprint the wing in a darker color.
- When the printing session is complete, wash the rubber stamps in warm soapy water. Let the stamps dry and store them flat.

Block-printing ink is available in a wide range of colors and unique patinas, such as neon and metallic. There are both water-soluble and oil-based ink formulations, but only water-soluble inks are considered in this section. The ink has a thick viscosity similar to gel toothpaste. When conditioned with a palette knife or plastic credit card and then spread into a smooth, thin layer with a brayer, the ink retains its consistency so that it can remain on a printing block without dripping. To thin a water-soluble ink, add a few drops of water or extender base and blend thoroughly until the ink is a creamy consistency. To slow drying, use a retarder. To increase transparency and lubricity, add a transparent base to the ink.

- **Printing paper**

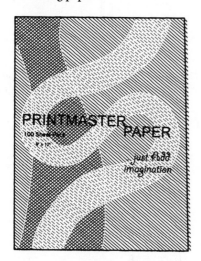

The paper used for block printing should be porous and smooth to the touch but have some tooth so that the ink adheres to its surface. Construction, drawing, charcoal, and pastel papers work well for most printing processes. Cardstock and 100 percent rag paper are ideal for pulling art prints as they absorb ink well. For block printing, use 20-pound weight paper and thicker cover stock. The slick surface of high-gloss papers, vinyl, and plastic-coated papers can cause an inked linoleum block to slide, smudging the print. When you are learning to block print or when you are pulling proofs or test prints, you can use any kind of paper, either sized or unsized. Paper without size is more absorbent, allowing ink to penetrate the paper's fibers without leaving a glossy coating on the surface. Heavily sized paper is less absorbent, so more ink remains on the surface.

- **Graphite paper**
This thin sheet of paper coated with powdered graphite is used to transfer line art to a flat surface, such as a printing block. A design printed on an inkjet printer can also be transferred onto most carving materials if the print is laid, ink side down, on the carving material before the ink dries.

## Working Tips: Three-Dimensional Effects with a High-Density Rubber Stamp

Instead of loading a stamp made from a slab of high-density rubber for each printed image, use the stamp to print several images before reloading it. As the paint on the pad diminishes, the sequence of prints will shift from heavy, saturated color to thinner, paler color. Darker images will appear to be in the foreground and paler images will recede, creating the impression of three dimensions. You could use a single stamp of a flying bird, for example, to suggest a flock of birds flying in the sky.

- **Set of cutters with a handle**

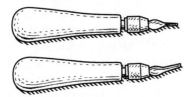

The handheld tools used to cut blocks of linoleum and slabs of soft-carve and high-density rubber are available in a convenient set containing a wood or plastic handle and several interchangeable cutters. The shape and size of the cutter and the angle at which the tool is held determine the width and depth of the carving. For a look at the kinds of cuts that can be made, see Choosing the Right Cutter (page 309).

- **Craft knife**

Handled like a pencil, a craft knife has a replaceable blade and is good for making fine cuts in the carving material.

- **Brayer**

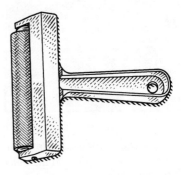

A brayer is a roller used to spread a thin even layer of ink on the printing surface of a hand-carved block. It can also be used to apply ink to a stamp that has a large printing area. The brayer has a central handle fitted with a roller. The roller

---

## Working Tips: Understanding Formulations of Printing Ink

Printing inks come in two basic formulations, those that can be thinned with water and those that can be thinned with a chemical solvent. Water-soluble inks include inks that are permanent when dry, such as acrylic inks made up of color pigment suspended in an acrylic resin, and inks that remain water-soluble when dry. Both types are easy to handle and clean up with soap and water when they are wet, but acrylic printing ink must be washed off immediately after use to prevent it from drying and caking in the gouges of the printing block or the mesh of the screen. Nonpermanent water-soluble inks printed on paper can be treated with a light coat of spray fixative after the printing ink has dried to provide some protection against moisture that could damage the print. Textile-printing inks are made permanent by heat-setting, usually with a hot iron at 275°F to 375°F (135°C to 190.6°C). Once the ink is heat-set and cured, the printed fabric can be washed.

material can be soft or hard, depending on the materials from which it is made. A soft roller picks up more ink than a hard roller, making it suited to printing on fabric; a hard roller picks up less ink, making it suited to printing on paper.

- **Ink slab**

Any flat, smooth nonporous surface can serve as a slab for the printing ink; glass, plastic, and acrylic are good surface choices. The slab holds the ink supply while it is being conditioned (worked into usable consistency) and also keeps an ink supply ready for the brayer, which is rolled across the inked surface, to reload.

- **Old credit card**

An expired plastic credit card that is firm and flexible is the ideal tool for spreading ink in a thin, even layer on a slab. A palette knife can also be used, but it has a shorter spreading edge.

- **Bench hook**

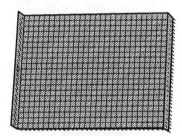

Laid flat on a work table, a bench hook is designed to keep a carving block that is placed on top from moving as it is cut. Made of wood or metal, a bench hook comprises a flat bed or platform with two lipped edges. The lip on one end points down and rests against the edge of the work table to keep the bench hook from sliding forward. A stop or fence at the opposite end points up and helps prevent the carving block from shifting as you cut. Available in a convenient 7½" × 10" (19.1 × 25.4 cm) size, a bench hook is suited to most small blocks of linoleum and slabs of soft-carve or high-density rubber. One or two C-clamps can be used instead to hold a block in place; the number needed depends on the size of the block. Use cardboard tabs to keep clamps from denting the block.

- **Baren**

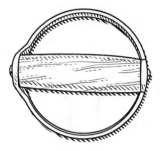

Another helpful printmaking tool, a baren is used to smooth the printing

## Working Tips: Practicing Cutting Mindfulness

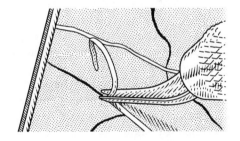

It may seem obvious, but it's worth restating. The parts of the drawing that you cut away are the parts that will not print. The parts that remain make up the printing surfaces. Remembering this little bit of wisdom can save you from having to begin your carving anew, which may be your only remedy once a wanted part of the block is cut away.

paper that is laid over an inked block. Having a subtle convex surface, the disk-shaped handheld baren has a mounted handle that spans its full diameter so that even pressure is distributed and the inked design is transferred uniformly to the paper. Available in a variety of sizes, the standard baren measures 5″ (12.7 cm) in diameter.

- **T square**

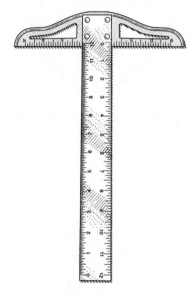

Adapted from its traditional drafting tasks, a T square is especially helpful for positioning a print on a piece of paper, such as a greeting card, or for registering several images that are printed in succession, as in a two-color design.

- **Printing frame**

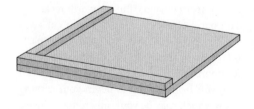

A printing frame is used to facilitate the accurate registration of one or more col-ors on a print. The wood frame is comprised of a flat rectilinear platform and two battens that are secured on a perpendicular to one corner. The printing block is set into this corner, and the edge of the printing paper is temporarily tacked to the frame. The paper is lowered onto the inked block to print and then raised; if a second color is being printed on the same paper, the next inked block in the sequence is inserted in the same spot. The result is a neatly registered print with two colors. An old wood frame can perform the same function.

---

## Quick & Easy: Making a Fleur-de-Lis Stamp

Use a slab of pink soft-carve or high-density rubber to make a printing block for the elegant fleur-de-lis motif (page 695). The fleur-de-lis design can be carved in one block as a positive image and in another block as a negative image. Use the blocks to print a border on a wall, alternating the motifs to accentuate the shape of their positive-negative spaces. Or, if you have some experience, you may wish to carve both motifs side by side on one block for more efficient printing.

---

## Designing and Marking a Block

The block-printing process requires that you visualize your design in a particular way while you are actively cutting your design. First, keep in mind that the parts of the design that are cut away will not pick up ink and therefore will not print. These cutaway areas are lower than the block's printing surface and will show up as white spaces on your print. The parts of the design that remain in relief on the block do pick up ink and will print. To avoid confusion or mistakes, use a colored pencil or a marker to fill in those areas on the block that do print before you begin cutting.

A second thing to remember is that the block will print a mirror image of the design that is cut. If the orientation of your design includes letters or numerals or is important for some other reason, make a reverse pattern before transferring the design to your block. Reversing the pattern will ensure that words or numerals are readable in the finished print.

## Technique: Transferring a Hand-Drawn Design to a Printing Block

This technique describes how to make a working drawing or tracing and transfer it to the surface of a printing block so it can be cut. Use this technique for linoleum, pink soft-carve, and high-density rubber blocks. A Tree and Moon design (page 695) is featured.

## Working Tips: Positive and Negative Space

Positive and negative space can be used to manipulate the perception of shape and to change the focal point of a print, an artistic effect that is most evident in a print with bold graphic shapes and strong contrast. Positive space is "occupied" space. Negative space is "unoccupied" space. In a print with a dark-colored shape on a white background, the dark shape is positive space and the white background is negative space. If the light and dark tones are reversed—the background is dark and the shape is light—then the background is "occupied" and commands attention while the shape itself is perceived as a negative space. The use of positive and negative space in a single design can produce interesting and unexpected visual effects by directing the eye to a particular area.

MATERIALS AND TOOLS
Paper
Printing block
Soft pencil
Graphite paper
Scissors

**Step 1**
Draw the design.
Place the block on a sheet of paper and trace around its perimeter with a pencil. Use the pencil to draw a design for printing within the marked area. Use scissors to cut out the working drawing. Cut a piece of graphite paper to the same size.

---

### Quick & Easy: Making a Reverse Pattern

If your design includes letters or numerals or if the orientation of your print is important—perhaps it shows your house or a familiar landmark—you'll need to reverse the pattern before transferring it to the printing block. Here are three ways to make a reverse pattern:

- Use a photocopier. Select the mirror image feature and then photocopy as usual.
- Use a computer, scanner, and printer. Scan the design, view it onscreen, and use your computer software to reverse the image. Print the mirror image design on your printer.
- Trace or draw the design onto tracing paper. Turn the tracing paper facedown on a light box and retrace the design lines on the reverse side to obtain a mirror image.

---

**Step 2**
Transfer the design.

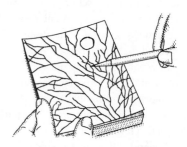

Lay the working drawing faceup on the printing block. Slip a piece of graphite paper, graphite surface facedown, between the drawing and the block. Trace over the lines with a pencil, applying medium pressure, to transfer the design to the block.

### Technique: Transferring a Design Printed with an Ink-Jet Printer

Designs printed with an ink-jet printer or copier are very easy to transfer to linoleum, high-density rubber, and pink soft-carve blocks while the ink is still fresh. Laying the printout ink side down on the carving surface reverses the transferred design, a desirable feature for letters or numerals that must be carved in reverse.

MATERIALS AND TOOLS
Working drawing or other artwork
Printing block
Ink-jet copier or printer
Tablespoon

**Step 1**
Copy the image.
Make a copy of the artwork using an ink-jet copier or printer, but do not use the mirror image feature.

**Step 2**
Transfer the image.
Lay the copy, ink side down, on the block. Rub the bowl side of a tablespoon over the

back of the copy to transfer ink from the copy to the surface of the block. Let the ink dry about 45 minutes, but test the ink by placing a finger on one of the lines in an obscure place on the block before beginning work. If the ink smears, it is still wet; wait another 15 minutes. The design on the block will appear in mirror image, but it will print right-reading as in the original drawing.

### Cutting a Block

If you are new to cutting, use a spare block to experiment with the cutting tool. Practice using the different blades, also called cutters or gouges, until you become familiar with the kinds of cuts each one makes. You will find that the character of a cut—its thickness, shape, direction, and depth—is determined by the angle at which you hold the tool and the amount of pressure you exert. Make certain the cutting edge of your cutter is sharp and that your fingers stay out of the way of the blade as you work. If you are having trouble cutting the block, make certain that the tool is not being held at too steep or too flat an angle. A bench hook is very helpful in keeping a carving block from sliding or shifting on the work surface, ensuring neat and precise cuts.

### Technique: Cutting the Design on a Block

Use a cutting tool with the desired cutter to cut out your design, following the marked lines on your block. This technique can be used for linoleum, pink soft-carve, and high-density rubber blocks.

#### MATERIALS AND TOOLS
Printing block, with transferred design
Set of linoleum cutters with different cutters
Bench hook
C-clamps (optional)
Cardboard tabs (optional)

### Step 1
Set up the bench hook.

To protect your hands and to stabilize your block during cutting, place a bench hook on your work table, resting the front downward-pointing lip of the block against the front edge of the table. If you are using C-clamps instead of a bench hook, insert small cardboard tabs between the block and the clamp to prevent the clamp from making indentations on the block's surface, depressions that could alter the surface enough to mar your print.

### Step 2
Install the proper cutter in the tool's handle. Choose a cutter according to the character

---

## Working Tips: Choosing the Right Cutter

Cutters or gouges designed for the handle of a cutting tool come in various shapes and sizes. You will discover that the size and shape of the cutter or gouge, the pressure that you exert on the tool, the angle at which you hold the tool, and the block material all affect the width and depth of the cut on a block.

- Use a flat blade or a narrow V-cutter to outline each of the printing parts on the block.
- Use a wide U-gouge to cut away the parts of the block that do not print, pushing the gouge away from the V-shaped cuts as you cut.
- Use a flat blade to incise fine lines or to create textural effects, such as cross-hatching; hold the tool's handle like a pencil and draw the blade toward you as if you were drawing or writing.

of the lines and shapes in your design. Install the cutter in the tool handle by loosening the chuck and putting the blunt end of the cutter blade into the space as far as it will go. Turn the chuck clockwise to secure the cutter.

**Step 3**

Cut the marked design.

Use the cutter to cut the design marked on the block. Hold the cutting tool at an angle (never in a completely vertical position) and apply even pressure to guide the blade, easing off the tool as you complete a cut. Change cutters as needed to cut the lines, grooves, and gouges you want.

**Step 4**

Assess the design cut into the block.

Stop cutting the block when all of the marked details are carved. Brush off all shavings from

## Working Tips: Cutting a Linoleum Block

- Choose a design that is bold and graphic with strong contrast. Linoleum can develop a rough edge along a cut, making the material unsuited to designs with fine details, congested line work such as cross-hatching, and intricate contours.
- Warm the linoleum with a hair dryer to make it softer and more receptive to cutting. Linoleum that feels cool to the touch is stiff and difficult to cut.
- Always work with a clean, sharp cutter, changing to a new blade when the working blade becomes dull or nicked.

- Don't wait until the blade is so dull, it doesn't cut easily; a dull blade can cause a slip of the tool that makes an injury and a miscut more likely.
- Cut slowly and methodically and apply moderate pressure. Forcing the tool or using excessive pressure can cause the blade to slip and make an errant cut that can ruin a block.
- If you make a mistake, try to incorporate the unplanned cut into your design. Remember that the areas you cut away won't print.

the block. Check that the cuts are deep and even to ensure that they will not get coated with ink.

You don't need a slew of different cutters to create designs for block prints. Only a few basic cutters will give you artistic flexibility, enabling you to create gouges in the carving material that vary in width, shape, and direction and that result in block prints with shapely contours, varietal texture, and movement. There is no substitute for practicing with the different cutters to get the feel for what they can do. When the subtle differences among the blade shapes and sizes become familiar to you, you will be able to wield the cutting tools in effective ways that facilitate your own artistic expression. For example, two blades with the same shape/silhouette, but in different sizes, will create cuts with similar topology, but with slightly different widths. A narrow U-cutter and a wide U-cutter will produce a rounded trough exhibiting slightly different widths in the carving material. However, when the pressure on the tool is changed, a whole new visual effect is created. These same cutters wielded delicately will scoop off shallow cuts. Pushed into the surface of the block, they will remove a deeper layer of material.

Here is a sampling of design effects and the cutters that produced them. Remember that varying the angle and force of the cutter, the type of carving material used, and the density and direction of the cuts will introduce a new set of printed effects.

Carved and Inked Block Print

Wide gouge

Narrow gouge

Wide V-cutter (or veiner)

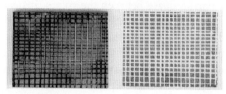

Narrow V-cutter (or veiner)

---

## Working Tips: Making a Test Print

After a block is cut, you will be eager to see how it prints. A test print on scrap paper lets you examine the design and refine the cutting. If an area on the block that is not supposed to print leaves an ink smudge on your test print, that area on the block is too high. Clean the ink off the block with warm soapy water and dry the block with paper towels. Then use a cutter to remove more of the unwanted area on the block. Make another test print to see if the results are better.

## Making Block Prints

The main reason for printing is to make more than one copy of a single design. Multiple prints of one design are called a print run or an edition. Registration ensures that all the images in a print run or edition print in the same position on each sheet of paper.

If you have a good spatial sense, you may feel comfortable simply eyeballing the placement of a print on the paper. Since it is unlikely that identical prints in a series will ultimately be viewed side by side, incremental differences will not be a problem. Printing a one-off—a single print not in a series—also grants you some leeway. If the print ends up somewhat askew on the paper and you've allowed an ample margin, you can trim the paper to square it off with the print. However, in general, I recommend that you register your prints for accurate printmaking. There are several straightforward approaches that you can use. The method presented here uses a T square, which acts as a stop for the block.

---

## Quick & Easy: Creating a Gradient Band of Color

One way to make a multicolor print is to blend different colors of ink on the slab before you roll the ink on the block for printing. Squeeze out two short ribbons of block-printing ink in two different colors, say lime green and turquoise, side by side on an ink slab, allowing a narrow space between the colors. Instead of rolling the brayer in a straight up-and-down motion, angle the roller slightly so that the adjacent edges of the colors blend in the middle. Use the inked roller to coat your linoleum block to make a print.

---

## Technique: Registering a Design with a T Square

This registration method requires very little in the way of setup and utilizes materials and tools you probably have. A self-healing cutting mat with a marked grid and a T square make it easy to align and mark multiple sheets of paper, one at a time, for each print in the edition.

### MATERIALS AND TOOLS

Printing paper
Printing block with cut design
Testing paper, in the same size as the printing paper
Self-healing cutting mat
T square
Masking tape
Pencil

### Step 1

Set up the cutting mat and paper.

Lay the cutting mat on a flat surface with the marked grid facing up. Place a sheet of testing paper on the mat, aligning one corner of the paper with the marked grid so the sheet is straight and square.

### Step 2

Add registration tabs.

Press two short strips of tape on the mat, aligning the inside edges of the tape with the outside edges of the paper to indicate the position of one corner of the paper. If desired, repeat at the opposite bottom corners.

### Step 3

Add the T square.

Position the carved block on the paper. Align the crossbar of the T square with the edge of the cutting mat. Slide the T square over until the long edge is aligned with one edge of the block. Use strips of masking tape to secure the ruler to the surface of the cutting mat.

**Step 4**

Mark the position of the block on the printing paper.

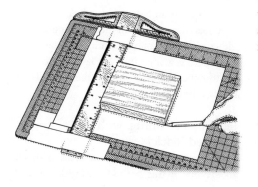

Use a pencil to make light ticks on either side of the block to indicate the position of the block on the paper.

**Step 5**

Mark all the printing paper in the edition.

Remove the printing block and the test paper from the grid. Slide a sheet of the printing paper under the T square, set the printing block in place, and use the setup to make registration marks on the new sheet. Repeat until every sheet for the print edition is marked. If you prefer, you can mark each sheet just before you print it instead.

### Technique: Preparing the Ink and Inking the Block

Inking a block for printing includes preparing the ink to ensure a smooth and even consistency.

#### MATERIALS AND TOOLS

Printing block with cut design
Tube of block-printing ink, water based or acrylic
Glass or plastic slab
Brayer
Expired credit card or palette knife

**Step 1**

Squeeze out the ink.

Lay the slab on a protected work surface. Squeeze out a ribbon of block-printing ink the width of the brayer roller on one end of the slab. Use a credit card to mix and flatten the ink but do not spread the ink over the slab.

---

## Quick & Easy: Using Gradient Color to Achieve Dimension

You can use the same block to make a series of prints, each with a different textural character, by blending inks in different proportions. Choose two different ink colors to produce a band of gradient color. Here, dark midnight blue and white are used in varying proportions to create the background sky in three different block prints. Even though an inked roller is usually rolled parallel to the cuts in the block, here the lightly coated brayer is rolled horizontally so that gradient color is applied horizontally across the block to suggest the growing darkness where the horizon darkens before the sky above. White was added to the blended color and applied in the area near the moon to suggest the luminous effects of moonlight on the night sky. Frame your finished prints individually or group all three in one frame to create a graphic tableau.

**Step 2**

Coat the roller.

Touch the roller of the brayer to the slab to pick up some ink; avoid overloading the ink, which will cause the roller to slide. Roll the brayer down the slab in a straight line from the top to the bottom and then lift the brayer, allowing the roller to turn. Roll the brayer back up to the top of the slab and lift it up. Continue the roll-and-lift motion until there is a thin, even, tacky layer of ink on the slab. If there is too much ink on the slab, use the credit card to scrape off some ink and return it to the top of the slab. When the layer of ink is workable, the roller will make a tick sound when it lifts off the surface.

**Step 3**

Roll ink onto the carved block.

Use the coated brayer to roll ink onto the block. The direction of the rolling should be parallel to the cuts in the surface, not across

---

## Working Tips: Setting Up a Print-Drying Line

Individual wet prints can be hung on a line to air-dry. To set one up indoors, mark two points at the same height on two opposite walls or points in the room. Screw in one eye hook at each marked point. Use a double knot to tie one end of a length of nylon cord to one eye hook. Thread the line through the other eye hook, pull it taut, and knot securely. As you pull wet prints, hang them on the line by the top edge with plastic spring-loaded clothespins or bulldog clips. Space the prints at a safe distance from one another to prevent wet ink from transferring.

---

them, to avoid depositing ink into the recessed areas.

**Step 4**

Reload the cut block, as needed.

Reload the roller from the slab, if necessary, and continue to roll more ink onto the block until there is a smooth, even layer. Be careful not to deposit gobs of ink in the gouged-out areas as these may print.

## Technique: Printing with an Inked Block

There are several ways to print with an inked block. In this method, the block is placed facedown on the paper to transfer the ink and make a print. Use the T square setup to make registration marks on the printing paper.

### MATERIALS AND TOOLS

Printing block with cut design
Block-printing ink
Printing paper with registration marks
Brayer
Slab of glass or plastic

**Step 1**

Ink the carved block.

Prepare the ink and use a brayer to apply a thin layer to the printing surface of the carved block. Two or three applications of ink on the block may be necessary for the first print.

**Step 2**

Make the print.

Lay the block, ink side down, within the registration marks on the paper, aligning one side of the block with the edge of the T square. Press down evenly on the block to transfer the ink to the paper. To ensure a clean print, do not rock or shift the block.

**Step 3**

Reveal the print.

Lift the block straight up and off the paper

to reveal the print. Lay the print, ink side up, on a flat surface to dry or use plastic clips to hang the print on a line.

## Technique: Flipping and Burnishing a Print

Unconventional, perhaps, and requiring some practice, this flipping method gives me greater assurance that I will achieve a complete print from an inked block that I have positioned by hand on the printing paper. After pressing the block against the paper, I carefully hold both pieces together and flip them over onto a hard surface so that the paper is on top. This new orientation allows me access to the reverse side of the print so that I can burnish it with a baren to ensure a complete and even transfer of the inked design. Practice a few times with scrap paper to get the knack of flipping and burnishing before you try it with good paper.

### MATERIALS AND TOOLS

Printing block, inked
Printing paper with registration marks
Baren

### Step 1

Make the print.

Set the block, ink side down, on the paper within the registration marks.

### Step 2

Prepare to flip the work.

Carefully slide the paper (with the block still on top) to the edge of the work surface. Bring one hand under the paper to support the weight of the block and place your other hand on top of the block to hold it against the paper. Carefully turn both hands simultaneously to flip over the work so that the paper is on top. Set the pieces back down on the work surface without shifting the paper.

### Step 3

Burnish the print.

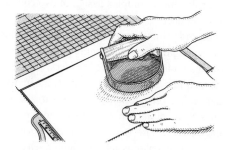

Move a baren or your hand in a circular motion with even pressure across the surface of the paper to transfer the ink. Avoid sliding the paper, which would smear the print.

### Step 4

Check the print.

Lay one hand flat on top of the paper and carefully lift up one corner at a time to examine the print. If a detail is weakly printed, lay the paper back down on the block and burnish it again to pick up more ink.

### Step 5

Lift the print off the block.

Lift up the paper at opposite sides in one continuous motion to remove the print from the block. Lay the wet print, ink side up, on a protected work surface or hang from a line. Let the ink dry completely.

Two-Color Printing

To print a more complex design in two colors, you will need to cut two blocks, one for each color, and print them one at a time in the same registered position on the same piece of paper. The main block, called the *key block,* contains the defining design lines and prints in the main color. The *secondary block* features select parts of the design only and prints in the secondary color. The secondary block is printed first, and its color is usually lighter. The key block is printed over it in a darker color, completing the design.

My earlier success with pink soft-carve material inspired me to try a more elaborate design for my two-color butterfly print. The secondary block with the wings is printed in hot pink, and the key block with the body details and wing pattern is overprinted in navy blue. I loved the challenge of carving the key block in a pattern of shapely islands. This degree of detail is time-consuming to cut and requires some previous experience with the cutting tool. If you are a beginner, you can cut and print the secondary block only or you might simplify the details on the key block to print the wing shapes as a graphic.

Registering the blocks of a two-color

design is essential for an overall neat, crisp print. Blocks printed out of register will show the lighter color extending like a pale halo beyond the basic outline of the darker color. To address this issue in the design stage, I drew the wings on the key block slightly larger and thickened the outline to provide some leeway during printing in case my registration of the key block was a little off. To register the images during printing, I use one of two registration methods: If I plan to pull four or five prints, I set up a printing frame, keep the paper stationary with pushpins, and slide the inked blocks into position one after the other. If I plan a one-off, I improvise with an unorthodox but effective method by registering the print with a T square, mat with a grid, and masking tape and keep the paper stationary with strips of double-sided tape.

### Technique: Cutting Blocks for a Two-Color Print

Cut away the nonprinting areas of the block gradually, making test prints as you go along to identify high areas that are inadvertently printing. It took me a half dozen test prints to refine my butterfly printing block. Although this cutting and testing process can be slow, it will prevent you from cutting away too much of the soft-carve material. If the block feels weak or flimsy after carving, mount it on a piece of chipboard for support. Pay attention to the angle of your cuts, too. Undercutting the walls on either side of a gouge can cause them to collapse and bottom out when you are printing.

---

## Working Tips: Cleaning the Printing Tools

Printing blocks and brayers should be cleaned thoroughly after printing. Because the medium used is water soluble, all you need is warm water and liquid soap to remove any ink from the block and the brayer. Dry them thoroughly before storing.

---

## MATERIALS AND TOOLS

Key block Butterfly Wing pattern
(page 696)
Color block Butterfly Wing pattern
(page 696)
2 soft-carve printing blocks, 8¼" × 5¾"
(21 × 14.6 cm)
Cutting tool and interchangeable cutters
Graphite paper
Bench hook
Pencil
Colored pencil

### Step 1

Transfer each pattern to a separate block.

Use a pencil and graphite paper to transfer the Butterfly Wing pattern to one soft-carve block and the Butterfly Color Block pattern to the other soft-carve block. Use a colored pencil to color in the printing areas of each block. These areas will not be cut out.

### Step 2

Cut out the design on each block.

Lay a bench hook on a flat surface with the hook part pushed against the front edge of the work surface. Place one block on the bed, pushing the block against the stop at the back of the hook. Use a cutting tool with sharp gouges to cut out each block, following the marked design. Choose a gouge according to the character of the lines and shapes in the design and change cutters as needed to cut grooves or V-shaped gouges. Repeat to cut out the second block. Make a test print using both blocks and refine the cutting, if necessary.

## Technique: Using an Ordinary Wood Frame to Register a Print with Two Colors

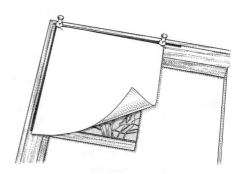

It is easy to adapt a frame that you can then use to accurately register a one or multi-colored print. The only requirement is that the frame and the carved printing block be of the same depth when both are laying flat. I adapted an old silk-screen frame, which conveniently was the same depth as my carved block, by removing the polyester screen. The printing paper, which is the same size as the block with a 1" (2.5 cm) margin all around, is secured at the top edge of the frame with pushpins. The inked block is set into the top inside corner of the frame and the paper is lowered onto it to make the print. If the print you plan is two-color, the frame makes it easy to install the key block in the same position as the secondary block to register and complete the print.

## MATERIALS AND TOOLS

Key block
Secondary block
Block-printing inks, water based, in two
colors (light and dark)
Printing paper, at least 1" (2.5 cm) larger
than the block
Testing paper, same size as printing paper
Frame, in a depth that matches the
printing blocks
Ruler
Pencil

2 pushpins
Ink slab
Old credit card
Brayer
Baren
Alligator clips
Masking tape

### Step 1

Register the print.

Lay the testing paper on the frame, aligning the edges of the top left corner so they are approximately ½" (1.3 cm) from the outside edges of the top left corner of the frame, which will establish the placement of the printing paper. Use a pencil and a ruler to draw two lines on the frame that define the edges of the top left corner of the paper.

### Step 2

Affix the printing paper.

Place the printing paper on the frame, aligning the edges of the paper with the marked lines on the corner of the frame. Use pushpins to secure the top edge of the paper at opposite corners to the frame.

### Step 3

Print the first color.

Prepare the lighter-colored ink on the ink slab and use a brayer to ink the secondary block. Lift the printing paper and hold it back with an alligator clip. Position the block, ink side up, inside the frame's top left corner, aligning two outside edges of the block with two inside edges of the frame. Remove the alligator clips. Carefully lower the paper onto the block. Smooth the paper with a baren to transfer the ink to the paper. Lift the printed paper, still pinned to the frame, and bend it away from the printing block. Attach an alligator clip to the edge of the print to hold it back. Remove the secondary block. Clean the brayer and the block. Let the print dry completely.

### Step 4

Print the second color.

Prepare the darker-colored ink on the slab and ink the key block. Position the key block in the corner of the frame, in the same orientation as the secondary block so the overlaid detail is correctly positioned on the first print. Remove the alligator clip from the printed paper and guide the paper over and onto the inked block. Smooth the paper with a baren to transfer the dark ink to the print. Lift up the print and remove the pushpins one at a time. Lay the print, ink side up, on a flat surface or clip it on a line. Let the ink dry.

## Quick & Easy:
## Making a Print Frame

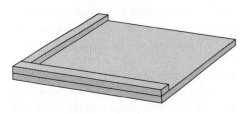

For the base of the frame, measure and cut a piece of plywood 3" (7.6 cm) longer and wider than your print paper. For example, if the print paper measures 8½" × 11" (21.6 ×27.9 cm), make the base of the print frame 11½" × 14" × ½" (29.2 × 35.6 × 1.3 cm). The extra margin accommodates the width of the battens that are added to hold and elevate the paper over the printing block. Choose battens that match the height of your block and cut them so they fit from edge to edge as shown. Attach them to the base with wood glue and clamp the pieces until the glue dries.

## Technique: Using a T Square and Self-Healing Cutting Mat to Register and Print in Two Colors

Although a rather unorthodox approach, this method works well for printing two-color one-offs. It combines elements of the T square method and the frame method. A T square, a cutting mat with a grid, and tape establish the registration of the paper, aided by strips of double-sided tape that form a hinge on the print so it can be lowered into position over the inked block as in the frame method.

### MATERIALS AND TOOLS
Key block
Secondary block
Block-printing inks, water based, in two colors (light and dark)
Printing paper, at least 1" (2.5 cm) larger than the block
Testing paper (same size as printing paper)
Self-healing cutting mat with grid
T square
Pencil
Permanent marker
Masking tape
Double-sided tape, low tack
Metal binder clips
Alligator clip
Ink slab
Expired credit card
Brayer

### Step 1
Set up the registration tools.

Align the T square at the bottom left corner of the cutting mat, with the crossbar of the T square pressed against the left vertical edge of the mat and the ruler portion laid on one of the horizontal lines on the mat's grid. Tape the ruler portion of the T square to the mat and the work surface. Lay the secondary block, faceup, on the mat, aligning the near edge of the block with the inside edge of the ruler. Use a marker to mark the position of the block

on the ruler. Lay the test paper over the block so that the edges align with the cross bar and inside edge of the ruler. With the test paper in position, run a long strip of masking tape on the mat that just touches the outer edge of the paper. Remove the test paper.

### Step 2
Apply ink to the secondary block.

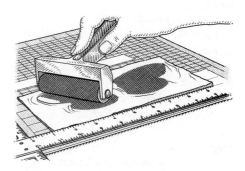

Squeeze out a ribbon of light-colored ink on the slab and condition it with an expired credit card. Use a brayer to roll the ink into a smooth, tacky layer. Use the inked brayer to apply a thin, even coat to the secondary block.

### Step 3
Lay the printing paper over the block.

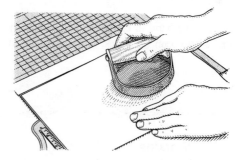

Check to make sure the secondary block is in position on the mat. Hold the printing paper in two hands, aligning the corners on the left side of the paper with the T square and the top edge of the paper with the inside edge of the long strip of tape, and lower the paper onto the inked block. Use a baren to smooth the paper against the block to transfer the print. To assist the registration for the second block, very carefully raise one edge of the paper, slide two short strips of low-tack double-sided tape under the edge, and press down until the paper adheres.

### Step 4
Ink the key block.

Clean the brayer. Squeeze out a ribbon of dark-colored ink on the slab and condition it with an expired credit card. Use a brayer to roll the ink into a smooth, tacky layer. Use the inked brayer to apply a thin, even coat to the key block; set the inked block aside.

### Step 5
Reveal the secondary block print.

Use one hand to carefully lift the print by one edge up off the block, keeping the taped

edge intact, and use your other hand to slide out and remove the secondary block from the mat.

### Step 6
Lay the print over the key block.

Position the key block, ink side up, against the marked ruler in the same position used for the secondary block. Lower the printing paper over and onto the key block, using the ruler and the long strip of tape to help guide the placement of the print.

### Step 7
Make the print.

Use a baren to smooth the paper against the inked block. Peel the paper off the block in one continuous motion, sliding your fingers under the taped edge to assist in releasing the tape. Lay the print, ink side up, on a protected surface or clip it on a line. Allow the print to dry, preferably overnight.

## Working Tips: Printing with More than One Color

Let the first color dry completely before over-printing a second color.

## Traditional Stenciling

Stenciled designs are easy to recognize by the defining silhouettes and telltale ladders that are manifest in the prints. A stencil is made of a nonporous flat material, such as coated paper or plastic film such as acetate. A design is made by pouncing or dabbing paint through cutouts in this material using a stiff brush or a fine-celled sponge.

Commercial stencils tend toward traditional motifs or feature border prints or single motifs with a theme, such as ducks and fish. If you prefer a more sassy selection, you can design your own stencils. Peruse the pages of magazines for items with distinct silhouettes, such as purses and shoes, or use whatever you are interested in. Use a copier or scanner and a printer to enlarge and print the pattern or picture of the item in a size that fits your design plan and then trace the outline, adding ladders to keep floating pieces together.

The pattern section includes two shoe designs, a Silver Spike Heel (page 698) and Red Shoe, a Strappy Sandal (page 697), for you to try. Neither stencil design has any telltale ladders to interfere with the stylish impression. Use a shoe stencil to print different colored shoes in a repeat pattern for a paper or wall border or make a solo print with textile ink to decorate a tote bag or a cloth-covered blank book. Instead of paint, you can apply thick craft glue and fine glitter within the cutout shape to make a fancy greeting card that sparkles.

### Materials and Tools

- **Plastic film**
  Acetate is a specific type of plastic material made from a polymer that comes in transparent, waterproof, sturdy film. It can be cut with a craft knife to make a custom stencil. An acetate stencil keeps its neat edges after many uses, producing a crisp impression many times over. Mylar plastic film can also be used to make stencils.

- **Acrylic craft paint or block-printing ink**
  The coloring agent used in stenciling must be thick enough to remain on the printing surface without bleeding or seeping under the edges of the stencil. Both acrylic craft paint and block-printing ink work well for stenciling and are available in a wide range of colors. Both acrylic media clean up with soap and water while wet but become permanent when dry.

- **Craft knife**

A craft knife is indispensable for cutting stencils. It has an extremely sharp point that cuts easily though thin plastic, nearly guaranteeing clean cuts and sharp lines on the print. It is important to change the blade on a craft knife as soon as it drags on the surface to avoid burrs or messy cuts. For a stencil with curves, consider a craft knife with a swivel head.

- **Stencil brush**

Used in a pouncing motion, a stencil brush has stiff bristles with a thick blunt end that leaves a film of color on the printing surface in the cutout areas of the stencil.

## Cutting and Using a Stencil

Cutting your own stencil designs is incredibly easy. You'll need a sheet of sturdy transparent plastic film. Slip your stencil pattern under the plastic film and trace the design on top using a permanent marker. With a fresh blade in your craft knife, make clean cuts through the plastic film.

After the stencil is cut, you can use it to print the design on any flat surface, such as a sheet of bristol or cardstock. Acrylic craft paint or block-printing ink is tamped onto the paper through the cutout areas, but the areas masked by the stencil remain unaffected. Stencil adhesive, applied to the reverse side of the stencil, can temporarily hold the stencil in place during painting. In lieu of adhesive, you can use a craft stick or the eraser end of a pencil to hold down loose appendages, such as the straps on either of the shoe designs, to prevent the paint from seeping under the edges and ruining the print. When you finish, wash the plastic stencil

in warm soapy water and dry it. A stencil made of plastic film can be used again and again.

## Technique: Cutting an Acetate Stencil

Every stencil has a few sections that require extra care during cutting to ensure that the plastic film remains intact.

MATERIALS AND TOOLS
Red Shoe, a Strappy Sandal pattern
(page 697)
Acetate film, in a size larger than the pattern
Craft knife with replaceable blades
Self-healing cutting mat
Masking tape
Cellophane tape

**Step 1**
Prepare the pattern.
Lay the pattern on the cutting mat and place a sheet of acetate over it, aligning the top edges. Tape down the edges to the keep the layers from shifting.

**Step 2**
Cut the stencil.
Use a sharp craft knife to cut completely through the acetate, following the pattern. Apply steady, firm pressure and draw the knife

toward yourself to ensure neat cuts. Turn the cutting mat as you work to keep the cuts going in the same direction. Hold down the acetate with your free hand and keep your fingers away from the path of the blade.

**Step 3**

Remove the cutout section from the stencil.

Carefully lift and remove the cutout section of the acetate, using the tip of the craft knife to sever any tiny connecting slivers. Inspect the cut edges on the stencil. Use the craft knife to carefully trim any ragged edges, staying within the outline. If you cut a ladder by mistake, repair the break with cellophane tape.

## Technique: Using a Stencil to Make a Print

### MATERIALS AND TOOLS

Stencil
Bristol or other printing paper
Block-printing ink or acrylic craft paint, in silver or desired color
Stencil brush
Small dish
Craft stick
Paper towels
Liquid stencil adhesive
Soap

**Step 1**

Prepare the paint.

Squeeze some block-printing ink or acrylic craft paint into a dish. Use a craft stick to stir it to a smooth consistency.

**Step 2**

Secure the stencil to the paper.

Turn the stencil, wrong side up, and apply stencil adhesive around the cutout edges. Set the stencil, adhesive side down, on the printing paper and press gently to tighten the bond. Let the adhesive dry. Apply strips of masking tape at the corners of the stencil to keep it from shifting.

**Step 3**

Apply paint to the cutouts.

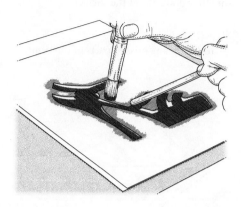

Pick up some ink or paint on the stencil brush. Gently stroke the bristles on a paper towel to shed the excess moisture; the bristles should be only lightly loaded. Use a gentle up-and-down pouncing motion to apply color to the cutout areas of the stencil, working the color from the outer edges to the interior of the cutout. Use a clean craft stick or the eraser

---

## Working Tips: Securing a Stencil with Stencil Adhesive

Masking tape is usually used to secure the perimeter of a stencil to the printing surface, but tape can't secure the edges of the interior cutouts without interfering with the quality of the print. To secure these interior cut edges, stencil adhesive can be applied to them on the reverse side. The adhesive is not permanent, but it is strong enough to hold the edges in place and prevent paint from seeping underneath. Stencil adhesive also makes it easier to stencil walls and other vertical surfaces.

end of a pencil to press down on any loose edges or slender sections of the stencil to make sure they don't lift off the surface.

## Step 4

Touch up any missed parts of the print.

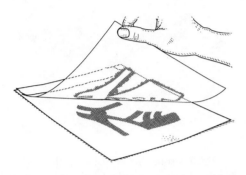

Lift up one corner of the stencil to examine the print. If parts of the image are not printed or the color is weak or missing, carefully lower the stencil, aligning the cut edges with the print, and apply more ink or paint to the areas that need it.

## Step 5

Let the print dry.

When the image is printed, lift the acetate and remove the print. Lay the print, ink side up, on a flat surface or hang it from a line to dry. Use a damp sponge or warm water and liquid soap to clean the ink or paint from the stencil, being careful not to distort or tear any floppy sections. Dry the stencil and lay it flat to store.

## Screen Printing

An advanced form of stenciling, screen printing is an amazingly satisfying way to create multiple prints. The technique requires a mesh screen, ink, and a squeegee. The mesh screen is treated with a mask that leaves some parts of the screen open or unblocked so ink can pass through to the printing surface set beneath it. The printing ink does not flow freely through the open areas of the screen by itself; it must be forced through the mesh by pulling the flexible rubber blade of a squeegee firmly across it. Different ink colors can change the graphic impact—a bird printed in bright chartreuse sings a different tune than one printed in pale blue.

The method used to make the stencil on the screen plays a major role in determining the visual character of the screen print. Three methods are featured in this section: using screen filler, using drawing fluid and screen filler, and using photo emulsion. These three methods provide a wide range of artistic effects, from flat, bold, bright graphics to images that are painterly and tonal in quality to those that rival engravings in their vitality and detail. Once the screen is prepared, the method for pulling a print is the same for all three.

Materials and Tools

- **Printing screen**

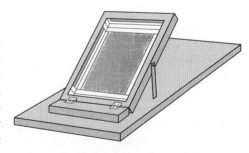

A printing screen is a wood frame across which a fabric mesh—woven from polyester or other fiber—is tightly stretched. The mesh is held in place with staples or by a cord embedded in a groove in the frame. The top surface of the screen is recessed to hold the ink, and the bottom or flat side hovers just slightly over the printing surface, until pressure from the squeegee being pulled across the screen forces the screen to momentarily touch down on the printing surface. The screen size is identified by the inside dimensions of the frame; the screen must be large enough to accommodate the image being printed plus any borders or margins. A screen can be used independently, that is, it can be set on a piece of fabric for printing, or it can be hinged to a wood base for accurate print registration of an edition. Removable hinge pins allow for easy cleaning. An optional kick leg holds the screen in a raised position, making it easy to load new paper onto the base of the screen unit.

- **Screen-printing ink**

Screen-printing ink has a thick creamy consistency that can pass through a mesh screen and produce a smooth layer of rich color on the printing surface. It is available in a wide variety of colors in formulations for paper and for textiles. Screen-printing inks that contain acrylic mediums will clean up with soap and water when wet but become water-resistant and permanent when dry. Some water-based inks suited to porous paper are not permanent when dry and can be affected by moisture, causing them to smudge even if they have dried completely. Textile screen-printing inks are specially formulated with acrylic emulsion and other additives to promote good ink flow and adhesion to any porous fabric. Textile inks do require heat setting with a hot iron to become washable and permanent, so choose a

fabric that will not scorch during the heat-setting process. The coat of thermoplastic textile ink must be protected by a press cloth if a hot iron is used to set (or cure) the ink or the ink may smear or melt. For specific heat settings, read the label on the jar or tube of textile ink. Fabric ink is not suitable for nonporous fabrics such as nylon.

- **Printing paper**

The paper you choose should be appropriate to your screen-printing project. The ideal paper for art prints is porous and has a smooth finish and high rag content, qualities that allow for fine details in the print. Use archival papers for art prints; archival papers are acid-free, are made to retard deterioration and yellowing, and can be identified by a watermark on the back of the paper. For printing greeting cards, use card stock or bristol in white or a soft pastel or any other color you wish. Cardstock is a good weight because it does not warp when exposed to moisture. Avoid paper with a high gloss or a coated surface. Keep in mind that dark ink shows up well against a light background, but light-colored ink may require more opacity on a dark background.

- **Waterproof tape**

Strips of wide waterproof tape are used to prevent ink from seeping between the edge of the frame and the screen, which can mar the prints. I like to tape the screen before coating it with any mask. The tape is applied along the edge of the screen where the fabric meets the wood. It is removed when the edition of prints is completed and as the screen is cleaned.

- **Registration tabs**
  Made from pieces of masking tape, registration tabs are short strips, about 1" × 2" (2.5 × 5.1 cm), that are adhered to the base of a screen unit or to the work surface to guide the placement of the printing paper. They ensure that the stencil on the screen prints images in the same place on each sheet of paper in an edition.
- **Extender base, transparent base, and retarder**
  Depending on the medium used, one can be mixed with the printing ink to change the consistency, lubricity, or opacity of the printing ink. When mixed with the printing ink, an extender base will thin the ink without making it runny and will also make the ink more transparent; a transparent base will increase the ink's lubricity and transparency; and a

## Working Tips: Choosing a Screen

Screens come in a variety of sizes; the inner dimensions of the screen determine the size of the print. I work with screens that have wood frames and a polyester mesh. As a rule, the more intricate the detail in my design, the higher the mesh count of my screen. Polyester screens are made from two kinds of thread: monofilament and multifilament.

- A monofilament mesh is woven from single strands of thread. Monofilament mesh screens are suited to printing on paper and are less prone to staining. The mesh comes in a range of sizes identified by the number of threads

per inch (or per centimeter). An ideal thread count for printing on paper with water-based inks is between 200 and 260 threads per inch (between 80 and 104 threads per cm).

- A multifilament mesh is woven from threads composed of many strands that are twisted together. Screens with multifilament mesh are suited to printing on fabric with textile inks. Screen filler and photo-emulsion liquid adhere better to a multifilament screen. The ideal thread count for printing on fabric with water-based textile inks is 10XX to 14XX.

retarder will keep printing ink from drying quickly, which can reduce the open time for printing and cause the screen to clog. When using any of these mediums, follow the manufacturer's recommendations to achieve the ratio needed to produce the desired effects.

• **Tapered paintbrush**

Any narrow paintbrush, such as a tapered watercolor brush, provides good control when applying screen filler and drawing fluid to the screen.

• **Squeegee**

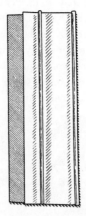

A squeegee has a flexible yet firm blade that when pulled across a screen, forces ink through the unmasked parts of screen's mesh fabric, depositing it on the paper or fabric laid beneath it. A squeegee blade can be made of rubber or polyurethane and comes in a range of lengths, cuts, and flexibility. The blade is clamped between two pieces of wood

## Working Tips: Using a Hole Punch to Register a Screen Print

Use an ordinary stationery paper punch with three holes to place three widely spaced holes on one edge of each sheet of printing paper. Stick on two or three registration pins to the base of the screen-printing unit that align with the desired position of the paper, spacing them so that the pins fit into the punched holes in the paper.

## Working Tips: Choosing a Squeegee

Squeegee blades come in different shapes for different tasks. A square blade is suited to basic printing on flat surfaces, such as paper and chipboard. A rounded blade is suited to laying down the thick layer of color needed for printing on fabric.

or plastic that act as a handle. Choose a blade length that fits within the top recessed dimensions of your screen with approximately 2" (5.1 cm) to spare on each side so that you can manipulate the squeegee easily. A blade that is at least 1" (2.5 cm) wider than your image is best as it will allow you to pass over open areas of the stencil in one stroke, resulting in a nonstreaky layer of ink.

The following materials and tools are specific to photo-emulsion printing.

- **Line art printed on acetate**
  The line art for photo-emulsion printing must have opaque lines that are strong enough to print on the light-sensitized screen without blurring or losing detail. Look for images with dark lines and high contrast. Visit a printing store to have the art printed onto the sheet of acetate to create your acetate positive.
- **Diazo photo emulsion and photo sensitizer kit**

A photo emulsion and a photo sensitizer are used together to create a light-sensitive coating that is applied to the screen's mesh fabric. Although these items can be purchased separately, it is very convenient and recommended to purchase the Diazo kit because the photo sensitizer and the photo emulsion are conveniently and accurately premeasured and ready to mix.

- **Reflector light**

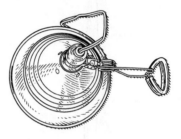

A clip-on lamp with a standard socket housed with a strong light and a reflector lampshade or a socket extension cord with a light and pie-pan reflector can be used to expose a screen that has been coated with photo emulsion. The reflector shade disperses the light evenly on the treated screen. The lamp or cord can be clamped to a stand or a pole and adjusted to a particular height over the screen, which will affect the quality of the stencil negative.

- **BBA No. 1 photoflood light**
  The light used to expose a screen treated with photo-emulsion liquid must be strong enough to instigate the photo process and harden the exposed areas of emulsion on the screen. The strength of the light, its distance from the screen, and the time it shines on the screen determine the quality of the stencil negative. A BBA No. 1 photoflood light (250 watts) is recommended to cut down on the exposure time, which would be more than twice as long with a clear incandescent 150-watt bulb. The photoflood bulb

is available in most photo-supply and art stores.

- **Timer**

A timer that can be set at 1-minute intervals is a convenient way to keep track of the exposure time of the screen coated with photo emulsion.

- **Black paper or cloth**
Black paper or cloth is a light-absorbing material that is laid underneath the screen so that reflected light from the lamp is absorbed instead of bouncing off and causing a blurred exposure on the photo-emulsion stencil negative.

- **Glass or Lucite sheet**
A thick, transparent sheet of glass or Lucite placed over the film-positive acetate ensures that all parts lay flat against the coated screen to prevent a blurred exposure of the lines and contours of the photo-emulsion stencil negative. The glass or Lucite should be ½" (1.3 cm) larger all around than the dimensions of the screen so that it can rest on the bottom (flat side) of the screen's frame.

- **Rubber or disposable vinyl gloves**

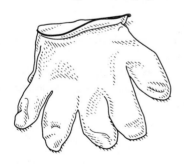

Rubber gloves provide protection for your hands while handling screen fluids and inks, keeping substances that can stain and irritate from reaching your skin.

## Preparing the Screen

Any mesh screen, whether new or previously used, should be cleaned before being prepared with a stencil or used for printing. Another recommended preparatory step is to seal the edge of the screen with tape to prevent ink from seeping through and marring the edges of the print.

## Technique: Cleaning a Screen before Use

Even if a screen has never been used before, it is important to scrub both sides of the screen before use to remove any residual grease or dust that could interfere with the smooth extrusion of ink through the mesh. If you are working with a screen attached to a base, detach the frame and take the screen to a sink with hot and cold running water. A spray hose attachment on the faucet is ideal.

### MATERIALS AND TOOLS
Screen, detached from frame
Dishwasher detergent
Measuring spoons
Mixing bowl
Rubber gloves
Soft scrub brush
Soft clean cloth

### Step 1
Prepare the detergent.
Put on rubber gloves. Mix 1 tablespoon of dishwasher detergent and 2 cups of warm water in a mixing bowl, stirring to dissolve the detergent.

### Step 2
Scrub the screen.
Working over a sink, use a scrub brush and the soap solution to clean one side of the screen.

Turn the screen over and clean the other side. Use the spray attachment and warm water to thoroughly rinse both sides of the screen.

**Step 3**

Dry the screen.

Use a clean, soft, lint-free cloth and a blotting motion to absorb as much moisture as possible from the screen and frame. Let the screen air-dry completely.

## Technique: Taping the Screen

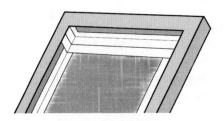

All screens should be taped before applying the stencil medium or ink. Tape prevents ink from seeping between the frame and the screen and marring the print or printing surface. Use waterproof packing tape with water-based inks. Water-resistant masking tape can also be used, but it is less resilient. I tape both sides of the screen to ensure that ink does not seep in from either side.

MATERIALS AND TOOLS

Screen, detached from screen unit
Waterproof packing tape, 2" to 3" (5.1 to
    7.6 cm) wide
Screen filler
Tapered watercolor paintbrush
Tablespoon
Scissors

**Step 1**

Apply the first tape strip.

Lay the clean, dry screen, flat side up, on a protected work table. Pull a length of tape from the roll that is several inches longer than one edge of the frame and cut the tape from the roll. Stretch the tape slightly and beginning at the middle of one short edge of the frame, press the tape along the crevice where the mesh and the wood portion of the frame meet to form a tight seal. Extend the tape at each end into and around the corners. Cut into the triangular lapped portion of the tape so that it lies flat against the mesh surface.

**Step 2**

Apply three more tape strips.

Repeat step 1 to apply tape to the opposite short edge and then to the two long edges, overlapping the tape ends at the corners. Use the bowl side of a tablespoon to press down the tape against the surfaces.

**Step 3**

Apply a second strip of tape to each short edge.

Add a second strip of tape to each short edge, overlapping the edge of the previously laid strip to create a holding area for the ink during printing.

**Step 4**

Seal the inside edges of the frame.

Turn the screen over so that the recessed side faces up. Use lengths of tape to seal the inside edges of the frame on all sides as in step 1. Make certain the tape is in the L-shaped groove and that the tape ends overlap at the corners. Use the bowl side of a spoon to press down the tape.

**Step 5**

Apply a second strip of tape to each short edge.

Add a second strip of tape to each short edge, overlapping the edge of the previously laid strip.

**Step 6**

Fill in any gaps.

Hold the taped screen up to the light to check for any gaps between the tape and the frame. Use a brush to apply screen filler to any gaps or open areas. Let the screen filler dry completely before using the screen.

### Using Screen Filler

The screen-filler method of screen printing refers to the application of a liquid mask by hand to the screen mesh. The screen filler is brushed onto areas that surround the design motifs. The design motifs themselves are left open, so that the ink can pass through and reach the printing surface.

Because the screen is translucent, you can place a pattern on the work surface, set the screen over it, and trace the design directly onto the mesh screen. Prints made with a screen-filler stencil are usually characterized by bold or well-outlined shapes, such as the print of the leafy branches shown above. Inspired by actual foliage, I drew the pattern on a sheet of paper first and when I was satisfied with the configuration, I traced it onto the screen.

### Technique: Making a Stencil with Screen Filler

As you create a stencil with screen filler, keep in mind that the areas or shapes you want to print are left open and all of the surrounding areas are filled. For a simpler pattern than the one shown, try Single Branch (page 700). Make sure that your screen is at least 1" (2.5 cm) larger all around than the pattern you choose.

#### MATERIALS AND TOOLS
Double Branches pattern (page 699)
Screen, cleaned and taped
Screen filler
Tapered watercolor paintbrush
Soft pencil
4 pushpins
Craft stick
Tape

#### Step 1
Trace the pattern onto the screen.

Lay the pattern on a protected work surface and tape down the corners to prevent shifting. Center the flat side of the prepared screen on the pattern so the image is centered. Use a pencil to trace the outline of the pattern directly onto the screen. It may be a little awkward to draw because the screen's raised frame will unavoidably be in your way.

#### Step 2
Elevate the screen.

Turn the screen over, flat side up, and press a pushpin into each corner of the frame. Turn the screen over again, recessed side up; the pushpins will act as little legs to elevate the flat side of the screen up and off the work surface.

**Step 3**

Apply the screen filler.

Use a craft stick to mix the screen filler until it is smooth. Avoid shaking, which will cause bubbles on the surface that can break and leave pinholes on the screen. Use a paintbrush to apply the filler to all of the nonprinting areas of the screen, extending the filler all the way to the tape. Work carefully around the edges of the shapes so they are neat. Press gently with the brush so that the flat side of the screen does not touch the work surface.

**Step 4**

Smooth out the screen filler.

When all of the designated areas on the screen are blocked out with screen filler, lift up the screen to inspect the flat side. Use the brush to carefully smooth out any screen filler that has collected. With the pushpins still inserted, set the screen in a horizontal position and allow the screen filler to dry overnight.

**Step 5**

Check for gaps and pinholes in the screen-filler coating.

Hold the screen up to the light to check for tiny pinholes, which will show as tiny points of light. If there are any pinholes, apply dabs of screen filler on either side of the screen to conceal them. Then let the screen filler dry completely. When the screen is dry, remove the pushpins from the bottom of the screen. The screen is now ready for printing.

### Using Drawing Liquid and Screen Filler

This screen-stencil method is suited to hand-drawn letters and images with smooth con-

---

### Working Tips: Removing a Screen-Filler Stencil

I never remove a stencil I have applied to a screen, preferring instead to save my screen designs for future use. However, if you do choose to remove the coating of screen filler from your screen, you will need to use a solvent designed for the job, such as Speed Clean by Speedball. Be sure to follow the manufacturer's recommendations and cautions.

---

### Fun for Kids: Using Tape and Stickers to Make a Screen Stencil

Children can easily get involved in screen printing and produce unique patterns while learning about the art. All they need to do is press strips of ordinary masking tape or adhesive-backed circles to the flat side of the screen in a random pattern. Lengths of masking tape can crisscross the screen, and circles can accent the spaces between the strips of tape. Once the screen is taped and stickered, you're ready to start pulling your prints.

tours and some fine detail. A working drawing or pattern can be placed underneath the screen as a guide and the art can be traced directly onto the screen using a pencil. Drawing freehand is a good way to add swirls, curlicues, and decorative strokes.

The stencil is created by a two-part layering of liquids. First, a water-soluble drawing liquid is applied to the screen in a freehand style that uses the marked design as a guide. Next, screen filler is applied over the entire screen, including those areas covered with drawing liquid. The screen filler is unable to come into contact with the parts of the screen mesh that are filled with drawing liquid. To complete the stencil, the coated screen is washed in cool water. The drawing fluid dissolves and washes away, opening up those areas of the design on the mesh, and the water-resistant screen filler that surrounds the opened areas remains behind as a mask, defining the line work. In the printing phase, ink is able to pass through the open areas of the screen and print as a positive image on the printing surface.

## Technique: Making a Positive Stencil with Drawing Liquid and Screen Filler

This stenciling method is referred to as positive printing because the design rendered on the screen with drawing fluid is the design that prints. Because the drawing fluid is applied with a brush, it is easy to vary the length and thickness of the strokes. You will love seeing prints

of your original drawings, especially those done by children like the one done by Gabrielle, two years old, although you may be surprised to find the printed lines slightly textured. For less texture, use a screen with a finer mesh.

### MATERIALS AND TOOLS
Bird in Flight pattern (page 701)
Screen, cleaned and taped
Drawing fluid
Screen filler
Tapered liner paintbrush
Squeegee
Rubber gloves
Scrubbing brush
4 pushpins
Soft pencil
Craft stick
Tape

**Step 1**
Make the bird pattern.
Detach the screen from the unit. Lay the pattern on a protected work surface and tape down the corners. Center the detached and prepared screen, flat side down, over the pattern so the image area is in the center of the screen. Use a pencil to trace the outline of the pattern directly onto the screen mesh. It may feel awkward to draw because the screen's frame will be unavoidably in your way.

**Step 2**
Trace the pattern and apply the drawing fluid.

Turn the screen over to the flat side, and press a pushpin into each corner of the screen, which will elevate the screen when you are painting it with drawing fluid. Use a craft stick to mix the drawing fluid. Use a paintbrush dipped in drawing fluid to trace over all the lines of the design. Work carefully around the lines so they are neat. Make certain not to allow the bottom of the screen to touch the work surface. If you make a mistake, you can simply wash out the drawing fluid and allow the screen to dry. Then you can apply the drawing fluid again to create a new design. When you are satisfied with your design, stand the screen horizontally on its pins and let the drawing fluid dry overnight.

### Step 3
Apply screen filler to the screen.

Use a craft stick to mix the screen filler until it is smooth. Do not shake the screen filler as this will cause bubbles, which can result in pinholes in the coating though which ink can seep, marring the print. Hold the screen on an angle with one hand, recessed side up, and use the other to pour a thin ribbon of screen filler on one end of the screen. Use a squeegee to smooth a thin coat of screen filler to the same side of the screen as the drawing fluid, passing the squeegee over the drawing fluid only *once* to avoid degrading the drawing fluid. (Note that the drawing visible in the illustration would in reality be concealed by the screen filler.) Do not let the screen bottom touch

down on the work surface. Allow the screen filler to dry completely overnight with the screen resting on its pushpins in a horizontal position.

### Step 4
Wash out the drawing fluid from the screen.

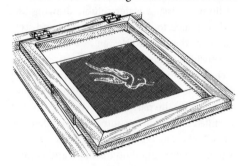

Put on rubber gloves. Bring the screen to a sink and use the spray attachment to direct a forceful spray of cold water over the design area of the stencil to wash out the drawing fluid and open the screen so that ink can pass through. Use a brush to gently scrub any blocked areas. Allow the screen to dry completely. Remove the pushpins. The screen is now ready for printing.

## Using Photographic Emulsion

This stencil-making method lets you reproduce photographic half-tone images, line drawings with intricate details, and other images that would be nearly impossible to copy freehand. It uses emulsion, a chemical used in photographic film processing, to transform a polyester screen into a negative that can be used to print a positive image.

In the photo-emulsion method, a positive image, such as a black-line drawing, is printed onto a sheet of transparent plastic film, such as acetate, using a computer scanner and laser printer. This acetate film positive is placed over a mesh screen made of polyester that has been coated with a light-sensitive emulsion. When the screen is placed under a light source for a timed period, the emulsion that is exposed to the light hardens and the emulsion that is blocked by the lines on the film positive remains soft and water-soluble. When the screen is washed, this softer emulsion washes out, leaving areas of open mesh for the ink to pass through. The resulting print is an exact replica of the film positive.

The overall method for making a photoemulsion stencil is straightforward but does require careful planning and timing. To prevent mishaps, make sure you understand the process and have everything you need on hand before you begin.

### Technique: Making the Acetate Positive

You'll need a scanner and laser printer or a laser copier to reproduce your chosen art on a sheet of acetate. Laser printers use thermal inks that are waterproof and that produce prints with crisp lines. Before doing this at home, make certain your printer will accept acetate; you may need to have the acetate positive printed at a copy shop. The size of the copy will be determined by the size of your screen.

MATERIALS AND TOOLS
Chrysanthemum original art (page 701)
Sheet of acetate
Laser copier, or scanner and laser printer
Black permanent marker

**Step 1**
Make the acetate positive.

Copy the Chrysanthemum original art onto acetate, using a laser photocopier or

---

### Fun for Kids: Making Multiples of a Drawing

There are several ways to make multiple prints of kids' drawings. One of the easiest is by hand-painting directly on a screen. Your child can use drawing liquid to paint an original face, figure, or design on the screen. Once the screen is prepared, you can do the printing steps together.

---

### Working Tips: Choosing Art for Photo-Emulsion Printing

The photo-emulsion method presents a unique opportunity to print line drawings and photographs with tonal variations—works of art that are beyond the skill level of most crafters. Readily available collections of copyright-free images are available for purchase or for free; Dover Publications has a vast collection of graphic art that is worth researching. You can browse online sources for art or search through old books for art that is in the public domain. Peruse family albums for images of a more personal nature.

a scanner and laser printer; size the image smaller than the mesh screen, understanding that any surrounding areas will be coated with emulsion and extra strips of waterproof tape to ensure an effective stencil.

**Step 2**

Touch up the acetate positive.

Inspect the acetate positive for imperfections. Use a black permanent marker to reinforce any weak or broken lines. Let the marker dry completely.

## Technique: Coating the Screen

The emulsion coating must be applied to both sides of the screen in a smooth layer, with the final smoothing done on the recessed side of the screen. Any dried pools or runny areas of emulsion can thicken the layer unevenly, preventing light from burning evenly through the emulsion, which can create breaks or missing parts in the design, causing a partial print.

### MATERIALS AND TOOLS

Polyester screen, cleaned and taped
Diazo system kit: premeasured photo
   emulsion and photo sensitizer
Squeegee
Rubber gloves
Craft stick
4 pushpins

**Step 1**

Elevate the screen.

Turn the screen over, flat side up, and insert a pushpin into each of the four corners of the screen. The pushpins will act as tiny legs to raise the screen off the work surface when the coating is applied and drying.

**Step 2**

Prepare the photo sensitizer.

Read the manufacturer's directions for the Diazo products. Put on rubber gloves. Working in a dimly lit area, open the small bottle of photo sensitizer, add cold water to the bottle, and mix thoroughly as directed.

**Step 3**

Mix the photo sensitizer and the emulsion.

Pour the photo sensitizer prepared in step 2 into the jar of emulsion. The emulsion will turn from blue to army green. Use a craft stick to stir the mixture thoroughly until it is smooth and the green color is consistent throughout.

**Step 4**

Coat the flat side of the screen with emulsion.

Hold the screen, flat side up, over a sink. Pour a thin ribbon of the emulsion mixture along the top end of the screen. Use a squeegee to spread the emulsion into a thin, even coat over the screen. Add more emulsion where necessary. Smooth away streaks and drips using the squeegee.

**Step 5**

Coat the recessed side of the screen with emulsion.

Turn the screen over so that the recessed side faces up. Repeat step 4 to coat this side of the screen with emulsion.

**Step 6**

Smooth the emulsion on the flat side of the screen.

Make a final check of the emulsion on the flat side of the screen, smoothing any excess emulsion. Then return any solution to the container by scraping the blade of the squeegee against the lip of the container.

**Step 7**

Let the emulsion dry in a dark closet.

Place the screen in a dark closet or drawer, away from heat and light. Stand it in a horizontal position on its pushpin legs. Let the screen dry completely, preferably overnight. Keep it in the dark until you are ready to expose it to the light.

## Technique: Exposing the Screen

The emulsion coating hardens when it is exposed to light. Any areas that are covered and not exposed will remain soft and will wash out to reveal the screen mesh. The first time I made a photo-emulsion stencil, I was worried that I wouldn't be able to balance all the variables—the distance between the light and the screen, the length of time needed to expose the screen—while working in complete darkness. I was happy to learn that I could work in normal room lighting, as long as I proceeded efficiently. That meant having everything ready and at my fingertips when I started the process of burning the screen. Work near a sink with hot and cold running water and a spray hose attachment.

### MATERIALS AND TOOLS

Polyester screen, prepared with emulsion
Acetate positive
Screen filler
Reflector shop light or socket extension cord with pie-pan reflector
BBA No. 1 photoflood bulb
Standing pole, such as a pole lamp
Clamp
Lucite sheet, ½" (1.3 cm) larger all around than screen
Black paper or fabric (larger than screen)
Small electric fan
Minute timer
Scrub brush
Paintbrush

### Step 1

Prepare the work space.

Refer to the instruction sheet and chart of exposure times that comes in the photo-

## Working Tips: Making a Pie-Pan Reflector

Use a commercial reflector shop light with the photoflood bulb to provide uniform illumination on screens that measure up to 10" x 14" (25.4 x 35.6 cm). A reflector shop light is not recommended for larger screens because the light will be most concentrated on the screen's center. For larger screens, use the photoflood bulb in a socket extension cord and make a reflector from a 10" (25.4 cm) diameter aluminum pie pan. Use a craft knife to cut an X in the pan's center and carefully spread the flanges apart. Feed the neck of the bulb through the opening so the pan rests on the bulb (and not on the socket) when the bulb is screwed into the socket.

## Checklist: Using the Photo-Emulsion Method

- Wear protective clothing, gloves, and safety glasses.
- Protect the work surface with black paper or fabric to avoid light bounce-back.
- Use a squeegee to apply the emulsion.
- Use Lucite or glass for a clean exposure.
- Watch the exposure time carefully and avoid overexposure.
- Use a BBA No. 1 photoflood bulb (250 W) for a shorter exposure time.
- Place the lamp at an appropriate distance from the screen.
- Use a small electric fan to prevent heat buildup.

emulsion kit. Screw the photoflood bulb into the socket of the reflector lamp or the extension cord and pie-pan reflector. Clamp the lamp or cord to a pole so that the bulb will be at the recommended distance from the surface of the screen when the screen is placed on a work surface. Lay the black fabric or paper on top of the work surface directly under the lamp. Set the acetate positive, the Lucite sheet, the timer, and the fan close by.

**Step 2**

Set up and expose the screen.

Retrieve the coated screen from the dark closet or drawer and remove the pushpins.

Place the screen, flat side up, on top of the black fabric, centering it under the lamp. Place the acetate positive, ink side down, on the screen, followed by the sheet of Lucite. Switch on the fan so it blows across the setup. Turn on the lamp and set the timer to the exposure time recommended on the chart.

**Step 3**

Thoroughly wash the screen.

When the allotted time is up, turn off the lamp. Remove the Lucite sheet and acetate positive from the screen and set them aside. Carry the screen to the sink. Use the spray attachment to direct a forceful stream of room-temperature (not hot) water on the lines of the design to stop the emulsion from reacting to light. Wash both sides of the screen until the emulsion washes off the areas of the screen that have line work; if necessary, use a soft scrub brush to nudge the emulsion out of the screen mesh. Hold the screen up to the light to check for clogged areas and continue washing until the mesh is open and the line work is completely clear. Spray the screen with cold water as a final rinse. Let the screen dry completely.

### Estimated Exposure Times According to Screen Size

Using a BBA No. 1 Photoflood (250 Watt) Bulb in a Reflector Shop Light
or Socket Extension Cord with a Pie-Pan Reflector

| Screen Size | Reflector Type | Lamp Height | Estimated Exposure Time |
|---|---|---|---|
| 8" × 10" (20.3 × 25.4 cm) | shop light | 18" (45.7 cm) | 1½ minutes |
| 10" × 14" (25.4 × 35.6 cm) | shop light | 18" (45.7 cm) | 1½ minutes |
| 12" × 18" (30.5 × 45.7 cm) | pie pan | 15" (38.1 cm) | 16 minutes |
| 16" × 20" (40.6 × 50.8 cm) | pie pan | 17" (43.2 cm) | 20 minutes |
| 18" × 20" (45.7 × 50.8 cm) | pie pan | 17" (43.2 cm) | 20 minutes |

Note that exposure times are approximate. Adjust the times according to your tests. Printed with permission of Speedball Art Products.

**Step 4**

Check the screen for pinholes.

Hold the screen up to the light to check for pinholes in the screen's mesh. If there are any, use a paintbrush and screen filler to conceal them. Allow the screen filler to dry completely.

### Making a Screen Print

Once the stencil is made, the steps for registering the printing paper, pulling the print, and cleaning the screen are the same.

## Technique: Registering a Screen-Printed Design

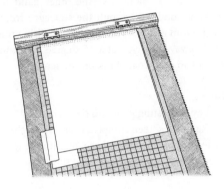

One of the easiest ways to ensure the registration of a series of prints made with a stenciled screen is to apply strips of tape representing one or two corners of the printing paper that are opposite the hinges on the screen of the screen-printing unit. The tape will guide the placement of each sheet of paper in the print run. Note that the illustration shows the screen removed from the unit to provide an unencumbered view of the registration.

### MATERIALS AND TOOLS

Polyester screen, with stencil
Baseboard unit
Printing paper
Masking tape
2 coins
Scissors

**Step 1**

Tape the screen.

Turn the screen so the flat side faces up. Use strips of tape to secure a coin to each bottom corner of the screen (the corners opposite the hinged edge). The coins will elevate the screen slightly and prevent it from bottoming out during printing.

**Step 2**

Test-fit the printing area on the base of the screen unit.

Attach the screen to the screen unit by inserting the hinge pins. Place a sheet of

---

### Working Tips: Registering a Print with Acetate and Register Pins

When you become more experienced in screen printing, you can try a different method of registration. The method requires that the first print be made on a sheet of acetate or other clear polyester film. A test sheet of paper is placed under the film so that the printed design can be seen; by moving the paper you can choose just where on the subsequent printing paper you may wish to locate your design. Once you have decided the design's placement, you can use metal register pins whose raised tabs are inserted into registration holes punched into the margin of the printing paper; if the paper hasn't a large enough margin to punch holes, you can affix adhesive-backed tabs that have holes in them onto the edge of the printing paper and then insert the raised tabs on the register pins that are adhered to the baseboard of the screen-printing unit into the hole to secure the registration of the paper.

printing paper on the baseboard unit and lower the screen. Adjust the paper position so that the screen image will print in the location desired.

**Step 3**

Register the printing paper on the base of the screen unit.

Lift the screen and prop it up on the kick leg. Use tape to create an L-shaped registration tab around the lower left corner of the paper. Press down tape strips, aligning the edges of the tape with the edges of the paper. If desired, create a second L-shaped registration tab at the lower right corner and use long strips of tape to register the midpoint of each long side of the paper. Remove the test paper from the base. Use the tape registration tabs to align each piece of printing paper in the series.

## Technique: Pulling Prints from a Screen Stencil

You have made your screen stencil using screen filler, drawing fluid and screen filler, or photo emulsion. You've made registration marks with tape on the baseboard unit of your screen-printing unit, and you've elevated the corners of the screen with coins. At last, you are ready to pull your first print!

○○○○○○○○○○○○○○○○○○○○○○

## Working Tips: Why Make a Test Print?

A test print allows you to check the quality of the print on less expensive paper before beginning a print run. Pinholes or other imperfections that appear in a test print can be corrected by locating the corresponding areas in the screen and applying screen filler to them on a cleaned screen. Let the filler dry completely before proceeding with your print run.

○○○○○○○○○○○○○○○○○○○○○○

### MATERIALS AND TOOLS

Screen, with stencil
Baseboard unit, with registration marks
Printing paper
Testing paper
Tube of screen-printing ink, water soluble, in desired color
Waterproof tape
Squeegee

**Step 1**

Make the flood stroke.

Hinge the screen to the base. Squeeze a ribbon of ink along the bottom end of the screen. Hold the screen up off the baseboard unit with one hand. Use the other hand to make a flood stroke: pull the squeegee from the bottom of the screen to the top, tilting the blade away from you at a 45-degree angle, to spread an even coat of ink on the screen.

**Step 2**

Lay the testing paper on the base unit.

Raise the screen completely and slip a sheet of testing paper on the base, aligning it with the registration tabs. Lower the screen.

**Step 3**

Make the print stroke.

Pull the squeegee toward you at 45-degree angle to force the ink deposited on the mesh by the flood stroke through the mesh and onto the printing paper.

**Step 4**

Examine the test print.

## Working Tips: Screen Printing with Textile Inks

The distinct properties of water-soluble textile-printing inks require some changes to your printing approach and methodology.

- Water-soluble textile inks must be heat-set to be permanent so that the printed fabric is washable. Choose a fine-weave fabric in a natural or synthetic fiber that can withstand the heat of an iron set to 275°F to 375°F (135°C to 190.6°C) for 3 or 4 minutes. (Avoid nylon, which will melt when exposed to the heat of a hot iron.) Always lay a sheet of heavy paper or fine-weave cloth over the printed design before lowering a hot iron on its surface to avoid melting the ink and smearing the design.

- Prewash all fabrics, especially those that have sizing, before printing on them. When printing layered fabrics, such as a T-shirt, place a sheet of chipboard between the layers to provide a flat and firm surface for even printing and to prevent ink from bleeding through the top layer onto the bottom layer.

- Use a removable screen to accommodate the nonstandard shape and thickness of the project and the desired position of the print on the fabric surface. Without the support of the screen unit, it will be necessary to find another way to keep the screen stationary during printing. Working with a partner is one way to ensure good results. A partner can hold the screen securely against the fabric as you squeegee the ink through the mesh onto the fabric underneath.

- Make a test print on a fabric that is similar to your project fabric to ensure accurate registration and the desired visual effect before printing the good fabric. For clean prints, use coins at all four corners of the screen to elevate the screen so it doesn't bottom out when printing.

- Water-soluble textile inks can be mixed with extenders, retarders, and transparent bases to thin the ink, slow the drying time (reducing the chance that ink will dry quickly and clog the screen), increase ink's lubricity, and create transparent color. Always follow the directions on the manufacturer's packaging for accurate measuring and mixing instructions. Always wash your tools and screen before the ink has dried; otherwise it may be difficult to remove easily, if at all.

Raise the screen and lower the kick leg to hold the screen off the print. Remove the wet print from the baseboard and place it on a flat, protected surface. Check the test print carefully. Although rare, you may see small holes or imperfections in the test print; to fix an imperfection, find the corresponding spot on the screen and move through the steps to remove and clean the screen and fill the hole with screen filler. Let the filler dry completely before using the screen to make additional prints. It may take several test prints before you are satisfied with the screen quality.

**Step 5**

Make multiple prints.

Repeat steps 1–4 to pull all prints in the series. Check the condition of the screen after each print, cleaning off any ink smudges from the screen to prevent marring the print. Set the prints on a flat surface or clip them to a line to dry.

---

## Fun for Kids: Learning to Screen-Print with Freezer Paper

Freezer paper makes an ideal stencil. One side is coated with plastic, so it is sturdy enough to hold up to water-based inks. Measure and cut a piece of freezer paper slightly larger than the outer dimensions of your screen. Have your child use a marker to draw big shapes on the dull side of the paper in the central area. The shapes should not overlap and there should be a 1" (2.5 cm) border around them. Cut out and discard the shapes, keeping the border intact for the stencil. Tape the stencil, shiny side down, to the flat side of the screen. Lay printing paper on a protected work surface and set the screen on it. Squeeze a ribbon of ink to the taped top of the screen and let your child spread the ink down the screen with a squeegee. Lift up the screen to reveal the print. Once your child has made the first pass with the squeegee, the ink will hold the stencil in place against the screen for further prints.

---

## Fun for Kids: Screen Printing a T-Shirt with a Friend

Screen printing a T-shirt is much the same as printing on paper. You will need a T-shirt (prewashed to promote adhesion of the ink), screen-printing ink for textiles, and a friend—printing a T-shirt is a fun two-person operation! One person needs to hold the screen firmly against the shirt so it doesn't shift and blur the print, while the other person squeegees the ink across the screen. Before you print a T-shirt, measure and cut a piece of foam core to fit snugly inside the shirt so that the fabric cannot stretch or wrinkle during printing and so no ink will leech through the front of the T-shirt fabric to the back. Let the T-shirt dry overnight and heat-set the ink with a hot iron set to 275°F to 375°F (135°C to 190.6°C), according to the manufacturer's directions.

---

## Working Tips: The Flood Stroke and the Print Stroke

Two strokes are used to apply ink to the screen: the flood stroke and the print stroke. Each is accomplished with a squeegee and requires a different degree of applied pressure, which determines how much ink is forced through the screen.

- **Flood stroke**

   The flood stroke is used to coat a clean screen with ink. It is made by pulling the ink in a thin, even coat from the bottom of the screen to the top. A narrow ribbon of ink will form at the top of the screen. The blade of the squeegee is tilted at a 45-degree angle away from your body.

- **Print stroke**

   The print stroke is made after the flood stroke. The squeegee jumps over the ribbon of ink that is at the top of the screen, coming down on the screen to spread the ink in a thin, even coat from the top of the screen to the bottom, forcing it through the screen mesh and onto the printing paper beneath the screen. The blade of the squeegee is tilted at a 45-degree angle toward your body.

## Technique: Cleaning a Screen after Use

It is essential to thoroughly clean the mesh screen of all printing ink before storing the screen or using it to print a second color. If you have used textile or acrylic inks, wash the screen immediately after you have pulled the last print, as these ink formulations are permanent when dry. Letting acrylic inks dry on the screen will block the mesh and make the screen unusable. Water-based inks should also be washed off as soon as possible, but you will have a bit more time to complete the job. Even if the ink dries, it won't clog the screen permanently, although it may stain the mesh.

MATERIALS AND TOOLS

Screen
Squeegee or old credit card
Nylon brush with long handle
Old toothbrush
Dishwashing gloves
Paper towels

### Step 1

Scrape off the excess ink.

Put on gloves. Use a squeegee or expired credit card to collect the excess ink from the screen. Transfer the ink back into its container by scraping the squeegee or credit card against the lip.

### Step 2

Gently scrub off the ink.

Place the screen in the sink. Use the spray attachment to run warm (not hot) water over both sides of the screen. Use a long-handled nylon brush to remove all traces of ink from the screen. Go gently, as vigorous scrubbing can tear or shorten the life of the screen.

### Step 3

Remove the tape and wash the screen.

Strip the tape from both sides of the screen and discard it. Use an old toothbrush to reach into the corners of the frame and clean out any trapped paint. Then continue washing the screen, turning it from top to bottom and back again to ensure that the screen and the frame are completely free of ink. Wipe both sides of the screen with paper towels and lay it flat to dry. Clean the squeegee or the credit card and brushes thoroughly in warm soapy water and dry with paper towels.

## Working Tips: Setting Up Your Hand-Printing Studio

You don't need a fancy studio for printmaking, but it does help to designate separate areas in your work space for various stages of the process, such as cutting a block or stencil and making a print. Keep your work surfaces clean and organized and provide good task lighting for detail work. Be sure to set up a good drying system, such as a clothesline with clips, to protect and separate the wet prints as you make them. In small runs, you can lay wet prints on an out-of-the-way flat surface or shelf so the papers don't overlap.

# PROJECTS

## Cord-and-Bead: Postcards

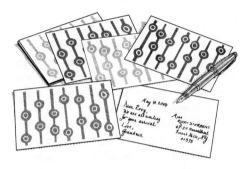

These postcards are easy to print using any sassy color combination of block-printing ink that you like. The design is organized in long vertical bars with bead-shaped accents. The design printed on each card was carved from a pink soft-carve block, which is easy to cut. Some of the featured cards are printed in hot pink and some are printed in leaf green. When mailing postcards, check with the post office to ensure that they have the correct postage.

MATERIALS AND TOOLS

    Cord-and-Bead pattern (page 702)
    Pink soft-carve block, 5¼" × 4" (13.3 × 10.2 cm)
    Cardstock, larger than the finished block
    Testing paper
    Set of cutters with handle
    Bench hook
    Tablespoon
    Ink slab, either glass or plastic
    Block-printing ink, water soluble
    Brayer
    Self-healing cutting mat
    Steel ruler
    Craft knife
    Pen
    Expired credit card
    Ink-jet copier or printer

**Step 1**

Transfer the pattern to the block.

Make an ink-jet copy of the Cord-and-Bead pattern. Lay the printout on a self-healing cutting mat and use a craft knife and steel ruler to trim it to 5¼" × 4" (13.3 × 10.2 cm). Lay the soft-carve block on a flat surface. Set the cutout, ink side down, on top. Burnish the back of the ink-jet printout with the bowl of a tablespoon to transfer the pattern to the soft-carve block. Let the ink dry.

**Step 2**

Cut the design on the printing block.

Place a bench hook on your work surface, pushing the front edge of the block against the front edge of your work table. Place the soft-carve block against the stop at the opposite end. Choose a cutter according to the character of the lines and shapes in the design. Use the tool to cut out the design on the block, changing cutters as needed to cut the grooves and gouges. Stop cutting when all of the marked details are carved. Brush off all shavings from the block.

**Step 3**

Make a test print.

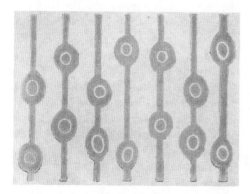

Use the carved block to make a test print on scrap paper. Examine the test print to make sure all parts of the bead-and-cord design are printing and the edges are clean. If an area of the design that is not supposed to print leaves

an ink smudge on your paper, that area on the block is too high. Clean the ink off the block and use a cutter to remove more of the soft-carve material in that area. Make another test print. Repeat this testing process until the print is good. Clean the block of all ink.

**Step 4**

Cut out the postcards.

Use a steel ruler and a craft knife to cut the sheet of cardstock into four equal pieces, each measuring 5½" × 4¼" (14 × 10.8 cm), working on a clean work surface; set the four cards aside.

**Step 5**

Ink the block.

Squeeze out a ribbon of block-printing ink the width of the brayer on one end of the ink slab. Use a plastic credit card to mix the ink to a smooth consistency. Use a brayer to spread the ink in an even, tacky coat on the slab, in a roll-and-lift motion. Lay the carved block on a protected flat surface. Use the loaded brayer to roll ink onto the carved side of the block, moving the roller parallel to the cuts in the surface.

**Step 6**

Make the prints.

Center one postcard over the inked block, lower it onto the block, and smooth it gently with your hands. Use a baren to transfer the inked pattern evenly onto the cardstock. Carefully lift up the printed postcard and lay it, ink side up, on a flat surface to dry. Continue to print the pattern onto the remaining three postcards. Let the prints dry overnight. Clean and store the block.

**Step 7**

Create the address side of the postcards.

Turn each postcard facedown and use a ruler and pen to draw a line that divides the card in half. Use the left side for your message; use the right side to address the card and adhere a stamp.

## Butterfly: A Gift Bag

Purchased gift bags, to fill with party favors or gifts, look extra-festive when decorated with a two-color butterfly print. The appeal of this project is that the butterflies are printed separately on plain white paper, cut out, then glued in place on the front of the bags. For more of a challenge, print the two-color design directly on the bags, using a registration frame to ensure that the colors line up. Add ribbon in a matching color to jazz up the handle.

### MATERIALS AND TOOLS

Key block Butterfly Wing pattern
 (page 696)
Color block Butterfly Wing pattern
 (page 696)
2 pink soft-carve printing blocks,
 8¼" × 5¾" (21 cm × 14.6 cm)
Block-printing inks, water soluble,
 in 2 colors
Printing paper
Testing paper, same size as printing paper
Gift bags
White glue
Bench hook
Cutting tool and interchangeable cutters
Frame, in a depth that matches printing
 blocks
Brayer
Baren
Self-healing cutting mat
Craft knife
Ruler
Tablespoon
Pencil
2 pushpins
Scissors
Tapered paintbrush
Alligator clip
Ink-jet copier, or scanner and ink-jet
 printer

### Step 1

Transfer the patterns to the blocks.

Make ink-jet laser copies of the Butterfly Wing and Butterfly Color Block patterns. Use a self-healing cutting mat, steel ruler, and craft knife to trim each printout. Lay the soft-carve blocks on a flat surface. Place each cutout facedown on a soft-carve block. Burnish the back of each printout with the bowl of a tablespoon to transfer the patterns to the blocks.

### Step 2

Carve the printing blocks.

Place a bench hook on your work surface, pushing the front edge of the hook against the front edge of your work table. Set the soft-carve block with the Butterfly Color Block pattern on the bench hook. Choose a cutter according to the character of the lines and shapes in your design and change cutters as needed. Stop cutting when all of the marked details are carved. Use a steel ruler and a craft knife to trim the edges of the block to size. Brush off all the shavings from the block. Repeat to carve the Butterfly Wing design for the key block.

## Step 3

Mark the registration on the frame.

Lay the testing paper on the top left corner of the frame, approximately ½" (1.3 cm) from the outside edges. Use a ruler and pencil to draw two perpendicular lines at one top corner of the frame, even with the edge of the scrap paper. Remove the testing paper. Place the printing paper on the frame in the same position, aligning the edges of the paper with the marked lines on the frame. Use pushpins to secure the top two corners of the paper to the frame.

## Step 4

Apply ink to the secondary block.

Squeeze out a ribbon of light-colored ink on the slab and condition it with an expired credit card. Use a brayer to roll the ink into a smooth, tacky layer. Lay the carved secondary block on a flat surface and roll the ink onto it in a thin, even coat.

## Step 5

Print the secondary block.

Lift the printing paper and hold it behind the frame with an alligator clip. Position the secondary block, ink side up, inside the frame's top left corner, aligning the two outside edges of the block with the two inside edges of the frame. Carefully lower the paper onto the block. Smooth the paper with a baren to transfer the light ink to the paper. Lift the printed paper, still pinned to the frame, and bend it away from the printing block. Attach an alligator clip to the edge of the print to hold it back. Remove the secondary block. Let the print dry completely. Clean the brayer and the block.

## Step 6

Overprint the secondary block using the key block.

Prepare the darker ink on the slab. Use a clean brayer to apply a thin, even coat of ink to the key block. Position the key block, ink side up, in the corner of the frame, in the same orientation as the secondary block. Remove the alligator clip from the printed paper and guide the paper over and onto the inked block. Smooth the paper with a baren to transfer the dark ink to the print. Use two hands to peel the paper off the block in one continuous motion. Remove the pushpins. Lay the print, ink side up, on a flat surface or clip it on a line. Allow to dry overnight. Repeat to make more two-color prints.

## Step 7

Decorate the gift bag.

Use scissors to cut out the two-color block print of the butterfly. Lay the cutout on a protected work surface, print side down, and brush a smooth coat of glue onto the reverse side. Position the cutout on the front of a gift bag and press to adhere.

## Leafy Branch: A Place Mat

You can use screen printing to make decorative accessories for your home. Here, a simple leafy branch design is printed on a fabric place mat. The same pattern can be used to stencil a random pattern of leafy branches on a larger surface, such as a tablecloth, a shower curtain, or even a wall. Remember to choose the right ink for your printing surface, whether it be textile or paper. For fabric place mats, I used water-soluble screen-printing ink designed for textiles. For more flexibility in positioning the screen print on the fabric place mat, I removed the screen from the screen-printing unit and worked with a friend.

### MATERIALS AND TOOLS

Single Branch pattern (page 700)
Screen
Screen filler
Water-soluble screen-printing ink for
    textiles, in red or desired color
Place mat, cream or white, in tight, flat
    weave 19" × 14" (48.3 × 35.6 cm)
Testing fabric in similar weave as
    place mat
Waterproof packing tape, 2" to 3"
    (5.1 to 7.6 cm) wide
Dishwasher detergent
Nylon scrub brush
Tapered watercolor paintbrush
Squeegee with U-shaped blade (for fabric)
Measuring spoons
Mixing bowl
Rubber gloves
Soft pencil
4 pushpins
8 coins
Craft stick
Scissors
Household iron

### Step 1

Wash the screen.

Put on rubber gloves. Scrub both sides of the screen in a sink, using a scrub brush and a solution of 1 tablespoon dishwasher detergent and 2 cups hot water. Use the spray attachment to thoroughly rinse both sides of the screen with warm water. Let the screen dry completely.

### Step 2

Tape the screen.

Apply lengths of tape to the edges of both sides of the screen so that the strips straddle the mesh and the wood frame on the bottom flat side and straddle the L-shaped join formed by the frame and the mesh on the top recessed side. Overlap the tape ends at the corners for a tight seal. Add a second length of tape across the top and the bottom of the screen on both sides.

### Step 3

Draw the pattern on the screen.

Lay the Single Branch pattern on a flat surface. Center the prepared screen, flat side down, over the pattern. Use a pencil to trace the branch outline.

### Step 4

Apply the screen filler.

Turn the screen flat side up and press a pushpin into each corner. Turn the screen over so it stands on the pushpin legs. Mix the screen filler until it is smooth. Use a paintbrush to fill in all of the nonprinting areas on the screen, extending the filler to the tape and making certain the bottom of the screen does not touch down on the work surface. Use the brush to smooth out any screen filler that has collected on the other side of the screen. Stand the screen horizontally on its pushpin legs and allow the screen filler to dry overnight. Inspect the screen for tiny pinholes and apply dabs of screen filler to conceal them; let the screen filler dry completely. Remove the pushpins from the screen.

**Step 5**
    Make a test print.

Lay the testing fabric on a flat protected surface, smoothing the fabric flat and taping the corners, using tape. Turn the screen so the flat side faces up. Stack and tape two coins to each corner of the screen. Pour a ribbon of ink along the bottom end of the screen, lift up that end of the screen, and make a flood stroke, tilting the squeegee at a 45-degree angle away from you and pushing it from the bottom of the screen to the top to spread an even coat of ink on the screen. Set the inked screen on the testing fabric. Make a print stroke, jumping over the ribbon of ink at the top of the screen and coming down on the other side, pulling the squeegee toward you at a 45-degree angle to spread the ink from the top to the bottom of the screen and forcing it through the screen and onto the fabric. Lift the screen and set it aside. Examine the test print for pinholes. Wash the ink from the screen and repair the stencil with screen filler as needed. Let the filler dry completely. Repeat the testing until you are satisfied with the quality of the print.

**Step 6**
    Print the place mat.
    Lay the place mat horizontally on a protected work surface. Tape down the corners. Working with a partner, one of you to hold the screen stationary and the other to work the squeegee. Use a flood stroke followed by a print stroke to ink the screen and print the place mat. Lift the screen off the place mat. Set the place mat, print side up, on a flat protected work surface or hang on a line to dry. Repeat to print additional place mats as desired. Check the screen for ink smudges after each print and clean the frame as needed.

**Step 7**
    Heat-set the ink.
    Lay a sheet of heavy paper over the inked design and use a hot iron to set the textile ink, following the manufacturer's directions.

## Chandelier: An Art Print

This large chandelier design is one of my favorites. The stencil is made using drawing liquid and screen filler to create a positive image. A multifilament polyester screen is recommended. Making the stencil is time-consuming and challenging, but it is extremely satisfying and the results are spectacular. Use your screen stencil to make an art print on rag paper, which looks beautiful when framed. Then, if you feel ambitious and you can inspire a friend to work with you, print the same design on the wall. Once the screen is made, it is easy enough to make multiple prints. You may need to practice printing on a vertical surface, which requires some dexterity and an ink that is just the right consistency—too thin and it will run down in drips. A friend helped me position and hold the frame against the wall while I ran the squeegee across the mesh. Keep the screen frame free of stray ink that could transfer onto the printing surface.

## MATERIALS AND TOOLS
Chandelier pattern (page 703)
Water-soluble screen-printing ink,
    in orange, or desired color
Archival printing paper, 100 percent rag
    stock
Testing paper, same size as printing paper
Screen, 14" × 20" (35.6 × 50.8 cm)
Baseboard unit
Screen filler
Drawing fluid
Waterproof packing tape, 2" to 3"
    (5.1 to 7.6 cm) wide
Dishwasher detergent
Soft scrub brush
Tapered liner paintbrush
Squeegee
Rubber gloves
Measuring spoons
Mixing bowl
Soft pencil
4 pushpins
8 coins
Craft stick
Scissors

### Step 1
Wash the screen.

Put on rubber gloves. Scrub both sides of the screen in a sink, using a scrub brush and a solution of 1 tablespoon dishwasher detergent and 2 cups hot water. Use the spray attachment to thoroughly rinse both sides of the screen with warm water. Let the screen dry completely.

### Step 2
Tape the screen.

Apply lengths of tape to the edges of both sides of the screen so that the strips straddle the mesh and the wood frame on the bottom flat side and straddle the L-shaped join formed by the frame and the mesh on the top recessed side. Overlap the tape ends at the corners for a tight seal. Add a second length of tape across the top and the bottom of the screen on both sides.

### Step 3
Trace the chandelier pattern on the screen.

Lay the Chandelier pattern on a flat surface. Center the prepared screen, flat side down, over the pattern so the image is in the center of the screen. Use a pencil to trace the outline of each of the elements of the chandelier.

### Step 4
Apply the drawing fluid.

Turn the screen, flat side up, and press a pushpin into each corner. Turn the screen over so it stands on the pushpin legs. Mix the drawing fluid with a craft stick until it is smooth. Use a paintbrush to fill in all of the shapes of the design, working carefully so the lines and contours are neat and making certain the bottom of the screen does not touch down on the work surface. Let the drawing fluid dry overnight with the screen resting on its pins in a horizontal position.

**Step 5**

Apply the screen filler to the screen.

Mix the screen filler until it is smooth. Pour a thin ribbon of screen filler along one end of the screen on the recessed side. Hold up one end of the screen and use a squeegee to make one pass to apply a thin coat of screen filler that covers the drawing fluid and the margins of the screen. Do not let the screen bottom touch the work surface. Stand the screen horizontally on its pushpin legs and allow the screen filler to dry overnight.

**Step 6**

Wash the drawing fluid out of the screen.

Put on rubber gloves. Set the screen in a sink and use the spray attachment to direct a forceful spray of cold water over the areas of the stencil on which the drawing fluid was applied. Use a brush to gently scrub any blocked areas. Allow the screen to dry completely.

## Working Tips: Getting Ready for an Ambitious Printing Project

You will find that after you have developed a foundation of screen-printing skills, you will look forward to projects of more complexity. Screen printing a wall will be a challenging and satisfying project when you are ready.

**Step 7**

Register the print.

Turn the screen so the flat side faces up. Remove the pushpins and stack and tape two coins to each corner of the screen. Turn the screen over and attach it to the screen unit by reinserting the hinge pins. Place the testing paper on the baseboard unit, lower the screen, and adjust the paper position so that the chandelier image is centered. Lift the screen and prop it up on the kick leg. Use tape to create L-shaped registration tabs around each corner of the paper. Use long strips of tape to register the midpoint of each long side of the paper, if desired.

**Step 8**

Pull a test print.

Pour a ribbon of ink along the bottom end of the screen, lift up that end of the screen, and make a flood stroke, tilting the squeegee at a 45-degree angle away from you and pushing it from the bottom of the screen to the top to spread an even coat of ink on the screen. Lower the inked screen onto the testing paper. Make a print stroke, jumping over the ribbon of ink at the top of the screen, and landing on the screen, pulling the squeegee toward you at a 45-degree angle to spread the ink from the top to the bottom of the screen and forcing it through the screen and onto the paper. Lift the screen and prop it on the kick leg. Remove the test print from the baseboard unit and examine it closely for pinholes or other imperfections. Wash the ink from the screen and repair the stencil with screen filler as needed. Let the filler dry completely. Repeat the testing process until you are satisfied with quality of the print.

**Step 9**

Make an art print.

Lay the printing paper on the baseboard unit, aligning it with the registration tabs. Use a flood stroke followed by a print stroke to in the screen and print the paper. Lift the screen and prop it on its kick leg. Remove the print and set it on a flat, protected work surface or hang it on a line to dry. Clean the screen of all ink. Set the screen in a horizontal position and allow it to dry completely.

## Chrysanthemum: Printed Fabric for a Box Book

The beauty of this design is in the fine-art engraving—actually, a small corner of a copyright-free print—that I enlarged to bring out the gorgeous line work. I used a fine marker to strengthen the lines to make them thick enough to burn onto the photo-emulsion screen. The level of detail was so dense, I wasn't able to thicken every line, and as a result, some of the very fine lines were lost. The resulting open spaces breathed some air into the design and created a nice tonal balance.

Once my screen stencil was made, I used it to print fabric for the cover of a box book; see Making a Box Book (page 273). To print on fabric, use a polyester screen with multifilament mesh with a tight weave; a good range for sharp details is 10XX to 14XX. You can use this screen to print on paper too, as I did for coordinating note cards.

### MATERIALS AND TOOLS

Chrysanthemum original art (page 701)
Laser copier, or scanner and laser printer
Acetate sheet, 7½" × 8½" (19.1 × 21.6 cm)
Permanent black marker
Polyester mesh screen, 12" × 16¼" (30.5 × 41.3 cm), and base unit
Waterproof packing tape, 2" to 3" (5.1 to 7.6 cm) wide
Screen filler
Diazo system kit: premeasured photo emulsion and photo sensitizer
Screen-printing textile ink, water based, in black, or as desired

Flat-weave cotton fabric, in white or a pale color, two 10" × 10" (25.4 × 25.4 cm) pieces for printing; also set aside one 10" × 4" (25.4 × 10.2 cm) piece for the spine of box book

Scrap fabric, several 10" × 10" (25.4 × 25.4 cm) squares for testing

Socket extension cord with pie-pan reflector

BBA No. 1 photoflood bulb

Standing pole, such as a pole lamp

Clamp

Lucite sheet, ½" (1.3 cm) larger all around than screen

Black paper or fabric (larger than screen)

Small fan

Minute timer

Squeegee with U-shaped blade (for fabric)

Tapered watercolor paintbrush

Masking tape

Dishwasher detergent

Soft scrub brush

Measuring spoons

Mixing bowl

Rubber gloves

Soft pencil

4 pushpins

4 coins

Craft stick

Scissors

Household iron

## Step 1

Prepare the screen.

Put on rubber gloves. Scrub both sides of the screen in a sink, using a scrub brush and a solution of 1 tablespoon dishwasher detergent and 2 cups hot water. Thoroughly rinse both sides of the screen with warm water. Let the screen dry completely.

## Step 2

Make an acetate positive of your design.

Copy the Chrysanthemum original art onto acetate, using a laser photocopier or a scanner and laser printer; size the image smaller than the mesh screen. Inspect the acetate positive for imperfections. Use a black permanent marker to reinforce any weak or broken lines. Let the marker dry completely.

## Step 3

Apply the photo emulsion to the screen.

Remove the screen from the baseboard unit and insert a pushpin into each corner on the flat side to create temporary legs. Follow the manufacturer's directions for the Diazo products. Put on rubber gloves. Mix the photo sensitizer and pour it into the jar of photo emulsion, stirring with a craft stick until smooth. Hold the screen, flat side up, over a sink. Use a squeegee to spread a thin, even coat of emulsion onto the screen, adding more solution where necessary and smoothing away streaks and drips. Turn the screen over so the recessed side faces up and coat this side with a thin layer of emulsion. Return to the recessed side of the screen and use a squeegee to make a final pass, smoothing the emulsion into a thin coat with no drips or uneven areas. Stand the screen horizontally on its pushpin legs in a dark closet. Let the screen dry overnight. Keep it in the dark until you are ready to proceed.

## Step 4

Prepare the work space.

Refer to the instruction sheet and chart of exposure times that comes in the photo-emulsion kit. Screw the photoflood bulb into the socket of the socket extension cord with pie-pan reflector. Clamp the cord to a pole so that the bulb will be the recommended distance from the surface of the screen when the screen is placed on the work surface. Lay the black fabric or black paper on top of the work surface directly under the lampshade. Set the acetate positive, the Lucite sheet, the timer, and the fan close by.

### Step 5

Expose the screen.

Retrieve the coated screen from the closet and remove the pushpins. Place the screen, flat side up, on the black fabric, centering it under the lamp. Center the acetate positive, ink side down, on the screen, followed by the sheet of Lucite. Switch on the fan so it blows across the setup. Turn on the lamp and set the timer to the exposure time recommended on the chart.

### Step 6

Thoroughly wash the screen.

When the allotted time is up, remove the Lucite sheet and acetate positive from the screen and set them aside. Carry the screen to the sink. Use the spray attachment to direct a forceful stream of room-temperature (not hot) water on the lines of the design to stop the emulsion from reacting to the light. Wash both sides of the screen, using a small scrub brush if necessary, until the emulsion washes off and the design is revealed. Spray clean with cold water and allow the screen to dry.

### Step 7

Make registration marks and a test print.

Turn over the prepared screen so the flat side faces up. Stack and tape two coins to each of the bottom corners of the screen. Turn the screen over and reattach it to the screen unit. Use a piece of scrap fabric to make registration marks on the baseboard unit. Make a test print on a piece of scrap fabric and check the quality of the print. Use screen filler to conceal any open areas or pinholes in the screen. Let the filler dry completely.

### Step 8

Print the fabric.

Raise the screen on its kick leg. Slip a piece of fabric on the base, aligning it with the registration marks and taping down the corners. Carefully pour a ribbon of ink along the bottom end of the screen. Hold the screen up off the baseboard unit with one hand. Use the other hand to make a flood stroke: pull the squeegee from the bottom to the top, tilting the blade away from you at a 45-degree angle, to spread an even coat of ink on the screen. Make the print stroke, pulling the squeegee toward you at 45-degree angle to force the ink deposited on the mesh by the flood stroke through the mesh and onto the fabric. Raise the screen on its kick leg. Peel up the tape, remove the fabric with the wet print from the base, and place it, printed side up, on a flat, protected work surface or hang it on a line to dry. Check the screen unit for ink smudges that could mar the prints and clean them before making the second print.

### Step 9

Set the ink.

Lay a clean scrap cloth over the print and use a hot iron to set the textile ink, following the manufacturer's directions.

# CHAPTER FIVE

# Decoupage

## THE HEART

### November Roses

"In happy hours, when the imagination
Wakes like a wind at midnight, and the
    soul
Trembles in all its leaves, it is a joy
To be uplifted on its wings, and listen
To the prophetic voices in the air
That call us onward. Then the work we do

Is a delight, and the obedient hand
Never grows weary . . . "
—Henry Wadsworth Longfellow,
    *Michael Angelo: Part First: II.*
    *Monologue: The Last Judgment,* 1884

While staying in London, I decided to take a
short detour north to the little village of Olney
in Buckinghamshire. After a long drive in a
torrential rain, I finally got settled in a cozy

bedroom in a pretty row house on one of the narrow lanes. It was well past midnight by the time I unpacked, but still on New York time, I couldn't sleep. I was standing at a window overlooking the neighbor's garden wall and there, rising above its edge, was a single pink rose, petals curled back to reveal a buttery center that glowed in the surrounding dark.

In the morning, I raised my umbrella against a steady drizzle and set off for Market Place to search for colorful prints for a decoupage project—a set of dessert plates. I planned to use a technique that I had learned several years before. It was called *potichomania*, a form of decoupage where prints are glued behind glass so that they gleam like fine porcelain. From the first time I saw the brilliant difference that a piece of glass could make in the appearance of a print, I wanted nothing else than to lay every print I found under glass.

I had set aside my entire afternoon in this small country village where row houses were stacked in narrow alleys with names like Cobbs Garden, Lace Mews, and Rose Court. I had no itinerary and could make any impulsive turn I wanted, but I was so unfamiliar with the notion of unscheduled time, I felt indecisive.

So I simply walked, allowing things that looked interesting to direct my steps. I took discreet looks through one picture window after another, each framing a tableau of English domestic life as I had always imagined it. Through parted gauzy curtains, I saw red roses lavishing the chintz fabric on a plump armchair in a small sitting room. In one home, a man wearing a vest leaned over a fireplace, poking the flames, which lit up his thin face; on the mantel were large porcelain vases, one emblazoned with oversize orange flowers. A sudden wind whipped fallen leaves into a swirling coil that collapsed when the wind subsided. I tightened my scarf and stopped at a windowsill lined with a china teapot and sugar bowl and large frames—a few were angled so that I could see photographs of a laughing child

in a pinafore and a formal portrait of Queen Elizabeth. The next window was bordered on one side by a tangle of twisted stems that climbed to the second story. A few pale yellow roses were low enough to cup in my hands, and I brought one to my nose and breathed in deeply. I was reminded that roses bloomed in November, and I decided I would search for rose motifs for my little plates. Imagining the designs, I pictured cutting out single blooms and placing one in the center of each plate, or perhaps I would cover each surface in an overall pattern of flowers, painting the backgrounds either blue or apricot—colors made famous by Madame de Pompadour, who so loved the cool blues and warm complementary tones that she decorated her personal suite at Versailles in the colorway, which came to be known as the Pompadour Palette.

I continued my wandering along High Street, Olney's main thoroughfare, and found myself in front of the historic house of Olney's favorite son and poet, William Cowper, who along with John Newton, the local curate, distinguished himself by composing a volume of hymns, among them one written in 1779 that became known as "Amazing Grace" after its opening verse.

As I stepped through the front door of Cowper's house, I heard a chorus of cheerful "good mornings." Two women were kneeling over several large cartons, unwrapping small sculptures of wild hares destined for the gift shop. It seemed that William Cowper had kept several pets, among them three wild hares, which he would release from their hutches on winter evenings so that they could play freely on the parlor carpet while he and his housekeeper Mary Unwin drank tea. The sculptures were a big seller. I began my tour, accompanied by one of the women who led me through a warren of first-floor rooms, all sparsely but tastefully furnished, as she explained the distinguished history of the home in a mellifluous voice.

The house tour ended outside in the back garden. The rain had stopped, but the sky remained low and brooding although a few patches of blue had appeared. I was sure that in earlier months the garden was well tended as visitors threaded their way through paths that outlined the flower beds, but today the garden looked dreary, unkempt, and over-grown—clusters of dried stems poked up from clumps of earth and rattled noisily in the wind. A rough brick wall surrounded the garden, interrupted by a wooden door that stood ajar, revealing Cowper's summerhouse—well, not a house per se, but rather a one-room structure so small that I could stand eye-level with its tiled roof and see the scattered colonies of green moss that freckled the orange tiles—a snow-white feather was caught in one of them. I peeked through the doorway. The low ceiling and all four walls were covered in a storm of signatures. Some of the names were written with curling flourishes that ended in looping underlines, transforming that particular graffiti into beautiful folk art. I imagined incorporating scripted passages into my decoupage, and for a split second I saw the finished design in its entirety. It was like looking through an aperture that opened and closed quickly, squeezing the image into a tiny dot that dis-

appeared into some part of my mind. I had these kinds of alchemical peeks at the future, although I rarely remembered them, if at all, until I was in the middle of a project and the picture would come back, leaving me awed and grateful. Before I left the garden, I visited the gift shop and browsed through the offerings in a spindled rack, collecting several post-cards and a brochure for their reproductions of the delicate watercolors of Cowper's pet hares, the little garden house, and a rural landscape.

On my way home, I stopped at a shop at the end of a cobblestone path where I bought gift wrap sprawling with English roses and a sheet of paper covered with a musical score written in a scratchy pen complete with smears of sepia-brown ink. I rolled up a large sheet of paper printed with fish cavorting in a pale turquoise ocean. I imagined them splashing in their own little aquarium—perhaps the inside of an oversized vase. I bought several birthday cards and picked up scrapbooking embellishments made of layered and glittered paper—frosted wedding cakes, gift boxes with ribbon bows, small birds in flight, and miniature wrapped candies. I knew even as I piled them on the counter that I was being immoderate,

but I had long ago accepted that these kinds of things were necessary to me.

By the time dark clouds were boiling up in a froth of white and gray behind the rooftops, I was turning the key in the lock on my door. Welcoming me home was the glow of a lamp that rested on a table completely covered in rose prints. I inspected the table's surface. Each blossom had been painstakingly cut and glued in place. It was an inspiring find, one that caused me to add it to my list of projects, which now numbered eight, but I knew even then that I wouldn't know what projects would actually remain of all those I had imagined until my scissors had clipped countless paths around the prints. I would spend a long night or two with my cutouts spread out over my worktable, configuring and reconfiguring the motifs. I would wait to see what new designs shuffled into place as if some magic were at work, knowing from experience that inspiration, like the November rose, could bloom unexpectedly—even at midnight—especially at midnight—or anytime I engaged my heart and allowed the creative prophecy of ordinary things to come forth, nudged out of some hidden place in me, and arrive full-blown and beautiful.

## A Brief History

The word *decoupage* is French (from *découper,* meaning "to cut out"), but the origin of the practice can be traced to twelfth-century China, where the peasants used colorful paper cutouts to decorate windows, lanterns, and small boxes. It was in the late seventeenth century that decoupage developed in Italy and gave rise to the form we know today. Italian city-states imported many products from China and Japan; especially popular among the Italian nobility were elaborately hand-painted Chinese lacquerware furnishings. When demand for the furniture outstripped the supply, enterprising Venetian guild cabinetmakers, printers, and lacquerers replicated the look. They began by constructing pieces of furniture, frequently cutting costs by using mismatched woods or papier-mâché and concealing the irregularities with gesso, a chalk-like substance that was mixed with rabbit-skin glue and applied to the entire surface. Once it hardened, the gesso was sanded to a satin finish and sealed. Hand-tinted prints were cut out and pasted onto the surface in an effort to mimic hand painting. The stunning transformation from crude cutouts to exquisite painterly decoration was made complete with the application of *lacca contrafatta.* In this "counterfeit lacquer" stage, as many as thirty to forty layers of lacquer were applied, seamlessly integrating the cutouts and the background into one smooth and lustrous veneer. This furniture, known as *l'arte povero* or "poor man's art," was a relatively cheap substitute for the expensive Oriental lacquerware that inspired it. The Venetian variations reflected such artistic vitality, originality, and fashionable opulence that *l'arte povero* became highly regarded in its own right, and by the eighteenth century, the craft had spread throughout Europe and the British Commonwealth.

Legalization of free trade led to the disbanding of formal craft guilds. Consequently, trade secrets were disseminated to a broader population of crafters of all levels of society—heralding a kind of golden age of decoupage. Decoupage became an amusing diversion for ladies of the royal court and high society and eventually for the growing middle classes. A hostess could entertain her guests by providing a few sheets of colored paper and a pair of scissors, which were in nearly every lady's sewing box. In social gatherings, ladies applied their appreciable training, patience, and creativity to transforming small trinket boxes, frames, trays, fans, and all manner of personal accessories into works of art.

In England, "japanning" (as decoupage was known) saw a burgeoning of popularity. Savvy businessman Robert Sayer compiled a collection of 1,500 engravings in a 200-page volume, published in 1780, entitled *Ladies Amusement Book; or Whole Art of Japanning Made Easy.* This book supplied *découpeurs* with a wealth of images—flowers, shells, birds, insects, landscapes, ships, and beasts—and border designs to hand-color and cut out. So valued was well-executed decoupage that many *découpeurs* became recognized as artists in their own right. Mrs. Mary Delaney, a hostess who began decoupage at the age of seventy-two, created botanical portraits of such high regard that she gained the respect and friendship of King George III and Queen Charlotte of Britain.

The new status of decoupage was evidenced by the proud display of increasingly larger pieces in the home. Dummy boards—large, flat pieces of wood—were decorated to look like life-size footmen, royal hounds, soldiers, and urns of flowers. Room screens, a particular English favorite, were adorned with lavish and colorful compositions of cutout prints. Lord Byron spent three years decorating both sides of a four-panel screen with prints of prominent boxers and theatrical prints. In Georgian England, entire "print rooms" were adorned with arrangements of fine engravings depicting botanical rarities, military and sporting life, imposing architecture, pastoral and urban scenes, and austere portraits of historical figures. Engravings were glued directly to painted ivory walls, "framed" with ornate paper borders, and linked to others by sumptuous garlands and ribbons in a composition that suggested a grand gallery of fine Baroque or Rococo art.

Across the Channel in eighteenth-century France, *lacquer pauvre* and *l'art scriban* were being practiced in a chinoiserie style that depicted idyllic scenes of Chinese life—women with parasols, graceful bridges and pagodas, and exotic monkeys. By the reign of Louis XVI, *découpeurs* included Marie Antoinette and ladies of her court, who cut up original works of art to transform personal accessories into fantasy objets d'art. In America, *découpeurs* imprinted their new national identity on their art, differentiating it from its European counterpart. As exuberance for the craft grew among amateurs and professional artisans alike, the scale of the American works grew larger. Crafters adorned fireboards that beautified cold hearths and decorated entire walls in the classic print-room style.

Germany's thriving printing industry mass-produced beautiful decorative borders that were applied to furniture using "intarsia," a technique that used marbleized paper to replicate the look of wood inlay. By the mid-nineteenth century, printers were embossing gold foil and colored paper cutouts and Godefroy Engelmann had patented chromolithography, a mechanized process that replaced hand tinting. These richly colored mass-produced prints were made up of countless dots of oil-based paints. The prints were exported and collected in scrapbooks, providing a ready source of embossed, precolored, and die-cut images. Sheets of the printed pictures, which were called scraps or chromos, could be cut out and combined with embossed gold-paper braid in sentimental arrangements that became emblematic of the Victorian style of decoupage.

Decoupage evolved further as artisans and crafters departed from the traditional rules. *Vue d'optique,* favored by Queen Victoria, used prints on thicker paper mounted in layers in a frame or deep box, creating architectural compositions with an illusion of depth. These "shadow boxes" were three-dimensional and might show a cathedral or a street scene. The potichomania style derived its name from the French words *potiche* ("porcelain vase") and *manie* ("craze"). Potichomania's look of hand-painted porcelain is created by gluing images behind glass.

*Découpeurs* the world over continue to explore new methods and applications, abandoning some of the traditional practices and adapting techniques from other crafts, to produce works of uncommon beauty from simple paper cutouts.

## Decoupage Materials and Tools at a Glance

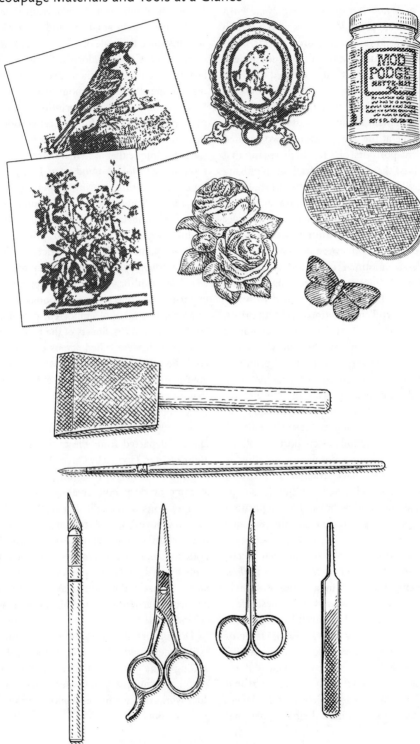

## THE SCIENCE

Decoupage is easy. It is essentially about imagination and good cutting. Cutting requires some manual dexterity and perhaps a little practice if you're not used to using small scissors, but otherwise the techniques are simple and few. The materials for decoupage are quite ordinary—printed images, glue, and a surface to apply them to. New materials and processes, such as synthetic adhesives and color laser printing, have made decoupage easier than ever to learn, and the wide range of art suitable for decoupage allows even total beginners to create beautiful or quirky designs of every description. If you've never done decoupage, I urge you to try it. Once you begin, you will find yourself snipping swaths through beautiful papers, applying silky paste and finishes to prints, and creating your own arrangements of the cutout images.

I have been doing decoupage for a long time. I have always loved working with beautiful paper, so it was natural that I would gravitate toward this art form. From my very first project—a small box with a hinge made when I was a Girl Scout—I enjoyed the freedom and the mystery of the decoupage process. By cutting up and rearranging the fine art of painters and draftsmen whose talents far exceeded my own, I could create completely new designs that frequently moved into place with little effort.

I don't actually remember deciding to take a holiday from decoupage; it simply slipped from view as other exciting and new crafts claimed my attention, time, and heart. Then, about ten years ago, I was introduced to potichomania, and my interest in decoupage soared. Potichomania is a form of decoupage in which prints are pasted under glass. The glass instantly forms a flawless finish over the prints, replacing the multiple layers of varnish that must be applied over prints glued to an opaque surface. My discovery of potichomania was liberating and inspiring; I became more and more involved in experimenting with decoupage under glass, and by extension, exploring special printing effects using a photocopier and my computer and printer.

Regardless of the project surface, I move through the same few stages each time I take up a print and my scissors: selecting and preparing the prints, laying out the design, preparing the surface, adhering the prints, and applying the finish. There is a small shuffle in sequence, depending on whether the paint is being applied to an opaque (wood or metal) or a transparent (glass) surface.

### Materials and Tools

The essential materials and tools for decoupage are relatively few. You probably have some of the more common items stashed away in a drawer, and the others are easily found at craft stores and through online sources. The items listed here are common to all decoupage projects regardless of the material from which the project is made. Additional materials and tools needed to prepare wood, metal, and glass surfaces for decoupage are described later in the chapter.

- **Item to decoupage**

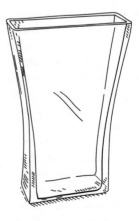

Any surface that is sturdy, clean, smooth, and not too porous is a candidate for decoupage. Suitable items can be made of wood, metal, or glass, so go with whatever captures your imagination. Decoupage is also possible on porous surfaces, such as paper and chipboard, and nonporous ceramic and plastic.

• **Printed images**

Any image that appeals to you can be used in decoupage as long as it is printed on one side of the paper only; an image that has ink on its reverse side is not suitable as the ink can bleed through and ruin your project. If a print does not meet this basic criterion, use a laser copier or a computer scanner and laser printer to make a one-sided print on light- to medium-weight uncoated paper, such as non-recycled copy paper.

• **Print sealer**
A print sealer, applied as a liquid or a spray, protects a paper print from damage caused by excessive handling or moisture during the decoupage process. Applied properly, the sealer stiffens the paper just enough to make it easier to cut out the image; a light even coat is very important because if the paper becomes too stiff and loses flexibility, the cutout

will be difficult to glue to a curved surface. It is essential to seal papers with short fibers, such as recycled copy paper; if left unprotected, these papers will tear and disintegrate when they come into contact with the wet decoupage medium. Sealer also provides a protective barrier over artwork that is hand-colored with inks, paints, or other media that bleed when exposed to wet glue and finishes.

• **Spray fixative**
Spray fixative is used primarily to stabilize the surface of original pencil, pastel, and charcoal drawings so that they can be handled safely without smudging or bleeding. Laser copies of this type of artwork, not the originals, would be used for decoupage.

• **Decoupage medium**

Decoupage medium is a water-soluble, viscous liquid that performs the function of three separate products needed in decoupage: a print sealer, an adhesive, and a final sealing coat. This three-in-one PVA-based medium is highly compatible with itself; it can be applied in layers that bond well without blistering or peeling, a distinct advantage in the decoupage process. Available in matte and gloss luster, the medium brushes on white, dries clear, and is permanent and waterproof. I use decoupage medium in all but the finishing stage of my projects, preferring instead acrylic medium-and-varnish for its superior transparency.

• **Surface sealer**

A surface sealer is used to coat a porous surface, smooth a rough surface, or stabilize a substrate in order to provide better adhesion for the successive layers of glue, paper, and cover coats of paint and sealer. It is important to choose a surface sealer that is compatible with the print sealer and the surface finish (i.e., all should be water-soluble) to prevent blistering or peeling that can disfigure the surface of the project. Surface sealers can be either brushed or sprayed on. Some popular surface sealers are primers, decoupage medium, acrylic varnish, and water-based acrylic gesso.

• **Acrylic medium-and-varnish**

I prefer acrylic medium-and-varnish to three-in-one decoupage medium for the finishing coat on a decoupage project. Easy to apply with a foam brush, it lays on thin, dries quickly, and remains transparent, a quality that enhances the depth of the print colors. Acrylic medium-and-varnish is slightly more viscous than straight acrylic varnish. It is available in matte, semigloss, and high-gloss finishes, and like all acrylic-based mediums, it cleans up with soap and water when it is still wet.

• **White craft glue**

White craft glue is not generally used in decoupage; however, in the unusual event that glue with extra tack is required for a hard-to-glue paper item, white glue is suitable. It should not be used on lightweight paper or on fragile, intricately cut sections of a print because it will weigh down the paper and cause it to tear. White craft glue is a PVA-based glue that goes on white, dries clear, and is permanent and waterproof. It has higher tack, so it can be used for fabrics and other absorbent or fuzzy materials.

• **Manicure (or cuticle) scissors**

While there are "official" decoupage scissors on the market, manicure or cuticle scissors can be used instead. The short, curved, sharp blades make it easy to cut intricate details with precision, and the pointed tips are good for nipping into tight corners. Thread-cutting scissors are a good substitute for cutting fine details. Somewhat larger than cuticle scissors, they are comfortable in a slightly larger hand and are easy to steer accurately, although they do not have curved blades.

• **Straight-blade scissors**

Scissors with straight blades are good for general-purpose cutting in decoupage. They are traditionally used for cutting paper borders and frames and for rough-cutting a print out of a larger piece of paper.

- **Craft knife**

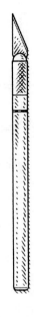

Handled like a pencil, a craft knife is good for intricate cutting; it has a replaceable blade and is often used with a self-healing cutting mat. A craft knife with a swivel head makes it easy to cut neat curves.

- **Assorted brushes**

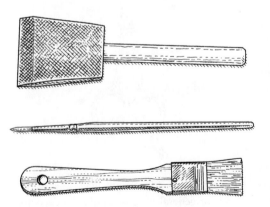

A small variety of good-quality brushes is needed to apply sealer, glue, paint, and finish, among other liquids, by hand. Suited to general crafting tasks, such as applying glue and paint to large prints or surfaces, foam brushes are disposable, come in a variety of widths, have flexible batons with beveled edges, and don't leave brush marks. In a pinch, a household sponge with fine cells can be used to apply paint. A stiff nylon brush is good for applying viscous glues. A soft, plump brush is good for applying thin, watery mediums, such as watercolor paints, and is especially effective in back-painting glass, being so soft as to leave the surface smoothly covered. A hake brush is made of soft animal hair that holds runny mediums well, and its long handle can reach inside tall containers. Other brushes that are nice to have are a large, round #12 brush (round ferrule with tapered end), a script liner (round ferrule with long point), and a 1"-wide (2.5 cm) flat brush (flat ferrule with square end). Add a few other all-purpose craft brushes of any kind according to your crafting style, and don't forget to get a few cheap brushes, such as chip brushes, to use for odd jobs without worry.

- **Self-healing cutting mat**
  Used with a craft knife, a portable self-healing cutting mat provides a firm surface on which prints can be cut without marring the work surface. Available in a variety of sizes, there is one that measures only 3" × 5" (7.6 × 12.7 cm), perfect for cutting small pieces of paper on a crowded work space because the mat can be easily rotated when making tight detailed cuts. A piece of glass will also provide a good cutting surface in a pinch, but do not cut on a thick magazine because it will quickly dull your cutting blade.

• Tweezers

An extension of your fingers, tweezers allow you to pick up and place glued prints on a surface.

Other items you may need for decoupage:

• **Cotton swabs**
  Convenient and readily available, cotton swabs are good for small mop-up jobs like cleaning wet glue from around the edges of a print.
• **Toothpicks**
  Especially helpful when gluing down the edges of a print that have lifted up, a flat wood toothpick can be used like a mini spatula to carry small amounts of glue and reach into narrow spaces without damaging a print.

---

## Working Tips: Making a Cardboard Drying Booth

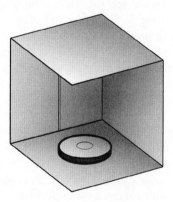

Use a utility knife to cut away two adjacent sides from a six-sided cardboard carton. Invert the carton so that the openings are at the front. Set a lazy Susan inside.

---

## Working Tips: The Case against Tinting

Tempted to tint decoupage medium or white glue? In a word, don't. Acrylic paint contains binders such as gum arabic that in larger quantities will interfere with the curing chemistry of the PVA ingredient in decoupage medium and white craft glue. Media that are mostly pigments with very little binder, such as watercolor paint, gouache, and tempera paint will technically mix with decoupage medium and white craft glue—but why bother mixing up viscous tints when you can apply color directly to the project as a separate, compatible layer of paint?

- **Set of watercolor paints, gouache, and/or colored pencils**
  A black-and-white print can be hand colored using watercolors (for a transparent wash of color), gouache (for opaque color), or wax or watercolor pencils (for light shading). Watercolors come in tube and tablet form, and each type is applied with a brush. Colored pencils come in an extremely wide spectrum of colors and look like standard graphite pencils.
- **Poster putty**
  This pliable plastic adhesive is used to temporarily hold small prints in place on a project or on a paper template during layout and design. Poster putty should not be oily to avoid transferring any residue to the prints. Always remove the putty from the print before gluing it down. Keep putty out of direct sunlight and away from heat so it doesn't get gummy.

## Selecting and Preparing the Prints

Finding the right images is the most important first step in decoupage, regardless of the kind of project you plan. Prints can be fantastic, abstract, or realistic in theme, but they need to be on the right paper and of sufficient resolution, with the image in sharp focus. In addition, your image needs to have a distinct silhouette when it is cut out so that it doesn't look truncated or chopped off (unless that jarring look is intentional). A bouquet and a medallion are examples of motifs that are easily silhouetted. If different motifs are going to be combined in a single project, choosing source art that is similar in style and scale is a must for a unified look. This holds true whether the prints are color or black-and-white.

The staggeringly large universe of sources for decoupage images guarantees that you will have no trouble finding what you like. Begin your search for images at home, looking through family albums or scrapbooks for photographs and mementos. Handwritten letters, greeting cards, and postcards with different styles of penmanship will add a unique graphic quality to your decoupage composition, as will children's art. When searching for art elsewhere, I prefer handling the actual artwork myself so that I can inspect the line work and coloration of the print at close range. For that reason, I frequent garage and estate sales and flea markets where browsing and serious snooping are expected. You can also visit shops specializing in old books and prints. Books can be a superb source of drawings and illustrations, especially children's books with illustrations that are charming and sentimental. I own several old children's books illustrated by Jessie Wilcox Smith and have made laser copies of her sensitive renderings of babies and young children and applied them to endearing gifts for baby showers and birthdays. I also inherited a book on European history; the front cover was missing but the pages were filled with engraved plates depicting historical figures, landscapes, and maps, surrounded by text in an old typeface that also became a usable element in my decoupage projects.

Wallpaper is another source of decorative designs. While wallpaper itself is too heavy to use in decoupage, you can easily harvest patterns you like by scanning the original wallpaper, resizing the motifs if desired, and making prints to use in decoupage. The repeat patterns and carefully articulated spacing in professionally designed wallpaper carries through when a pattern is sized smaller on a copier. A decoupaged lamp base or small table that coordinates with your walls becomes eminently doable. The availability of a laser printer has made me willing to try anything to get the visual effects I want on my decoupage projects, and despite some frustration now and then, I am usually serendipitously rewarded with surprisingly satisfying outcomes.

Another appealing source of decoupage images is gift wrap, which, like wallpaper, has a repeat pattern that offers multiple prints of the same motif. Gift wrap is generally made of thin paper, but it can be used for decoupage if is handled carefully or reinforced with several thin coats of print sealer. To strengthen gift wrap, consider using a spray sealer instead of a liquid medium as it is much easier to apply to large sheets. Liquid sealer will cause gift wrap to naturally curl and warp temporarily as moisture spreads through the fibers; applying too much sealer can oversaturate the paper and cause tears during handling.

Of course, there are collections of images amassed specifically for graphic application that can be found without a frustrating search; just check out the Internet. Online searches will yield an endless supply of images on every subject matter. Visit Flickr, DeviantArt, and Google Images for starters. Use any keyword that is in line with the theme of your decoupage project—flowers, roses, American Beauty—narrowing down your search as you go to locate something specific. Be prepared to spend a lot of time perusing the choices, which will appear endless. Some sites offer copyright-free clip art and others charge for use. Keep copyright laws in mind when you download any images for personal use. Dover Publications, a preservationist publisher, specializes in clip art and offers a broad selection of affordable books filled with images; some come with a CD that you can use right away.

---

## Working Tips: Testing Prints for Colorfastness

Prints made on a laser copier or laser printer are safe to use for decoupage, as the prints will not bleed when exposed to moisture. If you aren't sure about a print's origin or colorfastness, test it. Use a cotton swab to apply a small dab of liquid sealer, or spray a short blast of aerosol sealer, on an obscure place on the print. If a halo of color forms around the image where the sealer is applied, the color is prone to bleeding and you should not use the print as is. Make a color laser copy of the image for a print that is colorfast.

---

## Checklist: When to Make a Laser Copy

- Print is a fine or valuable original
- Paper is brittle or prone to crumbling
- Paper is too thick
- Image is not printed with colorfast inks
- Motifs need resizing
- You need multiples of a single image
- You want a different color ink

In addition to the many, many printed papers, there are also plain papers, such as marbled, rice, unryu, and Japanese origami papers, whose colors and fine textures can add decorative interest to a decoupage design. Colored papers that are not recommended include crepe paper and dyed tissue paper, which stain and bleed when exposed to moisture. Heavily textured and embossed papers, such as anaglypta and lincrusta, require careful handling because their relief patterns can crack or flatten when glued and folded over sharp corners. I don't recommend them for small projects.

## Making Laser Copies

Once you have selected an image, you have a decision to make—whether or not to use the original print directly on the project. Examine the paper on which the image is printed. Ideally, your image is printed on one side of lightweight to medium-weight paper, is easy to cut, and is flexible enough to lie flat against the decorative surface. Drawbacks to this ideal abound. Old originals can be brittle and may not bend well, let alone hold up to getting wet; the stresses of the decoupage process may well destroy an original. Some ink-jet papers are coated with clay and do not react well to wetting. The protective coating on photographic paper can prevent the back of a print from adhering properly to the project surface. Paper that is thin and fragile can tear or disintegrate when glue is applied; this is especially true of recycled paper made from short, chopped fibers (long-fiber recycled paper is fine to use), a distinction that only testing a paper sample will reveal. If a paper is too thick, it may be difficult to cut precisely and may require a great number of finishing coats to "bury" its cut edges against the surface of the project.

Issues can also arise with the print quality or artistic merits. A design in its original format may be too large or too small for your project. You might want to add color to a black-and-white print or change an old black-and-white photograph into one with a sepia tone.

The good news is that all of these drawbacks and more are easily remedied when you use a laser copier or a computer scanner and laser printer to make a reproduction of your chosen print. A computer scanner is particularly useful. You can manipulate the image on your screen, recoloring, silhouetting, or resizing it as you choose. Here is an easy formula for figuring out the percentage you will need to enlarge or reduce your print so it fits the decorative surface.

Desired finished size ÷ original size × 100 = % to enlarge or reduce

Example:
The original is 4" (10.2 cm) long and you want a reproduction that is 8" (20.3 cm) long.

8" (20.3 cm) ÷ 4" (10.2 cm) = 2
2 × 100 = 200%

Consult your scanner software manual for specific instructions on these and other types of customizing you can do. Make your laser printouts on uncoated laser copy paper, 20-pound, which is pliable yet stiff enough for intricate cutting and is sturdy enough to hold up to sealers and glues. If you don't have a laser

## Copyright Law

When making copies of any image, be aware of copyright laws. Get permission in writing from the copyright holder of any art that you intend to use for commercial purposes. Otherwise, use images that are in the public domain.

copier in your home office or studio, you don't have to buy one. Visit a neighborhood copy center to make laser copies at a reasonable cost.

### Hand-Coloring Laser Prints

There will be times when you find a black-and-white image you love, but you would prefer it in color. You can make a laser copy of the line art and then hand-color the copy, choosing from a variety of media. A laser print has crisp lines and good resolution that make coloring easy, and the ink is thermally set so it won't bleed when exposed to watery media. A light tint of color applied to a black-and-white image can replicate the look of old hand-colored lithograph. Once you have hand-colored a laser print, you can use it to make any number of additional copies on a color laser copier. You can print a single image on each sheet, or you can group rescaled images together on an 8.5" × 11" (21.6 × 27.9 cm) sheet of paper and then cut them apart to create a repeat pattern for a project.

It is equally important to choose a compatible paper on which to print an image for coloring with wet media. Watercolors applied to highly absorbent papers, identified by a feltlike texture, will bleed. On this type of paper, use gouache, which is thicker and more opaque, to prevent the color from running. Gouache can also be diluted and applied like

---

## Working Tips: Ink-Jet Printer Caution

Generally speaking, prints made on a home office ink-jet printer are not suited to hand coloring or, for that matter, any decoupage work. I have found that the ink used in my ink-jet printer bleeds and that the resolution of line work is fuzzier than I would like it to be. Enlarging the image simply brings out any flaws—lines are not sharp and some details merge together, leaving thick patches of dark ink. Professional ink-jet printers use archival inks that don't bleed or fade, but they are very expensive to buy and to use.

If you have an ink-jet printer at home and want to use it for decoupage prints, you'll need to do some experimenting. Allow the printing ink to dry at least 30 minutes before handling the print or applying any color. A very light coat of spray fixative or spray sealer can help minimize bleeding of the ink when wet media are applied. Do not use a liquid sealer applied with a brush—it will make the ink bleed. Allow the fixative or spray sealer to dry before attempting to hand-color the print.

watercolors to ordinary copy paper made with long fibers. Always pretest a paper to see how it reacts when wet; if the paper buckles or if watercolors bleed, upgrade the paper stock. I don't recommend acrylic craft paint or artist's acrylics in tubes for use on paper. Comprised of color pigment and binders for added body, acrylic paint will form a slick, unattractive, rubbery layer on top of a print. Its opacity can cover up delicate line work, and because the paint is permanent when dry, it is not possible to correct or alter the applied color.

Colored pencils are another option for hand coloring. They are available in a wide range of rich colors that you can buy in sets or as individual pencils. There are two kinds: watercolor and wax-based. If I want the look of a color wash, I simply use watercolor paint. However, you can experiment with watercolor pencils to see if this medium appeals to you. Draw in the color, fill the shapes, and then blend the color using a damp paintbrush to achieve a watercolor effect. Be ready with a paper towel to blot up excess moisture.

I prefer wax colored pencils to create shaded effects on my prints without covering up the black line work. I can easily vary the pressure on the pencil point to control the layer of color I apply. In the unlikely case that a hand-colored original will be glued directly to the project, you'll want to avoid a waxy buildup of color on the paper, which would interfere with the adhesion of water-based glues. A thin layer of color will leave thready bare patches of paper through which the glue can pass and adhere to the substrate. If you are going to make a laser copy of a hand-colored original, then you can lay down the color with relative freedom.

Be especially careful when selecting paper for your final laser-printed copies as well. Recycled paper with fibers that are chopped short will become soggy and disintegrate when moist. I found this out the hard way after organizing a family craft session to decoupage glass plates. Unfortunately, I copied the prints on inexpensive recycled paper, and we discovered just how short the fibers were when the liquid sealer was applied; even the most gentle handling caused the paper to split and fall apart.

As you collect images for decoupage, you may wish to hand-color them and build an archive of prints ready for copying and future use. A hand-colored copy can be reproduced on uncoated laser paper as many times as you wish.

## Technique: Using Watercolors to Color a Laser Copy

A small watercolor set of the basic colors and a watercolor brush are all you need to get started. The painting technique is easy and does not require freehand painting skills. Use the same basic approach to paint with gouache, which goes on thicker and produces color that is more opaque.

### MATERIALS AND TOOLS

Laser print of a black-and-white
  engraving
Set of watercolor paints
2 watercolor paintbrushes
Paint palette
Small dish of water
Paper towel

### Step 1

Dampen the print with water.

Lay the laser print on a flat surface. Use a watercolor brush to apply a very light wash of water over the print, staying within the inked outline. Let the paper rest a few minutes so that the dampness spreads evenly on the paper.

### Step 2

Apply color to the print.

Prepare gradient color by mixing a drop of paint with a few drops of water on a palette. Hold a folded paper towel in your non-dominant hand. Use the tip of the paintbrush to apply a tiny dab of full-strength watercolor paint at the inner edge of the printed outline and use a damp brush to bring in the gradient color to the center of the outlined area, filling it with soft shading. Use the paper towel to blot any watery color that accidently overruns the outlined area.

### Step 3

Blend the color.

Continue to apply color to your print, as desired. Use a damp brush to blend the watercolors. Let the area dry just slightly. Work on another area in the same way.

### Step 4 (optional)

Add more color.

Assess the intensity of the contrast in a damp section and apply another layer of color, if desired. If you want to strengthen the color or define the contours, brush the stronger color onto the edges and curves of the image.

This is a technique that requires some feel. With practice, you will be able to modulate the color from a hard line to a soft wash. Let the paint dry completely.

### Technique: Using Wax-Based Colored Pencils to Color a Laser Copy

Use wax-based colored pencils to hand-color a print with subtle, controlled shading.

### MATERIALS AND TOOLS

Laser print of a black-and-white engraving
Set of wax colored pencils
Handheld pencil sharpener

### Step 1

Lightly color in the shape.

Exerting light pressure on the pencil, fill in an entire outlined shape with a thin layer of color.

---

## Working Tips: Applying Watercolors

- Allow the paper to rest for a few minutes after you dampen it with water or a color wash to give the moisture time to spread out evenly.
- Apply the stronger color first at the edge of an outlined area and then use a damp brush to bring the gradient color to the center. Allow the water to do the work for you to achieve smooth shading.
- Wait until the paint has dried to see how intense the color is before augmenting it with more color. Many colors dry darker.
- Add more water to suspend the pigment and create a lighter color

wash. Experiment with different ratios of paint to water to gain an understanding of gradient color.
- Use a clean watercolor brush to apply moisture to the leading edge of any area where a softer, gradient color is desired.
- Avoid "scrubbing" the surface with the brush, which will make the paper soggy and cause it to fuzz, shred, or peel.
- Hold a folded paper towel in one hand and use it blot away errant color or too much water while painting. Use firm pressure but do not rub.

**Step 2**

Add more light color.

Apply a second thin layer of color to the edges and curves of the shape to make these areas darker to create shading and contour. Avoid laying down a thick, waxy layer.

**Step 3**

Moderate the colors to create perspective.

Continue to apply color to your print, as desired. Establish perspective in larger scenes by using richer, darker color in the foreground and paler, lighter color in the background. Blend different colors by lightly overlapping strokes.

## Sealing and Cutting Out the Prints

All prints have to be prepared in some way before they can be glued to a surface. Sealing used to be de rigueur to prevent printed and hand-colored images from bleeding when exposed to wet media, such as glue. However, modern technology has changed that. If you have created hand-colored art, it is likely that you will be applying not an original but a laser copy to the surface of your decoupage project. Prints made on a laser copier or laser printer have all but eliminated the problem of bleed-

ing ink, and for this reason, I usually don't seal my laser prints.

There is another reason that I do not recommend sealing a print. When a sealed print is glued to a surface, moisture becomes trapped under the layer of sealant, which is more or less impermeable. This slows down the evaporation of moisture in the glue and extends the drying time. If a colorfast paper is left unsealed, it is more porous and breathes, allowing moisture to pass through the paper fibers and into the air to promote drying.

If circumstances require that you seal your print—for instance, if you plan to use an original print on your decoupage project rather than a laser copy—use a spray print sealer, not a wet medium. A spray print sealer lightly coats the surface and still allows the paper to breathe. This is one of the rare occasions when I recommend an aerosol (the other is when priming metal surfaces). Always wear a chemical-cartridge respirator mask and work outdoors. To protect a pastel or charcoal drawing before making a laser print of it, use a spray fixative, which doesn't leave a lustrous layer on the work as a spray sealer can.

**Technique: Applying Spray Print Sealer to an Original Print (optional)**

Spray print sealer is dispensed in a fine mist that lightly coats the print surface to make it water-resistant. A spray fixative can also be used on paper in the same way. A spray sealer will add some luster to the print or artwork, whereas a spray fixative usually does not.

MATERIALS AND TOOLS

Print, roughly cut with a wide margin of paper
Spray print sealer
Poster putty
Chemical-cartridge respirator mask
Safety glasses
Disposable gloves
Cardboard carton (for spray booth; optional)

---

# Working Tips: Using Wax Grip

Watercolors will bead when applied to wet, slick surfaces. To create more surface tension, seal the paper with a clear liquid additive called *wax grip*. This surfactant solution breaks down the surface tension of waxy, water-resistant surfaces so that paints can flow and dry on them.

## Step 1

Secure the print to a protected work surface.

Work outdoors or in a well-ventilated area. Put on a chemical-cartridge respirator mask, safety glasses, and disposable gloves. Lay the print on a protected work surface or in a spray booth to contain the overspray. Secure the print with bits of putty so it doesn't shift during spraying. A lazy Susan inside the spray booth will allow you to gently rotate the print for more even coverage.

## Step 2

Apply a thin coat of sealer.

Following the manufacturer's directions and safety precautions, apply a light, even coat of sealer to the paper, spraying beyond the edges of the print to ensure full coverage. Let the sealer dry completely.

## Working Tips: Using a Spray-Can Product

- Before spraying, shake the can vigorously, continuing for several minutes until after you hear the ball inside rattling. Swirl the ball around the can's bottom where solids have settled to thoroughly mix the product.
- After spraying, turn the can upside-down and spray the product until only gas comes out of the nozzle, which will prevent the tip from clogging. If the nozzle becomes clogged, replace it with a new one made by the same manufacturer.

## Technique: Cutting Out a Print

Cutting out a print proceeds in several stages. First, straight-blade scissors are used to cut away most of the paper margin around the motif. Next, manicure scissors are used to cut out the more precise details. Finally, the print is placed on a cutting mat and a craft knife is used to refine any existing cuts and to access areas that are too tight or awkward to reach with a pair of scissors.

### MATERIALS AND TOOLS
Print
Straight-blade scissors
Manicure scissors
Craft knife with fresh blade
Self-healing cutting mat

## Step 1

Cut out the print, leaving a large margin.

Use straight-blade scissors to roughly cut away all the excess paper around the image, leaving a generous margin of paper approximately 1" (2.5 cm) wide.

## Step 2

Cut out the waste shapes.

Use manicure scissors to cut out any interior sections of the print. Hold the print in one hand and use the other hand to pierce a small pilot hole with the scissors through the waste area of the paper. Then bring the scissors underneath the print, insert the blade into the pilot hole, and proceed to cut out the waste shape. Repeat to cut out and remove each inside waste shape.

### Step 3

Cut out the outside shape of the print.

Use manicure scissors to cut the outside shape of the image, feeding the *paper* into the blades of the scissors and swiveling the paper, not the blades, to cut around curves or other details. For a slightly serrated edge, wiggle the paper back and forth as you cut. A serrated edge is "buried" in the decoupage finish coats.

### Step 4

Clean up all cuts.

Lay the cutout, image side up, on a cutting mat and assess your work. Use a craft knife to clean up any cuts or to remove any excess paper. Hold the craft knife by its handle as you would hold a pencil and use your other hand to hold the edge of the print. Draw the tip of the blade along the image lines, pulling the knife toward you to cut through the paper. Keep your fingers safely clear of the blade's path. Replace the blade at the slightest drag or resistance to avoid tearing the paper.

## Working Tips: Adapting Prints

Adaptations are part of the fun of cutting prints for decoupage. As you advance to larger projects, you'll find it practically impossible to use an image as is. Here are a few suggestions to inspire your imagination and confidence and liberate your creativity when cutting a print.

- Cut off extremely fragile elements, such as elongated stems, and reattach them when the print is glued to the decorative surface.
- Cut off entire elements from the image for a better fit on the decoupage surface.
- Make a series of cuts or slashes on large design elements, such as multipetal flowers, to enable a flat image to hug a curved decoupage surface. Small or deep cuts made

perpendicular to the cut edge can help the elements fit better when they are glued down.

- Choose a section of a beautiful engraving and enlarge it for decoupage to highlight the graphic quality. A whole print does not have to be used.
- Fill glaring voids in a composition by cutting motifs from one section of the print and grafting them onto the empty spaces. You can also introduce elements from a different print for the same purpose.
- Cut out a few unique shapes from the interior of an image to relieve the heavy quality of dense color. A few extra cutouts in the interior of a print will also provide convenient exits for trapped air bubbles and excess glue.

## Technique: Adding Ladders

Some prints have dangling or narrow elements that would otherwise tear away or be damaged if they weren't connected to other elements of the print. Ladders are paper connectors that hold these fragile sections of a print together during the cutting and handling of the print. Ladders prevent such elements as delicate petals and elongated stems from getting damaged, bent, or lost. The ladders are snipped off and discarded before the print is glued to the surface.

### MATERIALS AND TOOLS
Print
Colored pencil
Straight-blade scissors
Manicure scissors
Craft knife with replacement blades
Self-healing cutting mat

### Step 1
Draw in the ladders.

Lay the print faceup on a flat surface. Identify any fragile or narrow sections of the image that could accidentally be torn off the print during handling. Use a colored pencil to draw sets of parallel lines, or ladders, to connect these areas to one another or to the main body of the print.

### Step 2
Cut out the print.

Rough-cut the print and then proceed to cut it with manicure scissors. When you reach a ladder, place the print on a cutting mat and use a craft knife to cut along the marked lines to keep the print elements connected to one another.

## Decoupage on Wood and Metal

### Materials and Tools for Wood and Metal Surfaces

The materials and tools needed for wood and metal surfaces are predominantly those used to prepare their surfaces so they are ready for the application of prints and finishes.

- **Wood sealers: primers, acrylic gesso, and decoupage medium**

Of the wide variety of materials that can seal the wood surface, all are designed to ensure that the subsequent coat of paint or finish is evenly absorbed and to promote adhesion of paint or other finishes so they lay smoothly on the substrate (the surface under the coat of paint). If the wood is smooth but porous, use several coats of primer or a tinted primer, a thin liquid that has less of the expensive pigment component found in paint, thereby reducing the amount of the more costly paints that will be needed for full coverage. If the wood is rough or textured, has a very open grain, or is an end cut, use several coats of acrylic gesso, which comes in a spray or a thick liquid or gel, to smooth over and fill rough areas or gaps. If the wood needs light smoothing or filling in the grain, use decoupage medium, which has a high viscosity that

## Working Tips: Storing Your Prints

Assembling a collection of prints takes time. Proper storage ensures that the prints you collect over the years remain clean and ready for use in future projects. Choose a storage spot that is dry and out of direct sunlight. Avoid extremes in temperature. Collect small prints in envelopes, accordion files, and file folders. Lay larger prints on flat shelves. Roll poster-size prints loolsely and stand them upright in a partitioned box, making sure they have room to unfurl.

accomplishes both tasks well. Acrylic varnish or acrylic medium-and-varnish combination can also be used initially to seal and fill a wood surface, but I usually use it for the final sealing coat.

- **Metal primer**

  A metal primer promotes adhesion and provides a good bonding surface for paint and other finishes that are applied on top. Available in spray and brush-on versions, metal primers can be either water-based or oil-based. I much prefer oil-based primers because, if their solvents are allowed to evaporate fully, they provide good adhesion and establish a stable foundation for the paint, even acrylic craft paint, and prints that are glued on with acrylic medium. Spray primers can be transparent, white, pale gray, black, silver, or most commonly, rust red, aptly named "primer red." Acrylic primer is not recommended for metal because it can become rehydrated by top coats of acrylic paint and crawl off the metal. It can also cause some metals, such as iron, to rust.

- **Acrylic craft paint**

  Available in jars and bottles in a wide selection of colors in matte and gloss finishes, acrylic craft paints dry quickly, are permanent when dry, and clean up with soap and water as long as they remain wet. I don't recommend artists' acrylic paints, which traditionally come in tubes, because they are difficult to handle, especially those with a thick and pasty consistency; even a foam brush leaves marks on the painted surface.

- **Paint sealer**

  A paint sealer acts as a barrier between the paint and the print so that the pigment applied to the substrate does not leach into the paper. Acrylic varnish (thin and quick-drying) or acrylic medium-and-varnish (a combination product that is more viscous than varnish) can be used as a paint sealer.

- **Distilled white vinegar**

  Distilled white vinegar is an effective, eco-smart cleaning agent for organic oils. It cuts grease and removes fingerprints and grimy buildup from painted wood and metal surfaces. Equal parts water and vinegar can be combined in a solution, poured into a spray bottle, and applied as needed. Another all-purpose water-based cleaner to try is Simple Green.

- **Mineral spirits**

  Mineral spirits are especially effective for removing extra-stubborn grease from painted surfaces, especially from metals that are apt to be dressed or coated in mineral-derived oils, even silicone lubricants. Mineral spirits are toxic if ingested, but fairly benign as a vapor compared to other solvents and do not require a chemical-cartridge respirator mask to filter the spirits' fumes. However, wear disposable gloves and safety glasses and work outside in the fresh air or in a room with good cross-ventilation (for small projects) when using mineral spirits.

- **Sandpaper**

  Used alone or with a sanding block, sandpaper will smooth most flat or slightly curved wood surfaces. Sandpaper is available in coarse (#200), medium (#400), and fine (#600) grits that can be used in a progressive sequence to refine the condition of the wood surface to a buttery smoothness. Sandpaper is also available in a wet-or-dry version that is made with a specially treated waterproof paper.

- **Emery cloth**

  An abrasive cloth that works like sandpaper, emery cloth has a sturdy fabric backing. Available in coarse (40–70), medium (80–100), and fine (120, F, and FF) grits, emery cloth can be used alone or with a sanding block. The salient quality of emery cloth is its extremely hard, sharp abrasive corundum coating, which is very effective at abrading hard materials like metal. Emery cloth and water can be used to remove hairline scratches left by more coarse emery cloths or to abrade metal. Start by leveling a surface using coarse emery cloth and move progressively to medium and then to fine to achieve a very smooth finish.

- **Sanding block**
A sanding block is useful when sanding flat or slightly curved surfaces. The block, which can be made of wood or hard rubber, is wrapped with a piece of sandpaper or emery cloth that has been trimmed to size. I prefer the hard rubber because it is very useful for developing finishes, unlike a hard wood block. The hard rubber also has just enough give so that I don't flatten out any fine details I want to keep. Purchased sanding blocks come with flat and curved surfaces and include special pins to hold the sandpaper in place. In a pinch, a cellulose sponge can also be used as a sanding block, and it is especially useful on curved surfaces because it flexes easily.

- **Tack cloth**
A tack cloth is used to pick up particles of dust that remain on a surface after sanding. Purchased tack cloths are made of cheesecloth impregnated with resins, such as linseed oil. The cheesecloth surface is tacky enough to pick up fine particles but not so moist as to leave a residue. I make my own by dampening the cheesecloth with linseed oil and storing it in a coffee can to prevent drying. In a pinch, a soft cloth or paper towel misted with isopropyl (rubbing) alcohol can be used, but with special caution because paper can leave lint on a gummy surface that is not fully cured. Alcohol is used instead of water to moisten the paper towel because it vaporizes off a surface more quickly and will not raise the grain of wood.

- **Protective mask, safety glasses, and disposable gloves**
The kind of protective mask you wear will be determined by the matter you are trying to filter out when you breathe. For particulate matter, such as dust and smoke, wear a generic respirator mask. For vapors and gasses, such as paint VOCs and aerosol sprays, wear a chemical-cartridge respirator mask. Safety glasses are recommended when sanding to prevent fine dust particles from getting in your eyes and when working with harmful liquids or chemicals. Disposable gloves are also recommended to protect your hands.

## Preparing and Painting the Surface

Proper preparation of a wood or metal surface is vital for decoupage. The condition of the base material will affect the condition of all the other layers that are applied—from the paint to the layer of prints to the finish—and have a profound impact on the appearance and durability of the project. The projects in this chapter use new, unfinished wood and metal items, which require minimal preparation. Should you choose a previously finished wood or metal item to decoupage, perhaps something you pick up at a flea market or garage sale, you can expect the preparation to be more involved and time-consuming to make it ready for your prints. After your item is cleaned, sanded, and sealed, it can be painted in a background color that will enhance the silhouette of the prints. If the wood is nicely grained or you like the patina of vintage wood or old painted metal, you may wish to skip the paint coat.

### Preparing Wood Surfaces

Unfinished wood surfaces are prepared in a straightforward sequence of steps that begins with sanding, a stage which serves to smooth rough surfaces overall and especially those likely to be found at joined pieces or end cuts. Finished wood surfaces—those that are already painted and varnished—usually require a disparate set of procedures aimed at cleaning and stabilizing the treated wood before sanding is undertaken. Minimally, the surface needs to be cleaned of grease and fingerprints and be free of loose material. Flaking and peeling paint should be sanded down to the problem layer. (For tough jobs, you may need to use a stripper or heat gun.) Nail holes and cracks are filled. When the repairs are done, sandpaper is used to abrade all the surfaces, which will give them tooth for better adhesion of the next layer.

Your goal in sanding is a flawlessly smooth surface so that the successive layers of prints, paint, and finish show no roughness of texture. Sanding can be done with or without a block, according to the degree of sanding needed. The block, ideally made of hard rubber, provides support for the sandpaper as pressure is applied to abrade the wood's surface. Small sticks can also be wrapped with sandpaper to smooth hard-to-reach places. I have also used disposable emery boards (intended for nail care) to reach crevices and edges, but test them as they can smudge some surfaces. Generally, the coarser the sandpaper, the deeper the layer of wood that is removed; the finer the sandpaper, the shallower the abrasion. Sandpaper should be moved over the wood surface in a smooth oval shape as opposed to back and forth; a back-and-forth motion can wear the wood unevenly. Once the surface of the wood is smooth, lift off the dust with a tack cloth or by vacuuming (a DustBuster with a HEPA filter works well).

## Technique: Sanding Unfinished Wood

### MATERIALS AND TOOLS
Wooden item
Sandpaper, in coarse (#200), medium (#400), and fine (#600) grits
Sanding block, hard rubber
Squared rod, slat, or peg (for sanding hard-to-reach places)
Packing tape
Tack cloth
Respirator mask
Safety glasses

**Step 1**
Sand the surfaces smooth.
Put on a respirator mask and safety glasses. Use a sanding block wrapped with medium-grit (#400) sandpaper to smooth all of the flat wood surfaces, rubbing the wood along the grain. For more precise and targeted smoothing of narrow crevices and recessed areas, wrap a strip of fine-grit (#600) sandpaper around a squared rod and use it like a file in a rounded oval stroke. If the surface is flat, wrap a few winds of packing tape at the end of a rod to create an abrasion-free area, and then rub the sandpaper stick across the area, allowing the taped area to glide harmlessly across the object's flat side. Take care when working at the corners and edges of the item to avoid sanding off any sharp angles unless that is an effect you want.

**Step 2**
Clean off the dust.
Use a tack cloth and very gentle strokes in a tamping and pouncing motion to remove dust particles and wipe the wood clean. Pressing the cloth too firmly or dragging it along the bare wood will cause it to snag and leave pulled threads in the wood if it is at all grainy, especially at the corners. If your tack cloth has linseed oil, pressing too hard will leave traces of oily residue that will keep the paint from adhering.

**Step 3**

Refine the sanded surfaces.

Refine all of the sanded surfaces using a sanding block wrapped with fine-grit (#600) sandpaper. Then use a tack cloth as described in step 2 to wipe off any dust particles.

After the wood is sanded, a sealer is used to fill in the grain of the wood so that the paint layer lies smoothly on top. Different sealing strategies are recommended according to the condition of the wood. First, check the wood surface for imperfections before sealing and repair any cracks, nail or screw holes, and the like using wood-filler putty, making certain not to over-fill areas, which will mar the final result. (Do not use plastic wood or its equivalent because it is nonporous, cracks, and will not bond with the paint layer.) For shallow cracks, use a sharp knife, such as a putty knife, to deepen the crack into a wedge shape, which will hold the filler better. Sand down the filled area so it is even with the surrounding surface. Allow the wood-filler putty to dry before applying the first coat of sealer.

The sealing process is simple: Use a brush to apply two thin sealing layers, allowing the first coat to dry before applying the second coat. Let the sealer dry the specified time before handling the object. Use a very gentle touch and fine-grit (#600) sandpaper or emery cloth to smooth away the tiny motes on the surface. After wiping with a tack cloth, apply the third and final coat of sealer. This coat should be allowed to dry overnight.

For general-purpose sealing of a wood surface that is basically smooth, use decoupage medium or acrylic primer. Decoupage medium is an effective all-purpose transparent sealer that smooths the wood surface and makes it waterproof. To seal a wood surface and at the same time add a light coating of pigment, use a water-soluble primer, a non-transparent sealer that has some pigment in it. Some primer colors are white, gray, and black. A primer can be applied with a brush or sprayed out of a can, sealing the wood and establishing a color-compatible undercoat for the paint color that will follow. The number of coats of primer needed will depend on the absorbency of the wood, how well the primer conceals the surface, and whether the primer has to conceal a previously painted wood surface in a dark color. For distressed wood that has nicks or scratches or for wood with an open or end grain, use a filler, such as acrylic gesso, to seal the wood surface. Thicker than the other sealers mentioned, acrylic gesso will raise the grain, especially an end grain, so that it is smooth and level with the surrounding wood.

In most cases, two coats of a sealer are sufficient to seal the wood and achieve a smooth finish, but I use three coats to ensure a stable substrate. When the sealer dries completely, some sanding will still be necessary after the final coat to create tooth for the subsequent coats of paint or finish. Be sure the sealer is completely dry before doing this sanding.

## Working Tips: Concealing Knots in Wood

Exposed knots in either unfinished or previously finished wood should be concealed using silver paint, which is formulated with pigment that is ground into particles that are flat, allowing them to lie flat against the knot when the paint dries thereby blocking any sap that might otherwise leach through to the painted surface.

## Universal Guidelines for Applying Sealers, Paints, Varnishes, and Other Liquid Media

All liquid media should be applied in a thin, smooth coat. To achieve smooth and complete coverage, follow these basic protocols.

1. Place a small project on a lazy Susan for easy access to all sides. Elevate the item on flat sticks so that the chosen medium does not pool at the base.
2. Choose a brush suited to the medium.
   - For thin liquids, such as craft paints and wood stains, use a foam brush.
   - For thick liquids with a high particle load, such as acrylic gesso, use a bristle brush, such as a cheap chip brush or a springy nylon brush with feathered ends.
3. Apply the medium.
   - Load the brush sparingly (never completely submerge the foam pad or the bristles). If a brush is overloaded, too much paint will discharge onto the decorative surface, resulting in drips and rollovers.
   - Begin near one outside edge and pull the brush all the way across the surface; then lift the brush and brush in the opposite direction, crossing the bare edge where the stroke was started. To avoid bubbles, contact the surface lightly with the brush rather than pressing down hard.
   - Lift the brush in an upward arc or simply decrease pressure at the end of the stroke to prevent the liquid medium from pooling or forming drips or rollovers; this will also keep the brush from flicking a spray of liquid off the tip. Eliminate minor brushstrokes by very lightly touching the brush to the surface when painting the final strokes.
   - Begin each new stroke on a dry part of the item, working toward the area already coated. Make parallel strokes, overlapping new strokes just slightly. For the second coat, make the strokes perpendicular to the strokes in the first coat to help level out the brush marks.
   - Hold a foam brush at a 45-degree angle so that the beveled edge of the brush rests on the project. As the brush is drawn across the surface, the leading edge of the bevel wets the surface and the trailing edge deposits the liquid medium. Adjust the pressure on the brush to control the amount of fluid that flows out.

## Working Tips: Sanding and Leveling a Surface Sealed with a Liquid Medium

- *If you applied decoupage medium as a surface sealer,* the grain should be adequately and evenly covered; however, you may wish to sand it to smooth and refine the surface once the medium is completely dry. Use a sanding block wrapped with fine-grit (#600) sandpaper and medium pressure to smooth the sealed surfaces, rubbing along the grain using rounded oval stroking motions for best results and being careful not to rub through to the wood. Use a tack cloth to remove any dust particles.

- *If you applied a primer as a surface sealer,* it is likely that the primer is smooth; however, you may wish to further smooth and refine the surface. Use a sanding block wrapped with fine-grit (#600) sandpaper and medium pressure to smooth the primed surface, using a rounded oval stroking motion for best results and being careful not to rub through to the wood. Rubbing back and forth in a straight line will simply work over the same high spots repeatedly, which can cause blisters in the primer and cause filled spots on your sandpaper, which will be a sign that the primer is not thoroughly dry, although it's hard to avoid. Use a tack cloth to remove any dust particles.

- *If you applied gesso as a surface sealer,* it is an indication that the wood was rough or textured and thick filler was necessary to create a level surface. Unfortunately, because of its viscosity, a gesso-coated surface will almost unavoidably have brush marks and the gessoed surface must be sanded after it cures. Use a sanding block wrapped with fine-grit (#600) sandpaper and medium pressure to smooth the sealed surfaces, using a rounded oval stroking motion for best results and being careful not to rub through to the raw wood. Use a vacuum to remove any dust particles. Spray-on acrylic gesso is an alternative that goes on smoother, minimizing the need for sanding.

## Technique: Sealing Unfinished Wood with Decoupage Medium or Acrylic Primer

Decoupage medium is especially effective as a sealer when the prints, which are adhered with decoupage medium, form the next layer. Because the decoupage medium layers that touch one another are chemically identical, the adhesion is superior. Consider using acrylic primer if the wood piece will be painted to form the background for the prints.

### MATERIALS AND TOOLS
Wooden item, sanded and wiped clean
Decoupage medium or acrylic primer
Foam brush
Lazy Susan
Flat sticks

**Step 1**
Prepare the work area.

~~~~~~~~~~~~~~~~~~~~~~~~~~~~~~~~~~~~~~~~

## Working Tips: Cleaning a Surface with a Shellac Coating

Vintage wood items often have a shellac finish, recognizable by a yellow-orange color that ages to brown. The shellac coating must be removed because the acrylic mediums used in decoupage cannot bond to it. Sanding works to a certain extent, but old shellac is brittle and raises a crumbly dust when it is stripped. Denatured alcohol dissolves shellac easily and strips away built-up and ingrained grime, but it is toxic and flammable, requiring that you wear a chemical-cartridge respirator mask and work gloves and work in a very well-ventilated area, preferably outdoors. I recommend a professional furniture craftsmen for this job.

~~~~~~~~~~~~~~~~~~~~~~~~~~~~~~~~~~~~~~~~

Place the wooden item on a lazy Susan for easy access to all sides. Elevate it on flat sticks to keep the sealer from pooling or forming a hard ridge when dry.

**Step 2**
Apply the first coat.
Use a foam brush to apply a thin, even coat of decoupage medium or acrylic primer to the sides, bottom, and top of the wood item, both outside and inside. Work in several sessions if not all surfaces are accessible at the same time. Let the first coat dry completely.

**Step 3**
Apply the second coat.
Repeat step 2 to apply a second coat. Let the medium dry overnight.

**Step 4**
Apply a third coat.
Repeat step 2 to apply a third coat. Let the medium dry overnight.

## Technique: Sealing Unfinished Wood with Acrylic Gesso

Acrylic gesso has a high particle load that makes it an effective sealer on wood surfaces that are coarse or rough. It is applied with a bristle brush. You might also consider using spray acrylic gesso, which goes on easily in a thin coating in the same manner as spray metal primers.

### MATERIALS AND TOOLS
Wooden item, sanded and wiped clean
Acrylic gesso
Chip brush or nylon brush with feathered bristles
Sandpaper, fine-grit (#600)
Lazy Susan
Flat sticks

**Step 1**
Prepare the work area.
Place the wooden item on a lazy Susan for

easy access to all sides. Elevate it on flat sticks to keep the gesso from pooling or forming a hard ridge when dry.

**Step 2**

Apply the first and second coats.

Use a brush to apply a thin, even coat of gesso to the sides, bottom, and top of the wood item, both outside and inside. Work in several sessions if not all surfaces are accessible at the same time. Let the first coat dry for 2 hours. Apply a second coat in the same way and let the gesso dry.

**Step 3**

Sand the item.

Use fine-grit (#600) sandpaper to lightly sand and smooth all the coated surfaces, using an oval motion to avoid wearing down the gesso in an uneven layer.

**Step 4**

Apply the third coat.

Use a brush to apply thin, even coat over all surfaces. Let the gesso dry overnight.

Vintage wood items that have been previously painted or varnished do not need to be sealed, per se, but they do need to be cleaned and examined for damage in the sealed surface. Begin by removing any gummy or waxy residue. There are eco-smart ways to get rid of light grime, but you may need stronger solvent-based agents, such as mineral spirits or an orange cleaner, to lift off heavy, grimy deposits. Be aware that mineral spirits and like agents will strip wood of its natural oils; you may prefer to use an all-purpose water-based cleaner, such as Simple Green, to preserve the patina on a vintage piece. Note, however, that if the existing finish shows bare patches or cracks that expose the wood, you should avoid water-based cleaning agents as they can raise the wood grain and cause warping. Look for flaky, peeling, or bare spots and smooth them with sandpaper to remove loose pieces and add tooth to the surface. Be especially attentive to the sharp edges of the previous coats of paint, rubbing them carefully so the repaired section matches the surrounding area in texture and level. The sealer is applied

## Working Tips: A Final Treatment Option for Finished Surfaces

Of the many ways to further enhance a finished surface (once the coats of finish have been applied and dried thoroughly), there is an additional and worthwhile treatment that will positively affect the hand and appearance of your project. The method involves applying two additional coats of gloss finish, allowing the first coat to dry before applying the second. When the second coat is completely dry, the surface is abraded lightly using #0000 steel wool that has been coated with clear, carnuba-rich wax. Hold the pad of steel wool with the wire strands running parallel with your fingers and use light passes to remove the high-gloss luster only; be careful not to abrade the surface as is done when leveling. When the surfaces are dull (but not scratched), use a soft cloth to rub and buff the surfaces to a beautiful satin finish with a buttery hand.

to the damaged areas first, and then a second coat is applied to the entire surface. What you may wish to do next is to add a coat of paint if you are going to paint your item a new color anyway.

## Technique: Cleaning, Sanding, and Sealing Previously Painted or Varnished Wood

To begin the restoration of a previously treated wood surface, scrape or sand off peeling or flaking paint and fill in any holes and cracks. Then follow the steps below to assess your wood piece and prepare it for decoupage. The surface condition of your particular piece will determine what you need to do.

### MATERIALS AND TOOLS
Wooden item, previously painted
   or varnished
Surface sealer: decoupage medium or
   acrylic medium-and-varnish
Surface cleaner: distilled white vinegar
   or mineral spirits
Disposable gloves
Safety glasses
Sandpaper, fine-grit (#600)
Sanding block
Squared rod, slat, or peg
Packing tape
Foam brush
Soft cloth
Tack cloth
Respirator mask
Safety glasses
Disposable gloves
Carton larger than project (optional)
Flat sticks

### Step 1
Clean off oils and grime.

Use a soft cloth moistened with a 1:1 vinegar/water solution to wipe away grime and grease from the existing finish. If the finish has bare patches or cracks that expose the wood, use mineral spirits rather than vinegar for cleaning to avoid raising the wood grain or warping the wood.

### Step 2
Sand the wood surface.

Put on a respirator mask and safety glasses. Move a sanding block wrapped with fine-grit sandpaper over the surface, using a rounded oval stroke and applying light pressure; be very careful not to rub through to the raw wood or to sand down sharp corners and edges, unless you want those effects. To reach into narrow crevices or recessed areas, wrap a strip of sandpaper around a squared rod, slat, or peg and use it like a file in a rounded oval stroke. For smaller, flatter surfaces and for more precise, targeted smoothing (including getting rid of old drips of paint), wrap a few winds of packing or other thick tape at the end of the rod to create an abrasion-free area and then rub the stick across the surface with the taped area gliding harmlessly across the flat object's side. Replace the sandpaper when it gets filled. Use a tack cloth to remove dust particles.

### Step 3
Apply the sealer to the repaired sections.

Elevate the wooden item on flat sticks. Use a damp foam brush to apply a thin coat of surface sealer to the repaired areas, including any knots that were painted over. Let the sealer dry completely. Sand the surface using fine-grit (#600) sandpaper. Wipe clean with a tack cloth.

### Step 4
Apply sealer to all of the wood surfaces.

Elevate the wooden item on flat sticks. Use a damp foam brush to apply a thin, even coat of surface sealer to the sides, bottom, and top of the wood item, both outside and inside; work in several sessions if not all surfaces are accessible at the same time. Let the sealer dry. Repeat. Let the sealer dry overnight. Use fine-grit (#600) sandpaper to smooth all of the surfaces.

## Step 5

Apply the paint to the wood surfaces.

Use a damp foam brush to apply a thin, even coat of paint to the sealed surface. Let the paint dry completely. Apply a second coat, brushing perpendicular to brush strokes used in the previous coat. Let the paint dry overnight.

## Step 6

Lightly sand the painted surface.

Use a sanding block wrapped with fine-grit (#600) sandpaper. Rub in rounded ovals over the surface with medium pressure, being careful not to rub though to the raw wood. Replace the sandpaper when it gets filled. Use a tack cloth to remove dust particles.

### Preparing Metal Surfaces

Preparing metal for decoupage is a straightforward process. Metal is a nonporous, impermeable substrate, so the surface doesn't technically need to be sealed, but it should be clean and smooth. Traditionally, metal surfaces for decoupage are primed with a thin coat that promotes adhesion of the paint layer that follows.

The amount of effort needed for prepping will depend on the condition of the metal. Metal that is heavily rusted and corroded is obviously not suitable for decoupage. Even new metal probably has some grease and fingerprints on it; residue from the lubricants or coatings used in the manufacturing process may also be present. All greasy residue needs to be removed before applying a primer. Cleaning the metal may be as simple as using diluted liquid detergent on a soft kitchen sponge and brushing it gently over the surface or swabbing the surface with a vinegar solution. Isopropyl alcohol (rubbing alcohol) on a soft cloth is effective in removing light rust. Stronger agents are needed to remove the heavy surface grime.

If your metal item is super smooth, roughening the surface with an emery cloth to give it some tooth will help the primer and subsequent layers of paint, prints, and finish to adhere. You may wish to apply a new coat of paint over metal that already has an old coat

---

## Working Tips: Cleaning Slightly Flaky and Rusty Metal Surfaces

Wear a pair of disposable gloves throughout this cleaning process to prevent the fine metal particles from staining your hands. To remove flakes of rust or bits of crusty paint, start with a piece of coarse-grit (40) emery cloth. Moisten the cloth in a bowl of water and move it in a smooth circular motion to stroke the metal surface smooth. The cloth will be stiff at first, but it will soften after wetting. Dip your finger with the emery cloth into the water every 10 seconds or so to wash away loose particles and pick up some more water.

After removing the rough edges on the metal surface, switch to medium-grit (90) emery and continue smoothing the surface. Thoroughly mop off the project with a cellulose sponge and then repeat the process. When the metal is fully dry, wet a lint-free paper towel, such as Viva!, with isopropyl alcohol (rubbing alcohol) and wipe down the surface to remove all debris or residue. The alcohol will dry faster and smell less than mineral spirits, which emits toxic fumes.

on its surface. In this case, it is important to clean the painted metal first and then to sand it using emery cloth and a wet-and-dry method. See "Sanding Metal" below.

### Technique: Cleaning Metal

There are several different approaches to cleaning metal surfaces, depending upon how stubborn the residue is. Choose the cleaning agent that relates to the condition of your metal. I always start with the simplest, most natural eco-smart agents, such as soap and hot water or a distilled vinegar solution. If these don't prove sufficient, I upgrade to a stronger cleaner. You can use this cleaning approach for bare or previously painted metal.

MATERIALS AND TOOLS

    Metal item for cleaning
    Liquid dishwashing detergent
    Distilled white vinegar
    Mineral spirits
    Chemical-cartridge respirator mask
    Simple Green all-purpose cleaner
    Table salt
    Isopropyl alcohol
    Disposable gloves
    Wire brush
    Old toothbrush
    Sponge
    Soft cloth
    Lint-free paper towels

#### Step 1

Brush off heavy grime.

Put on gloves and work over a sink. Use a wire brush or an old toothbrush to scrape off any hard particles of grime or corrosion.

#### Step 2

Use cleaning agents to break up surface grime.

Use a soft cloth soaked in a 1:1 vinegar/water solution to remove light grime. Rub all of the metal surfaces, inside and out. Use an old brush and the vinegar solution to remove any minuscule eruptions of oxidation on the surface. Use table salt with the vinegar solution to deoxidize any oily buildup on a copper, brass, or bronze surface.

#### Step 3

Remove the surface grime.

Put on disposable gloves and the respirator mask. Swab down the metal surface with a paper towel doused in mineral spirits to dissolve the grease and make it liquid, but don't wipe it away. Spray the surface with Simple Green all-purpose cleaner, which will further dissolve and bind to the dissolved grease. With a new paper towel, pat down the metal surface to remove most of the now liquefied grime.

#### Step 4

Wash the metal.

Working at the sink, apply a liberal amount of liquid dishwashing detergent to the metal surface and use a sponge to spread it around; then wash it off under hot running water. The metal will be totally degreased, and the heated surface will also dry faster.

### Technique: Sanding Metal

Abrading a plain or painted metal surface gives it some tooth so the primer can adhere. However, you should not attempt to dry-sand a metal surface to achieve the abrasion as the dust produced can be highly toxic. Instead, work at your sink, using water as a lubricant and your gloved fingertip as a sanding pad to work off loose bits. Use a sanding block only if there are bumps that need to be leveled or nooks that your finger cannot reach. In addition to eliminating metal dust in the air, water helps the emery cloth cut the metal surface faster.

MATERIALS AND TOOLS

    Metal item for sanding
    Emery cloth, coarse-grit (40), medium-
       grit (90), and fine-grit (120)
    Flexible sanding block

Squared rod, slat, or peg

Fingernail brush, old toothbrush, or other mildly abrasive brush

Cellulose sponge

Dishwashing liquid

Disposable gloves

Safety glasses

### Step 1

Remove the metal dust.

Put on safety glasses and disposable gloves. Hold the metal item under running water and use your gloved finger or a brush (with water as a lubricant) to remove any metal dust from the metal surface. Use coarse-grit (40) emery cloth and a flexible sanding block to go over the entire surface under water running water to scrape and wash off any rust or crusty bits of paint.

### Step 2

Sand the metal surface.

Continue sanding with coarse-grit (40) emery cloth. The cloth will be stiff at first but will soften after the wetting. The water will wash away the particles so that they do not accumulate in the cloth. Move the emery cloth in a rounded oval over the surface. After removing the rough edges, switch to medium-grit (90) emery cloth. For an extra-fine finish, wrap a piece of fine-grit (120) emery cloth around a flexible sanding block, moisten with water, and sand all of the surfaces smooth.

### Step 3

Smooth hard-to-reach areas.

For more precise and targeted sanding of narrow crevices and recessed areas, wrap a strip of emery cloth around a squared rod, slat, or peg, and use it like a file in a rounded oval stroke. For smaller, flatter surfaces, wrap a few winds of packing or other thick tape at the end of the rod to create an abrasion-free area, and then rub the emery stick across the surface with the taped area gliding harmlessly across the flat object's side.

### Step 4

Wash the metal.

Apply a liberal amount of dishwashing liquid to the metal surface and use a sponge to spread it around; then wash it off under hot running water. The heated surface will dry faster.

After a metal surface is cleaned and abraded, it needs to be primed to set up good adhesion for the subsequent decoupage layers. A rule of thumb in priming and painting is to use like products with like—an oil-based primer with an oil-based paint, a water-based primer with a water-based paint—but I break the rules when it comes to priming metal and use an oil-based spray primer followed by a coat of water-based acrylic paint. I generally avoid using spray paint, especially those that require solvents that are not water-soluble, because of environmental concerns, but this is my

## Working Tips: Preparing Galvanized Metal for Decoupage

Galvanized metal is coated in zinc; its surface is resilient, weatherproof, and rustproof but unfortunately somewhat resistant to painting. To give the surface some tooth, use a soft sanding block and fine-grit (120) emery cloth dipped in a 1:1 solution of water and distilled vinegar. Prepare the solution carefully, as vinegar/acetic acid used straight is quite reactive with zinc and may cause toxic vapors. Rinse the metal item under water and dry it with paper towels. Let the metal dry completely. Choose a spray primer designed for galvanized surfaces to coat the metal.

## Working Tips: Figuring Out Drying Times

Assessing the exact number of minutes, hours, or days required for wet media to completely dry and cure is an imprecise science at best. A time range can attempt to capture the interrelated variables that affect the final outcome: the physical properties of the binders, resins, solvents, and pigments that make up the medium, the proportions in which they occur, and the ambient temperature and humidity. The more you work with a particular medium, the more you will become attuned to its drying properties in your craft environment. It is always advisable to read and follow the manufacturer's label before working with any medium. Here are some additional pointers that will help you work more effectively with water-soluble media.

- Water-based media dry through evaporation, so thickness and consistency of the applied coat and the ambient temperature and humidity will affect drying time. When humidity (the moisture in the air) is high, drying slows down. A thick layer of paint takes longer to dry than a thin one.
- Acrylic-based media dry through polymerization, a process that takes place on the molecular level. When one coat of acrylic medium is applied over another coat of acrylic medium, their bonding is facilitated if the second coat is applied over a first that has just reached a state of being dry to the touch.
- The temperature of the substrate and the surrounding air can affect drying and curing time. For example, a metal object left out in the sun will become

hot and may exceed the recommended temperature range for applying a particular medium. Follow the temperature guidelines on the product you are using to ensure proper and complete adherence.

- Compatibility of the layers of media will affect bonding and drying time. Media used together in one project should share a common solvent base (such as a water-soluble primer and a water-soluble paint). However, there are conveniences afforded when breaking this rule, especially when priming metal. An alkyd spray primer (soluble in paint thinner) is much easier for beginners to apply in a thin, even coat than a water-soluble paint, such as acrylic craft paint, which is brushed on. However, for a layer of acrylic craft paint to adhere properly to an alkyd primer, it is imperative that the primer's fumes dissipate completely before the paint is applied; otherwise the paint can peel or flake.
- Some media contain solvents (or solvents are added separately) that accelerate drying. Water is a solvent, and water-soluble media are featured almost exclusively in this book. (Paint thinner and denatured alcohol are two other solvents.) Water can be added to a water-soluble medium to increase the flow of the medium over a surface, to thin a medium, which can accelerate drying time, and to clean the water-soluble medium from tools and surfaces.

one exception because it is so much easier to apply than brush-on liquid metal primer and the results are superior. It works as a foundation for the acrylic paint layer as long as ample drying time is allotted. It is critical that the fumes of the alkyd spray primer evaporate completely, a time that varies from 30 minutes to 24 hours according to the ambient temperature and the size and texture of the primed surface area. Check the label on the can for drying time. Directions on the can of spray primer will explain that the primed metal surface will be dry to the touch after 10 minutes, but you must wait until the solvents are completely evaporated before applying acrylic paint to ensure a good bond. Even a trace of lingering solvent can interfere with the adhesion of the acrylic paint layer. Of course, if you use two oil-based products—an oil-based spray paint on top of an oil-based primer—the 10-minute drying time holds and compatibility is near guaranteed.

## Technique: Applying Oil-Based Spray Primer to Cleaned and Sanded Metal

Once a metal surface is clean and roughened, it is ready to accept primer. Read the directions on the spray primer can to choose the appropriate primer formulation for your type of bare metal. To avoid anodic corrosion, do not use silver aluminum primer on bare iron objects. I prefer oil-based spray primer because it is extremely easy to apply and lays down a smooth thin coat. Allow ample drying time for the solvent base to evaporate to provide a good foundation for the paint, glue, prints, and finish that are layered on thereafter.

MATERIALS AND TOOLS

Metal item, cleaned and sanded
Spray metal primer
Chemical-cartridge respirator mask
Safety glasses
Disposable gloves
Emery cloth, fine-grit (120) grit
Sanding block

Tack cloth
Lazy Susan (optional)
Cardboard carton (for spray booth; optional)

**Step 1**
Set up the work area.

Work outdoors, if possible, or in a well-ventilated space. For proper adhesion, read and follow the directions on the can of spray metal primer and work on a day when the temperature falls within the recommended range, for example, "not below 55°F (12.8°C) or above 90°F (32.2°C)." Proper ambient temperature is significant because metal has a high thermal conductivity that condenses moisture and retards evaporation of solvents, which can in turn interfere with the adhesion of paint. To contain the overspray, set the project in a spray booth fashioned from a cardboard carton. Placing the project on an old kitchen lazy Susan will allow you to rotate it as you spray to achieve a thin, evenly applied coat.

**Step 2**
Apply the primer.

Put on a chemical-cartridge respirator mask, safety glasses, and disposable gloves. Spray a thin, even coat of primer on all metal surfaces. Hold the spray can 12" to 16" (30.5 to 40.6 cm) from the object and use smooth overlapping strokes in a back-and-forth motion, turning the lazy Susan to access all sides. To prevent drips and runs, avoid aiming the spray in one place. Let the primer dry for as long as recommended before applying the next coat and before handling the metal object.

**Step 3**
Apply a second coat of primer.

As soon as the primer solvent is evaporated (usually within a few minutes), apply the second coat. If the window of opportunity is missed, wait 24 hours until the primer is completely dry before applying a second coat. If you buy the quick-drying kind of primer, wait

10 minutes or so between coats, then allow the final coat to dry the stated number of hours before handling.

**Step 4**

Sand the surface.

For an extra-fine finish, wrap a piece of fine-grit (120) emery cloth around a sanding block, moisten with water, and sand all of the surfaces smooth. Let the surface dry and wipe clean with a tack cloth.

**Step 5**

Apply a third coat of primer.

Apply the third coat of primer as before. Let the coat dry overnight.

*Painting Wood and Metal Surfaces*

Selecting paint is usually based on the size of the surface being painted. For anything small or made to hold up to repeated handling, buy acrylic craft paint. Acrylic craft paints have

---

## Working Tips: How to Clean Brushes

Brushes used to apply water-based mediums, such as acrylic paint and acrylic medium-and-varnish, are easy to clean.

- **Brushes with bristles**

  Off-load any paint by running the bristles over the rim of the original container or over the rim of a wide-mouthed jar and transfer the medium back into the original container. Rinse the brush's bristles in a container of water, swishing them around until any remaing paint or varnish is removed and refreshing the water as needed. Then mix liquid dishwashing detergent and water in a clean container and wash the bristles in this solution. Run the bristles over a layer of paper towels and use your fingers to straighten the bristles and shape them. Hang the brush by a hook with bristles facing down or lay the brush on a pad of paper towel to dry. When the brush is dry, hang it up or stand the brush,

  handle down, in a wide-mouth container until ready to use again.

- **Foam brushes**

  Off-load any paint or varnish by running the foam against the rim of the original container or other wide-mouthed jar and transfer the medium back into the original container. Rinse the foam section of the brush under running water. Apply a few drops of liquid dishwashing detergent to the foam, place it under running water, and squeeze the foam with your fingers to remove any lingering paint. Wash off the handle, rinse away all of the soap, and continue flushing the foam until the water runs clear. Wipe the foam section against a layer of paper towels and wipe off the handle. Lay the brush on a paper towel to dry. When the brush is dry, stand the brush, foam section up, in a wide-mouthed container until ready to use again.

good flow; are fairly thin so they are easy to apply; have good shrinkage so they dry to a nice smooth finish; and they are permanent when dry. Available in jars or bottles, acrylic craft paints are water-soluble and clean up with soap and water when still wet. They come ready-mixed in a broad variety of colors, and paint colors can be mixed together easily to create customized colors. The finish—matte, eggshell, satin, semigloss, and high gloss—doesn't really matter because the adhesion of one layer to another is accomplished on a chemical level through polymerization rather than surface tooth. The final coat of paint will be covered by surface sealer whose finish will determine the patina on the project's exterior surface.

I use acrylic craft paint for all of the projects featured in this chapter; they are so easy to use and produce such good results that I see no reason to use other paints, such as artist's acrylics that are sold in art stores. Acrylic paint for artists is formulated with color pigments and binders that give the paint body. The consistency ranges from pasty to runny, is hard to handle, and cures to a flexible, almost rubbery state, so for these reasons, I don't recommend artist's acrylics for painting a background color on a project. Another kind of paint that I don't use for small decoupage projects is household latex paint. Latex is reasonably stable under normal conditions, but moderate moisture or heat will cause latex paint to flex, which can cause the paint to blister and peel and the print to lift up. It is generally an unsatisfactory layer for anything that is applied on top of it that relies on a stable foundation layer.

## Technique: Painting Prepared Wood or Metal Surfaces

After being properly sealed or primed, a wood or metal surface is ready for painting. Water-based acrylic craft paint is used on both surfaces, and the painting technique is the same. If you are painting over an oil-based primer, allow ample time for all the solvents in the primer to thoroughly evaporate before applying the acrylic paint. Check the label on the can for drying time—quick-drying primers can take 30 minutes, others 24 hours. In addition, be aware that dry paint is not necessarily cured paint that has reached a final level of hardness. Some paint may be dry to the touch after 24 hours, but still take an impression of an object, even a fingerprint, after 3 days. Some longer-drying paints allow for some minor surface defects, such as brush marks, to level out. Refer to Universal Guidelines for Applying Sealers, Paints, Varnishes, and Other Liquid Media (page 380).

### MATERIALS AND TOOLS

Wooden or metal item, prepped for
  painting
Acrylic craft paint
Acrylic medium-and-varnish or
  decoupage medium
Foam brush
Sanding block
Sandpaper, fine-grit (#600)
Tack cloth
Safety glasses
Disposable gloves

### Step 1

Apply the first coat of paint.

Use a foam brush dampened in water to apply a thin, even coat of paint to the sealed wood or primed metal surface. Let the paint dry approximately two hours.

### Step 2

Apply the second coat of paint.

Apply a second coat of paint, brushing perpendicular to brush strokes used for the first coat. Let the paint dry completely.

### Step 3

Apply a paint sealer.

Use a damp brush to apply a thin, smooth coat of water-soluble acrylic medium-and-varnish or decoupage medium to the painted surface and allow the sealer to dry from 30 minutes to 24 hours. Then allow the sealer to cure to final hardness, which can take a minimum of one week or longer. The final curing time of any sealer is dependent upon the ambient temperature, the formula used, and the thickness of the applied layer. It is best to follow the label for drying and curing times.

### Laying Out and Adhering the Prints

Once the wood or metal surface is painted and sealed, the decorative stage of decoupage can begin. Before permanently gluing the prints to the surface of your project, take time to compose a pleasing arrangement. You can plan a design by arranging cutouts on the project itself, providing the surface is flat. For three-dimensional items, do your planning on an actual-size paper template. A template lets you view a project with multiple or curved surfaces as a flat plane. I like to use a template when planning a design with a lot of different design elements, especially those that flow from one section of a project to another.

After the design is laid out, the prints can be glued onto the surface of your project. The techniques for gluing prints on three-dimensional surfaces are easy to learn, and you'll be delighted with the results.

### Technique: Using the Project as a Template

This is my preferred method of working out a simple design, because it allows me to test-fit the prints and mark placement guidelines directly on my project. I use poster putty to hold the prints against the surface, and I arrange and rearrange the elements until I am happy with the design. During the gluing phase, I remove the putty and glue down the prints within the marked guidelines. There are times when I ignore the marked guidelines if another position works better. I have found that new ideas emerge in the process and I usually go with the flow.

### MATERIALS AND TOOLS
Cutout prints
Project surface, prepared for decoupage
Poster putty
Wax pencil

**Step 1**
Position the prints on the decorative surface.

Apply a tiny bit of poster putty to the back of each print. Stick the prints onto the project

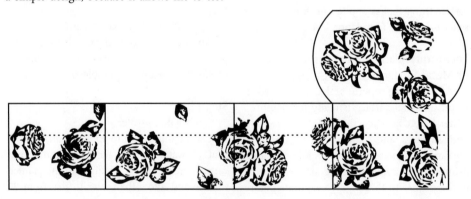

in a pleasing arrangement. Adjust the placement of the motifs until the design suits you.

**Step 2**

Mark the position of the prints on the decorative surface.

Use a wax pencil to mark short dash lines around the edges of each print to indicate its position on the surface. Keep the prints in place until you are ready to glue them down.

## Technique: Making and Using a Paper Template for a Box

The prints on all sides of a box must relate to one another; prints that fall on two adjacent sides help establish a flow of elements that moves the eye across the entire decorated surface. A print that folds over an edge or crosses the crevice between the lid and the box must be positioned in such a way that all parts can be securely glued (see page 392).

MATERIALS AND TOOLS
Cutout prints
Box, prepared for decoupage
Sheet of paper, larger than the project
Poster putty
Scissors
Pencil
Ruler
Wax pencil

**Step 1**

Make a paper template.

Use a pencil and ruler to draw an actual-size sketch of each side of the box on a sheet of paper. Draw the sides of the box first as a long band on the paper and then add the bottom of the box and the lid, if there is one. Add a line to indicate the lid opening, if there is one.

**Step 2**

Arrange the cutouts.

Lay the cutout prints on a clean, flat surface. Arrange the cutouts on the paper template, positioning the largest elements first,

then the smallest, to create a flow of prints from one box surface to the next, including the top of the box. Once you have a pleasing arrangement, use small bits of poster putty to stick the cutouts to the paper template.

**Step 3**

Transfer the cutouts to the box.

Using the template as a guide, transfer the cutouts to the corresponding area on the box, pressing down gently until the poster putty sticks. Use a wax pencil to mark the position of each cutout on the box. If you are comfortable working directly from the template, without positioning the pieces on the box before gluing, you can skip this step.

## Technique: Designing on a Paper Template for a Cylinder

On the softly contoured surface of a cylinder-shaped object, such as a bucket or pail, the design elements flow from one section to another in an unbroken flow. Plan the design so that contiguous motifs relate to one another. Pay special attention to the seam where the design comes full circle.

MATERIALS AND TOOLS
Cutout prints (for Poppy original art, see page 704)
Cylindrical item, prepared for decoupage
Sheet of paper, larger than the project
Poster putty
Scissors
Pencil
Ruler
Wax pencil

**Step 1**

Make a paper template.

Wrap a sheet of paper around the outside of the cylinder and press the paper against its edges to impress the dimensions into the paper. Lay the paper flat, and use a pencil to trace along the impressions in the paper to draw the shape of the design surface, making any corrections necessary.

**Step 2**

Arrange the cutouts on the template.

Lay the cutout prints on a clean, flat surface. Arrange the cutouts on the paper template, positioning the largest elements first, then the smallest, to create a flow of prints across the template. Once you have a pleasing arrangement, use small bits of poster putty to stick the cutouts to the paper template.

**Step 3**

Transfer the cutouts to the cylinder.

Using the template as a guide, transfer the cutouts to the corresponding area on the cylinder, pressing the print until it sticks to the surface. Make a few marks with a wax pencil to mark the position of each cutout on the cylinder. If you are comfortable working directly from the template, without positioning the pieces on the project before gluing, you can skip this step.

## Technique: Gluing Prints to a Prepared Surface

Decoupage medium has a slightly thick viscosity that goes on smoothly and easily. Use a tapered brush for small elements and a larger brush for large elements, such as borders. The liquid medium will cause the print to curl, but as the moisture spreads, the print will flatten out.

MATERIALS AND TOOLS

Project surface, prepared for decoupage
Cutout prints, in a design layout (on project or template)
Decoupage medium
Aluminum foil
Tapered paintbrush (for small prints)
Large paintbrush or foam brush (for large prints)
Tweezers (optional)
Small dish
Cellulose sponge
Cotton swabs
Pencil with eraser

**Step 1**

Set up the work area.

Pour decoupage medium into a dish. Lay a sheet of aluminum foil on your work surface.

**Step 2**

Apply the glue to the back of the print.

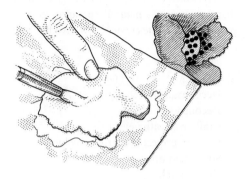

Lift a cutout print from the project surface or template, remove the putty, and set the print facedown on the foil. Hold down the print with your finger or the eraser end of a pencil and brush an even coat of decoupage medium onto the back, starting near the center and brushing beyond the outside edges to ensure full coverage. Move your finger or the pencil as needed. The print paper will curl and then flatten.

**Step 3**

Glue the print to the decorative surface.

Use gluey or moistened fingers or tweezers to pick up and position the print, glue side down, on the project surface. Use gluey fingers to smooth down the print, working from the center to the outside edges to move out any air bubbles and excess glue.

**Step 4**

Tamp to ensure good adhesion.

Use a damp sponge to tamp down the print. Make sure the edges of the print are glued down securely. Use a cotton swab to remove any excess glue from around the edges of the print. Repeat steps 2–4 until all of the prints are glued to the surface.

**Step 5**

Reglue any lifted edges.

Examine each print, looking for any edges that have bubbled or lifted up. Use damp fingers to gently tamp down any raised edges on the prints. If an edge is not sticking, use a narrow paintbrush or a toothpick to apply some decoupage medium under the edge and then press it down until it adheres. Let the medium dry completely.

## Technique: Gluing a Print over the Edges of a Box

Free-flowing design layouts are a signature characteristic of decoupage. It's not unusual for a print to fold over two or three edges at the corner of a box in such a way that part of the print will be lost. Here's how to trim the design to fit as you go.

MATERIALS AND TOOLS

Decoupage project in progress
Decoupage medium
Manicure scissors
Craft knife with new blade
Small tapered paintbrush
Pencil

**Step 1**

Partially adhere the cutout print.

Apply decoupage medium to the back of the print. Place the print, glue side down, on one flat surface of the project. Allow the part of the print that will fold over onto the adjacent surfaces to extend freely. Use gluey or

## Working Tips: Handling Wet Prints

Pick up a glue-moistened print with moist or gluey fingers or blunt-nosed tweezers to avoid tearing the paper.

wet fingers to press down the part of the print that is resting on the project. Smooth this part from the center to the outside edges, moving out air bubbles and excess glue.

### Step 2

Cut into the motif for easement.

Use manicure scissors to cut into the part of the print that extends beyond the edge. Cut along a line or contour in the image, stopping when you reach the edge of the project.

### Step 3

Press down each cut section of the motif.

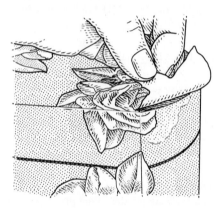

Fold one section of the extending piece onto the adjacent surface and press it lightly against the surface. Fold over and press down the second section, making light ticks with a pencil to roughly indicate the overlap on the first section. Lift up the second section and trim the first section to correspond to the overlap, so both sections will fit together like pieces in a jigsaw puzzle when they are pressed back into place. Use gluey or wet fingers to smooth both sections until they follow the contour of the object. Use a damp sponge to press the entire print flat, making sure the edges are glued down securely.

## Technique: Gluing a Print across a Break or Separation

Here's how to incorporate a design element that flows across a natural separation in your project, such as the crevice between a box and a lid.

### MATERIALS AND TOOLS

Decoupage project in progress
Decoupage medium
Craft knife with new blade
Paint, in project background color
Small paintbrush
Cotton swab

### Step 1

Glue the motif across the crevice.

Close the box so that the lid and box edge touch. Apply decoupage medium to the back of the print and position it, glue side down, across the area where the edges of the lid and the box meet. Use gluey or wet fingers to press down the print, smoothing from the center to the outside edges to move out air bubbles and excess glue. Tamp with a damp sponge and remove excess glue around the edges with a cotton swab. Let the glue dry overnight or longer, if necessary, to ensure it is completely dry.

**Step 2**

Slice through the print along the crevice.

Use a craft knife with a new blade. Push the blade of the craft knife through the print into the crevice between the lid and the box. Using the crevice as a guide, slowly pull the knife through the print, making a neat slice in the paper to separate the box and the lid.

**Step 3**

Touch up the cut edges.

Use a small paintbrush to carefully touch up the cut edges of the print, which will show as white, in a paint color that blends with the project background color.

## Applying the Finish

Three water-soluble mediums are suitable for the finish coat in decoupage: three-in-one decoupage medium (Mod Podge), which is the most viscous; a combination acrylic medium-and-varnish product, which is moderately viscous; and acrylic varnish, which is the thinnest of the three. All three products are applied with a brush, cover well, and add a lustrous, protective finish to wood and metal surfaces.

While I use three-in-one decoupage medium to seal and glue down the prints, I have had mixed results when using it as a finishing coat. It does not remain completely trans-parent, and the surface feels like plastic when many coats are layered over one another. Of the three finishes, I prefer the acrylic medium-and-varnish product. It remains transparent even when many coats are layered over one another, and it goes on thicker than straight acrylic varnish for fewer finish coats to create a level surface that conceals the edges of the print.

Selecting a finish coat for your project will depend on several factors: the patina you want (ranging from high gloss to satin), the degree of protection the project will need (depending on the amount of handling), and the aesthetics you prefer (whether a high-gloss finish for a modern piece or a satin finish for an antique look).

Whatever finish you choose, always read the label on the container; it explains how to use the product, the usual drying times, the number of coats needed for good coverage, and how to clean brushes or applicators. Work carefully and patiently. A finish that is smooth and unblemished brings out the beauty of the prints, reveals the quality of your painstaking cutting, and gives the impression that the many images you have brought together are a single hand-painted design.

## Technique: Applying Finish to Decoupage on a Wood or Metal Surface

Apply the finishing coats to your project on a cool, dry day. Work outdoors in a dust-free environment or in a room that has plenty of fresh air and cross-ventilation. I usually safeguard my wet finish by placing a clean, empty carton over the freshly coated project to protect it from settling dust as the finishing coats dry and cure. Refer to the Universal Guidelines (page 380) for pointers on keeping your brushwork smooth and even.

## MATERIALS AND TOOLS
  Acrylic medium-and-varnish
  Foam brush
  Small jar
  Sandpaper, fine-grit (#600; optional)
  Tack cloth (optional)
  Clean empty carton, larger than project
  Flat sticks (to elevate project)

### Step 1
  Apply the first coat of finish.

  Use sticks to elevate the project off the work surface. Pour some acrylic medium-and-varnish into a small jar. Dampen a foam brush in water and squeeze it out. Use the moistened brush to apply a thin, even coat of finish medium to the surface of your project, allowing it to dry 3 hours.

### Step 2
  Apply the second coat of finish.

  Repeat step 1 to apply a second coat of finish. Let the finish dry.

### Step 3 (optional)
  Refine the finish.

  Lightly sand the surface, moving fine-grit (#600) sandpaper in an oval motion over the surface. Wipe off the dust with a tack cloth.

### Step 4
  Apply a third coat of finish.

  Repeat step 1 to apply a third coat of finish.

### Step 5
  Allow the finish to cure.

  Set the project aside in a protected place, elevated on flat sticks and shielded with a carton to keep dust from settling on the still-sticky surface. Allow the finish to cure before handling the project, following the manufacturer's recommendations. Even though a medium is dry to the touch, it may need additional time to bond completely to the surface and cure to its final hardness.

## Decoupage on Glass

Decoupage can transform ordinary glass into a gleaming surface that enhances the look of the prints, creating an item of function and beauty and using a style of decoupage called potichomania. Several approaches are possible. Images can be applied to the underside of a glass platter or plate and then sealed so that food can be served on the top surface. Images can be applied to the outside of clear glass food containers, for effects that imitate the look of waterslide decals or fired enamel decoration. Images applied behind the glass can mimic the look of fine hand-painted porcelain. With a plastic liner safely inserted, a glass vase decorated in this way can be used to hold fresh flowers in water. The location of the prints on glass is determined, for the most part, by the intended use of the item. Prints obviously should not be glued to the side of the glass that will come into contact with food or water. It is also practical to position prints safely away from areas prone to wear and abrasion, such as the footed rim on a vase or platter.

### Cleaning and Preparing the Glass Surface

Glass items in good condition require very little preparation for decoupage. They should be cleaned thoroughly in a dishwasher or washed by hand using liquid detergent and hot water. If you use a liquid detergent, make sure you remove all the soapy residue by flushing the surface with hot water and then drying the glass thoroughly. For light grease and fingerprints, I use an eco-smart solution of equal parts distilled white vinegar and water in a spray bottle, although commercial products work fine. Just apply the degreaser and wipe the glass with a lint-free paper towel. I have found that non-embossed paper towels don't leave lint. After the glass item is clean and dry, continue to use fresh paper towels when handling the glass to avoid introducing new grease.

When dirt and grime are hard to remove, as they can be at the inside bottom of a glass vase, I use baking soda and a sponge or rag to scrub the glass surface clean. Baking soda is a gentle abrasive that won't scratch the glass. I use a wooden spoon to push a rag or sponge against the grime until it loosens, and then I wash and dry the glass item as usual.

Glass is nonporous and impermeable and does not require sealing. The glue used to adhere the prints is strong enough to bond them to glass. Some *découpeurs* apply a coat of spray fixative or a frosting agent to foster a better bond between the glass and the prints, but the bond will only be as strong as the coating's grip on the glass—if it is weak, an added coating can actually reduce the bond of the prints that are applied over it. Permanently etching the surface of the glass can help, but I forgo this added chemical step because I have found that if the glass surface is scrupulously clean and free of grease and fingerprints, decoupage medium adheres perfectly sufficient on its own.

## Laying Out and Adhering the Prints

You can take two basic approaches to planning a decoupage design for a glass object. One is to use the glass object itself as a template, temporarily laying the motifs in place. The other is to use a separate paper template to work out your ideas. Glass is a unique surface for decoupage, not only for the "instant" finish that glass provides, but also because its transparency allows you to lay out your design on one side of the glass and easily and accurately transfer the prints to the other side when you are ready to glue them in place. If you draw your design on a paper template, you place the template either under or inside the glass object and view the motifs through the glass to mark guidelines on the surface.

## Working Tips: Manipulating Depth and Color

The intensity of color and pattern on a surface that has decoupage can be manipulated by the choice of finish. A high-gloss varnish or medium will bring out the color and pattern of the applied prints and the ground color. Often dull colors that are barely discernible will emerge when light strikes the finish causing the light to refract through a layer of glossy finish, producing decoupage with greater depth and transparency.

## Working Tips: Toward a Clean Finish

Always use fresh acrylic-and-varnish medium. Pour the amount you need for immediate use in a jar to avoid contaminating the contents in the original container.

## Technique: Designing on a Flat Glass Surface

In this technique, the design is marked on the top surface of the glass. When you are ready to glue the prints, you simply transfer them, one image at a time, to the underside and glue them in place.

MATERIALS AND TOOLS

Cutout prints
Flat glass object for decoupage, such as a plate
Poster putty
Wax pencil
Paper towels

## Working Tips: Choosing a Vase for Decoupage

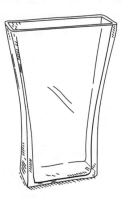

The opening in a vase for decoupage must be large enough for your hand to fit inside and move around. You will need some maneuverability in order to glue the prints to the inside walls and apply the paint and decorative finish. A long-handled paintbrush will allow you to reach the bottom of a tall vase without smearing the paint with your knuckles.

### Step 1

Place the prints on the glass.

Apply a tiny bit of poster putty to the back of each print. Stick the prints onto the top surface of the glass. Adjust the placement of the motifs until the design suits you.

### Step 2

Mark the placement of each cutout.

Use a wax pencil to mark the outline of each print, using short dash lines. You do not have to outline the whole print. Keep the prints in place until you are ready to glue them.

## Technique: Designing on a Paper Template for a Flat Glass Surface

A template for a flat glass plate can guide the placement of cutouts for both random and patterned designs. A template is drawn in the shape of the plate, and then the individual motifs are moved from one place to another until a design is created. Because the glass plate is transparent, a template can also serve to provide a fairly accurate pattern for the pieces that will be placed under the glass.

MATERIALS AND TOOLS

Cutout prints
Flat glass object for decoupage
Sheet of paper, larger than the project
Poster putty
Scissors
Pencil
Ruler
Wax pencil
Tape

### Step 1

Trace the shape of the plate.

Lay the plate on a sheet of paper, underside facing up, and use a pencil to trace around the rim. Use scissors to cut out the template along the marked line.

### Step 2

Lay out the design on a template.

Lay the prints on a clean, flat surface. Arrange the cutouts on the paper template, positioning the largest elements first, then the smallest. Once you have a pleasing arrangement, use tiny bits of poster putty to stick the cutouts to the paper template.

### Step 3

Mark the position of the cutouts on the glass.

Lay the plate, top side up, over the template, and use short strips of masking tape to hold the template against the glass. For plates with a slightly angled rim, adjust the paper by creasing it slightly. Then use a wax pencil and dash marks to mark the general shape and position of each of the prints on the top surface of the glass. Remove the template from the plate.

## Technique: Designing Directly on a Glass Vessel

In this approach, prints are positioned on the outside of a glass vessel during the design stage and are transferred, one at a time, to the inside of the glass vessel during the gluing stage. Stand at a distance to assess the arrangement of cutouts, squinting your eyes to get an idea of the positive areas of the design, formed by the prints, and negative areas of the design, formed by the spaces between the prints. The negative spaces will eventually be filled in with paint, which better reveals their own distinctive silhouettes.

### MATERIALS AND TOOLS

Cutout prints (for Roses original art, see pages 704 and 724)
Curved glass object for decoupage, such as a vase
Poster putty
Wax pencil

### Step 1

Arrange the cutouts on the outside of the glass vessel.

Lay the prints on a clean, flat surface. Apply a bit of poster putty to the back of each print. Stick the prints on the outside surface of the glass. Check the shape and size of the spaces between the prints—the negative spaces will form a secondary design field that will become more pronounced when the background glass is painted. The greater the space between the motifs, the more the background paint will show. Adjust the placement of the motifs as you assess the design for overall balance.

### Step 2

Mark the position of each cutout.

Use a wax pencil to outline each print on the glass. Use short dash marks; you do not have to outline the whole print. Keep the prints in place until you are ready to glue them to the inside surface of the glass.

## Technique: Designing on a Paper Template for a Glass Vessel

A paper template is especially useful when you are creating a design for a project piece that will be viewed from multiple angles. Laying out the motifs on a flat plane gives you an overview of the whole design. You can work out the relationships among the prints that are adjacent to one another and harmonize those that are noncontiguous, for a design flow that will draw the eye around the vessel. Pay special attention to the placement of motifs at the ends, for a design that comes full circle with a seamless join. You'll need a piece of paper that wraps all the way around the vessel plus some extra to form a small overlap.

## MATERIALS AND TOOLS

Cutout prints
Curved glass item for decoupage
Sheet of paper, larger than the project
Poster putty
Scissors
Pencil
Ruler
Wax pencil

### Step 1

Mark the paper template.

Wrap the sheet of paper around the outside of the glass, pressing the paper against the top rim and foot of the cylinder to impress its shape into the paper. Lay the paper flat. Use a pencil to trace along the impressions, making any corrections necessary to more accurately represent the dimensions of the vessel.

### Step 2

Arrange the cutouts on the template.

Lay the prints on a clean, flat surface. Arrange the cutouts on the paper template, positioning the largest elements first, then the smallest. Once you have a pleasing arrangement, use small bits of poster putty to stick the cutouts to the paper template.

### Step 3

Mark the design on the outside of the glass.

Roll the template into a tube, prints facing out, and insert the tube into the glass vessel. Let the tube unfurl so that the prints rest against the inside surface of the glass. Use bits of putty to hold the template against the glass for a more accurate placement of the cutouts. Use a wax pencil to mark the shape of each print on the outside of the glass with short dash marks. Remove the template from the glass vessel.

### Step 4

Stick the cutouts within the marked outlines.

Pick the cutouts off the template and stick them to the outside of the vase.

Once the design is mapped out, it is a simple matter to glue the motifs in place on or behind the glass. I prefer to apply decoupage medium to the prints because I can make sure that all parts, especially the edges, are coated. Another method is to apply the medium to the glass surface and press the dry print into place.

Decoupage is not such an exact science that you need to stick to your first idea; there's room for experimenting. You can use your wet finger pads to slide a wet cutout around.

## Technique: Gluing Prints to a Flat Glass Surface

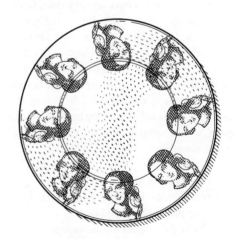

Gluing prints to a flat glass surface is very easy because the design area is so accessible. When I am decorating a small glass plate, I can position the prints on the underside and flip the plate over to see the effect. I can even reach my hand under the plate and use my wet or gluey fingers to slide the print around as I view it through the top. Try this technique using the Spanish Dancer art illustrated here (page 705) or a Marie Antoinette image, as shown on the front cover.

## MATERIALS AND TOOLS

Glass plate, marked with layout
Cutout print (for Spanish Dancer original art, see page 705)
Decoupage medium
Aluminum foil
Tapered watercolor paintbrush
Foam brush
Tweezers (optional)
Small dish
Household sponge
Cotton swabs
Paper towels
Large can (for propping plate)

## Step 1

Set up the work area.

Pour decoupage medium into a dish. Lay a sheet of aluminum foil on your work surface.

## Step 2

Apply glue to the image side of the print.

Lift a cutout print from the plate or template, remove the putty, and set the print on the foil, image side up. Hold down the print with your finger or the eraser end of a pencil and use a tapered watercolor paintbrush or a foam brush, depending on the size of the cutout, to brush an even coat of decoupage medium on the image side of the print, starting at the center and brushing past the outside edges.

## Step 3

Position the print on the glass.

Lay the plate facedown on a protected work surface. Use gluey or moistened fingers or tweezers to pick up and position the print, glue side down, against the glass within the corresponding marked outline or mark.

## Step 4

Adjust the position of the print.

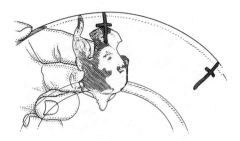

Turn the plate over and check the position of the print as it appears through the front side of the glass. Adjust the image, if necessary, using gluey fingers to avoid tearing or wrinkling the paper. Do not let the print traverse the edge of the plate or the foot rim; keep these sections plain.

## Step 5

Smooth the print onto the glass.

Lay the plate facedown on the work surface. Use a damp sponge to tamp down the print, pressing out excess glue or air bubbles from the center so they exit the nearest edge. Do not remove too much medium as any dry gaps between the paper and the glass will show up as silver streaks. Clean up the wet glue around the print.

---

## Working Tips: Adjusting the Position of the Glued Print

Decoupage medium is milky white when first applied, making it difficult to see the entire print through the coated glass. If you can't see a print well, hold the plate up to the light to see the print in silhouette.

---

**Step 6**

Glue down the remaining prints on the glass.

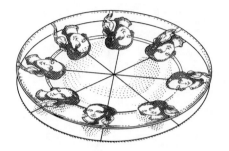

Repeat steps 2–5 to position and glue the remaining prints to the underside of the plate, following the marked outlines or marks. Use a damp sponge to clean off the excess glue on the glass, working carefully around the edges of the prints. Use a damp cotton swab to clean around intricate contours. If there is any decoupage medium on the rim of the plate or the foot rim, remove it with a moist cotton swab.

**Step 7**

Reglue any lifted edges.

Examine each print, looking for edges that have bubbled or lifted up. If an edge is not sticking, use a narrow paintbrush or a toothpick to apply some decoupage medium under the edge and then use your fingertip to press

## Fun for Kids: Decorating a Birthday Plate with Decoupage

Here is a decoupage project that can be made for or by a child. Featuring a laser color print of a child's face, the plate will become a favorite way to remember a birthday or other celebration that commemorates a milestone. Younger children can help apply the glue or the paint with supervision, while older kids can take off on their creative own.

- Make a color or black-and-white laser copy of the child's photograph. Cut out the image, but don't worry if some of white background paper shows around the cutout. It will be camouflaged when the plate is painted white!
- Glue the print to the underside of the glass, checking the position from the front. Add cutout circles made with a hole punch to the rim for a polka dot border. Let the medium dry completely.
- Pat white acrylic craft paint onto the back of the plate, let dry 30 minutes, and apply a second coat.
- Seal with two coats of decoupage medium.
- Add self-adhesive felt bumpers to the back.

it flat against the glass until it adheres. Let the glue dry completely.

### Step 8

Apply a sealer coat of decoupage medium.

Use a foam brush to apply a thin, even coat of decoupage medium over the underside of the glass plate, including the backs of all the prints, to set up a good bonding surface for the paint; do not coat the foot rim. Use a damp sponge to catch any drips or overflow. Set the plate facedown on the mouth of a large can and let the medium dry completely.

### Step 9

Clean the top surface of the plate.

Use a paper towel and glass cleaner to remove the wax pencil marks from the face of the plate.

## Technique: Gluing Prints to a Glass Vessel

Applying prints to a glass vessel, such as a vase, is similar, in principle, to applying prints to a glass plate, except the surface is a vertical wall of glass. Start with the largest prints and work from the bottom of the layout to the top. I always allow a longer drying time because there is less air circulation in the interior of a vessel, especially a tall one.

### MATERIALS AND TOOLS

Glass vessel, marked with layout
Cutout prints (for Roses original art,
    see pages 704 and 724)
Decoupage medium
Tapered watercolor paintbrush
Foam brush
Tweezers
Small bowl
Paper towels
Old bath towel
Small sponge
Toothpicks
Cotton swabs

### Step 1

Set up the work area.

Pour decoupage medium into a dish. Lay a sheet of aluminum foil on your work surface.

### Step 2

Apply glue to the image side of the print.

Select the largest cutout print from the bottom of the layout. Lift the print from the vase or template, remove the putty, and set the print on the foil, image side up. Use a tapered watercolor paintbrush or a foam brush, depending on the size of the cutout, to apply decoupage medium to the image side of the print, smearing the glue past the edges.

**Step 3**

Position the print against the glass.

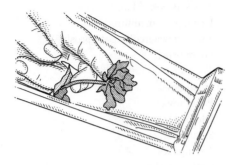

Use gluey or wet fingers to position and press the image side of the print against the interior surface of the glass, within the corresponding marked outline.

**Step 4**

Adjust the position of the print.

Check the position of the print as it appears through the front of the vase. Adjust the position, if necessary, by reaching gluey or moistened fingers inside the vase. Be careful not to tear or wrinkle the paper as you move it.

## Working Tips: Discovering the Negative Space

Large, colorful prints get all the attention when set against a nondescript pale or neutral background. To give that negative space a life of its own, try a background color that blends seamlessly with the background color in the prints. The eye will perceive the background as a continuous and distinct design element that is part of a unique webbery of colors and shapes.

**Step 5**

Smooth the print against the glass.

Use moistened fingers or a damp sponge to tamp the print against the glass, pressing out excess glue or air bubbles from the center so they exit the nearest edge. Do not remove too much medium as any dry gaps between the paper and the inside of the glass will show up as silver streaks when viewed from the outside of the glass. Clean up the wet glue around the print.

**Step 6**

Glue down the remaining prints on the glass.

Repeat steps 2–5 to position and glue the remaining prints, one at a time, to the inside of the vase; glue larger prints before smaller prints and work from the bottom to the top of the layout. Use a damp sponge to clean off the excess medium on the inside of the glass, working carefully around the edges of the prints. Use a damp cotton swab to clean around intricate contours.

**Step 7**

Reglue any lifted edges.

Examine each print, looking for edges that have bubbled or lifted up. Tilt the vase to get a better view of any gaps. Use your fingertip to coax extra glue under the edge and allow gravity to do the rest. Once the glue has flowed under the lifted edge, press it flat against the glass until it adheres. Let the glue dry completely.

**Step 8**

Apply a sealer coat of decoupage medium.

Use a foam brush to apply a thin, even coat of decoupage medium over the interior surface of the glass, including the backs of all the prints, to set up a good bonding surface for paint. Use a damp sponge to catch any drips or overflow. Let the medium dry completely.

**Step 9**

Clean the outside of the glass.

Use a paper towel and glass cleaner to

remove the wax pencil marks from the outside surface of the glass.

## Painting and Finishing

Paint provides an attractive background for your prints, especially when the chosen paint color works with the colors in the prints. When prints and a painted background are seen together, the glass takes on the appearance of hand-painted porcelain. The look is especially striking in a glass vase.

To choose a background color, I study the colors in the prints and decide if I want a paint color that coordinates or contrasts. For a seamless background, I choose a background color that matches the background of the cutouts. For an overall pattern of cutouts applied to the entire surface, I often pick a color that is common to most of the prints, to highlight and draw out that color in the prints. To accentuate a silhouetted cutout, I choose a background color that contrasts with the predominant color of the print. Of course, you can create a soft monochromatic flow of color from the prints to the background color, keeping the eye moving across the arrangement of prints and background. For inspiration, peruse a catalog of china patterns or take your cues from fashion, studying the colorways on fabric for ideas. Dress and drapery fabric, table linens, and sheets can inspire your color choices. If you do your designing on a computer, you can drop in different colors that appeal to you to see which one works best.

Choose a paint that offers good coverage. I use liquid acrylic craft paint on the background surface of glass because it adheres well, dries quickly, is water-soluble, and cleans up with soap and water. I have tried spray paints, but they seemed complicated to use. The paint goes on in a much thinner film, so more coats were required to cover a surface, and of course, I needed an outdoor setup to avoid breathing in the vapors.

The brush and the way you handle it are key to successful application of the paint. It is important to pat or buff on a thin, even coat until the glass and the back of the prints are concealed. More often than not, you will need a second coat for full opaque coverage. It is better to apply two thin coats of paint, allowing the paint to dry between coats, than to lather on one thick coat that can sag and run, take longer to dry, and have a greater chance of peeling off the glass.

I have used two kinds of brushes to apply paint to glass: a foam brush and a soft plump watercolor brush in the style of a Japanese hake brush. A foam brush holds paint well and will lay down a smooth coat if it is used gently in a patting motion; if moved in a vigorous or sweeping motion, the foam can scrape off some paint and leave streaks on the glass. A hake brush holds paint well in its soft, plump "bundle" of animal-hair bristles and lays down an even layer of paint without streaking when short circular strokes are used to buff or pat on the paint. Lay down the paint in moderate amounts, spreading it in overlapping patches and smoothing each area with the soft bristles before moving on to the next area. One coat covers approximately 90 percent of the area, and the second coat should catch any thin patches that remain.

In a pinch, I have also used an old blush brush (designed for applying cosmetic powders). If you want to recycle a blush brush, make sure its bristles are secure; loose bristles can get stuck in the paint and mar the finish. To test your blush brush, tug on the bristles to see if any come out in your hand. If they do, do not use the brush.

## Technique: Painting a Flat Glass Surface

A plate is perhaps the easiest glass surface to paint because the entire design area is within reach. When you are finished painting the underside of your plate, set it upside down on a can to elevate the rim off the work surface while the paint dries and cures.

## MATERIALS AND TOOLS

Glass plate, with sealed decoupage
  (for Spanish Dancer original art,
  see page 705)
Acrylic craft paint, in chosen background
  color
Acrylic medium-and-varnish
Self-adhesive felt bumpers
Foam brush
Soft, plump watercolor brush (Japanese-
  style hake brush)
Narrow paintbrush
Craft knife or single-edge razor blade
Small dish
Paper towels
Disposable gloves
Large can (to elevate plate)

**Step 1**

Apply the first coat of paint.

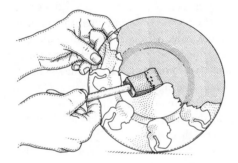

Use a foam brush or a plump watercolor brush to lay down a moderate amount of acrylic craft paint onto the entire back of the plate, except for the rim; do cover the backs of the prints. Use a gentle patting or buffing action so as not to leave brush marks or sweep paint under any print edges that may have lifted up. Apply paint in overlapping patches and pat each area smooth before moving on to the next area. Let the paint dry to the touch, approximately 2 hours.

**Step 2**

Apply a second coat of paint.

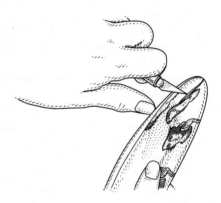

Repeat step 1 to apply a second coat of paint to the entire back of the plate. When the

---

## Working Tips: Removing Paint from a Plate Rim

There are several remedies when paint collects on the rim of a plate. Use a wet finger to carefully stroke a wet drip along the rim until the paint thins. Then wipe the rim clean with a moist cotton swab. If the paint is already dry to the touch, but not fully cured, it will still be somewhat elastic and you can shave off drips with a craft knife or single-edge razor blade. Slice diagonally downward for a clean trim line. Paint that has dried to a hard crust can also be shaved off, but it is likely to chip and flake in the process. Touch up chipped areas with a narrow brush, applying the paint in two thin coats.

paint is dry to the touch, but not fully cured, use a craft knife with a fresh blade or a single-edge razor blade to shave off any accidental drips on the edge of the plate, slicing diagonally downward to avoid chipping the paint. If necessary, touch up any bare spots on the shaved areas using matching paint and a narrow paintbrush. Elevate the plate off the work surface by setting it, paint side up, on top of a can. Let the paint dry overnight.

### Step 3

Apply a sealer to the painted surface.

Use a damp brush to apply a thin, smooth coat of acrylic medium-and-varnish to the back of the plate and the prints. Let the medium/varnish dry, but not cure, and then apply a second coat in the same way. Let the medium/varnish dry completely.

### Step 4

Protect the bottom of the plate.

Add self-adhesive felt bumpers to the flat part of the plate bottom just inside the rim to prevent abrasion.

## Technique: Painting a Glass Vessel

Painting the interior of a glass vessel can be tricky, especially if the opening is narrow or the item is tall. Use a long-handled brush and apply the paint from the bottom up to avoid bumping your hand against a previously painted surface. Allow for a slightly longer drying time because of the reduced air circulation.

### MATERIALS AND TOOLS

Glass vase, with sealed decoupage
   (for Roses original art, see pages
   704 and 724)
Acrylic craft paint, in chosen background
   color
Foam brush or soft, plump watercolor
   brush with long handle
Craft knife with fresh blade or single-edge
   razor blade

### Step 1

Apply the first coat of paint.

Use a long-handled foam brush or plump watercolor brush to pat or buff on a thin, smooth coat of paint to the interior of the vase, beginning at the bottom and moving up in a spiral pattern. Apply the paint in moderate amounts in overlapping patches, patting each area smooth before moving on to the next area. Avoid brushstrokes that could sweep paint under print edges that may have lifted up. Continue until you reach the top rim, but do not apply paint there. Let the paint dry for several hours.

### Step 2

Apply the second coat of paint.

When the first coat is dry but not cured, repeat step 1 to apply the second coat of paint. Applying the second coat before the first coat is allowed to cure promotes a good bond between the two layers.

### Step 3

Refine the finish.

When the second coat is dry to the touch but not fully cured, use a craft knife or single-edge razor blade to shave off any stray brushstrokes around the rim. Use a narrow paintbrush to touch up any bare or chipped spots. Let the paint dry completely.

## Technique: Sealing the Surface

The finish applied to the interior of a painted vase may not be seen, but it performs the essential function of protecting the painted surface from scratches and nicks that occur with normal handling. Apply a sealer on a cool, dry day, as humidity will prolong drying time. Work outdoors in a dust-free environment or in a room that has fresh air and cross-ventilation. An oversized empty carton can be adapted to protect the project from settling dust as the sealer dries and cures.

MATERIALS AND TOOLS

Glass vase, with decoupage prints, interior painted

Acrylic medium-and-varnish

Foam brush

Small dish

Oversize cardboard carton

Utility knife

**Step 1**

Make a cardboard drying booth.

Use a utility knife to cut away two adjacent sides from a six-sided cardboard carton. Invert the carton so that the openings are at the bottom and front and set the vase inside to see if it fits. For ample air circulation, there should be at least 3" (7.6 cm) clearance between the top of the vase and the ceiling of the booth.

**Step 2**

Apply two coats of sealer.

Pour some medium-and-varnish in a clean dish. Dampen a foam brush in water and squeeze it out. Use the moistened brush and light pressure to apply a thin, smooth coat of medium-and-varnish to the interior of the vase, beginning at the bottom and moving up in a spiral pattern. Avoid pressing hard to prevent bubbles from forming. Lift the brush in an upward arc at the end of each stroke to prevent the sealer from pooling or forming drips or rollovers. Overlap new strokes just slightly. Set the vase, mouth side up, in the drying booth. Let the sealer dry. Apply a second coat of sealer in the same way.

**Step 3**

Let the sealer dry completely and cure.

Set the vase in the drying booth and allow the sealer to dry completely and cure. Even though the medium feels dry to the touch, it will need additional time to cure and bond to the painted surface. Read the instructions on the jar of acrylic medium-and-varnish for the manufacturer's recommended drying times.

# PROJECTS

## Zebra: A Decorative Platter

This striking zebra design highlights the stark graphic contrast between black and white. The animal-print pattern is applied to a metal platter in two ways: as a central motif and as an enlarged stripe pattern used in the border.

MATERIALS AND TOOLS

Zebra original art (page 706)

Laser copier, or computer scanner and laser printer

Metal platter, 14" (35.6 cm) square with raised sides and 2"-wide (5.1 cm) flat rim

White acrylic spray paint

Oil-based spray metal primer
Decoupage medium
Acrylic medium-and-varnish
Black permanent marker
Foam brush
Tapered watercolor paintbrush
Emery cloth, fine-grit (120)
Sanding block, hard rubber
Tack cloth
Steel ruler
Self-healing cutting mat
Straight-blade scissors
Manicure scissors
Craft knife
Distilled white vinegar solution
Soft rag
Small dish

## Step 1

Make the copies.

Use a laser copier, or a computer scanner and laser printer, to copy the zebra, enlarging it to measure approximately 7½" (19.1 cm) from nose to tail. Enlarge any section of the zebra body at 300 percent to make a pattern of wide stripes for the border. Make four copies of the enlarged border pattern, each at least 2½" × 8½" (6.4 × 21.6 cm), to fit the border rims on the platter. If the borders on your platter are a different size, adjust the measurements accordingly.

## Step 2

Prepare the prints.

Use scissors to rough-cut the zebra print, leaving an ample margin around the figure. Use manicure scissors to cut out the zebra animal. Test-fit the zebra-patterned border strips on the platter. Use a craft knife, steel ruler, and cutting mat to trim the strips neatly to size.

## Step 3

Prepare the metal surface.

Use a rag soaked in the vinegar solution to clean off grease and fingerprints from the metal platter. Dry the platter thoroughly with paper towels. Working outdoors if possible and using a spray booth to contain the overspray, apply two thin, even coats of oil-based spray primer to all surfaces of the platter, working in sections. Let the primer dry for 2 hours so that the solvents evaporate completely. Then apply two coats of white acrylic spray paint to all the primed metal surfaces, allowing the first coat of acrylic paint to dry before applying the second. Let the second coat dry overnight. Use fine-grit (120) emery cloth to sand the painted surfaces. Remove the dust with a tack cloth. Use a foam brush to apply a coat of acrylic medium-and-varnish to seal the painted surfaces; let it dry.

## Step 4

Lay out the design and apply the prints.

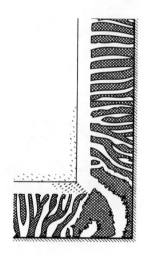

Lay the border strips, pattern side down, on a protected work surface. Apply a thin, even coat of decoupage medium to one strip. Position the strip onto a segment of the platter border and press gently to adhere. Position and glue the remaining strips to the platter border, trimming the ends so they butt one another. Let the decoupage medium dry. Then use a black marker to connect the stripes at each of the corners, widening or adding stripes, as desired. Adhere the zebra cutout to the center of the platter.

**Step 5**

Apply the finish.

Use a foam brush to apply two thin, even coats of acrylic medium-and-varnish to all surfaces, allowing the first coat to dry before applying the second. Let the finish dry overnight. Let the platter cure before displaying it.

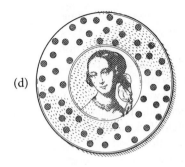
(d)

## Head Shots: Theme-and-Variation Dessert Plates

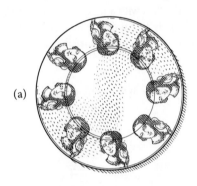
(a)

(b)

(c)

The appeal of decoupage plates is that you can make any quantity of plates in any style. You can bring together an eclectic mix of images or you can focus on a single motif, such as roses (my favorite), architecture, vegetables, or a monogram in a variety of typefaces. An image of a dancer inspired the dessert plates pictured here. Using a scanner and a laser printer, I copied only the dancer's head, rescaling it in several sizes to create a quirky but coordinated service for four. Plates with prints glued to the underside can be used to serve cookies and pastries, and the top glass surface wipes clean with a damp cloth. Hung on a wall in groups or in a row, a collection of decoupage plates can form an eye-catching display.

### MATERIALS AND TOOLS

Spanish Dancer original art (page 705)
Monogram original art (page 707)
Laser copier, or computer scanner and laser printer
4 dessert plates, 7" (17.8 cm) in diameter
Self-adhesive bumpers
Acrylic craft paint, in chartreuse, orange, white, pink, and black
Decoupage medium
Acrylic medium-and-varnish
Self-healing cutting mat
Manicure scissors
Craft knife
Narrow watercolor paintbrush
Foam brush
Poster putty
Glass cleaner

Paper towels
Pencil
Small dish
Cotton swabs

## Step 1

Prepare the prints.

Use a laser copier or a computer scanner and laser printer to make copies of the dancer's head and the initial or monogram of your choice. You'll need eight small heads 1½" (3.8 cm) high, one large head 6½" (16.5 cm) high, one extra-large head 8" (20.3 cm) high, one medium head 4" (10.2 cm) high, and an initial or monogram 1¼" (3.2 cm) high.

## Step 2

Prepare the glass plates.

Use glass cleaner and paper to remove any grease or fingerprints from the four glass plates. Dry the plates thoroughly.

## Step 3

Lay out the design and glue the prints.

Use poster putty to apply the head images and monogram to the top surfaces of the plates, referring to the illustrations for placement. Mark dash lines with a wax pencil on the glass surface to indicate the placement. Lift off one print, remove the putty, and use a foam brush to apply decoupage medium to the image side. Press the image side of the print against the underside of its plate. Use your wet or gluey fingertips to slide the image into position as you view it through the glass from the top. Continue until all of the prints are adhered. Let the glue dry completely.

## Step 4

Paint the plates.

Use a foam brush to apply two thin, even coats of paint to the back of three plates. Use chartreuse paint for the plate with eight heads (a). Use orange paint for the plate with the monogram (b). Use white paint for the plate with the extra-large head (c). On the plate

with the medium head (d), use a cotton swab to paint black polka dots in a random pattern around the print. Let the black paint dry completely and then use a foam brush to paint the background pink. Before the second coat on each plate is fully dry, use a craft knife or single-edge razor blade to remove stray paint from the rim. Use a fine paintbrush for touch-ups, if needed. Let all the paint dry overnight.

## Step 5

Seal the plates.

Use a foam brush to apply two thin, even coats of acrylic medium-and-varnish to the back of each plate, allowing the first coat to dry before applying the second. Let the sealer dry overnight. Let the sealer cure 2 to 3 weeks before using the plates.

## Step 6 (optional)

Protect the foot of each plate.

Add self-adhesive felt bumpers to the bottom of each plate's inner rim to prevent abrasion.

## Swimming Lessons: A Vase

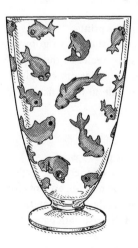

The decoupage design on this vase works on the principle of flow. Each individual fish motif is seen in relation to those around it, with the result that the fish appear to be swimming inside the vase. The same conceptual approach would work well with images of birds, butterflies, or insects. The fish on this vase range from 1½" to 3¼" (3.8 to 8.3 cm) long.

## MATERIALS AND TOOLS

Gift wrap, fish design, in apricot
  and steel blue
Glass vase, 13" × 7" diameter (33.0 ×
  17.8 cm), with clear plastic insert
Acrylic craft paint, in robin's-egg blue
Decoupage medium
Spray sealer
Acrylic medium-and-varnish
Self-healing cutting mat
Manicure scissors
Craft knife or single-edge razor blade
Tapered paintbrush
Foam brush
Poster putty
Wax pencil
Small dish
Glass cleaner
Paper towels
Cotton swabs

### Step 1

Prepare the prints.

Strengthen the gift wrap by applying two coats of spray sealer to the image side of the print. Let the sealer dry completely. Use scissors to cut out 30 to 35 fish motifs from the gift wrap.

### Step 2

Clean the glass vase.

Use glass cleaner and paper towels to remove grease and fingerprints from the glass vase. Thoroughly dry the interior and exterior surfaces of the vase with paper towels.

### Step 3

Lay out the design and glue the prints.

Use poster putty to stick the prints onto the exterior of the vase in a random pattern. Mark dash lines with a wax pencil on the exterior glass surface to indicate the fish placement. Pour some decoupage medium into a small dish. Lift off one print, remove the putty, and use a foam brush to apply decoupage medium to the image side. Press the image side of the print against the interior of the vase, using the wax pencil lines on the exterior as a guide. Continue until all of the prints are adhered. Let the glue dry completely.

### Step 4

Paint the vase.

Use a foam brush to pat a thin coat of acrylic paint onto the interior of the vase, beginning at the bottom of the vase and working upward in a spiral until you reach the top rim. Avoid sweeping strokes that would leave brush marks or force paint underneath any edges that may have lifted. Allow the paint to dry. Apply a second coat. Before the second coat is fully dry, use a craft knife or single-edge razor blade to remove stray paint from the rim. Use a fine paintbrush and matching paint for touch-ups, if needed.

### Step 5

Seal the vase.

Use a foam brush to apply two thin, even coats of acrylic medium-and-varnish to the painted surface, working from the bottom up in a spiral pattern; allow the sealer to dry after each coat. Use a paper towel to remove the wax pencil marks from the outside of the vase. Let the sealer cure before using the vase. Use the plastic insert to hold flowers in water to prevent damage to the decoupage surface.

# CHAPTER SIX

# Decorative Embellishing

## THE HEART

### One Pathway to Joy

"Art is not an end in itself. It introduces the soul into a higher spiritual order, which it expresses and in some sense explains."

—Thomas Merton,
*No Man Is an Island,* 1955

In popular crafting, embellishing is the art of adding ribbons, trims, passements, and like ornamentation to an object, particularly to soft furnishings and apparel. However, for me, embellishing encompasses more than the traditional techniques exacted by needle and thread. It includes any decoration added to beautify an object or a space—tying a ribbon bow to a gift box, festooning an office bulletin board with notes and souvenirs, or gluing wood appliqués to a frame. Embellishing is more than the materials and techniques we use; it is our way of making an object or a space our very own, adding touches that represent and connect us to the places where we live and work, revealing what we love and value.

How we choose our materials and techniques to embellish isn't unknown to us. We know what we like and respond to, and we are guided by our natural sensitivities, ones that cause us to lose ourselves in the chocolate-colored rivulets of grain that course through wood, to raise a piece of just-cut pine to our noses to breathe in the pitch of an ancient forest, to listen for the barely audible "tick" of size so we can begin to lay down gossamer-thin sheets of gold leaf, or perhaps, to run our fingertips over the surface of a piece of polished wood. We may not be able to explain all of the reasons why we do these things, but that is hardly the point. We surrender to our inclinations and see where they take us.

Before I start a project, I often lay out the materials. I will spread swaths of silk velvet, pristine and perfect, across my dining room table. I will be absorbed in the color—one an expanse of chartreuse with glowing pools of yellow so lemony they make my mouth water and another that looks like it was dipped in the juice of ripe berries. I will find myself wandering by the table simply to run my hand over the delicate nap of each shimmering piece, pushing the velvet into undulating folds. I know I am not alone in this. Ask any painter who works with oils and you will hear about the satisfying top note of turpentine or the subtle bounce of newly stretched canvas when the brush strokes its surface. Knitters who work beads into their designs are soothed by the familiar tug of yarn on their finger and the utter roundness of the pearl they move into place, producing not just a row of textured stitches, but a fabric that satisfies and protects.

By allowing our natural affinities to guide us to the materials and techniques we work with, we gain awareness of our creative selves and express it with more authenticity and joy. At least this has been my experience, but it wasn't until I was seven years old when a certain lesson in embroidery changed the locus of my hand crafting from outside to in. I didn't know it at the time, but the shift was transformative, changing my approach to learning, crafting, and living.

My mother was sitting next to me, teaching me to embroider. Our shoulders were touching, the sweet fragrance of her perfume sharing the space between us. As she handed me the needle, she said, "Measure the length of your thread by stretching it from here to here (she touched my breast bone with one hand and held the fingers on my outstretched hand with the other). When you fold the thread over, you will have a good working length."

I threaded my needle. It pierced the cloth and the floss emitted a hoarse whisper as it traveled through the linen stretched taut in an embroidery hoop. Untethered by a knot, the thread flew free. My mother explained, "You don't use a knot to begin or end a strand. Instead, sew a few stitches forward and then stitch back over them to secure your thread. It's neater that way." I struggled to make one careful stitch at a time, stopping to complain when the thread became trapped under the cloth. "Hold the thread against the back of the linen as you pull out the needle to keep the thread from tangling," she said as she gently pressed my finger under the cloth. I was very impatient, but there was no way to rush through this.

For reasons unknown to me then, I settled into the lesson, half of me in the room and the other half imagining that I was the embroidery floss, plunging beneath the woven fabric and parting the threads and then rising up and over them as I broke through to the linen's surface, leaving a wake of uneven stitches, bright blue and shining, on the cloth. It was not the last time I would find myself at one with my materials.

Ever since my mother taught me to

embroider, I have learned many other embellishing techniques and through them have experienced the same connection, resulting in embellishments that fill my home with color and pattern, sparkle and light. Unable to resist the pull of light-catching crystals—sharp-edged, water-clear, and accented with florets—and plump glass fruit in jewel colors, I attached every one I found or inherited to one chandelier, until it groaned under the excessive weight and we began to worry that one day the chandelier would rip out of the ceiling and land on our dog sleeping beneath it. Eventually, new chandeliers were hung to catch the glacial overflow. Corners, shelves, and tables were populated by embellished items drawn from a circulating collection of hand-painted vases, needlepoint and embossed-velvet pillows, animal print throws, etched glass, gilded statues, beribboned lampshades, and armloads of hand-painted roses. Some decorative embellishments were more permanent than others. A bold graphic of a chandelier remained as it was first screen-printed on the wall. Slabs of white marble, originally designed for rolling out pastry dough, had been pushed together on a mahogany hunt board and still held a mountain range of framed photographs of everyone in the family. A hand-painted screen emblazoned with baskets of lush fruit still formed the romantic backdrop of a pink couch. However, there were changes, too. The hand-painted silk roses that once filled an urn in the fireplace were separated into smaller bouquets—some held in vases, some bunched together on a wreath, and a few single blooms, stems cut short, pinned to the arm of a couch.

There have been many other necessary changes. Favorite projects continue to be rotated through different rooms, somehow taking on more character and meaning in their new settings, and some favorites have been given away to the kids, opening up new space that oftentimes went unadorned because I began to want less pretty clutter and more visually quiet space. When I set about clearing a space, I did not throw anything away, a vestige of the "waste not, want not" philosophy I was raised with. Instead, I always donated what I was ready to part with to a local charity or church.

My embellished things have brought me happiness, a return on my investment of so much pleasure in their making. Admittedly, it is joy that is most common to my creative experiences, the feeling that I am one with my work. It is as if there is some strange alchemy, enlarging me and transforming my handmade things to more than the sum of the materials I use.

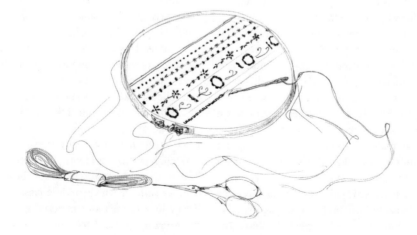

In crafting, there are moments when we abandon all effort and find our joy not simply in the materials or the procedures but in the state of crafting itself. In the end, it is this awareness, I believe, that elevates a craft project from an ordered assembly of materials to an artful expression of the human spirit.

## A Brief History

Embellishing is the art of applied ornamentation. It has been practiced throughout history for cultural, aesthetic, and spiritual reasons on everything from Egyptian gilded tombs to English embroidered ecclesiastical vestments, from costumes of the French court to Czechoslovakian etched glass. Materials for embellishing include metal leaf, passements, thread, chemical formulations, and tools, and the methods of application can involve the highest levels of artistry. Although embellishments historically benefited but a select few—the Pharaoh rather than the foot soldier—they helped define a culture. Only in the modern age has embellishing become an avenue of individual expression open to all.

Decorative embellishing has been a preoccupation of noble families for centuries, the perfect way to flaunt wealth, knowledge, and sophistication. Sculptural ornamentation, embroidery and needlepoint, lace and woven trims, beadwork, carving, etching, gilding, and painting were among the mediums the aristocracy used to adorn clothing, furnishings, and interior and exterior architecture. Motifs and materials varied from century to century and region to region; styles and colors that were popular in one age could easily be passé in the next. The Middle Ages showed a keen interest in signs and symbols; designs that incorporated animals, plants, persons, heraldry, and even numbers could tell a story or reveal a family history or motto. By the early eighteenth century, increased trade with China and India brought exotic birds and flowers, pagodas, and other chinoiserie into the height of fashion. The

Empire style celebrated the victories of Napoleon through Egyptian and contemporary military motifs: laurel wreaths, medallions, and imperial eagles, swans, and lions. The degree of embellishment considered fashionable also waxed and waned. Most notable is how the superabundance of the Baroque period, spanning one hundred fifty years beginning in 1600, gave way to the orderly, manicured, symmetrical ideal of Neoclassical design.

The middle and lower classes in Europe and the American colonies used various methods to emulate upper-class embellishments. Those who admired but could not afford relief statuary, ormolu, or architectural moldings and cornices used paint to replicate or reinterpret these features. Flowers, vines, shells, and other motifs painted on furniture could mimic more expensive three-dimensional decoration. A notable example is the painted furniture of eighteenth-century Sweden, which, like the rococo style that inspired it, is light in color and sometimes gilded. For those who couldn't afford hand-painted murals, there was wallpaper. For those who couldn't afford wallpaper, there was stenciling.

In many areas of Europe and Asia, distinctive embroidery motifs and techniques, handed down through generations of needleworkers among the peasantry, adorned folkloric dress worn for special occasions, such as weddings. Ethnic groups within Poland, Hungary, Russia, and Ukraine, for example, could each be identified by their own unique needlework style. This type of embellishment was pursued not as an avenue for individual creative expression but rather to display affinity and solidarity with one's cultural community.

Up through the eighteenth and nineteenth centuries, ordinary people did hand needlework largely for utilitarian purposes, such as making, repairing, or identifying clothing and linens. The Industrial Revolution brought a distinct shift in which middle-class families began to acquire more material goods and more luxury items. Lace, for example, once a luxury embellishment for the very wealthy, could now be factory made.

Embellishing as a hobby reached critical mass in ordinary people's lives during the Victorian era of the British Empire. For the first time in the history of the world, people had the leisure time, the materials, and the space to pursue needlework, drawing, watercolor painting, and other pastimes that in previous centuries were hallmarks of upper-class life; it was also an age of travel, cultural exhibitions, and scientific discovery, so inspiration was everywhere. Berlin woolwork and crazy quilting were two forms of needlework embellishment that were immensely popular.

In the early twentieth century, timesaving appliances for the homemaker put the accent on science and efficiency (think home economics), which allowed even more time (or at least the illusion of it) for needlework and crafts. Women's magazines from the 1920s through the 1950s kept readers well supplied with project ideas, patterns, and instructions for embellishing homes and wardrobes. By midcentury, people were seeing modern and historical home interiors in movies, magazines, and on television and coming away with ideas for their own dwellings. If they couldn't afford a brand-new decor, perhaps a few strategic embellishments, like ball fringe on the curtains or long strands of beads hung in an entrance, could give their interior a facelift.

The prosperity of the 1980s and 1990s generated a taste for luxury goods that spilled over into the craft market. True to the historical pattern, designs favored by the well-heeled could be replicated by middle-class do-it-yourselfers. Kits, classes, and instruction books on faux finishes, gilding, patinating, and glass etching reached the marketplace, and safe, modern formulas with soap-and-water cleanup enhanced their appeal. Activities once regarded as work had become leisure-time pursuits. In the early twenty-first century, salvaging and repurposing are the new embellishing bywords, as crafters and artists turn found objects, collections, and all manner of odds and ends into embellishments that both mimic the past and break new ground.

## THE SCIENCE

For sure, there is a science at work in decorative embellishing, evidenced in the prescribed sequence of steps to achieve a creative goal, but there is alchemy, too. Decorative embellishing is an invitation to allow those processes to unfold before your eyes, to practice them until they are second nature. When you follow your natural inclination to express yourself through materials and methods that mean something to you, your creativity reaches its full flowering. Decorative embellishing is about authenticity, about discovering who you are through your own unique choices, be they odd or conventional. In the end, the rules do not apply. You don't have to explain or figure out the underlying reasons for your kind of embellishing. Fanciful, seriously disciplined, or somewhere in between, what matters is that you decide what to do to make your projects and your space your own.

You'll enjoy ample technical support; the digital speed and facility of computers and laser copiers, along with improved products, such as water-based size and reformulated etching cream, provide shortcuts that do not compromise crafting results. You will find that you can make decorative embellishments that look rich but are well within your budget. Start anywhere in this chapter, choosing from a range of embellishments: glass etching, gilding, dry embossing, ribbons and trims, decals and heat-transfers, candle making and ornamentation, restoration of old chandeliers and picture frames, and picassiette. Each discussion begins with basic techniques and builds on the fundamentals.

### Glass Etching

The look of etched glass is unmistakable—the frosty patina of the etched design lays in contrast to the sparkling transparency of the glass. Glass has traditionally been etched in one of two ways: by physical abrasion, such as sandblasting or grinding, or by a chemical reaction. The chemical that comes in contact with the glass eats away the very top of the surface, microns thin, permanently changing its appearance from clear to frosted.

The chemical etching cream used today is effective after a minute of contact time. A stencil technique is used to mask some areas of the glass and leave others exposed to create permanently etched designs. The masks you apply can be free-form in nature, such as a random pattern of stars or flowers, or they can fall in strict, linear patterns, such as stripes or geometric shapes that are precisely arranged and spaced. If you are new to glass etching, start with a simple design that doesn't require measuring. You can practice your etching technique on a recycled glass jar before working on your project piece. Just about any glass item can be etched; exceptions to avoid are ovenproof glass (such as Pyrex), lead crystal, and glass with a coated surface.

Materials and Tools

- **Glass item to etch**

Most glass items with smooth surfaces can be etched. Examples include drinking glasses, votive candleholders, mirrors, glass plates, and glass vases. Three exceptions are Pyrex, coated glass, and lead crystal objects. Colored glass can be etched as long as the color is in the glass and not a coating on the surface. A colored surface coating will peel off or degrade when exposed to the chemicals in etching cream.

## Glass Etching Materials and Tools at a Glance

- **Etching cream**

- **Brushes**

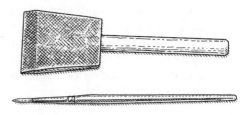

A creamy chemical compound, etching cream is formulated to etch most glass surfaces with which it comes into contact (exceptions are noted on page 420). The etching is permanent and appears as a fine frosting on the topmost layer of the glass. Caution is advised when using etching cream as it is a powerful chemical product. Etchants also come in liquid form; however, a liquid etching agent requires submersion of the glass item and raises safety issues beyond the scope of this chapter.

- **Masking material**

Any sturdy, water-resistant, self-adhesive material that can adhere tightly to a glass surface is suited to glass etching. A mask blocks access to the glass and determines the size and shape of the non-etched design. Strips of tape will block a linear section of the glass; stickers, such as stationery circles, will block round sections; and transfer stencils will conceal more defined areas of the glass, according to their motif.

A disposable foam brush is used to apply etching cream to large design areas with bold shapes. For small designs, use a tapered watercolor brush or other soft-bristle brush.

- **Timer or watch with second hand**
Any timer, especially one that is digital, or a watch that indicates the passing of seconds, will help you restrict the etching cream action to the time recommended by the manufacturer, usually 1 minute.

- **Disposable and rubber gloves**

Etching cream contains active ingredients (ammonium and sodium bifluorides) that are very caustic to the skin. It is extremely important to protect your hands and arms by wearing close-fitting disposable gloves and long sleeves so that the etching cream does not come into direct contact with your skin. While disposable gloves are convenient for such tasks as applying the etching cream, rubber gloves are recommended when using very hot water to clean a glass vase.

- **Other supplies**

  You will also need spray glass cleaner, liquid dishwashing soap, baking soda, a cellulose sponge, a plastic bucket, paper towels, and pH strips. Nonembossed towels are less linty. A test kit with pH strips is useful for testing waste water to ensure it can be disposed of properly.

## Working with Etching Cream

Etching cream contains ammonium and sodium bifluorides, strong chemicals that permanently etch the surface of glass, producing a frosted appearance. To ensure that the etching cream performs as intended, read and follow the manufacturer's directions and safety precautions.

You'll need to work in a well-ventilated room with ready access to running water. Protect your work space with newsprint or a disposable plastic bag that has been cut and taped to the work surface. Wear a long-sleeved shirt, rubber or disposable gloves, and safety glasses to avoid getting the cream on your skin or in your eyes. Always clean your work area and sink of any etching cream residue to prevent damage to those surfaces. Etching cream will not damage a stainless steel sink but it will remove the protective glaze from a ceramic sink. You can set a plastic bucket in the sink to collect the chemical-laden rinse water and then neutralize it with baking soda before pouring it down the drain—an eco-smart move that is easy on your ceramic sink as well as on the environment.

Ideally, the etching cream, the glass item to be etched, and the work environment should be above 70°F (21.1°C). If the bottle of etching cream is cold, submerge the closed container in a cup of hot tap water for 10 minutes to raise its temperature. Blend the etching cream before using it by shaking the closed container to evenly distribute the crystals suspended in the cream. The cream is patted onto the glass surface and covers any masks that have been applied. A tapered brush is useful to gently tamp the cream within the designated area should you discover a bare patch. Clock the etching time carefully and be prompt about rinsing off the etching cream when the allotted time is done. A large glass surface should be etched in small sections so that the time the cream remains on the surface is as close to the same time for all areas as possible; however, be aware that some areas may still show slight differences in the character of the etching. When working on several small projects, such as a set of matching glasses, etch one glass completely before beginning another.

Preparation is key when etching glass. The glass surface must be scrupulously clean before the masks or cream are applied. Grease and fingerprints, even faint traces, will prevent masks from adhering properly or the cream from etching uniformly. Use a lint-free cloth or a nonembossed paper towel to dry glass after cleaning it. Avoid using a glass cleaner formulated to resist fingerprints as the protective residue can interfere with the etching chemistry. Once a glass is cleaned, handle it with paper towels to avoid reintroducing trace amounts of oil from your fingers until the etching is complete.

---

## Caution: Safe Disposal of Rinse Water

Etching cream is corrosive even when diluted in water. When you are rinsing off the etching cream from your glass, work at the sink but let the rinse water drain into a plastic bucket. Add baking soda to the rinse water to neutralize it, testing it with a pH strip (used to test water in swimming pools). When the rinse water tests neutral, you can safely pour it down a drain.

---

Choosing etchable glass is also key to a satisfying outcome. Glass quality can vary widely, depending on how and for what purpose the glass item was manufactured, and etching tends to accentuate flaws and discolorations. If you are uncertain about whether a glass item is suited to etching, apply a tiny dab of etching cream on an obscure place, wait a minute, and wash it off. Glass that is ovenproof or coated will not etch well, and your test spot will reveal it.

## Technique: Basic Glass Etching

The basics of etching are straightforward but require your full attention. This exercise will acquaint you with the setup, sequence of steps, and timing of glass etching. An easy first project is a cube-style votive candleholder or other small glass item. The basic etching technique is the same whether or not a mask is applied. The foam brush must be narrow enough to fit into the opening of the jar of etching cream.

### MATERIALS AND TOOLS

Glass item to etch
Masking material
Etching cream
Foam brush, 1" (2.5 cm) wide
Tapered paintbrush
Timer
Small dish
Sink with hot and cold running water
Plastic bucket
Safety glasses
Disposable gloves (for applying the
    etching cream)
Rubber gloves (for washing the glass)
Spray glass cleaner
Dishwashing liquid
Baking soda
Test kit with pH strips
Paper towels, nonembossed (for less lint)
Newsprint or plastic sheet
Masking tape
Teaspoon

**Step 1**
Set up your work area.

Choose a well-ventilated room with access to a sink. The air temperature should be above 70°F (21.1°C). Protect your work surface with newsprint or plastic and tape down the edges. If the bottle of etching cream is cold, submerge the closed container in a cup of hot tap water for 10 minutes to raise its temperature. Set the plastic bucket in the sink. Have the other supplies close at hand.

**Step 2**
Clean the glass.

Use spray glass cleaner and lint-free paper towels to remove any fingerprints or grease from the glass. Dry the item thoroughly.

**Step 3**
Apply the mask.

Wash your hands to remove any surface oils and dry them completely. Use tweezers to lift and transfer the selected mask to the glass, smoothing the mask flat against the glass to remove any air trapped underneath and using the back of your fingernail or a teaspoon to press down the edges of the mask against the glass.

**Step 4**
Apply the etching cream to the glass.

Wear a long-sleeve shirt and put on disposable gloves and safety glasses. Shake the bottle of etching cream. Dip the foam brush a third of the way into the cream and use a patting motion to apply a thick layer of etching cream over the outside of the glass, covering the masks. Check for bare spots and use a tapered brush to redistribute the cream for even coverage. Immediately set the timer for 1 minute or for the etching time recommended by the manufacturer.

## Step 5

Complete the etching.

Let the cream stand on the surface of the glass for the allotted time. Put on rubber gloves. When the timer sounds, immediately wash off the etching cream under a gentle stream of warm water, letting it drain into the bucket without splashing. Use your gloved hand to gently wipe off the cream and masks as you continue to bathe the glass under the running water. Discard the used masks safely in a trash bag. Test and neutralize the rinse water before pouring it down the drain. Scrub the sink clean.

## Etching a Mirror

Etching a design on the surface of a glass mirror is no different than etching a sheet of plain glass. The etching cream must, of course, be applied to the front noncoated side of the mirror glass. If possible, remove the mirror from its frame and set the frame and any hardware aside. If the frame cannot be removed, tape off the sides of the frame, paying close attention to the edges where the mirror and frame meet to prevent etching cream from seeping under the frame. Cover all nonstenciled areas of the glass to protect them from the effects of the etching cream when it is rinsed off the mirror. Make sure to dry all of the surfaces thoroughly, using a cotton swab in crevices to absorb any moisture.

## Step 6

Clean and dry the glass.

Peel off and safely discard any remaining mask material. Use warm water and dishwashing liquid to clean the glass. Then use paper towels to dry the glass surface. The areas exposed to the etching cream will appear frosted and feel somewhat rough.

## Designing and Applying Masks

The principle of masking is straightforward. The mask blocks some areas of the glass and allows access to other areas. The mask for an etched design functions as a stencil with the cutouts allowing the etching cream to come into contact with certain parts of the glass and the non-cut areas of the mask blocking access to other parts, preventing the cream from coming into contact and etching the glass. Masks allow you to designate the size and shape of the frosted and unfrosted areas to create designs with positive and negative spaces. (When a motif is frosted and the surrounding area is transparent, the motif occupies positive space; when the area surrounding a motif is frosted, the motif occupies negative space.) Adhesive-backed materials can be used as masks. Stickers in bold shapes are perfect for creating simple graphic designs on glassware. Stationery supplies include circles, rectangular labels, stars, and doughnut-shaped loose-leaf reinforcements. All you need to do is peel the sticker off the backing sheet and stick it to the glass surface, making sure to burnish the edges so the etching cream doesn't seep under them, which will create a ragged etched line. Precut masks are not the only option. Motifs that are easily recognizable by their silhouettes can be cut from adhesive-backed vinyl; birds and flowers have simple outlines and work well in etching. Monograms and numerals can be drawn on the vinyl using a marker, then cut out and placed directly onto the glass; because the masks for etching are "right-reading," you will not need to cut a reverse image.

Masking tape, plastic tape, and vinyl tape (a graphic arts supply) can be used to make stripe patterns. Masking tape is the least resilient of the three and needs more careful handling, whereas plastic and vinyl tapes are very sturdy and can be stretched and pressed to promote firm adhesion to the glass surface without tearing. Attractive designs can be created by combining stripes (strips of tape) and shapes in silhouette (either die-cut stickers or those cut from shelving vinyl). If your glass item is cylindrical, wraparound patterns made of stripes or rows of dots can be very pretty. Stripes can intersect to make crisscross patterns or they can run in a swirl pattern that encircles a vase.

I love designs with linear clarity and decided to use stripes in a simple geometric arrangement to replicate that straightforward sensibility on a modern glass tumbler and decanter. Separate pieces with smooth transparent surfaces selectively etched can be mixed and layered to create the visual interplay. When a glass item with vertical stripes is placed over another glass item with horizontal stripes, a third grid pattern appears at the overlap. Achieving perfectly spaced parallel stripes in a mask pattern requires some measuring and a good eye. A T square can help you line up the critical first strip that will serve as a guide to align the others. For vertical stripes on a glass, rest the crossbar of the T square on the rim of the glass (to form a chord) and press the measuring bar against the side of the glass. Run a china marker along the edge of the measuring bar to mark the position of the first strip of tape; you can mark just the rim and foot if the glass is short, connecting the points with a length of tape; or you can mark the full length,

if you prefer. The tape is stretched slightly and placed onto the glass at the markings. If my stripe pattern has narrow intervals, I usually eyeball the placement of the subsequent strips, using a ruler to confirm my guesses as I work. For a design with more widely spaced stripes, I premeasure and mark the glass so that the tape masks are at even intervals and remain parallel throughout. One strip placed on even a slight tilt can produce a set of stripes that lists dramatically to one side or the other by the time you finish laying down the last strip of tape. If a strip of tape goes a bit off, pull the tape off the glass and start again, straightening the placement of a fresh strip to ensure good adhesion. Another approach for an all-linear design is to set up the first strip of tape on the glass using a ruler and a china marker, but then run strips of tape on the entire surface, pulling off every other strip to create stripes. In this way, the strips of tape become the measuring device, resulting in evenly spaced stripes.

## Technique: Using Stationery Supplies as Masks for Negative-Space Designs

Familiar shapes for this technique include circles, rectangles, stars, and doughnut-shaped loose-leaf reinforcements. An array of stickers on the surface forms a design. The visual effect is created by etching the space that surrounds and defines the chosen motifs. When the masks are removed, these areas appear as clear, transparent glass.

### MATERIALS AND TOOLS

Glass item
Adhesive-backed circles or other shapes, as desired
Tweezers
Spray glass cleaner
Paper towels, nonembossed (for less lint)
Craft stick

### Step 1

Clean the glass.
Use glass cleaner and lint-free paper towels

to remove any fingerprints or grease from the glass. Dry the item thoroughly.

### Step 2
Apply the first mask.

Use tweezers to lift and peel an adhesive-backed circle from its backing sheet. Place the circle, adhesive side down, on the outside of the glass. Use a craft stick or the back of your fingernail to press the edges of the circle against the glass.

### Step 3
Apply the remaining masks.

Repeat step 2 to apply more circles to the glass surface to create a random pattern of dots.

### Step 4
Check the edges.

Hold the glass up to the light to check for any gaps or tears in the edges of the circles and press them against the glass. If a circle is torn or won't stick down, lift it off the glass and clean that area of the glass with glass cleaner and a paper towel. Then affix a new circle in its place.

## Technique: Using Tape as a Mask for Striped Designs

The appeal of tape is that it is easy to apply to a smooth glass surface. Available in several widths, tape is sturdy and flexible and can be stretched slightly, creating a tight hold on a glass surface. Narrow tape is the most forgiving as it rounds soft contours without crinkling or gapping, nearly guaranteeing that etching cream will not seep under the tape and ruin the neat line of frosting. Strips of tape can be applied vertically or horizontally.

### MATERIALS AND TOOLS
2 drinking glasses
Tape, ⅛" (0.3 cm) wide
China marker (optional)
T square
Spray glass cleaner
Paper towels, nonembossed (for less lint)

### Step 1
Clean the glass.

Use glass cleaner and paper towels to remove any fingerprints or grease from the glass. Dry the glass thoroughly using paper towels.

### Step 2
Align and apply the first vertical tape strip.

Hold a T square against the glass, perpendicular to the rim and foot, and make ticks with a china marker at the rim and foot. Cut a length of tape slightly longer than the glass and stretch and press the tape to the glass between the two marks. Fold the extra tape at each end onto itself to make tabs for easy removal of the mask after etching.

### Step 3
Apply the remaining vertical strips.

Apply a second piece of tape alongside and parallel to the first piece so that the long edges are touching but not overlapping. Apply the remaining strips of tape in the same way. Peel off and discard every other strip to expose a pattern of vertical stripes. Use a craft stick or the back of your fingernail to press the edges of the tape against the glass.

### Step 4
Check the edges of the vertical strips.

Hold the glass up to the light and check each strip of tape for lifted edges or tears. Use the back of your fingernail to press any loose edges against the glass. If the tape won't stick down, pull it off the glass and clean that area of the glass with glass cleaner and a paper towel. Then position and press a new strip of tape in its place.

### Step 5
Apply the horizontal strips of tape.

Measure from the lip or bottom rim of the

glass for a horizontal stripe and make several ticks around the glass with a china marker. Cut a length of tape to go around the glass. Stretch and apply this tape around the glass, using the ticks as a guide and overlapping the tape ends when you come full circle. Apply a second piece of tape above and parallel to the first piece so that the long edges are touching but not overlapping. Apply the remaining strips of tape in the same way. Peel off and discard every other strip to expose a pattern of horizontal stripes.

## Step 6

Check the edges of the horizontal strips.

Repeat step 4 to check the edges of the horizontal strips and make any needed replacements.

## Technique: Using Transfer Stencils as Masks

Transfer stencils used as masks allow for intricate, traditional designs—ribbons, flowers, vines, fancy script, numerals—that would not be possible to render with tape or stationery supplies. Etching cream is applied through the open parts of the stencil to reproduce the cutout design as a positive image on the glass. A transfer stencil is made of a blue layer of sticky plastic carried on a backing sheet. When the stencil is placed against glass and burnished, the blue stencil material transfers and affixes to the glass. The carrier sheet is made of tough plastic that will not scratch or rip during burnishing, but it is important not to scrub too hard to avoid marring the delicate stencil material underneath. Each stencil is for one-time use only, so if you are planning to etch your monogram or a floral motif on a set of coasters, be sure to purchase enough stencils for repeats of your project. Choose a transfer stencil carefully, as the contrast between etched and clear surfaces on an article of glass is subtle, at best, and designs that are very delicate or finely detailed may not be easy to read.

MATERIALS AND TOOLS
Glass coaster to etch
Transfer stencil, such as a monogram and floral borders
Glass cleaner
Paper towels, nonembossed (for less lint), or a lint-free cloth
Craft stick
Masking tape

## Step 1

Clean the glass.

Use glass cleaner and paper towels to remove any fingerprints or grease from the glass. Dry the glass thoroughly.

## Step 2

Apply the stencil to the glass.

Press a strip of tape on the glass surface to mark a horizontal guideline. Place the monogram stencils side by side on the glass, blue side down and bottom edges aligned on the tape guideline. Apply additional strips of tape to the remaining three sides of the monogram to secure the stencils to the glass.

## Working Tips: Masking a Tapered Glass Object

A tape applied horizontally to a tapered glass vessel may form tiny wrinkles along one edge. If the etching cream creeps in to these tiny openings, the etched edge will appear wobbly or broken. To ensure a clean edge, stretch the tape slightly and press both edges against the glass. If you do it right, the edge of the tape on the broader end of the vessel will stretch a little more and the edge on the tapering end will stretch a little less, but both will lie flush against the surface with no gaps.

**Step 3**
Transfer the stencil to the glass.

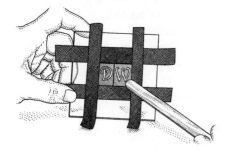

Use a craft stick to rub the shiny plastic surface of the carrier sheet and transfer the blue stencil material to the glass. Continue burnishing the plastic until all of the dark blue color changes to light blue, indicating that the whole stencil has adhered.

**Step 4**
Check the transfer.
Remove one strip of tape and lift off one side of the plastic sheet. Check to see if all

## Quick & Easy: Etched Glass Ornaments

Small projects are very satisfying to do. Etching lets you add easy elegance to a clear-glass tree ornament. Take extra care when using tape to mask a design on a fragile glass ball. Work with the stretch property of the tape as it will help to adhere the tape against the round shape without requiring undue pressure or burnishing. Also, be aware that when the metal cap that holds the hanging loop is removed for the technique, the stem's fragile and sharp edge becomes exposed. Watch your fingers and don't press on that part of the ornament. To safeguard the ornament

while applying the strips of tape, work over a padded surface.

- Remove the metal cap from the ornament.
- Clean the ornament with spray glass cleaner and a paper towel to wipe off grease or fingerprints.
- Apply strips of narrow tape in a swirl pattern around the ball, first in one direction and then in another direction. Carefully press down the tape using the back of your fingernail.
- Use a tapered paintbrush to apply an even coat of etching cream to the exposed areas of the glass. When the etching time has elapsed, turn the ornament upside down and rinse off the cream. Wash the ornament, draining any water that gets inside. Dry the outside surfaces with a paper towel.
- Replace the ornament cap. Your ornament is ready to display.

parts of the blue stencil material have adhered to the glass. If they haven't, reposition the plastic sheet and reburnish that area. When the stencil is completely transferred to the glass, remove the tape and the plastic carrier sheet and discard them.

## Technique: Using Peel-and-Stick Vinyl Letters as Masks

Vinyl type is another material suitable for masking a glass surface. A sheet of type typically includes all the letters of the alphabet in both uppercase and lowercase, numerals, and punctuation marks. The type comes in a variety of lettering styles, called typefaces or fonts, and sizes (measured in points). You can mix the typefaces and sizes any way you want to spell out words or monograms. Each letter is peeled off the backing sheet and pressed onto the glass individually. The letters have a strong adhesive backing and are made from a flexible plastic that stretches just enough for a good grip on the glass so that etching cream applied to the surrounding area cannot reach the glass, producing a negative print—the area surrounding the letters is frosted and the shape of each letter is transparent.

You can approach the design in several ways. Use presstype letters to create a monogram or spell out a slogan. If you prefer, you can place the letters in a random pattern so they seem to tumble across the glass surface.

### MATERIALS AND TOOLS
Glass item
Sheet of vinyl letters
Spray glass cleaner
Paper towels, nonembossed (for less lint)
Craft stick

**Step 1**
Clean the glass.
Use glass cleaner and paper towels to remove any fingerprints or grease from the glass. Dry thoroughly.

**Step 2**
Apply the first mask.
Use tweezers to lift and peel an adhesive-backed letter from its carrier sheet. Place the letter, adhesive side down, on the glass surface. Use a craft stick or the back of your fingernail to press the letter against the glass.

**Step 3**
Apply the remaining masks.
Repeat step 2 to apply more letters to the glass surface to create the desired design.

**Step 4**
Check the edges.
Hold the glass up to the light to check for any gaps in the edges of the letters and press them against the glass. If a letter is torn or won't stick down, lift it off the glass and clean that area of the glass with glass cleaner and a paper towel. Then affix a new letter in its place.

### Adhesive-Backed Vinyl by the Roll

Adhesive-backed vinyl by the roll offers a neat and efficient way of etching a design across a broad area without worrying about getting etching cream on parts of the glass that you don't want etched. The material has one side that is plain and one side that is coated with

## Working Tips: When a Transfer Stencil Doesn't Stick

If a transfer stencil does not stick when burnished, the glass surface or the stencil itself may be too cold. Use a hair dryer on a low setting to warm the layers (you can keep them taped together) and try burnishing again.

adhesive and covered with a paper backing sheet. The vinyl is sturdy, takes a clean cut, and provides superior coverage. I try to keep my designs of a manageable size; a large sheet of vinyl can become unwieldy and easily stick to itself once the protective backing is peeled off.

I adhere the vinyl to the project surface and do the cutting in situ directly on the glass. Although you can mark a design directly on the vinyl, I prefer to work out the design on a separate piece of paper, adjusting its scale and proportion, and adhering a printout of it (my design template) to the vinyl sheet. Then I simply cut out the stencil through both layers, using the lines on the template as a guide to expose the glass surface underneath. It is important that the stencil be marked and cut neatly; however, if you do make a mistake on one part of the stencil, you can easily graft in a completely new section and start again. As with all masks, the vinyl must adhere smoothly and tightly to the surface of the glass, especially on interior cut edges. Wrinkles, bubbles, or gaps in the sheet will cause the cut edges of the stencil to print a wobbly edged design.

---

## Working Tips: Using Transfer Stencil Motifs on a Mirror

You can configure identical or coordinating individual motifs found on transfer stencils to create a decorative design that spans the width of a glass mirror. First make a rough sketch of the design, using paper that is equal in measure to the design area. Map out the placement of the motifs on the paper. Use the sketch as a guide when placing the actual transfer stencils.

---

## Technique: Using Adhesive-Backed Shelf Vinyl as a Mask for Positive Designs

This etching technique offers many conveniences and safeguards. By adhering a sheet of vinyl (the stencil material) directly to the glass, you are provided two advantages: the underlying glass surface provides the needed support for cutting the stencil and the generous swath of stencil material provides freedom as you select and cut out only those shapes you want to etch, leaving the uncut vinyl to cover all of the surrounding areas of the glass you don't wish to etch. There is one caution, however, when cutting the stencil directly on the glass. When the knife blade, of necessity, cuts completely through the vinyl to make the cutout, it is possible for the knife blade to inadvertently incise the glass at the same time, depending on the angle of the blade and the pressure exerted on the tool during cutting. In most cases, the incision in the glass surface is extremely shallow, and because it also traces the line of the design, the etching texture will camouflage the scratch.

### MATERIALS AND TOOLS
Flower Stencil pattern (page 708)
Photocopier, or a computer scanner and printer
Flat glass item, such as a mirror
Adhesive-backed shelf vinyl
Spray adhesive
Craft knife
Steel ruler
Self-healing cutting mat
Chemical-cartridge respirator mask
Teaspoon
Pencil
Spray glass cleaner
Paper towels, nonembossed (for less lint)

### Step 1
Clean the glass.

Use glass cleaner and paper towels to remove any fingerprints or grease from the glass surface. Focus your attention on the area where the design will be etched. Dry the glass thoroughly and set it aside.

**Step 2**

Size and print the design template.

Scan the design, enlarging it to fit the design area on the glass, and make a printout. Use a pencil to mark the midpoint of the design on the printout.

**Step 3**

Cut and adhere the adhesive-backed vinyl to the glass.

Using a steel ruler, craft knife, and self-healing cutting mat, measure and cut a piece of adhesive-backed shelf vinyl to fit the design area of the glass. Use a pencil to mark the midpoint of the vinyl piece. Lay the vinyl on a flat surface and peel off the paper backing. Lift the sheet of vinyl at opposite ends to prevent it from sticking to itself and lower one edge into position on the glass until it adheres. Lower the rest of the vinyl piece so that it touches down on the glass in a rolling motion. Smooth the vinyl against the glass, removing any small bubbles or wrinkles as you work.

**Step 4**

Apply spray adhesive to the design template.

Work outdoors or in an area with good cross-ventilation. Put on a chemical-cartridge respirator mask. Lay the design template facedown on a protected work surface. Apply a thin, even coat of spray adhesive to the paper.

**Step 5**

Adhere the template to the vinyl.

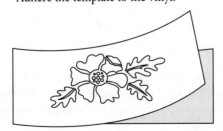

Center the design template, adhesive side down, on the vinyl, lining up the center marks and using your hands to smooth the design template against the vinyl surface.

**Step 6**

Cut out the vinyl stencil.

Use a craft knife to cut on the marked lines through both the template paper and the vinyl to make the stencil. Carefully peel up the cutout shapes, using the tip of the craft knife to lift the shape by one edge before peeling it off the glass. Cut out all marked shapes in the stencil design.

**Step 7**

Burnish the edges of the stencil.

Use the bowl of a teaspoon to press the cut edges against the glass. Simply press down hard; scrubbing or rubbing will cause the edges to stretch and lift away from the glass.

If you are planning to etch a larger glass surface, applying design motifs across a wide expanse or to a glass object with multiple sides, it is practical and advisable to etch small sections on one side of the project at a time. Etching cream is not designed for frosting large solid areas because of the difficulty in maintaining uniform timing, which affects etching results, such as blemishes or mottling in the frosted glass. The moment the cream touches the glass, the chemical reaction begins. You must be able to completely coat a section for etching within a few seconds. There is some debate about what constitutes "small" and "large" areas for quality etching, but after some trial and error, I find I can etch an area approximately 6" × 8" (15.2 × 20.3 cm) without sacrificing the quality of the frosted texture. When you are etching a glass item in sections, be sure to cover previously etched areas with wide bands of waterproof tape so a new application of etching cream does not mar the design already etched into the glass. This requires that you apply the masks carefully, aligning the edge of a mask with the edge of the etched surface. You can also experiment with overlapping or gapping seams, making them part of the design.

### Technique: Etching an Overall Design in Small Sections

Here is one approach to decorating a large vase with an overall random pattern of polka dots. The glass surface is too broad to be etched in a single application, so it is etched in sections. The one-time-use masks are stencils cut from adhesive-backed vinyl and taped to the glass surface. Use masking tape to mark off one small section of the design area at a time, etching each section in turn until the design is complete.

## MATERIALS AND TOOLS

Glass item, such as a vase
Etching cream
Adhesive-backed vinyl
Hole punch, 3¾" (1.9 cm) in diameter, or as desired
Foam brush
Scissors
Timer
Small dish
Sink with hot and cold running water
Plastic bucket
Safety glasses
Disposable gloves
Dishwashing gloves
Spray glass cleaner
Dishwashing liquid
Baking soda
Test kit with pH strips
Paper towels, nonembossed (for less lint)
Newsprint or plastic sheet
Masking tape
Cellophane tape
Wide waterproof tape

### Step 1
Clean the glass.

Use glass cleaner and paper towels to remove any fingerprints or grease from the glass surface. Dry the glass thoroughly and set it aside.

## Step 2

Make the stencils.

Cut several 2" (5.1 cm) squares of adhesive-backed vinyl. Use the hole punch to cut out a circle from the center of each square. The square piece with the hole is the stencil.

## Step 3

Apply the stencils to a section of the glass.

Lay the glass object on a protected flat surface. Carefully peel off the backing paper of one polka dot stencil. Position and press the stencil against the glass. Lay strips of cellophane tape on the four outer edges of the stencil, overlapping the ends at the corners. Do not tape over the cutout center. Repeat to add two or three more polka dot stencils to the glass in a tight, random pattern.

## Step 4

Tape off the stencil area and protect the bare glass.

Use strips of masking tape to mark off the area of the design. Then protect the bare glass *surrounding* the taped-off section using wide bands of waterproof tape, overlapping the strips of tape to prevent etching cream from coming into contact with the glass when the etching cream is rinsed off.

## Step 5

Etch the polka dots.

Put on disposable gloves and safety glasses. Use a foam brush to apply etching cream to the polka dot stencils. If there is a thin spot, add more etching cream. Allow the cream to remain on the glass for 1 minute or as recommended by the manufacturer. Rinse off the cream by holding the etched section under a gentle stream of warm water, allowing the rinse water to drain into a plastic bucket. Safely dispose of the rinse water.

## Step 6

Remove the tape and the stencils.

Pull off the wet protective bands of tape, the tape around the edges of the stencils, and the polka dot stencils and discard them safely. Rinse the vase. Clean the stenciled section, rubbing off any remaining residue using glass cleaner and paper towels. Dry the glass using paper towels to reveal the first area of the polka dot design.

## Step 7

Etch the remaining polka dots.

Repeat steps 3–6 on a new section of the glass surface. Cut new polka dot stencils as needed and mask off areas that are already etched with tape before applying the etching cream. Continue working on small areas, applying stencils and etching the design, until the entire surface is covered.

## Step 8

Clean the vase.

Thoroughly rinse the etched vase, dry it off, and set it aside. Continue to let the water run in the sink to rinse off any traces of the cream. Finish by scrubbing the sink.

## Technique: Etching Multiple Flat Surfaces

Use this technique to etch a glass item that has multiple flat surfaces, such as a cube-shaped votive candleholder. The surfaces are masked and etched one at a time. To create overall contrast, use the principles of negative and positive space to alternate the texture on adjacent surfaces—etched polka dots on one surface and transparent polka dots on the next. The frosted surfaces will appear to glow, and the light will shine brightly through the clear sections.

## MATERIALS AND TOOLS

Glass item with flat surfaces
Sheet of adhesive-backed letters
Adhesive-backed vinyl stencils, cut with
   ¾"-diameter (1.9 cm) hole punch
Etching cream
Foam brush
Scissors
Timer
Small dish
Sink with hot and cold running water
Plastic bucket
Safety glasses
Disposable gloves
Spray glass cleaner
Dishwashing liquid
Baking soda
Test kit with pH strips
Paper towels, nonembossed (for less
   lint)
Newsprint or plastic sheet
Masking tape
Cellophane tape
Wide waterproof tape

**Step 1**
Clean the glass.
Use glass cleaner and paper towels to remove any fingerprints or grease from the glass. Dry the glass thoroughly.

**Step 2**
Apply the masks to the first surface.
Peel off the chosen letters from the sheet, one at a time, and arrange them as desired on the first glass surface. Use a craft stick to

## Working Tips: Coasters from Plate Glass

Coasters can be made from ¼"-thick (0.6 cm) plate glass. Have a glass supplier cut the glass into squares and polish the edges so the pieces are safe to handle. Because the silica content is higher in plate glass than in other types of glass, the etching process takes longer, usually 10 to 15 minutes. Always test the material beforehand.

## Quick & Easy: Creating Frosted Glass Effects with Spray Frosting

You can create the look of a frosty windowpane or frosted glass candleholders with spray frost. This product is sold in hardware and home decorating stores. It can be used with a stencil or applied stickers to simulate the look of etched glass. As with etching, make certain to protect the areas you do not want frosted. Wait until the solvent in the spray evaporates and then carefully peel off the stencil or stickers from the glass, using a pin or tip of a craft knife to lift one edge of the sticker to avoid marring the surface or nicking the frosted coating.

press down firmly on each letter, especially the edges, to adhere it.

### Step 3

Etch the first surface.

Put on disposable gloves and safety glasses. Use a foam brush and a patting motion to apply a thick coat of etching cream to the masked surface only. Allow the cream to remain on the glass for 1 minute or as recommended by the manufacturer. Rinse off the cream by holding the etched section under a gentle stream of warm water, allowing the rinse water to drain into a plastic bucket. Safely dispose of the rinse water.

### Step 4

Clean and dry the glass.

Peel off and safely discard any remaining mask material. Use warm water and dishwashing liquid to clean the glass. Use paper towels to thoroughly dry the glass surface.

### Step 5

Mask and etch the remaining surfaces.

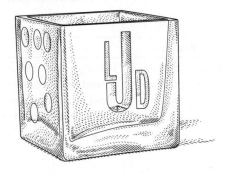

Apply tape to the etched surface until it is completely covered. Apply the adhesive-backed vinyl stencils to the second surface and tape down the edges. Repeat steps 3 and 4 to etch and reveal the second surface. Continue until all the surfaces are etched.

## Project Ideas for Glass Etching

- Glass coasters
- Glass vases
- Glass tumblers
- Martini and wine glasses
- Glass bowls
- Glass dessert plates

## Glass Etching Checklist

- Environment above 70°F (21.1°C)
- Etching cream warm, not cold
- Glass clean and dry, free of fingerprints, grease, or coating
- Masks firmly adhered, with no torn or lifted edges
- Etching cream applied evenly, to small areas at a time
- Proper etching time allotted
- All safety precautions observed

## Troubleshooting: Etching Glass

| Problem | Cause | Remedy |
|---|---|---|
| Edges of the etched motif are uneven and messy. | The edges of the mask were not pressed tightly against the glass, allowing the etching cream to seep under the stencil or tape. | Use the bowl side of a spoon, a craft stick, or the back of your fingernail to press down mask edges for tight adhesion to the glass surface. |
| | The mask was flawed. | Before etching, hold the glass item up to the light to check the mask for torn or lifted edges; peel off and replace a mask if these conditions are present. |
| | The glass had faint traces of grease or fingerprints that interfered with the mask adhesion. | Clean the glass with a 1:1 solution of distilled white vinegar and water and lint-free paper towels. |
| | The glass had a residue that interfered with the chemical action of the etching cream. | Avoid glass cleaners that leave a residue, such as fingerprint protection. Avoid coated glass, which does not etch. |
| Transfer stencil does not turn pale blue and adhere to the glass when burnished. | The stencil or the glass was too cold. | Tape the stencil to the glass and use a hair dryer on a low setting to warm the glass and the stencil before burnishing the carrier sheet. |
| The etched surface is mottled. | The etching cream was applied over too large an area, creating a gap in the exposure time. | Etch large glass items in sections no larger than 4" × 6" (10.2 × 15.2 cm). |
| | Traces of grease on the glass interfered with the chemical action of the etching cream. | Clean the glass with a 1:1 solution of distilled white vinegar and water and lint-free paper towels. |
| The glass does not etch at all or it etches very poorly. | Glass is a low-grade silica, lead crystal, or Pyrex—types of glass that do not etch well if at all. | Pretest the glass by applying etching cream to a small, unobtrusive spot on the glass and evaluate the result. |

## Gilding

Historically, the term *gilding* referred to a process in which thin sheets of genuine gold were applied to objects so they would appear to be made of solid gold, even though they were not. Today, *gilding* and *metal leafing* are used interchangeably to refer to a process done with leaf made of various metals—gold, silver, copper, alloys such as aluminum and composition gold leaf (also called Dutch metal), and metals with variegated surfaces.

Gilding an item requires several stages: preparing the surface, applying a size, preparing and adhering the metal leaf, and applying a protective finish. Contemporary gilding products have updated and simplified the tedious rigors of the traditional approach. For example, newer formulas of relatively fast-drying water-based size, such as Wunda size, can be used in place of the traditional oil-based size, which is slow-drying, has an odor that can persist for several days, and requires chemical

solvents for cleanup. Composition gold leaf is an alloy that looks like gold but is much less expensive and therefore a common substitute for the much more expensive sheets of real gold. With these new products and straightforward techniques, even beginners can achieve professional-looking results on their first try.

### Materials and Tools

- **Item to leaf**

Metal leaf can be applied to practically anything. The surface to be gilded can be nonporous (such as glass) or porous

## Gilding Materials and Tools at a Glance

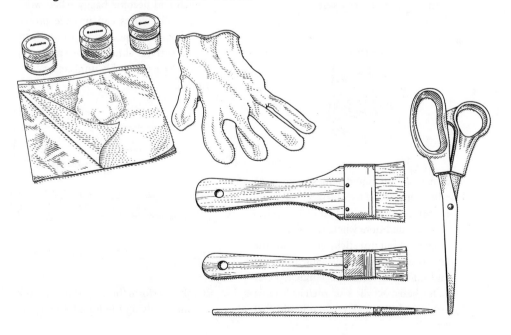

(such as wood). Decorative in nature, metal leaf adds luster and shine to the surface to which it is applied.

• **Metal leaf**

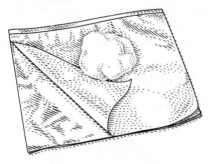

Metal leaf is available in sheets made of pure metals—gold, silver, and copper—and alloys, such as composition gold leaf and aluminum, which mimics the appearance of silver. Composition gold leaf is an affordable substitute for genuine gold and is available in a range of lustrous shades from reddish gold to lemony yellow. Most metal leaf is available in folios of twenty-five sheets, each 5½" (14.0 cm) square and interleaved with sheets of orange tissue paper.

• **Adhesive size**

Size is a thin liquid adhesive used to adhere metal leaf to a surface. After size is applied, it must rest until it reaches tack, a condition when the size is no longer wet but just sticky enough for the leaf to adhere. Size is available in water- and oil-based formulas. I much prefer water-based acrylic size, such as Wunda size, which is a milky white liquid that

dries clear, reaches tack in 15 to 30 minutes, and cleans up easily with soap and water. The low fume level makes it comfortable to use indoors. Oil-based sizes have a strong odor; their effectiveness in adhering leaf makes them especially recommended for items that will be displayed outdoors.

• **Cotton gloves and disposable gloves**

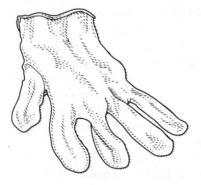

Nice to have, cotton gloves prevent natural skin oils from transferring to the metal leaf during handling. Unfortunately, the one-size-fits-all gloves tend to stretch and become baggy when worn. Disposable gloves can provide protection from the liquids used to finish the gilded surface, although for small projects, they are probably unnecessary.

• **Brushes**

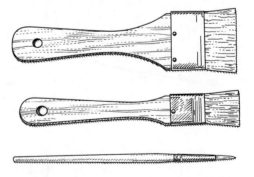

Brushes perform three basic functions in gilding: applying the liquid size, applying surface sealers and finishes, and sweeping up the flakes of leaf on a gilded surface. Size can be applied with either a soft-bristle brush or a high-density foam brush. Use a tapered watercolor brush to apply size to narrow crevices or along the edge of the sized area; the tip will give you control for applying size, paint, or finishes to minute areas. Use a separate soft-bristle brush, such as a recycled, good-quality brush used to apply blush or powder, to sweep away excess metal leaf, called *holidays* or *skewings*, from a leafed surface after the size is dry.

- **Items for surface preparation and sealing**

The essential items for preparing and sealing a surface include sandpaper and a sanding block, surface sealers, paint, and finishes. For a fuller description of these items, see Chapter Five.

- **Blunt-nose tweezers**

Tweezers with a blunt nose make it easier and safer to lift, carry, and position gold leaf when you are working on a project. The blunt nose protects the thin metal leaf from tearing.

- **Scissors**

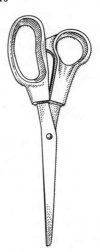

Depending on the visual effect you want, metal leaf can be cut with general-purpose scissors. The blades must be very sharp to produce clean, even cuts; dull blades will grind the metal leaf and the protective layers of orange paper. Ragged edges are more a nuisance than anything else, as careful burnishing and finishing will usually mitigate these flaws in the leafed surface.

- **100 percent cotton balls**

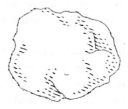

A ball made of 100 percent pure cotton fiber is a suitable (and handy) material for burnishing applied metal leaf. Conveniently sized and minimally abrasive, a standard cotton ball makes it easy to polish and smooth a leafed surface without leaving prominent abrasions on the metal. You will find that some hairline scratches do occur. To mitigate this tendency, burnish using a narrow oval motion in the same direction as you would when sanding a surface smooth. Then apply a neat and smooth finishing coat to make any fine lines disappear completely.

## Preparing the Surface

Foremost in any gilding project is surface preparation. The surface to be gilded must be clean and smooth so that the metal leaf adheres well and does not show any surface imperfections. Time invested in preparing the surface is time well spent. Metal leaf is not very forgiving—nicks, sanding scratches, and even brushstrokes on the surface of a project will be highlighted when metal leaf is applied over them.

Gilding on wood traditionally began with a coat of gesso, a creamy, chalky substance that sealed the wood and leveled out the surface in preparation for the metal leaf. Because gesso is porous, size could not be applied directly to it and still achieve proper tack, or stickiness; the gesso simply absorbed too much of the size for it to be effective. To remedy this, traditional gilders applied a coat of *bole*—a reddish-brown liquid clay—over the gesso. Bole formed a buffer between the gesso and the size. It allowed the size to remain on the surface and achieve tack so that the leaf would adhere. Over time, subtle faults and cracks formed in the leaf that allowed the bole to show through. The overall effect was of a colorful glow between the breaks in the gold leaf that added luminosity to the gilded finish. You can re-create this antique look by adding a coat or two of reddish-brown acrylic craft paint to your project before you gild it. Or you can paint an undercoat in any color you prefer for added flair.

After you have cleaned, sanded, and perhaps painted the surface of your project, use a foam brush or a bristle brush to apply a thin, even coat of sealer. Follow the directions on the container and allow the sealer to dry overnight or longer, depending on the humidity. Higher humidity will retard drying. When the sealer is completely dry, use a fine-grit (#600) sandpaper to further smooth and refine the finish. For instructions on how to prepare wood, metal, and glass surfaces, see the surface preparation techniques for decoupage in Chapter Five.

## Technique: Leveling and Smoothing a Wood Surface with Acrylic Gesso

Gesso is a good surface filler for porous wood. Use a nylon paintbrush with bristles that are feathered at the tips for the smoothest application. You'll still need to sand the surface after the gesso cures to achieve a silky smooth finish. Read Universal Guidelines: Applying Sealers, Paints, Varnishes, and Other Liquid Media (page 380) before you begin.

### MATERIALS AND TOOLS
Unfinished wood item, sanded
Acrylic gesso
Acrylic medium-and-varnish
Sandpaper, fine-grit (#600)
Sanding block
Squared rod, slat, or peg
Nylon brush with feathered bristles
Foam brush
Tack cloth
Respirator mask
Flat sticks

### Step 1
Apply the first coat of gesso.
Place the item on flat sticks to elevate it off the protected work surface. Use a bristle brush to apply a thin, even coat of gesso to the sanded surfaces of the wood item. Allow the gesso to dry for at least 2 hours.

### Step 2
Apply a second coat of gesso.
Repeat step 1 to apply a second thin, even coat of gesso to the item. Let the gesso dry overnight.

## Step 3

Smooth the gessoed surface.

Put on a respirator mask and safety glasses. Move a sanding block wrapped with fine-grit (#600) sandpaper over the surface, using a rounded oval stroke and applying medium pressure to smooth the sealed surfaces; be careful not to rub through to the raw wood. To reach into narrow crevices or recessed areas, wrap a squared rod, slat, or peg with fine-grit (#600) sandpaper and use it like a file in a rounded oval stroke. Use a tack cloth to remove the dust.

## Step 4

Apply the final coat of gesso.

Elevate the project on craft sticks. Repeat step 2 to apply the third and final coat of gesso to all surfaces of the item. Let the gesso dry overnight.

## Step 5 (optional)

Sand the gessoed surface.

Examine the gessoed surface and sand it very lightly, if needed, following step 3.

## Step 6

Apply two coats of sealer.

Use a foam brush to apply two even coats of acrylic medium-and-varnish, allowing 2 hours' drying time between coats. Let the second coat dry completely. Drying and curing times will be longer during periods of high heat or humidity.

## Technique: Painting a "Bole" Undercoat and Sealing the Painted Surface

Applying a coat of color to the gessoed surface before laying down metal leaf is one way to create textural effects and contrast. The painted undercoat shows through in a way that highlights the tiny jagged tears between the pieces of applied leaf. After the gesso or other sealer has dried and cured, apply a coat of color to all of the surfaces that will be gilded. The color you choose can be reddish-brown—the traditional color of bole—or another shade that you want to see peeking through the cracks in the leafed surface. For a subtle glow of color, choose a pale shade of paint, such as cream, ochre, or violet. For more contrast, consider turquoise or midnight blue. Read Universal Guidelines: Applying Sealers, Paints, Varnishes, and Other Liquid Media (page 380) before you begin.

### MATERIALS AND TOOLS

Wood item, prepared with gesso or other sealer
Acrylic craft paint, in reddish-brown or another color
Acrylic medium-and-varnish
Foam brush
Flat sticks

## Step 1

Apply the first coat of acrylic craft paint.

Place the item on flat sticks to elevate it off the protected work surface. Use a foam brush to apply a thin, even coat of acrylic craft paint over the gesso. Blot any drips that form near the base and do not allow paint to pool in narrow, carved areas of the wood. Let the paint dry 1 hour.

## Working Tips: Spray-on Gesso

Spray-on gesso is an alternative to conventional gesso medium applied with a brush. It goes on easily in a thin coating in the same manner as spray metal primers. Apply three thin coats, following the manufacturer's directions on the can.

## Step 2

Complete the painting.

Use a foam brush to apply a second thin coat of paint over the first coat. Let the paint dry 1 hour. Add a third thin coat of paint if necessary for even coverage. Let the paint dry overnight.

## Step 3

Apply one coat of sealer.

Use a foam brush to apply a thin, even coat of acrylic medium-and-varnish over the paint. Let it dry overnight or longer, if needed, until completely dry. Drying and curing times will be longer during periods of high heat or humidity.

### Applying Acrylic Size and Metal Leaf

The key to working effectively with size is to allow enough time for the size to get tacky, or sticky, before applying the metal leaf on top of it. Apply a thin, even coat of size with a foam brush or a pure-bristle paintbrush and then simply wait. You can tell the size is ready by touching a clean, dry finger to the sized surface and lifting it off. If you hear a tick sound or if the size surface feels sticky like cellophane tape, it is ready. Acrylic size reaches tack quite quickly (in 15 to 30 minutes) and remains open for the application of leaf 24 to 36 hours. Always read the manufacturer's directions on the product for more precise information.

Metal leaf comes in microns-thin sheets that are sandwiched between pages of orange-colored tissue paper bound into 5½"-square (14.0 cm) folios. There are twenty-five sheets of leaf in one bound folio, and they will cover a surface area of approximately 4 square feet (0.37 sq m). Metal leaf can be applied in one sheet, or it may be cut or torn into smaller pieces. Sheets of metal leaf should be handled with care. Work in a clean, draft-free environment, as even small air currents can send the delicate leaf aflutter. To avoid fingerprints and tarnish, wear cotton gloves and keep the leaf sandwiched between the sheets of protective tissue paper as long as possible. You can use a pair of blunt-nose tweezers (pointy ones can pierce the leaf) instead of your fingers to lift and move small pieces of leaf if it gives you more control. Metal leaf adheres easily to a sized surface, but it must be laid carefully to prevent wrinkling and buckling. Metal leaf cannot be repositioned once it touches the sized surface.

## Technique: Applying the Size and Testing for Tack

Size functions like an adhesive, going on wet and then becoming sticky, at which time metal leaf should be laid on top. The size proceeds to dry completely, creating a bond between the metal leaf and the surface to which it is applied.

### MATERIALS AND TOOLS

Surface prepared for leafing
Acrylic size
Pure-bristle brush or high-density foam
   brush
Flat sticks

## Step 1

Apply the size.

Set the project on flat sticks to elevate it. Use a pure-bristle brush or a foam brush to apply a thin, even coat of acrylic size to the prepared surface. Work on one side or surface of the project at a time to prevent the size from pooling or running off the project. Allow 15 to 30 minutes for the size to reach tack.

## Step 2

Test the size for proper tack.

Lightly touch a bare finger to the sized surface and remove it, listening for a tick sound. If you hear a tick, or if the surface feels like the sticky side of cellophane tape, you can begin applying leaf. The size should remain tacky for 24 to 36 hours, giving you plenty of time to apply leaf to even a large item.

## Technique: Cutting Metal Leaf into Squares

Metal leaf is very thin and easy to cut with sharp household scissors. It is also subject to tearing if the scissor blades shift sideways. For more control and to achieve clean cuts, it is best to cut the leaf while it is sandwiched between two pieces of the protective orange-colored tissue.

### MATERIALS AND TOOLS

Metal leaf
Cotton gloves
White paper
Scissors

### Step 1

Prepare the work surface and the protective paper cover sheets.

Choose a work area that is free of air currents. Cut three squares of white paper that are slightly larger than the square of metal leaf; set them aside. Put on cotton gloves. Lay a whole sheet of plain white paper on your work surface.

### Step 2

Transfer the metal leaf to the work surface.

Use scissors to snip along the spine of the folio to release the first two sheets of orange tissue. Carefully transfer the orange sheets and the sheet of leaf they carry to the work surface. Cover the exposed leaf in the folio with the square of white paper cut in step 1.

### Step 3

Cut the metal leaf.

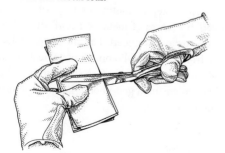

Hold the sandwiched layers in one hand and the scissors in the other hand. Cut all three layers into rough squares, allowing the pieces to fall onto the white paper. The precise size of the squares can vary, from ¾" (1.9 cm) for small projects up to 2½" (6 cm) for large projects.

## Technique: Tearing Metal Leaf

Tearing produces pieces of leaf that are random in size and have jagged edges. When the leafed surface is burnished, the loose pieces and rough edges of leaf virtually disappear, unless the pieces have been spaced so that the painted undercoat shows. You can tear metal leaf with your fingers but do wear cotton gloves to protect the surface of the leaf from grease and fingerprints.

### MATERIALS AND TOOLS

Metal leaf
Cotton gloves
White paper

### Step 1

Prepare the work surface.

Choose a work area that is free of air currents. Put on cotton gloves. Lay a sheet of plain white paper on your work surface.

## Working Tips: Using a Grid for Neat Cutting

For more precise cutting, draw a grid on the top sheet of tissue that covers the leaf before removing the sandwiched metal leaf from the folio. Use a ruler and a pencil to lightly mark a grid on the orange tissue that protects the gold leaf in the folio and then cut along the marked lines until you have the number of squares you need.

**Step 2**

Transfer the metal leaf to the work surface.

Place the folio flat on your work surface. Touch a gloved finger to one sheet of leaf and gently slide it onto the white paper. If you wish, you can transfer a single sheet of tissue paper and a sheet of leaf together to the white paper.

**Step 3**

Tear the metal leaf.

Use your gloved fingers and gentle pressure to tear the leaf into irregular shapes the size of a postage stamp.

### Technique: Adhering Squares of Metal Leaf to a Flat Surface

Squares of metal leaf are suited for gilding flat or large surface areas. The size of the squares can vary according to the size and proportion of the object being leafed—small squares for small items, larger squares for larger items. The larger the squares, the more quickly the surface will be leafed.

MATERIALS AND TOOLS

Item with flat surface, sized and at proper
    tack
Metal leaf, cut into squares
Blunt-nose tweezers
Tapered watercolor brush
Cotton gloves

**Step 1**

Position the first piece of metal leaf.

Wear cotton gloves. Use tweezers to carry one square of leaf, with its tissue-paper back-

ing underneath as support, to the sized surface. Position the leaf over the surface and allow its leading edge to touch down on the size. Slowly withdraw the tissue paper from under the leaf until the square of metal leaf lies flat against the surface. Lay the tissue paper over the metal leaf and use your gloved finger or a clean, tapered brush to tamp the leaf in place on the surface. Lift off the tissue paper and set it aside.

**Step 2**

Position the next piece of metal leaf.

Use tweezers to pick up another square of leaf and its tissue paper backing and carry them to the sized surface. Place the leading edge of the leaf over the leaf already laid, overlapping the edges by a scant ⅛" (0.3 cm). Ease the new square of leaf into place. Remove the tissue paper. Use the backing sheet of tissue paper to lightly tamp down the new piece of the leaf.

**Step 3**

Apply leaf to the entire surface.

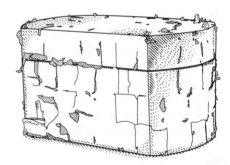

Repeat step 2, continuing to position and overlap squares of metal leaf until the entire sized surface is gilded. Lay the sheet of tissue from the leaf folio on the metal leaf; use a gloved fingertip, and buff the leaf through the tissue to ensure a good bond. Let the size dry completely.

## Technique: Adhering Torn Pieces of Metal Leaf to a Dimensional Surface

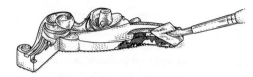

Torn pieces of metal leaf are suitable for small items, especially those with carved or dimensional surfaces. The size of the torn pieces of leaf can vary according to the size and proportion of the object or the characteristics of the carving—small pieces for grooves and crevices and larger pieces for areas with low-relief texture and minimal contour.

### MATERIALS AND TOOLS
Item with dimensional surface, sized
    and at proper tack
Metal leaf, torn into pieces
Blunt-nose tweezers
Tapered watercolor paintbrush
Cotton gloves

### Step 1
Position the first piece of metal leaf.

Wear cotton gloves. Use tweezers to carry one torn piece of leaf to the sized surface. (Because torn pieces are typically the size of a postage stamp, I do not use tissue paper to support them during carrying.) Position the leaf over the surface and allow its leading edge to touch down on the size. Use tapered brush to tamp the leaf in place on the surface.

### Step 2
Position the next piece of metal leaf.

Use tweezers to pick up another torn piece of leaf and carry it to the sized surface. Place the leading edge of the leaf over the leaf already laid, overlapping the edges by a scant ⅛" (0.3 cm). Use a tapered paintbrush to press the leaf into any narrow grooves or crevices.

If the leaf applied to a groove or crevice splits and reveals the painted undercoat, the split can be left as is or it can be patched with small flakes of leaf.

### Step 3
Apply metal leaf to the entire surface.

Repeat step 2, continuing to position and overlap torn pieces of metal leaf until the entire sized surface is gilded. Lay a sheet of tissue from the leaf folio on the metal leaf and use a gloved fingertip to buff the leaf through the tissue to ensure a good bond.

### Step 4
Fill in bare spots with metal leaf.

Examine the leafed surface, checking for any cracks or exposed areas that you would like to fill. Run the bristles of the dry paintbrush on your hair to create static electricity and then use the static-charged bristles to lift and transfer a small flake of metal leaf from your work surface to the project. Set the flake in position and tamp it down with a piece of tissue paper. If the size has lost tack, apply a new coat of size to the affected area, wait for it to reach tack, and proceed with the repair. Let the size dry completely.

After the leaf is applied, it is important to let the size dry completely, overnight or longer, to a hard coating, before burnishing the surface. Burnishing smooths out the leafed surface, removes loose bits of leaf that occur where two pieces of leaf overlap, and gives the leaf a lustrous and smooth finish. The rate of drying can be prolonged by high ambient temperature and humidity, so it is important to wait longer than recommended if you are unsure if the size has dried completely. Impatient as I am by nature, this is one process I have learned not to rush, as interfering prematurely can cause the leaf to creep and wrinkle, revealing a gummy undercoat underneath and spoiling the surface.

## Troubleshooting: Gilding

| Problem | Cause | Remedy |
|---|---|---|
| Size dried before the metal leaf was applied. | Misjudged the open window for tackiness. | Let the size dry completely. Reapply a thin coat of size to the unleafed areas, let it reach tack, and apply new leaf. |
| Size is pooling in the crevices of a carved area. | Size was applied too liberally. | Use a narrow watercolor paintbrush to soak up liquid size until only a light coat remains, and let it reach tack. |
| Size is gummy and does not reach tack, even after the recommended waiting time. | Air is warm and humid. | Allow more time for the size to reach tack. |
| Parts of the surface reach tack but parts are still gummy. | Size was applied unevenly or too heavily. | Strive for a very thin, even coat of size so the entire surface dries at the same rate. |
| Metal leaf has a dull appearance. | Too much size pooled and "drowned" the leaf. | Strive for a very thin, even coat of size and let it reach tack before applying the leaf. |
| Part of the leaf split and did not stick to surface. | The size dried before the leaf was adhered. | Reapply a thin coat of size to the "split," let it reach tack, and apply a new leaf. |
| The leafed surface has unwanted gaps where the base color shows through. | Pieces of leaf did not overlap when they were applied. | Always overlap pieces of leaf by a scant ⅛" (0.3 cm) (unless a gap is desired). |
| | Pieces of leaf were too small to cover the sized area. | Choose a larger piece of leaf. |
| Difficult to make a repair. | Pieces of leaf are too small and delicate to handle. | Rub a dry, tapered, watercolor paintbrush on your hair to generate static electricity and pick up the skewings with the brush and apply them with precision. |

## Technique: Burnishing the Applied Metal Leaf

Wait until the sized and leafed surface is completely dry—and then wait a little bit more—before burnishing the surface. Use a 100 percent cotton ball or a soft lint-free cloth to burnish the surface until the metal is smooth and lustrous.

### MATERIALS AND TOOLS

Item, leafed and completely dry
Soft-bristle brush
100 percent cotton ball
Soft lint-free cloth
Envelope

**Step 1**

Remove any loose pieces of metal leaf.
Use a dry soft-bristle brush to sweep off the skewings. Save the skewings in an envelope for another project.

**Step 2**

Burnish the leafed surface with a cotton ball.
Move a cotton ball in an oval shape over the leafed surface, using gentle pressure, to smooth out the leaf and remove any lingering skewings.

**Step 3**

Burnish the surface with a soft lint-free cloth.
Move a soft lint-free cloth gently over the surface in an oval motion to bring up the shine.

### Sealing Metal Leaf

Metal leaf is no more than a thin veneer of metal on the surface and is thus easily subject to nicks and scratches. Two thin, even coats of sealer, such as acrylic medium-and-varnish, will protect the metal leaf against abrasion and retard the damaging effects of humidity, oxidation, and ultraviolet light. Either a spray or a liquid sealer may be used; be aware that liquid sealers can dull the brilliance of the metal leaf just slightly. The only other care your gilded item will need is an occasional wipe with a soft cloth to prevent dust buildup.

## Technique: Applying Spray Sealer to a Leafed Surface

When the entire surface of the project is leafed, it will need a protective sealer coat. A spray sealer is very easy to apply in a thin, even coating because only a fine mist is dispensed from the can's nozzle. As you apply the coat, keep the can moving to avoid overcoating an area, which can cause drips and sags. Wear a chemical-cartridge respirator mask and work outdoors in a dust-free environment or in a well-ventilated space when applying a spray sealer. Use a spray booth to contain the over-spray and protect the surface as it dries.

### MATERIALS AND TOOLS

Leafed item
Clear spray sealer
Chemical-cartridge respirator mask
Safety glasses
Disposable gloves
Flat sticks
Lazy Susan (optional)
Cardboard carton (for spray booth)
Newsprint

## Gilding Checklist

- Draft-free environment
- Pet-free environment
- Wear cotton gloves
- Be patient as size reaches tack
- Size completely dry before burnishing
- Burnish with 100 percent cotton ball or soft, lint-free cloth
- Apply a protective sealer coat
- Save and use the skewings

**Step 1**

Set up the work area.

Work outdoors, if possible, or in a well-ventilated space. Lay newsprint on the work surface and set the leafed item on top, elevating it on craft sticks. Placing the project on an old kitchen lazy Susan will allow you to rotate it as you spray to achieve a thin, evenly applied coat. To contain the overspray, set the project in a spray booth fashioned from a cardboard carton.

**Step 2**

Apply the spray sealer.

Put on a chemical-cartridge respirator mask, safety glasses, and disposable gloves. Spray a thin, even coat of sealer on the leafed item. Hold the spray can 12" to 16" (30.5 to 40.6 cm) from the object and use smooth overlapping strokes in a back-and-forth motion, turning the lazy Susan to access all sides. To prevent drips and runs, avoid aiming the spray in one place. Let the sealer dry for as long as

recommended by the manufacturer before applying a second coat.

**Step 3**

Allow the sealer to dry.

Let the sealer dry completely. Read and follow the manufacturer's directions and recommendation for good results. The final coat may need several weeks to harden and fully cure.

**Technique: Applying Liquid Sealer to a Leafed Surface**

As effective as a spray-on sealer for providing a protective finish, a liquid sealer applied with a brush may be the preferred choice if you want to avoid using an aerosol sealer or if you enjoy the hand processes and simply want to take your time. After applying the liquid sealer, I usually safeguard my wet finish by placing a clean, empty carton over the freshly coated project to protect it from settling dust as the finish coat dries, hardens, and

## Working Tips: Caring for Gilded Plates

Metal leaf can be applied as a decoration to the back of a glass plate and protected by several coats of sealer. It is important to treat the gilded surface with care. Clean the food service side of the plate with a wet cloth and a drop of dishwashing liquid; never submerge a leafed plate in water. Stack gilded plates with pieces of soft cloth or wax paper placed between them to prevent abrasion.

## Project Ideas for Gilding

- Flat and carved frames, especially those with relief decoration such as carved molding
- Christmas tree ornaments, such as balls, cherubs, and angels, with details picked out in metal leaf
- Party favors, such as small decorative boxes
- Pressed botanicals, such as dried oak and beech leaves
- Metal wind chimes
- Sculptural home accents, such as curtain tiebacks and finials
- Recycled willow or wicker baskets
- Glass plates, gilded on the underside

fully cures. Read Universal Guidelines: Applying Sealers, Paints, Varnishes, and Other Liquid Media (page 380) for pointers on keeping your application smooth and even.

## MATERIALS AND TOOLS

Acrylic medium-and-varnish
Foam brush
Small jar
Clean empty carton, larger than project
Flat sticks

### Step 1

Apply the first coat of finish.

Use flat sticks to elevate the project off the work surface. Pour some acrylic medium-and-varnish into a small jar. Dampen a foam brush in water and squeeze it out. Use the moistened brush to apply a thin, even coat of finish medium to the surface of your project. Allow the coat to dry to the touch. Read and follow the manufacturer's directions for recommendations and best results.

### Step 2

Apply the second coat of finish.

Repeat step 1 to apply a second coat of finish. Let the finish dry.

### Step 3

Allow the finish to cure.

Set the project in a protected place, elevated on flat sticks and shielded with a carton to keep dust from settling on the still-sticky surface. Allow the finish to cure before handling the project, following the manufacturer's recommendations. Even though a medium is dry to the touch, it may need additional time to completely dry and bond to the surface.

## Dry Embossing

Dry embossing uses heat to impress a design into a piece of fabric with pile, such as velvet. The fine fibers of velvet stand upright. When velvet is embossed, the fibers are pressed down in the shape and texture of the heat-resistant

## Dry Embossing Materials and Tools at a Glance

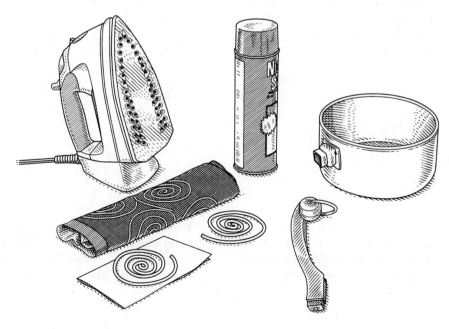

embossing object. The effect is beautiful, adding shimmering pattern to the fabric surface. Dry embossing can be done on your kitchen table using a household iron, a saucepan, and a coil of thick wire as the embossing object. After a length of velvet is embossed, it can be used to make soft home furnishings, such as pillows, bed throws, and curtain panels, or if you are fashion-minded, ravishing neck scarves.

## Materials and Tools

- **Velvet**

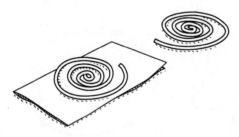

Velvet has a nap that makes it ideal for dry embossing. When laid over an embossing object—such as a coil of wire—and ironed, the velvet fibers flatten out, taking on the identical shape and pattern of the object as shown here. Silk and rayon velvet emboss well, whereas cotton velvet does not because the nap is too short and the fiber is resistant to the embossing effects.

- **Embossing object**

Any flat, heat-resistant object with an interesting shape or a texture that is raised above the background surface on an even plane can be used to dry-emboss velvet. Metal trivets, washers, and thick wire, such as armature wire, can be used for embossing. Thick chipboard can be cut into shapes and glued to a backing. Some rubber stamps are also suitable.

- **Chain-nose pliers**

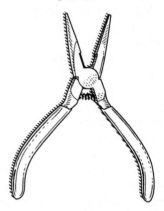

A pair of chain-nose pliers is suited to a wide range of tasks related to making an embossing object from wire, from gripping the end to make a hook to bending the wire to form the first tight coils. Chain-nose pliers have a slight curve on the outside of the nose, are tapered at the tips, and have smooth, flat inside jaws.

- **Wire cutters**

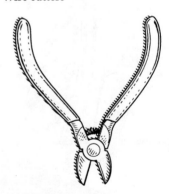

Wire cutters are specifically designed to cut wire in the neatest and most efficient way. Either end-cutters (with straight cutting edges across its wide, rectangular-shaped nose) or side-cutters, also called flush cutters (one side produces a flat, flush cut and the other side produces an angled cut), can be used to cut the armature wire used to make the embossing coil.

- **Household iron**

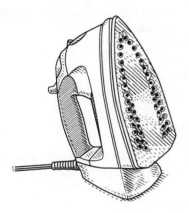

For the heat source, a dry household iron is applied with firm, downward pressure and then lifted straight up. The iron must be used without steam to prevent the vents on the faceplate from marring the surface of the velvet.

- **Metal pot**

The flat bottom of an overturned metal pot is an ideal staging surface for the embossing object. The pot provides a flat foundation and the metal conducts heat to the embossing object, helping to transfer its shape to the velvet. The pot should be large enough to accommodate the embossing object. Use a metal casserole or a pot with a removable handle so that it rests flat when inverted.

- **Spray starch**

Embossing velvet is easier when some controlled moisture is used. Applying a very fine mist of spray starch to the back of the velvet is just enough moisture to fix the embossing pattern on the velvet's surface. To avoid the flaky residue common to commercial spray starch, mix up a 1:1 ratio of liquid starch and water and pour it into a spray bottle so it is ready to use.

- **Square of cotton fabric (optional)**
  Used as a barrier between the slightly moist velvet and the hot iron, a piece of cotton placed over the back of the velvet will absorb the natural steam that forms when the hot iron comes into contact with the starch mist.

## Creating Your Own Embossing Objects

It is easy to create an overall pattern of individual silhouettes and bold textures using flat, heat-resistant objects that have simple shapes. Metal washers, flat metal buttons and coins, decorative trivets, wood blocks and ceramic tile, and coiled wire are just a few of many suitable embossing objects. Geometric shapes can be cut from thick chipboard. Rubber stamps can also be used to transfer more detailed designs onto the velvet. The embossing object can be used alone to make one impression at a time, or many embossing objects can be glued to a stiff, flat foundation, such as a square of thick chipboard, to make an embossing plate with a more complex pattern; just make sure that all of the relief objects are on the same level to avoid a partial print.

## Technique: Making a Single Motif from Coiled Wire

Aluminum armature wire is ideal for making a coiled design to use for embossing. It is thick yet lightweight and pliable and thus easy to shape with your hands. Armature wire can be found in hardware and craft stores and online in a range of thicknesses. Gauges that are easy to manipulate into an embossing object are 10-gauge or ⅛"-diameter (0.3 cm), 6-gauge or ³⁄₁₆"-diameter (0.2 cm), and 3-gauge or ¼"-diameter (0.6 cm).

### MATERIALS AND TOOLS
Armature wire, 10-gauge or ⅛" (0.3 cm) diameter
Wire cutters
Chain-nose pliers
Safety glasses
Ruler

**Step 1**
Cut the wire.
Put on safety glasses. Use wire cutters to cut a 24" (61.0 cm) length of armature wire.

**Step 2**
Shape a coil.

Use pliers to grip one end of the wire and twist it to form a hook. Twist the pliers again and then use your hands to bend the remaining wire around the hook until the coil measures about 3" (7.6 cm) across.

An embossing plate is a pattern of multiple motifs, made by gluing several embossing objects to a square of thick chipboard. An embossing plate makes it easier to emboss continuous designs over a larger surface of velvet.

The suitable materials for making single motifs cover a wide range, but I have found that chipboard and high-density rubber work well. Both are easy to cut into simple shapes with scissors or a craft knife, and some detail can be achieved by incising the surface with a craft knife. Thick, soft wire, such as armature wire, that can be manipulated into simple, geometric shapes is also suitable.

Embossing from a plate is a bit more difficult than impressing one embossed motif at a time because the design area on the embossing plate is larger than the face of the iron. Be sure to press the iron straight down and lift it straight up. Avoid moving the iron sideways, which can shift the velvet and cause an overlapping print.

## Technique: Making an Embossing Plate with a Coil Pattern

### MATERIALS AND TOOLS
Armature wire, 8-gauge or ⅛" (0.3 cm) thick
Chipboard
White craft glue, high-tack
Self-healing cutting mat
Steel ruler
Craft knife
Wire cutters

Scissors
Packing tape
Foam brush
Waxed paper
Heavy books

### Step 1
Make the embossing plate base.

Use a craft knife, steel ruler, and self-healing cutting mat to cut a 5½" (14.0 cm) square from chipboard. Lay the square on a flat work surface and press strips of tape on a diagonal to secure the corners of the square to the work surface.

### Step 2
Bend the wire coils.

Cut four 18" (45.7 cm) lengths of armature wire. Bend each length into a coil about 2½" (6.4 cm) to 3" (7.6 cm) across. The diameter of the coil will vary according to the space left between the coils.

### Step 3
Mount the coils on the base.

Brush a thick coat of white high-tack glue onto the large chipboard square, including the tape that crosses over the corners. Press the coils into the glue in a random pattern, making certain the top surface of each coil is accessible. Place a piece of wax paper over the pattern. Rest heavy books on top. Let the glue dry completely for several days. Then lift the chipboard square off the work surface, peeling up and snipping off the excess tape ends.

## Technique: Making an Embossing Plate with a Grid Pattern

### MATERIALS AND TOOLS
Chipboard
White craft glue, high-tack
Self-healing cutting mat
Steel ruler
Craft knife
Packing tape
Foam brush
Wax paper
Heavy books

### Step 1
Cut the chipboard squares.

Use a craft knife, steel ruler, and self-healing cutting mat to cut one 5½" (14.0 cm) square and nine 1½" (3.8 cm) squares from chipboard.

### Step 2
Mount the smaller squares on the base.

Lay the large square on a flat work surface and press strips of tape on a diagonal to secure the corners to the work surface. Brush a thick coat of white high-tack glue onto the large chipboard square, including the tape that crosses over the corners. Place the smaller squares in a grid pattern on the gluey surface, even with the outside edges and ½" (1.3 cm) apart. Place a piece of wax paper over the pattern. Rest heavy books on top. Let the glue dry completely for several days. Then lift the grid

off the work surface, peeling up and snipping off the excess tape ends.

## Technique: Making an Embossing Plate with a Leaf Pattern

### MATERIALS AND TOOLS
Leaf pattern (page 708)
High-density rubber
Chipboard
White craft glue, high-tack
Self-healing cutting mat
Steel ruler
Craft knife
Wire cutters
Scissors
Packing tape
Foam brush
Wax paper
Heavy books

### Step 1
Make the embossing plate base.

Use a craft knife, steel ruler, and self-healing cutting mat to cut a 5½" (14.0 cm) square from chipboard. Lay the square on a flat work surface and press strips of tape on a diagonal to secure corners of the square to the work surface.

### Step 2
Make the leaves.

Use the Leaf pattern to trace and cut six

leaves out of dense rubber using a craft knife or scissors. Use a craft knife to incise a pattern of veins in each leaf.

## Step 3

Mount the leaves on the base.

Brush a thick coat of white glue onto the large chipboard square. Press the leaves into the glue in a random pattern. Place a piece of wax paper over the pattern. Rest heavy books on top. Let the glue dry completely for several days. Then lift the grid off the work surface, peeling up and snipping off the excess tape ends.

Embossing Velvet

The difference between the texture of plain velvet and embossed velvet is so striking, you will love making the transformation. Embossing is an imprecise art in that it is difficult to fix the exact position of the embossed impression on the velvet. The reason for this is that the velvet being embossed is covering and concealing the embossing object during the process. This is not a problem when you are embossing single impressions, but on large swaths of fabric, you will find it easier to incorporate random overlapping patterns into your design rather than trying to fix a precise pattern of evenly spaced motifs.

## Technique: Dry-Embossing Velvet

Use a single embossing object to begin. When you are familiar with the embossing technique, try embossing more than one motif at a time, using an embossing plate with a fixed pattern of embossing objects.

MATERIALS AND TOOLS

Embossing object, such as a wire coil
Velvet, either rayon or silk
Spray starch
Square of cotton cloth
Household iron
Pot that lies flat when inverted

## Step 1

Heat the iron.

Empty the iron of all water, turning it upside down to shake out the drops. Make sure the steam function is turned off. Turn on the iron to its hottest setting and preheat for 10 minutes to vaporize any residual water.

## Step 2

Set up the embossing object.

Place the pot, bottom side up, on a protected, heat-resistant work surface. Set the wire coil on top.

## Step 3

Prepare the velvet for embossing.

Lay the area of the velvet you wish to emboss on top of the coil, nap side down. Apply a light mist of spray starch to the wrong side of the velvet. Lay the square of cotton cloth on top.

## Step 4

Emboss the first motif.

Press the hot iron down on the cloth for 6 seconds. Do not move the iron back and forth.

---

# Project Ideas for Embossed Velvet

Use embossed velvet to sew soft furnishings for your home, decorative accents, or personal accessories.

- Throw pillows
- Squares for a patchwork quilt, each with a different embossed pattern
- Table runner
- Scarf
- Small purse
- Tote bag

Lift the iron straight up off the surface and set it aside.

**Step 5**

Emboss the remaining motifs.

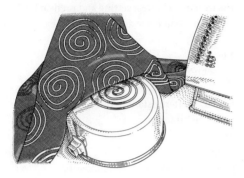

Slide the velvet across the pot, nap side down, so that a new section covers the wire coil. Repeat steps 3 and 4 to emboss another coil shape into the velvet. Continue to emboss the velvet until there is an overall random pattern of overlapping coils. Use the embossed velvet in any decorative way you wish.

## Ribbons and Trims

Using ribbons and trims to accent and revitalize home furnishings and decorative accessories is fairly quick and easy. Embellishments that use ribbons and trims require only the most fundamental hand or machine sewing skills to create, yet they can bring style and

## Troubleshooting: Dry-Embossing Velvet

| Problem | Cause | Remedy |
|---|---|---|
| Embossed impressions are blurred. | Embossing object or velvet shifted during the embossing process. | Press the iron straight down onto the surface and lift it straight up; do not move the iron back and forth or glide it along the velvet. |
| Velvet shows an embossed impression that is not from the embossing object. | The hot iron accidentally touched this area of the velvet or it pressed the velvet against the edge of the embossing plate or platform such as the pot. | Keep the iron level and flat against the embossing object. |
| | Steam vents released bursts of steam into the velvet. | Make sure iron is completely drained of water and steam feature is turned off before embossing. |
| A shape was embossed in the wrong area by mistake. | Embossing object is concealed underneath the velvet so exact position of shape is unknown. | Create a pattern of overlapping motifs that doesn't require precise spacing. |

color to a wide assortment of home furnishings, including pillows, runners, throws, and lampshades.

## Materials and Tools

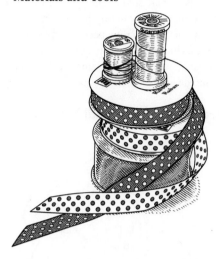

- **Ribbons**

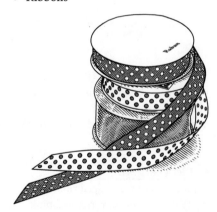

Ribbons are available in an enormous variety of fabrics, colors, widths, and styles; prices are based on the fiber content, surface detail, finishing, and overall quality. If you think of ribbon as an art supply, you will be able to imagine new uses for these strips of fabric. After you have chosen your ribbon, learn ways to manipulate it by wrapping, folding, crimping, or a combination of maneuvers, to create shapely decorations such as the featured ribbon rose and dainty bud.

- **Trims**
Trims include huge categories of tassels, fringe, and cord, among other types of prestitched dangling things that are available in a broad range of styles from opulent to plain. Although you can purchase any type of trim to suit your personal tastes and decorating needs, you can also make your own trims, including beaded trim.
- **Beads**
Beads add color and texture to whatever surface they are applied to, especially soft furnishings where even restrained use—such as a single pearl in the center of a pillow—can quickly and easily transform ordinary items into stylish accessories. Single beads can be added one at a time or in clusters, neat rows, and random scatterings. The variety of beads suited to accenting or loading onto home furnishings is nearly infinite; beads are available in a wide range of sizes, shapes, and materials, from semiprecious stones to plastic.
- **Thread**
Threads of varying weights and fibers are necessary to attach fabric trims and beads to your fabric project. Wound on spools, thread can be made of cotton, silk, polyester, nylon, filament, and other fibers. Polyester thread is easy to work with and versatile. It comes in a wide range of colors and is resistant to knotting and tangling. Monofilament is transparent and versatile, suited to attaching beads and trims in different colors to a single project. Heavier threads, such as twisted cotton and polyester, have the color range and hand of silk, making them suited to handmade tassels.

- **Sewing and cutting tools**

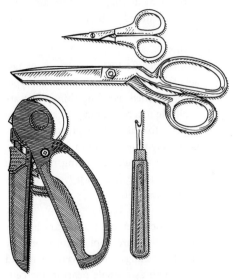

Various sewing and measuring tools are essential for securing embellishments neatly to soft furnishings. They include hand-sewing and embroidery needles, straight and ball-head pins, safety pins, a tape measure, and a yardstick. For cutting, you will need two types of scissors (thread scissors and dressmaker's shears). A rotary cutter will handle straight and slightly curving cuts in slippery fabrics with greater accuracy than scissors; your rotary-cutting equipment should include an acrylic grid ruler and self-healing cutting mat. Task-specific tools include a seam ripper and a thimble.

- **Sewing machine**

The sewing machine is an indispensable workhorse for sewing efficiently, accurately, and quickly. Even the most reasonably priced portable machine sews the straight stitch and the zigzag stitch. The zigzag stitch can be adjusted to a very short stitch length for satin stitch embroidery by machine. Presser foots that form ruffles are available, and some basic machines include a blind hem stitch.

## The Ribbon Rose

Using ribbon to make flowers, especially roses, is an economical and appealing way to take advantage of the wide selection of beautiful ribbons that are sold by the yard (or meter) or by the spool. You can buy ribbons in one colorway—pale pink, rose, peach, and cream—to make a cluster of roses on a pillow, or you can mix soft pastels or vivid primary colors to replicate the look of a country garden.

## Technique: Making a Ribbon Rose

A ribbon rose is made from a single length of wire-edged ribbon that is maneuvered into a series of folds and tacked in place. Using a variegated pink ribbon adds to the rose's lifelike appearance.

MATERIALS AND TOOLS

1 yard (0.9 m) wire-edged ribbon, 1½" (3.8 cm) wide, in variegated pink (for rose petals and bud)

Scrap of wire-edged ribbon, 1½" (3.8 cm) wide, in leaf green (for calyx)

Wire-edged ribbon, 6" (15.2 cm) long × 1½" (3.8 cm) wide, in leaf green (for stem with leaf)

Matching thread

Scissors

Hand-sewing needle

**Step 1**
Make the center bud.

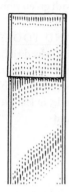

Lay the pink ribbon on a flat surface. Working from one end, fold down a 1" (2.5 cm) section of the ribbon.

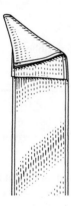

Fold down the right corner and flatten the fold.

Then fold over the top left point of the triangle, rolling it into a cone shape. Use a threaded needle to tack the ribbon in place.

**Step 2**
Make the first petal.

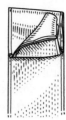

Hold the base of the cone and loop the long ribbon streamer around your finger to form the first petal. Pinch the ribbon at the base of the bud, tacking the petal to secure it.

**Step 3**
Make the second petal.

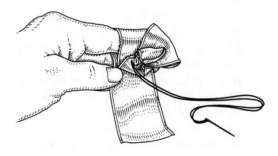

Turn the bud and the petal clockwise and make a second petal as before, overlapping the first petal slightly.

**Step 4**
Make the remaining rose petals.

Continue making petals, overlapping the sides of adjacent petals, until there are between 10 and 12 petals in all. Tack all of the petals at the base of the flower, sewing through all the layers of ribbon and anchoring the thread with several tiny stitches.

### Step 5

Add the calyx to the base of the rose.

Use a 1" (2.5 cm) length of green scrap ribbon to conceal the underside of the rose, pressing it over the calyx and folding under a narrow hem at each raw edge, using tiny stitches to secure it.

### Step 6

Shape the petals.

Use your fingers to shape each petal, rolling the straight fold at the top edge of the petal into a curl and folding down the corners until the construction resembles a real rose.

### Step 7 (optional)

Make a leaf with a stem.

For a pointed leaf, fold a 2¼" (5.7 cm) length of green ribbon in half widthwise and twist the bottom raw edges together, making a pointed shaft. Thread a needle and double-knot the thread. Sew tiny stitches to secure the leaf at the raw end, wrapping the thread around the shaft once and pulling tightly, and then securing the wrap with a few more tiny stitches. Fold in the top two corners of the ribbon on an angle to shape the leaf. For the stem, position the shaft of the leaf on the end of a 5" (12.7 cm) length of green ribbon, 1" (2.5 cm) from one raw end, allowing the leaf to extend above the top edge. Fold the raw edge of the green ribbon on an angle to conceal the leaf's shaft. Continue to wrap the green ribbon down and around itself to make a stem. When the stem is the desired length, cut off the excess green ribbon and tack the end. If desired, use tiny stitches to attach the stem of the leaf to the base of the calyx on the rose.

## Technique: Making a Ribbon Rosebud

The bud is made from folded pink ribbon that is wrapped with green ribbon and twisted.

### MATERIALS AND TOOLS

2" (5.1 cm) wire-edged ribbon, 1½" (3.8 cm) wide, in solid pink
6" (15.2 cm) wire-edged ribbon, 1½" (3.8 cm) wide, in leaf green
Matching thread
Scissors
Hand-sewing needle

### Step 1

Make a rosebud.

Fold the pink ribbon in half lengthwise and then again widthwise. Use a threaded needle to tack the raw edges at the base of the bud to secure it.

### Step 2

Prepare the stem ribbon.

Position the bud on the cut length of green ribbon, 1" (2.5 cm) from one raw end, allowing the head of the bud to extend above the top edge.

### Step 3

Wrap the rose and create a stem.

Fold the raw edge of the green ribbon on an angle to conceal the shaft of the bud. Continue to wrap the green ribbon down and around itself to make a stem. When the stem is the desired length, cut off the excess green ribbon and tack the end.

## Beaded Trim

Adding a border of beaded loops to the edge of a lampshade will maximize the lamplight and make the beads sparkle. Although there are many beautiful beaded trims to buy on the market, you can also make your own looped trim using seed beads, for a traditional look, or you can use any style of small bead that coordinates with the shade you are embellishing. See English Garden: A Ribbon-Rose Lampshade (page 551) for a lampshade with beaded trim.

## Technique: Making a Beaded-Loop Trim

A beaded-loop trim can be made in a custom length and sewn onto the edge of a lampshade or other item. A 26-gauge wire is used to make the beaded loops in this design because it is stiff enough to hold the beads in a round hoop shape. Although the featured design uses seed beads, you can use beads of any size as long as you adjust the size of the loops to accommodate the change. Larger beads will make larger loops.

MATERIALS AND TOOLS
Lampshade, 9" top diameter ×
  14" bottom diameter × 12½" high
  (22.9 × 35.6 × 31.8 cm)
Glass seed beads, size 11, in copper: 6
  ounces (170.1 g) or enough strands to
  total 800" (20.3 m)
Beading wire, brass, 28-gauge
Chain-nose pliers
Wire cutters
Ruler
Tape measure

**Step 1**
Measure the lampshade.
Measure the circumference of the lamp-

shade at the bottom edge and add ½" (1.3 cm). My lampshade measured 45½" (115.6 cm) + ½" (1.3 cm), or 46" (116.8 cm).

**Step 2**
Transfer the copper seed beads to the brass wire.

Lay a piece of fabric on your work surface to keep the seed beads from rolling and bouncing. Pull about 56" (142.2 cm) of 28-gauge brass wire from the spool; do not cut it. Transfer approximately 46" (116.8 cm) of copper seed beads (about 800 beads) from several threaded strands of seed beads onto the wire, 1" to 2" (2.5 to 5.1 cm) at a time.

**Step 3**
Make a beaded piece with loops that measures approximately 46" (116.8 cm).

Lay a ruler on the scrap fabric. Press your thumbnail against the wire 2" (5.1 cm) from the end, slide the beads against it, and measure a 1" (2.5 cm) segment of beads (approximately 17 beads). Bend this section back on itself to form a beaded loop, and then twist the wires twice at the base to secure the loop. Slide some loose beads up to the base, count off 5 beads, set your thumbnail against the wire, and measure a second 1" (2.5 cm) segment. Bend this segment into a loop and twist it once to secure it. Repeat the process to form a length of beaded loops that measures approximately 46" (116.8 cm), or your measurement from step 1, to go around the circumference of the shade's bottom edge. To end off, twist the wires twice and cut the wire 1" (2.5 cm) from the twisted base. The featured lampshade required 118 loops to encircle the bottom edge of the lampshade.

## Technique: Trimming a Lampshade with Beaded Loops

The principle of adding a beaded trim is simple. Make a length of beaded trim using beads and wire, and then attach it to the edge of a lampshade using a needle and thread.

### MATERIALS AND TOOLS

Lampshade, with fabric covering
Beaded-loop trim, to fit shade
Clear nylon thread
Ruler
Scissors
Wire cutters
Hand-sewing needle

### Step 1

Secure the thread to the lampshade.

Hold the lampshade upside down so the bottom edge faces up. Insert a threaded needle into the lampshade fabric about ⅛" (0.3 cm) from the edge. Sew a backstitch to anchor the thread end.

### Step 2

Sew on the beaded trim.

Lay the beaded edge of the loops against the edge of the lampshade. Reinsert the needle and exit at a point that is in line with the middle of the beaded loop. Pull the needle through. Bring the needle in front of the loop and catch a bit of the fabric on the shade. Pull the needle through to secure the first loop.

### Step 3

Continue to sew on the trim.

Reinsert the needle and exit the fabric at a point that is in line with the third bead in the row of five beads between the loops. Bring the needle behind the beads and catch a bit of the fabric on the shade. Pull the needle through.

### Step 4

End the trim.

Repeat steps 2 and 3, stitching along the length of the beaded loops to secure the trim to the shade. When you reach the starting point, overlap the beaded loops. End the thread with a few backstitches.

### Step 5

Bend the wire end.

Use wire cutters to cut the wire, leaving a ½" (1.3 cm) beaded tail. Remove two beads and bend the bare wire into a hook, using chain-nose pliers. Hide the hooked end behind a loop. The beaded loops will overlap one another all around.

## Technique: Adding Single Beads or Beaded Segments to a Lampshade

For maximum effect, combine several different beads and trims and sew them to the edge of a lampshade.

### MATERIALS AND TOOLS

Lampshade, with fabric covering
Seed beads, size 10, in any color
Glass diamond-shaped beads,
    14 mm long
Sequins, as desired
Matching thread
Tape measure
Ruler
Scissors
Beading needle

### Step 1

Secure the thread to the lampshade.

Hold the lampshade upside down so the bottom edge faces up. Insert a threaded needle into the lampshade fabric about ⅛" (0.3 cm) from the edge. Sew a backstitch to anchor the thread end.

**Step 2**

Add the first beaded segment.

Pick up two seed beads and one diamond-shaped glass bead on the needle and slide the beads down to the fabric. Place your thumb against the thread where it exits the beaded segment and take a tiny stitch next to the bead hole.

**Step 3**

Sew on the remaining beaded segments.

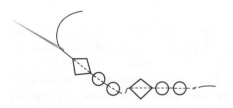

Pick up two more seed beads and one diamond-shaped glass bead and slide them down to the fabric. Anchor the bead segment as in step 1. Continue adding beading segments until the entire circumference of the shade's border is decorated. End with a backstitch and clip the thread.

**Step 4**

Sew seed beads above the first round.

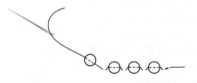

Anchor a new thread that is long enough to go around the lampshade plus 5" (12.7 cm) to the fabric above the beaded row. Pick up one seed bead on the needle and slide it down to the fabric. Place your thumb against the thread where it exits the bead and take a tiny stitch next to the bead hole. Continue working around the lampshade, tacking the beads until the border is decorated. Or, instead of sewing

one bead at a time, string seed beads on the full length of thread to make a strand. Wrap the strand around the lampshade, pushing the beads together, tack the strand to the lampshade where the thread was first anchored, and snip off the thread. Use a new thread to tack the strand of beads at even intervals using a whipstitch.

**Step 5**

Add a round of single seed beads and sequins above the strand of seed beads.

Anchor the thread with a backstitch, and sew a sequin and a seed bead onto the needle. Pass the needle around the seed bead and insert it back through the hole in the sequin, exiting the wrong side of the fabric. Insert the needle up through the fabric, exiting on the right side in a place next to the first sequin-and-bead combination. Continue working around the lampshade until the border is decorated.

## Tassels and Tassel Trim

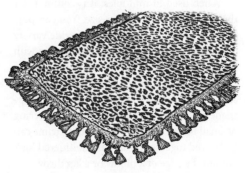

Making a tassel from scratch is a simple matter. Thread is wrapped multiple times around a piece of chipboard, tied off at one end, and trimmed evenly at the other end. The length of the tassel is determined by the size of the chipboard winding card; the tassel thickness is determined by the thread quality and the number of winds. The larger the chipboard, the longer the tassel; the greater the number of wraps, the thicker and plumper the tassel.

Choose the thread for the tassel according to the effect you want. I find rayon and silk embroidery threads very appealing because they make up into a tassel with movement. Threads that come in a wide range of colors are a plus for designing. Different shades in one colorway can be combined to create a tassel with an ombré effect. You can begin winding thread in deep apricot, for instance, and continue by winding lighter and lighter shades of the same color.

Single tassels can be sewn to each corner of a pillow or a lap throw, attached to a curtain tie back, or hung over to a knob for a pretty accent. Handmade tassels are suited to these decorative tasks, adding hints of color, movement, and style with little effort or expense. Sometimes small accents are all it takes to perk up the look of a familiar soft furnishing. Purchased single tassels can be elaborately configured, including those with ornamental heads with braided loops, intricately tied knots, and embroidery, and cut tufts of dangling beads and fine chain.

When used in multiples, it is common for the tassels to be smaller in size. You can purchase tassel trim by the yard in a wide variety of widths and styles. A thickly woven trim with tassels can be sewn to a soft furnishing, such as a table runner. A length of delicate tassel trim can be added to the bottom edge of a lampshade and accented with a random scattering of small beads. Several coordinating trims can be layered together for a rich, multitiered look around the edge of a pillow or a lap throw.

## Technique: Making a Basic Tassel

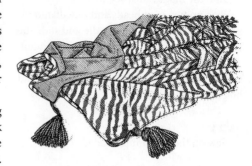

Tassels are very easy to make, requiring only the simple winding of thread around a card to make a skein (that is tied off at one end) and the snipping of the threads at the opposite end to make a loose tuft. Winding is a straightforward maneuver, but it helps to prepare the thread ahead of time by winding it into a ball and setting the ball in a bowl, which will keep it from bouncing around or tangling as you wind it around the card. A tassel can be made in any color, or it can be made with several colors as long as all of the threads used have the same fiber content.

### MATERIALS AND TOOLS

Four or five 70-yard (64.0 m) skeins of rayon or silk embroidery thread, in colors as desired

Glass bead (optional)

Beading glue (optional)

Chipboard, 5" × 7¼" (12.7 × 18.4 cm)

Craft knife

Self-healing mat

Tapestry needle

Scissors

Ruler

Large bowl

### Step 1

Prepare the winding card and balls of thread.

Use a craft knife and a self-healing mat to make a ½" (1.3 cm) slice into each long edge of the chipboard card just above the lower left and lower right corners. Wind each skein into a ball and place the balls in a large bowl.

## Step 2

Wind the threads onto the card.

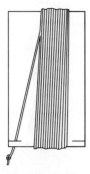

Pull a free end from each ball of thread. Hold the ends together and tie them in a loose overhand knot. Slip the knotted end into the slice on the lower left side of the winding card, allowing the knot to dangle 2" (5.1 cm) beyond the edge of the card. Wind the thread around the central area of the card, using even tension, until you achieve the desired thickness. I wound the threads 160 times around the card.

## Step 3

Secure the wraps.

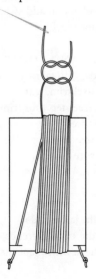

Slip the free ends of thread into the slice on the lower right side of the card. Make a loose overhand knot 2" (5.1 cm) below the edge of the card. Cut off the threads below the knot. Thread an 18" (45.7 cm) length of thread into the tapestry needle. Double the thread and slip the needle under the wraps at the top of the card, pulling the needle until the thread is centered. Tie a tight square knot to secure the wraps of thread. Cut off the needle.

## Step 4 (optional)

Add a decorative bead.

Pass the ends of the threads at the top of the tassel through a large-eye needle. String on a glass bead. Pull on the needle and thread so the knot lodges in the bead hole. Secure the bead with beading glue.

## Step 5

Cut the tassel free.

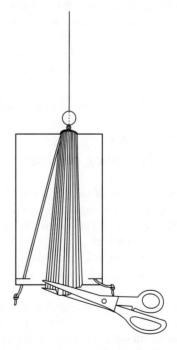

Use scissors to cut the thread loops along the lower edge of the card. Remove the tassel from the card.

**Step 6**
Bind the tassel.

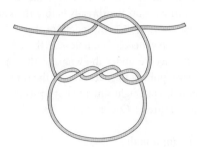

Thread an 18" (45.7 cm) length of thread into the tapestry needle. Hold the top of the tassel at the folded end and wind the thread three times around the tassel, approximately 1" (2.5 cm) below the folds. Tie a tight surgeon's knot to secure the wraps of thread. Continue to wrap the thread around the throat of the tassel to make a neat band. To end off, insert the needle back and forth through the tassel, hiding the passes between the threads. Cut

---

## Working Tips: Preventing Raveling

To prevent the ends of a length of twisted cord or braided trim from raveling, wrap a piece of clear tape around the cord or trim before you cut it. Cut through the center of the tape so that a bit of tape remains on both cut ends to prevent them from raveling. Depending on the application, the taped end can be concealed in a seam or overlapped and covered. You can also apply a liquid fray preventative to seal the cut ends of a trim. Drying usually takes 24 hours before the trim can be handled and the tape removed.

---

off the needle and allow the binding thread to hang down.

**Step 7**
Trim the tassel.

Hold the tassel in one hand with the threads hanging down and pull the threads through your other hand to compress the ends of thread into a bunch. Use scissors to trim the ends even.

## Technique: Adding Tassel Trim to a Lampshade

Available by the yard, tassel trim can be hand sewn to the bottom edge of a fabric-covered lampshade to add swingy movement and a decorator touch.

### MATERIALS AND TOOLS

Lampshade, with fabric covering
Beaded-tassel trim, with ½" (1.3 cm)
   tassels (see step 1 for trim length)
Matching thread
Straight pins
Tape measure
Scissors

**Step 1**
Measure the lampshade.
Measure the circumference of the bottom of the lampshade with a tape measure and add

2" (5.1 cm). Buy a length of beaded-tassel trim equal to that measurement.

**Step 2**

Sew on the trim.

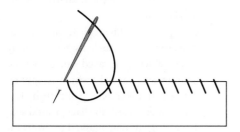

Use straight pins to secure the trim along the lower outside edge so that the tassels hang down. Use a threaded needle to sew the top edge of the woven trim to the shade's fabric, using the overcast stitch that gets lost in the woven trim. When you reach the starting point, tuck in the raw edge and tack the over-lap.

**Step 3**

Sew the lower edge.

Repeat step 2 to sew the bottom edge of the woven trim to the lower edge of the lampshade all around.

## Decals and Heat-Transfers

The appeal of decals and heat-transfers is that you can use artwork that would otherwise be difficult to create, unless you are particularly talented in drawing or painting, for embellishment. A special decal transfer paper allows you to transfer a drawing, engraving, or photograph to an object made of any smooth nonporous material, such as metal, glass, or ceramic. Similarly, you can use heat-transfer paper and an ordinary dry household iron to print artwork of every description on paper, fabric, and even wood. The most familiar use of heat-transfers is T-shirt art, but there are many more options.

Materials and Tools

- **Image for the decal or heat-transfer**

There are countless sources of images, in both black-and-white and color, that can be sourced from books and online for use as decals. Once you have chosen an image, make a copy of it on glossy paper to serve as your source art; the glossy patina will aid in creating a crisp reproduction of the image on the decal transfer paper or heat-transfer paper.

- **Decorative nonporous item**

Decals are transferred to nonporous items, such as glass vases and tableware, metal pots, and ceramic jugs and bowls. After you choose an object to embellish, the source art can be sized so that the decal is in scale, proportion, and balance with the dimensions of the piece.

- **Decal transfer paper**
  Decal transfer paper sheets measure a copier-friendly 8½" × 11" (21.6 × 27.9 cm). The paper comes in two kinds, according to the type of copier used to print the image, and each provides a different visual effect. The first type prints on an ink-jet printer. The background and non-printed areas remain white after the decal dries, making it well suited for items that have white or light-colored surfaces. The second type must be printed on a low-fusing laser copier that uses an oil-based toner. Its background and nonprinted areas remain transparent, making the decal suitable for application to glass and other transparent items. Read the package instructions carefully to make certain you choose the right decal transfer paper for your design and project surface, as well as the copier available to you.

- **Fabric item for heat-transfer**
  Cotton or polyester fabrics with a flat, tight, even weave or smooth cotton or polyester knits, such as T-shirt fabric, are suited for heat transfer. Napkins, tablecloths, pillowcases, and apparel can be decorated with this method. It is also possible to decorate wood and paper with cotton rag content with heat-transfers.

- **Heat-transfer paper**
  Heat-transfer paper comes in precut sheets that measure either 8½" × 11" (21.6 × 27.9 cm) or 11" × 17" (27.9 × 43.2 cm) to fit into a copier or printer paper tray. Some transfer papers are designed for ink-jet printers, others for laser printers, and still others for copiers. Be sure to use the type of copier or

printer recommended by the manufacturer of the transfer paper you are using. Read the package labels of transfer paper products and choose a type that is compatible with the machines available to you and the surface you wish to decorate.

- **Acrylic sealer**
  An applied decal benefits from a coat of protective finish, such as acrylic spray sealer, which is sprayed on, or acrylic medium-and-varnish, which is applied with a soft watercolor paintbrush. If a spray sealer is used, the background surface will need to be masked to protect it from overspray, unless you are coating the entire decorative surface.

- **Shallow bowl**
  A decal is soaked in water to separate the printed acrylic layer from the backing paper. Any shallow vessel that is large enough for the decal can be used.

- **Cutting tools**

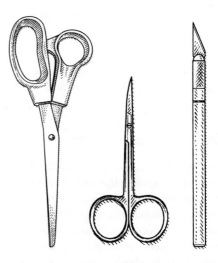

You will need a pair of general-purpose scissors, manicure scissors, and a craft knife and self-healing cutting mat, depending upon your choice of image. For more detailed descriptions of these cutting tools, see Chapter Five.

- **Photocopier or computer printer**
  You will need access to either an ink-jet printer or a toner-based laser photocopier, depending upon the transfer paper you choose.
- **Household iron**
  A household iron is used with dry heat to adhere heat-transfer images to fabric.

### Waterslide Method of Applying Decals

The term *waterslide* refers to transfer decals that are backed with a water-activated glue. When the decal is submerged in water, the sheet of acrylic imprinted with the image slides off the carrier paper and the water begins activating the glue that will enable the decal to adhere to the project surface.

You can use the waterslide technology to apply decals to any smooth nonporous surface, including metal, ceramic, or glass. The type of decal transfer paper you choose—ink-jet or laser—will depend on the project surface. A decal made on an ink-jet printer becomes temporarily transparent when it is soaked in water, but the decal dries white and remains opaque once it is applied to a decorative object. On white or light surfaces, a decal with a white background will virtually disappear. The look is similar to that of transferware, a style of fired ceramics developed in England in the mid-eighteenth century in which a decorative pattern was printed onto a piece of tissue paper and then transferred to bisque or a glazed piece of dinnerware.

Decals for glass and colored ceramic surfaces are specially formulated to remain clear after they have dried. The lines, shapes, and patterns of the artwork stand out, and the clear portion of the decal virtually disappears into the background. This type of decal transfer paper must be printed on a low-fusing laser copier that uses fuser oil. A visit to my local copy store ensured that I was using the right equipment for my decal transfer paper.

### Technique: Applying a Decal using the Waterslide Method

Choose a decal transfer paper that will result in either a white or a clear background—whichever is better for your project surface—and follow the manufacturer's instructions on the package to make sure you print the transfer paper on the appropriate equipment. Items decorated with waterslide decals can be wiped with a moist cloth but must not be submerged in water, as soaking will dissolve the glue and loosen the decal.

#### MATERIALS AND TOOLS

Monkey original art (page 710)
Decal transfer paper
Glossy copy paper
Ink-jet printer or low-fusing laser copier
Nonporous decorative object
Acrylic medium-and-varnish
Straight-blade scissors
Manicure scissors
Pencil or china marker
Sponge
Spray glass cleaner, or 1:1 vinegar-and-water solution
Shallow bowl
Paper towels, nonembossed (for less lint)
Tapered watercolor brush

#### Step 1

Print the decal.

Copy the monkey image onto glossy paper; note that it is not necessary to reverse the image as the decal will be applied face up to the decorative object. Follow the manufacturer's instructions to copy the image onto the eggshell, glossy side (the acrylic layer) of the decal transfer paper. Let the decal dry for 30 minutes before handling.

#### Step 2

Clean the decorative object.

Clean the surface of the decorative object of any grease or fingerprints, using glass cleaner or a 1:1 vinegar-and-water solution and paper towels.

**Step 3**
Cut out the decal.

Use scissors to rough-cut the decal from the sheet of transfer paper, cutting through both layers. Then use manicure scissors to cut the small details, following the general contour of the print and leaving a scant ⅛" (0.3 cm) margin.

**Step 4**
Mark the position of the decal.
Place the cutout decal on the surface of the object. Use a pencil or a china marker to make light ticks on the object to note the position.

**Step 5**
Soak the decal.

Pour warm water into a shallow bowl. Slip the decal under the surface until it is completely submerged, which will cause the paper to curl and then straighten. Wait a minute or two for the decal to release from the backing and then lift the decal out of the water, using the paper backing as support.

**Step 6**
Adhere the decal to the decorative item.

Place the decal, image side up, onto the item in the marked position, holding the top edge of the decal slightly off the surface with your fingers. Press one finger on the other hand against the bottom edge of the decal to stabilize it and use your fingers on the other hand to carefully slide the backing paper out from under the decal until it is off. Use wet fingers to pat the decal in place. Smooth the decal with a damp sponge, working from the center out to the edges to remove air bubbles. Blot away excess glue and water. Let the decal dry overnight.

**Step 7**
Apply acrylic sealer to the decal.

Use a tapered watercolor brush to apply two thin, even coats of acrylic medium-and-varnish to the surface of the decal, allowing the first coat to dry before applying the second.

## Baking Method of Applying Decals

Baking is an alternative to the waterslide method for decals that embellish glass and ceramic surfaces. The decal's transparent backing bakes on and becomes an integral part of the project surface. The item can be gently washed by hand without compromising the decal, making this method suited to glass and ceramic items of every description. Glass tableware can be embellished by applying the decal to a surface that will not come in contact with food—the outside of a drinking glass or mug, the underside of a plate or platter.

While straightforward to do, the baking method requires time and diligence to ensure good results. To adhere the decal, the item with decal adhered is placed into an ordinary home oven at a low temperature and the temperature is gradually increased in small increments over a period of several hours. The gradual rise in temperature prevents the glass or ceramic from cracking and prevents the decal from bubbling and blistering, which would result in incomplete bonding. Preparatory steps that lead up to baking include printing the image onto decal transfer paper, cutting out the decal, heat-setting the decal inks with a heat gun or in a home oven, and adhering the decal to the project item.

A few caveats are worth special mention. In the waterslide method, the decal is placed glue side down on the project surface. In the baking method, the decal is positioned ink side down on the surface and the water-activating glue is not needed. It is important to wipe off this

## Working Tips: Changing an Opaque White Decal to a Transparent Decal

It is possible to convert a decal from opaque to transparent after it has been applied to a porous object. Use a tapered watercolor paintbrush to apply two or three thin, even coats of clear, oil-based varnish, allowing one coat to dry before applying the next. Be aware that the method is not suited to objects that will come in contact with food or beverages.

## Distinguishing between a Color Laser Printer and a Color Laser Copier

It is important to note the difference between a color laser *printer* and a color laser *copier* before using decal transfer paper. Generally speaking, a copier operates at a low-fusing temperature and uses fuser oil; this type of machine is found in a copy shop. A color laser printer operates at a high-fusing temperature and does not use fuser oil. This high-fusing technology is found in newer color laser copiers entering the market. Each of these machines requires different decal transfer paper. If you run a paper with a low-fusing temperature through a high-temperature machine, the paper can melt on the print rollers.

unwanted glue before baking. Any glue that remains will turn brown when exposed to the oven heat and ruin the appearance of the decal.

Every oven works a little differently according to brand, type, and efficiency of insulation. I would recommend testing your oven before baking a decal onto a good item. The first time I used the baking method, I experimented with a small glass plate. I used an electric oven and kept careful track of the time increments, the changes in oven temperature, and the position of the plate in the oven. I made adjustments as needed, reducing the temperature increments or lowering the oven rack position, to avoid heating the glass too quickly or scorching the decal.

## Technique: Printing a Transparent Decal for the Baking Method

Choose a decal transfer paper designed for a low-fusing copier, as the inks are suited to the baking method. The finished decal will be placed face down on the glass or ceramic surface, which will reverse the image. To ensure the correct orientation, especially important for letters and numerals, you must print a mirror image of your original art to start.

### MATERIALS AND TOOLS
Image for decal
Glossy paper
Decal transfer paper
Low-fusing photocopier that uses fuser oil

**Step 1**
Copy the image.
Make a mirror image copy of your selected art onto glossy paper.

**Step 2**
Print the mirror image onto the decal transfer paper.
Photocopy the glossy print made in step 1 onto the eggshell, glossy side (or acrylic layer) of the decal transfer paper. Let the ink dry for 30 minutes.

## Technique: Cutting Out a Transparent Decal

The cutting path does not have to crop in close on a transparent decal. Motifs that are near one another can be cut out as a group to maintain the sturdiness of a transparent decal without sacrificing the look of the art.

### MATERIALS AND TOOLS
Decal image printed on decal transfer paper
Straight-blade scissors
Manicure scissors
Craft knife (optional)
Self-healing cutting mat (optional)

**Step 1**
Rough-cut the decal.
Use straight-blade scissors to cut the image from the sheet of decal transfer paper, leaving a generous border around the image and cutting through the layers of the transfer paper.

**Step 2**
Cut out the details.
Use manicure scissors to cut out the details on the decal, following the general contour of the print and leaving a scant ⅛" (0.3 cm) margin. For more precision or in tight areas, use a craft knife and self-healing mat.

## Technique: Heat-Setting a Transparent Decal with a Heat Gun

Heat-setting causes the copier ink to bond to the acrylic layer of the decal so that it does not bubble up during baking. Bubbles work against the smooth adhesion to the glass surface.

### MATERIALS AND TOOLS
Decal, printed and cut out
Heat gun

**Step 1**
Heat-set the decal.
Place the decal on a protected work surface. Plug in the heat gun, turn on the switch,

and let it run for a few seconds, giving it time to heat. Then wave the nozzle back and forth over the surface of the decal to set the toners in the printing ink. The printed image will appear shiny when the toner is set. Turn off the switch and unplug the heat gun. Let the decal cool.

### Step 2

Allow curing time.

Let the decal cool to room temperature.

## Technique: Heat-Setting a Decal in a Home Oven

Here is an alternative method for heat-setting a decal if you don't have a heat gun.

### MATERIALS AND TOOLS

Decal, printed and cut out
Home oven
Baking sheet
Parchment paper
Oven mitts
Wire rack

### Step 1

Prepare for heat-setting.

Preheat the oven to 350°F (176.7°C). Line a baking sheet with parchment paper. Place the decal ink side up on the parchment.

### Step 2

Heat-set the decal.

Place the baking sheet in the oven for 3 minutes, or until the decal's printed image is shiny.

### Step 3

Allow curing time.

Use oven mitts to remove the baking sheet from the oven and set it on a wire rack. Let the decal cool to room temperature.

## Technique: Applying a Decal to a Glass or Ceramic Surface

A key step in this technique is removing the glue, which is not needed for the baking method, from the back of the decal.

### MATERIALS AND TOOLS

Decal, cut out and heat-set
Ovenproof nonporous item
Spray glass cleaner
Paper towels, nonembossed (for less lint)
China marker
Sponge
Shallow bowl

### Step 1

Prepare the item for embellishing.

Use glass cleaner and lint-free paper towels to remove any fingerprints or grease from the glass or ceramic surface. Use a china marker to make light ticks on the object to note the position of the decal.

### Step 2

Soak the heat-set decal.

Pour warm water into a shallow bowl. Slip the decal under the surface until it is completely submerged, which will cause the paper to curl and then straighten. Wait a minute or two for the decal to release from the backing and then lift the decal out of the water, using the paper backing as support.

### Step 3

Apply the decal to the decorative item.

Position the decal ink side down on the marked area of the glass or ceramic surface.

Use your fingers to carefully slide the backing off the decal, being careful not to rip or tear any fragile parts of the decal. Use a moist sponge to gently wipe off the glue from the back of the decal and to remove any air bubbles, working from the center of the decal to the outside edges. Blot away any excess water.

## Technique: Baking a Decal on a Glass or Ceramic Surface

Gradual heating of the glass or ceramic object is critical in baking on a decal. If you use the oven method to heat-set the decal, open the oven door and allow the oven to cool before beginning the baking technique. As you move through the steps to increase the heat in the oven, be aware that the small increments are set to reduce the risks of overheating a glass or ceramic item, which can cause it to crack. To moderate the temperature at the higher level, 350°F to 380°F (176.7°C to 193.3°C), you may find that opening the oven door provides a thermal cushion. In all cases, let the texture and gloss on the decal determine the time your project remains in the oven.

### MATERIALS AND TOOLS

Ovenproof item in glass or ceramic with heat-set decal applied
Home oven
Baking sheet

Timer
Tablespoon

### Step 1

Preheat the oven.

Set the oven temperature to 200°F (93.3°C) or the lowest possible setting. Leave the oven door open.

### Step 2

Warm the decal for 30 minutes.

Place the glass or ceramic item on a baking sheet. Set the baking sheet on the middle rack in the oven. With the oven door open, bake the item for 15 minutes. Close the oven door and bake it for another 15 minutes.

### Step 3

Check the decal.

Open the oven door. Check to see that the decal is flat against the glass or ceramic surface. Use the bowl side of a tablespoon to gently tap down any parts of the decal that are not adhering. Close the oven door.

### Step 4

Bake the item for 80 minutes with the oven door closed.

Wearing oven mitts, transfer the baking sheet with the glass or ceramic object to the lower rack and close the oven door. Continue baking for another 80 minutes, increasing the oven temperature by 15°F (8°C) every 10 minutes until the oven temperature reaches 320°F (160.0°C).

### Step 5

Bake the item for the final 30 minutes more with the oven door open.

Put on oven mitts, open the oven door, and move the baking sheet with the glass or ceramic item to a lower rack in the oven to prevent overheating or browning of the decal. Continue baking the item for approximately 30 minutes more, increasing the oven temperature by 20°F (11.1°C) every 10 minutes. Keep a watchful eye during this stage. The decal should be baked onto the glass or ceramic by the time the oven reaches 380°F (193.3°C), although it may have bonded before. If the decal is shiny, it is bonded to the surface.

## Step 6

Allow the item to cool.

Turn off the oven and open the oven door but do not remove the baking sheet. Let the item rest inside the oven until it is cool. Use oven mitts, if needed, to carefully remove the item from the oven. Avoid touching the decal.

## Making Heat-Transfers

Heat-transfers are made on smooth woven or knit fabrics, paper, and even wood. Choose subjects for transfers that are appealing to you, keeping in mind the style and size of your project surface. I tend toward engraved art from the early nineteenth century when designing greeting cards, because the line work is so beautiful when viewed up close. I prefer more contemporary art for T-shirt designs, such as the simple drawings of a child.

Drawing by Yvan Guénot, age six

## Baking a Decal onto a Nonporous Surface

|  | Baking Time | Oven Condition | Oven Temperature |
|---|---|---|---|
| Stage One | 15 minutes | Open door Item on middle rack | Lowest setting |
|  | 15 minutes | Closed door | Lowest setting |
| Stage Two | 80 minutes | Closed door Item on lower rack | Increase by 15°F (8.5°C) every 10 minutes until the oven temperature reaches 320°F (160.0°C) |
|  | 30 minutes | Open door Item on lower rack | Increase by 20°F (11.1°C) every 10 minutes; decal should be baked on and shiny at 380°F (193.3°C) or before |
| Stage Three | 30 minutes | Open door Item left inside to cool | Oven off |

Heat-transfer paper is sized to fit a copier or printer paper tray, and the finished size of your art for most projects will fall within these standard dimensions. In fact, I like to copy an assortment of engravings, paintings, and original drawings onto a single sheet of transfer paper, placing as many images as will fit, and then cutting them apart for individual projects as needed. This strategy allows me to keep multiple illustrations at my fingertips for use on stationery of all kinds, from greeting cards to postcards. Should you happen to work with a larger design that exceeds the paper size, you can always copy the design in sections onto separate sheets of transfer paper and transfer them to the project surface one section at a time, until the complete image is reconfigured.

## Technique: Printing on Heat-Transfer Paper

You can use either a copier or a printer to print images onto heat-transfer paper. Just bear in mind that the different types of heat-transfer papers are machine-specific, so choose a paper and a machine that are compatible with one another. You can run heat-transfer paper through a copier or printer only once, so it is economical to copy as many images on one sheet at a time as possible. Refer to the manufacturer's instructions for the correct orientation when placing photo-transfer paper in the paper tray.

### MATERIALS AND TOOLS

Art, copyright-free, in color or black-and-white

Heat-transfer paper, for copier or printer

Photocopier, or computer scanner and printer

### Step 1

Prepare the art.

Copy the art, enlarging or reducing it as desired. Test-fit the art on your project surface, making additional copies as needed, until the size is confirmed. Print a copy of the final resized art.

### Step 2

Prepare to copy.

Lay the resized art face down on the glass of the copier or scanner bed and close the cover. Place a single sheet of photo-transfer paper in an empty paper tray, following the manufacturer's guidelines regarding orientation.

### Step 3

Make the photo transfer.

Copy the image onto the photo-transfer paper. Allow the ink to dry completely, about 1 minute or according to the information on the packaging, before handling.

## Applying Heat-Transfers to Paper and Fabric

Once the chosen image is printed onto the special paper, the image can be transferred to a porous surface using the heat of a household iron. For paper projects, such as handmade greeting cards and postcards, I prefer 100 percent cotton cardstock in a range of whites, from antique white to écru and ivory. The cotton fiber gives the paper an elegant hand, especially in the medium and heavier weights. Fabrics suitable for heat-transfer include smooth, even-weave cotton and polyester fabrics, 50/50 polyester-cotton blends, and knitted fabrics, such as T-shirts. You can print directly onto a garment or finished item, such as a tote bag, or you can print fabric to incorporate into a hand-sewn project. There is another kind of photo-transfer paper that is composed of a layer of photosensitive fabric adhered to a carrier sheet. This combination product can be placed in the paper tray of a copier or printer so that the image can be printed directly onto the fabric, without the need to iron.

Transferred images are sensitive to heat and can melt if they come into contact with a hot iron, so be careful.

## Technique: Using Heat-Transfer to Embellish Paper

The paper that receives a heat-transferred image must support the transfer layer and be able to withstand the heat of an iron without scorching. Medium-weight and heavy-weight 100 percent cotton cardstock satisfies both of these conditions. Once an image is transferred, never place a hot iron directly on it as the heat will smear or melt it. If transferring more than one image to a single sheet of transfer paper, do not remove the backing papers until all of the images have been transferred; or, make sure to protect the adjacent transfers when ironing nearby transfers by repositioning the backing sheets as you work. (See page 281, steps 6–7, in the Paper Crafting chapter for more detailed instructions for transferring multiple images.) In addition, because pressing times vary widely according to the size of the transfer and the kind of transfer paper used, it is important to read and follow the package directions.

### MATERIALS AND TOOLS

Photo-transfer paper with printed art
Medium-weight 100 percent cotton cardstock
Household iron
Craft knife
Steel ruler
Self-healing mat

### Step 1

Heat the iron.

Empty the iron of all water, turning it upside down to shake out the drops. Make sure the steam function is turned off. Turn on the iron to its hottest setting and preheat for 10 minutes to vaporize any residual water.

### Step 2

Cut the cardstock and the photo transfer.

Lay the cardstock on the self-healing mat. Use a steel ruler and a craft knife to cut the paper to the desired size. Cut the photo transfer to size in the same way.

### Step 3

Prepare to transfer.

Read the manufacturer's directions on the package of photo-transfer paper. Set the cardstock right side up on a flat, protected work surface. Lay the photo-transfer art on the cardstock print side down.

### Step 4

Complete the transfer.

Press the iron on the back of the photo transfer for about 15 seconds or according to the manufacturer's directions, constantly moving the iron in a circular motion to prevent scorching. Make sure to press the corners and edges of the transfer paper backing. While the paper backing is still hot, lift up one corner and slowly peel off the paper backing in one continuous motion, checking as you go to see that the print has transferred completely to the cardstock. If the paper does not lift off easily or if there is a partial print, return the backing paper to its original position and reheat the area, moving the iron until the paper peels off easily.

## Technique: Using Heat-Transfer to Embellish Light-Colored Fabric

Use this technique to transfer images to white or light-colored fabrics with an iron. Follow the same process for dark fabrics, except use an opaque photo-transfer paper. It is important to protect the print after it is on the fabric. Never place a hot iron directly on the transferred print as the heat will smear or melt it.

### MATERIALS AND TOOLS

Photo-transfer paper for light-colored fabrics
Smooth, even-weave polyester or polyester-cotton fabric, in white or a light color
Household iron
Craft knife
Steel ruler
Self-healing mat

**Step 1**

Heat the iron.

Empty the iron of all water, turning it upside down to shake out the drops. Make sure the steam function is turned off. Turn on the iron to its hottest setting and preheat for 10 minutes to vaporize any residual water.

**Step 2**

Cut the photo transfer.

Lay the photo transfer on a self-healing mat. Use a steel ruler and a craft knife to cut the photo transfer to the desired size.

**Step 3**

Prepare to transfer.

Read the manufacturer's directions on the package of photo-transfer paper. Lay the fabric on a protected work surface and use the hot iron to press it flat. Immediately lay the photo-transfer art, print side down, on the fabric.

**Step 4**

Complete the transfer.

Press the iron on the back of the photo transfer for about 15 seconds or according to the manufacturer's directions, constantly moving the iron in a circular motion to prevent scorching. Make sure to press the corners and edges of the transfer paper backing. While the paper backing is still hot, lift up one corner and slowly peel off the paper backing in one continuous motion, checking as you go to see that the print has transferred completely to the fabric. If the paper does not lift off easily or if there is a partial print, return the backing paper to its original position and reheat the area, moving the iron until the paper peels off easily.

## Quick & Easy: Homemade Transfer Textiles

At times, I have been inspired to begin a project late at night, long after the craft store had closed for the day. Such was the case one night when I discovered I was out of transfer textiles. After trial and error, I found that a sheet of freezer paper could support a piece of lightweight muslin in a secure layer that could be fed through my home printer (an Epson that consistently produced clean images). Here's what to do:

- Cut freezer paper into standard-size 8½" × 11" (21.6 × 27.9 cm) sheets.
- Cut pieces of muslin slightly larger than the freezer paper sheets and iron them flat.

- Lay one piece of muslin on a protected work surface, place a sheet of freezer paper on it shiny side down, and press with a warm household iron until the layers adhere.
- Carefully trim the muslin fabric even with the sheet of freezer paper. The edges must be crisp and clean so that they do not get stuck in the printer.
- Hand-feed the muslin transfer paper one sheet at a time into the printer to copy your art onto it.
- When you are ready to use the printed muslin, peel off the freezer paper backing.

## Quick & Easy: Photo-Transfer Faux Masterpiece

 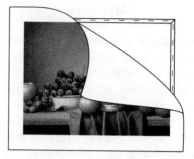

For a fun project, use photo-transfer and faux-finishing techniques to make your own antique masterpiece. I used a copyright-free image found online. Here's what to do:

- Photocopy your chosen image onto photo-transfer paper, sizing it to match a prestretched artist's canvas.
- Cut a rectangle of polyester-cotton fabric 4" (10.2 cm) larger in width and length than the canvas. Transfer the image to the fabric using a household iron.
- Brush white craft glue over the entire surface of the canvas, place the printed fabric on it, and smooth to adhere. Make a hospital corner at each corner for a neat finish.

- Hammer brass carpet tacks into the edge of the canvas. Trim off the excess fabric.
- Apply a coat of crackle finish with a foam brush, following the manufacturer's directions. Let the finish dry overnight.
- Apply a coat of thinned burnt umber craft paint with a foam brush or bristle brush, smoothing the paint into the cracks to simulate the look of age. Let the paint dry.
- Apply an even coat of acrylic medium-and-varnish to seal the painting. Let the sealer dry.

## Working Tips: Caring for Garments with Iron-On Transfers

Turn T-shirts and other embellished garments inside out before you wash them to protect the transfer from wear and abrasion during the wash cycle. Machine-wash on a gentle cycle, using cold water and a mild laundry soap; do not add bleach. Tumble-dry by machine or air-dry by laying the garment flat on a towel or a flat-mesh drying rack and smoothing out any wrinkles with your hands. If the garment requires pressing, use a non-stick press cloth; direct contact with a hot iron will cause the transfer to melt.

## Project Ideas with Photo Transfers

- Blank books with cloth covers
- Stationery, such as greeting cards and postcards
- T-shirts
- Tote bags
- Mouse pads
- Home furnishings in polyester, cotton, and polyester-cotton fabrics, such as fabric coasters, napkins, and children's sheets and pillowcases
- Quilt blocks

## Candle Making and Decorating

Candles possess a transformative power. The moment the wick of even the smallest votive flickers, the world of hard edges softens and the atmosphere feels tranquil. There are so many beautiful, reasonably priced candles in the market that it would seem to make sense to start your decorative embellishing using purchased candles, and you can. However, making candles in custom shapes, sizes, and colors, according to your own taste and style, is easy and fun to do. The basic steps are the same regardless of the design features: melt wax and pour it into a pretty container or a mold into which a wick is installed. Once the wax hardens, the candle remains in its container, or it is removed from its mold and displayed.

Candle making can begin in a simple way, using things you already have around the house. For example, you can melt down old candles and use a china teacup for a container or a waxed dairy carton for a mold. An old

candle stub already has a wick so it can be centered in a container with melted wax poured around it to make a new candle.

Of course, new wax can be purchased from a craft store, where you will find a wide variety, from straight paraffin and such natural waxes as soy, palm, and beeswax, to pre-blended waxes with special additives to help the wax retain its fragrance, increase its opacity, or introduce color and fragrance. With any new candle, you will need to install a wick in a container or mold before the wax is poured. Wicks are available in a wide and often confusing array, depending upon the type and size of candle you are making. Always read the recommendations on the package of wax to choose the proper wick.

Once you have your candle, whether it is one you have made yourself or one you have purchased, you will find it easy to add decorative embellishments. Embellishing is a way to customize candles for gift-giving and home decorating. Wax is an appealing surface for embellishers—it is receptive to paint and glue, soft enough to pierce, and colorful or textured enough to offer an appealing background for pressed flowers and foliage, pretty bands of paper, vellum, and passements such as ribbon, tassels, trims, and other baubles that add shimmer, shine, and personal style.

### Materials and Tools

The basic materials and tools for candle making are few, but they are related to one another. The particular candle you are making will determine the kind and amount of wax you will need, as well as the kind and size of the wick; the type of wax and the type, thickness, and length of the wick must be suited to the diameter of the candle. All of the information you need to make the proper pairings will be included on the package of wax or the wick, so be sure to read the directions carefully or to consult a reputable candle-making supplier to ensure good results.

- **Candle molds**

A mold is a sturdy, nonflammable vessel that temporarily contains the wick and the hot liquid wax until it cools and hardens. The cooled candle replicates the size and shape of the mold. Reusable molds can be made in hard or flexible materials, from sheet metal or aluminum to silicone, plastic, and latex rubber. The mold can produce a smooth or embossed surface on the candle. Candle molds are available in a wide variety of shapes—rectilinear, square, pyramid, and crenulated—and graduated sizes. A particularly convenient votive mold is made of metal and comes with a wick pin. The wick pin is centered in the mold as the molten wax is poured, forming a channel through which a pre-primed wick can be threaded when the wax hardens, obviating the need to center the wick in liquid wax using other means. Other molds suitable for wax include chocolate, candy, and soap molds. Many molds are available at craft stores, but you can also improvise with items found at home, such as empty dairy cartons and paper towel tubes, to make molded candles.

- **Candle containers**

Nonflammable vessels are used to hold the wick and the wax in a container-style candle. The candle remains inside the container while the candle burns. Such decorative containers as new or recycled glass, ceramic jars, small tins, and china teacups can be used to make container candles. Natural items such as eggshells, citrus fruit rinds, and seashells make good accent candles, although their burning time is shorter. Container candles use waxes with lower melt points, so added fragrance in a container produces good scent-throw.

• **Wax**

Wax for candle making comes either straight or preblended. A straight wax is one to which nothing has been added. The most common straight wax is paraffin, a petrolatum (think Vaseline) product available in slabs, small blocks, beads, and granules. Other straight waxes are made from such natural ingredients as soy, palm, and beeswax. Although straight waxes can be used solo to make candles—beeswax makes especially thick and aromatic tapers— it is common for candlemakers to combine different waxes and additives, manipulating the ingredients according to their own unique recipes, to improve the quality of the candle. Specially formulated preblended waxes have just the right proportion of additives, making them well suited to the beginning candlemaker.

• **Additives**
— **Vybar**

Vybar is a wax additive that enhances the fragrance-oil capacity of wax, increasing the scent throw of the candle. Vybar can be added to straight paraffin or to preblended waxes. Use ¼ to ½ teaspoon (1.2 to 2.5 mL) for 1 pound (0.5 kg) of wax, or 1.5 ounces (42.5 g) for 10 pounds (4.5 kg) of wax.

— **Stearic acid**

Stearic acid, or stearine, is an additive that aids in releasing the candle from a mold. It also increases the opacity and hardness of the wax and thus a candle's burn time. With a melt point of approximately 130°F (54.4°C), stearic acid is melted into the liquid wax in a 1:10 ratio, although it can be used in higher percentages according to the type of wax and candle being made. For hard wax, the ratio is 1 to 2 ounces (28.4 to 56.7 g) of stearic acid to 1 pound (0.5 kg) of wax.

— **Colorant**

Measured by weight, small highly concentrated chips of color pigment or drops of liquid dye are added to the colorless wax to give it a particular hue. Colors can also be blended to make new shades. With parental supervision, kids can use chunks of wax crayon to tint

## Quick & Easy: Instant Candles from Wax Crystals

Wax crystals, or granulated wax, come in a variety of colors. A candle can be made in mere minutes by layering different colored crystals in a glass container and installing a primed, pretabbed wick.

## Working Tips: Estimating Wax Amounts

To measure the amount of wax needed for a candle, pour water into the mold or container and then transfer the water to a measuring cup. Use 3 oz. (85.05 gm) of cold hard wax for every 3¹/₂ oz. (103.51 ml) of water held by the mold or container.

wax. Stearic acid enhances the blending of the colorant and the wax.

— **Fragrance**

Derived from essential oils and synthetic aroma chemicals, candle fragrances are specially formulated and approved so the candles burn safely and cleanly. The candle releases its scent, called "scent-throw," as the candle burns and the wax becomes hot. Sold by liquid weight, 1 ounce (29.6 mL) of fragrance can scent 1 pound (0.5 g) of wax. Vybar is an additive that helps wax retain fragrance. Fragrance is the last additive to be mixed into molten wax as prolonged heating can result in scent loss.

• **Wick**

A wick is the thin flammable cord that runs through the center of every candle. The wick determines a candle's burn time, scent-throw, and sooting (or smoking). Always follow the manufacturer's recommendations for wick size. A wick that is too large will cause the candle to burn quickly and to smoke; a wick that is too small will cause a tunnel effect, eventually drowning the wick in melted wax. Wick selection for a candle is based on the type of wax and additives, the kind of colorant, the amount of fragrance, the type of mold or container, and the candle diameter. The wicks for container and molded candles are anchored with a wick tab and have a core made of zinc, paper, or cotton that helps the wick remain upright, centered, and straight while liquid wax is poured. Flat-braided, square-braided, and round wicks do not have cores but are primed, or stiffened, with hot wax and anchored with a wick tab.

— **Round wicks**

Also called RRD wicks, round directional wicks have a cotton core and tension threads. The tension threads cause the wick to curl in the right direction to improve the burning characteristics of the wick. The wick is suited to solid-colored candles, scented votives, container candles, and candles made from viscous waxes, such as all natural soy and palm waxes.

— **Flat-braid wicks**

Also called LX wicks, flat-braid wicks have stabilized threads that help the wick curl while it burns. This type of wick is suited to candles made from paraffin and all natural soy and palm waxes, and to pillars, tapers, votives, and container candles.

— **Square-braid wicks**

Used for molded candles, square-braid wicks come in several widths. The wick for tapers is thinner than the wick used for chunky pillar candles. Square-braid wick is commonly used with beeswax candles and for paraffin and soy pillars.

## Working Tips: Choosing the Proper Wick Size

Selecting an appropriate wick for a candle can be difficult, even for veteran candlemakers. The right wick will burn at a proper flame height with minimal smoking and won't overheat a container. To begin, choose a wick that is suitable to the diameter of your container or mold and the type of wax you are using, following the manufacturer's guidelines on the package. As a general rule of thumb, use a small wick for a candle diameter of $2^1/_2$" to 3" (6.4 to 7.6 cm), a medium wick for a diameter of 3" to 4" (6.4 to 10.2 cm), and a large wick for a diameter of 4" to 5" (10.2 to 12.7 cm).

— **Papercore wicks**

Also called HTP wicks, or high-tension paper wicks, these wicks have a paper core wound into the wick, making them rigid and self-supporting while they burn. Used for votive and container-style candles, papercore wicks come in different sizes.

— **Cotton-core wicks**

These wicks have a cotton core wound into the wick, making them rigid and self-supporting while they burn. Suited to candles made of paraffin and soy waxes, the cotton-core wick has a low incidence of "mushrooming," which is caused by carbon buildup that leads to the production of soot.

— **Zinc-core wicks**

These wicks have a zinc core wound into the wick, making them rigid and self-supporting while they burn. Having a tendency to "mushroom," a zinc-core wick can be trimmed to reduce the incidence. These wicks are suited to paraffin and gel wax.

• **Wick tab**

Available in a variety of styles and diameters, from 15 mm to 20 mm, a wick tab (or wick sustainer) holds one end of the wick. It is placed inside the candle container on the center bottom and secured with mold sealer or hot glue. Wick tabs also come with preprimed wicks attached; these prewicked tabs are especially convenient to use when making candles in multiples, such as votives.

• **Wick pin**

A wick pin is one part of a two-part candle mold that is left inside the mold while the wax is poured inside. After the wax hardens, the candle is removed from the mold and the pin is removed from the candle, leaving a hollow channel the length of the wax column through which a pretabbed wick is inserted.

• **Thin rod**

A thin rod is used in two ways. One task is to span the rim of the mold or container to hold the wick taut and centered when the hot, liquid wax is poured in around it. Another is to pierce the skin of wax that forms around the wick as wax is cooling. Consider both functions when choosing a rod material. For small candles, use a wooden skewer. For large candles, use a chopstick, pencil, or thin dowel.

• **Mold sealer**

Mold sealer is used to seal the wick hole in a metal candle mold and any gaps around the wick. Several types are available: a claylike material that is torn into wads, a metal repair tape that is cut into strips, and a magnetic disk that is cut. Poster putty can also be used.

• **Wax or candy thermometer**

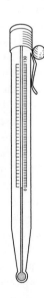

A thermometer with a range of up to 400°F (204.4°C) is essential for measuring and monitoring the temperature of wax during the heating process as it changes from a solid to a liquid state.

Wax will begin to smoke at approximately 270°F (132.2°C), which is dangerous as wax is flammable and can spontaneously ignite if it reaches its flash point. Other temperatures to monitor are the melt point (the temperature at which wax begins to liquefy) and the pouring temperature (a higher temperature when liquid wax is ready to be poured into a mold or container).

- **Double boiler setup**

A double boiler setup is used to heat wax safely on a stovetop. In a double boiler setup, a bottom pot holds water, which is brought to a boil and then allowed to simmer. The hot water heats a second pot, which is securely nested on top and holds the wax. This setup prevents the pot that is holding the wax from being in direct contact with the heat source. Double boiler setups can be improvised with other vessels to hold the wax. Items with pouring spots are especially convenient. Examples include a wax-pouring pitcher, a heatproof Pyrex measuring cup, and a recycled can.

- **Oven mitts**
Protective oven mitts should be used when holding hot items, such as a wax-filled mold or a metal tool, to avoid burning the skin. Do not use rubber gloves when working with hot wax; some melt when exposed to heat. A matter of personal style, it is probable that you will wear only one mitt on the hand that lifts or carries a vessel with hot liquid, leaving the other hand bare.

Optional items:

- **Wax-pouring pitcher**
This is a special pot designed for melting and pouring wax. I tend to rely on it because it is safe, convenient, and a versatile size (mine holds a column of wax for dipping tapers). Made from sturdy aluminum, the pot is seamless and has a handle and a pouring spout.
- **Kitchen scale**
A kitchen scale is a handy tool for weighing small amounts of wax and additives, such as Vybar and stearic acid, that are used in candle making.
- **Plastic bucket and pitcher**
Hot wax in a mold can be set into a cool-water bath to accelerate the cooling and hardening of wax. The size of the bucket holding the water must be large enough and deep enough to hold the candle mold; a bucket with a 3-quart (2.84 L) capacity is usually large enough. A pitcher is used to pour water into the bucket in a continuous stream. If the bucket is large, two pitchers might be needed to keep the flow going without interruption. A stop-and-start pour can cause unwanted seam marks on the candle.
- **Mold release**
A mold release applied to the inside walls of a mold aids in removing the wax candle. Nonstick cooking spray is a convenient, easy-to-use mold release. If you opt for a silicone spray, wear a chemical-cartridge respirator mask and work outdoors or in a well-ventilated space to apply it.

### Melting and Pouring Wax

Before wax can be made into a candle, it needs to change from a solid to a liquid state, a change made possible by heating the wax in a double boiler. The top half of a double boiler holds the wax, and the bottom half contains simmering water, which transfers heat to the wax, safely melting it. Hot wax should not be poured directly from the top half of a conventional double boiler into a container or candle mold as there is no safe pour spout (although small amounts can be scooped out and transferred with a ladle). Modern candlemakers have adapted the double boiler setup by substituting vessels with pouring spouts for the top half. A candlemaker's wax-pouring pitcher is the item I prefer to use.

The temperature of the wax as it is being heated, poured, and cooled directly affects the character and quality of the candle. In the beginning stages of the process, as the wax is being heated, there are two very important temperatures to monitor: the melt point and the pouring temperature. The melt point is the temperature at which the wax begins to liquefy; in most instances, the wax is not completely melted at its melt-point temperature and hence is not ready to be poured. The pouring temperature is a higher temperature at which the melted wax is thoroughly liquefied and blended so it flows smoothly and cleanly into the container or the mold. If wax is poured too cold, it can begin to harden as it is poured and produce air bubbles and blemishes that will mar the surface of the candle. If wax is poured too hot, it may shrink excessively and pull away from the walls of a container or mold.

Removed from its heat source, the poured wax begins to cool, shrink, and harden. Cooling takes place naturally and gradually in the ambient temperature of your work space over several hours or even several days, depending upon the size of the candle and the type of wax that is used.

### Technique: Melting Wax

My double boiler setup has a pot with straight sides for the water and a wax-pouring

---

### Working Tips: Breaking Up Wax Slabs

Wax comes in many solid forms—slab, block, pellet, granular. Slabs need to be broken into smaller pieces to fit into a pot, and because smaller pieces of wax melt more quickly in any case, it is a good idea to break up big chunks. Place your slab or large chunk of wax on a protected work surface and use an ice pick or screwdriver and a hammer to chip the wax into small pieces 1" to 2" (2.5 to 5.1 cm) across. Several pounds (kg) of wax can take 1 hour or more to melt.

---

### Quick & Easy: Making Your Own Pouring "Pitcher"

You can recycle an ordinary metal can into a pouring pitcher to melt small amounts of wax. Completely remove one end of the can, using a can opener. Thoroughly wash and dry the can. Use a pair of pliers to bend a pour spout in the rim of the open side of the can. Place small chunks of wax inside the can and set the can in a small pan of simmering water. The can should rest without wobbling when the wax is melted. When the wax is melted, mix in any additives, blending them with a metal spoon.

pitcher for the wax. If you don't have a wax-pouring pitcher, a standard double boiler will work if you pour or ladle the hot liquid wax into a heatproof vessel with a pouring spout. Use a wax or candy thermometer to monitor the temperature of the hot liquid wax, following the manufacturer's recommended temperatures for the specific wax being used.

## MATERIALS AND TOOLS

Solid paraffin, preblended wax, or other wax for melting
Double boiler setup with wax-pouring pitcher
Wax or candy thermometer
Wooden spoon
Oven mitt

### Step 1

Prepare the double boiler setup.

Fill the bottom half of a double boiler with water, bring it to a boil, and then lower the heat so that the water continues simmering. Place the solid wax in a wax-pouring pitcher and lower the pitcher into the simmering water. The pitcher may wobble a bit until the wax melts, but the walls of the bottom half of the boiler will keep it from tipping.

### Step 2

Melt the wax.

Heat the wax until it melts, stirring it thoroughly with a wooden spoon until it is a smooth and viscous liquid.

### Step 3

Measure the temperature.

Insert a wax or candy thermometer into the hot liquid wax to monitor the temperature, making certain it does not exceed the recommended pouring temperature.

## Technique: Mixing Additives into Hot Liquid Wax

When the wax is completely melted, additives can be introduced in the following sequence: stearic acid, Vybar, colorant (pigment tablet or liquid dye), and fragrance oil.

## Working Tips: Stabilizing the Melting Pitcher or Can

Choose the bottom pot for a double boiler setup with your wax-pouring pitcher or can in mind. The pot should have a flat, heavy bottom to support the pitcher or can that sits in it, without wobbling, especially if the pitcher is tall or lightweight. The pot diameter should not be so roomy that the pitcher or can is in peril of tipping over and spilling wax or taking on water.

## Working Tips: Safety First

Keep an ABC fire extinguisher nearby when you are melting wax and know how to use it. If hot liquid wax starts smoking, remove it from the heat source immediately! Smoking wax indicates that it is near its flash point, and it can spontaneously ignite. In the event of a small fire, use a pot lid to smother the flames. Never apply water, which will spread the fire.

# Wax Pouring Temperatures

When wax is heated, its temperature rises, progressing from room temperature to its melt point and then to its pouring temperature. The distinction between melt point and pouring temperature is significant. Pouring wax before it has reached the proper viscosity will compromise the performance and appearance of the candle.

The melt point and pouring temperature are not fixed numbers but vary according to the type of wax being used, the kind of candle being made, and the material from which a mold or container is made—and therein lies the art. Refer to the guidelines below and

use a wax or candy thermometer to monitor the temperature. In addition, you will want to consult the recommendations offered by the manufacturers of the molds and waxes you use in candle making. Unfortunately, the melt point of wax is not always given on product packaging, but the pouring temperature is usually stated. It is strongly recommended that you consult the information about a wax's pouring temperature on the package of wax as wax formulas differ from one manufacturer to another. If no instructions or guidance are provided on the package, start with a safe pouring temperature, about 170°F (76.7°C).

## Recommended Wax Pouring Temperatures by Wax Type

| Wax | Pouring Temperature |
|---|---|
| Paraffin, soft (low shrinkage) | 140°F (60.0°C) |
| Paraffin, hard (high shrinkage) | 170°F to 180°F (76.7°C to 82.2°C) |
| Soybean | 120°F to 140° F (48.9°C to 60.0°C) |
| Beeswax | 175°F to 185° F (79.4°C to 85.0°C) |

## Recommended Wax Pouring Temperatures by Candle Type

| Candle Type | Pouring Temperature |
|---|---|
| Container and one-pour candles | 150°F to 160°F (65.6°C to 71.1°C) |
| Votive | 155°F to 165°F (68.3°C to 73.9°C) |
| Taper | 160°F to 165°F (71.1°C to 73.9°C) |
| Molded | 170°F to 185°F (76.7°C to 85.0°C) |

## Recommended Wax Pouring Temperatures by Mold Material

| Mold Material | Pouring Temperature |
|---|---|
| Cardboard | 140°F to 150°F (60.0°C to 65.6°C) |
| Glass | |
| Plastic | |
| Rubber | |
| Metal | 190°F to 200°F (87.8°C to 93.3°C) |

If you are working with a preblended wax that already includes stearic acid or Vybar, skip step 2.

## MATERIALS AND TOOLS

Hot liquid wax in double boiler setup
Additives: stearic acid, Vybar, colorant, fragrance oil
Wax or candy thermometer
White ceramic plate
Long-handled metal spoon

**Step 1**

Monitor the temperature.

Use a wax or candy thermometer to check the temperature of the hot liquid wax. The wax is ready to receive additives when the temperature is around 190°F (87.8°C).

**Step 2**

Add stearic acid and Vybar.

Add stearic acid and Vybar, stirring slowly with a metal spoon until blended.

**Step 3**

Add color.

Add pigment chips or drops of dye, stirring slowly with a metal spoon until the pigment is dissolved and the color is blended evenly throughout the wax. Begin with a small amount of colorant and add more in small increments to intensify the hue. To assess the color during this process, drizzle some wax onto a white ceramic plate and let it cool.

**Step 4**

Add fragrance oil.

Add fragrance oil just before pouring the wax into a mold or container. Remove the wax-pouring pitcher from the double boiler, to avoid loss of fragrance due to heat. Add the oil in small increments, a few drops at a time; always follow the manufacturer's recommendations because fragrance oil comes in different concentrations. Blend thoroughly with a metal spoon after each addition. Additional drops will intensify the scent.

## Technique: Pouring Hot Liquid Wax into a Mold

Use this technique to fill a larger candle mold with hot, liquid wax. It is best to use a double boiler with a wax-pouring pitcher to melt and pour the wax. If you are using a conventional double boiler, pour or ladle the hot liquid wax into a heatproof vessel with a pouring spout, such as a large Pyrex measuring cup, and then use it to fill the mold. Wear oven mitts to protect your hands against accidental splashes.

## MATERIALS AND TOOLS

Hot liquid wax
Double boiler with wax-pouring pitcher
Large mold, prepared with wick
Wax or candy thermometer
Oven mitts

**Step 1**

Set up work area.

Set up a protected work area near the stove. Set oven mitts nearby to use when

---

## Working Tips: Olfactory Fatigue

As the air of your work space becomes suffused with the scent of candle oil, it becomes difficult for your nose to discern the kind or intensity of fragrance. Take a break to rest the sensory receptors in your nose and to regain your olfactory discernment or, as is done by some *parfumeurs,* take a whiff of coffee beans before assessing the scented wax.

handling objects and to protect your hands from accidental splashing of hot liquid wax.

## Step 2

Remove wax from heat.

Use the thermometer to test the temperature of hot liquid wax. When the appropriate pouring temperature is reached, remove the wax-pouring pitcher from the double boiler and set it on a heatproof surface.

## Step 3

Pour the wax.

Wearing an oven mitt, use one hand to tilt the mold at a slight angle. Use your other hand (with a mitt or not) to pour the hot liquid wax into the mold, funneling it along a wall or crevice in a slow continuous stream; without stopping or pausing the flow of wax, stand the mold upright when it is half full and continue pouring until the wax level is ½" to 1" (1.3 to 2.5 cm) from the rim. Tilting the mold at the beginning of the pour prevents air bubbles from forming. Continuous steady pouring prevents lines from forming on the surface of the candle.

As the wax in a poured candle cools, it shrinks and sinks down, forming a depression around the wick. The hotter the poured temperature, the greater the shrinkage and the smoother the candle's surface. To fill in and level off this hollow spot, more hot liquid wax is poured in. The "second pour" is reheated about 10°F (5°C) hotter than the initial pouring temperature to enhance the adhesion between the two wax layers and prevent an unattractive seam between them. The addition should be made as the wax in the mold is in the process of cooling, typically 30 to 40 minutes after the first pour. Deep vertical holes are poked into the wax with a rod to provide space for the shrinking wax. Check the wax around the wick every 30 minutes or so for new depressions and fill them as they occur.

## Technique: Filling in the Depression that Forms around a Wick

The technique is employed as the candle is cooling. You may need to perform this technique multiple times as a large candle is cooling.

### MATERIALS AND TOOLS

Hot liquid wax
Double boiler with wax-pouring pitcher
Large container or mold, with first pour of wax partially cooled
Wax or candy thermometer
Wooden skewer or chopstick

## Step 1

Create vent holes.

Use a wooden skewer or chopstick to pierce the wax skin in the depressed area around the wick to make vent holes. Push the skewer or chopstick deep into the candle, but be very careful not to touch the bottom of a candle mold, as this part of the mold forms the top of the candle. Let the candle cool to room temperature, 2 hours or longer, depending upon the size of the candle.

## Step 2

Reheat the wax.

Reheat the wax in the double boiler to a temperature that is 10°F (5°C) higher than the temperature of the first pour. The higher temperature helps improve the adhesion between the two layers of wax.

## Step 3

Fill in the depression around the wick.

Pour just enough hot liquid wax into the depression to form a level wax surface without overflowing the level of the first pour. Let the wax cool, checking every half hour for a newly formed depression and filling in the trough with hot wax as before. Let the wax cool and harden, 5 or 6 hours or overnight, depending upon the size of the candle.

*   *   *

Molten wax in a candle mold can be cooled more quickly by setting the mold inside a bucket where it is surrounded by water at room temperature or cooler. The value of a water bath is that water has a high capacity for absorbing heat. By surrounding the hot wax-filled mold with water, the heat is quickly drawn from the hot candle wax into the water, accelerating the wax's rate of cooling, which results in a smoother, glossier wax surface. The level of water must be even with the height of the column of liquid wax inside the mold; otherwise, a blemish line will appear on the surface of the hardened candle.

I like to place the candle mold inside the bucket, pour in the hot liquid wax, and then pour in the water bath around the mold, weighting the setup with a brick. For me, this approach is safer than carrying a mold filled with hot, liquid wax and placing it into a bucket already filled with water. It is important to add the cool water to the bucket in one continuous pour; a stop-and-start motion can create a seam, uneven coloration, or a frosty appearance on the surface of the candle. The pouring must be done with great care, to prevent water from coming in contact with the hot wax, which can mar the surface texture of the candle.

## Technique: Using a Water Bath to Accelerate Cooling in a Mold

Do a dry run with your materials before attempting the real thing with hot, liquid candle wax. You will need one or two large water pitchers to be able to pour water around the candle mold in a single continuous pour. You may find it helpful to work with a partner. Remember that wax is more buoyant than water so the wax-filled mold will be prone to floating or tipping over. To keep the mold resting on the bottom of the bucket, place a heavy weight, such as a brick, across the mouth of the mold. Be aware that this technique cannot be used to cool candles in hot glass containers as the stress caused by the difference in temperatures may cause the glass to break.

### MATERIALS AND TOOLS

Metal candle mold, prepared with wick, mold sealer, and skewer

Double boiler setup with wax-pouring pitcher

Deep plastic bucket, 3-gallon (11.4 L) capacity (to hold mold)

Brick (to weight mold)

Oven mitt

1 or 2 large pitchers, filled with water

Paper towels, nonembossed (for less lint)

### Step 1

Place the prepared mold into the bucket.

Set the prepared candle mold (with no wax) into the empty bucket. Set the brick next to the bucket.

### Step 2

Pour wax into the mold.

Wear an oven mitt to tilt the mold on an angle. Funnel hot liquid wax along a wall or a crevice of the mold in a steady stream, righting the mold when it is about half full but without stopping the stream of wax; continue pouring until the wax is 1" (2.5 cm) below the mold's rim. Save some wax in the pitcher for a second pour.

### Step 3

Pour water into the bucket.

Wear a mitt to hold the rim of the mold steady with one hand. Pour water from a pitcher into the bucket in a continuous stream until the water reaches the level of the wax inside the mold. Set the brick across the mouth of the mold to weight it down so that it doesn't tilt and take in water or spill wax.

### Step 4

Let the wax harden.

Check the candle as the wax cools, poking holes into the wax depression around the wick and adding more molten wax as needed to fill the holes without overflowing the level of the first pour. Let the wax harden completely overnight.

**Step 5**

Remove the candle from the mold.

Lift the mold out of the water bath and dry it off with paper towels. Cut the wick from the skewer and remove the mold sealer and the wick screw from the base of the mold. Turn the mold over and carefully slide the candle out of the open side. Use scissors to trim the wick, leaving a ¼" (0.6 cm) length. Keep the skewer for another project.

After a molded candle has cooled and been released from its mold, there is one more wax melting operation you may wish to perform. You may find that the base of the candle is uneven because of the way the wax settled as it cooled, but there is an easy way to smooth it out.

## Technique: Using Heat to Level the Base of a Small Molded Candle

This technique is used to even out the bottom surface of a molded candle, which distinguishes a candle with good workmanship. The leveling creates a candle that stands upright, but it also creates a smooth surface on the bottom of the candle.

### MATERIALS AND TOOLS

Candle, removed from mold
Flat, wide metal spatula
Cutting board
Aluminum foil
Oven mitt

**Step 1**

Set up the work surface.

Line a cutting board with aluminum foil, folding up the edges to catch any melted wax.

**Step 2**

Smooth the candle bottom.

Use an oven mitt to hold the handle of a wide metal spatula. Heat the flat blade of the spatula over a stove's burner until it is hot. Rest the blade on the foil and immediately set the

## Candle-Making Checklist

- Melt wax in a double boiler.
- Replenish the water in the double boiler.
- Use a wax or candy thermometer.
- Know the wax's melt point and pouring temperature.
- Never leave wax unattended on the stove.
- Remove smoking wax from the stove immediately!
- Read the manufacturer's recommendations when choosing wax, molds, and wicks.

- Allow ample ventilation when making candles, especially when using fragrance oil.
- Add scent to liquid wax just before pouring, when the wax is off-heat, to avoid dissipating the fragrance through evaporation.
- Preheat molds and containers before pouring in hot wax.
- Do not flush hot liquid wax down the drain. Let unwanted wax cool and harden for proper disposal.
- Do not microwave wax.

bottom of the candle on it, rotating the candle to allow the heat in the blade to melt and level off the wax.

### Step 3
Clean up.

Remove the candle from the spatula when the candle rests evenly on a flat surface. Do not return the spatula to the burner to reheat it because the residual wax on the blade can ignite! Save the wax in the foil tray for reuse or discard it in the trash.

## Technique: Using Heat to Level the Base of a Large Molded Candle
This technique is especially useful on broad pillar-style candles and chunky candle shapes with wide bases.

### MATERIALS AND TOOLS
Candle, removed from mold
Stockpot
Baking sheet with a lip
Oven mitt

### Step 1
Heat the water.

Bring a stockpot of water to a boil on the stovetop, then lower it to a simmer. Rest a baking sheet on the rim of the pot to heat it.

### Step 2
Smooth the candle bottom.

Put on an oven mitt and use that hand to hold the hot baking sheet steady. Use your free hand to set the base of the candle on the baking sheet and move it around in a circular motion until the bottom of the candle is smooth and level.

## Making Candles

Candle making is simple. Even if you have never made a candle before, you can melt and pour hot liquid wax into a container or a mold or dip a wick into hot wax to coat it. The easy, straightforward techniques ensure good results.

First you must decide on what kind of candle you wish to make. A container candle is perhaps the easiest of all candles to make. It is a candle and holder all in one—the container you choose becomes a featured part of the candle, forming the walls that contain the wax as it hardens. The container must be nonflammable, impermeable, and of course attractive. An old but pretty teacup, a silver bowl, an empty tin, even a seashell are possibilities. Once you have chosen a container, you can assemble the appropriate wax, additives, and wick to go with it. The wick must be primed, or stiffened with wax, before it can be used.

## Technique: Priming a Wick
Priming stiffens the wick, to help it stay upright and centered in the vessel when hot liquid wax is poured around it. I usually prime several wicks at one time in the hot melted wax, before coloring or additives are introduced. Long lengths or primed wick can be cut into shorter, custom lengths as needed according to the candles I am making.

### MATERIALS AND TOOLS
Wick, suited to the diameter and type of
  candle
Hot liquid wax in a double boiler setup
Aluminum foil
Tongs
Ruler
Scissors

### Step 1
Cut the wicks.

Use a ruler and scissors to measure and cut the wicks into the desired lengths.

### Step 2
Coat the wicks.

Lay a sheet of aluminum foil on your work surface near the stove. Reduce the heat under the double boiler to a simmer. Place the wicks in the hot liquid wax and let them remain until they are saturated, about 5 minutes.

### Step 3

Shape the wicks.

Use tongs to lift the lengths of wick from the hot liquid wax and set them on the aluminum foil. As soon as the wax is cool enough to touch, use your fingers to shape the wicks into straight rods. The wax cools quickly, but do exercise caution. Let the wicks harden.

Wicks do not float freely inside a container or mold when hot wax is poured into them; they are anchored in place. The wick in a container candle is held to the floor with a wick tab and small blob of mold sealer or hot glue. The wick in a candle mold is threaded through a hole in the base and secured with a screw and mold sealer. The upper end of the wick, in both cases, can be tied to the center of a rod—a skewer, chopstick, dowel, or pencil—that rests on the rim of the container or mold and helps keep the wick taut, straight, and centered as the wax cools around it. Wick tabs with attached wicks can also be inserted into hot liquid wax after it is poured, or a channel can be created for the wick using a wick pin.

## Working Tips: Attaching a Wick to a Crosscut Wick Tab

Insert one end of the primed wick into the crosscut in the tab. Press down the metal flanges to trap that end of the wick.

## Technique: Making a Container Candle

Follow this general technique to make a candle in a glass or metal container.

### MATERIALS AND TOOLS

Container, impermeable and nonflammable, in style as desired
Preblended wax, suited to container candles
Additives: color chips or dye, candle fragrance oil
Wick, primed, with a wick tab attached
Mold sealer
Double boiler with wax-pouring pitcher
Wax or candy thermometer
Wooden skewer
Oven mitt
Wooden spoon
Metal spoon
Pencil
Heat gun or warm oven

### Step 1

Prepare the container and wick.

Press a small blob of mold sealer onto the bottom center of the container. Tie the free end of the wick to a skewer. Push the tab end of the wick into the mold sealer, pressing it with the eraser end of a pencil to help it stick. Rest the skewer across the top rim of the container, rolling it so the wick is straight and taut.

### Step 2

Melt the wax.

Set up the double boiler, melt the wax, and blend in the additives, saving the fragrance oil for last. Use the thermometer to monitor the temperature as the wax heats and melts.

### Step 3

Preheat the container.

Use a heat gun to warm the container to approximately 120°F (48.9°C), which will improve the adhesion of the wax to the container. The container can also be placed in a warm oven.

## Step 4

Pour in the wax and let it cool.

When the wax has reached the proper pouring temperature, slowly pour it into the warmed container, tilting the container at the start of the pour to prevent air bubbles. If the wick becomes slack, gently reroll the skewer to make it straight and taut. Watch for the depression that forms as the wax cools. Pour in more wax, heated 10°F (5°C) higher than the first pour, to fill the sunken area. Let the wax cool completely, 5 or 6 hours or overnight, depending upon the size of the candle.

## Step 5

Trim the wick.

Use scissors to snip off the skewer and trim the wick, leaving a ¼" (0.6 cm) length. Keep the skewer for another project.

My favorite container candles use new or vintage teacups. The patterns on china cups, even on those with a tiny chip or two, add romance to a tablescape. Available in a broad spectrum of solid colors, gilded accents, and floral and geometric patterns, mismatched cups and saucers can be found at very reasonable prices at flea markets and garage sales. Teacup candles are lovely favors for wedding showers; add a teacup candle to each guest's place setting, attaching a place card to the handle of the cup using a narrow band of cardstock and a slender satin ribbon and inscribing the name of the guest on the card.

## Technique: Making a Container Candle with a Teacup

Warm a delicate china teacup with a heat gun or in a warm oven before introducing hot liquid wax to prevent cracks from a sudden change in temperature. Another precaution is to coat the inside of the cup with a thin layer of hot wax before doing the full pour.

### MATERIALS AND TOOLS

China teacup, with or without a saucer
½ pound (0.2 kg) preblended wax with additives, suited to container candles
Additives: color chips or dye, candle fragrance oil*
Primed 6" (15.2 cm) wick, suited to container candle, with wick tab
Mold sealer
Double boiler with wax-pouring pitcher
Wax or candy thermometer
Wooden skewer
Oven mitt
Wooden spoon
Metal spoon
Soup ladle
Pencil
Heat gun or warm oven

*Omit fragrance if candle will be used where food is served.

### Step 1

Prepare the teacup and wick.

Rinse and thoroughly dry the china teacup. Press a small blob of mold sealer in the bottom center of the cup. Tie the free end of the wick to a skewer. Push the tab end of the wick into the mold sealer, pressing it with the eraser end of a pencil to help it stick. Rest the skewer across the top rim of the cup, rolling it so the wick is straight, taut, and centered.

### Step 2

Melt the wax.

Set up the double boiler, melt the wax, and blend in the additives, saving the fragrance oil for last, if using. Use the thermometer to monitor the temperature of the wax as it heats and melts.

### Step 3

Preheat the teacup.

Use a heat gun to warm the teacup to approximately 120°F (48.9°C), which will improve the adhesion of the wax to sides of the cup. The cup can also be placed in a warm oven.

### Step 4

Coat the inside walls of the teacup with wax.

When the wax has reached the proper pouring temperature, put on an oven mitt and grasp the teacup, holding the skewer steady. Tilt the cup at an angle over the double boiler. Use your free hand and a ladle to scoop up some hot liquid wax and empty it into the cup. Swirl the cup very gently to lightly coat the inside walls.

### Step 5

Fill the teacup with wax and let it cool.

Stand the teacup on a level, protected work surface. Ladle in more liquid wax, filling the cup to within ¼" (0.6 cm) of the rim. If the wick becomes slack, gently reroll the skewer to make it straight and taut. Watch for the depression that forms as the wax cools. Pour in more wax, heated 10°F (5°C) higher than the first pour, to fill the sunken area. Let the wax cool completely, 2 or 3 hours or overnight, depending upon the size of the candle.

### Step 6

Trim the wick.

Use scissors to snip off the skewer and trim the wick, leaving a ¼" (0.6 cm) length. Keep the skewer for another project.

Seashell candles are made from old wax candles and found or purchased shells. Seashells collected on a beach walk can be made into candles within an hour and be lighting up your summer table by evening. They are perfect table accents for impromptu, casual suppers.

Choose a shell that is deep enough to hold ½" (1.3 cm) or more of wax. Clam, conch, and whelk shells have unique contours and coloration that add beauty to the candle. Set a lighted seashell candle on a flat surface and protect the flame from breezy drafts.

## Technique: Making a Container Candle with a Seashell

A recycled candle stub supplies a suitable wick and a wax core for a seashell tea light that will burn for 15 to 20 minutes. All you need to do is add a pool of wax around the stub to finish the candle.

### MATERIALS AND TOOLS

4 seashells, as desired
4 candle stubs, each the height of the shell cavity
1 pound (0.5 kg) preblended wax, suited to a container candle
Additive: color chip, in color that matches candle stubs, or as desired (optional)
Mold sealer
Double boiler with wax-pouring pitcher
Wax or candy thermometer
Large spoon or ladle
Paper towels
Oven mitt (optional)

### Step 1

Prepare the shells.

Wash and dry the shells. Check the shells for holes by filling them with water and examining them for leaks. Patch any holes on the outside of the shells using mold sealer. Dry the shells using paper towels and set them in a warm oven to dry completely.

### Step 2

Melt the wax.

Set up the double boiler, melt the wax, and blend in the color chip additive, if using. Use the thermometer to monitor the temperature of the wax as it heats and melts.

## Step 3

Install the candle stubs in the shells.

Lay the shells, cavity side facing up, on a level, protected work surface near the double boiler. Use a small wad of mold sealer to secure one candle stub to the center of each shell, to form the shell candle's wick.

## Step 4

Fill the shells with wax and let it cool.

When the wax has reached the proper pouring temperature, spoon hot liquid wax into each shell around the candle stub until it reaches the rim. Allow the wax to cool for 20 minutes, watching for depressions that may form. Use a skewer to pierce the wax skin at the lowest point and spoon in more hot liquid wax to fill the sunken area. Let the wax cool and harden completely. Remove the mold sealer from the outside of the shell. Let the candle stand for 3 to 4 hours before lighting the wick.

## Votive Candles

Inspired by the traditional prayer candles used in religious ceremonies, votive candles provide small hits of light on tables, mantels, windowsills, or wherever they are placed. For a container-style votive candle, consider tempered glass or other heatproof material, such as a small tin, a Pyrex bowl, or a ceramic ramekin. Because the wax remains in the container as the candle burns, it is important to avoid porous containers, such as cardboard and terra-cotta, as the hot liquid wax that forms when the wick is lit can leach through the material and pose a fire hazard.

One word about wicks for a votive candle: you will need a primed wick with a wick tab; however, because the column of wax in a votive candle is so short, I do not anchor the top of the primed wick to the skewer. To keep the wick centered and straight in larger votive-style candles, I lower a plastic drinking straw trimmed 1" (2.5 cm) taller than the container into the

wax right after the wax is poured, threading the wick through the straw at the bottom so that the wick comes up through the straw hole at the top. After 10 minutes, I withdraw the straw and let the wax fill in around the wick to cool and harden. A primed pretabbed wick can be lowered into the liquid wax and centered using the straw technique instead of being secured to the container before the wax is poured. Another unique approach is to use a metal votive mold with a wick pin. Used together, hot wax is poured into the mold and the wick pin prevents wax from filling in the mold. When the votive is removed from the mold and the wick pin is pushed out of the votive, an open channel remains into which a primed wick (on a wick tab) can be threaded. All three approaches work well for installing a wick in a votive candle.

## Technique: Making a Votive Candle in a Container

Votives are usually made in multiples because it is more practical to melt wax for more than one candle at a time—½ pound (0.2 kg) of wax will be enough to make four 2-ounce (56.7 g) votives. You may wish to gather a group of heatproof glass containers to make a small collection of votive candles. Preheating the glass will reduce the risk of cracking due to extreme or sudden changes in temperature.

### MATERIALS AND TOOLS

½ pound (0.2 kg) 100 percent beeswax or preblended wax, suited to votive candles

4 heatproof glass or ceramic votive containers

4 pretabbed, primed wick, suited to votive candles

Wax or candy thermometer

Double boiler setup

Soup ladle

Oven mitt

Heat gun or warm oven

4 plastic drinking straws

## Step 1

Prepare the glass or ceramic votive containers.

Rinse and thoroughly dry the containers. Press a pinch of mold sealer on the bottom center of the container. Press the wick tab into the sealer so the wick stands upright and extends above the rim of the container.

## Step 2

Melt the wax.

Set up the double boiler and melt the wax. Use the thermometer to monitor the temperature of the wax as it heats and melts.

## Step 3

Preheat the containers.

Place the glass containers in a warm oven to heat them to approximately 120°F to 125°F (48.9°C to 51.7°C), which will improve the adhesion of the wax to the containers.

## Step 4

Fill the containers with wax.

Stand the glass containers on a level, protected work surface. When the wax has reached the proper pouring temperature, ladle hot liquid wax into each container until it is ¼" (0.6 cm) below the rim.

## Working Tips: Reducing Wax Buildup

To keep the hardened wax that drips from a pillar or large votive candle from cementing the base to a holder, pour a shallow pool of water into the holder after the candle is placed. The water will make it easy to lift even the drippiest candle out of the container, bringing the hardened wax drips with it.

## Step 5 (optional)

Prepare the straws.

Use scissors to trim the straws so they are slightly shorter than the wicks.

## Step 6

Straighten the wicks.

Insert one straw into the center of the hot liquid wax in each votive container, threading the wick through its hole so the wick exits the top of the straw. Let the wax cool for 10 minutes and then withdraw each straw and discard it.

## Step 7

Fill in the depression around the wick.

Watch for the depression that forms as the wax continues to cool. Pour in more wax, heated 10°F (5°C) higher than the first pour, to fill the sunken area. Let the wax cool completely, 2 hours.

## Step 8

Trim the wick.

Trim the wick to ¼" (0.6 cm).

Votive candles can also be made by pouring hot liquid wax into molds, which are slipped off the candle when the wax is hard. The unmolded votive can be displayed in pretty, heatproof containers, such as colored-glass tumblers, which will protect the flame and keep wax from dripping on the display surface.

## Technique: Making a Votive Candle in a Metal Mold with a Wick Pin

The featured metal mold comes with a wick pin that forms a hollow channel the length of the column of wax, through which a pretabbed wick is inserted after the candle is cooled and hard. The two-part mold is a convenient substitute for molds that require wick priming and straightening.

### MATERIALS AND TOOLS

4 metal molds with wick pins for votive candles
100 percent beeswax or preblended wax, suited to votive candles
4 pretabbed, primed wicks, suited to votive candles
Nonstick cooking spray
Double boiler
Wax or candy thermometer
Soup ladle
Oven mitt
Heat gun or warm oven
Paper towels

### Step 1

Prepare the mold.

Rinse and thoroughly dry the molds and the wick pins. Apply a light coat of nonstick cooking spray to the interior of the mold and the wick pins, wiping off the excess with a paper towel.

### Step 2

Melt the wax.

Set up the double boiler and melt the wax. Use the thermometer to monitor the temperature of the wax as it heats and melts.

### Step 3

Preheat the molds.

Use a heat gun to warm the metal molds and wick pins to approximately 120°F to 125°F (48.9°C to 51.7°C), which will improve the adhesion of the wax to the components; the pieces can also be placed in a warm oven.

### Step 4

Pour in the melted wax.

Stand the metal molds on a level, protected work surface. When the wax has reached the proper pouring temperature, ladle hot liquid wax into each mold until it is even with the rim.

## Standard Candle Sizes

| Candle Type | Diameter | Height |
|---|---|---|
| Taper | 7/8" (2.2 cm) | 6" to 18" (15.2 to 45.7 cm) |
| Votive | 1½" (3.8 cm) | 2" (5.1 cm) |
| Pillar | 2" (5.1 cm) or more | 4" to 12" (10.2 to 30.5 cm) |

## Step 5

Fill in the depression around each wick.

Watch for the depression that forms around the wick pins as the wax continues to cool in each mold. Pour more wax, heated 10°F (5°C) higher than the first pour, into one mold to fill the sunken area. Repeat to fill the remaining votive molds, as necessary. Let the wax cool completely, 2 hours.

## Step 6

Remove the votive candles from their molds and pull out their wick pins.

Turn one votive mold over and tap it on a hard surface to release the candle from the mold. Turn the candle bottom side up and lean the wick pin on the work surface to push it out of the wax. Then grasp the circular base of the wick pin, pulling it completely out of the candle. Repeat to remove the wick pins from the remaining votive candles.

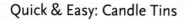

## Quick & Easy: Candle Tins

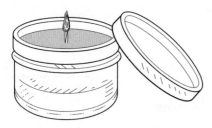

A thoughtful gift (and a super-easy project for beginning candlemakers), candle tins are small metal containers with wicks installed that can be filled with small amounts of wax left over from another project. Color can also be added to the liquid wax, if you wish.

## Step 7

Insert the pretabbed wicks.

Hold one votive candle and insert a wick through the channel made by the wick pin, pushing the tab until it rests on the base of the votive candle. Repeat to install the wicks in the remaining votive candles.

## Step 8

Trim the wicks.

Use a scissors to trim each wick to ¼" (0.6 cm). Set each votive candle into a pretty heat-proof container.

Other candle shapes and sizes besides the diminutive votive can also be made in molds. Commercially available molds are made of aluminum, plastic, silicone rubber, and other impermeable materials that contain the wax without seeping or leaching. Flexible mold materials show the greatest detail on the candle's surface. In fact, the beauty of using a mold is that the candle will take on its shape and surface texture exactly. Molds can be used to make bold geometric forms, such as pyramids and cylinders. For unique candle molds made from things you already have on hand, consider using a waxed dairy carton for a block-shaped candle, a cardboard tube (from a roll of paper towels) for a tall, cylindrical pillar candle, or a soup can lined in corrugated paper for a round, squat, rough-textured candle.

Just as with container candles, the wax must reach the appropriate temperature before being poured or ladled into a mold. The method of transfer will depend upon the size of the mold and the amount of liquid wax needed to fill it. Molds are inverted; the bottom of the mold forms the top of the candle. Preheating the mold so it is warm to the touch will evaporate any lingering moisture that can mar the candle's surface. Use a heat gun set on low or a warm oven to achieve a temperature of 120°F to 125°F (48.9°C to 51.7°C). Preheating is not necessary with disposable molds made from waxed dairy cartons or cardboard tubes.

## Technique: Making a Molded Pillar-Style Candle

I recommend a wax-pouring pitcher for this technique as it holds enough wax for a continuous pour, a decided advantage when making large candles, preventing lines on the candle's surface. Select the mold first and then determine the appropriate wax and wick according to the mold size.

### MATERIALS AND TOOLS

Metal mold, pillar style, or as desired
Preblended wax, suited to molded candles
Additives: color chips or dye, candle
    fragrance oil
Wick, suited to mold and wax, 8" (20.3
    cm) longer than height of mold
Mold sealer
Screwdriver
Nonstick cooking spray
Wooden skewer
Chopstick
Wax or candy thermometer
Double boiler setup with wax-pouring
    pitcher
Oven mitt
Heat gun or warm oven
Old nylon panty hose

### Step 1

Apply nonstick cooking spray to the mold.
Rinse and thoroughly dry the mold. Apply a light coat of nonstick cooking spray to the interior of the mold. Wipe off the excess with a paper towel.

### Step 2

Install the wick in the mold.
Use the screwdriver to remove the screw from the base of the mold and expose the wick hole. Thread one end of the wick through the wick hole from the outside of the mold and pull the wick through the mold until it exits the open end, leaving a 2" (5.1 cm) tail emerging at the wick hole. Replace the screw in the wick hole to trap the wick, but be careful not to overtighten the screw. Press a flat blob of mold sealer over the screw and the wick on the outside of the mold. Tie the free end of the wick to the center of a skewer and roll the excess wick onto the skewer until the wick is straight, taut, and centered in the mold. Set the mold upright on a heat-resistant work surface.

### Step 3

Melt the wax.
Set up the double boiler, melt the wax, and blend in the additives, saving the fragrance for last. Use the thermometer to monitor the temperature of the wax as it heats and melts.

### Step 4

Preheat the mold.
Use a heat gun to warm the metal mold to approximately 120°F to 125°F (48.9°C to 51.7°C), which will improve the adhesion of the wax to the mold. The mold can also be placed in a warm oven.

### Step 5

Pour in the melted wax.
Stand the metal mold on a level, protected work surface. When the wax has reached the proper pouring temperature, slowly pour it into the warmed mold, tilting the mold at the start of the pour to prevent air bubbles and finishing with the mold upright and the wax

## Working Tips: Removing a Candle from a Mold

If your candle does not easily slide out of a mold, put it into the freezer for 5 minutes or the refrigerator for 15 minutes. The chilled candle should slip out of the mold easily.

level 1" (2.5 cm) below the mold's rim. If the wick becomes slack, gently reroll the skewer to make it straight and taut.

### Step 6

Fill in the depressions.

Watch for depressions that form as the wax cools. Make vent holes with a chopstick around the wick and allow the wax to cool to room temperature, 2 hours or longer. Pour in more wax, heated 10°F (5°C) higher than the first pour, to fill the sunken area. Check the wax every half hour for newly formed depressions and fill them with hot liquid wax. Let the wax cool completely, 5 or 6 hours or overnight, depending upon the size of the candle.

### Step 7

Remove the candle from the mold.

Cut the wick from the skewer and remove the mold sealer and the wick screw from the base of the mold. Turn the mold over and carefully slide the candle out of the open side. Use scissors to trim the wick, leaving a ¼" (0.6 cm) length. Keep the skewer for another project.

### Step 8

Level the base of the candle.

Rest a baking sheet on a stockpot of simmering water. Set the base of the candle on the hot baking sheet and move it around in a circular motion until the bottom is smooth and level.

### Step 9

Polish the wax surface.

Use a wad of nylon panty hose to polish the sides and edges of the candle, rubbing in an oval motion to buff down any seams or corners and to give the surface a smooth, lustrous finish.

## Technique: Making a Molded Block-Shaped Candle with One Wick

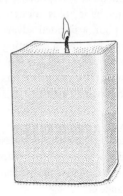

Use a disposable mold, such as a small recycled dairy carton, to make a simple block-shaped candle with one wick. This type of candle offers a beautiful, smooth surface for embellishing.

### MATERIALS AND TOOLS

Waxed 1-pint (0.47 L) dairy carton, empty, clean, and dry

Packing tape with nylon threads, 2" (5.1 cm) wide

2 pounds (0.91 kg) preblended wax, with additives

Color chip or dye, in desired color

Primed wick, suited to molded candles, 8" (20.3 cm) long

Metal washer

Double boiler setup with wax-pouring pitcher

Wax or candy thermometer

Mold sealer (optional)

Nonstick cooking spray

Awl

Wooden skewer

Chopstick

Oven mitt

Scissors

Craft knife

Paper towels

Baking sheet with lip
Stockpot (optional)
Old nylon panty hose

**Step 1**
Prepare the carton.

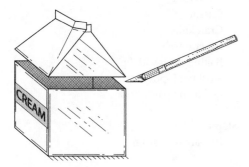

Use a craft knife to cut off the peaked section at the top of the carton, trimming the edges neatly to make an open box. Wrap packing tape snugly around the carton to reinforce the walls, pressing the tape against the sides of the carton without distorting its shape. Apply a light coat of nonstick cooking spray to the interior of the carton. Use a paper towel to wipe down the walls and floor of the carton so only a film of the cooking spray remains.

**Step 2**
Install the wick in the carton.
Use an awl to pierce a hole in the center bottom of the carton, working from the outside. Use a double knot to secure one end of the primed wick to the metal washer. Thread the opposite end through the hole in the carton from the outside and pull the wick through the inside until the washer rests against the carton bottom. Secure the washer flat against the container with a strip of tape or a flat wad of mold sealer. Turn the carton upright, rest a skewer across the top, and tie the free end of the wick to the center of the skewer, rolling the wick around the skewer until the wick is straight, taut, and centered in the mold.

**Step 3**
Melt the wax.
Set up the double boiler, melt the wax, and blend in the color additive. Use the thermometer to monitor the temperature of the wax as it heats and melts.

**Step 4**
Pour the melted wax into the carton.

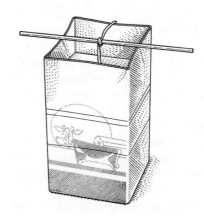

Stand the carton on a level, protected work surface next to the double boiler. When the wax has reached the proper pouring temperature, slowly pour it into the carton, tilting the carton at the start of the pour to prevent air bubbles and finishing with the carton upright and the wax level 2" (5.0 cm) below the carton's rim. If the wick becomes slack, gently reroll the skewer to make it straight and taut.

**Step 5**
Fill in the depressions.
Watch for depressions that form as the wax cools. Make vent holes with a chopstick around the wick and allow the wax to cool to room temperature, 2 hours or longer. Pour in more wax, heated 10°F (5°C) higher than the first pour, to fill in the sunken area. Check the wax every half hour for newly formed depressions and fill them with hot liquid wax. Let the wax cool completely, 3 or 4 hours.

### Step 6

Unmold the candle.

Cut the wick from the skewer, remove the tape or mold sealer, and cut off the washer. Peel off the tape, using scissors to snip through the bands. Tear the carton off the candle. Turn the candle to the smoothest end to establish the top of the candle. Trim the wick, leaving a ¼" (0.6 cm) length. Keep the skewer for another project.

### Step 7

Level the base of the candle.

Rest a baking sheet on a stockpot of simmering water. Set the base of the candle on the hot baking sheet and move it around in a circular motion until the bottom is smooth and level.

### Step 8

Polish the wax surface.

Use a wad of nylon panty hose to polish the sides and edges of the candle, rubbing in an oval motion to buff down any seams or corners and to give the surface a smooth, lustrous finish.

## Technique: Making a Molded Block-Shaped Candle with Three Wicks

Once you have poured a molded candle with one wick, it is easy to make a larger candle with several wicks. Instead of a small cream carton, use a milk carton and rest it on its side to make a long rectilinear candle with room for three wicks spaced at safe intervals.

### MATERIALS AND TOOLS

Waxed 1-quart (0.9 L) dairy carton
Packing tape with nylon threads,
    2" (5.1 cm) wide
2½ pounds (1.1 kg) preblended wax,
    with additives
Additives: color chip or dye, fragrance oil
    (optional)
3 primed wicks, suited to molded candles,
    each 8" (20.3 cm) long
3 metal washers
Double boiler setup with wax-pouring
    pitcher

Wax or candy thermometer
Mold sealer (optional)
Nonstick cooking spray
Awl
3 wooden skewers
Chopstick
Oven mitt
Scissors
Craft knife
Paper towels
Baking sheet with lip
Stockpot (optional)
Old nylon panty hose

### Step 1

Prepare the carton.

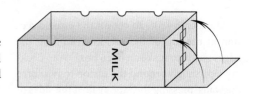

Rinse out the empty dairy carton with clean running water. Open up the pour spout at the top of the container and use a craft knife to cut off one side panel, including one section of the pour-spout flap. Fold in the short side flaps at the end of the carton, and bring up the third flap to close the end. Use strips of tape to secure the flaps. Mark and cut three half-circles on each long edge at the midpoint, and 2¼" (5.4 cm) to either side of the midpoint.

### Step 2

Reinforce the carton with tape.

Wrap packing tape snugly around the carton to reinforce the end flaps and the long walls, pressing the tape against the sides of the carton without distorting its shape. Apply a light coat of nonstick cooking spray to the interior of the carton. Use paper towels to wipe down the walls and floor of the carton so only a film of the cooking spray remains.

**Step 3**

Install the wicks in the carton.

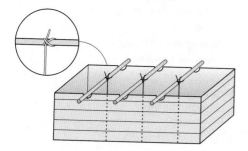

Use an awl to pierce a hole in the center bottom of the carton, working from the outside; then pierce two more holes in the carton, each 2¼" (5.4 cm) from the center hole. Use a double knot to tie one end of a primed wick to a metal washer. Thread the opposite end through the center hole in the carton from the outside and pull the wick through the inside until the washer rests against the carton bottom. Secure the washer with a strip of tape or a flat wad of mold sealer. Repeat to install the remaining two wicks in the other pierced holes. Turn the carton upright, rest three skewers across the top in the half-circle cutouts, and tie the free end of each wick to the center of the corresponding skewer, rolling the wick around the skewer until the wick is straight, taut, and centered.

**Step 4**

Melt the wax.

Set up the double boiler, melt the wax, and blend in the color additive. Use the thermometer to monitor the temperature of the wax as it heats and melts.

**Step 5**

Pour the melted wax into the carton.

Stand the carton on a level, protected work surface next to the double boiler. When the wax has reached the proper pouring temperature, slowly pour it into the carton, tilting the carton at the start of the pour to prevent air bubbles and finishing with the carton upright and the wax level 1" (2.5 cm) below the carton's rim. If a wick becomes slack, gently reroll the skewer to make it straight and taut.

**Step 6**

Fill in the depressions.

Watch for depressions that form as the wax cools. Make vent holes with a chopstick around the wick and allow the wax to cool to room temperature, 3 hours or longer. Pour in more wax, heated 10°F (5°C) higher than the first pour, to fill the sunken area. Check the wax every half hour for newly formed depressions and fill them with hot liquid wax. Let the wax cool completely, 5 or 6 hours or overnight.

**Step 7**

Remove the candle from the mold.

Cut the wicks from the skewers, remove the strips of tape or mold sealer, and cut off the washers. Peel off the tape, using scissors to snip through the bands, if necessary. Tear the carton off the candle. Turn the candle to the smoothest long side to establish the top of the candle. Trim the wicks, leaving ¼" (0.6 cm) lengths. Keep the skewers for another project.

**Step 8**

Level the base of the candle.

Rest a baking sheet on a stockpot of simmering water. Set the base of the candle on the hot baking sheet and move it around in a circular motion until the bottom is smooth and level.

**Step 9**

Polish the wax surface.

Use a wad of nylon panty hose to polish the sides and edges of the candle, rubbing in an oval motion to buff down any seams or corners and to give the surface a smooth, lustrous finish.

## Technique: Making a Molded Pillar Candle with a Cardboard Tube

This candle design is my all-time favorite! A cardboard tube from a roll of paper towels is the secret to the unique textural effect. The paper fibers of the cardboard emboss the surface of the candle as the wax hardens, leaving a frosty patina that reveals a spiral pattern from the construction seam of the tube. A cardboard tube, although porous, is sturdy enough to hold the molten wax as it hardens. This type of candle has poor scent throw, so fragrance is not recommended.

## MATERIALS AND TOOLS

Empty cardboard tube from paper towels
Plastic lid in same or slightly larger circumference than cardboard tube
2 pounds (0.9 kg) preblended wax
Additive: color chip or dye, as desired (optional)
Primed wick, suited to pillar candles, 20" (50.8 cm) long
Double boiler with wax-pouring pitcher
Wax or candy thermometer
Metal washer (optional)
Mold sealer
Awl
2 wooden skewers
Oven mitt
Baking sheet with lip
Stockpot (optional)

**Step 1**

Prepare the mold.

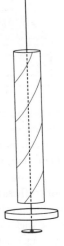

---

## Quick & Easy: Molded Candles from Eggshells

Eggshells are perfect molds for making candles for spring. All you need are hollow eggshells, wax, wicks, and a few extra items that you will have at home. Refer to Two Methods for Hollowing Out an Eggshell (page 672); use the two-hole method to prepare one eggshell for each candle desired. Make sure the eggshells are clean and dry before you begin.

- Thread a 5" (12.7 cm) length of primed papercore wick through each egg, so that a 1¹/₂" tail (3.8 cm) sticks out of the small hole in the shell (this will be the lighted end of the wick) and the rest exits the large hole. Press mold sealer on the wick at the narrow end of the egg to seal the hole.

- Set the eggshells in an egg carton, large holes facing up. Melt paraffin wax and pour it through a small metal funnel to fill each shell. Add more wax to fill in any depression that forms around the wick. Let the candles harden overnight.

- Carefully peel off the shell from each candle, beginning at the broad end.

- Glaze the egg-shaped candles by dipping each one in melted wax of any color for a smooth finish. Trim the wick even with the broad end of the candle and leave ¹/₄" (0.6 cm) length at the top of the egg candle.

Use an awl to pierce a hole in the center of the plastic lid. Tie one end of the primed wick to a metal washer, using a double knot, and thread the opposite end through the hole in the plastic lid and through the cardboard tube. Pull the wick taut so the washer rests on one side of the plastic lid and the base of the cardboard tube rests on the other side; press mold sealer around the edge of the tube and the lid to make a tight seal. Tie the free end of the wick to the center of the skewer, rolling the wick around the skewer until the wick is straight, taut, and centered inside the tube.

## Step 2

Melt the wax.

Set up double boiler, melt the wax, and blend in the color additive. Use the thermometer to monitor the temperature of the wax as it heats and melts.

## Step 3

Pour the melted wax into the tube.

Stand the tube on a level, protected work surface next to the double boiler. When the wax has reached the proper pouring temperature, slowly pour it into the tube, tilting the tube at the start of the pour to prevent air bubbles and finishing with the tube upright and the wax level ½" (1.3 cm) below the tube's rim. Add more mold sealer around the base of the tube assembly to keep it upright. If the wick becomes slack, gently reroll the skewer to make it straight and taut.

## Step 4

Fill in the depressions.

Watch for depressions that form as the wax cools. Make vent holes with a skewer around the wick, pushing the skewer deep down into the candle but without touching the bottom of the mold (which is the top of the candle). Allow the wax to cool to room temperature, 3 hours or longer. Pour in more wax, heated 10°F (5°C) higher than the first pour, to fill the sunken area. Let the wax cool completely, 2 or 3 hours.

## Step 5

Remove the candle from the mold.

Cut the wick from the skewer. Remove the

---

# Quick & Easy: Fire Starters from Recycled Candles

Here are two ways to melt down your old candle stubs and leftover wax and make novelty fire starters for a wood-burning fireplace, a fire pit, or campfire.

- **Glittering twig bundles**
  Gather fifteen to twenty 6"-long (15.2 cm) twigs into a bundle and bind them tightly with cotton string. Use tongs to place the twig bundle into hot liquid wax, rolling it to coat the sides and ends of the twigs. Lift the waxed bundle out of the pot, set it on wax paper, and immediately sprinkle with glitter.

- **Breakaway tabs**
  Hot-glue one end of a 3"-long (7.6 cm) wick in the bottom of each cavity of a cardboard egg carton. Fill each cavity with molten wax and let the wax harden completely. Break away one wax-and-paper section at a time, as needed.

## Fun for Kids: Sand Mold Candles

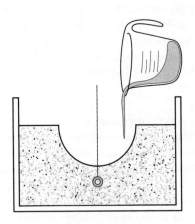

It is super easy to make candles using wet sand as a molding material because damp sand holds an impression. School-age kids can use a plastic bowl, a beach pail, even their hands to shape a well in the wet sand, making an instant mold for a free-form candle. A parent should melt and pour the wax into the sand mold, but a supervised child can add a peeled and broken crayon to color the wax. You may want to give an older child the opportunity to pour the wax; use a Pyrex measuring cup for safety. The basin that holds the sand should be about twice as large and twice as deep as the mold object.

MATERIALS AND TOOLS:
1 pound (0.5 kg) straight paraffin
Half of a wax crayon, in desired color
Primed wick, suited to container candle,
    10" (25.4 cm)
Plastic bowl or child's beach pail,
    approximately 5" diameter × 5" tall
    (12.7 × 12.7 cm)
12 cups (4.5 kg) sand
Large plastic basin
Metal washer
Skewer, chopstick, or pencil

Double boiler with wax-pouring pitcher
Pyrex measuring cup (optional)
Wooden spoon
Wax or candy thermometer
Oven mitt

**Step 1**
Prepare the sand.
Pour the sand into the plastic basin. Add ¼ cup (59.1 mL) of water at a time until the sand holds the imprint of a fist.

**Step 2**
Make the sand mold.
Scoop out the center of the sand to make a well that is slightly smaller than the small bowl or pail. Push the bowl, open side up, into the well of sand, packing the surrounding sand around the walls of the bowl. Carefully lift out the bowl to reveal the sand mold.

**Step 3**
Install the wick.
Use a double knot to tie one end of the wick to a washer. Tie the other end to the center of the chopstick, about 6" (15.2 cm) from the washer. Push the washer into the center of the sand mold, concealing it with more sand. Balance the chopstick across the rim of the sand mold.

**Step 4\*\***
Melt the wax.
Set up the double boiler and melt the wax. Use a thermometer to monitor the temperature of the wax as it heats and melts.

**Step 5**
Add the color.
Peel the paper off the piece of crayon. Add the crayon to the hot liquid wax and stir with a

wooden spoon until blended. Save the wooden spoon for another craft project and do not use it for food.

## Step 6**

Pour the wax into sand mold.

Slowly pour the hot liquid wax into the center of the sand mold, avoiding the walls to keep them from collapsing. Be aware that some wax will seep into the sand. Continue pouring until the wax is level with the rim of the sand mold. As the wax cools, it will sink down and develop a depression near the

wick. Use a skewer to poke a hole in the wax skin and pour in more wax to form a level surface. Let the wax cool for several hours or overnight.

## Step 7

Unmold the candle.

Untie the wick from the skewer and lift the candle out of the sand. Brush off the loose sand. Cut off the washer. Trim the wick, leaving ¼" (0.6 cm) length.

**For an adult to do

---

mold sealer, cut off the washer, and remove the plastic lid. Tear the tube off the candle by pulling along its construction seam. Trim the wick, leaving a ¼" (0.6 cm) length. Keep the skewer for another project.

## Step 6

Level the base of the candle.

Rest a baking sheet on a stockpot of simmering water. Set the base of the candle on the hot baking sheet and move it around in a circular motion until the bottom is smooth and level.

One of the most beautiful candles is the taper, named for its graceful and graduated contour. Tapers are traditionally made in pairs by dipping opposite ends of a long length of wick into the molten wax at the same time—the more dips, the thicker the candles. The method I used here is to cut separate lengths of wick for dipping. The level of hot wax in the melting pot or pitcher will determine the height of the candle; for example, a wax-pouring pitcher filled with a 6" (15.2 cm) column of wax will make a 6" (15.2 cm) candle.

To keep the wick straight and taut during

dipping, attach some kind of weight to the ends of the wicks, such as metal nuts or washers. You can remove the weights as soon as the tapers are thick and sturdy enough to hang straight and keep their shape on their own. Continue to dip the wicks until the tapers are the desired thickness. To ensure straight candles, do not store them flat, but rather, use their wicks to hang them upright until you are ready to use them.

There are many recipes for wax tapers. I love the fragrance of beeswax and have used it to make tapers. I have also mixed a blend of 60 percent straight paraffin with a medium melt point and 40 percent stearic acid to make tapers. As you work with preblended wax or blend your own, you will find out what you like. While fragrance is not recommended for tapers as they do not have sufficient scent-throw, you can add color by glazing, a process where you overdip the core into hot liquid wax to coat it with color.

## Technique: Making Tapers

If you don't have a tall wax-pouring pitcher for dipping long, slender tapers, try a large tomato juice can. Remove one end with a can opener and use pliers to bend the rim into a pour spout.

## MATERIALS AND TOOLS

3 lbs. (1.36 kg) preblended wax with additives, suited to tapers

2 wicks suited to tapers, primed, each 10" (25.4 cm)

Double boiler with wax-pouring pitcher or tall can

Wax or candy thermometer

2 metal nuts or washers

Adhesive tape

Dowel

Wooden spoon

Ruler

Scissors

**Step 1**

Melt the wax.

Set up the double boiler and melt the wax. Use the thermometer to monitor the temperature of the wax as it heats and melts. When the wax reaches 150°F to 155°F (65.6°C to 68.3°C),

it can be used to dip the wicks to begin the layering process.

**Step 2**

Tie each wick to a nut and the rod.

Measure and cut a length of wick that is twice as long as the height of the wax-pouring pitcher plus 6" (15.2 cm). Cut the wick in half and tie a nut to one end of each length. Use a double knot to tie the opposite end of each length to a rod, approximately 2" (5.1 cm) apart, using strips of tape to secure the knots to the rod.

**Step 3**

Dip the wicks.

Use one or two hands to hold the rod, and dip the wicks into the hot liquid wax in

---

## Working Tips:
## Keeping Tapers Upright

For style and safety, keep tapers standing upright in their holders by placing a small blob of photographer's prop wax in the base of each candle cup.

---

## Quick & Easy:
## Fresh Rose Tea Lights

For a beautiful centerpiece, nestle a tea light into the center of an open fresh rose and float the rose on water in a large crystal bowl.

one continuous down-and-up motion to coat them with wax. Wait about 10 seconds for the wax layer to cool and then dip the wicks again, using the same down-and-up motion. Repeat ten times until the wicks are coated with a thick layer of wax.

### Step 4

Finish dipping the tapers.

Cut off the nuts at the ends of the wicks. Continue dipping the wicks approximately 10 more times or until the tapers reach the desired thickness.

### Step 5

Use the tapers.

Trim each wick to ¼" (0.6 cm), and set the candles in a pair of matching candleholders.

### Technique: Glazing a Taper

You can add a thin or thick layer of wax to a pair of tapers in a custom color that coordinates or contrasts with the base color. Wear a mitt and use a sturdy pair of tongs or pliers to hold a single taper by the wick for dipping in hot wax.

### MATERIALS AND TOOLS

2 tapers with untrimmed wicks, at least 2" (5.1 cm) long
Clear wax, such as paraffin, or as desired
Color chip or dye, in color desired
Double boiler with wax-pouring pitcher or tall can
Wax or candy thermometer

### Step 1

Melt the wax.

Set up the double boiler, melt the wax, and blend in the color additive. Use the thermometer to monitor the temperature of the wax as it heats and melts.

### Step 2

Overdip the candle.

Put on a mitt and use a pair of pliers to hold

one of the tapers by the wick. Lower the taper into the hot liquid wax and lift it out in a continuous motion that coats the wax surface with colored wax; let the wax cool. Repeat until you are satisfied with the shade the overdipping creates. Repeat with the second taper.

### Decorating Candles

Any type of candle can be embellished as long as the decoration is at a safe distance from the burning wick. Round and square pillars, fruit-shaped candles, tapers, and votives are ready canvases for your creative ideas, with the embellishments changing in kind and position according to the size of the candle. Embellishment choices include fresh foliage, composition gold and silver leaf, acrylic paint, self-adhesive stickers or adhesive-backed vinyl (such as Con-Tact Brand paper), Diamond Dust glitter,

---

## Quick & Easy: Multicolor Glazing

Instead of glazing a taper with only one color of wax, melt two or three colors, each in its own can and at in different levels, and dip in succession, starting with the lightest color, to create a graduated pattern.

- Melt pale yellow, orange, and rose wax.
- For the first dip, submerge three-quarters of a white taper in pale yellow.
- For the second dip, submerge half of the taper in orange, overlaying the yellow.
- For the third dip, submerge one-quarter of the taper in rose, overlaying the orange. Experiment with different color combinations and different candle sizes and shapes.

∞∞∞∞∞∞∞∞∞∞∞∞∞∞∞∞∞∞∞∞∞∞∞∞∞∞∞∞∞∞∞∞∞∞∞∞∞

## Fun for Kids: Rolled Beeswax Candles

A safe way for kids to make candles is to use sheets of beeswax, which can be rolled around wicks to make candles of any size.

- Lay a sheet of honeycomb beeswax on a protected work surface. Use a ruler and craft knife to cut a 5" × 11" (12.7 × 27.9 cm) rectangle. Save the excess wax for another project.
- Use a hair dryer to warm the wax until it is flexible. Keep the nozzle moving to avoid overheating the wax, which will make it sticky.
- Lay the rectangle vertically. Center an 8" (20.3 cm) long primed wick suited to taper candles, such as a 24-ply flat-braid wick, on the bottom short edge. Press the wick gently against the warmed wax to adhere it.
- Roll the short edge of the wax against the wick. Continue rolling to form a fat rod shape until all of the wax is used.
- Use a hair dryer to heat the edge of the wax and press it against the candle to adhere it.
- Trim the wick even with the rolled wax at the end designated as the base of the candle and to $1/2$" (1.3 cm) at the other lighting end. Stand the candle upright with the $1/2$" (1.3 cm) wick pointing up.

∞∞∞∞∞∞∞∞∞∞∞∞∞∞∞∞∞∞∞∞∞∞∞∞∞∞∞∞∞∞∞∞∞∞∞∞∞

fine glitter, tissue paper, menus, photocopied images, and craft paper. Embossed metal charms, buttons, studs, and embossed sealing wax seal can add whimsy or sophistication, as you choose. Techniques and materials can be mixed and matched in a collage approach. Best of all, the results are instantly satisfying. Be aware that some decorative embellishments are made from flammable materials and should be used only on large pillar-style candles. As an extra precaution, place the embellishments on the lower part of the candle at a safe distance from the candle flame.

### Technique: Painting a Candle

Acrylic craft paint can be applied in patterns of dots or stripes, or it can be used in combination with a stencil to paint simple motifs. Wax is resistant to water-based liquids, but liquid detergent can make the wax surface hospitable to this opaque craft paint.

MATERIALS AND TOOLS
Candle to decorate
Acrylic craft paint, in desired colors
Dishwashing liquid
Tapered watercolor paintbrush
Stencil (optional)
Stencil brush (optional)
Sea sponge or makeup sponge (optional)
Saucer

**Step 1**
Prepare the paint.
Squeeze a small amount of acrylic craft paint onto a saucer. To improve the paint adhesion to the wax, add a drop of liquid dish detergent to the paint, stirring until blended.

**Step 2**
Apply the paint to the candle.
Use a tapered brush to paint a design freehand to the surface or a stencil brush to apply

the paint through a stencil. For an overall pattern, use a sea sponge or a small makeup sponge to dab paint onto the wax surface, altering the paint colors to create a mottled effect.

## Technique: Applying a Print with a Heated Spoon

Images cut from gift wrap or other printed papers can be applied to a candle using decoupage and a melting technique. Make sure to use a potholder when doing this project and follow safety precautions when working with a hot iron. This technique is not suited for children.

### MATERIALS AND TOOLS
Print or motif, cut from gift wrap
Candle to decorate
Acrylic spray sealer
Household iron
Silver tablespoon
Potholder
Large cardboard carton (for spray booth)
Chemical-cartridge respirator mask

**Step 1**
Seal the print.
Work outdoors or in a well-ventilated space. Put on a chemical-cartridge respirator mask. Turn the carton on its side and open the flaps to make a spray booth. Lay the cutout print or motif flat inside the booth. Apply a thin coat of acrylic spray sealer to both sides of the print; let the sealer dry.

**Step 2**
Position the print on the candle.
Lay the candle on its side. Position the print, image side up, on the wax. Use your fingers to rub the paper against the wax to temporarily adhere it.

**Step 3**
Adhere the print.
Heat a household iron to the hottest setting (linen). Use a potholder to hold the handle of a silver spoon. Press the bowl side of the spoon against the iron soleplate for about 20 seconds. Hold the bowl side of the hot spoon against the print, moving it from the center out to the edges, until the paper adheres to the wax.

## Technique: Making a Paper Message Band

Paper can be torn or cut into wide bands of any length or width and wrapped around a candle. Layering two bands, one in colored paper for the background and a second, overlapping band printed with a sentimental message is a nice way to commemorate a special occasion. Use your computer and printer to create the message band, choosing a pretty or quirky typeface to spell out your sentiment.

### MATERIALS AND TOOLS
Candle to decorate
Papers for two bands, such as colored
  paper and vellum
Steel ruler
Craft knife or scissors
Self-healing cutting mat
Cellophane tape

## Quick & Easy: Painting with Melted Wax

Melted wax in different colors can be used to add patterns to the surface of a candle. Melt clear wax in a double boiler and then spoon small quantities of hot liquid wax into the individual compartments of an egg poacher. Add a scant chip of individual color to each compartment according to the desired palette. Use tapered paintbrushes to paint the colored wax onto the candle.

**Step 1**

Cut a band of paper.

Using a cutting mat, steel ruler, and craft knife, measure and cut a band of paper that is approximately 2" (5.1 cm) wide and long enough to wrap around the candle plus 1" (2.5 cm) for the overlap.

**Step 2**

Tape the band to the candle.

Wrap the paper band around the candle, overlap the ends, and secure with tape.

**Step 3**

Make a message band.

Use your computer and printer to make a printout of a monogram, a person's name, or a short sentiment that will be readable when placed on the candle, such as "Congratulations" or "Good Luck." Cut a second band that incorporates the printed message, making this band ½" (1.3 cm) narrower than the first band but the same length.

**Step 4**

Overlay the message band on the first paper band.

Center the message band made in step 3 over the band applied in step 2, pulling the band snugly and overlapping the ends at the back of the candle. Use tape to secure the overlap.

## Technique: Wrapping a Candle with Ribbon and Trims

Ribbon, cord, trims, and like ornamentation can be wrapped around a candle and accented with an embossed charm. Choose a candle with a large diameter for safety when using flammable trims.

MATERIALS AND TOOLS

Large-diameter pillar candle

Ribbon or other trim

Embossed metal charm, or sealing wax embossed with a steel seal

Tape measure

Scissors

Hot-glue gun and glue sticks

**Step 1**

Cut the ribbon.

Measure the circumference of the candle with a tape measure and add ½" (1.3 cm). Cut a length of ribbon or trim to this measurement.

**Step 2**

Secure the ribbon to the candle.

Wrap the ribbon around the candle, overlap the ends, and secure the overlap with hot glue.

**Step 3**

Add the charm accent.

Glue an embossed metal charm or sealing wax embossed with a steel seal to the candle to conceal the overlap and to accent the ribbon.

## Technique: Applying Granular Materials

Fine glitter, Diamond Dust glitter, fine sand (natural or dyed), reflective glass beads, and similar materials can be used to add a layer of texture and sparkle to the exterior of a candle. Be aware that Diamond Dust glitter is finely ground glass and should be handled with care.

MATERIALS AND TOOLS

Pillar candle, 3" (7.6 cm) diameter

Fine glitter, sand, or other granular material

Foam brush

Tapered watercolor paintbrush

High-tack glue

Kraft paper

Cotton swabs

**Step 1**

Apply the glue.

Use a foam brush to apply a coat of high-tack glue to the candle's sides. If the glue beads up, work the brush in a scrubbing motion to roughen up the wax and improve the adhesion.

**Step 2**

Coat the candle with granules.

Pour the granular material onto a large sheet of kraft paper, spreading the swath of granules into a smooth layer that is large enough to coat the candle. Hold the ends of the candle at opposite ends, and roll the candle in the decorative material until the sides are fully coated.

**Step 3**

Clean off the excess granules from the candle.

Stand the candle upright to inspect the coverage for bare or thinly coated areas. A coating of fine sand will appear as a thin dusting, whereas a coating of glitter will be a thick layer. If there are any bare spots, patch them one at a time. Lay the candle on a protected work surface, one bare spot facing up. Use a dry tapered watercolor brush to sweep off any loose granules on the wax surface and the edges of the bare spot, and then reapply glue in a tamping motion, followed by a liberal sprinkling

of granules. Let the glue dry before patching the next bare area. Use a tapered brush or wet cotton swab to remove any granular material that is stuck to the top of the candle near the wick. Glitter especially is prone to sparking and igniting. Allow the glue to dry for several hours before lighting the wick.

**Technique: Applying Metal Leaf**

Metal leaf, such as composition gold, silver, and copper leaf, can be applied to the exterior of a large-diameter pillar candle using the natural static electricity between the wax and the leaf to adhere it. Be aware that metal leaf is flammable and should not come into contact with the burning wick.

MATERIALS AND TOOLS

Pillar candle, large diameter
Metal leaf
Cotton gloves
Blunt-nosed tweezers
100 percent cotton balls
Envelope

## Working Tips: Displaying Candles Safely

Lighted candles provide unique and glowing accents of illumination to any room, adding soft contour and alluring shadow to room settings. When displaying candles, follow a few simple precautions.

- Choose nonflammable decorative embellishments for your candles or make certain the candle to be decorated has a large enough diameter so a flammable decoration

remains at a safe distance from the flame.
- Display candles away from flammable materials.
- Never leave a lighted candle unattended.
- Keep children and pets away from a lighted candle.
- Avoid handling a glass or metal container that houses a lighted candle; it can be hot.

**Step 1**

Tear small pieces of metal leaf.

Put on cotton gloves. Open up the book of metal leaf. Use your gloved fingers to tear a sheet of leaf into small stamp-size pieces, allowing the leaf to remain on the orange tissue paper.

**Step 2**

Transfer the pieces of leaf to the candle.

Use blunt-nose tweezers to pick up and transfer one piece of leaf from the book to the candle. Tap the leaf in place with your gloved finger. Continue to position and press pieces of leaf onto the wax in an irregular pattern, allowing the wax color to show between pieces.

**Step 3**

Burnish the leaf.

Use a cotton ball to buff the leaf, smoothing the leaf against the candle's wax surface, allowing the skewings of leaf to flake off. Collect the skewings in an envelope and save them for another project.

## Troubleshooting: Removing Hardened Wax from a Surface

Wax drips on the candlesticks and tabletop are inevitable when candles are burned, especially when they are displayed in a drafty area. Here is how to remove wax that has hardened on different types of surfaces.

| Surface | Wax Removal Method |
| --- | --- |
| Fabric, with wax on the surface | Rub a wax blob with an ice cube to make it brittle. Break it up with your fingers and remove it from the cloth. |
| Fabric, with wax in the fibers | Sandwich the fabric between layers of paper towels and press with a warm iron. The towels will absorb the wax as it melts. Change the position of the towels frequently and avoid touching the iron to the wax until no more wax can be absorbed. Treat any residual wax with a wax removal spot cleaner and then launder as usual. |
| Metal, ceramic, or glass | Use a hair dryer or heat gun to melt the wax so it slides off the surface. Wash off residual wax in hot, soapy water, rinse well, and dry with a soft cloth. |
| Finished wood | Scrape off wax blobs with a thin plastic credit card held at a 45-degree angle, moving in the direction of the wood grain. Buff off residual wax with a soft cloth. Rub in beeswax or furniture polish to restore a uniform luster. |
| Plastic and laminates | Scrape off wax blobs with a plastic credit card. Remove the remaining waxy film with a cleaning agent suited to the surface. |

## Chandeliers: Restoring and Recycling

There was a time when, unable to resist the pull of light-catching crystals—sharp-edged, water-clear, and accented with florets and those plump orbs of colored glass in the shapes of cherries, pears, grapes, and apples— I attached practically every crystal and orb I could find to one chandelier, until it seemed to groan under the excessive weight and I began to worry that one day the chandelier was going to rip out of the ceiling and land on our little dog, LouLou, sleeping beneath it.

Since then I have added other chandeliers to our home, having a more trained eye so that I know what I like and what is fundamentally worth my embellishing efforts. Wandering through yard sales and flea markets and checking out curbside opportunities are just a few ways to uncover hidden treasures. You will find that if you look for a chandelier, you will begin to see them everywhere. Small (rea-sonably priced) chandeliers made from glass, brass, and cast metal are common enough in salvage and secondhand venues that it is nearly impossible not to come across a plain, if ugly, fixture that simply needs a little elbow grease and a vivid imagination to either restore it to its former grandeur or entirely reconceptualize its style. If you can see past the built-up dust and grime, the out-of-fashion style, or the parts that are broken or missing, you will embark on a restoration project that yields a lot of satisfaction and a one-of-a-kind decoration for your home. The most important aspect of recycling any lighting fixture is to make sure that the wiring is in safe working order and that the fixture is structurally sound. Always have a licensed electrician check out your find before investing your time and talent in a restoration.

There are several broad approaches to transforming any chandelier, depending upon its style and the material from which it is made. At its simplest, all a chandelier may need is a

## Working Tips: Determining if a Chandelier Is Solid Metal or Plated

Before you recycle a metal chandelier— whether by cleaning, polishing, painting, or patinating—it is a good idea to know what kind of metal lies beneath the layers of grime or tarnish. There are a few ways to make a good assessment. To determine if the metal is solid or plated, use a sharp nail to scratch the surface in an obscure place on the chandelier. If the color of the metal is the same but brighter, it is likely to be solid copper, bronze, or brass, in which case you may decide to clean and polish it to a high shine or hire a professional to dip it to restore the original luster. If the scratch test reveals a different color, the metal is most likely plated, in which case it should be primed and painted. Some solid metals, such as brass, are treated with a lacquer coating to maintain the shine and retard tarnishing, reducing the need for polishing. To test for lacquer, hold a single-edged razor blade on an angle and use the edge to shave the surface; if flakes kick up, the metal is coated with lacquer and must be stripped.

good cleaning and the addition of a silk shade on each candle cup. The next level of care may involve either polishing the metal by hand or having it dipped commercially to restore its gleaming patina.

If the metal armature has pits and abrasions that cannot be removed with vigorous polishing or abrading with fine emery cloth or steel wool, it is wise to consider concealing these imperfections under a coat of paint. Reminiscent of the shabby-chic style, several coats of chalky-white paint—applied over a coat of spray metal primer—will do the job, homogenizing all the parts (even a new replacement arm) to present a cohesive and updated style.

I rescued a cast-metal (of indeterminate composition) eight-arm chandelier from a neighbor's clutter of cellar junk, and was amazed at the transformation that careful cleaning and a few coats of paint achieved. First, I removed the bulbs and plastic candle sleeves and put them in plastic bags so that they didn't get misplaced. I used a soft cloth dipped in distilled vinegar to clean the metal surfaces, allowing the metal to dry completely thereafter. Then on the first cool day (humidity will retard the drying and curing of paint), I spread a plastic tarp on a patch of grass and set the chandelier on top. Donning a chemical-cartridge respirator mask and disposable gloves, I applied primer followed by several thin coats of white spray paint on all of the surfaces, turning the fixture upside down to reach all of the textural grooves and details underneath. (I must tell you, impatient as I was, I remembered to allow a respectable drying time between coats.) Finally, all I had to do was replace a few of the cracked plastic sleeves on the candlesticks, which took a quick trip to a home store. Not a conceit, but a satisfying indulgence, the recycled chandelier lights our laundry room, adding irony and charm to a common space, and with eight small bulbs blazing, the chandelier provides the brightest illumination you can imagine.

A glass chandelier has particular appeal because even unadorned, its transparent parts seem to breathe light. Easy to clean using mild liquid dishwashing soap and water (or spray glass or chandelier cleaner), the glass armature can be sponged clean if it isn't too grimy, although caked-on dirt on candle cups and loose crystals (if there are any) may need more effort. Grimy crystals can be soaked in hot water to which a tablet of denture cleaner or liquid soap has been added, which will help lift stubborn dirt. Never submerge the electrical parts of the chandelier in water—wires run through the arms and the central column and should not get wet. This cleaning job is better left to a professional, who can dismantle the chandelier for cleaning without jeopardizing the integrity of the wiring.

Once you have cleaned and/or painted the metal or cleaned the glass on your chandelier, examine the parts, replacing candle sleeves, if necessary, and adding new bulbs. Then add embellishments—from little bouquets of silk flowers or silk shades with swingy fringes to each candle cup, or beaded or crystal swags that swoop from one candle cup to the next. Or, hang mismatched crystals and glass fruit in small bunches to each armature. If you love the thrill of the hunt, take the time to find pretty and inexpensive elements—abandoned lead-crystal orbs from lobby-sized chandeliers, pear-shaped, elongated and cut-crystal teardrops, and gem-colored glass fruit—restoring and recasting the style of your chandelier, which may have come with a layer of dust, yes, but also with a sublime layer of happiness. Or rather than waiting for the next flea market, go to one of the online sources that can quickly satisfy your demands for reproduction crystals and glass decorations in every imaginable shape and color, and order them.

## The Parts of a Chandelier

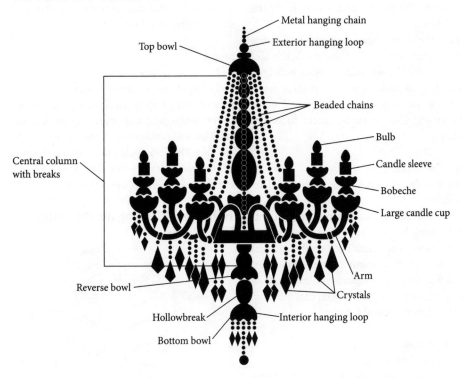

Metal hanging chain

Exterior hanging loop

Top bowl

Beaded chains

Bulb

Central column
with breaks

Candle sleeve

Bobeche

Large candle cup

Reverse bowl

Arm

Crystals

Hollowbreak

Interior hanging loop

Bottom bowl

### Technique: Dismantling and Cleaning an Old Glass Chandelier

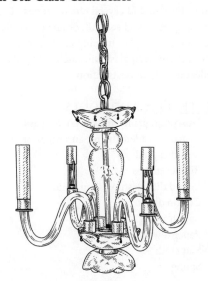

Chandeliers must be cleaned carefully to avoid breaking the glass or compromising the integrity of the wiring and the electrical components, such as sockets and plugs. First remove some of the pieces for easier access, but keep them in order for easy reassembly.

#### MATERIALS AND TOOLS

Glass chandelier in good working
    condition, with four or more arms
2 kitchen towels
1 bath towel
Plastic bags, sandwich size
Rubber bands
Spray glass cleaner
Paper towels
Liquid dishwashing soap, mild
Soft cloth
Cotton dish towel

### Step 1

Remove the loose components from the chandelier.

Rest the chandelier on an old bath towel on your work surface. Remove the lightbulbs, plastic candle sleeves, and the glass bobeches or candle cups from each arm; set them aside. Place a plastic bag over each exposed lightbulb socket, using a rubber band to secure the bag.

### Step 2 (optional)

Dismantle the glass components of the chandelier.

Unscrew the top hanging loop and the bottom hanging loop, twisting them in opposite directions to loosen their hold on the rod that runs through the length of the chandelier, which will allow you to disassemble the hollow glass components, called breaks, that make up the chandelier's central column.

### Step 3 (optional)

Remove the hardware.

Take off or unscrew any metal components—canopy, check rings, turned hexagon locknuts, cap—one by one and line them up on a clean towel in the same order

---

## Working Tips: Dismantling a Chandelier

Take digital photographs of a chandelier before you take it apart and during the stages of its disassembly to record the way it is put together. In this way, you will be able to reassemble the different components in the correct sequence. As an alternative, make a series of diagrams.

---

they are removed. The washers that protect the glass candle cups may be metal or plastic and should be removed too.

### Step 4

Clean the components.

For light grime, carefully clean each component, using spray glass cleaner, paper towels, cotton swabs, and a sponge, improvising any tool that will remove the grime and dirt in the crevices. Place the parts on a cotton dish towel in the same order in which they were removed. For heavy grime, see page 521, step 2.

## Technique: Cleaning the Decorative Glass Pieces

It is important to clean all the crystal pendants, beaded and crystal chains, ropes of cut crystal, pieces of glass fruit, or any other glass pieces that you plan to hang on your chandelier because clean glass will catch the light and reflect it without obstruction.

MATERIALS AND TOOLS

Dusty and grimy glass crystals, glass fruit, beaded chains, and ropes of cut crystal
Rubber gloves
Liquid dishwashing soap, mild
Cotton dish towel
Bath towel
Paper towels
Soft cloth
Sponge

**Step 1**

Soak and scrub the large, removable glass parts of the chandelier.

Plug the drain in your sink and lay a dish towel on the bottom. Run warm water into the sink and add several drops of dishwashing liquid, swishing the mixture to blend it. Turn off the water when the sink is half full. Soak the glass parts removed from the rod in warm soapy water and use a soft cloth or sponge to scrub them until all the accumulated grime has been removed. Rinse and dry the parts.

**Step 2**

Hand wash and dry the small decorative pieces.

Put on snug-fitting rubber gloves. Clean all of the loose glass pieces one at a time in the hot sudsy water, keeping your hands low in the water as you wash them to reduce the chance of damage should a piece drop. Use a sponge or soft cloth to loosen any dirt and grime. Rinse off each piece under warm water and lay it on a dry towel. Repeat until all of the loose glass pieces are clean. Dry with a soft cloth or paper towels.

Cleaning the decorative pieces is also important if you choose to add color to any of the glass surfaces. Color can be added to any glass or crystal using newly formulated water-based glass paints. Available in a broad variety of colors, the paint can be thinned to apply a sheer veil of color, allowing you to coordinate a chandelier with the colorway in the room in which it will hang. I applied glass paint to the inside of the candle cups only, because I planned to add glass fruit in a variety of Madame de Pompadour colors (pink, blue, and honey gold) and wanted only to suggest a foil for their sugary paleness. However, you can add color to the central column and the arms, accenting them with graphics—polka dots or stripes for a touch of whimsy—or with more prominent colors in the spectrum. Remember that what

you paint on one side of the crystal can be seen from both sides, so plan your designs accordingly.

There are many brands of water-based glass paint on the market. I chose one for its palette as well as for its sheer film of subtle color. I corrected errors when they occurred, using a moist cotton swab (or a full soak in warm water when I had a complete change of heart). The paint remains soluble when wet, but it becomes permanent and washable after it is cured in a home oven.

## Technique: Adding Color to Glass and Crystal

Glass paint should be applied to scrupulously clean glass with a soft brush that doesn't leave streaks. It must be allowed to dry for 24 hours before being heat-set to prevent the paint from bubbling.

### MATERIALS AND TOOLS

Clean, dry glass pieces to paint, such as candle cups
Transparent glass paint, such as Pebeo Vitrea 160
Thinner, such as Vitrea 160
Spray glass sealer
Soft natural-bristle brush
Gloss finish glaze (optional)
Rubber gloves
Chemical-cartridge respirator mask
Large cardboard carton (for spray booth)
Parchment
Baking sheet
Oven
Craft stick
Clear glass jar (to test color)

**Step 1**

Apply the sealer.

Work outdoors or in a well-ventilated space. Put on gloves and a chemical-cartridge respirator mask. Apply a light coat of sealer to one or both sides of the glass pieces, depending on which surfaces you are going to paint.

Use a spray booth to contain the overspray and spray several pieces at a time. If you are coloring the candle cups, spray the inside of the cups only. Let the sealer dry.

**Step 2**

Apply the paint to the pieces.

Stir the glass paint thoroughly using a craft stick, adding thinner if a light film of color is desired. Test the paint color on a clear glass jar. Use a soft-bristle brush to apply a light coat of paint to the sealed sides of each glass piece (or paint a design, if preferred). Let the paint air-dry for 24 hours, or for the time recommended by the manufacturer, until completely dry.

**Step 3**

Bake the painted pieces.

Distribute the painted glass pieces on a baking sheet lined with parchment so they do not touch one another. Place the sheet in a cold oven. Turn on the oven, setting the temperature to 325°F (162.8°C). Once the oven has reached that temperature, bake the glass pieces for 40 minutes. Open the oven door and leave the pieces inside the oven to cool slowly.

**Step 4**

Prepare to attach the painted pieces.

When the painted glass pieces are cool to the touch, transfer them one at a time to a bath towel or blanket laid on a table near the bare chandelier.

Hanging a chandelier is a job for a professional contractor and electrician. There are safety codes related to the electrical connection to ensure the fixture is grounded. The ceiling hook must be able to support the final weight of the chandelier after the cleaned and painted pieces are reattached, so don't forget to factor them into the equation. Once the chandelier is safely hanging overhead, move a table under it and pad it with a bath towel or thick

blanket so that any pieces that accidentally fall will not shatter. Then organize all of the glass pieces, pairing those you wish to attach to one arm or section and distributing like pieces in a balanced and symmetrical arrangement on the armature. You may find that as you attach the pieces, new ideas for their placement will come to you. Changing your mind is fine, because the decorative accents on a chandelier are so easy to move from one place to another.

## Technique: Hanging and Decorating a Glass Chandelier

Lay the cleaned chandelier and all loose glass pieces on a large towel or cloth to contemplate how you will hang them. After the chandelier is professionally mounted, you can begin bringing your design vision to life.

### MATERIALS AND TOOLS

1 glass chandelier in good working order with four arms, each with a painted candle cup

20 mismatched crystals and glass fruits, or hanging accents as desired
4 clear glass beaded chains or ropes of cut crystal, each 36" (91.4 cm) long
4 plastic candle sleeves, in good condition
4 chandelier lightbulbs
Wire, 26-gauge
Wire cutters
Soft cloth
Table covered in blanket or thick towels
Step stool

**Step 1**

Hang the chandelier.

Slip on the candle sleeves and install clean lightbulbs in the sockets. Have an electrician mount and test the chandelier in its new location.

**Step 2**

Wire all the decorative pieces.

Check all the loose decorative glass pieces to make sure each one has a hanging hook made from sturdy wire. If necessary, make replacement hooks using lengths of 26-gauge wire. Use wire cutters to cut the wire and use your fingers to bend it into hooks.

**Step 3**

Drape and secure the beaded chains.

Stand on a sturdy step stool to reach the chandelier. Add the crystal decorations to the arms, draping the beaded chains from one candle cup to the next; use short lengths of wire to secure the ends of the chains to the small hooks on the candle cups.

**Step 4**

Secure the loose glass pieces.

Distribute identical or like-shaped pieces of loose crystal and glass fruit evenly around the arms and the candle cups, aiming for some kind of symmetry and balance, if desired.

**Step 5**

Add more glass decorations as you collect them.

Continue to accumulate and clean new decorations for your chandelier. You can add them one at a time to the beaded chains or to the arms. Pay careful attention to the weight of the decorated chandelier; do not exceed the estimated weight capacity of the ceiling installation.

## Picture Frames: Restoring and Recycling

Recycling an old picture frame by adding embellishments is a satisfying way to give new life to an essential decorating accessory, while bringing it in line with your own taste and style. Of the many approaches possible, one straightforward and simple technique is to apply carved wooden appliqués (also called "onlays"), arranging them in a way that shows off their sculptural character and accentuates the shape and size of the frame. You do not have to carve the embellishments yourself. Wood appliqués are available in an alluring variety of sizes and motifs, from single scallop shells, rosettes, urns, Corinthian scrolls, and ribbons to swooping arabesques and woven baskets filled with flowers. Produced by hand and by machine, the carvings have one side raised in relief and one side that is flat to glue flush against the frame's surface. When the frame and the carved decoration are painted in the same color, they become beautifully unified.

The first criterion to look for when choosing a frame for recycling is a sound structure with tightly fitting corners and moldings that are glued securely. The frame must include flat sections that would be enhanced by the addition of ornate embellishment. These flat sections must be wide enough to accommodate the appliqués with "air" around them so they do not appear crowded, unless baroque is the look you are going for. Your frame may have either a mat or plastic strips to keep the glass from resting on the artwork, creating an air space that prevents moisture from building up between the artwork and the glass, which can cause mold. The aesthetic function of the mat is of course to highlight or dramatize the chosen artwork. Most picture frames have a rabbet at the back of the frame that holds the glass in place; the rabbet can be cut into the wood itself or it can be a separate piece of molding.

The restoration steps include disassembling the components—minimally the glass and mounting hardware—and cleaning, sand-

## Working Tip: Stripping Paint

You can remove the layers of old paint and varnish from your frame using a chemical stripper. When I choose this option, which is rare, I completely avoid any stripper containing methylene chloride (dichloromethane or DCM), which absolutely must be used outdoors while wearing a chemical-cartridge respirator, protective goggles, and gloves. Instead I choose one like Soy Green, which relies on soy esters to strip paint, posing fewer risks than paint removers formulated with volatile solvents and methylene chloride. Water-soluble strippers are almost always odor-free, are nonflammable, and clean up with soap and water. One complaint leveled against them is that they take longer to work, sometimes twice as long as chemical strippers; they also tend to dry up before they finish working, making multiple applications necessary. One unique product that addresses the drying problem is Peel Away 7 paint remover, a product that includes a fibrous, laminated paper that is laid over the coated surface, trapping moisture and keeping harmful particles from being released into the air. When the laminated paper is peeled off the treated surface, the stripper and the paint come off in one layer. Regardless of the product you choose, always read and follow the manufacturer's instructions. Be aware that any chemicals used for stripping paint are toxic and require extra care when working with them, including working outdoors while wearing gloves, safety glasses, and a mask.

ing, and refinishing the frame. An old frame in all likelihood is varnished, painted, or both—finishes that are usually stripped away as part of the restoration process. (For a fuller discussion on preparing and finishing wood surfaces, refer to Chapter 5: Decoupage.)

As you disassemble your frame, keep the components in a safe place so you can reinstall them, if in good condition, after the frame is restored. If a mat or backing board is marred, plan to replace it with new material. Keep mounting hardware, such as the screw eyes and picture-hanging wire, in a small plastic bag. Work outdoors when cleaning a frame with solvents, to avoid a concentration of the toxic fumes. Wear disposable gloves and a chemical-cartridge respirator mask when sanding painted surfaces as some old paint formulations contain lead, which is highly toxic.

## Technique: Disassembling and Cleaning a Recycled Picture Frame

You may be surprised by the condition of the components that are sandwiched within the dust protector and glass of your framed artwork. It is not uncommon for the protective paper and the mat to be torn or water damaged or to be infested (i.e., paper lice). For that reason, it is wise to disassemble the frame and examine closely all of the existing components, which protect valuable artwork.

MATERIALS AND TOOLS
    Frame with flat sections for appliqués
    Pliers
    Screwdriver
    Sandpaper, fine-grit (#600)
    Flexible sanding block
    Chemical-cartridge respirator mask
    Disposable gloves
    Soft rag
    Distilled white vinegar (for organic grease)
    Mineral spirits
    Sturdy folder or 2 sheets of chipboard
        (optional)
    Paper towels

**Step 1**
Disassemble the frame.

Lay the frame face down on a protected work surface. Use a staple remover or screwdriver and pliers to pry the staples or clips that hold the backing board. Set the backing board aside if it is in reusable condition; discard any backing paper. Lift out the artwork and the glass. Place the artwork in a sturdy folder or between two sheets of chipboard and lay it flat until you are ready to reframe it. Set the glass aside in a safe place.

**Step 2**
Clean the frame.

Turn the frame face up. Try distilled white vinegar first. If the grease cannot be removed, put on a chemical-cartridge respirator mask and gloves. Use a cloth dampened with mineral spirits to clean off any grime or grease from all sections of the frame. Wipe the frame with a dry cloth to remove any residue; let the surface dry.

**Step 3**
Sand the frame.

Wearing the respirator mask, use a sanding block wrapped in fine-grit (#600) sandpaper to smooth away areas of paint buildup or flaking paint. Wipe off the dust with a damp paper towel.

Once your picture frame is clean and smooth, it is ready to embellish. When choosing your appliqué motifs, consider their size and scale and how they relate to the frame and to one another. For example, to keep the eye from fixating on a central medallion spanning the top of your frame, you could add a decorative drop on each side of the center garland on the front of the frame. There are other ways to counterbalance an expansive decoration at the top and draw the eye down. You might choose a single accent on the center bottom of the frame or L-shaped accents, called "corner clips," at the two lower corners. Tackle the design by making a rough scale drawing of the frame so that you can freely experiment with the size and placement of the motifs. Visit websites that feature carved appliqués and make printouts of pieces that interest you, sizing them to your rough drawing. You will find that many appliqués come in a variety of lengths and widths, and your creative plans will not be thwarted when you are ready to actualize your design ideas.

You will notice a remarkable contrast in color and texture between the cleaned frame and the natural wood of the carvings that are glued to it. To ameliorate the disparity, you can paint the frame and the appliqués in one color so that the two surfaces blend together. Or you might play up the difference and choose a two-tone paint scheme, picking out the carved appliqués in one color and the frame in another. Antiquing and gilding are two more ways to finish a recycled-and-appliquéd frame so as to conceal the contrasting textures and colors and to unify the decorative elements or to highlight certain sculptural effects.

## Technique: Adding Carved Appliqués to a Frame

It continues to amaze me that crafters with little or no previous woodworking experience can transform ordinary frames into works of art using a few purchased onlays and paint. Requiring only the most rudimentary shop skills, finely carved decorations, which are available in abundance and stylistic variety, can be used to give new life to frames with good bones.

## Working Tips: Hanging a Picture Frame

Press a short strip of tape to the wall at the height where you are going to hammer in the picture-hanging hook. Install the nail in the hook, align the bottom edge of the hook with the tape's bottom edge, and hammer the nail to secure the hook to the wall.

## Preventing Rust from Ruining a Finish

Some old frames are secured with nails that, over time, will rust and stain the paint or finish. To remove the threat of rust completely, use pliers to carefully remove the nail from the frame and replace it with a nail made of nonferrous metal, such as brass. If you do not want to pull out the nail, carefully sand or scrape the nailhead, using a wire brush or steel wool to abrade the metal surface. Use a brush to apply a coat of red chromate primer or a stain-blocking primer to reduce the occurrence of rust.

## MATERIALS AND TOOLS
Wood frame, restored or new
Carved appliqués, as desired
Yellow carpenter's glue
Tape measure
Level
Pencil
Wood clamps
Scraps of thick chipboard

**Step 1**

Mark the positions of the appliqués.

Use a tape measure and a pencil to lightly mark the midpoint of each flat side of the frame. Measure and mark the midpoint of the wood appliqués planned for each of the key sections of the frame: the top, the two vertical sides, the two lower corners, and the bottom.

**Step 2**

Glue the top appliqué.

Apply glue to the back of the carved appliqué planned for the top central expanse of your frame, using an ample supply of glue at all points of contact. Center the appliqué horizontally on the frame, using a level to ensure that it is parallel with the frame's long edge. Press the appliqué, glue side down, onto the frame in the marked position, carefully wiping away any glue that oozes beyond the edges.

**Step 3**

Glue the remaining appliqués.

Glue the carved drops to opposite sides of the top central appliqué. Glue a corner clip to the bottom left and bottom right corners. Glue a small accent to the center bottom.

**Step 4**

Clamp the appliqués.

Clamp all of the glued-on pieces. Slip a scrap of chipboard between the clamp and the appliqué to avoid denting the wood. Wipe off any glue that oozes out beyond the edges. Let the glue dry overnight.

## Technique: Painting and Finishing a Recycled Picture Frame

The sealer applied in step 2 of this technique will also act as a primer coat under many paint colors. Make an exception and apply both a sealer and a primer if you are using a very light paint color, such as white, that would normally require two or more coats for full, even coverage.

## MATERIALS AND TOOLS
Frame, with glued-on carved appliqués
Water-soluble paint, such as acrylic craft paint, in white, or as desired
Acrylic medium-and-varnish, matte finish
Acrylic sealer
Water-soluble primer
Wood putty
Sandpaper, fine-grit (#600)
Respirator mask
Foam brushes
Tapered watercolor brush
Paper towels

**Step 1**

Fill in holes and breaks in the wood surface.

Following the manufacturer's directions, apply wood putty to any nail holes or across mitered corners of the frame, using your fingertips to smooth the putty even with the wood surface. Inspect the existing screw eye holes, located on the back of the frame along the facing sides of the frame, about one-third below the top edge. If the holes appear too large or too worn to be reused, fill in the original holes with wood putty and let it cure. After the putty cures, put on a respirator mask and use a handheld piece of fine-grit (#600) sandpaper to smooth the surfaces, wiping off the dust with a damp paper towel. If the putty shrinks and creates a depression as it dries, repeat the process until the surface is level and smooth.

## Quick & Easy: Faux Finish Effects for Wood

The term *faux finish* is used to describe textural surface effects that can be achieved using paint, abrasion, wax, and other means to simulate the effects of aging and wear on a wood surface. Here are two easy faux finishing techniques that can be used on wood frames. For more ideas and instruction, consult the bibliography for books on decorative painting.

- **Aging**
  This faux finish painting technique is designed to artificially confer the effects of passing time that would naturally occur when paintwork is exposed to light, moisture, and abrasion. The effects can be artificially created using beeswax or petroleum jelly to simulate faded color, chipped and scraped surfaces, peeling paint, and other signs of wear and tear. The painted finish depends on using grease to destabilize the layer of paint that is applied over it so the paint does not adhere evenly, if at all, to the coated surface. When different colors of paint are applied successively in layers and then abraded, the underlying coats of paint show through, creating the aging effect. Start with a clean sealed wood surface. Apply a liberal coat of water-soluble paint to the wood. Let dry for 12 hours. Use your hand or a rag to smear a narrow filmy streak of beeswax or petroleum jelly on random sections of the frame, applying it in the direction of the wood grain. Apply a second coat of paint in a different color, diluting it with water by one-third. Let the second coat dry for 1 hour. Use a narrow scraper or medium-grit (#400) sandpaper on a flexible sanding block to remove the paint in those areas where grease was applied which will expose the painted layer underneath. Wipe the surface with a damp cloth. Lightly sand all of the painted surfaces, wipe clean, and then apply a semigloss sealer to add soft satin luster and to protect the faux finish.

- **Pickling**
  This faux finish uses thinned white acrylic craft paint to highlight the wood grain of an unfinished wood piece. Although the effect is traditionally used on a hard wood with a prominent grain, such as oak, a pickled finish can also be used on a soft, closed-grain wood such as pine. Thin a water-soluble white paint with water so it is a milky consistency and apply it liberally to the wood, using a foam brush or paintbrush and brushing with the grain. Allow 15 to 20 minutes for the paint to penetrate the wood and raise the grain. Wipe the surface with a clean rag. Wiping will expose the wood grain and leave a wash of color deposited in the crevices and joinery. Finish the surfaces with a coat of matte sealer to protect the faux finish.

## Step 2

Seal the frame.

Lay the frame face up on a protected work surface. Use a foam brush to apply a thin, even coat of acrylic sealer to all wood surfaces, including the appliqués. Use the foam brush to blot up pools of sealer that collect in the crevices of the carvings. Let the sealer dry.

## Step 3

Prime the wood surfaces.

Use a foam brush to apply an even coat of water-soluble primer to all surfaces of the frame, including the carved appliqués. Let the primer dry 1 hour.

## Step 4

Paint the frame.

Use a foam brush to apply an even coat of paint to all surfaces of the frame, including the carved decorations. Do not allow paint to pool in the crevices. Let the paint dry 1 hour. Apply a second coat of paint and let it dry completely.

## Step 5

Apply the finish.

Use fine-grit (#600) sandpaper to lightly sand the painted surface of the frame to provide tooth for the sealer, using a damp paper towel to remove the dust. Use a foam brush to apply a thin, even coat of acrylic medium-and-varnish to all parts of the frame, including the

## Working Tips: Preparing Wood Frames

For more in-depth information and detailed instructions on preparing and treating wood surfaces, refer to Chapter 5.

carved appliqués. Do not allow the varnish to pool in the crevices. Let the sealer dry 1 hour. Apply a second coat for a more resilient finish and let the sealer dry completely.

## Technique: Painting a Two-Tone Picture Frame

Using paint in contrasting colors on a frame is one way to highlight or to minimize the appearance of the embellishments. To call attention to and unite the applied elements— the edge molding and the carvings—apply the same color paint to their surfaces and then use a contrasting color on the background. This will have the effect of delineating the frame's silhouette and moving the eye to the sculptural details that embellish it. To minimize the effect, use the same color to paint the frame and the appliqués.

### MATERIALS AND TOOLS

Frame with glued-on carved appliqués, sealed and primed
Acrylic craft paints, in white and robin's-egg blue, or as desired
Acrylic medium-and-varnish, matte finish
Sandpaper, fine-grit (#600)
Foam brush
Tapered watercolor brush
Paper towels
Low-tack masking tape

## Step 1

Paint the first color.

Use a damp foam brush to apply an even coat of white craft paint to the carved appliqués and the flat moldings. To paint small or hard-to-reach areas, use a tapered watercolor brush to apply the paint. Let the paint dry 1 hour. Apply a second coat of white paint as before. Let the paint dry completely.

## Step 2

Paint the second color.

Paint the remaining wood surfaces robin's-egg blue. First, run a strip of low-tack masking tape along the edge of the flat molding to avoid getting blue paint on it. Use a narrow foam brush to apply an even coat of blue acrylic craft paint to all wood surfaces except the wood appliqués and the flat molding. Let the paint dry 1 hour. Apply a second coat of blue paint as before. Let the paint dry completely.

**Step 3**

Seal the frame.

Use fine-grit (#600) sandpaper to lightly sand the painted surface to provide tooth for the sealer. Use damp paper towels to remove the dust. Use a foam brush to apply a thin, even coat of acrylic medium-and-varnish to all parts of the frame, including the carved appliqués. Do not allow the varnish to pool in the crevices. Let the varnish dry 1 hour. Apply a second coat for a more resilient finish and let the varnish dry completely.

Putting the frame back together is the final stage of your frame restoration project. Be sure the sealer is perfectly dry and cured before handling the frame. You will want to check the soundness of the mounting hardware, such as the screw eyes and the picture-hanging wire, which must be tightly secured and strong enough to support the weight of the frame when it is hung. Inspect the existing screw eye holes, located along the sides of the frame, about one-third below the top edge. If the holes appear too large or too worn to be reused, choose a new location nearby to install the screw eyes. Fill in the original holes with wood putty, let cure, and sand the surface smooth. The original glass, if it is in good shape, can be cleaned and reinstalled; if you need a replacement glass, take the frame to a glass store to be measured and fitted for a new piece. Any missing fillers, such as sheets of chipboard to elevate the artwork or kraft paper for a dust protector, must also be purchased and cut to fit the frame.

## Technique: Adding Mounting Hardware and a Dust Protector to a Restored Picture Frame

This technique involves framing a piece of artwork and preparing the frame for hanging and display. Use the originals or replacements of the picture glass, mounting hardware, and chipboard filler, depending upon their condition.

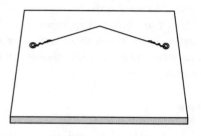

MATERIALS AND TOOLS

Artwork to frame
Frame, embellished, painted, and sealed
Picture glass
Mat or plastic strips
2 screw eyes
Picture-hanging wire
Brads or glazier points
Kraft paper
Chipboard, in two thicknesses
White craft glue
Awl
Hammer
Pliers
Screwdriver
Wire cutters
Tape measure
Steel ruler
Craft knife
Self-healing mat
Spray bottle with water
Hair dryer
Emery board
Pencil

**Step 1**

Cut the backing board.

Lay the artwork on a sheet of chipboard and use a pencil and a steel ruler to trace the outline. Lift off the artwork, lay the chipboard on a self-healing cutting mat, and use a craft knife and a steel ruler to cut the chipboard on the marked lines.

**Step 2**

Cut the dust protector.

Lay the frame on the sheet of kraft paper. Trace around it with a pencil, adding 4" (10.2 cm) on each side to the dimensions. Cut the kraft paper on the marked lines.

**Step 3**

Install the frame's components.

Turn the frame face down on a protected work surface. Set the glass, the mat, the artwork, and a sheet of chipboard inside the frame, making sure the stack of components is slightly lower than the edge of the frame when pressed together. If necessary, change out the chipboard for a thinner piece if the stack is too high. Use a hammer to tap small brads or glazier points into the rabbet to secure the components inside the frame.

**Step 4**

Glue on the dust protector.

Lay the sheet of kraft paper on a protected work surface. Apply a thin bead of glue along the four sides of the frame, smoothing the glue with your fingertip. Lay the frame, glue side down, onto the kraft paper (which is larger than the frame). Turn the frame right side up and smooth paper flat against the glued edge; let the glue dry completely. Use a sharp craft knife to trim the paper even with the frame, being careful not to slice into the wood.

**Step 5**

Shrink the dust protector and buff the edges.

Use a spray bottle to apply a heavy mist of water to the kraft paper, which will cause it to wrinkle. Use a hair dryer to dry the paper until it is taut across the frame. Use the fine-grit side of an emery board to abrade the edges of the paper so they are soft and even with the edge of the frame.

**Step 6**

Install the screw eyes.

Use an awl to pierce a starter hole through the dust cover and the wood. Insert the shank of the screw eye through the paper and into the wood and turn it by hand or with a pair of pliers; do not overtighten to avoid splitting the wood.

**Step 7**

Install the mounting hardware on the frame.

Use a tape measure to measure and cut a length of picture-hanging wire that is equal to the width of the frame plus 10" (25.4 cm). Thread one end of the wire through one of the screw eyes, pulling the wire so there is a 5" (12.7 cm) tail. Bring the wire end around and back through the screw eye and knot it; wrap the excess wire tail around the long wire. Repeat at the other screw eye, adjusting the tension according to how you wish the picture to hang on the wall, and tie and wrap the wire as before.

A large mirror, perhaps a vintage piece you are salvaging, is heavier than a piece of artwork and involves special framing considerations. A deep lip or rabbet, approximately ⅜" (1.0 cm), on the frame's inner edge will help hold the mirror in place and keep it from slipping out of the frame. To secure a mirror at the back, I use Z-shaped mounting clips, and as a precaution, I also run a bead of clear silicone between the mirror's edge and the wood frame. The extra weight of a mirror will be more evenly distributed and supported if you use D-rings (instead of screw eyes) and picture-hanging wire to mount it on the wall. Hang the D-rings on picture-hanging hooks with a test weight that is greater than the weight of the framed mirror or art.

## Technique: Installing a Mirror in a Frame

While a beveled mirror can be set into a frame and be supported by a rabbet (which is a channel cut into the inside edge of the wood frame using a table saw and a dado blade), a more convenient way is to secure the mirror in a frame using metal Z clips. The clips work because the lip on the beveled mirror makes the mirror slightly larger by about ½" (1.3 cm) than the inside dimensions of the frame, preventing the mirror from slipping through the frame's center opening. The Z clip is made of a crimped metal bar that has a shallow step in the middle that accommodates the thickness of the glass. One side of the clip is pressed flat against the inside of the edge of the frame and screwed into place, which forces the other side of the clip to press against the lip of the mirror, holding it securely in place. A backing board will protect the back of a mirror from scratches that will show on the right side and sturdy hardware will be attached to the frame and to the wall when it is mounted. Remember to use heavy picture hangers (30- or 50-pound test) according to the weight of your framed mirror; nail the hangers to the wall according to the directions on the package.

MATERIALS AND TOOLS

Frame, embellished, painted, and sealed
Beveled mirror
2-ply chipboard, larger than mirror
Offset Z-shaped mounting clips, with
    screws
2 D-rings
Brad
Hammer
Picture-framing wire, 10" (25.4 cm) more
    than the width of the frame
Wire cutters
2 picture-hanging hooks, tested at proper
    weight for mirror
Staple gun and staples
Clear silicone adhesive
Disposable gloves
Craft knife
Steel ruler
Self-healing cutting mat
Tape measure and ruler
Awl
Screwdriver
Masking tape
Pencil
Thick bath towels

### Step 1

Install the mirror in the frame.

Lay the frame face down on a work surface padded with thick towels. Set the mirror within the center opening, letting the lip of the mirror settle against the inside edge of the frame with the lip overlapping the edge by ½" on all sides. Position the offset Z-shaped mounting clips 5" to 6" (12.7 to 15.2 cm) apart on the frame, positioning the "step" on each clip on the edge of the lip and the other end (with the screw hole) resting on the frame's wood surface. Use a screwdriver and a screw to secure each Z clip to the frame. Do not overtighten the screw as it can distribute undue pressure from one end of the clip to the other part that rests on the mirror, causing the glass to break.

### Step 2

Apply silicone adhesive.

Put on disposable gloves. Read and follow the manufacturer's directions on the tube of silicone adhesive. Apply a thin bead of silicone between the edge of the mirror and the frame, using your gloved fingertip to gently smooth the adhesive into the gap. Let the adhesive cure completely, 12 to 24 hours.

### Step 3

Conceal the back of the mirror with backing board.

Use a steel ruler, craft knife, and self-healing cutting mat to measure and cut a sheet of chipboard 1" (2.5 cm) larger all around than the mirror. Use a pencil and ruler to draw a line on the chipboard ¼" (0.6 cm) from the edge all around. Center the chipboard on the back of the mirror and secure it temporarily with strips of tape. Staple the board to the wood frame along the marked lines. Avoid stapling near the edge of the mirror, which could cause the glass to chip or shatter. Remove the tape.

### Step 4

Install the D-rings on the back of the frame.

Measure the length of each side of the frame. Add the measurements together and divide the total by 4. For example, if the sum of the lengths is 60" (151.2 cm), divide that number by 4, giving you 15" (38.1 cm). Use a pencil and ruler to mark the positions of two D-rings on the sides of the frame, 15" (38.1 cm) down from the top edge of the frame. Use an awl to pierce starter holes in the wood and then use a screwdriver and the screws provided with the D-rings to secure the rings to the frame.

### Step 5

String on the picture-framing wire.

Mark the midpoint of the top width of the frame and use a hammer to tap the brad into the mark, sinking the nail to a depth of ¼" (6 mm). Thread one end of the picture-framing wire through one of the D-rings, leaving a 5" (12.7 cm) tail; wrap the wire tail around the long wire. Bring the wire over the top of the brad and thread the wire end through the other D-ring, pulling the wire taut. Cut off the excess wire, leaving a 5" (12.7 cm) tail. Wrap the wire tail around the long wire. Remove the brad.

### Step 6

Hang the mirror.

If possible, work with a partner if the framed mirror is heavy. Lift the mirror and place the picture wire over the hooks on the wall, slowly lowering the frame so the hooks are allowed to adjust to the weight of the frame. Adjust the frame so it is level.

### Technique: Painting an Unfinished-Wood Frame in a Single Color

A veritable blank canvas, an unfinished wood frame with appliqués can be treated in a variety of ways. Painting the entire surface in a single color helps unify the embellishments, which may be made from different woods and composites.

#### MATERIALS AND TOOLS

Frame with carved appliqués, sanded smooth
Acrylic sealer
Water-soluble primer
Water-soluble paint, in white or desired color
Sanding block
Sandpaper, fine-grit (#600)
Acrylic medium-and-varnish, matte finish
Foam brush

### Step 1

Seal the wood surfaces.

Lay the frame face up on a protected work surface. Use a foam brush to apply an even coat of sealer to all surfaces of the frame, including the carved appliqués. Let the sealer dry about 1 hour or according to the directions on the manufacturer's label.

### Step 2

Prime the wood surfaces.

Use a foam brush to apply an even coat of water-soluble primer to all surfaces of the frame, including the carved appliqués. Let the primer dry for 1 hour.

### Step 3

Paint the frame.

Use a damp foam brush to apply an even coat of white paint to the frame, including the wood appliqués and the flat molding. For small and narrow details, use a tapered watercolor brush to apply the paint. Let the paint dry for 1 hour. Apply a second coat of white paint as before; let the paint dry completely.

**Step 4**

Seal the frame.

Use a foam brush to apply a thin, even coat of matte acrylic medium-and-varnish to all parts of the front and sides of the frame, including the carved appliqués. Allow the sealer to dry for 1 hour. Repeat to add a second coat of acrylic medium-and-varnish for a more resilient finish. Let the sealer dry overnight.

## Picassiette: Restoring and Recycling

The art of using pieces of broken china to create a mosaic design is *picassiette*, which means, translating loosely from the French, "plate stealer." Whereas classical mosaics use uniformly sized tablets in individual colors to form a picture or pattern, picassiette employs pieces of china in irregular shapes and sizes and utilizes the patterns and motifs on the china itself to add color, texture, and detail to the overall design.

There are two basic stages to working the picassiette technique. The first involves acquiring the china and choosing a sturdy base, such as a table, for the mosaic design. The second is the execution stage, which includes breaking the plates into pieces, or *tesserae*, laying out the pieces and gluing them to the base, applying grout to fill in the mosaic, and finally sealing the surface to protect it.

### Materials and Tools

Unless you have done tilework before, it is unlikely that you will have the materials and tools for creating a mosaic on hand. The things you will need are readily available in hardware and craft stores and in tile stores that cater to tiling professionals.

• **Tesserae**

The term *tesserae* refers to pieces of ceramic that are used to compose a mosaic; a *tessera* is an individual tile, usually cube-shaped. In picassiette work, *tesserae* refers to broken pieces of china that are irregularly shaped, formed by breaking the china into pieces, and squares of ceramic tile.

• **Tile nippers**

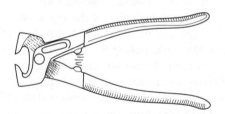

Designed with strong straight jaws for breaking ceramic tile, tile nippers are used in picassiette to break china plates into sections and to trim edges of small pieces in a moderately controlled way. The cutting edges of the tool are offset at the edge of the china or tile, and when pressure is applied to the handles, a fracture is created that runs across the piece, breaking it in two. There are several models of tile nippers. One type, designed for porcelain, has small blades that pinch without the need of excessive brute strength. Cut tesserae over a cardboard box to catch chips and shards.

- **Adhesive and mortar**

  Adhesives and mortars are used to secure the tesserae to a porous or nonporous base. Different formulations are available, according to whether the project will be used indoors or outdoors. Ceramic tile adhesives, also called "tile mastic" (Weldbond is one brand), are recommended for projects used indoors, whereas mortars, such as thinset bonding mortar that comes in a powdered form, is mixed with water, and is waterproof, are recommended for those used outdoors. Epoxy can be used to adhere tesserae to a project for both indoor and outdoor use, but it has a noxious odor and requires experience to use effectively as it cures quickly.

- **Palette knife or expired credit card**

  Any stiff, flexible, resilient blade-shaped tool that spreads adhesive on a base is suited to mosaics. Choose a blade according to the amount of adhesive you are applying to the base.

- **Grout float**

  A grout flout is a flat, rectangular metal plate with an attached handle. It is used to smooth grout evenly over the mosaic, filling in the spaces between the tesserae. A squeegee can perform the same function.

- **Grout**

  Grout comes in two different formulations. One blend contains portland cement and powdered pigments, and the other is the same formulation with sand added, which bulks up the substance to fill the spaces between the tesserae. The choice of grout is determined by the size of the gap between the tesserae. Sanded grout is recommended for a gap of more than ⅛" (0.3 cm) and nonsanded grout is recommended for a gap of less than ⅛" (0.3 cm). Picassiette projects use sanded grout because the irregularly shaped pieces of broken china and ceramic tiles leave gaps of slightly more than ⅛" (0.3 cm) when they are arranged in a mosaic. Having the consistency of thick, granulated cake frosting, grout is designed to permanently fill the gaps between the tesserae. Premixed sanded grout is easy to apply; powdered grout should be mixed outdoors and you should wear a respirator mask. Available in white and gray, grout can be tinted different colors, and two different colors of grout can be mixed together to create a new shade.

- **Grout sealer**

  Grout sealer provides essential protection to mosaics that will come into contact with moisture or liquids, such as an outdoor table or a serving tray. The sealer prevents the grout from absorbing moisture, which can in turn undermine the adhesive. There are two formulations, penetrating and membrane-forming, and both form a protective coating that keeps the grout from absorbing moisture and staining. I recommend the penetrating sealer because it allows the grout to breathe and doesn't get dingy as can a membrane-forming sealer. Some grout is already formulated with a sealer, so check the manufacturer's directions before taking the time to apply one separately.

- **Base**

  A suitable item for picassiette will have a flat or very slightly contoured rigid surface that can support the weight of the mosaic tesserae without sagging. If the base sags and stresses the grout, it can crack and pieces of tesserae can lift up off the surface. A base material can be porous (wood) or nonporous (metal or glass). Tables and trays are good bases for tesserae.

- **Safety glasses with side shields**

  Breaking glazed ceramic with either a tile nipper or a hammer can cause shards to fly out. It is imperative that you protect your eyes with safety glasses that have side shields.

- **Rubber gloves**
  Always wear rubber gloves when applying grout to protect your skin, as grout
  is caustic. Gloves also protect you from
  sharp edges on nipped pieces of ceramic
  that can cut you.

## Selecting the China

There are great sources of china in all kinds
of conditions that are ideal for use in mosaics:
garage sales, flea markets, thrift stores, antique
shops, and discount housewares chains are
places to look. China in these venues is sold
at reasonable prices because often only a few
pieces from a set or single pieces are available,
making them less desirable for normal use.
Look for any piece of china that has a broad,
flat area that is either a solid color or filled with
pattern. Dinner, salad, and dessert plates are
ideal because they have central, flat surfaces.
You may find a great-looking piece of china—
appealing in color and pattern—yet it may not
be suited to *picassiette*. Cups and bowls have
fewer usable sections for *picassiette,* especially
those areas around the foot, which have thick,
sloping ridges that are difficult to cut and too
contoured to adhere to a flat surface. Platters
may entice with their large central designs, but
they can be difficult to break.

Color is a more subtle indicator of suitability. Plates made before the 1950s that are
a pale cream color should break cleanly. It is
unlikely that the china will be stamped with
a date, but manufacturer names can help you
identify suitable pieces. Pope-Gosser, Myott,
and Johnson Brothers are but a few. Use an
online search engine and enter "dinnerware"
or "dishes" to find the names of American and
English china manufacturers that produced
china before 1950. China manufactured after
the 1950s will, in all likelihood, be break- and
heat-resistant. China stamped as safe for use
in a dishwasher or microwave is less suited to
picassiette. Bone china may be pretty, but it is
often so fragile that it shatters into unsalvage-
able pieces for a mosaic design.

If you are unsure about a piece—wondering
if it will break cleanly or if it is the right color—
I suggest you buy it anyway. Unmatched china
is usually priced reasonably and worth the
investment. You can test the china piece at
home. In addition, stocking up on mismatched
pieces will provide inspiration. Often as you
are breaking and assembling your tesserae,
you will come up with new ideas. Having a
wide selection of china will provide a broad
palette of patterns and colors that expand the
creative possibilities.

In all cases, make sure you have enough
tesserae to cover the surface of your project,
which will be determined by good guessing.
It is difficult to assess the actual number of
usable pieces a single plate will yield until you
break it as there are so many variables, from
the size of the image or pattern on the plate to
the size and shape of the broken pieces. Simple
rules of thumb: buy what you can afford and
buy more than you need.

## Planning a Design

The tesserae in a mosaic can be arranged randomly in an asymmetrical design or organized in a symmetrical pattern with repeat
sequences of color and pattern. The two design
approaches can be combined in one project,
with pieces of broken china arranged in one

pattern or color and tiles laid out in an orderly border around them. The design parameters are strongly influenced by the project base, which can be any shape and size as long as the surface is flat (or very softly contoured), stable, and sturdy. China pieces, tiles, and grout add significant weight to a piece, something to keep in mind when choosing a design surface. The surface must be rigid enough to support this extra weight without sagging, which can put stress on the grout and cause it to crack so that the tesserae break loose and lift up. Tables, trays, and counters are good choices. Delicate mosaics can be added to small accessories, such as frames and vases. Although jugs, bottles, and other items with curved and sloping contours can be used for mosaics, they require smaller tesserae that lay against the contoured surface without tilting up, exposing sharp edges that can cut you. One approach is to use tiles with narrow widths; they will round the curves and fit around the perimeter of a round shape without having to be trimmed.

The beauty of picassiette is that you can experiment with the arrangement of the tesserae until you are satisfied with the design and then permanently glue down the pieces to the project base. In general, a mosaic is easier to plan and execute when you can work out a design directly on a small surface, trimming the shapes of the china pieces to fit as you go along. For larger projects, I recommend using a paper template. Round shapes, such as a table or a mirror frame, demand more careful planning to fit the pieces around the curves. It is easy to go off-course if you are gluing down pieces on the fly. Mark the template and the project surface with a grid or with shapes that approximate or are identical to the design areas. For example, trace around a plate or other round object to mark a circle on the paper template and on the project surface to guide the placement of mosaic pieces.

### Creating the Mosaic

The goal of breaking a china plate into pieces is to create tesserae—mosaic "tiles"—that can be laid out in a pattern that is pleasing to the eye and that exploits the inherent beauty of each piece. Breaking up a china plate can be done in two different ways: by using a hammer, which makes irregularly shaped pieces, or by using tile nippers, for more uniformly sized pieces. (The use of a wet saw to cut tile is beyond the scope of this chapter.) The hammer approach is effective in general, but the shape and size of the pieces are impossible to control. Basically, you cover the back of a plate with a sheet of self-adhesive vinyl (think Con-Tact Brand paper), wrap the plate in newspaper and place it inside a brown paper bag; then you use a hammer to smash the plate. The more controlled approach is to use a pair of tile nippers, first splitting a plate into large segments and then making smaller, more even-edged pieces with irregular shapes and curves, as desired. Irregularities can often be camouflaged at the grouting stage when the spaces between the tesserae are filled. With a little practice, you will know what to expect when using the tile-nipping tool and be able to adjust the angle of the jaws and the pressure exerted to achieve the basic shapes you want. Be aware that the surface integrity of a plate may not reveal an internal hairline crack, which will result in an odd break when the tile nipper is used. If you are a total beginner, practice using the tile nippers on a few junky plates to understand how different kinds and thicknesses of china affect the results.

Once you are familiar with the mechanics of using a tile nipper, you will be able to create a supply of tesserae for your project. Your goal is to harvest and preserve as many flat pieces of china as you can. There are two basic areas to choose from: a flat central area and a rim. The central area will yield the most usable pieces, and you'll want to keep some motifs in one piece. Rather than breaking apart an attractive cluster of flowers into unrecognizable bits, keep the design intact, using the tile nippers to work around edges of the design to preserve it. As you turn your attention to the plate rim, remember that one of its original purposes is to visually frame the central motif, coordinating with it in both style and color. In all likelihood, the rim will be a good source of companion pieces for those harvested from the central area of the plate. The drawback is that the rim has a smaller usable area because of the thick ridge on the back of the plate, the rising slope, and an uneven thickness. You will need to use the tile nippers to nibble away at the unwanted slope and the ridge at the back of the plate until only the flat part remains.

## Technique: Breaking a China Plate with Tile Nippers

Suited to the controlled breaking of a china plate and to making incremental nips on the edge of a broken, irregularly shaped piece to refine it, tile nippers depend on brute strength and the careful positioning of the blades on the plate to split a large plate into wedge-shape sections and to refine the shape of smaller tesserae. Placed offset on a an angle to the plate

rim, a squeeze of the nippers will cause the cutting edges to begin a fracture in the ceramic that travels across the plate, usually splitting the plate into two sections, depending upon any flaws in the china, such as a hairline crack, which can send the break in a new direction. Tile nippers can also be used to "nibble" away at the edges of small pieces of tesserae, providing an easy way to harvest a great number of usable pieces from one plate.

## MATERIALS AND TOOLS
China plates, round, dinner size, or as desired
Tile nippers
Safety glasses with side shields
Rubber gloves

**Step 1**
Break the plate into four wedges.

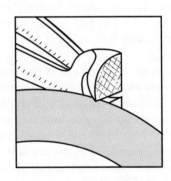

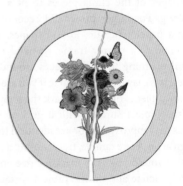

Put on safety glasses and rubber gloves. Position the tile nippers offset on the edge of the plate, on an angle to the rim, and squeeze the handles to break the plate into two pieces. Use the nippers to break each piece into two pieces. Set the four wedge-shaped pieces aside.

## Step 2

Separate the rims from the central flat sections.

Working one wedge-shaped piece at a time, use the tile nippers to carefully cut apart and separate the central flat section from each plate rim. Place the pieces in order on a flat surface, keeping the general shape of each wedge and rim.

## Step 3

Remove the thick ridge from the rim pieces.

Pick up and hold a rim section so that the rim faces away from you, the broken edge is near you, and the ridge that was on the underside of the plate faces up. Use the edge of the tile nippers to trim away the ridge, working from both sides of the rim and going as close to the ridge as possible until the ridge is completely removed and the remaining piece is flat. Repeat to break the thick ridge off the other rim pieces.

## Step 4

Cut apart the central flat sections of the wedge.

Use the tile nippers to break the flat sections of the wedge into smaller pieces. Set the cut pieces on a flat surface as you go, repositioning them as they were when still intact. Continue until all four flat sections are cut into pieces and organized on the work surface.

## Step 5

Assess the pieces of tesserae.

Examine all of your china pieces for uniform thickness, pattern, and usability. Further trim the pieces, as necessary, and arrange the pieces on the base of your project or a template in a way that best utilizes them.

## Technique: Breaking a China Plate with a Hammer

A piece of china can be broken using a hammer. Suited to this method are plates that are difficult to break with tile nippers, such as those made of modern dishwasher or microwave-safe ceramic. If a plate does not break with a pair of tile nippers, try the hammer method.

### MATERIALS AND TOOLS

China plate, round, dinner size, or as desired

Hammer

Sheet of clear, adhesive-backed vinyl (Con-Tact Brand paper) or packing tape, 2" to 3" (5.1 to 7.6 cm) wide

Paper grocery bag

Baking sheet

Safety glasses with side shields

Rubber gloves

Bath towel

### Step 1

Cover the plate with transparent adhesive-backed vinyl.

Protect the work surface with a thick towel. Invert the plate on the towel and cover it with a sheet of vinyl, pressing to adhere. Place the plate, vinyl side up, inside a paper grocery bag.

### Step 2

Break the plate.

Put on safety glasses and rubber gloves. Work on a sturdy workbench. Use your fingers to feel through the paper bag for the thick ridge on the underside of the plate that separates the plate center from the more fragile edge of the rim. Use a hammer to break the plate into pieces, aiming blows at the thick ridge. Do not aim for the center of the plate to avoid making a hammer-sized hole in the center. Check the size of the broken pieces. Hit the plate several more times, as necessary, according to the desired number and size of the broken pieces. Remove or tear off the paper bag. Carefully press down the vinyl to make certain all of the pieces are adhered. Some skinny shards may not adhere; pick these off with gloved fingers.

**Step 3**

Flip over the broken plate.

Lay a baking sheet on top of the vinyl-covered side of the plate. Slide the towel toward the edge of the work surface and flip the sandwich over so the towel is on top. Remove the towel to provide a view of the broken pieces from the color or pattern side. Slide the adhesive sheet with the broken pieces off the baking sheet and back onto the towel.

**Step 4**

Assess the tesserae.

Examine all of your china pieces for uniform thickness, pattern, and usability in the design. Lift the pieces off the adhesive backing, one at a time, and place them on the template, as desired. Use tile nippers to refine the size or shape of any piece or to cut off any thick ridges.

Once your pieces of china are broken into usable pieces and you have enough tesserae for your project, you can begin creating your mosaic design. Draw grid lines or other markings to map out the actual-size design on a paper template and on the base of your project. Lay out the key pieces of tesserae on the template, paying attention to the arrangement of colors and patterns. The space between the tesserae should be approximately ⅛" (0.3 cm). You can fine-tune the size or shape of a piece of china by trimming in small increments with the tile nippers.

The adhesive is applied to the base and the tesserae are set into it. It is important to choose an appropriate adhesive, because indoor and outdoor furnishings and accessories have different requirements. For indoor use, there are

## Designing a Mosaic for a Round Table

On a round table, the focal point can be a central medallion filled with broken pieces of china that reconstitute a pattern or image from a single plate before it is broken. A ring of square tiles around the central medallion and another border around the edge repeat the circular design. The field between the two borders is filled with random tesserae made from broken plates. Design the outer border, then the center design, and then the field in between. A circle is more technically demanding than a square design; careful cutting and fitting will ensure the tesserae fit around the curves.

effective, nontoxic, water-based PVA glues (such as Weldbond) that dry clear, are water-resistant, and clean up with soap and water. Products designated for outdoor use have to withstand the effects of moisture and temperature fluctuation. Adhesives (such as Liquid Nails) or bonding mortar (such as thinset) can be used on outdoor projects. Thinset is sold in large 25-pound (11.3 kg) bags; most manufacturers recommend wearing a respirator mask and mixing it outdoors, so it is not the most convenient option to use. Another option is epoxy. This adhesive can be used for indoor and outdoor applications. Epoxy has a noxious odor, which is unappealing to work with, and it hardens in a short time, which puts the pressure on to work quickly, so I don't recommend it for beginners. No matter what adhesive or mortar you choose, always read the manufacturer's directions before using it.

## Technique: Adhering Broken China Tessarae to a Square Wood Base

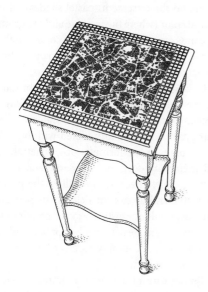

Porous surfaces, such as wood, must be sealed before the tessarae are adhered. Work out your design on paper and then transfer it to the wood base using a marker. Work out the design for a border first and then the rest of the design field.

### MATERIALS AND TOOLS

Broken china pieces and small square tiles
Flat square wood base, such as a side table with a square top
Adhesive for ceramic tile, premixed and designed for application to wood
Adhesive spreader, such as an expired credit card or a palette knife
Safety glasses with side shields
Disposable gloves
Permanent marker
Ruler
Shelf paper
Steel ruler

### Step 1

Make a design template.

Use a permanent marker to trace or draw the actual-size outline of the project surface on a large piece of shelf paper. Use the marker and a steel ruler to draw a grid pattern on the paper. Lay out the small square tiles around the edge of the template and lay the broken china pieces in the central part of the template. Mark the shape of key pieces on the paper template. If necessary, put on safety glasses and use the tile nippers to trim any pieces of tesserae to fit within the design area.

### Step 2

Reproduce the design template on the wood base.

Use a marker and a ruler to reproduce the grid pattern on the square tabletop.

### Step 3

Apply adhesive to one section of the wood.

Spread a ⅛"-thick (0.3 cm) layer of adhesive on a small border section, approximately 3" (7.6 cm) wide, of the square tabletop. Avoid overloading the adhesive, which will cause it to ooze from between the tiles and make it difficult to grout later.

**Step 4**

Position the tiles on the outer border of the wood base.

Using the paper template as a guide, transfer the tiles for the outer border from the template to the wood base, using some pressure and a twisting motion to ensure good contact with the adhesive and spacing them approximately ⅛" (0.3 cm) apart. Continue to apply adhesive and tiles in small sections until the entire border of the square is complete.

**Step 5**

Position the tesserae in the central part of the design.

Apply adhesive to a small area in the center of the design field. Pick up a piece of broken china from the corresponding area on the paper template and transfer it to the tabletop, pattern side up, and press it into the adhesive. Use some pressure and a twisting motion to ensure good contact between the adhesive and the china. Allow ⅛" (0.3 cm) between the pieces and align the cut edges of adjacent pieces as much as possible. Continue adhering broken pieces of china to the tabletop, one small section at a time and applying more adhesive as needed, until the design is complete.

After a mosaic design has been glued to the base of the project, you will need to wait 12 to 24 hours before filling in the gaps between the pieces of china and tiles with grout. Grout comes in two different formulations—one with a blend of portland cement and powdered pigments mixed with water and the other, the same formulation with sand. The choice of grout is determined by the gap between the tesserae—sanded grout for a gap of more than ⅛" (0.3 cm) and nonsanded grout for a gap of less than ⅛" (0.3 cm). Modern formulations have additives, such as polymers, that allow for color consistency and flexibility. Available in premixed and powder forms, grout should be the consistency of cake frosting and remain on the end of a knife without drooping. It may be applied with a stiff yet flexible plastic or rubber tool, such as a trowel or float, or with a gloved hand. Grout comes in white and gray, but it can be tinted to make new colors that coordinate with the colorway of the tesserae. More a question of style than function, there are several approaches to choosing the color of the grout. The grout can be in a contrasting color (where the tesserae is red and the grout white), a harmonizing color (where the grout is pale green and the tesserae in pastel shades), or a neutral color (where the tesserae and the grout appear as a continuous sweep of color). Make a small sample first before grouting your entire project to ensure a satisfying result.

Once grout has been applied to the mosaic and has been allowed to cure for several days, protect your work by applying a sealer, unless your grout is already formulated with one. A sealer comes in two formulations, penetrating and membrane-forming. I recommend penetrating sealers because they allow the grout to breathe and do not turn cloudy or peel off when exposed to moisture as can membrane-forming sealers. Sealers can be applied with a narrow brush or cotton swab, ensuring a finish that resists staining.

Taking care of a mosaic requires general housekeeping—wiping off spills and dust to keep the finish from getting dingy. For surface dirt or caked-on dirt on the grout, use a stiff bristle brush, such as an old toothbrush, and a nonabrasive cleaning agent to renew the grout. If any small areas in the grout need to be regrouted, carefully remove the old grout, using a pointed tool, and then proceed to fill the gap as before, matching the color, if necessary, and then seal the replacement grout.

## Technique: Applying Grout and Sealer to a Mosaic Design

Work steadily when applying grout, as the broken edges of the china are porous and will absorb moisture quickly, causing the grout to dry out and become difficult to spread. Frequent misting with water will ensure even hydration as the grout hardens and cures. Wear rubber gloves to protect your hands from caustic effects. If the grout is not formulated with a sealer, apply a sealer coat separately after the grout has dried and cured. The sealer will protect the grout from staining.

### MATERIALS AND TOOLS
Flat wood base with tesserae affixed
Sanded grout, premixed
Grout spreader, such as a squeegee
Household sponge
Disposable woven towels
Soft cloths
Safety glasses with side shields
Rubber gloves
Plastic bucket
Spray bottle with water
Sealer for grout, penetrating (optional)
Narrow brush (optional)

### Step 1
Smooth on the grout.

Put on rubber gloves. Scoop some grout from the container and spread it over a section of the mosaic, using your gloved hand to force the grout into the gaps between the pieces. Wipe off the excess with a damp sponge, working gently to avoid scraping out the grout already in the gap. Add more grout and work it into the spaces between the tes-

serae and tiles until the entire surface of the mosaic is covered.

### Step 2
Wipe off the excess grout.

Go over the mosaic with a damp sponge, cleaning as much grout off the surface as possible. Rinse out the sponge in a bucket of warm water when it becomes gritty. Continue wiping off the excess grout and rinsing out the sponge until the tesserae are clean. Let the grout cure, misting the surface if it begins to dry out.

### Step 3
Clean and polish the mosaic.

Use a series of disposable woven towels to remove the haze on the tesserae, changing to a new towel as one becomes dirty. Polish the surface using a soft cloth, switching to a clean cloth when one becomes filled.

### Step 4 (optional)
Mist the grout as it cures.

Use a spray bottle filled with water to apply a fine mist to the grout so that it doesn't dry out as it hardens; refer to the manufacturer's label on the grout package for specifics.

### Step 5 (optional)
Apply the sealer.

Use a narrow foam brush to apply a thin, even coat of sealer to the grout, following the directions on the manufacturer's label. Let the sealer dry completely.

# PROJECTS

## Tuxedo: An Etched Decanter and Tumbler

A modern glass decanter-and-tumbler set reveals a gridwork pattern of etching on the tumbler and parallel rings on the decanter, creating a pleasing juxtaposition of stripes that coordinates the pieces. The technique for applying the masks is simple: use tape as a spacer. Fill the design area with strips of tape so the edges of the adjacent pieces touch. Then pull off every other strip. The glass that is revealed is etched; the glass that is covered by the tape is not. The first strip of tape is marked, establishing the angle of every strip laid down thereafter.

### MATERIALS AND TOOLS

Glass decanter and tumbler
Masking tape, ⅛" wide (0.3 cm)
Washable marker
Safety glasses
Disposable gloves
Spray glass cleaner
Paper towels, nonembossed (for less lint)
Sink with hot and cold running water
Tapered watercolor paintbrush
Plastic bucket
Baking soda
Dishwashing liquid

### Step 1

Prepare the glass pieces.

Clean the glass pieces with spray cleaner and paper towels.

### Step 2

Mark and tape the vertical stripes on the tumbler.

Use a ruler and a marker to mark the position of one vertical stripe on the tumbler, making ticks at the rim and the bottom of the glass. Apply a piece of tape to the tumbler, aligning it vertically on the ticks. Apply a second piece of tape alongside and parallel to the first piece so that the long edges are touching but not overlapping. Apply 23 more pieces of tape in the same way. Peel off and discard every other strip to expose a pattern of 12 vertical stripes. Use the back of your fingernail to press the edges of the remaining tape pieces against the glass.

### Step 3

Mark and tape the horizontal stripes on the tumbler.

Use a ruler and marker to mark the position of one horizontal stripe 2½" (6.4 cm) below the lip of the tumbler. Apply a piece of tape around the tumbler, aligning it horizontally on the ticks. Apply four more pieces of tape, one at a time, below and parallel to the first piece so that the long edges are touching but not overlapping. Peel off and discard every other strip to expose a pattern of three horizontal stripes. Use the back of your fingernail to press the edges of the remaining tape pieces against the glass, paying particular attention to the strips of tape that overlap other strips.

### Step 4

Mark and tape the horizontal stripes on the decanter.

Apply a piece of tape around the belly of the decanter, aligning it horizontally on the ticks. Apply ten more pieces of tape, one at a time, above and parallel to the first piece, long edges touching but not overlapping. Peel off and discard every other strip to expose a pattern of five horizontal stripes. Use the back of your fingernail to press the edges of the remaining tape pieces against the glass.

## Step 5

Apply the etching cream to the tumbler.

Put on safety glasses and disposable gloves. Following the manufacturer's directions on the bottle of etching cream, use a tapered watercolor brush and a patting motion to apply a thick layer of etching cream between the strips of tape on the tumbler, dabbing carefully at the taped overlaps to prevent etching cream from seeping under the tape. Let the cream stand for 1 minute, or as long as recommended by the manufacturer.

## Step 6

Rinse off the etching cream.

Rinse the tumbler under a slow, steady stream of warm water, letting the water run into a plastic bucket without splashing and using your gloved hand to wipe off the cream. Pull off the strips of masking tape, discarding them safely in a trash bag. Use baking soda to neutralize the waste water before pouring it down the drain. Scrub the sink clean.

## Step 7

Etch the decanter.

Repeat steps 5 and 6 to etch the belly of the decanter.

## Step 8

Clean both pieces.

Use warm water and dishwashing liquid to clean the tumbler and decanter. Let them dry completely.

# Polka Dots: A Gilded and Bejeweled Glass Vase

Once you have some experience etching glass and gilding, you will be able to feature these effects together in a single project. The combination of techniques works because each is suited to a nonporous surface. The etched polka dots on the glass vase shown here were embellished with gold metal leaf and flat-backed molten glass jewels that bring warmth to the frosted glass surface. For a cooler palette with less contrast, combine frosted glass and silver leaf. To make an etched polka dot vase to start your project, see Technique: Etching an Overall Design in Small Sections (page 432) and then follow the steps here for gilding and adding the jewels.

## MATERIALS AND TOOLS

Glass vase, etched with polka dots
Composition gold leaf
Flat-backed glass jewels
Acrylic size
5-minute epoxy
2 tapered watercolor brushes
Blunt-nose tweezers
2 pairs of cotton gloves
Soft-bristle brush
Envelope
100 percent cotton ball
Disposable plastic lid
Toothpicks
Acrylic sealer (optional)

### Step 1

Apply size to the center of each frosted polka dot.

Lay or tilt the glass vase on its side on a protected work surface. Work in sections to prevent the size from dripping or running off the glass. Dip the tip of the watercolor brush into the size, picking up a scant drop of size. Apply a thin coat of size in the shape of a dot to the center of each frosted polka dot. Allow 15 to 30 minutes for the size to reach tack, or as the manufacturer recommends.

### Step 2

Tear the metal leaf and apply the pieces to the sized surface.

Put on the cotton gloves. Use your gloved fingers and gentle pressure to tear the gold composition leaf into rough irregular shapes the size of a postage stamp. Use tweezers to apply a piece of gold leaf to one polka dot of size. Lay the orange tissue paper from the book of leaf over the metal leaf and tamp the leaf in place. Continue to apply pieces of metal leaf to the sized polka dots, using a fresh sheet of tissue paper to lightly tamp down the pieces.

### Step 3

Fill in bare spots with metal leaf.

Examine the leafed surface, checking for cracks, exposed areas, or spots that you missed and would like to fill. Lay a small piece of leaf in position and tamp it down with a piece of tissue paper. If the size has lost tack, apply a new coat of size to the affected area, wait for it to reach tack, and then apply the leaf. Let the size dry completely overnight.

### Step 4

Burnish the leafed surface.

Use a dry soft-bristle brush to sweep off all of the skewings, saving them in an envelope for another project. Use a cotton ball and gentle pressure to lightly buff the leafed surfaces, which will smooth out the leaf and remove any lingering skewings.

### Step 5

Glue on the flat-backed glass jewels.

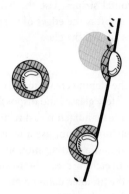

Use a toothpick to mix a small amount of 5-minute epoxy on a disposable lid, following the manufacturer's directions. Transfer a small bead of glue to the flat side of one glass jewel. Press the jewel onto the center of one gilded polka dot on the glass. Use a clean toothpick to remove any epoxy that oozes beyond the edge of the jewel. Continue to glue and press the remaining jewels to the glass surface. Let the epoxy cure.

### Step 6 (optional)

Apply the sealer.

Use a tapered watercolor brush to apply a thin coat of sealer to the exposed gilded areas around each of the glass jewels. Let the sealer dry completely.

### Step 7

Clean the vase.

Put on clean cotton gloves. Use your gloved fingers to clean off any grease or fingerprints from the glass, avoiding the gilded polka dots.

## The Golden Sparrow: A Gilded Bird

A project needn't be on a grand scale to be significant. It can be sentimental. I found this sculpture and it reminded me of a story I heard as a child about a golden sparrow. Granted, the bird is not a sparrow, but I enjoyed giving it a coat of gold leaf and when I look at it, it reminds me of my childhood home in Bellerose.

MATERIALS AND TOOLS

Carved bird on perch, or any desired
    sculpture
Composition gold leaf
Quick-drying water-based size
Acrylic sealer
Acrylic varnish
Sheet of plain white paper
Cotton gloves
Foam brush
Tapered watercolor brush
Blunt-nose tweezers
Envelope

**Step 1**
Apply sealer to the sculpture.
Use a brush to apply a thin coat of sealer to all parts of the bird sculpture. Let the sealer dry thoroughly.

**Step 2**
Apply the size.
Use a foam brush or watercolor brush to apply a thin, even coat of size to all sides of the sculpture. Allow the size to reach tack, normally 15 to 30 minutes, or as the manufacturer recommends.

**Step 3**
Tear the gold leaf.
Put on cotton gloves. Touch a gloved finger to one sheet of leaf and gently slide it onto the white paper. Carefully tear the composition gold leaf into rough irregular shapes the size of a postage stamp.

**Step 4**
Apply the gold leaf to the sized surface.
When the size has reached tack, use tweezers to lay the pieces of leaf on the sized surface, continuing to lay down leaf until the bird is covered. Use a dry narrow brush to tamp the leaf between carved sections and grooves. Lay a sheet of orange tissue paper over the gilded surface and press down the leaf, using a fresh sheet of tissue as needed.

**Step 5**
Fill in the gaps in the gold leaf.
Examine the sculpture and lay small pieces of leaf on any surfaces that haven't any leaf on them. If the size has lost tack, apply a new coat of size to the affected area, wait for it to reach tack, and then apply the leaf. Let the size dry overnight.

**Step 6**
Brush off the excess leaf.
Use a soft-bristle brush to sweep off all of the flakes of leaf, saving them in an envelope.

**Step 7**
Apply the sealer.
Use a watercolor brush to apply a thin, even coat of sealer to the leafed surface. Let the sealer dry for 1 hour, apply a second coat of sealer, and let it dry overnight.

## Golden Leaves: A Gilded Box with Embossed Leaves

Sometimes it is the small accents that pull a design together. Here, embossed metal leaves and a bumblebee in a gold finish create a textural layer on a box that is gilded in bright and lustrous gold leaf, creating a high-end contrast on this functional little vault.

### MATERIALS AND TOOLS

Wooden box with hinged lid, 7½" × 4¼" × 4" (19.1 × 10.8 × 10.2 cm)
4 embossed-metal leaves, each 3" (7.6 cm) long
Embossed-metal bumblebee, 1" long (2.5 cm)
20 to 25 sheets of composition gold leaf
Acrylic size
Acrylic craft paint, in gold metallic
Gesso
Soft-bristle brush
Clear acrylic spray sealer
Acrylic medium-and-varnish
High-tack adhesive
Sandpaper, fine-grit (#600)
Screwdriver (for screws on box lock and hinges)
Sanding block
Foam brush
Scissors
Nylon brush with feathered bristles
Respirator mask
Chemical-cartridge respirator mask
Safety glasses
Disposable gloves
Tack cloth, or paper towels, nonembossed (for less lint)
Envelope
Soft-bristle brush
Gold paint
100 percent cotton balls
Flat sticks (to elevate box)
Large cardboard carton (for spray booth)
Lazy Susan

### Step 1

Remove the hardware.

Use a screwdriver to remove the hardware on the box, keeping the parts in a safe place. Separate the box bottom and lid.

### Step 2

Sand the box bottom and lid.

Work outdoors or in a well-ventilated space and wear a respirator mask. Use a sanding block wrapped with fine-grit (#600) sandpaper to sand all the exterior surfaces of the box bottom and lid until they are satiny smooth. For interior surfaces, hold a folded piece of fine-grit (#600) sandpaper and use the fold to abrade the rough surfaces. Use a tack cloth to remove the dust.

### Step 3

Apply the spray sealer to the box bottom and lid.

Work outdoors or in a well-ventilated space and wear a chemical-cartridge respirator mask, safety goggles, and disposable gloves. Set up a spray booth with a lazy Susan inside. Spray the box bottom and box lid separately, elevating each piece on flat sticks and turning the lazy Susan to achieve a thin, evenly applied coat. Let the first coat of sealer dry and then apply a second coat. Let the sealer dry overnight.

### Step 4

Sand the box bottom and lid.

Repeat step 2.

## Step 5

Apply two coats of gesso.

Working the box lid and the box bottom separately, use a soft-bristle brush to apply a thin, even coat of gesso to all surfaces of the box bottom, propping up the box on flat sticks. Let the gesso dry 2 hours. Apply a second coat of gesso. Let the gesso dry overnight.

## Step 6

Sand the gessoed surface.

Put on a respirator mask. Working in a well-ventilated space, use a sanding block wrapped with fine-grit (#600) sandpaper to smooth all of the surfaces of the box lid and box bottom, making certain the surface is satiny smooth; use a tack cloth to remove any dust.

## Step 7

Apply one more coat of gesso.

Apply one more coat of gesso as in step 5. Then repeat step 6 to sand all surfaces smooth.

## Step 8

Apply the acrylic medium-and-varnish.

Use a foam brush to apply a thin coat of acrylic medium-and-varnish to the box bottom and lid. Let the parts dry overnight.

## Step 9

Cut the gold leaf into squares.

Put on cotton gloves. Use scissors to snip along the spine of the folio to release four or five sheets of orange tissue interleaved with gold leaf. Cut through all the layers to rough-cut 1" (2.5 cm) squares. Repeat until you have cut 16 to 21 sheets of gold leaf.

## Step 10

Apply size to the box bottom and lid.

Work in a draft-free, dust-free space. Use a foam brush to apply a thin, even coat of size to the exterior surfaces of the box bottom. Work on one side or surface at a time to prevent the size from pooling or running off the project. Elevate the piece on flat sticks. Repeat to apply size to the box lid. Allow 15 to 30 minutes for the size to reach tack. Touch a dry finger to the surface; if it feels tacky or if you hear a tick sound, the size is ready for the metal leaf.

## Step 11

Apply gold leaf to the box.

Use tweezers to pick up and transfer squares of gold leaf to the sized areas on the box bottom and the lid. Overlap the leading edge of the new squares of leaf on the edge of the previously laid squares, overlapping the edges by a scant ⅛" (0.3 cm). Allow edge of the box bottom and lid to dry completely.

## Step 12

Burnish the gold leaf.

Use a soft-bristle brush to sweep off the skewings. Save them in an envelope for another project. Burnish each gilded surface with a cotton ball, moving it in an oval shape to remove any lingering skewings.

## Step 13

Paint the interior of the box.

Use a paintbrush to apply two coats of gold paint to the interior surfaces of the box bottom and lid, allowing the paint to dry between coats. Let the final coat dry completely.

## Step 14

Apply the sealer.

Use a foam brush to apply two thin, even coats of sealer to all sides of the exterior and interior surfaces of the box bottom and the lid, allowing the sealer to dry between coats. Let the sealer dry completely.

## Step 15

Glue the metal leaves and the bumblebee to the box.

Following the manufacturer's directions, use small blobs of high-tack adhesive to affix the embossed-metal leaves and the bumblebee to the sides of the box in positions as desired. Let the adhesive dry and allow to cure.

## Wind: An Embossed-Velvet Pillow

A coil of armature wire is embossed onto velvet in a random, allover pattern that fills the space with sweeping movement. The finished fabric is sewn into a pillow cover.

### MATERIALS AND TOOLS

Armature wire, 8-gauge or ⅛" (0.3 cm) thick
Rayon or silk velvet, 36" × 18" (91.4 × 45.7 cm), in magenta, or as desired
Matching thread
Pillow form, 16" × 16" (40.6 × 40.6 cm)
Piece of cotton fabric, 18" × 18" (45.7 × 45.7 cm)
Household iron
Pot that lies flat when inverted
Spray starch
Rotary cutter
Plastic ruler
Safety glasses
Wire cutters
Chain-nose pliers
Tape measure
Straight pins
Sewing machine
Hand-sewing needle

### Step 1

Make the wire coil.

Put on safety glasses. Use a tape measure and wire cutters to cut a 24" (61.0 cm) length of armature wire. Use the chain-nose pliers to make a small rounded hook in one end of the wire. Then use your fingers to bend the wire into a coil that measures approximately 3" (7.6 cm) across.

### Step 2

Prepare to emboss.

Empty the iron of all water and preheat on the hottest setting for 10 minutes. Place the pot, bottom side up, on an ironing board. Set the wire coil on top. Lay the area of the velvet you wish to emboss on top of the coil, nap side down. Apply a light mist of spray starch to the wrong side of the velvet. Lay the square of cotton cloth on top.

### Step 3

Emboss the coil shape into the velvet.

Press the hot iron down on the cloth for 6 seconds. Do not move the iron back and forth. Lift the iron straight up and off the surface and set it aside. Slide the velvet across the pot, nap side down, so that a new section covers the wire coil and press with a hot iron for 6 seconds. Continue to emboss the velvet until there is an overall random pattern of overlapping coils.

### Step 4

Sew the pillow cover.

Cut the embossed layer in half to make two 18" (45.7 cm) squares. Layer the embossed squares right sides together and edges even. Pin around the edges. Machine-stitch ⅝" (1.6 cm) from the edge all around, pivoting at each corner and leaving an 8" (20.3 cm) opening in the middle of one side for turning. Clip the corners diagonally and turn the pillow cover right side out. Insert a pillow form and slipstitch the opening closed, using a needle and matching thread.

# Zebra: A Throw with Tassels

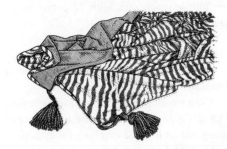

Low-pile animal prints are available in zebra, tiger, leopard, and cheetah. The fabric is sold in 54" (137.2 cm) widths. Easy to make from two layers of fabric and four fat tassels, the zebra throw is a four-season blanket.

## MATERIALS AND TOOLS

2 yards (1.8 m) low-pile cotton fabric, 54" (137.2 cm) wide, in animal print

2 yards (1.8 m) wool flannel, 54" (137.2 cm) wide, in pink or desired color

4 tassels, 4" (10.2 cm) long, in black

Matching thread

Tape measure

Scissors

Straight pins

Sewing machine with heavy-duty needle

## Step 1

Even up the fabrics.

Layer the two fabrics, right sides together and selvages matching, on a large flat work surface. Use scissors to trim and even up the cut edges so that the layered fabric rectangle measures 72" × 54" (182.9 × 137.2 cm).

## Step 2

Pin the edges together.

Use straight pins to pin together the edges of the fabric on all four sides.

## Step 3

Add the tassels.

Insert the fringe end of one tassel between the layers of fabric at one corner. Make sure

the hanging cord of the tassel emerges exactly at the corner. Pin the corner, trapping the hanging cord of the tassel. Repeat at each corner with the remaining tassels.

## Step 4

Sew the throw.

Machine-stitch ⅝" (1.6 cm) from the edge all around, pivoting at each corner to trap the tassel hanging cords in the seam. Leave an 18" (45.7 cm) opening in the middle of the last side for turning.

## Step 5

Finish the throw.

Clip the corners diagonally and turn the throw right side out. Slip-stitch the opening closed. Press the seams flat. Topstitch 1" (2.5 cm) from the edge all around, if desired, using a machine basting stitch.

# English Garden: A Ribbon-Rose Lampshade

Any plain fabric lampshade can be the backdrop for a lush garden of handmade and purchased ribbon roses and beaded trims. The fabric on the lampshade should be sturdy, yet have some give, so you can stitch each rose in place. Follow the color suggestions listed or choose your own colorway. Refer to Making a Beaded-Loop Trim (page 461) for step 1 and Making a Ribbon Rose (page 458) for steps 2–5.

MATERIALS AND TOOLS

Lampshade, top circumference 30" (76.2 cm), bottom circumference 45½" (115.6 cm)

Wire-edged ribbon, 1½" (3.8 cm) wide
   5½ yards (5.0 m), in variegated pink
   2 yards (1.8 m), in ivory
   1½ yards (1.4 m), in variegated green/lavender/purple
   2½ yards (2.3 m), in green

6 purchased rosebuds, in pale blue, pink, and peach

Assorted trims
   2½ yards (2.3 m) braided trim with beaded tassels, ½" (1.3 cm) wide with ¾" (1.9 cm) drop
   2½ yards (2.3 m) beaded strand with diamond-shape glass beads
   2½ yards (2.3 m) beaded loops

Clear nylon thread

Scissors

Hand-sewing needle

## Step 1

Secure beaded trims to the lampshade.

Use a needle threaded with nylon filament to apply the beaded and braided trims to the top and the bottom of the lampshade, as desired.

## Step 2

Make nine large ribbon roses, each with a green stem and leaf.

Use a piece of ribbon approximately ⅔ yard (0.61 m) long for each large rose and a piece of green ribbon 6" (15.2 cm) long for each stem and leaf. Make six variegated pink roses, two ivory roses, and two variegated green/lavender/purple roses, each with 12 petals and a green stem and leaf.

## Step 3

Make four small ribbon roses, each with green stem and leaf.

Use a piece of ribbon approximately ½ yard (0.5 m) long for each small rose and a piece of green ribbon 6" (15.2 cm) long for each stem and leaf. Make two variegated pink roses, two ivory roses, and two variegated green/lavender/purple roses, each with seven petals and a green stem and leaf.

## Step 4

Make buds with stems.

Use the leftover ribbon to make buds with stems. You will need a 2" (5.1 cm) length of ribbon for each bud and a 6" (15.2 cm) length of green ribbon for each stem.

## Step 5

Sew the ribbon roses to the lampshade.

Arrange all of the large and small roses and the rosebuds on a flat work surface. Referring to the lampshade illustration on page 551, use a needle threaded with nylon filament to tack the roses and buds to the fabric of the lampshade. Tack the large roses first and then add the small roses, the rosebuds, and the even smaller purchased buds.

## Juliet: A Vase with Rose Decals

Even without any fresh flowers to hold, this embellished vase is lovely to look at. Line drawings and engravings add delicate beauty to a glass vase, yet keep the design open and light. The pattern is designed for a flat, tapered glass surface measuring 6" (15.2 cm) across the top, 4½" (11.4 cm) across the bottom, and 9¾" (24.8 cm) tall, but you can easily adapt the pattern, or introduce other line drawings and engravings, to create a design that fits the shape of your vase.

### MATERIALS AND TOOLS

Juliet Rose original art and pattern
   (page 709)
Paper (for adapting original art)
Decal transfer paper (such as regular
   Lazertran decal transfer paper)
Low-fusing photocopier that uses fuser oil
Ovenproof glass vase, with tapered flat
   sides, or as desired
Home oven
Large shallow dish
Oven mitts
Baking sheet
Parchment paper
Scissors
Heat gun

Minute timer
Glue
White correction tape or fluid
Scissors
Pencil

### Step 1

Adapt the pattern to your vase.

The Juliet Rose original art is designed to fit the tapered rectangular shape of the featured vase. To adapt the pattern, lay your glass vase on a sheet of paper and trace the outline with a pencil. Make several photocopies of the Juliet Rose artwork, adjusting the size and making some in mirror image. Neatly cut out individual flowers and arrange them in a new way within the outline of your vase. When you are satisfied, glue the flowers to the paper template. Photocopy the pattern, using white correction tape or fluid to remove unwanted join lines on the printout. Use the corrected pattern to make a good print on glossy photo paper.

### Step 2

Make the photo transfer.

Take your glossy pattern and several sheets of decal transfer paper to a copy store. On a copier that uses fuser oil, make a black-and-white mirror-image print of the pattern on the glossy side (acrylic layer) of the decal transfer paper. Make a second print on another sheet of decal paper at a different ink level and decide which tonal effect you prefer.

### Step 3

Heat-set the decal.

Place the decal on a protected work surface. Plug in the heat gun, turn on the switch, and let it run for a few seconds, giving it time to heat. Then wave the nozzle back and forth over the surface of the decal to set the toners in the printing ink. The printed image will appear shiny when the toner is set. Turn off the switch and unplug the heat gun. Let the decal cool.

**Step 4**

Cut out the decal.

Use scissors to cut out the decal, cutting just inside the marked line so that the line does not remain on the decal, which will be as large as and in the shape of the front of your vase.

**Step 5**

Soak the decal.

Use a spray glass cleaner and lint-free paper towels to clean the vase. Lay the vase on a flat work surface, with the flat side intended for the decal facing up. Set a shallow dish of warm water next to the vase. Slip the decal under the surface until it is completely submerged, which will cause the paper to curl and then straighten. Wait a minute or two for the decal to release from the backing and then use both hands to lift the decal out of the water, using the paper backing as support.

**Step 6**

Adhere the decal to the vase.

Position the decal on the front of the vase, ink side down and edges even. Carefully lift up the bottom edge of the backing paper and press one finger against the bottom edge of the decal. Lift off the backing paper. Carefully use your fingers to smooth the decal flat to remove any air bubbles, working from the center of the decal to the outside edges. Use a moist sponge to wipe off the glue from the back of the decal and to remove any air bubbles, working from the center of the decal to the outside edges. Blot away excess water. Any residual glue on the decal will turn brown during baking.

**Step 7**

Preheat the oven.

Set the oven temperature to 200°F (93.3°C) or the lowest possible setting. Leave the oven door open.

**Step 8**

Warm the decal for 30 minutes.

Place the glass vase on a baking sheet. Set the baking sheet on the middle rack in the oven. With the oven door open, bake the item for 15 minutes. Close the oven door and bake it for another 15 minutes.

**Step 9**

Check the decal.

Open the oven door. Check to see that the decal is flat against the glass surface. Use the bowl side of a tablespoon to gently tap down any parts of the decal that are not adhering. Close the oven door.

**Step 10**

Bake the vase for 80 minutes with the oven door closed.

Continue baking the vase for another 80 minutes, increasing the oven temperature by 15°F (8.5°C) every 10 minutes until the oven temperature reaches 320°F (160.0°C).

**Step 11**

Bake the vase for the final 30 minutes more with the oven door open.

Put on oven mitts, open the oven door, and move the baking sheet with the vase to a lower rack in the oven to prevent overheating or browning of the decal. Continue baking the vase for approximately 30 minutes more, increasing the oven temperature by 20°F (11.4°C) every 10 minutes. Keep a watchful eye during this stage. The decal should be baked onto the glass by the time the oven reaches 380°F (193.3°C), although it may have bonded before. If the decal is shiny, it is bonded to the surface.

**Step 12**

Allow the vase to cool.

Turn off the oven and open the oven door but do not remove the baking sheet. Let the vase rest inside the oven until it is cool. Use oven mitts, if needed, to carefully remove the vase from the oven. Avoid touching the decal.

## Portrait: A Block-Shaped Candle

Sentimental but practical, a block-shaped candle with a portrait print is a lovely way to commemorate a special occasion, from a child's birthday to a friend's engagement. An ordinary photocopy of a favorite photograph is adhered to a handmade candle for this special gift.

### MATERIALS AND TOOLS

Laser photocopy of portrait, sized to fit one surface of candle
1-pint (0.47 L) waxed dairy carton, empty, clean, and dry
2 pounds (0.91 kg) preblended wax, with additives
Color chip or dye, in desired color
Primed papercore wick, 8" (20.3 cm) long
White craft glue
Packing tape with nylon threads, 3" (7.6 cm) wide
Metal washer, 1" (2.5 cm) in diameter
Double boiler setup with wax-pouring pitcher
Wax or candy thermometer
Nonstick cooking spray
Awl
Wood skewer
Oven mitts
Old nylon panty hose
Scissors
Household pliers
Baking sheet with lip
Stockpot

### Step 1
Prepare the carton.

Use a craft knife to cut off the peaked section at the top of the carton, trimming the edges neatly to make an open box. Wrap packing tape snugly around the carton to reinforce the walls, pressing the tape against the sides of the carton without distorting its shape. Apply a light coat of nonstick cooking spray to the interior of the carton. Use a paper towel to wipe down the walls and bottom of the carton and discard the paper towel.

### Step 2
Install the wick in the carton.

Use an awl to pierce a hole in the center bottom of the carton, working from the outside. Tie one end of the primed wick to a metal washer, making a double-knot to secure it. Thread the opposite end through the hole in the carton and pull the wick through the inside until the washer rests flat against the carton bottom. Secure the washer with a strip of tape or a flat wad of mold sealer. Turn the carton upright, rest a skewer across the top, and tie the free end of the wick to the center of the skewer, rolling the wick around the skewer until the wick is straight, taut, and centered in the mold.

### Step 3
Melt the wax.

Set up the double boiler, melt the wax, and blend in the color additive. Use the thermometer to monitor the temperature of the wax as it heats and melts. When the temperature registers 155°F (68.3°C), turn off the heat.

## Step 4

Pour the melted wax into the carton.

Stand the carton on a level, protected work surface next to the double boiler. Put on oven mitts. Slowly pour the hot liquid wax into the carton, tilting the carton at the start of the pour to prevent air bubbles and finishing with the carton upright and the wax level 1" (2.5 cm) below the carton's rim. If the wick becomes slack, gently reroll the skewer to make it straight and taut. Check every 30 minutes or so for newly formed depressions in the cooling wax. Poke deep vertical channels with a skewer and pour in more hot liquid wax to form a level surface. Let the wax cool completely, 3 or 4 hours or overnight.

## Step 5

Unmold the candle.

Cut the wick from the skewer, remove the tape or mold sealer, and cut off the washer. Peel off the tape, using scissors to snip through the bands. Tear the carton off the candle. Turn the candle so the smoothest side faces up. Trim the wick, leaving a ¼" (0.6 cm) length. Keep the skewer for another project.

## Step 6

Level the base of the candle.

Rest a baking sheet on a stew pot of simmering water. Set the base of the candle on the hot baking sheet and move it around in a circular motion until the bottom is smooth and level.

## Step 7

Polish the wax surface.

Use a wad of nylon panty hose to polish the sides and edges of the candle, rubbing in an oval motion to buff down any seams or corners and to give the surface a smooth, lustrous finish.

## Step 8

Adhere the portrait to the candle.

Use a laser copier to make a black-and-white photocopy of a favorite photo, sizing it to fit the front of the candle. Center and glue the photocopy to the front of the candle.

## Step 9

Glaze the candle.

Reheat the wax in the double boiler setup until it is completely melted. Put on oven mitts. Use pliers to hold the wick of the candle and submerge the candle in a down-and-up motion to coat the candle and portrait with a thin translucent layer of wax. Let the candle cool overnight. Repeat step 7 for a lustrous finish.

## Hopewell: A Cottage-Style Mirror Frame

The cottage-style mirror is an accent piece inspired by my family's summers in upstate New York. The frame is a reproduction of a frame that lay under coats of varnish and wax. I love the frame because of the memories but wanted to freshen up and contemporize its style.

You will need four pieces cut from a 1" × 4", a nominal term for a piece of wood that actually measures ¾" × 3½" (1.9 × 8.9 cm) × the board length. The 3½"-wide (8.9 cm) board provides an ample flat surface for embellishing with carved wood appliqués. Select an even-grained clear pine board that is free of large knots. Begin with straight cuts and proceed to the miter cuts—or have a lumber store do the cutting and mitering so that you can indulge even sooner in the embellishing and painting. The featured frame was custom-made for a 16" × 20" (40.6 × 50.8 cm) beveled mirror. If your mirror is a different size, adapt the dimensions accordingly. Refer to Technique: Installing a Mirror in a Frame (page 532) to mount and hang your mirror.

MATERIALS AND TOOLS

    Knot-free clear pine board, 1" × 4"
        (see step 1 for sizes)
    Flat L-profile molding, ½" (1.3 cm) deep
        (see step 5 for sizes)
    1 carved wood shell and scroll appliqué,
        24" × 5¼" (61.0 × 13.3 cm)
    2 carved wood corner appliqués
    Finishing nails
    Brads, ½" (1.3 cm) long
    Water-based paint in matte white or
        as desired
    Acrylic sealer
    Acrylic varnish, satin finish
    Wood putty
    Yellow carpenter's glue
    Miter box
    Backsaw
    Drill
    Hammer
    Tackhammer
    Awl
    Craft knife
    Ruler
    Pencil
    Strong twine
    Wood blocks or thick chipboard
    Foam brush
    Tapered paintbrush
    Sandpaper, fine-grit (#600)
    Sanding block
    Countersink

**Step 1**

Measure and miter-cut four pieces of clear pine.

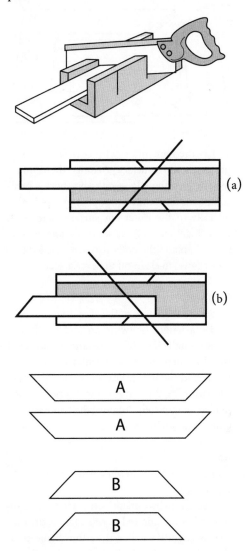

From the 1" × 4" pine board, cut two pieces 30" (76.2 cm) long and two pieces 26" (66.0 cm) long. Use a miter box and a backsaw to miter-cut the ends, following diagrams (a) and (b), to make two A and two B pieces as shown.

**Step 2**

Glue the miter-cut pieces together.

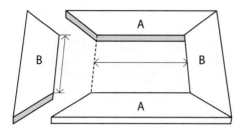

Lay the four miter-cut pieces face up on a protected work surface. Arrange them into a rectangle so the edges with the shorter measurements form the frame opening. Apply glue liberally to the miter-cut surfaces and push them together, making sure the angled surfaces align and the ends are even. Use a damp paper towel to clean off the excess glue.

**Step 3**

Secure the frame as the glue dries.

Tie a length of twine around the frame, positioning scraps of chipboard or blocks of wood at each corner as a buffer between the frame and the twine. Use a slipknot to secure the twine tightly around the frame. Let the glue dry completely. Remove the twine and the chipboard or blocks.

**Step 4**

Reinforce the mitered corners with finishing nails.

Use an awl to make two starter holes on one side of a mitered corner. Use a drill bit that is slightly smaller than the diameter of the nails. Start the drill and then place the bit into a starter hole, drilling diagonally through the first piece of wood and one-half to three-quarters through the second piece of wood without exiting on the other side. Repeat to drill a second pilot hole. Use a hammer to drive a nail into each pilot hole, stopping before the nailhead touches down on the wood. Use a countersink to drive each nail below the sur-

face of the wood. Repeat to add two nails to each of the three remaining corners.

**Step 5**

Measure and miter-cut four pieces of L-profile molding for the rabbet.

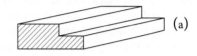

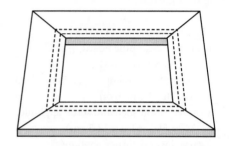

From the ½" (1.3 cm) L-profile molding (a), cut two pieces 24" (61.0 cm) long and two pieces 20" (50.8 cm) long. Use a miter box and a backsaw to miter-cut one end of each piece. Align one piece on the inside edge of the frame and use a pencil to mark for the second miter. Repeat for each piece. Cut the miters and test-fit the pieces. Make small adjustments until the mitered ends meet neatly at the corners.

**Step 6**

Measure and miter-cut four pieces of L-profile molding for the trim.

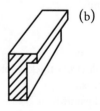

Repeat step 5 to cut two pieces 30" (76.2 cm) long and two pieces 25" (63.5 cm) long for the L-profile molding (b); miter-cut to fit the outside edge of the frame.

## Step 7

Attach the L-profile molding to the frame.

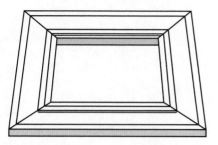

Hammer brads partway into each short and long strip of the rabbet and trim molding pieces, spacing them 5" (12.7 cm) apart. Apply glue all around the outside edge of the frame and to the L-shaped lip of the molding. Reposition the strips on the frame, matching up the miter-cuts at each corner. Tap in the brads, leaving the nail heads slightly exposed to avoid denting the wood with the hammer. Use a countersink to recess the nails. Let the glue dry.

## Step 8

Fill in the nail holes and crevices and sand smooth.

Use your finger to smear wood putty to fill in the holes and separations between the mitered sections at the corners of the frame. Let the putty dry. Let the glue dry. Use fine-grit (#600) sandpaper to smooth the putty even with the wood surface.

## Step 9

Sand the frame.

Use fine-grit (#600) sandpaper and a sanding block to smooth the molding and all sections of the frame, removing the dust with a damp paper towel.

## Step 10

Glue on the appliqués.

Add the appliqués to the frame in a pleasing arrangement, using a liberal amount of glue on all contact points.

## Step 11

Finish the frame.

Use a foam brush to apply an even coat of white paint to the frame. Let the paint dry for 1 hour and then apply a second coat. Let the paint dry overnight. Use fine-grit (#600) sandpaper and a sanding block to sand the flat sections of the frame.

## Step 12

Fill and hang the frame.

Add D-rings to the back of the frame. Install the mirror and add a protective backing board. See pages 532–33, steps 3–4, for more details. String on the picture-framing wire. Position and attach picture hangers according to the weight of your frame; nail the hangers to the wall according to the directions on the package. Hang the framed mirror.

# CHAPTER SEVEN

# Children's Arts
# and Crafts

## THE HEART

### Home for Christmas

". . . he loved them. He loved them!
. . . As he thought of [his children],
they seemed to be the furniture of
his soul, its lintel and rooftree."
—John Cheever,
"The Geometry of Love," 1966

My children are grown, yet they still come
home before Christmas to make a gingerbread house. The tradition began a few dozen
years ago when Genevieve was nine years old,
Rodney was seven, and Gabrielle was three. It
was the year we moved into a pretty Victorian
house by the bay in Huntington, New York. The
house had an old-fashioned, cozy kitchen that
was filled with the mingled scents of cinnamon
and cloves carried by the warm air of an afternoon fire. After the sections of gingerbread

had cooled, I used thick cords of royal icing to join the pieces of the house together. We gathered around a large oak table, which was set with bowls of sugar sprinkles, candy canes, chocolate, and small plastic bags filled with royal icing.

I placed the house—that year in the style of a Danish farmhouse—in the middle of the table. Genevieve and Rodney stood at its edge and leaned over the house as they lathered icing into snowy drifts on the roof, using butter knives to smooth the sugary layer. Then they added more detail using plastic bags filled with tinted icing, squeezing it through a tiny hole in one corner, forming neat lines, squiggles, and curls. Genevieve made rows of icicles along the roofline, the windows, and the door with the same careful precision that would distinguish her later design work. Rodney pushed bright red and green M&Ms into blobs of icing to simulate the look of outdoor Christmas lights, and with characteristic wit that would become a hallmark of his writing, squeezed a thick layer of icing along the house's foundation, crashing his Matchbox car against it and grinning as he added a liberal sprinkling of pepper for skid marks! Gabrielle sat on my lap, fascinated by the stream of icing that was oozing out of her little bag. I placed my hands around hers and together, we squeezed a scribble of icing on a gingerbread shutter placed on the table in front of her.

I watched my children, amazed at their dexterity and the intense concentration they brought to the very smallest details they added to the house. How was it that only yesterday I held them in my arms and couldn't leave the house without thinking I had left pieces of my heart behind? I remember Genevieve, my firstborn. She was only days old when I wrote in her baby book, "I heard your faint cry and padded into your bedroom. Day was just breaking, but there was enough light to see you lying in your cradle, which was swaying slightly as if a thin thread of wind was pulling it gently back and forth, but no, it was you, Genevieve, mov-

ing under your blanket. I whispered, 'You are home,' as I picked you up and held you against my chest. At first you seemed to startle, but as quickly, you refolded yourself into a small and peaceful bundle. 'Good morning, Genevieve Aimée. Good morning, bright new day.' "

Motherhood changed me in profound ways. Each time one of my children was born, I discovered that another new space opened up in me filled with an immense love I didn't know I was capable of. I didn't think my heart could grow and stretch any more, but it did and continued to do so as we grew close as a family. Parenting also heightened my awareness of how important it was to provide room for each child's individuality to grow. It would be up to my husband John and me to provide a good garden of sorts, one with plenty of sunshine (freedom and opportunity) and enough rain (rules and discipline) so they could grow strong and bloom. I had some wisdom in me, inherited from my parents and gained from my wonderful years as a teacher of elementary school kids, and I made a promise that my children would live in a home filled with boundless love and laughter and protection, stories at bedtime, and plenty of craft supplies.

Looking back, I can see that I got most of it right, but if anything drew us together and enriched our time together, it was working on crafts. For me, it certainly provided creative fun (and extended my childhood), but more important, it became one way for me to spend time with my children, to be in their presence and observe up close the workings of their imaginations and the logic of their young minds. The hard framework of parenting fell away as we mooshed clay or painted or added glitter to paper. All the while, I was aware of this sacred gift—that I was actually witnessing their evolution through these scribbles, self-portraits, and whatever else they thought important enough to represent. I saw them change and develop before my eyes; their attention spans grew longer and their level of engagement deepened. We never rushed during these creative times. We got lost in the activity and time seemed to slow down, but never enough for me. I so wished their childhoods would last and last, but of course, that wasn't possible. I knew with an aching love that we were being moved swiftly through time as the earth spun on its axis and the sun moved soundlessly past our window, and with each revolution another year of watching my children change and grow was given to me, deepening my understanding of who they were and sharpening the broad experiences of my own life into distinct moments filled with love and belonging.

Of course, I often grappled with the inevitable—the time when the kids would move onto independent paths, heeding the call to fulfill their own distinct destinies. Children naturally assert themselves when they are ready, and I accepted that. I remember when Gabrielle was five. She appeared at breakfast every morning from autumn through winter wearing a gold lamé bathing suit under her school clothes; no amount of coaxing convinced her to change. Sometimes in the evening, when she visited me in my workroom, she would be wearing the gold lamé suit over her pajamas. She claimed she had better dreams, and I believed her.

Growing up and away was the natural order of things, and in later years, I would hint that perhaps we might skip a year of gingerbread-making, but the kids insisted we continue getting together, making me believe that the tradition had gained some personal significance. This year, we gathered in Westchester County, New York, where John and I had moved. As in previous years, we prepared carefully. Handmade decorations that had been tucked away all year—little bears in wool jackets and caps, an opossum in a plaid vest with a fishing rod, and a Father Christmas with a bag filled with toys—were unwrapped, one by one, and arranged on the mantel knee-deep in fresh evergreen twinkling with tiny lights. Gifts made by our children when they

were young were lifted from boxes or taken from a glass shelf in the French armoire and set on side tables—Genevieve's paper house with Santa and his sleigh floating over a snowy rooftop; Rodney's necklace for me, a sawed-off clothespin on a knotted cord that was colored with markers to resemble Superman; and Gabrielle's greeting card made from iridescent foil, her first, middle, and last names printed in large capital letters with fake pearls stuck in pools of glue—each creation precious to me still.

But this year there was no gingerbread baking in our oven, no scent of ginger, cloves, and cinnamon wafting through the air. Instead we waited for it to arrive, fresh from Gabrielle's oven at her apartment in New York City where she had baked the gingerbread sections, calculating the exact scale and proportion of each piece and matching it to a numbered blueprint she had drawn after weeks-long planning; there were sixty-two separate pieces in all. However, these precisely cut, baked, and numbered pieces would not come together as a house, but rather as l'Arc de Triomphe, the monument in Paris that commemorates Napoleon's victories and that had come to symbolize our love of France. Because the structure was complicated and the pieces large and unwieldy, each of us helped in our own way as Gabrielle used a glue gun to attach them together until the monument was standing, golden brown and majestic. The fun of decorating began immediately thereafter. Genevieve placed symmetrical rows of colored candy across one arch. Rodney stood behind his daughter, Maxx, who added a modern design in peanut butter cups, while he cradled his infant daughter, Roxy, in his arms. My tears surprised me as memories of Rodney as a baby broke through. He was only two days old and I was holding his strong body, which stretched from my open palms, which cradled his head, to the folds at my elbows. How I marveled at his peaceful face, his little mouth murmuring in sounds learned in amniotic seas. What was he saying? I didn't know. I kissed the fine hair on his head that felt like satin on my lips. "Time, go slow," I said to myself.

Here, decades later, our family was together again. We were the same and we were different. The children had lives of their own, carried their own memories and secrets and stories, had their own concerns. John and I had changed, too. I knew that I had been transformed by my children. From them, I learned a way to embrace and a way to let go. When our tradition of making a gingerbread house began, I did not know what the future would hold, but I was living in that future now and could see with poignant clarity how the joys and sorrows of my life had unfolded perfectly. A durable strand extending from my past and threading itself through our family connected us all, both loosely and closely, in a timeless web, represented this time around by a Parisian arch that shone with tiny lights and bright color.

## A Brief History

Throughout history, children have crafted with their hands in order to learn essential life skills. In ancient civilizations, children mingled with adult society and began learning skills such as weaving, sewing, and pottery at an early age. Creative play, such as making dolls out of scraps of cloth, was not the special province of childhood but a way for everyone, young and old, to take a break from daily work. As the centuries unfolded, artisan training in the fields like stained glass, embroidery, and painting began in late childhood and developed over a lifetime. By the mid-twentieth century, this paradigm for childhood art education had shifted. Research in psychology and medical science, such as the pioneering work of Dr. Maria Montessori, redefined childhood as a unique phase of human development, and technological and societal changes allowed the "new" childhood to flourish. It is in this modern environment that children's crafting as a purely creative venture emerges.

Personal creativity was not the paramount objective of most artisanal training. In the Middle Ages, dyers, knitters, weavers, tanners, papermakers, and many other trades formed guilds to ensure and protect their financial enterprises and to train the next generation of artisans. The boy apprentice began with menial chores and advanced gradually over three to eleven years. The goal was the mastery of set designs, techniques, and materials, rather than innovation or self-actualization. Vestiges of the guild system with its childhood learning lingered on into the nineteenth century in female lacemakers' groups in Europe.

Prior to modern clothing manufacture, needlework was a vital survival skill for girls. Depending on the region, girls as young as four and five learned knitting, crocheting, hand sewing, quilting, and embroidery from their mothers or other female relatives.

Day schools specializing in needlework were extremely popular for girls in nineteenth-century America, especially across the northeast. Sampler making taught girls how to label their future household linens. Surviving samplers can often be traced to a particular instructress or school—another example of this era's focus on technique and execution, rather than on creativity and innovation.

The groundwork for change was laid in the nineteenth century. Viewed through this century's romantic, sentimental lens, the childhood ideal was serene, protected, and unencumbered by adult cares and responsibilities. Children in flourishing middle class homes received more years of formal education and had more time to indulge in play. The manufacture of toys, games, and children's periodicals mushroomed, and do-it-yourself leisure projects became popular. Boys and girls alike enjoyed the projects in *St. Nicholas Magazine*, published from 1873 to 1941. Other co-ed magazines would follow, including *Jack and Jill*, first published in 1938, and *Highlights*, first published in 1946. Another avenue of crafting for children was through the Boy Scouts and the Girl Scouts, founded in 1910 and 1915 respectively, clubs such as 4-H, and religious organizations, such as the YMCA. Crafts of all kinds were offered at club-sponsored summer camps. While club craft projects encouraged entrepreneurship and pride in one's work, merit badges and county fair competitions rewarded excellence in the product.

In the first half of the twentieth century, art classes in American public schools generally concentrated on mechanics, such as drawing dimensional objects in perspective or rendering illustrations for industrial design, fashion, or architecture. Art was approached like a science. There were exercises in light and shadow, color theory, and the realistic drawing of limbs and facial features. Art "lessons" emphasized technical skill and accuracy, not creativity.

This began to change after World War II, as movements and schools within the larger art world, such as Impressionism, filtered down to the popular culture and began to influence how art teachers were trained.

The 1950s and 1960s mark a turning point in public school art education for American children. Educators envisioned art classes that would be interesting for everyone, not just those who were naturally gifted at drawing. The focus in the classroom shifted from creating a product to immersing in a process. Art would engage the child in spatial relations, use of color, tactile sensations, and other right-brain functions later identified by psychologists as essential to clear thinking and overall functioning. Educators believed that children who expressed creativity and independence in art classes would succeed in other subjects as well. The goal was to help each student tap into his or her natural creativity at a young age. As described by art professor F. Louis Hoover, "From the first day of school, children should take it for granted that whatever they produce with art materials will reflect their own thinking, their own feelings, their own seeing."

The new art curriculum explored a wide variety of media. The mainstays were paper, drawing and painting media, and clay. Paper art in two dimensions included weaving, collage, and mosaics; the paper pieces could be torn or cut with scissors. Paper art in three dimensions included flowers, stabiles and mobiles, dioramas, geometrical shapes such as cubes and cones, and papier-mâché. Different types of paper, such as colored tissue paper and crepe paper, provided experiences with more creative potential. Teachers were encouraged to develop art projects that used simple, affordable art materials, scrap paper, old magazines and newspapers, and household items like buttons, yarn, and dry macaroni.

Art in the classroom spawned a new generation of consumer art supplies. Chain stores like Michael's, founded in 1976, and A. C. Moore, founded in 1985, stock a huge variety of materials, from glitter-glue and polymer clay to paints and paper. Today's affordable, readily available supplies make it easy for children and adults to craft for leisure enjoyment or to explore new media with creative abandon—the raison d'être of contemporary arts and crafts.

## THE SCIENCE

On one level, arts and crafts appear to be simple play activities that keep kids occupied, but on a deeper level, they are so much more. As a child goes about the work of scribbling or drawing or pinching salt dough or sculpting clay, he is creating a tangible expression of his imaginative thinking and learning life lessons that will reach far into his future. As parents, we can make arts and crafts a meaningful part of our children's lives, the earlier the better, because it is through these seemingly ordinary experiences that children enlarge their creative wingspan, grow their skills, discover their potential, and prepare for the future.

Drawing by Genevieve A. Sterbenz, age four

The traditional arts and crafts in this chapter are designed with children in mind. The chapter is filled with creative ideas, activities, and projects that will lead your child through an exciting continuum of experiences in paper, crayons, paint, chalk, markers, clay, and mixed media. The activities are introduced in a sequence that roughly follows the four stages of child development: birth to 18 months; 18 to 36 months; 3 to 6 years; and 6 to 9 years and up. In the beginning, the activities are purely sensory in nature, ones that immerse a young child in the creative process for its own sake. For the child, this is a time when the enjoyment is purely in the doing, and a splotch of paint or a scribble with a crayon does not have to *mean* anything. Over time, the child who has been exposed to simple art experiences will grow accustomed to self-expression in many media and will acquire a foundation of skills that leads to the making of actual craft projects. The craft projects in this chapter span the creative spectrum and are designed to be fun and to promote learning, from making and using finger paint to marbling paper, constructing a kaleidoscope, and assembling a robot. Use your own judgment to assess your child's interests and capabilities when planning any creative activity, always keeping safety and fun in mind.

### Getting Started

Providing meaningful arts and craft activities for children involves imagination and preparation. By keeping a few important principles in mind, you can ensure safe and happy crafting experiences. Although the principles are presented individually, you will recognize that they are interconnected in fundamental ways.

- **Always put safety first.**
  Supervise a child's crafting activities by joining in the experience, especially

when a child is young. Guide children when they are learning a new skill but allow them to function independently as much as possible so that they can make their own choices and move at their own pace. Older children still appreciate supervision; while you may not need to sit right next to them, it is a good idea to be nearby.

Select materials and tools according to a child's age and skill level. Always read the manufacturer's labels on purchased supplies and follow the printed directions. If your little artist is still putting things in the mouth, be sure to use only child-safe, nontoxic materials. Keep age-appropriate supplies accessible in a child's arts and crafts starter kit or in a separate drawer and keep tools a child cannot handle safely out of reach. Do not give young children access to sharp knives, straight-blade scissors, or a household iron or oven. Always keep the tools utilized in arts and crafts activities separate from those used for food.

Drawing by Gabrielle Sterbenz, age three

Read the setup section for each craft activity in this chapter; it will alert you to the preparation stage of a project that might involve tools or techniques beyond your child's ability to handle or recommend tasks you can perform ahead of time to keep a project from running beyond the limits of your child's attention span. Use your own best judgment as far as involving a child in the setup steps, such a stirring cooked ingredients as they cool.

- **Make creative experiences fun.**
Make the creative experience a fun sharing time that leaves a child feeling happy and satisfied to have done or made something independently. Give a child the freedom to choose a craft activity from among several alternatives. Once a project is chosen, encourage a child to follow his or her personal preferences when choosing materials. When possible, personalize the creative experience; for example, you might put your child's picture on a cookie that you are making together.

Set aside a span of time in which a child can work without rushing. Seeing results in a comfortable time frame is important, especially for toddlers and preschool kids who have a shorter attention span. A child who is older and can work on his own needs the opportunity to choose a time that suits his schedule.

Approach every experience with excitement and openness and with no prejudice about its difficulty. Select a variety of experiences, some that you know a child can do with ease and some that will offer more challenge. Children pick up valuable problem-solving skills when they have to figure things out for themselves. Children will lose interest if a project is too hard or if it takes too long to see the finished product, so be patient and step in with encouragement or a helping hand without actually completely the project yourself.

Older crafters will have gained enough working experience in different media, techniques, and processes and have the analytical skills to choose new projects that they feel they can handle comfortably or that pose an exciting challenge.

Plan for the unexpected. Overt educational goals are fine and recommended, but remember that there are countless ways to achieve a desired result—children will always surprise us with their unique and imaginative approaches and discoveries, conjuring creative solutions that adults might never think of. This is true learning.

Drawing by Yvan Guénot, age six

- **Use good-quality materials and tools.**
Good-quality supplies can always be purchased from specialty and craft stores and online but do not overlook the value of items that are already in your pantry or that can be "harvested" from a junk drawer and re-purposed for arts and crafts.

Be discerning when purchasing arts and crafts materials. You do not have to buy the most expensive supplies to produce pleasing results but do be aware of the link between cost and quality in crafts materials designed for children. Materials and tools geared to kids are often less expensive and of an inferior quality. The nylon-bristle brush in an inexpensive paint set is a floppy disappointment that does not come close to providing a satisfying, realistic painting experience. Artist-grade supplies may be your best buy from the start. Good paintbrushes last a long time; quality synthetic bristles can withstand the learning curve of a young painter. Artist-quality colored pencils are known for their intense pigment-rich colors, good coverage, and ease of blending—properties that reward a child's early drawing efforts. You don't have to buy a whole set of pencils; you can buy one pencil at a time, if you prefer.

Keep a child's arts and crafts supplies in a special place, such as a shelf that he or she can reach, or in an arts and crafts starter kit. All children take pride in owning and organizing a personal stash of supplies.

Upgrade materials and tools as a child shows interest and ability. As children mature, they seek tools and materials that give them better, more consistent results. A foundation in arts and crafts makes children more aware of their own artistic intentions; they begin to understand for themselves the connection between the materials they use and the effects they are able to produce. Expose children to local art exhibits, especially school shows that display a wide range of media and creativity. These kinds of experiences will widen your child's knowledge and offer a new set of choices.

See the value in ordinary things and be willing to improvise. No childhood is complete without the ubiquitous appliance-box stove or playhouse. Kids have a high level of imagination and will overlook the crude nature of corrugated cardboard structures, remembering instead the enjoyable experience of playing with them. Look around your home for nontraditional art supplies, such as shoe boxes, old CD cases, toothbrushes, birthday invitations, colorful photos and illustrations from magazines, short lengths of ribbon, trim, and yarn, scraps of gift wrap, and old greeting cards—"finds" like these can spark creative experiences.

Seek intriguing new uses for common recyclables. Many recycled items make convincing substitutes for the real thing, such as using odd nuts and bolts to simulate cogs and gears on a toy robot. Disposable items can function like their authentic counterparts—a mailing tube can be used as the reflective chamber of a kaleidoscope, and a toothbrush can be an effective paintbrush for a spatter-paint effect. Use empty yogurt containers for cleaning brushes or for mixing paint. A Styrofoam egg carton makes a great palette for liquid paint.

Make your own art materials. Commercially prepared art supplies, such as finger paint and clay, are convenient to buy, but relatively expensive for the quantities offered. Making your own concoctions from ingredients on your pantry shelves ensures a ready supply.

- **Avoid judgment; praise often.**
Children thrive in an atmosphere that prizes their individuality. Praise a child's efforts, but avoid going to extremes— a child will think you don't mean your compliments. Don't focus on the end product. Acknowledge rather that the path the child took to get to a finished project was filled with thinking and imagination—efforts that are unseen but extremely valuable. To encourage children to talk about their art, say, "Tell me about your drawing" rather than ask "What is that?" Children glow with pride when you acknowledge their creativity and talk about the unique ways they approached their projects.

Drawing by Genevieve A. Sterbenz, age three

Children need to learn that some tasks require practice and that there are truly no wrong answers in arts and crafts. If a child expresses disappointment in an outcome, ask what he or she would like to try next time. Trial-and-error is one productive approach to learning something new. Avoid comparing the work of one child to that of another or to your own expectations. No two children are alike; each must find a personal pathway to expressing his or her own ideas. However, be aware that imitating the work of others is a natural part of learning for a child.

- **Prepare the work space and your child before any activity.**
Arts and crafts involve messy procedures that can splash and stain a child, clothing, or the immediate surroundings. You can prepare for the inevitable creative mess and, more important,

## Troubleshooting: Stain Removal Remedies for Fabrics

The following remedies, recommended for an adult to do, are suggested for removing stains caused by arts and crafts supplies on washable and nonwashable fabrics. It is always a good idea to test the chosen method on an obscure section of any fabric first.

| Stain | Washables | Nonwashables |
|---|---|---|
| Ball-point pen | Apply liquid detergent directly to the stain; wash and rinse the item. | Apply glycerin directly to the stain, soaking up the ink with a rag. Then treat the stain with an oil solvent. [Note: Hair spray removes some ball-point pen marks, but test it first.] |
| Pencil | Use a clean section of an eraser to rub off the pencil mark. Apply any liquid soap directly to the stain; wash and rinse the item. | Apply an oil solvent to the stain. |
| Crayon | Scrape off the loose wax; spread the waxy area of the fabric over a bowl or pot and pour boiling water through the fabric from a height of 12" (30.5 cm). Apply vinegar, lemon juice, or diluted bleach to the remaining stain. | Lay a thick pad of paper towels on a heat-proof surface, place the area of the fabric with the crayon wax on top, and cover with a double layer of paper towels. Use a warm iron to melt off the wax. Change to clean paper towels as needed. Apply an oil solvent to the remaining stain. |
| Wet acrylic craft paint | Apply any liquid soap and lightly scrub the stained area; rinse the fabric with water. Repeat the process as needed. | Try the directions for washables, being aware that a nonwashable fabric may be altered by the cleaning process. |
| Dried acrylic craft paint | No remedy. | No remedy. |
| Wet oil paint | Apply an oil solvent, such as turpentine, to the stain, allowing the solvent to soak through the fabric and onto a clean rag held underneath; blot out as much of the paint as possible. Apply liquid soap and lightly scrub the stained area; rinse the fabric with water. Repeat the process as needed. | Working outdoors or in a very well ventilated space, apply mineral spirits to the stain, gently blotting the fabric with a clean rag to absorb the paint. Then apply an oil solvent. Repeat the process as needed. |
| Dried oil paint | No remedy. | No remedy. |

accustom a child to taking responsibility for all aspects of the creative experience, including cleanup.

Have a child wear a smock or put on old clothes before beginning any experience. Older children will be served by changing out of school clothes or wearing an apron. Even paint that is labeled "washable" can stain some fabrics.

Prepare a work space that you do not have to worry about, indoors or outdoors—a kitchen table, a corner in the playroom, or a patio table all work well. The younger your child, the more vigilant you will need to be to safeguard the surroundings. Spread a recycled shower curtain (trimmed to a desired size) or a painter's drop cloth over the floor, walls, or work surface.

- **Encourage a child's imagination.**
The most valuable resource in any arts and crafts experience is a child's imagination. Provide a broad range of mixed-media experiences with no preconceived notions or expectations attached to the outcome of the creative activity. Kids are naturally intuitive and with some basic instruction are eager to express themselves freely.

Set the stage for creativity by establishing an atmosphere of free thinking. Don't wait for a formal "art" activity to encourage originality and self-expression. Turn common everyday situations into a quest for out-of-the-box thinking. Be silly, asking, "What does a monkey wear to the movies?" Or turn a familiar photograph or picture from a magazine upside down and have a child draw from it. Use familiar fictional characters and pretend scenarios to inspire dramatic play. Tell stories and let a child paint an ending scene. Show a closed box and ask a child to draw a picture of what can fit inside. Seemingly straightforward activities will reveal a lot about a child's view

of the world. Play music while children do arts and crafts and encourage them to use color and line to paint their own "symphony." Visit local art galleries—kids in strollers enjoy the oversized canvases and sculptures. These and myriad other exercises that you devise will develop a child's creative thinking and ability to look at ordinary things in completely new ways.

- **Get into good crafting habits.**
Children are served by structure, and they relax when they know what is expected of them. Prepare all of the materials that a young child needs before the activity begins. A child who is old enough can help you organize and set up. Older kids can manage setup and cleanup on their own if they have early experiences of taking on these responsibilities.

Work in a well-lit and well-ventilated room and provide for plenty of air circulation.

Organize and store supplies in marked boxes or on shelves. Labels are key to keeping a wide assortment of supplies identified, organized, and usable for another time. Use both drawings and words to identify what is in a box or on a shelf. Separate out those supplies that need refrigeration, such as homemade finger paints, marking the current date on the container before storing them. Get children into the habit of managing their own art supplies, recapping glue bottles and paint tubes, wiping drips off jars to keep them from seizing shut, and keeping supplies that tend to dry out, such as markers and tubes of paint, in resealable airtight jars or reclosable plastic bags. Take the green approach by using nontoxic, biodegradable supplies. Look for eco-smart alternatives, eschewing overconsumption or tossing out half-used supplies.

- **Display children's artwork and craft projects.**
Children enjoy seeing their artwork displayed in a prominent place—on walls, refrigerators, or bulletin boards—and take pride in sharing their work with relatives, friends, and visitors. I've even secured a long curtain rod along a wall as a permanent home gallery.

When a child decides to make room for new work, remove the old display, selecting special "masterpieces" for sav-

## Working with Safe Arts and Crafts Materials

When we are crafting with children, we want to be sure that the products they use are safe. The best way to ensure safety is to read the product label. The label tells you which ingredients in the product, if any, are potential hazards, explains how to use the product properly, and outlines first-aid remedies for improper use. Products endorsed by the Art & Creative Materials Institute (ACMI) have seals that indicate that the product has been evaluated and certified by a qualified toxicologist for both acute and chronic hazards.

medical expert for any known health risks and with information on the safe and proper use of these materials.

Conforms to
ASTM D 4236

Conforms to
ASTM D 4236

The CL seal identifies a product that is certified to be properly labeled in a program of toxicological evaluation by a

The AP seal (with or without a Performance Certification that states a material is certified to meet specific requirements of material, workmanship, working qualities, and color) identifies art materials that are safe and that are certified in a toxicological evaluation to contain no materials in sufficient quantities to be toxic or injurious to humans, adults and children, or to cause acute or chronic health problems. (Source: Art and Creative Materials Institute, www.acminet.org)

ing in a large manila folder, a shelf, a flat drawer, or an artist's zippered case. Revisit the collection at a later time to hear the child describe the time in which the work was done. Such a retrospective will enlarge a child's understanding of time, growth, and development. Scan or photograph pieces of art, if possible, and store them on a separate disk. Visit a website that offers easy-to-use programs for creating digital scrapbooks and keepsake gifts, such as plates, ornaments, and bed linen that use a child's artwork.

Drawing by Maxx Hamilton, age seven

## Children's Ages and Developmental Stages

Each child grows gradually at his or her own rate on a basically predictable, yet complex, course of developmental stages. Drawing on a general understanding of child development and adding your personal insight gained through firsthand observation, you can plan arts and crafts activities for any child that are both developmentally appropriate and also sensitive to a child's individual preferences and leanings. An environment that meets a child's basic developmental needs provides time and space to create and to be, and prizes individuality allows a child to become self-actualized and grow into the adult he or she is meant to become.

### Birth to 18 Months

In the first year and a half of life, infants make quantum leaps in cognitive and physical development, learning about their world through observation, tactile touching experiences, and interaction with attentive parents and loved ones. While infants are not yet ready for formal arts and crafts experiences, you can provide an array of spontaneous and unstructured sensory experiences. Touching, looking, and tasting are typical ways that babies and toddlers learn about themselves and the world around them.

An adult can take a leading role in fostering a child's future creativity by making a baby's first learning toys. Play is the serious work of early childhood. A mobile of plush forms in vivid colors can introduce a baby to color and shape and how to focus the eyes on moving objects. For the young toddler, an adult can create a soft book of textures that includes samples of low-pile shearling, smooth vinyl, fine-weave cotton, fabrics with embossed textures, and other textural samples that are colorfast and have finished edges with no loose threads. Young children naturally want to put everything into their mouths, so it is very important, of course, to provide creative playthings that are nontoxic and don't have small or breakable parts, such as small balls, balloons, and toy figures, or dangling strings or cords that can pose a choking hazard.

As a child moves through the early developmental stage, his or her motor skills are developing quickly. Suddenly, the child is walking! Fill a low cabinet that gives a child access to colorful plastic containers, small pots with lids, and measuring cups and spoons. A child who handles small tools will develop stronger muscles and better eye-hand coordination. You can provide plenty of opportunities to develop a child's power of observation and thinking skills through little "art" experiences. Give a child a jumbo-size crayon to grasp and tape a piece of paper to the floor or an easel for scribbling. A piece of paper taped to a rough-textured surface can be rubbed with a crayon to produce a print. Children who have access to these types of experiences will begin to recognize their emerging power to make things change—a *ta-da* moment that will inspire repetition and new learning.

The fantastic adventures of this stage of development are even more exciting when a child begins to use language and is able to elicit responses from others, express emotion, and set the wheels of interpersonal communication whirring. The use of language will ignite the imagination and unlock the door to learning and self-awareness. Use the words a child can say or understand, such as the names of loved ones, to make a first scrapbook: slip computer-generated photographs of family members, friends, and pets into separate plastic pages, zigzag the edges on a sewing machine to keep the photos from slipping out of the sleeves, and sew the pages together along one side to make a sturdy album.

## Age 18 to 36 Months

The child between ages eighteen and thirty-six months old is learning to talk, feed, dress, and wash independently. The child alternates between drawing close to familiar, warm comforts and venturing wherever curiosity leads.

When I was raising my own children, I found that arts and crafts, which carried low risks and promised high rewards, provided both protection and guidance. You can begin with creative play and use pretend scenarios such as playing house or driving a car to encourage creativity. With an adult to help, a child can construct a playhouse, a little stove, or a tunnel out of a cardboard box. In the kitchen, children can make artful patterns in a mixing bowl of leftover chocolate pudding, knead bread clay, or help put berry eyes on bunny-shaped pancakes—simple two-step operations that build memory and concentration for later crafting experiences.

As soon as a child seems ready, you can begin introducing short creative experiences that use child-safe, nontoxic materials, such as fat crayons, sponges, and water-soluble paints. (Do not yet offer sharp-pointed pencils and markers; they can be dangerous to rambunctious toddlers.) A child will love helping to stir homemade concoctions, such as bubble soap and finger paint, in simple processes that develop orderly thinking. Instead of being overly concerned about the mess, plan for it. A child can finger-paint in the bathtub where the inevitable mess can be quickly dealt with.

For children who do not like the sticky mess of finger paint on their hands, there are less messy alternatives, such as pasting collages, weaving with strips of colored paper, or squeezing play clay, a recipe you can mix up using pantry staples. A three-year-old can make a simple puzzle using play clay, gaining firsthand experience in problem-solving and reasoning. Take advantage of a child's growing attention span by providing art activities that teach the letters of the alphabet, numbers, and basic colors. Make a little book about one of the colors, say, orange or any other color the child likes, and have a child paste drawings or pictures of orange things inside. Pictures can be torn from a magazine.

One-on-one creative experiences with an adult will satisfy a young child's need for undivided attention. In all cases, the aim of arts and crafts at this stage is to engage a child in creative experiences that are fun and process-driven rather than aimed at the end product (although the simple elegance of a child's early artistic expressions may surprise you). If a child indicates a desire to do or try something, stand by at a distance to oversee the enterprise but otherwise let the child's creative energy flow out. Allow for some frustration to encourage a child to find a way to solve a problem. At the end of an arts and crafts experience, the only tangible output may be a lump of clay or a tangled scribble of color on a sheet of paper, but hidden within are unseen life lessons that will continue to motivate the child to seek joy, self-discovery, and self-mastery through creative work.

## Age 3 to 6 Years

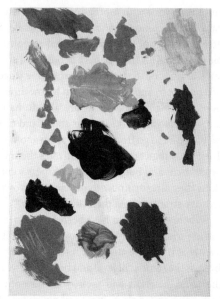

Finger painting by Katie Anne Kulikowski, age four

Collage by Nicholas Guider, age four

This stage of development is an especially exciting one as children begin to explore the world beyond home. Children in this age group are often in a preschool or elementary school setting. They are crossing new thresholds and moving toward greater autonomy every day. They use language effectively and enjoy imaginary play. Three-year-olds enjoy serving tea to their dolls and teddy bears, using clay constructions of food in their dramatizations. They love to pretend and use their imaginations to "live" in a castle they build from sand or to become the magician that waves a magic wand—props that are easily made from common arts and crafts materials and tools.

A three-year-old child brings a unique perspective to a finished craft project, such as a free-form collage, a Calder-style mobile, or an arrangement of pretty leaves. To encourage collage-making, place a variety of embellishments, such as stickers, glue, and colored paper, on a table. A child will become engrossed in the creative process, pondering which materials to use and how to apply them, and then evaluating the result in the finished project—a worthy road map for working through many life experiences. With every new creative activity that is tackled, a child develops the confidence to try more complex techniques, such as block printing, embossing, and weaving.

This is a perfect time to help a child assemble supplies for a personal arts and crafts starter kit. A starter kit can contain any items the child has shown interest in or has enjoyed using. Start with such items as crayons, nontoxic and washable paint, and a variety of papers. Add a glue stick or a jar of paste with a brush and a roll of masking tape for three-dimensional creations. Consider buying a coloring book with "invisible" paint that is activated by a wet brush and add a foam trim roller and stiff bristle brushes for more free-form painting on blank paper. It is also a good idea to consult with a child about new interests that might warrant new supplies.

## Age 6 to 9 Years and Up

Drawing by Genevieve A. Sterbenz, age six

Drawing by Kazio Kulikowski, age seven

Children in a later stage of development are cognitively, physically, and socially ready for more independence. The older child's approach to new experiences extends more and more from personality and temperament. Children of this age gravitate to arts and crafts that give them an opportunity to express their personal view of the world. They like being encouraged to follow their own paths to discovery and appreciate having wider creative choices. Often kids will seek outlets such as journals, diaries, and scrapbooks to record their experiences. This is the perfect time to offer a disposable camera or a video camera to create a "My Life" retrospective that allows a child to film family and friends.

A child at this age level understands that different art materials produce different results and convey different meanings. Color, form, and line are understood intuitively, and the child can work with a broad variety of materials and techniques and begin to handle a greater variety of tools in a safe and responsible manner. Kids this age have enough of a creative arts foundation to move from one stage of a project to another—they can follow directions and plan ahead. They are able to handle projects with three or four stages and can switch gears to go from one skill set to another. Their growing competence motivates them to experiment and build on craft techniques and skills they already know to develop their own creative strategies and their own designs.

Where crafts might have been gender-neutral in earlier stages, girls and boys differ significantly at this stage and their interests diverge. Even at the same skill level and beginning with the same materials and tools, you will notice that boys and girls begin to show different preferences for certain subjects and craft techniques (for example, girls may draw kittens and puppies and boys may draw monsters and airplanes). What is important is that your child expresses his or her own interests and ideas.

Drawing by Rodney T. Sterbenz

## Children's Arts and Crafts Materials and Tools at a Glance

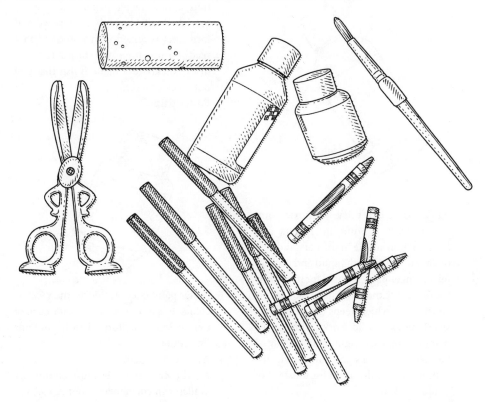

The materials and tools that provide a stimulating arts and crafts environment for a child are extremely varied. Begin with the basics, selecting items according to the child's age and developmental stage and add more sophisticated media and tools as the child's skills develop or as particular interests or talents emerge.

• **Crayons**

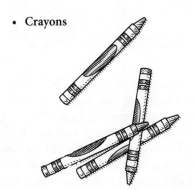

Crayons are sticks of colored wax composed of paraffin, dry pigment, and clay. The components are mixed together, liquefied by heat, poured into a mold, cooled, and wrapped with labels. Crayons for children should be nontoxic. Available in bright, lightfast colors, crayons come in various sizes and formulations. A fat, stubby style is easy for young hands to grasp. A water-soluble version allows a child to draw on wet paper to create watercolor effects. Some crayons are made in extra-large sizes or in formulations that can be washed off walls with warm water and a sponge. Triangular-shaped crayons guide a toddler's fingers into a tripod position for more control in preparation for writing with a pencil.

- **Finger paint**

Finger paint is a thick, nontoxic paint that is worked with the fingers and hands. It is available in primary and secondary colors in both liquid and powder form. Finger paint is noted for its slightly translucent texture and its thick, creamy consistency, which keeps the paint from splashing as a child works with it. The paint can be used right from the jar or be transferred to a small pump-style dispenser, such as that used for mustard or liquid hand soap.

- **Watercolors**
Watercolor paints are available in a hard cake form, in tubes, in creamy liquids, and as watercolor pencils. All forms enable good mixing capabilities. Applied with a brush, watercolors can be manipulated to produce a subtle gradation of color in delicate, transparent washes and thick opaque layers, depending upon the paper used and the amount of water added to the paint. Watercolor pencils contain color pigment mixed with a water-soluble binder that allows the color to adhere to paper; this binder also enables the color to spread when water is applied to it, making it easy to manipulate according to the amount of water added.

- **Tempera**
Tempera is a pigment paint that provides opaque coverage on absorbent, nongreasy surfaces, including construction and drawing paper and papier-mâché. Available both in a powdered form that is mixed with water and in a ready-to-use premixed form, tempera dries quickly to a matte finish that will not crack or flake.

- **Poster paint**

Poster paint goes on thicker than watercolors to lay down an opaque coat of rich color. One formulation contains fine glitter.

- **Acrylic craft paint**
Acrylic craft paint is most commonly available in convenient 2-ounce (57.3 g) plastic containers in a full range of colors. Having a fast drying time, acrylic craft paint is washable when wet. It becomes permanent but remains slightly flexible when dry.

- **Chalk**

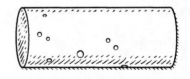

Common chalk is made by baking a mixture of pigment, water, and calcium carbonate, a form of gypsum, into a hard stick. Chalk offers a convenient and inexpensive tool for drawing on a range of surfaces, including chalkboards, sidewalks, charcoal and construction paper, drawing paper, and other media with sufficient tooth, or surface texture, to hold the chalk dust in place. Plain chalk is hard, brittle, and prone to breaking, so break long pieces of chalk in half for a child to use. Chalk is suitable for children who are beyond the stage of putting things into their mouths, usually 3 years old and older. Big and chunky sticks are easy to hold and use.

- **Pastels**

Pastels are composed of a pigment and a binder, and it is the proportion of the color pigment to the kind of binder that determines their type and the effects they produce. Soft pastels, available as sticks and in pencil form, are made of calcium sulfate, clay, and oils that are mixed together and air-dried. The high ratio of powdered pigment to the clay and oil binders makes them bright in color but also prone to splintering and producing dust. Spray fixative prevents unwanted smudging and makes a pastel drawing permanent. Hard pastels have a greater proportion of binders to pigment, making them suited to adding sharp details to drawings rendered in soft pastels. Oil-based pastels are made with powdered pigment, a nondrying oil, and a wax binder, which gives the sticks a soft malleability that produces rich and dense color, but no dust. Oil-based pastels are suitable for older children. However they do not blend well, although they can be used in combination with watercolors to create wax-resist pictures.

- **Colored pencils**

Unlike the traditional school pencil, which has a thin rod of black or gray graphite, a colored pencil has a rod of color—numerous shades are available—made from chalk and clay or wax and mixed with binders and pigments. Colored pencils made from wax are not water-soluble and are usually good for drawing. Colored pencils are particularly suited for use by children who are familiar with using a graphite pencil.

- **Markers**

Markers are versatile drawing tools that carry their own supply of dye or color in a thin rod made of synthetic fibers. The dye flows through the fiber, keeping the tip of the marker supplied with color. Variations include the thickness of the plastic barrel that houses the tube; the shape, diameter, flexibility of the fibrous

Drawing by Katie Anne Kulikowski, age four

drawing tip; the degree of transparency, translucency, or opacity of the dye; and the permanency or washability of the dye once it is placed on a surface. Markers can be used for drawing only or they can be used with water like paintbrushes to make washes and gradient color.

- **White craft glue**

Also called PVA (polyvinyl acetate), white craft glue is an all-purpose glue that creates a smooth, strong bond when used to secure porous surfaces, such as paper, chipboard, and wood, together.

## Working Tips: Working with Glue, Paste, and Tape

Many kinds of glues, pastes, and adhesive tape are used to adhere paper projects, depending upon the size of the job and the desired finished effect. Choose an adhesive that is child-safe and easy for a child to use. Keep bottles and sticks of glue and paste that have removable caps away from children under 3 years old.

The glue is washable when wet, and it dries to a transparent, flexible finish that is not completely waterproof. It can be squeezed directly from the bottle or it can be applied to large areas with a brush. After use, always replace the cap and wipe the tip with a damp cloth; if glue is allowed to remain and dry inside the tip, it will become difficult to squeeze out the glue.

- **Paste**

The consistency of paste ranges from runny (homemade flour or cornstarch paste) to thick (school paste). Nontoxic and inexpensive, paste can warp and curl paper. If pasting paper to cardboard, apply the paste to the paper first, let the paper curl and then flatten. Then apply the coated paper to the cardboard.

- **Glue sticks**

Suited to small jobs, such as tacking together pieces of paper and adhering picture corners, glue sticks are nontoxic and available in washable and permanent versions. Colored glues are visible during application. Another type of glue stick is used with a glue gun. Low-temperature glue guns are preferable to hot-glue guns for use by or around children.

- **Tape**

Children can use many types of tape effectively. Cellophane tape has a glossy or translucent finish; it comes with one sticky side or two. Children should be careful when using the dispenser as the cutting edge is sharp. Masking tape comes on rolls that can be very sticky (high tack) or barely sticky (low tack).

- **Paper**

All types of paper can be used in children's arts and crafts projects: copier paper, drawing paper, construction paper, tissue paper, brown kraft paper, watercolor paper, finger painting or other glossy coated paper (such as freezer paper), bristol, crepe paper, cardstock, cardboard, mat board, corrugated paper, vellum, and tracing paper.

- **Scissors**

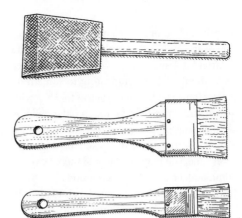

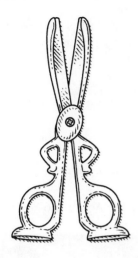

Scaled in size with finger and thumb loops to fit a child's hand, children's safety scissors have precision-ground, hardened stainless steel blades that are set at an effective and safe cutting angle and that have blunt tips. Safety scissors are always recommended for use by young children. School-age children can use many models with adult supervision, including scissors with decorative edges.

- **Paintbrushes**

A wide variety of paintbrushes are used in children's arts and crafts projects. A tapered watercolor brush allows coverage of small areas that require careful, precise handling. A foam brush gives smooth coverage of large areas and is easy to handle. Inexpensive chip brushes are good for large or textured surfaces.

- **Clay**

Clay for children should be nontoxic and selected according to the ease with which it can be worked. There are air-dry and heat-set clays, as well as types that remain permanently pliable. Most air-dry clays are suited to young children because they require little to no conditioning and are so easy to manipulate and shape; however, the color choice is limited to white or gray. Heat-set clays are available in a wide range of colors and lusters, but being somewhat difficult to condition, they are more suited to older children. A nondrying modeling clay made from pigmented wax in a range of bright colors is also easy for children to work. (Casting and solid clays used by artists and sculptors, such as plastilene, which is oil-based, and porcelain, which is kaolin-based, are beyond the scope of this chapter.)

\* \* \*

To help a child organize and care for a collection of arts and crafts supplies and tools, create a starter kit. Use a shoe box or plastic container for a younger child, graduating to something fancier (and a bit heavier), such as tool box with a latch and separate trays, for an older child. A child can display pride of ownership by personalizing a starter kit with stickers or drawings. Over time, you may need to add more boxes or commandeer a shelf to accommodate a growing collection of supplies. Use labels to identify containers or shelves and their contents.

### Starter Kit: Ages 18 to 36 Months

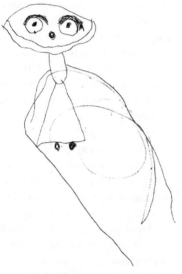

Drawing by Elka Pinny, age three

Keep the starter kit out of a toddler's reach until you are ready to spend time together doing a creative activity. Always supervise the use of these materials.

MATERIALS AND TOOLS
FOR A STARTER KIT
Freezer paper, cut into sheets, rolled, and
  secured with a rubber band
Coloring book (with partial drawings to
  be completed by child)

Watercolor book with water-activated
  paint
Jumbo-size wax crayons
Jumbo-size chalk
Finger paint in small plastic jars
Tempera in small plastic jars
Air-dry clay
Smock
Plastic measuring spoons
Large-hole salt shaker
Foam brush
Foam roller (for painting trim)
Clothespins
Large refrigerator magnets

### Starter Kit: Ages 3 to 6 Years

Collage by William Guider, age four

Children in this age group have the skills and cognitive development to handle a more varied selection of materials and tools and will let you know about the kinds of materials they wish to add to their starter kit. Provide careful supervision, but allow the child to do the work as much as possible.

MATERIALS AND TOOLS
FOR A STARTER KIT
Drawing paper
Colored construction paper
Tissue paper
Metallic foil
Cardboard
Lunch-sized paper bags

Chenille stems (pipe cleaners)
Stickers and labels
Feathers
Scraps of yarn, felt, and fabric
Large-particle glitter
Metallic stars, moons, and assorted shapes
Recycled and natural items, such as
    pinecones, pods, and leaves
Oven-bake clay
White craft glue
Glue stick
Cellophane tape
Masking tape
Colored pencils with thick lead and large-
    diameter barrels
Water-soluble markers
Watercolor set
Poster paints
Household paintbrushes, 1" (2.5 cm) and
    2" (5.1 cm) wide
Kitchen sponge
Hand-pump and spray-mist bottles
Cotton swabs
Craft sticks
Toothbrush
Drinking straws
Safety scissors

## Starter Kit: Ages 6 to 9 Years and Up

Painting by Jonah Pinny, age seven

Children in this age group have widely dif-
fering skills and interests and enjoy experimenting with a broad range of papers, paints,
markers, clays, and craft tools. Because they
are beginning to develop interests along
gender lines, their choices may reflect some
typical stereotypes. Provide moderate supervision.

## MATERIALS AND TOOLS
## FOR A STARTER KIT

Watercolor paper
Bristol
Cardstock
Vellum
Origami paper
Crepe paper
Recycled paper: greeting cards, gift wrap,
    magazines
Blank scrapbook
Stickers
Sheet protectors
Foam core and foam sheets
Embellishments: large-hole beads, ribbon,
    trims, feathers, glitter, yarn
Metal hardware: nuts, bolts, washers,
    springs
Office supplies: paper clips, double-sided
    tape, rubber bands
Grommets and a grommet punch
Oven-bake clay
Air-dry clay
Plaster tape
Acrylic paint in bottles and tubes
Chalk pastels
Oil-based pastels
Waterproof markers in a wide range of
    colors
Hole punch
Paper punches
Soft-bristle paintbrushes, in size 4 for
    detail, size 12 for larger areas
Foam brushes
Chip brushes
Brayer
Straight-blade scissors
Decorative-edge scissors
Ruler
Color wheel

## Working with Paper

Introduce paper to a child as early as possible. Paper will provide a welcoming door to many other creative materials and foster confidence in working with the hands. Children can go through volumes of paper fast, so economize by giving them recycled copy paper, chipboard cut from the back of a notepad, or gently used gift wrap. Buy a roll of inexpensive kraft paper or a pad of plain newsprint for a child to use at will. As children gain dexterity and their spatial understanding matures, they will proceed from making simple wrinkles and folds to creating dimensional sculptures from papier-mâché. They may even want to make their own paper. All of the techniques in this section are straightforward and require few, if any, tools. They will provide a springboard to countless innovations a child will make on his or her own.

### Manipulating Paper

Children are fearless when working with paper of any kind. Its malleability and versatility provide a variety of satisfying experiences for children. As children grow and develop, they can learn to cut and pierce paper, as well as to weave, roll, and tear paper into every imaginable shape, all without putting pen or brush to its surface. These activities change the shape and texture of paper.

### *Wrinkling*

Babies know intuitively how to wrinkle paper, even if they discover the technique by accident. Children as young as 8 months old find it fun and easy to wrinkle the pages of a catalogue—its thin paper yields easily to the effortless scrunching and makes a delightful sound. With a little guidance, an older child can learn to wrinkle paper in a controlled way to make textural pictures and small stages for imaginative play.

## Activity: Making a Wrinkled "Mountain"

Crumpled paper can be pushed into the shape of mountains and moonscapes and glued to cardboard. Used together with action figures, paper landscapes add dramatic context to your child's creative play. Very young children can use a glue stick instead of white craft glue.

Recommended age: 3+ years
Skill level: Easy
Supervision: Careful
Mess factor: Moderate

### MATERIALS AND TOOLS
Construction paper in any color
Chipboard, cut 1" (2.5 cm) smaller on all
    sides than construction paper
White craft glue
Foam brush, 1" (2.5 cm) wide

### SETUP
None

**Step 1**
Crumple the paper into a ball.
Use your hands to crumple a piece of construction paper into a small ball.

**Step 2**
Crumple the paper again.
Open the paper as flat as possible. Crumple it up again to make another ball shape and open it as flat as possible. Repeat one more time or until the paper has fine creases and is soft to the touch. Gently open the paper, keeping as many wrinkled contours as possible.

**Step 3**
Glue the wrinkled paper to chipboard.
Use a foam brush to apply a thin coat of glue to a piece of chipboard. Center the opened wrinkled paper on the chipboard and push the creased sections close together to make "mountains." Let the glue dry.

## Folding

A simple fold can instantly transform a sheet of paper from two dimensions to three! A fold can be soft or hard, wide or narrow; paper can be folded in a forward or backward direction or in a combination of them. With a little practice, folded paper can be used effectively to create fans, books, greeting cards, and fortune games.

### Activity: Making an Accordion (or Pleated) Fold

Several parallel folds, made to fall in alternating directions, will produce accordion-style pleats.

Recommended age: 6+ years
Skill level: Intermediate
Supervision: Moderate
Mess factor: Low

MATERIALS AND TOOLS
Bristol or construction paper
Ruler
Dry ball-point pen
Pencil
Teaspoon

SETUP
None

**Step 1**
Mark the folds.
Lay the paper on a flat work surface with the paper's grain running from top to bottom. Use a ruler and a pencil to mark off 1" (2.5 cm) intervals along the top and bottom edges.

**Step 2**
Indent the folds.
Align the ruler on one set of marks and use a dry ball-point pen to indent a vertical line in the paper. Repeat for each set of marks to indent parallel vertical lines across the paper. Press hard so that the indented lines show on both sides of the paper.

**Step 3**
Make the pleats.

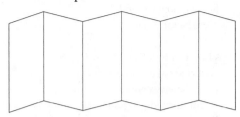

Fold the paper along the indented lines, one at a time, alternating the direction of the folds so that they bend forward and backward to create a pleated fan shape. Use a ruler or the straight edge of a table to help guide the paper into neat folds, if needed.

## Cutting and Punching

Cutting is a skill a young child loves to practice. The fine motor skills must be developed so that the child can hold a pair of scissors and coordinate the grinding/cutting action of the scissor blades. With a little practice, cut paper can be incorporated into such projects as paper masks, boxes, and dolls replete with fashion wardrobes. Cutting and folding can be combined to create pop-up cards.

Handheld paper punches offer another way to cut paper. Some punches are designed to cut a decorative edge and some cut out single shapes, from flowers to frogs to geometrics, in the interior edge of paper. The most common hole punches have two handles that are squeezed together or two long bars that are pressed down. Punches are designed to be maneuvered easily; however, many styles require hand strength that is beyond that of a young child, so be ready to help. For a project that uses a paper punch, see Polka Dot: A Kaleidoscope (page 643).

### Activity: Making Artful Cuts in Paper with Scissors

Here are a few of the basic cuts that a child can make with scissors.

Recommended age: 5+ years
Skill level: Easy
Supervision: Careful
Mess factor: Low

## MATERIALS AND TOOLS
Assorted papers, as desired
Child-safety scissors
Decorative-edge scissors
Pencil

## SETUP
Prepare the work space.
Arrange all of the sheets of paper and the scissors on a clean, dry work surface

## Step 1
Cut 1—Short and long cuts
Use the tips of the scissor blades to make short cuts in the edge of a piece of paper. Run your finger along the short narrow strips to create texture and dimension. Fun applications of snipped paper are making mown grass, fringe, and short bangs and adding them to paper sculptures. Use more of the scissor blades to make longer cuts in the edge of the paper for strands of hair, a horse's mane, or ribbon streamers.

## Step 2
Cut 2—Curls
Make long, narrow cuts in the edge of a piece of paper. Use a pencil to curl each strip, wrapping the strip snugly around the barrel of the pencil to make a curl and then gently pulling the pencil free. Fun applications of curled paper are making flower petals, antennae on bugs, and curly ringlets on paper dolls.

## Step 3
Cut 3—Decorative edges
Use scissors with decorative edges to add scallops, points, or curves to the edge of a piece of paper. Fun applications of decorated edges are making signs for a child's room, thank-you notes, picture frames, and birthday party invitations.

## Activity: Making a Pop-Up Cut
Children can achieve a clever pop-up feature on a sheet of paper by combining cutting and folding techniques. More complex pop-up designs require precise measuring and folding, techniques covered in books dedicated to the subject. Fun applications of the pop-up technique are greeting cards and dioramas; see Technique: Making a Pop-Up Card (page 232).

Recommended age: 6+ years
Skill level: Easy
Supervision: Moderate
Mess factor: Low

## MATERIALS AND TOOLS
Bristol, 8½" × 11" (21.6 × 27.9 cm)
Watercolors
Watercolor brush
Colorful stickers (optional)
Ruler
Pencil
Scissors
Teaspoon

## SETUP
None

## Step 1
Fold the bristol.
Fold the bristol in half widthwise to make a 5½" × 8½" (14.0 × 21.6 cm) rectangle, using the rounded bowl of a teaspoon to press the fold flat.

## Step 2
Mark the pop-up fold.
Open the paper flat so the fold runs vertically down the middle. Use a ruler and a pencil to mark two parallel horizontal lines that extend from the center fold to the middle of each panel.

## Step 3
Cut the pop-up fold.
Fold the card neatly in half with one half of the marked band facing up. Hold the card

in one hand, fold facing you, and scissors in the other, and cut along each marked line through both layers to make a band. Open the card and ease the paper band forward as you begin to close the card. Make a crease to mark the fold that forms when the band moves completely forward as the paper is folded flat. Use the bowl side of the teaspoon to reinforce the crease. Use paint or stickers to decorate the pop-up band. You can also glue drawings, magazine images, or photos to the pop-up.

## Perforating

Piercing a single hole or a series of tiny holes in a sheet of paper can be the beginning of many imaginative textural designs. Young paper engineers will have no trouble using common household tools, such as toothpicks, straightened paper clips, or a tailor's tracing wheel to pierce holes in a piece of paper. Holes can be placed at random or form organized patterns. Just remember to leave some margin of paper between and around the holes so the paper doesn't tear or form unwanted gaps that spoil the perforated design. Hold a perforated paper up to a light or tape it to a window to see the design more easily. Perforated art can also be used to make greeting cards.

## Quick Activity:
## Perforating with a Tailor's
## Tracing Wheel

This nifty dressmaker's tool is very easy for a child to use. All a child needs to do is grip the handle and roll the wheel along the paper in any direction. The serrated edge on the wheel will perforate the paper along the rolled line. A folded towel, carpet, or a blanket can be used instead of a foam sheet as a support under the paper.

Recommended age: 5+ years
Skill level: Easy
Supervision: Moderate
Mess factor: Low

## MATERIALS AND TOOLS

Sheet of drawing paper
Layer of foam, ½" to 1" thick (1.3 to 2.5 cm)
Masking tape
Tailor's tracing wheel

## SETUP

A yielding surface is required to produce the effect. Lay a 1"-thick (2.5 cm) sheet of foam larger than the sheet of paper on the work surface.

## Step 1

Lay a sheet of paper over the foam.
Place the working sheet of paper on top of the foam-covered work surface. Use strips of tape to secure the paper to the foam.

## Step 2

Perforate the paper.
Use the tailor's tracing wheel to impress lines across the surface of the paper in any pattern, running new lines in the same or in crisscross directions. Avoid tracing over the same line twice as the extra perforation can split the paper.

# Working Tips: For Adults Only

While a utility or craft knife is effective in making clean, straight cuts in paper, it is *not* recommended for use by children. If you choose to make a cut with a craft knife for a child, be sure to put on the safety cap and store the knife in a safe place after you have finished.

## Weaving

Weaving cut or torn strips of paper is an extremely easy way for a child to learn about sequence and direction, as well as improve dexterity and motor coordination. Adults can precut the strips with scissors or by tearing the paper against a steel ruler placed along the grain. Older children can cut or tear their own strips for weaving.

## Quick Activity: Making an Artful Weaving

With a little practice, a child can learn to weave unique patterns by varying the width and length of the strips, the pattern on the cut or torn edge of the strips, and the number and sequence of the colors. Completed weavings can be used as place mats for playtime snacks. For a pretend picnic, a child can draw images of food directly on paper plates, draw and cut out utensils and napkins from plain paper, and glue the pieces to the woven place mat.

Recommended age: 5+ years
Skill level: Easy to intermediate
Supervision: Careful
Mess factor: Low

### MATERIALS AND TOOLS

2 sheets of construction paper, in different colors, 9" × 12" (22.9 × 30.5 cm)
Chipboard, 9" × 12" (22.9 × 30.5 cm)
Cellophane tape
Scissors
Ruler

### SETUP

Arrange all of the sheets of paper on a clean, dry work surface.
Cut or tear the construction paper along the grain into approximately 1"-wide (2.5 cm) strips (the edges will be ragged).

### Step 1

Lay out the vertical strips.
Arrange six strips side by side in a vertical orientation on a sheet of chipboard. Use tape to secure each strip at both ends. These vertical strips form the warp.

### Step 2

Weave the first horizontal strip.
Weave from bottom to top and from right to left (or left to right, for a left-handed child). Thread one end of a new paper strip over the first vertical strip and under the second vertical strip. Continue weaving over and under across the warp until the first horizontal row is complete. Tape the ends of the strip to the chipboard.

### Step 3

Weave the second horizontal strip.
Thread the end of a new strip under the first vertical strip and over the second vertical strip. Continue weaving under and over across the warp until the second horizontal row is complete. Tape the ends of the strip to the chipboard.

### Step 4

Weave the remaining horizontal strips.
Repeat steps 2 and 3 to weave four more horizontal strips. The horizontal strips form the weft.

### Step 5

Bind the edges.
Run lengths of tape along four sides of the woven edge to secure the weaving.

## Tearing

Tearing is a straightforward technique that children intuitively know how to do. With no previous experience, a child can make surprisingly intricate designs using torn paper. Relatively straight tears can be made by tearing paper along its grain, using the edge of a ruler or the edge of a table as a guide. Curved tears can be made along an indented line or the edge of a curved object, such as a can. A jagged edge will naturally occur on those parts of the paper that are torn across the grain.

## Activity: Making a Paper Bird with a Curly Tail

The curly tail on this bird is made from torn strips of copy paper.

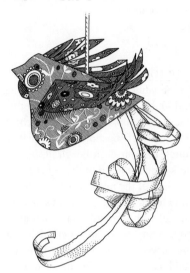

Recommended age: 6+ years
Skill level: Easy
Supervision: Moderate, with some steps for an adult to do
Mess factor: Low

### MATERIALS AND TOOLS

Bird and Wing patterns (page 711)
Scrapbook paper, 12" × 12" (30.5 × 30.5 cm), in pattern, as desired
2 sheets of white copy paper
½ yard (45.7 cm) yarn
White craft glue
Tape
Ruler
Scissors
Stapler
Large-eye needle with sharp point*
Craft knife and self-healing cutting mat*
Pencil*

*For adult use only

### SETUP

None

### Step 1**

Mark and cut out the pattern pieces.

Fold a piece of scrapbook paper in half. Place the Bird Body and Wing patterns on the paper, aligning the Bird Body on the fold, and trace around the outlines. Use a needle to pierce dots through both layers of paper to mark the wing tabs on the bird's body. Use scissors or a craft knife and self-healing cutting mat to cut out the body and wing pieces. Cut slots for the wing tabs on each side of the body section.

### Step 2

Shape the wings.

Make freehand cuts in the ends of the wings to resemble feathers. Use your fingers or a pencil to press the paper feathers into soft curves. Fold the wing along the marked lines to make tabs A and B.

### Step 3

Attach the wings to the body.

Slide tabs A and B on one wing into the slots on the body of the bird. Repeat for the other wing. Use tape to secure the wing tabs on the wrong side of the body. Repeat to secure the second wing. Fold the bird in half so the wings are on opposite sides of the body.

### Step 4

Make the tail.

Tear a piece of copy paper along the grain from top to bottom to make a long strip, which will naturally curl. Repeat to make eight strips in all. Hold the torn strips in an even stack, straight edges even, and staple together at one end.

### Step 5

Attach the tail to the bird's body.

Slip the stapled end of the tail between the fold at the tail section of the body. Use white craft glue to secure the tail in place.

**Step 6***

Add a hanging cord.

Thread the needle with yarn and make a double knot at one end. Insert the needle up through the center of the fold in the bird's body and pull the yarn taut to lodge the knot on the inside. Pull the needle off the yarn. Use the yarn to hang the bird, as desired.

**Adult activity

## Activity: Making Animal Collages using Straight, Jagged, and Curved Tears

This tearing activity requires some patience and dexterity. Colored construction paper is torn into the shape of an animal. Prominent features, such as the spots on a giraffe or leopard, can be added in a contrasting color. When choosing colors, think in terms of fantasy combinations—pink polka dots on a brown giraffe, orange stripes on a lime green tiger, or pale blue stripes on a red zebra.

❮◦◦◦◦◦◦◦◦◦◦◦◦◦◦◦❯

## SmART ideas:
## Fun with Tissue Paper

Children love working with tissue paper, a light-weight translucent paper with a slight sheen that comes in a fabulous range of rich and vibrant colors. Tissue paper can be torn easily into fantastic shapes that resemble fish scales and bird feathers and applied in overlapping layers to stiff paper or papier-mâché forms to create a shimmering layer of color. Tissue paper can also be wrinkled into tight balls and used to cover an object in a "carpet" of puffy-shaped color. For a fantasy chick made this way, see Using Papier-Mâché to Make "Hilarious Hen" (page 602).

❮◦◦◦◦◦◦◦◦◦◦◦◦◦◦◦❯

Recommended age: 5+ years
Skill level: Intermediate
Supervision: Moderate
Mess factor: Low

### MATERIALS AND TOOLS

2 sheets of construction paper, in different colors
Pencil
Glue stick

### SETUP (OPTIONAL)

For an adult to do: Young children aged 4 and under may want you to draw the outline of the animal on the sheet of construction paper. If so, choose an animal with a simple contour, such as a giraffe with a long neck. Use the grain of the paper to line up the lines of the neck, which will help your child tear a relatively straight shape. For an animal with a round body, such as a hippopotamus, mark an indented line along the curved contour, which will help your child tear curves. Individual features, such as ears, legs, and a tail can be torn from scraps.

**Step 1**

Sketch the shape of the animal.

Use a pencil to sketch the basic shape of an animal, such as an elephant, on a sheet of construction paper.

**Step 2**

Tear the shape.

Use your hands to tear the paper along the outline, doing small sections at a time.

**Step 3**

Tear the features.

Use a second sheet of construction paper in another color to tear shapes for special features or details of the animal, such as big floppy ears, eyes, toenails, and a fringed tail. Tear polka dots or stripes to make patterned coats.

*Rolling and Sculpting*

Rolling refers to shaping paper into open or closed curves, to make curls and tubes. Sculpting takes rolling to the next level, combining it with cutting, folding, and pasting to create three-dimensional paper sculptures, mobiles, and stabiles that are filled with texture and movement and are fast and easy to do. It's easier to create sculptural effects, such a curled fringe, first and then glue the paper to the larger project.

### Quick Activity: Making a Paper Chain

Use scissors to cut fifteen 4" × 1" (10.2 × 2.5 cm) strips of construction paper. Use a glue stick to apply a dab of glue to one end of each strip. Overlap the ends of one strip and press to adhere to form a ring. Thread a new strip through the ring, glue and overlap the ends of the new strip, and press to form a ring. Continuing in this way to make a chain of interlocking rings. Cut more strips to make a paper chain in any length desired.

### Quick Activity: Making a Gigantic Necklace

Cut three 8½" × 11" (21.6 × 27.9 cm) sheets of colored construction paper in half widthwise. Roll each rectangle of paper into a tube until one short edge overlaps the other and secure with cellophane tape. String the six tubes on a length of yarn. Then add craft jewels or feathers to the necklace for added glamour. For smaller beads, reduce the size of the paper rectangles.

### Quick Activity: Making a Curl

Wrap a narrow strip of paper tightly around a pencil, dowel, or knitting needle, pressing it tightly with your fingers. Withdraw the tool to reveal a curl of paper. Make as many curls as you need. Glue the curls to a hand drawing of a boy or girl to create a fun hairdo of curls and ringlets. Add little ribbon bows, if you wish.

### Quick Activity: Adding Height to Flat Paper Embellishments

Glue small pieces of foam core or a kitchen sponge between a paper embellishment and the base of a sculpture to raise the embellishment up off the surface. If the light is right, the raised piece will cast a shadow.

### Quick Activity: Sculpting a Bowl Shape with a Spoon

Lay a sheet of paper on a piece of felt or a folded flat-weave cotton towel. Beginning at the center and working out toward the edges, press down on the paper with bowl of a stainless steel spoon. Move the spoon in an oval motion, burnishing the paper into a soft bowl shape.

## SmART ideas: Making a Gigantic Fringed Tube

Lay a newspaper on a flat surface and open it to the middle page. Taking one or two sheets at a time, use scissors to cut a 4"-long (10.2 cm) fringe along the top edge of each sheet. Continue until all of the pages are cut. Roll all of the pages of a newspaper into a thick tube, one sheet of paper at a time, fringe facing up, and overlapping the end of one sheet with the beginning of the next. When you have a fat tube, use thick rubber bands to hold it together. Hold the outside of the tube with one hand, and use your other hand to pull the edge of the innermost sheet (the first one you rolled) out of the tube. Continue to pull the paper into a tall spiral, allowing the subsequent sheets of paper to emerge from the center of the tube.

## Quick Activity: Making Twisted Pop-up Strips

Glue down one end of a paper strip. Twist the strip once or twice and glue down the other end.

### Origami

A subject worthy of an entire book, origami is only touched upon here. This section presents a few basic folds and the symbols used to denote them. Before attempting a complicated sequence of folds, practice the simple folds—the mountain and the valley—upon which all origami designs are based and then work side by side with a child to fold a "penguin parade" (page 596). This introduction may inspire children to seek out more complex designs. Look through origami books cited in the source section to learn more about this fascinating art form.

Ultimately, copy paper and recycled paper will prove too bulky to maintain neat creases in a model that has multiple layers and multiple folds. The fibers of recycled paper have been cut many times in the process of shredding and reconstituting it, making it prone to tearing. You will want to switch to paper that is strong and won't tear easily. Paper sold as origami paper in specialty and craft stores comes in packages of 5⅞" (14.9 cm) squares and larger. It is available in hundreds of varieties, from solid colors and repeating patterns that depict flowers and geometrics to specialty foils and woven papers. Some origami papers are printed on both sides in different patterns.

Every fold begins as a bend in the paper that finally flattens to a crease. In origami, you are positioning a fold and the paper's edge at the same time. It is important to direct the edge of the paper as the paper is being folded so that the fold is neat and positioned precisely and the edges come together perfectly. Neatness is the hallmark of origami. It is suggested that a child have the requisite coordination and attention span before attempting origami. Beginners will find the basic origami folds easy to make.

## Technique: Making the Mountain Fold and the Valley Fold

Mountain and valley folds are essential paper-folding techniques that are the bases of all origami folds.

The mountain fold is formed when a single fold bends the paper backward.

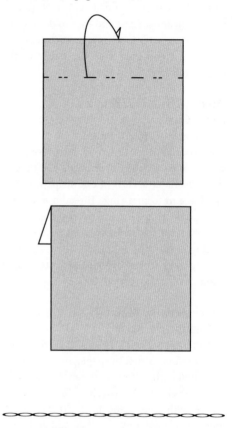

## The Meaning of Origami

Origami comes from two Japanese words: *oru,* meaning folding, and *kami,* meaning paper. A revered art form, origami is based on using one sheet of paper to create a three-dimensional item by making a sequence of folds and crease patterns—no cutting or gluing allowed, at least in the strict interpretation of the tradition!

The valley fold is formed when a single fold bends the paper forward.

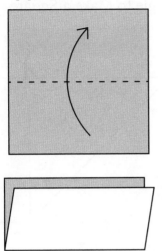

## Technique: Making a Crease

Sometimes a fold is made (a) and then the paper is opened out again (b), leaving a crease in the paper that guides the position of subsequent folds. Together with mountain and valley folds, the crease is one of the essential paper-folding techniques in origami.

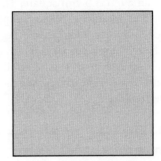

# SmART ideas: Making a Paper Mobile

Hold a wire hanger at opposite ends and twist to form a helix shape; set the hanger aside. Cut out six to eight random shapes from construction paper in different colors, each approximately 4" × 4" (10.2 × 10.2 cm). Add a different texture to each piece by cutting, folding, piercing, and burnishing. For example, use a spoon to burnish one piece of paper so that it forms a soft arch; use a T-pin to perforate a different shape; make snips or long cuts to decorate the edge of another shape; roll long cuts into curls in another. Use lengths of yarn to attach each sculpted-paper shape to the hanger, suspending each shape at a different level. Hang the mobile using the hook on the hanger.

# Working Tips: Parts of a Piece of Origami Paper

A colored side indicates the front of the paper. A white side indicates the back of the paper.

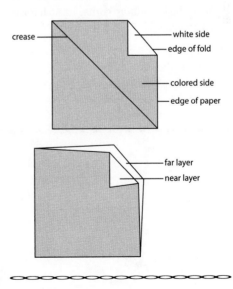

## smART ideas: Trimming a Rectangle to Make a Square

Origami paper is square, but you may not want to buy pricey origami paper for practice folding. Ordinary copy paper can be trimmed to make an $8^1/_2$" (21.6 cm) square. This size is larger than traditional origami paper, but it makes for easier folding for a beginner. When the rectangular paper is folded corner to corner to establish the square, it will make a diagonal crease in the paper when the paper is opened out again.

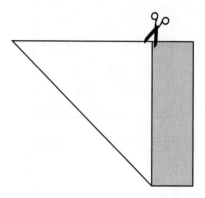

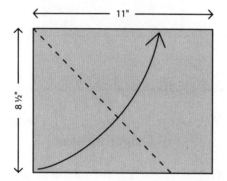

Lay a sheet of copy paper on a flat surface. Bring the left bottom corner up so it forms a diagonal fold. Flatten the fold.

Use a ruler and pencil to mark a line along the edge of the paper. Unfold the paper. Use scissors to cut along the marked line.

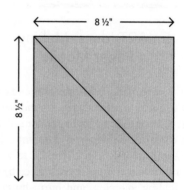

Smooth the crease.

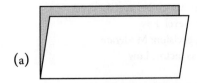

(a)

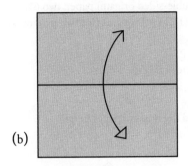

(b)

## Technique: Following a Sequence of Origami Diagrams

Origami diagrams are supported by symbols and a few words of explanation and proceed through an orderly sequence of folds and manipulations. Following the diagrams produces the desired model. Before beginning to fold the paper, look at the diagrams and read the short directions. Pay attention to the symbols, which explain what kind of fold to make or what kind of action to take. Look ahead to the next diagram to understand where you are heading.

- **Kinds of folds and features:**

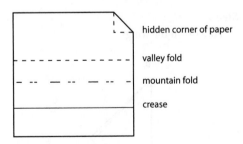

hidden corner of paper

valley fold

mountain fold

crease

A dash line indicates a valley fold, or a fold in front.

A long dash and two short dash lines indicates a mountain fold, or a fold in back.

A thin line indicates that the paper was folded and unfolded to make a crease.

A dash line indicates hidden features, such as a hidden edge.

- **Kinds of actions:**

## fold in front

An V-shaped arrowhead with an arching line means fold in the direction of the arrow.

## fold behind

A half-hollow arrowhead with an arching line means fold the paper behind.

## fold and unfold

An arching line with a V-shaped arrowhead on one end and a whole hollow arrowhead on the other end means fold and unfold the paper.

## repeat behind

An arrowhead with a crossbar means repeat the action behind.

## Technique: Making an Origami Penguin

Perfect for beginners, the penguin model introduces two kinds of folds, providing a fun origami project for a child. While traditional origami paper has a colored side and a white side, it is fun for a child to use double-sided origami paper, which is colored or patterned on both sides in two contrasting hues. Both sides show as the folding progresses.

○○○○○○○○○○○○○○○○○○○○○○○○

### smART ideas:
### Making Neat Folds

- Rest the paper on a flat clean surface.
- Fold the paper away from your body, bending your head over the fold so that you can look straight down at the edges of the paper.
- Start any crease in the middle of the fold, smoothing the crease from the center of the fold to one outside edge and repeating the action from the center to the opposite edge.
- Burnish a crease using the back of your thumbnail, the bowl side of a teaspoon, or a bone folder.

○○○○○○○○○○○○○○○○○○○○○○○○

Recommended age: 6+ years
Skill level: Easy
Supervision: Moderate
Mess factor: Low

### MATERIALS AND TOOLS
Double-sided origami paper, two 6¾"
(17.1 cm) squares (for two penguins)

### SETUP
None

**Step 1**
Fold the origami paper in half.

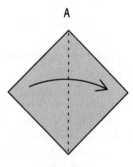

Fold in half

Use a single large sheet of origami paper. Lay the paper flat so the paper shape appears as a diamond. Fold the paper in half, corner to corner.

**Step 2**
Fold down the wings.

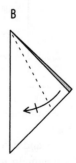

Repeat behind

Fold down the upper edge of the paper in the near layer by about one-quarter. Repeat for the far layer so both sides are the same.

**Step 3**
    Open up the body.

C

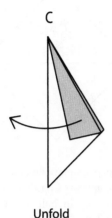

Unfold

Unfold the paper at the center fold and lay it flat.

**Step 4**
    Fold up a triangle at the bottom.

D

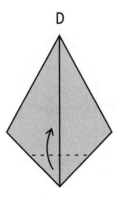

**Step 5**
    Fold back a smaller triangle at the top.

E

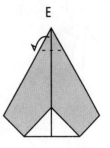

Fold behind

**Step 6**
    Fold in half.

F

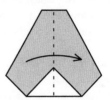

**Step 7**
    Ease up the small triangle for the head and beak.

G

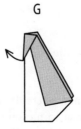

Slide up the head

## Step 8

Stand the penguin upright.

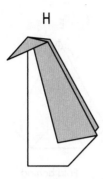

H

Finished penguin

Splay the halves until the penguin stands on its own.

### Technique: Making an Origami Fish

A challenge to fold, but enjoyable to do, the origami fish can be suspended from filament to make a mobile or it can be used as an embellishment on a card or gift box.

Recommended age: 10+ years
Skill level: Intermediate
Supervision: Moderate
Mess factor: Low

### MATERIALS AND TOOLS

Any light-weight paper, such as gift wrap
Glue stick
Pencil
T square
Craft knife
Steel ruler
Self-healing cutting mat

### SETUP

Use a craft knife, steel ruler, and self-healing cutting mat to measure and cut a 9" (22.9 cm) square from gift wrap. Use a T square to confirm that the corners are true.

## Step 1

Make the first folds.

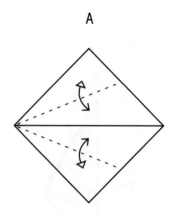

A

Lay the paper square flat, colored side up, so the shape appears as a diamond. Fold the square diagonally in half and then unfold. Bring the top left edge down to meet the fold, make a crease, and then unfold. Repeat for the bottom left edge.

## Step 2

Begin the fin triangles.

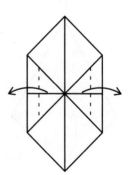

B

Fold the square diagonally in half in the other direction. Bring each side corner to the center and fold. Fold out each corner by two-thirds, so that a small triangle extends at each side.

**Step 3**

Shape the fins.

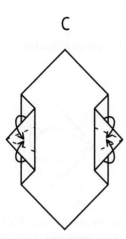

C

Push in the midpoint of each side edge of one small triangle to nearly meet each other. Flatten the paper to resemble the next diagram. Repeat for the other small triangle

**Step 4**

Fold the fish body.

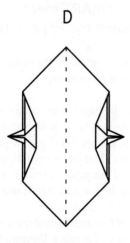

D

Fold the shape lengthwise in half, enclosing all but the tips of the triangles.

**Step 5**

Continue folding the fish body.

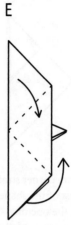

E

Fold down the top corner along the dash line. Fold back the bottom corner along the dotted line.

**Step 6**

Isolate the fins.

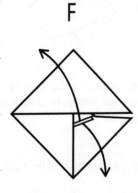

F

Pull the tiny triangles in the center out and away from each other, then flatten the entire piece.

**Step 7**
  Shape the fish body.

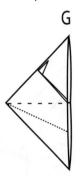

Pull the bottom corner straight up, perpendicular to the rest of the shape. Place a couple of fingers inside the opening. Open the shape, pulling the sides out, and flatten into a kite shape.

**Step 8**
  Repeat on the reverse side.

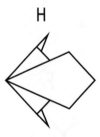

Turn the piece to the reverse side and repeat. Fold one part of the kite back and to the inside.

**Step 9**
  Form the bottom part of the tail fin.

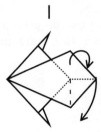

Pull the opposite part of the kite under, pulling the corner straight down to form a bottom tail fin.

**Step 10**
  Form the top part of the tail fin.

Repeat on the reverse side, but fold the top part of the kite down first, to create a tail fin pointing in the opposite direction. Although not traditional, you may want to apply a dab of glue between the tail fins to secure them.

---

## smART ideas:
## Finding the Paper Grain

Here are some ways to determine the grain direction on a piece of paper.

- Hold the paper at opposite edges and make a soft bend. If the paper bends easily, the bend is along the grain.
- Make a short tear perpendicular to the edge of the paper. A straight tear runs along the grain. A jagged tear runs across the grain.
- Tear off a small square from one corner of the paper. Dampen the square with water. It will curl into a soft tube shape that runs in the direction of the grain.

## Papier-mâché

Children enjoy the convenience and ease of working with traditional papier-mâché to make three-dimensional sculptures. Derived from the French words for "paper" and "chew," traditional papier-mâché involves diluting wallpaper paste (or white craft glue or flour paste) and applying it to torn strips of paper. The glued strips are applied over a base mold or an armature. The layers of glued paper build up, taking on the shape of the mold or armature. A mold used to support the shape during construction can either be removed or be allowed to remain inside the sculpture permanently. A balloon mold can be removed by slicing through the dried paper layers and pulling it out. The slice in the papier-mâché is then sealed with strips of paper. A foam shape, such as a Styrofoam ball, is a permanent mold that remains inside the sculpture.

Once the papier-mâché has dried, its surface can be painted using acrylic craft paint or tempera. It can also be finished with strips of thin decorative paper, such as tissue paper and gift wrap. Either way, a finishing coat of acrylic sealer will protect the surface and add shine.

### Activity: Using a Permanent Mold to Make a Fat Bumblebee

In this fun activity, a Styrofoam ball is used as a mold for the body of the bumblebee, and chenille stems and paper cutouts help to add realistic features. The black stripes are painted and coated with transparent glitter; for shiny stripes, apply black electrical tape instead.

Recommended age: 6+ years
Skill level: Easy to intermediate
Supervision: Moderate, with some steps done by an adult
Mess factor: High

MATERIALS AND TOOLS
10 sheets of newsprint or other absorbent paper
White copy paper
Styrofoam ball, 4" (10.2 cm) in diameter
2 wiggly eyes
9 chenille stems (pipe cleaners), in black
Transparent glitter
Elastic, 10" (25.4 cm) long, in black
Tempera, in yellow and black
White craft glue
Scissors
Shallow bowl
Foam brush
Tapered watercolor brush
Knitting needle*
*For adult use only

SETUP
Tear newsprint into 20 narrow strips, each approximately 1" × 3" (2.5 × 7.6 cm).
Draw four large eye-shaped wings freehand on a sheet of copy paper. Use scissors to cut them out.
Squeeze some white craft glue into a shallow bowl and thin with water to the consistency of light cream.

**Step 1**
Coat the paper strips.
Dip a paper strip into the thinned glue, coating both sides. Use your fingers to smooth away any excess.

**Step 2**
Apply the strips to the ball.
Starting at the middle of the ball, apply the glued strip to the surface, smoothing it flat. Apply glue to a second strip and lay it on the ball, overlapping the long edge of the first strip and smoothing the strip flat. Continue gluing and applying new strips of paper, overlapping and smoothing the strips in place until the ball is covered completely. Use your hands to smooth all of the layers flat; let the glue dry completely.

**Step 3\*\***
Add the elastic for hanging.
Use a knitting needle to carefully pierce a

hole straight through the center of the ball. Tie one end of the elastic onto the capped end of the needle. Tie a double knot into the other end of the elastic. Use the knitting needle to pull the elastic through the hole in the ball until the knot lodges flush with the surface of the ball. Secure with glue. Tie the free end into a small skein to keep it neat while you work.

**Step 4**

Paint the ball yellow.

Rest the ball on a protected surface. Use a foam brush to apply a coat of yellow paint. Let the paint dry completely.

**Step 5**

Make holes for the legs and the antennae.

Use the knitting needle to poke three deep holes into each side of the ball for the legs, two holes in the top of the head for the antennae, and one hole at the back of the ball for the stinger.

**Step 6**

Add the legs and antennae.

Cut one chenille stem in half; insert and glue a half stem into the back of the ball for the stinger. Insert and glue full-length chenille sticks into the remaining holes for the legs and antennae. Let the glue dry.

**Step 7**

Paint the black stripes.

Use a tapered watercolor brush to paint black stripes on the yellow body. Sprinkle glitter over the wet paint. Let the paint dry.

**Step 8**

Glue on the eyes and the wings.

Position and glue on two eyes; let the glue dry. Position and glue two white paper wings to each side of the bumblebee; let the glue dry.

**Step 9**

Bend the chenille sticks.

Bend the legs, the stinger, and the antennae so they look realistic.

**Adult activity

### Activity: Using Papier-Mâché to Make "Hilarious Hen"

Papier-mâché bird by Isabel Johnson, age four

## smART ideas: Making Flour Paste

To make flour paste for a papier-mâché project, combine 3 tablespoons (24.0 g) of plain white flour and 2 cups (473.2 mL) of water in a stainless steel saucepan. Slowly bring the mixture to a boil and stir until the mixture is smooth and lump-free. Remove from the heat and let the paste cool to room temperature before using. Store flour paste in an airtight jar in the refrigerator and use it within 3 or 4 days.

Recommended age: 5+ years

Skill level: Intermediate

Supervision: High, with some steps for an adult to do

Mess factor: High

## MATERIALS AND TOOLS

Beak, Wing, Comb, and Foot patterns (pages 712–13)

15 sheets of tissue paper, in yellow and orange

2 wiggly eyes, ¾" (1.9 cm) in diameter

5 sheets of newsprint

Masking tape

White craft glue or flour paste

Styrofoam ball, 6" (15.2 cm) in diameter

Wire hanger

T-pins

Scrap cardboard

Shallow bowl

Scissors

Pliers*

Wire cutters*

Tape measure*

Foam brush

Craft stick

Low-temperature glue gun and glue sticks

*Adult use only

## SETUP

Cut a plastic bag along two long sides, lay it flat on your work surface, and use masking tape to secure the corners

Use your hands to rip newsprint into long strips

Use scissors to cut ten sheets of tissue paper into 1" × 4"-long (2.5 × 10.2 cm) strips; rough-cut five sheets into 5" (12.7 cm) squares

Use the patterns to mark and cut out one beak, two wings, one comb, and four feet from cardboard. Roll the nose/beak section into a cone and secure with tape. Press the cone in half to make a beak,

bend it into a soft arch, and use tape to hold the shape

Use wire cutters to cut off the straight wire on a wire hanger so you have a piece 16" (40.6 cm) long.

Lay the Styrofoam ball on a protected work surface. Insert the wire through the bottom third of the ball so that an equal length of wire extends out each side. Use pliers to bend down the extending wires so that they are perpendicular to the wire that is inside the ball. Bend the end of each wire into L-shaped foot that is 2" (5.1 cm) long. Wrap a piece of newsprint around the top of each wire (where it exits the ball) to shape a thigh and use masking tape to secure the wraps.

Sandwich and glue each wire foot between two cardboard foot pieces. Let the glue dry.

## Step 1

Cover the ball and the legs with papier-mâché strips.

Pour thinned white craft glue or flour paste into a shallow bowl. Wet a strip of newsprint with the mixture and apply the glued strip to the ball, smoothing down the edges. Apply a second glued strip to the ball, overlapping the strips slightly. Continue applying glued strips to the ball and the legs until they are concealed with paper strips; let the glue dry.

## Step 2

Cover the ball and the legs with tissue paper.

Use a foam brush to apply a light coat of glue to a section of the papier-mâché ball. Lay a square of tissue paper on top of the glue and use the brush to smooth it in place over the papier-mâché layer. Continue to glue sections of paper to the ball and the thighs, overlapping tissue paper squares until the ball and the thighs are concealed. Let the glue dry.

**Step 3**

Cover the wings and the beak with tissue paper.

Use tissue paper squares to conceal both sides of each wing, folding the paper over the cardboard edges so they are smooth. Repeat to cover the comb piece. Use more squares of tissue paper to cover the beak piece, folding the tissue paper over the cardboard edges so they are smooth.

**Step 4\*\***

Pin the beak, wings, and comb to the ball.

Pin one piece at a time, using T-pins, and allow the child to layer it with tissue paper strips. Alternate back and forth between steps 4 and 5 until all the pieces are attached.

**Step 5**

Secure the beak, wings, and comb to the ball.

Use a foam brush to apply glue or flour paste to the foam ball and the pinned piece. Layer tissue paper strips over the glued areas and smooth in place with a brush. Let the glue dry.

**Step 6**

Add the tissue paper "feathers."

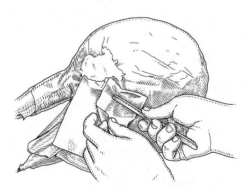

Use a craft stick to tamp down the edge of a tissue paper strip to each leg, making a row of feathers. Continue to glue on the feathers, overlapping each new layer on the layer already glued.

**Step 7**

Add feathers to the remaining parts of the hen.

Continue to apply the tips of the tissue paper strips in layers to the chick's body, wings, and head until the chick is covered completely.

**Step 8**

Add the eyes.

Use a low-temperature glue gun to secure a wiggly eye to each side of the hen's head.

\*\*Adult activity

## Plaster Tape

Plaster tape is a convenient substitute for papier-mâché strips. The plaster tape is pretreated with a coating of plaster of Paris, enabling you to wet the ready "adhesive" using wet fingers and apply it to a mold, such as a Styrofoam ball. The wet strips of plaster are easy to apply and the plaster sets to a hard finish that is smooth and easy to paint. Keep the plaster tape dry until you are ready to use as the plaster begins setting up immediately. Plaster tape is sold in several widths and lengths.

## Activity: Using Plaster Tape to Decorate a Fish

Plaster-tape fish by Maxx Hamilton, age ten

A child can wear disposable gloves to handle the wet plaster tape. If the gloves are floppy, tape them around the wrists.

Recommended age: 9+ years

Skill level: Intermediate

Supervision: Moderate to high, with some steps for an adult to do

Mess factor: High

## MATERIALS AND TOOLS

Fin, Tail Fin, and Nose patterns (pages 712–13)

2 rolls of plaster tape, 4" wide × 180" long (10.2 × 457.2 cm)

Styrofoam ball, 6" (15.2 cm) in diameter

2 wiggly eyes, ¾" (1.9 cm) in diameter

Cellophane tape

Acrylic craft paint, in light and dark colors

Liquid acrylic sealer, high-gloss

T-pins*

Scrap cardboard

Small dish

Paper towels

Disposable gloves

Masking tape

Scissors

Low-temperature glue gun and glue sticks

Foam brush

*Adult use only

## SETUP

Cut a plastic bag along two long sides, lay it flat on your work surface, and use masking tape to secure the corners.

Use scissors to cut the entire length of plaster tape in half lengthwise; then rough-cut each length into 5"-long (12.7 cm) strips.

Use the patterns to mark and cut out two dorsal fins, one tail fin, and one nose from chipboard. Roll the nose section into a cone and secure with tape.

## Step 1**

Pin the nose and fins to the ball.

Pin the nose, dorsal fins, and tail fin to the ball, one piece at a time, using T-pins.

## Step 2

Apply the plaster strips.

Put on the disposable gloves and tape the wrists. Pour water into a shallow bowl. Pick up one plaster strip and dip it in and out of the water without saturating it, which will cause it to twist or stick together, making it unusable. Working on the nose first, apply a plaster strip to secure the edges of the nose cone to the foam ball. Continue to apply plaster strips, overlapping and smoothing the strips until the nose is concealed. Repeat to cover the dorsal fins and tail fin, overlapping and smoothing the strips until the fins are secure. Then apply plaster strips to the entire ball until it is covered completely. Let the plaster cure so that it is dry and stiff.

## Step 3

Reinforce the nose and fins.

When the plaster is dry, apply a second layer of plaster strips to the entire fish, reinforcing the fins, as necessary. Let the plaster harden and cure, following the manufacturer's recommendations.

## Step 4

Paint the fish.

Use a foam brush to apply a coat of paint in the lighter color to the entire surface of the fish; let the paint dry. Use a tapered paintbrush to add stripes or other pattern to the fish; let the paint dry.

## Step 5

Apply sealer.

Use a foam brush to apply two coats of acrylic sealer to the fish, allowing the first coat to dry before applying the second coat. Let the sealer dry completely.

**Step 6**

Attach the eyes.

Use a low-temperature glue gun to secure a wiggly eye to opposite sides of the fish.

\*\*Adult activity

## Making Paper

Children are especially fascinated by the process of turning a colorless mush into single sheets of paper that they can write and paint on or use to make greeting cards, frames, and album covers. The materials and tools for paper making are simple—paper fiber and a two-part screen, called a mold and deckle. Recycled paper—telephone books, copy paper, newspapers, tissue paper, and paper towels—can be used for the paper fiber. A mold and deckle can be purchased from a craft store or made from recycled picture frames and pantyhose (see page 608).

Making paper at home is straightforward and fun. Reconstituted paper is chewed into a pulp using an old kitchen blender. The prepared pulp, called *slurry,* is suspended in a vat of water. The deckle is held on top of the mold and both are submerged in the slurry and then lifted up, capturing some of the paper pulp on the mesh screen of the mold. After the excess water drains off, the deckle is lifted off the mold and the layer of pulp is transferred, or couched, onto a sheet of absorbent fabric or paper, called the felt. More water is pressed out, and over time the pulp dries out, contracts, and becomes a sheet of paper.

## Activity: Making Paper from Recycled Paper

This is a great project for an adult and a child to do together. Work at the kitchen counter near a sink or set up a sturdy child-size table if the child cannot reach the kitchen counter comfortably. You can also blend the paper pulp ahead of time and bring it outdoors to work on a picnic table. You don't have to buy anything special for this technique. For white paper, you can use uncoated copy paper, paper towels, tissues, or a combination. A single sheet of red construction paper adds a pink tint, but other colors can be chosen as well. The slurry is mixed with water in a large, low plastic container, such as a kitty litter box or an under-the-bed storage box. The container should be about 4" (10.2 cm) larger all around than the mold and deckle. White cotton couching cloths can be cut from an old clean sheet and should be about 2" (5.1 cm) larger all around than the mold and deckle.

Yield: 6 to 8 sheets of paper, 8" × 10" (20.3 × 25.4 cm), in pale pink

> Recommended age: 5+ years
> Skill level: Easy to intermediate
> Supervision: Careful to moderate
> Mess factor: High

MATERIALS AND TOOLS

> 12 sheets of uncoated white drawing paper, 8½" × 10" (21.6 × 25.4 cm)
> 1 sheet of construction paper, 9" × 12" (22.9 × 30.5 cm), in red
> Liquid starch
> Mold and deckle, for paper size 8" × 10" (20.3 × 25.4 cm)
> Large, low plastic container, about 16" × 18" (40.6× 45.7 cm)
> 20 white cotton couching cloths, about 12" × 14" (30.5 × 35.6 cm)
> Electric blender
> 2 terry cloth bath towels
> Cotton kitchen towels
> Measuring spoons
> Old newspapers
> Large bowl

Spray bottle with water

Pressing board (plastic cutting board or heavy books wrapped in plastic)

## SETUP

One day before:

Tear the white paper and the red construction paper into 1" (2.5 cm) squares and put them into a large bowl. Add warm water, covering the paper completely. Add 2 tablespoons (29.6 mL) liquid starch and stir the mixture thoroughly. Let the paper soak overnight.

A few hours before crafting:

Layer two bath towels on the kitchen counter next to the sink or on a sturdy child's table. Set the large plastic container on top. Layer the table with sheets of newspaper and top with cotton kitchen towels.

Transfer two or three handfuls of wet paper pulp to the blender jar. Add warm water to fill the jar halfway. Cap the blender jar.

Pulse the pulp into tiny pieces. Continue blending to make a fine slurry. Transfer the slurry to the large plastic container. Repeat the process, filling the container until the plastic container is three-quarters full.

Lay a cotton cloth on a bare work surface. Spray the cloth liberally with water until it is fully dampened. Use your hands to smooth out any wrinkles.

## Step 1

Add a layer of pulp to the mold and deckle.

Hold the mold mesh side up and fit the deckle on top. Holding the mold and deckle together as a unit, dip the front edge into the vat, submerging the frames in a horizontal position on the vat's bottom. Then raise the frames straight up, allowing the fibers to settle on the mesh screen in an even layer.

## Step 2

Distribute the pulp.

Lift the frames completely out of the vat and gently shift them side to side to drain off the water and evenly distribute the pulp. Hold the frames over the sink to let more water drain off, using a sponge to absorb drips from the underside of the frame.

## Step 3

Lift the deckle off the mold.

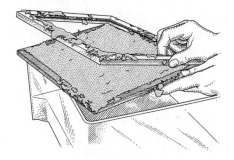

Carefully lift off the deckle to reveal the wet sheet of pulp on the mesh screen.

## Step 4

Release the sheet of pulp.

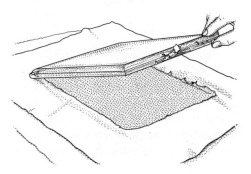

Stand the mold upright on its short edge, pulp side facing the cotton cloth. Treating the short edge as a hinge, lower the mold onto the damp cloth until the mold lies flat. Use a sponge to blot the water coming through the screen. Tap the frame gently to release the sheet of pulp onto the cotton cloth. Lay a second cotton cloth over the paper. Use the sponge to blot up more water.

### Step 5

Make more sheets of paper.

Repeat steps 1–4 to make more sheets of paper, stirring the slurry just before dipping the mold and deckle into it to evenly distribute the pulp. Add more pulp to the container when the sheets begin to look thin or have bare spots. Discard any remaining pulp in the trash, draining off the liquid beforehand.

### Step 6

Release the sheets of paper from the cotton cloths.

When the paper is almost dry, pull the cotton cloth at opposite ends to release the paper layer. Stack all of the sheets of paper on a flat surface and set a plastic cutting board on top to keep the papers flat. Check periodically for dryness; when the papers are completely dry, remove the cutting board. The paper is ready to use.

## Technique: Making a Mold and Deckle for Rectangular Sheets of Paper

It is easy to make a mold and deckle using two same-size picture frames and a pair of pantyhose. The pantyhose forms a double layer of mesh when it is pulled around one of the frames to make the mold. Some wet pulp may get trapped between the mesh layers, but this will not affect the shape of the handmade paper. The frame's rabbet may cause some pulp to build up at the inside edge of the deckle. You can thin the buildup at the edge after you have lifted the frames completely out of the vat by gently shifting them from side to side as the water drains off.

Recommended age: 7+ years
Skill level: Easy
Supervision: Minimal
Mess factor: Low

### MATERIALS AND TOOLS

2 picture frames with flat sides, 8" × 10" (20.3 × 25.4 cm)
Waterproof packing tape
Pair of pantyhose, large size
2 rubber bands
Scissors

### Step 1

Prepare the frames.

Disassemble each picture frame, removing the backings and glass. Use a strip of packing tape to cover each outside corner of the frame. The tape will keep the sharp corners from tearing the sheer pantyhose.

### Step 2

Make a mesh sleeve for one of the frames.

Cut off one of the legs from the pantyhose. Stretch the stocking with your hands and slowly work the opening over one frame until the frame is inside the stocking leg. Use a rubber band to secure the mesh at each side, pulling the mesh taut over the frame. Use scissors to trim the mesh within 1" (2.5 cm) of the rubber band.

**Step 3**

Lay the frames together.

Hold the frames together, back sides facing one another, to use as a mold and deckle.

## Collages and Assemblages

A collage is made by arranging and gluing an assortment of paper in different sizes, shapes, and textures to a background surface, such as a sheet of thick chipboard or a piece of Masonite. Traditionally, a collage uses only one kind of material, such as paper, but children enjoy mixing all sorts of materials together to make their collage designs. Pieces that combine scraps of paper, lengths of ribbon, trims, feathers, and found items such as buttons and dried beans are typical of the work children produce.

When a mix of materials is used to make the arrangement, it is called an "assemblage."

Finding items is always fun. Allow a child to spend some time browsing through junk drawers or button boxes to locate interesting items. You can take a walk together and gather small, light-weight leaves, pods, pebbles, and other natural items that have texture and color. Children love to leaf through old magazines and newspapers (don't forget junk mail) for illustrations and photographs with bold lines and contrasting shapes and colors.

**Activity: Making a Collage**

This collage activity uses colored tissue paper. Choose contrasting colors such as orange and blue, or analogous colors, such as bright aqua, purple, and pink. The finished piece could easily become the foundation for an assemblage.

Recommended age: 4+ years

Skill level: Easy

Supervision: Careful to moderate

Mess factor: Moderate

## smART ideas: Making Paper with Even Thickness

If the wet pulp is unevenly layered on the screen, turn the mold over and touch the wet pulp to the surface of the slurry. It will instantly release into the water, clearing the screen so that you can try again.

## smART ideas: Making Round Sheets of Paper

You can make a round sheet of paper using a mold you make yourself. Bend and pull a wire coat hanger with your hands to form a circle. Insert the wire circle into a cutoff pantyhose leg, bind the ends tightly with rubber bands, and trim off the excess mesh. Use the hook of the hanger as a handle to scoop the mold into the slurry and lift it out. The wet pulp can remain on the screen until it dries or it can be couched onto a cloth (as if you were flipping over a fried egg). Because this handmade mold has no deckle, some of the pulp will run over the edges. If you don't like the wobbly edge, you can trim it when the paper is dry.

## MATERIALS AND TOOLS

Thick chipboard, any size
Tissue paper, in assorted colors
White craft glue
Small bowl
Child safety scissors
Craft stick
Foam brush, any width

## SETUP

A few hours ahead:

Pour ¼ cup (59.1 mL) white craft glue into a bowl. Add water, a little bit at a time, until the glue is the consistency of light cream.

Use a foam brush to apply a coat of the diluted glue to both sides of the cardboard. Set it aside to dry. The glue will act as a size to prevent the chipboard from warping.

Cover the unused glue solution with plastic wrap and set aside.

Wash the foam brush and let it dry.

### Step 1

Apply glue to the chipboard.

Lay the prepared chipboard on a protected work surface. Use a foam brush to apply an even coat of diluted glue to one side, brushing from the center to the outside edges.

### Step 2

Line the chipboard.

Center a sheet of tissue paper on the wet surface and press and smooth it in place, knowing that the paper will get somewhat wrinkled. Apply a coat of diluted glue over the entire surface of the tissue paper. Let the glue dry.

### Step 3

Arrange the collage design.

Use scissors to cut random shapes, both large and small, from several sheets of tissue paper. Arrange the shapes on the dry chipboard, moving them about until you are pleased with the arrangement.

### Step 4

Glue down the tissue paper.

Press the tip of a craft stick on one tissue paper shape to hold it in place against the surface. Use a foam brush to pat a thin coat of glue on the top surface. The glue will seep through the thin tissue and hold it in place. Repeat to glue down the remaining shapes.

## Working with Crayons, Paint, Chalk, and Markers

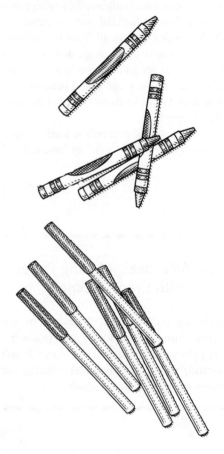

Color is integral to most arts and craft activities. This section examines ways that children can use crayons, paint, chalk, and markers to grow experientially in their understanding and use of color.

Drawing and painting are two major visual

arts that children love to do, regardless of age level or experience. When I was in first grade, I was given a set of watercolors that had separate tins filled with tablet-shaped cakes of paint. I could use the paints whenever I wanted to, although it was usual that my father would sit next to me and show me how to mix colors or how to create a three-dimensional effect by applying saturated color at the edge of an object and a pale wash in the center. I painted small pictures on folded paper to make greeting cards for holidays and birthdays. At Christmas, I painted tree boughs and ornaments; for birthdays, I painted hearts and balloons. I painted details on the envelopes. I was, like most young children, content to produce simple, even random, effects, but as I got older, I demanded more of myself and my materials and wanted to replicate what I saw more realistically.

Learning to draw and paint is an ongoing process that requires practice and interest. Much like learning a spoken language, children learn to draw and paint by imitating what they see and by using marks and visual symbols that they learn or invent themselves. In the beginning, babies have no idea what a circle or a square is, but they can learn quickly by being exposed to simple line drawings. Start simply. Draw a shape on a piece of paper, using a crayon, and name the shape. Babies will begin to associate the visual symbol, or shape, with the linguistic symbol, or name. Sit with a child and talk through the drawing experience, asking the child to add marks to a blank page or to a drawing that you have begun. For example, draw a round circle and add the features of a face one at a time as you name them—eyes, a nose, and a smiley mouth. Relate the drawing to the features on the child's face. Small art experiences that enable a child to connect visual symbols and verbal expression spur cognitive development. As the months and years unfold and eye-hand coordination develops, a child will draw and paint shapes, faces, people, pets, houses, trees,

and other subjects, placing them in compositions of his or her own conjuring.

Drawing by William Guider, age four

Drawing by Yvan Guénot, age six

## Multimedia Art Activities

Children of all ages enjoy creating special effects using crayons, paint, markers, and chalk, alone or in combination. As long as the motor and cognitive skills are present, a child can be introduced simultaneously to a wide variety of coloring tools and techniques. A child does not need to "graduate" from one medium to another, say, from crayons to paintbrushes and paint. Through practice and experimentation, interchanging markers for crayons, for example, or trying out a stencil or mask, a child will develop a repertoire of drawing and painting skills that can be applied spontaneously to other arts and crafts activities.

Given the wide range of readiness and interests among children, I suggest that you use your own best judgment to assess which of the activities are appropriate for a particular child. All of the activities are designed to provide near-instant gratification, but if a child is very young or has a limited attention span, you can introduce a new activity in two shorter sessions to keep it fun.

### Quick & Easy Activity: Making Triple Patterns

MATERIALS AND TOOLS
   3 markers or new wax crayons
   Paper
   Tape or wide rubber band
   Crayon sharpener

Hold the markers or crayons together and rest the tips on a flat surface so that they are on the same plane. Secure the bundle with tape or a rubber band. Use the triple points to draw lines, plaids, crosshatch designs, or other patterns on paper. Sharpen the tips of the crayons when they become too blunt to use.

### Quick & Easy Activity: Making Scribbled Stained-Glass Patterns

MATERIALS AND TOOLS
   Markers or wax crayons
   Paper

Use a dark-colored marker or a wax crayon to make a loopy pattern of overlapping scribbles. Go back and fill in the loopy shapes using a variety of light colors.

### Quick & Easy Activity: Making Polished Patterns

MATERIALS AND TOOLS
   Wax crayons
   Drawing paper
   Soft cloth (such as an old sock)

Use wax crayons to draw on sturdy drawing paper, pressing hard to apply a thick waxy layer of color. Use a soft cloth to polish the layer of wax crayon to a lustrous shine.

### Quick & Easy Activity: Making Crackle Patterns

MATERIALS AND TOOLS
   Wax crayons
   Watercolor paint
   Kraft paper
   Paintbrush

Use wax crayons to draw a picture that takes up a sheet of kraft paper. Wrinkle the paper into a ball to make tiny creases all over the paper and smooth the paper flat. Apply watercolor paint in a contrasting color to the crayon design, using light pressure to make a crackle design.

### Quick & Easy Activity: Making Wax-Resist Patterns

Wax-resist drawing by Maxx Hamilton, age ten

MATERIALS AND TOOLS
   Wax crayons or candle
   Paint thinned with water

Smooth paper
Foam brush

Use crayons or a wax candle to scribble or draw a simple figure or object on a sheet of smooth paper. Then use a foam brush to apply thinned paint over the entire paper to reveal the drawing.

## Quick & Easy Activity: Making an Oil Pastel and Watercolor Pattern

MATERIALS AND TOOLS
Oil pastels
Paint thinned with water
Smooth paper
Foam brush

Use oil pastels in rich colors to draw favorite shapes on a sheet of smooth paper. Then use a foam brush to apply thinned paint over the entire drawing to make the drawing pop.

## Quick & Easy Activity: Making a Random Droplet Splash Pattern

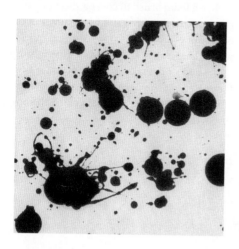

MATERIALS AND TOOLS
Poster paint
Drawing paper
Paintbrush

Put a sheet of drawing paper on a protected floor. Dip a paintbrush into thinned poster paint, hold it by the end of the handle, and stand over the paper. Use your free hand to tap the handle of the brush so that droplets of paint fall onto the surface of the paper in a random splash pattern.

## Quick & Easy Activity: Making a Watery Splash Pattern

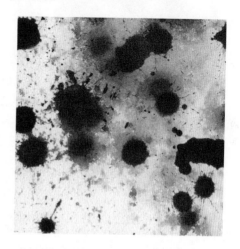

MATERIALS AND TOOLS
Poster paint
Drawing paper
Sponge
Paintbrush

Use a wet sponge to coat a piece of drawing paper until the paper is very damp, but not dripping. Put the paper on a protected floor. Dip a paintbrush into any color poster paint and stand over the paper. Hold the brush by the end of the handle and use your free hand to tap the handle so that droplets of paint fall onto the surface of the paper. The droplets will spread into unique watery splash patterns.

## Quick & Easy Activity: Making a Multicolor Splash Pattern

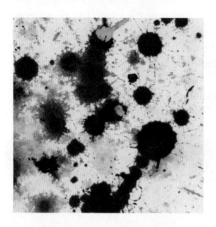

MATERIALS AND TOOLS
Poster paint, any two colors
Drawing paper
Sponge
Paintbrush

Follow the activity on page 613 to make a splash pattern in one color. Then add drops of paint in a second color to create a multicolor splash pattern.

## Quick & Easy Activity: Making a Spreading Splash Pattern

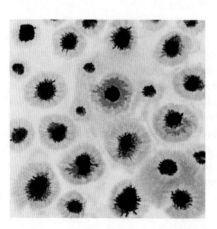

MATERIALS AND TOOLS
High-gloss acrylic enamel
Drawing paper
Foam brush
Paintbrush

Use a foam brush to dampen the surface of a sheet of paper. Put the paper on a protected floor. Dip a paintbrush in thinned high-gloss acrylic enamel and then touch the tip of the brush to the surface of the damp paper. The dot of paint will spread in a small burst of color. Repeat to create a random pattern of spreading polka dots. Use more than one color enamel, if desired.

## Quick & Easy Activity: Making a Reverse Splash Pattern

MATERIALS AND TOOLS
Finger paint
Glossy white paper
Foam brush
Paintbrush
Dish of water

Use a foam brush to cover a sheet of glossy paper with a thin layer of finger paint. Put the paper on a protected floor. Working quickly while the paint is still wet, dip a paintbrush into water and shake droplets of water onto the surface of the paper. Wherever the droplets land, the paper's original color will show through.

## Quick & Easy Activity: Making Blown Paint Patterns

### MATERIALS AND TOOLS
Watercolor paint
Glossy white paper
Drinking straw
Brush

Use a brush loaded with watercolor paint to tap drops onto a piece of glossy paper. Aim a drinking straw at the center of one paint drop and blow through the straw to spread the paint in all directions. Then aim at a nearby drop and blow through the straw so that the blown patterns intersect.

## Quick & Easy Activity: Making a Grainy Pattern

### MATERIALS AND TOOLS
Tempera paint
Smooth paper
Regular salt
Paintbrush

Use a brush and tempera paint to paint a simple shape on a sheet of smooth paper. Sprinkle salt over the wet paint to create a grainy pattern of color. Let the paint dry.

## Quick & Easy Activity: Making a Two-Toned Pattern

### MATERIALS AND TOOLS
Tempera
Drawing paper
2 small sponge rollers
Paintbrush

Use a paintbrush to apply a horizontal band of tempera in one color along the top left edge of a piece of drawing paper. Apply a second color band of color along the top right edge so that the bands of color overlap in the middle. Use a separate small sponge roller to roll each color down the paper. Use either roller to roll down and overlap the middle section.

## Quick & Easy Activity: Making a Spatter Pattern

### MATERIALS AND TOOLS
Tempera
Paper
Toothbrush or stiff paintbrush
Craft stick

Set the paper on a protected work surface or the floor. Dip the bristles of a toothbrush or stiff paintbrush into tempera. Run a craft stick across the bristles from back to front to spatter paint droplets onto the paper.

## Quick & Easy Activity: Making a Masked Pattern

### MATERIALS AND TOOLS
Tempera
Drawing paper
Masking tape
Toothbrush

Use strips of low-tack masking tape to form a letter of the alphabet on a piece of drawing paper. Use a toothbrush to spatter-paint all over the paper and the tape (see previous activity, Making a Spatter Pattern). When the paint is dry, peel off the tape to reveal the letter of the alphabet.

## Quick & Easy Activity: Making a Spray Pattern

### MATERIALS AND TOOLS
Food coloring
Spray bottle
Drawing paper
Sheet of medium-weight paper
Scissors
Poster putty or masking tape

Cut out a desired shape from a sheet of medium-weight paper to create a paper mask. Use a pinch of poster putty or a rolled piece of masking tape to secure it to the drawing paper. Fill a spray bottle with ½ cup (118.3 mL) water, add 15 drops of food coloring, and replace the sprayer cap. Swirl the bottle to mix the solution. Spray the tinted water over the paper and the paper mask. Allow the color to dry. Lift off the mask and remove the putty to reveal the cutout design on the paper.

## Quick & Easy Activity: Making a Stenciled Pattern

### MATERIALS AND TOOLS
Tempera
Drawing paper
Decorative punch
Sheet of medium-weight paper
Glue stick
Sponge

Cut a sheet of medium-weight paper into rough squares. Use a decorative punch to cut out a shape in the middle of each square to make a stencil. Use dabs of a glue stick to adhere the stencils to a sheet of drawing paper in a random pattern. Use a sponge dipped in tempera to dab a light coating over the paper and the shapes. Let the paint dry completely and lift off the stencils to reveal the prints.

## Quick & Easy Activity: Making a Layered Collage

### MATERIALS AND TOOLS
Poster paint, in blue and orange
Bristol, 2 sheets
White craft glue
Foam brush or roller
Comb
Scissors

Use a foam brush or roller to cover a sheet of bristol with blue poster paint. Run a comb through the paint to make wavy lines across the paper. Let the paint dry completely. Repeat to paint a second sheet of bristol with orange poster paint and let dry. Use scissors to cut out shapes for several goldfish from the orange paper. Glue them to the patterned blue paper.

## Quick & Easy Activity: Making a Tie-dye Pattern

### MATERIALS AND TOOLS
5 markers
Drawing paper
Spray bottle with water
Rubber band

Stand five markers on a flat surface so their points are even. Use a rubber band to secure the bundle. Press the marker tips against a sheet of paper, making a tight web of tangled lines or feathery strokes. Use the spray bottle to mist the design so the colors bleed, for a tie-dye effect.

## Quick & Easy Activity: Making a Crosshatch Pattern

### MATERIALS AND TOOLS
Markers or colored pencils
Paper

Use markers or colored pencils to draw tic-tac-toe patterns all over a sheet of paper, overlapping the patterns until there is a thick layer of color.

## Quick & Easy Activity: Making a Disappearing Pattern

### MATERIALS AND TOOLS
Jumbo-size chalk
Garden hose

## Quick & Easy: Making a Tie-dye T-shirt in a Sunburst Design

Tie-dying is a very easy technique that enjoyed great popularity in the 1970s. I remember working alongside my kids in our yard as we created colorful patterns in T-shirts using a technique that required absolutely no previous experience to achieve a one-of-a-kind masterpiece. An infinite array of tie-dye designs is possible, but one of the simplest is the sunburst, which is produced using string to tightly bind off parts of the T-shirt fabric so that they don't come into contact with the dye. The pattern is revealed when the strings are removed. For a two-color design, dip the lightest color first and then overdye a selected section with a darker color. Choose two colors that are near one another on the color wheel so that when the colors are overdyed, a third pretty color will result.

- Wash and dry a white cotton T-shirt.
- Lay the T-shirt on a protected flat surface. Yank up the center top layer of fabric to form a peak, gathering the fabric into tight folds. Use lengths of string to tie off the fabric, spacing the bindings at even intervals, or as desired, and tying tight knots.
- Wearing disposable gloves and following the manufacturer's directions, mix the cold-water dye in a sink or an old plastic basin (dye will stain plastic) that is large enough for the T-shirt to move around freely. Immerse the T-shirt in the dye, stirring it gently.
- Rinse the T-shirt until the water runs clear.
- Use scissors to carefully snip through the string bindings.
- Wash the T-shirt by hand with mild detergent and rinse thoroughly in cool water. Squeeze out the excess water. Tumble-dry on a low setting.

## Working Tips: Removing Gooey, Greasy, Sticky Stuff

If your crafter has worn his "good" clothes while crafting, you may find gooey, greasy, sticky stuff, such as permanent marker and wax crayon, grease, adhesive residue from stickers, and even gum, ground into the fabric. To remove the toughest stains, I use Goo Gone, a citrus-scented, acetone-free solvent that is available in a spray gel that clings to most surfaces, such as upholstery, carpet, wood, glass, and most fabrics, and removes soil without staining.

Use jumbo-size chalk to draw patterns of any kind on a smooth sidewalk. Hose them off when you are finished or wait for the next rain to wash them off.

## Quick & Easy Activity: Making a Glow-in-the-Dark Pattern

MATERIALS AND TOOLS
    Fluorescent chalk
    Black construction paper

Use fluorescent chalk to draw shapes on a sheet of black construction paper. Expose the drawn shapes to bright light. Darken the room to see the pattern.

## Quick & Easy Activity: Making a Blended Pattern

MATERIALS AND TOOLS
    Soft pastels in the colors of the rainbow
    Drawing paper
    Cotton swabs

Use a soft pastel to draw a band of color in an arc shape on a sheet of drawing paper. Choose another color and draw a second band, overlapping the first one slightly. Continue until all of the colors are used. Use cotton swabs to softly smudge and blend the overlapping areas to create a continuous band of color.

## Quick & Easy Activity: Making an Oil-Resist Pattern

MATERIALS AND TOOLS
    Oil pastels
    Watercolor paints
    White textured paper or charcoal
        drawing paper
    Paintbrush

Use oil pastels to draw a series of patterns—dots, short and long strokes, and solid shapes—on the paper to make an abstract design. Then use a brush to apply a light wash of watercolor over the drawing.

## Quick & Easy Activity: Making an Invisible Oil-Resist Pattern

MATERIALS AND TOOLS
    Oil pastel, in white
    Watercolor paints
    White textured paper or charcoal
        drawing paper
    Paintbrush

Follow the activity above using a white oil pastel to draw and write "invisible" messages on the white paper. Then use a brush to apply a light wash of watercolor to reveal the design.

### Pastel Chalks

Kids love drawing with pastels on textured paper or on sidewalks outdoors. Adults can mix up a batch of pastels using paint and plaster of Paris to keep them well supplied. The process is easy enough, but it is an adult-only operation. Children should not take part because of the dangers associated with breathing in the plaster dust or getting it on the skin.

### Technique: Making Jumbo Chalks

Use cardboard tubes from paper towels or toilet tissue to mold these jumbo chalks. The tubes are lined with freezer paper for easy release. Be sure to wear disposable gloves and a respirator mask. You can use soap and water to clean up, but dispose of leftover liquid plaster in the garbage can, not down the drain.

Yield: Three sticks, each 3½" long × 1½" in diameter (8.9 × 3.8 cm)
    Mixing ratio: 2:1 plaster to liquid

INGREDIENTS
    2 cups (441.6 g) plaster of Paris
    ½ cup (118.3 mL) liquid tempera
    ½ cup (118.3 mL) water

## MATERIALS AND TOOLS
3 cardboard tubes, each 3½" (8.9 cm) long
3 pieces of freezer paper, each 3½" × 6"
    (8.9 × 15.2 cm)
Respirator mask
Disposable gloves
Disposable container
Large spoon
Disposable plastic bag
Rubber band
Scissors
Skewer

**Step 1**
Prepare the paper tubes.

Roll up a freezer paper rectangle, shiny side in, and place it inside a cardboard tube. It will naturally unfurl and fit inside the tube. Use a strip of wide packing tape to close one end of each tube.

**Step 2**
Mix the plaster.

Put on the respirator mask and disposable gloves. Use a large spoon to carefully transfer

---

# smART ideas: Art Experiences

- Guide your child in an art activity by working on your own sheet of paper and using your own paintbrush, pencil, or marker to show how to make washes and lines of color. Don't worry if you think you cannot draw or paint, just begin.
- Work together on a story picture. Begin by drawing a shape or figure on one sheet of paper, telling your child some details about the drawing or the story you have in mind. Ask him to add to the story or drawing by adding his own details, taking turns until the story is complete.
- Have your child draw or paint a self-portrait using any coloring media. Scan the portrait and print copies to create postcards, greeting cards, and informal note cards. For a long-range activity, a child can do a self-portrait on each birthday. Display the portraits gallery-style or in an album, adding a new portrait every year.

Drawing by Nicholas Guider, age five

- Give a child a blank sketchbook for recording personal impressions of the world. Bring the sketchbook along on walks to the park or other outings for spontaneous drawing. Most drawing tools are light-weight, neat, and portable. Travel paint kits include a collapsible paintbrush and a water bottle.

the measured plaster of Paris to a disposable plastic bowl; work slowly, to avoid sending up plaster dust. Keeping your face away from the top of the bowl, slowly pour in the tempera and the water. Stir the mixture with a large spoon until it is smooth.

**Step 3**

Fill a plastic bag with colored plaster.

Use a large spoon to transfer the colored plaster into a plastic bag, pushing the mixture to a bottom corner of the bag. Twist the top of the bag shut and secure it with a rubber band.

**Step 4**

Fill each cardboard mold with plaster.

Line up the prepared chalk molds on a flat surface. Use scissors to snip off a corner of the plastic bag to make a ½"-diameter (1.3 cm) hole. As if using a pastry bag, gently squeeze the plaster mixture into one prepared tube, stopping halfway from the top. Repeat for the remaining tubes. Tap the bottom of each tube against a hard surface to settle the contents. Then fill up the tubes to their brims.

**Step 5**

Let the plaster cure.

Use a skewer to stir the plaster in each tube to break up any air pockets. Let the tubes stand upright until the plaster is hard. It will become warm as it hardens and cures. When the plaster is cool to the touch, peel off the cardboard tubes and the freezer paper. The pastels are ready to use.

Finger Painting

Finger painting by Charlotte Kulikowski, age four

Finger painting doesn't require innate art ability, just a willingness to get a bit messy. It is the quintessential beginning art experience that lets a child create textures in the paint, erase the impressions, and try again. The focus on process, rather than result, is especially appealing to young children, who can't wait to roll up their sleeves and give these techniques a try. Store-bought finger paint is used in these directions, but you can also mix up your own batch (see page 622).

**Activity: Making Textured Prints and Patterns with Finger Paint**

Ordinary objects can be pressed or swiped across wet finger paint to create unique and interesting patterns. Some objects to try include a craft stick, plastic fork, expired credit card, pencil with eraser tip, sponge, comb, jar lids, cardboard tubes, and string or cord.

Recommended age: 2+ years

Skill level: Easy

Supervision: High

Mess factor: High

## MATERIALS AND TOOLS

Finger paint

Finger painting paper with glossy
surface

Sponge roller, 2" (5.1 cm) wide
(for painting trim)

Assorted objects

## SETUP

Cut open a plastic trash bag and tape the
plastic to the work surface. Lay a sheet
of newsprint on top.

## Step 1

Coat the paper.

Use a sponge roller or your hand to apply
an even coat of finger paint over the sheet of
paper.

## Step 2

Add pattern.

Choose an object for making a design in
the wet finger paint. Here are some suggestions:

Comb—Run the teeth of the comb through
the finger paint, from the top to the bottom
edge of the paper, to make vertical lines
across the paper. Then run the comb from
left to right, crossing over the vertical lines,
to make a plaid pattern.

Plastic fork—Run the tines of the fork through
the finger paint, moving from left to right
in a wavy pattern to suggest river currents
or the bark of a tree. Do not push down so
hard as to rip the paper.

Plastic credit card—Rest one long edge of the
credit card on the coated paper. Hold the
opposite edge of the card at the middle.
Rotate the card partway to make a bow-tie
pattern. Do a complete rotation to make a
circular pattern.

New pencil with eraser tip—Press the eraser
tip straight down into the finger paint multiple times to make a polka dot pattern.

Sponge—Press the large flat side of a damp
sponge onto the finger paint and lift up. The
sponge will pick up paint, leaving behind a
cellular pattern.

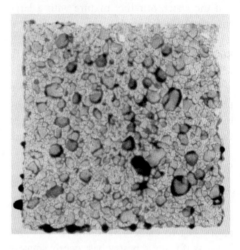

## Step 3

Make a new design.

Roll a sponge roller over the design to
smooth the paint so that you can begin again.
Make a new design on the same sheet of paper.
Set aside a finished design on a flat surface to
dry.

## Activity: Making Finger Paint

The appeal of making your own finger paint
is that you and a child can mix up a batch anytime in any color, quickly and inexpensively.
The finger paint formula that follows has a
thicker consistency than the store-bought
variety, making it easy for a child to create
designs with texture. Store homemade finger
paint in a sealed jar or plastic bag in the refrigerator. It will keep for 4 or 5 days.

Yield: ¾ cup (177.0 mL)

Recommended age: 3+ years

Skill level: Easy

Supervision: Careful, with some steps done
by an adult

Mess factor: Low

## INGREDIENTS

1 tablespoon (8 g) cornstarch

2 tablespoons (29.6 mL) + ½ cup (118.3 mL) cold water

¼ cup (59.1 mL) tempera, in desired color

1 tablespoon (14.8 mL) light corn syrup or white craft glue

## EQUIPMENT

Measuring cup

Measuring spoons

Stainless steel saucepan

Wire whisk

Plastic screw-top container or resealable plastic bag

### Step 1

Combine the water and cornstarch.

Stir the cornstarch and 6 teaspoons (29.6 mL) of cold water together in a measuring cup until the cornstarch is dissolved. Transfer the mixture to a saucepan and add ½ cup (118.3 mL) of water to the mixture. Stir until fully combined.

### Step 2**

Cook and cool the mixture.

Bring the mixture to a boil, stirring constantly with a whisk until it thickens to the consistency of pudding. Remove the pan from the heat and continue to whisk the mixture until it is smooth and cool.

### Step 3

Add paint and syrup or glue.

Add tempera to the mixture and stir it in. Add the light corn syrup or white craft glue and stir until fully blended.

### Step 4

Store the paint until ready to use.

Transfer the finger paint to a plastic container or resealable bag and close tightly. Store the mixture in a refrigerator and use within 4 to 5 days.

**Adult activity

## Monoprinting with Paint

A monoprint is a single print made by smoothing a sheet of paper over a painted surface while the paint is still wet. The paper picks up the wet paint in a reverse image. Only one truly clear print can be made from the printing surface, called the "plate"; any successive prints that are pulled will be lighter in color and have less definition. The same principle is used to pull soap bubble prints and one-of-a-kind marbled designs.

## Activity: Making a Monoprint with a Plastic Cutting Board and Acrylic Paint

This activity is recommended for older children. It uses acrylic craft paints, which dry fairly quickly to a permanent, waterproof finish. Younger children can produce monoprints with similar textural effects using finger paint or tempera paint, which remain wet for a longer period, and applying the paint through a squeeze bottle.

Recommended age: 6+ years

Skill level: Easy to intermediate

Supervision: Careful

Mess factor: Moderate to high

## MATERIALS AND TOOLS

Acrylic craft paint, in dispenser-tip containers, in desired colors

Bristol, cut to size of cutting board

Plastic cutting board

Scissors

Old newspapers

## SETUP

Lay the plastic cutting board on a protected work surface.

Layer newspapers near the work area.

Use scissors to cut the dispenser tip of the paint container to a ⅛" (0.3 cm) diameter.

Be prepared to wash the cutting board before the acrylic paint dries.

## Step 1

Draw the designs on the cutting board.

Gently squeeze the paint container and use the dispenser tip to draw a simple outline, such as a face, a flower, or a dog, on the surface of the cutting board. Use a second container in a different color to make another line drawing, keeping the lines at least 1" (2.5 cm) apart. The paint will flatten and spread during the printing, filling in the design.

## Step 2

Lay the bristol on the painted design.

Center the bristol over the wet paint. Press down a corner of the paper with one hand and use your other hand to gently smooth the paper against the painted surface. Be very careful not to shift the paper, which will cause a smudged design.

## Step 3

Remove the print from the cutting board.

Pick up two adjacent corners of the paper and carefully peel the paper off the board in one smooth motion. Lay the finished monoprint paint side up on newspaper. Allow the paint to dry completely.

## Activity: Making a Monoprint with Bubble Wrap

MATERIALS AND TOOLS
Acrylic craft paint
Bristol
2 plastic cutting boards
Bubble wrap
Cellophane or masking tape
Sponge roller

Lay a rectangle of bubble wrap on one cutting board, taping down the corners to keep it from shifting. Apply a blob of paint to the second cutting board and use the sponge roller to spread it into a thin coat. Use the loaded sponge roller to coat the surface of the bubble wrap with paint. Lay a sheet of bristol onto the painted sur-

face, smooth gently with your hands, and peel up the paper to reveal the transferred design.

## Activity: Making a Monoprint with Found Objects

MATERIALS AND TOOLS
Acrylic craft paint
Bristol
Plastic cutting board
Cotton swabs, expired credit card, new
    pencil with eraser tip
Sponge roller

Use a sponge roller to apply paint to the surface of the cutting board. Use a cotton swab, the edge of a credit card, the eraser end of a pencil, or your finger to draw a design in the paint. Lay a sheet of bristol onto the painted surface, smooth gently with your hands, and peel up the paper to reveal the transferred design.

## Activity: Making a Monoprint with Colored Soap Bubbles

Use a drinking straw to build a little "mountain" of colorful bubbles and transfer the design onto paper. Add as many bubble layers as you wish. Make a bubble mixture in a second color and print on the same paper for a two-toned picture.

Recommended age: 3+ years
Skill level: Easy
Supervision: Careful
Mess factor: Moderate

MATERIALS AND TOOLS
1 cup (236.6 mL) liquid dishwashing soap
¼ cup (59.1 mL) light corn syrup
½ cup (118.3 mL) tempera
Bristol
Measuring cup
2 bowls
Spoon
Plastic straw
Straight pin*

*For adult use only

Use a straight pin to make a tiny air hole in the straw, halfway from one end. The air hole should prevent a child from accidentally sucking in the soap mixture.

**Step 1**
Combine the ingredients.
Pour the soap and corn syrup into a bowl. Use a spoon to gently stir the mixture. Add the tempera and gently blend the ingredients together.

**Step 2**
Blow bubbles in the mixture.
Pour 1 cup (236.6 mL) of the mixture into a second bowl. Insert the prepared straw into the mixture. Blow through the straw until a tall mound of bubbles forms and rises above the rim of the bowl.

**Step 3**
Make a print.
Immediately lay a sheet of paper over the bubbles to make a print. Repeat steps 2 and 3 to add more printed patterns to the same paper. When you are satisfied with the print, set it aside on a flat surface to dry.

## Activity: Marbling in Two Colors

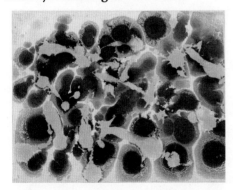

In this activity, paint is dropped onto a bath of thick gelatin and floats on the surface. Encourage a child to experiment with different paint combinations and the order in which the colors are added. A skewer or chopstick helps move the floating paint globules in different directions, to make completely new patterns. When the floating pattern is as desired, lay a sheet of paper on top to permanently capture it on the paper.

Recommended age: 7+ years
Skill level: High, with some steps done by an adult
Supervision: High
Mess factor: Moderate to high

### MATERIALS AND TOOLS
High-gloss acrylic enamel paint, in cherry red and light blue
Oxgall*
Cornstarch*
Alum*
Sheets of white paper
Disposable roasting pan, larger than the paper
Shallow soup bowl
Ladle
2 watercolor paintbrushes
Measuring cup*
Measuring spoon*
Large pot*
Large spoon*
Clean sponge
Pencil
Wooden skewer
Craft sticks
Disposable gloves*
2 disposable plastic cups
Scissors*
Masking tape
Freezer paper*
Plastic bag*
Newspapers
Paper towels
Heavy books*
*For adult use only

### SETUP
A few hours ahead:
Prepare the gelatin bath, or "size." Bring 3

quarts of water to a boil in a large pot. Combine 1 cup (236.6 mL) cold water and ½ cup (64 g) cornstarch in a disposable cup and add it to the hot water. Stir the solution with a large spoon. Let it stand for a few hours until warm.

Prepare the paper. Combine 2 tablespoons (27.6 g) alum and 2 cups (473.2 mL) warm water, stirring to dissolve. Use a clean sponge to apply the solution to one side of a sheet of paper (the side that will be marbled). Use a pencil to lightly mark an X on the opposite side of the paper (the side that will not be marbled). Prepare the remaining sheets of paper in the same way. Stack the papers, interleaving them with sheets of freezer paper cut to size with scissors. Place the papers inside a plastic bag and weight with books to keep the paper damp, for better color adherence.

Prepare the paint. Put on disposable gloves. Dilute one paint color by mixing equal parts of paint and water in a plastic cup, stirring with a craft stick until the mixture is smooth and the consistency of thin cream. Repeat to dilute and mix the second paint color. To increase the dispersion, add 8 drops of oxgall for every 2 teaspoons (9.9 mL) of diluted paint. Use a ladle to transfer some size to a shallow bowl. Test a drop of the solution on a corner of the size: If the drop of paint does not spread, add another drop of oxgall and test it again. If the drop of paint spreads too much, add more diluted paint.

### Step 1

Prepare the work surface.

Lay newspaper over the work surface. Tape extra sheets of paper to nearby walls and place some on the floor, to protect the surfaces from getting spattered with paint.

### Step 2**

Prepare the gelatin bath.

Set roasting pan on the protected work surface. Pour the cornstarch solution into the pan.

**Adult activity

### Step 3

Spatter drops of paint onto the gelatin bath (size).

Dip a paintbrush into one of the containers of thinned paint. Hold the paintbrush by the end of the handle over the surface of the gelatin bath. Gently tap the handle of the brush against your wrist to spatter a random pattern of paint droplets over the surface of the bath. Use a clean paintbrush to spatter drops of the second paint color, aiming at areas of the bath with no drops of paint.

### Step 4

Manipulate the paint spatters.

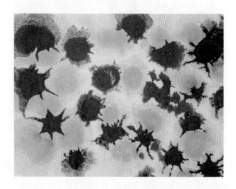

Spidery shapes can be created by treating each paint drop separately. Place the end of a wooden skewer into the center of one drop of red paint and move the skewer through the edge of the drop to make an "arm." Continue to make four to eight "arms" in a radial pattern. Do not stir the paint as the color may turn muddy.

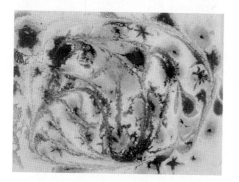

A swirling pattern can be created by cutting through all of the paint drops. Place the end of a wooden skewer into one end of the vat of floating paint drops and move the skewer from side to side in a continuous pattern of loops without lifting the skewer until you have worked from the top of the floating paint to the bottom. Do not stir the paint as the color may turn muddy.

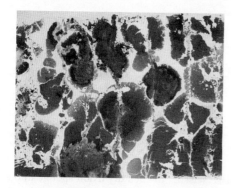

A broken stone pattern can be created by cutting through the surface that surrounds each drop of paint. Use a wooden skewer to cut through the second color (or the size), moving the skewer vertically in straight lines from top to bottom to disturb the perimeter of the paint drops. Do not stir the paint as the color may turn muddy.

**Step 5**

Print the paper.

Remove one sheet of paper from the plastic bag. Hold the paper at opposite corners over the gelatin bath, with the X facing up. Lower the center of the paper onto the surface and then roll each corner of the paper onto the bath's surface in a continuous motion, making certain that no air bubbles get trapped between the bath and the paper. Air bubbles will create an unprinted section on the paper. Gently pat the paper against the size. After 2 or 3 seconds, lift up the paper by opposite corners in a reverse rolling motion. Lay the marbled paper face up on newspaper and allow the paint to dry.

**Step 6**

Print more paper.

To reuse the size for another print, skim off the paint residue from the size, using torn strips of newspaper. Then repeat steps 3–5 to marble another sheet of paper. To keep the paper moist, remove one sheet at a time and reseal and weight the bag.

**Step 7**

Press the prints flat.

When the marbled papers are completely

dry, sandwich each one between two sheets of freezer paper, stack the papers, and set heavy books on top to flatten them.

### Block Printing with Paint

Kids of any age who have worked with rubber stamps or made prints of their own hands will have no trouble understanding the principle of block printing. Printing with a block allows you to transfer the shape or design of the block, which is coated with paint, to a piece of paper or fabric time after time. In the child-friendly techniques presented here, cut fruits and vegetables are substituted for the more traditional blocks made of linoleum and soft carve, allowing even very young children to take part and reproduce textural motifs with ease. (More easy printing techniques suitable for children are in Chapter Four.)

There are two ways to apply paint to the surface of the printing block. Either the face of the block is pressed onto a thin layer of paint or a sponge roller or brayer is rolled over the face of the block to deposit a thin layer of paint. The paint-coated block is then pressed onto a sheet of paper, printing a mirror image of the painted areas that touch the paper.

Pressing a painted block onto a piece of paper makes a positive print. For a negative print, a clean block is pressed onto a wet painted surface to lift off some paint in the shape of the block.

### Activity: Making a Print with a Fresh Lemon

Using a cut piece of citrus fruit as a printing block will produce a replica of the fruit's cellular pattern. For a print with soft definition, cut a lemon in half and let a child print with it right away. The juice from the lemon will cause the paint to spread a little. For a print with stronger, cleaner lines, blot the cut surface with a paper towel or allow the lemon to dry out for a few days before printing with it. The fruit pulp will pull slightly away from the fibrous sections as it dries, resulting in a print with clear lines and definition.

Recommended age: 2+ years
Skill level: Easy
Supervision: Careful
Mess factor: Low to moderate

### MATERIALS AND TOOLS
Fresh lemon
Tempera
Bristol, freezer paper, or drawing paper
Waterproof paper plate
Paper towels
Knife*
Cutting board*
Paintbrush
*For adult use only

### SETUP
Lay the printing paper on a flat, protected work surface. If using freezer paper, place it glossy side up. Lay a piece of paper towel next to the paper.

---

## smART ideas: Making a Printing Block with a Kitchen Sponge

Use scissors to cut a dry nylon sponge into a simple shape, such as a square or diamond. Glue the sponge shape to a little box, a jar lid, or a piece of chipboard that is slightly larger than the shape. Make a handle for the block by pressing a ball of poster putty or hot-gluing an empty spool of thread onto the other side of the box, lid, or chipboard.

---

Cut the lemon in half using a knife and a cutting board.

Pour a small pool of paint onto the surface of a paper plate. Use a paintbrush to spread the paint into a thin, even layer.

**Step 1**

Load the paint.

Press the cut, flat side of lemon into the paint.

**Step 2**

Make the print.

Position the lemon, painted side down, onto the paper. Press and lift up to make a print.

**Step 3**

Make more prints.

Blot the cut surface of the lemon on a paper towel. Press it onto the paint in the paper plate and make a second print on the paper. Repeat as many times as desired. Lay the paper flat to dry.

## Activity: Making a Two-Tone Apple Print

More than one color can be applied to different parts of the same surface of a printing block. After you cut an apple in half, use a brush to pat a thin layer of paint in two different colors onto the flat side of the apple. For example, apply yellow paint to the center of the apple (avoiding the core) and apply red paint to the remaining surface, stopping at the apple peel. When the painted apple is pressed on to the paper, it will leave a two-tone print with blended color, giving the print added dimension.

MATERIALS AND TOOLS

Fresh apple

Acrylic craft paint or fabric paint, in two colors

Paper or smooth fabric

Foam brushes

Paper plate

Paper towel

Knife*

Cutting board*

*For adult use only

Cut an apple in half, through the core. Blot the cut surface of one piece with a paper towel. Use a foam brush to apply paint to half of the cut surface. Use a clean foam brush to apply a different color paint to the other half of the cut surface. Keep the brush horizontal to prevent paint from filling the seed cavity. Press the painted surface onto paper or fabric to make a two-tone print.

## Activity: Making a Print with a Carved Potato

Potato printing is a classic arts and crafts activity that has remained popular for children of all ages. Potato prints most closely resemble traditional block prints in appearance. A young child can use a fork to scratch random patterns into the cut surface of a potato. The older child can carve simple shapes with a plastic knife. Areas that are not carved away will stand higher, and it is these high areas that will print.

Recommended age: 6+ years

Skill level: Intermediate

Supervision: Moderate

Mess factor: Low to moderate

## MATERIALS AND TOOLS

Fresh potato
Tempera or acrylic craft paint
Bristol, freezer paper, or drawing paper
Waterproof paper plate
Plastic knife
Plastic fork
Paper towels
Scrap of paper
Pencil
Skewer
Scissors
Knife*
Cutting board*
Paintbrush

*For adult use only

## SETUP

Lay the printing paper on a flat, protected work surface. If using freezer paper, place it glossy side up. Lay a piece of paper towel next to the paper.

Use a knife and a cutting board to cut the potato in half, exposing the broadest cut surface as possible.

**Step 1**

Draw a pattern.

Use pencil and paper to draw a simple shape, such as a triangle or square, in a size that fits on the cut surface of the potato. Use scissors to cut out the shape.

---

## smART ideas: Printing with Disposable Foam Plates and Trays

Make a negative print using foam plates and trays. Use a ball-point pen to draw on the surface, pressing firmly to create an indentation. Apply paint with a foam roller, being careful not to get paint into the recessed areas. Lay a sheet of paper over the painted surface and smooth with your hands to make a print. Hang the print or lay it flat to dry.

---

## The Gift Within

Drawing by Emily Centino, age four

Every child has a rich and active imagination that can be nurtured and enlarged through arts and crafts activities. Albert Einstein once said that "Imagination is more important than knowledge." Encourage your child to use his imagination; it will be a resource that increases the quality and meaning of life.

### Step 2

Mark the pattern on the potato.

Lay the paper cutout on the flat cut surface of the potato. Use a pencil to trace around the shape, pressing firmly to make a dented line.

### Step 3

Cut the potato.

Use a plastic knife to cut or scrape away the flat part of the potato that is outside the marked line. Cut to a depth of ¼" (0.6 cm) below the flat surface. Blot the potato on a paper towel to remove moisture. Use a skewer or a plastic fork to poke holes or scratch lines in a random pattern on the remaining flat surface.

### Step 4

Prepare the paint.

Pour a small pool of paint onto the surface of a paper plate. Use a paintbrush to spread the paint into a thin, even layer.

### Step 5

Make a print.

Blot the potato on a paper towel to remove any moisture. Press the cut, flat side of the potato into the paint. Position the potato, paint side down, onto the paper. Press and lift up to make a print. To print again, blot the face of the potato on a damp paper towel and reload with fresh paint. Repeat as many times as desired. Lay the paper flat to dry.

## Working with Clay

Children of all ages love working with clay because it is so responsive to handling. As long as the clay is soft enough to work and resilient enough to hold a shape or pattern, children are rewarded for making the slightest pinch or the most careful tooling. The youngest child will enjoy the simple tactile experience of working with clay and will be extremely satisfied to pound a lump of clay with his fists or squeeze it through his fingers.

As children begin to understand that they can make things from clay, they can engage their hands and imaginations to shape simple figures, pots, and other small structures. If they don't like what they have shaped, they can collapse it and start again. With more experience, children will seek simple tools to help them add texture and details to their creations. The tools can be as elementary as a craft stick, a pencil, or a butter knife or as sophisticated as professional sculpting tools like a modeling knife, a double-ended dental tool, and a wire-loop sculpting tool.

Clay is easy and inexpensive to make in small batches at home. Of the commercial clays found in craft and hobby stores, two types are suitable for use by children: air-dry and heat-set. Each type has its own distinct properties, which in turn affect the working qualities of the clay in its raw state and the characteristics of the project when it is finished. Properties to consider when choosing clay are malleability, quality and ease of hand modeling or pressing into a mold, drying or curing methods, available colors, and finishing options. Significant differences between the types have to do with the hand of the raw clay—basically, how it feels in the hands and how it responds to touch. Is it easy or difficult to impress details into its surface? Is it easy to shape and does the shape hold? Air-dry clays made from cellulose are not as suited to embossing fine details; the clay tends to shrink when completely dried, whereas heat-set polymer clay keeps its size and shape and retains even small details debossed into its surface. The deciding factor may well be the age of the child. Younger children, who are still developing dexterity, prefer clays that are soft and easy to work. Older children have the hand strength to manipulate heat-set clay and the patience and dexterity to use sculpting tools. Their priorities run to color options and clay that allows them to sculpt shapes and fine details.

Homemade Clay

Early clay modeling experiences do not have to involve store-bought clay of any kind. Instead, you can make moldable nontoxic clay using ingredients from your pantry. Clays made from salt and flour or white bread are easy to mix, and children can help. Clays that require cooking on the stove will, of course, require a grown-up's supervision. Homemade clay concoctions have a limited shelf life, but they provide good experiences that prepare a child for working with commercial air-dry and oven-set clays.

### Activity: Making Cooked Play Clay from Cornstarch and Salt

A child can help mix the ingredients for this clay, but an adult should do the cooking at the stove. Older children can participate in the cooking with continuous supervision and at your discretion. Keep a batch of this homemade clay in the refrigerator (it will keep for about 2 weeks) and pull out small amounts when your child wants to work with clay. Molded pieces that are fully dry can be sealed with an acrylic sealer and painted with acrylic craft paint.

INGREDIENTS
1 cup (128 g) cornstarch
2 cups (576.0 g) salt
½ cup (118.3 mL) water
4 or 5 drops liquid food coloring

EQUIPMENT
Saucepan
Bowl
Wooden spoon
Dishcloth
Reclosable plastic bag

SETUP
None

Step 1
Mix the dry ingredients.
Place the cornstarch and salt in a saucepan and stir them together with a wooden spoon.

Step 2
Add the water and food coloring.
Add the water slowly and stir until mixed. Add the food coloring or cake-decorating gel and stir until the color is fully blended.

## Working Tips: Cornstarch-and-Salt Clay Drying Time

Pieces molded from cornstarch-and-salt clay will air-dry in 1 to 3 days, depending upon their thickness and the ambient temperature and humidity. To accelerate the drying time, small or thin shapes may be placed on a baking sheet in a 200°F (93.3°C) oven for approximately 2 hours.

## smART ideas: Making Your Own Sealer

To make homemade sealer for air-dried clay creations, mix 3 parts white craft glue and 1 part water to a consistency of thin cream. Use a brush to apply several coats of the mixture to seal the clay, allowing the glue to dry between coats.

**Step 3**

Cook the mixture.

Cook the mixture over medium heat, stirring continuously until it is the consistency of thick mashed potatoes.

**Step 4**

Let the clay cool.

Transfer the cooked clay to a bowl. Lay a clean, damp dishcloth over the bowl to keep the clay moist. If not using the clay, store it in an airtight plastic bag or container in the refrigerator for up to 2 weeks.

## Activity: Making Uncooked Play Clay from Flour and Salt

Because no cooking is involved, kids can help make this clay.

Recommended age: 2+ years
Skill level: Easy
Supervision: Careful
Mess factor: Moderate to high

INGREDIENTS

1 cup (128.0 g) flour, plus more for
  kneading
1 cup (288.0 g) salt
1½ cups (354.9 mL) water
1 teaspoon (4.9 mL) vegetable oil
Food coloring

EQUIPMENT

Reclosable plastic bags
Wooden spoon
Bowl
Plastic place mat

SETUP

Lay a plastic place mat on the work surface.

**Step 1**

Mix the dry ingredients.

Place the flour and salt in a bowl and stir them together with a wooden spoon.

**Step 2**

Add the water and the oil.

Slowly add the water, ¼ cup (59.1 mL) at a time, to the dry ingredients, and mix until well combined. Continue mixing in water until the clay is the consistency of thick mashed potatoes. Add the oil and mix until the clay is smooth and blended.

**Step 3**

Divide and knead the clay.

Transfer the mixture to a plastic place mat. Begin kneading the clay. If the clay feels gummy and wet, add more flour and knead it in. If the clay feels dry and crumbly, knead in a few drops of water at a time. Continue working the clay until the consistency is firm yet pliable.

**Step 4**

Tint the clay.

Divide the clay into four roughly equal portions. Flatten each portion, using your fingers to make a shallow trough in the middle of the clay. Add a few drops of food coloring in one color to one trough and fold the sides of the clay over and into the center. Knead the clay, which may stain hands, until the color is blended throughout the clay. Repeat to add a different color to each remaining portion. Store each clay portion in its own plastic bag.

## Activity: Making Play Clay from White Bread and Glue

The sheer convenience of this little concoction is perfect for spontaneous clay projects. The white bread makes fine-grained clay that works up to a smooth finish.

Recommended age: 3+ years
Skill level: Easy to intermediate
Supervision: Careful
Mess factor: Moderate

INGREDIENTS

2 or 3 slices of white bread
1 to 1¼ teaspoons (4.9 to 6.2 mL) white
  craft glue

EQUIPMENT
Measuring spoons
Mixing bowl

SETUP
None

**Step 1**
Tear the bread.
Tear the crusts off of each piece of bread (discard the crusts or keep them for stuffing). Tear the bread into tiny pieces.

**Step 2**
Combine the bread and glue.
Put half of the torn bread into a bowl. Add the smaller amount of white craft glue. Use your fingers to knead the bread and glue together to make a clay.

**Step 3**
Continue kneading.
Add more torn bread bits, kneading the clay until it is smooth and shiny and you can make a small neat ball. If the clay is too dry, add the remaining ¼ teaspoon (1.2 mL) of glue and knead the clay with your fingers until it is pliable. If the clay is too wet, add bits of dry bread.

**Step 4**
Store the clay.
Store the clay in its own reclosable plastic bag and place it into the refrigerator. Use it within a week.

Air-Dry Clays

As its name implies, air-dry clays harden as the moisture in them evaporates. The clay ranges from white to gray in color with some brands being heavy and dense in their moistened state and others being light and fluffy. I recommend trying many different brands so that a child can experience the special properties of each.

Always read the package directions and notes. Some brands are malleable straight out of the package and are comfortable for small hands to manipulate. Some clays are formulated for larger items that do not require sharp detailing, and some are better suited for projects with fine detail, textures, lines, and impressions made by rubber stamps, needle tools, or other delicate instruments. Clay made from cellulose fiber must be mixed with water before it is worked. This small inconvenience aside, the clay itself is pulpy, soft, and mushy, qualities that young children enjoy. Finely ground particles suspended in the clay allow for the capture of simple impressions and shaping by hand.

Air-dry clay should be stored in an airtight plastic bag to remain malleable for a longer period, but even then it will slowly harden. The hardened surface is porous and absorbent even after hardening. Cellulose clay can be rough and bumpy to the touch, but other types can be smoothed with a moist finger, making it easy to touch up dents, wrinkles, or fingerprints. All types require sealing with an acrylic sealer before paint can be applied.

**Activity: Making a Slab Sculpture with Air-Dry Clay**

This easy construction technique uses a rolling pin to flatten a blob of air-dry clay into a thick slab. The secret to achieving a uniform thickness is same-size wood sticks, which are placed on either side of the clay to support the rolling pin as the clay as it is rolled out.

Choose the thickness of the sticks according to how thick you want the slab to be. Once the slab is rolled out, shapes or figures can be cut from it freehand or by tracing around a pattern that is laid on top of the clay. After the clay dries, fun details can be glued on to give the shape texture and character. Children can use this technique to create a menagerie of zoo animals with wheels made from empty thread spools.

Recommended age: 6+ years
Skill level: Intermediate
Supervision: Moderate
Mess factor: Low

## MATERIALS AND TOOLS

Dinosaur pattern (page 714)
Butterfly original art (page 694)
Air-dry clay (in vacuum-sealed package)
2 wooden spools
Acrylic sealer
Acrylic craft paint in turquoise blue, or as desired
20 small yellow pom-poms
4 paper flowers, same diameter as end of spool
2 wiggly eyes
Colored pencils
White craft glue
Low-temperature glue gun and glue sticks
Plastic cutting board
Rolling pin
Two rulers or strips of wood ¼" thick
Pointed skewer or plastic knife
Cotton swab
Foam brush

## SETUP

Enlarge the dinosaur pattern and cut it out with scissors. Make two copies of the butterfly original art.

## Step 1

Roll out the clay.
Remove the clay from the sealed pack-age. Flatten the clay into a pancake shape and lay it on a protected work surface. Place one flat stick on each side of the pancake. Lean a rolling pin on the flat sticks, one on each side of the roller, and roll the clay flat, moving the sticks as the clay pancake gets larger with rolling.

## Step 2

Cut out the dinosaur.

Center the dinosaur pattern on the flattened clay. Use a pointed stick or knife and follow the edges of the pattern to cut the dinosaur shape in the clay. Lift away the clay that surrounds the dinosaur, using the point of the skewer to cut through any clay that remains attached. Leave the dinosaur lying flat.

## Step 3

Let the clay dry and apply the sealer.
Peel the pattern off the clay dinosaur. Use a wet finger to smooth any flaws. Use a wet cotton swab to smooth any rough edges, especially around the feet. Place a flat cutting board over the dinosaur to keep the clay from warping. Let the clay air-dry for 48 hours. Use a foam brush to apply sealer to both sides of the clay. Let the sealer dry.

## Step 4

Attach the spools and apply the paint.
Use a low-temperature glue gun to attach the dinosaur's feet to the spools, centering one spool under each foot. Use a foam brush to apply a thin even coat of paint to the dinosaur and the spools; let the paint dry. Glue a

paper flower to each side of the spools, adding a pom-pom to the centers.

**Step 5**

Add the pom-poms and wiggly eyes.

Use white craft glue to secure one pom-pom to each point in the dinosaur's back. Use a low-temperature glue gun to attach a wiggly eye to each side of the dinosaur's head.

**Step 6**

Add the paper butterfly.

Use colored pencils to color in the butterflies. Cut out the butterflies and glue them together, back to back. Glue the butterfly to the dinosaur's tail.

Heat-Set Clays

Heat-set clays, or polymer clays, can be hardened by exposure to low heat, under 300°F (148.9°C) in a home oven. This type of clay is made of plastic and a softening agent and comes in an exciting palette of mixable colors—rich and vibrant primary colors, soft and powdery pastels, glow-in-the-dark pigments, and pearlescent and metallic textures. If the base color of the clay isn't to your liking, you can paint over it with acrylic craft paint or you can blend two colors to make a third color. The ease with which polymer clay can be shaped is important for projects that require fine detail. The clay holds its overall shape, and details can be etched, carved, or impressed into the surface with clay sculpting tools or implements borrowed from sewing and cooking. If a child feels his or her work isn't ready for final baking, not to worry: polymer clay won't dry out, even if left uncovered, and it can be reused in another project.

Polymer clay does require conditioning, or kneading, to make it pliable and workable. The kneading time can be anywhere from 2 to 20 minutes, depending on the brand and temperature of the clay and the hand strength

used to knead it. Some polymer clays are easy to condition but have a tendency to become too soft after a lot of manipulation. Others crumble when you begin to condition them but soften up with prolonged exposure to the warmth of your hands. Of course, an adult can always knead polymer clay and present a young child with a workable lump. One type of polymer clay remains flexible after it is cured, allowing children to make figures with limbs that bend and move. For super easy conditioning, a pasta machine can be a big help, creating sheets of uniform thickness and blending different colors of clay into patterned sheets.

**Activity: Making a Dimensional Sculpture with Heat-Set Clay**

Mixed-media doll by
Genevieve A. Sterbenz, age twelve

Heat-set or oven-baked clays are fun to work with; with practice, an older child will find its properties easy to exploit, especially its plasticity, to sculpt small details. Here, Rosie the Riveter, an American icon who represented women who worked in factories during World War II, is depicted in a doll made from clay and fabric scraps. The clay head is defined by a few simple features—a nose, a mouth, and a pair of welding goggles—making Rosie a good first project for a child with dexterity. The clay head is attached to the top of a wire armature that is wrapped with aluminum foil to give the body dimension. Clothes are fashioned from scraps of fabric.

Age group: 10+ years
Skill level: Intermediate to advanced
Supervision: Moderate
Mess factor: Low

## MATERIALS AND TOOLS

Two 2-ounce (56 g) packages of heat-set
    polymer clay, in skin tone
Small bale of aluminum wire, 12-gauge
Wire cutters
Aluminum foil
Acrylic craft paint, in black
Fabric scraps: blue denim and red cotton
Baking sheet
Oven mitts
Scissors
Paintbrush
Home oven

## SETUP
None

## Step 1
Condition the clay.
Knead the clay until it is soft and smooth.

## Step 2
Make an armature from wire and foil.
Unwind a 12" (30.5 cm) length of wire from the bale; do not cut the wire. Use your hands to bend the length into a stick figure. When the figure is shaped, use wire cutters to cut the wire from the bale. Wrap the armature with pieces of aluminum foil to shape a head, a torso, legs, and arms.

## Step 3
Make a head and neck, hands, and shoes from clay.

For the head and a neck, wrap a thick strip of soft clay around the foil-covered wire at the top of the armature. Add a nose and mouth and any other facial features desired. Add accessories such as welding goggles. For the hands and shoes, wrap short strips of soft clay around the ends of the foil-covered arms and legs on the wire armature.

## Step 4
Bake the clay doll.
Lay the figure on a baking sheet. Set the oven between 265°F and 275°F (129.4°C and 135°C) according to the package directions. Bake 15 minutes for every ¼" (0.6 cm) thickness of the clay.

## Step 5
Dress the doll.
Remove the figure from the oven and allow it to cool. Use scraps of fabric to fashion a pair of pants, a shirt, and a pair of gloves in blue denim and secure them to the figure with hot glue. Cut a triangle of red fabric for a babushka and tie it to the doll's head.

## Step 6
Paint the goggles and any other details.
Use a tapered paintbrush and black paint to paint the goggles. Let the paint dry.

## Working with Glitter

Glitter nearly instantly transforms ordinary objects, from a plain sheet of cardboard to an old pair of kid's shoes, into fantasy items that sparkle and shimmer. Made of tiny particles, some microns thin, glitter is available in several materials, the most popular being glass and polyester. Children should use the polyester glitter as it is safer to handle. (Glass glitter is geared to adult projects and is often chosen when a vintage look is desired.)

Plastic glitter is available in a wide range of grades, shapes, colors, and textures. Microfine glitter is only 50 microns thin and resembles and behaves like powder. Coarse glitter looks like large granular sugar. Shapes include squares, circles, hexagons, and rectangles. Colors range from bright primaries to pastels to jewel tones; there are gradient colors that move from light to dark. Glitter can be clear, iridescent, holographic, or phosphorescent. A key characteristic of all glitters is the way they sparkle. Glitter is highly reflective. A coarse grade is the best choice for children to use.

Glitter can be applied in many ways to make sparkling things. It can be sprinkled liberally over wet glue or paint or stuck to one side of double-sided tape that is applied to a surface. The glue can be applied over the entire surface of a three-dimensional object or through the cutout in a stencil. Glitter in several colors can be laid side by side on a surface (wait until the glue for one color is set before beginning an application of a new color). Different colors of glitter can be mixed together to make a new hue or lighter and darker versions of the same hue, an activity older children like to perform; the finer the glitter, the more successful this type of color blending will be. Glitter can be mixed into white craft glue, which will show as sparkling flecks when the glue dries.

The way in which the glue is applied affects the crafting outcome. A foam brush gives fast, efficient coverage of large areas. If the glue is unevenly applied, a bare patch can result.

Wait until the glue is completely dry and then apply a light coat of glue over the bare area and sprinkle it with glitter. A patched area may look bumpy and uneven. A narrow bristle brush is useful for small areas and to add detail. A coat of glue does not have to be heavy to attach light-weight particles of glitter. White craft glue, applied too heavily, is prone to sagging and forming drips on three-dimensional objects; you may actually prefer high-tack glue for these types of surfaces. Glue can also be dispensed from the tip of a small plastic squeeze bottle, giving children the opportunity to write their names or other messages in glue and follow up with a liberal application of glitter.

Once the glue is applied, glitter is sprinkled directly from the vial or from a spoon over the wet surface. The object is held over a wide shallow dish or bowl that both holds the supply of glitter and catches the excess glitter as it falls. To apply glitter to larger items, cover the work surface with a sheet of scrap paper to catch the overflow. When the project is finished, the paper can be picked up and rolled into a cone to funnel the excess glitter back into the dish or its original container. Glitter goes a long way, so it is worth it to recapture and use the excess.

# Working Tips: How to Prevent Glitter from Falling Off a Glittered Surface

To help glitter stay attached to a project, apply a coat of acrylic varnish to all the glittered surfaces. Choose a gloss finish to maintain the sparkling patina. Let the varnish dry completely before handling the project.

Particles of glitter are sometimes sharp, so keep the containers and utensils used for glitter activities separate from those you use for food preparation. A child's craft kit can contain sturdy paper plates and an old stainless steel or a disposable plastic spoon for glitter work. Cleaning up after a glitter project can be tedious. A light coating of coarse glitter remaining on the work surface can be wiped up with a moist paper towel. However, because glitter particles are so tiny, it is likely that you will continue to find them long after a project or activity session is finished. Glitter also tends to flake off projects over time, as sometimes only a scant edge of the particle is actually adhered.

## Glitter Activities

The glitter activities that follow are suitable for young children with supervision and for older school-age children with some adult oversight. To prepare the work area, put each color of glitter in a wide, shallow dish and provide teaspoons for sprinkling. Provide glue in separate dishes.

## Quick & Easy Activity: Making Glitter String

### MATERIALS AND TOOLS
Glitter, in any color
Long string
White craft glue
Wax paper

Dip a long string into the white craft glue. Use your fingers to smooth the coat of glue along the full length of the string. Hold the coated string at opposite ends and lower it into the glitter, running its entire length through the glitter. Lay the glitter string on a sheet of wax paper and let dry overnight. Use the string to accent a wrapped gift box or to suspend a paper mobile.

## Quick & Easy Activity: Making Glitter Ornaments

### MATERIALS AND TOOLS
Glitter, in any color
Christmas ball ornament, in any color
Double-sided tape
Tapered paintbrush

Wrap a length of double-sided tape around the equator of a ball ornament, overlapping the ends. Press the tape against the ornament to ensure good adhesion. Apply more pieces of tape, as desired, to create a striped, checkerboard, or plaid pattern. Roll the ornament in glitter to coat the bands of tape. Use a dry tapered paintbrush to remove any excess glitter at the edges of the tape.

## Quick & Easy Activity: Stenciling with Glitter

### MATERIALS AND TOOLS
Stencil
Glitter, in any color
Cardstock
High-tack glue
Stencil brush
Teaspoon
Tape

Lay a sheet of cardstock on a protected flat surface. Center a stencil over the cardstock and tape down the corners to prevent shifting. Use a stencil brush to apply high-tack glue to the cutout areas of the stencil, being careful not to get glue underneath the edges of the stencil. Use a teaspoon to pour glitter over the cutout areas. Let dry for 10 minutes, just enough to set the glitter, but not so long that the layer of glitter lifts up when the stencil is removed. Carefully remove the tape and lift up the stencil. Hold the stencil over a sheet of scrap paper and tap the excess glitter off the stencil; return the glitter to the container. If necessary, use a soft cloth to wipe off any excess from the stencil. Let the glue dry completely before handling the cardstock.

## Quick & Easy Activity: Coating Animal Figurines with Glitter

### MATERIALS AND TOOLS

Small figurine, plastic or papier-mâché,
 of a bird, fish, or zoo animal
Glitter, in assorted colors
High-tack glue
Tapered watercolor brush
Teaspoon

Choose glitter colors for the figurine that are realistic or fanciful (think lavender giraffe!). Use a tapered watercolor brush to apply glue to one section of the figurine. Hold the figurine over the dish with the appropriate color glitter and use a teaspoon to sprinkle glitter over the wet glue area. Tap off the excess glitter back into the dish. Continue to apply glue and different colors of glitter in sections, allowing some blending where the sections touch. Let the glue dry completely.

## Quick & Easy Activity: Making Butterflies with Glittery Wings

### MATERIALS AND TOOLS

Butterfly print (page 696)
Glitter
Adhesive-backed vinyl
String
Markers or paint
White craft glue
Scissors
Tapered brush
Teaspoon

Use a laser photocopier to make two copies of the butterfly print. Apply each print, image side up, to the sticky side of a sheet of adhesive-backed vinyl, pressing and smoothing the paper flat with your hands. Cut out each butterfly with scissors. Use markers or paint to color in the butterflies; allow the paint to dry. Use a tapered brush to apply glue to the wing design of each butterfly. Use a spoon to sprinkle glitter over the wings. Shake off the excess glitter back into the dish. Let the glue dry completely. Glue the butterflies back to back, sandwiching a hanging string between them.

## Quick & Easy Activity: Making Glittery Petals and Wings

### MATERIALS AND TOOLS

Silk flower
Artificial bird, with flocking and feathers
Glitter, clear or in colors to match flower
 and bird
High-tack glue
Tapered watercolor brush
Teaspoon

Artificial flowers and birds are sold as party favors or package decorations. Use a tapered watercolor brush to apply glue to the edges of the flower petals. Hold the flower over the dish of glitter and use a teaspoon to sprinkle a dusting of glitter over the wet glue areas. Shake off the excess glitter back into the dish. Then apply glue to the wings and tail of the bird, followed by a dusting of glitter. Let the glue dry completely.

## Quick & Easy Activity: Making a Two-Tone Glitter Fish

### MATERIALS AND TOOLS

Glitter, in two colors
Flexible plastic fish, about 3½" (8.9 cm)
 long
High-tack glue
Teaspoon
Tapered paintbrush

Use a tapered paintbrush to apply a light coat of glue to both sides of a flexible plastic fish. Hold the fish over a dish of glitter and use a teaspoon to sprinkle glitter over the wet glue area.

Tap off the excess glitter back into the dish. Set the fish on wax paper and let dry. Use a tapered paintbrush to apply a thin, wavy line along the full length of the body on both sides of the fish. Sprinkle on a different color glitter and tap off the excess. Let the glue dry completely.

## Quick & Easy Activity: Glitter Animals with Patterns

### MATERIALS AND TOOLS

Glitter, in assorted colors
Medium-weight paper
Acrylic craft paint, in assorted colors
Pencil
White craft glue
Tapered paintbrush
Teaspoon

Draw a picture of a zoo animal on a sheet of medium-weight paper. Use acrylic craft paints and a tapered paintbrush to color in the animal; let the paint dry. Use a tapered paintbrush and glue to "paint" polka dots or other simple patterns that mimic the natural markings of the animal, such as stripes for a zebra. Use a teaspoon to sprinkle glitter onto the wet glue areas. Let the glue dry completely. Tap off the excess glitter.

## Quick & Easy Activity: Making Glitter Snowflakes

### MATERIALS AND TOOLS

Chenille stems
Glitter, in silver
White craft glue
Tapered paintbrush
Scissors
Wide, shallow dish
Small dish
Spoon
Wax paper

Twist chenille stems together to make snowflakes. Cut shorter lengths of stems with scissors and twist them onto the main piece to simulate snow crystals. Pour glitter into a wide, shallow dish. Pour white craft glue into a small dish. Use a tapered paintbrush to apply a coat of white craft glue to the chenille snowflake. Hold the snowflake over the dish of glitter and use a spoon to sprinkle glitter over the wet glue areas. Tap off the excess. Set the snowflake on a sheet of wax paper to dry.

While a child is busy working with glitter, you may be inspired to create a glitter project of your own.

## Fun for Mom: Glitter Stars for a Christmas Tree

You can top your family's Christmas tree with a large two-part star that glitters with lustrous color. The secret to its intricate shape is simple: the smaller star is cut out of the center of the larger star, and both stars are decorated with different colors of glitter. The stars are rotated and glued together to show off the many pointed arms. The tips of the large star are accented with filigree beads.

## MATERIALS AND TOOLS
Glitter Stars pattern (page 715)
White mat board, two 16" (40.6 cm)
    squares
8 filigree balls, each 18 mm
Glitter, in ice blue and silver, or as desired
Acrylic varnish, gloss finish
8 extra-long straight pins
Steel wire, 18-gauge
Pliers
High-tack tape
5-minute epoxy

White craft glue
Contact cement
Tracing paper
Steel ruler
Craft knife
Self-healing cutting mat
Paintbrush
Wire cutters
Broom handle
Plastic lid
Toothpicks

**Step 1**
Cut out the stars.
Lay one square of mat board on a self-healing cutting mat, taping the edges to the cutting mat to prevent the piece from shifting. Lay the second square of mat board on top of the mat board, all edges even, and tape down the corners to the cutting mat. Tape the Glitter Stars

## smART ideas: Making Your Own Glitter

Kids will love making their own sparkling glitter using salt and food coloring. An adult should do the steps involving a hot oven and baking sheet. Do note that as attractive as granulated sugar looks, it will not work for this process. Even though sugar can be tinted, it will melt and caramelize under high heat.

- Combine 4 tablespoons (72.0 g) salt and 4 drops of food coloring in a bowl, using the back of a soup spoon to mash and blend the color into the

salt. When the color is distributed thoroughly and there are no colored blobs of salt remaining, spread the tinted salt on a baking sheet lined with aluminum foil.

- Bake in a preheated 350°F (176.7°C) oven for 15 minutes. Use potholders to remove the hot baking sheet from the oven and let the salt cool.

- Transfer the tinted "glitter" into a salt shaker with large holes. Use the homemade glitter as you would any store-bought glitter.

pattern to the top mat board. Use a steel ruler and a craft knife to cut through both boards along the marked lines. Cut out the small star first, along the fine line, through both layers. Then cut out the large star along the heavy line.

**Step 2**

Apply the glue and the glitter.

Separate the cutout stars, keeping the same-size stars together. Lay the smaller stars on a piece of scrap paper on a protected work surface. Use a paintbrush to apply a thick, even coat of white craft glue to the top surface and edges of each one. Sprinkle ice blue glitter liberally over the wet glue areas and let dry. Return the excess glitter to its container. Repeat to apply silver glitter to the larger stars.

**Step 3**

Stabilize the glitter.

Use a soft brush to apply a coat of gloss acrylic varnish to all glittered surfaces; let the varnish dry.

**Step 4**

Attach the stars.

Lay a large star on the work surface, glitter side up. Align a smaller star on the original cutout shape, glitter side up, and then rotate it 15 to 20 degrees as illustrated. Following the manufacturer's directions, use a toothpick to mix up a small batch of 5-minute epoxy. Apply dabs of epoxy to secure the smaller star to the larger one. Repeat to join the remaining small and large stars.

**Step 5**

Assemble the stars.

Use a ruler and wire cutters to measure and cut a 30" (76.2 cm) length of steel wire. Fold the wire in half. Hold the bend with one hand and twist the lengths together, using pliers to hold the wire ends steady, if necessary. Wind the bottom 4" (10.2 cm) of wire around a broom handle to make a coil (to fit on the tree top). Lay the stars wrong side up on a flat work surface. Center the twisted wire along the dash line on one star and secure with a long strip of tape. Use the brush in the can of contact cement to apply a coat of glue to the wrong sides of both stars. Let the glue dry and then position and press them together, all edges even, to adhere them and to trap the wire stem inside.

**Step 6**

Attach the filigree balls to the points of the large star.

Insert one pin into each gold ball. Insert the pins between the mat boards at each point of the large star and secure with a dab of epoxy.

# PROJECTS

## Polka Dot: A Kaleidoscope

This clever kaleidoscope is made from a mailing tube, three plastic mirrors, and some beads. The beads are held in a small plastic container with a screw-on lid that is pushed into the end of the tube. The beads can be replaced with other little treasures—tiny seashells, confetti, sequins, assorted dry pasta—to change the configuration seen through the viewing hole at the opposite end of the tube. The sections of mirror are plastic and can be cut to size at your local glass and mirror store, making this project safe for older children to assemble.

Age group: 10+ years
Skill level: Moderate
Supervision: Moderate
Mess factor: Low

## MATERIALS AND TOOLS

White mailing tube, 12" × 2" diameter
(30.5 × 5.1 cm)
Assorted paint chip samples
Clear plastic container with screw cap,
1¼" × 1⅞" diameter (2.9 × 4.8 cm),
or to fit snugly inside tube
24 to 36 assorted glass beads
3 plastic mirrored strips, each 11¼" × 1½"
(28.6 × 3.8 cm)
White paper
White craft glue
Low-tack tape
Paper punch, ¾" diameter (1.9 cm)
Hole punch, ¼" diameter (0.6 cm)
Awl

## SETUP

None

## Step 1

Make the mirror prism.

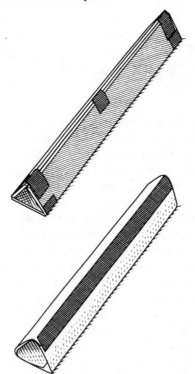

Lay the plastic mirrors facedown on the work surface, side by side with long edges touching. Use short pieces of tape to join the edges together in the middle and at each end. Do not move the tape once it is applied to prevent lifting off the reflective coating. Pick up the joined mirrors and collapse them into a three-dimensional triangular shape. Tape the remaining touching edges to hold the shape. Wrap white copy paper around the entire piece to protect the mirror backing; tape the white paper to itself along one long edge.

## Step 2

Make and install the eyepiece.

Remove and discard one plastic endcap from the mailing tube. Use an awl to pierce a hole through the center of the other endcap, working the awl until the hole is about ¼" (0.6 cm) in diameter. Insert the eyepiece into one open end of the tube.

## Step 3

Add the colored circles.

Use the paper punch to cut 50 to 60 circles from the assorted paint chip samples (I cut 14 light blue, 5 green, 3 chartreuse, 11 red, 3 dark orange, 5 orange, 6 yellow, and 6 brown). Use the hole punch to cut 60 to 70 circles from the paint chip samples (I cut 33 purple and 33 light green). Glue the circles at random to the outside of the tube.

## Step 4

Assemble the kaleidoscope.

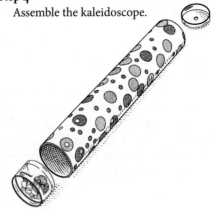

Insert the mirror prism into the open end of the tube, wrapping extra tape or white paper around it, if necessary, to achieve a snug fit. Add glass beads to the clear plastic container and screw on the cap. Insert the plastic container bottom first into the open end of the tube and wedge it in place.

## Katie and Charlotte: Pom-Pom Chicks

To sculpt yarn pom-poms, all you need are scissors and your imagination. Cut a little bit at a time to turn fluffy yarn balls into chicks with personality. Make the pair, one in blue and one in pink. Add-ons like the felt beaks, poseable legs, and paint chip eyes give kids lots to do.

Recommended age: 10+ years
Skill level: High
Supervision: Moderate
Mess factor: Moderate

MATERIALS AND TOOLS
Yarn, in blue and pink
Scrap of yellow felt
Two 14" (35.6 cm) chenille stems
Feathers
Polymer clay
Brown paint chips
Acrylic craft paint in blue, pink, and yellow
Black marker
White craft glue
Cardboard, 3½" × 3" (8.9 × 7.6 cm)
Tapestry needle
Scissors
Paintbrush
Clay sculpting tools (optional; see step 3)
Baking sheet
Home oven
Paper clips or clamps

SETUP
None

**Step 1**
Make the yarn wraps.

Cut an 18" (45.7 cm) length of blue or pink yarn and thread the tapestry needle. Wind the remaining yarn of the same color around the 3" (7.6 cm) width of the cardboard 110 times. Slip the tapestry needle between the cardboard and the yarn wraps on one side and draw the yarn through, leaving a 4" (10.2 cm) tail. Draw the needle around the yarn wraps a second time in the same location, pull the ends snug, and tie in a knot. Clip off the loose ends. Turn the cardboard over and repeat on the other side. Slide the yarn off the cardboard. Hold the tied-off middle sections together and wrap the yarn in the tapestry needle three times tightly around the sections. Then insert the needle back and forth through the wraps to reinforce the join. Clip off the yarn ends.

**Step 2**
Trim and sculpt the bird body.

Use scissors to cut the yarn loops a few at a time until the entire pom-pom is released. Fluff up the fibers with your fingertips. Use scissors to trim the yarn ends, cutting slowly and carefully to gradually sculpt the pom-pom into an oval. Trim one end of the oval narrower to make a pointy egg shape (the narrow end will be for the tail feather). Shape the larger end to suggest a head.

**Step 3**

Make the shoes.

Condition the polymer clay and roll into two ¾" (1.9 cm) balls. Flatten each ball slightly into an oval shape. Use your fingers or a clay sculpting tool to flatten one side for the sole of the shoe. Shape the shoe upper, making a hole about two-thirds from the toe for the leg. Drag a narrow tool or the tip of the embroidery needle along the upper to mark the tongue opening. Pierce three holes on either side for shoelace eyelets. Place the shoes on a baking sheet and bake in a preheated 275°F (130°C) oven for 15 minutes or as the manufacturer directs. Allow to cool. Paint the soles of the shoe blue or pink, to match the bird body. Paint the uppers yellow. Allow to dry.

**Step 4**

Attach the legs and shoes.

Apply glue to one end of a chenille stem. Wind yellow yarn firmly around the gluey section and secure with a paper clip or clamp. Continue applying glue and wrapping the yarn until the entire stem is wrapped. Clip or clamp the other end, trim off the excess, and allow to dry overnight. Bend the chenille stem in half. Use a tapestry needle and yarn to join the legs to the center wrap of the bird's body. Glue the shoes to the two ends.

**Step 5**

Complete the face and tail.

Fold the scrap of yellow felt in half and cut a narrow triangle through both layers for the beak. Cut two small circles from a brown paint chip for the eyes; use a black marker to make a dot on each eye circle. Glue the beak and eyes to the bird body to make a face. Glue a few feathers to the back. Allow to dry.

# Robert: The Nuts-and-Bolts Robot

Remember Erector sets? Here's a robot project to engage today's budding mechanical genius. The body is an open-mesh drawer organizer with a magnetic strip on top, and the metallic parts include nuts, bolts, washers, and springs. Follow the exploded diagram to put them all together.

Recommended age: 8+ years

Skill level: Moderate, with some steps to be done by an adult

Supervision: High

Mess factor: Low

## MATERIALS AND TOOLS

Open mesh box, 3½" × 2¼" × 2½" (8.9 × 5.7 × 6.4 cm) (a)

Wire spring, ⅜" diameter × 5¾" long (1.0 × 14.6 cm) (b)

Alligator clip with spring lead (c)

Sawtooth picture hanger, 1½" (3.8 cm) long (d)

2 hex tap bolts, ¼" × 1" (0.6 × 2.5 cm) (e)

2 connecting bolts, ¼" × 2" (0.6 × 5.1 cm) (f)

1 carriage bolt, ¼" × 2" (0.6 × 5.1 cm) (g)

14 machine nuts, ¼" (0.6 cm) diameter (h)

Flat washers in three sizes:

21 small, ⅝" (1.6 cm) in diameter (i)

19 medium, 1" (2.5 cm) in diameter (j)

4 large, 1½" (3.8 cm) in diameter (k)

Lock washers in two sizes:

2 small, ⅜" (1.0 cm) in diameter (l)

3 medium, ⅝" (1.6 cm) in diameter (m)

Thin wire

Instant glue (cyanocrylate)

Awl

Pliers

Adjustable wrench

Wire cutters

Marker

Ruler

SETUP

None

## Step 1

Prepare the mesh box.

Place the mesh box face down on a protected work surface. Use the ruler and marker to mark two dots on the bottom of the box, about 1¼" (3.2 cm) from each short edge, for the eyes. Mark one dot in the center of one long edge for the neck. Mark two dots on the opposite long edge for the legs. Use an awl to pierce through the mesh at each dot to open up a ¼" (0.6 cm) hole.

## Step 2

Add the eyes.

Referring to the exploded diagram, thread a small flat washer and a medium flat washer onto a hex tap bolt. Insert the end of the bolt into an eye hole in the mesh box. On the inside of the box, thread a small flat washer and a machine nut onto the bolt. Use pliers or an adjustable wrench to screw the nut tight against the washer. Make and attach a second eye in the same way.

## Step 3

Add the antenna.

Screw a machine nut onto the carriage bolt. Add a medium washer and another machine nut to hold the washer snug. Slip both ends of the coil spring onto the bolt to form a ring.

Screw on a nut to hold the spring in place. Screw on another nut but leave a ½" (1.3 cm) space between it and the nut above. Add a washer and then insert the end of the bolt into the neck hole of the mesh box. On the inside of the box, thread a small flat washer and a machine nut onto the bolt and tighten with pliers or an adjustable wrench.

## Step 4

Add the legs.

Thread two large flat washers, eight medium flat washers, and four small flat washers onto a connecting bolt. Screw on two machine nuts to hold the washers snug. Thread on a small flat washer. Insert the end of the bolt into a leg hole of the mesh box. On the inside of the box, thread on another small flat washer and a machine nut and tighten with pliers or an adjustable wrench. Make and attach a second leg in the same way.

## Step 5

Add the arms.

Use a ruler and wire cutters to measure and cut two 4" (10.2 cm) lengths of wire. Slip one wire through the spring end of the alligator clip with spring lead. Pass both wire ends from outside to the inside of one side of the mesh box. On the inside of the box, twist the wire ends together to hold the arm in place. Attach the second arm in the same way.

## Step 6

Add the details.

Cut four 4" (10.2 cm) lengths of wire. Following the wiring method in step 5, turn a machine nut on its side and wire it to the mesh box between the eyes for a nose. Wire the sawtooth picture hanger below the nose for a mouth. Wire two medium lock washers to the top of the box so that they stand up. Glue a small lock washer to each eye and let dry. Give the robot a flat washer and a lock washer to hold.

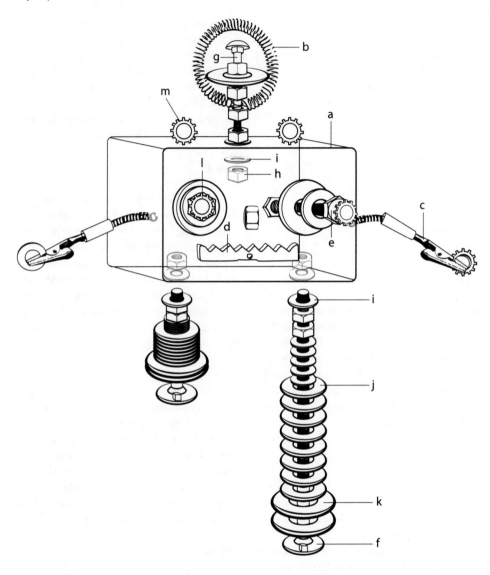

## Sox Martin: Sock Monkey

A sock monkey is a friendly soft toy for any age. Babies and toddlers love to grasp the long arms, legs, or tail and make the monkey "dance"—a wonderful way to experience the magic of cause and effect. Older children will enjoy exploring how to sculpt with needle and thread. Dexterity and patience are required; be prepared to lend a hand with some of the more challenging areas, such as the lips and muzzle. Use a small tapestry needle with a blunt tip for easier sewing in the knit fabric.

Recommended age: 10+
Skill level: Difficult
Supervision: High
Mess factor: Low

### MATERIALS AND TOOLS

Mitt, Ear, Muzzle, and Lips patterns (page 716)

Women's size 9–11 knee socks in coordinating colors:

3 single argyle
1 pair striped
1 single aqua
1 single red
1 single white

1 pom-pom
2 buttons, ⅝" (1.6 cm) in diameter
Sewing thread, in colors to match socks

Fiberfill
4 or 5 small tapestry needles, size 26
Long straight pins with ball heads
Scissors
Tape measure

### SETUP

Thread each tapestry needle with a doubled length of thread about 18" (45.7 cm) long. Rethread the needles as needed so that you always have a ready supply of different colors at hand.

**Step 1**

Make the body and head.

Lay an aqua sock flat. Using a tape measure and scissors, cut off the foot and the ribbing to make a tube about 11" (27.9 cm) long. Turn the tube inside out. Use a needle and matching thread to sew the ribbing end closed. Tie off the thread and clip the ends. Turn the tube right side out and stuff it with fiberfill to make a body about 6" (15.2 cm) long. Sew a running stitch through one layer of the sock fabric all around and pull gently to shape the neck. Tie off and clip the ends. Continue stuffing with fiberfill to make a head about 4" (10.2 cm) long. Tuck in the edges at the top of the head and sew closed. Tie off and clip the ends.

**Step 2**

Make the ears and mitts.

Use the patterns to cut four ears and four mitts from the leftover aqua sock foot. Layer the pieces right sides together in pairs and sew the curved edges together with matching thread, making a ¼" (0.6 cm) seam. Turn each piece right side out. Stuff them gently with fiberfill. Turn in the raw edges of the ears and sew them closed. Sew an ear to each side of the head. Stuff the mitts with fiberfill, pin each opening closed, and set aside.

**Step 3**

Make the face.

Use the patterns to cut two lips from the

red sock and one muzzle from the heel of a white sock. Stuff the muzzle with fiberfill, position it on the head, and secure with a few straight pins. Sew the muzzle to the head, tucking in the raw edges all around as you go. Remove the pins. Lay the lips right sides together and sew one long edge, making a ¼" (0.6 cm) seam. Open up the lips and pin them to the muzzle. Sew all around, tucking in the raw edges as you go. Remove the pins. Sew two buttons to the head for the eyes.

### Step 4

Make the arms.

Lay an argyle sock flat and cut 8" (20.3 cm) from the ribbing edge to make a tube. Cut the tube in half lengthwise through both layers to make two arm pieces. Fold each piece in half lengthwise, right side in, and sew the long edges together, making a ¼" (0.6 cm) seam. Turn right side out. Remove the pins from the mitts and sew a mitt to the ribbing end of each arm. Stuff each arm with fiberfill. Pin the open end.

### Step 5

Make the legs.

Lay a striped sock flat and cut 10" (25.4 cm) from the ribbing edge to make a tube. Follow step 4 to cut, sew, and stuff the leg pieces; sew the ribbing end closed and pin the open end.

### Step 6

Make the tail.

Lay a striped sock flat and cut 12" (30.5 cm) from the ribbing edge to make a tube. Cut 2¼" (5.7 cm) in from a folded edge for the tail. Sew and stuff the tail as for the legs in step 5.

### Step 7

Make the shirt.

Lay two argyle socks flat and cut 6½" (16.5 cm) from the ribbing edge to make two tubes. Cut each tube along one fold and open out into one piece. Stack the pieces right sides together

and trim to 6½" × 6" (16.5 × 15.2 cm) for the shirt front and back. Sew the side edges and the shoulder part of the top edges together, leaving a large opening at the ribbed bottom edge and a smaller neck opening at the top.

### Step 8

Make the hat.

Cut a leftover argyle foot piece 5½" (14.0 cm) from the toe. Tuck in the raw edges. Sew a pom-pom to the toe end.

### Step 9

Assemble the pieces.

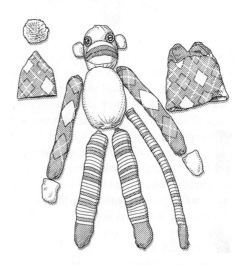

Remove the pins and sew the legs and tail securely to the body. Slip the shirt onto the body and tack in place at the shoulders. Turn in and sew the neck edge. Sew the arms to the shirt just below the shoulders. Place the hat on the monkey's head, turn in the raw edges, and sew in place.

## Izzie and Andrew: Jointed Clay Dolls

The fun of making these dolls is that the clay pieces are joined loosely together to move like marionettes. With a little imagination, children can refashion the clothing, add clay polka dots in a contrasting color, or create hairstyles that match their own.

Recommended age: 8+ years

Skill level: Easy

Supervision: Moderate; adult should do oven baking

Mess factor: Moderate

### MATERIALS AND TOOLS

Izzie and Andrew patterns (pages 717–18)

Polymer clay, in 2-ounce (56 g) packages:
2 packages each, in blue, red, and skin tone
1 package each, in light orange, white, and brown

Cotton embroidery floss, in peach

Acrylic craft paint, in pink

Instant glue (cyanocrylate)

Thin wire

6" (15.2 cm) dollmaking needle

Round-nose pliers

Wire cutters

Small rolling pin

Clay sculpting tools

Butter knife

Scissors

Small paintbrush

Baking sheet*

Home oven*

*For adult use only

### SETUP

Photocopy the head, dress, and wig patterns for Izzie and the head, shirt, pants legs, and wig patterns for Andrew. Cut out the paper patterns with scissors.

**Step 1**

Make the flat clay pieces.

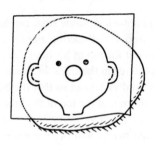

Work with one color clay at a time on a protected work surface, washing your hands when switching colors. Condition the clay until it is soft and malleable. Use a rolling pin to roll out the conditioned clay to a ¼" (0.6 cm) thickness. Place a cutout paper pattern on top and use a butter knife to cut the clay piece, following the pattern outline. For Izzie, make one skin-tone head, one red dress, and one light orange wig. For Andrew, make one skin-tone head, one blue shirt, two red pants legs, and one light orange wig.

**Step 2**

Pierce channels in the heads and add the wigs.

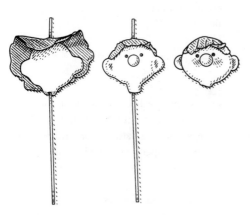

Working with Andrew first, carefully and slowly insert a dollmaking needle into the neck and out the top of his head, keeping the needle centered in the clay's thickness. Align a wig over Andrew's head so that the black dot on the pattern is at the top of the head. Lower the wig into position until it is pierced by the dollmaking needle and press the wig against the back of Andrew's head. Use a clay sculpting tool to curl the bangs forward and then tweak them upward. Pull the needle through the head, wiggling it slightly to open up the hole. Repeat the process to add the wig to Izzie's head, shaping and curling Izzie's long locks at the back of her head and around her forehead. Pull the needle through Izzie's head, wiggling it slightly to open up the hole. Roll two pea-size balls of clay and press one on each face for a nose. Use a tool to shape the ears. Press a pointed tool into the clay to make holes for the eyes.

**Step 3**

Make the arms.

Work some skin-tone clay into a sausage shape about 1" × ⅜" (2.5 × 1.0 cm). Sculpt one end into a mitt shape to suggest fingers and a thumb. Roll the part above the hand slightly thinner for the forearm. Make four arms, reversing the thumb position on two of them.

**Step 4**

Make Izzie's legs and shoes.

Roll two white sausages about 1½" × ½" (3.8 × 1.3 cm) each. Roll out some very skinny ropes from blue clay and wrap them around the sausages in rings, trimming off the excess. Reroll each sausage to a ⅜" (1.0 cm) diameter to press the blue ropes flat, creating striped stockings. Shape a small piece of brown clay into an oval, flatten the bottom and the two short ends to make a shoe, and attach to a leg. Repeat on the other leg. Continue shaping the shoes to make broad, slightly upturned toes.

**Step 5**

Make Andrew's ankles and shoes.

Follow step 4, starting with two 1" (2.5 cm) white sausages. Add blue stripes and make brown shoes. Trim the ankles if they appear too long. Attach the ankles to the bottom of the red pants legs.

**Step 6**

Attach the wire hooks and eyes.

Cut 16 pieces of wire, each 1¼" (2.9 cm) long. Use needle-nosed pliers to hold each wire near the middle; use round-nose pliers to bend one end into a U shape and the other end into a zigzag. Insert eight wires, zigzag end first, into the blue clay shirt and the red dress at the sleeves and lower torso so that the hook remains open. Insert the other eight pieces, zigzag end first, into the arm and leg pieces so that the hook is closed.

**Step 7**

Pierce channels in the bodies.

Carefully and slowly insert a dollmaking needle through the center of each body, beginning at the lower edge and emerging at the neck and keeping the needle centered in the clay's thickness. Pull the needle through,

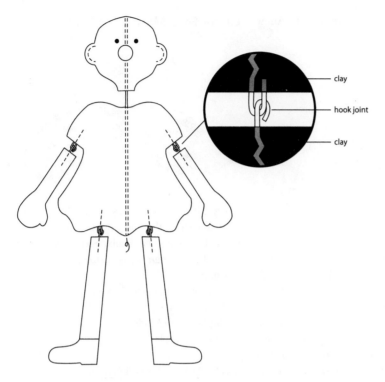

clay

hook joint

clay

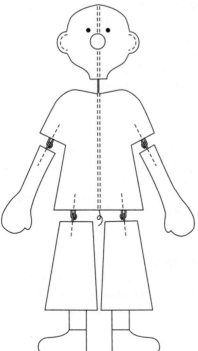

wiggling it slightly to open up the hole. Repeat for the other body.

**Step 8**

Add a pocket to Andrew's shirt and a dot pattern to Izzie's dress.

Use a rolling pin to roll out a piece of blue clay to a ¹⁄₁₆" (0.6 cm) thickness. Use a tool to cut it into a ½"-wide (1.3 cm) × ½"-high (1.3 cm) pocket. Position and press the pocket to the shirt. Use a tool to poke "stitches" along the borders. Add a three-dot pattern to Izzie's dress, using a tool to poke a row of three-hole clusters along the hem and sleeves of the dress, working both sides of the clay dress for a continuous pattern.

**Step 9***

Bake and assemble the pieces.

Lay all the clay pieces on a baking sheet. Bake in a preheated 275°F (130°C) oven for 15 minutes or as the manufacturer directs. Allow to cool.

**Step 10**

Assemble the pieces.

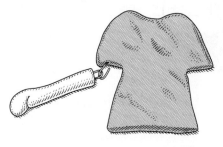

Join the arms and legs to the bodies by slipping each wire hook through the corresponding wire eyelet and closing with needle-nosed pliers. Cut an 18" (45.7 cm) length of floss. Thread the dollmaking needle, doubling the floss and knotting the ends together. Insert the needle into the hole at the bottom of Izzie's dress and then into the hole at the neck; draw the thread through so that the knot lodges at the bottom opening and the opposite end exits the top of her head. Clip the threads, releasing the needle, and tie the ends together to form a hanging loop. Add a drop of instant glue (cyanocrylate) to each opening to secure the floss. Join Andrew's body and head with floss in the same way. Blush the checks with pink acrylic craft paint thinned with water. Allow the glue and paint to dry.

**Adult activity

## Glitter Feet: Mary Jane Shoes

Every little girl imagines wearing a pair of sparkling shoes that just might help her create magic by clicking her heels together. Creating the wished-for pair is easy using a special glue and glitter.

Recommended age: 5+ years
Skill level: Easy
Supervision: Moderate
Mess factor: High

### MATERIALS AND TOOLS

Pair of Mary Jane shoes, in any fabric
Glitter, in magenta or desired color
Glitter glue in dispenser bottle
Paintbrush
Acrylic varnish, gloss finish
Container with shaker top
Newsprint

### SETUP

Cut open a plastic trash bag and tape the plastic to the work surface. Lay a sheet of newsprint on top.
Transfer the glitter to a container with a shaker top.

**Step 1**

Apply the glitter glue.

Use a tapered paintbrush and a patting motion to apply a thick coat of glue to the exterior of one shoe, including the strap.

**Step 2**

Apply the glitter.

Working over a sheet of newsprint, use the shaker to apply a liberal layer of glitter to the entire shoe. Set the shoe aside. Roll the newsprint into a cone shape to funnel excess glitter back into the shaker. Repeat steps 1 and 2 for the second shoe. Wash the paintbrush and let it dry. Let the glittered shoes dry overnight.

**Step 3**

Varnish the shoes.

Tap the shoes over a sheet of paper to shake off the excess glitter onto a sheet of newsprint. Return the glitter to the shaker. Use a soft brush to apply a coat of acrylic varnish to all of the glittered surfaces. Let the varnish dry completely.

## Harry: A Jumpy Spider

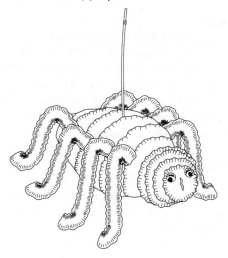

This plump spider is the perfect accessory for a child's scary Halloween costume. Suspended from an elastic band tied to a dowel, the furry spider will naturally "jump" up and down when the stick is moved—the perfect spooky companion for a young witch, ghost, or goblin making trick-or-treat rounds. To use the spider as a party decoration, just hang it from a doorway and/or make one land in the center of a table.

Recommended age: 6+ years
Skill level: Easy
Supervision: Careful to moderate
Mess factor: Low

### MATERIALS AND TOOLS

19½" (5.9 m) chenille stem roping, in black
Styrofoam egg, 3 ⅞" × 5 ⅞" (9.8 × 14.9 cm)
Styrofoam ball, 2½" (6.4 cm) diameter
Elastic band, 14" (35.6 cm) long, in black
2 dowels, ⅜" (1.0 cm) diameter, 24" (61 cm) and 4" (10.2 cm) long
2 wiggly eyes, ¾" (1.9 cm) diameter
20 large metal paper clips
Low-temperature glue gun and glue sticks
Wire coat hanger
Wire cutters*
Goggles*
Pencil
Ruler
*For adult use only

### SETUP

Make 40 jumbo-size staples. Put on goggles. Bend each paper clip in half, widthwise, and rock the sections back and forth until the wires break and there are two separate U-shaped sections. Use wire cutters to straighten the wire ends.

Make a long heavy-duty needle. Use wire cutters to cut a straight section of wire from a wire coat hanger. Use pliers to bend a 1" (2.5 cm) hook at one end. Flatten the hook against the stem, leaving an opening just wide enough for the strand material to pass through. This sturdy homemade needle is used to draw material through Styrofoam shapes.

Cut the spider's legs. Use a ruler and wire cutters to measure and cut eight 8" (20.3 cm) pieces from the chenille roping.

**Step 1\*\***

Make the spider's segmented body.

Use the 4" (10.2 cm) dowel to make 1"-long (2.5 cm) pilot holes in the Styrofoam ball and the broad end of the Styrofoam egg. Use the same dowel to join the pieces, squeezing some melted glue on the ends of the dowel and between the foam surfaces and then pushing the foam pieces tightly together; let the glue harden.

**Step 2\*\***

Install the elastic band.

Lay the segmented body on a flat surface. Use the 24" (61 cm) dowel to make a hole through the Styrofoam egg, pushing straight down from the top until it exits the bottom. Snip off a short piece from the chenille rope and tie it to one end of the elastic band. Use the homemade wire needle to thread the elastic band through the hole, inserting the straight end into the bottom hole and exiting the top.

**Step 3**

Mark the leg holes.

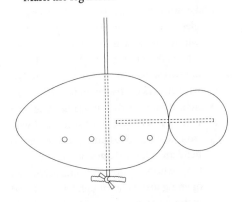

Use a pencil to mark four holes in a row on each side of the foam egg, approximately 1½" (3.8 cm) apart. Push a jumbo staple into each mark.

**Step 4**

Wrap the foam spider with chenille roping.

An adult and child can work together on this step. Unfurl the length of chenille roping and use your hands to straighten it. Insert one end of the roping 1" (2.5 cm) deep into the center back of the foam egg, using a dab of glue to secure it. Wind the chenille around that fixed point at the end of the egg, pressing the chenille against the foam in a snug coil until the end is concealed; use jumbo staples to secure the chenille roping as needed. Continue wrapping the chenille roping around the foam, starting a new length of chenille when the previous length is used up by inserting the end into the foam where the previous chenille left off. Use jumbo staples to secure the wraps as you go. Cover the foam ball in the same way for the head.

**Step 5**

Insert and shape the chenille legs.

Locate the eight marker staples in the foam body. Insert one end of a precut leg piece into the foam approximately ¼" (0.6 cm) above each staple. Bend a ¾" (1.9 cm) length at the end of the chenille leg to make a foot. Bend the leg in half to form a knee.

**Step 6**

Add the eyes.

Set the spider on a flat surface. Glue a wiggly eye to each half of the spider's head as shown or as desired.

**Step 7**

Attach the spider to the stick.

Tie the end of the elastic band to the end of the long dowel, using a tight double knot. Hold the stick and move it up and down to make the spider jump.

\*\*Adult activity

# Little Miss Muffet:
## Small Spider on a Spiderweb

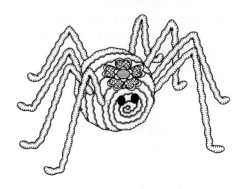

A costume with a Miss Muffet theme is easy to put together using wardrobe pieces in your little girl's closet—a few flouncy skirts, a blouse and sweater, and a wide satin hair bow. For a finishing touch that adds to the nursery rhyme, make a pink spider and portable spiderweb for your trick-or-treater to carry. It is easy to make a spiderweb by knotting lengths of string to a wire-hanger frame in a radial pattern and then weaving and knotting more to make the lacy web. When glue is applied to the web, it gets stiff enough to support the weight of a little spider, and when the web is painted pink, it will coordinate with the sweet theme. The spiderweb can also be cut from the frame and hung in front of a window or placed on the table.

*Stage One: The Spider*
Recommended age: 6+ years
Skill level: Intermediate
Supervision: Careful to moderate
Mess factor: Moderate

MATERIALS AND TOOLS
14 chenille stems, 12" (30.5 cm) long, in pink
Styrofoam ball, 1¾" (4.4 cm) diameter
Wood skewer
Blue construction paper
Hole punch, ¼" (0.6 cm) diameter
Die-cut flower (optional)

Low-temperature glue gun and glue sticks
Wire cutters

**Step 1**
Wrap the ball with chenille stems.
Insert ½" (1.3 cm) of the end of one chenille stem into the center of the foam ball and secure it with a dab of glue. Wind the chenille around that fixed point, pressing it against the foam in a snug coil and securing with it dabs of glue. Continue wrapping, starting a new stem where a previous one left off by inserting ½" (1.3 cm) of the end of the new chenille stem into the foam and then wrapping it around the foam until the entire ball is covered. End in a tight coil, just as you started.

**Step 2**
Insert chenille stems and shape them into legs.
Use wire cutters to cut four chenille stems in half, making eight pieces. Use a wood skewer to poke a row of four evenly spaced holes on each side of the ball, gently parting the wrapped stems to reach the foam. Push ½" (1.3 cm) of one end of a half chenille stem into the foam. Bend a ¼" (0.6 cm) length at the end of each stem to make a foot. Bend each leg in half to form a knee.

**Step 3**
Add the eyes.
Use a hole punch to cut out two circles from blue construction paper. Set the spider on a flat surface and glue the blue circles to the front of the ball for the eyes.

**Step 4**
Add the flower.
Glue the flower to the top of the ball just above the eyes to make a hat.

*Stage Two: The Spiderweb*
Recommended age: 6+ years
Skill level: Moderate
Supervision: High
Mess factor: Moderate

## MATERIALS AND TOOLS

    2 yards (1.8 m) ribbon, ½" (1.3 cm) wide, in pink
    2 wire coat hangers
    Ball of cotton string
    Floral tape
    Acrylic craft paint, in medium pink
    White craft glue
    Small bowl
    Foam brush
    Pliers
    Scissors

### Step 1

Prepare the wire hoop.

Use your hands to pull open each wire hanger into an open hoop. Hold the wire hoops together, matching the hanger hooks, and wrap with floral tape all around except for the hooks to make a nonskid surface for the string.

### Step 2

Make a bundle of strings for the web's central radial design.

Measure and cut eight pieces of string long enough to span the wire hoop at its widest point plus 5" (12.7 cm). Lay the pieces of cut string in a neat bundle on a flat surface with ends even. Grasp all of the strands and tie a single overhand knot in the center, pulling the string ends taut to tighten the knot.

### Step 3

Attach the bundle of strings to the wire hoop.

Lay the wire hoop on a flat surface. Set the knot in the center of the hoop. Referring to the diagram, arrange the ends of the strings in a radial design. Tie one string end to the hoop with a double knot and then tie the opposite end of the same string so that the string is taut across the hoop. Repeat for each string. Snip off the excess string.

### Step 4

Attach the first row of the web.

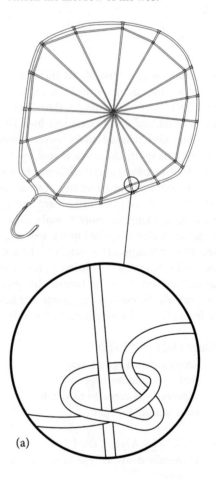

(a)

Cut an 18" (45.7 cm) length of string. Tie one end to one of the radial spokes, close to the wire hoop, making a double knot. Bring the free end of the string across an adjacent spoke and tie a single overhand knot (a). Continue to the next radial spoke and tie a single overhand knot. Continue around the spokes of the radial design until the first round of the web is formed.

**Step 5**

Attach the remaining rows of the web.

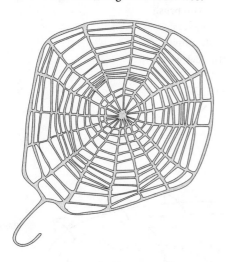

Repeat step 4 to add more knotted rounds to the radial design, spiraling in toward the center. Feel free to go over the same strings to move to a desired spot on the web that is forming. End each string by tying a double knot and snipping off the excess.

**Step 6**

Apply glue to the web.

Lay the finished web flat on a protected work surface. Pour white craft glue into a small bowl and use a foam brush to apply it to one side of the string web, including the hoop. Turn the web over and repeat, catching any drips of glue with the brush. Let the glue dry completely.

**Step 7**

Paint the web.

Apply two coats of pink paint to the web and the hoop. Use a foam brush to paint both sides, allowing the paint the dry after each coat.

**Step 8**

Bend the wire hooks and wrap them with ribbon.

Use pliers to flatten the wire hook into a handle. Use scissors to cut the ribbon in half widthwise. Wrap one length of ribbon around the handle, overlapping the wraps until the wire is concealed; secure with dabs of glue. Tie the remaining piece into a bow at the handle.

## Mardi Gras: A Feather Mask

A feather mask can be made to match a wide range of costumes, from an elegant ball gown (an adult-size fancy dress tacked or pinned to fit) to a down-to-earth bird, such as a chicken, duck, or swan. The technique for the mask is simple: glue layers of feathers to a store-bought mask, changing the colors of the feathers, ribbons, and sequins according to the theme or your imagination. A low-temperature glue gun is used to attach the feathers, so much of the decorating is designed for an adult to do; however, with moderate supervision an older child who has worked with a glue gun before can decorate the mask. Always keep a bowl of

ice water nearby should melted glue accidentally touch the skin.

Recommended age: 6+ years
Skill level: Moderate
Supervision: High
Mess factor: Low

## MATERIALS AND TOOLS

Satin mask, 7" (17.8 cm) across, in white
or another color, as desired
¼ ounce (7.1 g) feathers, in red, orange,
and yellow or other colors, as desired
Scrap of felt, in turquoise or another color,
as desired
Dowel, ³⁄₁₆" diameter × 12" (0.5 × 30.5 cm)*
Empty spool*
3 yards (2.7 m) ribbon, ½" (1.3 cm) wide
Acrylic craft paint, in red or another color,
as desired
Tacky white craft glue
Low-temperature glue gun and glue sticks
Foam brush
Scissors
Toothpick
*For adult use only

## SETUP
None

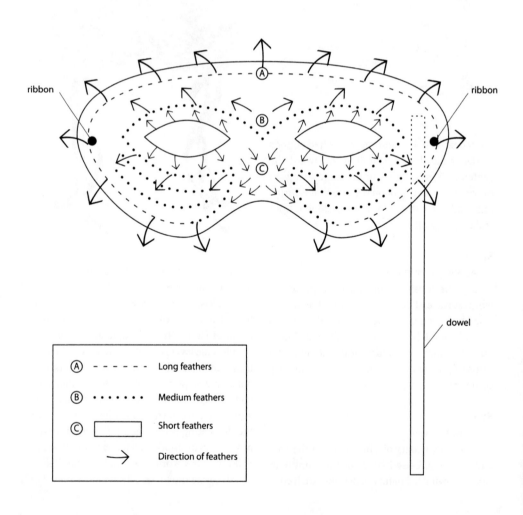

ribbon                                                                ribbon

dowel

| | | |
|---|---|---|
| (A) | - - - - - - | Long feathers |
| (B) | • • • • • • • | Medium feathers |
| (C) | [ ] | Short feathers |
| | → | Direction of feathers |

**Step 1\*\***

Make the handle for the mask.

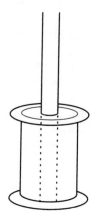

Set the empty spool on a protected work surface, hole facing up, and drizzle melted glue into the hole. Immediately insert one end of a dowel into the hole, holding the dowel straight and perpendicular until it is secure. Use a foam brush to apply two thin coats of paint to all parts of the handle, letting the paint dry between coats. Glue the top of the handle to the back of the mask on either side, depending on which hand you want to use to hold the mask. Position the dowel ½" (1.3 cm) from and perpendicular to the edge.

**Step 2**

Sort the feathers.

Divide the feathers by length into three separate piles, one for long, one for medium, and one for short feathers.

**Step 3\*\***

Glue the long feathers to the edge of the mask.

Lay the mask, front side up, on a flat surface. Referring to the arrows on the diagram for the feather direction, hold the quill of one long feather against the mask so the plume extends out and beyond the edge of the mask. Secure the quill to the mask with a dab of melted glue. Continue to position and glue long feathers around the edge of the mask (A), excluding the nose section.

**Step 4\*\***

Glue the medium-length feathers to the middle of the mask.

Following the diagram and key, glue the quills of the medium-length feathers to the middle section of the mask (B), so that the plumes overlap the quills of the long feathers. Refer to the arrows on the diagram for the direction of the feathers.

**Step 5\*\***

Glue the short feathers to the mask.

Following the diagram and key, glue the short feathers around the eyeholes and over the bridge of the nose (C), observing the arrows for the feather direction. Fill in any remaining bare spots.

**Step 6\*\***

Add the eyelashes.

Cut sixteen 1" × ³/₁₆" (2.5 × 0.5 cm) strips from felt. Use scissors to snip one end of each strip into a point to mimic a thick eyelash. Lay the mask, feathers facing up, on a flat surface. Apply a dab of melted glue to the straight edge of one eyelash and immediately position and press it to the top rim of the eyehole, using a toothpick to press it down. Continue to add seven more eyelashes side by side across the top rim of the eyehole. Repeat on the other eyehole.

**Step 7**

Add the decorative ribbons.

Cut the ribbon into six 18" (45.7 cm) lengths. Turn the mask face down and glue the ends of three ribbons to each side of the mask.

\*\*Adult activity

## Starlight: A Magic Wand

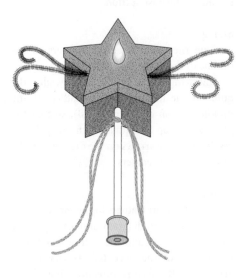

A golden wand with a shimmering light is truly a dream come true for a princess or a wizard. Made from a star-shaped papier-mâché box that is covered in glitter, the actual glow comes from a small LED light installed in the lid. The wand requires that an adult make some cuts with a craft knife, but once the cuts are made, kids of all ages will love painting and glittering the components of this Starlight wand. The wand can be used year to year, but check that the LED light illuminates before beginning a walk through the neighborhood. For extra security, have a spare battery handy.

    Recommended age: 7+ years
    Skill level: Moderate
    Supervision: Moderate
    Mess factor: Moderate

### MATERIALS AND TOOLS
    Papier-mâché star-shaped box with lid, 4" (10.2 cm) across
    4 metallic gold stems, each 12" (30.5 cm) long
    LED flame-shaped bulb, flickering, in housing 1½" high × 1½" diameter (3.8 × 3.8 cm)
    Dowel, $^{3}/_{16}$" diameter × 12" (0.5 × 30.5 cm)

    Empty spool, 1" diameter × 1¼" high (2.5 × 3.2 cm)
    Acrylic paint, in white and turquoise or other colors, as desired
    Fine glitter, in gold or another color, as desired
    Acrylic varnish, high gloss
    1 yard (0.9 m) twisted cord, in gold
    White craft glue
    2 foam brushes, 1" (2.5 cm) wide
    Tapered paintbrush
    Craft knife with replaceable blades*
    Tapestry needle
    Pencil
    Hot-glue gun and glue sticks*
*For adult use only

### SETUP
None

**Step 1**\*\*
    Make a hole in the lid for the LED light.

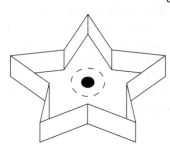

    Following the diagram, use a pencil to mark a hole in the center of the lid. Place the lid, wrong side up, on a protected work surface. Position the tip of a craft knife firmly on the center mark and rotate the knife blade to make a pilot hole. Pick up the lid and hold it by the sides with your free hand. Insert the blade of the knife into the pilot hole and rotate the blade to bore a ¼"-diameter (0.6 cm) hole in the center of the lid. Test-fit the LED lightbulb in the hole; the fit should be snug. For a larger hole, continue to turn the knife blade in the hole, removing scant bits of the box material and stopping often to test the fit.

**Step 2\*\***

Make two more holes in the lid.

Use a pencil to mark a hole on each side of the lid for the metallic gold stems. Use the craft knife blade to bore a ⅛"-diameter (0.3 cm) hole at each mark. Test-fit metallic gold stems in these holes; two stems should fit snugly. Bore larger holes if necessary.

**Step 3\*\***

Make three holes in the box.

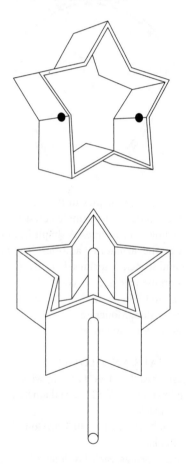

Set the lid on the box. Following the diagram, use a tapestry needle to pierce two starter holes in the box, even with the holes in the box lid. Remove the lid. Use a craft knife as in step 1 to bore a ⅛"-diameter (0.3 cm) hole at each starter hole for two metallic gold stems.

Then, measure down 1⅝" (4.1 cm) from the rim of the box, or the height of the LED bulb housing plus ⅛" (0.3 cm), and pierce a starter hole for the dowel. Use a craft knife to bore a ³⁄₁₆"-diameter (0.5 cm) hole, test-fitting it with the dowel as you go. The dowel must be positioned low in the box to provide clearance for the LED light housing that will be attached to the underside of the lid.

**Step 4**

Paint the handle and the inside of the box.

Use a foam brush to paint the dowel white. Rinse out the brush. Use the foam brush to paint the spool, the inside of the box, and the inside of the lid turquoise blue. Rinse out the brush. Let the paint dry. Glue the spool to one end of the dowel for the wand handle.

**Step 5**

Apply glitter to the outside of the box and the lid.

Use a foam brush to apply a layer of white craft glue to the outside of the box lid. Immediately apply a liberal sprinkling of gold glitter to the wet glue areas. Repeat to apply glue and glitter to the outside of the box. Return the excess glitter to its container. Set the lid and the box on a flat surface, glitter side facing out, and let dry. When the glue is completely dry, pick up the box and lid and tap each one gently over a sheet of scrap paper to dislodge the loose glitter. Return the excess glitter to the container.

**Step 6**

Apply a coat of varnish to the glitter.

To keep the glitter from shedding, use a tapered brush to apply a thin coat of high-gloss varnish to all glittered surfaces. Let the varnish dry completely.

**Step 7\*\***

Install the handle.

Place the box on a flat surface. Insert the plain end of the handle through the hole in the outside of the box, pushing the dowel straight through the box's interior until it touches the opposite side of the box. Make sure the dowel is level and then secure it with hot glue; let the glue harden.

**Step 8\*\***

Install the LED light in the lid.

Working from the inside, gently guide the flame-shaped bulb through the hole in the lid until the housing comes to rest on the painted surface. Apply a few drops of hot glue around the edge of the plastic housing to secure the light; let the glue harden.

**Step 9 (optional)**

Decorate the handle.

Cut two 18" (45.7 cm) lengths of cord and knot them around the handle where the dowel meets the box. Use a scant dab of hot glue to secure the knot.

**Step 10**

Assemble the wand.

Use your fingers to coil one end of each chenille stem. Switch on the LED light, following the manufacturer's instructions. Set the lid on the box, aligning the small holes on the lid with the small holes on the box. Insert the straight ends of two metallic gold stems into each side hole to secure the lid to the box. Arrange the coils as desired.

\*\*Adult activity

# Bumblebees and Ladybugs: Halloween Headgear

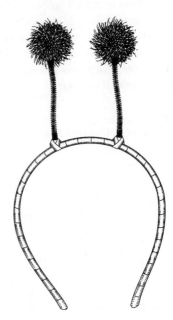

A bit of ingenuity comes to the rescue when kids need to make last-minute accessories for their Halloween costumes. A simple headband provides the armature; add-ons like pom-poms and stretched springs do the rest.

Recommended age: 5+ years

Skill level: Moderate

Supervision: Moderate

Mess factor: Moderate

## MATERIALS AND TOOLS

Plastic headband, ⅜" (1.0 cm) wide

2 pom-poms, 1⅛" (2.9 cm) diameter, in black

2 chenille stems, 12" (30.5 cm) long, in black

2 brass springs, each 1¾" long × ⅛" diameter (4.4 × 0.3 cm)

1 yard (9.1 m) satin ribbon, ½" (1.3 cm) wide, in black

Low-temperature glue gun and glue sticks

Permanent marker

Ruler

Wire cutters
Scissors

SETUP
None

**Step 1**

Stretch the springs.

Pull the ends of each spring in opposite directions to make a piece 5" (12.7 cm) long. The stretched coils should remain separated, so that you can see through them.

**Step 2**

Make the antennae.

Insert a chenille stem into each stretched spring. Hold the spring and stem even at one end and clip the stem 1½" (3.8 cm) beyond the spring at the other end. Nuzzle the coil end of each piece between the tufts of a pom-pom and secure with a dab of glue.

**Step 3**

Attach the antennae to the headband.

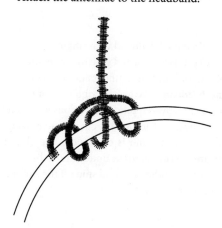

Mark the midpoint of the headband. Measure and mark two points 1¼" (2.9 cm) from the midpoint in each direction. Wrap a chenille stem extension around the headband at each mark so that the springs and pom-poms stand up above the headband. Secure each one with a dab of glue.

**Step 4**

Wrap the headband with ribbon.

Use melted glue to secure one end of the ribbon to the underside of one end of the headband. Wrap the ribbon around the headband, overlapping the previous wraps and going over and around the chenille stem wraps until the headband is concealed. Use melted glue to secure the ribbon to the underside of the headband at the other end and snip off the excess.

## Monster with Wiggly Eyes: Halloween Headgear

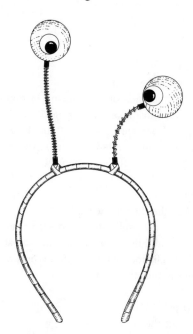

A bit googly, but in good fun, adding a pair of wiggly eyes to the top of your head can be the beginning of an imaginative costume that is put together at the last minute, especially one that uses children-safe makeup to conjure chalky-faced skeletons, green-faced monsters, and the like.

Recommended age: 5+ years
Skill level: Moderate
Supervision: Moderate
Mess factor: Moderate

## MATERIALS AND TOOLS

Plastic headband, ⅜" (1.0 cm) wide

2 Ping-Pong balls

2 wiggly eyes, ¾" (1.9 cm) diameter

2 brass springs, each 1¾" long × ⅛" diameter (4.4 × 0.3 cm)

2 chenille stems, 12" (30.5 cm) long, in white or desired color

1 yard (91.4 cm) satin ribbon, ½" (1.3 cm) wide, in black or desired color

Low-temperature glue gun and glue sticks*

*For adult use only

## SETUP

None

### Step 1

Stretch the springs.

Pull the ends of each spring in opposite directions to make one spring 6" (15.2 cm) long and one spring 4" (10.2 cm) long. The stretched coils should remain separated, so that you can see through them.

### Step 2

Add the chenille stems.

Insert a chenille stem into each stretched spring. Hold the spring and stem even at one end and clip the stem 1½" (3.8 cm) beyond the spring at the other end.

### Step 3**

Make the monster eyes.

Rest the heated tip of the glue gun nozzle for a second or two anywhere on the surface of a Ping-Pong ball to make a ³⁄₁₆"-wide (0.5 cm) hole. Insert the coil end of a stretched spring/chenille stem into the hole and secure with glue. Repeat for the second ball. Glue a wiggly eye to each ball.

### Step 4**

Attach the monster eyes to the headband.

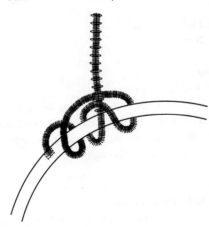

Mark the midpoint of the headband. Measure and mark two points 1¼" (2.9 cm) from the midpoint in each direction. Wrap a chenille stem extension around the headband at each mark so that the springs and monster eyes stand up above the headband. Secure each one with a dab of melted glue.

### Step 5**

Wrap the headband with ribbon.

Use a dab of melted glue to secure one end of the ribbon to the underside of one end of the headband. Wrap the ribbon around the headband, overlapping the previous wraps and going over and around the chenille stem wraps until the headband is concealed. Use glue to secure the ribbon to the underside of the headband at the other end and snip off the excess.

**Adult activity

## Flower Girl: Halloween Headgear

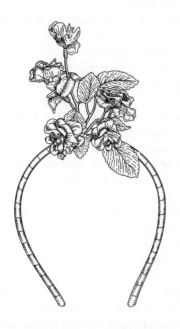

A sweet cluster of roses can be the finishing touch to a flower girl costume. Pair a pretty dress and a handheld bouquet or a basket filled with rose petals to complete the picture.

    Recommended age: 5+ years
    Skill level: Moderate
    Supervision: Moderate
    Mess factor: Moderate

## MATERIALS AND TOOLS

    5 small fabric roses with 1" (2.5 cm) leafy
        stems
    1 small fabric rose with 4" (10.2 cm) stem
    Wire, medium-gauge, thread-wrapped
    Floral tape, in green
    1 yard (9.1 m) satin ribbon, ½" (1.3 cm)
        wide, in green
    Low-temperature glue gun and glue
        sticks*
    Wire cutters
*For adult use only

## SETUP

    None

### Step 1

    Make a rose bouquet.

    Hold the stems with leaves together to form a cluster of roses, placing the long-stemmed rose in the middle. Use thread-wrapped wire to bind the bottom ½" (1.3 cm) of the shorter stems. Wrap floral tape around the stems to conceal the wire.

### Step 2**

    Attach the rose bouquet to the headband.

    Hold the wrapped stems against the mid-point of the headband. Wrap a 5" (12.7 cm) length of thread-wrapped wire around the headband and stems and secure with a dab of melted glue. Use wire cutters to trim off the excess.

### Step 3**

    Wrap the headband with ribbon.

    Use a dab of melted glue to secure one end of the ribbon to the underside of one end of the headband. Wrap the ribbon around the headband, overlapping the previous wraps and going over and around the chenille stem wraps until the headband is concealed. Use glue to secure the ribbon to the underside of the head-band at the other end and snip off the excess.

**Adult activity

## Imperial: Eggshell Gift Boxes

Empty eggshells painted in jewel colors make unique gift packaging for small gifts and trinkets. Two shell halves are hinged with a ribbon to enclose a small but thoughtful gift—a sentimental remembrance inscribed on a strip of paper and rolled into a coil, an embossed charm or memento, or any other token you choose.

### MATERIALS AND TOOLS
3 white eggs
Assorted embellishments: ribbon roses, metallic charms, and beads
Assorted ribbons, ⅛" (3 mm) wide, in green, pale blue, and pink
Acrylic craft paint, in jewel colors, such as robin's-egg blue and magenta
Acrylic spray sealer, gloss or matte finish (optional)
White craft glue
Jordan almonds or other small token (to enclose in shells)
Empty egg carton
Disposable gloves
Respirator mask
Paintbrush
Scissors

### Step 1
Prepare the eggs for painting.
Carefully crack each raw egg into two more or less equal halves (refrigerate the yolks and

---

## smART ideas: Making a Chick using a Cracked Shell

If your egg cracked apart while you were trying to make the holes to empty it, you can use the shell in another way. Rinse the shells under warm water, color with egg dye (page 670), and allow the shells to dry completely. Make a pom-pom chick (page 645) with yellow yarn but skip the legs and the shoes. Install the pom-pom chick in the larger section of the eggshell, place the other section on top of the chick's head, and secure the pieces with hot glue.

whites for cooking later). Rinse the eggshells carefully in warm soapy water and air-dry. Store the pairs of halves in an empty egg carton.

## Step 2

Paint the eggs.

Use a paintbrush and acrylic craft paint to paint the interior of each half eggshell. Set the shell halves in the empty cavities in the egg carton to dry. Repeat to paint the exterior of each half eggshell, choosing a color that matches or contrasts with the interior color of the shell; let the paint dry.

## Step 3 (optional)

Seal the outside of the eggshells.

Work outdoors or in a very well ventilated space and wear a respirator mask. Invert the shells on a protected work surface, keeping the pairs together. Apply a thin coat of spray acrylic to the exterior surface of each shell; let the sealer dry. Repeat to apply a second coat of sealer.

## Step 4

Glue on the ribbon hinge.

Cut a short strip of ribbon, about ½" (1 cm) long. Hold two eggshell halves together, lining up the cracked edges as closely as possible. Glue the ribbon across the crack to make a hinge, pressing gently to adhere it and to neaten any frayed ribbon edges. Set the eggshell back into the egg carton, keeping the edges aligned; let the glue dry completely. Repeat to add a ribbon hinge to the remaining pairs of shells.

## Step 5

Enclose the gift and decorate the egg.

Carefully open the eggshell and place a couple of Jordan almonds or other token gift in the bottom half. Lower the top shell, matching the edges on both shells so they close neatly. Glue a length of ribbon around the egg, perpendicular to the joined edges, thread a charm onto the ribbon, and tie the ends in a bow. Use white craft glue to affix a ribbon rose to the bow, as desired.

## Easter Parade: Hollowed-Out Eggshell Ornaments

Color and decorate blown-out eggshells to make these delicate ornaments. Each eggshell remains intact (except for a small hole at each end) and is light enough to be suspended by a pretty ribbon. With careful handling, the hollow shells can be decorated to resemble a lively cast of characters to decorate an Easter egg tree.

Recommended age: 5+ years
Skill level: Easy
Supervision: Careful to moderate
Mess factor: High

### MATERIALS AND TOOLS

9 to 12 blown-out eggshells, holes at both ends
Narrow ribbon, about ⅛" to ¼" (0.3 to 0.6 cm) wide
Self-adhesive loose-leaf reinforcements
Decorative elements (see individual items under step 8)
Liquid food coloring, in red, green, blue, and yellow
White vinegar
Ceramic or glass cups
Measuring cup
Measuring spoons
Disposable gloves
Medium-gauge wire (for needle)
Wire cutters
Ruler
Scissors
Egg carton
Paper towels

## Step 1

Prepare the egg carton.

Tear small pieces of paper towel and line the bottom of each trough in the egg carton, pushing the towel down so it conforms to the shape of the trough.

**Step 2**

Prepare the liquid colors.

For each color desired, mix 20 drops of liquid food coloring, ½ cup (118.3 mL) warm water, and 3 tablespoons (44.4 ml) white vinegar in a clean cup. Refer to the chart below for different colors to try or experiment with your own combinations. Each cupful of dye can color six to eight eggshells.

| Color | Number of Drops |
|---|---|
| Red | 20 red |
| Blue | 20 blue |
| Green | 20 green |
| Yellow | 20 yellow |
| Turquoise | 5 blue + 15 green |
| Purple | 12 red + 8 blue |
| Rose | 15 red + 5 blue |
| Chartreuse | 15 yellow + 5 green |

**Step 3**

Color the hollow eggs.

Put on disposable gloves. Float a hollow egg on the surface of the egg dye and immediately begin rolling the shell with your gloved hand so that all surfaces touch the liquid. Do not try to push the egg under the color solution as the force can cause the shell to crack; instead, just keep the egg rolling until the desired color intensity is achieved. The longer the egg is exposed to the dye, the deeper the color will be. If a dye color is too concentrated, it can be lightened by adding more water. I usually break an extra eggshell into pieces for testing my colors. This way, I can see exactly what a mixed color will look like before I color an entire egg.

**Step 4**

Drain and dry the colored eggs.

When the color is right, use a spoon to lift the hollow eggshell from the liquid dye. Hold the eggshell upright in your gloved hand and allow the liquid color to drain out into an empty cup. Set the colored eggshell upright in one trough of the egg carton. Repeat steps 3 and 4 to color each eggshell.

Stage One: Installing the Hanging Ribbon in a Hollowed-Out Eggshell Ornament

**Step 1**

Prepare the wire needle and ribbon.

Measure and cut a 10" (25.4 cm) length of wire. Bend the wire in half and gently twist the wires together, leaving a narrow eye at the bend. Thread one end of a 16" (40.6 cm) length of ribbon through the eye of the wire needle and pull through until the ends are even.

**Step 2**

Thread the ribbon through the egg.

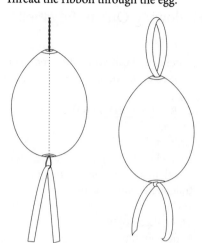

*Chicken*

Center a loose-leaf reinforcement over each hole and gently press down the edges to adhere it to the eggshell. Carefully guide the twisted wire needle so that it enters through the bottom hole and emerges out the top hole. Gently pull the needle through the eggshell until the ribbon loop at the top is about 2½" (6.4 cm) long and ribbon tails extend at the bottom. Untwist the wires and remove the needle (you can retwist them for the next eggshell). Tie the ribbon ends at the bottom hole into a knot. Hold the knot against the eggshell and secure the ribbon at both holes with melted glue.

## Stage Two: Decorating the Hollowed-Out Eggshell Ornament

Use the patterns to cut out the required shapes from laminated fabric. Use paper punches to cut shapes from cardstock. Attach all the pieces to the eggshells using a low-temperature glue gun and glue sticks.

Comb, Wing, Tail, and Beak patterns
  (page 719)
Laminated fabric
5" (12.7 cm) metal spring
Chenille stem
Black permanent marker

Use the patterns to cut out four comb pieces, two wings, one tail, and one beak from laminated fabric. Curl the ends of the feathers with your fingers. Use melted glue to affix the fabric components to the egg as shown. Use wire cutters to cut the metal spring in half. Glue one end of each spring to the bottom of the egg. Cut six ¾"-long (1.9 cm) pieces from the chenille stem. Glue three pieces to the end of each spring for feet. Use a black permanent marker to add the eyes.

ᴏᴏᴏᴏᴏᴏᴏᴏᴏᴏᴏᴏᴏᴏᴏᴏᴏᴏᴏᴏᴏᴏᴏᴏᴏᴏᴏᴏᴏᴏᴏᴏᴏᴏᴏᴏᴏᴏᴏᴏᴏᴏᴏᴏᴏᴏᴏ

## smART ideas: Two Methods for Hollowing Out an Eggshell

The appeal of extracting the contents of an egg is that the intact hollow shell can be used to create a palm-size work of art. The shell's surface can be colored with food coloring or commercial color tablets diluted in water and then they can be embellished with feathers, chenille stems, punched paper, laminated-fabric shapes, and much, much more.

Removing the egg white and yolk can be accomplished in two ways; both methods require that a hole (or two) be made in the eggshell through which the contents can be extracted or blown. The hole can be made with a piercer (available in a kit) or the sharp tip of a metal skewer. The contents can be removed by forcing air into the egg, pushing the egg through and out of the hole. Air can be introduced into the egg using a blunt hollow needle attached to a plastic bellows (available in a kit) or by blowing through a straw that is inserted into the egg. If you are planning to thread a ribbon through the hollow eggshell, use the two-hole method; otherwise, either the one-hole or the two-hole method is fine for hollowing out an egg in preparation for decorating it.

- **One-hole method: Using an egg piercer and bellows**
  The kit for this method includes a shell piercer and a bellows with a blunt hollow-needle attachment. Both tools make it very easy to make a hole in the eggshell and force out the yolk and egg white through the same hole. The hole diameter of approximately $^3/_{16}$" (0.5 cm) is large enough for the hollow needle and the egg, which will flow out around the needle and out of the hole. If a hole is accidentally made larger than recom-

mended, it can always be concealed with a decoration.

### MATERIALS AND TOOLS
Raw eggs
Cardboard egg carton
Egg-hollowing kit: piercer and bellows
    with hollow-needle attachment
Straightened jumbo paper clip
Bowl
Baking sheet (optional)
Home oven (optional)

**Step 1 (optional)**
Preheat oven.
Preheat an oven to 300°F (148.9°C). You can also air-dry blown eggshells.

**Step 2**
Make a hole in an eggshell.
Hold an egg in one hand with the wide end of the egg facing up. Use the other hand to place the piercing tool on the top center of the egg, putting just enough pressure on the tip while turning the tool to make a $^3/_{16}$"-diameter (0.5 cm) hole in the shell.

**Step 3**
Pierce the contents in the eggshell.
Cradle the egg in one hand. Use your other hand to insert one end of a straightened paper clip into the hole in the egg, gently poking and stirring the egg's contents to break the membrane enveloping the yolk.

**Step 4**
Pump out the contents of the shell.
Working over a bowl, cradle the egg in the palm of one hand, hole facing downward, and use the other hand to carefully insert the end of the hollow needle attached to the bellows

tool into the hole. Squeeze the bellows several times to force air into the egg, expelling all of the egg contents out of the same hole and into the bowl. Withdraw the needle from the egg.

### Step 5
Clean the inside of the egg.

Run warm tap water into the egg hole. Shake the egg to agitate the water so it rinses the inside of the shell. Set the eggshell, hole side down, in the egg carton to allow the water to drain out.

### Step 6
Hollow out the remaining eggs.

Repeat steps 2–5 to remove the contents of the remaining eggs. Rinse out the eggshells and set them in the cardboard egg carton. Wash the bellows tool.

### Step 7
Dry the eggs.

To oven-dry the eggshells, place the cardboard carton onto a baking tray and place the tray on the lowest rack in the preheated oven for 10 minutes. Remove the carton from the oven and let the eggs cool, about 5 minutes. Or let the eggs air-dry, about 3 days.

- **Two-hole method: Using a metal skewer and a drinking straw**

  This method is used to make the holes in the eggs for Easter Parade: Hollowed-Out Eggshell Ornaments (page 669). The eggshells have two holes at opposite ends, through which a ribbon is threaded to make a hanging loop. The holes are made by tapping the sharp tip of a metal skewer against the shell, using a pecking action much like a baby chick would use to crack a shell and emerge from it. Both holes are made with the egg yolk and white still inside; the contents absorb the force of the taps and distribute it through the liquid, helping to keep

the shell from shattering. An ordinary drinking straw is used to blow air into the eggshell and force out the contents. Be aware that the raw contents of the egg should not be ingested or used for cooking.

### MATERIALS AND TOOLS
Raw eggs
Cardboard egg carton
Metal skewer
Straightened jumbo paper clip
Plastic drinking straw, ³⁄₁₆" (0.5 cm) diameter
Poster putty pinched into a skinny 1"-long (2.5 cm) snake
Bowl
Baking sheet (optional)
Home oven (optional)

### Step 1 (optional)
Preheat oven.

Preheat an oven to 300°F (148.9°C). You can also air-dry blown eggshells.

### Step 2
Make two holes in an eggshell.

Hold an egg in one hand with the wide end of the egg facing up. Use the sharp tip of a skewer to tap a ¼"-diameter (0.6 cm) hole in the top center of the shell. Turn the egg so the narrow end faces up. As before, tap a 1¼"-diameter (0.6 cm) hole in the shell.

### Step 3
Pierce the contents in the eggshell.

Cradle the egg in one hand. Use your other hand to insert one end of a straightened paper clip into the hole in the egg, gently poking and stirring the egg's contents to break the membrane enveloping the yolk.

### Step 4
Blow the contents out of the shell.

Hold the egg, wide end facing up, and insert one end of a straw into the hole, stopping midway in the egg. Seal the gaps between the straw and the eggshell with a snake-shaped piece of putty. Working over a bowl, hold the egg in one hand and the straw in the other and blow through the straw to force the contents of the egg out through the hole at the opposite end and into the bowl. Discard the yolk and egg white down a sink drain. Remove the putty and withdraw the straw from the egg.

### Step 5

Clean the inside of the egg.

Run warm tap water into the egg hole. Shake the egg to agitate the water so it rinses the inside of the shell. Set the eggshell, hole side down, in the egg carton to allow the water to drain out.

### Step 6

Blow the contents out of the remaining eggs.

Repeat steps 2–5 to blow out the contents of the remaining eggs. Rinse out the eggshells and set them in the egg carton.

### Step 7

Dry the eggs.

To oven-dry the eggshells, place the carton onto a baking tray and place the tray on the lowest rack in the preheated oven for 10 minutes. Remove the carton from the oven and let the eggs cool, about 5 minutes. Or let the eggs air-dry, about 3 days.

---

## smART ideas: Laminating Fabric

Although eggshell ornaments can be decorated with ordinary construction paper, they will be more unique if design components are made from cotton fabric. The wings and tail feathers of small birds and the ears and paws of small animals are especially endearing in tiny prints or patterns. Fabric is made sturdier and reversible by laminating two layers together using acrylic varnish. Intricate details can be cut with precision and shapes can be rolled or curled without tearing. Use a brush to coat both sides of a 4" × 6" (10.2 × 16.2 cm) piece of even-weave cotton fabric with acrylic varnish. Fold the coated fabric in half, wrong side in, and press the layers together. Let the varnish dry completely, 10 to 15 minutes, and cut out the desired shapes.

## Making an Easter Egg Tree for Indoor Display

Gather fresh-cut stems of pussy willow or flowering branches, such as forsythia or apple blossoms. Place a layer of pebbles in the bottom of a bucket and fill the container with water. Strip off the bottom foliage from each of the branches so the plant matter isn't below the water line and insert the stems in the container. Use the loop on each hollowed-out eggshell ornament to hang the decorated eggs, distributing the eggs throughout the arrangement.

*Flowers*

*Mouse*

Paper punch, ½" (1.3 cm) flower
Cardstock, in assorted colors

Use a paper punch to cut 20 to 24 flowers from cardstock in assorted colors. Use dabs of melted glue to affix the flowers in a random pattern to the surface of the egg.

Ear, Nose, and Paws patterns (page 720)
Black thread
3 mm pearl
Black permanent marker

Use the patterns to cut out two ears, one nose, and two sets of paws from laminated fabric; also cut one 4" × ¼" (10.2 × 0.6 cm) strip for the tail. Roll and glue the nose piece into a cone. Use dabs of melted glue to affix the fabric components to the egg as shown. Add snippets of black thread to the nose for whiskers. Glue a pearl to the tip of the cone to finish the nose. Use a black permanent marker to add the eyes.

*Little Boy*

*Little Girl*

Infant-size sock
String or yarn
Permanent markers
Pink cosmetic blush

Cut off the sock cuff to make a tube 2½"
(6.4 cm) wide. Slip the tube onto the eggshell,
having one edge at the top and the other edge
hugging the eggshell all around. Use dabs of
melted glue to affix the bottom edge to the
eggshell. Pull the ribbon loop through the top
opening of the tube and tie the tube closed
with string or yarn, approximately ½" (1.3 cm)
from the raw edge, to make a hat. Cut a 3" × ½"
(7.6 × 1.3 cm) strip from the foot of the sock.
Wrap and glue the strip around the ribbon
at the bottom of the eggshell for a scarf. Use
permanent markers to sketch in the facial features. Smudge on pink cosmetic blush for the
cheeks.

Infant-size sock
Small fabric rose, ½" (1.3 cm) in diameter
Permanent markers
Pink cosmetic blush

Cut off part of the sock cuff to make a
½"-wide (1.3 cm) band. Slip the band over
the egg and use dabs of melted glue to affix a
small fabric rose to the front of the headband.
Use permanent markers to sketch in facial features. Smudge on pink cosmetic blush for the
cheeks.

*Airplane*

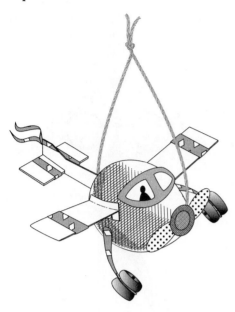

to the back of the plane for a streamer. Glue the small button to the center of the propeller piece. Glue the components to the egg as shown.

*Humpty Dumpty*

Wing, Tail A, Tail B, Windshield, and
    Propeller patterns (page 721)
Cardstock, in white or color, as desired
Laminated fabric or narrow ribbon
Four ⅝" (1.6 cm) buttons
Button, 1 mm diameter
Yarn, 12" (30.5 cm) length
Black permanent marker

Instead of a ribbon hanger, thread yarn through the eggshell and tie the ends in a double knot. Hold the egg horizontally so that the yarn extends from the holes on the left and right sides. Use the patterns to cut two wings, one tail A, one tail B, one windshield, and one propeller from cardstock; cut slits or tabs and make folds as indicated on the patterns. Decorate the wing and tail pieces with ⅛"-wide (0.3 cm) strips of laminated fabric or ribbon. Use a permanent marker to draw a pilot figure on one side of the windshield piece as shown. Cut two 2" × ¼" (5.1 × 0.6 cm) strips from laminated fabric. Sandwich the end of one strip between two ⅝"-wide (1.6 cm) buttons to make each landing gear. Glue the other strip

Hat, Mitt, and Shoe patterns (page 722)
Laminated fabric
Felt
Yarn
Ribbon
Construction paper
Wire spectacles (page 679)
Hole punch, ¼" (0.6 cm) in diameter

Use the pattern to cut one hat from laminated fabric; also cut two 2½" × ⅜" (6.4 × 1.0 cm) strips for arms and two 3" × ⅜" (7.6 × 1.0 cm) strips for legs. Roll the hat into a cone shape and secure with glue. Trim the brim and peak with ribbon, as desired. Use the remaining patterns to cut four mitts and four shoes from felt. Glue two mitts back to back, sandwiching the end of an arm strip in between; make a second arm to match. Glue the shoes to the legs in the same way. Glue the arms and legs to the eggshell. Cut 1¼" (3.2 cm) pieces of yarn and glue them around the top of the eggshell for hair; glue on the hat at a slant, covering the ends of the yarn but allowing the ribbon loop to emerge. Glue the wire spectacles to the face; punch paper circles from construction paper to make white eyes with dark pupils and glue them to the wire rims. Cut a nose and mouth from construction paper and glue in place.

## Circles

Paper punch, ⅝" (1.6 cm) circle
Cardstock, in assorted colors

Use a paper punch to cut 20 to 24 circles from cardstock in assorted colors. Glue the circles in a random pattern to the surface of the egg.

## Owl

Wing, Tail, and Ear patterns (page 723)
Laminated fabric
Construction paper
Paper punches
   1" (2.5 cm) circle
   ¾" (1.9 cm) circle
   ½" (1.3 cm) flower
Chenille stem
Wire spectacles

Use the patterns to cut out two wings, one tail, and two ears from laminated fabric; cut a beak freehand. Curl the ends of the feathers with your fingers. Cut two pieces from construction paper with each paper punch; layer and glue the pieces to the eggshell, with the flower shape on top, for the eyes. Use wire cutters to cut two ¾" (1.9 cm) long pieces of pipe cleaner; bend each piece in half to make a V-shaped foot and glue at the bottom of the eggshell. Glue on wire spectacles.

# smART ideas: Making Wire Spectacles

Wire spectacles for decorated eggs are made from 24-gauge brass wire. The directions are easy to adapt to larger or smaller sizes to make spectacles for dolls and stuffed animals.

- Measure and cut an 18" (45.7 cm) length of 24-gauge brass wire. Use your thumb to hold the wire against a $\frac{1}{2}$"-diameter (1.3 cm) dowel 3" (7.6 cm) from one end. Wrap the wire around the dowel three times to make a coil. Carefully slide the coil off the dowel.

- Hold the wire coil in one hand. Use your other hand to bring the shorter end through the center of the coil. Pull the short end taut, securing it to the coil at the 9 o'clock position.

Make a second wrap at the same position.

- Bring the longer wire end through the center of the coil and pull it taut at the 3 o'clock position. Make a second wrap at the same position.

- Straighten the long wire. Beginning $\frac{1}{2}$" (1.3 cm) from the first coil, hold the long wire against the dowel and wrap three times to make the second coil. Slide the coil off the dowel. Repeat the process to make a wrap at the 9 o'clock position and then at the 3 o'clock position.

- Use wire cutters to snip off any excess wire, leaving a 3" (7.6 cm) tail. Bend the end of each tail into a C shape. Bend the wire ends toward the back.

# Patterns and Original Art

This section contains patterns and original art used in the techniques and projects. Given with each piece are page references for the original citations and a suggested percentage for photocopying.

## Enlarging and Printing a Pattern

Use a laser copier or a computer with a scanner and a laser printer to enlarge the pattern by the percentage indicated. Here's a formula you can use to figure out the percentage for any size you may require:

Desired finished size ÷ original size × 100 =
    % to enlarge or reduce

Example:
The printed pattern is 4" (10.2 cm) long and
    you want a reproduction that is 8" (20.3
    cm) long.
8" (20.3 cm) ÷ 4" (10.2 cm) = 2
2 × 100 = 200%

Copy the resized pattern onto noncoated laser copy paper, #20, which is pliable, yet sturdy enough for handling. If the pattern is larger than the printer paper, copy the pattern in sections and piece them together, using a glue stick to secure the matched edges, to create one large pattern.

## Transferring a Pattern Printed on an Ink-Jet Printer

The ink on a print made using most ink-jet printers goes on wet and takes time to dry. An ink-jet print that is still wet can be used to transfer a pattern to paper and to linoleum and soft-carve blocks used for printing. Simply place the printed copy facedown on the project surface to transfer the line work to it, as if you were stamping with an inked stamp, and burnish the back of the pattern using your hand or the bowl side of a spoon. Pick up a corner of the print as you work to ensure that all of the pattern lines have transferred completely. Remove the pattern. If any of the lines of the pattern are light or broken, go over them with a marker or pencil.

Keep in mind that the ink-jet print will transfer a reverse pattern. If the orientation of the pattern is important, make a mirror-image print to start.

## Transferring a Pattern Using Graphite Paper

Graphite paper comes in thin, precut sheets. The sheet is coated with powdered graphite that transfers to the surface material when rubbed or pressed. Graphite paper is a convenient, albeit slightly messy, way to transfer a pattern to another surface material.

Lay a sheet of graphite paper facedown on the chosen surface and lay the printed pattern, faceup, on top. Use a pencil or ball-point pen and medium pressure to trace over the lines on the pattern to transfer them to the surface material. Check that the line work is complete. Remove the pattern and the graphite paper and then work with the transferred pattern as desired.

## Transferring a Pattern by Tracing and Cutting

Make a copy of the pattern and cut out the shape on the marked lines. Lay the paper cut-out on the chosen material and trace around it.

Some projects require that the same pattern be used several times, which can cause wear and tear on its cut edges. In that case, make a sturdy template. Trace the pattern onto clear, medium-weight plastic or glue the paper pattern to chipboard and cut it out using general-purpose scissors.

## Using a Pattern

Lay the pattern faceup on the chosen material, orienting its placement according to the symbols or guides printed on the pattern.

## Pattern Symbols

 Direction of grain of paper or fabric

Indicates the direction of the grain of paper or the straight of the fabric. Lay the pattern on the surface material, aligning the double arrows and the grain of the surface material.

———————— Exterior cutting line

Indicates an exterior cutting line that usually delineates the shape of the template. Lay the pattern on the surface material, using strips of low-tack tape or straight pins to secure it, and then use scissors or a craft knife to cut along the marked heavy, unbroken line.

- - - - - - - - - - Fold or interior cutting line

Indicates a fold or an interior cutting line. Use pin pricks or ticks made with a pencil to indicate short dash lines on the surface material. Fold or cut along this broken line, according to the written instructions.

– – – – – – – Half or quarter pattern

Indicates a half-pattern or a quarter-pattern. Complete these patterns by printing a reverse copy of the pattern and joining the sections together, matching the marks and using tape to secure the sections. Tape the mirror images together along the long dash lines and work with that, or use the taped pattern to make a new print out of the complete pattern.

Page 221   Elephant; Fun for Kids: Elephant Parade
Shown Actual Size

Page 223   Quick & Easy: Decorating a Card with Sewing
Shown Actual Size

Page 227   Envelope; Technique: Making an Envelope

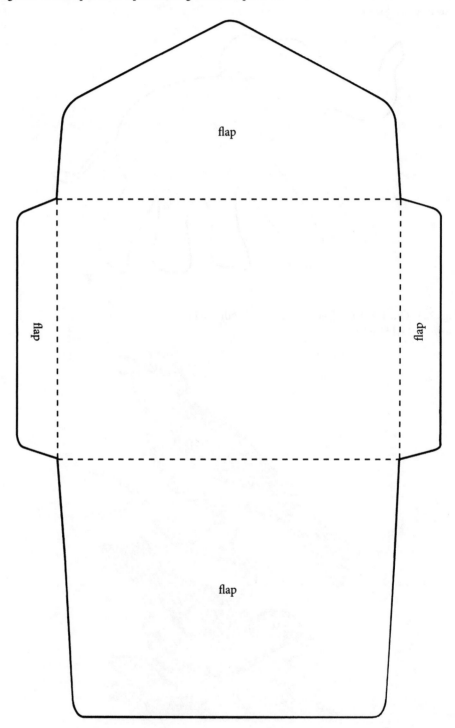

Page 231   Key to My Heart; Technique: Making a "Die-Cut" Card
Enlarge 200 Percent

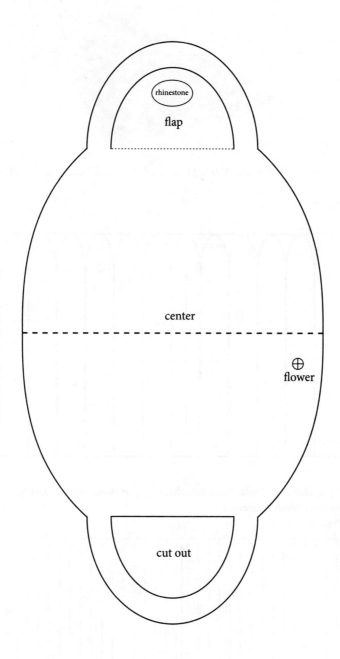

Page 234  Seashell; Technique: Making a Side Pop-Up
Shown Actual Size

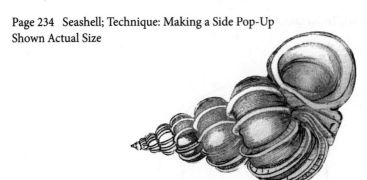

Page 261  Daisy Petals; Technique: Making Daisies, Black-Eyed Susans, and Sunflowers with
Button Stamens
Shown Actual Size

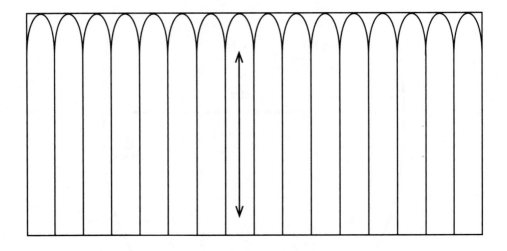

Page 261  Chrysanthemum Petals; Technique: Making Chrysanthemums, Zinnias, Cornflowers,
and Carnations with Brush Stamens
Enlarge 200 Percent

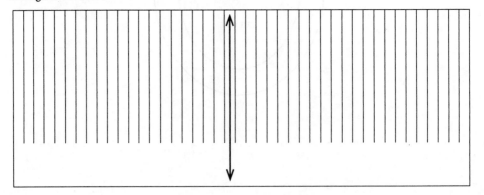

Page 262 Poppy Petal; Technique: Making a Poppy with a Combination Button and Anther-and-Filament Stamen
Shown Actual Size

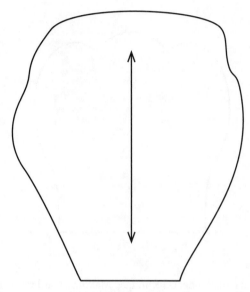

Page 263 Lily Petal; Technique: Making a Lily with an Anther-and-Filament Stamen
Shown Actual Size

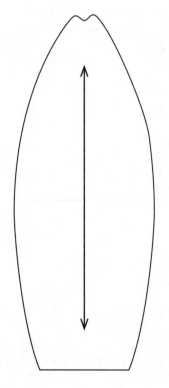

Page 263   Gardenia Petal (large outer); Technique: Making a Gardenia with a Bud Stamen
Shown Actual Size

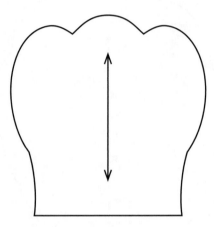

Page 263   Gardenia Petal (small inner); Technique: Making a Gardenia with a Bud Stamen
Shown Actual Size

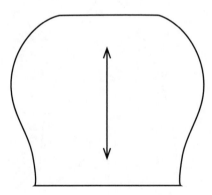

Page 264   Rose Petal; Making an Oversize Crepe Paper Rose
Shown Actual Size

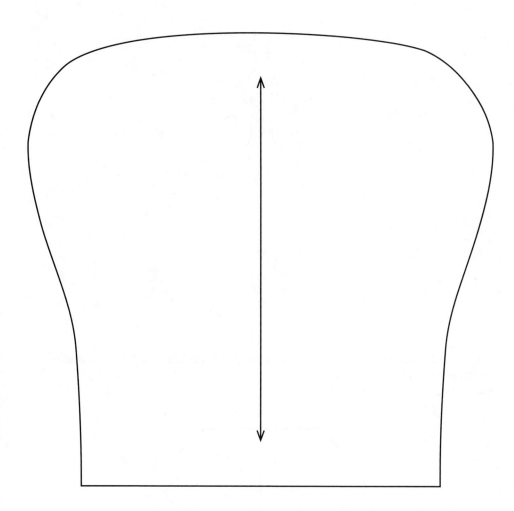

Page 261 Daisy Leaf; Technique: Making Daisies, Black-Eyed Susans, and Sunflowers with Button Stamens
Shown Actual Size

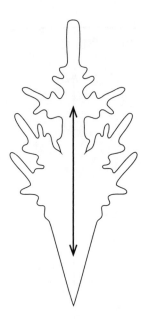

Page 261 Chrysanthemum Leaf; Technique: Making Chrysanthemums, Zinnias, Cornflowers, and Carnations with Brush Stamens
Shown Actual Size

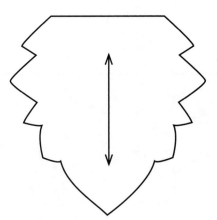

Page 262  Poppy Leaf; Technique: Making a Poppy with a Combination Button and Anther-and-Filament Stamen
Enlarge 125 Percent

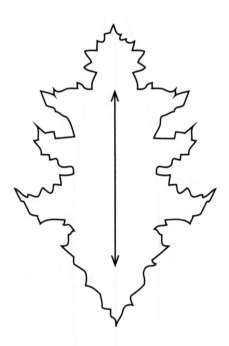

Page 263  Gardenia Leaf; Technique: Making a Gardenia with a Bud Stamen
Enlarge 120 Percent

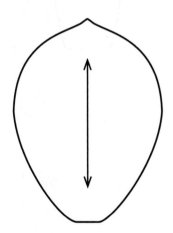

Page 263  Lily Leaf; Technique: Making a Lily with an Anther-and-Filament Stamen
Shown Actual Size

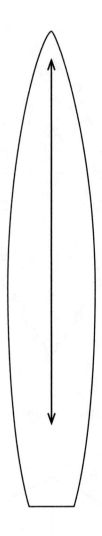

Page 277   Woven Heart: A Paper Basket
Enlarge 130 Percent

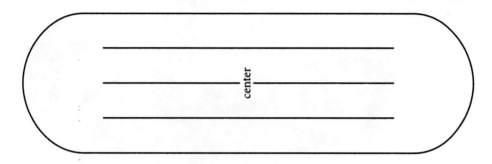

Page 279   Memories: Mini Photo Album
Enlarge 230 Percent

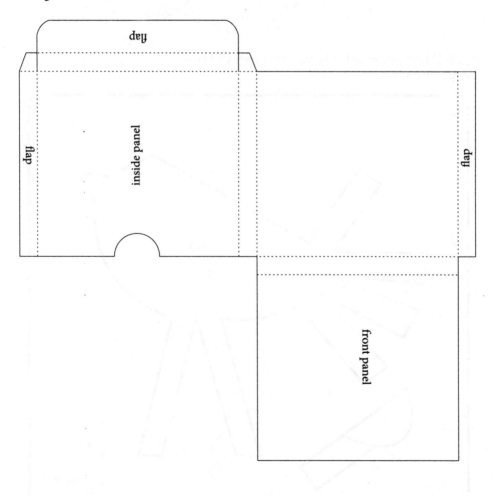

Page 634  Butterfly; Activity: Making a Slab Sculpture with Air-Dry Clay
Reduce 44 Percent

Page 282  Butterfly; The Deluxe Book of Butterflies: A Flag Book
Size as desired

Page 302  Bird; Fun for Kids: Making a Multicolor Bird Print
Enlarge 130 Percent

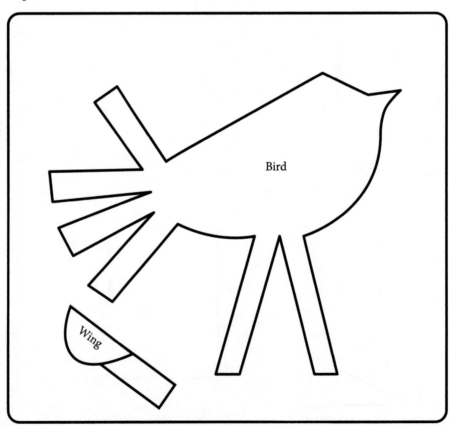

Bird

Wing

Page 306   Fleur-de-Lis; Quick & Easy: Making a Fleur-de-Lis Stamp
Enlarge 150 Percent

Page 226   Technique: Making a Single-Fold Card
Page 307   Tree and Moon; Technique: Transferring a Hand-Drawn Design to a Printing Block
Shown Actual Size

Page 319   Key Block and Color Block; Technique: Using a T Square and Self-Healing Cutting
Mat to Register and Print in Two Colors
Page 346   Butterfly Wing and Butterfly Color Block; Butterfly: A Gift Bag
Size as desired

Key Block

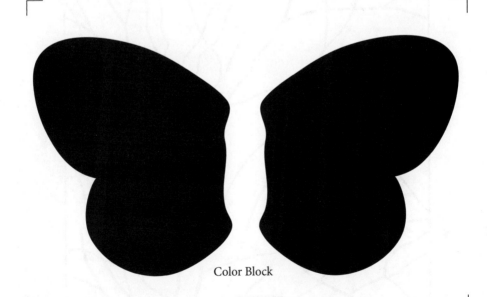

Color Block

Page 278   Red Shoe, a Strappy Sandal; Priceless: A Die-Cut Card
Page 322   Technique: Cutting an Acetate Stencil
Shown Actual Size

Page 278 and front cover   Silver Spike Heel (design by Rex Bonomelli);
Priceless: A Die-Cut Card
Shown Actual Size

Page 331  Double Branches; Technique: Making a Stencil with Screen Filler
Page 340  Technique: Pulling Prints from a Screen Stencil
Enlarge 140 Percent

Page 348  Single Branch; Leafy Branch: A Place Mat
Enlarge 140 Percent

Page 333   Bird in Flight; Technique: Making a Positive Stencil with Drawing Liquid and
Screen Filler
Enlarge 120 Percent

Page 273   Chrysanthemum; Technique: Making a Box Book
Page 335   Technique: Making the Acetate Positive
Page 352   Chrysanthemum: Printed Fabric for a Box Book
Enlarge 140 Percent

Page 344   Cord and Bead: Postcards
Shown Actual Size

Page 349   Chandelier: An Art Print
Enlarge 180 Percent

Page 393   Poppy; Technique: Designing on a Paper Template for a Cylinder
Page 394   Technique: Gluing Prints to a Prepared Surface
Enlarge 270 Percent

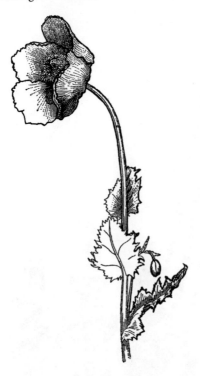

Page 369   Hand-Coloring Laser Prints
Page 401   Roses; Technique: Designing Directly
on a Glass Vessel
Page 405   Technique: Gluing Prints to
a Glass Vessel
Page 409   Technique: Painting a Glass Vessel
Enlarge 150 Percent

Page 402   Technique: Gluing Prints to a Flat Glass Surface
Page 412   Head Shots: Theme-and-Variation Dessert Plates
 Top (a): Enlarge 150 Percent
 Middle (b): Enlarge 500 Percent
 Middle (c): Enlarge 800 Percent
 Bottom (d): Enlarge 300 Percent

Page 410   Zebra: A Decorative Platter
Enlarge 175 Percent

Page 412 Monograms and Numerals; Head Shots: Theme-and-Variation Dessert Plates, Middle (b)
Enlarge 250 Percent

$$A\ B\ C\ D\ E\ F\ G$$

$$H\ I\ J\ K\ L\ M$$

$$N\ O\ P\ Q\ R\ S\ T$$

$$U\ V\ W\ X\ Y\ Z$$

$$1\ 2\ 3\ 4\ 5\ 6\ 7\ 8\ 9\ 0$$

Page 430   Flower Stencil; Technique: Using Adhesive-Backed Shelf Vinyl as a Mask
for Positive Designs
Enlarge 250 Percent

Page 454   Leaf; Technique: Making an Embossing Plate with a Leaf Pattern
Reduce or enlarge the size as desired

Page 474  Juliet Rose; Technique: Baking a Decal on a Glass or Ceramic Surface
Page 553  Juliet: A Vase with Rose Decals
Enlarge 150 Percent

Page 373 Technique: Cutting Out a Print
Page 467 Decals and Heat Transfers
Page 469 Monkey; Technique: Applying a Decal using the Waterslide Method
Shown Actual Size

Page 589 Bird and Wing; Activity: Making a Paper Bird with a Curly Tail
Enlarge 130 Percent

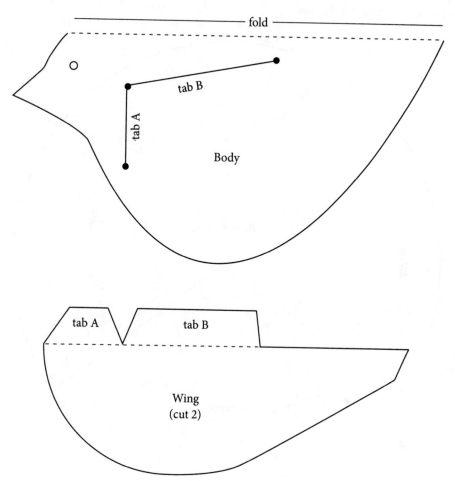

Page 602   Activity: Using Papier-Mâché to Make "Hilarious Hen"
Page 604   Activity: Using Plaster Tape to Decorate a Fish
Beak & Nose: Enlarge 140 Percent

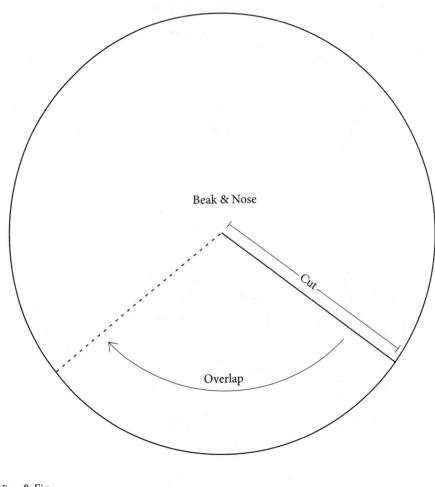

Beak & Nose

Wing & Fin
Enlarge 130 Percent

Wing & Fin
(make 2)

Pages 602 and 604 (*continued*)
Comb & Tail Fin
Enlarge 140 Percent

Comb & Tail Fin
Tail & Comb

Page 602   Hen's Foot; Activity: Using Papier-Mâché to Make "Hilarious Hen"
Enlarge Wing & Fin
      (make 2)

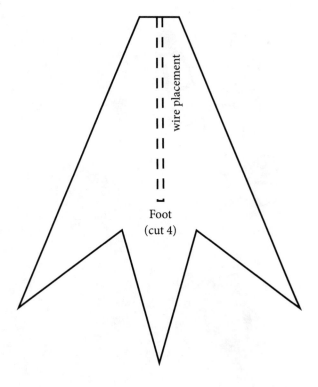

wire placement

Foot
(cut 4)

**Page 634** Dinosaur; Activity: Making a Slab Sculpture with Air-Dry Clay
**Enlarge 160 Percent**

**Page 240** Children's Original Drawings; Technique: Making Multiple Prints from Original Art

Page 641   Glitter Stars; Fun for Mom: Glitter Stars for a Christmas Tree
Enlarge 250 Percent

Glitter Stars
(cut 2)

**Page 649** Sox Martin: Sock Monkey
Enlarge 130 Percent

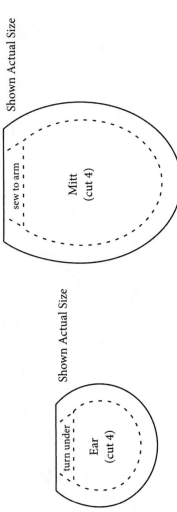

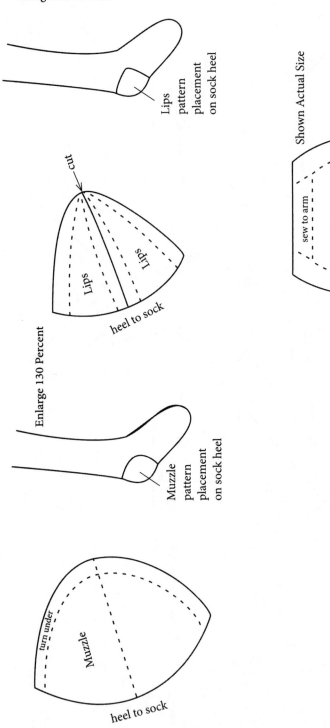

Page 651  Izzie and Andrew: Jointed Clay Dolls
Shown Actual Size

Izzie's Wig

Shown Actual Size

Andrew's Wig

Page 651   Izzie and Andrew: Jointed Clay Dolls (*continued*)
Enlarge 110 Percent

Izzie's Dress

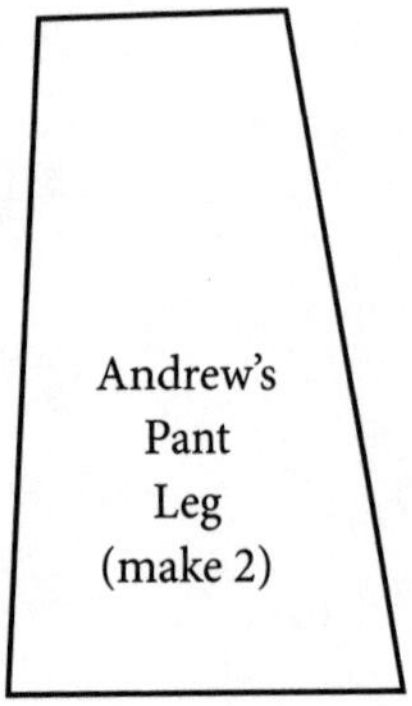

Andrew's
Pant
Leg
(make 2)

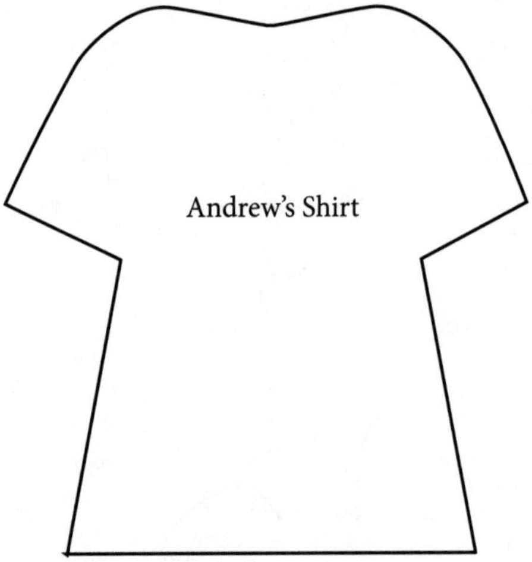

Andrew's Shirt

Izzie's Head

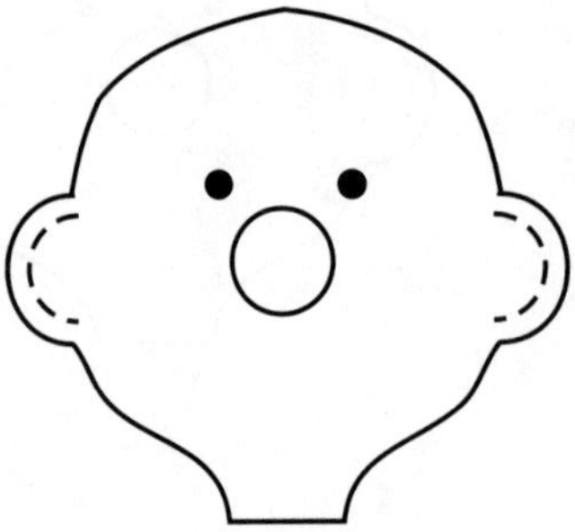

Andrew's Head

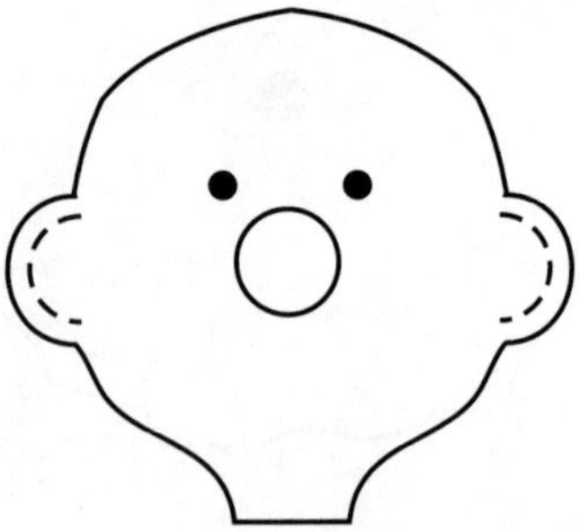

Page 671  Chicken
Shown Actual Size

Comb
(cut 4)

Tail

Wing
(cut 2)

Beak

Page 675  Mouse
Shown Actual Size

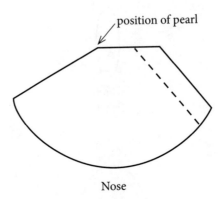

position of pearl

Nose

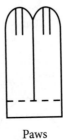

Paws
(cut 2)

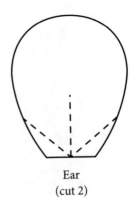

Ear
(cut 2)

Page 677 Airplane
Shown Actual Size

Windshield

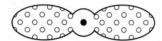

Propeller

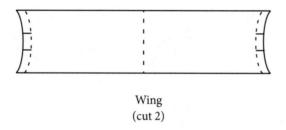

Wing
(cut 2)

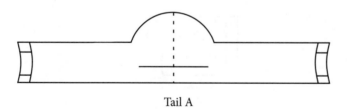

Tail A

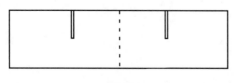

Tail B

Page 677   Humpty Dumpty
Shown Actual Size

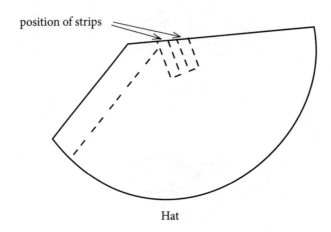

position of strips

Hat

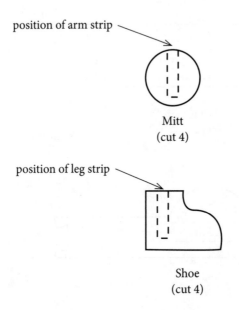

position of arm strip

Mitt
(cut 4)

position of leg strip

Shoe
(cut 4)

Page 678   Owl
Shown Actual Size

Wing
(cut 2)

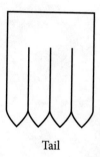

Tail

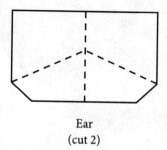

Ear
(cut 2)

Page 335  Technique: Making the Acetate Positive
Choose any section on the image or choose the whole image, reducing or enlarging
the size as desired.

# Resources

To find more crafting information, ideas, and original projects, feel free to visit my website, www.makeithomemade.com. Many of the arts and crafts supplies used for the techniques and projects in this book are available in retail craft stores. Visit the individual websites listed below or check out Qwest's Dex Online directory at www.dexknows.com to find suppliers in your area. A chapter-by-chapter listing follows to help you locate more specialized or technique-specific items that are sure to enhance your crafting experiences.

## General Craft Supplies

A. C. Moore Arts & Crafts
www.acmoore.com

Art Supply Warehouse
www.artsupplywarehouse.com

Craft King
www.craftking.com

Dick Blick Art Materials
www.dickblick.com

Hobby Lobby
www.hobbylobby.com

Jerry's Artarama
www.jerrysartarama.com

Jo-Ann Fabric & Crafts
www.joann.com

Michael's Arts and Crafts
www.michaels.com

Pearl Paint
www.pearlpaint.com

Ragshop
www.ragshop.com

Save-On-Crafts
www.save-on-crafts.com

Sunshine Discount Crafts
www.sunshinecrafts.com

## Chapter One: Beading

Each source offers a broad range of beads, findings, tools for jewelry making, glues and adhesives, stringing material, wire, organizers, and videos and books. Additional materials of special note are listed with the source reference. For a worldwide index of retail bead stores, go to www.guidetobeadwork.com.

Beadalon
www.beadalon.com
Offers wire-wrapping supplies, including colored copper wire, and Scrimp findings.

Beadazzled
501 North Charles Street
Baltimore, MD 21201
Phone: 410-837-2323
www.beadazzled.net
Offers African beads, beads in Chinese porcelain, resin, Lucite, cinnabar, and polymer clay, and finished dharma items (malas).

Beads and Gems International
66 West 37th Street
New York, NY 10018
Phone: 212-904-1690
Email: beadsandgems@verizon.net
Offers precious and semiprecious stones, and pearls on strands.

Beads on Fifth Inc.
376 Fifth Avenue
New York, NY 10001
Phone: 212-244-6616
www.artbeads.com
Offers a wide selection of Swarovski crystals and findings in sterling and gold fill.

Beads World, Inc.
1384 Broadway
New York, NY 10018
Phone: 212-302-1199
www.beadsworldusa.com
Offers loose and strung beads, precious and semiprecious stones, and sequins.

Beadworks
149 Water Street
Norwalk, CT 06854
Phone: 203-852-9108
www.beadworks.com

Bovis Bead Co.
www.bovisbeadco.com
Offers all types of French glass seed beads and French white-heart beads, as well as Native American Indian, rendezvous, mountain man, and historical reenactment craft supplies.

Bright Gems & Beads, Inc.
62 West 47th Street, Suite #706C
New York, NY 10036
Phone: 212-869-5520
www.brightgemsbeads.com
Offers wide selection of precious and semiprecious stones.

Cartwright's Sequins & Vintage Buttons
www.ccartwright.com
Offers wide range of sequins and buttons.

Charm Factory
www.charmfactory.com
Offers sterling silver charms and bracelets.

Creativityinc.com
(Blue Moon Beads)
www.creativityinc.com
Offers natural and acrylic beads, charms, and pendants.

Crystal Beads of Boston
31 Hayward Street, Suite A-1
Franklin, MA 02038
Phone: 866-70BEADS
www.crystalbeadsofboston.com
Offers Swarovski crystals, Miyuki and Toho seed beads, sterling silver and gold-filled findings, Venetian/Murano glass beads, and freshwater pearls.

Earthstone Co.
www.earthstone.com
Offers a helpful annotated and illustrated glossary of a wide range of beads.

Fire Mountain Gems and Beads
www.firemountaingems.com
Offers Swarovski crystal, Czech fire-polished beads, Czech glass beads, and pendants.

Fun 2 Bead
1028 Sixth Avenue
New York, NY 10018
Phone: 212-966-2748
www.fun2bead.com

Fusion Beads
www.fusionbeads.com
Offers sterling silver blank charms and links for stamping.

Genevieve Sterbenz Designs
www.genevievesterbenz.com
Offers free downloads of beading projects with illustrated directions.

Genuine Ten Ten
1010 Sixth Avenue
New York, NY 10018
Phone: 212-221-1173
www.j-genuine.com

Jewelry-Design-Gemstone.com
www.jewelry-design-gemstone.com
Offers information on birthstones, precious metals, and designs by Leslie Leirness Jewelry Designs for Shabocon.

Jewelry Supply Company
www.jewelrysupply.com

Margola
48 West 37th Street
New York, NY 10018
Phone: 212-695-1115
www.margola.com
Offers wide selection of Preciosa crystals, Czech beads, rhinestones, and trimmings, including vintage glass buttons.

Master Wire Sculptor, Inc.
www.wire-sculpture.com
Offers broad range of wire—sterling silver, gold-filled, argentium, copper, brass, and gold- and silver-enameled copper—along with helpful jewelry tutorials.

Metalliferous
34 West 46th Street
New York, NY 10036
Phone: 212-944-0909
www.metalliferous.com
Offers high-quality tools and embossed metal charms and onlays.

Modern Tibet
103 Sullivan Street
New York, NY 10012
Phone: 646-613-0600
www.moderntibet.com
Offers exotic beads, including turquoise and yak bone in bezel settings, yellow amber with silver endcaps, and sterling silver pendants.

New York Beads
1026 Sixth Avenue
New York, NY 10018
Phone: 212-382-2994
www.newyorkbeads.com

Nina Designs
www.ninadesigns.com
Offers silver and gold pendants, charms, and findings.

Prima Bead
2860 Roosevelt Boulevard
Clearwater, FL 34620
Phone: 727-531-7533
www.primabead.com
Offers faceted beads and rhinestones in acrylic and glass.

Stormcloud Trading Co.
www.beadstorm.com
>Offers seed beads, crystals, Czech pressed-glass beads, needles and threads, metal charms, and chain by the foot.

Toho Shoji
990 Sixth Avenue
New York, NY 10018
Phone: 212-868-7466
www.tohoshoji-ny.com

White Cloud Co.
2 West 46th Street, #808
New York, NY 10036
Phone: 212-840-3899
Email: whitecloud@hotmail.com
>Offers handcrafted gold findings and precious and semiprecious beads.

Whole Bead Shop
www.wholebeadshop.com
>Offers wide selection of Knopfen Strasse buttons and beads, German metal, embossed-glass flowers, and findings in a range of metals, including 22-karat gold, fine silver, antiqued copper, and oxidized fine silver.

## Chapter Two: Floral Arts

Craft chains, local craft stores, and garden centers carry a broad range of floral supplies, including wire, wreath frames, foam, adhesives, tape, and wraps, as well as vases, baskets, and unique containers. See below for retail and online vendors with products of special interest, including ingredients to make potpourri and beauty and bath potions.

Arnold Gummer
www.arnoldgrummer.com
>Offers an easy-to-use portable botanical press for pressing fresh flowers and foliage for use in card making and paper making.

Center of Floral Design and Supply, Inc.
145 West 28th Street
New York, NY 10001
Phone: 212-279-5044
>Offers high-quality silk flowers, plants, and trees.

D. Blumchen & Company
www.blumchen.com
>Offers rare and vintage floral supplies, including artificial flowers, foliage, stamens, lacquer-composition fruits, berries, vegetables and mushrooms, and floral items, some made of flocked velvet, goose feathers, and foil.

Dried Flowers Direct from Keuka Flower Farm
www.driedflowersdirect.com
>Offers dried wreaths and flowers, wheat, grasses, pods, and foliage shipped directly from this upstate New York family-run farm.

Flowers by Design
470 Mission Street, Unit #11
Carol Stream, IL 60188
Phone: 800-833-SILK
www.flowers-by-design.com

Hanken Imports
7140 North Dixie Drive
Dayton, OH 45414
Phone: 800-783-0852
www.hankenimports.com
>Offers artificial birds, butterflies, chickens, flowering bushes, eggs, and nests, and wreath forms and baskets.

Jamali Garden Hardware
149 West 28th Street
New York, NY 10001
Phone: 212-244-4025
www.jamaligarden.com
>Offers glass for bouquets, arrangements, and centerpieces; bamboo and willow;

garden pots in wood, fiberglass, and ceramic; and decorative man-made sea glass, glass nuggets, and acrylic gemstones.

Lavender Lane
www.lavenderlane.com
Offers a variety of essential and fragrance oils, lotions, gels, powders, waxes, potpourri, candle and soap molds, bottles, and books.

Mountain Rose Herbs
P.O. Box 50220
Eugene, OR 97405
Phone: 800-879-3337
www.mountainroseherbs.com
Offers organic herbs and spices, organic teas, essential oils, and containers and packaging.

Oxford Grove Premium Artificial Plants
P.O. Box 308
Klamath Falls, OR 97601
Phone: 503-922-0546
www.oxfordgrove.com
Offers handcrafted artificial trees, plants, flowers, topiary, flowers, cactus, ficus, ferns, and shrubbery.

Pressed Flower Store
www.pressedflowerstore.com
Offers a wide variety of pressed flowers, as well as supplies for pressing flowers, including pads, filters, and a flower press.

Prudence Designs and Events
228 West 18th Street
New York, NY 10011
Phone: 212-691-1356
www.prudencedesigns.net
Offers one-of-a-kind arrangements by nationally distinguished floral designer Arturo Quintero and full-service event planning led by creative director Grayson Handy.

Richters Herbs
357 Highway 47
Goodwood, ON LOC 1A0 Canada
Phone: 905-640-6677
www.richters.com
Offers a wide variety of organic and wild-crafted dried herbs, plus seeds, plants, roots, extracts, and oils.

San Francisco Herb Company
250 14th Street
San Francisco, CA 94103
Phone: 415-861-3018
www.sfherb.com
Offers gourmet spices, botanical herbs, roots, berries, tea, essential oils, and potpourri.

Scentsational
259 Main Street
Huntington, NY 11743
Phone: 631-549-2090
www.escentsational.com
Offers custom-blended and preblended fragrances, including a wide selection of fragrance oils, essential oils, eau de toilette, and moisturizers, and items for skin, hair, hand, and foot care.

Sugar Plum Sundries
www.diannassundries.com
Offers soapmaking and cosmetic supplies, including clear soap base and essential oils, colorants, molds, and cutters.

Teddy's Florist
22–41 31st Street
Astoria, NY 11105
Phone: 718-728-7307
www.teddysflorist.com
Offers a wide selection of cut flowers and foliage in a broad seasonal range, and provides a full-service florist with arrangements of every description for all events and occasions.

White Flower Farm
Box 50
Route 63
Litchfield, CT 06759
Phone: 800-503-9624
www.whiteflowerfarm.com
Offers a wide selection of plants, shrubs, bulbs, and gardening supplies.

Willow Way, LLC
www.soapequipment.com
Offers soapmaking equipment and supplies for the beginner and professional soap maker, including soap cutters, molds, and bath-bomb presses.

## Chapter Three: Paper Crafting

Suppliers of items for paper crafting provide a wide range of unique brands of paper, stationery, sundries, and tools, including 100 percent rag papers, vintage chromolithographs, and stamps.

Addicted to Rubber Stamps
www.addictedtorubberstamps.com
Offers a huge variety of rubber stamps from over 150 stamp companies in all artistic styles and themes: love, home, flowers, animals, wedding, baby, holiday; stamp types include wood-mounted, foam-mounted, clear, unmounted, pre-inked, cling, and rolling-style. Other products include coloring tools, paints, inks and pads, mounts, tools, transfers, stencils, and paper.

All Things Ukrainian
www.allthingsukrainian.com
Offers items created by Ukrainian artists and artist's supplies. Also carries the Blas Fix egg-hollowing kit, which will help clean out the contents of an egg without breaking the shell.

Archivers
www.archiversonline.com
Offers creative ways to organize, display, and preserve photographs.

Artist & Craftsman Supplies
www.artistcraftsman.com
Offers paper in rolls and reams, including kraft paper, poster board, construction paper, tag board, tissue paper, and drawing paper.

Brassworks Embossing
www.brassworksembossing.com
Offers brass embossing templates for dry embossing and a wide range of eyelets, brads, and buttons for scrapbooking.

D. Blumchen & Company
www.blumchen.com
Offers Christmas tree ornaments, decorations, and old-time crafting supplies from Europe and America, including embossed die-cut scraps and vintage chromolithographs, embossed Dresden foil trims, German Lametta tinsels; unique offerings for Valentine greetings, Christmas, Halloween, and Easter.

Dover Publications, Inc.
www.doverpublications.com
Offers over 800 books of illustrations, plus clip art on CD-ROMs, for use by artists and crafters, including decorative leaf, floral, plant, bird, and animal designs; traditional Chinese designs; and royalty-free Art Nouveau graphics, from simple medallions and borders to elaborate panels and vignettes.

The Ink Pad
22 Eighth Avenue
New York, NY 10014
www.theinkpadnyc.com
Offers a wide selection of stamps, papers, embellishments, inks, crafting tools,

magazine and books; also has in-store classes.

Kate's Paperie
72 Spring Street
New York, NY 10012
Phone: 212-941-9816
www.katespaperie.com
Offers stationery and paper by Cavallini, Crane, Kate Spade, Vera Wang, and Retro 51; also offers invitations, gift wrap, ribbon, photo albums, journals and notebooks, writing instruments, unique decorative paper by the sheet, and items and gifts for holidays, birthdays, weddings, and baby showers.

Lasting Impressions for Paper
www.lastingimpressions.com
Offers a complete line of card making and scrapbooking products, including die-cut metal embossing templates in a vast range of motifs and embossing styluses. Consult the website to find a local retailer.

New York Central Art Supply
62 Third Avenue
New York, NY 10003
Phone: 212-473-7705
www.nycentralart.com
Offers a wide assortment of papers in different sizes, textures, colors, and weights.

Packaging Specialties
515 South Michigan Avenue
Seattle, WA 98108
Phone: 206-762-0540
www.packagingspecialties.com
Offers decorative silver- and gold-bullion wire.

Papermart
www.papermart.com
Offers a wide selection of paper packaging supplies, including gift wrap, tissue,

recycled paper, kraft paper, corrugated and colored-mesh sheets, fabric and paper bags, boxes and containers (for heavy-duty shipping, gifts, jewelry, favors, and food), ribbons, tape, loose fill, and baskets.

Paperzone
www.memories.com
Offers an extensive variety of fine paper, card making and scrapbooking supplies, gift wrap, invitations, stamps, boxes, and adhesives, as well as a wide range of crafting tools.

Rubber Monger
www.rubbermonger.com
Offers a wide selection of rubber stamps in over twenty categories, including original art and vintage illustrations of birds, animals, Native American designs, faux postage, celestial designs, household themes, and people.

Rycraft, Inc.
www.rycraft.com
Offers ceramic cookie stamps and cutters in a wide variety—Americana, animals, holiday, music, and home—as well as some craft materials for casting with paper and clay.

Stamp Francisco
www.stampfrancisco.com
Offers a vast collection of mounted and unmounted rubber stamps in ninety-nine categories, including holidays, animals, romance, rabbits, and travel; manufactured by Art by Moonlight, Bartholomews Ink, D.O.A., Eclectic Omnibus, Fruit Basket Upset, Gumbo Graphics, Hippo Heart, Imagine, Ivory Coast Trading Poste, Renaissance Art Stamps, Rubber Baby Buggy Bumpers, and Rubber Stamp Madness.

Stampington & Company
www.stampington.com
Offers a wide variety of wood-mounted and transparent unmounted stamps through the publisher of *Somerset Studio* and other crafting magazines focused on paper crafting, mixed-media art, and doll making.

Talas
330 Morgan Avenue
Brooklyn, NY 11211
Phone: 212-219-0770
www.talasonline.com
Offers materials and tools for professional archival storage, bookbinding, conservation, and restoration.

Thomson's Art Supply
184 Mamaroneck Avenue
White Plains, NY 10601
Phone: 800-287-4885
www.thomsonsart.com
Offers a broad range of artist's materials, drafting supplies including Chartpak tape, and papers, and provides conservation and custom framing.

## Chapter Four: Hand Printing

Dennis Johnson Photography
Phone: 201-445-6213
Offers a wide range of services, including portraiture (especially babies and children in natural settings) and still-life photography.

Dover Publications, Inc.
www.doverpublications.com
Offers over 800 books of illustrations, plus clip art on CD-ROMs, for use by artists and crafters, including decorative leaf, floral, plants, birds, and animal designs, traditional Chinese designs, and royalty-free Art Nouveau graphics, from simple medallions and borders to elaborate panels and vignettes.

New York Central Art Supply
62 Third Avenue
New York, NY 10003
Phone: 212-473-7705
www.nycentralart.com
Offers a wide assortment of papers in different sizes, textures, colors, and weights.

Pearl Paint
308 Canal Street
New York, NY 10013–2572
Phone: 800-451-7327
www.pearlpaint.com
Offers a broad line of materials and tools for block printing and screen printing, including inks, brayers, linoleum blocks, and screens; carries Speedball Art Products.

Speedball Art Products Company
www.speedballart.com
Offers a broad selection of supplies and tools for block printing and screen printing, including instructional videos on hand-printing methods, Speedy-Cut rubber blocks, and the Diazo Photo-Emulsion Kit.

Stamp Francisco
www.stampfrancisco.com
Offers a vast collection of mounted and unmounted rubber stamps in ninety-nine categories, including holidays, animals, romance, rabbits, and travel, manufactured by Art by Moonlight and Rubber Stamp Madness, among others. Stamp Francisco's Fleur-de-Lis rubber stamp design is featured on pages 306 and 695.

Stampington & Company
www.stampington.com

    Offers a wide variety of wood-mounted and transparent unmounted stamps through the publisher of *Somerset Studio* and other crafting magazines focused on paper crafting, mixed-media art, and doll making.

## Chapter Five: Decoupage

Supplies for decoupage are available from a wide variety of vendors, from national retail chains to one-of-a-kind shops, most of which offer online shopping.

D. Blumchen & Company
www.blumchen.com

    Offers old-time crafting supplies from Europe and America for decoupage—embossed, die-cut scraps, and vintage chromolithographs, including embossed Dresden foil trims and German Lametta tinsels.

Découpage Online
www.decoupage-online.com

    Offers sealers, varnish, paint, brushes, gesso, and tack cloths.

Dover Publications, Inc.
www.doverpublications.com

    Offers over 800 books of illustrations for use by artists and crafters, including decorative leaf, floral, plants, birds, and animal designs, traditional Chinese designs, and royalty-free Art Nouveau graphics, from simple medallions and borders to elaborate panels and vignettes.

Krylon
www.krylon.com

    Offers a wide selection of spray paint in a full chromatic spectrum and in metallic colors; products include paint formulations for application to plastic and metal, protective finishes for paper, spray adhesives and fixatives, and smaller-size cans for painting small projects. Consult the website to find a local retailer.

Paper Source
www.paper-source.com

    Offers a full range of fine and artisanal papers, gift wrap, and gift boxes; imported papers from Japan, India, Lokta/Nepal, and Italy; as well as vellum and paper crafting tools (for blind and heat-embossing; paper punches).

Walnut Hollow
Phone: 800-950-5101
www.walnuthollow.com

    Offers unfinished wood products, tools, and accessories, including basswood keepsake boxes. Consult the website to find a local retailer.

Woodcrafter.com
www.woodcrafter.com

    Offers a wide selection of unfinished wooden items, from boxes and frames to beads, bracelets, buckets, and containers.

www.1stockphoto.com

    Offers a central index of online sources of stock photography, including a wide selection of clip art, some free.

## Chapter Six: Decorative Embellishing

Supplies for embellishing are available from a wide variety of vendors, from national retail chains to one-of-a-kind shops, most of which offer online shopping.

## Glass Etching

**Crate & Barrel**
www.crateandbarrel.com
Offers glass items suitable for etching. Consult the website to find a local retailer.

**Etchworld**
www.etchworld.com
Offers Armour Etching Cream, etch bath, Rub 'N' Etch stencils, cutting tools, and glass items, including mirrors, vases, bottles, and frames, to etch.

**Pier 1 Imports**
www.pier1imports.com
Offers glass items suitable for etching. Consult the website to find a local retailer.

**Pottery Barn**
www.potterybarn.com
Offers glass items suitable for etching. Consult the website to find a local retailer.

## Gilding

**Artist & Craftsman Supplies**
www.artistcraftsman.com
Offers a full line of gilding supplies, including leaf in sheets and rolls and mica powders.

**Speedball Art Products Company**
www.speedballart.com
Offers a broad selection of metal-leafing supplies, including gold, silver, and copper leaf in sheet, flake, and powder forms, adhesives, mediums, cotton gloves, and sponges. Consult the website to find a local retailer.

## Dry Embossing

**B & J Fabrics**
525 Seventh Avenue
New York, NY 10018
Phone: 212-354-8150
www.bandjfabrics.com
Offers a wide selection of fabric, including brocade, faux fur, chenille, novelty, silk, Ultrasuede, velvet, wool, and vinyl.

**Dick Blick Art Materials**
www.dickblick.com
Offers aluminum armature wire in a range of sizes, from 4- to 16-gauge.

**New York Elegant Fabrics**
222 West 40th Street
New York, NY 10018
Phone: 212-302-4980
www.nyelegantfabrics.com
Offers a wide range of fabric, including velvet, silk, and wool, and also provides personal service, gives advice, and answers questions concerning fabrics through Facebook and Twitter.

## Ribbons, Trims, and Fabric

**B & J Fabrics**
525 Seventh Avenue
New York, NY 10018
Phone: 212-354-8150
www.bandjfabrics.com
Offers a wide selection of fabric, including brocade, faux fur, chenille, novelty, silk, Ultrasuede, velvet, wool, and vinyl.

**Bellochio**
10 Brady Street
San Francisco, CA 94103
Phone: 415-864-4048
www.bellochio.com
Offers antiques and curiosities, including vintage ribbons, gift boxes, cards, and stationery items.

Full Swing Textiles Collections, Inc.
474 Thames Street
Newport, RI 02840
Phone: 401-849-9494
www.fullswingtextiles.com
  Offers vintage- and retro-inspired drapery
  and upholstery-grade barkcloth.

Hyman Hendler & Sons
21 West 38th Street
New York, NY 10018
Phone: 212-840-8393
www.hymanhendler.com
  Offers wide selection of cotton, velvet,
  taffeta, satin, and wire-edged ribbons,
  including vintage ribbons in floral,
  jacquard, plaid, stripes, and other novelty
  weaves.

Lou Lou Buttons
69 West 38th Street
New York, NY 10018
Phone: 212-398-5498
  Offers a huge selection of buttons made of
  various materials, including bone, metal,
  plastic, resin, and glass, in a wide range of
  styles and sizes. Retail shop only.

M & J Trimming
1008 Sixth Avenue
New York, NY 10018
Phone: 800-965-9595
www.mjtrim.com
  Offers wide selection of appliqués,
  buttons, cords and tassels, fringe, ribbons
  and jacquards, rhinestones and crystals,
  sequins and sew-ons, trims and braids,
  flower pins and pendants, and craft
  supplies and tools.

Mountain of Fabrics
227 West 40th Street
New York, NY 10018
Phone: 212-354-8442
www.mountainoffabrics.com
  Offers a broad range of fabrics, including

silk, wool, cotton, and upholstery, plus
trimmings.

New York Elegant Fabrics
222 West 40th Street
New York, NY 10018
Phone: 212-302-4980
www.nyelegantfabrics.com
  Offers a wide range of fabric, including
  velvet, silk, and wool; in addition, provides
  personal service, gives advice, and answers
  questions concerning fabrics through
  Facebook and Twitter.

Reproduction Fabrics
205 Haggerty Lane, Suite 190
Bozeman, MT 59715
Phone: 800-380-4611
www.reproductionfabrics.com
  Offers a wide range of cotton reproduction
  fabrics in the period from 1775 to 1950.

Tinsel Trading Company
47 West 38th Street
New York, NY 10018
Phone: 212-730-4030
www.tinseltrading.com
  Offers an eclectic assortment of new and
  vintage passementerie, ribbons, metallic
  trims, and flowers.

Decals and Heat-Transfers

Dover Publications, Inc.
www.doverpublications.com
  Offers over 800 books of illustrations
  for use by artists and crafters, including
  decorative leaf, floral, plants, birds, and
  animal designs, traditional Chinese
  designs, and royalty-free Art Nouveau
  graphics, from simple medallions and
  borders to elaborate panels and
  vignettes.

**Electric Quilt Company**
www.electricquilt.com
Offers printable peel-and-stick fabric sheets for use with an ink-jet printer that can be used as printed appliqués.

**Lazertran**
www.lazertran.com
Offers waterslide decal papers and transfer paper for both light- and dark-colored textiles for use with ink-jet printers, transfer paper for use with laser printers and color photocopiers, and embossed decals for use with stamps and laser transfers for silk, satin, polymer clay, and metal foil.

## Candle Making and Decorating

**Candlewic**
www.candlewic.com
Offers candle making materials and tools, including wax, wicks, fragrances, coloring, containers and molds, thermometers, and packaging. Also offers soapmaking materials and tools, including melt-and-pour bases, essential oils, natural additives, and molds.

**Crate & Barrel**
www.crateandbarrel.com
Offers quality-made tapers, cathedral candles, and pillars to decorate. Consult the website to find a local retailer.

**Pier 1 Imports**
www.pier1imports.com
Offers quality-made tapers, cathedral candles, and pillars to decorate. Consult the website to find a local retailer.

**Pottery Barn**
www.potterybarn.com
Offers quality-made tapers, cathedral candles, and pillars to decorate. Consult the website to find a local retailer.

## Chandeliers: Restoring and Recycling

**Chandelier Parts**
www.chandelierparts.com
Offers wide range of chandelier parts, prisms, candle covers, Strass crystal parts, bulbs, sockets, shades, chains, and replacement parts and accessories.

**Cheap Joe's Art Stuff**
Phone: 800-227-2788
www.cheapjoes.com
Offers a wide array of fine art supplies, including a full line of paints suited to adding color to glass surfaces.

**City Knickerbocker**
665 11th Avenue, 2nd Floor
New York, NY 10019
Phone: 212-586-3939
www.cityknickerbocker.com
Offers antique, reproduction, and contemporary lighting fixtures of every description along with a wide range of parts for lighting fixtures; also offers repair services, from wiring single electrical sockets to replacing the arms of large ballroom crystal chandeliers.

**Grand Brass Lamp Parts**
51 Railroad Avenue
West Haven, CT 06516
Phone: 212-226-2567
www.grandbrass.com
Offers lamp, lighting, and chandelier parts, including glass lampshades suited to vintage lighting fixtures.

**Just Bulbs**
936 Broadway
New York, NY 10010
Phone: 800-544-4877
www.justbulbs.com
Offers a wide range of bulbs and lights.

## Picture Frames: Restoring and Recycling

Artists Frame Service
1867 North Clybourn Avenue
Chicago, IL 60614
Phone: 773-248-2800
www.artistsframeservice.com
Offers a full range of framing services, including conservation framing, museum-quality matting, and ultraviolet-protective glass.

Decorative Millwork Products
www.decorativemillworkproducts.com
Offers traditional and embellished hardwood moldings, wood carvings, full-surround mantels, mantel shelves, and adornments for cabinetry and furniture. Source for the long scrolls and corner clips featured on page 523. Consult the website to find a local retailer.

Home Depot
Phone: 800-HomeDepot
www.homedepot.com
Offers supplies for making or refurbishing a picture frame; consult the website for a retailer near you.

Janovic Plaza
30–35 Thomson Avenue
Long Island City, NY 11101
Phone: 718-392-3999
www.janovic.com
Offers wide selection of supplies for home and commercial painting, including supplies used in restoration and preservation work, such as strippers, tapes, solvents and cleaners, disposable gloves, rollers, and drop cloths.

Lowe's
www.lowes.com
Offers supplies for making or refurbishing a picture frame; consult the website for a retailer near you.

3M
www.3m.com
Manufacturer of 3M Safest Paint Stripper and Varnish Remover and Magic Goo Gone; consult the website to find a retailer near you.

## Picassiette: Restoring and Recycling

Glass Mosaic Tile
www.glassmosaictile.net
Offers instructions for using mosaic tiles, plus links to mosaic suppliers and artists.

Happycraftn's Mosaic Supplies
www.happycraftnsmosaicsupplies.com
Offers mosaic glass tiles, Van Gogh glass, millefiori, gems, grout, glues, and cutters.

Opus Mosaics
www.opusmosaics.com
Offers broad range of mosaic tiles, including Italian millefiori, tools, and supplies, including adhesives.

# Chapter Seven: Children's Arts and Crafts

The range of arts and crafts supplies suited for children's creative activities is near limitless. Here are some suppliers that offer materials and tools suited to young hands.

Activa Products
www.activaproducts.com
Offers plaster cloth in rolls for use in covering papier-mâché models. Consult the website to find a local retailer.

**All Things Ukrainian**
www.allthingsukrainian.com
> Offers the Blas Fix egg-hollowing kit, which will help clean out the contents of an eggshell without breaking the shell.

**American Science & Surplus**
www.sciplus.com
> Offers a selection of scientific supplies and mechanical items, including micromotors, optical toys and illusions, semiautonomous bug bots, jointed animals, and glow-in-the-dark wall decorations. Caution is advised as some items are not suited to young children and may contain parts that present a choking hazard; check out the menu to narrow the selections.

**Arnold Gummer**
www.arnoldgrummer.com
> Offers kits and supplies for paper making, including additives like pressed flowers and glitter; also offers molds and presses for paper casting, supplies for making cards and books, and how-to books and instructional videos on paper making.

**Artist & Craftsman Supplies**
www.artistcraftsman.com
> Offers a wide range of children's crafts supplies and tools, including paints, brushes, pastels, markers, crayons, and paper in rolls and reams, including kraft paper, poster board, construction paper, tag board, tissue paper, and drawing paper. Use the website to locate a store near you.

**Cincinnati Cake & Candy Supplies**
1785 East Galbraith Road
Cincinnati, OH 45215
Phone: 800-304-4536
www.cincicakeandcandy.com
> Offers baking, cake decorating, and candy making supplies for all occasions, including wide selection of cookie cutters that can be adapted for use in clay projects.

**The Container Store**
www.thecontainerstore.com
> While not a child-oriented store per se, this chain offers specific products that can be used in children's arts and crafts projects, including a wide selection of plastic boxes, the plastic stacking organizer used in the kaleidoscope project (page 643), and Three by Three Seattle magnets used in robot (page 646). Consult the website to find a store near you.

**CR's Bear and Doll Supply Catalog**
Box 8
Leland, IA 50453
Phone: 515-567-3652
www.crscraft.com
> Offers teddy bear and doll-making supplies, patterns, and kits, including the doll-making needle used in making jointed clay dolls.

**IFobot**
www.ifobot.com
> Features the work of Amy Flynn, a North Carolina artist and illustrator, who makes one-of-a-kind robots from found objects. A good source of inspiration.

**Jamali Garden Hardware**
149 West 28th Street
New York, NY 10001
Phone: 212 244 4025
www.jamaligarden.com
> Offers artificial birds, butterflies, seashells, ribbon, and cord that can be used as project bases for decorative applications of glitter.

**Jo-Ann Fabric & Crafts**
www.joann.com
> Offers a wide selection of fabric, including small amounts of precut pieces, and general craft supplies.

Jones Tones
33865 United Avenue
Pueblo, CO 81001
Phone: 800-397-9667
www.jonestones.com
Offers a wide range of glitter in a broad spectrum of color and texture, and specialty glues that are suited to adhering glitter. Consult the website to find a local retailer.

Kitchen Krafts
P.O. Box 442
Waukon, IO 52172–0442
Phone: 800-298-5389
www.kitchenkrafts.com
Offers supplies for the food crafter: cake decorating, baking and canning, and candy-making, plus cutters and molds that can be adapted for use in clay projects.

Neatstuff Collectibles
www.neatstuff.net/space-robots
Offers a large selection of new and vintage tin toys, collectible record albums, board games, toy cars, and antiques, such as miners' lamps and old radios. A good source of inspiration.

New York Cake & Baking Distributors
56 West 22nd Street
New York, NY 10010
Phone: 212-675-CAKE
www.nycakesupplies.com
Offers a broad range of tools and equipment for baking that can be adapted for use in cutting and molding clay.

Off the Beaten Path, Inc.
6601 D Royal Street
Pleasant Valley, MO 64068
Phone: 866-756-6543
www.cookiecutter.com
Offers wide selection of cookie cutters that can be adapted for use in cutting and molding shapes in clay.

Paper Clay
www.creativepaperclay.com
Offers an air-hardening, nontoxic, light-weight clay that can be shaped, carved, and sanded after it dries. Consult the website to find a local retailer.

Rycraft, Inc.
9234 E. Valley Road, Suite D
Prescott Valley, AZ 86314
Phone: 800-479-2723
Fax: 800-479-7911
www.rycraft.com
Offers ceramic cookie stamps and cutters in a wide variety of themes—Americana, animals, holiday, music, and home—as well as some craft materials for casting with paper and clay and tools that can be adapted for use with cutting and debossing clay.

Streich's Cake and Candy Supply
www.streichs.com
Offers a large selection of cake and candy supplies, including over five hundred chocolate and candy molds that can be adapted to clay projects and soapmaking.

Target
www.target.com
Offers Cherokee brand canvas Mary-Jane shoes that can be decorated with glue and glitter.

Walnut Hollow
www.walnuthollow.com
Offers a clay-extruder tool with easy-to-turn crank-style handle with twenty unique disc designs to use with conditioned clay.

Online Fun

Crayola
www.crayola.com
Offers a wide range of age-compatible arts and crafts ideas for children of all ages.

Disney's Family Fun
www.familyfun.go.com
   Offers a wide range of age-compatible arts
   and crafts ideas for children of all ages.

Everything Preschool
www.everythingpreschool.com
   Offers a wide range of lesson plans,
   alphabet ideas, coloring pages, and
   product reviews geared to activities for the
   preschool-age child.

Paul Neave
www.neave.com/imagination
   Offers unique computer experiences
   designed by Paul Neave, an English
   interactive designer who makes tools
   and toys. This site allows a child to
   participate in and create interactive art,
   such as original light shows and sound
   experiences. Click on the various icons,
   such as imagination, strobe, fractal, and
   anaglyph, and assess the suitability for a
   particular child.

Products Databases

http://www.acminet.org
   The Art & Creative Materials Institute
   (ACMI) use their seals (see page 572) to
   let the consumer know that a particular
   product has been evaluated and certified
   by a qualified toxicologist for both
   acute and chronic hazards, and that it is
   endorsed for use by children.

http://householdproducts.nlm.nih.gov
   Compiled by the U.S. Department of
   Health & Human Services of the National
   Library of Medicine, the Household
   Products Database provides health
   and safety information on over 10,000
   consumer brands. The information is
   taken from the product label and/or
   the Materials Safety Data Sheet (MSDS)
   prepared by the manufacturer. The
   organization does not test products, nor
   does it evaluate information from the
   product label or the MSDS.

# Bibliography

## General

Martha Stewart Living Magazine. *Martha Stewart's Encyclopedia of Crafts: An A-to-Z Guide with Detailed Instructions and Endless Inspiration.* New York: Potter Craft, 2009.

Weiss, Daniel, cont. ed. *Reader's Digest Crafts & Hobbies: A Step-by-Step Guide to Creative Skills.* New York: Reader's Digest, 1979.

## Chapter One: Beading

Alden, Nancy. *Simply Pearls: Designs for Creating Perfect Pearl Jewelry.* New York: Potter Craft, 2006.

Coles, Janet, and Robert Budwig. *Beads: An Exploration of Bead Traditions around the World.* New York: Simon & Schuster Editions, 1997.

Crabtree, Caroline, and Pam Stallebrass. *Beadwork: A World Guide.* New York: Rizzoli International Publications, 2005.

Durant, Judith, and Jean Campbell. *The Beader's Companion.* Loveland, CO: Interweave Press, 1998.

Franchetti Michaels, Chris. *Teach Yourself Visually: Jewelry Making and Beading.* Hoboken, NJ: John Wiley Publishing, Inc., 2007.

Geary, Theresa Flores, Ph.D. *The Illustrated Bead Bible: Terms, Tips & Techniques.* New York: Sterling Publishing, 2008.

Lambert, Marjie. *Microwave Craft Magic.* New York: Crescent Books, 1992.

Mann, Elise. *The Bead Directory: The Complete Guide to Choosing and Using More than 600 Beautiful Beads.* Loveland, CO: Interweave Press, 2006.

Meng, Kaari. *French-Inspired Jewelry: Creating with Vintage Beads, Buttons & Baubles.* New York: Lark Books, 2007.

Ryan, M. T. *Glamorous Beaded Jewelry: Bracelets, Necklaces, Earrings, and Rings.* Upper Saddle River, NJ: Creative Homeowner, 2006.

———. *More Glamorous Beaded Jewelry: Bracelets, Necklaces, Earrings, and Rings.* Upper Saddle River, NJ: Creative Homeowner, 2008.

Sterbenz, Genevieve. *Bead Style: Fabulous Chunky Jewelry.* Upper Saddle River, NJ: Creative Homeowner, 2006.

———. *The Color Book of Beaded Jewelry.* Upper Saddle River, NJ: Creative Homeowner, 2007.

———. *Mastering the Art of Beading: Essential Tools and Techniques Every Jewelry Maker Must Know.* San Francisco: Chronicle Books, 2010.

## Chapter Two: Floral Arts

Frankel, Candie. "Christmas Potpourri Demystified." *Handcraft Illustrated,* November/December 1995: 14–15.

———. "The Best Way to Dry Roses." *Handcraft Illustrated,* May/June 1995: 20–21.

Grosso, Alicia. *The Everything Soapmaking Book: Recipes and Techniques for Creating Colorful and Fragrant Soaps.* 2nd ed. Avon, MA: Adams Media, 2007.

Guzzo, Suzanne. "Artificial Fruits and Berries." *Handcraft Illustrated,* November/December 1993: 30–31.

Handcraft Illustrated. "Weaving Your Own Wreath." *Handcraft Illustrated,* November/December 1995: 5.

Handy, Grayson, and Tracey Zabar. *Flowers for the Home: Inspirations from the World Over by Prudence Designs.* New York: Rizzoli International Publications, Inc., 2009.

Hanneman, Cellestine. "Perfectly Pressed Flowers." *Handcraft Illustrated,* Spring 1996: 32–34.

Lachter, Sylvia. "Home-Grown Dried Flowers." *Handcraft Illustrated,* July/August 1995: 31.

Pryke, Paula. *Paula Pryke's Flower School: Mastering the Art of Floral Design.* New York: Rizzoli International Publications, 2006.

Quintero, Arturo. *Faux Florals: Easy Arrangements for All Seasons.* Upper Saddle River, NJ: Creative Homeowner, 2007.

Reader's Digest. *The Complete Illustrated Book of Herbs.* New York: Reader's Digest Association, 2009.

Sheen, Joanna. *Microwaved Pressed Flowers.* New York: Watson-Guptill Publications, 1998.

Stark, David, and Avi Adler. *To Have and To Hold.* New York: Artisan, 2005.

Tukua, Deborah. *Making and Using a Flower Press.* North Adams, MA: Storey Publishing, 1999.

## Chapter Three: Paper Crafting

Bunkers, Traci. *Print & Stamp Lab: 52 Ideas for Handmade, Upcycled Print Tools.* Beverly, MA: Quarry Books, 2010.

Dawson, Sophie. *The Art and Craft of Paper-Making: Step-by-step Instructions for Creating Distinctive Handmade Paper.* London: Quarto, Inc., 1992.

Drucker, Johanna, Krystyna Wasserman, and Audrey Niffenegger. *The Book as Art: Artists' Books from the National Museum of Women in the Arts.* Princeton, NJ: Princeton Architectural Press, 2007.

Fleck, Becky. *Scrapbook Page Maps.* Cincinnati, OH: F+W Publications, 2010.

Frankel, Candie. "The Best Way to Tie Multiloop Bows." *Handcraft Illustrated,* November/December 1995: 34–35.

Gear, Adam D., and Barry L. Freestone. *The Complete Guide to Stamping*. New York: Reader's Digest, 2004.

Grummer, Arnold. *Arnold Grummer's Complete Guide to Easy Papermaking*. Iola, WI: Krause Publications, 1999.

Jackson, Paul. *The Pop-up Book*. New York: Henry Holt and Company, LLC, 1993.

Johnson, Pauline. *Creating with Paper: Basic Forms & Variations*. Mineola, NY: Dover Publications, Inc., 1991.

———. *Creative Bookbinding*. Mineola, NY: Dover Publications, 1990.

Kate's Paperie with Bo Niles. *Paperie: The Art of Writing and Wrapping with Paper*. New York: Simon & Schuster Editions, 1999.

Klanten, R., and B. Meyer, eds. *Papercraft II: Design and Art with Paper*. Berlin: Gestalten, 2011.

Klanten, R., au. and ed., S. Ehmann and B. Meyer, eds. *Papercraft: Design and Art with Paper*. Berlin: Gestalten, 2009.

Leisure Arts, Inc. *Creating Keepsakes' Encyclopedia of Scrapbooking*. Little Rock, AR: Leisure Arts, Inc., 2005.

Smyth, Esther K. *How to Make Books*. New York: Potter Craft, 2007.

Sokol, Dawn De Vries. *1000 Artist Journal Pages: Personal Pages and Inspiration*. Beverly, MA: Quarry Books, 2008.

Taylor, Terry. *Eco Books: Inventive Projects from the Recycling Bin*. New York: Lark Books, 2009.

## Chapter Four: Hand Printing

Ayres, Julia. *Printmaking Techniques*. New York: Watson-Guptill Publications, 1993.

Corwin, Lena. *Printing By Hand: A Modern Guide to Printing with Handmade Stamps, Stencils, and Silk Screens*. New York: Stewart, Tabori & Chang, 2008.

Eichenberg, Fritz. *Lithography and Silkscreen Art and Technique*. New York: Harry N. Abrams, Inc., Publishers, 1978.

Gear, Alan D., and Barry L. Freestone. *The Complete Guide to Stamping*. New York: Reader's Digest, 2004.

Gupta, Amit, and Kelly Jensen. *Photojojo*. New York: Potter Craft, 2009.

Hardy, Francoise. "Buyer's Guide to Rubber Stamps." *Handcraft Illustrated,* November/December 1995: 38–40.

Lassiter, Frances, and Norman Lassiter. *Screen Printing: Contemporary Methods and Materials*. Philadelphia, PA: Hunt Manufacturing, Co., 1978.

Martin, Judy. *The Encyclopedia of Printmaking Techniques*. Philadelphia, PA: Running Press, 1993.

Robertson, Bruce, and David Gormley. *Learn to Print Step by Step*. London: Macdonald Orbis Diagram Visual Information Ltd., 1987

Saff, Donald, and Deli Sacilotto. *Printmaking: History and Process*. New York: Holt, Rinehart Winston, 1978.

Stromquist, Annie. *Simple Screenprinting: Basic Techniques & Creative Projects*. Asheville, NC: Lark Books, 2004.

Walker, John R. *Graphic Arts: Fundamentals*. Tinley Park, IL: Goodheart-Willcox Company, Inc., 1986.

Westley, Anne. *Relief Printmaking*. New York: Watson-Guptill Publications, 2002.

## Chapter Five: Decoupage

Cochrane, Lyn. *The Fine Art of Découpage*. Binda, NSW, Australia: Sally Milner Publishing, Ltd., 2001.

Davis, Dee. *Découpage: Paper Cutouts for Decoration and Pleasure*. New York: Thames and Hudson Inc., 1995.

Innes, Jocasta, and Stewart Walton. *The Decoupage Sourcebook*. North Pomfret, VT: Trafalgar Square Publishing, 1995.

Johnson, Nancy. "Field Guide to Watercolor Brushes." *Handcraft Illustrated*, November/December 1994: 28–29.

Lang, Donna, and Lucretia Robertson. *Decorating with Paper: Creative Looks with Wallpapers, Art Prints, Gift Wrap, and More*. New York: Clarkson Potter Publishers, 1993.

Nimocks, Patricia. *The Craft of Decoupage*. New York: Charles Scribner's Sons, 1972.

Rawlings, Eleanor Hasbrouck, ed. *Découpage: The Big Picture Sourcebook*. New York: Dover Publications, Inc. 1975.

## Chapter Six: Decorative Embellishing

Altschuler, Chris. "3 Simple Techniques for Weathering Furniture." *Handcraft Illustrated*, July/August 1994: 18–20.

Colgrove, Debbie. *Teach Yourself Visually: Sewing*. Hoboken, NJ: Wiley Publishing, 2006.

Cutbill, Stu, and Vi Cutbill. "Grape Arbor Mural." *Handcraft Illustrated*, September/October 1994: 13–15.

Dupuy, Celine. *Simple Sewing with a French Twist*. New York: Potter Crafts, 2007.

DuVal, Elizabeth. *Beyond the Basics: Mosaics*. New York: Sterling Publishing Co., Inc., 2004.

Franklin, Lily. "Decorative Painted Plates." *Handcraft Illustrated*, Spring 1997: 22–24.

The Editors of Consumer Reports Books with Monte Florman and Majorie Florman. *How to Clean Practically Anything*, 4th ed. New York: Consumer Reports Books, 2006.

Haupert, Debba. *The New Book of Image Transfer: How to Add Any Image to Almost Anything with Fabulous Results*. New York: Lark Books, 2004.

Kelsey, Barbara. "How to Make a Decorative Tassel." *Handcraft Illustrated*, Winter 1996: 23–25.

La Ferla, Jane. *Gilding, Easy Techniques & Elegant Projects with Metal Leaf*. New York: Sterling Publishing Co., Inc., 1997.

Lucasso, Sonia. *Remake, Restyle, Reuse: Easy Ways to Transform Everyday Basics into Inspired Designs*. New York: Watson-Guptill Publications, 2008.

Marx, Ina Brosseau, Allen Marx, and Robert Marx. *Professional Painted Finishes: A Guide to the Art and Business of Decorative Painting*. New York: Watson-Guptill Publications, 1991.

McCloud, Kevin. *Decorative Style: The Most Original and Comprehensive Sourcebook of Styles, Treatments, Techniques, and Materials*. New York: Simon & Schuster, 1990.

Meng, Kari. *French General Home Sewn: 30 Projects for Every Room in the House*. San Francisco, CA: Chronicle Books, 2008.

———. *French General Treasured Notions: Inspirations and Craft Projects Using Vintage Beads, Buttons, Ribbons, and Trim from Tinsel Trading Company*. San Francisco, CA: Chronicle Books, 2010.

Miller, Judith. *The Style Source Book: The Definitive Illustrated Directory of Fabrics, Wallpapers, Paints, Flooring, Tiles*. New York: Firefly Books, Ltd., 2003.

Miller, Judith and Martin. *Period Finishes and Effects: A Step-by-Step Guide to Decorating Techniques*. New York: Rizzoli International Publications, 1992.

Rixford, Ellen. "Miter-Box Frame." *Handcraft Illustrated,* March/April 1995: 17–19.

Ryan, Michio. "French Tinware Cachepot." *Handcraft Illustrated,* March/April 1995: 6–8.

———. "How to Gild Any Surface." *Handcraft Illustrated,* March/April 1995: 10–11.

———. "Star Frost Vase." *Handcraft Illustrated,* January/February 1995: 24–25.

———. "The Secrets of Quick Gilding." *Handcraft Illustrated,* November/December 1993: 26–28.

## Chapter Seven: Children's Arts and Crafts

Dewar, Andrew. *Origami Airplanes*. North Clarendon, VT: Tuttle Publishing, 2007.

Florman, Monte, and Marjorie Florman, eds. *How to Clean Practically Anything,* 4th ed. New York: Consumer Reports Books, 2006.

Friesen, Christi. *Polymer Clay and Mixed Media—Together at Last*. Minneapolis, MN: Creative Publishing, Inc., 2008.

Hoover, F. Louis. *Art Activities for the Very Young*. Worcester, MA: Davis Publications, Inc., 1961.

Lang, Hillary. *Wee Wonderfuls: 24 Dolls to Sew and Love*. New York: Stewart, Tabori & Chang, 2010.

Partain, Jessica and Susan. *The Polymer Clay Cookbook*. New York: Watson-Guptill Publications, 2009.

Ryan, Michio. "Marionette Tree Ornaments." *Handcraft Illustrated,* Fall 1997: 18–21.

———. "Testing Air-Dry and Heat-Set Clays." *Handcraft Illustrated,* September/October 1995: 26–29.

Sims, Laura. "How to Make Marbled Paper." *Handcraft Illustrated,* September/October 1994: 28–29.

Van Sicklen, Margaret. *The Joy of Origami*. New York: Workman Publishing, 2007.

# Advisory Board

## Genevieve A. Sterbenz

### Beading

Genevieve A. Sterbenz is a lifestyle expert and author of eleven craft and home decorating books. Her book *Mastering the Art of Beading: Essential Tools and Techniques Every Jewelry Maker Must Know* (Chronicle Books, 2010) is an authoritative guide to making beaded jewelry that follows two best-selling previous beading titles: *The Color Book of Beaded Jewelry* (Creative Homeowner, 2007) was a 2007 ForeWord Magazine Book of the Year Award Finalist, a USA Book News Best Books Award Winner, and a Next Generation Indie Book Award Finalist; *Bead Style: Fabulous Chunky Jewelry* (Creative Homeowner, 2006) was the Independent Publisher Book Awards' silver medalist in 2007. Ms. Sterbenz has appeared on national television programs on CBS, The Discovery Channel, and HGTV. She lives in Manhattan.

## Grayson Handy

### Floral Arts

Grayson Handy is a founding partner, along with noted floral designer Arturo Quintero, of the award-winning Prudence Designs & Events, a full-service florist. Mr. Handy is the creative director of Prudence Events. Known for their artistic vision and exclusive one-of-a-kind floral arrangements, Mr. Quintero and Mr. Handy have been recognized by The Knot (www.theknot .com) for Best of Weddings and by Citysearch (newyork.citysearch.com) as Best Florist in New York City. They have been featured on *The View* and *Today,* as well as in the *New York Times, New York, Modern Bride, InStyle,* and *Martha Stewart Living,* among other distinguished publications. Previous to his work at Prudence Designs & Events, Mr. Handy had a visual career at the prestigious retail stores Takashimaya (where he was the visual director), ABC Carpet and Home, and Barneys New York. Mr. Handy is the author of *Flowers for the Home: Inspirations from the World Over by Prudence Designs* (Rizzoli International Publications, Inc., 2009).

## Sarah Latham

### Floral Arts

Sarah Latham is a founding creator of Scentsational company and co-owner, along with partner Janice Hubers, of this thriving service-oriented business in Huntington, New York, established in 1980. Scentsational's perfumers create custom-blended fragrances using innovative formulas and natural-based bath and body products that can be custom-scented with perfume oils. They also offer a wide selection of preblended perfumes and body and skin care products. All formulations are not tested on animals.

## Clare Petropoulos

### Floral Arts

Clare Petropoulos is a well-known floral designer and co-owner, along with her brother George, of Teddy's Florist, a full-service florist established in 1922 in Astoria, New York—"the heart of Queens." Ms. Petropoulos attended La Guardia College before following in the footsteps of her father and uncle, who became the new owners of the shop in 1984, providing Clare with a unique opportunity to learn the art of flower arranging from a very young age and from the ground up. With a career that has spanned twenty-six years, Clare has a well-cultivated understanding of flowers and plants and a genuine gift for design, which she has been instrumental in passing on to the interns who come to the shop to learn the floral arts. Well known for her distinct wedding flowers, especially the cascade and nosegay style arrangements, Clare also designs for all occasions, including sweet sixteen celebrations, baby showers, christenings, and funerals. She is married and has four children.

## Phillip Sohn

### Paper Crafting

Phillip Sohn is the manager of Thomson's Art Supply in downtown White Plains, New York. This family-owned and -operated business offers an extensive range of fine artist materials, drafting supplies, and crafts materials and tools in all media, as well as conservation and custom framing of works of art through archival materials and expert craftsmanship. Mr. Sohn joined the company after graduating from the University of Pennsylvania and has been bringing his in-depth knowledge and firsthand experiences of all arts and crafts media to a base of specialized professionals and local art students for nearly a decade. Phillip enjoys working in watercolors whenever he can.

## Bud Martin

### Hand Printing

Bud Martin holds a bachelor of science degree in chemical engineering from Texas Tech University. He has been the director of research and development for Speedball Art Products since 2005. Prior to that, he worked for Hunt Corporation for fourteen years in various technical and product development roles related to paper and art products. He has focused his development efforts toward meeting the product needs of the artist and has provided training in printmaking to artists and teachers throughout North America. He lives in Hamptonville, North Carolina, with his wife and two daughters.

## William Binder

### Candle Making

William Binder is the president and owner of the Candlewic Company, one of the largest and oldest suppliers of candle making equipment in the United States, established by his parents in his childhood home in 1970. William was a Cub Scout when he made his first molded candle by pouring hot liquid wax into a milk carton; his experience inspired a passion for candle making that would last a lifetime. Today, he directs the manufacturing and processing of the Candlewic product lines, continuing his family's tradition of developing materials, tools, and easy and innovative ways to make candles as a hobby or as a business. With a dedication to crafters and a commitment to ensuring good results, William developed a company website that provides free information, instructional videos, a newsletter, and unique projects.

## Amanda Stanford

### Children's Arts and Crafts

Amanda Stanford is an art teacher for grades K–5 in the White Plains School District in Westchester County, New York, where she encourages children to express their ideas uniquely through painting, drawing, sculpture, and other visual art media. Amanda graduated from Boston University, where she earned a bachelor of fine arts degree in graphic design and a master of fine arts degree in studio art teaching. She began her teaching career in the Bronx, a borough of New York City, where she taught grades 1–5 for four years before relocating to White Plains. A dedicated educator, Amanda believes that art is essential to the overall growth of children because it provides experiences and opportunities for developing human values that are fundamental to their well-being. Amanda and her husband welcomed the birth of their first son, and she looks forward to nurturing his creativity.

# Acknowledgments

I am filled with grateful appreciation and affection for the many talented individuals who generously contributed their expertise, insight, and goodwill to the making of *Homemade: The Heart and Science of Handcrafts.*

I consulted with an advisory board of experts, whose in-depth knowledge, insight, and first-hand experience in their chosen fields helped to cohere the technical information in each of the chapters. I am especially indebted to Genevieve A. Sterbenz, jewelry designer and author (Chapter One: Beading); Grayson Handy, founding partner of Prudence Designs & Events and creative director of Prudence Events; Clare Petropoulos, floral designer and co-owner of Teddy's Florist; Sarah Latham, co-owner of Scentsational and an expert in fragrances and essential oils (Chapter Two: Floral Arts); Phillip Sohn of Thomson's Art Supplies (Chapter Three: Paper Crafting); Bud Martin of Speedball Art Products (Chapter Four: Hand Printing); Bill Binder of Candlewic Company (Chapter Six: Decorative Embellishing); and Amanda Stanford, elementary school art teacher, with special thanks to Gary West, coordinator of fine arts of the White Plains School District (Chapter Seven: Children's Arts and Crafts).

Many companies and their representatives generously contributed exactly those materials and tools I needed to ensure good crafting results. With appreciation, I thank Susan K. Jones for glitter, specialty glues, foils, and stickers; Rita Madsen at Speedball Art Products Company for gilding and block- and screen-printing supplies and tools; Lazertran for decals and photo transfers; Chris Kuppig and Susan Barell at Dover Publications, Inc., for the fine prints used for decoupage and decorative embellishing; Cynthia Gotuzzo at Decorative Millwork Products for the carved wood onlays for the embellished frame; Nelson Glass and Mirror for the plastic mirrors for the children's kaleidoscope; Katie Hoy at Singer for a Confidence 7470 sewing machine; and General Electric for a rechargeable battery-operated electric drill. I am especially grateful to Ott Light for providing a Shelby floor lamp and flexible stem with magnifier attachment, Model #S6237T, which saw me through many hours of concentrated crafting.

As I look back on a lifetime of crafting, I remember with gratitude and affection the mentors who inspired me on the long and winding path that eventually led me to write *Homemade*: Hazel Davis, Margaret Gilman, Jane Hamada, Lena Tabori, Lois Brown, Chris Kimball, Deborah Broide, and colleagues Anne Alexander, Elizabeth Viscott Sullivan and Rebecca Atwater Bricetti, who have become my close friends. Mary Green of Martingale & Company graciously granted permission to reprint the memoirs previously published in *Handcraft Illustrated.* I also want to recognize the great friends in Bay Hills who shared hours and hours of crafting camaraderie and friendship: Mary Frazier, Mary Gale, Maryanne Pettit, Ruth Sansiviero, Woodie Sims, Edie Staib, Heather Tucker, and Bonnie Williamson.

The extraordinary pen-and-ink renderings by illustrator Harry Bates beautify every page they grace, and I know they will enhance the reader's understanding of the technical aspects of the work. Maureen Mulligan, graphic designer and dear friend, converted complicated drawings, patterns, and diagrams into readable, easy-to-follow graphics. I so value her ever-enduring spirit and artistic perspective. Dennis Johnson's trained eye, expertise, and good nature prevailed through days and days of shooting the thousands of photographs on which the illustrations are based, and his wife, Laura, and darling children, Izzie and Andrew, provided hospitality beyond measure. (Dennis is also the young photography student and dear nephew featured in the memoir in Chapter Four: Hand Printing.) Christina Haskin, illustrator, drew the sensitive pen-and-ink renderings that began and ended the Introduction and each of the memoirs, making visible the most meaningful contextual details of my personal stories and recollections.

The young and ebullient artists who joyfully made and contributed their work are Emily Centino, Yvan Guénot, Nicholas Guider, William Guider, Maxx Hamilton, Isabel Johnson, Charlotte Kulikowski, Casimir (Kazio) Kulikowski, Katie Anne Kulikowski, Elka Pinny, Jonah Pinny, and, of course, my own children, Genevieve, Rodney, and Gabrielle. Charged with wonderment and innocence, each of the works was executed with remarkable certainty and provided a comprehensible view of the young artist's star-filled imagination.

Thanks to Susan Moldow, publisher, and Nan Graham, editor-in-chief, at Scribner, who believed in *Homemade*; especially heartfelt thanks go to my editor, Alexis Gargagliano, whose deep understanding of the editorial process and sensitivity to my vision allowed me the creative wingspan I needed to make the book what I had imagined it could be; to Kelsey Smith, editorial assistant, whose good cheer and support made the editorial process all the more efficient and enjoyable; to Rex Bonomelli, art director extraordinaire, for his unerring eye and his stunning plate, shoe, and topiary designs featured on the cover of the book; to Erich Hobbing, design director, whose courage and vision shaped beautiful, peaceful, and informative spaces for myriad elements whose intrinsic characters differed so widely; to Mia Crowley, production editor, who shepherded everything so that the bound book now rests in your hands; and thanks to Maria Massie at Lippincot Massie McQuilken. Candie Frankel, technical editor, brought her erudition and craftsmanship to focus and clarify the enormous wide scope and breadth of the work. Our professional camaraderie has turned into a deep friendship.

I am deeply grateful to those who made contributions large and small at the draft stage: Anne Alexander, Steven Mays, Annie Guénot, Adrienne Johnson, Christina Haskin, Nancy K. Johnson, Olivia Just, Gabrielle A. Sterbenz, and Genevieve A. Sterbenz.

Words cannot express how blessed I feel to have the love and support of my family—my husband John and our kids, Genevieve, Gabrielle, and Rodney, together with his young family, Leni, Maxx, and Roxy—who always let me know how much I was missed when I disappeared for even short stretches of time to make *Homemade* the book it was meant to be. I offer special thanks to my sisters, Nancy and Joan, and to our parents, Aune Sivia and Jorgen Gustav Endler, who provided us with a loving and creative environment that always encouraged my dreams.

# Credits and Notes

Personal recollections of the author that originally appeared in whole or in part in *Handcraft Illustrated*, Boston Common Press, are reprinted with permission of Martingale & Company. Introduction: Adapted from *Handcraft Illustrated* January/February 1995, 1, and Fall 1998, 1. Chapter Two: "Family Roots" excerpted from *Handcraft Illustrated*, July/August 1994, 1. Chapter Three: "Woven Baskets" adapted from *Handcraft Illustrated*, Christmas, 1997, 1. Chapter Four: "Through Immigrant Eyes" adapted from *Handcraft Illustrated*, May/June 1995, 1. Chapter Six: "One Pathway to Joy" adapted from *Handcraft Illustrated*, Fall 1996, 1; Chapter Seven, "Home for Christmas" excerpted from *Handcraft Illustrated*, September/October 1994, 1, November/December 1994, 1, Winter 1996, 1, and Fall 1997, 1.

Projects noted in the following previously published works by the author were sources of inspiration for several of the new and original designs featured in *Homemade: The Heart and Science of Handcrafts*. *The Gnomes Book of Christmas Crafts* (New York: Harry N. Abrams, Publishers, 1980), Gingerbread Farmhouse, 46–47, Woven Heart Ornament, 80. *Ornaments: Creating Handmade Tree Decorations* (Kansas City, MO: Andrews McMeel Publishing, 2000), Etched Glass Balls, 38–41, Beaded Bugs, 62–65, Tree-top Star, 110–113. *Wreaths, Garlands, Topiaries and Bouquets* (New York: Rizzoli International Publications, Inc., 1993), Holiday Door Wreath, 17, Table Topiary, 57, Door Garlands, 93, Billowy Door Wreath, 118–119. "The Traditional Beaded Christmas Tree," *McCalls' Needlework & Crafts Magazine*, Spring 1979. "Dried Rosebud Pineapple," *Handcraft Illustrated*, Fall 1997, 38–39. "Gilded Candles," *Handcraft Illustrated*, Winter 1996, back cover. "Gold and Silver Leaf Plate Chargers," *Handcraft Illustrated*, January/February 1995, 26–27. "Hand-Painted Parrot Tulips," *Handcraft Illustrated*, Spring 1997, 25. "How to Make an Infinite Variety of Wreaths," *Handcraft Illustrated*, November/December 1995, 8–11. "Notes From Readers: Weaving a Heart Basket," *Handcraft Illustrated*, November/December 1993, 3. "Embossed Velvet Pillow," *Handcraft Illustrated*, Winter 1997, 17. *Instant Gratification: Candles* (with Genevieve Sterbenz) (San Francisco, CA: Chronicle Books, 2001), Retro Daisies, 14–15, Floating Rose, 42–43, Portrait, 52–53, China Cup, 76–77, Seashells, 84–85, Faux Alabaster, 94–95, Beach Light, 100–101. *The Home Spa: Creating a Personal Sanctuary* (with Genevieve A. Sterbenz) (Kansas City, MO: Andrews McMeel Publishing, 1999): Herbal Paper Sachets, 32–33, Scented Bath Oil, 44–45, Scented Bath Salts, Scrub, and Gel, 49–51, Etched Carafe and Tumbler, 71–73, Decorative Glycerin Soaps, 88–90, Index to Base Oils and Essential Oils, 104–107.

Illustrations: All illustrations by Harry Bates, including the author's portrait on the book jacket, except as noted.

Maureen Mulligan, 14, 15, 16, 17, 18, 35, 36, 37, 38 (top left), 40 (top left), 41 (top right), 42, 43, 44 (top left), 47, 48, 49, 50, 51, 53, 56, 57, 59, 61, 76 (bottom), 81 (lower right), 82, 83, 84, 85, 95, 97, 98 (lower left, right), 99, 100, 101, 102, 103, 104, 108, 122, 129 (lower left), 130, 132, 143, 145, 150 (top left), 152, 153, 172, 194, 195, 215, 218 (top right), 221 (lower left), 229 (lower right), 230, 232, 235, 245 (right), 246, 247 (lower right), 248 (lower left, right), 250 (bottom), 252 (bottom), 255, 256, 257, 258, 259, 260, 261, 262, 263, 267, 268 (top left), 270, 277 (right), 294 (lower right), 301 (lower left), 302 (bottom), 306 (lower left, lower right), 307, 318, 324 (lower right), 330, 361, 365 (bottom), 394 (left), 400, 404 (bottom), 420 (top right), 424, 428 (bottom), 431, 432, 433, 439 (lower right), 461, 462, 463 (left, top right), 465, 466, 467 (top left), 479, 481 (lower left), 484, 485, 498, 500, 503 (top left), 504, 505, 506, 508, 510, 519 (top), 530, 534 (lower right), 545, 546, 585, 592, 593, 594, 595, 596 (right), 597, 598, 599, 600, 618, 641, 648, 650, 653, 654 (left), 655, 656, 657, 658, 659, 660, 661, 662, 663, 664, 665, 666, 667, 668 (bottom), 670, 671, 675, 676, 677, 678, 679, 683 (top), 684, 685, 686, 687, 688, 689, 690, 691, 692, 693, 694 (bottom), 695, 696, 697, 698, 699, 700, 701 (top), 702, 703, 707, 708, 711, 712, 713, 714 (top), 715, 716, 717, 718, 719, 720, 721, 722, and 723.

Christina Haskin, xi, xviii, 1, 3, 87, 89, 201, 203, 285, 288, 355, 357, 415, 417, 561, and 564.

Denis Johnson, 221 (lower right), 295, 311, 313 (right), 316, 328 (top left), 331 (top left), 338 (left), 345, 347, 349, 351, 453, 454, 467, 566, 567, 569, 573, 575, 576, 582, 583, 612, 613, 614, 615, 616, 617, 621, 622, 625, 626 (lower right), 627, 629, and 714 (bottom).

The illustrations on pages 362, 366 (author adaptation), 369 (author adaptation), 467 (author adaptation), 694 (top), 704 (author adaptation), 705, 706, 709 (author adaptation), 710 (author adaptation), and 724 are reprinted with permission of Dover publications.

The ACMI seals on page 572 are reprinted with permission of the Art & Creative Materials Institute.

Epigraphs and Dedication: Robert Hass, *The Apple Tree at Olema* (New York: HarperCollins Publishers, 2010), 10. Introduction: Laurens van der Post, *Jung and the Story of Our Time* (New York: Vintage Books, 1975), 123. Chapter One: Margaret Laurence, *The Stone Angel* (Chicago: University of Chicago Press, 1964), 120. Chapter Two: Edward F. Murphy, ed., *The Crown Treasury of Relevant Quotations* (New York: Crown Publishers, Inc., 1978), 270. Chapter Three: Harriet Doerr, *The Tiger in the Grass: Stories and Other Inventions* (New York: Penguin Books, 1995), 184. Chapter Four: Danish saying as told to the author by her father, Jorgen Gustav Endler. Chapter Five: Henry Wadsworth Longfellow, *Michael Angelo: Part First: II. Monologue: The Last Judgment* from *The Complete Poetical Works of Henry Wadsworth Longfellow* (Gutenberg ebook, Kindle edition, 2004), location 12425; originally published in Cambridge, MA, by The Riverside Press, 1884. Chapter Six: Thomas Merton, *No Man Is an Island* (Boston: Shambhala Publications, Inc., 1983), 36; originally published by The Abbey of Our Lady of Gethsemani in 1955. Chapter Seven: John Cheever, "The Geometry of Love" from *The Stories of John Cheever* (New York: Vintage International, 1978), 596; short story originally published in *The Saturday Evening Post*, January 1, 1966. Page 775: Ann Dillard, "Write Till You Drop," *New York Times*, May 28, 1989.

Other credits and notes: Chapter One: Birthstone chart on page 10 © 2006–2007 is reprinted with permission of Jewelry-Design-Gemstones.com. Chapter Four: Exposure Time according to Screen Size on page 338 courtesy of Speedball Art Products. Chapter Five: Die-cut roses on pages 393–94 © Wallee. Gift wrap for Swimming Lessons: A Vase by Cavallini Papers & Co., Inc. © 2006. Printed in Korea. Chapter Seven: Quote on page 561 from F. Louis Hoover, *Art Activities for the Very Young* (Worcester, MA: Davis Publications, Inc., 1961), 11. The code number for this work is 57187.

# Index

accordion folds, 214–16, 585

acetate:
    line art printed on, 328
    registering a print with, 339

acetate stencils, 322, 697, 698, 701, 724

acrylic craft paint, 321, 376, 578

acrylic gesso, 375, 382–84, 440–41

acrylic medium-and-varnish, 363, 375–76

acrylic spray sealer, 216, 468

acrylic varnish, 375–76

adhesive-backed vinyl, 429–32

adhesives, 210
    stencil, 323
    tile, 535

aging, of wood finish, 528

air-drying plants, 111–13

air fresheners, 183–85

albums:
    making covers for, 271–72
    photo, 268, 279–82, 693

alkyd spray primer, 388

almond oil, 174

animal collages, 590

animal figurines, glitter-coating, 640

anise, 175

annuals, 105

anther-and-filament stamen, 253–54, 256–57, 262–63

appliqués, carved, 526–27

apricot kernel oil, 174, 178

AP seal, 572

Art & Creative Materials Institute (ACMI), 572

l'arte povero, 358

artificial fruit, 123
    adding shimmer and shine to, 128
    creating false stem on, 129–30

Artist Trading Cards (ATCs), 205

art prints, 349–52, 702

autumn wreath, 197

avocado oil, 178

badges, ribbon, 272–73

bails, 22

Bakelite, 5

bangle bracelet, 63–65

baren, 305–6, 315

basil, 175

bathing products, 174–82

BBA No. 1 photoflood light, 328–29

beaded bugs, 42

beaded-loop trim, 462–63

bead holes, 18

beading, beads, 1–85
    beading needles and other tools for, 31–33
    brief history of, 4–5
    children's projects for, 42
    common finishes for, 19
    common hole placements in, 18
    coordinating crimp bead sizes and nylon-coated beading wire in, 53
    for decorative embellishing, 457

beading, beads (*cont.*)
  determining loop size in, 35
  eye loops in, 35
  findings for, 20–23
  finishes of, 19
  hand tools for wire work in, 24, 25–28
  heart of, 1–5
  making and using beaded-loop trim in, 461–63
  matching months and birthstones in, 10
  materials and tools for, 19–33
  metal wire for, 23–25
  nylon-coated beading wire for, 30–31
  off-loom weaving in, 5, 55–61
  projects for, 62–85
  resources for, 725–28
  science of, 5–61
  securing bead stations in, 54
  sizes and shapes of, 14–18
  standard lengths for jewelry in, 52
  stops for, 34–38
  stringing and off-loom weaving supplies for, 28–33
  stringing of, 6, 46–54
  techniques for, 34–54, 57–61
  thread and cord for, 29–30
  threading needles in, 32
  tying knots in, 48
  types of, 6–13
  wiring of, 6, 33–38
  working tips for, 7, 30, 32, 35, 48, 51, 52, 53, 54
  wrapped-wire loops in, 38–46
beading boards, 27–28
beading needles, 31–32
bead reamer, 27
bead tips, 22
bench hook, 305
bent-nose pliers, 27
bergamot, 175
berries, 107, 149
biennials, 105
biogenic (organic) beads, 12–13
birthstones, 10
black paper or cloth, 329
black pepper, 175

block printing, 300–320, 695–96
  for children, 628–31
  cleaning tools for, 316
  cutting a block for, 309–11, 316–17
  design effects in, 311
  designing and making a block for, 307–9
  facedown printing in, 314–15
  flipping and burnishing a print in, 315
  gradient color in, 312, 313
  inking a block for, 313–14
  making a test print in, 311
  making prints in, 312–15
  materials and tools for, 301–6
  papers for, 303
  registering colors in, 306, 317–20
  registering designs in, 312–13
  setting up a print-drying line for, 314
  three-dimensional effects in, 303
  transferring a hand-drawn design in, 307–8
  transferring an ink-jet design in, 308–9
  two-color printing in, 316–20, 696
  working tips for, 303, 304, 305, 306, 307, 308, 309, 314, 317
  *see also* printing blocks
block-printing ink, 302–4, 313–14, 321
block-shaped portrait candle, 555–56
bole, 441–42
bone and horn beads, 12
bone folder, 212
books:
  altered, 275–76
  box, 273–74, 352–54, 701
  flag, 216, 282–83, 694
bouquets:
  binding vine wreaths with, 150–51
  container arrangements of, 136–44
  floral arch pitcher, 191
  for garlands, 156–59
  handheld, 133–36
boutonnière, 129
bowls, 167
box books, 273–74, 352–54, 701
boxes:
  applying decoupage to, 395–97
  gift wrapping of, 245–46
  templates for, 392–93

boxwood, 162–63
bracelets:
    bangle, 63–65
    beaded, 63–65, 71–73, 76–78, 79–80
    charm, 71–73
    peyote, 76–78
brayers, 296, 304–5
bread and glue play clay, 633–34
brushes
    for children, 581
    cleaning of, 390
    for decoupage, 364, 407
    for gilding, 438–39
    for glass etching, 421
    stencil, 322
    tapered, 327
brush stamens, 258–61
bud stamens, 257–58, 263
bugle beads, 9
bullion, 51
burnishing, 447
buttonholes, in beading, 61
button stamens, 253, 255–58, 261–63
Byron, George Gordon, Lord, 359

candle containers, 481–82
candle making and decorating, 480–516
    children's projects for, 508–9, 512
    materials and tools for, 481–85
    safety in, 487, 515
    techniques for, 486–87, 489–507, 509–16
    troubleshooting for, 516
    working tips for, 486, 487, 489, 494, 498,
        501, 510, 515
candle molds, 481
candles:
    applying granular materials to, 514–15
    applying prints to, 513
    block-shaped, 502–4
    container, 495–99
    decorating of, 511–16
    instant, 482
    molded, 486–94, 499–509
    multicolor glazing of, 511
    multi-wick, 504–5
    old, recycling of, 507

    painting of, 512–13
    paper message bands for, 513–14
    pillar, 501–2, 505–9
    rolled beeswax, 512
    standard sizes for, 499
    tapers, 509–11
    votive, 497–500
    wrapping with ribbons and trims, 514
candle tins, 500
candy cane ornament, 84
canola oil, 178
cardboard tube, as candle mold, 505–6
cards, see greeting cards and invitations
carpet needles, 31–32
carrier oils, 179
cedarwood, 175
cellophane tape, 210
centerpieces, 194–96
Centino, Emily, 630
chain-nose pliers, 26–27, 104, 450
chains, 21
chalcedony quartz, 11
chalks, 578–79
    pastel, 619–21
chamomile, 175
chandeliers:
    adding color to glass on, 521–22
    dismantling and cleaning of, 519–21
    hanging and decorating of, 522–23
    parts of, 519
    restoring and recycling of, 517–23
charm bracelets, 3–4, 71–73
charted designs, in off-loom weaving, 56
Cheever, John, 561
children's arts and crafts, xiv–xv, 561–679
    activities for, 584–93, 601–10, 612–17,
        619, 621–37, 639–43
    ages and developmental stages in, 573–76,
        582–83
    in author's childhood, xi–xii, 88–89,
        201–2
    of author's children, 561–64
    brief history of, 564–66
    color in, 610–31
    creating experiences for, 620
    displaying art and craft projects in, 572–73

children's arts and crafts (*cont.*)
  encouraging imagination in, 571
  getting started in, 566–73
  good habits in, 571
  judgment and praise in, 569
  making creative experiences fun in, 567–68
  materials and tools for, 577–82
  multimedia activities for, 611–19
  original art in, 566, 567, 568, 569, 573, 575, 576, 579, 582, 583, 611, 612, 620, 621, 630, 636, 714
  patterns for, 683, 694, 711–23
  preparing a work space for, 569, 571
  projects for, 643–79; *see also children's projects and activities in specific crafts*
  resources for, 737–40
  safety precautions for, 566–67, 572
  science of, 566–643
  smART ideas for, 590, 591, 593, 594, 596, 600, 602, 609, 620, 628, 630, 632, 642, 668, 672–74, 679
  starter kits for, 582–83
  troubleshooting for, 570
  using good quality materials and tools in, 568–69
  working tips for, 580, 587, 593, 618, 632, 638
  working with clay in, 631–37
  working with crayons, paint, chalk, and markers in, 610–31
  working with glitter in, 638–43
  working with paper in, *see* paper crafts for children
china, for picassiette, 536, 539–43
chokers, 65–66
Christmas ornaments:
  beaded, 84–85
  etched glass, 428
  glitter, 639, 641–43, 715
Christmas traditions, 201–3, 561–64
Christmas tree beading project, 81–84
chromolithography (color printing), 204, 359
cinnamon, 175
citronella, 175

citrus fruit slices:
  in decorating soap, 189
  drying of, 114
clamps, 27
clamshell with hook, 22
clary sage, 175
clasps, 21
clay, 581, 631–37
  air-dry, 634
  heat-set, 636
  homemade, 632–34
  making your own sealer for, 632
clay beads, 4, 13
cloisonné, defining, 13
clove, 175
CL seal, 572
coasters, 434
cold-pressed paper, 207
collages and assemblages, 609–10
  animal, 590
colorant, for wax, 482–83
colored pencils, 366, 370–72, 579
colorfastness, testing for, 367
color printing (chromolithography), 204
conditioning, for fresh flowers and foliage, 104–8
container arrangements, 136–44
  adjusting span of tripod in, 138
  floral arch pitcher bouquets, 191
  tape grids for supporting tall stems in, 141
containers, for flowers, 98
continuous-petal flowers, 260
cooking spray, 187
copyright laws, 367, 368
coral beads, 12
cornstarch and salt play clay, 632–33
cottage-style mirror frame, 556–59
cotton balls, 439–40
cotton-core wicks, 484
cotton fabric, 451
cotton swabs, 365
Cowper, William, 356
cowslip knot, 250
crafters, crafting:
  author's reflections on, 1–5, 87–91, 201–3, 285–88, 355–58, 415–18

creativity of, xvi–xvii
family bonding through, 561–64
kindred spirit among, xv–xvi
making mistakes in, xvii
resources for, 725–40
*see also specific crafts*
craft knife, 211, 220–22, 304, 321, 364, 468, 587
crayons, 577
credit cards, craft uses for, 305, 535
crepe paper, 253
crepe paper rose, oversize, 263–66, 689
crimp bead covers, 22
crimp beads and tubes, 22
crimping pliers, 26
crimp-style fold-over clamps, 22
crow beads, 9
crystal beads, 9
cubic zirconia (CZ) beads, 9
cultured pearls, 12
cutters:
    for decorative embellishing, 458
    for printing blocks, 304, 309, 311
cutting boards, 187
cutting mat, self-healing, 212, 319–20, 364, 468
cyanoacrylate (instant glue), 33
cylinder (tubular) beads, 9
cylinders, templates for, 393–94
cypress, 175
Czech seed beads, 8–9

decals, 467–75
    baking (heat-setting) method of applying, 471–72, 709
    choosing items for, 457–68
    images for, 467
    materials and tools for, 467–68
    techniques for, 469–75
    waterslide method of applying, 469–71, 710
decal transfer paper, 468
decanter and tumbler, etched, 544–45
deckle, 207, 608–9
    faux, 214
decorative accents, 98

decorative decoupage platter, 410–12
decorative embellishing, 415–559
    candle making and decorating as, 480–516
    of chandeliers, 517–23
    dry embossing as, 449–56
    gilding as, 437–49
    glass etching as, 419–36
    heart of, 415–18
    individuality expressed through, 416, 418, 419
    picassiette in, 534–43
    of picture frames, 523–34
    projects for, 544–59
    resources for, 733–37
    in restoring and recycling, 517–43
    science of, 419–543
    using decals and heat-transfers in, 467–80, 709, 710
    using ribbons and trims in, 456–67
decoupage, 355–414
    adapting prints for, 374
    adding ladders in, 375
    applying the finish to, 397–99
    brief history of, 358–59
    children's projects for, 404
    cutting out prints for, 373–74
    depth and color in, 399
    discovering negative space in, 406
    drying times for, 388
    final treatment for, 383
    on glass, *see* glass, decoupage on
    gluing prints for, 394–97
    golden age of, 358–59
    heart of, 355–58
    items for decoration with, 361–62
    laying out prints for, 392–94
    materials and tools for, 360–66, 375–98
    origin of term, 358
    painting on, 390–92, 407–10
    papers for, 357, 366–68, 369–70
    preparing prints for, 368–75
    projects for, 410–14
    science of, 361–410
    sealing prints for, 372–73
    selecting printed images for, 362, 366–68
    storing prints for, 375

decoupage (*cont.*)
   techniques for, 370–75, 378–79, 382–87, 389–98, 400–410
   using templates in, 392–94, 400–402, 704
   on wood or metal, 375–98; *see also* metal, for decoupage; wood, for decoupage
   working tips for, 365, 367, 369, 371, 372, 374, 375, 379, 381, 382, 383, 385, 387, 388, 390, 395, 399, 403, 406, 408
decoupage medium, 362–63, 375–76, 382
*découpeurs,* 359
Delaney, Mary, 359
Delicas, 5
desiccant, desiccating, 113–16
   common flowers for, 115
dessert plates, 412–13, 705
Diazo kit, 328
die-cut cards, 231–32, 278–79, 685, 697
dimensional clay sculpture, 636–37
Doerr, Harriet, 201
dolls, jointed clay, 651–54, 716–17
dome topiaries, 163
double boiler, 485
double-fold cards, 230–31
double overhand knot, 48
double-sided tape, 210
dowels, wood, 99
drawing liquid, 332, 701
dried and preserved flowers and foliage, 109–23
   adding false stems to, 127
   air-drying of, 111–13
   caring for, 117–18
   and common choices for drying by any method, 113
   decorative citrus fruit slices, 114
   desiccant for drying of, 113–16
   and fresh plant materials for drying in place in long-lasting displays, 149
   good choices for growing of, 111
   harvesting of, 109–10
   microwave-drying of, 116–17
   preserving foliage in, 118
   pressing of, 118–23
   in topiary project, 199–200

dry embossing, 213, 218–19, 449–56
   creating your own objects for, 452–55
   grid pattern in, 454
   leaf pattern in, 454–55, 708
   materials and tools for, 449–51
   objects for, 450–51
   project ideas for, 455
   techniques for, 452–56
   troubleshooting for, 456
   using coiled wire in, 452–53
   of velvet, 455–56
drying booth, 365
dry mounting, 216–17

earring clasps and hooks, 21
earrings, beaded, 62–63, 73–74
Easter crafts, 668–79
Easter egg tree, 674
ebony beads, 5, 13
editions (print runs), 312
eggshell gift boxes, 668–69
eggshell ornaments, 669–79, 719–21
eggshells:
   as candle molds, 506
   how to hollow out, 672–74
embedded soap, 189
embossed-velvet pillow, 550
embossing, 218–20, 297
   *see also* dry embossing
embossing powder, 294, 297
emery cloth, 27, 376–77
Engelmann, Godefroy, 359
enlarging or reducing, formula for, 368
envelopes, 227, 684
erasers, making stamps from, 298
essential oils, 167, 186
   allergic reactions and, 169
   in bathing products, 174–82
   fragrance chart of, 170
   fragrance oils vs., 164
   health and safety precautions for, 190–91
   popular, characteristics of, 175–78
   in potpourri, 166–74
etched decanter and tumbler, 544–45
etched glass ornaments, 428

etching, *see* glass etching
etching cream, 421, 422–23
Etsy, 205
eucalyptus, 175
exposure times, for screen printing, 338
extender base, 326
eye beading needles, 31
eyedroppers, 168, 186
    equivalent measures for drops in, 179
    using and cleaning of, 165
eye pins, 21

fabric:
    badge, 272–73
    covering a box book with, 273–74, 701
    heat-transfers on, 476–80
    ink for, 304, 341
    removing stains and soil from, 570, 618
    screen printing on, 326, 341, 342, 352–54, 701
    *see also* velvet
facial scrubs and masks, 182–83
faience, 4
fat bumblebee, 601
faux deckle, 214
faux finish, 528
faux masterpiece, 479
faux pearls, 12
feather mask, 659–61
felt mats, 28
fennel, 175
fiberfill padding, 122
findings, for beading, 20–23
fine art prints, 291
finger paint, finger painting, 578, 621–23
fire-polished beads, 8
fire starters, 507
fixatives, 167
flag books, 216, 282–83, 694
flamework (lampwork) beads, 8
flat-braid (LX) wicks, 483
flat-weave cotton towel, 28
fleur-de-lis stamp, 306, 695
flood stroke, 342–43
floral arch pitcher bouquets, 191

floral arts, 87–200
    adding false stems in, 127–31
    adding food to water in, 93
    air fresheners, 183–85
    artificial fruit in, 123, 128, 129–30
    bathing products, 174–82
    bouquets to carry and display in, 133–36
    brief history of, 90–91
    caring for dried floral arrangements in, 117–18
    children's projects in, 143, 152
    cleaning containers in, 140
    conditioning in, 104–8
    container arrangements in, 136–44, 191
    cutting of stem ends in, 109
    decorating wreath frames in, 148–55
    decorative citrus fruit slices in, 114
    dried and preserved flowers and foliage in, 109–23, 127, 149, 199–200
    drying techniques in, 110–17
    essential oils used in, *see* essential oils
    facial scrubs and masks, 182–83
    floral picks in, use of, 131–33, 154
    fresh flowers and foliage in, 104–9, 149, 189
    garlands in, 155–59, 198–99
    green floral foam and, 94–95, 99, 139–40, 162
    harvesting of plant material in, 109–10
    heart of, 87–91
    herbs for, 105
    live flower arranging in, 89
    making or preparing wreath frames in, 144–48
    materials and tools for, 97–104
    moss-covered balls in, 147
    natural care for body and soul with, 165–91
    potpourri, 166–74
    preserving foliage in, 118
    pressing flowers and foliage in, 118–23
    preventing premature aging in, 108–9
    principles of, 92–96
    projects for, 191–200
    resources for, 728–30
    science of, 91–191

floral arts (*cont.*)
    seasonal guide to, 106–7
    silk flowers in, 123–25, 140–42, 189
    soapmaking in, 185–90
    tape grids for supporting tall stems in, 141
    topiaries in, 159–65, 199–200
    two types of arrangements in, 96
    using plant material at various stages of
        growth in, 136
    wiring stems in, 125–27
    working tips for, 93, 94–95, 96, 120, 122,
        129, 137, 140, 158, 164, 165, 168, 179,
        187
    wreaths in, 144–55, 191–93, 196–97
floral foam, 94–95, 98–99, 139–40
floral knives, 102
floral picks, 101
    making your own, 132
    using of, 131–33, 154
floral pins, 101
    on straw wreath base, 154–55
floral scissors, 102–3
floral tapes, 101
flour and salt play clay, 633
flour paste, 602
flowers and foliage, 98, 104–23
    air-drying of, 111–12
    conditioning for, 104–8
    cutting stem ends of, 109
    desiccating of, 113–16
    dried and preserved, 109–23, 127, 149,
        199–200
    dried, caring for, 117–18
    fresh, 104–9, 149, 189
    harvesting of, 109–10
    microwave-drying of, 116–17
    paper, *see* paper flowers
    pressing of, 118–23
    preventing premature aging in, 108–9
    protecting endangered species of, 110
    seasonal guide to, 106–7
    silk and artificial, 123–25, 128, 129–30,
        140–42, 189
    in soap decorating, 189
    topiary-making with, 164–65
    *see also* floral arts

foam anchor, 99
foam brushes, 390, 421
foam sheets, 299
foam tape, 211
foam wreath frames, 153
fragrance, for candles, 483
fragrance oils, essential oils vs., 164
frames:
    for block printing, 306, 317, 318
    picture, 523–34
    wreath, 99–100
France, author's visits to, 1–4, 89–90
frankincense, 175
freezer paper, 342, 476
fresh flowers and foliage, 104–9
    for drying in place in long-lasting displays,
        149
    in soap decorating, 189
    topiary-making with, 164–65
freshwater pearls, 12
fringed tube, 591
Froebel, Friedrich, 204
frosted glass effects, 424, 434
fruit, 107, 149, 189
    adding false stems to, 128–30
    artificial, 123, 128, 129–30
    drying decorative, 114
fused beads, 8

galvanized metal, 387
gardens, 88–89
garlands, 155–59
    with central spray of flowers, 158
    monogram, 158
    summer, 198–99
geranium, 176
gesso, acrylic, 375, 382–84, 440–41
gift bags, 346–47, 696
gift packages, 243–52
    gift bags, 346–47, 696
    gift tags, 248–52
    gift wrap, 243–46
    ribbons and bows for, 246–48, 250, 252
    wrapping technique for, 245–46
gifts, of potpourri, 172–73
gift tags, 248–52

gift wrap, 216, 243–46
    for decoupage, 357, 367
gigantic necklace, 591
gilded and bejeweled glass vase, 545–46
gilded bird, 547
gilded box with embossed leaves, 548–49
gilding, 237–38, 437–49
    applying acrylic size and metal leaf in, 442–49
    bole undercoat in, 441–42
    choosing items for, 437–38
    leveling and smoothing surface for, 440–41
    materials for, 437–40
    preparing the surface for, 439, 440–47
    project ideas for, 448
    sealing metal leaf in, 447–49
    techniques for, 440–45, 447–49
    troubleshooting for, 446
    working tips for, 441, 443, 448
ginger, 176
glass, 448
    applying decals to, 471–75
    in chandeliers, 519–23
    gilding on, 448
    see also glass etching
glass, decoupage on, 359, 361, 398–410, 704, 705
    choosing a vase for, 400
    cleaning and preparing surface for, 398–99
    on a flat surface, 400–401, 402–5, 407–8
    gluing prints to, 402–7, 704, 705
    laying out prints for, 399–402
    painting on, 407–10
    removing paint from a plate rim in, 408
    sealing of, 410
    templates for, 400–402
    on a vessel, 401, 402, 405–7, 409–10
glass beads, 4, 8
glasses, safety, 28, 377, 535
glass etching, 419–36
    checklist for, 435
    items for, 420, 423
    masks for, 421, 424–32
    materials and tools for, 420–22
    on a mirror, 424, 430, 432
    multiple flat surfaces in, 433–35
    overall design in, 432–33
    project ideas for, 435
    techniques for, 423–35
    troubleshooting for, 436
    working tips for, 427, 429, 430, 434
glass jars, 167
glass or Lucite sheet, 329
glitter, 236, 638–43
    making your own, 642
glitter animals, 641
glitter ornaments, 639, 641–43, 715
gloves:
    cotton, 438
    disposable, 377, 421, 438
    rubber or vinyl, 329, 421, 536
glue, 206
    instant (cyanoacrylate), 33
    novelty, 211
    rubber cement, 210–11
    spray adhesive, 210–21
    sticks, 102, 210, 580
    white craft (polyvinyl acetate; PVA), 101, 209, 363, 580
    writing with, 236
glue guns, 102
glue sticks, 102, 210, 580
gold-filled wire, 23
gold-plated wire, 23
gold wire, 23
gouache, 366
grapefruit, 176
grapeseed oil, 178
graphite paper, 303, 681
green floral foam, 94–95, 99, 139–40
    sculpting topiary head out of, 162
greeting cards and invitations, 223, 225–43, 683–85
    die-cut, 231–32, 278, 685, 697
    double-fold, 230–31
    embellishments for, 235–39
    hand-cut features for, 228–35
    hand-drawn, 237–38, 695
    insert folios for, 242–43
    machine-sewn, 223, 683
    magnified letters in, 239

greeting cards and invitations (*cont.*)
 making an envelope for, 227–28, 684
 paper choice for, 225
 photo transfer and printing on, 239–42
 pop-up, 228, 232–35
 postcards, 344–45, 702
 single-fold, 226, 695
 using paint chips in, 238–39
grids, 443
grout, 535
grout float, 535
grout sealer, 535
gsm, g/m2 (grams per square meter), 207
Guénot, Yvan, 475, 568, 611
Guider, Nicholas, 620
Guider, William, 575, 582, 611

Halloween crafts, 655–59, 663–67
Hamilton, Maxx, 573, 604, 612
hammers, 103
hand-coloring, 369–70, 704
hand-cut cards, 228–35
handheld bouquets, 133–36
handmade paper, 207
hand-molded soaps, 186
hand printing, 285–354
 block printing in, 300–320, 695
 brief history of, 288–90
 children's projects for, 301, 302, 332, 335,
  342, 623–28
 heart of, 285–88
 ink for, 304
 materials and tools for, 292–93
 monoprinting with paint in, 623–28
 projects for, 344
 resources for, 732–33
 rubber stamping in, 292–300
 science of, 291–344
 screen printing in, 324–44
 stenciling in, 321–24
 techniques for, 295–300, 307–20, 322–24,
  329–40, 343–44
 using positive and negative space in, 300,
  307
hand sewing, 222–23
headgear, decorative, 664–67

head pins, 21
heat embossing:
 in paper crafting, 218
 in rubber stamping, 297
heat gun, 218, 294, 297, 472–73
heat-transfer paper, 468, 476–77
heat-transfers, 467–69, 475–80
 applying of, 476–78
 caring for fabrics with, 480
 choosing items for, 466
 from freezer paper, 476
 images for, 467
 making of, 475–76
 materials and tools for, 467–69
 project ideas for, 480
 techniques for, 476–78
herbs, 105
high-density rubber, 299–300
high-density rubber printing block, 301–2
"hilarious hen" figure, 602–4, 712–13
holiday crafts:
 Christmas, 81–85, 428, 639, 641–43,
  716
 Easter, 668–79
 Halloween, 655–59, 663–67
 Mardi Gras, 659–61
Hoover, F. Louis, 565
hot-pressed paper (H.P.), 207
hydrangea wreath, 193–94

ink:
 block-printing, 302–4, 313–14
 screen-printing, 325, 341
 textile, 341
ink-jet printers and copies, 308–9, 369,
  681
ink pads, 294
ink slab, 305
inscribed soap, 189
insert folios, 242–43
instant glue (cyanoacrylate), 33
intaglio, 291
intarsia, 359
Internet, 367
iron, 451, 469
ivory beads, 12–13

jade, 11
Japanese seed beads, 8–9
"japanning" (decoupage), 358
jasmine, 176
jet beads, 5, 13
jewel cases, 279
jointed clay dolls, 651–54, 716–17
jojoba oil, 178
journals, 269–70
jumbo chalks, 619–21
jumping spider, 655–59
jump rings, 20–21
juniper, 176

kaleidoscope, 643–45
kindergarten movement, 204
*kirigami,* 205
knives, 187
    craft, 211, 220–22, 304, 321, 364, 468, 587
    floral, 102
    palette, 535
    serrated, 103
knots, tying of, 48
knots, wood, 379
Kulikowski, Charlotte, 621
Kulikowski, Katie Anne, 575, 579
Kulikowski, Kazio, 576

ladders, in decoupage, 375
*Ladies Amusement Book; or Whole Art of Japanning Made Easy* (Sayer), 359
laminating, 216–18
lamps, magnifier, 28
lampshades, trimming of, 462–63, 466–67, 551–52
lampwork (flamework) beads, 4, 8
laser printer copies, 224–25, 334–35, 362, 367–68
    coloring of, 369–72
    for decals, 471
    when to use, 367
Laurence, Margaret, 1
lavandin, 176
lavender, 176
leaves, paper, 266–68, 690–92
lemon, 176

lemongrass, 176
letters:
    magnified, 239
    peel-and-stick vinyl, 429
lime, 176
linings, for envelopes, 228
linoleum blocks, 301
    cutting of, 310
liquid media:
    drying times for, 388
    guidelines for applying, 380
    sanding and leveling of a surface sealed with, 381
    *see also specific media*
lithography, 291
litsea, 176
Little Miss Muffet spider, 657–59
loaf soap, 188

machine sewing, 224–25
magic wand, 662–64
magnifier lamps, 28
mandarin, 176
marbling, 625–28
marjoram, 176
markers, 579–80
Mary Jane shoes, sparkling, 654–55
masking, masks, 296
    in glass etching, 421, 424–32
masking tape, 210, 421
masks:
    for Mardi Gras, 659–61
    protective, 377
measuring cups, 187
measuring spoons, 168
melissa, 176
memory keeping, 205, 268–76
    albums, 271–72, 279–82, 693
    altered books, 275–76
    box books, 273–74
    journals, 269
    organizing elements for, 270
Merton, Thomas, 415
metal, for decoupage, 375–98
    applying primer to, 389–90
    cleaning of, 385–86

metal, for decoupage (*cont.*)
    flaky and rusty surfaces of, 385
    painting of, 391–92
    preparing surfaces of, 385–90
    sanding of, 386–87, 389
metal beads, 13
metal leaf, 237–38, 438
    adhering of, 444–45
    applying to candles, 515–16
    burnishing of, 447
    cutting and tearing of, 443–44
    *see also* gilding
metal primer, 376
metal wire:
    for beading, 23–25
    common gauges of, 24
microwave-drying, 116–17
mineral spirits, 376
mini photo album, 279–80, 693
mirror:
    etching of, 424, 430, 432
    installing in picture frame, 532–33
mobiles, paper, 593
Mod Podge, 397
mold, as terra cotta finish, 160
mold, paper, 207
molded (pressed) beads, 8
mold release, 485
mold sealer, 484
molds, soapmaking, 186–87
monofilament mesh screen, 326
monogram garlands, 158
monograms and numerals, 707
monoprinting with paint, 623–28
Montessori, Maria, 564
mosaic round table, 540
mosaic, *see* picassiette
moss, 160
    decorating topiary head with, 163–64
moss-covered ball, 147
mountain and valley folds, 592
multicolored bird print, 302
multifilament mesh screen, 326
multiloop bows, 247
multimedia art activities for children, 611–19
myrtle, 176

nacre, defining, 11
nail polish, 33
narrow gouge cutter, 311
narrow V-cutter (veiner), 311
natural pearls, 11–12
necklaces, beaded, 69–71, 75
needle file, 27
needles:
    beading, 31–32
    stiffening strand material for making of,
        32
    threading of, 32
needle threader, 32
negative space, 300, 307, 406, 425–26
neroli, 176
niobium wire, 23
nuts, 107
nuts-and-bolts robot, 646–48
nylon-coated beading wire, 30–31
nylon thread, 29

off-loom weaving, 55–61
    charted designs in, 56
    peyote stitch in, 55
    supplies for, 28–33
olfactory fatigue, 489
olive oil, 178
one-ply leaves, 266–67
orange, 177
oregano, 177
organic (biogenic) beads, 12–13
origami, 205, 592–600
    fish, 598–600
    penguin, 596–98
ornaments, Christmas:
    beaded, 84–85
    etched glass, 428
    glitter, 641–43
oven mitts, 485
ovens, for heat-setting decals, 473–75, 709
overprinting, 298

paint:
    acrylic craft, 321, 376, 578
    block printing with, 628–31
    finger, 578

guidelines for applying, 380
monoprinting with, 623–28
poster, 578
stripping of, 524
tempera, 578
watercolor, 366, 370–71, 578
paint-chip polka dots, 238–39
painting:
  of candles, 512–13
  in decoupage, 390–92, 407–10, 704
  finger, 619–21
  of picture frames, 527, 529–30, 533–34
paint sealer, 367
palette knife, 535
palmarosa, 177
paper beads, 13
paper bird with curly tail, 589–90, 711
paper chains, 591
papercore wicks (HTP), 484
paper crafting, 201–83
  brief history of, 204–5
  children's projects for, 221
  folding, 212–14; see also origami
  gift packages in, 243–52
  greeting cards and invitations, 225–43
  handling paper in, 209
  heart of, 201–3
  Japanese, 205
  making multiple prints from original art
    in, 240–41
  materials and tools for, 208–12
  memory keeping through, 205, 268–76
  paper flowers, 253–68
  papers for, 206–7, 209–10
  Polish, 205
  product safety in, 210–11, 216
  projects for, 277–83
  resources for, 730–32
  science of, 205–76
  scoring in, 212–16
  techniques for, 212–52, 255–76
  working tips for, 209, 210, 214, 216, 222,
    238, 242, 253, 254, 266
  woven baskets, 201–3, 277–78
paper crafts for children, 584–610
  activities for, 584–92, 601–10

collages and assemblages, 609–10
cutting and punching in, 585–87
folding in, 585
manipulating paper in, 584–600
origami, 592–600
paper making, 606–9
papier-mâché, 601–6
perforating in, 587
rolling and sculpting in, 591–92
tearing in, 588–90
techniques for, 593–600, 608–9
weaving in, 588
wrinkling in, 584
paper flowers, 253–68
  adjusting petal size in, 266
  choosing papers for, 253
  making and attaching leaves for, 254,
    266–68, 690–92
  petals of, 253–54, 259–66, 686–89
  stamens of, 253–54, 255–65
  stems of, 253–54
  wire for, 254
paper making, 606–9
paper mobile, 593
papers:
  absorbency of, 207, 209
  for block printing, 303
  for children, 580–81
  color in, 204, 209
  for crafting, 204–5, 206–7, 209–10
  cutting of, 220–21, 222
  for decoupage, 357, 366–68, 369–70
  embellishments of, 235–39
  grain of, 207, 600
  graphite, 303
  handmade, 207, 606–9
  heat transfers on, 476–77
  laminating of, 216–18
  manufacture of, 204–5, 207
  for origami, 593
  for paper flowers, 253
  rag, 206, 219
  recycled, 606–8
  round shape for, 609
  for screen printing, 325
  sewing on, 221–25

papers (*cont.*)
  for stamping, 295
  strengthening of, 216
  texture in, 207
  weight of, 207
paper satchels, 173–74
papier-mâché, 601–6, 712–13
papyrus, 204
parchment, 204
Parkes, Alexander, 5
paste, 209–10, 580
  flour, 602
pastel chalks, 619–21
pastels, 579
patchouli, 177
pattern designs, quick and easy children's
    activities in, 612–19
patterns and original art, 681–724
  enlarging and printing of, 681
  transferring of, 681–82
  using, 682
  *see also* children's arts and crafts, original
    art in
pattern symbols, 682
pearls, 11–12
pendants, 66–67
peppermint, 177
perennials, 105
petals, 253–54, 259–66, 686–89
petitgrain, 177
peyote bracelets, 76–78
peyote rings, 68–69
peyote stitch, 55, 58–60
photo albums, 268, 279–82, 693
photocopiers, 239–40, 469
photo emulsion, 328
photo-emulsion printing, 328–29, 334–39
  choosing art for, 335
  coating the screen in, 336
  exposing the screen in, 337–40
  making an acetate positive for, 335–36
photography, xiii–xiv, 285–88
photo sensitizer, 328
photo transfers, 239–42
picassiette, 534–43
  adhering tesserae in, 541–43

applying grout and sealer in, 543
breaking china for, 538–41
creating a mosaic for, 537–43
materials and tools for, 534–36
planning a design for, 537
selecting a base for, 535
selecting china for, 536
techniques for, 539–43
pickling, 526
picks, floral, 101
picture frames, 523–34
  adding appliqués to, 526–27
  adding mounting hardware and dust
    protectors to, 530–31
  disassembling and cleaning of, 525–26
  hanging of, 526
  installing a mirror in, 532–33
  painting and finishing, 527, 529–30,
    533–34
  rusting as threat to, 526
pine, 177
pineapple floral centerpiece, 194–96
pinecones, creating false stems for, 130–31
pink soft-carve printing block, 301
Pinny, Elka, 582
Pinny, Jonah, 583
pins, floral, 101
place mats, 348–49, 700
plaster of Paris, 99
plaster tape, 604–6, 712
plaster tape fish, 604–6
plastic beads, 5, 13
plastic film, 321
plastic liners, 101–2
plastic wrap, 187
platter, 410–12, 706
play clay, 632–34
pliers, 450
  for wirework, 26–27
pods, 107, 149
polymerization, 388
polyvinyl acetate (PVA; white craft glue), 101,
  209, 363, 580
pom-pom chicks, 645–46, 668
pony beads, 9
pop-up cards, 228, 232–35, 686

pop-ups for children, 586–87
portrait decoupage, 189
positive space, 300, 307, 430–32
postcards, 344–45, 702
poster paint, 578
poster putty, 366
potichomania, 356, 359, 361
potpourri, 166–74
    mellowing scent of, 172
    safeguarding fragrance potency of, 168
pots, metal, 451
pounds (lbs.) per ream, 207
precious and semiprecious stones, 9–10
pressed (molded) beads, 8
pressing flowers, 118–23
    common choices for, 121
    fiberfill padding for, 122
    newsprint vs. newspaper in, 120
    troubleshooting in, 119
pressure embossing, 218–19
primer:
    alkyd, 388
    metal, 376, 389
    wood, 375, 382
priming, of wicks, 493–94
print-drying line, 314
printers, 239–40, 469, 476
    vs. copiers, 471
    see also laser printer copies
print frame, 306, 317, 318
printing, on cards and invitations, 239–42
printing blocks, 301–2
    for children, 628–31
    cutters for, 304
    cutting of, 309–11, 316–18
    designing and marking of, 307–9
    mindfulness in cutting of, 305
    for two-color prints, 316–18
printing frame, 306
printing screen, 324–25
print runs (editions), 312
print sealer, 362
print stroke, 343
pruning shears, 103
punches, 299, 327
puppets, paper, 221

quartz, 11
quilling, 205

rag paper, 206, 219
raveling, prevention of, 466
recycled paper, for paper making, 606–8
reflector shop light, 328
register pins, 339
registration:
    in block printing, 306, 312–13, 317–20
    in rubber stamping, 296–97
    of screen prints, 327, 339–40
registration tabs, 326
relief printing, 291
resin beads, 12
restoring and recycling, 517–43
    of chandeliers, 517–23
    picassiette in, 534–43
    of picture frames, 523–34
    techniques for, 519–23, 525–27, 529–34,
        538–43
    working tips for, 517, 520, 524, 526
retarder, 326–27
ribbon, stringing beads with, 30
ribbon bow, 252
ribbon rose, 458–61
ribbon-rose lampshade, 551–52
ribbons and bows, 246–48, 457
    badges, 272–73
    for gift tags, 250, 252
    working tips for, 246
ribbons and trims, embellishing with, 456–67
    making and using beaded-loop trim in,
        461
    making a ribbon rose, 458–60
    materials and tools for, 457–58
    tassels and tassel trim in, 463–67
    techniques for, 458–63
    wrapping a candle with, 514
right-angle rulers, 296
rings:
    beaded, 68–69, 78–79
    peyote, 68–69
rock crystal, 11
rose, 177
    oversize crepe paper, 263–66, 689

rose decal vase, 553–54, 709
rosemary, 177
rosewood, 177
round-nose pliers, 26
round (RRD) wicks, 483
rubber cement, 210–11
rubber or vinyl gloves, 329, 421, 536
rubber stamping, 292–300
    beginner techniques for, 295–97
    materials and tools for, 293–95
    overprinting with a mask in, 296
    paper for, 295
    registering a print in, 296–97
    three-dimensional effects in, 303
    working tips for, 296, 298, 300, 303
rubber stamps, 293–94
    cleaning and storing of, 298
    making your own, 298–300
rulers, 27, 211–12
    right-angle, 296
rust, removal of, 526
rutilated quartz, 11

safety glasses, 28, 377, 535
sage, 177
sand, 160
sandalwood, 177
sanding, 378–79, 386–87, 389
sanding block, 377
sand mold candles, 508–9
sandpaper, 376
satin cord, 29
Sayer, Robert, 358–59
scales, 485
scanners, 239–40, 334
scherenschnitte (scissor snipping), 205
scissors, 103, 439, 458, 468
    for children, 581
    floral, 102–3
    manicure (cuticle), 363
    paper, 211
    straight-blade, 363–64
    thread, 32–33, 363
screen filler, 331–35, 699
screen printing, 291, 324–44
    on fabric, 326, 341, 342, 352–54

with freezer paper, 342
making prints in, 339–44
materials and tools for, 324–29
papers for, 325
photo-emulsion method of, 328–29,
    334–39
pulling prints in, 340–43, 699
registering a design in, 327, 339–40
screen filler method of, 331–34, 701
stencils for, 331–39
testing a print in, 340
on a T-shirt, 342
on a wall, 351
working tips for, 225, 326, 327, 332, 337,
    339, 340, 341, 343
screen-printing ink, 325
screens:
    choosing of, 326
    cleaning after use of, 343–44
    cleaning before use of, 329–30
    preparing of, 329–31
    taping of, 330–31
scrimp findings, 22
sealer:
    guidelines for applying of, 380
    liquid, 448–49
    paint, 376
    print, 362
    spray, 216, 447–48, 468
    surface, 363
    wood, 375–76
seashell, candle in a, 496–97
seed beads, 5, 8–9, 18, 461
    transferring of, to wire, 33
self-healing cutting mat, 212, 319–20, 364
semiprecious beads, 11
serrated knives, 103
sesame oil, 178
sewing machines, 458
sewing, on paper, 221–25, 683
shears, pruning, 103
shellac, 382
shell beads, 12
silhouette cutting, 205
silica gel, 113–16
silk cord, 29, 49–51

silk flowers, 123–25
   container arrangements of, 140–42
   in soap decorating, 189
silk thread, 29
silver-plated wire, 23
single-fold cards, 226, 695
single overhand knot, 48
single-petal flowers, 262
size, 207, 209, 438, 442
slab clay sculpture, 634–36, 694, 712
slurry, 206
snowball ornament, 85
snowman ornament, 85
soapmaking, 185–90
   removing soap skin in, 187
   swirling loaf, 188
   textural and colorful variations in, 189
sock monkey, 649–50, 716
soft-cover photo album, 280–82
soft-cover travel journal, 269
*Somerset Studio,* 205
spacer beads, 22–23
spearmint, 177
Speed Clean, 332
spoons, 168
spray adhesive, 210–11
spray booth, 216–17, 373
spray fixative, 362
spray frosting, 434
spray mister, 101
spray starch, 451
square-braid wicks, 483–84
square knot, 48
squeegee, 327–28
stainless steel wire, 24
stamens, 253, 255–65
stamping, *see* block printing; rubber
      stamping
stamp positioner, 296
stationery supplies, as masks for etching,
      425–26
stearic acid, 482
stems:
   adding false, 127–31
   wiring of, 125–27
stencil adhesive, 323

stencil brush, 322
stenciling, 697–701
   with glitter, 639–40
   materials and tools for, 321–22
   screen printing, *see* screen printing
   traditional, 321–24
   working tips for, 323
stencils:
   acetate, 322–23, 697, 698, 724
   cutting and using, 322–24
   photo-emulsion, 334–39
   positive, 333
   screen filler, 331–34, 699, 701
   for screen printing, 331–39
Sterbenz, Carol Endler:
   childhood of, 88–89, 201–2
   family heritage of, xi–xiv
   father of, xiii–xiv
   friendships of, xv
   motherhood of, 561–64
   mother of, xii–xiv
   reflections on crafting by, 1–5, 87–91,
      201–3, 355–58
   in visits to France, 1–4, 89–90
   in visit to England, 355–58
Sterbenz, Gabrielle, xiv–xv, 87–88, 202,
      561–64, 566
Sterbenz, Genevieve, xiv–xv, 87–88, 202,
      561–64, 566, 569, 576, 636
Sterbenz, John, xiv, 87–88, 202, 562–64
Sterbenz, Maxx, 563
Sterbenz, Rodney, xiv–xv, 87–88, 202,
      561–64, 576
Sterbenz, Roxy, 563
sterling silver wire, 23
storage boxes, 28
straw wreath frames, 153–55
stretch cord, 29–30
string, waxed, 100
stringing beads, 6, 46–54
   with ribbon, 30
   supplies for, 28–33
   tying knots in, 48
   working tips for, 48, 51, 53, 54
striped designs, 426–27
stylus, 212

summer garlands, 198–99
summer wreath, 196
surface sealer, 363
surgeon's knot, 48
swirling loaf soap, 188

tack, 442
tack cloth, 377
tailor's tracing wheel, 587
tangerine, 177
tape grids, 141
tape measures, 27
tapered paintbrush, 327
tapes:
    for children, 580
    floral, 101
    masking, 296, 421, 580
    for paper, 210, 211
    plaster, 604–6
    waterproof, 326
tassels and tassel trim, 463–67
teacup, candle in a, 495–96
tea tree, 177
tempera, 578
templates, 392–94, 400–402, 704
terra-cotta pots, 160
tesserae, 534
thermometers, 484–85
thin rod, 484
thread and cord, 29–30, 457
thread conditioner, 33
thread scissors, 32–33
thyme, 178
tie-dying, 618
tile adhesives, mortar, 535
tile nippers, 534
tilework, see picassiette
timers, 329, 421
tinting, 365
tissue paper, 253, 590
titanium wire, 23
toothpicks, 365
topiaries, 159–65
    dome, 163
    dried, 199–200
tracing and cutting, of patterns, 682

transfer stencils, 427–30
transparent base, 326–27
transparent decals, 471–75
travel journal, 269
trims, 457
T-shirt, 468
    screen printing on, 342
    tie-dyed, 618
T square, 306, 312, 319
tubes, water, 102
tubular (cylinder) beads, 9
tweezers, 33, 365, 439
twine, 100
two-ply leaves, 267–68
tying knots, 48

valerian, 178
van der Post, Laurens, xi
vanilla, 178
varnishes, applying of, 380
vase, for decoupage, 400, 413–14, 709
vegetable ivory, 13
vellum, 204, 229, 242
velvet, 450, 455–56
velvet pillow, embossed, 550
vials, 28
vine wreaths, 150–51
vintage wood, 383–85
vinyl, adhesive-backed, 429–32, 708
vitamin E oil, 178
votive candles, 497–500
vue d'optique (shadow boxes), 359
vybar, 482, 483

wallpaper, for decoupage, 366–67
wampum, 4
watercolors, 366, 370–71, 578
waterproof tape, 326
waterslide method of applying decals,
    469–71
water tubes, 102
wax, 482–83
    cooling of, 491–92
    leveling of, 492–93
    melting of, 484–88
    mixing additives into, 487, 489

pouring of, 486, 489
  removal methods for, 516
  temperature chart for, 488
wax-based colored pencils, 370–72
wax buildup, reducing of, 498
waxed cotton cord, 29
waxed string, 100
wax grip, 372
wax or candy thermometer, 484–85
wax-pouring pitcher, 485, 487
Weldbond, 535
wet embossing, 219–20
wet mounting, 217–18
wheat germ oil, 178
white craft glue (PVA; polyvinyl acetate), 101,
  209, 363, 580
white vinegar, distilled, 376
wick pins, 484, 494
wicks, 483–84
  filling depression around, 490–91
  priming of, 493–94
wick tabs (wick sustainers), 484, 494
wide gouge cutter, 311
wide V-cutter (veiner), 311
window cards, 228–31
winter wreath, 191–93
wire, 100, 254
  for dry embossing motifs, 452–53
wire cutters, 25–26, 103, 450
wire gauge, 24
wire spectacles, 679

wirework tools, 25–28
wiring beads, 6, 33–46
  determining loop size in, 35
wiring stems, 125–27
wood:
  concealing knots in, 379
  for decoupage, 375–98
  faux finish effects for, 528
  gilding on, 440–41
  painting of, 391–92
  preparing surface of, 377–85
  previously painted or varnished, 384–85
  sealing surface of, 382–84
wood dowels, 99
wooden spoons, 168
wood primer, 375
wood sealers, 375–76
woven heart basket, 201–3, 277–78, 693
wrapped-wire loops, 38–46
wreaths, wreath frames, 99–100
  decorating of, 148–55
  making or preparing of, 144–48
  projects for, 191–94, 196–97
Wunda size, 437, 438
wycinanki, 205

ylang ylang, 178

zebra platter, 410–12, 706
zebra throw with tassels, 551
zinc-core wicks, 484

Thornton Wilder cited the words of an unnamed writer of sonnets:

One line of the sonnet falls from the ceiling, and you tap in the others around it with a jeweler's hammer. Nobody whispers it in your ear. It is like something you memorized once and forgot. Now it comes back and rips away your breath. You find and finger a phrase at a time; you lay it down as if with tongs, restraining your strength, and wait suspended and fierce until the next one finds you: yes, this; and yes, praise be, then this.

–Ann Dillard, "Write Till You Drop"
*The New York Times,* May 28, 1989

# DICTIONARY OF CHRISTIAN BIOGRAPHY

## Edited by Michael Walsh

A Michael Glazier Book
THE LITURGICAL PRESS
Collegeville, Minnesota
*www.litpress.org*

First published in Great Britain in 2001 by
**Continuum**
The Tower Building, 11 York Road
London SE1 7NX

First published in the United States of America and Canada in 2001 by
THE LITURGICAL PRESS,
St John's Abbey, Collegeville,
Minnesota 56321

ISBN 0 8264 5263 9 (Continuum)
ISBN 0 8146 5921 7 (The Liturgical Press)

Typeset by CentraServe Ltd, Saffron Walden, Essex
Printed and bound in Great Britain by The Bath Press

# CONTENTS

Introduction
vii

Contributors
xi

Works of Reference
xiii

## The Dictionary
1

Index of Dates of Death
1169

Index of Places of Death
1206

# INTRODUCTION

There are, within this dictionary, the brief biographies of rather more than 6500 Christians. They have been selected for inclusion in this volume because, in their public lives, their commitment to Christianity played an important part. Simply to state that there are, herein, 6500-plus lives of prominent Christians does not quite reflect what the contributors and I have been trying to do when constructing this *Dictionary of Christian Biography*. To say that we were going to include the lives of as many prominent Christians as the size of the book – some 810,000 words – would allow, in a world in which hundreds of millions of men and women have been Christians of one sort or another, would not have been very helpful. It would not have defined the specific character of this collection of biography. On the other hand, I wanted to get away from the notion that only 'professional' Christians – theologians, that is to say, or saints and other spiritual gurus, or bishops and pastors – were worthy of inclusion.

People of this kind are, of course, to be found in their thousands within these pages, but they are interspersed with people whose professional lives may well have been fundamentally affected by their Christian faith, but who did not earn their keep from the profession of their religion. Barbara Ward, Lady Jackson, is my own personal hero in this category, but there are many more – lawyers, politicians, architects, educationalists. And, of course, there are, above all, artists – composers and painters in particular – who so often relied upon the Church for patronage, or produced music for liturgical use. One of the delights of compiling this book has been the entirely accidental juxtaposition of people from different walks of

life, and from different centuries and continents. Two other criteria operated: all those included are deceased; and everyone included lived after the close of the New Testament era.

The problem was never so much who was to be included, but who was to be left out. The first task placed before me by the publishers when commissioning this book was to produce a list of the 6000 men and women I would want to cover in the text. I had reached that figure long before I had got to the letter S, which is why, I confess, there is something of an over-representation of letters A and B. I take comfort in the lesson of that extraordinarily valuable work, the *Biographisch-bibliographisches Kirchenlexikon*, which rather went the other way. It is now up to ten volumes, and publishing supplements, but in its first volume, which appeared in 1975, it covered significant Christians from A to F.

Of course, not all of those on that first list made it to the final version. Some had their lives written, and then were dropped because, when I came to read what had been written about them, they did not meet the criteria laid down above. Some were dropped for the same reasons even before their biographies had been commissioned from contributors. On the other hand, many new names were added – those from S onwards, naturally, but more significantly, those suggested to us by contributors, who were specialists in different periods of Christian history, or in different regions of the Christian world, or in different varieties of the Christian faith.

The number of entries proposed determined what style of book this was to be. To cover the number suggested meant that the lives had to be fairly short – for the most part between one hundred and two hundred words, with only a few very important individuals running into the several hundred-word category. Only the most basic information could be given – dates of birth and death, when known (which is not always), and places of birth and death, education, roles and writings, feast days (if saints or blesseds), and so on.

Even with entries as short as this, there were some seemingly obvious candidates who did not make the final version. Take saints, for example. The most thorough listing of saints readily available is the *Bibliotheca Sanctorum* (see the list of reference works for publication details), which is an Italian-language production despite its Latin title, and well overdue for translation into English. Under the month of January alone it has listed in its index a thousand saints whose feasts fall within the first month of the year. The invaluable *Book of Saints*, which has room for only the briefest of notices, covers some 10,000 saints and blesseds of the Roman Catholic Church. This dictionary, therefore, could never be an exhaustive listing of those publicly venerated by the Church down the ages. Many – the majority – have simply had to be omitted.

But some saints have been more important than others in our shared history, not necessarily because they have helped to shape history, even the history of the Church, but because they have, for some reason, entered our culture in other ways. There is an obvious example in St Nicholas of Bari who, by an extraordinary transmutation, has become Santa Claus. Or there is St Cecilia, the patron saint of music, whose story has inspired painters and composers, and who has left her name behind in innumerable societies and choirs, and yet is entirely mythical.

For the first millennium of Christianity there was, in theory at least, a single Christian Church. The mutual excommunication of patriarch by pope (or at least by the papal representative) and of pope by patriarch, in 1054, ended all that. Long before, however, Rome and Constantinople had gone their different ways, and the history of the Church of the East has not been as well known in Europe and the Americas as has the history of the Church of the West. Though the excommunications have happily now been rescinded, the Eastern Church remains something of an unknown quan-

tity. It is, therefore, I feel, represented rather less well in these pages than it ought to have been. To take an obvious example: the lives of all the bishops of Rome – the popes – have been included, but not the lives of all the patriarchs of Constantinople, much less of Alexandria or Moscow. Another edition, were there to be one, would, I trust, redress this imbalance. None the less, the lives of the major figures of Byzantium have been covered, and we have had specialist advice from some more contemporary representatives of Orthodoxy, for which I am very grateful.

Looking at the list of people to be found in these pages, one or two of our contributors have commented on the large number of Roman Catholics. But the Roman Communion still has more adherents than all the other Christian denominations put together – Orthodoxy included. It is hardly surprising, therefore, that they predominate. But other denominations are certainly represented, and not just the mainline churches – the Lutherans and Anglicans, the Methodists and the Presbyterians – Mary Baker Eddy, founder of Christian Science, is to be found here. I have been much helped in expanding my horizons by the publication of Donald Lewis's *Dictionary of Evangelical Biography* and by specialist advice on the Pentecostal Churches, on the Free Churches, and also on African and Asian Christianity that I have received from the contributors.

While in compiling this dictionary it has been my aim to cover not just all varieties of Christianity, but all parts of the world, there is no escaping the fact that for three-quarters of its history, the Christian Church has been a European and Near-Eastern phenomenon, with modest – in terms of numbers at least – outposts in India and China. I have attempted to escape this in-built historical bias by a mite of positive discrimination in favour of the New World. It is now well represented in these pages, particularly through heroic missionaries and – I have noticed – through a remarkable number of clerical patriots in Latin American countries who were as active in the politics of their nations as they were in providing for the spiritual sustenance of their flocks; sometimes (I could not help feeling, as I read their lives) rather more so.

One of the more curious aspects of this compilation, as I have observed it developing, is how often the individuals mentioned are interlinked. It has occasionally struck me that, were a reader to follow all the links in a particular article, he or she might emerge from the process with a fairly detailed history of a period, even though the individual entry is short. To aid this kind of research, individuals mentioned in the body of an article who have a separate entry themselves are indicated in bold type.

When I first embarked on this project it seemed simple. I had 800,000 or so words to produce, so I needed 80 postgraduate students each writing c.10,000 words, or approximately 100 lives, apiece. That was the thought with which I started. I put up notices, I contacted friends at several universities and asked them to put up notices. They were kind enough to do so, and there were indeed lots of volunteers. There is a full list of contributors on another page, but I ought to make special mention of Donald Moorman, a mature student at my own College, Heythrop, who contributed more lives than anyone else, and who was at work until the day before the final text was handed over. Some contributors came aboard by way of notices distributed through the Association of British Theological and Philosophical Libraries, and through the Ecclesiastical History Society. I am very grateful to ABTAPL and the EHS for their assistance.

This project was languishing until, two years or so ago, Kate Walsh took over its management. Lists appeared; new contributors were engaged; new names were added to the database. She wrote entries and edited others. She also involved our daughters, Clare and Alex, both of whom typed up entries on the computer. But my special thanks goes to Alex, who turned her computing skills to good use, not only scanning in text on paper from contributors, but also helping to render the result into usable form.

I would also like to thank Tony Corley, Heythrop College's network manager, for his advice on sundry computer problems, and for his handling of the database on which the entries are all listed. Indeed, I feel I ought to thank the Internet as a whole. Had it not been for the invention of e-mail I cannot imagine how this project would ever have been completed.

When I first embarked upon this book I wrote for advice to another editor of a biographical dictionary, at that point just about to appear. 'You won't have enough time,' he told me gloomily, and 'you won't have enough money.' The book was indeed delivered late, so he was right on the first count; but not on the second. The contributors to this *Dictionary of Christian Biography* have been a remarkably generous group. They have given of their time and their expertise for very little financial reward, and many, if not quite all, of them seem positively to have relished the experience. My very grateful thanks go to them all.

Michael J. Walsh
Heythrop College, University of London
May 2001

# CONTRIBUTORS

Ana Abrams, Heythrop College

Richard Bartholomew, London

Niki Bartram, London

Margaret Batty, Edinburgh

Nancy Benvenga, New York

John Briggs, Westhill College, Birmingham

Stuart Burns, Leicester

James Conlon, London

Noreen Conway-Morris, London

Stephen Copson, Hitchin, Hertfordshire

Leonard W. Cowie, London

Rhonda Crutcher, Africa Nazarene University, Nairobi

Timothy Crutcher, Africa Nazarene University, Nairobi

Ivor Davidson, University of Otago, New Zealand

Michael Dawney, Poole, Dorset

John Dick, Catholic University of Louvain

Stella Fletcher, King Alfred College, Winchester

Avril Furneaux, Wales

Alex Gilmore, University of Sussex

James Girdwood, University of Wolverhampton

Linda Gottschalk, University of Louvain

John Harwood, Mill Hill Institute, London

Stan Ingersoll, Nazarene Archives

Ian Jones, Birmingham

Deslea Judd, Darlington, New South Wales, Australia

Rene Kollar, St Vincent's University, Latrobe, Pennsylvania

Abraham Kovacs, Edinburgh

Colin Lawlor, University of Brighton

Johan Leemans, Catholic University of Louvain

Sr Jessica Leonard, s.m. Hythe, Kent

Alan Linfield, London Bible College

Elizabeth Longley, London

John McGurk, Co. Mayo, Ireland

Barbara Melaas-Swanson, Illinois, USA

Donald Moorman, Heythrop College

Michael Morgan, Heythrop College

Gregory Morris, St Deinols Library, Hawarden

Adriana Piacentini, Heythrop College

Jon Porter, Indianapolis, Indiana

John Roxburgh, Bible College of New Zealand

Ann-Marie Sharman, London

Debra Snoddy, University of Louvain

Simon Valentine, Bradford

Kate Walsh, London

James Webb, Heythrop College

Emma Wild-Wood, Edinburgh/The Congo

# WORKS OF REFERENCE

The following list contains only those works which were regularly used, by the editor or by contributors, in the production of this text. They can be referred to for further information on most of the individuals whose lives are briefly recounted in this book.

*Acta Sanctorum*, Brussels, The Bollandists

*Bibliotheca Sanctorum*, Rome, Lateran University/ Città Nuova, 1961–87

*Biographical Dictionary of American Cult and Sect Leaders*, J. Gordon Melton, 1986

*Biographical Dictionary of Christian Missions*, edited by Gerald H. Anderson, New York, Macmillan, 1998

*Biographisch-bibliographisches Kirchenlexikon*, edited by F. W. Bautz, Hamm, Traugott Bautz, 1975–99

*Butler's Lives of the Saints* (edited by Herbert Thurston and Donald Attwater), London, Burns and Oates, 1926–38

*Cambridge Biographical Encyclopedia* (edited by David Crystal), Cambridge University Press, 1994

*Catholic Encylopedia*, New York, Encyclopedia Press, 1914

*Catholicisme*, Paris, Letouzey, 1948–

*Chambers Biographical Dictionary*, edited by Magnus Magnusson, Edinburgh and New York, 1990

*Contemporaries of Erasmus* (edited by Peter G. Bietenholz), University of Toronto Press, 1989

*Dictionary of American Biography*, New York, Scribner, 1964

*Dictionary of American Catholic Biography* (edited by John J. Delaney), Garden City, NY, Doubleday, 1984

*Dictionary of Art* (edited by Jane Turner), London, Macmillan, 1996

*Dictionary of Catholic Biography* (edited by John J. Delaney and J. E. Tobin), Garden City, NY, Doubleday, 1961

*Dictionary of Christian Biography* (edited by William Smith and Henry Wace), London, John Murray, 1877–87

*Dictionary of Evangelical Biography* (edited by Donald M. Lewis), Oxford, Blackwell, 1995

*Dictionary of National Biography*, Oxford University Press, 1917–

*Dictionary of Saints* (edited by John J. Delaney), Tadworth, Kaye and Ward, 1980

*Dictionary of Scottish Church History and Theology* (edited by M. de S. Cameron), Edinburgh, T & T Clark, 1993

*Dictionary of the Ecumenical Movement* (edited by Nicholas Lossky et al.) Grand Rapids, Eerdmans; Geneva, WCC, 1991

*Dictionary of the Middle Ages* (edited by J. R. Strayer), New York, Scribner, 1982–9

*Dictionary of American Catholic Biography* (edited by John J. Delaney), 1984

*Dictionnaire de Biographie Française*, Paris, Letouzey, 1933–

*Dictionnaire de histoire et de géographie ecclésiastiques*, Paris, Letouzey, 1912–

*Dictionnaire de théologie catholique*, Paris, Letouzey, 1909–67

*Dizionario Biographico Degli Italiano*, Rome, Istituto Enciclopedia Italiana, 1960–

*Encyclopaedia Judaica*, Jerusalem, Keter Publishing, 1972

*Enciclopedia Cattolica*, Vatican City, Enciclopedia Cattolica, 1948–1954

*Encyclopedia of American National Biography*, Oxford University Press, 1999

*Encyclopedia of Early Christianity* (edited by Everret Ferguson), 1990

*Encyclopedia of Religion* (edited by Mircea Eliade), New York, Macmillan, 1987

*Encyclopedia of the Early Church* (edited by A. Di Berardino, translated by A. Walford), Cambridge, James Clarke, 1992

*Encyclopedia of American Catholic History* (edited by M. Glazier and T. Shelley), Collegeville, MN, Liturgical Publications, 1997

*Evangelical Dictionary of Theology* (edited by W. A. Elwell), Baker Book House, 1984

*Heresies of the High Middle Ages* (edited by Walter L. Wakefield and Austin P. Evans), New York, Columbia University Press, 1981

*Lexikon für Theologie und Kirche*, Freiburg, Herder, 1993–

*Macmillan Dictionary of Biography*, London: Macmillan, 1986

*Mission Legacies: Biographical Studies of Leaders of the Modern Missionary Movement* (edited by Gerald H. Anderson et al.), Maryknoll, Orbis, 1994

*Neue Deutsche Biographie*, Berlin, Duncker and Humblot, 1952–

*New Catholic Encyclopedia*, Washington DC, Catholic University of America Press, 1967

*New Grove Dictionary of Music and Musicians* (edited by Sir George Grove and Stanley Sadie), London, Macmillan, 1980

*New International Dictionary of the Christian Church* (edited by J. D. Douglas), Exeter, Paternoster Press, 1974

*Oxford Classical Dictionary* (edited by S. Hornblower and A. Spawforth), Oxford University Press, 1996

*Oxford Companion to English Literature* (edited by Margaret Drabble), Oxford University Press, 1996

*Oxford Dictionary of Byzantium* (edited by A. P. Kazhdan et al.), Oxford University Press, 1991

*Oxford Dictionary of Popes*, J. N. D. Kelly, Oxford University Press, 1986

*Oxford Dictionary of Saints*, D. H. Farmer, Oxford, Clarendon Press, 1998

*Oxford Dictionary of the Christian Church* (edited by F. L. Cross, and E. A. Livingstone), Oxford University Press, 1997

*Oxford Encyclopedia of the Reformation* (edited by Hans J. Hillerbrand), Oxford University Press, 1996

*Penguin Dictionary of Saints* (edited by Donald Attwater and C. R. John), London, Penguin Books, 1995

*Personenlexikon für Religion und Theologie* (edited by M. Greschat), Vandenhoeck & Ruprecht, 1998

*Theologische Realenzyklopädie* (edited by Gerhard Krause and Gerhard Müller), Berlin, De Gruyter, 1975–

*Westminster Dictionary of Church History* (edited by Jerald C. Bauer), Philadelphia, Westminster Press, 1971

**Aaron, Pietro** Monk, music theorist, born Florence, Italy, c.1489, died after 1545. His career in music began by founding a choir school for Pope **Leo X** in 1516. He moved to Imola in 1521, Rimini in 1523, Venice to work for the Knights of Malta in 1525. He himself entered the Knights in 1529 and then joined the Cross-Bearers in Bergamo. His best work is *Toscanello in Musica* (first 1523, last 1539). His solution to the problem of temper, to flatten the fifth, anticipated the well-tempered tuning of the eighteenth century. He is also known for asking composers to write the different singing parts together ('vertically') and to specify all accidentals.

**Abad y Sánchez, Diego José** Jesuit scholar, born La Lagunita, Mexico, 1 June 1727, died Bologna 30 September 1779. He entered religious life in 1727, and after a successful career as educator in rhetoric, philosophy, theology and law (canon and civil), as a Jesuit he was expelled from the Spanish Empire in 1767 and took to writing in Ferrara, Italy. His noted work *De deo deoque homine heroica* (1773) is a verse treatise on God intended for young Mexicans. His scholarly dedication extended to studying medicine and thereby prolonging his life when the doctors were powerless.

**Abbatini, Antonio Maria** Music theorist, composer, born c.1597 Tiferno, Italy, died there, c.1679–80. He studied with the brothers **Nanino** and extended their style in much music. He married Dorotea Giustini in 1631. His career started as chapel master of St John Lateran (1622–8) and he spent much time at St Mary Major. He composed an opera on a libretto by the future Pope **Urban** VIII and worked with Athanasius **Kircher** on *Musurgia Universalis* (1650). His major theoretical work *Discorsi e lezioni accademiche* is kept in the Bologna Conservatory.

**Abbelen, Peter** Priest and spiritual director, born Germany, 8 August 1843, died Milwaukee, USA, 24 August 1917. He was ordained in Milwaukee in 1868 but joined the La Crosse Diocese. After eight years of pastorate he became spiritual director to the School Sisters of Notre Dame in Milwaukee where they had been established since 1850. This congregation had come to the USA from Germany in 1847 to minister to German-speaking immigrants. Abbelen became embroiled in a dispute over jurisdiction in nationalistic parishes and the use of English in schools. The subsequent decision of the Congregation for the Propagation of the Faith is considered unfavourable to him. He was made a domestic prelate in 1907.

**Abbeville, Claude d'** French Capuchin missionary and historian, born c.1575, died 1616. Having entered the order in 1593, he joined the French expedition to Brazil in 1611 as a missionary, and became the first to write about the Brazilian lands conquered by the French. He is best known for *Histoire de la mission des Perès Capuchins en l'isle de Maragnan et terres circonvoisines* (Paris, 1614); he was involved in this mission (Maranhao).

**Abbo of Fleury** Benedictine abbot, saint, born c.945 near Orléans, France, died at Fleury-sur-Loire, France, 13 November 1004, from a wound received while trying to resolve a monastic dispute in Gascony. This monk was known for learning and sanctity, having studied philosophy, mathematics and astronomy. He calmed those who foresaw the end of the world in the millennium year 1000. He served for two years in England from 965 as director of the newly founded Ramsey monastery school in Huntingdon. Gerbert (later Pope **Sylvester II**) intervened when his election as abbot of Fleury was contested. His disciple Aimoin, in whose arms he died, recorded his labours and virtues.

**Abbo of Metz** Bishop, born Aquitaine, died 647. He succeeded his kinsman St **Arnulf** as bishop of Metz in 629, and built St Peter's there. He is named Abbo in the will of King Dagobert but he is also known as Goericus.

**Abbott, Lyman** Congregational clergyman and editor, author, born Roxbury, Massachusetts, USA, 13 December *c.*1835, died Cornwall-on-Hudson, NY, 22 October 1922. He was ordained in 1860 after studying theology and law. An abolitionist, he served as secretary of the American Freedman's Union. He was editor for *The Illustrated Christian Weekly and the Christian Union* (later *Outlook*), popularized his teaching on religion in *Dictionary of Christian Knowledge*, and tried to reconcile Christianity with Darwinism. He wrote the official biography and edited the papers of Henry Ward **Beecher**, whom he succeeded at the Plymouth Church, Brooklyn, NY. After the Civil War he worked for reconciliation.

**'Abdallah Zahir** Goldsmith, printer, lecturer, polemicist, deacon, born Aleppo, Syria, 1680, died monastery of Mar Hanna, Shuwair, Lebanon, 20 August 1748. He became a lay deacon of Melkite rite in the monastery of Mar Hanna (St John) after persecution in Aleppo. He defended the rights of the Melkite Church against Latinizers, and set up a printing press to provide religious material for Arabic-speaking Christians. He was also involved in composing the religious constitutions of the Basilian Shuwairite Order.

**Abdias of Babylon** Saint, the supposed first bishop of Babylon appointed by SS Simon and Jude, and ascribed author of *Historia Certaminus Apostolici*, now considered a sixth-century Latin work.

**Abdisho IV (Ebedjesu)** Chaldean patriarch from 1555 to 1567, succeeding John Sulaqa. He had been a monk at the monastery of SS Acha and John, and then bishop of Gezirah, Mesopotamia. He received the pallium from Pope **Pius IV** in Rome in 1562. He attended the third session of the Council of Trent, where he read a profession of faith. He tried to bring India's Thomas Christians under his jurisdiction but was resisted by the Portuguese. He wrote hymns about the martyrs and poems about his predecessor and Pius IV.

**'Abdisho bar Berika (Ebedjesu)** Nestorian writer and metropolitan of Nisibis (Soba) and Armenia, died November 1318. Known as one of the last writers in Syriac, he wrote many religious and philosophical works, sometimes in Arabic. He became metropolitan in 1291 after being bishop in Sighar and Bet 'Arabaje.

**Abel, Felix Marie** Dominican priest, biblical scholar and geographer of Palestine, born Saint-Uze (Droame), France, 24 December *c.*1878, died Jerusalem, 24 March 1953. After studies in Jerusalem he was ordained a Dominican priest in 1902, and remained there to become a foremost expert on Palestinian geography and history, extending his talents to a tourist guide for 1932. He taught at the Ecole Biblique of Jerusalem for more than 50 years, being named by **Pius XII** Consultor to the Pontifical Biblical Commission in 1940.

**Abelard, Peter** Philosopher, theologian, well-known lover, then monk, born near Nantes, Brittany, 1079, the son of a knight, died at Chalon-sur-Saône, France, on 21 April 1142. After five years at the school of Ste Geneviève in Paris he held the chair of rhetoric and dialectic at the important Nôtre Dame School of Paris, which became part of the eventual university, and where he had previously studied. In 1118 he had to abandon his prodigious academic career in Paris as a result of the scandal surrounding his relationship with **Héloïse**, niece of Canon *Fulbert*, in whose house he had lodgings. His *Story of my Calamities*, recounting the growing affection, consummation, secret marriage, eventual castration and the joy of a son – whom he named Astrolabe after the instrument for measuring the heavens – has become part of the classic love-theme literature. He also describes his pride and temerity which led to disputes all through his life. After some twenty years in a monastery he returned to Paris as a teacher. His writings on the Trinity eventually brought him into conflict with **Bernard of Clairvaux**. Although condemned, first by the French bishops, then by the Pope, he was defended by Peter of Cluny and was allowed his freedom. He ended his days as a teacher at the Chalon-sur-Saône priory. His final resting place with Héloïse at the Père Lachaise cemetery, Paris, is frequented by courting couples. In his studies he laid the foundations of method, leaning more towards the scholastic principle 'Reason aids Faith' than to 'Faith aids Reason'. The *Sentences* of his student **Peter Lombard** and others extended his influence into the thirteenth century. He is also known for examining the role of the subjective intention in determining the moral value of human action.

**Abell, Robert**  Missionary, born Nelson County, Kentucky, USA, 25 November 1792, died Louisville, Kentucky, 28 June 1873. Ordained in 1818 this tall priest (6ft 4in) worked in a huge Kentucky mission field among the native population. He built churches in Louisville and Lebanon, and became vice-principal of St Joseph's College, Bardstown, where he had taught earlier.

**Abell, Thomas**  Blessed, martyr, royal chaplain, born late fifteenth century, martyred at Smithfield on 30 July 1540. He became chaplain to Queen **Catherine of Aragon** before 1528 and in 1529 went to Spain on her behalf carrying two letters: one officially asking for an original document concerning the dispensation for the marriage to **Henry VIII** to be sent to England, the other (her true mind) asking for it not to be sent. In this and other ways, including the anonymous *Invicta Veritas*, Thomas defended the queen's marriage. For his pains he was committed to the Tower; later released he was rearrested a year later for misprision; accused in 1540 of treason for refusing to acknowledge the king's supremacy, he was sentenced to be hanged, drawn and quartered. Feast day 30 July.

**Abelly, Louis**  Anti-Jansenist writer, born 1603, died 1691. He became bishop of Rodez in 1664 after being vicar general in Bayonne and parish

priest in Paris. He abdicated in 1666 to work with St **Vincent de Paul** of whom he wrote the life. He wrote against Jansenism and in favour of submission to the Pope. He is well known for his useful *Modulla Theologica*.

**Abercromby, Robert**  Jesuit missionary who brought Queen **Anne of Denmark**, wife of James VI of Scotland (later **James I** of England), into the Catholic faith, born 1532, died in self-imposed exile at Braunsberg, Prussia, 27 April 1613. He met the queen after her Lutheran chaplain became a Calvinist on arriving in Scotland. She, however, preferred the Catholic faith with which she was familiar through a niece of Emperor **Charles V.** A price was put on Abercromby's head when the queen's conversion (*c.*1600) became known, but his temporary refuge England was no safer after the 1605 Gunpowder Plot and accusations against the Jesuits.

**Abhishiktananda**  *see* **Le Saux, Henri**

**Abington, Thomas**  Antiquarian, born England 1560, died in exile accused of complicity in the aftermath of the Gunpowder Plot, 1647. His father was treasurer to Queen **Elizabeth I**. He spent six years in the Tower of London with his brother Edward, accused of complicity in the Babington plot, the scheme of Queen Elizabeth's head of security Walsingham to implicate Catholics in an attempt to free **Mary Queen of Scots** and perhaps overthrow the English queen's government. Then he harboured two Jesuits, Henry Garnett and Oldcome, at Hinlop Castle, Lancaster. Their link to the Gunpowder Plot led to Abington's sentence to death, commuted to exile on the intervention of his son-in-law, Lord Monteagle.

**Abra de Raconis, Charles François d'**  French bishop, born 1580 at the chateau of Raconis, died 1646. Born into a noble Calvinist family he converted to the Catholic faith with his family in 1592. After teaching philosophy and theology he was appointed court preacher and royal almoner for the seventeen-year-old **Louis XIII** in 1618 during the rise to influence of Cardinal **Richelieu.** He was consecrated bishop of Lavaur in 1639. In this epoch of religious controversy, with the eventual encouragement of St **Vincent de Paul** he defended the Catholic faith notably against Jansenism and in 1646 wrote a tract in favour of frequent Communion, a topic which brought him into conflict even with his fellow French bishops.

**Abraham Ecchellensis**   A learned Maronite, born in Ecchel, a Lebanon village, 1600, died in Rome, 1664. After studies in the Maronite College, Rome, he taught Syriac and Arabic, first at the College of Propaganda and then from 1630 in the Royal College, Paris. In Paris he helped to edit Le Hay's *Polyglot Bible* but disagreed with his collaborator **Gabriel Sionita** over work on the Syriac and Arabic texts and their Latin translation. He returned to Rome in 1642, to Paris in 1645 and back to Rome in 1653. He published a *Synopsis of Arabic Philosophy*, and various works on dogma, liturgy, canon law, history and mathematics.

**Abraham Kidunia**   Saint, hermit, sixth century. Born of a wealthy family living near Edessa, Abraham left home on the day of his arranged marriage to become for fifty years a hermit in the desert near the town of Beth Kiduna. However, at the request of his bishop, he spent three years preaching to a settlement close by until the villagers were converted to Christianity. There is a story that he rescued his orphaned niece from a brothel. She had lived in a hermitage beside his own, but had run away in shame after a visiting monk raped her. Abraham discovered where she was and went there, disguised as a customer. He persuaded her that, whatever her supposed sins, God loved her and she returned with him. Abraham died when he was some 70 years old. Feast day 16 March.

**Abraham of Sancta Clara**   Discalced Augustinian friar, preacher and popular author, born Messkirch, 1644, died Vienna, 1 December 1709. The eighth son of a well-to-do serf, John Ulrich Megerle entered the Augustinian friars in 1662 taking the name Abraham, presumably after his uncle, and adding 'a Sancta Clara'. He had roles as prior and eventually provincial and definitor. His preaching was witty and charming. His writings spoke to the situation of his day such as the plague and the Turks' second siege of Vienna (1683). His masterpiece was *Judas, the Archknave*, full of moral reflections. His clever and original writings, with

some influence from Sebastian **Brant**'s *Narrenschift* (*Ship of Fools*), in turn influenced Schiller.

**Abraham of Smolensk**   Saint, Russian monk, born at Smolensk in the late twelfth century, died there 21 August 1221. After the death of his parents he entered the monastery of the Mother of God at Smolensk, and, apart from a particular devotion to the Eucharist, celebrating Mass daily, which was then uncommon, lived the usual life of a monk, combining contemplation and preaching with caring for the poor and sick. But his prophetic messages, in which he called for repentance and warned about the judgement of God, aroused the anger of the rich and of some of the clergy. He was accused of heresy and misconduct with women, arrested and publicly humiliated. Two courts refused to convict him and his bishop ruled the charges to be false. On his release he was appointed abbot of a small monastery. Feast day 21 August.

**Abrantovic, Fabijan**   Archimandrite of the Byzantine-Slavonic rite, born Navahradak, Byelorussia 14 September 1884, died 1940 in unknown circumstances after arrest by Communists. Ordained in 1908 he taught theology at the Catholic Academy of St Petersburg and contributed to the Byelorussian renaissance. He became a Marian Father in 1926 and went to Harbin, Manchuria, in 1928 to organize a Catholic diocese where the Christians were predominantly Orthodox. In 1939 he returned to his native Byelorussia from Rome but was accused of being a Vatican spy.

**Absalon of Lund (Axel)**   Also known as Axel, archbishop, born 1128 in Seeland, died in Soroe, 21 March 1201. After graduating from the University of Paris he taught at the school of Ste Geneviève. He returned to Denmark to become bishop of Roskilde in 1158. In 1178 he was made archbishop of Lund, primate of Denmark and Sweden and eventually papal legate. Absalon waged war on paganism in Scandinavia which was losing its influence, with its last stronghold held by the Wendish pirates on Rugen. He encouraged Saxo Grammaticus to write a history of the Danes. He had great influence with the kings of Denmark and resisted the German yoke, but he could not prevent Valdemar I rendering fealty to **Frederick I Barbarossa** in 1162. His stature is shown in leading a group of twelve men plus the bishop of Aarhus past 6000 warriors to overturn the idols in the Wendish temple.

**Abu 'l-Barakat**  Coptic priest and author, died 10 May 1324. Attached to the church called al-Mu'allaqa in Cairo, Shams al-Riasa abu 'l-Barakat also held the post of secretary to the prince and Mameluke officer Ruqn al-Din Baibars al-Mansuri. His principal work is the theological encyclopedia: *The Lamp of Darkness and the Exposition of the Service*. He also wrote a Coptic–Arabic dictionary and collaborated with Prince Ruqn on his history of Islam.

**Abu 'l-Faraj 'Abdallah ibn at-Tayyib**  Nestorian philosopher, physician, monk, died Baghdad 1043. A secretary to two patriarchs, Catholicos Yuhanna ibn Nuzuk (1012–22) and Elias I (1029–49), he was in favour also with the Muslim authorities. He wrote commentaries on Aristotle which were quoted by Avicenna and Averroes. He also wrote on medicine and ecclesiastical subjects, including a commentary on the Psalms.

**Acacius of Beroea**  Bishop, born *c.*322 in Syria, died Beroea, 434. In his century-long life he was never far from controversy and was excommunicated on two occasions. He defended orthodoxy against Arianism, and from being a monk was made bishop of Beroea in 378 by **Eusebius of Samosata**. He attacked the errors of **Apollinarius**, then those of the Pneumatomachians, and then helped to consecrate Flavian as bishop of Antioch, an act which led to excommunication for ten years by Pope **Damasus**. With claims he had been badly received in Constantinople he fell out with St **John Chrysostom**, and his attempt to get Pope **Innocent I** on his side led to another spell of excommunication. He advocated leniency for **Nestorius** and when that failed he tried to have **Cyril of Alexandria** accused of Apollinarianism, but then he worked to defuse the tension caused by this dispute. In spite of controversy he was remembered as an 'athlete of virtue'.

**Acacius of Caesarea**  Bishop, died 366. Probably a Syrian, he became bishop of Caesarea in Palestine in 340, succeeding his teacher **Eusebius** the historian, and was eventually deposed by the Council of Sardica in 347, although he refused to accept this judgement and organized the court faction into promulgating a similar deposition with excommunication of his opponents including Pope **Julius I**. He was of Arianizing tendency and fought against the precisions of the Nicene Creed. He was also remembered for his opposition to **Cyril of Jerusalem** whose exile he obtained. Matters came to a head at the non-canonical Council of Seleucia. He did later accept the Nicene formula for a time but changed his mind under an Arian emperor.

**Acca**  Saint, bishop of Hexham, born *c.*660, died 742. A disciple of **Wilfrid**, he was made abbot of St Andrew's Monastery, Hexham, when Wilfrid was reinstated bishop. He eventually succeeded Wilfrid in 709. He built up the Church materially, liturgically and in learning. He brought to the north a famous cantor Maban, encouraged Eddius to write the life of St Wilfrid and was patron of St **Bede** for some biblical works. Since he was honoured as a saint after his death, two high stone crosses were erected at the ends of his grave.

**Acciaioli, Angelo**  Cardinal, born 1349, died near Pisa 31 May 1408. A member of an illustrious Florentine family which was to produce two more cardinals (see next entries), Angelo became archbishop of Florence in 1383 and cardinal in 1385 by Pope **Urban VI**. He defended Pope Urban's rights to the Papacy against the antipope **Clement VII**, and in the consistory after Urban's death was favourite to succeed him until he directed the election to **Boniface XI**. The new Pope made him cardinal-bishop of Ostia. Later he became governor of Naples.

**Acciaioli, Filippo**  Cardinal, archbishop of Ancona, born 12 March 1700, died in Ancona 4 July 1766. He had been nuncio in Portugal.

**Acciaioli, Niccolò**  Cardinal, bishop of Ostia, born 1630 at Florence, died in Rome 23 February 1719.

**Accolti, Benedetto (the younger)**  Cardinal-archbishop of Ravenna and papal secretary, born Florence 29 October 1497, died there 21 September 1549. He is not to be confused with fifteenth-century jurist and historian (1415–66) of same name, nor with his uncle Pietro from whom he inherited some bishoprics. After being secretary to **Clement VII** he was made a cardinal by him in 1527, and succeeded his uncle Pietro at Ravenna in 1532. He fell out with **Paul III** when he returned to Rome after 1535. He is known as a poet.

**Accolti, Michele** Jesuit missionary, born Bari, Italy, 29 January 1807, died San Francisco, USA, 7 November 1878. Of noble birth he started training as an ecclesiastic in Rome before entering the Jesuits in 1832. In 1843, a year after ordination, he joined Pierre du Smet in a Jesuit mission to the Flathead Indians in the north-west of North America. He eventually refounded the Jesuits in California in 1849, after the expulsion in 1768. He helped to found St Ignatius College in San Francisco, now the University of California.

**Accolti, Pietro** Cardinal-bishop of Ancona, instrumental in condemnation of **Luther**, born Florence, 15 March 1455, died Rome, 12 December *c.*1532. (See **Accolti, Benedetto**.) After studies in jurisprudence he became Dean of the Rota in 1500 and from there went to Ancona as bishop in 1505. Named cardinal by **Julius II** on 10 March 1515, as well as the titular church of St Eusebius he took two more bishoprics and later others including Ravenna in 1524. An important participant in the Lateran Council V he later helped to draw up the document *Exsurge Domine* published on 15 June 1520 by **Leo X** to condemn Martin Luther on 41 points of heresy.

**Achard of Saint-Victor** Blessed, bishop, born English or of a noble Norman family early twelfth century, died Avranches, France, March 1172. After studies in England he entered the Canons Regular at Saint-Victor, Paris, and in 1155 became second abbot (on death of Gilduin). Elected bishop to Seez in 1157 he did not obtain royal approval, but the Plantaganet Henry II allowed him to become bishop of Avranches in 1162. Achard met **Thomas Becket** in Tours in 1163 and supported him in his persecution. He is known for a treatise *De Trinitate* preserved in a Padua MS.

**Achery, Jean Luc d'** Benedictine monk, librarian and editor, born 1609 in Picardy, France, died in the monastery of St-Germain-des-Prés at Paris, where he had spent nearly 50 years of his life, on

29 April 1685. He entered the Benedictines at Vendome but soon moved to Paris for health reasons. As librarian at St-Germain-des-Prés he was responsible for several original manuscripts including monastery correspondence, and edited authors such as **Guibert of Nogent** (Paris) and Grimlaicus. His principal work is *Spicelegium, sive collectio veterum aliquot scriptorum qui in Galliae bibliothecis, maxime Benedictinorum, latuerunt* (Paris, 1655–77).

**Achterfeldt, Johann Heinrich** Theologian, born 17 June 1788 at Wesel (Germany), died at Bonn, 11 May 1877. His academic career was marked by a conflict with church authorities over the doctrines of **Hermes**, which he supported in the review *Zeitschrift für Philosophie und Katholische Theologie* founded with his colleague J. W. J. Braun. He was professor of theology at Bonn from 1826 to 1843 and again from 1873 but he was suspended in the intervening time for refusing to sign a declaration of faith after Pope **Gregory XVI** placed the writings of Hermes, including *Christkatholische Dogmatik* edited by Achterfeldt, on the Index (1835).

**Acosta, José de** Jesuit scholar and South American missionary, born 1540 at Medina del Campo, Spain, died Salamanca, 15 February 1600. A Jesuit novice at thirteen, he taught theology first at Ocana and then in the new mission of Lima, Peru. In 1576 he was elected provincial and he founded a number of colleges. As well as in western South America, he studied flora and Indian customs also in Mexico. On returning to Europe he taught theology in Rome and eventually became the rector of the college at Salamanca. His best-known work is *Historia natural y moral de las Indias* (Seville, 1590), but from a missiological view *De procuranda Indorum salute* is better. His *De Natura Novi Orbis* is also significant. His 1583 Indian catechism was the first book printed in Peru.

**Acquaviva, Claudius** Fifth general of the Society of Jesus, born Atri, October 1543, died Rome, 31 January 1615. He provided strong leadership at a time of great turmoil after being elected general at the age of 37 on 19 February 1581. Alongside the internal threats of schism in the Society and of suppression by the Pope, he had to deal with persecution in England (where he once wanted to go as missionary); the crushing of Christianity in Japan; the Huguenot troubles in France; expulsion from Venice and oppression elsewhere. He is counted the second best administrator of the Society after the founder, St **Ignatius**, and is known for preparing the *Ratio Studiorum* (a study guide for training Jesuits) and a commentary on the Ignatian Exercises. With his encouragement many famous Jesuit saints and scholars flourished, schools educated statesmen in Europe, the China mission prospered with Jesuits becoming the emperor's astronomers, the Indian population of Paraguay was organized in reductions. The controversy with the Dominicans over grace flared up but discussion was allowed to die away.

**Acquaviva, Guilio**  Cardinal, born 1546 at Naples, died 1574. After being nuncio to Philip of Spain, he was made cardinal by St **Pius V**.

**Acquaviva, Ottavio (the elder)**  Cardinal, born 1560 at Naples, died 1612. He was cardinal-legate in the Campagna and at Avignon. In 1605 he was made archbishop of Naples by **Leo XI**.

**Acquaviva, Ottavio (the younger)**  Cardinal, born 1608 at Naples, to the family of the dukes of Atri, died at Rome, 1674. **Innocent X** made him a cardinal in 1654, and then legate in Viterbo and Romagna.

**Acquaviva, Rudolf**  Blessed, Italian Jesuit martyr. Born Ati, Naples, 2 October 1550; died Goa, 25 July 1583. Son of the duke of Atii and nephew of Claudio Acquaviva, general of the Society, Rudolf went to Goa in 1578 and led a mission to the court of the Great Mogul Akbar, near Agra; he returned to Goa as superior of the Salsette mission. With four companions, Rudolf went to Cuncolini to select ground for a church and to mark the area with a cross. Some Hindus, aroused by this threat to their beliefs, killed them and threw their bodies into a well; they were later recovered and are now venerated in Goa City. The martyrs were beatified in 1893. Feast day 27 July.

**Acquaviva, Trojano**  Cardinal, born 1694 at Naples, died in Rome, 1747. After being involved in the administration of the Papal States he was made cardinal by **Clement XII** in 1732. He became archbishop of Toledo, and later of Montereale.

**Acton, Charles Januarius**  Cardinal, born at Naples, 6 March 1803, died there, 23 June 1847. The second son of Sir John Francis Acton, Bart, Charles studied in London with Abbé Queque, then in Westminster School which was unusual for a Catholic, then at Magdalene College, Cambridge, which in principle was forbidden to Catholics. He was made an attaché to the Paris nunciature by **Leo XII**. Then **Pius VIII** made him legate of Bologna. **Gregory XVI** made him assistant judge to the Civil Court of Rome, and then auditor to the Apostolic Chamber as well as cardinal-priest of Santa Maria della Pace in 1842. He gained a reputation for succinct writing, careful judgement and heartfelt charity to the poor.

**Acton, John Emerich Edward Dalberg**  History professor, Member of Parliament, later Lord, Catholic scholar and editor, born 10 January 1834 at Naples, died at Tegernsee, Bavaria, 19 June 1902. His grandfather had been prime minister of Naples and his father, Sir Richard, had a diplomatic post there. John got to know the German historian **Döllinger** well but did not eventually follow him in leaving the Catholic Church after the definition of papal infallibility at Vatican I. He was MP for Carlow, Ireland, 1859–65. He succeeded J. H. **Newman** in 1859 as editor of the Catholic periodical *The Rambler* which became the quarterly *The Home and Foreign Review*, discontinued in 1864, under pressure from the ecclesiastical authorities for its liberal stance, and so as not to come under the strictures of the papal *Syllabus of Errors*. In 1865 he married Countess Marie, daughter of Count Arco-Valley of Bavaria, and they had one son and three daughters. He was made the first Baron Acton in 1869. He remained somewhat bitter towards Roman authority after Vatican I, although his uncle Charles J. E. **Acton** had been a cardinal. As Cambridge regius professor of modern history (1845–1902) he began organizing the *Cambridge Modern History*, the first volume of which appeared after his death. His friendship with Liberal leader **Gladstone** was noted by Matthew **Arnold** for its influence on Gladstone. A learned man but without many publications he is known for the dictum: 'Power tends to corrupt and absolute power corrupts absolutely.'

**Acuña, Cristobal de** Jesuit missionary and explorer, born Burgos, Spain, 1597, died Lima, Peru, 14 June 1670. A Jesuit from 1612, he passed from the province of Spain to the vice-province of Chile in 1620. In 1634 he passed to the vice-province of Ecuador having been since 1630 founder and first rector of the College of Cuenca. His previous travels through South America led to his being chosen for a 1639 scientific expedition with Pedro Texiera down the Amazon, with findings published in *Nuevo descubrimiento del Grand Rio de las Amazonas* (Madrid, 1641), translated into English, 1661. He explained his work at court in Spain and then returned to South America in 1644.

**Adalar** Saint, priest and martyr, martyred at Dokkum, The Netherlands, with St **Boniface**, 5 June 754. Listed as a companion of St Boniface and fellow martyr, he is known only as a priest. However there is an unsubstantiated tradition that he was bishop of Erfurt, where his remains are in the cathedral. He would have been consecrated by St Boniface in 741. Feast day 20 April (translation).

**Adalard** Benedictine abbot and saint, born *c.*751, died 2 January 827. After education at the court of **Charlemagne**, of whom he was a relation, he entered the Benedictines at Corbie in Picardy. After a spell in Monte Cassino, he was elected abbot at Corbie, and appointed by Charlemagne prime minister to Pepin who was half-brother to Adalard's father. Exiled for suspected involvement in Pepin's son Bernard's bid to be emperor, he was later reinstated and helped to found the monastery at Corvey in Westphalia.

**Adalbald (of Ostrevant)** Saint, nobleman, assassinated near Perigueux, Aquitaine, by antagonistic in-laws *c.*652. Husband of St Rictrude, whose ninth-century Life exists, he met his future wife on an expedition sent by King Dagobert against the Gascons. Their four children were all monastic saints. He helped his fellow Fleming St **Amandus** to set up the monastery of Marchiennes. His maternal grandmother was St Gertrude of Hamage. Feast day 2 February.

**Adalbero I (of Metz) (Auberon)** Bishop, statesman, monastic reformer, born beginning of tenth century, died Saint-Trond, Belgium, 26 October 962. Of noble Lorraine family, he succeeded **Benno** as bishop of Metz in 929, after the latter had been blinded. He played a certain political role, at first resisting **Otto I** of Germany but later becoming his faithful servant. He intervened in ecclesiastical disputes, for example, about the bishop of Rheims. He instigated monastic reforms, especially in Gorze, and was known as the 'father of monks'.

**Adalbero II (of Metz)** Blessed, bishop, monastic reformer, born between 955 and 962, died Metz 14 December 1005. A nephew of **Adalbero I**, he became bishop of Metz in 984 after a short time in Verdun, under pressure of his mother Beatrice on the empress Adelaide. He avoided political activity, but still defended church rights. Against the canons, however, he is known to have ordained sons of secular priests. He pushed the Cluniac reforms in the monasteries, and founded two monasteries at Metz.

**Adalbero of Augsburg** Blessed, bishop, died 28 April 909. Bishop of Augsburg from 887 to his death, he is buried in the church of St Afra in Augsburg. Monk (850) and afterwards abbot of Ellwanger, abbot restorer of Lorsch, he is known for his scientific knowledge and musical ability. He helped to educate Louis the Child, King of East Frankland, who called him a 'spiritual father'; he later served as his advisor. He kept a close spiritual connection with the monastery of Sankt Gallen, and encouraged the monastic discipline at the abbey of Lorsch. Feast day 9 October.

**Adalbero of Rheims** Benedictine abbot then archbishop, statesman, born Lorraine *c.*920, died Rheims, 23 January 988. Like **Adalbero II** of Metz, a nephew of **Adalbero I** of Metz, he became a monk at Gorze and eventually abbot. Approved archbishop of Rheims (the most important see in France) by King Lothaire in 969, he first set about building, reforming and defending ecclesiastical rights against the feudal lords. He put Gerbert of Aurillac, the future Pope **Sylvester II**, in charge of the cathedral school. Already a chancellor of King of Lorraine from 975, in 984 he changed allegiance, defending the Ottonian dynasty of Robertians, in particular Hugh of Capet, against the Carolingians.

**Adalbero of Würzburg** Saint, bishop, born c.1010, died Lambach Abbey, 6 October 1090. The son of Count Arnold of Lambach-Wells, Austria, he studied at Paris with St **Altmann** of Passau, and became a canon of Würzburg Cathedral. Emperor Henry II named him bishop and he was consecrated 30 June 1045. He at first sided with the Emperor **Henry IV** when in dispute with Pope **Gregory VII**, but broke with him when Henry 'excommunicated' the Pope (1076). An antibishop Meginhard took his see so he retired to Lambach, a Benedictine monastery in his ancestral home which he had helped to found. Feast day 6 October.

**Adalbert of Hamburg-Bremen** Archbishop, born c.1000, died at Goslar 1072. His ecclesiastical career was mixed with **Henry III**'s imperial favours, and from archbishop of Hamburg-Bremen (1043 or 1045) would have become Pope after accompanying the emperor to Rome to sort out a schism. Instead his friend Suidger became **Clement II**. Adalbert concentrated on a dream of a northern patriarchate which would strengthen his see against that of Cologne. He was influential with the next emperor **Henry IV**.

**Adalbert of Prague** Saint, oftentime bishop, 'Apostle of Prussia', born 939 of a noble Bohemian family, died 997, murdered near Gdansk at the instigation of a pagan priest. From Magdeburg, centre for the apostolate to the Slavs, he went to Prague, Hungary, Poland and Prussia, inspired by St Adalbert of Magdeburg whose name he assumed. He met resistance both within and without the Christian fold, and spent some time in Rome.

**Adalbert the Deacon** Saint, monk, missionary, born Northumberland, England, late seventh century, died Egmond, The Netherlands, 25 June 705. Possibly a grandson of King Oswald of Deira, Adalbert became a monk at Rathmelgisi and in 690 accompanied St **Willibrord** in the evangelization of the Frisians. Assigned to the northern Netherlands in 702 he preached in Kennemaria as archdeacon of Utrecht. He built the church at

Egmond where he is buried. The tenth-century bishop of Trèves, Egbert, had Adalbert's life written after a miracle attributed to his favour. Feast day 25 June.

**Adaldag** German saint and archbishop, born some time in 900, died in Bremen, Germany, 28 or 29 April 988. In 937 when the Emperor **Otto** succeeded Unni as archbishop of Bremen, Adaldag was elected his chancellor and in 964 when Otto removed Pope **Benedict V** from his office, Adaldag was appointed guardian of the deposed Benedict. Fulfilling his role as archbishop of Hamburg-Bremen, Adaldag was particularly known for his missionary activity, especially in founding the sees of Schleswig, Ribe, Aarhus and Odense in Denmark. He was also directly responsible for resisting the archbishop of Cologne's assertion of leadership over Bremen. The life of Adaldag was characterized by various diplomatic duties and great missionary zeal. Feast day 28 April.

**Adalgar of Bremen** German saint and archbishop, date of birth unknown, died in Bremen, Germany, 9 May 909. Originally a monk and deacon at Corvey, Adalgar was well known for his spirit of prayer and wisdom. In 865 his own bishop, also named Adalgar, appointed him assistant to Archbishop **Rembert** of Hamburg-Bremen. His subsequent succession of Rembert was confirmed by King **Louis II**, his two sons, the Emperor Arnulf and the abbot and community of Corvey by means of a local synod. Though the Norman wars restricted his missionary activity, Adalgar did travel throughout his see and assisted the royal court. Following the Synod of Tribur (895) Archbishop Herman of Cologne reduced Bremen to the rank of suffragan, a decision which was only revoked at Adalgar's death. Though there appears to be no written documentation of his canonization, he was first called a saint by Trithemius and is buried at St Michael's Basilica, Bremen.

**Adalgis of Novara** Italian saint and bishop, date of birth unknown, died some time between 849 and 850. Adalgis was appointed bishop of Novara c.830 and held his office for eighteen years. He is thought to have been related to the last Lombard king, **Desiderius**, and it remains unclear as to whether his appointment to the episcopacy was due to personal qualities or family connections. He is named in various imperial and ecclesiastical documents of his time, indicating his particular concern in political matters. He is especially believed to have been Lotario's councillor. This is evinced in correspondence to Lotario in 840 urging him to react against ongoing violence to the Church, and in a document in which Lothair gave over St Michael in Lucedio and St Genuario's Abbey to the church of Novara. Originally buried at the church of St Gaudence, where he had probably been canon, his remains were moved on 22 October 1553 to the church of St Vincent of Novara. Feast day 6 October.

**Adalgott I**   Swiss saint and abbot, date of birth unknown, died 1 November 1031. Originally a Benedictine monk of Einsiedeln's abbey, he was appointed abbot of Disentis in 1016. In this office he proved himself true to the Benedictine spirit, concerning himself primarily with the promotion of monastic reform and the liturgy. Though little else is known of him, success in his endeavours can be assumed since an extract from the Einsiedeln Chronicle reveals that he was venerated as a saint subsequent to his death. In 1672 his relics were entombed in a new church of the abbey. Feast day 26 October.

**Adalgott II**   Swiss saint, abbot and bishop, date of birth unknown, died 3 October 1160 at the abbey of Disentis. He was appointed abbot and bishop in 1150 and appears to have been very dedicated to both these offices. He is particularly remembered for his generous financial support to Münster and Schannis' religious communities and it seems he was closely connected with Emperor **Frederick I Barbarossa** and Pope **Stephen III**, with the latter of whom he was a co-student. His relics are to be found alongside those of **Adalgott I** at Disentis Abbey. Feast day 3 October.

**Adam, Karl**   Roman Catholic priest, theologian, born Pursruck, Bavaria 22 October, 1876, died Tübingen, 1 April, 1966. Studied in Bavaria and was ordained priest in 1900. He did pastoral work and some teaching at the University of Munich and in 1918 was made professor at Strasburg, and the following year at Tübingen, where he remained for the next 30 years. His theology was in line with Roman Catholic orthodoxy but he was liberal and modern in his outlook, and appealed to the increasing numbers of lay readers of theology. His writings include *Das Wesen des Katholizismus* (1924), *Christus unser Bruder* (1926), *Jesus Christus* (1933), *Una Sancta in Katholischer Sicht* (1948) and *Der Christus des Glaubens* (1954).

**Adam Easton**   English theologian and cardinal, born at Easton, England, some time in 1330, died in Rome 20 September 1397. Easton studied at Oxford in 1363–6 and became a master in theology. He was a well-known fourteenth-century biblical scholar and wrote various spiritual and liturgical works. He is best known, however, for his *Defensorium ecclesiastice potestatis*, written in 1373 to refute **Marsilius of Padua** and John **Wycliffe**'s works against the Papacy. Easton was also present at, and defended, Pope **Urban V's** election, whose validity had been the subject of much questioning. He was appointed cardinal in 1381 when he also wrote the *Office of the Visitation of the Blessed Virgin Mary* to enhance unity within the Church. His *Defensorium s. Birgittae* helped to bring about **Bridget** of Sweden's canonization in 1381. A learned theologian, Easton was an able defender of the Papacy and promoter of church unity.

**Adam Marsh**   English Franciscan theologian, born in the diocese of Bath and Wells some time in 1180, died 18 November 1258. Marsh studied arts at Oxford under **Robert Grosseteste** and gained his master's degree in 1226. After joining the Franciscan community of Worcester in 1232–3, he returned to Oxford to study theology and in c.1247 became its first Franciscan master. Subsequently, Marsh taught there until 1250. Having been made bishop of Lincoln in 1235, he was called on by King Henry III for help in court affairs and became councillor to **Boniface of Savoy**, archbishop of Canterbury. The Pope also enlisted his help in refereeing local disagreements. A man of high regard, he was given the title *Doctor illustris* while still alive. Though theological and biblical works attributed to him remain unpublished, J. S. Brewer has published some 247 of his letters. Writing of Marsh and Grosseteste, Roger Bacon described them as among the 'greatest clerics of the world'.

**Adam Mulieris Pulchrae** Born some time in 1200, died 1250. Known as Master Adam, this enigmatic figure obtained his master's degree in theology at Paris, and in 1234–5 read the *Sentences* there under Peter Lamballe. Between 1210 and 1240 he wrote *De intelligentis* (also known as *Memoriale rerum difficilium*) and in this demonstrated extensive knowledge of Aristotle's *Metaphysics*. He is also believed to have been influenced by pseudo-Dionysius' theme of hierarchical illumination. Though little is known regarding the identity of Adam, he was a contemporary of Eudes Rignauld (fl. 1236–75), Peter the Archbishop (fl. 1245–8), Stephen of Poligny (fl. 1242–8) and John Pagus (fl. 1231–46). Writings ascribed to him include those of **Adam of Buckfield** (or Bouchermefort), though these remain unedited.

**Adam of Bremen** German chronicler and geographer, date of birth unknown, died in Bremen, Germany, 1081. During his lifetime his main achievement was a four-volume historical work of Bremen-Hamburg's archbishops. The first two volumes deal with the events of the 250 years prior to **Adalbert of Bremen's** time as archbishop (1045–72). The third and most important of the four consists of a detailed biography of him. The fourth volume is an epilogue outlining the geography of the northern seas. Though Adam's career began in Franconia, he moved to Bremen in 1066 where he remained canon and headteacher of the school attached to the cathedral for the rest of his days.

**Adam of Buckfield** English Aristotelian philosopher, born at Bockenfield, Northumberland, *c.*1220, died some time between 1279 and 1294. Adam studied at Oxford and gained his MA in 1243. In 1249, already a subdeacon, he went to the rectory of Iver, Bucks, at the recommendation of **Robert Grosseteste**. Renowned for his learning and devout nature, by 1264 he also became canon at Lincoln. Various writings under different names – Adam Buckfield, A. Bouchermefort and Magister Adam Anglius – are ascribed to the one and same. There are some 45 extant texts of his, demonstrating his influence and popularity. In particular, his study of Aristotle was very clear, succinct and thorough. Adam of Buckfield represented a major figure of Aristotelian thought of the thirteenth century.

**Adam of Dryburgh (Dryborough)** Scottish preacher and writer, born in Berwickshire, Scotland, in 1140, died in Somerset, England, in 1212. As a young man Adam joined the Premonstratensians at Dryborough. Historically, it remains uncertain whether he became abbot there or not; certainly he did hold some position of authority. Between 1179 and 1180 he wrote his greatest work, *De tripartito tabernaculo* and in his latter *De triplici genere contemplationis* evinced his deeply mystical theology. He also wrote one work on the monastic life, *De instructione animae*. On a visit to France he became attracted to the Carthusians and on his return to England in *c.*1188 entered their Witham Charterhouse. Only one of his works on Carthusian spirituality is extant, *De quadripartito exercitio cellae*. Adam was a profoundly spiritual character who gave a particular witness to the values of the monastic way of life.

**Adam of Ebrach** Blessed, a German abbot, born near Cologne in 1100, died 20 November 1166. Adam was clearly an associate of **Bernard of Clairvaux** who addressed two extant letters to a certain Adam of Morimond, commonly acknowledged to be the same. Initially a monk of Marmontier, Adam joined the Cistercian community at Foligny in 1121 and went on to become abbot at Morimond. In 1125 Adam, alongside other monks, left the abbey (the reason for this is unclear) and returned only under Bernard of Clairvaux's pressure. Clearly successful and popular in his living out of the monastic life, Adam founded and became abbot of Ebrad Abbey in 1127 and went on to found at Rheims (1129), Heilsbronn and Langheim (1133), Nepomuk (1145), Alderspach (1146) and Bildhausen (1158). Adam's holiness and wise council is also evinced in his correspondence with the great mystic **Hildegard of Bingen.** He also proved a firm supporter of the Crusades. Feast day 25 February (Cistercian communities).

**Adam of Fulda** German composer of liturgical music and author, born in Fulda, Germany, 1445, died a victim of the plague at Wittenberg, 1505. A valued composer and musician, Adam was placed at the Benedictine monastery of Vormbach and was also 'ducalis musicus' at the court of Savoy in 1490. From 1492 to 1498 he excelled himself as poet, chronicler, composer and master in Torgan. In 1502 he was made professor of music at Wittenberg University, a position that he held until his tragic death. In addition to composing an array of liturgical pieces, three popular songs are also ascribed to him. These are of particular historical value since in theme he uses the methods of Burgundy's composers, evincing a link between these and the composers of southern Germany.

**Adam of Houghton**   English bishop and servant of the royal court, born Pembroke at an unknown date, died at St David's, on 13 February 1389. Adam obtained a doctorate in civil law from Oxford in 1340 and was appointed bishop of St David's by the Pope himself on 20 September 1361. A man of great tact and intelligence, Adam fulfilled various important diplomatic duties between France and England. In 1377 he reached the peak of his career when he was appointed chancellor of England. He held this office until 1378. In 1365 he founded the College of St Mary at St David's and along with it a choir. As a bishop, Adam devoted himself to community and patriotic service and would appear to have enjoyed considerable success.

**Adam of Orleton**   English bishop, born in 1280, died at Farnham Castle, Hampshire, 18 July 1345. A student of Oxford, Adam obtained a doctorate in canon law in 1310 and went on to receive appointment to three bishoprics; Hereford in 1317, Worcester in 1327 and Winchester in 1333. Clearly a politically minded person, he was charged with treason because he went against the wishes of Edward II in his involvement in the escape of Roger Mortimer of Wigmore from the Tower in 1323. Though he refused to attend his hearing, he was condemned nonetheless. His rebellion against the king continued in his affiliation with Queen Isabelle in plotting his abdication in 1327. Despite this, Adam went on to serve on **Edward III**'s council and represented him in various matters with Pope **John XXII** and France. Thus his previous conviction was revoked in 1329. A subsequent disagreement with Archbishop John **Stratford** in 1341 led many to believe that Adam authored the king's response to Stratford's condemnation of the

government. Although a man of significant political capability, modern writers generally agree that he was an individual somewhat lacking in integrity.

**Adam of Perseigne**   French abbot and spiritual writer, date of birth unknown (Champagne), died at Perseigne, 1221. As a Cistercian, Adam put his substantial theological and philosophical training to good use, being appointed abbot of Perseigne in 1188. Under the service of **Innocent III**, Adam revealed himself an able diplomat. Of his achievements, among the most notable are: his mediation of a disagreement subsequent to the death of King **Richard I** in 1199, his role in organizing the Fourth Crusade in 1200, his ability to quell controversy surrounding an episcopal election at Rheims in 1203 and in 1208 a particular role in facilitating peace between Philip II Augustus of France and King John of England. His immense success was believed to be the fruit of his piety, so much so that he was venerated as 'blessed' by his community. Unfortunately, few of his manuscripts are extant. Adam's holiness was evinced, above all, by his wise handling of delicate religious and political matters.

**Adam of Saint-Victor**   Poet, born in either Britain or Brittany in 1110, died 1180. Historically little is known of Adam's life. The first biographical account of him was written by William of Saint-Lô who died some 69 years after Adam's death. He was certainly a canon and a gifted liturgical poet. His theological background would appear to have been Augustinian as is evidenced in his celebrated poem on humankind, *Haeres peccati*. Composer of some 45 liturgical sequences approved by Pope **Innocent III**, he is acknowledged as perfecter of the style of sequence poetry initiated by **Notker Balbulus** and ongoing at Saint-Victor before Adam's birth. A man of great religious sensitivity, Adam was clearly concerned with rendering the Christian faith accessible through his works.

**Adam Wodham**   English Franciscan theologian, born *c*.1295, died at Babwell, England, some time in 1358. After completing theological studies at Oxford in 1319, Wodham went on to lecture on the *Sentences* of **Peter Lombard** in London's Franciscan priory in 1328–30, revised and presented them at Oxford in 1330–2 and lectured on his revised edition at Norwich in 1332–4. Having written the prologue to **William of Ockham**'s *Summa logicae*, he was commonly deemed an Ockhamist. In truth, his thought was free and independent of any one school. Peter of Candia thought him due the same regard as **Thomas Aquinas**, **Duns Scotus**, Ockham and **John of Ripa**.

**Adamnan of Iona**   Irish saint and abbot, born at Drumhome, Co. Donegal, Ireland, 625, died at Iona, Scotland, 704. Having moved to the island of Iona, Adamnan succeeded **Columba**, becoming the ninth abbot of the abbey there in 679. On a mission to help the cause of Irish captives held in England in 685, he was converted to the Roman position regarding the date of Easter and to the Roman tonsure. Back in Scotland, Adamnan did much work to ensure the application of this and in many places – though not in Iona – succeeded. A deeply pastoral man, he expressed his concern that women should have no part in fighting (Synod of Tara 697). The Canon of Adamnan (Cain Adamnain) is ascribed to him and he wrote the first biography of Columba of Iona. An ancient Irish biography of him, *Betha Adamnain*, still exists. Feast day 23 September.

**Adams, Henry Brooks**   American chronicler and author, born Boston, Massachusetts, 16 February 1838, died at Washington, DC, 27 March 1918. Born of impressive ancestry – two of his relatives had been presidents of their country – Henry was raised a Unitarian, but later chose to abandon this particular tradition. A prolific writer, he was educated at Harvard (1854–8), where Louis **Agassiz** proved influential in his devotion to study. When his father was appointed minister to Great Britain, Henry moved to London and after marrying in 1872, returned to Boston in 1877. Though his writing career flourished, his wife sadly took her life in 1885. This traumatized Adams, who looked to travel for solace. His two greatest works – *Mont-St-Michel and Chartres* and *The Education of Henry Adams* – witness his fundamental concern to make sense of the ages and events of history. After suffering a heart attack in 1912, he moved to France until 1914. Back in the United States in 1918, he died a successful writer and prominent figure in religious reform.

**Addai** (also known as **Thaddeus**)   Saint, dates of birth and death unknown. According to Christian tradition, he was one of Jesus' 72 disciples and, along with St **Mari**, brought Christianity to Syria and Persia, founding the churches there. Addai is mentioned in **Eusebius**' *History of the Church* which contains the *Acta Eddesa*. This document recounts some of the Doctrine of Addai, a fourth-century apocryphical work describing how Christianity reached Edessa. The Nestorians claimed that SS Addai and Mari were the source of their liturgy.

**Adela**   Saint and Benedictine abbess, born 675, died near Trier, 734. It is thought that Adela was the daughter of Dagobert II and her name is first mentioned in Abbess Adela's letter to Abbess Alfield. Adela is known for her foundation of a Benedictine abbey at Trier. Her grandson – **Gregory of Utrecht** – was educated under **Boniface** who took him away with him on a visit to Adela in 722. Curiously, though she died in 734, her remains were not discovered until 1072. She is not commonly venerated and her cult never received official confirmation. Feast day 24 December.

**Adelaide of Turin**   Marchioness, born 1020, died at Canischio, Italy, 29 June, 1091. Twice widowed, three times married and the mother of five children, Adelaide was the subject of controversy during her lifetime. Despite this, she was an influential figure, especially in her efforts to counter hostility to Pope **Alexander II**. Adelaide's relationship with the Papacy was at times strained. Whilst enjoying the respect of **Peter Damian** on the one hand, she was once summoned to Rome for reconciliation and absolution. The marriage of **Henry IV** and one of Adelaide's daughters, Bertha, is indicative of her status and connections. An exceptionally politically minded and astute woman, she even managed to reconcile Pope **Gregory VII** and Henry IV.

**Adelaide of Vilich**   Saint, Benedictine abbess, born Cologne, 960, died there 5 February 1015. Born of a noble family, Adelaide's father was Count Megingoz of Gelder. Generous and devout by nature, she entered St Ursula's Convent. Here she introduced the practice of the Benedictine Rule, deeming it more fitting and demanding than the previous one of St Jerome. Her love of prayer led her to urge her community to learn Latin in order that they might better understand the Breviary. She became abbess of Vilich (which her own parents had founded) and of St Marie im Kapitol, Cologne, simultaneously, where she succeeded her sister Bertrande. A confidant of Herbert, archbishop of Cologne, Adelaide was renowned for her generosity towards the poor in times of famine. She was buried and her remains enshrined at Vilich. Feast day 5 February.

**Adelard of Bath**   Philosopher, writer and translator, born *c.*1070, died some time after 1142–6. A Benedictine monk, Adelard studied at Tours and later went on to pursue a teaching career at Laon. A man of great culture and scientific learning, he travelled through Jerusalem, Italy and perhaps Spain throughout a seven-year period. Among his most notable works are: *De eodem et diverso, Questiones naturales, Rules for the Abbacus* and *The Function of the Astrolabe*. In the twelfth century, he played a significant role in the integration of the sciences and nature into England's learning system. his works were of special inspiration to Roger **Bacon** and **Robert Grosseteste**.

**Adelelm of Burgos** (or **Lesmes**)   Saint and abbot, date of birth unknown (probably Loudon, close to Poitiers), died 30 January 1097 at Burgos. A man renowned for his holiness, he is patron saint of Burgos and one of the four eleventh-century Benedictine abbots in Castile. The main source of the information we have on his life comes from the biographical work of the Auvergnese monk Rudolph. Adelelm gave up great wealth and the military life to pursue his religious calling. The fruits of his ardent prayer life were evinced in a number of miraculous works, especially involving the use of bread or water blessed by him and by curing the sick. He successfully rid the Queen of England (Matilda of Flanders) of her lethargy when she ate blessed bread sent by him. He is also believed to have crossed the river Tagus without getting wet. Feast day 30 January.

**Adelhelm**   Blessed, Benedictine abbot, date of birth unknown, died 25 February 1131. Originally a Benedictine of the community of Sankt Blasien,

he was appointed the first abbot of Engelberg Abbey, Switzerland (founded by Conrad of Switzerland), *c.*1122. Once in office, Adelhelm strove to obtain complete autonomy of the abbey from exterior management. In 1124, he received papal and royal confirmation of this. Renowned for his prayerful nature, miracles are reputed to have occurred at his tomb. He became the object of popular veneration from the mid-twelfth century. His relics were entombed at Engleberg in 1744. Feast day 25 February.

**Adelmannus**   Bishop of Brescia, northern Italy, theologian and writer, date of birth unknown, died *c.*1061. Adelmannus received his education under **Fulbert of Chartres** and was a co-student of **Berengarius of Tours**. From *c.*1028 to 1050 he pursued a teaching career first at Liège, then at Spire. He produced a number of works during this time. In 1050 he was consecrated bishop of Brescia and held this office to his death. There are two extant works of his: *Rhytmi alphabetici de viris illustribus* (a poem) and a letter to Berengarius in which he expounded the eucharistic doctrine of his time. Another letter, to Archbishop Hermann of Cologne (1036–56), containing an exhortation against general absolution, is also ascribed to him.

**Adelphus of Metz**   Saint and bishop, date of birth unknown, died 29 August 460. Very little is known about this saint, who remains an enigmatic figure to this day. He appears to have been venerated at Metz soon after his death. It is believed he succeeded St Rufus as archbishop of Metz; a position which he held for some seventeen years. In 836 his relics were transferred to Neuweiler and in the eleventh century a new church was purpose-built to enshrine them. During the Reformation, however, the relics were returned to their original place in the old abbey church. Feast day commonly celebrated on 29 August, but in Neuweiler 1 September.

**Adenauer, Konrad**   German Roman Catholic lawyer and politician, born Cologne, 5 January 1876, died Rhondorf 19 April 1967. He was a member of the Catholic Centre Party, and served on the city council of Cologne in 1906, being made mayor in 1917. He held that office, and from 1921 the post of President of the Prussian Council of State, until dismissed by the Nazi Party in 1933, at which point he retired to Rhondorf. He was arrested in the aftermath of the 1944 attempt on Hitler's life, though he had not been implicated. The Americans restored him as mayor of Cologne in 1945, but he was dismissed by the British. He was instrumental in creating the Christian Democratic Union, and was, from 1950 to 1966, its chairman. He presided over the German constitutional assembly preparing the way for the Federal Republic, and became the first Chancellor, retiring in 1966.

**Adenulf of Anagni**   Italian priest and scholar, born 1225, Anagni, died Paris, 26 August 1289. A nephew of **Gregory IX**, he studied theology and arts at Paris, excelling in theology. A prolific writer he produced, among others, two works on Aristotle and several homilies. Commentaries on the Psalms and the Book of Revelation from the same period and written under the name **Albert the Great** also appear to have been the work of Adenulf. Himself a wealthy and learned man, he understood the importance of education and did much to foster the promotion of studies. Though a candidate for the bishopric of Paris and Narbonne, he refused the offer, preferring to work at Saint-Victor. Saint-Victor and the Sorbonne must have been particularly dear to Adenulf since he left around forty of his works to them.

**Adeodatus I**   See **Deusdedit I**

**Adeodatus II**   Pope, date of birth unknown, elected 7 April 672, died 17 June 676. When the Church was confronted with the threat of Monothelitism, Adeodatus appears to have had a role in ridding the Church of this heresy. Originally a Benedictine monk, he was generous by nature and during his papacy contributed greatly to the refurbishment of St Erasmus' Monastery. A religious at heart, he wrote two letters in which he expressed his wish that monasteries be permitted to rely on internal jurisdiction only. Adeodatus is also renowned for initiating the papal tradition of dating events according to his reign. Though the Bollandists refused to accept Adeodatus ever having been venerated, some celebrate his feast on 26 June.

**Adhemar of Chabannes**   French monk and chronicler, born into a noble family near Limoges 989, died in Jerusalem in 1034. When some seven years old he was sent to the monastery of Saint-Cybard at Angoulême where he was trained as a scribe. About the year 1007 he moved to the abbey of St Martial at Limoges to be under the direction of his uncle Roger. There he continued his studies in the scriptorium, and also learned to draw. He returned to Saint-Cybard c.1014 where, a decade or so later, he began his *Historia*, the greater part of which was a reworking of earlier annals and which exists in several different recensions. He returned to St Martial c.June 1028 at the request of its abbot to work on a new liturgical manuscript, where he helped to promote the abbey by claiming, especially through the liturgy, that St Martial had been an apostle. This assertion was challenged, and Adhemar left Limoges to return to his own monastery in August 1029 but he did not give up his claim. In order to defend it he produced a number of forgeries, including one of a papal letter, asserting the apostolicity of St Martial. He left on pilgrimage for Jerusalem probably in 1033.

**Adhemar of Puy**   Bishop, date of birth unknown, died at Paris, 1 August 1098. Of noble stock, Adhemar is believed to have been related to the counts of Valentinois. He was elected bishop of Puy some time after 1080, and in this time he succeeded in regaining territory that had originally been part of his see. On **Urban II**'s announcement of the First Crusade on 27 November 1095, Adhemar was the first bishop who vowed to take part in it. Consequently, he was made councillor to Urban and deputy to two of his armies. Together with the army of **Raymond IV** of Saint-Gilles, he set out on crusade in October 1096. Especially renowned for his success in mediating various battles, Adhemar revealed himself as a true ecumenist in his attempts to foster peaceful rapports between the crusaders and the eastern Christian inhabitants of the places they conquered. He also did much to strengthen unity between Eastern and Western churchmen.

**Adjutor**   Saint, born Vernon, in the late eleventh century, died 30 April 1131 at Tiron, France. From an early age, Adjutor was well known for his kindness and prayerful spirit; a fact attested by his close friend and eventual biographer **Hugh of Amiens**, archbishop of Rover. Eager to defend and spread his faith, Adjutor was one of the first Normans involved in the 1095 Crusade. His prayer life reaped much fruit, especially in the form of miracles. The most noted of these was his own miraculous flight from Muslim captivity during the First Crusade. He was deeply affected by his experience of the Crusades, so much so that on his return to France he devoted himself to becoming a monk at Torin Abbey. In his latter years Adjutor's love of prayer and silence increased and he lived as a hermit near the monastery in a cell built by himself. Feast day 20 April, he is venerated in several French parishes.

**Ado of Vienne**    Saint, archbishop and chronicler, born 800 at Sens, Paris, died 16 November 875 at Vienne, France. After entering the Benedictines and receiving his formation from Abbots **Lupus of Ferrières** and Markward, Ado went to Italy for a five-year period. On his return to France he was made parish priest at Lyons and then archbishop of Vienne. He remained in this office from 6 July 859 to 22 October 860. He was successful in his ecclesiastical endeavours and well respected by Popes **Nicholas I** and **Adrian II**, King **Charles** the Bald and **Louis the German**. A great pastor, Ado was particularly concerned to promote fervour among the priests of his diocese and was an enthusiast of the Divine Office. His writings include a history of the world (*Chronicum sive Breviarium de sex mundi aetatibus ab Adamo usque ad annum 869*) and the disputed martyrology, *passionum codices undecumque collecti*. Most of this latter was taken from the writings of **Florus of Lyons** and the remainder is largely thought to be plagiarized. At the time, this led to further speculation regarding other such works.

**Adragna, Antonio Maria**    Franciscan priest and theologian, born 1 October 1818 at Trapani, Italy, died 14 October 1890, Rome. After entering the Conventual Franciscans at the age of sixteen, Antonio was ordained in 1841 and pursued a teaching career in Würzburg and Assisi. We can presume success in his endeavours since in 1861 he was a councillor of the Holy See and in 1866 he was made a member of the Vatican Council I's dogmatic commission. Success also ensued for Anto-

nio within his religious order where from 1872 to 1879 he fulfilled the office of general. Rome's hostile religious climate led him to move to Holland some time between 1876 and 1878. Sadly, none of his works appear to have been published and much of the information regarding his life has been lost.

**Adrian**    Saint, martyr and bishop, date of birth unknown, died (Hungary?) 875. According to legend, Adrian was of royal blood, but there is no reliable historical information to back this up. After his appointment as bishop of Hungary, Adrian went to Scotland where he preached to the Fifeshire Picts. Some say he was archbishop of St Andrew's, Scotland, but it is more likely that this was the Irish St Odrhan. Adrian built a monastery on the Isle of May and received his martyrdom on Holy Thursday 875 during the fighting between the Danes and the Scots that took place on the Firth. Many Scots were killed during these battles and the Aberdeen Breviary of 1509 is dedicated to those martyred at the monastery.

**Adrian I**    Pope, born of a wealthy family in Rome, died 25 December 795 in Rome. Still a deacon when unanimously elected to the Papacy, Adrian held this office from 1 February 772 until his death. During his turbulent Papacy, Adrian strove principally to preserve and maintain an appropriate relationship between the Church and the state. At a time when **Desiderius**' troops plagued Rome and continually took land from the Church, Adrian proved himself a successful peacemaker and his dialogue with Charlemagne led to the formation of the Church States that were to remain so until 1860. As well as restoring the Roman Church, Adrian also engineered a magnificent agricultural zone. The excess alone that this produced daily fed around one hundred people. Adrian was also very involved in the preservation of orthodoxy. This was evinced in his successful handling of Adoptionism in Spain and in the support he lent to Empress **Irene** in calling the second Council of Nicaea (787). This council pronounced iconoclasm anathema. An exceptionally gifted Pope, Adrian was a source of unity in the much troubled first-century church.

**Adrian II**    Pope, born 792 in Rome, died some